*Modern Literatures of
the Non-Western World*

Modern Literatures of the Non-Western World

WHERE THE WATERS ARE BORN

Jayana Clerk and *Ruth Siegel*
City University of New York

HarperCollins*CollegePublishers*

Acquisitions Editor: Lisa Moore
Developmental Editor: Tom Maeglin
Project Coordination: Ruttle, Shaw & Wetherill, Inc.
Text and Cover Design: Mary Archondes
Art Studio: RR Donnelley Receivables, Inc.
Electronic Production Manager: Valerie A. Sawyer
Desktop Administrator: Hilda Koparanian
Manufacturing Manager: Helene G. Landers
Electronic Page Makeup: RR Donnelley Barbados
Printer and Binder: RR Donnelley and Sons Company
Cover Printer: The Lehigh Press, Inc.

For permission to use copyrighted material, grateful acknowledgment is made to
the copyright holders on pp. 1207–1216, which are hereby made part of this
copyright page.

Modern Literatures of the Non-Western World: Where the Waters Are Born

Copyright © 1995 by HarperCollins College Publishers

Library of Congress Cataloging-in-Publication Data

Modern literatures of the non-Western world : where the waters are born/
    [compiled by] Jayana Clerk and Ruth Siegel.
       p.   cm.
    Includes bibliographical references and index.
    ISBN 0-06-501269-0
     1. Developing countries—Literatures—History and criticism.
2. Literature, Modern—History and criticism.   I. Clerk, Jayana.
II. Siegel, Ruth.   III. Title: Where the waters are born.
PN849.U43M63 1995
809'.891724—dc20   94-5832
                                                  CIP

95 96 97 98 9 8 7 6 5 4 3 2 1

Contents

Preface   *xvii*

Part 1: *East Asia—Japan, Korea, and China*   3

Introduction   3

Yosano Akiko *(1878–1942) Japan*   **15**
Three modern *tanka*   16
The Day When Mountains Move   16

Han Yongun *(1879–1944) Korea*   **17**
Ferryboat and Traveler   17
On Reading Tagore's "The Gardener"   18

Lu Xun *(Lu Hsun, 1881–1936) China*   **19**
My Old Home   20

Tanizaki Junichiro *(1886–1972) Japan*   **28**
The Tattooer   29

Akutagawa Ryunosuke *(1892–1927) Japan*   **35**
In a Grove   36

Mao Zedong *(Mao Tse-tung, 1893–1976) China*   **43**
Swimming   44

Mao Dun *(Mao Tun, 1896–1982) China*   **45**
Spring Silkworms   46

Kawabata Yasunari *(1899–1972) Japan*   **65**
The Silver Fifty-Sen Pieces   66

Kim Sowol *(1902–1934) Korea*   **70**
The Road   70

Ding Ling *(Ting Ling, 1904–1986) China*   **71**
A Certain Night   72

Enchi Fumiko *(1905–1986) Japan*   **76**
Boxcar of Chrysanthemums   77

Hirabayashi Taiko *(1905–1972) Japan*   **90**
A Man's Life   91

Kato Shuson *(b. 1905) Japan*   **103**
Three modern *haiku*   104

Yi Sang *(1910–1937) Korea*   **105**
Wings   105

Xiao Hong *(Hsiao Hung, 1911–1942) China*   **119**
The Crossroads   120

Hwang Sunwon *(b. 1915) Korea*   **124**
Cranes   125

So Chongju *(b. 1915) Korea*   **129**
The Huge Wave   130

Ch'i Chun *(b. 1918) Taiwan*   **130**
The Chignon   131

Abe Kobo *(1924–1993) Japan*   **135**
The Red Cocoon   136

Mishima Yukio *(1925–1970) Japan*   **139**
The Damask Drum   140

Kim Namjo *(b. 1927) Korea*   **156**
Having Come to the Mountain   156

Ariyoshi Sawako *(1931–1984) Japan*   **157**
The Tomoshibi   157

Ko Un *(b. 1933) Korea*   **171**
Lee Chongnam   172

Tomioka Taeko *(b. 1935) Japan*   **173**
Just the Two of Us   174

Pai Hsien-yung *(b. 1937) Taiwan*   **175**
A Sea of Bloodred Azaleas   175

Jialin Peng *(b. 1948) China*   **185**
What's in a Name   186

Bei Dao *(b. 1949) China*   **191**
Electric Shock   192
Language   192

Part 2: *South Asia, Southeast Asia, Australia,*
and New Zealand 195

Introduction 195

Rabindranath Tagore (1861–1941) India 207
Chandalika 208
Where the Mind Is Without Fear 216

Ho Chi Minh (1890–1969) Vietnam 217
Noon 219
Transferred to Nanning 219

R. K. Narayan (b. 1906) India 219
Trail of the Green Blazer 220

Raja Rao (b. 1909) India 224
Companions 225

Faiz Ahmed Faiz (1911–1984) Pakistan 231
Ghazal 231

Umashankar Joshi (1911–1988) India 233
The Universal Man 234

Bienvenido N. Santos (b. 1911) Philippines 235
Footnote to a Laundry List 236

Amador Daguio (1912–1966) Philippines 245
Wedding Dance 245

Saadat Hasan Manto (1912–1955) Pakistan 252
The Dog of Titwal 253

Amrita Pritam (b. 1919) India 257
The Weed 258

Oodgeroo Noonuccal (Kath Walker, 1920–1993)
  Australia 263
Municipal Gum 264

Mochtar Lubis (b. 1922) Indonesia 264
Harimau! 265

Nissim Ezekiel (b. 1924) India 277
Night of the Scorpion 278

Pramoedya Toer (b. 1925) Indonesia 279
Inem 280

Mahasweta Devi (b. 1926) India   **290**
Dhowli   291

Thich Nhat Hanh (b. 1926) Vietnam   **312**
The Pine Gate   312

Jayanta Mahapatra (b. 1928) India   **320**
30th January 1982: A Story   320

Hyllus Maris (1930–1986) Australia   **322**
Spiritual Song of the Aborigine   322

Abdullah Hussein (b. 1931) Pakistan   **323**
The Tale of the Old Fisherman   323

Tan Kong Peng (b. 1932) Malaysia   **331**
A Jungle Passage   331

Ranjini Obeyesekere (b. 1933) Sri Lanka   **337**
Despair   337

Edwin Thumboo (b. 1933) Singapore/Malaysia   **341**
Christmas Week 1975   341

Kevin Gilbert, Wiradjuri (b. 1933) Australia   **343**
Kiacatoo   343

Kamala Das (b. 1934) India   **345**
An Introduction   346

Anita Desai (b. 1937) India   **348**
A Devoted Son   348

Patricia Grace (b. 1937) New Zealand   **356**
It Used to Be Green Once   357

Khalida Asghar (b. 1938) Pakistan   **361**
The Wagon   362

Shashi Deshpande (b. 1938) India   **371**
My Beloved Charioteer   372

Mudrooroo Nyoongah (Colin Johnson, b. 1938)
 Australia   **378**
Poem Two   379

Catherine Lim (b. 1942) Singapore/Malaysia   **380**
Ah Bah's Money   380

Witi Ihimaera (b. 1944) New Zealand   **384**
Yellow Brick Road   384

M. A. Nuhman (b. 1944) Sri Lanka   **390**
Murder   390

Salman Rushdie (b. 1947) India   **391**
An Iff and a Butt   392

Sally Morgan (b. 1951) Australia   **400**
Arthur Corunna's Story   401

Part 3: *The Middle East*   417

Introduction   417

Kahlil Gibran (1883–1931) Lebanon   **422**
On Children   422

Nazim Hikmet (1902–1963) Turkey   **423**
12 December, 1945   424

Sadiq Hidayat (1903–1951) Iran   **425**
Seeking Absolution   426

Ya'akob Yehoshua (b. 1905) Israel   **433**
Childhood in Old Jerusalem   434

Fadwa Tuqan (b. 1917) Palestine   **435**
Song of Becoming   436

Simin Danishvar (b. 1921) Iran   **437**
The Half-Closed Eye   438

Etel Adnan (b. 1925) Lebanon   **450**
In the Heart of the Heart of Another Country   451

Ahmad Shamlu (b. 1925) Iran   **457**
The Gap   457

Abdallah al-Baraduni (b. 1929) Yemen   **458**
Answers to One Question   459

Shimon Ballas (b. 1930) Israel   **459**
Imaginary Childhood   460

Mohammed Khudayyir (b. 1930?) Iraq   **466**
Clocks Like Horses   466

Forugh Farrokhzad (1935–1967) Iran   **476**
The Wind-Up Doll   477

Ghassan Kanafani (1936–1972) Palestine   **479**
The Slave Fort   479

Hushang Golshiri (b. 1937) Iran **483**
The Wolf 484

Abd al-Aziz al-Maqalih (b. 1939) Yemen **490**
Sanaa Is Hungry 490

Muhammad Abd al-Wali (1940–1973) Yemen **491**
Abu Rubbiya 492

Saeed Aulaqi (b. 1940) Yemen **496**
The Succession 497

Mahmoud Darwish (b. 1942) Palestine **503**
Guests on the Sea 504

Erez Bitton (b. 1949) Israel **506**
Something on Madness 507

Fawziyya Abu Khalid (b. 1955) Saudi Arabia **508**
A Pearl 508

Shelley Elkayam (b. 1956) Israel **509**
The Crusader Man 509

Abd al-Hameed Ahmad (b. 1957) United Arab
  Emirates **510**
Khlalah SEL 511

Part 4: *Africa* **521**

Introduction **521**
Jomo Kenyatta (1891–1978) Kenya **526**
The Gentlemen of the Jungle 526

Jean-Joseph Rabearivelo (1901–1937) Madagascar **529**
Flute Players 529

Yahya Haqqi (b. 1905) Egypt **531**
The Tavern Keeper 531

Leopold Sedar Senghor (b. 1906) Senegal **534**
Prayer to Masks 534

Naguib Mahfouz (b. 1911) Egypt **536**
Half a Day 536

Es'kia Mphahlele (b. 1919) South Africa **539**
Interlude 540

Amos Tutuola (b. 1920) Nigeria   **545**
The Gentleman of Complete Parts   545

Gabriel Okara (b. 1921) Nigeria   **553**
You Laughed and Laughed and Laughed   554

Augustinho Neto (1922–1979) Angola   **555**
Kinaxixi   556

Nadine Gordimer (b. 1923) South Africa   **557**
Good Climate, Friendly Inhabitants   557

Christopher Okigbo (1923–1967) Nigeria   **568**
Come Thunder   568

Sembene Ousmane (b. 1923) Senegal   **569**
The March of the Women   570

Dennis Brutus (b. 1924) South Africa   **582**
Nightsong: City   583

Camara Laye (1924–1980) Guinea   **584**
The Goldsmith   585

Efua Sutherland (b. 1924) Ghana   **589**
New Life at Kyerefaso   590

Can Themba (1924–1968) South Africa   **595**
The Suit   596

Noemia de Sousa (b. 1927) Mozambique   **604**
If You Want to Know Me   604

David Diop (1927–1960) Senegal   **606**
The Vultures   606

Yusuf Idris (b. 1927) Egypt   **607**
The Chair Carrier   608

Chinua Achebe (b. 1930) Nigeria   **612**
The Madman   613

R. Sarif Easmon (b. 1930) Sierra Leone   **619**
Bindeh's Gift   620

Grace Ogot (b. 1930) Kenya   **628**
The Rain Came   629

Nawal El Saadawi (b. 1931) Egypt   **637**
She Has No Place in Paradise   637

Flora Nwapa (1931–1993) *Nigeria* **643**
The Chief's Daughter   643

Tchicaya U Tam'si (1931–1988) *Congo* **651**
Brush-Fire   652

Athol Fugard (b. 1932), *John Kani* (b. 1943), *and*
  Winston Ntshona (b. 1942?) *South Africa* **653**
The Island   654

Okot p'Bitek (1931–1982) *Uganda* **679**
Song of Lawino   680

Lenrie Peters (b. 1932) *Gambia* **695**
Isatou Died   696

Kofi Awoonor (b. 1935) *Ghana* **696**
The Weaver Bird   697

J. P. Clarke Bekederemo (b. 1935) *Nigeria* **698**
The Leader   698

Wole Soyinka (b. 1935) *Nigeria* **699**
The Strong Breed   700

Costa Andrade (b. 1936) *Angola* **729**
Fourth Poem of a Canto of Accusation   729

Assia Djebar (b. 1936) *Algeria* **730**
There Is No Exile   731

Bessie Head (1937–1986) *South Africa* **740**
The Collector of Treasures   741

Keorapetse Kgositsile (b. 1938) *South Africa* **757**
The Air I Hear   757

Ngugi Wa Thiong'o (b. 1938) *Kenya* **758**
Wedding at the Cross   758

Ayi Kwei Armah (b. 1939) *Ghana* **770**
Halfway to Nirvana   770

Molara Ogundipe-Leslie (b. 1940) *Nigeria* **775**
song at the african middle class   776

Ama Ata Aidoo (b. 1942) *Ghana* **777**
In the Cutting of a Drink   777

Syl Cheney Coker (b. 1945) *Sierra Leone* **783**
The Philosopher   784

Jack Mapanje (b. 1945) Malawi   **785**
On African Writing   785

Charles Mungoshi (b. 1947) Zimbabwe   **786**
Shadows on the Wall   787

Zoe Wicomb (b. 1948) South Africa   **791**
You Can't Get Lost in Cape Town   792

Part 5:   ***Latin America and the Caribbean***   **807**

Introduction   **807**
Antonio Gonzalez Bravo (1885–1962) Bolivia   **816**
Kori Pilpintu   816

Gabriela Mistral (1889–1957) Chile   **817**
Song   818

Claude McKay (1890–1948) Jamaica   **819**
Crazy Mary   820

Cesar Vallejo (1892–1938) Peru   **825**
The Eternal Dice   826

Jesus Lara (1898–1980) Bolivia   **827**
Incallajta Jarahui   827

Miguel Angel Asturias (1899–1974) Guatemala   **828**
Legend of "El Cadejo"   829

Jorge Luis Borges (1899–1980) Argentina   **833**
The Gospel According to Mark   834

Carlos Drummond de Andrade (1902–1987) Brazil   **839**
An Ox Looks at Man   839

Nicolas Guillen (b. 1902) Cuba   **840**
Arrival   841

Silvina Ocampo (b. 1903) Argentina   **842**
The Servant's Slaves   843

Alejo Carpentier (1904–1980) Cuba   **849**
Like the Night   850

Pablo Neruda (1904–1973) Chile   **860**
The Heights of Macchu Picchu, III   861
The Chilean Forest   861

Jacques Roumain (1907–1944) Haiti   **870**
Delira Delivrance   871

Joao Guimaraes Rosa (1908–1967) Brazil   **878**
The Third Bank of the River   879

Juan Bosch (b. 1909) Dominican Republic   **883**
The Beautiful Soul of Don Damian   884

Juan Carlos Onetti (b. 1909) Uruguay   **890**
A Dream Come True   891

Maria Luisa Bombal (1910–1980) Chile   **901**
Sky, Sea and Earth   902

Rachel de Queiroz (b. 1910) Brazil   **905**
Tangerine Girl   905

Jorge Amado (b. 1912) Brazil   **910**
Of Dice and Unshakable Principles   911

Leon Damas (1912–1978) French Guiana   **915**
Poems   916

Walter Montenegro (1912–1991) Bolivia   **917**
The *Pepino*   918

Aime Cesaire (b. 1913) Martinique   **924**
To Africa   925

Julio Cortazar (1914–1984) Argentina   **927**
Our Demeanor at Wakes   928

Julia de Burgos (1914–1953) Puerto Rico   **931**
To Julia de Burgos   932

Octavio Paz (b. 1914) Mexico   **934**
Return   935

Joseph Zobel (b. 1915) Martinique   **937**
Mr. Medouze   937

Murilo Rubiao (b. 1916) Brazil   **942**
Teleco, the Rabbit   943

Juan Rulfo (1918–1986) Mexico   **949**
Tell them not to kill me   950

Wilson Harris (b. 1921) Guyana   **955**
Yurokon   956

Rubem Fonseca (b. 1922) Brazil **967**
Night Drive 968

Jose Donoso (b. 1924) Chile **969**
Paseo 970

Lygia Fagundes Telles (b. 1924) Brazil **983**
The Ants 984

Ernesto Cardenal (b. 1925) Nicaragua **990**
The Filibusters 991

Rosario Castellanos (1925–1978) Mexico **992**
Daily Round of the Spinster 993

Martin Carter (b. 1927) Guyana **994**
Listening to the Land 995

Carlos Fuentes (b. 1928) Mexico **995**
Chac-Mool 996

Gabriel Garcia Marquez (b. 1928) Colombia **1004**
The Handsomest Drowned Man in the World 1005

Derek Walcott (b. 1930) Saint Lucia **1009**
I Once Gave My Daughters . . . 1010
The Season of Phantasmal Peace 1011

V. S. Naipaul (b. 1932) Trinidad **1012**
My Aunt Gold Teeth 1013

Manuel Puig (1932–1990) Argentina **1020**
Kiss of the Spider Woman 1020

Austin Clarke (b. 1934) Barbados **1060**
Leaving This Island Place 1060

Earl Lovelace (b. 1935) Trinidad **1067**
The Fire Eater's Journey 1068

Mario Vargas Llosa (b. 1936) Peru **1077**
A Shadow of Gnats 1077

Maryse Conde (b. 1937) Guadeloupe **1087**
Mira 1088

Nelida Pinon (b. 1937) Brazil **1097**
Brief Flower 1097

Simone Schwarz-Bart (b. 1938) Guadeloupe   **1103**
Toussine   1104

Olive Senior (b. 1941) Jamaica   **1114**
Do Angels Wear Brassieres?   1115

César Verduguez (b. 1941) Bolivia   **1124**
The Scream in Your Silence   1125

Isabel Allende (b. 1942) Chile   **1135**
Our Secret   1136

Antonio Cisneros (b. 1942) Peru   **1139**
After the Battle of Ayacucho: A Mother's Testimony   1140

Rosario Ferré (b. 1942) Puerto Rico   **1141**
The Youngest Doll   1141

Ana Lydia Vega (b. 1946) Puerto Rico   **1146**
ADJ, Inc.   1147

Rigoberta Menchu (b. 1951) Guatemala   **1155**
The Death of Dona Petrona Chona   1156

Opal Palmer Adisa (b. 1954) Jamaica   **1159**
Duppy Get Her   1159

Appendix A: Alternate Table of Contents by Theme   *1169*
Appendix B: Alternate Table of Contents by Country   *1177*
Appendix C: Alternate Table of Contents by Genre   *1187*
Appendix D: Selected Further Readings   *1193*
Credits   *1207*
Index   *1217*

Preface

We know where the waters are born,
and love them for they pushed our canoes under the crimson skies.
"Arrival"
NICOLAS GUILLEN

The purpose of *Modern Literatures of the Non-Western World: Where the Waters Are Born* is to balance the Eurocentric emphasis in literary studies and to expand the canon. Many courses currently offered in universities, however, use the term "non-Western" or "Third World" in their titles, sometimes "Post-Colonial," or "International." Ironically, in the process of redressing the imbalance and directing our anthology to the appropriate courses, we faced the dilemma of using a negative term that derives from a Western perception. Our subtitle embodies the true spirit of this collection.

Included here are modern literatures from Latin America, the Caribbean, Africa, the Middle East, East, South, and Southeast Asia, as well as aboriginal literatures from Australia and New Zealand.

Until very recently, the academy has paid attention mainly to the Western tradition. Universities now design courses—in most disciplines and at all levels—that incorporate material from distinct cultures. Our anthology addresses these new needs. The selections are appropriate for advanced electives as well as introductory literature and composition courses. The readings are also suitable for area studies, interdisciplinary programs, and the social sciences.

Modern Literatures of the Non-Western World presents the twentieth-century literatures of the world that extends from Asia to the Pacific Rim through Africa to the lands south of the Rio Grande and the Caribbean. The anthology offers poetry, fiction, plays, and memoirs written by 180 women and men from 61 countries, and translated from some 23 languages. It brings together established authors who speak primarily from the center of their cultures. They are the giants who created a literary awakening and contemporary writers who have enlarged on their predecessors. Many have received prestigious national and international prizes, including the Nobel Prize. But while a handful of the authors have attained international renown, many are still unknown outside their own society, except among small cadres of scholars, intellectuals, and fellow writers around the world.

This is the first anthology of its kind, the first to focus solely on the literatures of these countries. Its convenience is that it makes this rich body of literature available in one collection. By providing access to this aspect of our human heritage, our anthology opens the way to a fresh, more comprehensive view of world literature. Thus, it helps adjust the perceptions of the academy and fills a void.

We see our book as a means to transcend ethnocentricity in general and Eurocentricity in particular. And we contend, like Carlos Fuentes, that "literature [is] not of linear progression but of circles and simultaneities, capable of receiving the ec[-]centric contributions of our total humanity." All of us, from the East or the West, need to open our perceptions outward, understanding the limitations of our own visions of reality since we all too often remain trapped within the specific modes of our perceptions. We need to acknowledge that we all are "others" to one another. The literature in this anthology offers an opportunity to readers to appreciate and respect diverse centralities; it helps cultivate an awareness that honors different cultural perspectives. It is in this sense that our anthology breaks barriers, opening the boundaries of the Western literary canon.

The literatures included are spirited in every way, and the image of water in our subtitle, *Where the Waters Are Born,* captures this sense of vitality. Water, which is the source of all life, represents fertility as well as rebirth. And according to ancient philosophies, the waters carry the word into existence, thus evoking the ages-old concept of the power of literature. The waters also suggest the distinctiveness and connectedness of diverse literatures. While most cultures, however disparate, perceive water as regenerative, each body of water is peculiar to its native land, changing from well to well, river to river, and yet the waters gather in the oceans of the world.

Our book attests to an interconnected global history. Since the rise of European nations with their expansion into the rest of the world, a Eurocentric vision has come into conflict with the perspectives of other societies. This vision has impinged on the world's consciousness and created a division between a so-called first and third world. As a result, our selections depict the similarities of colonial history: imperialism, resistance, and postcolonialism. But we have not concentrated on political and economic themes alone. The readings also illustrate traditional cultural differences. Our intention is to discourage any monolithic perceptions, and so we have provided a generous sampling of distinct voices.

Several criteria governed our selections. We were guided throughout by the importance of the writers, their significance in their own cultural and literary history, their contribution to literature in general, and their influence on other writers. But the quality of the translation was always a primary criterion. Another major consideration was how the readings fit into and reflected their cultural context. Since we do not focus solely on political or historic concerns, we looked for a wide stylistic and thematic range in the material. We also looked for readings that would connect with each other, both within their own and across cultures.

In the process of collecting the literature, we were faced with the necessity of excluding material that, in spirit, belongs in this anthology. One of the problems relates to our dependence on the availability of translated materials. We have had to exclude some eminent authors, either because no translations of their works exist or those that do are weak and do not reflect the authors' styles or interests. A second problem concerns excerpted materials. We have included intercolated tales and self-contained episodes, but we have had to omit many important novelists whose intentions and narrative lines would be broken by excerpting. The integrity of the piece has been our determining factor. Finally, since the anthology does not cover readings from Europe and North America, we have, with deep regret, not included the literatures of Native and African Americans (or of immigrants of color).

We have integrated the selections and study apparatus to make this anthology a self-contained text. Since our purpose is to help generate a new awareness, the readings are set in a context that will help readers enter unfamiliar worlds. The introductions to the various sections, author headnotes, and study questions, all open up the literature, placing each piece and author within their own milieu and emphasizing the culture that informs them. We intend the introductions and headnotes to provide enough information so that readers will not need secondary sources to understand the selection; the questions help open up the selections. Furthermore, maps as well as the bibliography of suggested readings provide additional support for understanding and exploring writers and their worlds further. We hope, of course, to whet everyone's appetite for more literature from and information about these areas of the world.

The introductory essays to each section reach into the distant past to provide historic and cultural background. Even though the twentieth-century experience of many nations reflects colonialism, imperialism, and their aftermath, the recognition of a precolonial past creates a true sense of time and place. This sweep of history explains the present and provides a sense of continuity for understanding the selection. In addition, the discussions of ancient times in the regional introductions illuminate common concerns among the writers within the same region as well as across cultures.

As the writers developed their art, many synthesized Western traditions with their own, while many others rejected the West. But both groups have maintained their separateness from Europe and asserted their national and cultural identities. They have sought their past, often stretching back thousands of years, insisting on its integrity. Their work frequently has evolved from and incorporated ancient oral traditions. And the philosophical underpinnings of the work have derived in good part from indigenous concepts. In this way, the writers began to articulate national voices and reassert their unique literary traditions as well as to express their personal visions.

Each section introduction is organized differently, and each is determined by the distinct history of the region. The diversity and magnitude of Asia is such that we have separated the area into several regions adopting a different approach for each. For Japan, the essay focuses on literary history, while for China, it emphasizes the tremendous political upheaval of the twentieth century. The South Asian introduction concentrates on ancient historical and philosophical background, while the shared history of European colonization and Japanese occupation is discussed in the essay on Southeast Asia. In the essay on the Middle East, the focus is on its history from ancient times. The introduction to Australia and New Zealand reflects their indigenous heritage, just as the African essay highlights the literary. For Latin America and the Caribbean, we have considered their common political history and distinctive literary traditions.

Headnotes, providing a brief biographical preface to each selection, accent the special features of each writer, creating a sense of the person. In some cases, however, the inaccessibility of biographical material has limited our drawing as full a picture as we would like. Focusing on the salient literary and personal concerns of the authors, we have noted whatever illuminates their sensibilities, be it literary, political, or philosophical. These notes place the writers within their cultural contexts. For consistency, we have left out all diacritical marks.

In posing a set of questions, we have tried to avoid imposing our point of view, attempting, instead, to draw out individual interpretations. The questions are intended to encourage the appreciation of and respect for diverse perspectives and sensibilities, assisting readers to observe the literature from within the culture that shaped it. The Discussion and Writing questions are detailed and aid in understanding the text. From these questions, instructors can develop writing exercises suited to their courses. The Research and Comparison topics propose several subjects, some of which are listed as Interdisciplinary Discussion Questions. These topics lead to critical inquiry into the different societies and a deeper understanding of their literatures. By examining the same theme across regions and cultures, moreover, readers can perceive the particular— sometimes antithetical—approaches to the same issues. General in nature, all these topics are offered as possibilities for developing more focused themes that correspond to the objectives of any course. They also help the reader notice differences within as well as between cultures.

The anthology follows a basic geographical order, dividing the text into sections along continental rather than political or cultural lines. Each section is divided into regions and the literature placed within it. Each reading is then organized chronologically according to the author's date of birth. In its overarching organization, the anthology follows the sun's track, beginning in East Asia, dipping down into Australia and New Zealand, and traveling across the Asian continent through the Middle East into Africa, moving then to South and Central America, Mexico, and the Caribbean.

We offer this text as a beginning, an opening into the richness of our world's plenty.

For us, as teachers and students of these literatures, the book is the realization of a long-held dream. Many people—colleagues looking for such an anthology, scholars in the various areas, general readers—have been as exhilarated as we at the prospect of seeing this material finally available and studied in universities. They have given their unstinting and generous assistance in a way that spoke to their pleasure and belief in our endeavor. Even as the anthology goes into print, we are receiving suggestions for additional selections: another volume, perhaps. This enthusiasm and generosity has enriched the text and our undertaking.

Several people have translated material for this volume and we are immensely appreciative: Ammiel Alcalay; Clifford E. Landers; David McCann; Rebecca Louise Siegel; and Carolina Udovicki.

We are grateful to all our colleagues—several newly found during the process of putting the manuscript together—who offered their assistance. We would especially like to thank those who helped guide us in their special fields: Ammiel Alcalay, Queens College; Corrine Jennings, Queens College; Clifford E. Landers, Jersey City State College; David McCann, Cornell University; Bahman Maghsoudlou; Irwin J. Schulman, University of Pittsburgh; Carol Sicherman, Lehman College; Barbara Webb, Hunter College.

We are also grateful to all those professors whose advice guided us: Agha Shahid Ali, University of Massachusetts, Amherst; Ali Behdad, University of Rochester; Steve Belcher, Pennsylvania State University; Norman R. Cary, Wright State University; Ferida Cassimjee, University of Illinois at Urbana-Champaign; Joni Adamson Clarke, University of Arizona; Bill Clemente, Peru State College; Carlo Coppola, Oakland University; Kevin Griffith, Wartburg College; Norma Jenckes, University of Cincinnati; Diane M. Kammeyer, Anoka-Ramsey Community College; Ketu Katrak, University of Massachusetts, Amherst; Martha E. Kendall, San Jose City College; Amitava Kumar, University of Florida; Michael Liberman, East Stroudsburg University; Lucy Maddox, Georgetown University; Adrienne

Perez Melgosa, University of Rochester; David Chioni Moore, Duke University; Donald Morton, Syracuse University; Rhoads Murphy, University of Michigan; Rajagopal Parthasarathy, Skidmore College; Beatrice Pita, University of California-San Diego; Aparajita Sagar, Purdue University; Joseph Sarfoh, SUNY, Albany; Carol Schaffer-Koros, Kean College of New Jersey; Chuck Schuster, University of Wisconsin, Milwaukee; George Sebouhian, State University of New York, Fredonia; Bede Ssensalo, California State University, Long Beach; Nancy Topping-Bazin, Old Dominion University; Pennie Ticen, University of Massachusetts; Albert Wertheim, Indiana University; Gay Wilentz, East Carolina University; and Cynthia Wong, University of Colorado at Denver.

Our special thanks, too, to those who advised us and helped us track down sources and resources. Their pleasure in assisting us buoyed our spirits, and their knowledge was invaluable: David Brownstone; Irene Frank; Amy Vladeck Heinrich; Peter Johnson; Edgar Kann; Frances LaFleur; Panna Naik; Linda Oppenheim; John Schulman; and Hasan Wazani.

We thank Leona James, Parul Jariwala, and Benjamin Karp, who cheerfully helped us research copyright information. Among the staff at HarperCollins, we are indebted to Lisa Moore, Tom Maeglin, and Lynn Huddon for all their assistance and to Mark Getlein for his fine editorial insights.

Our continuing thanks go to our families and friends for their fortitude and their support as we worked on this hugh project. Finally, we thank Ruth's husband, Jacques Sartisky, who read and reread drafts, fed us, and lived through our anxieties with unparalleled patience, but also with pride in the book.

Jayana Clerk and Ruth Siegel

*Modern Literatures of
the Non-Western World*

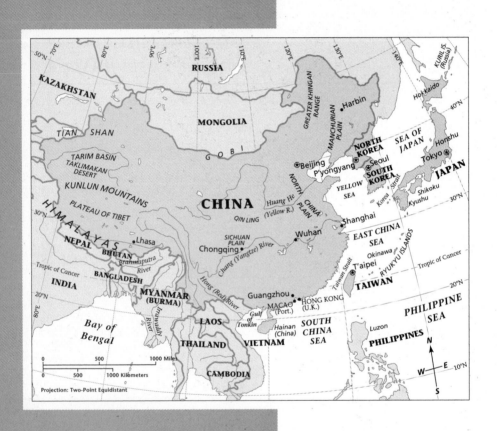

PART

1

East Asia—
Japan, Korea,
and China

Japan

The Japanese date the beginning of their literary history to the compilation of the *Manyoshu* (Collection of 10,000 Leaves) in the late eighth century. The *Manyoshu* contains about 4500 poems by women and men at all levels of society—commoners, beggars, soldiers, aristocrats, and emperors. The *Tanka,* or short poem, was already the preferred, though not the only, form. Written in a 31-syllable pattern of alternating lines (a pattern that became the basic rhythm of prose), *tanka* distilled a personal, lyrical response to the world. One aspect of *tanka* came to be associated with highly refined declarations of love within the courtly tradition of classical Japan, and by the middle of the Heian period (794–1192), contests were held at court to judge the elegance of both the poetry and the calligraphy in which it was written. But Japanese poetry has essentially remained the province of all classes. What Ki no Tsurayuki said in 905 still holds true: "Japanese poetry has for its seed the human heart"; people still turn to poetry, "when they [are] startled into thoughts on the brevity of their lives by seeing the dew on the grass or the foam on the water."

   The world view of classical Japanese literature was informed by three religious-philosophical traditions: Shinto, Buddhism, and Confucianism. Shinto was the ancient state religion of Japan. Its customs and rituals permeated Japanese life. Encompassing a wide range of beliefs, Shinto incorporates the worship of numerous deities and spirits, ancestral homage, and pilgrimages to the shrines inhabited by helpful deities. Chief among the spirits is Amaterasu, the sun goddess, who is held to be the ancestor of the emperors of Japan. The term Shinto, deriving from the Chinese *shen* and *dao* (or *tao,* "the way of the gods"), was officially coined in the sixth century to distinguish the native Japanese religion from foreign religions entering Japan. Confucianism and Buddhism were brought to Japan as part of the "New Learning"—ideas imported during Japan's first sustained contact with Chinese civilization. Confucianism remained largely on the periphery of Japanese thought. Buddhism, however, quickly became an important religious, artistic, and literary force as the Buddhist emphasis on the transi-

3

tory nature of existence struck a sympathetic chord in Japanese lyrical aesthetics.

Chinese merchants and missionaries brought to Japan the philosophies, arts, language, and writing system of their culture. Chinese was soon established as the scholarly language. Education meant learning classical Chinese language and literature, and Chinese continued as a scholarly language into the nineteenth century. Most important, however, these foreign philosophies and aesthetics were transformed into something essentially Japanese, an example of the process of absorption and metamorphosis that has characterized Japanese culture in general, and the modern period of Japanese literature in particular.

Although only men were scholars, the Heian period of imperial rule marked the great age of women writers. Women became the masters of the major classical prose genres—the memoir, the diary, and *monogatari* (a fictional storytelling similar to the novel). These prose genres incorporated lyrical poetry, and it is believed that the novel may in part have originated with the practice in which poets wrote lengthy prefaces to introduce each poem. Poets as well as writers of prose, the Heian authors created works of keen psychological and social astuteness. The greatest of these—indeed, the single greatest work of Japanese literture and a classic in its own day—is the *Tale of Genji* by Lady Murasaki (d. 1031), the pen name chosen by a woman of the Heian court. A *monogatari* of epic dimensions and infused with Buddhist philosophy, the *Tale of Genji* has endured as a source of inspiration for twentieth-century Japanese writers, several of whom have produced highly praised translations in modern Japanese.

As the Heian period drew to a close, the shoguns (or generals) took control of the government. Society gradually became totalitarian as a warrior caste, the *samurai*, rose to dominance. Women's lives grew more and more circumscribed, although women's education became a means for advancing their families' social status. An educated woman was prized, and, thus, her family's rank rose through advantageous marriage.

There was a flurry of writing during the twelfth and thirteenth centuries, but poetry seemed to have lost its vitality. In the fourteenth and fifteenth centuries, however, *noh* drama blossomed, evolving from various popular entertainment forms, particularly Shinto song and dance recitals, into a highly esteemed literary genre. *Noh* incorporated all elements of theatrical performance: poetry, music, dance, mask, makeup, and gesture. Emphasizing the perfection of the performance itself, *noh* demanded an almost religious intensity from its actors, whose training was extremely rigorous. Zeami Motokiyo (1363–1444) has been generally regarded as the master classical *noh* dramatist. His plays embraced such diverse influences and subjects as Buddhist philosophy, history and legend, and theories of poetry and calligraphy.

Around 1600, after some two centuries of internal warfare, the Tokugawa clan rose to power. The Tokugawa embarked on 250 years of feudalistic control: the emperor retained a merely ceremonial role in Kyoto, while actual power was wielded by a succession of Tokugawa shoguns who ruled from Edo (present-day Tokyo). Wary of European expansion throughout Asia, the Tokugawa initiated *sakoku*, a policy of isolationism. Among other prohibitions, people could not travel outside Japan; Christianity was banned; and except for the Dutch and the Chinese, foreign ships were forbidden entry into Japanese ports. And the Dutch and the Chinese were only allowed to enter the harbors of an island near Nagasaki. Shinto, which had been almost obliterated after the eighth century, re-emerged as an important social force and Neo-Confucianism became the official state ideology. In the 1600s, principles from Shinto and Neo-Confucianism were combined to create *Bushido* ("the way of the fighting knight"), the *samurai* or warrior code.

At the beginning of the Edo period (1603–1868), the *samurai* were, for the most part, uneducated men with rough ways; they gradually became an elite class of highly accomplished poets, painters, and scholars. Women, however, lost status in Neo-Confucianist Edo society. Although there were conflicts between the ruling conservative feudal class and a rising, newly rich merchant class, the Edo Period was remarkably peaceful, and the arts flourished. In poetry, the courtly *tanka* gave way to the 17-syllable *haiku*. Basho (Matsuo Munefusa, 1644–1694), who imbued his *haiku* with Zen Buddhist philosophy, established and developed the subtlety of the genre. With nature as the most common subject and frequently emphasizing the evanescence of life, the poems resonated evocatively by setting up associations and comparisons. In drama, the *kabuki* theater with live actors and the *joruri* (a puppet theater) emerged, often producing the same plays. Mainly concerned with the "floating world" (the world provided for men, from geisha conversation to licensed sexual encounters with prostitutes), *kabuki* has remained an extremely popular entertainment.

By the 1840s, Europe and the United States had become more determined in their efforts to gain a foothold in Japan, sending warships and treaty missions. U.S. Commodore Matthew C. Perry finally sailed into lower Tokyo Bay with his warships in 1853, and forced a trade agreement between the United States and the Tokugawa shogunate in 1854. Japan signed a series of treaties, first with the United States and then with Europe, but all unfavorable to Japanese interests. The nobles and their *samurai* felt that Japan had been betrayed. They rebelled, the Tokugawa shogunate fell, and in 1868, formal power was returned to the Meiji emperor. The Meiji Restoration defines the beginning of the modern period, marking the end of isolationism as Japan moved from feudalism to an industrialized nation.

Japan became fascinated by Western technology and culture, and transmuted aspects of Western thought into indigenous Japanese culture, as it had previously done with Chinese philosophies. The two major Meiji novelists, Mori Ogai (1862–1922) and Natsume Soseki (1867–1916), lived in Germany and England, respectively, absorbing the current Western literary attitudes. Mori Ogai created a new form of autobiographical writing with the *shi-shosetsu*, or "I-novel," which remained a prevalent genre through much of the twentieth century. Natsume Soseki followed his lead, and along with other Meiji writers, they also initiated the "romantic" movement. While such movements were new, they were also an extension of tradition, for autobiographical writing, with its emphasis on the individual, on emotions, on capturing the psychological moment—whether in prose or poetry—had dominated Japanese literature from the Heian poetic diaries and *tanka* on.

During the decade following the victory of the Russo-Japanese War (1904–1905), many of the great twentieth-century novelists began their careers, including Akutagawa Ryunosuke and Tanizaki Junichiro. Literary schools multiplied, branching off into subcategories: "neoromantic," "neorealist," "neosensualist," and so forth. They all challenged "naturalism." Though these categories were Western, the process itself was not: group affiliation (here, schools) had long served as a means of identification in most areas of life. The writers, moreover, not only recast the Western principles, they continuously reaffirmed their Japanese literary heritage. Akutagawa began his career as a "neorealist" writer, rejecting the "I-novel" and concentrating on an objective stance rather than an authorial presence. In his later work, however, he turned to autobiographical fiction—such was the pull of tradition. The "neoromantic" novelist Tanizaki came to question Western influence in his later work, but even in his early explorations of the psyche, he had implicitly placed himself within the conventions of the Japanese novel.

Women resurfaced as writers in this new cultural climate. Yosano Akiko's early "romantic" *tanka* hearkened back to Heian courtly conventions even as she struck out as a modern woman, speaking explicitly about a woman's sexuality. An outspoken feminist, she prepared the way for later writers, such as Enchi Fumiko, who focused on the lives of women. As the first to use literature to address political issues, Yosano Akiko also paved the way for writers such as Hirabayashi Taiko, a novelist associated with the "proletarian" school, and Ariyoshi Sawako, who wrote about social and political problems.

The unrest of the twenties and thirties, generated by economic disparities and rising militarism, led to the "proletarian" movement with its focus on class and everyday lives. Such writers as Kawabata Yasunari, however, reacted against both "neorealism" and the "proletarian" school. A "neosensualist," Kawabata merged modern psychological insights with Heian conventions. But whatever school they belonged to, most twentieth-century Japanese writers were affected by the rising militarism. They saw the dangers inherent in their country's occupation of Korea (1910) and Manchuria (1931). Indeed, Japan's new territorial ambitions led to war with China (1937), which in turn led directly to Japanese participation in World War II as an Axis power (called the Pacific War) and the occupation of Southeast Asia. Atom bombs dropped on Hiroshima and Nagasaki in

1945 by the United States brought those dangers that had been feared to their terrible conclusion. Ironically, Nagasaki had been the first of the Japanese islands to open its port to Western trade.

The carnage of the bomb and the subsequent seven-year occupation of Japan by the United States stood as tragic inescapable reminders of defeat. After the war, some writers rejected nationalism altogether. Abe Kobo, for example, published innovative novels and plays drained of nostalgia for the past. Instead, he probed contemporary society, focusing particularly on the issue of alienation. Mishima Yukio, on the other hand, embraced nationalism. He espoused a return to traditional mores, specifically to the *samurai* culture, as a resolution to contemporary ills. All of the postwar and post-occupation writers, in one way or another, have sought to regain an equilibrium, to evoke the Japanese spirit, philosophy, and aesthetic in genres that are also essentially Japanese, whatever Western elements have been absorbed. They play out Ki no Tsurayuki's belief that "Japanese poetry has for its seed the human heart, and grows into countless leaves of words."

Korea

Korean legend speaks of Tangun, known affectionately as "Grandpa Tangun," who became the first Korean king in the second millennium B.C.E. In the 1200s C.E., a Son (Zen) Buddhist master recorded this tale in Chinese. His transcription exhibits continuing characteristics of Korean culture and literature. It merges the indigenous and the foreign—Korean and Chinese philosophies; Korean and Chinese languages. And it brings together a popular and an elite art—lyrics by ordinary people and poems by scholars.

Historically, Korea was first unified in the seventh century by the kingdom of the Silla, one of the three kingdoms that had arisen on the peninsula during the first centuries of the common era. Neighboring China, which had backed the Silla, had long furnished a powerful cultural model for the developing Korean civilization. The Chinese writing system was known in Korea from at least the fourth century; Buddhism and Confucianism took root not long after.

Buddhism mingled with indigenous beliefs, informing Korean poetry from the time of its arrival. Buddhism became the state religion in 527, and Buddhist monks played a key role in the society. They participated in the education of future administrators and served as secular and sacred counselors. The Silla people had borrowed Chinese characters to transcribe the vernacular (spoken) language, and Buddhist monks preserved early Korean poetry by means of the Silla script. Only a few examples of this poetry survive—some two dozen *hyangga* (or "local songs"), written largely by the monks themselves—along with a handful of later folksongs and poems composed by ordinary people. These poems, all of which were meant to be sung, have remained a source of inspiration for twentieth-century writers. Educated Koreans also wrote voluminously—but in classical Chinese, which the ruling elite had adopted wholeheartedly as the language of literature and scholarship. And women contributed prolifically, especially during the thirteenth and fourteenth centuries.

With the advent of the Yi dynasty (1392–1910), Confucianism supplanted Buddhism as the state philosophy, and remained the official ideology for the entire 518 years of Yi rule. Early in the fifteenth century, scholars working under royal patronage devised the Korean alphabet. Although the Chinese language continued to hold a higher status among scholars and continued to be a vehicle for literary works, a body of literature written in Korean now began to emerge. In poetry, two forms became especially popular, the three-line *sijo* and the narrative *kasa*. *Sijo* poems sang about the court—now praising, now satirizing it—about nature, love and mutability, about the contemplative life as opposed to the engaged. *Kasa* poetry celebrated equally the lives of farmers and monks, but women of the upper classes also wrote *kasa* to protest against the restrictions of their lives. In addition, Yi authors pioneered the *sosol*—lengthy prose narratives that have evolved in the twentieth century to resemble the Western novel. Incorporating Buddhist as well as Confucian philososophy, some Yi *sosol* created dreamlike worlds, while others drew pictures of society.

Toward the end of the Yi dynasty, in the late 1800s, China and Japan coerced Korea into opening its doors to the West. The Korean government began a program of Western-style modernization, and Korean writers turned to Western literature and theory as they attempted to break through traditional Confucian constraints. Ultimately, however, Korean writers found rejuvenation in the vitality of their own popular tradition, which offered an antidote to rigid literary conventions.

At the turn of the century, Korea became a pawn in a regional power struggle between Russia, China, and a newly militaristic Japan. The First Sino-Japanese War (1894–1895) brought dramatic political and social change as Japanese troops moved onto the Korean peninsula. The U.S.-brokered treaty that ended the Russo-Japanese War (1904–1905) allowed Japan to enter Korea as an occupying force. Finally, in 1910, Japan annexed Korea. Japan imposed harsh regulations, and in 1919, Korean discontent with Japanese rule fueled the short-lived March First Independence Movement. Thirty-three artists and intellectuals signed a "Declaration of Independence," and 2 million people across the nation protested against Japanese occupation. Many people were imprisoned.

As Japan increased its ventures into China, conditions in Korea worsened. The Japanese drive to industrialize Korea broke up the self-sufficient rural economy based in a traditional mode of communal farming. Farm families moved to the cities, where they entered an ever-growing urban poor population. New laws aimed at suppressing Korean culture exacerbated this social disruption: Koreans were required to take Japanese names and to worship at Shinto shrines, and schools were forbidden to teach the Korean language. The imprisonment of large numbers of dissidents increased, especially of those who refused to participate in the war with China that grew into World War II, known in Asia as the Pacific War.

Having suffered deprivation and humiliation, the Korean people rejoiced when the war ended in 1945 and they were liberated, but their joy was short-lived. Promised independence, they received a divided country: Soviet troops occupied the mineral-rich land north of the Thirty-eighth Parallel, and U.S. troops occupied the industrial lands to the south. Two governments emerged in 1948 and war followed (1950–1953), during which as many as 3 million Koreans—10 percent of the population—were killed. The conflict ended in a stalemate, and the Korean peninsula remained divided into two countries at the Thirty-eighth Parallel, leaving the buffering demilitarized zone (DMZ) as a bitter reminder of the fratricidal Korean War.

This century-old history of violence and disorder, of nationalistic hope and frustrated despair, became the setting and the subject of twentieth-century literature. As writers responded to each event, dynamic literary schools arose. To frame their urgent denunciations of colonization, poets turned to the innate strengths of the Korean language, to its colloquial simplicity and terseness. Some looked to Buddhism and traditional folksongs for inspiration as they voiced their concern for the Korean people. Other writers organized the Korean Artist Proletariat Federation (1925) in reaction to the terrible poverty of the growing lower class. A body of fiction centered on class issues developed over the next decade, before the Federation was summarily disbanded. During the war years, a poetry of resistance emerged; after the liberation, writers confronted the Partition. Ironically, the Partition has generated a still more vigorous body of work, even as the DMZ, that barren strip of wasteland, tragically continues as an emblem of the Korean predicament.

China

Originating in the North China plain and the western reaches of the Yellow River, and spreading south from there to the Yangtze River and beyond, Chinese civilization has a continuous history of more than four thousand years. Since the time of the Qin[1] dynasty (221–206 B.C.E.) when its separate

---

[1]Pinyin is the official system of romanization in the People's Republic of China, the United Nations, and other world agencies, replacing the older Wade-Giles system. Persons and places relating to China are, for the most part, in Pinyin, and those relating to Taiwan are in Wade-Giles. Readings retain the romanization of the originals. Such well known names as Peking, Canton, and Chiang Kai-shek either retain the Wade-Giles or vary in the romanization system, depending on the context within the introductory material.

kingdoms were first brought together under a single ruler, China has generally been a unified country, governed by an elaborate bureaucratic state. Most people have worked the land, living in villages where they have barely eked out a subsistence. Historically, a small fraction of this population has been literate. Yet over the centuries, China has produced a cultural legacy of immense depth, complexity, and influence, a legacy comprising philosophy, history, poetry, and fiction; paintings, sculptures, architecture, bronzes, and ceramics; music, dance, and drama.

While the Qin established the characteristic mechanisms of China's centralized bureaucracy, it was the ensuing Han dynasty (206 B.C.E.–221 C.E.) that gave Chinese culture its definitive form. Perhaps the most enduring legacy of Han rule was the institution of Confucian philosophy as state doctrine. From the Han onward, Confucian principles served as the standards for government, society, and the arts. The Five Classics—five works associated with Confucius—became and remained the core texts of a scholarly education until the founding of the Chinese Republic in 1912. But the most revered Confucian text was the *Analects,* a collection of the master's teachings compiled by his followers. Routinely committed to memory by educated men all over East Asia, the sayings of the *Analects* formed a virtual encyclopedia of common reference and literary allusion for two millennia. Even today, Confucian influence remains profound.

Confucius (c. 551–479 B.C.E.) lived on the cusp of an extended period of unrest known as the Warring States. According to traditional Chinese histories, the famous "one hundred schools of philosophy" of his day blossomed in response to these troubled times. Confucius was a moral reformer, and he structured his ideas on concepts already considered classic. He believed that the right way of government was based on the ancient principles, in good part because they were ancient. A humanist, Confucius maintained that study led to wisdom, and wisdom to a more correct society, that moral education could reform government and that conduct was the distinguishing mark of a person.

Ancient Chinese thought explained all life, human and cosmic, as an opposition and alternation of the principles of *yin* and *yang:* darkness and light, moisture and heat (or earth and sky), contraction and expansion, feminine and masculine. Long before Confucius, the concept of the *dao* had been added: the principle of the connectedness and correlation of the *yin* and the *yang.* These principles came to be associated with Daoism (Taoism), another philosophy of the Warring States period that has had a lasting impact on Chinese thought. While not considered canonical in quite the same way as Confucian texts, Daoist writings have been prized for their inventiveness and beauty. Dating back to the third or fourth century B.C.E., the texts focus on the rhythm of life and the unity of all phenomena, on the individual and the nature of the universe. Although a few explicitly concern issues of government, most concentrate on mystical and meditative experience. The third formative influence on Chinese thought was

Buddhism, which entered China from India between the second and sixth centuries C.E. Taking much of its terminology from Daoism, Buddhism evolved into a vital cultural, intellectual, and literary force.

It is the Confucian classics, however, that are recognized as the basis of Chinese literature. Comprising philosophy, history, poetry, and anecdote, the Classics set the standards for exellence as well as for subject matter in the various genres. The *Shi Jing* (Book of Songs), for example, established the ideal in poetry that persisted into the twentieth century. Compiled in the sixth century B.C.E., the *Shi Jing* contains 305 poems, many already ancient at that time. Though touched up in varying degrees by the poet-scholars who recorded them, most of the poems were traditional folksongs, and they speak of common experience: love and marriage, daily work, the sufferings of war, the pain of separation. There are also poems of social and political protest, as well as poems celebrating work on the land:

> *Ah! They are clearing the land! Their ploughs are opening up the earth.*
> *Thousands of couples are digging up roots, some in the lowlands, others on the*
> *high ground.*

For the next thousand years, classical Chinese, the written language formalized during the Han period, remained the medium considered appropriate for literature, even as it became increasingly remote from the language people actually spoke. A vibrant literature written in a mixture of classical and vernacular (spoken) Chinese eventually developed, however, emerging first during the Tang dynasty (618–907) with the Daoist-inspired tales of the supernatural. The colloquial novel evolved during the Yuan dynasty (1280–1368). Springing from a long tradition of storytelling in village markets and teahouses, these works reached a broad audience and became immensely popular. Overcoming the Confucian precept that prose was the appropriate medium for philosophical writings, such works were outside the Confucian aesthetic realm. Indeed, from about 1400 on, it was in prose, in the vernacular, that the most vibrant and innovative writing was to be found. Written in the 1700s, *The Dream of the Red Chamber* is the most famous in the long line of Chinese novels, and it is a work that has a Buddhist flavor.

Except for Buddhism, Chinese literary and artistic traditions have owed comparatively little to outside influences. This is not to imply, however, that China had no outside contacts. Long before 105 B.C.E., the accepted date of the opening of the Silk Road, traders had journeyed back and forth between China, India, Persia, and Rome. In East and Southeast Asia, contact with China deeply influenced the developing cultures of Korea, Japan, and Vietnam. Within its own borders, commerce generated a small but thriving landowning and mercantile class as well as colonies of foreign traders like the community in Canton (now Guang Zhou) of Arab and Persian merchants that flourished in the thirteenth century. European traders, such as the Venetian Marco Polo, began to trickle into China at the time when it formed part of the Mongol empire under Kublai Khan (c. 1215–1294). Marco Polo's descriptions in *The Book of Ser Marco Polo* (1298) fascinated Europeans for centuries.

Toward the end of the 1500s, Jesuit missionaries were admitted to the Chinese court, where they were admired for their vast learning. A century later, the British East India Company established a trading post in Canton. Although China ordered the expulsion of missionaries during the 1700s, this was the century when trade with England began to develop. The balance in trade fluctuated, but by the end of the century, England had introduced opium as a commodity to shift the balance to its favor.

In the 1800s, pressure mounted for further entry into the potential markets of China. England launched the first campaign in the Opium Wars (1839–1842), and with its victory acquired Hong Kong and forced the opening of several coastal cities to Western trade. During the decades that followed, coastal cities like Shanghai, Tianjin, and Canton became, in large part, Western outposts. Imperialism basically took the form of the successful extraction of privileges: concessions to build railroads and open coal mines; opportunities to engage in missionary work; exemptions from Chinese legal jurisdiction; control over China's economy. Japan gained control of Taiwan and trading rights to China's coastal cities as a result of the first Sino-Japanese War (1894–1895). Then, between 1898 and 1900, in a last, ultimately futile, attempt to oppose foreign intervention and Christian intrusion, millions of peasants rebelled. Known as the Boxer Rebellion, the uprising was finally crushed by an international army from eight nations, including the United States.

Followers of the revolutionary leader Sun Yat-sen overthrew the last imperial dynasty, the Qing (or Manchu), in 1911 and established a republic. Thirty-eight years of intermittent civil war and foreign invasion followed, however: a turbulent time known as the Warlord period. In 1924, the newly founded Chinese Communist Party formed an alliance with the Nationalist Party of Sun Yat-sen in an effort to liberate China from the control of the warlords and foreign imperialists. The alliance ended in 1927 when Chiang Kai-shek, successor to Sun Yat-sen, turned on the Communists, ordering the massacre of his former allies. These purges, in effect, were the driving force behind the Long March: between 1934 and 1936, Mao Zedong led some 80,000 Communists across 6,000 miles, pursued by Chiang Kai-shek, to establish a new base at Yan'an in the northwestern province of Shaanxi. Only eight to nine thousand survived.

Japan had occupied the Chinese province of Manchuria in 1931, and full-scale war erupted between China and Japan in 1937. During this second Sino-Japanese War that ended with the defeat of Japan in World War II in 1945, the Communists became increasingly powerful as they successfully organized the resistance to the Japanese invasion and occupation. The Nationalists retained some hold in the southwest, but after Japan's surrender, attempts at a coalition government failed and the terrible civil war resumed. With the Communist victory in 1949, Chiang Kai-shek shifted his government to the island of Taiwan (Formosa), and Mao Zedong became the first chairman of the People's Republic of China.

Mao Zedong remained committed to two major issues: the condition of the peasants and the unification of China. He instituted land reform, which meant the destruction of the landlord class and the distribution of its land to poor and landless peasants. Following the Soviet model at first, he organized agriculture into collectives and nationalized industry; then turning to more revolutionary methods in the Great Leap Forward (1958–1959), he created the people's communes and mass campaigns. The Cultural Revolution, from 1966 to 1976, was an even more radical attempt to restore revolutionary enthusiasm as well as to reassert Mao's central role. Both schemes had disastrous results. After his death, his radical colleagues, including his wife, were arrested and collectivism abandoned. The one-party bureaucracy remained in place, sometimes encouraging but mostly suppressing a vital democratic movement.

With domestic disorder and foreign threats as the background for China's modern cultural life, nearly every modern writer has been concerned with national salvation. How, writers have asked, can one account for China's present humiliation in the light of its past greatness; how can China be saved? These overtly political questions have ramifications in issues of family structure, religion, sexuality, the meaning of life, issues that have become central to the literature. For many writers and intellectuals, China's long history, its achievements, and, above all, its Confucian heritage, have served as both a reproach and a barrier in the search for solutions to present problems.

As they have sought solutions, along with larger audiences, twentieth-century writers have increasingly worked in a colloquial idiom, shunning the stylized, classical, literary language of the past. The first great flowering of this vernacular literature was in the May Fourth movement. Taking its name from the May 4, 1919, student demonstrations in Tiananmen Square that denounced the Treaty of Versailles, the movement covered a period of great intellectual ferment that lasted until 1928. With many university-trained writers coming together, journals were founded; an assortment of ideologies, from Buddhism to Marxism, was expounded; and a mass readership began to form. Many of the writers attacked the Confucian legacy, seeing it as a barrier to resolving China's difficulties.

The history, mostly catastrophic, that followed the May Fourth movement has provided these and younger authors with their subjects: the brutal Japanese invasion and occupation and the equally brutal civil war; the hope of Communism and the bitter frustration of its promise; the calamitous events occurring between 1950 and 1976. History has been no kinder since the death of Mao, and the uneasy relations between the intellectuals and the government as well as the June 1989 massacre in Tiananmen Square have found their way into more contemporary works. The post–May Fourth writers have explored issues of authority, corruption, and survival. In a once-revolutionary society that seems depleted of idealism and purpose, these writers continue to address fundamental questions of justice, morality, and meaning, as writers and intellectuals always have throughout China's recorded history.

Taiwan

Taiwan, an island about a hundred miles off the China coast, was colonized by the Chinese in the seventeenth and eighteenth centuries and became a province of China in the mid-nineteenth century. In 1895, it was ceded to Japan and remained under Japanese rule until 1945. In 1949, as the Communists seized control of the Chinese mainland, over a million refugees, mostly remnants of the Nationalist government and army and their dependents, fled to Taiwan. The Nationalists have governed Taiwan to this day, although in recent years the local population, or Taiwanese, who far outnumber the mainlanders, have gained increasing control over the political system. In the last half century, Taiwan has been transformed from a sleepy, largely rural island into an advanced industrialized society, its prosperity derived from an ever-expanding export economy. The issue of its future relations with China has yet to be resolved.

Yosano Akiko
(1878–1942)
Japan

Yosano Akiko (Ho Shoko) was born in Osaka Prefecture in what is now the port city of Sakai, Japan, two months after the accidental death of a brother. Angered because the new baby was a girl, her father left home rather than celebrate the traditional seven-day commemoration of a birth. Her mother so feared his and his mother's anger that she sent her baby daughter away, seeing her occasionally at night when it was possible to slip out of the house without being noticed. Raised by her mother's sister until she was three years old, Yosano Akiko was able to return home only after the birth of another brother. While her intelligence eased her father's hostility, and he provided her with the best education that was available for women at that time in Osaka, she experienced the traditional restrictions imposed on women of the wealthy merchant class.

Her father's confectionery was frequented by the emperor's household. But as he preferred the arts to shopkeeping, and as her brother was sent to Tokyo to continue his studies, it was she who managed the confectionary, becoming the family's main provider. While she was allowed access to her father's library, she was accompanied by a servant or family member whenever she left the house during the day, and she was locked into her bedroom at night. Outmaneuvering her father's strategies, she joined a group of young poets and married one of its central figures, the poet Tekkan (Yosano Hiroshi). Together they established the "New Poet Society" and the journal *Myojo* (Morning Star), but eventually she supported him and their many children. To this end, she published novels, essays, and children's books along with poetry. As her fame grew, she became an acknowledged master.

Yosano Akiko has been credited with revolutionizing the *tanka.* She began publishing in 1896 and by 1901 had published her famous book *Midaregami* (Tangled Hair), a collection of 399 *tanka.* Not confining herself to such conventions as the beauty of nature and the moment of enlightenment, she focused on the psychologically dramatic moment. She spoke of the experience of women, of their loneliness and sexuality; she spoke of madness and of revolution. The title, *Midaregami,* embodies these points as the term evokes sexuality, sexual freedom, beauty, women's emancipation, and madness. A pacifist as well as a feminist, she protested against the Russo-Japanese War in a poem that was the first of its kind to be published, and she memorialized the socialists and anarchists executed in 1912.

Three modern tanka*

Purple butterflies
fly at night through my dreams.
Butterflies, tell me,
have you seen in my village
the falling flowers of the wisteria?

* * *

My heart is like the sun,
drowned in darkness,
soaked with rain,
beaten by the winds.

* * *

Last autumn
The three of us tossed acorns
To the scattering carp.
Now in the cold morning wind off the pond
He and I stand hand in chilling hand.

The Day When Mountains Move†

The day when mountains move has come.
Though I say this, nobody believes me.
Mountains sleep only for a little while
That once have been active in flames.
But even if you forgot it,
Just believe, people,
That all the women who slept
Now awake and move.

❋ Discussion and Writing

1. Comment on the implications of purple butterflies in dreams.
2. Describe the feelings captured in the three *tanka*.
3. Examine the impact of the image of the moving mountains.
4. Interpret the metaphor of the volcano with regard to women.

❋ Research and Comparison

Examine Yosano Akiko's life and literary works to explore her views and concerns about women's position in the first half of twentieth-century Japan.

Translated by Kenneth Rexroth and Ikuko Atsumi
†Translated by Kenneth Rexroth and Ikuko Atsumi*

Han Yongun
(1879–1944)
Korea

Han Yongun was born in the village of Hongsong, Korea, where he astonished the schoolmaster with his precocity. When he was 14, he entered a
traditional marriage, but after participating in the Tonghak (Eastern Learning) rebellion (1896), he joined a Buddhist monastery and in 1905
became a monk. This year marked the end of the Russo-Japanese War
(1904–1905), in which Russia and Japan fought for control of Manchuria
and Korea, and the beginning of Japanese colonial rule. Han Yongun
visited Japan in order to bring modern concepts to Korean Buddhism, but
at the same time, he rejected Japanese influence in the religion. Committed to reviving Korean Buddhism, he wrote essays and published a digest
in vernacular Korean. Equally dedicated to overthrowing the Japanese, he
helped draft and signed the "Declaration of Independence." The Independence movement (1919) was defeated, and Han Yongun was imprisoned
until 1922. When a translation of Rabindranath Tagore's *Gitanjali*
appeared, its themes, use of language, and tone inspired many poets,
including Han Yongun: Tagore himself represented the hope for liberation
from Japanese domination.

Considered one of the major modern poets, Han Yongun continued
writing essays and speaking about freedom until his death. He also wrote
novels and Buddhist studies. His volume of poetry *Nim ui ch'immuk* (The
Silence of Love, 1926), written at the Paektam Monastery, set forth a revitalized concept of *nim. Nim* (meaning love) evoked country, king, god,
Buddha, and the beloved—depending on the particular type of poetry:
love, allegorical, religious. Essentially Buddhist, *nim* informed Han's concern for Korea as well as his spiritual quest. *Nim* is inherent in the images
of the ferry boat, symbolizing the body, and the traveler, symbolizing the
self. These images represent the Buddhist experience, an experience that
can only be realized, not explained.

Ferryboat and Traveler*

I am the ferryboat

You, the traveler.

---

*Translated by David McCann

You tread on me with muddy feet.
I hold you and cross over the water.
Holding you, deep or shallow, or sudden rapids I cross over.

When you do not come I am waiting for you
under the wind, borne down by snowy rains, from night until day.

When you have crossed over the water you do not turn and look
    back at me but go on.
But I know that you are coming always.
Waiting for you day by day I grow older.

I am the ferryboat
you, the passenger.

On Reading Tagore's "The Gardener"*

O my friend, dearest friend, you who cause me to weep
    like the flowers blooming on my love's grave;
like the love encountered suddenly on a desert night
    with no trace of the rare bird, you gladden me.
You bring the fragrance of bones from an ancient grave mound,
    fragrance that pierces the heavens.

To weave a garland you gather up the fallen flowers and set it
    on another branch. Put aside the fallen flowers
    to become a song sung out in despair becoming hope.

Dear friend of mine, friend who cries out at shattered love:
Tears will not bring the fallen flowers to bloom once again on the branch;
So do not let tears wash over the fallen ones, but in the dust instead
    at the base of the flowering tree.

Friend, my dear friend!
No matter how sweet death's fragrance, the bones' white lips cannot be
    kissed
Do not fly the golden net of song around the grave, but set instead
    the blood-soaked flag upon it.
Spring wind will tell of how the dead earth moved at the touch of the
    poet's song.

---

*Translated by David McCann

I am so ashamed, my friend. Hearing your song
   I tremble in shame.
That is because I hear your song alone—I, who have parted
   from my love.

❋ Discussion and Writing

Ferryboat and Traveler
1. Describe the relationship between the ferryboat and the traveler.
2. What is the significance of the ferryboat's patient waiting? Why is it sure the traveler will come back?
3. Interpret the mystical bonding between the ferryboat and the traveler.

On Reading Tagore's "The Gardener"
1. What is the persona's overpowering emotions as he reads Tagore's *"The Gardener"*; what is the significance of the juxtaposition of love and the grave?
2. What does the persona urge his friend to do? What is the implication of setting the flag upon the grave?
3. Who is the persona's love in the last stanza: his dead comrade, his beloved, or his country?

❋ Research and Comparison

Compare the theme of nationalism in the poems of Han Yongun and Faiz Ahmed Faiz.

Lu Xun
(Lu Hsun, 1881–1936)
China

Lu Xun (Zhou Shuren) was born in Shaoxing in the rich south China province of Zhejiang. His family, members of the gentry, lost their wealth and prestige when his grandfather spent seven years in prison—indicted for accepting a bribe while presiding over civil service examinations. Lu Xun's father, a frustrated scholar who turned to opium and to drink, was bedridden much of the time, most likely from tuberculosis, which was not correctly identified. His mother's strength, on the other hand, caused Lu Xun to choose her name, Lu, as his pseudonym. A child of a gentry family, she was a progressive woman who taught herself to read and broke the old tradition of keeping her feet bound, a practice followed by upper-class Chinese women. Lu Xun never forgot the misdiagnosis of his father's illness, however, and after attending schools that offered sciences, he studied medicine in northern Honshu, Japan, since Japan offered Chinese students a doorway to Western thought and medical science. He lived a fairly isolated life there. Within four years he abandoned medicine to devote himself to literature, deciding that the best means to nurture the spirit was through literature.

Lu Xun worked on translations and articles before his return to China in 1909, when he concentrated on researching classical literature. Considered one of the major writers of the May Fourth movement, he also taught literature at various universities. In addition, his protests against injustice—whether the closing of the Beijing (Peking) Women's Normal University or Chiang Kai-shek's massacres of Communists—were legendary. Called by Mao Zedong "not only a great writer but a great thinker," Lu Xun became a mentor to countless young writers, such as Xiao Hong. He was one of the founding members of the League of Left-Wing Writers, but the factionalism, along with the restrictive criteria, tormented him, and he felt persecuted during his last years. When he died of tuberculosis, he left wry instructions to "get the funeral done quickly, bury me and get it over with."

Lu Xun's first story, "Kuangren riji" (Diary of a Madman), published in 1918 in the magazine *Xin qinqnian* (New Youth), was hailed in China as the first "modern" story. In his fiction, he experimented with methods of narration and the use of the vernacular, lyricism, and irony, and he depicted traditional culture and perspectives with a sardonic pen, creating keen psychological pictures. Deeply committed to the possibilities of literature, he wrote essays, poetry, and stories that illuminated his continuing concern with apathy and superstition, class attitudes and change. The ending of "My Old Home" muses on the nature of hope, expressing not only his thinking but that of the May Fourth movement as well.

*My Old Home**

Braving the bitter cold, I traveled more than seven hundred miles back to the old home I had left over twenty years before.

It was late winter. As we drew near my former home the day became overcast and a cold wind blew into the cabin of our boat, while all one could see through the chinks in our bamboo awning were a few desolate villages, void of any sign of life, scattered far and near under the somber yellow sky. I could not help feeling depressed.

Ah! Surely this was not the old home I had remembered for the past twenty years?

---

*Translated by Yang Hsien-yi and Gladys Yang

The old home I remembered was not in the least like this. My old home was much better. But if you asked me to recall its peculiar charm or describe its beauties, I had no clear impression, no words to describe it. And now it seemed this was all there was to it. Then I rationalized the matter to myself, saying: Home was always like this, and although it has not improved, still it is not so depressing as I imagine; it is only my mood that has changed, because I am coming back to the country this time with no illusions.

This time I had come with the sole object of saying good-bye. The old house our clan had lived in for so many years had already been sold to another family, and was to change hands before the end of the year. I had to hurry there before New Year's Day to say goodbye forever to the familiar old house, and to move my family to another place where I was working, far from my old home town.

At dawn on the second day I reached the gateway of my home. Broken stems of withered grass on the roof, trembling in the wind, made very clear the reason why this old house could not avoid changing hands. Several branches of our clan had probably already moved away, so it was unusually quiet. By the time I reached the house my mother was already at the door to welcome me, and my eight-year-old nephew, Hung-erh, rushed out after her.

Though mother was delighted, she was also trying to hide a certain feeling of sadness. She told me to sit down and rest and have some tea, letting the removal wait for the time being. Hung-erh, who had never seen me before, stood watching me at a distance.

But finally we had to talk about the removal. I said that rooms had already been rented elsewhere, and I had bought a little furniture; in addition it would be necessary to sell all the furniture in the house in order to buy more things. Mother agreed, saying that the luggage was nearly all packed, and about half the furniture that could not easily be moved had already been sold. Only it was difficult to get people to pay up.

"You must rest for a day or two, and call on our relatives, and then we can go," said mother.

"Yes."

"Then there is Jun-tu. Each time he comes here he always asks after you, and wants very much to see you again. I told him the probable date of your return home, and he may be coming any time."

At this point a strange picture suddenly flashed into my mind: a golden moon suspended in a deep blue sky and beneath it the seashore, planted as far as the eye could see with jade-green watermelons, while in their midst a boy of eleven or twelve, wearing a silver necklet and grasping a steel pitchfork in his hand, was thrusting with all his might at a *zha* which dodged the blow and escaped between his legs.

This boy was Jun-tu. When I first met him he was just over ten—that was thirty years ago, and at that time my father was still alive and the family well off, so I was really a spoilt child. That year it was our family's turn to take charge of a big ancestral sacrifice, which came round only once in thirty years, and hence was an important one. In the first month the ancestral images were presented and offerings made, and since the sacrificial vessels were very fine and there was such a crowd of worshippers, it was necessary to guard against theft. Our family had only one part-time labourer. (In our district we divide labourers into three classes: those who work all the year for one family are called full-timers; those who are hired by the day are called dailies; and those who farm their own land and only work for one family at New Year, during festivals or when rents are being collected are called part-timers.) And since there was so much to be done, he told my father that he would send for his son Jun-tu to look after the sacrificial vessels.

When my father gave his consent I was overjoyed, because I had long since heard of Jun-tu and knew that he was about my own age, born in the intercalary month,[1] and when his horoscope was told it was found that of the five elements that of earth was lacking, so his father called him Jun-tu (Intercalary Earth). He could set traps and catch small birds.

I looked forward every day to New Year, for New Year would bring Jun-tu. At last, when the end of the year came, one day mother told me that Jun-tu had come, and I flew to see him. He was standing in the kitchen. He had a round, crimson face and wore a small felt cap on his head and a gleaming silver necklet round his neck, showing that his father doted on him and, fearing he might die, had made a pledge with the gods and buddhas, using the necklet as a talisman. He was very shy, and I was the only person he was not afraid of. When there was no one else there, he would talk with me, so in a few hours we were fast friends.

I don't know what we talked of then, but I remember that Jun-tu was in high spirits, saying that since he had come to town he had seen many new things.

The next day I wanted him to catch birds.

"Can't be done," he said. "It's only possible after a heavy snowfall. On our sands, after it snows, I sweep clear a patch of ground, prop up a big threshing basket with a short stick, and scatter husks of grain beneath. When the birds come there to eat, I tug a string tied to the stick, and the birds are caught in the basket. There are all kinds: wild pheasants, woodcocks, wood-pigeons, 'blue-backs.'. . . "

Accordingly I looked forward very eagerly to snow.

"Just now it is too cold," said Jun-tu another time, "but you must come to our place in summer. In the daytime we'll go to the seashore to look for shells, there are green ones and red ones, besides 'scare-devil' shells and 'buddha's hands.' In the evening when dad and I go to see to the watermelons, you shall come too."

---

[1]The Chinese lunar calendar reckons 360 days to a year, and each month comprises 29 or 30 days, never 31. Hence every few years a 13th, or intercalary, month is inserted in the calendar.

"Is it to look out for thieves?"

"No. If passers-by are thirsty and pick a watermelon, folk down our way don't consider it as stealing. What we have to look out for are badgers, hedgehogs and *zha*. When under the moonlight you hear the crunching sound made by the *zha* when it bites the melons, then you take your pitchfork and creep stealthily over. . . ."

I had no idea then what this thing called *zha* was—and I am not much clearer now for that matter—but somehow I felt it was something like a small dog, and very fierce.

"Don't they bite people?"

"You have a pitchfork. You go across, and when you see it you strike. It's a very cunning creature and will rush towards you and get away between your legs. Its fur is as slippery as oil. . . ."

I had never known that all these strange things existed: at the seashore there were shells all colors of the rainbow; watermelons were exposed to such danger, yet all I had known of them before was that they were sold in the greengrocer's.

"On our shore, when the tide comes in, there are lots of jumping fish, each with two legs like a frog. . . ."

Jun-tu's mind was a treasure-house of such strange lore, all of it outside the ken of my former friends. They were ignorant of all these things and, while Jun-tu lived by the sea, they like me could see only the four corners of the sky above the high courtyard wall.

Unfortunately, a month after New Year Jun-tu had to go home. I burst into tears and he took refuge in the kitchen, crying and refusing to come out, until finally his father carried him off. Later he sent me by his father a packet of shells and a few very beautiful feathers, and I sent him presents once or twice, but we never saw each other again.

Now that my mother mentioned him, this childhood memory sprang into life like a flash of lightning, and I seemed to see my beautiful old home. So I answered:

"Fine! And he—how is he?"

"He? . . . He's not at all well off either," said mother. And then, looking out of the door: "Here come those people again. They say they want to buy our furniture; but actually they just want to see what they can pick up. I must go and watch them."

Mother stood up and went out. The voices of several women could be heard outside. I called Hung-erh to me and started talking to him, asking him whether he could write, and whether he would be glad to leave.

"Shall we be going by train?"

"Yes, we shall go by train."

"And boat?"

"We shall take a boat first."

"Oh! Like this! With such a long moustache!" A strange shrill voice suddenly rang out.

I looked up with a start, and saw a woman of about fifty with prominent cheekbones and thin lips. With her hands on her hips, not wearing a skirt but with her trousered legs apart, she stood in front of me just like the compass in a box of geometrical instruments.

I was flabbergasted.

"Don't you know me? Why, I have held you in my arms!"

I felt even more flabbergasted. Fortunately my mother came in just then and said:

"He has been away so long, you must excuse him for forgetting. You should remember," she said to me, "this is Mrs. Yang from across the road. . . . She has a beancurd shop."

Then, to be sure, I remembered. When I was a child there was a Mrs. Yang who used to sit nearly all day long in the beancurd shop across the road, and everybody used to call her Beancurd Beauty. She used to powder herself, and her cheekbones were not so prominent then nor her lips so thin; moreover she remained seated all the time, so that I had never noticed this resemblance to a compass. In those days people said that, thanks to her, that beancurd shop did very good business. But, probably on account of my age, she had made no impression on me, so that later I forgot her entirely. However, the Compass was extremely indignant and looked at me most contemptuously, just as one might look at a Frenchman who had never heard of Napoleon or an American who had never heard of Washington, and smiling sarcastically she said:

"You had forgotten? Naturally I am beneath your notice. . . ."

"Certainly not . . . I . . . " I answered nervously, getting to my feet.

"Then you listen to me, Master Hsun. You have grown rich, and they are too heavy to move, so you can't possibly want these old pieces of furniture any more. You had better let me take them away. Poor people like us can do with them."

"I haven't grown rich. I must sell these in order to buy. . . ."

"Oh, come now, you have been made the intendant of a circuit, how can you still say you're not rich? You have three concubines now, and wherever you go out it is in a big sedanchair with eight bearers. Do you still say you're not rich? Hah! You can't hide anything from me."

Knowing there was nothing I could say, I remained silent.

"Come now, really, the more money people have the more miserly they get, and the more miserly they are the more money they get . . ." remarked the Compass, turning indignantly away and walking slowly off, casually picking up a pair of mother's gloves and stuffing them into her pocket as she went out.

After this a number of relatives in the neighborhood came to call. In the intervals between entertaining them I did some packing, and so three or four days passed.

One very cold afternoon, I sat drinking tea after lunch when I was aware of someone coming in, and turned my head to see who it was. At the first glance I gave an involuntary start, hastily stood up and went over to welcome him.

The newcomer was Jun-tu. But although I knew at a glance that this was Jun-tu, it was not the Jun-tu I remembered. He had grown to twice his former size. His round face, once crimson, had become sallow and acquired deep lines and wrinkles; his eyes too had become like his father's, the rims swollen and red, a feature common to most peasants who work by the sea and are exposed all day to the wind from the ocean. He wore a shabby felt cap and just one very thin padded jacket, with the result that he was shivering from head to foot. He carried a paper package and a long pipe, nor was his hand the plump red hand I remembered, but coarse and clumsy and chapped, like the bark of a pine tree.

Delighted as I was, I did not know how to express myself, and could only say:

"Oh! Jun-tu—so it's you?. . . "

After this there were so many things I wanted to talk about, they should have poured out like a string of beads: woodcocks, jumping fish, shells, *zha*. . . . But I was tonguetied, unable to put all I was thinking into words.

He stood there, mixed joy and sadness showing on his face. His lips moved, but not a sound did he utter. Finally, assuming a respectful attitude, he said clearly:

"Master! . . . "

I felt a shiver run through me; for I knew then what a lamentably thick wall had grown up between us. Yet I could not say anything.

He turned his head to call:

"Shui-sheng, bow to the master." Then he pulled forward a boy who had been hiding behind his back, and this was just the Jun-tu of twenty years before, only a little paler and thinner, and he had no silver necklet.

"This is my fifth," he said. "He's not used to company, so he's shy and awkward."

Mother came downstairs with Hung-erh, probably after hearing our voices.

"I got your letter some time ago, madam," said Jun-tu. "I was really so pleased to know the master was coming back. . . ."

"Now, why are you so polite? Weren't you playmates together in the past?" said mother gaily. "You had better still call him Brother Hsun as before."

"Oh, you are really too. . . . What bad manners that would be. I was a child then and didn't understand." As he was speaking Jun-tu motioned Shui-sheng to come and bow, but the child was shy, and stood stock-still behind his father.

"So he is Shui-sheng? Your fifth?" asked mother. "We are all strangers, you can't blame him for feeling shy. Hung-erh had better take him out to play."

When Hung-erh heard this he went over to Shui-sheng, and Shui-sheng went out with him, entirely at his ease. Mother asked Jun-tu to sit down, and after a little hesitation he did so; then leaning his long pipe against the table he handed over the paper package, saying:

"In winter there is nothing worth bringing; but these few beans we dried ourselves, if you will excuse the liberty, sir."

When I asked him how things were with him, he just shook his head.

"In a very bad way. Even my sixth can do a little work, but still we haven't enough to eat . . . and then there is no security . . . all sorts of people want money, there is no fixed rule . . . and the harvests are bad. You grow things, and when you take them to sell you always have to pay several taxes and lose money, while if you don't try to sell, the things may go bad. . . ."

He kept shaking his head; yet, although his face was lined with wrinkles, not one of them moved, just as if he were a stone statue. No doubt he felt intensely bitter, but could not express himself. After a pause he took up his pipe and began to smoke in silence.

From her chat with him, mother learned that he was busy at home and had to go back the next day; and since he had had no lunch, she told him to go to the kitchen and fry some rice for himself.

After he had gone out, mother and I both shook our heads over his hard life: many children, famines, taxes, soldiers, bandits, officials and landed gentry, all had squeezed him as dry as a mummy. Mother said that we should offer him all the things we were not going to take away, letting him choose for himself.

That afternoon he picked out a number of things: two long tables, four chairs, an incense burner and candlesticks, and one balance. He also asked for all the ashes from the stove (in our parts we cook over straw, and the ashes can be used to fertilize sandy soil), saying that when we left he would come to take them away by boat.

That night we talked again, but not of anything serious; and the next morning he went away with Shui-sheng.

After another nine days it was time for us to leave. Jun-tu came in the morning. Shui-sheng did not come with him—he had just brought a little girl of five to watch the boat. We were very busy all day, and had no time to talk. We also had quite a number of visitors, some to see us off, some to fetch things, and some to do both. It was nearly evening when we left by boat, and by that time everything in the house, however old or shabby, large or small, fine or coarse, had been cleared away.

As we set off, in the dusk, the green mountains on either side of the river became deep blue, receding towards the stern of the boat.

Hung-erh and I, leaning against the cabin window, were looking out together at the indistinct scene outside, when suddenly he asked:

"Uncle, when shall we go back?"

"Go back? Do you mean that before you've left you want to go back?"

"Well, Shui-sheng has invited me to his home. . . ." He opened wide his black eyes in anxious thought.

Mother and I both felt rather sad, and so Jun-tu's name came up again. Mother said that ever since our family started packing up, Mrs. Yang from the beancurd shop had come over every day, and the day before in the ash-heap she had unearthed a dozen bowls and plates, which after some discussion she insisted must have been buried there by Jun-tu, so that when he came to remove the ashes he could take them home at the same time. After making this discovery Mrs. Yang was very pleased with herself, and flew off taking the dog-teaser with her. (The dog-teaser is used by poultry keepers in our parts. It is a wooden cage inside which food is put, so that hens can stretch their necks in to eat but dogs can only look on furiously.) And it was a marvel, considering the size of her feet, how fast she could run.

I was leaving the old house farther and farther behind, while the hills and rivers of my old home were also receding gradually ever farther in the distance. But I felt no regret. I only felt that all round me was an invisible high wall, cutting me off from my fellows, and this depressed me thoroughly. The vision of that small hero with the silver necklet among the watermelons had formerly been as clear as day, but now it suddenly blurred, adding to my depression.

Mother and Hung-erh fell asleep.

I lay down, listening to the water rippling beneath the boat, and knew that I was going my way. I thought: although there is such a barrier between Jun-tu and myself, the children still have much in common, for wasn't Hung-erh thinking of Shui-sheng just now? I hope they will not be like us, that they will not allow a barrier to grow up between them. But again I would not like them, because they want to be akin, all to have a treadmill existence like mine, nor to suffer like Jun-tu until they become stupefied, nor yet, like others, to devote all their energies to dissipation. They should have a new life, a life we have never experienced.

The access of hope made me suddenly afraid. When Jun-tu asked for the incense burner and candlesticks I had laughed up my sleeve at him, to think that he still worshipped idols and could not put them out of his mind. Yet what I now called hope was no more than an idol I had created myself. The only difference was that what he desired was close at hand, while what I desired was less easily realized.

As I dozed, a stretch of jade-green seashore spread itself before my eyes, and above a round golden moon hung in a deep blue sky. I thought: hope cannot be said to exist, nor can it be said not to exist. It is just like roads across the earth. For actually the earth had no roads to begin with, but when many men pass one way, a road is made.

❋ Discussion and Writing

1. What precipitates the narrator's visit to his village; what are the narrator's feelings as he approaches his old home; what images indicate the narrator's distance from his past?
2. Contrast Jun-tu as a young boy and a grown-up man. Analyze the reasons for his transformation. Explain how the narrator has changed over the years.
3. Comment on the role of the narrator's mother in the narrative.
4. Examine the importance of the two young children, Hung-erh and Shui-sheng. What is the significance of the last paragraph?
5. Analyze the depiction of the contrasts: rural and urban; rich and poor; young and old. Comment on the correlation of the past, present, and future.

❋ Research and Comparison

Examine Lu Xun's "Diary of a Madman," focusing on the major social concerns depicted in it. Also comment on Lu Xun's influence on twentieth-century Chinese fiction.

Tanizaki Junichiro
(1886–1972)
Japan

Tanizaki Junichiro was born in the low-lying Tokyo district of Nihombashi, the old trade area near Tokyo Bay in Japan. His mother—a beautiful, strong-willed, sensuous, yet sometimes reserved woman—was a model of complexity. She passed this image of a woman along with her love of *kabuki* theater on to her son. His father's repeated business failures left a different legacy: because of the family's economic difficulties, Tanazaki had to help with household chores when he was a child and work as a houseboy while he was going to school. He despised the work. During his years at Tokyo Imperial University, where he studied Japanese classical literature and continued reading avant-garde and Western works, financial constraints forced him to live in his family's house. His sister suffered from tuberculosis, and the acrimonious and apprehensive environment created by her condition contributed to his experiencing a period of neurasthenia. During his student days at the university, he collaborated with a group of friends in the publication of a literary journal, *New Thought.* The journal became associated with the "neoromantic" school. Tanizaki published his early stories, including "Tattoo," in *New Thought* and was quickly identified as one of the leaders of "neoromanticism."

His move to Kyoto (the ancient capital of Japan) after the 1923 earthquake that ravaged Tokyo was a symbolic migration. In a sense, Kyoto represented his pursuit of tradition, of the Japanese past, while Tokyo represented his interest in Western ideas and modernization. Whether he was concerned with the old or new ways or with the conflict arising from the Western influence in Japan, a deep, frequently dark and frequently erotic, psychological strain runs through his work, as does a mordant sense of humor. And from the very beginning, the figure of women recur as prominent complex characters.

The Tattooer*

It was an age when men honored the noble virtue of frivolity, when life was not such a harsh struggle as it is today. It was a leisurely age, an age when professional wits could make an excellent livelihood by keeping rich or wellborn young gentlemen in a cloudless good humor and seeing to it that the laughter of Court ladies and geisha was never stilled. In the illustrated romantic novels of the day, in the Kabuki theater, where rough masculine heroes like Sadakuro and Jiraiya were transformed into women—everywhere beauty and strength were one. People did all they could to beautify themselves, some even having pigments injected into their precious skins. Gaudy patterns of line and color danced over men's bodies.

Visitors to the pleasure quarters of Edo [Tokyo] preferred to hire palanquin bearers who were splendidly tattooed; courtesans of the Yoshiwara and the Tatsumi quarter fell in love with tattooed men. Among those so adorned were not only gamblers, firemen, and the like, but members of the merchant class and even samurai. Exhibitions were held from time to time; and the participants, stripped to show off their filigreed bodies, would pat themselves proudly, boast of their own novel designs, and criticize each other's merits.

There was an exceptionally skillful young tattooer named Seikichi. He was praised on all sides as a master the equal of Charibun or Yatsuhei, and the skins of dozens of men had been offered as the silk for his brush. Much of the work admired at the tattoo exhibitions was his. Others might be more

Translated by Howard Hibbet

noted for their shading, or their use of cinnabar, but Seikichi was famous for the unrivaled boldness and sensual charm of his art.

Seikichi had formerly earned his living as an ukiyoye[1] painter of the school of Toyokuni and Kunisada, a background which, in spite of his decline to the status of a tattooer, was evident from his artistic conscience and sensitivity. No one whose skin or whose physique failed to interest him could buy his services. The clients he did accept had to leave the design and cost entirely to his discretion—and to endure for one or even two months the excruciating pain of his needles.

Deep in his heart the young tattooer concealed a secret pleasure, and a secret desire. His pleasure lay in the agony men felt as he drove his needles into them, torturing their swollen, blood-red flesh; and the louder they groaned, the keener was Seikichi's strange delight. Shading and vermilioning—these are said to be especially painful—were the techniques he most enjoyed.

When a man had been pricked five or six hundred times in the course of an average day's treatment and had then soaked himself in a hot bath to bring out the colors, he would collapse at Seikichi's feet half dead. But Seikichi would look down at him coolly. "I dare say that hurts," he would remark with an air of satisfaction.

Whenever a spineless man howled in torment or clenched his teeth and twisted his mouth as if he were dying, Seikichi told him: "Don't act like a child. Pull yourself together—you have hardly begun to feel my needles!" And he would go on tattooing, as unperturbed as ever, with an occasional sidelong glance at the man's tearful face.

But sometimes a man of immense fortitude set his jaw and bore up stoically, not even allowing himself to frown. Then Seikichi would smile and say: "Ah, you are a stubborn one! But wait. Soon your body will begin to throb with pain. I doubt if you will be able to stand it. . . ."

For a long time Seikichi had cherished the desire to create a masterpiece on the skin of a beautiful woman. Such a woman had to meet various qualifications of character as well as appearance. A lovely face and a fine body were not enough to satisfy him. Though he inspected all the reigning beauties of the Edo gay quarters he found none who met his exacting demands. Several years had passed without success, and yet the face and figure of the perfect woman continued to obsess his thoughts. He refused to abandon hope.

One summer evening during the fourth year of his search Seikichi happened to be passing the Hirasei Restaurant in the Fukagawa district of Edo, not far from his own house, when he noticed a woman's bare milk-white foot peeping out beneath the curtains of a departing palanquin. To his sharp

---

[1]Genre painting depicting the "floating world" or transitory world. [eds.]

eye, a human foot was as expressive as a face. This one was sheer perfection. Exquisitely chiseled toes, nails like the iridescent shells along the shore at Enoshima, a pearl-like rounded heel, skin so lustrous that it seemed bathed in the limpid waters of a mountain spring—this, indeed, was a foot to be nourished by men's blood, a foot to trample on their bodies. Surely this was the foot of the unique woman who had so long eluded him. Eager to catch a glimpse of her face, Seikichi began to follow the palanquin. But after pursuing it down several lanes and alleys he lost sight of it altogether.

Seikichi's long-held desire turned into passionate love. One morning late the next spring he was standing on the bamboo-floored veranda of his home in Fukagawa, gazing at a pot of *omoto* lilies, when he heard someone at the garden gate. Around the corner of the inner fence appeared a young girl. She had come on an errand for a friend of his, a geisha of the nearby Tatsumi quarter.

"My mistress asked me to deliver this cloak, and she wondered if you would be so good as to decorate its lining," the girl said. She untied a saffron-colored cloth parcel and took out a woman's silk cloak (wrapped in a sheet of thick paper bearing a portrait of the actor Tojaku) and a letter.

The letter repeated his friend's request and went on to say that its bearer would soon begin a career as a geisha under her protection. She hoped that, while not forgetting old ties, he would also extend his patronage to this girl.

"I thought I had never seen you before," said Seikichi, scrutinizing her intently. She seemed only fifteen or sixteen, but her face had a strangely ripe beauty, a look of experience, as if she had already spent years in the gay quarter and had fascinated innumerable men. Her beauty mirrored the dreams of the generations of glamorous men and women who had lived and died in this vast capital, where the nation's sins and wealth were concentrated.

Seikichi had her sit on the veranda, and he studied her delicate feet, which were bare except for elegant straw sandals. "You left the Hirasei by palanquin one night last July, did you not?" he inquired.

"I suppose so," she replied, smiling at the odd question. "My father was still alive then, and he often took me there."

"I have waited five years for you. This is the first time I have seen your face, but I remember your foot. . . . Come in for a moment, I have something to show you."

She had risen to leave, but he took her by the hand and led her upstairs to his studio overlooking the broad river. Then he brought out two picture scrolls and unrolled one of them before her.

It was a painting of a Chinese princess, the favorite of the cruel Emperor Chou of the Shang Dynasty. She was leaning on a balustrade in a languorous pose, the long skirt of her figured brocade robe trailing halfway down a flight of stairs, her slender body barely able to support the weight of her gold crown studded with coral and lapis lazuli. In her right hand she held a large wine cup, tilting it to her lips as she gazed down at a man who was about to be tortured in the garden below. He was chained hand and foot to a hollow copper pillar in which a fire would be lighted. Both the princess and her victim—his head bowed before her, his eyes closed, ready to meet his fate—were portrayed with terrifying vividness.

As the girl stared at this bizarre picture her lips trembled and her eyes began to sparkle. Gradually her face took on a curious resemblance to that of the princess. In the picture she discovered her secret self.

"Your own feelings are revealed here," Seikichi told her with pleasure as he watched her face.

"Why are you showing me this horrible thing?" the girl asked, looking up at him. She had turned pale.

"The woman is yourself. Her blood flows in your veins." Then he spread out the other scroll.

This was a painting called "The Victims." In the middle of it a young woman stood leaning against the trunk of a cherry tree: she was gloating over a heap of men's corpses lying at her feet. Little birds fluttered about her, singing in triumph; her eyes radiated pride and joy. Was it a battlefield or a garden in spring? In this picture the girl felt that she had found something long hidden in the darkness of her own heart.

"This painting shows your future," Seikichi said, pointing to the woman under the cherry tree—the very image of the young girl. "All these men will ruin their lives for you."

"Please, I beg of you to put it away!" She turned her back as if to escape its tantalizing lure and prostrated herself before him, trembling. At last she spoke again. "Yes, I admit that you are right about me—I *am* like that woman. . . . So please, please take it away."

"Don't talk like a coward," Seikichi told her, with his malicious smile. "Look at it more closely. You won't be squeamish long."

But the girl refused to lift her head. Still prostrate, her face buried in her sleeves, she repeated over and over that she was afraid and wanted to leave.

"No, you must stay—I will make you a real beauty," he said, moving closer to her. Under his kimono was a vial of anesthetic which he had obtained some time ago from a Dutch physician.

The morning sun glittered on the river, setting the eight-mat studio ablaze with light. Rays reflected from the water sketched rippling golden waves on the paper sliding screens and on the face of the girl, who was fast asleep. Seikichi had closed the doors and taken up his tattooing instruments, but for a while he only sat there entranced, savoring to the full her uncanny beauty. He thought that he would never tire of contemplating her serene masklike face. Just as the ancient Egyptians had embellished their magnificent land with pyramids and sphinxes, he was about to embellish the pure skin of this girl.

Presently he raised the brush which was gripped between the thumb and last two fingers of his left hand, applied its tip to the girl's back, and, with the needle which he held in his right hand, began pricking out a design. He felt his spirit dissolve into the charcoal-black ink that stained her skin. Each drop of Ryukyu cinnabar that he mixed with alcohol and thrust in was a drop of his lifeblood. He saw in his pigments the hues of his own passions.

Soon it was afternoon, and then the tranquil spring day drew toward its close. But Seikichi never paused in his work, nor was the girl's sleep broken. When a servant came from the geisha house to inquire about her, Seikichi turned him away, saying that she had left long ago. And hours later, when the moon hung over the mansion across the river, bathing the houses along the bank in a dreamlike radiance, the tattoo was not yet half done. Seikichi worked on by candlelight.

Even to insert a single drop of color was no easy task. At every thrust of his needle Seikichi gave a heavy sigh and felt as if he had stabbed his own heart. Little by little the tattoo marks began to take on the form of a huge black-widow spider; and by the time the night sky was paling into dawn this weird, malevolent creature had stretched its eight legs to embrace the whole of the girl's back.

In the full light of the spring dawn boats were being rowed up and down the river, their oars creaking in the morning quiet; roof tiles glistened in the sun, and the haze began to thin out over white sails swelling in the early breeze. Finally Seikichi put down his brush and looked at the tattooed spider. This work of art had been the supreme effort of his life. Now that he had finished it his heart was drained of emotion.

The two figures remained still for some time. Then Seikichi's low, hoarse voice echoed quaveringly from the walls of the room:

"To make you truly beautiful I have poured my soul into this tattoo. To-day there is no woman in Japan to compare with you. Your old fears are gone. All men will be your victims."

As if in response to these words a faint moan came from the girl's lips. Slowly she began to recover her senses. With each shuddering breath, the spider's legs stirred as if they were alive.

"You must be suffering. The spider has you in its clutches."

At this she opened her eyes slightly, in a dull stare. Her gaze steadily brightened, as the moon brightens in the evening, until it shone dazzlingly into his face.

"Let me see the tattoo," she said, speaking as if in a dream but with an edge of authority to her voice. "Giving me your soul must have made me very beautiful."

"First you must bathe to bring out the colors," whispered Seikichi compassionately. "I am afraid it will hurt, but be brave a little longer."

"I can bear anything for the sake of beauty." Despite the pain that was coursing through her body, she smiled.

"How the water stings! . . . Leave me alone—wait in the other room! I hate to have a man see me suffer like this!"

As she left the tub, too weak to dry herself, the girl pushed aside the sympathetic hand Seikichi offered her, and sank to the floor in agony, moaning as if in a nightmare. Her disheveled hair hung over her face in a wild tangle. The white soles of her feet were reflected in the mirror behind her.

Seikichi was amazed at the change that had come over the timid, yielding girl of yesterday, but he did as he was told and went to wait in his studio. About an hour later she came back, carefully dressed, her damp, sleekly combed hair hanging down over her shoulders. Leaning on the veranda rail, she looked up into the faintly hazy sky. Her eyes were brilliant; there was not a trace of pain in them.

"I wish to give you these pictures too," said Seikichi, placing the scrolls before her. "Take them and go."

"All my old fears have been swept away—and you are my first victim!" She darted a glance at him as bright as a sword. A song of triumph was ringing in her ears.

"Let me see your tattoo once more," Seikichi begged.

Silently the girl nodded and slipped the kimono off her shoulders. Just then her resplendently tattooed back caught a ray of sunlight and the spider was wreathed in flames.

❁ Discussion and Writing

1. Examine the opening paragraph: what is implied by "beauty and strength were one" in that age of leisure; describe the various phases of Japanese culture that encouraged the creation of beauty.
2. Analyze Seikichi as a tattooer: what is the source of his pleasure in tattooing men; what is the significance of his power as an artist?
3. Explain his ultimate desire to tattoo a woman: define the nature of his obsession and his notion of a perfect woman. Explain his conduct when he finds woman.
4. How does the woman Seikichi wants to tattoo relate to the two women in the picture scrolls? Comment on the influence of the picture scrolls on the woman.
5. Analyze Seikichi's passion that is manifested in the figure of the black-widow spider: comment on its influence on the girl; what are the implications of the ending.
6. Analyze the fusion of the concepts of: present, past, and future; pleasure and pain; beauty and ugliness; fantasy and reality; victim and victor.

❁ Research and Comparison

Examine Tanizaki's place in twentieth-century Japanese literature. Analyze any one of his major works.

Interdisciplinary Discussion Question: Research the association among the various art forms—music, painting, dance, poetry, drama—in the Japanese tradition.

Akutagawa Ryunosuke
(1892–1927)
Japan

Akutagawa Ryunosuke was born in Tokyo, Japan, where his father owned a modest business. Called Ryunosuke (dragon-child) because of the time of his birth, he came to be haunted by the significance of his name. That his parents sent him to a wet-nurse because their ages were considered unlucky also tormented him. Most disturbing of all was his mother's mental breakdown when he was less than a year old, compounded by her early death when he was about ten. His mother's brother raised him from the time of her breakdown, giving him the family name, Akutagawa, two years after her death. Akutagawa grew up obsessed with the fear of insanity and the idea of displacement. He was raised (and spent his short life) in Tokyo in the midst of a family that retained the ethics of its feudal past. Although the hypocrisies and class pretensions annoyed, even offended, him, the family's old-fashioned interest in the arts accommodated his own aesthetic sensibility and passion for reading. This interest offered him an early acquaintance with classical Japanese literature. By the time he was ten, he was learning Chinese and English and within a few years was not only reading Meiji and Edo writers, but Chinese classics and English translations of European literature as well. He entered Tokyo Imperial University as an English major, wrote his thesis on the British poet William Morris, and taught English for a few years. In the meantime, Akutagawa had begun publishing translations and his own stories.

During his years at the university, he and a group of friends created a new literary journal in which he published his first story, a work that came to the attention of one of the great novelists, Natsume Soseki, who became his mentor. "Rashomon" was published in another university magazine in 1915, and it established his reputation among his fellow writers. Quickly recognized as a leader in the "neorealist" school, he rejected the naturalists by turning away from autobiographical writing and concentrating on style. While he frequently turned to traditional material or medieval feudal tales as a frame, he always experimented with methods of narration and informed his stories with psychological insight. He sought the appropriate mode to project simultaneously a sense of complete objectivity and the machinations of the psyche, always ambiguous and often ridiculous. His was a fundamentally ironic voice as he raised questions regarding destiny and the nature of reality. (Kurosawa Akira captured these qualities in his film *Rashomon,* based on Akutagawa's "Rashomon" [the Rasho gate built in 789] and "In a Grove.") Given to self-doubt, haunted by the phantoms of his childhood, and dreading the possibility of his own insanity, he took his own life when he was 35.

In a Grove*

The Testimony of a Woodcutter Questioned by a High Police Commissioner

Yes, sir. Certainly, it was I who found the body. This morning, as usual, I went to cut my daily quota of cedars, when I found the body in a grove in a hollow in the mountains. The exact location? About 150 meters off the Ya-mashina stage road. It's an out-of-the-way grove of bamboo and cedars.

The body was lying flat on its back dressed in a bluish silk kimono and a wrinkled head-dress of the Kyoto style. A single sword-stroke had pierced the breast. The fallen bamboo blades around it were stained with bloody blossoms. No, the blood was no longer running. The wound had dried up, I believe. And also, a gad-fly was stuck fast there, hardly noticing my foot-steps.

You ask me if I saw a sword or any such thing?

No, nothing, sir. I found only a rope at the root of a cedar near by. And . . . well, in addition to a rope, I found a comb. That was all. Apparently he must have made a battle of it before he was murdered, because the grass and fallen bamboo blades had been trampled down all around.

"A horse was near by?"

No, sir. It's hard enough for a man to enter, let alone a horse.

The Testimony of a Traveling Buddhist Priest Questioned by a High Police Commissioner

The time? Certainly, it was about noon yesterday, sir. The unfortunate man was on the road from Sekiyama to Yamashina. He was walking toward Sekiyama with a woman accompanying him on horseback, who I have since learned was his wife. A scarf hanging from her head hid her face from view. All I saw was the color of her clothes, a lilac-colored suit. Her horse was a sorrel with a fine mane. The lady's height? Oh, about four feet five inches. Since I am a Buddhist priest, I took little notice about her details. Well, the man was armed with a sword as well as a bow and arrows. And I remember that he carried some twenty odd arrows in his quiver.

Little did I expect that he would meet such a fate. Truly human life is as evanescent as the morning dew or a flash of lightning. My words are inade-quate to express my sympathy for him.

---

*Translated by Kojima Takahashi

The Testimony of a Policeman Questioned
by a High Police Commissioner

The man that I arrested? He is a notorious brigand called Tajomaru. When I arrested him, he had fallen off his horse. He was groaning on the bridge at Awataguchi. The time? It was in the early hours of last night. For the record, I might say that the other day I tried to arrest him, but unfortunately he escaped. He was wearing a dark blue silk kimono and a large plain sword. And, as you see, he got a bow and arrows somewhere. You say that this bow and these arrows look like the ones owned by the dead man? Then Tajomaru must be the murderer. The bow wound with leather strips, the black lacquered quiver, the seventeen arrows with hawk feathers—these were all in his possession; I believe. Yes sir, the horse is, as you say, a sorrel with a fine mane. A little beyond the stone bridge I found the horse grazing by the roadside, with his long rein dangling. Surely there is some providence in his having been thrown by the horse.

Of all the robbers prowling around Kyoto, this Tajomaru has given the most grief to the women in town. Last autumn a wife who came to the mountain back of the Pindora of the Toribe Temple, presumably to pay a visit, was murdered, along with a girl. It has been suspected that it was his doing. If this criminal murdered the man, you cannot tell what he may have done with the man's wife. May it please your honor to look into this problem as well.

The Testimony of an Old Woman Questioned
by a High Police Commissioner

Yes, sir, that corpse is the man who married my daughter. He does not come from Kyoto. He was a samurai[1] in the town of Kokufu in the province of Wakasa. His name was Kanazawa no Takehiko, and his age was twenty-six. He was of a gentle disposition, so I am sure he did nothing to provoke the anger of others.

My daughter? Her name is Masago, and her age is nineteen. She is a spirited, fun-loving girl, but I am sure she has never known any man except Takehiko. She has a small oval, dark-complected face with a mole at the corner of her left eye.

Yesterday Takehiko left for Wakasa with my daughter. What bad luck it is that things should have come to such a sad end! What has become of my daughter? I am resigned to giving up my son-in-law as lost, but the fate of my daughter worries me sick. For heaven's sake leave no stone unturned to find her. I hate that robber Tajomaru, or whatever his name is. Not only my son-in-law, but my daughter. . . . (Her later words were drowned in tears.)

---

[1]Of the warrior aristocracy.

Tajomaru's Confession

I killed him, but not her. Where's she gone? I can't tell. Oh, wait a minute. No torture can make me confess what I don't know. Now things have come to such a head, I won't keep anything from you.

Yesterday a little past noon I met that couple. Just then a puff of wind blew, and raised her hanging scarf, so that I caught a glimpse of her face. Instantly it was again covered from my view. That may have been one reason; she looked like a Bodhisattva.[2] At that moment I made up my mind to capture her even if I had to kill her man.

Why? To me killing isn't a matter of such great consequence as you might think. When a woman is captured, her man has to be killed anyway. In killing, I use the sword I wear at my side. Am I the only one who kills people? You, you don't use your swords. You kill people with your power, with your money. Sometimes you kill them on the pretext of working for their good. It's true they don't bleed. They are in the best of health, but all the same you've killed them. It's hard to say who is a greater sinner, you or me. (An ironical smile.)

But it would be good if I could capture a woman without killing her man. So, I made up my mind to capture her, and do my best not to kill him. But it's out of the question on the Yamashina stage road. So I managed to lure the couple into the mountains.

It was quite easy. I became their traveling companion, and I told them there was an old mound in the mountain over there, and that I had dug it open and found many mirrors and swords. I went on to tell them I'd buried the things in a grove behind the mountain, and that I'd like to sell them at a low price to anyone who would care to have them. Then . . . you see, isn't greed terrible? He was beginning to be moved by my talk before he knew it. In less than half an hour they were driving their horse toward the mountain with me.

When he came in front of the grove, I told them that the treasures were buried in it, and I asked them to come and see. The man had no objection— he was blinded by greed. The woman said she would wait on horseback. It was natural for her to say so, at the sight of a thick grove. To tell you the truth, my plan worked just as I wished, so I went into the grove with him, leaving her behind alone.

The grove is only bamboo for some distance. About fifty yards ahead there's a rather open clump of cedars. It was a convenient spot for my purpose. Pushing my way through the grove I told him a plausible lie that the treasures were buried under the cedars. When I told him this, he pushed his laborious way toward the slender cedar visible through the grove. After a while the bamboo thinned out, and we came to where a number of cedars

---

[2] A compassionate being concerned for the spiritual salvation of others.

grew in a row. As soon as we got there, I seized him from behind. Because he was a trained, sword-bearing warrior, he was quite strong, but he was taken by surprise, so there was no help for him. I soon tied him up to the root of a cedar. Where did I get a rope? Thank heaven, being a robber, I had a rope with me, since I might have to scale a wall at any moment. Of course it was easy to stop him from calling out by gagging his mouth with fallen bamboo leaves.

When I disposed of him, I went to his woman and asked her to come and see him, because he seemed to have been suddenly taken sick. It's needless to say that this plan also worked well. The woman, her sedge hat off, came into the depths of the grove, where I led her by the hand. The instant she caught sight of her husband, she drew a small sword. I've never seen a woman of such violent temper. If I'd been off guard, I'd have got a thrust in my side. I dodged, but she kept on slashing at me. She might have wounded me deeply or killed me. But I'm Tajomaru. I managed to strike down her small sword without drawing my own. The most spirited woman is defenseless without a weapon. At least I could satisfy my desire for her without taking her husband's life.

Yes, . . . without taking his life. I had no wish to kill him. I was about to run away from the grove, leaving the woman behind in tears, when she frantically clung to my arm. In broken fragments of words, she asked that either her husband or I die. She said it was more trying than death to have her shame known to two men. She gasped out that she wanted to be the wife of whichever survived. Then a furious desire to kill him seized me. (Gloomy excitement.)

Telling you in this way, no doubt I seem a crueler man than you. But that's because you didn't see her face. Especially her burning eyes at that moment. As I saw her eye to eye, I wanted to make her my wife even if I were to be struck by lightning. I wanted to make her my wife . . . this single desire filled my mind. This was not only lust, as you might think. At that time if I'd had no other desire than lust, I'd surely not have minded knocking her down and running away. Then I wouldn't have stained my sword with his blood. But the moment I gazed at her face in the dark grove, I decided not to leave there without killing him.

But I didn't like to resort to unfair means to kill him. I untied him and told him to cross swords with me. (The rope that was found at the root of the cedar is the rope I dropped at the time.) Furious with anger, he drew his thick sword. And quick as thought, he sprang at me ferociously, without speaking a word. I needn't tell you how our fight turned out. The twenty-third stroke . . . please remember this. I'm impressed with this fact still. Nobody under the sun has ever clashed swords with me twenty strokes. (A cheerful smile.)

When he fell, I turned toward her, lowering my blood-stained sword. But to my great astonishment she was gone. I wondered to where she had run away. I looked for her in the clump of cedars, I listened, but heard only a groaning sound in the throat of the dying man.

As soon as we started to cross swords, she may have run away through the grove to call for help. When I thought of that, I decided it was a matter of life and death to me. So, robbing him of his sword, and bow and arrows, I ran out to the mountain road. There I found her horse still grazing quietly. It would be a mere waste of words to tell you the later details, but before I entered town I had already parted with the sword. That's all my confession. I know that my head will be hung in chains anyway, so put me down for the maximum penalty. (A defiant attitude.)

The Confession of a Woman Who Has Come to the Shimizu Temple

That man in the blue silk kimono, after forcing me to yield to him, laughed mockingly as he looked at my bound husband. How horrified my husband must have been! But no matter how hard he struggled in agony, the rope cut into him all the more tightly. In spite of myself I ran stumblingly toward his side. Or rather I tried to run toward him, but the man instantly knocked me down. Just at that moment I saw an indescribable light in my husband's eyes. Something beyond expression . . . his eyes make me shudder even now. That instantaneous look of my husband, who couldn't speak a word, told me all his heart. The flash in his eyes was neither anger nor sorrow . . . only a cold light, a look of loathing. More struck by the look in his eyes than by the blow of the thief I called out in spite of myself and fell unconscious.

In the course of time I came to, and found that the man in blue silk was gone. I saw only my husband still bound to the root of the cedar. I raised myself from the bamboo blades with difficulty, and looked into his face; but the expression in his eyes was just the same as before.

Beneath the cold contempt in his eyes, there was hatred. Shame, grief, and anger . . . I don't know how to express my heart at that time. Reeling to my feet, I went up to my husband.

"Takejiro," I said to him, "since things have come to this pass, I cannot live with you. I'm determined to die, . . . but you must die, too. You saw my shame. I can't leave you alive as you are."

This was all I could say. Still he went on gazing at me with loathing and contempt. My heart breaking, I looked for his sword. It must have been taken by the robber. Neither his sword nor his bow and arrows were to be seen in the grove. But fortunately my small sword was lying at my feet. Raising it over head, once more I said, "Now give me your life. I'll follow you right away."

When he heard these words, he moved his lips with difficulty. Since his mouth was stuffed with leaves, of course his voice could not be heard at all. But at a glance I understood his words. Despising me, his look said only,

"Kill me." Neither conscious nor unconscious, I stabbed the small sword through the lilac-colored kimono into his breast.

Again at this time I must have fainted. By the time I managed to look up, he had already breathed his last—still in bonds. A streak of sinking sunlight streamed through the clump of cedars and bamboos, and shone on his pale face. Gulping down my sobs, I untied the rope from his dead body. And . . . and what has become of me since I have no more strength to tell you. Anyway I hadn't the strength to die. I stabbed my own throat with the small sword, I threw myself into a pond at the foot of the mountain, and I tried to kill myself in many ways. Unable to end my life, I am still living in dishonor. (A lonely smile.) Worthless as I am, I must have been forsaken even by the most merciful Kwannon.[3] I killed my own husband. I was violated by the robber. Whatever can I do? Whatever can I . . . I . . . (Gradually, violent sobbing.)

The Story of the Murdered Man, as Told Through a Medium

After violating my wife, the robber, sitting there, began to speak comforting words to her. Of course I couldn't speak. My whole body was tied fast to the root of a cedar. But meanwhile I winked at her many times, as much as to say "Don't believe the robber." I wanted to convey some such meaning to her. But my wife, sitting dejectedly on the bamboo leaves, was looking hard at her lap. To all appearances, she was listening to his words. I was agonized by jealousy. In the meantime the robber went on with his clever talk, from one subject to another. The robber finally made his bold, brazen proposal. "Once your virtue is stained, you won't get along well with your husband, so won't you be my wife instead? It's my love for you that made me be violent toward you."

While the criminal talked, my wife raised her face as if in a trance. She had never looked so beautiful as at that moment. What did my beautiful wife say in answer to him while I was sitting bound there? I am lost in space, but I have never thought of her answer without burning with anger and jealousy. Truly she said, . . . "Then take me away with you wherever you go."

This is not the whole of her sin. If that were all, I would not be tormented so much in the dark. When she was going out of the grove as if in a dream, her hand in the robber's, she suddenly turned pale, and pointed at me tied to the root of the cedar, and said, "Kill him! I cannot marry you as long as he lives." "Kill him!" she cried many times, as if she had gone crazy. Even now these words threaten to blow me head long into the bottomless abyss of darkness. Has such a hateful thing come out of a human mouth ever before? Have such cursed words ever struck a human ear, even once?

---

[3]Buddhist Goddess of Mercy.

Even once such a . . . (A sudden cry of scorn.) At these words the robber himself turned pale. "Kill him," she cried, clinging to his arms. Looking hard at her, he answered neither yes or no . . . but hardly had I thought about his answer before she had been knocked down into the bamboo leaves. (Again a cry of scorn.) Quietly folding his arms, he looked at me and said, "What will you do with her? Kill her or save her? You have only to nod. Kill her?" For these words alone I would like to pardon his crime.

While I hesitated, she shrieked and ran into the depths of the grove. The robber instantly snatched at her, but he failed to grasp her sleeve.

After she ran away, he took up my sword, and my bow and arrows. With a single stroke he cut one of my bonds. I remember his mumbling, "My fate is next." Then he disappeared from the grove. All was silent after that. No, I heard someone crying. Untying the rest of my bonds, I listened carefully, and I noticed that it was my own crying. (Long silence.)

I raised my exhausted body from the root of the cedar. In front of me there was shining the small sword which my wife had dropped. I took it up and stabbed it into my breast. A bloody lump rose to my mouth, but I didn't feel any pain. When my breast grew cold, everything was as silent as the dead in their graves. What profound silence! Not a single bird-note was heard in the sky over this grave in the hollow of the mountains. Only a lonely light lingered on the cedars and mountains. By and by the light gradually grew fainter till the cedars and bamboo were lost to view. Lying there, I was enveloped in deep silence.

Then someone crept up to me. I tried to see who it was. But darkness had already been gathering round me. Someone . . . that someone drew the small sword softly out of my breast in its invisible hand. At the same time once more blood flowed into my mouth. And once and for all I sank down into the darkness of space.

❀ Discussion and Writing

1. What information do the testimonies of the Buddhist priest and the old woman provide? How vital are they?
2. Examine the woodcutter's testimony to determine whether it corroborates (or contradicts) any other.
3. What does the policeman's testimony illustrate?
4. Analyze the characters of Tajomaru and Takehiko: why would Tajomaru confess to murdering Takehiko, who, through a medium, claims to have committed suicide? Discuss their motivations.
5. Describe the character of the wife as it emerges from all testimonies, including her own.
6. What is achieved by the distinct narrative points of view of the same event? What is the significance of the hand pulling the sword from the man's breast at the end; was it a murder or suicide?

✸ Research and Comparison

Examine Akutagawa's work, paying particular attention to his literary experimentation.

Interdisciplinary Discussion Question: Analyze *Rashomon*, the movie based on the stories "In a Grove" and "Rashomon," and directed by Kurosawa Akira, to compare the presentation in two different media.

Mao Zedong
(Mao Tse-tung, 1893–1976)
China

Mao Zedong was born in Shaoshan in Hunan Province, China, into a peasant family of comfortable means. He did not remain on the family farm or in the marriage arranged by his father, but became a student at the famous First Normal School in Changsha, where he majored in ethics, studying European as well as Chinese philosophers. After a brief period at Beijing (Peking) University, he returned to Hunan, organized the United Students Association of Hunan, and founded and edited the *Xian River Review.* He also began a drive to oust the Hunan warlord. In 1921 when the Chinese Communist Party was inaugurated, he was one of the two Hunanese delegates to the first congress. He immediately started organizing labor unions and establishing classes for peasants and workers. From the beginning, he was concerned with land reform and with the lives of peasants. He worked with Sun Yat-sen's Nationalist government under the auspices of the United Front (established in 1923) in an attempt to unify China. After the 1927 massacre of Communists in Shanghai, ordered by Chiang Kai-shek, Mao initiated the series of battles and counterattacks that led to the "Long March" (1934–1935). Throughout the years of World War II and the civil war that followed, Mao's political power fluctuated. But he was a brilliant military strategist in guerrilla warfare, and with his successes peasants flocked to him and Nationalist troops defected to join the Red Army. He became the first chairman of the People's Republic of China in 1949. And he remained passionately committed to reforming Chinese society.

Mao had been publishing essays and articles since 1924. "Snow"— written in 1936 during the drive to fend off the Japanese invasion—was his first published poem (1945). In his poetry, he used classical forms from the Tang (618–907) and Song (960–1127) dynasties. He implicitly set his poems within the context of emperor-art. A tradition of emperor-art began during the 700s with an emperor who was known for his wisdom and who could write elegant poetry in graceful calligraphy, paint equally exquisite pictures, and play beautiful music. Because of his abilities, people expected every emperor to be wise, literate, and artistic. Both Mao Zedong and Chiang Kai-shek used a similar image of the sage emperor as a means of legitimatizing their claims to head the government.

While Mao's allusions frequently called up legendary and historic figures in the manner of classical Chinese prosody, he avoided nostalgia and melancholy, evoking instead the contemporary spirit of revolution. Thus, "Swimming" hearkens back to his own poem "The Tower of the Yellow Crane," written in the spring of 1927 about the time of the massacre of the Communists. The same rivers figure in both poems. In "Swimming" the allusions to ancient kingdoms illustrate his hope of uniting China.

Swimming*
(June 1956)

Yesterday I drank the water of Changsha;
Today I taste the fish of Wuchang.
As I swim across the mighty Yangtze,
I gaze at the horizon where lies the land of Chu,
And marvel at the immensity of the heavens.
Though whipped by waves and wind,
I continue my way,
Enjoying the crossing
Far better than a courtyard stroll.
For today I have shed all cares!
Today I am free!
As I watch the river flow on ceaselessly,
I remember the Master once said,
"Swiftly and irrevocably time flows,
Just as the water of the river rushes out to sea!"

Yonder, a forest of tall masts is moving.
Buoyed by the wind, they glide through the channel
Where Tortoise and Snake stand guard in solemn silence.
What wonderful plans we have!
What an ambitious enterprise we are to undertake!
We will fly a bridge across the river to join north and south,
Making a thoroughfare out of nature's awesome barrier.

*Translated by Ma Wen-yee

Upstream we will build a precipice of stone to hold back
    Mount Wu's clouds and rains,
Creating a shimmering lake between the steep walls of the gorge.
Should the Goddess of Mount Wu live still in the clouds,
How surprised would she be to find her world so changed!

❋ Discussion and Writing

1. Analyze the effect of Mao's activities alluded to in the first five lines.
2. What is implied by the comparison between swimming the Yangtze and a stroll in the courtyard?
3. Discuss the relevance of the master's (Confucius's) words for Mao.
4. Analyze the significance of combining the images of ships and bridges with traditional ones of the guard and the goddess.

❋ Research and Comparison

Interdisciplinary Discussion Question: Examine Mao's writings in relation to his life as a military leader up to the time he became chairman of the People's Republic of China. Discuss the historical developments from the beginning of the century to that point.

Interdisciplinary Discussion Question: Research Mao's political career as expressed in his writings and analyze the course of ideological and political events in China since the late 1940s.

Interdisciplinary Discussion Question: Research the historical and literary material on the major revolutions in China and discuss their impact on people's lives.

Mao Dun
(Mao Tun, 1896–1982)
China

Mao Dun (Shen Yanbing) was born in Dong County in Zhejiang Province, China. As a young man, he organized one of the first associations to promote the new literary approaches and philosophy, the Literary Research Society. He took over the editing of the literary journal *Fiction*, radically altering its traditional perspective. In 1921, he moved from Shanghai, where *Fiction* was published, to Hankow to edit *Minguo Ribao*, a revolutionary daily newspaper. In 1927, however, when Chiang Kai-shek ordered the massacre of the Communists in Shanghai, Mao Dun returned to Shanghai. It was at this time that he took his pen name and concentrated his attention on exposing the Kuomintang (or Nationalist Party) as a reactionary government and Chiang Kai-shek as having abandoned the revolution. He portrayed the revolutionary struggle, and thus focused on social and economic issues, such as the effect of the Great Depression on a silk-producing village in "Spring Silkworms." In 1936, he and his associates conducted a massive survey, asking people to describe what had occurred on a particular day. Three thousand people of all classes and occupations throughout the entire country replied, and their letters indicated overwhelming dissatisfaction with and distrust of Chiang and the Kuomintang. His poll served to validate his past and fire his future work. (The study was translated into English as *One Day in China, May 21, 1936* and published in 1983.)

Mao Dun was one of the leading writers to follow the League of Left-Wing Writers' tenets of revolutionary realism. These tenets dictated the portrayal of precise class relationships in contemporary fiction, and his 1932 novel *Midnight,* in which he delineated the exploitation and corruption of the capitalistic society in Shanghai, was one of his major works following League criteria. During the war years (1937–1945), identified as the War of Resistance Against Japan, he continued writing essays and fiction, and he edited the important periodical *The Literary Front.* After the civil war, with the defeat of Chiang and the establishment of the People's Republic of China in 1949, he became minister of culture and subsequently served in various political capacities.

Spring Silkworms*

I

Old Tung Pao sat on a rock beside the road that skirted the canal, his long-stemmed pipe lying on the ground next to him. Though it was only a few days after "Clear and Bright Festival"[1] the April sun was already very strong. It scorched Old Tung Pao's spine like a basin of fire. Straining down the road, the men towing the fast junk wore only thin tunics, open in front. They were bent far forward, pulling, pulling, pulling, great beads of sweat dripping from their brows.

The sight of others toiling strenuously made Old Tung Pao feel even warmer; he began to itch. He was still wearing the tattered padded jacket in

---

Translated by Sidney Shapiro
[1]Qing Ming Jie (Clear and Bright) is a festival day honoring the ancestors. This ancient festival is still practiced in the 1990s. [eds.]

which he had passed the winter. His unlined jacket had not yet been re-deemed from the pawn shop. Who would have believed it could get so hot right after "Clear and Bright"?

Even the weather's not what it used to be. Old Tung Pao said to himself, and spat emphatically.

Before him, the water of the canal was green and shiny. Occasional pass-ing boats broke the mirror-smooth surface into ripples and eddies, turning the reflection of the earthen bank and the long line of mulberry trees flank-ing it into a dancing grey blur. But not for long! Gradually the trees reap-peared, twisting and weaving drunkenly. Another few minutes, and they were again standing still, reflected as clearly as before. On the gnarled fists of the mulberry branches, little fingers of tender green buds were already bursting forth. Crowded close together, the trees along the canal seemed to march endlessly into the distance. The unplanted fields as yet were only cracked clods of dry earth; the mulberry trees reigned supreme here this time of the year! Behind Old Tung Pao's back was another great stretch of mulberry trees, squat, silent. The little buds seemed to be growing bigger every second in the hot sunlight.

Not far from where Old Tung Pao was sitting, a gray two-story building crouched beside the road. That was the silk filature, where the delicate fibers were removed from the cocoons. Two weeks ago it was occupied by troops; a few short trenches still scarred the fields around it. Everyone had said that the Japanese soldiers were attacking in this direction. The rich people in the market town had all run away. Now the troops were gone and the silk fila-ture stood empty and locked as before. There would be no noise and excite-ment in it again until cocoon selling time.

Old Tung Pao had heard Young Master Chen—son of the Master Chen who lived in town—say that Shanghai was seething with unrest, that all the silk weaving factories had closed their doors, that the silk filatures here probably wouldn't open either. But he couldn't believe it. He had been through many periods of turmoil and strife in his sixty years, yet he had never seen a time when the shiny green mulberry leaves had been allowed to wither on the branches and become fodder for the sheep. Of course if the silkworm eggs shouldn't ripen, that would be different. Such matters were all in the hands of the Old Lord of the Sky. Who could foretell His will?

"Only just after Clear and Bright and so hot already!" marvelled Old Tung Pao, gazing at the small green mulberry leaves. He was happy as well as surprised. He could remember only one year when it was too hot for padded clothes at Clear and Bright. He was in his twenties then, and the silkworm eggs had hatched "two hundred percent"! That was the year he got married. His family was flourishing in those days. His father was like an experienced plough ox—there was nothing he didn't understand, nothing he wasn't willing to try. Even his old grandfather—the one who had first started the family on the road to prosperity—seemed to be growing more hearty with age, in spite of the hard time he was said to have had during the years he was a prisoner of the "Long Hairs."[2]

Old Master Chen was still alive then. His son, the present Master Chen, hadn't begun smoking opium yet, and the "House of Chen" hadn't become the bad lot it was today. Moreover, even though the House of Chen was of the rich gentry and his own family only ordinary tillers of the land, Old Tung Pao had felt that the destinies of the two families were linked together. Years ago, "Long Hairs" campaigning through the countryside had captured Tung Pao's grandfather and Old Master Chen and kept them working as prisoners for nearly seven years in the same camp. They had escaped together, taking a lot of the "Long Hairs'" gold with them—people still talk about it to this day. What's more, at the same time Old Master Chen's silk trade began to prosper, the cocoon raising of Tung Pao's family grew successful too. Within ten years grandfather had earned enough to buy three acres of rice paddy, two acres of mulberry grove, and build a modest house. Tung Pao's family was the envy of the people of East Village, just as the House of Chen ranked among the first families in the market town.

But afterward, both families had declined. Today, Old Tung Pao had no land of his own, in fact he was over three hundred silver dollars in debt. The House of Chen was finished too. People said the spirit of the dead "Long Hairs" had sued the Chens in the underworld, and because the King of Hell had decreed that the Chens repay the fortune they had amassed on the stolen gold, the family had gone down financially very quickly. Old Tung Pao was rather inclined to believe this. If it hadn't been for the influence of devils, why would a decent fellow like Master Chen have taken to smoking opium?

What Old Tung Pao could never understand was why the fall of the House of Chen should affect his own family. They certainly hadn't kept any of the "Long Hairs'" gold. True, his father had related that when grandfather was escaping from the "Long Hairs'" camp he had run into a young "Long Hair" on patrol and had to kill him. What else could he have done? It was "fate"! Still from Tung Pao's earliest recollections, his family had prayed and offered sacrifices to appease the soul of the departed young "Long Hair" time and time again. That little wronged spirit should have left the nether world and been reborn long ago by now! Although Old Tung Pao

---

[2]In the middle of the 19th century, China's oppressed peasants rose against the feudal Ching dynasty in one of the longest (1851–1864) and bitterest revolutions in history. Known as the Taiping Revolution, it was defeated only with the assistance of the interventionist forces of England, France and the United States of America.

The Ching rulers hated and feared the "Long Hairs," as they slanderously called the Taiping Army men, and fabricated all sorts of lies about them in a vain attempt to discredit them with the people.

Old Tung Pao, although steadily deteriorating economically, was typical of the rich peasants. Like others of his class, he felt and thought the same as the feudal landlord rulers.

couldn't recall what sort of man his grandfather was, he knew his father had been hard-working and honest—he had seen that with his own eyes. Old Tung Pao himself was a respectable person; both Ah Sze, his elder son, and his daughter-in-law were industrious and frugal. Only his younger son, Ah To, was inclined to be a little flighty. But youngsters were all like that. There was nothing really bad about the boy. . . .

Old Tung Pao raised his wrinkled face, scorched by years of hot sun to the color of dark parchment. He gazed bitterly at the canal before him, at the boats on its waters, at the mulberry trees along its banks. All were approximately the same as they had been when he was twenty. But the world had changed. His family now often had to make their meals of pumpkin instead of rice. He was over three hundred silver dollars in debt. . . .

Toot! Toot-toot-toot. . . .

Far up the bend in the canal a boat whistle broke the silence. There was a silk filature over there too. He could see vaguely the neat lines of stones embedded as reinforcement in the canal bank. A small oil-burning river boat came puffing up pompously from beyond the silk filature, tugging three larger craft in its wake. Immediately the peaceful water was agitated with waves rolling toward the banks on both sides of the canal. A peasant, poling a tiny boat, hastened to shore and clutched a clump of reeds growing in the shallows. The waves tossed him and his little craft up and down like a see-saw. The peaceful green countryside was filled with the chugging of the boat engine and the stink of its exhaust.

Hatred burned in Old Tung Pao's eyes. He watched the riverboat approach, he watched it sail past and glared after it until it went tooting around another bend and disappeared from sight. He had always abominated the foreign devils' contraptions. He himself had never met a foreign devil, but his father had given him a description of one Old Master Chen had seen—red eyebrows, green eyes, and a stiff-legged walk! Old Master Chen had hated the foreign devils too. "The foreign devils have swindled our money away," he used to say. Old Tung Pao was only eight or nine the last time he saw Old Master Chen. All he remembered about him now were things he had heard from others. But whenever Old Tung Pao thought of that remark—"The foreign devils have swindled our money away"—he could almost picture Old Master Chen, stroking his beard and wagging his head.

How the foreign devils had accomplished this, Old Tung Pao wasn't too clear. He was sure, however, that Old Master Chen was right. Some things he himself had seen quite plainly. From the time foreign goods—cambric, cloth, oil—appeared in the market town, from the time the foreign riverboats increased on the canal, what he produced brought a lower price in the market every day, while what he had to buy became more and more expensive. That was why the property his father left him had shrunk until it finally vanished completely; and now he was in debt. It was not without reason that Old Tung Pao hated the foreign devils!

In the village, his attitude toward foreigners was well known. Five years before, in 1927, someone had told him: The new Kuomintang government says it wants to "throw out" the foreign devils. Old Tung Pao didn't believe it. He heard those young propaganda speechmakers the Kuomintang sent when he went into the market town. Though they cried "Throw out the foreign devils," they were dressed in Western-style clothing. His guess was that they were secretly in league with the foreign devils, that they had been purposely sent to delude the countryfolk! Sure enough, the Kuomintang dropped the slogan not long after, and prices and taxes rose steadily. Old Tung Pao was firmly convinced that all this occurred as part of a government conspiracy with the foreign devils.

Last year something had happened that made him almost sick with fury: Only the cocoons spun by the foreign strain silkworms could be sold at a decent price. Buyers paid ten dollars more per load for them than they did for the local variety. Usually on good terms with his daughter-in-law, Old Tung Pao had quarrelled with her because of this. She had wanted to raise only foreign silkworms, and Old Tung Pao's younger son Ah To had agreed with her. Though Ah Sze didn't say much, in his heart he certainly had also favored this course. Events had proved they were right, and they wouldn't let Old Tung Pao forget it. This year, he had to compromise. Of the five trays they would raise, only four would be silkworms of the local variety; one tray would contain foreign silkworms.

"The world's going from bad to worse! In another couple of years they'll even be wanting foreign mulberry trees! It's enough to take all the joy out of life!"

Old Tung Pao picked up his long pipe and rapped it angrily against a clod of dry earth. The sun was directly overhead now, foreshortening his shadow till it looked like a piece of charcoal. Still in his padded jacket,he was bathed in heat. He unfastened the jacket and swung its opened edges back and forth a few times to fan himself. Then he stood up and started for home.

Behind the row of mulberry trees were paddy fields. Most of them were as yet only neatly ploughed furrows of upturned earth clods, dried and cracked by the hot sun. Here and there, the early crops were coming up. In one field, the golden blossoms of rapeseed plants emitted a heady fragrance. And that group of houses way over there, that was the village where three generations of Old Tung Pao's family were living. Above the houses, white smoke from many kitchen stoves was curling lazily upward into the sky.

After crossing through the mulberry grove, Old Tung Pao walked along the raised path between the paddy fields, then turned and looked again at that row of trees bursting with tender green buds. A twelve-year-old boy came bounding along from the other end of the fields, calling as he ran:

"Grandpa! Ma's waiting for you to come home and eat!" It was Little Pao, Old Tung Pao's grandson.

"Coming!" the old man responded, still gazing at the mulberries. Only twice in his life had he seen these finger-like buds appear on the branches so soon after Clear and Bright. His family would probably have a fine crop of silkworms this year. Five trays of eggs would hatch out a huge number of silkworms. If only they didn't have another bad market like last year, perhaps they could pay off part of their debt.

Little Pao stood beside his grandfather. The child too looked at the soft green on the gnarled fist branches. Jumping happily, he clapped his hands and chanted:

Green, tender leaves at Clear and Bright,
The girls who tend silkworms
Clap hands at the sight!

The old man's wrinkled face broke into a smile. He thought it was a good omen for the little boy to respond like this on seeing the first buds of the year. He rubbed his hand affectionately over the child's shaven pate. In Old Tung Pao's heart, numbed wooden by a lifetime of poverty and hardship, suddenly hope began to stir again.

II

The weather remained warm. The rays of the sun forced open the tender, finger-like, little buds. They had already grown to the size of a small hand. Around Old Tung Pao's village, the mulberry trees seemed to respond especially well. From a distance they gave the appearance of a low gray picket fence on top of which a long swath of green brocade had been spread. Bit by bit, day by day, hope grew in the hearts of the villagers. The unspoken mobilization order for the silkworm campaign reached everywhere and everyone. Silkworm rearing equipment that had been laid away for a year was again brought out to be scrubbed and mended. Beside the little stream which ran through the village, women and children, with much laughter and calling back and forth, washed the implements.

None of these women or children looked really healthy. Since the coming of spring, they had been eating only half their fill; their clothes were old and torn. As a matter of fact, they weren't much better off than beggars. Yet all were in quite good spirits, sustained by enormous patience and grand illusions. Burdened though they were by daily mounting debts, they had only one thought in their heads—If we get a good crop of silkworms, everything will be all right! . . . They could already visualize how, in a month, the shiny green leaves would be converted into snow-white cocoons, the cocoons exchanged for clinking silver dollars. Although their stomachs were growling with hunger, they couldn't refrain from smiling at this happy prospect.

Old Tung Pao's daughter-in-law was among the women by the stream. With the help of her twelve-year-old son, Little Pao, she had already finished washing the family's large trays of woven bamboo strips. Seated on a stone beside the stream, she wiped her perspiring face with the edge of her tunic. A twenty-year-old girl, working with other women on the opposite side of the stream, hailed her:

"Are you raising foreign silkworms this year too?"

It was Sixth Treasure, sister of young Fu-ching, the neighbor who lived across the stream.

The thick eyebrows of Old Tung Pao's daughter-in-law at once contracted. Her voice sounded as if she had just been waiting for a chance to let off steam.

"Don't ask me; what the old man says, goes!" she shouted. "He's dead set against it, won't let us raise more than one batch of foreign breed! The old fool only has to hear the word 'foreign' to send him up in the air! He'll take dollars made of foreign silver, though; those are the only 'foreign' things he likes!"

The women on the other side of the stream laughed. From the threshing ground behind them a strapping young man approached. He reached the stream and crossed over on the four logs that served as a bridge. Seeing him, his sister-in-law dropped her tirade and called in a high voice:

"Ah To, will you help me carry these trays? They're as heavy as dead dogs when they're wet!"

Without a word, Ah To lifted the six big trays and set them, dripping on his head. Balancing them in place, he walked off, swinging his hands in a swimming motion. When in a good mood, Ah To refused nobody. If any of the village women asked him to carry something heavy or fish something out of the stream, he was usually quite willing. But today he probably was a little grumpy, and so he walked empty-handed with only six trays on his head. The sight of him, looking as if he were wearing six layers of wide straw hats, his waist twisting at each step in imitation of the ladies of the town, sent the women into peals of laughter. Lotus, wife of Old Tung Pao's nearest neighbor, called with a giggle:

"Hey, Ah To, come back here. Carry a few trays for me too!"

Ah To grinned. "Not unless you call me a sweet name!" He continued walking. An instant later he had reached the porch of his house and set down the trays out of the sun.

"Will 'kid brother' do?" demanded Lotus, laughing boisterously. She had a remarkably clean white complexion, but her face was very flat. When she laughed, all that could be seen was a big open mouth and two tiny slits of eyes. Originally a slavey in a house in town, she had been married off to Old Tung Pao's neighbor—a prematurely aged man who walked around with a sour expression and never said a word all day. That was less than six months ago, but her love affairs and escapades already were the talk of the village.

"Shameless hussy!" came a contemptuous female voice from across the stream.

Lotus' piggy eyes immediately widened. "Who said that?" she demanded angrily. "If you've got the brass to call me names, let's see you try it to my face! Come out into the open!"

"Think you can handle me? I'm talking about a shameless, man-crazy baggage! If the shoe fits, wear it!" retorted Sixth Treasure, for it was she who had spoken. She too was famous in the village, but as a mischievous, lively young woman.

The two began splashing water at each other from opposite banks of the stream. Girls who enjoyed a row took sides and joined the battle, while the children whooped with laughter. Old Tung Pao's daughter-in-law was more decorous. She picked up her remaining trays, called to Little Pao and returned home. Ah To watched from the porch, grinning. He knew why Sixth Treasure and Lotus were quarrelling. It did his heart good to hear that sharp-tongued Sixth Treasure get told off in public.

Old Tung Pao came out of the house with a wooden tray-stand on his shoulder. Some of the legs of the uprights had been eaten by termites, and he wanted to repair them. At the sight of Ah To standing there laughing at the women, Old Tung Pao's face lengthened. The boy hadn't much sense of propriety, he well knew. What disturbed him particularly was the way Ah To and Lotus were always talking and laughing together. "That bitch is an evil spirit. Fooling with her will bring ruin on our house," he had often warned his younger son.

"Ah To!" he now barked angrily. "Enjoying the scenery? Your brother's in the back mending equipment. Go and give him a hand!" His inflamed eyes bored into Ah To, never leaving the boy until he disappeared into the house.

Only then did Old Tung Pao start work on the tray-stand. After examining it carefully, he slowly began his repairs. Years ago, Old Tung Pao had worked for a time as a carpenter. But he was old now; his fingers had lost their strength. A few minutes' work and he was breathing hard. He raised his head and looked into the house. Five squares of cloth to which sticky silkworm eggs were adhered, hung from a horizontal bamboo pole.

His daughter-in-law, Ah Sze's wife, was at the other end of the porch, pasting paper on big trays of woven bamboo strips. Last year, to economize a bit, they had bought and used old newspaper. Old Tung Pao still maintained that was why the eggs had hatched poorly—it was unlucky to use paper with writing on it for such a prosaic purpose. Writing meant scholarship, and scholarship had to be respected. This year the whole family had skipped a meal and with the money saved, purchased special "tray pasting paper." Ah Sze's wife pasted the tough, gosling-yellow sheets smooth and flat; on every tray she also affixed three little colored paper pictures, bought at the same time. One was the "Platter of Plenty"; the other two showed a militant figure on horseback, pennant in hand. He, according to local belief, was the "Guardian of Silkworm Hatching."

"I was only able to buy twenty loads of mulberry leaves with that thirty silver dollars I borrowed on your father's guarantee," Old Tung Pao said to his daughter-in-law. He was still panting from his exertions with the tray-stand. "Our rice will be finished by the day after tomorrow. What are we going to do?"

Thanks to her father's influence with his boss and his willingness to guarantee repayment of the loan Old Tung Pao was able to borrow the money at a low rate of interest—only twenty-five percent a month! Both the principal and interest had to be repaid by the end of the silkworm season.

Ah Sze's wife finished pasting a tray and placed it in the sun. "You've spent it all on leaves," she said angrily. "We'll have a lot of leaves left over, just like last year!"

"Full of lucky words, aren't you?" demanded the old man, sarcastically. "I suppose every year'll be like last year? We can't get more than a dozen or so loads of leaves from our own trees. With five sets of grubs to feed, that won't be nearly enough."

"Oh, of course, you're never wrong!" she replied hotly. "All I know is with rice we can eat, without it we'll go hungry!" His stubborn refusal to raise any foreign silkworms last year had left them with only the unsalable local breed. As a result, she was often contrary with him.

The old man's face turned purple with rage. After this, neither would speak to the other.

But hatching time was drawing closer every day. The little village's two dozen families were thrown into a state of great tension, great determination, great struggle. With it all, they were possessed of a great hope, a hope that could almost make them forget their hungry bellies.

Old Tung Pao's family, borrowing a little here, getting a little credit there, somehow managed to get by. Nor did the other families eat any better; there wasn't one with a spare bag of rice! Although they had harvested a good crop the previous year, landlords, creditors, taxes, levies, one after another, had cleaned the peasants out long ago. Now all their hopes were pinned on the spring silkworms. The repayment date of every loan they made was set for the "end of the silkworm season."

With high hopes and considerable fear, like soldiers going into a hand-to-hand battle to the death, they prepared for their spring silkworm campaign!

"Grain Rain" day—bringing gentle drizzles—was not far off. Almost imperceptibly, the silkworm eggs of the two dozen village families began to show faint tinges of green. Women, when they met on the public threshing ground, would speak to one another agitatedly in tones that were anxious yet joyful.

"Over at Sixth Treasure's place, they're almost ready to incubate their eggs!"

"Lotus says her family is going to start incubating tomorrow. So soon!"

"Huang 'the Priest' has made a divination. He predicts that this spring mulberry leaves will go to four dollars a load!"

Old Tung Pao's daughter-in-law examined their five sets of eggs. They looked bad. The tiny seed-like eggs were still pitch black, without even a hint of green. Her husband, Ah Sze, took them into the light to peer at them carefully. Even so, he could find hardly any ripening eggs. She was very worried.

"You incubate them anyhow. Maybe this variety is a little slow," her husband forced himself to say consolingly.

Her lips pressed tight, she made no reply.

Old Tung Pao's wrinkled face sagged with dejection. Though he said nothing, he thought their prospects were dim.

The next day, Ah Sze's wife again examined the eggs. Ha! Quite a few were turning green, and a very shiny green at that! Immediately, she told her husband, told Old Tung Pao, Ah To . . . she even told her son Little Pao. Now the incubating process could begin! She held the five pieces of cloth to which the eggs were adhered against her bare bosom. As if cuddling a nursing infant, she sat absolutely quiet, not daring to stir. At night, she took the five sets to bed with her. Her husband was routed out, and had to share Ah To's bed. The tiny silkworm eggs were very scratchy against her flesh. She felt happy and a little frightened, like the first time she was pregnant and the baby moved inside her. Exactly the same sensation!

Uneasy but eager, the whole family waited for the eggs to hatch. Ah To was the only exception. We're sure to hatch a good crop, he said, but anyone who thinks we're going to get rich in this life is out of his head. Though the old man swore Ah To's big mouth would ruin their luck, the boy stuck to his guns.

A clean dry shed for the growing grubs was all prepared. The second day of incubation, Old Tung Pao smeared a garlic with earth and placed it at the foot of the wall inside the shed. If, in a few days, the garlic put out many sprouts, it meant the eggs would hatch well. He did this every year, but this year he was more reverential than usual, and his hands trembled. Last year's divination had proved all too accurate. He didn't dare to think about that now.

Every family in the village was busy "incubating." For the time being there were few women's footprints on the threshing ground or the banks of the little stream. An unofficial "martial law" had been imposed. Even peasants normally on very good terms stopped visiting one another. For a guest to come and frighten away the spirits of the ripening eggs—that would be no laughing matter! At most, people exchanged a few words in low tones when they met, then quickly separated. This was the "sacred" season!

Old Tung Pao's family was on pins and needles. In the five sets of eggs a few grubs had begun wriggling. It was exactly one day before Grain Rain. Ah Sze's wife had calculated that most of the eggs wouldn't hatch until after that day. Before or after Grain Rain was all right, but for eggs to hatch on the day itself was considered highly unlucky. Incubation was no longer necessary, and the eggs were carefully placed in the special shed. Old Tung Pao stole a glance at his garlic at the foot of the wall. His heart dropped. There were still only the same two small green shoots the garlic had originally! He didn't dare to look any closer. He prayed silently that by noon the day after tomorrow the garlic would have many, many more shoots.

At last hatching day arrived. Ah Sze's wife set a pot of rice on to boil and nervously watched for the time when the steam from it would rise straight up. Old Tung Pao lit the incense and candles he had bought in anticipation of this event. Devoutly, he placed them before the idol of the Kitchen God. His two sons went into the fields to pick wild flowers. Little Pao chopped a lamp-wick into fine pieces and crushed the wild flowers the men brought back. Everything was ready. The sun was entering its zenith; steam from the rice pot puffed straight upward. Ah Sze's wife immediately leaped to her feet, stuck a "sacred" paper flower and a pair of goose feathers into the knot of hair at the back of her head and went to the shed. Old Tung Pao carried a wooden scale-pole; Ah Sze followed with the chopped lamp-wick and the crushed wild flowers. Daughter-in-law uncovered the cloth pieces to which the grubs were adhered, and sprinkled them with the bits of wick and flowers Ah Sze was holding. Then she took the wooden scale-pole from Old Tung Pao and hung the cloth pieces over it. She next removed the pair of goose feathers from her hair. Moving them lightly across the cloth, she brushed the grubs, together with the crushed lamp-wick and wild flowers, on to a large tray. One set, two sets . . . the last set contained the foreign breed. The grubs from this cloth were brushed on to a separate tray. Finally, she removed the "sacred" paper flower from her hair and pinned it, with the goose feathers, against the side of the tray.

A solemn ceremony! One that had been handed down through the ages! Like warriors taking an oath before going into battle! Old Tung Pao and family now had ahead of them a month of fierce combat, with no rest day or night, against bad weather, bad luck and anything else that might come along!

The grubs, wriggling in the trays, looked very healthy. They were all the proper black color. Old Tung Pao and his daughter-in-law were able to relax a little. But when the old man secretly took another look at his garlic, he turned pale! It had grown only four measly shoots! Ah! Would this year be like last year all over again?

III

But the "fateful" garlic proved to be not so psychic after all. The silkworms of Old Tung Pao's family grew and thrived! Though it rained continuously during the grubs' First Sleep and Second Sleep, and the weather was a bit colder than at Clear and Bright, the "little darlings" were extremely robust.

The silkworms of the other families in the village were not doing badly either. A tense kind of joy pervaded the countryside. Even the small stream seemed to be gurgling with bright laughter. Lotus's family was the sole exception. They were only raising one set of grubs, but by the Third Sleep their silkworms weighed less than twenty catties.[3] Just before the Big Sleep, people saw Lotus's husband walk to the stream and dump out his trays. That dour, old-looking man had bad luck written all over him.

Because of this dreadful event, the village women put Lotus's family strictly "off limits." They made wide detours so as not to pass her door. If they saw her or her taciturn husband, no matter how far away, they made haste to go in the opposite direction. They feared that even one look at Lotus or her spouse, the briefest conversation, would contaminate them with the unfortunate couple's bad luck!

Old Tung Pao strictly forbade Ah To to talk to Lotus. "If I catch you gabbing with that baggage again, I'll disown you!" he threatened in a loud, angry voice, standing outside on the porch to make sure Lotus could hear him.

Little Pao was also warned not to play in front of Lotus's door, and not to speak to anyone in her family.

The old man harped at Ah To morning, noon and night, but the boy turned a deaf ear to his father's grumbling. In his heart, he laughed at it. Of the whole family, Ah To alone didn't place much stock in taboos and superstitions. He didn't talk with Lotus, however. He was much too busy for that.

By the Big Sleep, their silkworms weighed three hundred catties. Every member of Old Tung Pao's family, including twelve-year-old Little Pao, worked for two days and two nights without sleeping a wink. The silkworms were unusually sturdy. Only twice in his sixty years had Old Tung Pao ever seen the like. Once was the year he married; once when his first son was born.

The first day after the Big Sleep, the "little darlings" ate seven loads of leaves. They were now a bright green, thick and healthy. Old Tung Pao and his family, on the contrary, were much thinner, their eyes bloodshot from lack of sleep.

No one could guess how much the "little darlings" would eat before they spun their cocoons. Old Tung Pao discussed the question of buying more leaves with Ah Sze.

"Master Chen won't lend us any more. Shall we try your father-in-law's boss again?"

"We've still got ten loads coming. That's enough for one more day," replied Ah Sze. He could barely hold himself erect. His eyelids weighed a thousand catties. They kept wanting to close.

"One more day? You're dreaming!" snapped the old man impatiently. "Not counting tomorrow, they still have to eat three more days. We'll need another thirty loads! Thirty loads, I say!"

Loud voices were heard outside on the threshing ground. Ah To had arrived with men delivering five loads of mulberry branches. Everyone went out to strip the leaves. Ah Sze's wife hurried from the shed. Across the

---

[3]A catty equals 1.102 lbs. [eds.]

stream, Sixth Treasure and her family were raising only a small crop of silk-worms; having spare time, she came over to help. Bright stars filled the sky. There was a slight wind. All up and down the village, gay shouts and laughter rang in the night.

"The price of leaves is rising fast!" a coarse voice cried. "This afternoon, they were getting four dollars a load in the market town!"

Old Tung Pao was very upset. At four dollars a load, thirty loads would come to a hundred and twenty dollars. Where could he raise so much money! But then he figured—he was sure to gather over five hundred catties of cocoons. Even at fifty dollars a hundred, they'd sell for two hundred and fifty dollars. Feeling a bit consoled, he heard a small voice from among the leaf-strippers.

"They say the folks east of here aren't doing so well with their silk-worms. There won't be any reason for the price of leaves to go much higher."

Old Tung Pao recognized the speaker as Sixth Treasure, and he relaxed still further.

The girl and Ah To were standing beside a large basket, stripping leaves. In the dim starlight, they worked quite close to each other, partly hidden by the pile of mulberry branches before them. Suddenly, Sixth Treasure felt someone pinch her thigh. She knew well enough who it was, and she suppressed a giggle. But when, a moment later, a hand brushed against her breasts, she jumped; a little shriek escaped her.

"Aiya!"

"What's wrong?" demanded Ah Sze's wife, working on the other side of the basket.

Sixth Treasure's face flamed scarlet. She shot a glance at Ah To, then quickly lowered her head and resumed stripping leaves. "Nothing," she replied. "I think a caterpillar bit me!"

Ah To bit his lips to keep from laughing aloud. He had been half starved the past two weeks and had slept little. But in spite of having lost a lot of weight, he was in high spirits. While he never suffered from any of Old Tung Pao's gloom, neither did he believe that one good crop, whether of silkworms or of rice, would enable them to wipe off their debt and own their own land again. He knew they would never "get out from under" merely by relying on hard work, even if they broke their backs trying. Nevertheless, he worked with a will. He enjoyed work, just as he enjoyed fooling around with Sixth Treasure.

The next morning, Old Tung Pao went into town to borrow money for more leaves. Before leaving home, he had talked the matter over with daughter-in-law. They had decided to mortgage their grove of mulberries that produced fifteen loads of leaves a year as security for the loan. The grove was the last piece of property the family owned.

By the time the old man ordered another thirty loads, and the first ten were delivered, the sturdy "little darlings" had gone hungry for half an hour. Putting forth their pointed little mouths, they swayed from side to side, searching for food. Daughter-in-law's heart had ached to see them. When the leaves were finally spread in the trays, the silkworm shed at once resounded with a sibilant crunching, so noisy it drowned out conversation. In a very short while, the trays were again empty of leaves. Another thick layer was piled on. Just keeping the silkworms supplied with leaves, Old Tung Pao and his family were so busy they could barely catch their breath. But this was the final crisis. In two more days the "little darlings" would spin their cocoons. People were putting every bit of their remaining strength into this last desperate struggle.

Though he had gone without sleep for three whole days, Ah To didn't appear particularly tired. He agreed to watch the shed alone that night until dawn to permit the others to get some rest. There was a bright moon and the weather was a trifle cold. Ah To crouched beside a small fire he had built in the shed. At about eleven, he gave the silkworms their second feeding, then returned to squat by the fire. He could hear the loud rustle of the "little darlings" crunching through the leaves. His eyes closed. Suddenly, he heard the door squeak, and his eyelids flew open. He peered into the darkness for a moment, then shut his eyes again. His ears were still hissing with the rustle of the leaves. The next thing he knew, his head had struck against his knees. Waking with a start, he heard the door screen bang and thought he saw a moving shadow. Ah To leaped up and rushed outside. In the moonlight, he saw someone crossing the threshing ground toward the stream. He caught up in a flash, seized and flung the intruder to the ground. Ah To was sure he had nabbed a thief.

"Ah To, kill me if you want to, but don't give me away!"

The voice made Ah To's hair stand on end. He could see in the moonlight that queer flat white face and those round little piggy eyes fixed upon him. But of menace, the piggy eyes had none. Ah To snorted.

"What were you after?"

"A few of your family's 'little darlings'!"

"What did you do with them?"

"Threw them in the stream!"

Ah To's face darkened. He knew that in this way she was trying to put a curse on the lot. "You're pure poison! We never did anything to hurt you."

"Never did anything? Oh yes, you did! Yes, you did! Our silkworm eggs didn't hatch well, but we didn't harm anybody. You were all so smart! You shunned me like a leper. No matter how far away I was, if you saw me, you turned your heads. You acted as if I wasn't even human!"

She got to her feet, the agonized expression on her face terrible to see. Ah To stared at her. "I'm not going to beat you," he said finally. "Go on your way!"

Without giving her another glance, he trotted back to the shed. He was wide awake now. Lotus had only taken a handful and the remaining "little darlings" were all in good condition. It didn't occur to him either to hate or pity Lotus, but the last thing she had said remained in his mind. It seemed to him there was something eternally wrong in the scheme of human relations; but he couldn't put his finger on what it was exactly, nor did he know why it should be. In a little while, he forgot about this too. The lusty silkworms were eating and eating, yet, as if by some magic, never full!

Nothing more happened that night. Just before the sky began to brighten in the east, Old Tung Pao and his daughter-in-law came to relieve Ah To. They took the trays of "little darlings" and looked at them in the light. The silkworms were turning a whiter color, their bodies gradually becoming shorter and thicker. They were delighted with the excellent way the silkworms were developing.

But when, at sunrise, Ah Sze's wife went to draw water at the stream, she met Sixth Treasure. The girl's expression was serious.

"I saw that slut leaving your place shortly before midnight," she whispered. "Ah To was right behind her. They stood here and talked for a long time! Your family ought to look after things better than that!"

The color drained from the face of Ah Sze's wife. Without a word, she carried her water bucket back to the house. First she told her husband about it, then she told Old Tung Pao. It was a fine state of affairs when a baggage like that could sneak into people's silkworm sheds! Old Tung Pao stamped with rage. He immediately summoned Ah To. But the boy denied the whole story; he said Sixth Treasure was dreaming. The old man then went to question Sixth Treasure. She insisted she had seen everything with her own eyes. The old man didn't know what to believe. He returned home and looked at the "little darlings." They were as sturdy as ever, not a sickly one in the lot.

But the joy that Old Tung Pao and his family had been feeling was dampened. They knew Sixth Treasure's words couldn't be entirely without foundation. Their only hope was that Ah To and that hussy had played their little games on the porch rather than in the shed!

Old Tung Pao recalled gloomily that the garlic had only put forth three or four shoots. He thought the future looked dark. Hadn't there been times before when the silkworms ate great quantities of leaves and seemed to be growing well, yet dried up and died just when they were ready to spin their cocoons? Yes, often! But Old Tung Pao didn't dare let himself think of such a possibility. To entertain a thought like that, even in the most secret recesses of the mind, would only be inviting bad luck!

IV

The "little darlings" began spinning their cocoons, but Old Tung Pao's family was still in a sweat. Both their money and their energy were completely spent. They still had nothing to show for it; there was no guarantee of their earning any return. Nevertheless, they continued working at top speed. Beneath the racks on which the cocoons were being spun fires had to be kept going to supply warmth. Old Tung Pao and Ah Sze, his elder son, their backs bent, slowly squatted first on this side then on that. Hearing the small rustlings of the spinning silkworms, they wanted to smile, and if the sounds stopped for a moment their hearts stopped too. Yet, worried as they were, they didn't dare to disturb the silkworms by looking inside. When the silkworms squirted fluid in their faces as they peered up from beneath the racks, they were happy in spite of the momentary discomfort. The bigger the shower, the better they liked it.[4]

Ah To had already peeked several times. Little Pao had caught him at it and demanded to know what was going on. Ah To made an ugly face at the child, but did not reply.

After three days of "spinning," the fires were extinguished. Ah Sze's wife could restrain herself no longer. She stole a look, her heart beating fast. Inside, all was white as snow. The brush that had been put in for the silkworms to spin on was completely covered over with cocoons. Ah Sze's wife had never seen so successful a "flowering"!

The whole family was wreathed in smiles. They were on solid ground at last! The "little darlings" had proved they had a conscience; they hadn't consumed those mulberry leaves, at four dollars a load, in vain. The family could reap its reward for a month of hunger and sleepless nights. The Old Lord of the Sky had eyes!

Throughout the village, there were many similar scenes of rejoicing. The Silkworm Goddess had been beneficent to the tiny village this year. Most of the two dozen families garnered good crops of cocoons from their silkworms. The harvest of Old Tung Pao's family was well above average.

Again women and children crowded the threshing ground and the banks of the little stream. All were much thinner than the previous month, with eyes sunk in their sockets, throats rasping and hoarse. But everyone was excited, happy. As they chattered about the struggle of the past month, visions of piles of bright silver dollars shimmered before their eyes. Cheerful thoughts filled their minds—they would get their summer clothes out of the pawnshop; at Dragon-Boat Festival perhaps they could eat a fat golden fish. . . .

They talked, too, of the farce enacted by Lotus and Ah To a few nights before. Sixth Treasure announced to everyone she met, "That Lotus has no shame at all. She delivered herself right to his door!" Men who heard her laughed coarsely. Women muttered a prayer and called Lotus bad names. They said Old Tung Pao's family could consider itself lucky that a curse hadn't fallen on them. The gods were merciful!

Family after family was able to report a good harvest of cocoons. People visited one another to view the shining white gossamer. The father of Old Tung Pao's daughter-in-law came from town with his little son. They

---

[4]The emission of the fluid means the silkworm is about to spin its cocoon.

brought gifts of sweets and fruits and a salted fish. Little Pao was happy as a puppy frolicking in the snow.

The elderly visitor sat with Old Tung Pao beneath a willow beside the stream. He had the reputation in town of a "man who knew how to enjoy life." From hours of listening to the professional story-tellers in front of the temple, he had learned by heart many of the classic tales of ancient times. He was a great one for idle chatter, and often would say anything that came into his head. Old Tung Pao therefore didn't take him very seriously when he leaned close and queried softly:

"Are you selling your cocoons, or will you spin the silk yourself at home?"

"Selling them, of course," Old Tung Pao replied casually.

The elderly visitor slapped his thigh and sighed, then rose abruptly and pointed at the silk filature rearing up behind the row of mulberries, now quite bald of leaves.

"Tung Pao," he said, "the cocoons are being gathered, but the doors of the silk filatures are shut as tight as ever! They're not buying this year! Ah, all the world is in turmoil! The silk houses are not going to open, I tell you!"

Old Tung Pao couldn't help smiling. He wouldn't believe it. How could he possibly believe it? There were dozens of silk filatures in this part of the country. Surely they couldn't all shut down? What's more, he had heard that they had made a deal with the Japanese; the Chinese soldiers who had been billeted in the silk houses had long since departed.

Changing the subject, the visitor related the latest town gossip, salting it freely with classical aphorisms and quotations from the ancient stories. Finally he got around to the thirty silver dollars borrowed through him as middleman. He said his boss was anxious to be repaid.

Old Tung Pao became uneasy after all. When his visitor had departed, he hurried from the village down the highway to look at the two nearest silk filatures. Their doors were indeed shut; not a soul was in sight. Business was in full swing this time last year, with whole rows of dark gleaming scales in operation.

He felt a little panicky as he returned home. But when he saw those snowy cocoons, thick and hard, pleasure made him smile. What beauties! No one wants them?—Impossible. He still had to hurry and finish gathering the cocoons; he hadn't thanked the gods properly yet. Gradually, he forgot about the silk houses.

But in the village, the atmosphere was changing day by day. People who had just begun to laugh were now all frowns. News was reaching them from town that none of the neighboring silk filatures was opening its doors. It was the same with the houses along the highway. Last year at this time buyers of cocoons were streaming in and out of the village. This year there wasn't a sign of even half a one. In their place came dunning creditors and government tax collectors who promptly froze up if you asked them to take cocoons in payment.

Swearing, curses, disappointed sighs! With such a fine crop of cocoons the villagers had never dreamed that their lot would be even worse than usual! It was as if hailstones dropped out of a clear sky. People like Old Tung Pao, whose crop was especially good, took it hardest of all.

"What is the world coming to!" He beat his breast and stamped his feet in helpless frustration.

But the villagers had to think of something. The cocoons would spoil if kept too long. They either had to sell them or remove the silk themselves. Several families had already brought out and repaired silk reels they hadn't used for years. They would first remove the silk from the cocoons and then see about the next step. Old Tung Pao wanted to do the same.

"We won't sell our cocoons; we'll spin the silk ourselves!" said the old man. "Nobody ever heard of selling cocoons until the foreign devils' companies started the thing!"

Ah Sze's wife was the first to object. "We've got over five hundred catties of cocoons here," she retorted. "Where are you going to get enough reels?"

She was right. Five hundred catties was no small amount. They'd never get finished spinning the silk themselves. Hire outside help? That meant spending money. Ah Sze agreed with his wife. Ah To blamed his father for planning incorrectly.

"If you listened to me, we'd have raised only one tray of foreign breed and no locals. Then the fifteen loads of leaves from our own mulberry trees would have been enough, and we wouldn't have had to borrow!"

Old Tung Pao was so angry he couldn't speak.

At last a ray of hope appeared. Huang the Priest had heard somewhere that a silk house below the city of Wusih was doing business as usual. Actually an ordinary peasant, Huang was nicknamed "The Priest" because of the learned airs he affected and his interests in Taoist "magic." Old Tung Pao always got along with him fine. After learning the details from him, Old Tung Pao conferred with his elder son Ah Sze about going to Wusih.

"It's about 270 *li* by water, six days for the round trip," ranted the old man. "Son of a bitch! It's a goddam expedition! But what else can we do? We can't eat the cocoons, and our creditors are pressing hard!"

Ah Sze agreed. They borrowed a small boat and bought a few yards of matting to cover the cargo. It was decided that Ah To should go along. Taking advantage of the good weather, the cocoon selling "expeditionary force" set out.

Five days later, the men returned—but not with an empty hold. They still had one basket of cocoons. The silk filature, which they reached after a 270-*li* journey by water, offered extremely harsh terms—Only thirty-five dollars a load for foreign breed, twenty for local; thin cocoons not wanted at any price. Although their cocoons were all first class, the people at the silk house picked and chose, leaving them one basket of rejects. Old Tung Pao and his sons received a hundred and ten dollars for the sale, ten of which had to be spent as travel expenses. The hundred dollars remaining was not even enough to pay back what they had borrowed for that last thirty loads of mulberry leaves! On the return trip, Old Tung Pao became ill with rage. His sons carried him into the house.

Ah Sze's wife had no choice but to take the ninety-odd catties they had brought back and reel the silk from the cocoons herself. She borrowed a few reels from Sixth Treasure's family and worked for six days. All their rice was gone now. Ah Sze took the silk into town, but no one would buy it. Even the pawnshop didn't want it. Only after much pleading was he able to persuade the pawnbroker to take it in exchange for a load of rice they had pawned before Clear and Bright.

That's the way it happened. Because they raised a crop of spring silkworms, the people in Old Tung Pao's village got deeper into debt. Old Tung Pao's family raised five trays and gathered a splendid harvest of cocoons. Yet they ended up owing another thirty silver dollars and losing their mortgaged mulberry trees—to say nothing of suffering a month of hunger and sleepless nights in vain!

❋ Discussion and Writing

1. What is the significance of the economic, political, and social issues in the first section regarding the family history of Chen and Tung Pao? What is implied by ending the section with Little Pao?
2. Discuss the philosophical code of bad deeds and expiation that informs Tung Pao's sensibility.
3. Analyze the depiction of Tung Pao's authority in his family: be it the control of the two dissimilar sons or his business policy.
4. Comment on the character of the nameless daughter-in-law: in her dealings with the village women; her involvement in family affairs; her responsibilities; her father's assistance to her husband's family; her position in the family.
5. What do Clear and Bright, Grain Rain, and such refer to? Comment on the various traditions that permeate the life of the community.
6. Describe the process of harvesting the spring silkworms. Discuss its effect on the lives and minds of the villagers.
7. Analyze the nature of taboos and superstitions that are integral parts of people's lives. Discuss Mao Dun's treatment of the subject. Is he critical, conciliatory, neutral?
8. Discuss the multiple ironies inherent in the narrative.

❋ Research and Comparison

Interdisciplinary Discussion Question: Mao Dun's story describes the typical experience of a farmer in the so-called "third world," overpowered by perpetual debt, hard work, and starvation. Examine a major literary work from another "third world" country, and discuss the predicament of the farmer who has to contend with natural as well as man-made catastrophes in the process of modernization.

Kawabata Yasunari
(1899–1972)
Japan

Kawabata Yasunari, who was orphaned when he was quite young, was born in Osaka, Japan. When he was three years old, his father—a physician with a keen interest in the arts—died. Kawabata's mother died the next year, followed within five years by his only sister and his grandmother. When he was 14, his grandfather, who had raised him for about six years, also died, an event that marked a shift in Kawabata's professional ambitions. He had been studying painting, but as he watched his grandfather becoming more and more ill, Kawabata began recording his feelings of ambivalence about the impending death. These notes were subsequently published as *Diary of a Sixteen-Year-Old* (1925). He matriculated in the English Literature Department at the Tokyo Imperial University and, with other students, started a magazine to which he contributed his early stories. Before his graduation, he became a staff writer on one of the leading literary journals, *Bungei Shunju,* and it was here he began his work as a reviewer and major critic, work that later in his life led him to discover, and support, younger writers like Mishima Yukio.

In 1924, the year of his graduation, Kawabata founded *Bungei Jidai* as a voice for the new literary movement, the lyrical *shinkankaku-ha* (variously translated as neosensationalist and neosensualist). The "neosensualist" movement derived, in part, from *haiku* poetry and its precursor, the linked verse *renga*. Kawabata was concerned with immediacy. His interest was in presenting a series of psychologically charged moments unmarked by sequential transitions; his aesthetic was *shinkankaku-ha*. Throughout his life, he wrote tiny stories that resemble *haiku* which he called *tanagokoro no shosetsu* or "palm-of-the-hand stories." Despite their brevity, they incorporate the themes that dominated his work: loneliness, solitude, transience, the vanity of existence. Modeling his work on Heian literature (794–1192), the great age of classical women writers, he also centered much of his fiction on women. Kawabata was awarded the Nobel Prize in literature in 1968, the first Japanese author to receive this honor. His suicide in 1972 has never been explained: he died alone in his studio without revealing his reasons.

*The Silver Fifty-Sen Pieces**

It was a custom that the two-yen allowance that she received at the start of each month, in silver fifty-sen pieces, be placed in Yoshiko's purse by her mother's own hand.

At that time, the fifty-sen piece had recently been reduced in size. These silver coins, which looked light and felt heavy, seemed to Yoshiko to fill up her small red leather purse with a solid dignity. Often, careful not to waste them, she kept them in her handbag until the end of the month. It was not that Yoshiko spurned such girlish pleasures as going out to a movie theater or a coffee shop with the friends she worked with; she simply saw those diversions as being outside her life. She had never experienced them, and so was never tempted by them.

Once a week, on her way back from the office, she would stop off at a department store and buy, for ten sen, a loaf of the seasoned French bread she liked so much. Other than that, there was nothing she particularly wanted for herself.

One day, however, at Mitsukoshi's, in the stationery department, a glass paperweight caught her eye. Hexagonal, it had a dog carved on it in relief. Charmed by the dog, Yoshiko took the paperweight in her hand. Its thrilling coolness, its unexpected weightiness, suddenly gave her pleasure. Yoshiko, who loved this kind of delicately accomplished work, was captivated despite herself. Weighing it in her palm, looking at it from every angle, she quietly and reluctantly put it back in its box. It was forty sen.

The next day, she came back. She examined the paperweight again. The day after that, she came back again and examined it anew. After ten days of this, she finally made up her mind.

"I'll take this," she said to the clerk, her heart beating fast.

When she got home, her mother and older sister laughed at her.

"Buying this sort of thing—it's like a toy."

But when each had taken it in her hand and looked at it, they said, "You're right, it *is* rather pretty," and, "It's so ingenious."

They tried holding it up against the light. The polished clear glass surface and the misty surface, like frosted glass, of the relief, harmonized curiously. In the hexagonal facets, too, there was an exquisite rightness, like the meter of a poem. To Yoshiko, it was a lovely work of art.

Although Yoshiko hadn't hoped to be complimented on the deliberation with which she had made her purchase, taking ten days to decide that the paperweight was an object worth her possession, she was pleased to receive this recognition of her good taste from her mother and older sister.

Even if she was laughed at for her exaggerated carefulness—taking those ten days to buy something that cost a mere forty sen—Yoshiko would

*Translated by Lane Dunlop

not have been satisfied unless she had done so. She had never had occasion to regret having bought something on the spur of the moment. It was not that the seventeen-year-old Yoshiko possessed such meticulous discrimination that she spent several days thinking about and looking at something before arriving at a decision. It was just that she had a vague dread of spending carelessly the silver fifty-sen pieces, which had sunk into her mind as an important treasure.

Years later, when the story of the paperweight came up and everybody burst out laughing, her mother said seriously, "I thought you were so lovable that time."

To each and every one of Yoshiko's possessions, an amusing anecdote of this sort was attached.

This Sunday, unusually allured by the charm of a shopping trip with her mother, Yoshiko had come to Mitsukoshi's. It was a pleasure to do their shopping from the top down, descending regularly from floor to floor, so first they went up to the fifth floor on the elevator. Although their shopping for the day was done, when they'd descended to the first floor, her mother, as a matter of course, went on down to the bargain basement.

"But it's so crowded, Mother. I don't like it," grumbled Yoshiko, but her mother didn't hear her. Evidently the atmosphere of the bargain basement, with its competitive jockeying for position, had already absorbed her mother.

The bargain basement was a place set up for the sole purpose of making people waste their money, but perhaps her mother would find something. Thinking she'd keep an eye on her, Yoshiko followed her at a distance. It was air-conditioned so it wasn't all that hot.

First buying three bundles of stationery for twenty-five sen, her mother turned around and looked at Yoshiko. They smiled sweetly at each other. Lately, her mother had been pilfering Yoshiko's stationery, much to the latter's annoyance. Now we can rest easy, their looks seemed to say.

Drawn toward the counters for kitchen utensils and underwear, Yoshiko's mother was not brave enough to thrust her way through the mob of customers. Standing on tiptoe and peering over people's shoulders or putting her hand out through the small spaces between their sleeves, she looked but nevertheless didn't buy anything. At first unconvinced and then making up her mind definitely no, she headed toward the exit.

"Oh, these are just ninety-five sen? My . . . "

Just this side of the exit, her mother picked up one of the umbrellas for sale. Even after they'd burrowed through the whole heaped-up jumble, every single umbrella bore a price tag of ninety-five sen.

Apparently still surprised, her mother said, "They're so cheap, aren't they, Yoshiko? Aren't they cheap?" Her voice was suddenly lively. It was as if her vague, perplexed reluctance to leave without buying something more had found an outlet. "Well? Don't you think they're cheap?"

"They really are." Yoshiko, too, took one of the umbrellas in her hand. Her mother, holding hers alongside it, opened it up.

"Just the ribs alone would be cheap at the price. The fabric—well, it's rayon, but it's so well made, don't you think?"

How was it possible to sell such a respectable item at this price? As the question flashed through Yoshiko's mind, a strange feeling of antipathy welled up in her, as if she'd been shoved by a cripple. Her mother, totally absorbed, opening up one after the other, rummaged through the pile to find an umbrella suitable to her age. Yoshiko waited a while, then said, "Mother, don't you have an umbrella at home?"

"Yes, that's so, but . . . " Glancing quickly at Yoshiko, her mother went on, "It's ten years, no, more, I've had it fifteen years. It's worn out and old-fashioned. And, Yoshiko, if I passed this on to somebody, think how happy they would be."

"That's true, It's all right if it's for a gift."

"There's nobody who wouldn't be happy."

Yoshiko smiled. Her mother seemed to be choosing an umbrella with that "somebody" in mind. But it was not anybody close to them. If it were, surely her mother would not have said "somebody."

"What about this one, Yoshiko?"

"That looks good."

Although she gave an unenthusiastic answer, Yoshiko went to her mother's side and began searching for a suitable umbrella.

Other shoppers, wearing thin summer dresses of rayon and saying, "It's cheap, it's cheap," were casually snapping up the umbrellas on their way into and out of the store.

Feeling pity for her mother, who, her face set and slightly flushed, was trying so hard to find the right umbrella, Yoshiko grew angry at her own hesitation.

As if to say, "Why not just buy one, any one, quickly?" Yoshiko turned away from her mother.

"Yoshiko, let's stop this."

"What?"

A weak smile floating at the corners of her mouth, as if to shake something off, her mother put her hand on Yoshiko's shoulder and left the counter. Now, though, it was Yoshiko who felt some indefinable reluctance. But, when she'd taken five or six steps, she felt relieved.

Taking hold of her mother's hand on her shoulder, she squeezed it hard and swung it together with her own. Pressing close to her mother so that they were shoulder to shoulder, she hurried toward the exit.

This had happened seven years ago, in the year 1939.

When the rain pounded against the fire-scorched sheet-metal roof of the shack, Yoshiko, thinking it would have been good if they had bought that umbrella, found herself wanting to make a funny story of it with her mother. Nowadays, the umbrella would have cost a hundred or two hundred yen. But her mother had died in the firebombings of their Tokyo neighborhood of Kanda.

Even if they had bought the umbrella, it probably would have perished in the flames.

By chance, the glass paperweight had survived. When her husband's house in Yokohama had burned down, the paperweight was among those things that she'd frantically stuffed into an emergency bag. It was her one remembrance of life in her mother's house.

From evening on, in the alley, there were the strange-sounding voices of the neighborhood girls. They were talking about how you could make a thousand yen in a single night. Taking up the forty-sen paperweight, which, when she was those girls' age, she had spent ten days thinking about before deciding to buy, Yoshiko studied the charming little dog carved in relief. Suddenly, she realized that there was not a single dog left in the whole burned-out neighborhood. The thought came as a shock to her.

❋ Discussion and Writing

1. Discuss the significance of Yoshiko's hesitation in buying the paper-weight and the reactions of her mother and sister.
2. Describe the shopping scene at Mitsukoshi's. What does it reveal about Japan in 1939?
3. Analyze the images portraying the changes in 1946 Japan. What histor-ical events precipitated them?
4. Comment on the symbolism of the silver fifty-sen pieces, the paper-weight, and the umbrella.

❋ Research and Comparison

Interdisciplinary Discussion Question: Explore the post–World War II Japanese literature created in the wake of the dropping of the atom bomb on Hiroshima and Nagasaki.

Interdisciplinary Discussion Question: Research the political history leading to the dropping of the atom bomb on Japan. Discuss the U.S. justifica-tion for using the bomb: comment on the controversy surrounding this issue from the U.S. and Japanese perspectives.

Kim Sowol
(1902–1934)
Korea

Kim Chongsik Sowol was born in Kwaksan, Korea, northwest of the city of P'yongyang, in North P'yongan Province. He studied in Seoul at Paejae High School where the poet Kim Ok was his mentor and helped him publish his poems the year before his graduation in 1923. While Kim Ok's melodic translations of the French Symbolists and other Western poets set a standard for the development of younger poets, he nonetheless praised Kim Sowol's formulating poems in "the purest Korean" mode. The most popular modern poet, Kim Sowol often worked in the traditional folksong style. His manipulation of its versification and motifs frequently evoked the sense of defeat that permeated Korean society during the Japanese occupation. He, like Han Yongun, was roused by Rabindrinath Tagore and contemplated the meanings of *nim* (love). Kim Sowol, too, sought to perpetuate and revitalize the language. But he was an unhappy man. Although he achieved recognition as a poet, he tried other possible careers, going to Japan to study at the Tokyo Commercial College, then returning to Seoul when he failed the entrance examination for another attempt at letters. He left Seoul for the province of his birth, North P'yongan, where he managed the Namsi town office of a daily newspaper. He was 32 when he took his own life.

The Road*

Again last night
at a country inn
grackles screeched at dawn.

Today
how many miles
again lead where?

Away to the mountains,
to the plains?
With no place that calls me
I go nowhere.

---

*Translated by Peter Lee

Don't talk of my home,
Chongju Kwaksan,
for the train and the boat go there.

Hear me, wild geese in the sky:
Is there a road of the air
that you travel so sure?

Hear me, wild geese in the sky:
I stand at the center of the crossroads.
Again and again the paths branch,
but no way is mine.

❋ Discussion and Writing

1. What do the grackles' screech symbolize for the poet? How does his condition differ from theirs?
2. What is the significance of the train and the boat going to Kwaksan, the poet's hometown? Why does the poet not want to talk about home? What is he searching for?
3. What is suggested by the poet's standing at the center of the crossroads?
4. Comment on the tone of the poem. Which feelings are evoked?

Ding Ling
(Ting Ling, 1904–1986)
China

Ding Ling was born in Linfeng in Hunan Province, China, into a gentry family. She was educated in the modern schools of Changsha (where Mao Zedong also studied) during the time of the intellectual ferment of the May Fourth movement. Both she and her mother responded enthusiastically to the movement, and they counted among their friends many of the students who left China in 1919 to study in France. When Ding Ling was 18, she left Hunan, an emancipated woman, traveling to several cities before she joined the poet Hu Yepin, whom she later married, and a group of avant-garde artists in Beijing. Her story "The Diary of Miss Sophie" (1927) brought her recognition, for in it she had captured her generation's sense of alienation. The work also portrayed a woman's unhappiness, establishing her lifelong commitment to feminism.

Both Ding Ling and her husband were political activists, he as a member of the Communist Party. She joined the party in 1931 after the Kuomintang executed him along with 22 fellow party members. Leaving her newborn baby with her mother in Hunan, she dedicated herself to the League of Left-Wing Writers, serving as the editor-in-chief of its magazine, *The Dipper*. Between 1933 and 1936, the Kuomintang held Ding Ling under house arrest in Nanjing. "A Certain Night," written during this time, describes the execution of her husband in 1931: he is the young poet in the narrative. When she escaped, fleeing to Yan'an, she reproached the party for its lack of concern for women's rights in general, and women workers in particular, despite its slogans. As a result, in 1942, she was sent to the countryside to work and learn from the peasants as part of Mao Zedong's Yan'an "Rectification Campaign," a program intended to crack the class structure by re-educating the traditionalist intellectual elites. Her 1948 novel *The Sun Shines over the Sanggan River,* with its description of land reform during the civil war, won the Stalin Prize in literature in 1951, indicating the official restoration of her reputation.

When she said, "a writer is not like a child who cannot leave his mother, he must be independent," the party did not challenge her. During the period of openness known as the "Hundred Flowers" movement of 1957, there was no dispute about her loyalty, but by the end of the year, she was exiled to a border farm in the northeast province of Heilongjiang, a year she remembered as "a time of spiritual suffering." With her prestige re-established, she was later promoted to the position of deputy chair of the Chinese Writers' Association. In 1984, she wrote of her desire for greater European "understanding of China" and for reconciliation. She remained committed throughout the fluctuations of her life to her early dream of a vibrant China.

A Certain Night*

A muffled tramp of feet.

A group of figures, too many to be counted, came into the square from the hall that was lit with bluish electric lights. The heavy tramp of boots and shoes in the thick snow. The ferocious wind of a winter's night lashing their faces with the rain that had been falling for a fortnight and with large snowflakes. The sudden onslaught of the cold wind made them all shiver in their hearts, but they tramped on.

Another howling blast of wind mercilessly flailed their bodies and faces. In the middle of them all, surrounded and driven along by a huge escort, came one man, a slight young man looking handsome and at the same time drawn. The shock seemed to wake him up. Everything that had happened in the past or just a moment ago seemed set out before him, at a great distance

---

*Translated by W. J. F. Jenner

and very clearly. That cunning face, malicious and smug, a round face, a face with a revolting mustache of the sort imperialists wear; and an evil voice giving a forced laugh. From where he sat up on high he had given him such an arrogant and uninhibited stare. "Have you anything else to say?" he had asked, then continued, "You have been given your sentences and they will be executed immediately." When the young man remembered this a fire that could have consumed him started up in his heart. He had wanted to rip that face to shreds and smash the voice to smithereens. In his wild fury he almost longed to push his way out through the men crowding round him and start walking fast and vigorously. Just now, when he had been suddenly condemned to death without any trial, he had not stayed calm like the rest of his comrades, but had passed out, overwhelmed by extreme anger and pain.

He was a passionate poet, loyal and hard-working.

A rifle butt thudded hard into his chest, which was even more emaciated than usual after twenty days of being kept on short rations and going hungry in the dark and sunless prison.

"What are you in such a hurry for, f— you? Death's waiting for you. You'll get yours." A murderous-looking soldier started swearing at him after breaking the silence by hitting him.

The manacles and fetters on his hands and feet clanked repulsively, as did those on other hands and feet. Then there was even more noise around him as iron-soled boots tramped harder in the snow.

He now understood some more, and realized where he was now being taken. A strange thought came into his head. Above his eyes he could see another pair of eyes, a pair of beloved and unforgettable eyes that could always see his soul. He was very clearly aware of something deep in his heart that was pricking him then agonizingly tearing his flesh and blood inch by inch.

The sky was black, boundlessly black, and from it fell rain and snow while the north wind howled. The world was gray, like fog, and the deathly gray was reflected in the night by the snow. The people were black figures moving silently across the snow. Amid the sound of shackles and bayonets none of the escorts or prisoners spoke, groaned, sighed or wept. They moved without interruption to the square that had been secretly turned into a temporary execution ground.

"F— them, the swine," thought some of them. "Where are they taking us to bump us off?"

A woman comrade in the second rank kept shaking her thick mop of hair as if she were angry. It was because the wind kept blowing her short hair across her forehead and eyes.

The young man forced himself by biting his lips hard not to give a wild and rending final shout. He was shaking with a fury that he could not express and glaring all around with a look of hatred so fierce that it hurt him, looking for something as if he wished he could devour it all, looking at one person and then at another.

The dim light of the snow shone on the man next to him, a fierce-browed soldier, and on another stupid soldier with his mouth and nostrils open wide, and on. . . . Suddenly he saw a familiar and friendly face, which showed him a calm, kindly expression, an expression that spoke volumes, an expression of consolation and encouragement that only comrades can give each other as they face their death. Most of his hatred and regrets disappeared. Affection and something else that can only be called life filled his wounded chest. All he wanted to do was to hug that face and kiss it. He replied to the expression with a much braver and a resolute nod.

The tramp of feet, a loud and untidy noise in the darkness, was like the irregular pounding of victory drums crowded all around them, the twenty-five of them, as they walked ahead. Above their heads the wind was roaring and soughing, as if a great red banner were waving above them.

"Halt! This is the place. Where d'you think you're going, you f—ers?" The chief executioner was armed and struck his Mauser pistol hard as he shouted in a firm voice with all his intimidating might.

"We're there," was the thought that echoed in many minds.

"Line the criminals up! Tie them up." The loathsome and vicious order came from the chief executioner's throat, and the soldiers in their padded greatcoats pushed them clumsily and hard, hitting them with rifle butts and putting ropes round their chests to tie them to the stakes behind them. There was an even louder noise of leather boots and shoes in the snow.

They said not a word, holding hard to their anger and their silence because they could no longer find any way of expressing their hatred for these enemies. Their hands and feet were now shackled and they were each tied fast to a wooden post that had been driven in days earlier.

Darkness stretched out in front of them, wind, rain and snow kept blowing into their faces, and the bone-chilling cold was mercilessly lashing their bodies, from which the warm scholars' gowns and overcoats had been ripped off in the hall. But they did not feel cold.

They were standing in a close-packed row.

"Here, over here a bit. Aim straight. . . ."

In the darkness of the night a group of men could just be made out in front of them carrying and moving around something heavy.

"Right. Here will do. Count the criminals."

"One, two, three. . . ." A soldier walked up to them and started counting.

The chief executioner, his face set in an ugly cast, followed the soldier along the row of prisoners, bending his fingers as he counted.

At the sight of that ugly and vicious face, which seemed to symbolize the cruelty of all the rulers to the oppressed, an angry fire started to burn in his heart again. The fire hurt his eyes and his whole body. He longed to be able to punch and kill the cur, but he had been tied up tightly with his hands behind him. All he could do was to grind his teeth in hatred, his whole body shaking with fury.

"Courage, comrade," said a comrade standing to his right.

He turned and saw that it was a familiar face: the man with whom he had talked a great deal at supper.

'It's not that. I'm rather worked up."

". . . twenty-three, twenty-four, twenty-five. Correct. Right. . . ."

The men who were counting started yelling and stamping hard in the snow as they moved toward the object that had been set up.

Boundless emptiness, wind, snow, grey, darkness. . . .

Human forms looked big and heavy against the deathly pale gray.

"Very well. Ready. Wait for my order."

So shouted the chief executioner.

All hearts tensed, pulled tight like bowstrings. The heavy death-like thing stood in front of them, carefully guarded by several soldiers. The sky was about to fall and the darkness to crush them, the twenty-five.

Someone started shouting in a loud voice:

"Arise, comrades. Don't forget that although we're going to die now a great congress is being held elsewhere today, and our government is going to be formed today. We must celebrate the creation of our government. Long live our government!"

With that they all broke out into wild shouts. There had been many things in their minds that they had forgotten to say or express. Only now did they suddenly realize, which was why they were all shouting at the tops of their voices the slogans they wanted to shout, dispelling the darkness. What spread out in front of them was the brilliance of a new state being founded.

As a whistle blew shrilly a mighty sound rose from twenty-five voices starting to sing:

"Arise, ye prisoners of starvation. . . ."

There was a rattle of fire as the heavy object raked along the whole length of the row, firing several dozen rounds.

The singing was quieter, but some voices were now even louder:

"It is the final struggle. . . ."

The whistle blew again.

Another rattle of fire as the row was raked for a second time with several dozen more rounds.

The more bullets that were fired, the quieter was the singing. There were now only a few voices still shouting.

"The Interna. . . ."

The whistle blew for the third time and the third burst of firing began. With the sound of the bullets the singing stopped.

"Try singing now, you c—ts, you bastards."

The chief executioner swore at them with an air of satisfaction, then walked back the way they had come, giving his orders:

"Put the gun away, and get back to barracks as soon as you can. The bodies can be buried tomorrow morning. The dead can't run away."

With that he walked back towards the hall.

Several dozen soldiers once again tramped noisily through the snow as they returned.

The night was silent, hushed, solemn. Large snowflakes and fine drops of rain were swirling around. The wild, winter wind blew first one way then another. Snow piled up on the head that hung forward, only to be dispersed by the wind. None of them said anything, tied there in silence. In a few places, in one, two, three . . . places, blood was flowing and falling on the snow in the darkness.

When will it be light?

❀ Discussion and Writing

1. Who are the prisoners? What are they guilty of? Who are their escorts? Construct the political situation depicted in the narrative.
2. Interpret the strange thought of the young poet.
3. What is the significance of the scene where the young man silently converses with his comrades?
4. Comment on the behavior of the escorts. What is the implication of their conduct in the description of the execution?
5. Examine the effect of the poetic description of nature and human behavior.

❀ Research and Comparison

Interdisciplinary Discussion Question: Research the early history of Communist ideology in China, and discuss its positive contributions to Chinese society.

Enchi Fumiko
(1905–1986)
Japan

Enchi Fumiko, whose father was a noted scholar and professor of literature at Tokyo University, was surrounded with classical literature and encouraged in her reading from the time she was a little girl. She also frequently accompanied her grandmother, a devotee of the art of *kabuki*, to the theater. Dissatisfied with the curriculum, she left high school when she was 17 to study classical Chinese, English, and French with a tutor. Osanai Kaoru, considered the progenitor of modern drama, accepted her as a student and she began her career by writing plays. She turned in the late

1920s to fiction when she became associated with the literary journal *Nichireki*. Although her friends in the early years were leftist writers, she herself was never a political activist. She wrote prolifically and experimented continually with various types of stories. Having lost her house in an air raid in 1945, she became quite poor. During the late 1940s, she fell seriously ill and was unable to write, and when she resumed writing in 1949, her work took on a new resonance, imbued now with her suffering. Turning to the feminist tradition, she focused on the nature and fate of women, concerning herself with a woman's state of being, her psyche, passions, and sexuality. Her many awards, including the highest honor, the Bunka Kunsho (cultural medal), have verified her place in Japanese letters as an essayist and literary critic as well as a writer of fiction.

Boxcar of Chrysanthemums*

It must have been seven or eight years ago, since the highway wasn't as good as it is now, and traveling by car wasn't easy.

I was still staying in my summer house in Karuizawa even though it was mid-September. One day a women's group in the nearby town of Ueda asked me to give a talk. I've forgotten what kind of group they were, but I left my house in the late afternoon and spoke to the audience right after dinner, for less than an hour. If my memory is correct, it was a little after nine when I got on a train to go home.

It was too late for the express train that ran during the summer, but I heard there was a local that went as far as Karuizawa, and I decided to take it since I wanted very much to return home that night. There was no second class (in those days seats were divided into second and third class); the third-class cars were old and looked to be of prewar vintage. There were only a few passengers.

Although I said, "How nice, it's not crowded," to the people who came to see me off, I realized after the train started to move how uncomfortable it is to ride on an old train that makes squeaky noises every time it sways, and that has dirty, frayed, green velveteen upholstery.

Well, even if this is a local I'll be in Karuizawa in two hours or so for sure, I said to myself as I turned to look out the window. The moon was nearly full and boldly silhouetted in dark blue the low mountains beyond the fields beside the tracks. The plants in the rice paddies were ripe, so of course I couldn't see the moon reflecting on the water in the fields. Plastic bird rattles here and there glittered strangely as they reflected the moonlight. The clear dark blue of the sky and the coolness of the evening air stealing into the deserted car made me realize keenly that I was in the mountain region of Shinshu, where fall comes early.

---

*Translated by Ukiko Tanaka and Elizabeth Hanson

I was thinking that I wanted to get home quickly when the train shuddered to a stop at a small station. We had been moving for no more than ten minutes. I couldn't complain about the stop since the train wasn't an express, but it didn't start up for a long time even though no one was getting on or off. It finally moved but then stopped again at the next station, took its time and wouldn't start again, as it had done before.

The four or five passengers in my car were all middle-aged men who looked as though they could be farmers from the area. There was no one sitting near me, and I didn't feel like standing up to go and ask about the delay. I looked out the window and saw several freight cars attached to the rear of the car I was in. It seemed that the cars were being loaded with something.

I realized then that this was a freight train for transporting cargo to Karuizawa that also happened to carry a few passengers. If I had known this earlier, I would have taken the local-express that left an hour before, even if I had had to rush to catch it. But it was too late for regrets; I told myself it would do no good to get off at an unfamiliar station late at night and resigned myself to the situation. The train would get me to Karuizawa sometime that night, no matter what; with that thought in mind, I felt calmer.

I took a paperback book from my bag and tried to read, but the squeaking noise of the car made it difficult to concentrate. I was tired, but I couldn't sleep because of the chilly air that crept up my legs and also because of my exasperation with a train that stopped so often.

When the train stopped for the fourth time at a fairly large station, I got off to ease my irritation. It would probably stop for ten minutes or so, and even if it started suddenly I thought I could easily jump on such a slow-moving train.

A few passengers got off. Some long packages wrapped in straw matting were piled up near one of the back cars, and the station attendants were loading them into the car as if they were in no big hurry. The packages were all about the same size, bulging at the center like fish wrapped in reed mats, but the station attendants were lifting them carefully in both hands, as if they were handling something valuable, and loading them into the soot-covered car.

I was watching the scene and wondering what the packages were when I suddenly noticed a moist, plant-like smell floating in from somewhere. Then I heard a woman's voice ask hesitantly, "Have you already loaded ours?"

I turned toward the voice. A middle-aged woman with her hair pulled into a bun was standing behind me. She wasn't alone; beside her was an old man with white hair and sunken cheeks. The moment I saw the pupils of his eyes with their strangely shifting gaze, and his slightly gaping mouth with its two long buck teeth and fine white froth at the corners, I was so startled that I stepped back a few paces.

"The Ichiges," one of the station attendants said to another, motioning with his eyes, and then he turned to the old man. "Yes, I loaded them. I put them in the best spot. They'll be in Tokyo tomorrow and will be the best flowers at the flower market," he said, speaking to the man as if he were a child.

The old man nodded with a dignified air.

"Oh, that's nice, isn't it? Now you don't have to worry. Well, let's go home and go to bed," the woman said, also as if she were humoring a child, and patted the old man's shoulder, which looked as stiff as a scarecrow's.

The old man stood there and said nothing. Meanwhile the packages were being loaded one after another, and by then I realized that the fragrance in the air was coming from them.

"Oh, that one over there! Those are our mums!" the old man yelled suddenly, extending his arms as if he were swimming toward the package the station attendant was about to load on the train. The old man's little nose was twitching like a dog's . "That smell . . . It's the Shiratama mum."

"Is it? Well, then, we'll ask them to let you smell them. The train's leaving soon, so you only smell once, all right?" the woman said and gave the station attendant a meaningful look. He put down the package the old man was trying to press his nose against and loaded another one first.

"That's enough now. You said good-bye to Shiratama, didn't you?" The woman spoke as if she were talking to a small child and put her arm around the stooping old man. She then took his hand and placed it gently on her lips. The old man let go of the package as if he were under a spell and stood up with his wife.

The door of the freight car finally closed, and the starting signal sounded. I got on the train in a hurry but didn't know quite what to make of the strange scene I had just witnessed. I couldn't believe that what I'd seen wasn't an illusion, like a scene from a movie.

"I feel sorry for them. Living on into old age like that."

I turned around. A middle-aged man in a gray jacket was sitting across the aisle from me. His face was dark and wrinkled from the sun, but he didn't look unpleasant. I realized that he hadn't been on the train before we stopped at the last station.

"That man—is he mentally ill?" I asked, unable to suppress my curiosity.

"Not mentally ill, more like an idiot. I think the term they use nowadays is 'mentally retarded.'" The man spoke without using any dialect. "The old man himself doesn't understand a thing, so he's okay, but I feel sorry for his wife. She's been married to that man for over twenty years now. If he'd been born into a poor family, marriage would have been out of the question, but simply because his family was wealthy, all kinds of cruel things happened."

Not only did the man speak without an accent, but his manner of speaking was smooth and pleasant. The name Ichige that the station attendant had mentioned turned my consciousness to some troublesome, submerged memory, but instead of mentioning this, I said, "Were those chrysanthemums they were loading in that boxcar? That old man was smelling them, wasn't he?"

"Yes, those were the chrysanthemums they grow in their garden. Mums are the only thing the old man cares much about. When they send some off he comes with his wife to watch, whether it's late at night or early in the morning."

"Then all of the packages are chrysanthemums?"

"That's right. Most of the flowers that go to Tokyo at this time of year are. Lots of farmers around here grow flowers, but they're all sold in Tokyo, so it's a big deal. Not only flowers, either. The people who work in the mountains around here collect tree roots, branches and other stuff, put prices on them and send them to Tokyo. Once they get them to market they can sell them, I guess, because money is always sent back. Tokyo's a good customer that lets the landowners around here earn money that way."

"I see. I was wondering why we were stopping so often to load things. It's a mistake for people to take this train," I said, smiling.

"You're right. It takes a good three hours to get to Karuizawa on this train."

"Oh, that's awful! No one told me that at Ueda when I got on."

"I don't think the people around here know that there's a train running at this hour that carries mums. Well, you might as well just get used to it and consider it an elegant way to travel."

My family would worry if I got to Karuizawa after midnight, but as the saying goes, there's nothing you can do once you're on board; even if no one had told me that I'd have to resign myself to the situation, I had no choice but to do so.

And so our conversation returned to the couple who grew chrysanthemums. The man across from me, whose name was Kurokawa, said he used to teach at an agricultural institute in Tokyo, but after he was evacuated to this region during the war he bought an orchard and settled down. He made extra income by collecting alpine plants, something he liked very much. He was taking this train because he had decided on an impulse to go to the town of Komoro and then climb Mt. Asama early the next morning.

It was the year after the end of the war when Kurokawa learned about Ichige Masutoshi and Rie.

Luckily Kurokawa didn't have to leave the country to do his military service, so as soon as the war was over he went to a village where his family had been evacuated. The village wasn't far from where he was born, and since he had never been particularly fond of city life and had also been hit hard by the war, he decided to settle there. At first he taught at a middle school in a nearby town. It was quite a while later that he bought an orchard and began to grow grapes and apples for a livelihood.

Food was scarce for most people in those days. No one grew fruit or flowers; everyone was busy growing potatoes and corn on the plots of land that weren't suitable for rice paddies. Kurokawa's father was still alive and healthy then and worked hard with his wife and daughter-in-law to grow vegetables. After living there for a while, Kurokawa noticed a new Tokyo-style house on a fairly large piece of land not far from his house. On his way back from school he often saw a woman in her thirties busily working in the garden behind the house. She wore a kerchief over her head and work pants, but her fair, unburned complexion and fine features had a calm sadness that reminded him of classic Korean beauties.

"That house is built in a different style from the others around here. Was it built during the war?" Kurokawa asked his father one evening during supper.

"That one? That's the house Ichige from Tokyo built during the war." His father, born and raised in that region, said this as if his son would know who Mr. Ichige was even if he didn't explain.

"Who's Ichige?"

"Ichige? He's the owner of a big paper company in Tokyo. I heard that he went bankrupt after the war. His father was the famous Ichige Tokuichi."

"Oh, I see." Kurokawa finally remembered the name. "But he's been dead for a long time, hasn't he?" Kurokawa had heard of Ichige Tokuichi of the Shinshu region, one of the success stories of the Meiji era.

"Right. Tokuichi was the father of Hanshiro, who was also known as a fine man. Hanshiro built the house, but his only son, Masatoshi, and his wife live there now."

With this as a beginning, Kurokawa's father then continued: Masatoshi was Ichige's legitimate heir, but he had contracted meningitis as a child, and although he was not actually an idiot, he was capable of only a few simple words. When he reached adulthood, however, it was decided that he should have a wife. Rie, who had come from the city of Iida to work as one of the Ichige's servants, was chosen as the human sacrifice.

"That's ridiculous, like a feudal lord and his serf. There's something wrong with any woman who would go along with it, too," Kurokawa snapped, but secretly he couldn't comprehend how the ladylike woman he saw when he passed the back of Ichige's house each morning and evening could be so lacking in expression and yet also give an impression of innocence and purity.

"That's what everyone says at first. When I heard the story, I despised the woman for agreeing to marry a man like that, no matter how much money was involved. But you know, after we came here that house was built nearby, and so I've seen a lot of Rie. She always showed up for volunteer work days and air raid drills, and ever since I was head of the volunteer guards I've known her well. Your dead mother and your wife, Matsuko, would agree that there's nothing wrong with Rie. She works harder than anyone else and doesn't put on the airs of a rich person. The catty local women used to sit around and drink tea and make fun of the Tokyo women who were evacuated here, but they stopped at Rie. They agreed that she took good care of that idiot husband of hers and only pitied her.

"It was like that for two or three years, and then before the war ended Hanshiro died of a stroke. His mother and son-in-law were careless and used up what money there was. They say only that house is left. In these times when there isn't much food, Rie has a hard time finding enough potatoes and flour to feed that glutton of a husband. She knits things for the farmers and sews clothes for their kids. You can't do that much for others if you're a fake and just trying to make a good impression. Sometimes I even wonder if she's a reincarnation of Kannon.[1] . . . "

Kurokawa's father spoke earnestly. He seemed to believe what he was saying. He was the kind of old-fashioned man who would want to believe that a person like Rie was a Kannon, or at least her reincarnation; at the war's end and in the years that followed he had seen whatever trappings human beings find to wrap themselves up in cruelly pulled off to reveal their naked, shameful parts.

Kurokawa certainly understood his father's feeling. He realized that he too wanted to purify his image of Rie and think of her as a reincarnated Kannon. Rie had lived up to the expectations of Kurokawa's father and had continued to be a devoted wife for more than ten years. She had converted most of Ichige's land into apple orchards and supported her husband and herself with this income. Growing chrysanthemums was partially for income but partially because Masatoshi enjoyed looking at flowers. Kurokawa said there didn't seem to be much money in it.

"It was two years ago, I think. Rie won some kind of prize. Hmm, what was it called? It was to commend her for having devoted herself to her mentally retarded husband for so many years; you might say for being the model of the faithful wife. In any case, it's a rare thing these days, and I think she deserved the praise."

While I listened to Kurokawa's long story, the train kept stopping at every station, and it looked as though chrysanthemums wrapped in straw mats were being loaded into the freight cars.

Between Komoro and Oiwake the train picked up speed. The moon seemed to be high in the middle of the sky; I couldn't see it from the train window, but the rays of moonlight had become brighter, and they shone upon the scene along the tracks with the coppery glow of an old mirror. This copper color changed to the smoky silver of mica when we reached a plateau and a mist settled onto the ground. After Kurokawa got off at Komoro, the only passengers left were a pair of men sitting near the far en-

---

[1]Kannon is the Buddhist Goddess of Mercy—Translator.

trance to the car. Since it was late at night when we reached the high land, a chill that was enough to shrivel me crept up from the tips of my socks as I sat there and quickly permeated my lower body.

I didn't actually mind the chill, even though I shrugged my shoulders now and then and pressed my knees together tightly, shivering. I was too absorbed in adding some facts from my own memory to the story that Kurokawa had told me about Ichige Masatoshi and his wife.

When I heard the names Ichige Tokuichi and Hanshiro, I was reminded of the story I had almost forgotten about the retarded son of the Ichiges. I had barely stopped myself from saying to Kurokawa, "Yes, of course, I've heard about him too."

I happened to have heard about the marriage between Masatoshi and Rie just about the time it took place. It was a year or so after the outbreak of the China Incident, when the image of the red draft notice calling soldiers to the army burned like fire in young men's minds. I had a friend whose husband was a psychiatrist, and although he practiced primarily in one of the private hospitals, he spent a few days a week at the Brain Research Institute of S Medical School. Interns and volunteer assistants who worked at this Institute often gathered at my friend Nagase's house to talk. I became acquainted with this group in the course of writing a play that dealt with a mental patient; I visited the hospital to ask the doctors questions about their experiences. One day when I met with three or four of these young doctors at Nagase's house, I noticed that Kashimura, who had always been with the group, was missing.

"Where is Dr. Kashimura? Is he on duty tonight?" I asked. The young doctors looked at each other and laughed before saying things like, "I guess you could call it 'duty,'" or "He sure is on duty," or "It's some duty."

I thought he might have gone to see a lover, and so I kept quiet, but then Nagase interrupted and said, "It's all right to tell her. It might be helpful to her."

"It's not a very respectable story, though."

"But a job's a job. Maybe she'll write a story about how we have to do this kind of work to support ourselves."

One of them sat up straight and said, "Kashimura is on night duty tonight at the home of one of the patients."

"I see. Does the patient get violent?" I asked without hesitation, since such cases are common among psychiatric patients.

"Yes, you couldn't say he *doesn't* get violent, but it's a tricky point." The young man who spoke, Tomoda, looked at another and said, "How was it when you were there?"

"Nothing happened, fortunately. You always had bad luck, didn't you?"

Tomoda nodded. "Yeah, my luck is bad. I'll probably die first if I go to war."

"I don't agree. You got a chance to see things you can't usually see. A voyeur would even pay for the chance."

"Idiot! Who said I'm a voyeur?"

"If everybody talked like that, no one would understand. I'll tell the true story in a scientific way without any interpretation," Nagase said, and he then told me the story of Ichige Masatoshi's marriage. Of course he didn't mention the name, but I learned of it quite a while later.

When Masatoshi reached physical maturity, his father consulted with a professor of psychiatry because he was troubled about how to find a partner to meet his son's sexual needs.

"The best way would be to provide him with one woman who would be kind to him. You should disregard her family background and her appearance and find someone who would take care of him like a mother," the professor told the father.

Masatoshi was particularly pitiful because his mother, Shino, had always disliked her retarded eldest child and had barely tolerated living in the same house with him. When she was young, Shino had been a hostess at Koyo-kan, a famous restaurant of the Meiji period, and had been popular among aristocrats and wealthy merchants because of her beauty.

Ichige Hanshiro had won her and made her his wife. For Shino the marriage meant an elevation in her own status, but her own background made her unyielding and vain, and she was determined not to be outdone by anyone. Her daughter was normal and married a man who was adopted into the family, but Shino was ashamed because she couldn't show off her only son in public. This shame turned into a hatred that she vented on Hanshiro.

Since Hanshiro had a sense of responsibility as a father, Masatoshi was raised at least to give the impression of being a son of the Ichige family. If the matter had been left to Shino's discretion, he probably would have been confined to one room and treated like a true moron.

When Masatoshi reached puberty he would sometimes become excited like a dog in heat and chase the maids and his sister. When Shino saw this happen, far from feeling sad, she would grow so livid that the veins would stand out at her temples.

"It's your responsibility! You let him wander around the house like an animal! Let's hurry and put him in a hospital. If we don't, all of our maids will leave us, I assure you," she shrieked at her husband.

"You don't have to shout for me to understand. I have my own thoughts about this," Hanshiro said calmly. Shino, who had given birth to Masatoshi, had no comprehension of the pain and unseverable strength of the parental bond Hanshiro felt in his very bones.

The next day Hanshiro went to see the psychiatry professor again and asked him to arrange for his son to be sterilized before he was married.

"I know a woman who might become my son's wife, but I can't imagine bringing the subject up to her whenever I think of the possibility of a child being born. Once the operation is finished, though, I think I can hope for a marriage. I feel sorry for the woman who'll be my son's wife, but from a father's viewpoint, I would at least like to give him the experience of living with a woman."

The professor agreed to Hanshiro's request, and the operation for sterilizing Masatoshi was performed in the surgery department of the hospital where he worked. It was a very simple procedure and was guaranteed not to interfere with the performance of the sex act.

It was said that after this Hanshiro talked to Rie about marriage. No one knew how Rie had reacted, or how long it had taken her to accept the proposal, or what sort of conditions Hanshiro had promised. It was clear only that Rie was not promised a bright future. The young couple began their married life in a small house that was fixed up for them in a corner of the grounds. It was originally built as a retreat. Rie took care of Masatoshi by herself, without any help from the household maids.

On formal occasions like weddings and funerals, Hanshiro and his wife attended with their daughter and her husband—their adopted son and an executive at Hanshiro's company—and their second daughter, who was also married. Of course Masatoshi didn't go along and neither did Rie.

"When they were married, he gave Rie a lot of stock in the company," one of Hanshiro's employees said, as if he had been there and seen this happen.

What I had heard at Nagase's house, that several young psychiatrists were hired to oversee the married relations of Masatoshi and Rie, was true; they were dispatched because it was assumed that there would be some times when Rie would be subjected to some violence. Hanshiro had heard from the psychiatrists that retarded men like his son sometimes perform the sexual act interminably, beyond a normal limit, since they are unable to control themselves, and that in some cases women had been killed as a result. To assure Rie's safety, Hanshiro had arranged for young doctors from S Medical School to take turns standing by every night in a room next to the couple's.

In teaching hospitals before the war, many young doctors worked for nearly nothing after receiving their degrees before they found a position somewhere. Of course not all of them had fathers who owned private clinics, so even if they were single it wasn't easy for them to support themselves unless they did some moonlighting.

The job at the Ichiges' was unusual even for psychiatrists, and the pay was much more than the average. There were many applicants. The professor chose several whom he felt could keep a secret; three of them were among the five or six young doctors who came to Nagase's.

"Rich people do such awful things. In fact, that woman was bought, but to have a doctor waiting on them like that. . . . It's like some kind of show. Even if the father did want his son to enjoy sex, it's too big a sacrifice. Why didn't he have them castrate his son instead of sterilizing him? I think that father is perverted." I spoke forcefully. I couldn't control my anger while listening to the story. Looking back on it now, I realize that at age thirty or so I knew little of life's unavoidable bitterness. I feel ashamed that I was so naive, but at that time I detested not only Hanshiro—though I didn't know his name then—but also Rie, the woman bought to be Masatoshi's wife, for her cowardice.

"Hey, don't get upset so fast. All of that made life a little easier for these guys," Nagase said, trying to act the mediator.

"That's true," I said, but I still felt revulsion, even toward Tomoda and Kashimura, who had worked for the Ichiges.

They say that when the wind blows, the cooper prospers; applying this logic, I could find no reason to criticize a man like Ichige Masatoshi, who had in fact helped the poor young doctors. Leftist ideology would probably explain this as the contradiction inherent in capitalistic society. Still, I simply could not feel comfortable with a situation where young, single doctors watched a young couple in bed from beginning to end, paying diligent attention until the two fell asleep. If one does not make a fool of himself when doing such things, then he is making a fool of his charges. The doctors were too young and well educated to see themselves as fools, and if they were making fun of someone else, it was of the woman who was the victim of this marriage. Obviously I didn't like their making fun of her or their seeing her as an object of erotic stimulation. At the same time that they were ridiculing her, they were acting like fools who couldn't see the spittle on their own faces. Someone had used the word "voyeur," but I had thought at the time that there was a basic difference between a voyeur and someone who kept such a nightly vigil.

After that I heard nothing more about the Ichiges from the young doctors, but through Nagase I learned there were in fact times when what had once seemed an absurd possibility had come to pass; Rie had fainted once, and there was a big row when Kashimura went to take care of her. It turned out that Masatoshi had forced himself on Rie when she was menstruating, and as a result she had lost a great deal of blood.

The interns from S Hospital must have stood duty at the Ichiges' for about a year when they decided there was no longer any danger and so stopped going there. A few years later, in the spring after the outbreak of the Pacific War, Kashimura was drafted as a military doctor and left to go to the South Seas. At the party to see him off, he came to me with a sake cup in his hand.

"I've been wanting to talk with you, but it seems like time is running out. If I return safely I'll tell you. It's about the family where I did night duty," he said.

"Oh yes, that family," I said, nodding. It was better not to mention the Ichiges' name in a place where there were so many people.

"The wife—Rie, I mean—I fell in love with her. To tell the truth, I wanted to marry her and talked to her about it." Kashimura spoke loudly, without concern for the people around him. Going to the battlefield seemed to have made him free from the petty restraints of normal times.

"Did you really?" I was intrigued and looked into Kashimura's eyes. I remembered that I had once secretly scorned the trio who had done that night duty for the Ichiges, including Kashimura. Now that I heard from Kashimura himself words that seemed to prove he had not been making a fool of either himself or Rie, I couldn't help reacting with a tense curiosity.

"What did she say?"

"She said no. She really loves her husband. But she said she was grateful for my having asked. She said it was more than she could have expected, after I had seen her in such unsightly circumstances. Masatoshi couldn't go on living, and probably wouldn't live for very long if she left, she said, and when she thought of this she felt sorry for him and couldn't possibly leave. Then she cried and cried. I thought there was nothing else I could do, and so I gave up," he said. Kashimura's face was flushed with sake, and tears welled up in his bloodshot eyes.

"I got married after that and have children now, but I haven't forgotten her. For a while I thought I had to rescue her from that place, but now it seems natural she stays with that husband," he said.

"Why were you attracted to her in the first place?" I asked Kashimura impatiently, trying to make sense of a situation I could not comprehend in many ways.

"Well . . . " After thinking for a moment, Kashimura said, "I felt the same as I would if my mother were in an animal cage. It was like a bad dream."

"Does she look like your mother?"

"No, not at all." Kashimura shook his head vigorously.

"What are you two talking so seriously about?" said a colleague of Kashimura's, patting his shoulder. Seeing this as a chance to excuse himself, Kashimura stood up to leave. He didn't seem particularly interested in talking with me anymore.

I thought about my brief conversation with Kashimura more than once after I returned home that night, and I tried to imagine what this woman Rie, whom I had never met, looked like. His words about his mother being in a cage excited my imagination, but in truth I couldn't picture Rie herself.

She was the daughter of a quilt merchant in the city of Ida. Her father had not been very well off, and although she only finished grammar school, like many children in those days, she was smart, wrote neatly, learned to sew and knit after arriving at the Ichiges', and acquired the knowledge of a high school graduate. Nagase said he had not heard any rumors about her family receiving a large sum of money when she married.

I suspected that she might have had something physically wrong with her as a woman, but when I learned that Kashimura had proposed to her after doing that strange nightwatch, I decided Rie must be normal.

It was extraordinary that a man who had witnessed a most private part of her life would ask her to divorce Masatoshi and marry him. Kashimura was a quiet, scholarly type—tall, well-built, and handsome. He was popular among the nurses and patients at the hospital, and I wondered how Rie felt when she was proposed to by a man who was beyond comparison with her husband. It puzzled me that she could calmly refuse such a proposal, since she was only twenty-four or twenty-five.

Four or five years after the end of the war, I learned from Tomoda, an old friend of Kashimura's, that Kashimura had died of malaria in the South Seas. Since my friends the Nagases had moved to the Kansai region after the destruction of the war, I heard almost nothing about that group of friends.

I myself went to Karuizawa to live after I lost my house in the bombings. A year after the end of the war when I returned to Tokyo, I became very ill, and for a year or two after having surgery I struggled to keep going during the hard times, even though I was still not completely well. In those days of rapid change after the war, I might have heard about the death of Ichige Hanshiro and the subsequent collapse of his family business, but it was not until I heard the news of Kashimura's death that I remembered Rie and her husband, whom I had forgotten; I thought at the time that I might write a story with Rie as the central character.

By then I had gained firsthand experience with the extreme situations of life, having gone through a war and a serious illness that had been a matter of life and death. I had lost the naiveté that had made me feel indignant about Hanshiro for having married his retarded son to a girl like Rie, as if it were a privilege of the bourgeois class. Nevertheless, Rie still remained a mystery to me.

When I thought about the story I would write about Rie, I imagined Masatoshi as the young kleptomaniac owner of an old established shop. His wife, ashamed of her husband, had an abortion, but unable to get a divorce, she continued to live with him as the lady of the household. She then fell in love with a young employee and in the end poisoned her husband.

This was all my own fabrication, but since it had been Kashimura's death that prompted me to start writing it, the metamorphosis of the main female character into a malicious woman left a bad taste in my mouth for this would surely have made Kashimura sad.

Later I thought off and on of writing down just what Kashimura had told me that night, a more lucid account that would convince even me, but the limits of my own imagination simply did not include a woman like Rie. I felt that if I forced myself to write, the character of Rie would end up being like a listless, white cat. Meanwhile the months and days passed, and once again I almost forgot the name Ichige.

Only one or two other passengers, shrugging their shoulders as if they were cold, got off the train with me. The chrysanthemums were still shut in the freight cars, so their penetrating fragrance didn't reach the platform.

I didn't see a taxi in front of the station, so after I called home from a public phone and asked someone to meet me with a flashlight at the corner of a dark field, I started walking alone through the town.

The moon was at its zenith, and the night mist was hanging low under the cloudless sky, spreading its thin gauze net over the pine trees and the firs. I could see the swirling motion of the mist underneath the street lamps, where the light made a circle. As I walked along, treading on the dark shadows that seemed to permeate the street, my footsteps sounded clear and distinct. Between the stores with their faded shutters I could hear the thin, weak chirping of some insects. It felt like autumn in the mountains.

Now I recalled fondly that I had been riding on a freight train full of chrysanthemums. In those dark, soot-covered cars hundreds and thousands of beautiful flowers were sleeping, in different shades of white, yellow, red, and purple, and in different shapes. Their fragrance was sealed in the cars. Tomorrow they would be in the Tokyo flower market and sold to florists who would display them in front of their shops.

"She's a white chrysanthemum, that's what she is," I said, and wondered the next moment to whom I was speaking. I realized immediately, however, that I was addressing the dead Kashimura. The words had come out so effortlessly that I felt vaguely moved.

That evening at O Station I had seen Rie with her husband for the first time, though only for a few minutes. Then by chance I had heard from Kurokawa about her recent life. Twenty years had passed since I had heard about Rie at Nagase's house. After that I had heard Kashimura's brief confession at his farewell party, and after the war I learned of his death. Did Rie know that he had died in the war? It didn't really matter now. I felt that Kashimura wouldn't mind if she was uninterested in his life and death.

Seeing Rie that night and hearing Kurokawa's story didn't add anything new to my image of her. Rie was the same as she had been; I was the skeptical one who hadn't believed she was like that.

Rie's devotion to Masatoshi had seemed absurd to me. I had no reason to say she was a fake, but I simply couldn't accept a way of thinking that was so different from my own. What I mean is that I couldn't accept what she did without imagining that some handicap was part of her devotion—she must have been jilted or raped or experienced something to make her unhappy. I even wondered if religion had motivated her, an inclination to follow an authority higher than that of human beings. That was why, when I had intended to write about Rie, I had explored the psychology of a woman who would kill her husband, and who was not at all like Rie. Even though Kashimura had said he had had no difficulty accepting Rie's refusal, I couldn't.

But now I was humbly reaching out to Rie. I wanted to accept the Rie who had lived with Masatoshi as she was and to disregard her background, any misfortunes she had had before her marriage, or any religious inclinations. I wanted to take her hand and say "I understand."

Did this mean that I had grown old? Should I be grateful that I had reached an age when I could accept without explanation the fact that human beings have thoughts and behavior that seem beyond rational comprehension? I felt a sense of joy in thinking of the flat features of Rie's melancholy, middle-aged face as being somehow like the short, dense petals of a modest white chrysanthemum.

✻ Discussion and Writing

1. Examine the life of the Ichiges as viewed by their neighbors and townspeople: what is their estimation of the father, the retarded son, and his wife; how do the people differ in their perceptions?
2. Analyze the involvement of the psychiatry department in the lives of Rie and Masatoshi. Discuss the complex issues of ethics and practicality mixed up in this case.
3. Discuss the portrayal of Kashimura: as a doctor, lover, and fighter. What is the significance of Kashimura's role in the narrative?
4. Analyze the character of Rie as a sacrificial lamb and/or a goddess of mercy. Discuss the narrator's final comments about Rie, and relate them to the title of the story.
5. Examine the slow train journey as a setting for the leisurely narration of incidents and past memories; what is the final impact of the journey on the narrator?

✻ Research and Comparison

Interdisciplinary Discussion Question: Research the Japanese cultural mores informing this story. Compare the issue of the woman as a victim and savior from the perspective of any other culture.

Hirabayashi Taiko
(1905–1972)
Japan

Hirabayashi Taiko was born in Sunawa in Nagano Prefecture, the beautiful mountain country of central Japan. Her grandfather, who had run a silk mill and served as a conservative politician, left his family impoverished.

After he had squandered his holdings, the only available work was small-scale farming. Unlike her brothers and sisters, she managed to go beyond primary school. Secretly taking the examination for high school, she passed with the highest score and somehow found the fees. During her school years, she read Russian literature and socialist philosophy; thus when she moved to Tokyo, the groundwork for her joining the anarchist movement had already been laid. In Tokyo, she worked briefly as a telephone operator, a waitress, and a maid, but she had also been writing fairy tales and detective stories for many years. Turning now to the novel and short story, she published her work in *Bungei sensen* (Literary Front), the journal of the "proletarian" school. By winning a Literary Association prize in 1926, she established her reputation as a "proletarian" writer. She was arrested several times, and contracted tuberculosis during the last eight-month imprisonment. Bedridden for eight years, she could not work. She resumed writing after World War II, still concerned about human distress and still concentrating on detailed pictures of experience. She eventually focused more and more on the experiences of women and received the Women's Literature Prize twice, for *Ko iu onna* (Such Women) in 1946 and *Himitsu* (Secret) in 1968.

A Man's Life*

"I wonder if conversion is a word that anyone can use. If it doesn't sound too funny for a fellow like me to be using it . . . well, I suppose I've experienced a sort of conversion too."

We'd been talking about something else when Sei, an ex-gangster, said this to me.

"What?"

Noting my bewilderment, Sei hesitatingly began to tell me his story, one which he apparently had kept to himself for a long time, and one which in its telling seemed most natural.

Now let me tell it in my own way. Because if you don't understand what kind of fellow I am, the story won't make much sense.

It was when things were beginning to turn bad for Japan in the Pacific War and people's lives were being increasingly upset by conscription and forced labor. As for me, for about a year I'd been a prisoner at Sugamo—a convicted murderer.

In the spring of the year before I'd knifed a fellow named Shida. He ran a little hotel in Togoshi-Ginza. In my own mind, there were two motives for the killing. But even today I don't know which of the two provided the decisive strength to drive me to murder.

---

*Translated by George Saito

Both the police and the public procurator's office were convinced that I did away with Shida to eliminate his influence in the Ebara district and thus strengthen the power of the Kawanaka gang.

As you probably know, my boss, Kawanaka, was an old man of eighty. Taking this fact into consideration, it seemed only natural that I, who was the real power in the Kawanaka gang, should kill Shida to expand my own influence. The assumption wasn't far wrong.

To tell the truth, however, there was one thing else. Working in that hotel run by Shida there was a woman I'd fallen in love with. Her name was Machiko. She had a face likely to draw attention, and she had a gentle disposition. When I had to make duty calls on Shida for my boss, it was she who would attend to me and pour the wine.

Without quite realizing it, I'd become attracted to this woman and I found myself speaking to her affectionately. But I never laid a hand on her, nor asked her to marry me. Maybe I'm not the passionate type—the kind that falls blindly in love.

Then by chance I learned that Machiko was Shida's woman. With the feeling of having been betrayed by a woman, a livid anger surged in me against Shida . . . whom, of course, I had no reason to resent.

It was on a dark night not very long after I'd learned about Machiko that I called Shida outside the kitchen, where I was hiding behind a large trash bin, and killed him with a single knife thrust.

As was our standard practice, I turned myself in and exaggerated Shida's supposed breach of faith into an unpardonable betrayal. Where gang wars are concerned, even in case of a killing, one can usually expect to get off with a sentence of five or six years at the most.

But the times were bad; my attempts to escape the draft came to light; and a previous police record didn't help either.

At the first trial they handed down a heavy sentence of eleven years at hard labor. Naturally I appealed, but because of the indifferent efforts of my lawyer, the verdict of the higher court was little better—ten years.

Ordinarily another appeal to a still higher court would have been made. But, besides being short-tempered, I found the whole thing unbearably tiresome and, out of spitefulness toward the fellow Kawanaka had provided to defend me, I decided, in a moment of youthful folly, to accept the verdict.

It was the day after the sentence. Breakfast over, my attention was vaguely directed to things going on outside—beyond the door of my cell. Morning at the prison begins with a guard's crying: "Sick call, breakfast; sick call, breakfast," Different voices can be heard passing by. It takes at least two months of cell life to distinguish the words "sick call" and "breakfast" from what at first seems an unintelligible mumbling. And it takes at least that long to realize that the affable, white-robed person who shouts "Sweets! Magazines!" and appears to be a peddler as he walks beside a trusty with a pushcart is, in fact, also a guard.

This one must have been working on a percentage basis, for he was quite good in his high-pressure salesmanship. The Prison Association, which at that time was still putting out a prison paper called *Man,* apparently had thought up this business for the guards to implement their meager pay.

Occasionally the cry "Rub that beard!" could be heard. After an application of ice-cold water from the spigot, beards would be vigorously massaged. Soon the turn for a shave would come. The process was swift and simple. It required only three of four strokes with a blunt-edged instrument called a razor, once down each side of the face, under the nose, and beneath the chin. It goes without saying that the whole operation was little short of torture.

On that particular morning, my ears were tuned for a sound I was waiting for with something more than ordinary expectation. Sure enough, the guard's footsteps came to a halt outside my cell door.

"No. 178! Ready for cell change!"

"Yes, sir! Ready, sir!"

The answer came out with a youthful bounce as I gave a glance at the cloth-bound bundle containing my personal belongings. Custom had it that those sentenced by courts of second instance, unless for ideological offenses, would be transferred from solitary confinement to a general cell. It is hard to imagine what this change of cells can mean to a young and gregarious fellow like me who has suffered from the loneliness of solitary confinement.

Already bundled in an arabesque-patterned green cloth were my earthly belongings, all bought since I had come here—a mirror, a bar of soap, toothpaste, a toothbrush, some underwear, a two-volume life of Hideyoshi, and three letters from Machiko. Snatching the bundle up, I stepped outside as the heavy door swung open. Now that I was leaving the place where I'd lived for a whole year, recollections flashed through my head of all the anguish, remorse, and irritation which had been breathed into the air of this cell. With an uncommon consciousness of human vanity, I'd been laughing at my own case; but as a matter of fact, I'd been awakened by the guard on many a night in the throes of a terrible nightmare.

Padding along in my straw sandals, I walked from my solitary cell on the second floor of Block Six to a general cell in Block Five. Block Five was an extension of Block Six, and the general cell was also on the second floor. The guard opened the door of the large cell.

"New man."

To these words I entered the cell. So from today I'd be with the inmates of this cell. It measured about twelve by fifteen feet. On either side of the two-foot-wide planked walk which ran from the door to the end of the room there were four mats, a total of eight for the room.

At the end of the walk, up against the wall, there was a box for personal effects; beside that, a glass-enclosed toilet; and above the latter, a window looking out over the shrubbery in the courtyard. On each of the mats on the two sides of the passage was a man, squatting on his mat in his own particular fashion.

This not being the first time I'd been in such a place, I knew immediately that the fiftyish-looking man squatting closest to the door was the cell boss. I lost no time in giving him the customary greeting of respect.

The fellow let out a grunt that was hardly audible and turned his ashen face aside. His airs annoyed me. I can see now how stupid I was, but at the time I was cut to the bone by a sudden feeling of resentment toward this old man who, I presumed, was nothing more than a petty criminal and who apparently didn't think much of me.

In the angry stare I shot at the old man, my thoughts were apparent: "Better make no mistake about the fellow you see in front of you," I was saying. "He's in here for murder. He's a little different from the sneak thieves you've got here, and you'd better not try to make a fool of him!"

But the old man apparently took no notice of the stripling in his twenties with the bright look in his eyes. His parched and restless glance shot here and there into the void. A shudder passed through me as I watched those eyes. They seemed starved, hungering for a spot on which to fix themselves. My random thoughts, however, did not pursue that impression to any great extent. It was for only one brief instant that I thought; "What queer people there are in this world."

Speaking of queer people, there was another one in that cell. He was about thirty-five, and he seemed well-bred and intellectual. Ever since I had entered the cell—and it was now close to the noon meal, for the meal cart could be heard in the distance as it moved along on its rails—this fellow had kept polishing the lid of his utensil box with a dirty rag. He had not stopped for an instant. The cloth made a queer, squeaking noise as it rubbed against the lid.

Until the war, these boxes for holding one's food utensils had been painted brown. Now, however, with the war situation so grave, they were made of just plain, unpainted wood. Without pause and without a glance elsewhere, the intellectual kept polishing the lid of his box, now old and gray from having been soaked in water so many times. The lid already had a brilliant sheen, yet with the same regular motion he continued his polishing. Soon, louder noises could be heard from the nearby cells as the trusty passed out the noon meal. Lightheartedly the men began arranging their boxes on the planked walk and taking out bowls and plates.

When I had been in here before, these bowls and plates had all been of aluminum, but the metal utensils had been turned in for use by the armed forces, and now we ate from chinaware, unmatched bowls and plates, large and small, which inmates had once bought as personal belongings from the prison sales stand. Of course, this stand no longer had such things to sell. The utensils that were being used were therefore quite old, left behind by previous inmates who had had full use of them. So there were all kinds, some chipped and some cracked, large ones and small ones. It was a little pathetic to note that even here one could see evidence of the hard times onto which the government had fallen.

When the curd soup was ladled out, those with small bowls naturally were at a disadvantage. Those who had foresight would offer whole lunches to some inmate due to leave soon, with the understanding that the large bowl he had been using would be left behind. But those who could not bear to part with an entire lunch had to be content with a small bowl, thereby incurring a loss with each meal.

As the cell door was opened from the outside, the cell boss turned and growled:

"Lid!"

"Here," someone answered and held out the lid of his box.

"Filthy! It's filthy!"

I turned at the sound of this different voice and its scathing comment. I saw the intellectual holding out his own shiny lid. The cell boss took it without a word. Using the lid as a tray, he placed each man's bowl on it in turn and held it out. The trusty scooped the rice from a bucket with a round, wooden implement resembling a ladle. After leveling the rice with the palm of his hand, he dumped it into the bowl. The rice was mixed with barley and soybeans.

I noticed that the guard who accompanied the trusty had suddenly moved a couple of yards away and looked off in another direction, apparently feigning ignorance. During this brief time, three lunches more than the number of inmates came into the cell.

"Well, this cell boss has a little pull."

With this thought I took a second look at the fellow. Beside him, the intellectual, with a satisfied look on his face, was now busily engaged in scraping into one corner of his box lid the grains of rice that had fallen on it. One at a time, he conveyed the grains to his mouth.

How well I understood now! To make these few dozen grains of rice his own—that was why he worked to polish his utensil box so much shinier than the others. But this was not particularly comical; nor was it particularly serious. It was quite ordinary here, and it impressed me little more than the touch of air.

While my thoughts thus wandered, the trusty at the entrance to the cell was handing in the last lunch. It was mine.

"No. 178—that you?"

The guard glanced at his notebook, peered into the darkness of the cell, and pointed at me with his chin.

"Yes, sir, sorry to trouble you, sir."

After getting my thumb print as a receipt, the guard shut the heavy door and followed the trusty to the next cell.

The cell boss, who had received my lunch from the guard, sat for some time with the lunch in his lap, apparently enjoying the whiteness of the grains of rice. His parched eyes darted hither and thither.

"Looks good. Think I'll keep this lunch for myself."

He'd no sooner mumbled these words than he got up to put the lunch with his personal effects.

"Hey, you! What d'ya think you're trying to do! Who d'ya think I am!"

I began hurling out the usual invective, but remembering that the fellow had quite a bit of influence, I immediately changed my tone:

"Course, if I was getting out of here in six months or a year, I wouldn't mind giving an old fellow like you something good to eat, but since I've got to stay in this hole for ten years . . . "

It was almost as if I were talking to myself. My words seemed to carry a note of sympathy, but in reality they were designed to let the men know that I was the possessor of a considerable criminal record.

There was every likelihood that by noting my number—the low number 178—people who knew the place would see that I was in for murder. But I hadn't been able to discern even the slightest suggestion of awe. Prodded on by a certain desire for distinction, I'd seen the need for intimidating this old man from the very beginning. I'd been deeply conscious of every word I'd spoken and every move I'd made, down to the motions of my eyes.

Though I raved and ranted, it had made little impression on this man. He went right on and put my lunch with his personal effects.

"Damn you! You still don't understand what I'm trying to tell you!"

In a fit of rage, I knocked the cell boss down from behind. His scrawny back felt like a piece of lumber through his dirty jacket, the only upper garment he wore.

Because of this commotion, I was the last to have lunch. Just as I finished, the cell boss was called outside for exercise.

"Queer fellow! What's he in for anyway?" I lost no time in asking a fortyish-looking fellow nearby.

"Sentenced to death." Two men spoke in unison. Their faces were thrust forward, alight with a sort of pride for having revealed something which would surprise me.

"So—sentenced to death." I acknowledge the information with a slight nod. But it set me to thinking, and my face no doubt paled a little.

"What did he do?"

"A long list: robbery, rape, murder, public indecency." The fortyish-looking fellow deliberately enunciated each word. His precise mode of expression was indicative of the intense respect the men with light sentences had for the older prisoner.

"Is it final?"

"Yes, it's been some time now since his appeal was turned down, and any day now, it's—this! You see, it's supposed to be carried out within a hundred days after it becomes final."

I felt myself in a strange vacuum and again fell silent.

Noting my youthful agitation, the fortyish one sidled up as if taking pity on me.

"Yes, you were hasty. You know, men condemned to death can get an extra lease on life, maybe three months or half a year—at least while the trial's going on—if they commit another murder. So you can never tell when they'll try it."

I knew that well enough. When I was in the station detention cell, my cellmate was a swindler. He had been imprisoned once with a fellow who'd killed his adopted child and been condemned to death. This child-killer also had a way of wanting other people's lunches. And when somebody would refuse, he'd take out his towel and twist it in his hands. "Since it's come to this, one or two more won't matter." As he mumbled the words, his sinister eyes would be directed at the throat of the man he was talking to. Everyone would contribute a part of his lunch.

Noticing my dejection, the intellectual, still polishing his utensil box, spoke from his place several mats away:

"Apologize. You've got to apologize."

"That's right! You've got to do it tactfully, Then there's—"

For some reason, the fortyish fellow cut himself short. Suddenly, a crafty light in his eyes, he gave me a sidelong glance.

"Long as a fellow sentenced to death is here, extra lunches come in. We won't lose anything by humoring him."

I realized that what these men were saying out of apparent kindness was certainly so. But knowing myself as I did, I was convinced it would hardly be possible for me to apologize to a man at whom I'd been shouting curses only a few moments before. In this perplexed state I passed the afternoon.

Presently, the boss was returned to the cell. The color had returned to his face, and he began to talk more freely.

Soon it was night. When the time came to go to sleep, I didn't know what to do. In the daytime, a sort of unwritten law prevailed within the cell. In accordance with their seniority, the men had places near the cell door: the cell boss at the door, the next oldest inmate beside him, and so on. At night, however, the prison regulations called for the prisoners to sleep according to their numbers.

This meant that the cell boss, No. 170, would be sleeping at the very end of the room, and that I, No. 178, would be next. I'd have to sleep next to him.

Sound sleep was out of the question that night. Whether he was sleeping or not, I never knew. He didn't twist or turn. He just lay there, his gaunt frame with its sallow, rough skin exposed to the glare of the electric light. His breathing was like air going in and out of a bellows.

I'd heard that there were two other men in Block Five who'd been condemned to death but whose sentences were not yet final. The sounds seemed to come from their direction, shrieks of men having nightmares.

Each time they would be followed by the footsteps of the guards going to rouse the sleepers.

Morning came. We could stay in bed till the guard shouted "Get up! Get up!" but No. 170 next to me was already awake and sitting up.

I struggled awake. I took one glance at his face and was shocked into disbelief. So ashen was the face that the skin seemed transparent. It wasn't the face of a living person.

With the command to get up, the men began folding their thin bedding, sweeping the floor with short-handled brooms, and wiping the planked walk. But No. 170, the cell boss, remained motionless, squatting and facing the cell door.

"What's wrong with him anyway?" I whispered to the fortyish fellow with whom I'd become acquainted the day before.

"You never know when the order for execution will come. If it comes, it should be before the change of guards at nine o'clock. No wonder he's worried."

I muttered something as if I'd understood, but I felt myself paling and beginning to tremble.

In all likelihood, a single minute of this man's life now was equivalent to more than an entire year of the life he'd spent like water. The poor all look older than they really are, but he couldn't have been much over fifty. If he were to live out his normal lifetime, he'd still have another fifteen or twenty years. He was trying to live those fifteen or twenty years in the next hour.

Soon it was time for breakfast. Once again, the intellectual shoved aside the box lid offered by the man of the day before and handed the cell boss his own shiny one, as if this were his own personal prerogative. As had happened at supper the night before, this man and the intellectual engaged in a bit of rivalry. The intellectual again pushed aside that dirty cover, and I felt somehow that the fellow who would again and again offer his dirty cover, knowing it would be shoved aside, was a great deal greedier and more to be pitied than the intellectual who pushed it aside.

The trusty dished up the soup with a ladle. The ladle was big, the bowls small, and the soup spilled over onto the lid. By the time all the men had been served, there was a considerable amount of spilled soup in the lid.

After getting his lid back from the cell boss, who continued to sit in stony silence, the intellectual walked cautiously back to his own mat. He then tilted the cover and drank down the soup, his lips smacking with unutterable delight.

I turned to look at the cell boss. In front of him, lined up in a row, were his own meal and the two extra meals that had found their way into the cell. He made no move to take up his chopsticks and remained leaning against the door. I wondered whether he'd soon share his food with some of his favorites, but he didn't. In a little while he rose, took up the three meals, and placed them with his personal effects.

Time passed. It must have been after nine, for the voice of the day-shift guard could be heard down the corridor. Though we heard it each morning, the voice of the new guard always sounded as fresh as the chirping of sparrows.

"It's after nine," one of the men said, to let the cell boss know that the hour of danger had passed.

But the cell boss already knew. He didn't trouble to answer, but rose swiftly and took out the food he had put away only moments before.

To have to look at the hideous color and manner of the man was to have an enormous weight on top of one's head. We all wanted intensely to move away with him from that dangerous hour.

He began eating. Only a moment ago he had been unable to eat a single mouthful, and now he shoveled the food into his mouth with amazing relish. Quickly he disposed of one meal, and not many minutes later he'd finished the other two. His was indeed a formidable appetite. His spirits had recovered completely.

It began when somebody asked me: "And what're you in for?"

For some minutes, the talk was of my criminal record.

"Say, old man, today why don't you finally tell us the details of that rape, murder, and public indecency of yours?" Seeing the cell boss in a good humor, someone asked him this question. As a matter of fact, this was exactly the lurid account I too had been wanting to hear.

The beaming face of the cell boss suddenly turned grim.

"That's one thing I don't want to be asked."

His tone was heavy. For some time now I'd been darting glances in his direction, my face alight with a conscious youthfulness. I was giving him these meaningful little glances to let him know I'd be interested in making peace with him. For the life of me, I couldn't make myself say the words outright. So I'd taken this rather crafty way of making amends.

Soon he was taken out again for exercise.

"'Robbery, rape, murder, public indecency.' What did he do anyway?" I asked the fortyish fellow. I'd memorized the list of crimes attributed to the cell boss though I'd heard it only once.

"Well, he seems bent on keeping that a secret if it's the last thing he does, but as a matter of fact, there's this."

He pulled a document from among the personal effects of the cell boss. It was the decision on a preliminary hearing.

The other men apparently had seen it already and I was the only one to extend my hand. It was couched in the stilted language of official documents, but as I read it, an image of the event formed itself, piece by piece, in my mind.

The season was spring; the scene, the lush pine woods of northern Kanto. Among the evergreens could be seen spring flowers, and to the nostrils came the strong odor of chestnut blossoms. From somewhere not far off sounded the song of a thrush. The time was just past noon and the air had the breath of late spring, almost like the soft touch of flesh.

For some time now the shrill voices of young girls had been coming from the other side of the woods. Soon, glimpses of school uniforms could be seen as the girls came filing down the hill through the straight-standing spruces.

"Looks like a picnic."

Two construction workers, on their way up the hill to where a power station was being built, were sitting on rocks by the road and smoking.

"There still must be snow at the top."

"No, not any more. The azaleas are in bloom."

The two fell silent. It was a meaningful silence.

Just then: "Go on. Go ahead. Don't look back. Don't."

Waving toward the group she'd just left, a schoolgirl of about eighteen ran behind some trees. Before the spot where the two workers were sitting there was a tangled thicket of withered pampas-like grass. The stems were graying and broken, but there were traces of green at the roots. The schoolgirl, worried only about whether she could be seen by her companions, pulled down her underpants and crouched down. Only the white calico showed clearly.

One of the workers whispered something to the other. Without replying, the latter rose and hurried off. The first jumped in front of the schoolgirl, who was still squatting down. The snapping of grass stems could be heard. In an instant she was overpowered. Her shrieks only echoed through the spruce branches. It was over in a matter of minutes. Then the other worker, who had been standing watch, came back and changed places with the first. It was No. 170, our cell boss.

The schoolgirl lay face upward, her soft hair wet from the oozing mire. The second worker did as the other had done. The schoolgirl had lost consciousness. The breath came from her dainty nostrils like a soft whisper.

With his big hands, the worker strangled her. And as he stood up, he saw the girl's tiny red purse lying a couple of feet away. It had so many bills in it that its clasp would not close. He picked it up and put it inside his waistband.

The two men dragged the body to soft ground and buried it. Cautiously, they left in different directions. Probably the other man hadn't thought of killing the girl.

When night begins to fall, there comes a moment when everyone becomes a bit emotional. I noticed the cell boss sitting perfectly still, facing the wall and murmuring a Buddhist prayer.

I slept little better that night. Occasionally, he'd roll over and kick me. I'd awake with a start, as if dashed with cold water. Even if he'd forgiven me, he hardly needed a pretext to commit another murder. It was I, close at hand, who had the greatest chance of becoming the victim.

But nothing unusual happened. With the morning there came again those terrible agonies we could hardly bear to watch. And yet at noon he'd be able to eat not only his own but other people's lunches too.

One day my chance came to make peace with him.

"Don't worry," I said. "We'll win this war soon, and then everyone will get a pardon."

It was nonsense. But if I was to say anything to him at all, what else could I say?

"Think so? But even if I should get out, I wouldn't have anything to wear."

"Oh, you don't have to worry about things to wear. A long time ago they had an amnesty when the Constitution was promulgated, and they say a market was set up outside the prison. I'll lend you a little money."

But one morning, at about eight o'clock:

"No. 178—visitor!"

Almost immediately the door opened. I'll never forget the look on No. 170's face as the guard said "one seventy. . . " and then added "eight." His face became chalk white, his eyes jerked upward, his whole body started to tremble. But it was just that one of the fellows in the Kawanaka gang had come to see me.

On the following morning, the same thing happened again. The shock was the same as it had been the day before. I could hardly stand to watch him.

Without saying why, I told the fellow from the Kawanaka gang not to visit me again. I'd begun to have a strange liking for the cell boss. You may laugh when I tell you the reason. You may not be able to understand. In a word, it was because he wasn't going to kill me.

I'd been thinking over and over again the frame of mind in which I'd killed Shida, and the frame of mind the cell boss must have been in when he'd killed the schoolgirl. They were deeds that couldn't be undone. But isn't it remarkable that this man would forego killing me, who slept beside him, and thus forego his chance to live longer? Isn't it wonderful that man is unable to kill without reason, even given his burning desire for life?

I asked that erudite fellow in his forties: "I've heard that men who've been sentenced to death think of killing someone else in prison. I wonder if anything like that has ever actually happened?"

"Well, it's something they often talk about, but I've never heard of an actual case."

I don't know why, but I thought happily: "Why, of course."

It was one morning some days later. An order was shouted by a guard to a man who had gone out to write a letter.

"Stop writing!"

I was the first to start up. When I was still in solitary, I had once heard that same order: "Stop writing!" I had wondered what it meant and later had asked one of the trusties.

"Yesterday, the janitor went in to sweep out the cellar room just under the gallows trap. That means there'll be a hanging today. Guess it'll be the German spy whose sentence was confirmed the other day."

As I recalled this, I thought: "Well, this is it!" I stole a glance at No. 170. In Cell Block Five there were three men sentenced to death, but it was only No. 170 whose sentence had been confirmed.

"Could be a news bulletin," someone was saying. Decidedly it couldn't be anything like that, however.

Soon there were footsteps and two guards stood at the entrance to our cell.

"No. 170. Visitor!"

The cell boss was ashen. He sat transfixed.

"Out, No. 170! Out! Visitor!"

The guards came inside without removing their shoes. They pulled No. 170 to his feet, supporting him from both sides. Swaying and staggering, No. 170 reached the cell door. One of the guards urged him to put on straw sandals, but his feet trembled so he couldn't keep them on.

He went off down the passage toward the women's cells, supported by two guards. The straw sandals lay on the concrete corridor where he had dropped them, a pace or so apart.

"Well, I wonder which guard will pull the rope today. He just has to pull that rope and he gets a whole bottle of saké, some eats, and the rest of the day off."

The fortyish fellow seemed quite proud of his store of knowledge. My face felt pale, I had an urge to slap him. But I fell silent, my head bowed.

✸ Discussion and Writing

1. Discuss Sei's character as a gangster, murderer, and prisoner. What aspects of his personality are reflected in his narrative?
2. Analyze Sei's conflict with the cell boss. Examine the significance of his treatment by the other men in the cell.
3. Describe the condemned man and his behavior, noting particularly the nature of his daily routine.
4. Comment on Sei's conversion. What is the function of the prefatory dialogue between Sei and the narrator? What is implied in the last sentence of the story? Discuss the effect of a narrative within another narrative.
5. Evaluate Hirabayashi Taiko's (a woman's) portrayal of the strictly male prison world.

❊ **Research and Comparison**

Interdisciplinary Discussion Question: Research the proletarian movement during the early and mid-twentieth century in Japan: its history, literary criteria, and effect. Examine various writers' involvement in this movement.

Kato Shuson
(b. 1905)
Japan

Kato Shuson, who was born in Yamanashi Prefecture in Japan, was the son of a government official. He taught in elementary and middle school after his graduation from Kanazawa Middle school and began writing *haiku* when he was 25. His mentor was an influential member of the conservative *Hototogisu* group that named itself for the *hototogisu,* or cuckoo, a bird whose song is heard at dusk and hence carries an association of sadness. Its name established the group's traditional aesthetic. Kato Shuson soon broke with his teacher's group and became known as an avant-garde poet. He infused his work with compassion. His poems were down-to-earth, concerned with common experience and daily life. From 1939 on, he was identified as a poet of *Ningen Tankyu-ha* or the "human quest" school. In 1940 he graduated from Tokyo Bunri University, where he studied Japanese literature, and two years later he founded the journal *Kanrai* as a voice of *Ningen Tankyu-ha* poetry. Continuing to teach, he became a mentor to the next generation of *haiku* poets.

The old genres like *haiku* have remained popular as twentieth-century poets have sought to express personal experience. Kato Shuson is one of the major poets to inform the compression of *haiku* with contemporary interests and reality. Translating *haiku,* however, presents a challenge. The compactness of the Japanese language allows for so much to be implied in so few words: there are no articles, prepositions, or relative pronouns, and few plurals. Moreover, the language is highly homophonic; words not only sound alike, they each contain many nuances, one word suggesting several connotations. The language itself is highly suggestive, and *haiku* depends on overtones for creating an evocative picture. The versification, moreover, demands a 17-syllable, 5-7-5 pattern and allows for fragmentation of the grammar. In that same vein, in Japanese syntax, adjective clauses precede the noun and sentences end with the verb.

Successful *haiku* depends on the association of ideas and comparison, both of which hinge on the fullness of meaning in each word. The implicit comparison projects a philosophic significance; thus, the poem not only paints a picture or evokes a feeling, but presents a moment of truth. And just as reading *haiku* has been viewed as an art in itself, so too is translating the poems.

Three modern haiku

In the depths of the flames*
I saw how a peony
Crumbles to pieces.

* * *

The winter sea gulls–
In life without a house,
In death without a grave.

* * *

Sad and forlorn: the shrike†
Bears on its back
The gold of the sunset.

❀ **Discussion and Writing**

1. Describe the feelings evoked by the images of the flames and a peony. What do the flames refer to?
2. Explore the implications of the images pertaining to the winter sea gulls.
3. Elaborate on the word picture created in the third *haiku*. Given the habit of the shrike to pin other birds on thorns to eat later, what do the shrike's sadness and loneliness suggest? What does "the gold of the sunset" symbolize?

❀ **Research and Comparison**

Interdisciplinary Discussion Question: Examine *haiku* in relation to painting within the Japanese aesthetic tradition, focusing on the work of any major poet.

Interdisciplinary Discussion Question: Research the nature and history of the development of *haiku*. Examine the impact of this genre on the literary works of American writers.

Translated by Donald Keene
†*Translated by Geoffrey Bownas and Anthony Thwaite*

Yi Sang
(1910–1937)
Korea

Yi Sang (Kim Haegyong) was born in the capital city of Seoul, Korea. He studied architecture at the College of Engineering and, after graduating in 1929, took a position in the government as a civil engineer. He tried various types of work: managing a tearoom one year and a café the next, but these occupations satisfied neither his financial nor his artistic needs. He edited journals and tried painting and design, and in 1931 he published a series of poems in which he experimented with style. He became known as a controversial writer, in part because of his experimentation and in part because of his revolutionary ideas. Still restless and ill with tuberculosis, in 1936 he went to Tokyo, where he was imprisoned because of his opposition to Japanese control of Korea. In his famous story "Wings," published the same year, he explored the sense of hopelessness brought about by the occupation, portraying the struggle to free the spirit from despair and questioning complicity. He found the short story a liberating genre: in the year before he died, he wrote a dozen stories in which he continued to experiment with methods of narration.

Wings*

Do you know the "genius who became a stuffed specimen"? I'm cheerful. Even love is cheerful at such a time.

My spirit shines like a silver coin, even when my body is tired till my joints creak. My mind prepares a blank sheet of paper whenever the nicotine filters into my roundworm-ridden stomach. On the blank sheet I spread out my wit and paradoxes, as if placing the pieces in strategic positions in a game of chess. This is a horrible ailment of common sense.

Again, with a woman, I draw up a plan of life, a scheme of one whose spirit has gone mad after a glimpse of the ultimate of reason, a man whose skill in making love has become awkward. What I mean is that I plan to design a life in which I own half a woman—a half of everything. The two halves, like two suns, will keep on giggling face to face, with only one foot in life. I must have been fed up with all mankind. Goodbye.

Goodbye. It may do you some good if you practice the irony of devouring food that you detest the most. Wit and paradoxes . . .

*Translated by Peter Lee

It is worth your trouble if you put on your mask. Your mask will feel at ease and noble—think of something ready-made no one has seen before.

Shut off the nineteenth century if you can. What is called Dostoevsky's spirit is probably a waste. It is well said (although I don't know by whom) that Hugo was a slice of French bread. Why should you be deceived by the details of life or of its pattern? Don't let disaster catch you. I'm telling this to you in earnest.

If the tape breaks, blood will flow. The wound will heal itself before long. Goodbye.

Emotion is a kind of pose (I suspect I'm pointing out only the elements of the pose).

The supply of feeling comes to a sudden stop when the pose advances to an immobile attitude.

I've defined my purport of viewing the world by recalling my extraordinary growth.

The queen bee and the widow . . . is there any woman in the world who has not become in daily life a widow? No. Would my theory of looking at every woman as a widow offend women? Goodbye.

This number thirty-three looks like a house of ill fame . . . eighteen families live in this compound labeled thirty-three, where all rooms are lined up shoulder to shoulder, their paper windows and furnaces identical. And everyone who lives in them is young, a budding flower.

No sun ever shines into the rooms, because they ignore the sun. On the pretext that they have to hang their soiled bedding on the clothesline in front of their rooms, they shield the sun from the sliding doors. They take naps in the dark rooms. Don't they sleep at night? I don't know, because I sleep day and night. The daytime for eighteen families is quiet in the compound numbered thirty-three.

But they keep quiet only in the daytime. At dusk they take the bedding down. And when the lights come on, eighteen families become much more brilliant than in the daytime. And then I hear the doors opening and closing all through the night. I begin to notice all sorts of odors: the smell of broiling herrings, the odor of women's makeup, the smell of water after washing rice, and the fragrance of soap.

What amuses me most here are the name plates posted on each door.

Standing all by itself there is a front gate that represents the eighteen families. But the gate, like a thoroughfare, has never been closed; so through it all sorts of peddlers come in and out at any hour of the day or night. None of the eighteen families bother themselves to go out to buy bean curd: they do their buying in their rooms, just by sliding the door open. It would be meaningless for the eighteen families to post their name plates at the gate that indicates number thirty-three. So they have devised a system of pasting their name cards on their doors, bearing such names as "The Hall of Patience" or "The Hall of Blessing."

On top of the sliding doors of my room—my wife's room, I mean—there is her small name card, a quarter the size of a playing card, just to follow the custom around the compound.

I do not play with anyone in the compound. I never greet anyone. I don't want to greet anyone other than my wife.

I think it would hurt my wife's reputation if I were ever to greet others or play with any of them. My devotion to her goes to that extent. The reason for my devotion is that she is, like her name card, the smallest and the most beautiful of the women of all the eighteen families. Because she is the most beautiful flower among all the eighteen flowers, she shines radiantly, even in this area with no sunshine under a galvanized roof. And I keep this most beautiful flower; no, I live clinging to her, and my existence has to be an indescribably awkward one.

I like my room very much. Its temperature is comfortable for me, and the semidarkness suits my eyes. I don't want a room cooler or warmer, brighter or darker. I have kept on thanking the room that keeps such an even temperature and darkness. I have been pleased to think that I was born to enjoy this kind of room.

But I don't want to calculate whether I'm happy or unhappy. I do not need to think about that problem. All went well as long as I spent day after day in idleness, with no reason. Wanting to be happy or unhappy is a mundane calculation. This way of living is the most convenient and comfortable condition.

This unconditionally suitable room is the seventh from the gate—"lucky seven." I love number seven like a decoration. Who would have guessed that the partition of a room into two with sliding doors was a symbol of my fate?

The lower part of the divided room sees sunshine. In the morning, it enters in the shape of a wrapping cloth; in the afternoon, it goes out the size of a handkerchief. I do not need to tell you that I live in the upper half of the room that sees no sun. I don't remember who decided that I should occupy the sunless part and my wife the sunny part. But I don't complain.

As soon as my wife goes out, I go into her room and open the window to admit the sun. The sunlight on her dressing table makes the bottles display their colors. Watching the bright colors is my best amusement. I play by singeing tissue paper, which only my wife uses. If I gather the parallel sunrays into focus with a magnifying glass, the light becomes hotter and begins to scorch the paper. Presently a small flame accompanied by thin smoke begins to spread. The process is quick, but the anxious state of mind until that moment, akin to wishing oneself dead, interests me.

If I get tired of this game, I play with my wife's small hand mirror, which has a handle. A mirror has utility only when one looks into it; otherwise it is nothing but a toy. Soon I get fed up with the mirror. And my zeal for play leaps from the physical to the mental. Throwing the mirror down, I go to my wife's dressing table and look into the beautifully colored cosmetic bottles lined up in a row. These are more attractive to me than anything else in the world. Selecting and uncorking one, I bring it close to my nose and inhale it as softly as if I were holding my breath. My eyes close themselves at the exotic sensual fragrance. Surely it is a fragment of my wife's body fragrance. After corking the bottle, I reflect: from which part of her body have I detected this particular smell? But it is unclear, because her body fragrance is a composite of many odors.

My wife's room is always splendid. In contrast to my bare room, without even a nail on the wall, her wall has a row of hooks under the ceiling on which are hung her colorful skirts and blouses. All sorts of patterns regale me. Dreaming of her naked beneath her skirts and of the various poses she would take, my mind loses its dignity.

However, I have no clothes to speak of. My wife doesn't give me any. The Western suit I wear serves at once as my Sunday best, my ordinary clothes, and my pajamas. My upper underwear through all the seasons is a black turtleneck sweater. The reason for black, I presume, is that it does not require washing. Wearing soft shorts with elastic bands around the waist and the two legs, I play without complaint.

Without my knowing it, the sun went down, but my wife has not returned. Tired of playing my own games and knowing that it's time for her return and that I should vacate her room, I creep back to my room. It is dark. Covering myself with a quilt I take a nap. The bedding, which has never been stowed away, has become a part of my body. I normally fall asleep right away; but sometimes I cannot sleep, even if I am dead tired. At such times, I choose a theme and think about it. Under the damp bedding I invent and write. I have also composed poems. But as soon as I fall asleep, all these achievements evaporate into the stagnant air that floods my room.

When I wake up, I find I am a bundle of nerves, like a pillow stuffed with cotton rags or buckwheat husks.

I loathe bedbugs. Even in winter I find a few in my room. If I have any problem in the world, it is my hatred of bedbugs. I scratch the bitten spots till blood oozes.

In the midst of a contemplative life in bed, I seldom thought about anything positive. There was no need for me to. If I had, I would have had to consult with my wife, and she would always scold me. Not that I feared her scolding, but it bothered me. Trying to do something as a social being or being scolded by my wife—no, idling like the laziest animal suited me. If possible, I sometimes wished to tear off my mask, this meaningless human mask.

To me, human society was awkward. Life itself was irksome. All things were awkward to me.

My wife washes her face twice a day.

I don't wash at all.

At three or four in the morning, I go to the lavatory across the yard. On moonlit nights I used to stand in the yard for a while before returning to the room. Although I have never met any one of the eighteen families, yet I remember the faces of almost all the young women in the compound. All of them fall short of my wife's beauty.

My wife's first washing, at eleven in the morning, is simple. Her second washing, at seven in the evening, is more complicated, and she puts on far cleaner dresses at night than she does in the daytime. And she goes out day and night.

Does my wife have a job? Perhaps, but I don't know what it is. If, like me, she has no job, there is no need for her to go out, but she does. And she has a lot of visitors. When she has many visitors, I have to stay in my room all day long, covered with a quilt.

On such days I cannot play at making flames, or smell her cosmetics. And I am aware of being gloomy. Then my wife gives me some money, maybe a fifty-chon silver coin. I like that. But not knowing how to spend them, I put them beside my pillow and they accumulate. Seeing the pile, she bought me a piggy bank that looked like a safe. I fed the coins into it one by one, and then my wife took away the key.

I recall putting silver coins into a box thereafter, but I was too lazy to count them. Sometime thereafter I spied a hairpin in the shape of a beehive in her chignon; does this mean that my safe-shaped piggy bank has become lighter? However, in the end, I never again touched that piggy bank beside the pillow. My idleness did not call my attention to such an object.

On days she has visitors I find it hard to fall asleep, as I do on rainy days. On such days, I used to investigate why my wife has money all the time, and why she has a lot of money.

It seems that the visitors are unaware of my presence behind the sliding doors. Men tell jokes so easily to my wife, ones that I would hesitate to tell her. Some visitors, however, seem comparatively more gentlemanly than others, leaving at midnight, while others stay on the whole night, eating. In general, things went smoothly, however.

I began to study the nature of my wife's job, but found it difficult to fathom because of my narrow mental vision and insufficient knowledge. I'm afraid I may never find it out.

My wife always wears new stockings. She cooks meals too, though I've never seen her cooking. She brings me three meals a day in my room without fail. There are just the two of us, so it is certain that she herself has prepared the meals.

I eat my meals alone and sleep alone. The food has no taste, and there are too few side dishes. Like a rooster or a puppy, I take the feed with no complaints. But deep within me I sometimes feel her unkindness. I became skinny, my face grew paler, my energy visibly weakened day by day. Because of malnutrition, my bones began to stick out. I have to turn my body dozens of times a night, unable to remain for long on one side.

Meanwhile I kept on investigating the provenance of her money and what kind of food she shares with her guests. I could not fall asleep easily.

I perceived the truth at last. I realized that the money she uses must be given her for doubtful reasons by the visitors who appeared to me nothing less than frivolous.

But why should they leave money and why should she accept it? I could never understand the notion of such etiquette.

Well, is the transaction merely for etiquette's sake? Would not the money be a kind of payment or honorarium? Or did my wife seem to them one who deserved sympathy?

Whenever I indulge in such probing, my head swims. The conclusion I had reached before I fell asleep was that the subject was unpleasant. But I have not asked her about it, not only because it would be a nuisance but also because, after a sound sleep, I used to forget everything.

Whenever visitors go away or when she returns from outside, she changes into her negligee and pays me a visit. Lifting my quilt, she tries to console me with strange words I cannot understand. Then with a smile that is neither sneering, nor sardonic, nor hostile, I watch her beautiful face. She gives me a gentle smile. But I do not fail to notice a hint of sadness in her smile.

I know she notices that I am hungry. But she never gives me the leftovers in her room. It must be that she respects me. I like her respect, which is reassuring even when I am hungry. When she leaves me alone, not a word she has spoken remains with me. I see only the silver coin she has left behind, shining brightly in the electric light.

I've no idea how full the piggy bank is now. I never pick it up to feel its weight. I keep on feeding the coins through a slit, like a buttonhole, with no volition, no supplication.

Why she should leave me a coin is as difficult to solve as why her visitors leave money with her. I do not dislike the coin she gives me, but the feel of it in my fingers from the moment I pick it up till it disappears through the slit of the piggy bank gives me a brief pleasure. That's all there is to it.

One day I dumped the piggy bank into the latrine. I did not know how much money was in it. How unreliable everything seemed to me when I realized that I was living on an earth revolving fast like lightning through endless space. I wished I could quickly get off the speedy earth that makes me dizzy. Having pondered thus inside my quilt, putting the silver coins into the piggy bank became bothersome. I had hoped my wife would carry the piggy bank away. In fact, the piggy bank and money are useful to her, but they were meaningless to me from the start. I hoped she would take it away, but she didn't. I thought of putting it in her room myself but I had no chance because of her numerous guests. Having no alternative, I dumped it into the latrine.

With a heavy heart I awaited my wife's scolding. But no. She kept on leaving a coin in my room. Without my knowing it, the coins began to pile up in a corner of the room.

I resumed my probing—the reason for my wife's giving me coins and her guests' leaving her money. It dawned upon me at last that it had no other reason than a sort of pleasure. Pleasure, pleasure . . . unexpectedly I began to acquire interest in the subject. I wanted to experience the existence of pleasure.

Taking advantage of my wife's absence, I went out to the streets. I brought along all my coins and changed them into paper notes—five won. Pocketing them, I walked and walked, heedless of direction, in order only to forget the reason for my walk. The streets that came to view after a long time stimulated my nerves. I began to feel tired in no time, but I persisted. Until late at night I kept walking, heedless of direction and oblivious of my original purpose. Of course I did not spend a penny; I could not conceive the idea of spending money. I've completely lost the ability to spend.

I could not stand the fatigue any longer. I staggered home. To reach my room, I had to pass through my wife's. Thinking she might have a visitor, I stopped before the door and clumsily cleared my throat. To my consternation, the door slid open, and my wife and a man behind her glared at me. The onrush of bright light blinded me, and I fidgeted.

Not that I didn't see my wife's angry eyes, but I had to pretend I didn't, because I had to pass through her room to get to mine.

My legs gave out, and I could not stand. I covered myself with my quilt. My heart throbbed, and I was on the verge of fainting. I was out of breath, though I had not been aware of it on the streets. Cold perspiration broke out on my back. I regretted my adventure. I wanted to sleep in order to forget the fatigue. I wanted a sound sleep.

After a rest, lying on my belly, my heart's wild beating subsided. I thought I was living again. Turning to lie on my back, I stretched my legs.

However, my heart again began to beat fast. I listened through the sliding doors to my wife and her man whispering. In order to sharpen my auditory sense, I opened my eyes and held my breath. But by that time I heard my wife and the man getting up, the man putting on his coat and hat, then the noise of the door opening, the loud thuds of the man's leather shoes on the ground, followed by my wife's rubber shoes softly treading, and their steps finally receding toward the gate.

I've never seen my wife acting this way before. She had never whispered to a man. Lying in my room, I used to miss the men's talk when they were drunk, but I always caught every word my wife spoke in an even clear voice, not too loud nor too low. Even when she said something that was against my grain, I felt relieved at her composed tone.

But there had to be some reason for her present attitude, I thought, and I felt displeased. But I made up my mind not to probe anything that night and tried to sleep. Sleep did not come for a long while, and my wife did not return until late. I must have been sleeping at last. My dream roamed amid the incoherent street scenes I had been witnessing.

Someone shook me violently. It was my wife after she had sent off her guest. I opened my eyes and stared at her. There was no smile on her face. After rubbing my eyes, I looked at her more attentively. Her eyes were filled with anger, and her lips trembled convulsively. It seemed her anger would not go away easily. So I closed my eyes. I awaited her tirade. But presently I heard her rise, breathe gently, swish her skirt, and then there was the opening and closing of the sliding doors. Lying still like a frog, I repented my sortie more than my hunger.

Inside the bedding, I begged her pardon. I told her it was a misunderstanding. I had returned home thinking it was past midnight—indeed not before midnight, as she had said. I was too tired. I had walked too far and too long, and that was my fault, if fault there must be. I wanted to give five won to someone in order to feel the pleasure of giving away money. That was all there was to it. If you think that sort of wish is wrong, it's all right with me. I concede I was wrong. Don't you see I am repenting?

If I could have spent five won, I would not have returned before midnight. But I could not. Because the streets were too complex, swarming with people. Indeed I could not figure out to whom I should give five won. And in the midst of it all, I ended by staggering with exhaustion.

The first thing I wanted was rest. I wanted to lie down. Hence I returned home. I'm sorry I miscalculated—I thought it was past midnight. I am sorry. I'm willing to apologize a hundred times. But if I failed to dispel her misunderstanding, what good is my apology? What a disheartening thing!

For an hour I had to fret like this. I put aside the quilt, rose, slid open the door, and staggered into my wife's room. I almost lost consciousness. I remember throwing myself down on her quilt, producing five won from my trouser pocket, and shoving it at her.

The following morning when I woke up, I found myself inside her bedding. It was the first time I had slept in my wife's room since we moved to compound number thirty-three.

The sun's rays were filtering through the window, but my wife was already out. Well, she might have gone out last night when I lost consciousness. I did not want to investigate. I was out of sorts, had no strength left to move my fingers. A sunny spot the size of a wrapping cloth dazzled my eyes. In the bright sunbeam countless particles of dust danced wildly. I felt my nostrils blocked. I closed my eyes, covered myself with the quilt, and tried to take a nap. But her body odor was provocative. I twisted and turned, and in the midst of recalling all the cosmetic bottles lined up on her dressing table and the perfume that wafted up the moment I uncorked them, I could not fall asleep, however desperately I tried.

Unable to calm down, I kicked the quilt to one side, got up with a jerk and returned to my room. I found a tray of food neatly arranged, already cold. She had gone out, leaving my feed behind. At first, I was hungry. But the moment I scooped up a spoonful of rice, I felt a sensation akin to putting cold ashes into my mouth. I threw the spoon down and crept into the quilt. The bedding that had missed me the previous whole night welcomed me. Covered with my quilt, this time I slept a deep sleep for a long while.

It was only after the sunlight came in that I awoke. My wife seemed not yet home. Or she might have returned but gone out again. But what was the use of examining the matter carefully?

I felt refreshed. I began to recall what had happened the night before. I cannot adequately tell of the pleasure I had felt when I thrust five won into her hand. I think I've discovered the guests' psychology when they leave money for my wife, and my wife's state of mind when she leaves coins for me. I was delighted beyond measure. I smiled to myself. How ludicrous I've been not to know such a state of mind. My shoulders began to dance.

Therefore I want to go out again tonight. But I've no money. I regretted having given my wife five won all at once. I regretted having thrown the piggy bank into the lavatory. Disappointed, but out of habit, I put my hand into the trouser pocket that had once contained five won and searched. Unexpectedly my hand caught something. Only two won. It doesn't have to be much money. I mean, any amount will do; I was grateful.

Oblivious of my only shabby suit and the assaulting hunger, I went out to the streets swinging my arms. Going out, I wished time would fly like an arrow so that it would soon be past midnight. Handing money to my wife and overnighting in her room are fine in every respect, but to return home mistakenly before midnight and to provoke her into looking daggers at me is terribly frightening. I kept watching the street clocks while roaming about, heedless of direction. I did not get tired easily this time. Only time's slow progress frustrated me.

After ascertaining by the Seoul railway station clock that it was past midnight, I turned toward home. That night I encountered my wife and her man standing at the gate talking. Assuming an unconcerned air, I brushed by them and went straight into my room. Presently my wife returned to hers. Then she began to sweep the floor, which she had hitherto never done. As soon as I heard her lying down, I slid open the door, went into her room, and thrust two won into her hand. She stole a glance at me as if she thought it strange that I returned home again without spending the money. At last

she allowed me to sleep in her room. I would not exchange that joy for anything in the world. I slept well.

When I woke up, my wife was already out again. I then went to my
room and took a nap. When she aroused me by shaking me, light was already streaming in. My wife asked me to come to her room, the first time
she had ever bestowed such a favor. With an unending smile, she dragged
me by the arms. I was apprehensive, lest a terrible conspiracy lurk behind
her changed attitude.

Leaving everything to her, I let her drag me into her room. There was a
neat supper table. Come to think of it, I had gone two days without food.
Forgetting that I was starved, I equivocated.

I began to think. I would not regret it even if she raised hell soon after
this last supper. In fact, I have been bored to death by the world of man.
With my mind at ease and in peace, I ate the strange supper with my wife.
We two seldom exchange a word, so after supper I returned to my room.
She did not detain me. I sat leaning against the wall, and lit a cigarette. And
waited for a thunderbolt. Let it strike me if it must.

Five minutes, ten minutes . . .

But no thunderbolt. Gradually tension loosened. I thought of going out
again tonight and wished I had money.

Of course I had none. What pleasure would there have been had I gone
out? I felt giddy. Incensed, I covered myself with a quilt and tossed and
turned. My supper seemed to rise up in my throat. I felt nauseated.

Why does not paper money—even a small amount—rain down from
heaven? Sadness overtook me. I knew no means of obtaining money. I must
have wept in the bed, asking why I didn't have money.

My wife came into the room once more. Startled, I crouched like a toad
and held my breath, anticipating her thunderbolt. But the words she spoke
were tender and friendly. She said she knew why I wept. I wept because of
the lack of money, she said. I was taken aback. How does she read others'
minds? I was a trifle frightened, but hoped that she might from the way she
talked intend to give me money—if so, how happy I would be. Wrapped in
the quilt, I did not raise my head, and waited for her next move. "There,"
followed by the sound of something falling beside the pillow. Judging from
its light sound, it must be paper notes. Then she whispered into my ear that
she would not mind if I returned a bit later than last night. That wouldn't be
too difficult; what made me happy and grateful in the first place was the
money.

At any rate, I went out. Since I am night-blind, I decided to walk around
the brightly lit streets. Then I dropped in at the coffee shop next to the first-
and second-class passengers' waiting room at Seoul station. That shop was a
great discovery.

First, no acquaintances of mine patronize the place. Even if they came
in, they left right away. I made up my mind: henceforth I would while away
my time there.

Also, the shop's clock, more than any other in the city, must tell the correct time. If I tactlessly trusted incorrect clocks and returned home ahead of time, I would faint again.

Occupying a whole booth, I drank a cup of hot coffee. Travelers seemed to be enjoying their coffee in the midst of rushing. They drank it quickly, gazing at the walls as if they were meditating, and then went out. I felt sad. But the sad mood here pleased me more than the cumbersome atmosphere of other tearooms in the city. Occasional shrill or thundering steam whistles were louder than the Mozart played in the shop. I read and reread, up and down, down and up, the menu with its list of few dishes. Their exotic names, like the names of my childhood playmates, came in and out of my vision.

I had no idea how long I had sat there, my mind meandering, when I noticed that the place was almost deserted, and the boys were tidying up the shop. It must be the time to close. A little after eleven. This is no haven after all! Where could I spend one more hour? Worrying, I left the coffee shop. It was raining. Heavy streaks of rain fell, intending to afflict me who was without a raincoat and an umbrella. Loitering in the waiting room with my weird appearance was out of the question. A bit of rain would not do me harm. I stepped out.

Soon I felt an unbearable chill. My suit began to drip, and in no time the rain soaked through to my skin. I tried to keep on wandering about the streets braving the rain, but I reached the point where I could no longer endure a chill. I shivered with cold, and my teeth chattered.

I quickened my gait and thought: probably my wife would have no visitor on a wet night like this. I decided to go home. If unfortunately there were guests, I would explain the unavoidable circumstances. They would understand my problem.

No sooner had I got home than I discovered my wife had a guest. I was cold and wet and, in the confusion, forgot to knock. I witnessed a scene that my wife would have liked me not to. With drenched feet I strode across her room and reached mine. Casting off my dripping garments, I covered myself with a quilt. I kept on shivering; the cold became intense. I felt as if the floor under me were sinking. I lost consciousness.

The following day when I opened my eyes, my wife was sitting beside my pillow, looking concerned. I had caught cold. The chill and headache persisted, and my mouth was full of bitter water.

Pressing her palm on my forehead, she told me to take some medicine. Judging from the coolness of her palm, I must have fever. She reappeared with four white pills and a glass of lukewarm water. "Take them and have a good sleep. You'll be all right," she said. I gulped them down and covered myself with the quilt; I fell asleep at a stroke, like a dead man.

I was laid up for several days with a running nose, during which time I kept on taking pills. I got over the cold, but a bitter taste like sumac lingered in my mouth.

I began wishing to stir out again. But my wife advised me not to. She told me to keep on taking the pills every day and rest. "You got a cold by roaming about to no purpose, causing me trouble," she said. She had a point. So I vowed not to go out, and planned to swallow the pills just to build up my health.

I kept on sleeping day and night. Strangely, I felt sleepy day and night and could not stand the feeling. I believed it to be a sure sign of regained strength on my part.

Thus I must have spent almost a month sleeping. My overgrown hair and moustache were uncomfortable, so I went to my wife's room while she was away and sat before her dressing table. I decided to have my hair cut and to smell her bottles of cosmetics at random. In the midst of the various odors. I detected her body fragrance, which made me feel entangled. I called her name to myself, "Yonsim!"

Once again after a long while I played with her glasses. And I played with her hand mirror. The sun filtering through the window was very warm. It was May, come to think of it.

I took a good stretch, laid myself down on her pillow, and wished to boast to the gods of my comfortable and joyful existence. I've no traffic with the community of man. The gods probably could neither punish nor praise me.

But the next moment I caught sight of a strange thing: a box of adalin— sleeping pills. I discovered the box under her dressing table, and thought they looked much like aspirin. I lifted the lid and found four tablets missing.

I remember taking four pills this morning. I slept yesterday, the day before yesterday, the day before that . . . I was unable to withstand sleep. My cold was over, but she kept on feeding me aspirin. Once, fire had broken out in the neighborhood while I was sleeping, but I slept through the fire. I slept that soundly. I must have been taking adalin for a month, thinking it was aspirin. This was too much!

All of a sudden I felt giddy, and I almost fainted. Pocketing the adalin box, I left home. I climbed up a hill. I loathed seeing all the things in the world of man. Walking, I resolved not to think about anything related to my wife. I thought about flat rocks, about azaleas I've never seen before, about larks, and about the rooks laying eggs to hatch. Fortunately I did not faint on the way.

I found a bench. I sat in meditation, thinking about aspirin and adalin. My head was too confused to think coherently. In five minutes, I got frustrated and became cross. Producing the adalin case from my pocket, I chewed all six tablets. What a funny taste! I then laid myself down on the bench. Why did I do such a thing? I do not understand. I just wanted to. I fell asleep right there. In my sleep, I heard the faint gurgling of a brook among the rocks.

When I woke up, it was broad daylight. I had slept one day and one night. The scene around me looked yellowish. Even in such a state, a thought flashed through my mind: aspirin, adalin.

Aspirin, adalin, aspirin, adalin, Marx, Malthus, Madras, aspirin, adalin.

My wife had cheated me into taking adalin for a month. Judging from the adalin box I had discovered in her room, the evidence was indisputable.

For what purpose did she put me to sleep day and night? After putting me to sleep, what did she do day and night?

Did she intend to kill me bit by bit?

On the other hand, it might very well be possible that what I took for a month was aspirin. She might have taken it herself in order to sleep away something that troubled her. If so, I am the one to be sorry. I was sorry to have harbored such a great suspicion.

I hurriedly climbed down the hill. My legs gave in, my head was dizzy, and I barely made my way home. It was shortly before eight.

I intended to apologize about my perverse thought. I was in such a hurry the words failed me.

Oh what a disaster! I witnessed something I should absolutely never have laid my eyes on. In confusion, I closed the door and stood leaning against the post, head lowered and eyes closed, trying to allay my dizziness. In a second, the door opened, and out came my wife, her clothes still in disarray. My head swam, and I fell head over heels. Astride me, she began to bite me all over. Pain almost killed me. Having neither intention nor energy enough to protest, I remained prostrate, awaiting what would come next. A man came and lifted my wife in his arms and carried her into the room. I loathed her for so docilely submitting to his arms. I loathed him.

"Are you spending the night prowling or whoring around?" she reviled me. I was mortified. Dumbfounded, words failed me.

I wanted to shout back at her. Didn't you try to kill me? My allegation might prove to be groundless, which would bring a disaster. I'd rather keep silent in spite of my undeserved treatment. I stood up, dusted, and emptied my trouser pocket—God knows what made me do it—and stealthily pushed a few paper notes and coins under her doorsill. Then I ran out.

Narrowly escaping a few collisions with passing cars, I managed to find Seoul station. Sitting in an empty booth, I wanted to remove the bitter taste in my mouth.

Oh for a cup of hot coffee! As soon as I stepped into the station hall, I realized that I had forgotten the fact that I was penniless. Dazed, I loitered helplessly, heedless of direction, not knowing what to do. Like a half-wit, I wandered here and there . . .

I could not recall where I'd been. The moment I realized that I was on the top floor of the Mitsukoshi department store, it was almost noon.

I sat down at the first place I spied and recalled the twenty-six years of my life. In dim recollection nothing emerged clearly.

I asked myself: What desire have I had in life? I did not want to answer yes or no. I disliked such a question. It was hard for me to recognize even my own existence.

Bending over, I looked at some goldfish in a bowl. How handsome they were! The little ones, the big ones—all of them looked fresh and wonderful. They cast their shadows in the bowl under the May sun. The movement of their fins imitated people waving handkerchiefs. Trying to count the number of fins, I stayed bent over. My back was warm.

I looked down on the merry streets. The tired pedestrians, like the goldfish fins, jostled wearily. Entangled by a slimy rope, they could not free themselves. Dragging along my body crumbling from fatigue and hunger, I too must be swept away into the merry streets.

Coming out, a thought flashed through my mind: Where would my steps lead me?

We're misunderstanding each other. Could my wife feed me adalin in place of aspirin? I could not believe it. There is no reason for her to do so. Then, did I steal and whore around? Certainly not!

As a couple we are destined to go lame. There is no need to see logic in my and my wife's behavior. No need to defend ourselves either. Let fact be fact, misunderstanding be misunderstanding. Limping through life endlessly. Isn't that so?

However, whether or not I should return to my wife was a trifle difficult to decide. Should I go? Where shall I go?

At the moment, a shrill noon siren sounded. People were flapping their limbs like chickens; the moment when all sorts of glass, steel, marble, paper currency, and ink seemed to be boiling up, bubbling—the noon with extreme splendor.

All of a sudden my armpits began to itch. Ah, these are traces of where my man-made wings had once grown. The wings I don't possess today. Torn shreds of hope and ambition shuffled like dictionary pages in my mind.

I halted, wanting to shout:

Wings, grow again!
Let me fly, fly, fly, let me fly once more.
Let me try them once again.

❈ Discussion and Writing

1. Comment on the description of the man, his personality, and his surroundings. Examine the significance of splitting everything in half in the narrative.

2. Describe the games the man and his wife play. What does the mirror signify? Comment on other images that enhance the reader's understanding of their games.

3. What is signified by the reversal of the man's relationship with his wife: examine the symbolism of the coin (money) and interpret its importance for the man.
4. What are the implications of incidents involving: the aspirin/adalin mix-up, the Mitsukoshi department store, and the goldfish?
5. Explain the reference to growing wings. What do they represent?
6. Analyze the nature of wit, paradox, and mask in the prelude to the story. Why is emotion described as "a pose" and common sense as "an ailment"? In what way is the prelude pertinent to the narrative?

Xiao Hong
(Hsiao Hung, 1911–1942)
China

Xiao Hong (Zhang Naiying) was born in the town of Hulan, near the city of Harbin (at the time, in Manchuria), just at the close of the Qing dynasty. The residents called the town Hulan River, the name she used in her autobiographical work *Tales of Hulan River*. She came from a wealthy traditional family but because of her father's strictness, she frequently turned to her grandfather for comfort. She left Manchuria at the time of the Japanese occupation, and died in Hong Kong ten years later of complications from a throat infection. Xiao Hong traveled and wrote a good deal during those ten years, remaining devoted to the memory of her beloved grandfather and to Lu Xun, her mentor and benefactor. In *Huiyi Lu Xun* (Remembering Mr. Lu Xun, 1940) she recorded her warm memories of his many kindnesses, among them his sponsoring the publication of her work and that of her husband Xiao Jun, who was also a writer.

Acclaimed as a masterpiece, *Tales of Hulan River* was begun in the city of Chongqing, the capital during the war, and completed shortly before her death. Xiao Hong depicts small-town life in Manchuria as the Qing dynasty, with its brutality and devastation, was drawing to a close. She portrayed the inherent complexity of the society, while at the same time evoking the innocence of her childhood perspective. This innocence also generates a good deal of horror. Mao Dun called the work "a narrative poem, a colorful genre painting, a haunting poem," Xiao Hong remains known as a master of description and stylistic simplicity. *Tales of Hulan River* opens, appropriately, with a picture of the weather, included here as "The Crossroads," for in Hulan River the temperature often drops to −50°.

The Crossroads*

I

After the harsh winter has sealed up the land, the earth's crust begins to crack and split. From south to north, from east to west; from a few feet to several yards in length; anywhere, anytime, the cracks run in every direction. As soon as harsh winter is upon the land, the earth's crust opens up.

The severe winter weather splits the frozen earth.

Old men use whisk brooms to brush the ice off their beards the moment they enter their homes. "Oh, it's cold out today!" they say. "The frozen ground has split open."

A carter twirls his long whip as he drives his cart sixty or seventy *li* under the stars, then at the crack of dawn he strides into an inn, and the first thing he says to the innkeeper is: "What terrible weather. The cold is like a dagger."

After he has gone into his room at the inn, removed his dogskin cap with earflaps, and smoked a pipeful of tobacco, he reaches out for a steamed bun; the back of his hand is a mass of cracked, chapped skin.

The skin on people's hands is split open by the freezing cold. The man who sells cakes of bean curd is up at dawn to go out among the people's homes and sell his product. If he carelessly sets down his square wooden tray full of bean curd it sticks to the ground, and he is unable to free it. It will have quickly frozen to the spot.

The old steamed-bun peddler lifts his wooden box filled with the steaming buns up onto his back, and at the first light of day he is out hawking on the street. After emerging from his house he walks along at a brisk pace shouting at the top of his voice. But before too long, layers of ice have formed on the bottoms of his shoes, and he walks as though he were treading on rolling and shifting eggs. The snow and ice have encrusted the soles of his shoes. He walks with an unsure step, and if he is not altogether careful he will slip and fall. In fact, he slips and falls despite all his caution. Falling down is the worst thing that can happen to him, for his wooden box crashes to the ground, and the buns come rolling out of the box, one on top of the other. A witness to the incident takes advantage of the old man's inability to pick himself up and scoops up several of the buns, which he eats as he leaves the scene. By the time the old man has struggled to his feet, gathered up his steamed buns—ice, snow, and all—and put them back in the box, he counts them and discovers that some are missing. He understands at once and shouts to the man who is eating the buns, but has still not left the scene: "Hey, the weather's icy cold, the frozen ground's all cracked, and my buns are all gone!"

Passersby laugh when they hear him say this. He then lifts the box up onto his back and walks off again, but the layers of ice on the soles of his

---

*Translated by Howard Goldblatt

shoes seem to have grown even thicker, and he finds the going more diffi-cult than before. Drops of sweat begin to form on his back, his eyes become clouded with the frost, ice gathers in even greater quantity on his beard, and the earflaps and front of his tattered cap are frosting up with the vapor from his breath. The old man walks more and more slowly, his worries and fears causing him to tremble in alarm; he resembles someone on iceskates for the first time who has just been pushed out onto the rink by a friend.

A puppy is so freezing cold it yelps and cries night after night, whim-pering as though its claws were being singed by flames.

The days grow even colder:
Water vats freeze and crack;
Wells are frozen solid;

Night snowstorms seal the people's homes; they lie down at night to sleep, and when they get up in the morning they find they cannot open their doors.

Once the harsh winter season comes to the land everything undergoes a change: the skies turn ashen gray, as though a strong wind has blown through, leaving in its aftermath a turbid climate accompanied by a constant flurry of snowflakes whirling in the air. People on the road walk at a brisk pace as their breath turns to vapor in the wintry cold. Big carts pulled by teams of seven horses form a caravan in the open country, one following closely upon the other, lanterns flying, whips circling in the air under the starry night. After running two *li* the horses begin to sweat. They run a bit farther, and in the midst of all that snow and ice the men and horses are hot and lathered. The horses stop sweating only after the sun emerges and they are finally turned into their stalls. But the moment they stop sweating a layer of frost forms on their coats.

After the men and horses have eaten their fill they are off and running again. Here in the frigid zones there are few people; unlike the southern re-gions, where you need not travel far from one village to another, and where each township is near the next, here there is nothing but a blanket of snow as far as the eye can see. There is no neighboring village within the range of sight, and only by relying on the memories of those familiar with the roads can one know the direction to travel. The big carts with their seven-horse teams transport their loads of foodstuffs to one of the neighboring towns. Some have brought in soybeans to sell, others have brought sorghum. Then when they set out on their return trip they carry back with them oil, salt, and dry goods.

Hulan River is one of these small towns, not a very prosperous place at all. It has only two major streets, one running north and south and one run-ning east and west, but the best-known place in town is The Crossroads, for it is the heart of the whole town. At The Crossroads there is a jewelry store, a yardage shop, an oil store, a salt store, a teashop, a pharmacy, and the office of a foreign dentist. Above this dentist's door hangs a large shingle about the size of a rice-measuring basket, on which is painted a row of oversized teeth. The advertisement is hopelessly out of place in this small town, and the people who look at it cannot figure out just what it's supposed to represent. That is because neither the oil store, the yardage shop, nor the salt store displays any kind of advertisement; above the door of the salt store, for example, only the word "salt" is written, and hanging above the door of the yardage shop are two curtains that are as old as the hills. The remainder of the signs are like the one at the pharmacy, which gives nothing more than the name of the bespectacled physician whose job it is to feel women's pulses as they drape their arms across a small pillow. To illustrate: the physician's name is Li Yongchun, and the name of his pharmacy is simply "Li Yongchun." People rely on their memories, and even if Li Yongchun were to take down his sign, the people would still know that he was there. Not only the townsfolk, but even the people from the countryside are more or less familiar with the streets of the town and what can be found there. No advertisement, no publicity is necessary. If people are in need of something, like cooking oil, some salt, or a piece of fabric, then they go inside and buy it. If they don't need anything, then no matter how large a sign is hung outside, they won't buy anything.

That dentist is a good case in point. When the people from the countryside spot those oversized teeth they stare at them in bewilderment, and there are often many people standing in front of the large sign looking up at it, unable to fathom its reason for being there. Even if one of them were standing there with a toothache, under no circumstances would he let that dentist, with her foreign methods, pull his tooth for him. Instead he would go over to the Li Yongchun Pharmacy, buy two ounces of bitter herbs, take them home and hold them in his mouth, and let that be the end of that! The teeth on that advertisement are simply too big; they are hard to figure out, and just a little bit frightening.

As a consequence, although that dentist hung her shingle out for two or three years, precious few people ever went to her to have their teeth pulled. Eventually, most likely owing to her inability to make a living, the woman dentist had no recourse but to engage in midwifery on the side.

In addition to The Crossroads, there are two other streets, one called Road Two East and the other called Road Two West. Both streets run from north to south, probably for five or six *li*. There is nothing much on these two streets worth nothing—a few temples, several stands where flatcakes are sold, and a number of grain storehouses.

On Road Two East there is a fire mill standing in a spacious courtyard, a large chimney made of fine red brick rising high above it. I have heard that no one is allowed to enter the fire mill, for there are a great many knobs and gadgets inside which must not be touched. If someone did touch them, he might burn himself to death. Otherwise, why would it be called a fire mill? Because of the flames inside, the mill is reportedly run neither by horses nor donkeys—it is run by fire. Most folk wonder why the mill itself doesn't go up in flames since only fire is used. They ponder this over and over, but are unable to come up with an answer, and the more they ponder it, the more confused they become, especially since they are not allowed to go inside and check things out for themselves. I've heard they even have a watchman at the door.

There are also two schools on Road Two East, one each at the southern and northern ends. They are both located in temples—one in the Dragon King Temple and one in the Temple of the Patriarch—and both are elementary schools.

The school located in the Dragon King Temple is for the study of raising silkworms, and is called the Agricultural School, while the one in the Temple of the Patriarch is just a regular elementary school with one advanced section added, and is called the Higher Elementary School.

Although the names of these two schools vary, the only real difference between them is that in the one they call the Agricultural School the silkworm pupae are fried in oil in the autumn, and the teachers there enjoy several sumptuous meals.

There are no silkworms to be eaten in the Higher Elementary School, where the students are definitely taller than those in the Agricultural School. The students in the Agricultural School begin their schoolwork by learning the characters for "man," "hand," "foot," "knife," and "yardstick," and the oldest among them cannot be more than sixteen or seventeen years of age. But not so in the Higher Elementary School; there is a student there already twenty-four years old who is learning to play the foreign bugle and who has already taught in private schools out in the countryside for four or five years, but is only now himself attending the Higher Elementary School. Even the man who has been manager of a grain store for two years is a student at the school.

When this elementary school student writes a letter to his family he asks questions like: "Has Little Baldy's eye infection gotten better?" Little Baldy is the nickname of his eldest son, who is eight. He doesn't mention his second son or his daughters, because if he were to include all of them the letter would be much too long. Since he is already the father of a whole brood of children—the head of a family—whenever he sends a letter home he is mainly concerned with household matters: "Has the tenant Wang sent over his rent yet?" "Have the soybeans been sold?" "What is the present market situation?" and the like.

Students like him occupy a favored position in the class; the teacher must treat them with due respect, for if he drops his guard, this kind of student will often stand up, classical dictionary in hand, and stump the teacher with one of his questions. He will smugly point out that the teacher has used the wrong character in a phrase he has written on the board.

✺ Discussion and Writing

1. Analyze the effect of the description of the harsh winter in the opening paragraph.
2. What are the implications of the description of life at the Crossroads? Why is advertising absurd in Hulan River?
3. What is implied by the townspeople's perception of the fire mill?

Hwang Sunwon
(b. 1915)
Korea

Hwang Sunwon was born in Taedong, South P'yongan Province, Korea, at the time of the Japanese occupation, when men were obliged to join the Japanese army or forced to work in labor camps. His father was imprisoned for eighteen months because of having taken part in the Independence movement of 1919. As a child, Hwang Sunwon attended Japanese-language schools, and as a young man he studied at Waseda University in Tokyo, graduating with a degree in English literature in 1939. After first trying his hand at poetry—publishing poems in the P'yongyang newspapers in the early 1930s—he turned to fiction, and his first collection of stories was published in 1940, soon after his return from Japan. Although writing was banned during the Pacific War, he continued to work, and his stories of this period reflect the national despair. Because Korea was divided after World War II at the 38th parallel into a Soviet-dominated North and a U.S.-dominated South, the despair deepened as the two superpowers fought for control. During the ensuing Korean War (1950–1953), he left his home in the North. His experiences as a refugee informed the body of work he wrote at this time.

After the war, with Korea still divided, the area identified as the Demilitarized Zone stood as a bitter symbol of brother against brother. In "Cranes" (1953), Hwang Sunwon captured the bewildering painfulness of the end of the war that brought no peace. The sense of loneliness projected in "Cranes" pervaded his subsequent stories and novels. Still, he sought moments of connection. Considered the master of the modern short story, he has said that while the "writer should seek beauty," one should also "seek the salvation of man." Whether as a professor at Kyonghui (Kyung Hee) University or as a writer, he has remained committed to his belief in the power of literature.

Cranes*

The village just north of the thirty-eighth parallel was quiet beneath the clear, lofty autumn sky.

A white gourd lay where it had tumbled, leaning against another on the dirt-floored space between the rooms of an abandoned house.

An old man Songsam happened to meet put his long tobacco pipe behind his back. The children, as children would, had already fled from the street to keep their distance. Everyone's face was masked with fear.

Overall, the village showed few signs of the conflict that had just ended. Still, it did not seem to Songsam to be the same village where he had grown up.

He stopped walking at a grove of chestnut trees on the hill behind the village. He climbed one of the trees. In his mind, from far away, he could hear the shouts of the old man with a wen.[1] Are you kids climbing my chestnut tree again?

Had that old man died during Songsam's absence? He had not seen him among the men he had met so far in the village. Hanging onto the tree, Songsam looked up at the clear autumn sky. Though he did not shake the branch, some of the remaining chestnut burrs burst open, and the nuts fell to the ground.

When he reached the house that was being used temporarily as the Public Peace Office, he found someone there bound tightly with rope. This was the first young man he had seen in the village. As Songsam drew closer and examined his face, he was taken aback. It was none other than his boyhood friend Tokjae.

Songsam asked one of the security guards from his detachment who had accompanied him from Ch'ont'ae what the situation was. The guard answered that the prisoner had been vice-chairman of the Communist Farmers' Alliance and that he had just been captured while hiding in his own house here in the village

Songsam squatted by the house and lit a cigarette. Tokjae was to be escorted to Ch'ongdan by one of the young security guards.

After a while Songsam lit a cigarette from the one he had been smoking, then stood up.

"I'll take the guy myself."

Tokjae kept his face turned away; he did not even glance at Songsam.

They left the village.

Songsam kept smoking, but he could not taste the tobacco. He just sucked and puffed. He suddenly realized that Tokjae might like a smoke. He

---

*Translated by J. Martin Holman
[1] A benign skin tumor. [eds.]

recalled when they were boys how they had shared a smoke of dried pumpkin leaves, hiding from the adults in the corner of the wall around the house. But how could he offer a guy like this a cigarette?

Once, when they were boys, he had gone with Tokjae to steal chestnuts from the old man with the wen. Songsam was taking his turn climbing the tree when suddenly they heard the old man shouting. Songsam slid down the tree and got chestnut burrs stuck in his rear end. Yet he dashed off without doing anything about them. Once they had run far enough that the old man could not catch them, he turned his backside toward Tokjae. It hurt even more to have the prickly chestnut spines pulled out. Tears ran freely down Songsam's face. Tokjae held out a fistful of his own chestnuts, then thrust them into Songsam's pocket.

Songsam had just lit a cigarette from the last one he had smoked, but he tossed it away. He made up his mind not to smoke anymore while he was escorting this bastard Tokjae.

They reached the mountain ridge road. He had often come to the ridge with Tokjae to cut fodder before Songsam moved to the area around Ch'on-t'ae, south of the thirty-eighth parallel, two years before the Liberation in 1945.

Songsam felt an inexplicable urge. He burst out shouting. "You bastard, how many people have you killed?"

Tokjae glanced toward Songsam, then looked away again.

"How many people have you killed?"

Tokjae turned his face toward Songsam and glared. The light in his eyes grew fierce and his mouth, which was surrounded by a stubble beard, twitched.

"So, is that what you've been doing? Killing people?"

That bastard! Still, Songsam felt a clearing in the center of his chest, as if something caught there had been released. But then he said, "Why wouldn't someone like the vice-chairman of the Farmers' Alliance try to escape? You must have been hiding out because you had been given some assignment."

Tokjae did not respond.

"Well? Answer me. What kind of mission were you hiding out to do?"

Silent, Tokjae just kept walking. The guy certainly seems cowed. At a time like this, it would be good to get a look at his face. But Tokjae did not turn toward Songsam again.

Songsam took hold of the pistol in his belt.

"It's no use trying to explain your way out of it. You'll have to be shot anyway, so go ahead and tell the truth."

Tokjae began to speak. "I'm not trying to get out of anything. First and last, I'm the son of a dirt farmer. I was made vice-chairman of the Farmers' Alliance because they said I was a hard worker. If that's a crime worthy of death, there is nothing I can do. The only skill I've got is tilling the ground."

After a moment he continued. "My father is sick in bed at home. It's been six months now."

Tokjae's father was a widower, a poor farmer who had grown old with only his son by his side. Seven years ago his back had already been bent, and his face had dark age spots.

"Are you married?"

"Yes," Tokjae answered after a moment.

"Who to?"

"To Shorty."

Not Shorty! Now that's interesting. Shorty, a fat little girl who knew the breadth of the earth but not the height of the sky. Always such a prig. Songsam and Tokjae had hated that about her. They were always teasing and laughing at her. So that's who Tokjae had married.

"And how many kids do you have?"

"Our first is due this fall."

Songsam tried to stifle a smile that rose to his lips in spite of himself. Asking how many children Tokjae had and having him answer that the first was due in autumn was so funny he could not stand it. Shorty—holding up her armload of a belly on that little body. But Songsam realized that this was not the place to laugh or joke about such things.

"Anyway, don't you think it looks suspicious that you stayed behind and didn't flee?"

"I tried to go. They said if there was an invasion from the south, every last man who was a man would be captured and killed, so all the men between seventeen and forty were forced to head north. I really didn't have any choice. I thought I would carry my father on my back and go. But he wouldn't stand for it. He said if a farmer leaves the fields he has already tilled and planted, where can he go? My father has always depended on me alone. He's grown old farming all these years, and I have to be the one to close his eyes when the end comes. The truth is, people like us who just till the ground wouldn't be any better off even if we *did* flee . . . "

Songsam himself had fled the past June. One night he secretly spoke to his father about escaping, but his father had said the same thing as Tokjae's. How could a farmer flee and leave his work behind? Songsam fled alone. As he wandered along the strange roads through strange towns in the south, he never stopped thinking of the farm work he had left to his old parents and his wife and children. Fortunately, then as now, his family was healthy.

They crossed the ridge. Now, somehow, Songsam was the one who kept his eyes averted. The autumn sun was hot on his forehead. What a perfect day this would be for harvesting, he thought.

After they had gone down the far side of the ridge, Songsam hesitated.

It looked like a group of people wearing white clothes were stooped over working in the middle of the field. It was actually a flock of cranes, here in the so-called Demilitarized Zone at the thirty-eighth parallel. Even though people were no longer living here, the cranes remained as before.

Once when Songsam and Tokjae were about twelve years old, they had secretly set a snare and caught a crane. They even bound its wings with a straw rope. The two boys came out to the place they kept the crane almost every day; they would hold the crane around the neck and raise a ruckus trying to ride on its back. Then one day they heard the adults in the village talking in whispers. Some people had come from Seoul to hunt cranes. They had special permission from the Japanese governor-general to collect specimens of some kind. When they heard this, the two boys raced off to the field. They were not worried about being caught by the adults and scolded. Now they had only one thought: their crane must not die. Without stopping to catch their breath, they scrambled through the weeds. They took the snare off the crane's leg and loosened the straw rope from its wings. But the crane could hardly walk, probably because it had been tied up for so long. The boys held the crane up between them and tossed it into the air. They heard a gunshot. The bird flapped its wings two, three, four times, but fell back to the ground. It was hit! But in the next instant, another crane in the grass nearby spread its wings. Their own crane, which had been lying on the ground, stretched out its long neck, gave a cry, and rose into the sky, too. They circled over the boys' heads, then flew off into the distance. The boys could not take their eyes off the spot in the blue sky where the cranes had disappeared.

"Let's go catch a crane." Songsam said abruptly.

Tokjae was bewildered. He did not know what was going on.

"I'll make a snare out of this, and you drive the cranes this way." Songsam untied Tokjae's bonds and took the cord. Before Tokjae knew it, Songsam was crawling through the grass.

At once. Tokjae's face went white. The words "you'll have to be shot" flashed through his mind. At any moment a bullet would come from wherever Songsam had crawled.

Some distance away, Songsam rose and turned toward Tokjae. "What do you mean standing there like an idiot! Go drive some cranes this way!"

Only then did Tokjae realize what was happening. He started crawling through the weeds.

Above, two cranes were soaring, their vast wings spread against the high, blue autumn sky.

❋ Discussion and Writing

1. What is the origin of desolation and fear in the village?
2. Comment on the political and personal situations Songsam and Tokjae face and the disparate decisions they make. Describe the implications of the times they lived in.
3. Explain the dichotomy between Songsam's memory of the past and his treatment of Tokjae in the present. What is the impact of the dialogue between the two men?
4. What does the childhood incident involving the crane reveal about each in the past? What motivates Songsam's last action? What is its implication?
5. Analyze the intertwined narrative of the past and the present. Comment on the fusion of the two times in the concluding part of the narrative.

❋ Research and Comparison

Compare the theme of alienation in Hwang Sunwon's "Cranes" and in "The Red Cocoon," by his Japanese contemporary Abe Kobo.

Interdisciplinary Discussion Question: Research the history of the Korean War, its causes and impact. Examine the writings of any two Korean writers as they reflect the social and political issues that affect people's lives.

So Chongju
(b. 1915)
Korea

So Chongju was born in Sonun, a village in North Cholla Province in southwestern Korea. The southwest is noted for religious zeal and rebellions: for farmers' rebellions at the end of the nineteenth century and for guerrilla warfare in the twentieth. In his early poetry, he worked in the dialect of the southwest. He also spoke of his father as a "serf," a declaration that pointed to Japanese occupation of Korea and to So Chongju's literary independence as well. Respected for the depth of feeling evoked throughout his career, he experimented with form and theme, gravitating in midlife toward older literary motifs: nature, the legendary past, and Buddhism. In his later poetry, however, he turned once again to daily life and to Sonun. Thus in "The Huge Wave" (1972), there is a reverberation of "Self Portrait," a poem in his first collection, *Flower Snake* (1938). In "The Huge Wave," he described his grandfather, a "fisherman," and his old grandmother with an intensity augmented by the evolution of his own aesthetic and by a linguistic simplicity.

The Huge Wave*

There was a day when the sea overflowed, climbing back up the stream, sliding through gaps in the hemp-stalk hedge, crossing over the corn patch to gather brimming in the yard of my grandmother's house. On such a day I would have been visiting for minnows or shrimp fry, and hopping around chirping, happy as a lark. Grandmother, who always seemed able to spin the stories out as long as the silkworm's thread, this time for some reason was utterly still. She stood there, her old face turned reddish, like the sunset, staring mutely out to sea. I did not understand, that day, but now that she has passed away I have at last begun to. Grandfather was a fisherman, sailing far out to sea, and one autumn, before the time I was born, they say that in a sudden storm he was swept away overboard and forever lost. There was simply nothing grandmother could say, though her face flushed red, when she saw the waters of her husband's sea returning to the yard of his own home.

❀ Discussion and Writing

1. Analyze the imagery that describes the movement of the overflowing sea.
2. Describe the grandmother: comment on the implications of the silkworm thread, the sunset, and her mute stare.
3. What is the importance of the grandson in the scene?
4. Examine the impact of the personification of the sea; discuss how the beginning of the poem relates to its end.

Ch'i Chun
(b. 1918)
Taiwan

Ch'i Chun (P'an Hsi-chen) was born in Zhejiang (Chekiang) Province in China and graduated from Zhe Jiang University in Hangzhou, where she studied in the Chinese Language Department. She emigrated to Taiwan,

*Translated by Peter Lee

and subsequently taught in several universities in Taipei and the United States before retiring. She has published many highly regarded volumes of essays as well as anthologies of short stories. In "The Chignon," she portrays the retention of feudal mores and their effect on women. Seen through the eyes of a young girl, the story of a woman's role, her sexuality, and male power becomes all the more bitter and, at the same time, poignant.

The Chignon*

When Mother was young, she would weave her tresses into a long thick braid. During the day she wound it into a shell-like spiral and piled it high on the back of her head. Evenings she undid it and let it hang down her back. When I slept I would snuggle up close to Mother's shoulder and playfully wrap my fingers around the tip of her braid. My nose was continuously assailed by whiffs of "Twin Sister" hair oil mingled with the smell of her hair. Though the odor was rather unpleasant, it was part of the security I felt in lying by Mother's side, and I would fall quickly off to sleep.

Once a year, on the seventh day of the seventh lunar month, Mother would thoroughly wash her hair. According to rural custom, hair could never be washed on ordinary days, as the dirty water would flow down to where the king of the underworld would store it up to make one drink after death. Only if the hair was washed on the seventh day of the seventh lunar month could the dirty water pass harmlessly out to the Eastern Sea.

So on that day, all the women in the village let their hair hang loose to dry over their shoulders. Some of the women with flowing hair were as beautiful as vineyard fairies,[1] others as hideous as monsters. Take my fifth uncle's wife for example—a squat, withered old hag. On her nearly-bald head she used black ash to draw in a square hairline, and then painted her scalp pitch black. Thus when shampooing her hair, the charcoal was completely washed away, and out shone the half-bald, shiny crown of her head, fringed with thin wisps of hair fluttering down her back. She would hobble to and fro helping my mother fix dinner. I never dared glance her way.

But Mother's raven hair was like a length of satin falling over her shoulders. When a breeze blew, locks of shorter hair would sometimes sweep against her soft white cheeks. She would squint, gather the hair in her hand, and smooth it back, but soon another puff of wind would pass by. Mother was near-sighted, and when she narrowed her eyes in a squint, she was remarkably beautiful. I thought, if only Father were at home to see Mother's glossy black hair, he certainly would go out and buy a pair of sparkling dia-

---

*Translated by Jane Parish Young
[1]The vineyard fairies are described in a popular children's song.

mond hair clips for her to wear. Mother probably would have worn them a while, then, embarrassed, have taken them out. That pair of diamond clips would then become part of my headdress when I played bride.

Father returned home soon afterward, bringing not the diamond clips, but a concubine. Her skin was white and delicate, her head of soft cloud-like hair even blacker, shinier than Mother's. The hair on her temples seemed like folded cicada wings half-concealing her ears. Her hair, brushed back and knotted in a horizontal "S" chignon, covered the back of her head like a huge bat. She presented Mother with a pair of emerald earrings, but Mother just kept them in a drawer and never wore them, not even once. She wouldn't let me play with them, though. I thought she was probably saving them because they were too nice.

After the family moved to Hangchow, Mother didn't have to work in the kitchen anymore. Frequently Father would want her to come out and entertain guests. Her severe hairstyle really seemed out of place, so Father insisted that she change. Mother asked her friend Aunt Chang to style an "Abalone Fish" for her. At that time, the "Abalone Fish" was the style old ladies wore. Mother had just turned thirty, yet she wanted to look like an old lady. When the concubine saw it, she would only smirk, while Father would constantly wrinkle his brow. Once when we were alone, I quietly implored, "Mother, why don't you also do your hair into an 'S' twist and wear the emerald earrings that 'Auntie'[2] gave you?" Mother replied solemnly, "Your mother is a country woman, unsuited for that kind of modern fashion. How can I wear such fancy earrings?"

When "Auntie" washed her hair, she would never select the seventh day of the seventh lunar month. Within one month she washed her hair many times. After washing, a maidservant standing to one side would lightly swing a large pink feather fan to and fro. Her soft hair would float out, making me feel light and dizzy. Father would sit on a sandalwood lounge chair, puffing away on his water pipe. He often turned around to look at her, and his eyes sparkled with laughter. "Auntie" dressed her hair with "Three Flowers" oil, and the perfume floated in all directions. Then she sat straight up facing the mirror, and entwined a glossy "S" chignon around her head. I stood to one side, entranced. She handed me a bottle of the "Three Flowers" oil and asked me to take it to Mother. But Mother just put it in the back of the closet saying. "The smell of this new hair oil turns my stomach."

Mother couldn't always trouble Aunt Chang, so she styled a taut "Abalone Fish" herself. It turned out about the same as her first twist. Father didn't like it; even I thought it was awful.

At that time, "Auntie" had already hired a Mrs. Liu to dress her hair. Mrs. Liu wore a huge red bamboo pin in her hair and puffed and panted as her large duck feet carried her short plump body along. She came every

---

[2]According to the author, this is what her father wanted her to call his concubine.

morning at ten to fashion all different kinds of coiffures for "Auntie"—the "Phoenix," "Feather Fan," "Entwined Heart Twist," "Swallow Tail," etc.— she was always changing the style. The coiffures accentuated "Auntie's" delicate skin and willowy waist, which more and more drew delighted smiles from Father. Mrs. Liu advised Mother, "Madam, why don't you dress your hair a little more fashionably?" But Mother, shaking her head, pursed her thick lips, and just walked away without saying a word.

Soon afterward Aunt Chang brought a regular hair dresser, a Mrs. Chen, to Mother. She was older than Mrs. Liu, and had a huge flat yellowish face with two protruding shiny gold teeth. At a glance one could tell she was the kind of woman who liked to gossip. She would ramble on about people from old Mr. Chao's elder daughter-in-law down to General Li's third concubine, all the while dressing Mother's hair. Mother sat wilted in her chair, not uttering a single word, but I listened with great relish. Sometimes Mrs. Liu and Mrs. Chen came together. Mother and the concubine would sit back to back in front of the breezeway and have their hair dressed. One could hear "Auntie" and Mrs. Liu talking and laughing; on our side Mother just sat resting with her eyes closed. Mrs. Chen brushed and combed with less and less vigor, and soon quit altogether. I distinctly heard her tell Mrs. Liu, "This antique of a country hick—she still wants her hair combed and dressed." I was so angry that I cried, but didn't dare tell Mother.

From then on, I stood on a low stool and brushed Mother's hair into the simplest "Abalone Fish." I would stand on tiptoe and watch Mother in the mirror. Her face was already not as plump and radiant as when we lived in the country and she hurried about in the kitchen. Her eyes fixed on the mirror, she gazed at herself absent-mindedly, never again squinting and smiling. I gathered Mother's hair a lock at a time and brushed, but I already knew that one little yellow willow comb couldn't brush away Mother's heartsickness—because from the other side of the breezeway came floating across the occasional tinkling sound of Father's and "Auntie's" laughter.

After I grew up I left home to pursue my studies. When I returned home for summer and winter vacations, I would sometimes dress Mother's hair. I gathered her hair together in the palm of my hand and felt it becoming sparser and sparser. I remembered back in my childhood when on the seventh day of the seventh lunar month I saw Mother's soft raven tresses flowing over her shoulders, her face filled with joy, and I couldn't help but feel heartbroken. When Mother saw me return home, her distressed look occasionally gave way to smiles. No matter what, the happiest time was when Mother and daughter were together.

When I was studying in Shanghai, Mother wrote to say she had rheumatism and couldn't lift her arms. Even the simplest twist came out all wrong, so she just cut her sparse locks off. I clutched her letter in my hands, and as I sat bathed in desolate moonlight beside the dormitory window, I cried in loneliness. The late autumn night breeze blew over me and I felt cold. I draped the soft sweater that Mother had knit for me over my shoulders and warmth crept over me from head to toe. But Mother was old now, I couldn't always be at her side. She had cut off her thinning hair, but how could she trim away a heart full of sorrows?

Soon afterward, "Auntie" came to Shanghai on business and brought me a picture of Mother, I hadn't seen her for three years—her hair had already turned silvery white. Saddened, I stared dumbly at the picture, yet had no way of pouring out my feelings to "Auntie," who stood before me. Almost as if sympathizing with my thoughts of Mother, she rambled on and on about Mother's present condition, saying her heart was weak and she was troubled again with rheumatism, so she was not as strong as before. I bowed my head and listened in silence, thinking that it was she who had made my mother unhappy all her life. But I didn't hate her anymore, not even a little bit, because since Father's death, Mother and "Auntie" had unpredictably become friends in their mutual suffering. Mother had stopped hating her long ago.

I looked at her closely. She wore a gray padded cloth gown, with a white flower tucked in her hair. Her nape no longer was draped with the rich and versatile "Phoenix" or "Entwined Heart" twists of days past, but was covered by a very simple "Banana Roll." She didn't apply any makeup, and appeared sad and lonely. I couldn't help feeling unlimited pity for her, because she wasn't a woman like Mother, contenting herself with a tranquil life. Having followed Father close to twenty years, she had enjoyed honor and wealth, but once her support was gone, her feeling of emptiness and loss was even greater than Mother's.

After coming to Taiwan, "Auntie" became my only relative, and we lived together for many years. In the breezeway of our Japanese-style house I watched her sit by the window brushing her hair. She occasionally pounded her shoulder blade with her fist saying, "My hands are really stiff. I'm truly old now." Old—she too was old. Her black hair, like a silken cloud in those days, had now gradually thinned out, only a wisp remained, and that was speckled with gray. I remembered the days of their rivalry in Hangchow, when she and Mother sat back to back in the corridor, having their hair coiffured, not exchanging a word. In a flash all that was past. In the human world, what then is love and hate? Old decrepit "Auntie" had finally started on a vague journey in an unknown direction. Her life at this time was lonelier than anyone else's.

Startled, I stared at her, and remembering her lovely horizontal "S" chignon, said, "Let me brush it into a new style, all right?" But she gave a nervous little laugh saying, "What do I still want to wear fancy styles for? That's for you young people."

Can I stay forever young? What she had said is already more than ten years past. I'm far from being young anymore, already callous and wooden toward the love, hate, greed and foolishness in this world. The days with Mother slip farther and farther behind me. "Auntie's ashes," too, are deposited in a lonely temple somewhere. What, after all, is eternal in this world, and what is worth being serious about?

❀ Discussion and Writing

1. Discuss the distinct positions of the two wives: what does one have that the other could not; explain their initial discomfort and their subsequent closeness with each other. What is the function of Father in the narrative?
2. Analyze the implications of the different hairstyles of Mother and "Auntie": why does each woman adopt or reject a style; what do the hairstyles represent about them and their attitudes?
3. Examine the young narrator's (a daughter's) perspective. How would the story change if told by one of the older women?
4. Analyze the symbolic significance of the hair, the hairoil, and the diamonds/emeralds. What does the last paragraph imply?
5. What is suggested by the fact that a woman's hair is a part of a legend and a ritual? Discuss how and why hair is important for women (in any culture), especially in the old Chinese tradition portrayed in the story.

❀ Research and Discussion

Compare any two stories in this anthology that concern the issue of polygamy, preferably from different cultures.

Interdisciplinary Discussion Question: Survey the old Chinese practice of men taking concubines and the responses of different women about sharing their men. How does the old tradition affect relations between women and men in modern times?

Abe Kobo
(1924–1993)
Japan

Abe Kobo (Abe Kimfusa) was born in Tokyo, Japan; his family's place of origin was Hokkaido; and he was raised in Manchuria in the ancient city of Mukden (now called Shenyang) during the Japanese occupation. Captivated by the strong Chinese influence in Mukden and disturbed by the Japanese army's aggressive conduct, he changed his name to the Chinese-sounding Kobo. His position not only as an outsider but as a child of the occupying army distressed him. This position, along with his three places of origin, led to a sense of displacement, and he called himself "a man without a hometown." In addition, the passionate nationalism and fascism preceding and during the war years, when he was still in school, so affected him that he remained profoundly antinationalist and antifascist throughout his life. After the war, he studied medicine, following in the footsteps of his father—who was a doctor—though he never practiced medicine. Abe decided to become a writer while in medical school, and his first novel was published in 1948, the year of his graduation from Tokyo University. Along with writing fiction, he wrote plays and turned in 1964 to screenplays—the first of which was his famous film *Woman in the Dunes* (1964), his adaptation from his novel *Suna no onna* (The Woman in the Dunes, 1962). He also directed and produced plays for his own acting company in Tokyo, the Kobo Theatre Workshop.

Always an inventive, ironic writer, Abe continually played with the concept of transformations and experimented with techniques. In early writing such as *Aka mayu* (*The Red Cocoon,* 1949), written when he was a political activist, he directly confronted social questions, but throughout his life, he continued to explore social and philosophical issues. Projecting a fundamental morality, his work contemplates the problem of displacement. While he focused on alienation and isolation in modern society, however, he never proposed a return to a glorified past. Rather, he said, people "had to deal with the stranger who is not an enemy."

*The Red Cocoon**

The sun is starting to set. It's the time when people hurry home to their roosts, but I don't have a roost to go back to. I go on walking slowly down the narrow cleft between the houses. Although there are so many houses lined up along the streets, why is there not one house which is mine? I think, repeating the same question for the hundredth time.

When I take a piss against a telephone pole, sometimes there's a scrap of rope hanging down, and I want to hang myself. The rope, looking at my neck out of the corner of its eye, says: "Let's rest, brother." And I want to rest, too. But I can't rest. I'm not the rope's brother, and besides, I still can't understand why I don't have a house.

Every day, night comes. When night comes, you have to rest. Houses are to rest in. If that's so, it's not that I don't have a house, is it?

Suddenly, I get an idea. Maybe I've been making a serious mistake in my thinking. Maybe it's not that I don't have a house, but that I've forgotten it. That's right, it could be. For example, I stop in front of this house I happen to be passing. Might not this be my house? Of course, compared to other

---

*Translated by Lane Dunlop

houses, it has no special feature that particularly breathes out that possibility, but one could say the same of any house. That cannot be a proof canceling the fact that this may be my house. I'm feeling brave. OK, let's knock on the door.

I'm in luck. The smiling face of a woman looks out of a half-opened window. She seems kind. The wind of hope blows through the neighborhood of my heart. My heart becomes a flag that spreads out flat and flutters in the wind. I smile, too. Like a real gentleman, I say:

"Excuse me, but this isn't my house by any chance?"

The woman's face abruptly hardens. "What? Who are you?"

About to explain, all of a sudden I can't. I don't know what I should explain. How can I make her understand that it's not a question now of who I am? Getting a little desperate, I say:

"Well, if you think this isn't my house, will you please prove it to me?"

"My god . . . " The woman's face is frightened. That gets me angry.

"If you have no proof, it's all right for me to think it's mine."

"But this is my house."

"What does that matter? Just because you say it's yours doesn't mean it's not mine. That's so."

Instead of answering, the woman turns her face into a wall and shuts the window. That's the true form of a woman's smiling face. It's always this transformation that gives away the incomprehensible logic by which, because something belongs to someone, it does not belong to me.

But, why . . . why does everything belong to someone else and not to me? Even if it isn't mine, can't there be just one thing that doesn't belong to anyone?

Sometimes, I have delusions. That the concrete pipes on construction sites or in storage yards are my house. But they're already on the way to belonging to somebody. Because they become someone else's, they disappear without any reference to my wishes or interest in them. Or they turn into something that is clearly not my house.

Well then, how about park benches? They'd be fine, of course. If they were really my house, and if only he didn't come and chase me off them with his stick . . . Certainly they belong to everybody, not to anybody. But he says:

"Hey, you, get up. This bench belongs to everybody. It doesn't belong to anybody, least of all you. Come on, start moving. If you don't like it, you can spend the night in the basement lockup at the precinct house. If you stop anyplace else, no matter where, you'll be breaking the law."

The Wandering Jew—is that who I am?

The sun is setting. I keep walking.

A house . . . houses that don't disappear, turn into something else, that stand on the ground and don't move. Between them, the cleft that keeps changing, that doesn't have any one face that stays the same . . . the street.

On rainy days, it's like a paint-loaded brush, on snowy days it becomes just the width of the tire ruts, on windy days it flows like a conveyor belt. I keep walking. I can't understand why I don't have a house, and so I can't even hang myself.

Hey, who's holding me around the ankle? If it's the rope for hanging, don't get so excited, don't be in such a hurry. But that's not what it is. It's a sticky silk thread. When I grab it and pull it, the end's in a split between the upper and sole of my shoe. It keeps getting longer and longer, slippery-like. This is weird. My curiosity makes me keep pulling it in. Then something even weirder happens. I'm slowly leaning over. I can't stand up at a right angle to the ground. Has the earth's axis tilted or the gravitational force changed direction?

A thud. My shoe drops off and hits the ground. I see what's happening. The earth's axis hasn't tilted, one of my legs has gotten shorter. As I pull at the thread, my leg rapidly gets shorter and shorter. Like the elbow of a frayed jacket unraveling, my leg's unwinding. The thread, like the fiber of a snake gourd, is my disintegrating leg.

I can't take one more step. I don't know what to do. I keep on standing. In my hand that doesn't know what to do either, my leg that has turned into a silk thread starts to move by itself. It crawls out smoothly. The tip, without any help from my hand, unwinds itself and like a snake starts wrapping itself around me. When my left leg's all unwound, the thread switches as natural as you please to my right leg. In a little while, the thread has wrapped my whole body in a bag. Even then, it doesn't stop but unwinds me from the hips to the chest, from the chest to the shoulders, and as it unwinds it strengthens the bag from inside. In the end, I'm gone.

Afterward, there remained a big empty cocoon.

Ah, now at last I can rest. The evening sun dyes the cocoon red. This, at least, is my house for sure, which nobody can keep me out of. The only trouble is now that I have a house, there's no "I" to return to it.

Inside the cocoon, time stopped. Outside, it was dark, but inside the cocoon it was always evening. Illumined from within, it glowed red with the colors of sunset. This outstanding peculiarity was bound to catch his sharp policeman's eye. He spotted me, the cocoon, lying between the rails of the crossing. At first he was angry, but soon changing his mind about this unusual find, he put me into his pocket. After tumbling around in there for a while, I was transferred to his son's toy box.

❋ **Discussion and Writing**

1. What does the protagonist's search for the house connote? What else is he searching for? Analyze the nature of his rationalization.
2. What roles do the woman and the policeman play in the story?

3. Examine the significance of such inanimate objects as the house, the rope, the pipe, the bench, the street.
4. What is the symbolism of the protagonist's turning into a cocoon: why is it red; what is the significance of the last sentence?
5. What does Abe Kobo criticize in this story?

❈ Research and Comparison

Examine Abe Kobo's literary works to explore the fusion of the fantastic with the actual as he portrays the individual's alienation.

Interdisciplinary Discussion Question: Compare Abe Kobo's *Woman in the Dunes,* the novel and the film, exploring the theme of the individual and society in two different genres.

Mishima Yukio
(1925–1970)
Japan

Mishima Yukio (Hiraoka Kimitake) was born in Tokyo, Japan, in a household managed and dominated by his paternal grandmother. She claimed him as her own when he was 50 days old, and he slept in her bedroom until he was 12. His mother, distraught and jealous, had no option in the matter. His grandfather, once a colonial governor, had fallen into debt and spent his days playing the game *go.* In the meantime, his father, a government official and a stern, rigid man, struggled to pay the debts and the extravagant upkeep of the house. Mishima's mother was a sensitive, educated woman whose family had been scholars for generations. She had a fine appreciation of literature, and, in fact, from the age of 12 to the very end of his life, Mishima immediately brought her his writing before showing it to anyone else. He was sent to the aristocratic Peer's School (originally established for the imperial family and the aristocracy) where he, as a not-too-wealthy commoner, learned about the precise distinctions of class. Graduating with the highest honors, including the award of a silver watch from the emperor, Mishima began studying law at Tokyo University the same year he became a published author.

Mishima's work spoke to the generation of postwar young people, to their turmoil and bewilderment. He illuminated the hollowness of contemporary society, often by manipulating traditional genres such as *kabuki* and *noh* drama or using material from ancient chronicles, informing the traditional with modern psychology. He wrote frankly about sexuality, about homosexuality and heterosexuality; he focused on beauty, merging it with motifs of the erotic and death; he portrayed ecstasy, despair, obsession, suicide, and his writing was dazzling.

Mishima's exploration of the older genres was both aesthetic and philosophical: the aristocratic *noh* drama, which developed during the fourteenth century as an ideal form, thus symbolized this beliefs. He took the title *The Damask Drum* from the play of the same name by Zeami Motokiyo (1363–1444) who had established the *noh* aesthetic. His answer to the sterility of modern Japanese culture resided in a return to traditional values, to an idealized aristocratic and *samurai* (warrior) ethic. He organized a private, uniformed army of devoted ultraconservative patriots, and, in accordance with *samurai* custom and doctrine, committed *seppuku* (ritual suicide) in 1970, after dramatically taking over the Tokyo headquarters of the army's Self-Defense Force.

*The Damask Drum**

CHARACTERS

IWAKICHI, *an old janitor*
KAYOKO, *a girl of about 20, a clerk*
SHUNNOSUKE FUJIMA, *a teacher of Japanese dance*
TOYAMA, *a young man*
KANEKO, *a member of the Ministry of Foreign Affairs*
MADAME, *owner of a fashionable dressmaking establishment*
SHOP ASSISTANT, *a girl*
HANAKO TSUKIOKA

The center of the stage is a street between buildings. Windows and signboards face each other on the third floors of the buildings on either side.

Stage-right is a third-floor law office. A musty-looking room. A room in good faith, a forthright room. There is a potted laurel tree.

Stage-left is a third-floor couturiere. A room in the most modern style. A room in bad faith, a deceitful room. There is a large mirror.

Spring. Evening.

(In the room to the right)

IWAKICHI *(He is sweeping the room with a broom. He sweeps up to the window):*
    Out of the way, out of the way. You act as if you're trying to protect the dirt around your feet:
KAYOKO *(She takes a mirror from her cheap handbag and stands in the light applying a fresh coating of lipstick): Just a minute. I'll be finished in just one minute*

---

*Translated by Donald Keene

now. (IWAKICHI *pushes up* KAYOKO's *skirt from behind with his broom.*) Oh-h-h —you're dreadful. Really. The old men these days are getting to be horrible lechers. (*She finally moves aside.*)

IWAKICHI (*sweeping*): And what about the young ladies? A girl of nineteen or twenty looks better when her lips aren't covered with all the paint. I'll bet your boyfriend thinks so too.

KAYOKO (*glancing at her watch*): I can't afford expensive clothes. Lipstick's the best I can do. (*She looks at her watch again.*) Oh, I'm really sick of it. I wonder why he and I can't both get off from work at the same time. Heaven help me if I tried to kill time waiting for him anywhere outside the office. The first thing you know it'd cost money.

IWAKICHI: I've never once set foot in any of those fashionable drinking places. But they know my face in all the counter restaurants. If you want to know where the bean soup is good, just ask me. (*Pointing at the desk*) Once I invited the boss and he said it was first rate. I couldn't have been more pleased if he'd praised the bean soup in my own house.

KAYOKO: Business has not been good for the boss lately.

IWAKICHI: There're too many laws. That's why there're more lawyers than anybody knows what to do with.

KAYOKO: I wonder—when he's got such a stylish place for an office.

IWAKICHI: The boss hates anything crooked. I'm sure of that. (*Looking at a picture on the wall*) It bothers him even if that picture frame is a quarter of an inch crooked. That's why I've decided to spend the rest of my days working for him.

KAYOKO (*opening the window*): The wind's died down since evening.

IWAKICHI (*approaching the window*): I can't stand that dusty wind that blows at the beginning of spring. . . . The calm of evening. Oh, there's a good smell coming from somewhere.

KAYOKO: It's from the Chinese restaurant on the ground floor.

IWAKICHI: The prices are too high for me.

KAYOKO: Look at the beautiful sunset. It's reflected in the windows of all the buildings.

IWAKICHI: Those are pigeons from the newspaper office. Look at them scatter. Now they've formed a circle again. . . .

KAYOKO: I'm glad you're in love too. It's made you young again.

IWAKICHI: Don't be silly. My love is a one-sided affair, not like yours.

KAYOKO: You're in love with a great lady whose name you don't even know.

IWAKICHI: She's the princess of the laurel, the tree that grows in the garden of the moon.

KAYOKO (*pointing at the potted tree*): That's the tree you mean, isn't it? There's nothing so wonderful about a laurel.

IWAKICHI: Oh! I've forgotten to water my precious laurel.

  (*Exits*)

KAYOKO: Isn't he the sly one? Running off to cover his embarrassment.

IWAKICHI *(enters with a watering can):* Laurel, I'm sorry I forgot to water you. One more effort now and you'll be covered with glossy leaves. *(As he waters the plant he strokes the leaves fondly.)* Poets often talk about hair glossy as leaves. . . .

KAYOKO: You still haven't got any answer?

IWAKICHI: Mmmm.

KAYOKO: I call that disgusting. It makes me sick. Not to have the decency to send you an answer. Nobody else but me would go on being your messenger. How many letters has it been? Thirty, isn't it? Today makes exactly thirty.

IWAKICHI: If you count in all the love letters I wrote without sending them, it'd make seventy more. For seventy days—every day I wrote her one and every day I burned it. That's what it was like before you were kind enough to take pity on me and become my postman. Let's see, that makes a total of . . . *(Thinks)*

KAYOKO: A hundred, of course. Can't you count any more?

IWAKICHI: Unrequited love is a bitter thing.

KAYOKO: You haven't the sense to give up.

IWAKICHI: Sometimes I think I'll try to forget. But I know now that trying to forget is worse than being unable to. I mean, even if being unable to forget is painful in the same way, it's still better.

KAYOKO: How did you ever get into such a state, I wonder.

(As she speaks a light is lit in the room to the left.)

IWAKICHI: They've switched on the light. Every day at the same time . . . when this room dies that one comes to life again. And in the morning when this room returns to life, that one dies. . . . It was three months ago. I'd finished sweeping and I just happened to look at the room over there, with nothing particular on my mind. . . . Then I saw her for the first time. She came into the room with her maid. The Madame was showing her the way. . . . She was wearing a coat of some kind of golden fur, and when she took it off, her dress was all black. Her hat was black too. And her hair, of course, it was black, black as the night sky. If I tried to describe to you how beautiful her face was—It was like the moon, and everything around it was shining. . . . She said a few words, then she smiled. I trembled all over. . . . She smiled. . . . I stood behind the window staring at her until she went into the fitting-room. . . . That's when it began.

KAYOKO: But she's not all that beautiful. It's her clothes—they're exquisite.

IWAKICHI: Love's not that sort of thing. It's something that shines on the one you love from the mirror of your own ugliness.

KAYOKO: In that case, even I qualify.

IWAKICHI: There's nothing for you to worry about! You look like a great beauty to your boyfriend.

KAYOKO: Does that mean there's a moon for every woman in the world?

IWAKICHI: Some women are fat, and some are thin. . . . That's why there's both a full moon and a crescent.

(*Three men appear in the room to the left.* FUJIMA, TOYAMA, KANEKO.)

IWAKICHI: It'll be time soon. I've got to finish the rest of today's love letter.

KAYOKO: Hurry, won't you? I'll read a book while I wait.

(IWAKICHI *goes to the desk and finishes his letter.* KAYOKO *sits and begins to read.*)

(*In the room to the left*)

FUJIMA (*He carries a parcel wrapped in a purple square of cloth*): I am Shunnosuke Fujima. Very pleased to meet you.

TOYAMA: How do you do? My name is Toyama. And this is Mr. Kaneko from the Ministry of Foreign Affairs. (*Introduces the men*) Mr. Fujima.

KANEKO: How do you do?

FUJIMA: You and Mr. Kaneko seem to be old friends.

TOYAMA: Yes. He was at the same school, but ahead of me.

FUJIMA: Oh, really? . . . My pupils are about to put on a dance-play. (*Hands them leaflets.*) Please take these. . . . Mrs. Tsukioka said she would buy a hundred tickets.

TOYAMA (*jealously*): Mrs. Tsukioka wouldn't do that unless she were sure of making a profit.

KANEKO: No, she's not like you. She's the kind who makes losses, never a profit.

FUJIMA: Yes, that's the kind of person she really is.

KANEKO (*firmly*): I am perfectly well aware what kind of person she is.

FUJIMA (*changing the subject*): The plot of the dance-play is charming, if I must say so myself.

TOYAMA (*looking at his watch*): She's late, isn't she? Summoning people here like that. . . . It's bad taste to keep a man waiting in a dress shop.

KANEKO: In the reign of Louis XIV they used to receive men in their boudoirs. And when a man wanted to compliment a woman he'd say something like "Who does the shading under your eyes?" (*He says it in French.*)

FUJIMA: Excuse me? What was that?

(KANEKO *translates word for word.* TOYAMA *looks the other way.*)

FUJIMA: Shading under a woman's eyes is a lovely thing, isn't it? Like clouds hovering under the moon, you might say.

KANEKO (*interested only in what he himself has to say*): That's the secret of all diplomacy. To ask who did the shading under a woman's eyes when you know perfectly well she did it herself.

TOYAMA: Mr. Kaneko is about to become an ambassador.

FUJIMA (*bowing*): Congratulations.

(*In the room to the right*)

IWAKICHI: I've written it. It's done. And very good this time.

KAYOKO: It must be a terrific strain always thinking up new things to say.

IWAKICHI: This is one of the more agreeable hardships of love.

KAYOKO: I'll leave it on my way home.

IWAKICHI: Sorry to bother you, Kayoko. Please don't lose it.

KAYOKO: You talk as if it wasn't just across the street. I couldn't lose it even if I wanted to. . . . Good night.

IWAKICHI: Good night, Kayoko.

KAYOKO (*waving the letter as she stands in the door*): Maybe I will forget about the letter after all. I'm in a big hurry myself, you know.

IWAKICHI: You mustn't tease an old man like that.

(In the room to the left)

KANEKO: She certainly is late.

TOYAMA (*He stands in front of the mirror and fiddles with his necktie*): Mrs. Tsukioka's taste in neckties always runs to something like this. I really hate loud ties.

FUJIMA: This is a tobacco case Mrs. Tsukioka gave me when I succeeded as head of the company. The *netsuke*[1] is more valuable than the case itself. Just have a look at it. (*He holds it up to the light.*) You'd never think it was made entirely of wood, would you? It's exactly like ivory, isn't it?

KANEKO: We civil servants must refuse all presents. There's always the suspicion of bribery. I envy artists.

FUJIMA: Everybody says that.

TOYAMA (*in a tearful voice*): Damned old woman! Why should she have invited everybody except me?

KAYOKO (*out of breath*): Oh, excuse me. Is the Madame here?

TOYAMA: She went to the shop a couple of minutes ago. I think she had some business to do.

KAYOKO: Now what am I going to do?

TOYAMA: Is it something urgent?

KAYOKO: Yes. It's a letter. I give one to Madame every day, at somebody's request. . . .

KANEKO (*haughtily*): I'll take care of it.

KAYOKO (*hesitantly*): It's very kind of you. . . .

KANEKO: I'll accept responsibility.

KAYOKO: I'm much obliged. Please.

(Exits)

TOYAMA: What a terrific hurry that girl is in!

KANEKO (*He reads the address on the envelope*): Well, I never! It says "To the princess of the laurel of the moon."

---

[1]A small piece of sculpture fastened onto a pouch or case.

FUJIMA: Very romantic, isn't it?

KANEKO: You didn't write it yourself, by any chance?

FUJIMA: You're joking. When a dancing teacher has the time to write love letters, he holds hands instead.

KANEKO: The sender is one Iwakichi.

FUJIMA: He writes a very good hand, whoever he is.

TOYAMA: Just imagine—calling the Madame a "princess of the laurel of the moon"! I don't think I've ever seen a laurel. Is it a very big tree?

FUJIMA: Only around the middle, I think.

KANEKO: There's no accounting for tastes, is there? Let's see—there's a French expression something like that—

MADAME (*Enters. She is unusually tall):* It's so good to find you all here.

TOYAMA: A love letter's come for you.

MADAME: I wonder who it can be from. There are five or six gentlemen who might be sending me one.

KANEKO: Your affairs are touch-and-go, I take it?

MADAME: Yes, that's right. I never forget my defenses.

TOYAMA: Your armor must take a lot of material.

MADAME: Darling boy! You always say such amusing things.

FUJIMA (*dramatically):* "The princess of the laurel of the moon," I presume?

MADAME: Oh, is *that* the love letter you're talking about? In that case, it's not for me.

KANEKO: Don't try to fool us.

MADAME: You're quite mistaken. It's for Mrs. Tsukioka.

ALL: What?

MADAME (*sitting):* These letters are driving me simply frantic. They're from the janitor who works in the building across the street. An old man almost seventy. He's fallen in love with Mrs. Tsukioka, from having seen her through the window.

KANEKO: That doesn't surprise me. They say that the aged tend to be far-sighted. (*He laughs, amused at his own joke.*) I can't wait to grow old. It must be very convenient being far-sighted.

MADAME: The old man has sent her dozens—no, hundreds—of letters.

TOYAMA: If he sent out all his letters to different women, one of them might have been successful.

KANEKO: There's something in what you say. But if, after all, love were a question of probability, the probability for one woman might be the same as the probability for innumerable women.

FUJIMA: Have you shown her the letters? Mrs. Tsukioka, I mean.

MADAME: How could I possibly show them to her? I've used them all as comb wipers.

TOYAMA: Do combs get as dirty as all that?

MADAME: They're for my dogs' combs. I have five wire-haired fox terriers. They shut their eyes in positive rapture when I comb them.

KANEKO: Which runs faster—love or a dog?

FUJIMA: Which gets dirty faster?

MADAME: It makes me quite giddy to talk with such enchanting men.

KANEKO: Sidetracked again. What's happened to the love letters?

MADAME: This is what has happened. The one who's been delivering the letters is that sweet girl from the office across the way.

TOYAMA: The girl who was just here? What's sweet about her?

MADAME: She's a well-behaved, good girl, and I've become so fond of her that I've been accepting the letters every day. But I've never dreamed of giving one to Mrs. Tsukioka.

KANEKO: If the girl knew that, she'd never give you another one.

MADAME: You'll have to excuse me. Just put yourself in my place. If Mrs. Tsukioka should read them and get upset—

(Knock at the door)

MADAME: Now what shall I do? It's Mrs. Tsukioka.

KANEKO: Attention. *(HANAKO enters.)* Salute!

TOYAMA *(clutching her):* It's cruel of you. To be late again.

FUJIMA: We were expecting you at any minute.

MADAME: You always look lovely, no matter how often I see you.

(HANAKO does not answer. She smilingly removes her gloves.)

MADAME *(trying to take the initiative):* Everybody's been waiting so impatiently I don't want to waste another minute. We'll start the fitting at once. *(She examines HANAKO from the front and from behind.)* A dressy model really suits your naturally elegant line best, Mrs. Tsukioka. But in a spring suit, you know, I think we should try for a different effect. With your figure you can carry off something sporty. This time I've been really daring in the cut. The lines are simple, divinely simple. Just the barest of pleats on the sides of the waist, as you suggested. Very effective in bringing out the accents. . . . And now, would you mind stepping into the fitting-room? We can have a leisurely cup of coffee afterward.

KANEKO: A love letter came for you, Mrs. Tsukioka. Guess how old the man is who sent it. Twenty? Thirty? Older?

(HANAKO holds up one finger.)

TOYAMA: No, no. He's not a high-school student.

(HANAKO with a smile holds up two fingers. The others shake their heads. She holds up one more finger each time until finally, with a look of incredulity on her face, she holds up seven.)

KANEKO: You've guessed it, at last. A blushing seventy. I'm told he's the janitor in the building across the street.

(The MADAME, *flustered, lowers the blinds.* IWAKICHI, *in the room to the right, stares fixedly at the shut window. During the interval* KANEKO *hands the letter to* HANAKO. *She opens it. The others stand behind her and read over her shoulder.)*

TOYAMA *(reads):* "Please read this thirtieth expression of my love, and take it to your heart," it says. Madame's been lying again. She said there were hundreds of letters. You know, Mrs. Tsukioka, the Madame has embezzled all the previous letters.

KANEKO *(reads):* "My love grows only the stronger as the days go by. To heal the scars of the whip of love which torments my aged body from morn to night, I ask for one, for just one kiss." Isn't that touching? All he wants is one little kiss.

(They all burst into laughter.)

TOYAMA: Just one kiss? He's very modest in his demands.

FUJIMA: It really surprises me. The old men nowadays are younger at heart than we are.

MADAME: Is that the sort of thing he's been writing? I confess I haven't read any of his other efforts. *(The letter is passed to her.)* Oh, dear. *(Reads)* "That which we call love is an eternal, unending sorrow." Trite, isn't it? He might just as well say: "That which we call vinegar, unlike honey, is an unending source of bitterness."

KANEKO: This old man thinks he's the only one who's suffering. Such conceit is detestable. All of us are suffering in exactly the same way. The only difference is that some people talk about it and others don't.

FUJIMA: That's because we have self-respect, isn't it?

TOYAMA: Even I can understand that much. I can't bear that tone which implies that he's the only one who knows real love, and the rest of us are all frivolous and fickle.

KANEKO: I'd be glad to show anyone who's willing to be shown how much repeated suffering we have to endure just in order to fool ourselves, all of us who are living in these depraved times.

FUJIMA: There's nothing you can do about people who are set in their ways. He must think there are special reserved seats for love.

TOYAMA: A romanticist.

MADAME: Little boys should not interfere in the conversation of grown-ups. The argument has become serious. *(She rings a bell.)* Isn't it enchanting, Mrs. Tsukioka, how heated men get over an argument?

KANEKO *(as if he were delivering a speech):* I believe I may state without fear of contradiction that we are convinced that entities like this old man are abhorrent, and that such entities cannot further be tolerated by us—entities, that is, who believe in genuine feelings. There is not a village, no matter how remote, where the genuine and original Nagasaki sponge cake is not sold. I despise any shopkeeper who would really believe such nonsense and fatuously sell the cake as the genuine article. It is far better to sell it knowing all along that it is fake. That makes the sale a cheat and a fraud, the splendid product of a conscious human mind. We have tongues to recognize the taste of the sponge cake. Our loves begin from the tongue.

MADAME: How erotic!

KANEKO: The tongue admits the existence of no "genuine," of no "original." What it depends on is the sense of taste common to all men. The tongue can say: "This tastes good." Its natural modesty forbids it to say more. The "genuine and original" is merely a label people paste on the wrapping. The tongue confines itself to determining whether or not the sponge cake tastes good.

SHOP ASSISTANT (enters): Did you ring?

MADAME: It wasn't for sponge cake. What was it? Oh yes, please bring five cups of coffee immediately.

ASSISTANT: Yes, Madame.

KANEKO: All questions are relative. Love is the architecture of the emotion of disbelief in genuine articles. That old man, on the other hand, is impure, polluted—he's making fools of us. He is delighted with himself, inflated with pride.

FUJIMA: I'm afraid what you say is much too difficult for someone like myself, who's never had an education, to follow, but I was told by my teacher that all disputes about who was the senior member of a company or which was the oldest tradition in a dance have nothing whatsoever to do with art. He said that the only true atmosphere for the dance is one where the gesture to the front and the gesture to the rear can be performed in absolute freedom. . . . That old man is so anxious to found a school for himself that he (mimes dance action) . . . one and two and over to the side . . . neglects the free, unconfined realms of the ecstasy of love.

TOYAMA: And what do you think about all this, Mrs. Tsukioka? It isn't very nice of you to keep so silent. But I suppose it isn't entirely distasteful to receive love letters even from such an old man. Isn't that the case? Say something, laurel of the moon.

MADAME: Mrs. Tsukioka had a refined upbringing, and I'm sure she dislikes arguments.

TOYAMA: But she's very fond of tormenting people all the same.

MADAME: That's a taste common to all beautiful women.

FUJIMA: And one which only becomes beautiful women, they say.

MADAME: When it comes to colors, the ones which suit her best are the difficult ones like green.

KANEKO: Those, of course, are the colors she doesn't wear in public. She saves them for her nightgowns, and pretends she doesn't know they become her.

TOYAMA: I can testify that Mrs. Tsukioka never wears green nightgowns.
KANEKO: You've become increasingly cheeky of late.
MADAME: Come, come.

(*THE ASSISTANT enters with the coffee. They all drink unhurriedly.*)
(*In the room to the right*)

IWAKICHI: I wonder what's the matter. Why don't they open the curtains? Oh, the suspense. All I could get was just the barest glimpse of her. . . . And I was so sure that tonight she would take pity on me and at least stand at the window and smile at me, like a picture in a frame. . . . But I'm still not giving up hope. . . . No, I won't give up hope.

(*In the room to the left*)

KANEKO: Well, now.
FUJIMA: Oops. (*He spills coffee on his lap and wipes it.*).
KANEKO: What is it?
FUJIMA: Just now as I was drinking my coffee, a fine idea came to me.
KANEKO: I have also been considering what we might do to teach that old man a little lesson. What do you say, Mrs. Tsukioka? In general . . .
FUJIMA: My plan was . . .
KANEKO (*paying him no attention*): In general, such entities are incapable of seeing the light unless they have once been administered a sound thrashing. We need show him no pity simply because he's an old man. It is essential to make him realize that where he lives is a little room nobody will enter.
TAYOMA: You mean, human beings won't go in a dog's house?
KANEKO (*recovering his good mood*): Yes, exactly.
FUJIMA: My plan is this. (*He unfolds the parcel wrapped in purple silk, revealing a small hand drum.*) Do you see this?
MADAME: It's a drum, isn't it?
FUJIMA: It's a prop for my forthcoming dance-play. Oh, since I mentioned the play, I must thank you, Mrs. Tsukioka . . . the tickets. . . . At any rate, about the drum. Shall I beat it for you? (*He beats it.*) You see, it doesn't make the least sound. It looks exactly like a real drum, but instead of a skin, which is essential of course, it's covered with damask.
TOYAMA: You mean they've invented a drum that doesn't make any noise?
FUJIMA: No, as I was saying, it's a prop.
KANEKO: And what do you propose to do with it?
FUJIMA: To attach a note to this drum and throw it into the old man's room. I've had the most wonderful idea about what to write in the note.
MADAME: That sounds fascinating. Tell us.
FUJIMA: In the note we should write: "Please beat this drum." Do you follow me? "Please beat this drum. If the sound of your drum can be heard in this room above the street noises, I will grant your wish." That's all.

TOYAMA: Excellent idea! That will take the old man down a peg or two.

KANEKO: Don't you think you ought to add: "If the sound doesn't reach me, your wish will not be granted"?

FUJIMA: There's such a thing as an implied meaning.

KANEKO: In diplomatic correspondence you can't be too careful.

FUJIMA (*excitedly*): Don't you think it's a good plan, Mrs. Tsukioka? I'll be glad to sacrifice this prop to protect you.

TOYAMA: For a customer who buys a hundred tickets, what's one drum?

FUJIMA: I'll thank you not to interpret it in that way. Mrs. Tsukioka, you do agree, don't you? (*HANAKO nods smilingly.*)

MADAME: It will be a great relief to me too. This will probably be the last day the old man will bother us.

FUJIMA: Let's have some paper and a pen.

(*They set about their preparations with animation. FUJIMA writes a note to attach to the drum. The MADAME draws the curtains. HANAKO is led to the window, which KANEKO opens.*)

KANEKO: His room is pitch dark. Are you sure the old man is there?

MADAME: The girl who comes as his messenger says that he stares at this window until Mrs. Tsukioka leaves.

KANEKO: Still, I wonder if our voices will reach him.

TOYAMA: That'll be my responsibility. Oh, doesn't it look pretty up here to see the neon lights everywhere?

FUJIMA: Who will throw the drum?

KANEKO: I will. I was quite a renowned pitcher in my high-school days.

(*He limbers his arm by way of preparation.*)

TOYAMA: Hey! Iwakichi! Open your window!

(*The window opens. IWAKICHI timidly shows himself.*)

TOYAMA: Can you hear me? We're going to throw you something. Be sure to catch it.

(*IWAKICHI nods. KANEKO throws the drum. IWAKICHI barely gets it. He takes the drum to the desk.*)

IWAKICHI: What can this mean? She's sent me a drum. She's standing at the window looking at me. It's strange, when she looks straight this way it's all I can do to keep from hiding myself. I wonder if she's always hidden herself from me because I stared too much. . . . Oh, there's a note attached. (*Reads.*) At last my wish will be granted! What carries better than the sound of a drum, even above the traffic noise? It must be her elegant way of saying things—she can't pronounce a simple yes, but has to say it in some roundabout manner. . . . Oh, my heart hurts. It's never known such joy before. It's weak, like the stomach of a poor man's child before a feast. It hurts because it's been struck by happiness. . . . They're all waiting in the window over there. It must be for the fun of it. They think it will be amusing to hear an old man play the drum for the first time. . . . Ah, I've a good idea. I'll hang the drum on my laurel tree and beat it there. *(He kneels before the tree.)* Laurel, lovely, dear laurel, forgive me. I'm going to hang the drum in your green hair. Heavy, is it? Just be patient for a while. It becomes you. It becomes you very well, like a big beautiful ornament that has fallen from heaven into your hair. . . . It's all right, isn't it? Even when I begin to beat the drum, I won't shake your leaves. I've never before been so happy before you. Whenever I've seen you I've thought: My unhappiness has made you more beautiful, has made you put forth your leaves more abundantly. And it's true, my laurel, it's true.

TOYOMA: Hurry up and beat the drum. We're standing in the cold waiting for you.

IWAKICHI: All right! I'm going to beat it now, so listen! *(He strikes the drum. It makes no sound. He strikes the other side. It is also silent. He strikes frantically but to no avail.)* It doesn't make a noise. They've given me a drum that doesn't make a noise! I've been made a fool of. I've been played with. *(He sinks to the floor and weeps.)* What shall I do? What shall I do? A refined lady like that—to play such a low trick on me. It's something that should never have happened. It couldn't have happened. *(The people at the window to the left laugh. The window is slammed shut.)* Laugh! Go ahead and laugh! Laugh all you like! . . . You'll still be laughing when you die. You'll be laughing when you rot away. That won't happen to me. People who are laughed at don't die just like that. . . . People who are laughed at don't rot away. *(He opens the window at the back. Climbs out on the window sill. He sits there motionlessly for a minute, sadly staring below. Then he pushes himself over the edge in a crumbling gesture. Shouts from below. Inarticulate cries from the crowd continue awhile.)*

(In the room to the left they are all chatting and laughing. They cannot see the window from which the old man committed suicide, and they are unaware what has happened. Suddenly the door opens.)

ASSISTANT: The janitor from the building across the way has just jumped out of the window and killed himself.

(They get up with confused outcries. Some rush to the window, others run toward the stairs. HANAKO stands alone rigidly in the center of the stage.)

(Late at night. The sky between the two buildings is now full of stars. A clock on a shelf in the room to the left gives forth two delicate chimes. The room is pitch dark. Presently there is a scratching sound of a key in the door. The door opens. A flashlight beam shines in. HANAKO enters. She wears a half-length coat thrown over

the shoulders of her evening gown. In one hand she holds a key, in the other a flashlight. She puts the key in her handbag. She goes to the window, opens it, and stares motionlessly at the window on the right.)

HANAKO *(Her voice is low. She talks as if to someone present):* I've come. You told me to come and I've come. I slipped out of a party, even though it was the middle of the night. . . . Answer me, please. Aren't you there?

(The window at the back of the room to the right opens. The ghost of IWAKICHI *climbs in the window from which he jumped. He walks to the left. The window facing left gradually opens as he approaches it.)*

HANAKO: You've come. . . . You've really come.

IWAKICHI: I've been going back and forth between your dreams and this room.

HANAKO: You summoned me and I am here. But you still do not know me. You don't know how I was able to come.

IWAKICHI: Because I drew you here.

HANAKO: No. Without human strength no door opens for human beings to pass through.

IWAKICHI: Do you intend to deceive even a ghost?

HANAKO: Where would I get the strength? My strength was enough only to kill a pitiful old man. And even in that all I did was to nod. I did nothing else. *(IWAKICHI does not answer.)* Can you hear me? *(IWAKICHI nods.)* My voice carries even when I speak as low as this. But when I talk to people they can't hear me unless I shout. . . . It would have been better if voices had not carried between this room and yours.

IWAKICHI: The sky is full of stars. You can't see the moon. The moon has become covered with mud and fallen to earth. I was following the moon when I jumped. You might say that the moon and I committed suicide together.

HANAKO *(looking down at the street):* Can you see the corpse of the moon anywhere? I can't. Only the all-night taxis cruising in the streets. There's a policeman walking there. He's stopped. But I don't think that means he's found a corpse. The policeman won't meet anything except the policeman who comes from the opposite direction. Is he a mirror, I wonder?

IWAKICHI: Do you think that ghosts meet only ghosts, and the moon meets only the moon?

HANAKO: In the middle of the night that's true of everything. *(She lights a cigarette.)*

IWAKICHI: I'm not a phantom any more. While I was alive I was a phantom. Now all that remains is what I used to dream about. Nobody can disappoint me any more.

HANAKO: From what I can see, however, you still aren't precisely the incarnation of love. I don't mean to criticize your growth of beard or your janitor's uniform or your sweaty undershirt—There's something lacking, something your love needs before it can assume a form. There's insufficient proof that your love in this world was real, if that was the only reason why you died.

IWAKICHI: Do you want proof from a ghost? *(He empties his pockets.)* Ghosts don't own anything. I've lost every possession which might have served as proof.

HANAKO: I am teeming with proofs. A woman simply crawls with proofs of love. When she has produced the last one, she is full of proofs that the love is gone. It's because women have the proofs that men can make love empty-handed.

IWAKICHI: Please don't show me such things.

HANAKO: A little while ago I opened the door and came in, didn't I? Where do you suppose I got the key to the door?

IWAKICHI: Please don't ask me such things.

HANAKO: I stole the key from Madame's pocket. My fingers are very nimble, you know. It gave me great pleasure to discover my skill at pick-pocketing has still not left me.

IWAKICHI: I understand now. You're afraid of my tenacity, and you're trying to make me hate you. That must be it.

HANAKO: Then shall I show you? You gave me a very appropriate name, princess of the moon. I used otherwise to be known by the nickname of Crescent, from a tattoo on my belly. The tattoo of a crescent.

IWAKICHI: Ah-h-h.

HANAKO: It wasn't that I asked to have it tattooed myself. A man did it, violently. When I drink the crescent turns a bright red, but usually it is pale as a dead man's face.

IWAKICHI:. Whore! You've made a fool of me twice. Once wasn't enough.

HANAKO: Once wasn't enough. Yes, that's right, it wasn't. For our love to be fulfilled, or for it to be destroyed.

IWAKICHI: You were poisoned by men who were untrue.

HANAKO: That's not so. Men who were untrue molded me.

IWAKICHI: I was made a fool of because I was true.

HANAKO: That's not so. You were made a fool of because you were old.

(The room to the right becomes red with the wrath of the ghost. The laurel tree on which the drum had been hung appears in the glow.)

IWAKICHI: Don't you feel ashamed of yourself? I'll place a curse on you.

HANAKO: That doesn't frighten me in the least. I'm strong now. It's because I've been loved.

IWAKICHI: By whom?

HANAKO: By you.

IWAKICHI: Was it the strength of my love that made you tell the truth?

HANAKO: Look at me. It's not the real me you love. *(She laughs.)* You tried to place a curse on me. Clumsy men are all like that.

IWAKICHI: No, no. I am in love with you, passionately. Everybody in the world of the dead knows it.

HANAKO: Nobody knows it in this world.

IWAKICHI: Because the drum didn't sound?

HANAKO: Yes, because I couldn't hear it.

IWAKICHI: It was the fault of the drum. A damask drum makes no noise.

HANAKO: It wasn't the fault of the drum that it didn't sound.

IWAKICHI: I yearn for you, even now.

HANAKO: Even now! You've been dead all of a week.

IWAKICHI: I yearn for you. I shall try to make the drum sound.

HANAKO: Make it sound. I have come to hear it.

IWAKICHI: I will. My love will make a damask drum thunder. *(The ghost of* IWAKICHI *strikes the drum. It gives forth a full sound.)* It sounded! It sounded! You heard it, didn't you?

HANAKO *(smiling slyly):* I can't hear a thing.

IWAKICHI: You can't hear this? It's not possible. Look, I'll strike it once for every letter I wrote you. Once, twice, you can hear it, I know, three, four, the drum has sounded. *(The drum sounds.)*

HANAKO: I can't hear it. Where is a drum sounding?

IWAKICHI: You can't hear it? You're lying. You can't hear this? Ten, eleven. You can't hear this?

HANAKO: I can't. I can't hear any drum.

IWAKICHI: It's a lie! *(In a fury)* I won't let you say it—that you can't hear what I can. Twenty, twenty-one. It's sounded.

HANAKO: I can't hear it. I can't hear it.

IWAKICHI: Thirty, thirty-one, thirty-two. . . . You can't say you don't hear it. The drum is beating. A drum that never should have sounded is sounding.

HANAKO: Ah, hurry and sound it. My ears are longing to hear the drum.

IWAKICHI: Sixty-six, sixty-seven. . . . Could it possibly be that only my ears can hear the drum?

HANAKO *(in despair, to herself):* Ah, he's just the same as living men.

IWAKICHI *(in despair, to himself):* Who can prove it—that she hears the drum?

HANAKO: I can't hear it. I still can't hear it.

IWAKICHI *(weakly):* Eighty-nine, ninety, ninety-one. . . . It will soon be over. Have I only imagined I heard the sound of the drum? *(The drum goes on sounding.)* It's useless. A waste of time. The drum won't sound at all, will it? Beat it and beat it as I may, it's a damask drum.

HANAKO: Hurry, strike it so I can hear. Don't give up. Hurry, so it strikes my ears. *She stretches her hand from the window.)* Don't give up!

IWAKICHI: Ninety-four, ninety-five. . . . Completely useless. The drum does-
n't make a sound. What's the use of beating a drum that is silent? . . .
Ninety-six, ninety-seven. . . . Farewell, my laurel princess, farewell. . . .
Ninety-eight, ninety-nine. . . . Farewell, I've ended the hundred
strokes. . . . Farewell.

*(The ghost disappears. The beating stops, HANAKO stands alone, an empty look
on her face. TOYAMA rushes in excitedly.)*

TOYAMA: Is that where you've been? Oh, I'm so relieved. . . . We've all been
out searching for you. What happened to you? Running off like that in
the middle of the night. What happened to you? *(He shakes her.)* Get a
hold on yourself.

HANAKO *(as in a dream):* I would have heard if he had only struck it once
more.

Curtain

❋ Discussion and Writing

1. Analyze the details of the opening description. What is symbolized by
   the center street and a large mirror?
2. Compare the two offices and the businesses carried out in each.
3. What is Kayoko's function in the play? Comment also on the roles of
   Fujima, Toyama, Kaneko, and the Madame.
4. What are the outstanding qualities of Iwakichi? Discuss his concept of
   love and dedication to people and objects. Interpret the significance of
   his suicide?
5. Comment on the class distinctions portrayed in the play, especially between Iwakichi and Hanako Tsukioka?
6. What is the significance of Hanako's silence throughout the play and
   her dialogue with the ghost of Iwakichi in the final scene?
7. The central force of a *noh* play is more a state of feeling than the action:
   what feelings are dramatized in this play; what does the damask drum
   symbolize; why does Iwakichi give up drumming; what is the significance of Hanako's last words?
8. Examine the play as Mishima's commentary on Westernized Japan.

❋ Research and Comparison

Research the biographical material on Mishima to examine the influence
of the East-West conflict on his ideology and life. Examine his short stories and
novels as a denunciation of modernity in Japan.

Interdisciplinary Discussion Question: Research the history of traditional
noh drama and *kabuki,* focusing on the use of these forms in the works of any
twentieth-century Japanese writer.

Kim Namjo
(b. 1927)
Korea

Kim Namjo was born in Taeju, Korea, and attended high school in Japan. After returning to Korea, she graduated from the Seoul National University Teachers College. She taught for 30 years at Soongmyong Women's College in Seoul before retiring. Her first book of poetry was published in 1953, and she has published numerous collections since then, receiving many awards in Korea and elsewhere. Highly acclaimed, she is most known for her profound inquiry into the nature of love.

Having Come to the Mountain*

In the rain, Mount Sorak
wears the cloud band on its forehead
and fog below its bosom.
Those who know one another
beyond words, touched
in the flesh
as in a hazy dream.

Trees
and rocks
are without names,
like the unknown soldiers
or the early saints
who lost their names.

Living on the green mountain,
those who have forgotten their own names,
just as their bodies stand naked in the rain
are at peace
and warm.

Today I have learned the reason,
why a person who has died
comes to be held in the mountain's embrace.

❀ Discussion and Writing

1. What image does Mount Sorak in the rain evoke for the persona?
2. Explain the significance of the association among the soldiers, the early saints, and the people who have forgotten their own names.

---

*Translated by David McCann

3. Elaborate on what the persona learns as she looks at the mountain.
4. Comment on the symbolism of: the rain, the fog, trees, and rocks.

Ariyoshi Sawako
(1931–1984)
Japan

Ariyoshi Sawako was born in the port city of Wakayama, Japan. When she was a child, recurrent illness caused her to be absent from school but did not prevent her from accompanying her parents on their frequent travels. Her meeting people of different cultures and living for four years in Java during her childhood laid the groundwork for her mature preoccupations. A graduate of Tokyo Women's College, she began her prolific writing career when she was 25. Her first stories suggested a yearning for traditional Japanese culture in their depiction of modern society. These stories were followed by novels about traditional women. She ultimately evolved into a novelist concerned explicitly about the effect of political and social changes on Japanese culture. In addition to describing the experience of women, she depicted the condition of the elderly in contemporary life and the effects of pollution on the environment. She wrote about the bias against people with radiation disease caused by fallout from the atom bombs dropped on Hiroshima and Nagasaki, and protested against subsequent missile testing. She also portrayed the prejudice against women and people of different races. At the time of her sudden death, she was a successful, highly respected author. Although "The Tomoshibi" (*tomoshibi* means gentle light) is a story from 1961, it contains the seeds of her later work.

The Tomoshibi*

It was almost incredible that a small, quiet bar like The Tomoshibi should exist in the Ginza. Although it was located on an alley branching off a back street of Higashi Ginza, a noisy place where bars stood side by side in a row, it was still part of the Ginza. To the right, there was a large coffee shop, and to the left there was a well-known men's clothing store. The three shops across the street—a restaurant, a coffee shop, and an accessories store—were famous, and so, this one corner overflowed, with a true Ginza-like atmosphere, almost as if it were on the main street itself.

However, The Tomoshibi was inconspicuous in all respects. It was only natural that it wasn't noticeable during the day, since the bar opened at five

*Translated by Keiko Nakamura

in the afternoon; but in any case, since the frontage was narrow—only about six feet wide—it was overwhelmed by the imposing appearance of the neighboring stores on both sides. It didn't seem likely that there would be such a bar in a place like this.

There was a small lantern placed outside, above the door, and on this "The Tomoshibi" was written in quaint lettering. In the evening, even when it became both in name and in reality a *tomoshibi*, it did not shine very boldly.

When the night grew late and all the neighbors had closed shop, the street became silent. Even people looking for a place to drink would go right past it, not noticing that the street even had a bar.

The fact was, then, that the patrons of The Tomoshibi were an exceedingly limited group of regular customers. However, The Tomoshibi hadn't many of what one usually thinks of as "regular customers," the type of people who gather together out of affection for the proprietress and barmaids.

There were few customers who came to The Tomoshibi every night; neither were there many stray customers who wandered in. Nevertheless, the bar was always filled to capacity, and although the popularity of the proprietress, who was called "Mama-san," might have helped a little, the patrons and the barmaids all knew the exact reason why.

It is true that the bar was small. In a space of about ninety square feet, there was a cramped restroom, a large refrigerator, a tiny counter behind which Mama-san and one barmaid could stand, and just enough chairs and tables for the other barmaid to entertain customers. Even with only the three of them, when none of the customers had showed up yet, a dry wind did not blow in the bar. Thus anyone who casually entered The Tomoshibi alone would be enveloped by a warm atmosphere, and immediately feel at home.

Here, no one felt like chasing away the blues by noisily badmouthing their superiors while under the influence; nor were there any customers who told vulgar jokes to first get into a state of mind sufficiently disillusioned to bring on a quick drunk.

"Hello there!" Mama-san greeted a customer who hadn't come for several months. Speaking as if he had come the day before yesterday, the customer asked, "It's been a while since I've seen the girl who used to work here—what's happened to her?"

"She got married," Mama-san replied quietly.

"Hmm, got married, huh?" The customer spoke as if he were surprised and impressed, and he looked around the bar once again.

"I see. . . . I guess if she were from this bar, a barmaid could really get married decently." As if he were quite convinced, he sipped his whiskey-on-the-rocks and sighed.

Mama-san and a barmaid known as Shizu-chan, who were seated quietly on chairs away from the counter, exchanged furtive smiles.

The girl, Eiko, who had been helping Mama-san behind the counter, had committed suicide about three weeks ago.

Any girl who decides to come to work in a bar has her own complex reasons. And, while she works, her life usually becomes even more complicated. Although she had found employment in a quiet bar like this, Eiko probably suffered from more hardships than the average person. It had looked as if she was confiding everything to Mama-san, and had been seeking her advice. Yet there was probably something she had not been able to confide, and maybe that had become unbearable. One night, she took some pills and died. Since she was a quiet girl, perfectly suited for The Tomoshibi, there had not been anything out of the ordinary in her conduct, and even the worldly-wise Mama-san had not noticed anything.

Since it was a whole day before the suicide was discovered, nothing could be done. There was no will, and her humble one-room apartment was left neatly in order. There was a savings passbook left for her younger brother, her only blood relative, but it certainly did not contain an extraordinary sum of money. That a young, nameless barmaid had died one night was such a small happening that it wouldn't even be mentioned in an obscure corner of a newspaper.

That is why Mama-san did not want to do anything that would cast a shadow on the memories of the customers who remembered Eiko.

"Is that so? She got married Hmmm. . . ." The customer, perhaps because the alcohol had begun to take its effect, re-articulated his initial surprise, but Mama-san only commented gently, "Quite so, she got married."

"What kind of guy was he? Was he a customer here?"

"There's no use in being jealous. It's already too late." When Mama-san laughed in her sweet voice, the customer also gave a forced laugh, and at that point they ended the conversation.

"Another drink, please."

"Coming! Coming! Isn't it cold today?"

Although there were peanuts and smoked squid on the narrow counter, with the second glass of whiskey Mama-san provided some fresh cucumber with a dash of lemon, free of charge. The customer picked up a slice with his fingers, and while eating with a crunching sound, asked, "Did you choose all those paintings by yourself?" He was examining the inside of the bar again.

"Yes, but they're all reproductions!"

Several framed pictures, none of them any larger than fifteen square inches, were hung on the wall. Among these, two were Chagalls, one was a Miro, one was an oil painting by Takayama Uichi, and one was a woodblock print by Minami Keiko.

Those by Takayama and the Minami were originals, and those by Chagall and Miro were lithographs, but Mama-san always said that they were replicas and didn't care to elaborate further.

Mama-san had bought them only because they were pictures that she had liked, and not because they were the works of famous artists. But if some customers didn't like the pictures, that was that, no matter what she said.

A picture in which lovers embraced on the roof of a small house in the moonlight. And a sweet, dream-like picture of a young girl singing, enveloped by a bird of fire. Next to the two Chagalls hung a surrealistic picture, with bright colors like a child's scribbles. It was the Miro. This was Mama-san's greatest pride, for she had thrown caution to the winds and bought it, although it was extremely expensive. Yet since the customers who came to the bar could barely appreciate the Chagalls, the Miro seemed even more incomprehensible to them.

However, when one looked at all of them, including the Takayama painting of greenery and butterflies, and the Minami woodblock print of autumn leaves and fish, even the Miro became part of a coherent whole which created a fairy tale-like, innocent, and happy atmosphere throughout the bar. Perhaps it was because of this atmosphere that customers were convinced that barmaids from this bar could become brides after all.

"Last night I had such a beautiful dream."

All of a sudden, Shizu-chan started to speak. Since it was a small bar, whatever anyone said could be overheard by everyone else, so there was no need to turn their heads. The good thing about this bar was the fact that both Mama-san and Shizu-chan had beautiful voices. Some customers said flatly that it was better just to listen to their voices when they started to speak, rather than to look at their faces.

"What kind of dream?" Mama-san responded in a leisurely tone.

"In my dream, I met a boy whom I had been extremely fond of when I was small."

"How incriminating!"

Because Shizu-chan had started to tell her story in such a passionate manner, one of the customers tried to tease her, but Mama-san waited patiently for her next words.

"This boy was the village headman's son. Since we were the children of tenant farmers, in spite of being in the same class at school, we didn't dare go near him. Even so, all the girls liked the young master. When he came close, I could hardly breathe!"

"It must have been your first love!"

"Yes, I guess it was. But it's been over ten years since I left the village. I've never had such a dream in all these years, so I wonder why I should have one now. Last night's dream just came out of the blue. It really surprised me!"

"Was the young master a child? Or had he grown up?"

"I'm not too sure. I'm not even sure whether I was a child or whether I was like I am now. . . . ."

"Isn't that nice!"

"In any case, it was incredibly beautiful. There were birds of fire flying around us."

The Chagall painting had apparently made its way into Shizu-chan's dream. Yet while she was talking, she seemed to enter a dreamy state of mind once again. Even after she had finished talking, she remained staring into space as if entranced.

"I'll go home after one more drink. I think I'll go to sleep early tonight and dream of my first love, too."

Customers would be engulfed by the mood of the bar before they knew it. Shizu-chan was skillful at telling her life story in this fragmentary way, under the pretense of relating, for example, a story about her dreams. Since she differed from the many barmaids who allure customers by going over their sad life stories in great detail, from childhood to more recent hardships, there were quite a number of customers who came to the bar wanting to talk to her.

"And so, Shizu-chan, you haven't returned home ever since you came out to Tokyo?"

"No, even though my father and mother are there, and they've been asking me to come home soon."

"Don't you like the countryside?"

"That's not the point. There are many reasons why I have to stay in Tokyo."

"Is some man giving you a hard time, then?"

"No man would ever give me a hard time!"

Although she was replying seriously, it still sounded so funny that the customers would unexpectedly burst out laughing. It was probably because of Shizu-chan's natural virtue that nobody would think of teasing her by saying. "Would you like me to give you a hard time?"

Only Mama-san knew that Shizu-chan's parents had died when she was still a child, and that she was having a rough time of it at her aunt's into whose family she had been adopted. When Shizu-chan said her parents were awaiting her return, only Mama-san sensed the truth behind the lie.

In the back streets of the Ginza, drunken men would usually spend their time speaking loudly and amorously of women, and drunken women would speak similarly of men. Yet in this bar, even if conversations of that type did get started, they never lasted very long. Strangely enough, though, conversations about pet dogs or cats would continue on and on endlessly.

There was a Siamese cat at The Tomoshibi. It was Mama-san's pet, and every day she carried it with her to work. It had a light gray, slender body, and its legs and the tip of its tail were dark sepia. Since it had a straight, shapely nose, Mama-san believed that it was a beautiful cat.

"Don't be ridiculous! Don't you know that the flatter a cat's nose is, the more attractive it's supposed to be?"

"Impossible! Cats or human beings, it's the same. The higher the nose is, the better."

"You're wrong!"

"Well then, please look carefully. Use your aesthetic sense to judge this. Here. . . ."

Mama-san picked up her beloved cat and thrust it out in front of the customer's nose.

"I still think it's funny. . . ."

If the customer should persist in this manner, things would get serious. In high spirits, Mama-san would refill the glass of whiskey and say, "Here, pull yourself together with this, and look carefully once again. Here Chika, Chika, make a nice face. . . ."

One might wonder whether the customer or Mama-san would be the first to give in, but it was the always the cat in question who, hating to stay still, got bored with trying to outstare the customer, yawned out loud, scratched Mama-san's hand, and jumped down. The area on top of the window above the heater was Chika's seat, and once she retreated there, she would not come out, no matter how one called or invited her.

"Mama-san, don't you like dogs?"

"I like them, but you can't keep a dog in a bar."

"I really like dogs. Even when I get home late after drinking, I always wake up at seven in the morning, since I have to take Hachiro out for a walk."

"Is his name Hachiro? How cute!"

"Is it an Akita?" Shizu-chan interrupted.

"How did you know?" the customer asked in surprise.

"Oh, it's just a lucky guess. I thought a name like Hachiro might be quite appropriate for an Akita."

With this boost to his spirits, the customer drew out a billfold from the inside pocket of his suit and, produced a photograph from it.

He was a customer who perfectly matched the proprietress and barmaids. The snapshot was of his dog.

"See, look, isn't he a handsome one?"

His eyes and mouth were certainly those of an Akita, but the line between the ears and the neck was rather questionable. Yet even so, Mama-san was charmed by the eyes and mouth and said, "How adorable! He looks like a fine, lively dog."

Her manner of praise was clever, but young Shizu-chan, who was peering over from the side, was too honest.

"Hmm, is this really an Akita?" she questioned in a loud voice.

"It's an Akita, all right. This dog's father, you know, has quite a pedigree."

"What about the mother?"

"Well, you see. . . ." he said regretfully, drinking up the remaining whiskey. "It's a case of 'a woman of humble birth marrying into royalty.'"

In other words, Hachiro was a mutt. However, if lineage were to be determined patrilineally, as in the imperial family, then without doubt he would be a descendent of the noble Akita breed.

Being quick with her wits, Mama-san said, "They were quite gallant parents, weren't they?" and saved the customer from his predicament.

With this, the customer regained his balance. Ordering a double-on-the-rocks, he began to speak in great detail of how Hachiro was such a fine dog that he didn't bring disgrace to his father's name.

Birds of a feather flock together, and that night as many as four dog-lovers had gathered there. Since each of them had to introduce the pedigree, name, personality, and distinguishing features of his pet, The Tomoshibi didn't close until quite late.

"Since it's late, Shizu-chan, I'll take you home," Mama-san said to Shizu-chan, who was waiting with her collar pulled up. Mama-san locked the door and stopped a taxi.

"Please take us first to Higashi Nakano, then Shibuya." No matter how tiring a night she might have had, her manner of speaking was always kind.

As the car drove along through the night streets, Shizu-chan started to giggle about something she remembered.

"What is it?"

"Oh, I was just thinking of the dog contest we had."

"Wasn't it funny—everyone thought his own was the best."

"But they were all mongrels!"

"That's why we didn't get into a fight."

Mama-san was smiling serenely, the purebred Siamese cat fast asleep on her lap. It was a conceited cat with a picky appetite. None of the customers who boasted about their half-breed dogs dared to show their antipathy toward Chika, because she was protected by Mama-san's goodness.

"You know, Shizu-chan. . . ."

"Yes?"

"If these late nights continue, we'll surely need a replacement for Eiko."

"I think so, too."

"Unless we find someone who will take turns with you working late, you'll get too tired. Do you know of anyone who would be good?"

"Well, I don't have too many friends, so. . . ."

After a while, Mama-san, looking out of the window, murmured, "What a fool Eiko was to die!"

Almost ready to cry herself, Shizu-chan said hurriedly to the taxi driver, "Oh, please stop here. That corner will be fine. Yes, right here."

Although Mama-san had taken her home on several occasions in the past, Shizu-chan would always get off by the main road and avoid being taken by car to the front of her house. Since there must have been some reason, Mama-san didn't insist on accompanying her any farther. She would quietly see Shizu-chan off, turning around in the taxi, which had started to move, and would watch her figure disappear into the darkness. Small dirty houses stood clustered, side by side.

"Position for barmaid. A young person, with or without experience. The Tomoshibi."

Mama-san wrote this with a brush on a small piece of paper. For three days her routine was to put up the sign at night when leaving, and take it down before eight in the evening when the customers came. Three or four applicants came knocking at the door, despite the fact that it was such a tiny advertisement and for such an inconspicuous bar.

During the hours before her customers came, Mama-san held "interviews" in the bar, and when there were customers, in the coffee shop next door.

One girl was so young she seemed like a firm plum still attached to a branch. It appeared that she had come to the accessories store across the street and read the advertisement by chance. Her family was apparently well-off, and she had been casually thinking that she wanted to work. Mama-san shuddered at her naive boldness.

"When you discuss this matter with your parents, please make sure that you tell them I said this is not the sort of place you should be coming to."

"Oh, then there's no use in discussing it with them. Am I unqualified?"

In the eyes that asked "Am I unqualified?" shone fearless, youthful, as yet unblemished pride. Hoping that this child would be able to grow up just as she was, Mama-san gently smiled and nodded.

"Yes, you're unqualified."

"Oh, shucks!"

Since she stuck her tongue out and left without seeming too disappointed, Mama-san felt greatly relieved.

On another occasion, a sickly, tired woman came by.

"Why did you quit the other bar?"

"The proprietress scolded me too often. About not being lively and boisterous. She complained a lot, but how could I help it? After all, that's my nature!"

"That's true."

"But I have my own good customers. That's why the proprietress didn't want to let me go, but I don't like working under someone I have personality conflicts with."

Realizing quite clearly that she wouldn't get along with her either, Mama-san smiled and stood up.

"As you can see, our bar is rather small, isn't it? We don't need any more customers than we already have. If fate so ordains, I'll see you again."

It seemed as if the many layers of grime from the woman's harsh daily life were smeared across her coarse skin. Wishing she had the confidence to try and wash away this person's unhappiness at The Tomoshibi, Mama-san was sad that she couldn't hire her.

However, even if Mama-san invited this person to come and work at the bar, sooner or later she would leave of her own accord.

Mama-san had always hired the type of barmaids who would stay only at The Tomoshibi.

"Good evening!" a voice called cheerfully.

A figure dressed in bright colors entered the door, and the bar became crowded at once. It was the madam of one of the five largest bars in the Ginza.

"My, I haven't seen you for such a long time!"

Mama-san, in her usual manner, invited her in warmly. Mama-san's smile never changed according to whom she was talking to. Some ten years ago, Madam and Mama-san had worked in the same bar. They both became independent in the same Ginza area around the same time. However, Madam had been quite a businesswoman. Therefore, after moving from place to place, her bar and her name had become so noted that any person who dealt with the Ginza could not have failed to hear of them.

"This bar hasn't changed at all!"

"I guess it's been two years since you last came."

"How I envy you! I suppose if you don't have to make alterations in the interior of your bar for two whole years, you don't have to spend much money. As for my place, since the customers are so demanding, we frequently have to change the wall hangings and the paintings. . . ."

It was probably because Madam had some good qualities that her constant complaining about her financial situation, as well as her total envy of this small bar, were not intolerably offensive. Drinkers are very honest with themselves, so unless the proprietress is somewhat good-natured, customers won't be attracted to the bar.

"I have something to talk with you about." Madam said suddenly in a low voice, pulling Mama-san out to the coffee shop next door.

"Don't you have an opening at your place?"

"Well, I am looking for someone right now, but there aren't very many people who would come to work at a bar like ours."

Madam took Mama-san's modesty seriously, and after firmly nodding, leaned forward.

"I know of a nice girl. . . . Will you take a look at her?"

"But isn't she one of the girls at your place?"

"That's true, but she won't last there. She's just too nice. I don't know what to do, because whenever a customer teases her even a little bit, she starts to cry. I tell her over and over again that unless you strike back when you're teased you can't survive in the Ginza, but it's completely useless. The girls at my place are always being offered positions at rival bars whenever I'm not paying close attention, except for that one. She's fairly popular with the customers, but she still has an inferiority complex. Touch upon that complex and she gets depressed. I just haven't any idea what to do!"

"What kind of inferiority complex?" Mama-san attempted to pursue the matter further, but Madam waved her hands dramatically and ignored the question.

"Well, in any case I'll tell her to stop by and see you after work, so take a look at her. She's the perfect girl for your place. It would be easy for me to fire her, but she's such a nice girl that I don't have the heart to kick her out. Do it for me, all right?"

Madam pulled out a one-thousand yen bill and picked up the check from the table in one swift move. Having finished her business, she hastily paid for the coffee and left.

Forced to accept the proposition, Mama-san returned to the bar. She didn't feel so badly after she remembered that Madam always behaved in the same way.

Since the two bars belonged to such different categories, they were not in competition with each other, and even if Madam tried to pass off a secondhand article that was of no use at her place, Mama-san would not be offended. On the contrary, she rather enjoyed going over in her mind what Madam had said, "She's such a nice girl that she can't work at my bar." That she was such a nice girl she was not even appropriate for the very best bar in the Ginza district certainly pleased Mama-san.

Therefore, when the night grew late and Momoko appeared—quietly opening the door and inquiring, "May I come in?"—Mama-san said almost by reflex, "Oh, I've heard all about you. Everything's all set. Please start working here from five tomorrow evening."

Shizu-chan seemed to take in Momoko's round face and lovely lips immediately, as well as the fact that her dark blue overcoat was very becoming.

Just before leaving for home, Shizu-chan asked nonchalantly, "Is the person who came by a little while ago working with us from tomorrow?" But Mama-san, who was busy getting ready to close up and go home, answered without going into great detail, "Yes, I'll introduce her to you tomorrow."

Mama-san was rather noisily occupied in the restroom.

"Shizu-chan."

"Yes?"

"It's quite late, so you can go home first."

"Are you sure it's all right?"

Shizu-chan wondered what Mama-san could be up to, but anxious to head for home just as soon as she could, she left straight away.

The next day, having been delayed by collecting bills, Shizu-chan arrived at the bar a little later than usual and found Mama-san cleaning here and there inside the bar with the new girl.

"Good morning!"

"Oh, good morning! This is Shizu-chan, and this is Momoko-chan."

Mama-san introduced them in an intimate manner, as if she were bringing together two of her children. Momoko bowed humbly, and Shizu-chan felt slightly embarrassed. Deep inside, she had received quite a shock.

Dimly aware of the fact that Madam, who was an old friend of Mama-san, had spoken to Mama-san about this matter, Shizu-chan had been worried about what kind of person was going to come. Yet unlike last night's impression of her, the minute she looked at Shizu-chan today, Shizu-chan was taken aback.

She's cross-eyed, Shizu-chan realized at once. To use a Japanese expression, her eyes were "London-Paris"—her right eye was focused on London, while her left eye looked toward Paris. Furthermore, one of her eyes was a bit too close to the other. Besides these, there were no other faults in her appearance.

When Momoko went to the restroom, and there were still no customers, Shizu-chan found her chance to speak. "Mama-san," she began.

Mama-san, in a low, yet sharp voice, said firmly, "Shizu-chan, the subject of her eyes is taboo." Since Shizu-chan was also a nice girl, she accepted this immediately. Something deep within moved her to tears.

Perhaps because there was one more person in the bar than before, thus making it more lively, many customers turned up that night. The regular customers quickly took notice of Momoko. But since, unlike Eiko, she stood further behind the counter than Mama-san and was occupied with diligently opening and closing the refrigerator door, they couldn't talk to her very much.

Very few customers came to this bar simply for the barmaids, however, so no one was very dissatisfied with her behavior. The Tomoshibi remained completely the same as it had been. The customers quietly sipped their drinks, and when once in a while they did say something, Mama-san would take up the conversation, with Shizu-chan in her carefree and easy-going manner joining in.

One customer did find something different from before. This man, who had been chugging his beer, returned from the restroom with a strange expression on his face and asked, "What happened to the mirror?"

"Oh, someone broke it," answered Mama-san.

"You must have had some rough customers!"

"We can get a new mirror, but it might be broken again. Besides, we really ought to be able to put up with the inconvenience."

Probably only Shizu-chan noticed that Mama-san, upon realizing the source of Momoko's inferiority complex, had taken her in only after removing the mirror from the restroom.

"Anyway, our customers aren't the type that have to feel guilty when they look at their drunken faces in the mirror," Mama-san said in her mellow voice.

"Right! That's right!"

This cheered the customers; there was no chance of them being put out by it. Although the type of customer who got drunk and became boisterous rarely came to The Tomoshibi, there were, among the regular customers some young men who liked to sing quiet songs. However, once they started to get tipsy, they demanded that Mama-san and the girls sing, too. Mama-san would say, "No, I can't because I'm tone-deaf," and escape, refusing to sing under any circumstances. If one flattered Shizu-chan, though, telling her that she was good, she would sing a number of songs in her melodious voice. Since she made every popular song come out like an elementary school tune, her specialty had become nursery songs. Everyone was impressed by her specialty. Her singing was popular probably because it was most appropriate for the atmosphere of the bar. She could certainly not have been called very talented.

"Mama-san, wasn't Eiko-chan pretty good, too? Wasn't she?" With his eyes half closed as if trying to remember, a customer asked, "Didn't she go away to get married? Is she happy?"

"Yes, yes, she's very happy."

Shizu-chan began to sing:

When she was fifteen Nanny got married
Letters from home
No longer came.

"In this present age, what do you think we lack the most and need the most?"

In one corner of the room there were customers discussing serious topics while drinking their whiskey.

"Hmmm, let's see, . . . how about dreams? As far as I'm concerned, right now that's what I lack the most and need the most."

"Well, I agree, but I don't call them 'dreams.'"

"Then what are they?"

"Fairy tales."

"Hmm, fairy tales. I guess you're right."

While that conversation was going on, Shizu-chan was singing away in front of customers in another corner.

"Well, what do you think about being able to listen to nursery rhymes in a Ginza bar?"

"Now I'm beginning to understand why you said you wanted to come here."

Sometimes a dreadfully tone-deaf person in high spirits would sing along with Shizu-chan.

After four or five days, Momoko was in a state of total astonishment. She wondered if this, too, could possibly be a bar.

Some types of people aren't affected by hardships; Momoko was the type who wasn't affected by past experiences. Even though this was the fourth time she had found herself employed in a bar, she possessed naive qualities which made it seem as if she had only worked in a bar for the first time yesterday. Shizu-chan began to act as if she were Momoko's elder sister all the time, and on occasions when Mama-san wasn't present, she would ask, "Well, do you think you'll be able to handle working here?" and peer into Momoko's face.

"Yes, I look forward to coming to work. And also, it almost seems like this isn't a bar, but some other kind of place."

"Well, if it's not a bar, what is it?"

"A kindergarten!"

Shizu-chan almost fell out of her chair, laughing. Before very long, Mama-san returned and Shizu-chan presented her with this masterpiece. Mama-san was reminded of the fact that the Chagalls and the Miro, all hanging on the wall, were also childlike. Even the small, low chair in the corner was appropriate for a kindergarten, she thought.

Around Christmas and at the end of the year, The Tomoshibi was not affected by irregular waves of customers. Just as there were never times when the bar was full and customers couldn't come in, so there was never a day when there were absolutely no customers. Momoko was most grateful for the fact that she wasn't compelled to wear a fancy kimono just because it was Christmas or New Year's.

Mama-san casually wore lovely, unobtrusive things, but she did not force her pleasure in clothes on other people.

"Happy New Year!"

"We value your patronage and hope to see you again this year."

Early in the new year, one customer dashed in as soon as they opened the bar crying "Happy New Year!" Mama-san politely repeated her New Year's greetings, and without waiting for any prompting from him, asked, "Well?"

"They were born!"

"Well, that is an auspicious event indeed! How many of them?"

As usual, they were discussing dogs.

"Six. . . . I went out of my way to make sure that only purebreds got to her, but I failed again. Half of them are spotted. Even their faces are quite different from their mother's"

"That's probably the aftereffects of a previous mate."

"I've heard that's so . . . once you've made a mistake, you can't breed purebreds."

"But aren't the puppies cute?"

"Cute things are cute, even if they're mutts. There are too many of them, but I can't bring myself to give them away. My son also says that they're his children and loves them very much. It's a nice feeling."

As they spoke, another person who shared their interest wandered in, and leaning forward, commented, "Even though you may think they're mongrels, sometimes it happens that while you're rearing them, they become purebreds, just like one of their parents."

"Isn't that a miracle!"

"A miracle, indeed. In my experience, this is where the owner's character plays a great part!"

"I see. . . ."

"Yes, it's really true. Was it in Aesop that the ugly duckling became a white swan?"

"Wasn't that Hans Christian Andersen?"

"Whichever! In any case, things like that happen."

"So then, will you try to raise all six of them? A miracle might happen to at least one."

For a while after that, miracles were the topic of conversation. After those customers had gone their merry ways, and before the next wave of customers arrived, Momoko said, "Mama-san, miracles really do happen, don't they?" She started to speak very seriously.

When Shizu-chan asked "Have you ever seen one?" Momoko nodded in assent, saying, "My eyes are getting better!"

Momoko continued in front of her two listeners who were holding their breath.

"From when I was small, I was always teased about my eyes. As I got older, it was even harder to bear, and I was always crying. Since I could make better money in a bar than at other jobs, I was able to help my family, but the customers always mentioned my eyes. It was really painful."

Looking up suddenly, Momoko's eyes lost the correct balance between right and left, and one side inclined outward.

"Even since I came to this bar, nobody has commented on my eyes. In the beginning, I thought that you were purposely avoiding the subject. But even the customers didn't say anything. When I came to think of it, nobody seemed to even notice my eyes. On New Year's Day, I went to the mirror and was almost too scared to look—until then, I had always disliked large mirrors and had used a compact to do my makeup. Then, well, miraculously, my eyes were cured! I don't know why they got better, but I think that miracles do happen after all."

Mama-san, who had been listening attentively to Momoko's story, said, "Really? How wonderful!" She spoke with great feeling, placing her hand on Momoko's shoulder. Shizu-chan looked as if she were going to cry if she spoke, so she quickly turned her back to Momoko and said in a deliberately dry tone, "How wonderful!"

To the two of them, it did not seem as if the miracle Momoko had spoken about had taken place, but if that was what Momoko believed, then a miracle had definitely occurred.

"Hello there!"

Once again familiar customers were coming through the door.

"Welcome! Happy New Year!" Momoko greeted them cheerfully.

✸ Discussion and Writing

1. Describe The Tomoshibi, its locale, and the decor. In what ways does it differ from the other bars in the Ginza?
2. Explain Mama-san's treatment of the barmaids. Discuss her rationale for the lies about them.
3. Why does Madam ask Mama-san to hire Momoko? What does the incident reveal about the three individuals involved?
4. Analyze the impact of the atmosphere of the bar: the talks about dreams, cats, dogs; the singing with customers; the bar being called a kindergarten.
5. To whom is the *tomoshibi* applicable: discuss its implications.

✸ Research and Comparison

1. Examine the works of two contemporary women writers of Japan, focusing on the social concerns that inform their writings. Explore the experience of women in regard to the conflict between traditional mores and modern life depicted in these works.
2. Compare two women writers from different cultures included in this anthology, concentrating on the portrayal of any specific issue concerning women.

Ko Un
(b. 1933)
Korea

Ko Un was born in Kunsan, Korea, in North Cholla Province at the time of the Japanese occupation. He was an unusually precocious child and sensitive young man. During the Korean War, he was conscripted into the People's Army and became despondent over the fratricidal bloodshed. Leaving the army before the war ended, he became a Zen Buddhist monk and cofounder of the *Buddhist Newspaper,* serving as editor-in-chief and publishing his poems and essays. When the eminent poet Cho Chihun recommended that Ko Un's work be published in an important review, *Modern Poetry,* Ko Un's career as a poet officially began, for according to custom, to be accepted one must first be praised by an established author. For ten years he practiced Zen Buddhism: as a monk living on alms, as the head priest of two temples, as education director, as a member of the National Monks' Association. After teaching for a time at a charity school, there followed a period of political activity when he took a leading role in the protest against President Park Chung Hee. Imprisoned several times, he remained active and a recognized leader for some 20 years in the fight for democracy and human rights, even after his life was threatened at the time of the Kwangju massacre. (The government quelled a protest over martial law in the city of Kwangju in May 1980.)

Ko Un's poetry, novels, and essays reflect the many turns his life has taken. He has been a prolific poet, publishing more than 20 collections of poems, and his work has ranged from epigrams to discursive poems; he has also written epic and pastoral poetry and created the popular-historical poem. Respected as Korea's leading contemporary poet for his sensitivity, humanity, and philosophical breadth; he is noted also for the deftness with which he manipulates the language. He was honored in 1993 with a festival in Seoul, celebrating his dedication to the people and literary arts of Korea.

Lee Chongnam*

When children cry, if you tell them:
A roaring tiger will come,
a big tiger will come
and carry you off if you cry!
the crying goes on;
but if you say:
They'll take you to Sinpung-ri police box!
then the crying stops as if by magic.
And grown-ups too,
when they pass before Sinpung-ri police box
with the three trays of eggs they're selling,
they feel as if they've stolen them somewhere, and
their hearts beat two or three times faster than normal.
One fellow who simply took to his heels
as he went by was called in: Hey, you!
by a Japanese cop, and had a hard time.
I had a fright going by there once, too,
as I was following uncle Hongsik
on the way to sell dried pine branches down at the wood store.
A man was coming out with a messed-up face,
his hands tied behind his back.
He was being transferred to Kunsan central police station.
Someone was marching along behind him, holding the rope.
And who was that? The police box cat's paw, that's who,

---

*Translated by Brother Anthony of Taize, Young-Moo Kim

Lee Chongnam, brother-in-law to our grandfather's niece.
That wicked man!
He kicked his wife in the stomach and made her abort.
He turned on his own father and pulled his beard.
But where the Japs were concerned, he was down on his knees,
on his knees and crawling, he was so crazy about them!
At Liberation he should have been first to get it,
but he hid for a while, and when he came out
he was put in charge of Sinpung-ri police box.
He dressed himself up in a policeman's cap and uniform,
and put on airs riding around the district on a bicycle:
tring-a-ling, tring-a-ling, Out of my way!

❄ Discussion and Writing

1. Comment on the resemblance between the tiger and the Sinpung-ri police box. Explain the people's (children's and adults') anxiety.
2. Analyze the social and political framework the persona and his community are placed in. To what extent does this background determine the behavior of both the police and the people?
3. Describe Lee Chongnam and his dealings with the family, community, and authority. Explain his successful political moves.
4. Elaborate on Ko Un's statement about the innocent and the guilty during the Japanese occupation of Korea.
5. What is the tone of the poem: what is the effect of the various scenes and the colloquial use of language?

❄ Research and Comparison

Interdisciplinary Discussion Question: Research the history of Japanese expansion in Korea, focusing on its impact on people's self-esteem and identity. Explore the question of the search for identity and self-assertion in the works of any major Korean writer.

Tomioka Taeko
(b. 1935)
Japan

Tomioka Taeko was born in a working-class neighborhood in Osaka, Japan. She was the eldest child and a great favorite of her father, who was originally a scrap iron dealer. After building a foundry and becoming modestly affluent, he rejected family life and left the home. Tomioka graduated from Osaka Women's College, where she majored in English. She then taught briefly in high school, and also won a major poetry prize for her first volume of poetry, *Henrei* (Reciprocal Courtesy, 1957). While involved in a passionate, but ultimately disastrous, love affair with an impoverished painter, she traveled to the United States. Having already published several volumes of poetry, she turned to writing short stories and novels. Fiction allowed her the scope to depict the fragmentation of modern society and to portray the nameless, strong unlettered people who spoke the dialects of Kyoto and her native Osaka. She experimented with form and methods of narration. In "Family in Hell"—the title story of the collection that earned her the Women's Literature Prize in 1974—she based the narrative on her unhappy love affair but told the tale from different points of view. Inventive in her poetry as well as in her fiction, she displays an openness and analytic discrimination that have become characteristic. She manipulates syntax and form to reveal the demoralization of contemporary society, confronting issues of class conflict and traditional values as well as the effect of modernity on women.

*Just the Two of Us**

You'll make tea,
I'll make toast.
While we're doing that,
at times, early in the evening,
someone may notice the moonrise dyed scarlet
and at times visit us
but that'll be the last time the person comes here.
We'll shut the doors, lock them,
make tea, make toast,
talk as usual about how
sooner or later
there will be a time
you bury me,
and I bury you, in the garden,
and go out as usual to look for food.
There will be a time
either you or I
bury either me or you in the garden
and the one left, sipping tea,
then for the first time, will refuse fiction.

Translated by Hiroaki Sato and Burton Watson

Even your freedom
was like a fool's story.

❄ Discussion and Writing

1. What does the scarlet moonrise suggest?
2. Describe the three phases of the couple's life.
3. What is implied by the surviving person's refusing fiction for the first time? Why is freedom a fool's story?
4. What is the tone of the poem: loving, angry, sarcastic, other?

Pai Hsien-yung
(b. 1937)
Taiwan

Pai Hsein-yung was born in China the year the Japanese invaded and began its occupation (1937–1945). His father served as a leader in the Nationalist army and in the government as a high-level defense official during this period when the nationalist Kuomintang and Communists united to wage war against Japan. The family immigrated to Taiwan after the war. At the time, Pai Hsein-yung was in middle school; he subsequently took his degree at National Taiwan University. He began publishing his short stories at the end of his freshman year at the university. Regarded as one of the finest contemporary writers in the Chinese language, he has drawn on memories of his childhood experiences during the war in Guilin in Southwest China for much of his fiction. Thus, his work depicts displacement and the indignities frequently attendant on exile, and with his careful attention to detail, his characters remain indelibly, often poignantly, etched in the memory.

A Sea of Bloodred Azaleas*

According to Chinese mythology, in ancient times Tu Yu, the king of Shu, had a love affair with the wife of one of his ministers. Ashamed, he fled his kingdom and turned into a *tu-chuan*, a cuckoo.

The cuckoo is said to sing unceasingly through the spring for his tragic love, until he spits blood, which is transformed into *tu-chuan* flowers, or azaleas.

The Chinese literary tradition also maintains that the singing of the cuckoo evokes homesickness in the exile.

Translated by Pai Hsien-yung and Patia Yasin

It was on a remote, deserted beach near Keelung that they found Wang Hsiung. His body was swept back in among the rocks and stuck there in a crevice; he never got to drift out to sea after all. When my aunt, my mother's brother's wife, sent me to identify the body, Wang Hsiung had been in the water for days. His whole body had turned black and blue; his belly was so swollen it had burst through his shirt; the fish had been eating at his head and it had turned into rotten pulp with little holes all over, some dark red, some inky black; even the eyes and eyebrows were gone. Even when you were yards away, the stench of the decaying corpse carried on the breeze and nauseated you. If it hadn't been for those gigantic hands of his with their round, stubby fingers, still unaltered, I would never have suspected that the huge monster lying there on the ground could be Wang Hsiung, the manservant at my aunt's house.

The death of Wang Hsiung caused a great stir. That very night, my aunt burned a big wad of paper money in the garden; she squatted on her heels, burning the money and muttering prayers to appease his soul. She said that with a violent death like Wang Hsiung's you never knew if the house would remain peaceful. When I told my aunt that Wang Hsiung's body had already decomposed, Happy, the maid who was standing nearby, overheard me and let out a shriek of terror. My aunt tried hard to get her to stay, but Happy wouldn't remain another instant; then and there she threw her belongings together and fled back to her home in I-lan. My cousin Little Beauty was the only one we kept in the dark about all this; we never told her, we were afraid it would frighten her. When my aunt and I went to Wang Hsiung's room to collect the things he had left behind, she swore to me that after this lesson she'd never again, not as long as she lived, hire another manservant.

The first time I saw Wang Hsiung was two years ago, in the spring. I had been in the ROTC on Quemoy and had just been transferred back to Taipei to work in an administrative job at Supply Headquarters. My home was in Taichung; my only relatives in Taipei were my aunt and her family. As soon as I had reported for duty, I went to my aunt's to pay them a visit. My uncle had owned a big business; he died young—he had had only one child, my cousin Little Beauty. He left a considerable estate, so my aunt and my cousin had always lived a luxurious life. At that time my aunt had just moved, and now they lived on a half-acre of land, in a huge Western-style house with a garden, on Jen-ai Road, Section 4. The day I went to my aunt's she was in the living room, in the middle of a game of mah-jong; she gave me a casual greeting and told me to go out into the garden and look for Cousin Little Beauty. My mother had told me my aunt watched over Little Beauty like a mother cat; she was still personally spoon-feeding the child at the age of six. Little Beauty was so spoiled that even though she was now in the sixth grade in primary school she still refused to tie her own shoelaces. But she was such an adorable child, with such winsome features, that everyone doted on her. I had never seen any other child with such snow-white skin, and so roly-poly; her face, her eyes, even her nose and mouth were round and cute-looking. When she shook her short hair and giggled, that baby-girl innocence of hers couldn't help but win you over. She was like a jade doll. On the other hand, very few children had her willful and imperious temperament either. At the least provocation, she'd grab something, no matter how valuable, and dash it to the ground. Then she'd sit on the floor rubbing her plump legs and cry and cry until her voice was gone; she simply wouldn't stop, and nobody, not even may aunt, could make her come round.

My aunt's garden was very spacious, the new-grown grass, flowers, and trees all carefully tended; in the center of the garden there was a lush green lawn of downy Korean grass; surrounding it were flower beds filled with azalea bushes—many were beginning to bud—all of them would be flaming red when in bloom. The minute I came into the garden, I heard tinkling, rippling laughter that went on and on. When I walked around the grove of banana trees, I was surprised to see Little Beauty astride a large man on all fours who was trotting around the lawn like a beast. Little Beauty was sitting straight up on his back, her plump little hand holding an azalea branch which she swished in the air like a riding crop. She was wearing a red corduroy skirt. Her bare white legs kicked and flailed; her head bobbed up and down; her short hair flopped to and fro; she was so happy she couldn't stop her shrill laughter.

"Cousin! Look at me riding my horsie—" When Little Beauty saw me, she threw away the branch and waved at me with both her hands; then she jumped off over his head and ran to me.

"Young Master-Cousin." The man scrambled to his feet, smiled at me, and murmured the greeting sheepishly.

I hadn't realized he would be such a giant, well over six feet, with an enormous head, his scalp shaved to a green-blue glow, his face swarthy, his whole body gleaming like black bronze. He grinned at me, showing a mouthful of white teeth; he kept rubbing those gigantic hands of his together bashfully; his stubby fingers looked clumsy and somewhat comical. He wore a pair of soldiers' pants washed to a faded white, the knees plastered with mud and grass.

"Cousin!" said Little Beauty, pointing at the man, "Wang Hsiung said he could crawl like that for miles and miles!"

"That was in the war, lo-ong ago-o—" Wang Hsiung hastened to explain; he had the very heavy accent of a native of Hunan.

"Nonsense!" Little Beauty cut him short with a frown. "You *did* say it, that day. You said you would let me ride on your back all the way to school."

Wang Hsiung looked at Little Beauty sheepishly; he seemed unable to get a word out; he even started to blush through his swarthy skin, as if some secret between Little Beauty and him had been revealed.

"Cousin! Let's go look, Wang Hsiung's caught me a whole lot of big green crickets." Little Beauty went running ahead of me, leading me toward the house; after a few steps she stopped, as if she'd suddenly thought of something; she turned around and stretched out her round, white arm at Wang Hsiung.

"Come, Wang Hsiung," she called out.

Hesitating for a moment, Wang Hsiung finally came shuffling up. Little Beauty snatched his dark, brawny arm; hand in hand with him; hopping and leaping about, she ran toward the house. Wang Hsiung lumbered off after her, pulling his colossal body along.

That night, after my aunt finished playing mahjong she sat around and chatted with me; she told me Wang Hsiung was the manservant she'd just hired. He had been a soldier all his life and was recently discharged. "You simply couldn't find a more honest fellow!" my aunt declared approvingly. "Not a peep out of him all day long, he just buries himself in his work. And you should see the way he takes care of the trees and flowers! Amazing for such an uncouth fellow. He certainly has his own idea of how to go about it." My aunt told me that every single one of the hundred or so azaleas in the garden had been planted by Wang Hsiung with his own hands. Why so many azaleas? "For Little Beauty, of course," my aunt explained with a sigh. "What else? Just because that little imp is crazy about azaleas."

"I've never seen such a thing in all my born days!" Suddenly my aunt laughed behind her hands. "A forty-year-old great big hunk of a man letting a baby-doll of a little girl lead him around by the nose! Why, he caters to her every wish." It's a miracle, my aunt wondered out loud with a shake of her head; the two of them must be fated for each other.

Indeed Little Beauty and Wang Hsiung must have been fated for each other. Every time I went to my aunt's I saw them playing together. Each morning Wang Hsiung would carry Little Beauty to school in his pedicab; in the afternoon he would bring her home. He always polished his pedicab bright and shiny; he had little bamboo sticks topped with woollen balls of rainbow hues, paper-cut phoenixes and little pinwheels stuck all across the handlebar; the vehicle was decorated like an Imperial Palace carriage. Each time Wang Hsiung went out to transport Little Beauty he made himself spic-and-span; even on the hottest days he was always respectably attired. As Little Beauty marched through the gate, chin in the air, hair shaking, haughty as a little princess, Wang Hsiung brought up the rear, holding her schoolbag, his back straight and his face solemn, every inch the Imperial Guard to her Royal Highness. The minute she got home Little Beauty would drag Wang Hsiung out into the garden to play. Wang Hsiung would dream up a hundred little games to delight her. Once I saw him seated by himself under the eaves, at his feet a multicolored pile of glass beads; he was holding a golden thread and stringing the beads with the utmost concentration. As he reached out to catch the glass beads that were rolling in all directions, his gigantic paws looked really clumsy, yet rather engaging. When Little Beauty got home that day and came to the garden, Wang Hsiung decorated her from head to foot with bracelets and necklaces of glass beads. She wore a double-ringed crown on her head and five or six bracelets on each arm; she kicked off her shoes and, barefoot, her skirt tucked up showing her white legs, she had her ankles ringed with several rainbow-colored bangles. She was chanting—"*ee-yah-oo-yah*"—and laughing, her plump pretty arms waving aloft two bouquets of azaleas, and dancing on the lush green lawn the aborigine dance she had learned in school. Wang Hsiung was circling around her, bounding up and down, clapping his hands, his swarthy face flushed crimson, his mouth wide open in a toothy grin. The two of them— one big, one small, one dark, one white—leaping and gamboling, sang and danced against a sea of flaming red azaleas.

During my tour of duty at Supply Headquarters, I'd stay overnight at my aunt's two or three days a week. My aunt wanted me to tutor Little Beauty, because she was going to take the entrance exam for middle school in the summer. As a regular visitor at my aunt's I became better acquainted with Wang Hsiung, and on occasion he'd tell me something about himself. He told me that originally he was a peasant boy from the Hunan countryside; during the Anti-Japanese War a press gang got him and put him in the army. He said he was only eighteen then; one day he was trotting off to town to sell the two baskets of grain on his carrying pole; the minute he stepped outside his village he was taken away.

"I thought I might still get back in a few days," he said with a chuckle. "Who'd have dreamt? Before you know it, so many years have gone and I never made it back to home."

"Young Master-Cousin," Wang Hsiung once asked me, as if something were on his mind, "Can you see the mainland from Quemoy?"

I told him that through a telescope you could practically see people moving on the other side.

"That close up?" He stared at me, disbelieving.

"Why not?" I said. "Very often bodies of people who have died of hunger drift over to our side."

"They come over to look for their kinfolk," he said.

"Those people have died of hunger," I said.

"No, Young Master-Cousin, you don't know." Wang Hsiung stopped me with a wave of his hand. "Down in our Hunan countryside we got zombie-raisers; when people die outside and they got some kinfolk at home they're attached to, you wouldn't believe how fast them zombies run home."

When I was on Quemoy, there were a number of old soldiers in our battalion; they must have been in the army for almost twenty years, but it seemed to me they had still kept a childlike innocence; their joy, anger, sorrow, and happiness were just like the burning sun and sea storms of Quemoy, primitive and direct. Sometimes I'd see a whole lot of them naked in the ocean having a water fight; from time to time one or another of their wrinkled faces would suddenly break into a child's smile, the kind of smile you never see on grownup faces. One night when I was out on patrol, on a rock by the beach near our barracks I found an old soldier sitting there all by himself playing the *erh-hu*.[1] The moon was bright that night; there was almost no breeze off the ocean; I don't know if it was that pensive posture of his or the mournful sound of his Tartar violin that made me associate his nostalgia with that of those sentries of olden days along the frontier, so profound and ancient.

"Wang Hsiung," I asked him one night when we were sitting outside to cool off, "who is left of your family?" He'd been telling me about his old home in the countryside of Hsiangyin in Hunan.

"Oh, there's my mamma, don't know if she's still alive or not," said Wang Hsiung. "And there's—."

At this point he suddenly became shy and tongue-tied; then, with a lot of hemming and hawing, he told me that before he left home he'd been engaged at an early age; his mother had bought him a little Sissy from the next village.

"She weren't more than ten, only that high—" Wang Hsiung made a gesture with his hand. How that Sissy of his loved to eat and hated to work! His mamma would pick up a broomstick and give her a licking for it; when she got spanked she'd turn and hide herself behind his back. "Sissy was right white and plump, a very silly little gal." Wang Hsiung bared his teeth and started chuckling.

"I've got a nice lot of squid for you!" Happy, the maid, had sneaked up behind Wang Hsiung; abruptly she thrust out a string of barbecued squid and dangled it right in front of Wang Hsiung's face. She had just washed her hair and come out to the garden to cool off. She was a big-breasted female who was particularly fond of wearing skintight clothes, so tight you could see her flesh jiggling around in them. She always painted her face oily white, and pencilled her eyebrows heavily. She would ogle people with her small eyes and purse her lips defiantly, fancying herself very seductive. My aunt said the two of them, Happy and Wang Hsiung, must have their horoscopes crossed in some way; from the first moment Wang Hsiung set foot in the house they were deadly enemies. Whenever Wang Hsiung saw her he would try to avoid her, but Happy took a perverse delight in provoking

---

[1]From *Hu-ch'in*, "Tartar violin," a viol of the rebab family, of Central Asian origin. The *erh-hu*, "second *Hu-ch'in*," is the viola to the violin.

him, and whenever she made him turn red as a beet she would laugh in his face with great glee.

Wang Hsiung rudely brushed her hand away and growled; he jerked his head away with a frown and wouldn't talk any more. Happy, laughing out loud, threw back her head and lowered the barbecued squid into her mouth; then, tossing her long, dripping-wet hair, she strutted over to the rattan lounge under the banana trees and stretched out on it. The big, round yellow moon had just climbed up over the garden wall and shone on the fat banana leaves till they gleamed. Happy was fanning herself with a large rushleaf fan; she kept slapping at her legs to chase away the mosquitoes. In a shrill voice she began to sing a Taiwanese "sob-tune," "Tossing and Turning till Dawn." Brusquely Wang Hsiung stood up; without so much as turning his head he dragged himself off to the house.

Little Beauty was a bright child, all right; after I'd tutored her for only a few weeks during the summer vacation, she passed the entrance examination without much effort and was admitted to the Provincial Middle School Number Two for Girls. My aunt was so happy she could hardly close her mouth for laughing; as soon as the names of the successful candidates were posted she took Little Beauty to a tailor and had her measured for her school uniform and took her out shopping for her schoolbag and other supplies. The day school started, the whole household was in a dither; my aunt personally packed Little Beauty's schoolbag and ironed her uniform. As Little Beauty marched triumphantly to the front gate dressed in her smart Girl Scout uniform with all the accessories, her cap at a jaunty angle and a brand new black leather schoolbag under her arm, it seemed as if she had changed in the twinkling of an eye from a little girl into a real middle-school student. Wang Hsiung had already wheeled the pedicab to the gate and was waiting there; when Little Beauty emerged, Wang Hsiung looked awestruck and gaped at her, utterly speechless. Little Beauty tossed her schoolbag into the pedicab and nimbly jumped in after it; she waved at us and gave her driver a push, saying:

"Let's go, Wang Hsiung!"

Little Beauty became totally fascinated with her middle-school life. The first few days she simply wouldn't take off her uniform after school; she stood in front of the mirror and kept looking at herself this way and that. Whenever she got the chance, she would pick up her *Far East English Reader* and read aloud in English with great pride. One day she was standing on the stone steps leading to the garden, holding the English reader in her hand; Wang Hsiung was down below, his head raised, listening intently to the young lady read English.

"*I am a girl.*" Little Beauty pointed at her chest; then she pointed at Wang Hsiung.

"*You are a boy.*" Wang Hsiung's mouth hung open, his face full of admiration.

"I am a student," Little Beauty read on; she cast a glance at Wang Hsiung; suddenly she pointed at him and shouted, *"You are a dog!"*

Little Beauty went off into a fit of laughter, giggling and swaying to and fro, her short hair flying in all directions. Wang Hsiung blinked his eyes in bewilderment, totally at a loss; then he opened his mouth and laughed happily with his little mistress.

Three weeks after school started, one Saturday around noon Little Beauty returned home where we were all waiting for her so we could eat lunch together. The girl flung open the living-room door and walked in, her face stormy; Wang Hsiung was following behind with her schoolbag.

"Beginning next week, I don't want Wang Hsiung to take me to school any more!" she said to my aunt the minute she sat down. We were all very surprised; quickly my aunt asked her whatever was the matter.

"Everybody laughs at me!" Little Beauty threw up her head, her face reddened.

"Why should they laugh?" My aunt went over and tried to comfort her; wiping the perspiration from Little Beauty's forehead with her handkerchief, she said gently, "Lots of other people ride to school in pedicabs, don't they?"

Little Beauty pushed my aunt's hands away; suddenly she pointed her finger at Wang Hsiung. "All my schoolmates are talking—they say he looks like a big gorilla!" She glanced at Wang Hsiung; all at once her face was full of disdain. My aunt stared at Wang Hsiung for a moment and burst out laughing. Happy nearly doubled up with laughter, her face buried in her skirt. Holding onto Little Beauty's schoolbag, Wang Hsiung just stood there, completely mortified, his swarthy face turning purple; he stole a glance at Little Beauty, his lips quivering as if he wanted to give her a smile in apology, but the smile just wouldn't come out.

After Little Beauty began riding her bicycle to school she was seldom with Wang Hsiung. She was very active in school and would often invite a whole bunch of schoolmates home to play. One Sunday afternoon Little Beauty brought seven or eight schoolfriends—all twelve- or thirteen-year-old girls—home to play kick-the-shuttlecock in the garden. Little Beauty was a champ at this game; she could kick up to a hundred nonstop. As I was standing on the stone steps watching the little girls, who had their skirts tucked up and were kicking the shuttlecock with great enthusiasm, I saw Wang Hsiung steal out of the banana grove. Beckoning to Little Beauty, he called her in a hushed voice:

"Little Beauty—"

"What are you doing here?" Little Beauty came over, somewhat annoyed.

"See? What I've got for you?" From a brown paper bag Wang Hsiung pulled out a fragile glass bowl with two goldfish swimming around in it. I had once bought a bowl of goldfish for Little Beauty. She was very fond of it and hung it in the window; every day she asked Wang Hsiung to feed the goldfish red worms; later a cat from next door tipped the bowl over, and ate up the fish. Little Beauty cried her heart out; I tried to comfort her and I promised to buy her another bowl, but I'd forgotten all about it.

"Who wants to play with that stuff any more?" said Little Beauty scornfully, her chin in the air.

"It took me a powerful long time to find these two," Wang Hsiung said earnestly.

"I'm going back to play shuttlecock!" Little Beauty turned to run off.

"These here two are phoenix-tails—" Wang Hsiung caught Little Beauty's arm; he held the bowl close to Little Beauty's face to let her see.

"Let go of my arm!" Little Beauty cried out.

"Please, just take a look, Little Beauty—" Wang Hsiung pleaded; he held Little Beauty tight and wouldn't let her go. Little Beauty twisted around and couldn't free herself; her other arm shot up and struck the bowl and crack! the bowl was knocked to the ground and smashed to pieces. Little Beauty flung Wang Hsiung's hand away and ran off without looking back. The water in the bowl was splashed all over the ground, and the two bright red goldfish kept leaping up and down. Wang Hsiung uttered a cry of alarm; he squatted down, his fists clenched, and looked helplessly at the two struggling goldfish, not knowing how to rescue them. The two delicate goldfish gave a couple of final desperate jumps and fell to the ground inert. His head lowered, Wang Hsiung stared at the two dying fish for a long time; then he picked them up by their tails, laid them in his palms, and holding them carefully, walked out of the garden.

From then on, Wang Hsiung grew more reticent than ever. Whenever he had time, he would retreat into the garden and water the flowers. Every day he would sprinkle every one of the hundred or so azaleas in the garden; early in the morning or late in the afternoon you could see that giant form of his moving back and forth among the flowers, alone. His head bowed, his body slightly stooped, with a long-handled bamboo dipper, one after the other, splash after splash, very slowly, very carefully, he watered those azaleas he had raised with his own hands. No matter who spoke to him, he would ignore them. Sometimes when my aunt called urgently for him, he would just answer in a raspy voice: "Yes, Ma'am," and at once quietly flee back into the garden. Then, the day before it all happened, Happy went into the garden to get water from the faucet to do her washing; Wang Hsiung had already hung a bucket under the tap to get water for the flowers. Happy took Wang Hsiung's half-filled bucket off and set her own washtub under the tap. Wang Hsiung came over; without a word he kicked over the tub and sent the water flying, splashing all over Happy. The maid flared up, her face turned a dark red; she threw back her long hair, one step and she was blocking Wang Hsiung's way to the faucet.

"Nobody's using this water today!" she yelled.

Head in the air, arms akimbo, breasts thrust high, her face sprinkled with beads of water, the hem of her skirt still dripping, she kicked off her wooden clogs and stood in her bare feet confronting Wang Hsiung challengingly. His lips tightened, Wang Hsiung glared at her. Happy looked him up and down; suddenly she broke out laughing, sassy and wild, her whole body trembling.

"Big gorilla!—Big gorilla!—" she shrieked through her laughter.

The words were barely out of her mouth when Wang Hsiung reached out his gigantic hands, seized her by her fleshly shoulders and began to shake her violently, growling and snarling like a mortally wounded beast letting out its howl of fury and anguish. Happy's face twisted in pain; she was probably so shocked that for a moment she couldn't utter a sound. Just as I ran over to stop Wang Hsiung, Happy let out a scream; Wang Hsiung relaxed his grip and Happy picked up her skirts and took to her heels. As she ran she kept massaging her shoulders; not until she was a safe distance away did she turn and spit. "Rot your parents!" she cursed.

Wang Hsiung stood there, motionless, panting heavily, beads of sweat rolling down his face one after the other, his eyes red enough to spit fire. I suddenly saw that Wang Hsiung was a completely changed man. He had stubble all over his face, his unshaven hair had grown an inch, sticking out stiffly, his head looked like a porcupine, and his eyes had sunk way back in, the rings blackened as if he hadn't slept for days. I could hardly believe that in a few days Wang Hsiung could have turned so withered, so savage.

Even so many days after it happened, my aunt still refused to believe it. She said she would never have dreamed an honest fellow like Wang Hsiung would do that kind of thing.

"That damned ghost—" Happy would bury her face in her skirt and burst into tears whenever Wang Hsiung's name was mentioned; she would caress her neck with a look of lingering fear.

That morning when we found Happy, we thought she was dead. She was lying in the garden under the azalea shrubs, unconscious, her skirt ripped to shreds, naked to the waist, her breasts covered with bruises and scratches, a ring of finger-marks around her neck. That same day, Wang Hsiung disappeared. My aunt asked me to distribute the belongings he'd left behind among those old soldiers in my company. Rummaging through his trunk we found a big package of colored beads left over from the time he made bracelets for Little Beauty.

After I was discharged, I went back home to Taichung. It was not until the following spring when I returned to Taipei to look for a job that I visited my aunt's house again. My aunt had been ill in bed for a long time; she looked pale and listless. She said that ever since that unlucky thing had happened in her house she hadn't had a single day of good health; she simply couldn't sleep at night. She struggled to sit up and caught my hand.

"Every night," she said in a hushed voice, "I hear someone watering the garden."

Mother had told me my aunt was a hopeless neurotic—all her life she loved to talk about ghosts. When I walked out into the garden, I was stunned to see those hundred or so azaleas, one mound piled on another mound, one wave churning up another wave, all exploding in riotous bloom as if a chestful of fresh blood suddenly had shot forth from an unstanchable wound and sprayed the whole garden, leaving marks and stains everywhere, bloodred. I had never seen azaleas bloom with such abandon, and so angrily. Little Beauty and a bunch of girls were playing hide-and-seek in the garden; they cut to and fro through the sea of bloodred azaleas. Peal after peal, with ever-heightening insistence, the little girls' shrill, ringing laughter reverberated through the bright spring day.

❀ Discussion and Writing

1. Examine Wang Hsiung's early life and its influence on his present behavior. In what ways is the story of old soldiers relevant to the narrative?
2. Analyze Wang Hsiung's attachment to Little Beauty: why does he allow her to control him; what is the importance of the beads and the gold fish; what is the effect on him of her rejection?
3. Comment on Happy's personality and her behavior. What is the significance of Wang Hsiung's attack on her? Discuss the cause of his disappearance and death.
4. Interpret the symbolism of the blood, the sea, and the azaleas. What is the significance of abundant azaleas after Wang Hsiung's death?
5. Discuss the pertinence of the ancient Chinese myth, included at the beginning of the story, to this narrative.

❀ Research and Comparison

Explore how "A Sea of Bloodred Azaleas" differs from the myth of Beauty and the Beast and its variations in many cultures.

Jialin Peng
(b. 1948)
China

Jialin Peng came of age during the 1960s, hence the title of his collection, *Wild Cat: Stories of the Cultural Revolution.* Initially a struggle for power among the leaders of the Chinese Communist Party (CCP), the Cultural

Revolution (1966–1976) was launched at a rally in Tiananmen Square. However idealistic its beginnings, over time a condition close to anarchy evolved as the newly formed Red Guards were caught up in the local struggles for power that victimized innocent people. Anyone could be identified as an enemy, but professionals, intellectuals, scholars, and artists were particularly vulnerable. It was a time of violence and fear. Those who were denounced could be sent to labor camps or to prison, where execution was not unusual. Those authors who survived, whether or not they themselves had been victims, developed the school of Wound or Scar literature. "What's in a Name," from *Wild Cat: Stories of the Cultural Revolution,* belongs to this tradition.

What's in a Name

What's in a name? That which we call a rose
By any other name would smell as sweet.
W. SHAKESPEARE

I adore Shakespeare, but in China a rose smells different when you give it another name. My names—family name, given name and adopted name—caused me no end of trouble.

My name was Chou Dexiao. Chou was my family name; Dexiao, the name given me by my father. *De* means "virtue" and *xiao* means "filial obedience." From the name you may deduce my father's high expectations. With this name I lived eighteen years without mishap. When people used my name, they were not conscious of its literal meaning. A rose is a rose.

But a rose can decay. The Great Cultural Revolution began, and suddenly we found everything had the smell of social class: the girls' long braids stank of the capitalist class, so they had them cut short. My name reeked of the ruling class of feudalist times. Virtue and filial obedience—the Revolutionary Proletariat did not like them. Therefore, I had to change my name to a revolutionary one. But that was more easily said than done, because for each revolutionary name, there might be thousands of people who wanted to use it. And it was inconvenient to share the same name with so many people, especially with your schoolmates.

In our class alone, there had already been two Zaofans (rebel), two Gemings (revolution), two Weibiaos (defenders of Lin Biao) and three Weidongs (defenders of Mao Zedong). I didn't want to share any of these names with my classmates. So I thought and thought, then I had an idea: why not call myself Weiqing (the defender of Jiang Qing)? Comrade Jiang Qing was the wife of our "great leader, great teacher, great commander and great helmsman" Chairman Mao Zedong. And she herself was the "standard-bearer of the Great Proletarian Cultural Revolution."

I was thrilled to have found a name so thoroughly revolutionary. I immediately started going through the name-changing procedures. All I had to do was to write a *dazibao* and put it on a wall at school. *Dazibao* literally meant a public poster handwritten in big fat characters. In the first days of the Cultural Revolution, millions upon millions of *dazibaos* appeared all over China, stuck to walls, pasted on doors and windows and hanging from wires. They denounced the enemies of the Revolution, criticized the corruption of Capitalism, Revisionism and Feudalism, and even made proclamations such as: A REVOLUTIONARY CROSSES THE STREET ON A RED LIGHT! and CAPITALIST SONS OF BITCHES ARE NOT SERVED IN THIS RESTAURANT!

I had hardly finished writing my new name for the first time when a voice thundered over my shoulder, "Do you want to be a counter-revolutionary?" I was astounded, and gazed in bewilderment at the speaker, Wang Zaofan, the head of a major Red Guard organization in our school. The name Zaofan meant "rebel" but his original name was Wenbin, meaning "gentle."

"Look," he said. "Your family name is Chou; it means 'hate.' What does 'Chou Weiqing' mean?"

I was so scared that I broke out in a cold sweat. My new name could imply that I hated Chairman Mao's wife! My God! If I had not shared the same desk all through school with Zaofan and if I had not let him copy from my papers in examinations, the consequences would have been too ghastly to contemplate!

Obviously, if I wanted to give myself a revolutionary name, I'd have to change my family name as well. I had read a report in a newspaper about a boy who, in order to express his boundless respect for the great leader Chairman Mao, had changed his own family name Mu to Mao. I was going to use him as my example. But this time I first consulted Wang Zaofan.

"You want to name yourself *Mao* too? Hah! Pee on the ground and look at your image to see if you're worthy of the name Mao. What kind of person was your father?" he snarled with curled lips. Zaofan was seven inches shorter than I, so for greater emphasis he jumped up on a chair and continued, "What kind of person was your grandfather?"

I knew what he was getting at. Before their deaths, my father had been a rightist and my grandfather a landlord. I was not worthy of so great and honorable a family name as Mao; absolutely not.

Finally, I adopted my mother's family name, Qin, as my own. Before the decision was made, I carried out as thorough a research as possible. I consulted three different dictionaries. They all defined the character *Qin* as follows: the Qin Dynasty (221–207 B.C.); another name for Shaanxi Province; a surname.

None of the definitions looked like a potential trouble-maker. I also investigated my maternal history. My mother's parents were poor peasants, her father's father was a poor peasant, and so was her father's father's father. Therefore, I concluded with relief, Qin should be a safe surname for me.

To be honest, I was glad to change my old family name. My father had divorced my mother after he became a rightist in 1957. Then he'd died somewhere. I'd been raised by my mother, who earned her living as a primary school teacher. I could hardly remember what my father looked like. It was shameful and painful to be a rightist's son! So it was not simply that I had no affection for my father, I positively hated him. By discarding his name, I intended to make a clean break from him, and wash his reactionary taint off myself.

With this thoroughly new name. Qin Weiqing, I lived another ten years. Before long I found the name was far from being as good as I had thought. People began to hate Jiang Qing. Scandalous rumours about her spread from mouth to mouth throughout the country. Even the threat of imprisonment did not stop people from whispering. Could you expect them to be nice to a fellow who'd named himself Jiang Qing's defender? And in fact, I myself had also come to hate this woman. So after the downfall of the Gang of Four, headed by Jiang Qing, the first thing I did was to apply to resume my old given name, Dexiao. I continued to use the surname Qin, for it showed my love for my mother.

The year I turned thirty-two, the government removed the label "rightist" from just about everyone. My father was among the rehabilitated. So I was finally free of his reactionary mark.

I was now a skilled turner in a factory. Some people said I was quite handsome. However, with a wage of only 36 yuan per month and without powerful and rich parents, I found it very hard to find a wife. My mother was so anxious about me that her hair turned white. An old Chinese woman suffers untold anxiety until she sees her son married. She asked all her acquaintances to look for a girl for me. Thanks to an introduction by an aunt of one of my mother's former pupils, I was finally brought together with a potential marriage partner. Her name was Yue Meihua. Though *Meihua* meant "beautiful flower," she wasn't beautiful at all. The girl, an unskilled laborer in a cotton mill, was twenty-eight. Her parents were peasants who lived in a village far from our city. All of which meant that she was not a girl with a high "selling price."

All the same, I liked her very much. Perhaps it was because she was so gentle, even shy. She would always blush before she started to speak to a strange man, and one never heard her speak or laugh loudly. I didn't agree with the aesthetic standard of ancient China which required a woman not to show her teeth while smiling; still I preferred a gentle, timid girl, for I'd been frightened by a few neighbors' wives. They enjoyed quarrelling too much, and for them the greatest pleasure in life was to bad-mouth their husbands. I could often hear them, in the small hours of the morning, cursing their husbands instead of making love to them. But my Meihua was quieter than a sleeping flower.

Besides, for my sake, my mother had suffered too much already and I didn't want to hurt her by marrying a shrewish girl. As some of my married friends had told me, the most unbearable business, for a man, was to be a buffer in clashes between his mother and his wife.

Evidently, Yue Meihua liked me too. So I wrote a letter and proposed to her. A few days later, the go-between—the aunt of my mother's former pupil—told me that the girl liked me but could not accept until she got her parents' approval, and it was very likely that her mother would come and have a look at me.

Of course, the news gave my mother hope. But it added to her worries because it was said of people in the country that they didn't marry off their daughters, but sold them at high prices. It happened that a couple of days earlier, my mother had read a tragic story reported in the newspaper. A bride refused to go into the bridal chamber because the bridegroom was unable to satisfy her parents' additional economic demands. The poor bridegroom, who was up to his ears in debt already, killed the bride and then himself. If Meihua's parent's asked for extravagant betrothal gifts, what would we do?

When her mother arrived, Meihua took me to see her. All I remember about the meeting was that the top button of my new shirt seemed determined to strangle me. The day was sweltering and I was terribly thirsty. But I do recall what happened at the end of the interview. Her mother filled the pockets of my new jacket with peanuts which she had grown herself. I was half-paralyzed and murmured some words no one could understand. Meihua blushed and said softly, "Say thank you to Mama, you foolish man." I came to my senses at once. Wonderful! The old lady was fond of me!

Then her mother and my mother met. Exceeding our hopes, the negotiations went off without a hitch. Although Meihua's mother was unable to read or write, she had an enlightened mind. She did not ask for betrothal gifts.

Now what we needed was her father's approval. That would be no problem, Meihua assured me. Her father had never questioned any decision made by her mother. Therefore, no sooner had her mother departed than we began to prepare for the wedding. My close friends and relatives went into action. Three friends asked for a few days sick leave to make a bed and a wardrobe for us. A cousin who was a truck-driver made plans to go to some out-of-the-way town to fetch food for the wedding feast. My mother withdrew all her savings from the bank and went on a shopping spree. How happy and excited she was!

Then came the blow. Meihua's parents suddenly refused to let me marry her. The wedding was off. It was not her mother nor her father but some elders of the clan who had exercised their veto. They made a declaration: if Meihua marries the man named Qin, we will expel her from the clan. And after the marriage, if she appears in our village, we will break her legs.

Why? All they knew about me was my name. But it was nothing else than my name that killed the wedding!

To understand, one must go back more than 800 years, to the year 1142. That year, an evil Prime Minister, Qin Hui, concocted a charge against a great national hero, Marshal Yue Fei, and had him put to death. But people loved Yue Fei very much. Soon he was rehabilitated, and from then on, Yue Fei's tomb has become a scenic spot in Huangzhou City. Out of indignation, people cast two iron effigies in a kneeling position, to represent Qin Hui and his conspiratorial wife. Since then the two have been humbling themselves in front of the tomb for hundreds of years. And since Yue Fei's execution, people named Yue have adopted an unwritten prohibition against marrying people named Qin.

So, I remain a bachelor. What's in a name? That which we call a rose by any other name may smell of stinkweed.

❁ Discussion and Writing

1. Why do the protagonist and many of his contemporaries feel compelled to change their names? Discuss what else may change along with people's names. Comment on the influence of politics on one's identity.
2. What are the major considerations of the family in arranging the marriage of the protagonist? Who are the decision-makers? What is the rationale for such communal participation?
3. Comment on the impact of the community invoking an 800-year-old history to oppose a marriage alliance. What is the writer's stance regarding this issue: serious, humorous, neutral, critical?
4. Discuss the implications of the quotation from Shakespeare. Comment on the effect of the humorous treatment of a serious subject?

❁ Research and Comparison

Interdisciplinary Discussion Question: The tradition of arranged marriages prevails in many cultures around the world. Research the rationale for this widely followed practice and its consequences in any culture. Examine how different individuals react to it. Discuss the result of trying to view a tradition from someone else's perspective.

Interdisciplinary Discussion Question: Research the importance of family in Chinese social structures. Develop a paper on how individual identities and responsibilities hinge on family loyalties. What may be the positive and negative aspects of such a system?

Interdisciplinary Discussion Question: Review the Wound or Scar literature that grew out of the Cultural Revolution in China to examine its effect on
people's lives.

Bei Dao
(b. 1949)
China

Bei Dao (Zhao Zhenkai) was born in Beijing, China. His father, a member
of neither the Communist Party nor the Kuomintang, was an administrator
of one of the opposition parties, and his mother was a physician. During
his last year in secondary school—at one of the most prestigious institutions established for the elite—Bei Dao joined the newly formed Red
Guard movement. Like many young people of his background, Bei Dao
enlisted in the movement with high expectations of revitalizing his class;
he soon left, disillusioned. In light of the persistence of the Cultural Revolution, Bei Dao became a subversive poet. Early on, he wrote a poem, "An
End or a Beginning," dedicated to "the martyr Yu Luoke," one of the
poems that confirmed his reputation as a spokesman for his generation. As
one of the underground poets of the 1970s, he sought a new aesthetic,
rejecting the conventions established at the beginning of the People's
Republic in 1949. He experimented with language, syntax, and structure
to evoke "un-reality," a term that expressed both his poetics and the world
of the Cultural Revolution. He formulated a kind of free verse that resembled classical versification while, at the same time, abridging grammatical
usage, omitting punctuation, compressing images, and clouding transitions.

Bei Dao's participation in the 1976 Tiananmen Square demonstrations and his famous poem "The Answer" represented his appearance as a
dissident. Cofounder and coeditor of the journal *Today*, he also contributed poetry voicing the principles of the "Democratic movement" of
1978–1979. These were hopeful days, as new writing and journals prolif-
erated. With the fluctuating positions of the Deng Xiaoping government
and with the mounting evidence of corruption, however, the promise of
the "Democratic movement" was short-lived. Moreover, during the times
of repression, Bei Dao was frequently censured. Despite the criticism, he
remained committed to a new aesthetic and to the illumination of conditions of suffering. Thus, the poetry of the 1980s, like "Electric Shock" and
"Language," took on a bitter tone in light of the hollowness of Deng's re-
forms.

*Electric Shock**

I once shook hands with
an invisible man, a cry of pain
a brand was left
on my burning hand
when I shake hands with
visible men, a cry of pain
and a brand is left
on their burning hands
now I dare not shake hands
but hide my hands behind my back
yet when I pray
to heaven, palms pressed together
a cry of pain
and a brand is left
deep in my heart

Language†

many languages
fly around the world
producing sparks when they collide
sometimes of hate
sometimes of love

reason's mansion
collapes without a sound
baskets woven of thoughts
as flimsy as bamboo splints
are filled with blind toadstools

the beasts on the cliff
ran past, trampling the flowers
a dandelion grows secretly
in a certain corner
the wind has carried away its seeds

many languages
fly around the world
the production of languages

---

*Translated by Bonnie S. McDougall
†Translated by Bonnie S. McDougall

can neither increase nor decrease
mankind's silent suffering

✺ Discussion and Writing

1. Analyze the three actions and their implications in "Electric Shock."
2. What is suggested by the shift in tenses for shaking hands. Why is the prayer painful?
3. Comment on the metaphors used to describe the collision of languages.
4. Explain the symbolism of a dandelion.
5. What is the connection between languages and mankind's silent suffering?

✺ Research and Comparison

Interdisciplinary Discussion Question: Research the movements for democracy in the recent history of China, paying special attention to the role of students.

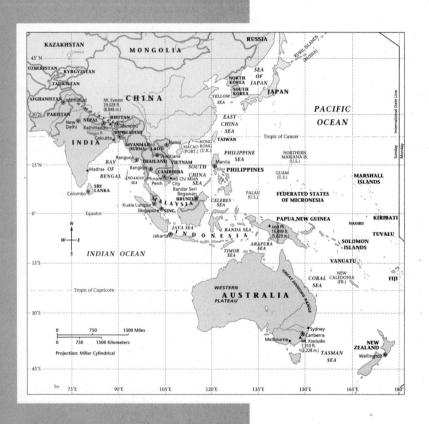

South Asia, Southeast Asia, Australia, and New Zealand

South Asia

South Asia, also known as the Indian subcontinent, describes the great triangular landmass extending south from the Himalayas and comprising the present-day countries of Nepal and Pakistan, India, Bangladesh, and Sri Lanka. (See map.)

Toward the end of the third millennium B.C.E., in what is now Pakistan, thriving cities arose along the Indus River Valley and flourished for many centuries. This civilization disappeared mysteriously and its writing has yet to be deciphered. Nevertheless, archeological finds suggest that elements of its culture persisted in the vibrant civilization to come.

Somewhere between 1700 and 1200 B.C.E., a nomadic people who referred to themselves as Aryans entered the subcontinent from the northwest and settled in the Indus Valley. Their influence was basic to subsequent South Asian civilization. Mingling with indigenous customs and beliefs, the Aryan social-religious order gradually evolved into the numerous forms of religious life that later came to be known as Hinduism.

Aryan priests were composing the *Vedas* in Sanskrit, the sacred texts that set forth the ritual of religious practice. The earliest of these texts is the *Rig Veda* (c. 1200–900 B.C.E.), comprising 1028 hymns dedicated to the Aryan gods. Toward the end of the Vedic period (c. 500 B.C.E.), the *Upanishads* were formulated—philosophical treatises that interpreted Vedic ritual— exploring the nature of the soul and the relation of humankind to the universe. The *Vedas* and the *Upanishads* became, and have remained, the basic scriptures of Hinduism.

The Vedic texts also mention four groups that were part of the Aryan social order and ultimately gave rise to the hierarchical caste system that became a basic element in Indian society: *brahmin* (priests), *kshatriya* (warriors), *vaishyas* (landowners and traders), and *shudra* (laborers and craftspeople). Divisions along caste lines had begun when the Aryans subjugated and later intermarried with indigenous people of darker color. (In Sanskrit, caste is *varna*, or color.) The system was thus founded as much on racial distinctions as on the exigencies of economic control. Over the centuries, the four castes shifted in status and spawned hundreds of subcastes, no longer determined by occupation, but by birth. Beneath them all was an out-caste, menial laborers, whose members cleaned up garbage, skinned dead animals, and disposed of dead bodies. Because they touched pollution, they were themselves considered impure—literally untouchable. Among many other restrictions, they were denied access to education and forbidden to worship in temples.

During the sixth century B.C.E., various social-religious communities developed, rising in opposition to Vedic culture. The two most important and lasting were the communities of the Jains and the Buddhists, both of which incorporated the idea of reincarnation set out in the *Upanishads*. Jainism preached nonviolence and self-discipline as its central teachings. Avoiding the extremes of Vedic ritualism and the austerity of Jainism, Buddhism advocated a middle way. Believing that life was suffering, Buddha taught the eightfold path to reach *nirvana,* the release from the cycle of birth and death. The two religions spread throughout the subcontinent. While Jainism has continued within small but vital communities, Buddhism waned in India, after an early period of strong influence. Buddhism, however, traveled beyond Indian borders into Sri Lanka and Southeast Asia, China, Korea, and Japan, evolving into one of Asia's most powerful religions.

The philosophical revelations of the *Upanishads* and the new religious thinking of the Jains and Buddhists influenced the development of Hinduism. Hindu ideology incorporated complex beliefs, merging various, often divergent, philosophies and religious practices. Among these beliefs are: the concept of female, male, and androgynous gods; the theory of *karma* and reincarnation; and the doctrine of nonviolence. The mother goddess is the highest form of *shakti* (energy) and not solely the consort of a male god. *Karma* means deeds, which determine one's life; together, reincarnation and *karma* form a theory of cause and effect controlling the cycle of birth, death, and rebirth. Within the diversity of Hinduism, the *Upanishadic* concept of the oneness of all creation has endured.

With the rise of mighty kingdoms in the sixth century B.C.E., religious culture swept through much of what is present-day India, flowing eventually into Southeast and Northeast Asia. In India itself, where, from time immemorial, social and religious institutions have been considered inseparable, ancient beliefs became inextricably entwined in society, and they have persisted.

This formative period of South Asian civilization also produced the founding works of its literature, the two great Sanskrit epics, the *Mahabharata* and the *Ramayana*. The longest epic in the world, the *Mahabharata* (c. 400 B.C.E.–400 C.E.), takes as its central subject a civil war that is thought to have occurred around 900 B.C.E. Incorporated into the epic is the famous *Bhagavad Gita* (Song of the Lord), a philosophical poem in which Lord Krishna, a Hindu deity, explains the path of spiritual wisdom. The *Ramayana* (c. 200 B.C.E.–200 C.E.) is based on events surrounding the ancient king, Rama, and his wife, Sita (c. 1950 B.C.E.). Along with the *Vedas* and the *Puranas* (the stories of the gods), the two epics carry the essence of Hindu thought, and they continue to provide writers with richly reverberating tales and images, mythological motifs, and philosophic material.

Toward the end of the first century C.E., Sanskrit, the language of the *Vedas* and the epics, blossomed into South Asia's first transregional literary language. Over the next centuries, the exceedingly rich and varied body of Sanskrit literature developed. Local dialects related to Sanskrit, meanwhile, evolved into the numerous modern languages of northern India such as Bengali, Gujarati, Hindi, Punjabi, Oriya and others. Oriya gave rise to Sinhala, the official language in Sri Lanka. Each eventually generated its own literature. In the south of India, Tamil, a member of the Dravidian family of languages, created its own literary tradition early on alongside other Dravidian languages such as Kannada, Telugu, and Malayalam. All of these, along with English, are currently among the 16 to 18 languages recognized in India's constitution, and all continue as vehicles for literature. There are also hundreds of dialects spoken in the different regions, and a proto-Dravidian language is not only still spoken by tribal hill people but is also the idiom of an important (untranslated) oral literature.

Islam entered the subcontinent soon after its founding in the seventh century C.E., first via Arab trading ships that plied the southwest coast of India, and then overland from the north. During this same period, Zoroastrian Persians arrived and established self-contained communities in western India. They were eventually known as Parsees.

It was the raids on Hindu temples at the beginning of the eleventh century by Turkic Muslim leader Mahmud of Ghaznin that initiated antagonism between the followers of the two religions. Within two hundred years, Islamic rule was established in Delhi and Islamic influence spread throughout the northern regions. The empire reached its peak with the accession of the Mughal ruler Akbar in 1556. He assembled leading figures from among the Sunni Muslims and Sufi mystics, from the Parsees, Hindus, and Jains, and he included Portuguese Catholic priests, who, by this time, had settled on the island of Goa. Thus, he was able to bring together rival religious factions. In his eclecticism, Akbar had the New Testament translated into Persian. Along with honoring Hindu practices, he also ordered the translation of one of the *Vedas,* the *Ramayana,* and the *Mahabharata.* A new religious path called Sikhism evolved, reflecting both Hindu and Islamic thought in India during the Mughal period.

Persian, then the favored literary language of eastern Islam, became the second transregional literary language of the subcontinent. During the seventeenth century, this linguistic convergence produced Urdu, which eventually formed a literary tradition of its own. Now the official language of Pakistan, Urdu is Hindi in structure, Turkish and Persian in vocabulary, and written with the Arabic alphabet.

European presence on the subcontinent began tentatively in 1498, when Vasco da Gama, sailing under the Portuguese flag, landed on the Malabar coast (present-day Kerala). The Portuguese established a stronghold on Goa, where they introduced Catholicism, missions, and the Inquisition. Their priests allowed no Hindu temples. While the Portuguese economic venture succeeded, this first Western cultural advance failed. During the 1500s, however, other European traders made their assault on the subcontinent, and in 1600, the English queen, Elizabeth I, established the British East India Company, granting a charter to "certain adventurers for the trade of the East Indies." During the following two centuries, the British, French, Dutch, and Portuguese literally battled each other for control of the Indian trade. The turning point came when the British East India Company obtained privileges from the Mughals in exchange for protection, in effect becoming the maritime auxiliary of the empire.

As the Mughal empire weakened during the 1700s, events in Europe, and rising antagonism on the part of Hindu nobles toward the Muslim rulers, brought about more intrusive British intervention. By 1818, the Company had control over the subcontinent. The Company instituted a British system of jurisdiction; and English, already the language of trade, supplanted Persian as the official state language and the medium of the higher courts. And with a growing wealthy middle class, an English education became not only a symbol of social status; it was key.

In 1858, the British crown claimed the Indian subcontinent as its colony. This change in status came about partially as a result of the soldier's mutiny of 1857, known today as India's first war of liberation. The following fifty years marked the heyday of British rule and, subsequently, the rise of the Indian National Movement. Progressive intellectuals derived inspiration from both Western and Asian science, philosophy, and literature. They initiated social reform, challenging such customs as child marriage, female infanticide, the ban on widows' remarrying, and the seclusion of women. They also denounced the caste system that had completely woven itself into the social fabric from the Vedic period on.

Early in the twentieth century, three important leaders emerged: Mohandas Gandhi, Jawaharlal Nehru, and Muhammad Ali Jinnah. Along with many nationalists, they led the drive for independence, initially under the aegis of the Indian National Congress, a political party formed in 1885 to foster economic reform. Gandhi, called Mahatma (or great soul) and father of the nation, named the out-caste people *harijan* (children of God) in his campaign against caste restraints, in general, and to end discrimination against the out-caste, in particular. In the struggle for independence, he organized the noncooperation movement and his strategy of passive resistance (*satyagraha*, literally, "insistence on truth") was instituted. Accordingly, he accepted imprisonment several times.

The Congress advocated Hindu-Muslim unity, and Gandhi remained dedicated to this ideal. Jinnah, however, joined the Muslim League in 1934. Founded in 1906 to address Muslim issues, the League did not originally hold a separatist ideology. In fact, it initially joined forces with the Indian National Congress to present a united front against the British. Yet Jinnah ultimately led the struggle for an independent Muslim state, and when the British finally withdrew in 1947, the subcontinent was divided along religious lines into India and Pakistan. To Gandhi, this was a bitter solution. He was assassinated in 1948 by a Hindu radical who opposed his concessions to Muslims. Jawaharlal Nehru became the first prime minister of India, which invoked its ancient glory by taking the name Bharat in the constitution. Jinnah served as the first president of Pakistan.

The partition caused great suffering: countless refugees, flowing in both directions, told stories of rape and plunder. Moreover, under the Indian Independence Act, Pakistan emerged in two parts, West and East Pakistan. West Pakistan included the site of the original Indus Valley civilization; and one thousand miles away, East Pakistan covered the region of East Bengal. United only by religion, East and West Pakistan were racially and linguistically diverse. Along with several wars between Pakistan and India, a bloody civil war—in which one million Bengalis were killed—erupted between East and West Pakistan. East Pakistan finally achieved independence as Bangladesh in 1971. Thus, religious, ethnic, class, and caste animosities have intensified on the subcontinent over the century.

Nor has the island of Sri Lanka, lying off the southern tip of the subcontinent, avoided recent problems of factionalism. In late twentieth-century Sri Lanka, the Buddhist Sinhalese constitute a majority of the population and Hindu Tamils a significant minority. The Sinhalese from North India had migrated to the island, then called Lanka, in the sixth century B.C.E. By the third or fourth century B.C.E., a world-renowned center of Buddhism was established there. Coveted during the expansion of European trade from the sixteenth century on, the island fell into Portuguese, then Dutch, and finally British hands. In 1798, it was named the British crown colony of Ceylon. A nationalist spirit awakened during World War I, and Ceylon achieved independence in 1948, subsequently renaming itself Sri Lanka in 1972.

Each action has caused a reaction, growing more violent as the years have passed. Nationalism, political ideologies, and contention over power have exacerbated the volatile situation. This long, immensely complex history has both generated and permeated a rich modern literature. Twentieth-century authors from the subcontinent have portrayed their history, even as they have been caught up in it. Their British education has stimulated them; their Vedic literary heritage has inspired them; their various religious and political philosophies have roused them. In their work, they have described, clarified, and analyzed the established roles of women and men, religious and social constrictions, colonial and postcolonial structures. On the one hand, they have illuminated the ways in which traditional mores persist and continue to impinge upon the individual; on the other hand, they have illustrated the ways in which colonialism, by invading cohesive traditions, has caused a keen sense of displacement and bitter fratricide. At the same time, however, a literature celebrating the human spirit endures, encompassing love and joy, as Rabindranath Tagore has so abundantly revealed:

When I bring you colored toys, my child, I understand why there is such a play of colors on clouds, on water, and why flowers are painted in tints.

The Crescent Moon (1913) "When and Why"

Southeast Asia

Southeast Asia traces an arc through the Malay archipelago and up onto the mainland of the Asian continent. Its eastern boundary is marked by the more than seven thousand islands that make up the Philippines. To the south, Indonesia—encompassing more than four thousand islands—lies along the equator. Malaysia comprises Peninsular Malaysia, which brings the western curve of the arc onto the mainland, and the island states of East Malaysia. The tiny countries of Singapore and Brunei sit at the tip of the Malay peninsula and the top of the island of Borneo, respectively. Sharing a border with China and India, the Southeast Asian mainland includes the countries of Vietnam, Laos, Cambodia, Thailand, and Burma.

Largely tropical, Southeast Asia contains thick forests where once the fearsome tiger ranged. Fertile plains of rich alluvial soil, deposited over the millenia along the major rivers—the Irrawaddy in Burma, the Chao Phray in Thailand, the Red River and Mekong in Vietnam—have historically spawned the most prosperous and densely populated areas, drawing rice farmers, merchants, landowners, and invaders. The region's ample mineral resources and strategically located maritime territory have also attracted foreign intervention over the centuries. And the tiger, now threatened with extinction, has remained a recurrent image, a powerful symbol in twentieth-century literature.

The history of Southeast Asia is long and many-layered. When the Malay people emigrated to the region from China some four thousand years ago, they encountered communities already of long standing, whose descendants, it is believed, still live today for the most part in remote mountain forests. The Malays settled the region from the Philippines (where they are known as Filipino). Various ethnic groups of Mongolian and Polynesian descent also came and populated the mainland. Over the centuries, people of Papuan, Indian, and Chinese descent, among others, also formed lively communities.

Beginning almost two thousand years ago, a thriving trade brought cultural influence from India and, to a lesser extent, from China. Buddhist pilgrims on their way from China to India introduced Buddhism into Vietnam, where it has continued to flourish. Temples dedicated to Hindu and Buddhist deities sprang up along the coasts of Cambodia and Indonesia. By the ninth century, major Hindu-Buddhist empires had arisen in which the religions coexisted harmoniously. The city of Angkor in present-day Cambodia, for instance, was a leading Hindu-Buddhist center of the Khmer Empire (sixth to fifteenth century). It was also a leading artistic center. Hindu and Buddhist kings built famous "temple-mountains," the most glorious of which was the great temple complex of Angkor Wat, completed about 1150. Indonesia also had a long history of Indian influence, and by the thirteenth century prominent Hindu and Buddhist kingdoms had emerged on the island of Java.

During the fourteenth century, Muslim Arab, Persian, and Indian traders began to arrive in greater numbers. Islam gradually spread through the islands and onto the Malay Peninsula, becoming the principal religion of Indonesia and Malaysia, which had been a Buddhist kingdom for five centuries. Buddhism emerged as the dominant force on the mainland, while Hinduism survived only on the Indonesian island of Bali.

In 1511, Portugal began the race for European dominion in Southeast Asia when it occupied the Islamic state of Malacca on the west coast of Malaysia, which commanded the approach to the Indonesian archipelago and its lucrative spice trade. Sea-faring traders had traveled this route for more than a thousand years. Long a source of wealth, the rare spices from the easternmost Molucca islands of Indonesia now became a source of conflict as Spain and Holland sought to challenge Portugal's position.

After the 1550s, Spain turned its attention to the Philippines, where it created plantations and established Catholic missions. As time passed and the Spaniards infiltrated the islands, the Philippines became a Catholic country. Spanish control lasted until the defeat of Spain in the Spanish-American War (1898), at which point the Philippines came under U.S. rule.

Holland persisted in the battle for dominance on the islands of the Indonesian archipelago, and its increasing military and commercial strength prevailed by the seventeenth century. At first, the territories were administered by the United East India Company, which operated under Dutch authority. At the end of the 1700s, however, the government of the Netherlands assumed direct rule, appropriating the Company's holdings, and renaming the area the Netherlands (or Dutch) East Indies. Of all the Indonesian islands, only Sumatra, a land of vast mineral wealth and remunerative plantations, did not fall under colonial jurisdiction until the twentieth century.

The British were also tempted by Southeast Asia. They purchased Singapore in the early 1800s, and it quickly became one of the world's most prosperous ports. (In contrast to the other Southeast Asian countries, Singapore's population is mainly urban; the people speak Malay, Chinese, Tamil, and English, along with many other languages, and follow Buddhism, Islam, Hinduism, and Christianity.) Over the course of the century, Great Britain annexed Burma as a province of British India and consolidated control over much of the Malay Peninsula. But the greatest European presence on the Southeast Asian mainland was French. Beginning with their capture of Saigon (Vietnam) in the mid-1800s, the French drove steadily forward and by 1887 had formed French Indochina, roughly comprising Vietnam, Laos, and part of Cambodia. Thus, by the beginning of World War II, all of Southeast Asia, with the single exception of Thailand, found itself colonized.

In the late 1800s, nationalism spread in varying degrees of intensity across Southeast Asia, everywhere eliciting a similarly repressive response. When, for instance, the United States took over control of the Philippines from Spain, the transfer of power led to an armed uprising (1899–1901). The United States forcefully quelled the revolt, but not the spirit of the resistance. In Malaysia, writers published under various pseudonyms to protect themselves from imprisonment. Throughout Southeast Asia, colonial governments frequently imprisoned—often without trial—artists and intellectuals (such as Indonesian writers Mochtar Lubis and Pamoedya Toer) who opposed them. Ironically, the jails became schools for resistance as prisoners studied Marxist political and economic philosophy and contrasted it with the colonialist's philosophy of capitalism. They were especially exhilarated by the Chinese (1911) and Russian (1917) revolutions, which they adopted as potential models.

During World War II, Japan occupied the entire region of Southeast Asia. Many nationalists entered the war alongside their colonizers—all Allied powers—in order to rid their country of the occupying forces. It was a period of great suffering, of harsh oppression and deprivation, as well as of brutal fighting. Nevertheless, the war decisively disrupted Western colonial rule, and with its end, independence was inevitable. In 1946, the United States granted the Philippines independent status, but retained its hold on the country; the struggle in the Philippines to rid itself of U.S. military and political constraints continues. Britain granted independence to Burma in 1947 and to Malaya ten years later. Indonesia won its independence in 1949 after a four-year war with the Dutch.

With the protracted dissolution of French Indochina, imperialism in Southeast Asia took on new meaning. For eight years after World War II, Vietnam fought for its independence from the French. With the defeat of France in 1953, Vietnam was divided: the Soviet Union and China supported the North; the United States supported the South. The battle was joined in the contention for political and economic power, escalating into the Vietnam War. Over the next two decades, Vietnam became a symbol as well as one of the bloodiest battlegrounds of the cold war's ideological face-off. The conflagration ended officially only in 1975; the effect on the people persists.

While all Southeast Asian countries fought for their independence, all found the postcolonial situation a bitter disappointment. Political corruption and dictatorship, ethnic divisions, class disparities, and poverty have been the rule rather than the exception. For intellectuals and writers, the danger of protesting against the state remains unchanged: prison awaits them, sometimes death, and thousands still sit in what used to be colonial jails.

The beginning of modern Southeast Asian literature coincided with the rise of nationalism, and the issue of which language would be the appropriate medium for a national literature immediately arose. The question was complicated, for in each country numerous indigenous languages coexisted with that of the colonizers. Works have been written in Malay, Japanese, Tamil, Chinese, to name a few, as well as in English and Dutch.

The dominant subject matter for twentieth-century Southeast Asian writers has been their history: colonization, economic and social oppression, class conflicts, and ethnic strife. After World War II and independence, they wrote about the occupation, the struggles for nationhood, and the catastrophic postcolonial turmoil. They have also written about traditional experiences, about village life: the mores, the characters, the social and religious hierarchy. Working within ancient philosophical systems, they have explored the question of moral responsibility. Speaking of the challenges and the internal tigers people must face, Mochtar Lubis has claimed,

> Some acquiesce to the tiger; some try to tame it and live in uneasy peace with it; still others, stronger and with greater courage, subdue it; but only a very few ever succeed in killing it.

Australia and New Zealand

Aboriginal peoples, who have lived in Australia for some twenty thousand years, say "we have *always* been here." However distinct their languages and mores, the various Aboriginal peoples have always shared, and lived in accordance with, the central concept of the Dreaming and its Laws. The Dreaming is an all-encompassing concept: it is the beginning when the land was given its form; it is also the record of that creation, as well as the Laws themselves. It is the culture, and it is renewed in the present day whenever the ancient stories are evoked in painting, song, story, or dance. The Laws, immutable and sacred, established the social and spiritual system: the principles of marriage customs and land rights that allowed the people to live peaceably. This Dreaming and these Laws have continued to nourish the people, even during the past two hundred years when they were almost anihilated.

In 1770, Captain James Cook landed on the eastern coast of Australia, named the harbor he had found Botany Bay because of the interesting flowers growing there, and claimed the entire coast for England. In 1788, Great Britain founded its first Australian settlement in Sydney, a penal colony for transported convicts. The British government used the continent as a jail until 1840, when the policy (which was called transportation, as opposed to colonization) was offically ended.

Populated by former convicts, free settlers, and Europeans with capital to invest, the Australian colony at first expanded slowly, confining itself mainly to the coasts. Huge land grants were given, and a pastoral industry evolved. In 1851, however, the discovery of gold brought a large wave of immigrants. Settlers pushed further and further into the interior; railways were built; and while fluctuations in the market or severe weather conditions occasionally caused economic distress, the colonists generally prospered.

As Europeans moved inland, laying claim to millions of acres, they frequently rounded up the people living there and marched them away, sometimes killing them, sometimes abandoning them in places where they did not belong according to their Law. Those who survived became a source of almost free labor as entire families were forced to work the colonists' plantations. When Aborigines offered any resistance to this treatment, Europeans described them as "treacherous," "violent," "implacably hostile and shamelessly dishonest." Those who remained near the settlements became figures of ridicule; Europeans portrayed them in literature as "dirty," "ugly," "ignorant," "racially inferior." This is the image that has lasted into the twentieth century, the perception that children, both black and white, learned from their earliest years.

According to the constitution, moreover, "the Aborigine shall not be counted." When the British landed in Botany Bay, there were 350,000 people living on the continent; the descendants of these people, omitted from the official 1961 census, numbered only 40,000 two hundred years later. In the late twentieth century Aboriginals have insisted that they be counted. People like Oodgeroo Noonuccal, whose book of poems *We Are Going* (1964) brought the oppression of her people to worldwide attention, have dedicated their work and their lives to social and political change, to equal human rights, to restoring Aboriginal dignity. Poets as various as Kevin Gilbert, Mudrooroo Nyoongah, and Hyllus Maris have followed in her footsteps.

Now, in the final quarter of the century, Aboriginals are writing their stories of colonization, of slave conditions, humiliation, injustice, and decimation, giving voice to their own experience. In narratives such as Sally Morgan's *My Place* (1987), they tell of the forced separation of families by white authorities earlier in the century: children of black and European descent who showed European coloring were raised in mission orphanages and trained to be servants; and as every social institution indicated the disadvantages of Aboriginal ancestry, people of racially mixed backgrounds living in the towns and cities hid their origins.

There is a nobility to the narratives and the poetry. This nobility lies in the spiritual undercurrent and pride that spill out into explicit statements of love and good humor. In the narratives, people speak of their lives in the mode of their ancient oral tradition in which the story was at once spiritual, humorous, serious, and entertaining: their lives become a telling. In keeping with the oral tradition, the poets, too, follow the ancient modes: repeating phrases, emphasizing images, calling on the spiritual presence of these images. The poetry and prose have thus entered the Dreaming and restored health and dignity to the Aboriginal peoples.

Colonization proceeded at a different pace in New Zealand, which until the 1840s was considered part of New South Wales, or Australia. When Captain Cook sailed around the islands that make up New Zealand in 1769, he met fierce opposition from the Maoris. Although there were subsequent skirmishes, the Maoris finally received the British, trading with them, selling them land that had traditionally been held communally. Colonization moved slowly, with Australian cattle grazers and runaway convicts coming over into New Zealand. By the middle of the 1800s, larger numbers of European colonizers had begun arriving, and relations between the races had deteriorated. With much of the best land in the hands of the Europeans, Maoris in several areas resisted, and wars lasted through the 1860s. They feared losing the land they still retained, a fear that was largely realized over the course of the next forty years. The discovery of gold gave rise to an increase in European population, but New Zealand remained a pastoral country with tracts for grazing in European hands. Maoris who continued to resist, particularly those who opposed the religion of the missionaries, finally retreated to the center of the island.

Maori peoples had been living on the islands for more than a thousand years before the arrival of the British. A Polynesian people, they tell of their ancestry and origins, of the time when the Maori had sailed across the seas in canoes to what is now New Zealand. This story is an important element in the culture; another is a particular concept of family. The family simultaneously exists within and consists of a complex social structure, for the family includes an extended family that reaches out into a larger social grouping. It is this Maori sense of family that has become emblematic of the retention of Maori culture.

The loss of land and the rise of urbanization have left Maoris vulnerable, fearing cultural domination. They have, therefore, insisted on being identified as Maori. They have stressed their rights to their family land and to belonging to their ancestral village, emphasizing the importance of the extended family, the respect and love due those of common descent, and the demands of hospitality. They have stressed the old traditions: the speeches in the Maori language, the action songs, the carvings, the rituals. Just as twentieth-century Maori writers have spoken of the Maori family, of the loss of land, and of the illusions of the urban promise; they have given implicit voice to the central issue: the injustices of the nineteenth-century land sales and confiscations.

Rabindranath Tagore
(1861–1941)
India

Rabindranath Tagore (Rabindranath Thakur) was born in Calcutta, India, where as the fourteenth child of an affluent Bengali family that had been influential since the seventeenth century, he was hardly permitted to leave the house without being accompanied. Both his father and his grandfather were members of the Brahmo Samaj movement, one of the first religious reformist associations to propose that the human rights of all women and men were inherent in the spirit of Hinduism. Tagore's father served as the society's second leader. Thus, Tagore grew up in a household noted for its philosophers and its progressive attitudes; it was also famous for its artists, musicians, and writers. He never earned a university degree, either in India or in England, where he was sent to complete his education in law. In 1901, however, he founded the experimental school Shantiniketan (the abode of peace), based on the open-air schools of ancient India, because of his dissatisfaction with the British educational system. It evolved into an international university, Visva-Bharati, that emphasized social reform and world unity. A man of immense energy, he published his first poem when he was 14 and turned to painting when he was 70.

Throughout his life, Rabindranath Tagore wrote prolifically in all genres: poetry, fiction, and drama; he wrote critical, historical, political, and metaphysical works, and he was a journalist. Manipulating Western genres and material, he drew on classical Indian literature as the source of his literary writing, thereby providing an implicit philosophical continuum. As part of his belief in the necessity of exchanging ideas between the East and West, he also translated his own work. He wrote *Gitanjali* (Offerings of Songs, 1912) in his native Bengali and translated it into English: *Gitanjali*, which includes "Where the Mind Is Without Fear," earned him the Nobel Prize in literature in 1913. In *Chandalika* (the feminine form of *chandal*, meaning the wretched one, an untouchable; see the introduction to this section), he integrated the revolutionary spirit of the times: as a religious reformist, he censured social discrimination; as a philosopher, he created a metaphor for the soul's conflict between passion and spirituality. (*Prakriti* is innate human nature; *Ananda* is the ultimate joy.) The play is a dance-drama, combining the Indian tradition of music and dance with Western theater. Much of the dance sequence has been omitted from this translation.

The British knighted him in 1915, the same year Mohandas Gandhi returned to India and Tagore named him Mahatma, or great soul, the title Gandhi carried for the rest of his life. In 1919, when the British massacred hundreds of people at Amritsar, Tagore renounced the title the British had bestowed on him. He remained committed to a humanitarian internationalism that respected racial equality, as he illustrated in *Crisis in Civilization* (1940). Tagore's life, his lecture tours, and writing inspired people throughout the world. It is not surprising, therefore, that India and Bangladesh each adopted a poem of his as its national anthem.

*Chandalika**

Act I

(The setting can be in front of a village house, in a courtyard, or on a path. When the play opens the mother is on stage.)

MOTHER: Prakriti! Prakriti![1] *(There is no answer)* Where could she have gone? She is never to be found at home!

PRAKRITI *(from a distance):* Here I am, Mother, I'm here.

MOTHER: Where?

PRAKRITI: Here, at the well.

MOTHER *(calling):* Come here. I must talk with you. *(To herself)* At the well at this time of the day when the earth is burning like a furnace, and water for the day already brought from the well! *(Prakriti enters)* All the other girls of the village have gotten on with their work, and you sit and melt in the sun for no reason—unless you wish to repeat Uma's[2] penance. Is that why you sit there?

PRAKRITI: Yes, Mother.

MOTHER: Good Heavens! And for whom?

PRAKRITI: He who has called me.

MOTHER: Who has called you?

PRAKRITI: His words are ringing in my mind: "Give me water."

MOTHER: "Give me water!" God grant it was not someone outside our caste!

PRAKRITI: He said he was one of us.

MOTHER: Did you tell him you are a *chandalini*?[3]

PRAKRITI: Yes, but he said, "Do not deceive yourself with names. If you call the black cloud a *chandal*, does it cease to be what it is? Does the water it carries lose its value for our earth? Do not degrade yourself, for self-degradation is a greater sin than suicide." I can remember every word he spoke to me. He spoke so beautifully to me.

MOTHER: What nonsense are you saying? Or are you remembering a story from some former birth?

---

*Translated by Krishna Kripalani; revised by Marjorie Sykes; revised by Robert Steele and Donald Junkins

[1]Lit., innate human nature; also the female principle of creation (*Purusha* is the male). [eds.]

[2]Wife of Hindu god Shiva; through penance she won Shiva's love. [eds.]

[3]Fem. form of *chandal*, one of the untouchable groups, lit. the wretched [eds.]

PRAKRITI: I am telling you the story of my new birth.

MOTHER: Your new birth? You are no more my daughter, Prakriti? Tell me. When did this happen?

PRAKRITI: That noontime while I was washing the motherless calf at the well a yellow-robed monk came and stood before me and said, "Give me water." I sprang up and did obeisance. When I found my voice I said, "I am a daughter of the *chandals* and the water of this well is polluted by my family's use." He said, "You and I are of the same family. All water that quenches thirst and relieves need is pure." I never heard such words before, and with these *chandal* hands, which never before would have dared touch the dust of his feet, I poured water for him.

MOTHER: You silly girl, how could you dare such an act? Do you forget who you are and the destiny of your birth?

PRAKRITI: No, but the cup of water he took from my hands seemed to become an infinite ocean in which all the seven seas flowed together. They drowned my family, my caste, and my birth.

MOTHER: How strange! How strange you are! Even your language is changed. It's not your own. You are under someone's spell. What are you saying? Do you understand your own words?

PRAKRITI: Was there no water to be had anywhere else in this whole village? Why did he come to this particular well? Why did he come, Mother, if not to bless me with a new life? Surely, he was seeking an occasion for such a deed. In a holy place he could not have found water that would give him the opportunity to further the mission of his life. He said, "So Seeta[4] bathed in water such as this, which was fetched by a *chandal*, Guhak, at the beginning of her exile in the forest."

MOTHER: Child, listen to me. I do not like this. These monks have a way of changing other people's minds by words. Today I can hardly understand you. Tomorrow your very face may seem foreign to me. I am frightened.

PRAKRITI: You have never really known me, Mother. But he knows me. Every day I watch for him at the well, long after the other girls have gone home with their water.

MOTHER: Watch for whom?

PRAKRITI: For the monk.

MOTHER: What monk will come to you, you sick girl?

PRAKRITI: That one monk, Mother, the only one. Without saying a word he told me he would come. Why then does he not keep his word? My heart is burning dry and there is no water to quench it. Day after day I have waited, and he has not come. Oh, why has he not come? (*Prakriti seems to be talking to herself in near delirium.*)

MOTHER: Prakriti, you talk like someone drunk. Come into the house at once.

---

[4]Wife of Rama, a Hindu god and the hero of the *Ramayana;* Guhak was the water carrier and of a low caste. [eds.]

PRAKRITI: *(Prakriti continues as if not hearing)* I want him, who came unknown and revealed to me that I, too, am acceptable. He has lifted me up from dust and placed me by his heart.

MOTHER: Don't forget, Prakriti, that pleasant words are not necessarily true. Because of some unknown sin you have been born in a caste whose barrier no one can break. You are untouchable. This is the truth. Accept it. Believe it. The sun has made you ill. Come in I say.

PRAKRITI: *(Sings)*
Blessed am I says the flower who belongs to the earth,
For I serve you my God in my lowly home.
Make me forget that I am born of dust,
For my spirit is free.
When you bend your eyes down to me my petals tremble;
Let the touch of your feet fill this dust with heavenliness,
For the earth offers worship through me.

MOTHER: I begin to follow you a little. Worship where you love and find there your kingdom of freedom. Caste does not bind a woman if fortune blinds a man to her caste. Such good fortune did come to you once, Prakriti, when the prince had strayed here, deer-hunting, and offered to take you. Do you remember?

PRAKRITI: Yes, I remember.

MOTHER: Then why did you refuse to go with him? He was blind with love. He would have taken you away.

PRAKRITI: Blind! Yes, he was blind to me! He was hunting an animal and could only see the animal in me.

MOTHER: Even though it was a hunt, he saw the beauty of your form. But this monk, how do you know he has seen you as more than just a woman?

PRAKRITI: Hush, Mother! You won't understand, Mother, you won't! I know that it was he who first loved me. And it is he I love and shall always love. I will take to him the worship of my life and offer it at his feet. And his feet shall not be polluted. I yearn to tell him with pride, "If I am not to stay in the dust as everybody's servant, I must be devoted to you."

MOTHER: Do not get so excited, Prakriti. We are servants by birth. We cannot wipe out what providence has ordained.

PRAKRITI: No, no, Mother. Do not wrong yourself by self-degradation. A princess may be a slave, a Brahmin a *chandal*. I am Prakriti—neither slave nor *chandal*.

MOTHER: I am no match for you today. Your tongue is new. I myself will go to him and beg him that even if he goes to other houses for food, he will come to ours for a cup of water.

PRAKRITI: [Not hearing her mother and deeply disturbed] *(Sings)*
No, I will not call him with my voice,
I will call him with my heart and bring him near.
My heart aches to give to him

But I know not where he goes, he who will receive me.
How can this union come about?
Can my pain touch his pain, and mingle
As the Ganges mingles with the dark Jamuna?
The music comes and goes
But leaves its word of hope behind.

Mother, when the earth is parched with drought, what good is one cup of water? Won't the clouds be drawn by this thirst, and won't the rain then fall to the dry earth?

MOTHER: This talk is futile. If the clouds do not come of their own accord and the fields burn up, what else can we do but gaze helplessly at the sky?

PRAKRITI: No! Mother, please listen to me and help me. You know the art of magic. You can cast a spell and bring him here.

MOTHER: Hush, Prakriti! My magic is not for play, and this is playing with fire. These monks are not ordinary men. One does not risk spells on them. You frighten me with your madness.

PRAKRITI: Who dared to think of casting a spell on the king's son?

MOTHER: I do not fear the king. The worst he can do is put me on the gallows.

PRAKRITI: I fear nothing, or only one thing: a falling back into the body of the dead Prakriti, losing my new self and again being lost in the darkness. That would be worse than the gallows or any death. Drag him here, Mother, you must! I must have him. Is not this desire of mine a miracle in itself? He worked one miracle and will work a greater one when he comes here to be at my side.

MOTHER: I am frightened and I may be doing you and him a great wrong. It may be I can draw him here, but can you stand the ordeal? Another of the monk's miracles and nothing of you may remain.

PRAKRITI: No, nothing shall remain. That is my one wish—that I have the chance to give, to pour out my being and be fulfilled. That is the consummation I have been waiting for. The world has conspired to make me forget what I *can* give. Now I know and I *shall* give—everything that I have! I will wait for him. Please bring him, Mother, at once.

MOTHER: Do you fear God?

PRAKRITI: I do not fear what does not fear me. A god that insults, debases, and blinds is no god. Men have conspired to make my god evil. Now I see and am not afraid. Begin your chant and make the monk sit by me. I will exalt him.

MOTHER: Do you fear no curse?

PRAKRITI: The real curse has clung to me by my birth, the monk shall redeem me. I will listen to no delays, Mother. Begin your chant!

MOTHER: I do this for you. Tell me his name.

PRAKRITI: Ananda! His name is Ananda.

MOTHER: Ananda? The Buddha's close companion?

PRAKRITI: Yes, that is he.

MOTHER: It is a sin to work a spell on him.

PRAKRITI: Why a sin?

MOTHER: The Buddha and his companions attract with virtue; I force by magic, as a hunter ambushes game. It is like churning mud.

PRAKRITI: Then churn mud. How else can mud be purified?

MOTHER: Only because I love you, Prakriti. Oh, Ananda, you who art great in soul, forgive my sin. Your power to forgive is greater than my strength to wrong. Accept my adoration as I begin my sacrilege.

PRAKRITI: Do not be so afraid, Mother. It is I who work the spell through you. If to drag him by the anguish of my yearning is wrong, then I do that wrong.

MOTHER: You are daring, Prakriti.

PRAKRITI: Daring? Consider him daring when he said so simply what no one had dared to say before, "Give me water." These simple words illumined my whole life. If you had seen him, you would know your fear is baseless. He had finished begging in the city, and still he walked across the wasteland, past the cremation ground, then he crossed the river, all in the scorching sun, for what? Just to say to me, "Give me water." Such tenderness and grace to shower on a worthless creature! "Give me water!" Water has welled up within me and I must pour it out. "Give me water!" In an instant I knew of a reservoir within me. Now I must give it. That is why I call him night and day. Chant your spell. He will hear it.

(From a distance come the sounds of a Buddhist chant)

MOTHER: Look, Prakriti! There go some monks.

PRAKRITI: See, Mother, see! He is at the head of the procession! *(Both look for what seems like a long time)* He did not look back at the well. He did not look this way once! He might have come and said, "Give me water." How could he pass me up like this? I who am his own creation? *(She falls to the ground weeping)* This earth, this earth, this earth alone is mine. For an instant he raised me up in light, miserable creature that I am! Could this be grace? To let me sink back into my mud and be mixed with it forever, and to be trampled upon by everyone.

MOTHER: Quiet, child. Forget him. It's best that your moment's illusion is shattered. Let what cannot endure vanish as soon as it may.

PRAKRITI: Illusion? This longing from day to day, this insult from year to year, this bird's imprisonment beating wings forever against a cage, do you call this all an illusion? Do you call something which strains every nerve in my body only a dream? Those who have no earthly burdens, no joys or sorrows, who float along like autumn clouds—are they the only ones without illusion? No, I know what is real for me.

MOTHER: I can't see you suffer like this. Get up. Dress your hair. I will drag him here with a spell. I will break his vow of "I desire not" and I will make him moan and crave, "I want, I want, I want."

PRAKRITI: Mother, your spell is as ancient as life itself; thin *mantras* are merely crude and recent words. They cannot match your power.

MOTHER: Where are they going?

PRAKRITI: They are going nowhere. During the rains they fast and do penance for four months, and then they are off again to who knows where. They call this being enlightened.

MOTHER: Then why talk about spells, you crazy girl? If he is going so far away, how can I bring him back?

PRAKRITI: Your spells can overcome distance. He showed no pity for me; I'll show none for him. Work your spell, Mother. Wrap him in a coil he can never escape from.

MOTHER: Hold this mirror in your hand and dance; it will reflect what happens to him.

PRAKRITI: (*Looks into the mirror and dances*) The clouds, Mother, are gathering in the west. They are storm clouds. The spell will work. His dry meditations will be swept away like dry leaves, his vow extinguished, his path turned toward me. He will be blown here as a bird which falls into a dark courtyard when its wing is broken. I see the lightning flash and the sea pound.

MOTHER: It is not too late, Prakriti to stop. Consider. Shall I go on? Will you be able to bear it? This spell will not subside until it has burnt his vow to ashes. To undo this spell may cost me my life.

PRAKRITI: Let him pass through the whole fire. I see his end approaching, and our stormy union will make destruction a bliss. He will give himself to save me, and I will save you.

Act II

(*A few days have elapsed*)

PRAKRITI: (*She is dancing*) I can bear no more. (*Her steps falter*) I am choking. I cannot look into the mirror anymore. What a whirlwind of agony is raging in that noble man.

MOTHER: Speak to me Prakriti. It is not too late to revoke the spell. Though my own life be extinguished, let me spare this great soul.

PRAKRITI: All right, Mother, stop the spell. . . . No, no, don't. I must have him. Try a little longer. Let him come a bit nearer. Let him go through with it and come to me. When he enters my house, I shall wash away his suffering. My surrender will comfort and heal him. The fire in me will illumine the darkness of his fall, and the fountain of my life will bathe and refresh his tortured soul. Once more he shall say. "Give me water." Until that moment let the spell work.

MOTHER: Oh, it takes so long! Wait! The spell is triumphing. I think I have won. But I cannot breathe.

PRAKRITI: Go on with it, Mother. I beg you, a little more.

MOTHER: The rainy season is coming, and their fast is at hand.

PRAKRITI: They have gone to the monastery at Vaisali.

MOTHER: But that is so far away. You have no pity, Prakriti.

PRAKRITI: It is only seven days' journey. Fifteen days have already gone. His meditation has been shaken—he is coming! And that which was so many million miles away is coming with him.

MOTHER: Prakriti, I have worked the spell to its utmost. Such force would have brought down Indra, wielder of the thunderbolt. And still he had not come! What a struggle! You could not have told me all you saw in the mirror.

PRAKRITI: I saw the heavens covered over with mist which here and there was pierced by lightning. I saw gods as they lay exhausted after the war with the demons. That passed. Then I saw black clouds gathering. There was terrifying lightning. And then I saw my life-giving monk. He looked as if he were on fire. Flames were searing him from every direction. I looked and I froze. I rushed to tell you to break the spell and found you unconscious. I came back to look into the mirror and saw only intolerable agony on his face.

MOTHER: It did not kill you? His suffering burned into me until I couldn't stand it any longer.

PRAKRITI: The suffering I saw was of us both. My own suffering mingled with his like copper and gold in a furnace.

MOTHER: Now, finally, you have known fear.

PRAKRITI: I knew something greater than fear. I felt like a witness to creation, something mightier than destruction. It all seemed to be for some purpose. Was it life or death? A feeling of release came over me, and I could not contain myself. My whole being leapt up like a joyous flame.

MOTHER: And the monk?

PRAKRITI: He gazed into the distance. He was as steadfast as the sun in its orbit.

MOTHER: Did he look as if he felt your presence?

PRAKRITI: I shudder when I think of it. His eyes went red with anger, as though he was about to curse. Then he stamped out his flaming passion and like a javelin it seemed to re-enter his soul and become fixed there.

MOTHER: And you endured it?

PRAKRITI: I was amazed at myself. A nobody from nowhere—and his suffering and mine were one.

MOTHER: How long will this horror drag on?

PRAKRITI: Until my suffering is soothed. How can he be freed when I am not?

MOTHER: When did you look into the mirror last?

PRAKRITI: Yesterday evening. Some days before, in darkness, he had passed the lion-gate of Vaisali. After that I saw him, sometimes crossing rivers or mountain passes, sometimes trudging along forest paths, alone in the night. At times he seemed more and more in a dream, forgetful of everything, even of the conflict raging in him. His face looked like death, his eyes were fixed on nothing, and his body seemed old and shrunken.

MOTHER: Where is he now?

PRAKRITI: Yesterday at sunset he was at the village Patal on the Upali River, and it was overflowing with the rains. On the bank was an old peepul tree, glimmering with fireflies, beneath which an altar was overgrown with moss. He looked stunned when he reached that spot, recognizing it as the one where the Buddha had preached to the King Suprabhas. He turned his face away. I could not look a moment longer. I threw away the mirror. *(Prakriti hears the nightwatchman pounding with his stick.)* Now the watchman is calling. It must be past midnight. This night may be wasted. Mother, he may be near. Hurry and cast the spell more powerfully. He must find me.

MOTHER: I am no longer able to. My strength is weakening.

PRAKRITI: No, you cannot weaken, Mother! Keep trying. Don't give up. He may have turned backward and the chain holding may snap and I will lose him forever. I could not endure it. I beg you, Mother, repeat your earth chant and make the steadfastness of my monk tremble.

MOTHER: Are you prepared for the ending?

PRAKRITI: I am.

MOTHER: Then begin your dance of welcome while I repeat my chant. *(Prakriti dances.)* Prakriti, find your mirror. Look into it again. Tell me when a shadow descends on the altar. Can you see it?

PRAKRITI: No, I will not look. I will only listen and wait. I shall look only when I can look at him.

MOTHER: I can stand it no longer. Something stops my breath, I. . . .

PRAKRITI: Carry on a little longer, Mother! Pull him here. He will come, I know! See? There comes the storm announcing his approach. I feel the earth trembling.

MOTHER *(gasping)*: . . . Coming to curse you, you wretched girl. I am nearly done. My veins are snapping. I can't. . . .

PRAKRITI: Not to curse, no, not to curse! My beloved comes with lightning to smash down the gate of death and to give me a new life. The darkness is breaking. The walls of my prison are giving way, and the great delusion of my life is exposed. I am trembling with fear, but my heart is pounding with joy. Oh my destroyer, you have come! I will seat you on the summit of my degradation and will fashion your throne from my shame, my fear, and my joy!

MOTHER: Look into the mirror. Quick. My time is up.

PRAKRITI: I am afraid to, Mother. His path is nearing the end. How will he look at me? Will I be able to make up for his long torture?

MOTHER: Don't delay, Prakriti, look into the mirror. I want to know. Quick, I can bear it no longer.

PRAKRITI: *(Picks up the mirror, looks in it as if transfixed, and then flings it away.)* Break the spell, Mother, break it. Undo your spell. Revoke it. Immediately! How wicked of me to have dragged him down to this! That heavenly light on his face! Where has it all gone? He comes with his head bowed, his face pale, his body bearing the load of the soul's defeat. What have I done to him *(She kicks away the apparatus of magic.)* I am a wretch, a *chandalini*—how else could I have desecrated my lover? *(Ananda enters. Prakriti falls at his feet.)* You have come, my master, to redeem me. I have caused you much suffering for which I ask forgiveness. Forgive me. I have dragged you down to my earth. But how else could you have raised me? Oh, pure one, the earth under your feet is made pure. You are blessed.

MOTHER: *(Lifting her head and attempting to kneel.)* You are blessed and ever victorious, O Lord. At your feet my sin and my life are both at an end. *(She dies)*

ANANDA: *(Chants)* I honor the Enlightened One, most pure, an ocean of mercy, the Buddha, endowed with the vision of pure and supreme knowledge, who destroys all sin and suffering in this world.

*Where the Mind Is Without Fear**
(Song XXXV from *Gitanjali*)

Where the mind is without fear and the head is held high;
　Where knowledge is free;
　Where the world has not been broken up into fragments by narrow
domestic walls;
　Where words come out from the depth of truth;
　Where tireless striving stretches its arms towards perfection;
　Where the clear stream of reason has not lost its way into the dreary
desert sand of dead habit;
　Where the mind is led forward by thee into ever-widening thought and
action—
　Into that heaven of freedom, my Father, let my country awake.

❋ **Discussion and Writing**
Chandalika
1. What feelings does the monk evoke in Prakriti: what is symbolized by her being asked to give water? Interpret her new perception of herself.
2. Discuss the implications of Mother's concerns regarding: caste distinction; her acceptance of the prince as a suitable match for her daughter but not the monk; her concept of rebirth.
3. Contrast the two spells, Mother's and the monk's, as the central conflict in the play.
4. Explain Prakriti's intense desire to recall the monk: her reasoning; her reaction to what she sees in the mirror. Comment on the irony of her calling herself a *chandal* and the context of the title.

*Translated by Rabindranath Tagore

5. Interpret the ending of the play: what does Mother's death symbolize; what is the meaning of Ananda's sacrifice; what is the nature of Prakriti's realization?
6. Discuss the play as a critique of social practices.
7. Given the meanings of their names, Prakriti and Ananda, what is the religious and spiritual significance of the play? Identify the use of the images that reflect Hindu, Buddhist, and Christian traditions. What does Tagore accomplish by the blending of traditions?

Where the Mind Is Without Fear
1. Define the poet's concept of freedom for India. What kind of bonds does he want his countrymen to shatter?
2. Elaborate on the impact of the poem as a prayer.
3. Which countries can be called free according to Tagore's definition? Is his concept of total freedom an achievable ideal? What is the value of a utopian ideology?

❀ Research and Comparison
Chandalika
Examine Rabindranath Tagore's short stories focusing on the vivid depiction of women, men, and children.

Interdisciplinary Discussion Question: Research the issue of discrimination against the untouchables in India and Mahatma Gandhi's contribution to the improvment of their status.

Where the Mind Is Without Fear
1. Examine Tagore's *Gitanjali* (Offering of Songs), *Fireflies,* or *The Gardener.* Comment on the use of the child and nature in his poems.
2. Explore Tagore's prose and poetic writings as they transcend narrow bounds of nationalism and center on the essential humanity of all. Define Tagore's concept of patriotism.

Interdisciplinary Discussion Question: Research the early history of India's independence, going back to the nineteenth-century Indian Renaissance. Examine the role of the Indian National Congress and the Muslim League.

Ho Chi Minh
(1890–1969)
Vietnam

Ho Chi Minh (Nguyen Sinh Cung) was born in the province of Nghe An in northern Vietnam, an area noted for resisting colonialism. His mother died when he was ten. His father, a dissident, left the children with their maternal grandparents and served as a magistrate in the south until a French colonial official discovered he was not applying French law. Ho Chi Minh's brother and sister also rebelled against the French, and both were imprisoned numerous times. By the time Ho left secondary school to teach in a fishing port in the south (1911), he had participated in the 1908 revolts and the police had recorded his activities. He taught for eight months. Then, in an attempt to avoid police detection, he took on the first of many pseudonyms, setting sail for France as an assistant cook: he did not return for 30 years. In France, he associated with many of the leading left-wing intellectuals, read widely, and worked as a journalist, editing several publications and writing anticolonialist articles. He tried to hand Woodrow Wilson his Eight-Point Program calling for self-determination (in what was then Indochina) at the Versailles Peace Conference (1919), but while the European powers ignored him, Ho gained the respect of socialists. He became one of the founding members of the French Communist Party.

Ho Chi Minh called himself a "professional revolutionary" and traveled to Moscow, where he extended the network of friends that continued to expand throughout his life, friends who supported his endeavors to bring peace and unification to Vietnam. He returned to Asia, setting up schools and introducing anticolonialist philosophy into the Buddhist monasteries. Captured by the police in Hong Kong, he was imprisoned. When he was hospitalized with tuberculosis, the warmth of his personality endeared him to the staff, and they helped him to escape from the prison ward. He was pronounced dead for unknown reasons, and thus evaded the police. After a series of daring feats, he returned to Moscow and, finally, in 1941 to Vietnam. There in Bac Bo, close to the northern border with China, he formed the Vietminh League, but when he re-entered China the following year he was imprisoned for 14 months. It was here he wrote his famous *Prison Diary*, a collection of 120 poems he composed in classical Chinese. He created pictures of prison life, his suffering from the extreme cold and from starvation, and he described being shifted from jail to jail, often in chains.

When he was able to return to Vietnam, he raised the army that fought against the Japanese invasion during the Pacific War (World War II) and that defeated French colonialism in the Indochina War (1946–1954). After he became president of North Vietnam when the country was divided at the Geneva Conference in 1954, he sought to avoid war with the United States. But when his offers of negotiation were rejected, he continued to lead the fight against any colonial control during the Vietnam War (1954–1975). He remained committed to unifying Vietnam but died before the end of the war. His integrity and the power of his conviction led his compatriots to call him Bac Ho, or Uncle Ho, and when he died, even his adversaries honored him.

Noon*

A snooze in a cell: how lovely.
The sleep-dragon runs for hours,
Runs to Heaven.
Then I wake up.

Transferred to Nanning*

No rope—iron chains, now,
Jingling like jade rings.
I may be a jailbird but I walk
Like a parade of judges.

❋ Discussion and Writing

1. Analyze the significance of the images of the sleep-dragon and the jade rings. Comment on the tone of the poems.
2. What are the political implications of a Vietnamese political leader in a prison cell?

❋ Research and Comparison

Interdisciplinary Discussion Question: Examine Ho Chi Minh's life, his writings, and his impact on world politics. Compare his writings with those of nationalist writer or political leader from another country.

R. K. Narayan
(b. 1906)
India

Rasipuram Krishnaswamy Narayan, one of eight children, was born in Madras, South India, where his father taught English. Although Narayan himself was not academically inclined, when he decided to become a writer, he chose to work in the English of his schooling rather than in his native Tamil. He employed a simple fluid idiom that reflected the quality of life and the characters he depicted, characters who frequently would not have spoken or understood English. Portraying the lower middle class,

---

*Translated by Burton Raffel

he set most of his work in a small South Indian town, named Malgudi, that combined traits of Madras and Mysore, the two cities Narayan knew well. In his 15 novels and several collections of short stories, he created a world of Malgudi that captured the nuances of India. Although he also worked in other genres—the memoir and the essay—and retold legends from ancient scriptures and the epic *Ramayana,* the pervading note in all his writing has been the natural blending of opposites. He yoked the comic and sad, naive and tricky, material and spiritual, and because of his compassion for his characters, his work exhibits an underlying comic-seriousness, providing a kind of meditation on life. Thus, the political turmoil and social changes emerge as elements in Malgudi life, tinged with ironic humor, not as central issues. In 1964, the Indian government awarded Narayan the title of *Padma Bhushan,* an official title, awarded yearly for exemplary achievement.

Trail of the Green Blazer

The Green Blazer stood out prominently under the bright sun and blue sky. In all that jostling crowd one could not help noticing it. Villagers in shirts and turbans, townsmen in coats and caps, beggars bare-bodied and women in multicolored saris were thronging the narrow passage between the stalls and moving in great confused masses, but still the Green Blazer could not be missed. The jabber and babble of the marketplace was there, as people harangued, disputed prices, haggled or greeted each other; over it all boomed the voice of a Bible-preacher, and when he paused for breath, from another corner the loudspeaker of a health van amplified on malaria and tuberculosis. Over and above it all the Green Blazer seemed to cry out an invitation. Raju could not ignore it. It was not in his nature to ignore such a persistent invitation. He kept himself half-aloof from the crowd; he could not afford to remain completely aloof or keep himself in it too conspicuously. Wherever he might be, he was harrowed by the fear of being spotted by a policeman; today he wore a loincloth and was bare-bodied, and had wound an enormous turban over his head, which overshadowed his face completely, and he hoped that he would be taken for a peasant from a village.

He sat on a stack of cast-off banana stalks beside a shop awning and watched the crowd. When he watched a crowd he did it with concentration. It was his professional occupation. Constitutionally he was an idler and had just the amount of energy to watch in a crowd and put his hand into another person's pocket. It was a gamble, of course. Sometimes he got nothing out of a venture, counting himself lucky if he came out with his fingers intact. Sometimes he picked up a fountain pen, and the "receiver" behind the Municipal Office would not offer even four annas for it, and there was always the danger of being traced through it. Raju promised himself that someday he would leave fountain pens alone; he wouldn't touch one even if it were presented to him on a plate; they were too much bother—inky, leaky and next to worthless if one could believe what the receiver said about them. Watches were in the same category, too.

What Raju loved most was a nice, bulging purse. If he saw one he picked it up with the greatest deftness. He took the cash in it, flung it far away and went home with the satisfaction that he had done his day's job well. He splashed a little water over his face and hair and tidied himself up before walking down the street again as a normal citizen. He bought sweets, books and slates for his children, and occasionally a jacket-piece for his wife, too. He was not always easy in mind about his wife. When he went home with too much cash, he had always to take care to hide it in an envelope and shove it under a roof tile. Otherwise she asked too many questions and made herself miserable. She liked to believe that he was reformed and earned the cash he showed her as commission; she never bothered to ask what the commissions were for; a commission seemed to her something absolute.

Raju jumped down from the banana stack and followed the Green Blazer, always keeping himself three steps behind. It was a nicely calculated distance, acquired by intuition and practise. The distance must not be so much as to obscure the movement of the other's hand to and from his purse, nor so close as to become a nuisance and create suspicion. It had to be finely balanced and calculated—the same sort of calculations as carry a *shikari*[1] through his tracking of game and see him safely home again. Only this hunter's task was more complicated. The hunter in the forest could count his day a success if he laid his quarry flat; but here one had to extract the heart out of the quarry without injuring it.

Raju waited patiently, pretending to be examining some rolls of rush mat, while the Green Blazer spent a considerable length of time drinking a coconut at a nearby booth. It looked as though he would not move again at all. After sucking all the milk in the coconut, he seemed to wait interminably for the nut to be split and the soft white kernel scooped out with a knife. The sight of the white kernel scooped and disappearing into the other's mouth made Raju, too, crave for it. But he suppressed the thought; it would be inept to be spending one's time drinking and eating while one was professionally occupied; the other might slip away and be lost forever. . . . Raju saw the other take out his black purse and start a debate with the coconut-seller over the price of coconuts. He had a thick, sawing voice which disconcerted Raju. It sounded like the growl of a tiger, but what jungle-hardened hunter ever took a step back because a tiger's growl sent his heart racing involuntarily!

---

[1]A hunter. [eds.]

The way the other haggled didn't appeal to Raju either; it showed a mean and petty temperament . . . too much fondness for money. Those were the narrow-minded troublemakers who made endless fuss when a purse was lost. . . . The Green Blazer moved after all. He stopped before a stall flying colored balloons. He bought a balloon after an endless argument with the shopman—a further demonstration of his meanness. He said, "This is for a motherless boy. I have promised it him. If it bursts or gets lost before I go home, he will cry all night, and I wouldn't like it at all."

Raju got his chance when the other passed through a narrow stile, where people were passing four-thick in order to see a wax model of Mahatma Gandhi reading a newspaper.

Fifteen minutes later Raju was examining the contents of the purse. He went away to a secluded spot, behind a disused well. Its crumbling parapet seemed to offer an ideal screen for his activities. The purse contained ten rupees in coins and twenty in currency notes and a few annas in nickel. Raju tucked the annas at his waist in his loincloth. "Must give them to some beggars," he reflected generously. There was a blind fellow yelling his life out at the entrance to the fair and nobody seemed to care. People seemed to have lost all sense of sympathy these days. The thirty rupees he bundled into a knot at the end of his turban and wrapped this again round his head. It would see him through the rest of the month. He could lead a clean life for at least a fortnight and take his wife and children to a picture.

Now the purse lay limp within the hollow of his hand. It was only left for him to fling it into the well and dust off his hand and then he might walk among princes with equal pride at heart. He peeped into the well. It had a little shallow water at the bottom. The purse might float, and a floating purse could cause the worst troubles on earth. He opened the flap of the purse in order to fill it up with pebbles before drowning it. Now, through the slit at its side, he saw a balloon folded and tucked away. "Oh, this he bought. . . ." He remembered the other's talk about the motherless child. "What a fool to keep this in the purse," Raju reflected. "It is the carelessness of parents that makes young ones suffer," he ruminated angrily. For a moment he paused over a picture of the growling father returning home and the motherless one waiting at the door for the promised balloon, and this growling man feeling for his purse . . . and, oh! it was too painful!

Raju almost sobbed at the thought of the disappointed child—the motherless boy. There was no one to comfort him. Perhaps this ruffian would beat him if he cried too long. The Green Blazer did not look like one who knew the language of children. Raju was filled with pity at the thought of the young child—perhaps of the same age as his second son. Suppose his wife were dead . . . (personally it might make things easier for him, he need not conceal his cash under the roof); he overcame this thought as an unworthy side issue. If his wife should die it would make him very sad indeed and tax all his ingenuity to keep his young ones quiet. . . . That motherless boy must have his balloon at any cost, Raju decided. But how? He peeped over the parapet across the intervening space at the far-off crowd. The balloon could not be handed back. The thing to do would be to put it back into the empty purse and slip it into the other's pocket.

The Green Blazer was watching the heckling that was going on as the Bible-preacher warmed up to his subject. A semicircle was asking, "Where is your God?" There was a hubbub. Raju sidled up to the Green Blazer. The purse with the balloon (only) tucked into it was in his palm. He'd slip it back into the other's pocket.

Raju realized his mistake in a moment. The Green Blazer caught hold of his arm and cried, "Pickpocket!" The hecklers lost interest in the Bible and turned their attention to Raju, who tried to look appropriately outraged. He cried, "Let me go." The other, without giving a clue to what he proposed, shot out his arm and hit him on the cheek. It almost blinded him. For a fraction of a second Raju lost his awareness of where and even who he was. When the dark mist lifted and he was able to regain his vision, the first figure he noticed in the foreground was the Green Blazer, looming, as it seemed, over the whole landscape. His arms were raised ready to strike again. Raju cowered at the sight. He said, "I . . . I was trying to put back your purse." The other gritted his teeth in fiendish merriment and crushed the bones of his arm. The crowd roared with laughter and badgered him. Somebody hit him again on the head.

Even before the Magistrate Raju kept saying, "I was only trying to put back the purse." And everyone laughed. It became a stock joke in the police world. Raju's wife came to see him in jail and said, "You have brought shame on us," and wept.

Raju replied indignantly, "Why? I was only trying to put it back."

He served his term of eighteen months and came back into the world— not quite decided what he should do with himself. He told himself, "If ever I pick up something again, I shall make sure I don't have to put it back." For now he believed God had gifted the likes of him with only one-way deftness. Those fingers were not meant to put anything back.

❋ Discussion and Writing

1. In what ways is Raju's vocation as a pickpocket a calculated business venture: what aspects of his maneuver parallel those of business management?
2. Analyze the use of the image of hunting as Raju follows the trail of the Green Blazer.
3. Discuss the significance of references to Mahatma Gandhi and the Bible preacher in the narrative?

4. Why (not how) does Raju get arrested?
5. R. K. Narayan captures an idiosyncracy of a character, as does a cartoonist, and carefully weaves a story around it. Analyze the comic irony of this narrative about a pickpocket.

❋ Research and Comparison

Examine any one of Narayan's works, for instance, *The Man-Eater of Malgudi, The Tiger of Malgudi,* or *Malgudi Days,* paying particular attention to his creation of Malgudi and to his art as a master of irony.

Raja Rao
(b. 1909)
India

Raja Rao was born in Hassana, India. His father was a teacher of English in Hyderabad. Rao studied in France at the University of Montpellier and at the Sorbonne, and has taught at various universities throughout the world, and he has lectured frequently on Indian philosophy. Considering himself and his compatriots bilingual, he has said that English "is the language of our intellectual make-up—like Sanskrit or Persian was before—but not of our emotional make-up." He worked, therefore, in English. In his novel *Kanthapura* (1938), a precursor to much recent Asian and African Anglophone literature, he experimented with the spoken idiom. Regarded as a classic, *Kanthapura* depicts the influence of Mahatma Gandhi's noncooperation movement on a small South Indian village through a woman narrator who had no formal education. Raja Rao was himself inspired by Gandhi's ideology of nonviolence, and in this novel he portrayed the political mobilization of the village, capturing the quality of life during this turbulent period by permeating his English sentences with Indian manners of expression. A philosophical writer, Rao has drawn on the intellectual ethos of classical India. In "Companions," he intertwines two conflicting religious traditions in the two characters. In 1969, the Indian government awarded him the title of Padma Bhushan.[1]

---

[1]An official title, awarded yearly for exemplary achievement. [eds.]

Companions

Alas till now I did not know
My guide and Fate's guide are one.
Hafiz

It was a serpent such as one sees only at a fair, long and many-colored and swift in riposte when the juggler stops his music. But it had a secret of its own which none knew except Moti Khan who brought him to the Fatehpur Sunday fair. The secret was: his fangs would lie without venom till the day Moti Khan should see the vision of the large white rupee, with the Kutub Minar on the one side and the face of the Emperor on the other. That day the fang would eat into his flesh and Moti Khan would only be a corpse of a man. Unless he finds God.

For to tell you the truth, Moti Khan had caught him in the strangest of strange circumstances. He was one day going through the sitaphul[1] woods of Rampur on a visit to his sister, and the day being hot and the sands all scorching and shiny, he lay down under a wild fig tree, his turban on his face and his legs stretched across a stone. Sleep came like a swift descent of dusk, and after rapid visions of palms and hills and the dizzying sunshine, he saw a curious thing. A serpent came in the form of a man, opened its mouth, and through the most queer twistings of his face, declared he was Pandit Srinath Sastri of Totepur, who, having lived at the foot of the Goddess Lakshamma for a generation or more, one day in the ecstasy of his vision he saw her, the benign Goddess straight and supple, offering him two boons. He thought of his falling house and his mortgaged ancestral lands and said without a thought, "A bagful of gold and liberation from the cycle of birth and death." "And gold you shall have," said the Goddess, "but for your greed, you shall be born a serpent in your next life before reaching liberation. For gold and wisdom go in life like soap and oil. Go and be born a juggler's serpent. And when you have made the hearts of many men glad with the ripple and swing of your shining flesh, and you have gone like a bird amidst shrieking children, only to swing round their legs and to swing out to the amusement of them all, when you have climbed old men's shoulders and hung down them chattering like a squirrel, when you have thrust your hood at the virgin and circled round the marrying couples; when you have gone through the dreams of pregnant women and led the seekers to the top of the Mount of Holy Beacon, then your sins will be worn out like the quern with man's grindings and your flesh will catch fire like the will-o-the-wisp and disappear into the world of darkness where men await the birth to come. The juggler will be a basket-maker and Moti Khan is his name. In a former life he

---

[1]Custard-apple; a fruit tree. [eds.]

sought God but in this he sits on the lap of a concubine. Wending his way to his sister's for the birth of her son, he will sleep in the *sitaphul* woods. Speak to him. And he will be the vehicle of your salvation." Thus spoke the Goddess.

"Now, what do you say to that, Moti Khan?"

"Yes, I've been a sinner. But never thought I, God and Satan would become one. Who are you?"

"The very same serpent."

"Your race has caused the fall of Adam."

"I sat at the feet of Sri Lakshamma and fell into ecstasy. I am a brahmin."

"You are strange."

"Take me or I'll haunt you for this life and all lives to come."

"Go, Satan!" shouted Moti Khan, and rising swift as a sword he started for his sister's house. He said to himself, "I will think of my sister and child. I will think only of them." But leaves rustled and serpents came forth from the left and the right, blue ones and white ones and red ones and copper-colored ones, long ones with short tails and short ones with bent tails, and serpents dropped from tree-tops and rock-edges, serpents hissed on the river sands. Then Moti Khan stood by the Rampur stream and said, "Wretch! Stop it. Come, I'll take you with me." Then the serpents disappeared and so did the hissings, and hardly home, he took a basket and put it in a corner, and then he slept; and when he woke, a serpent had curled itself in the basket. Moti Khan had a *pungi*[2] made by the local carpenter, and, putting his mouth to it, he made the serpent dance. All the village gathered round him and all the animals gathered round him, for the music of Moti Khan was blue, and the serpent danced on its tail.

When he said good-bye to his sister, he did not take the road to his concubine but went straight northward, for Allah called him there. And at every village men came to offer food to Moti Khan and women came to offer milk to the serpent, for it swung round children's legs and swung out, and cured them of all scars and poxes and fevers. Old men slept better after its touch and women conceived on the very night they offered milk to it. Plague went and plenty came, but Moti Khan would not smell silver. That would be death.

Now sometimes, at night in caravanserais, they had wrangles.

Moti Khan used to say: "You are not even a woman to put under oneself."

"But so many women come to see you and so many men come to honor you, and only a king could have had such a reception though you're only a basket-maker."

---

[2] A kind of flute. [eds.]

"Only a basket-maker! But I had a queen of a woman, and when she sang her voice was all flesh, and her flesh was all song. And she chewed betel-leaves and her lips were red, and even kings. . . ."

"Stop that. Between this and the vision of the rupee. . . ."

Moti Khan pulled at his beard and, fire in his eyes, he broke his knuckles against the earth.

"If only I could see a woman!"

"If you want God forget women, Moti Khan."

"But I never asked for God. It is you who always bore me with God. I said I loved a woman. You are only a fanged beast. And here I am in the prime of life with a reptile to live with."

But suddenly temple bells rang, and the muezzin was heard to cry *Allah-o-Akbar.*[3] No doubt it was all the serpent's work. Trembling, Moti Khan fell on his knees and bent himself in prayer.

From that day on the serpent had one eye turned to the right and one to the left when it danced. Once it looked at the men and once at the women, and suddenly it used to hiss up and slap Moti Khan's cheeks with the back of its head, for his music had fallen false and he was eyeing women. Round were their hips, he would think, and the eyelashes are black and blue, and the breasts are pointed like young mangoes, and their limbs so tremble and flow that he could sweetly melt into them.

One day, however, there was at the market a dark blue woman, with red lips, young and sprightly; and she was a butter woman. She came and stood by Moti Khan as he made the serpent dance. He played on his bamboo *pungi* and music swung here and splashed there, and suddenly he looked at her and her eyes and her breasts and the *nagaswara*[4] went and became *mohaswara,*[5] and she felt it and he felt she felt it; and when night came, he thought and thought so much of her and she thought and thought so much of him, that he slipped to the *serai*[6] door and she came to the *serai* gate, flower in her hair and perfume on her limbs, but lo! Like the sword of God came a long, rippling light, circled round them, pinched at her nipples and flew back into the bewildering night. She cried out, and the whole town waked, and Moti Khan thrust the basket under his arm and walked northward, for Allah called him thither.

"Now," said Moti Khan, "I have to find God. Else this creature will kill me. And the Devil knows the hell I'd have to bake in." So he decided that, at the next saint's tomb he encountered, he would sit down and meditate. But he wandered and he wandered; from one village he went to another, from

---

[3]Allah is great. [eds.]
[4]Lit., lord of the serpent; also Shiva. [eds.]
[5]Lit., lord of love; also Krishna. [eds.]
[6]An inn. [eds.]

one fair he went to another, but he found no *dargah*[7] to meditate by. For God always called him northward and northward, and he crossed the jungles and he went up the mountains, and he came upon narrow valleys where birds screeched here and deer frisked there but no man's voice was to be heard, and he said, "Now let me turn back home;" but he looked back and was afraid. And he said, "Now I have to go to the North, for Allah calls me there." And he climbed mountains again, and ran through jungles, and then came broad plains, and he went to the fairs and made the snake dance, and people left their rice-shops and cotton-ware shops and the bellowing cattle and the yoked threshers and the querns and the kilns, and came to hear him play the music and to see the snake dance. They gave him food and fruit and cloth, but when they said, "Here's a coin," he said, "Nay." And the snake was right glad of it, for it hated to kill Moti Khan till he had found God, and it himself hated to die. Now, when Moti Khan had crossed the Narbuda and the Pervan and the Bhagirath, he came to the Jumna, and through long Agra he passed making the snake dance, and yet he could not find God and he was sore in soul with it. And the serpent was bothersome.

But at Fatehpur Sikri, he said, "Here is Sheikh Chisti's tomb and I would rather starve and die than go one thumb-length more." He sat by Sheikh Chisti's tomb and he said, "Sheikh Chisti, what is this Fate has sent me? This serpent is a very wicked thing. He just hisses and spits fire at every wink and waver. He says, 'Find God.' Now, tell me, Sheikh Chisti, how can I find Him? Till I find Him I will not leave this spot."

But even as he prayed he saw snakes sprout through his head, fountains splashed and snakes fell gently to the sides like the waters by the Taj, and through them came women, soft women, dancing women, round hips, betel-chewed lips, round breasts—shy some were, while some were only minxes—and they came from the right and went to the left, and they pulled at his beard—and, suddenly, white serpents burst through the earth and enveloped them all, but Moti Khan would not move. He said: "Sheikh Chisti, I am in a strange world, But there is a darker world I see behind, and beyond that dark, dark world, I see a brighter world, and there, there must be Allah."

For twenty-nine days he knelt there, his hands pressed against his ears, his face turned toward Sheikh Chisti's tomb. And people came and said, "Wake up, old man, wake up"; but he would not answer. And when they found the snake lying on the tomb of Sheikh Chisti they cried, "This is a strange thing," and they took to their heels; while others came and brought *mullahs* and *maulvis*[8] but Moti Khan would not answer. For, to speak the truth, he was crossing through the dark waters, where one strains and splashes, and where the sky is all cold, and the stars all dead, and till man come to the other shore, there shall be neither peace nor God.

---

[7]The tomb of a Muslim holy man. [eds.]

[8]*Mullahs* and *maulvis* are Muslim religious leaders. [eds.]

On the twenty-ninth night Sheikh Chisti woke from his tomb and came, his skull-cap and all, and said: "My son, what may I give you?"

"Peace from this serpent—and God."

"My son, God is not to be seen. He is everywhere."

"Eyes to see God, for I cannot any more go northward."

"Eyes to discern God you shall have."

"Then peace from this serpent."

"Faithful shall he be, true companion of the God-seeker."

"Peace to all men and women," said Moti Khan.

"Peace to all mankind. Further, Moti Khan, I have something to tell you; as dawn breaks Maulvi Mohammed Khan will come to offer you his daughter, fair as an oleander. She has been waiting for you and she will wed you. My blessings on you, my son!"

"Allah is found! Victory to Allah!" cried Moti Khan. The serpent flung round him, slipped between his feet and curled round his neck and danced on his head, for, when Moti Khan found God, his sins would be worn out like the quern-stone with the grindings of man, and there would be peace in all mankind.

Moti Khan married the devout daughter of Maulvi Mohammed Khan and he loved her well, and he settled down in Fatehpur Sikri and became the guardian of Sheikh Chisti's tomb. The serpent lived with him, and now and again he was taken to the fair to play for the children.

One day, however, Moti Khan's wife died and was buried in a tomb of black marble. Eleven months later Moti Khan died and he was given a white marble tomb, and a dome of the same stone, for both. Three days after that the serpent died too, and they buried him in the earth beside the *dargah*, and gave him a nice clay tomb. A *peepal* sprang up on it, and a passing brahmin planted a *neem*[9] tree by the *peepal*, and some merchant in the village gave money to build a platform round them. The *peepal* rose to the skies and covered the dome with dark, cool shade, and brahmins planted snake-stones under it, and bells rang and camphors were lit, and marriage couples went round the platform in circumambulation. When the serpent was offered the camphor, Moti Khan had the incense. And when illness comes to the town, with music and flags and torches do we go, and we fall in front of the *peepal* platform and we fall prostrate before the *dargah*, and right through the night a wind rises and blows away the foul humors of the village. And when children cry, you say, "Moti Khan will cure you, my treasure," and they are cured. Emperors and kings have come and gone but never have they destroyed our village. For man and serpent are friends, and Moti Khan found God.

---

[9]Peepal and neem are kinds of trees; peepal is a holy tree. [eds.]

Between Agra and Fatehpur Sikri you may still find the little tomb and the *peepal*. Boys have written their names on the walls and dust and leaves cover the gold and blue of the pall. But someone has dug a well by the side, and if thirst takes you on the road, you can take a drink and rest under the *peepal*, and think deeply of God.

❈ Discussion and Writing

1. Why is the brahmin born as a serpent: what is the brahmin's role in determining his destiny; what is his function as a serpent?
2. What is Moti Khan's role: as a vehicle for the serpent's salvation; as a follower of Allah; in his weaknesses for women?
3. Analyze the mingling of the authorities of the Hindu goddess and Allah: describe the human weaknesses castigated through the divine intervention. In what ways is the quotation of Hafiz relevant to the story?
4. What is the implication of the companionship of the reborn serpent and Moti Khan, who, as a Muslim, does not believe in rebirth?
5. Explain the duality of the serpent's benevolent role (consistent with the Hindu tradition) and his being Satan (according to Muslim tradition). What is the significance of connecting the two antithetical traditions?
6. Discuss the significance of the holy *peepal* tree (according to Hindu tradition) and the graves of the pious (in Muslim tradition) in the village square. Elaborate on the importance of the trio's monument in people's life.
7. Analyze Raja Rao's mingling of the disparate aspects of two religious traditions, without diminishing or altering the basics of either.

❈ Research and Comparison

Interdisciplinary Discussion Question: Research the twentieth-century history of the Hindu-Muslim conflict in India. Keeping in mind this rift, discuss the significance of "Companions" and its central idea of harmonious coexistence. Comment on the more recent conflicts of the 1980s and 1990s.

Interdisciplinary Discussion Question: Research the mythic image of the serpent in various cultures of the world, its importance, its diverse meanings. Compare any two or more traditions as portrayed in any two or more stories in this anthology.

Faiz Ahmed Faiz
(1911–1984)
Pakistan

Faiz Ahmed Faiz was born in the Punjab, India, and came of age during the struggle for independence from British rule. After that battle was won in 1947, however, came the division of India; he settled in the new nation of Pakistan, where he became editor of the *Pakistan Times*. He was a student of literature, holding two master's degrees: one in Arabic literature and the other in English. An immensely humane person, he was a student of history and a dedicated Marxist. Because of his public stature, the various Pakistani governments viewed him as potentially dangerous; he was imprisoned twice, once for four years when he was sentenced to death and kept in solitary confinement. After his release, he gained and lost several positions, depending on the government in power, was imprisoned again, and lived in exile for many years before returning to Lahore, Pakistan. While in exile in Beirut, Lebanon, he edited *Lotus,* the journal of the Afro-Asian Writers Association.

Considered one of the major twentieth-century poets, Faiz Ahmed Faiz was exceptionally popular. He wrote in his native Urdu, manipulating the rich traditions of Urdu poetry. In the nineteenth century, for instance, poets always concealed their political intentions: when the British hanged some thirty thousand people in response to the 1857 war of resistance, the British were not identified in poems describing the event. It was too risky. In similar fashion, Faiz extended the conventional significance of the Beloved to include the Revolution as well as friend, woman, God. Faiz also wrote traditional love poetry. In addition, he turned to older forms of versification, and was acclaimed a master of the *ghazal.* The *ghazal,* a medieval genre, calls for a strict pattern of at least four rhymed couplets, linked by rhyme and a repeated phrase, and following a set meter. Since it is very difficult to maintain these requirements in translation, many translators prefer to adjust the form in order to project the feeling and ideas of the poem, as in this example of Faiz's *ghazals.*

Ghazal*

We all were killed
this our final
triumph

---

*Translated by Agha Shahid Ali

for we did reach the destination
we met your challenge
Beloved Revolution

and returned after dying
Oh victory

Whether eyes aflame
or minds lit up by suns
or a solitary heart in ashes

Love
each final fire
emerged from your door

shaped thus
by your grace or disdain

As such I came away from the evening
everyone still there with you
among the lights

only the heart felt
its terrible defeat

only it knew its desolation

and it could speak
only to itself

Each footstep meant death
and even the promise of life

for I've returned from the lane
where the executioner lives

I've loitered there
as if to get some air

casually
I've strolled by his door

Faiz
be grateful to autumn

to its cold winds

that are seasoned postmen
carrying letters as mere habit

from spring

its custom to announce thus
that it will surely come

❋ **Discussion and Writing**

1. To whom is the *ghazal* addressed? Explain the paradox of death and victory.
2. Why does the persona feel defeated and isolated despite the victory in the revolution?
3. What do the antithetical images in the last two verses signify?
4. Elaborate on the implications of the juxtaposed paradoxes in the entire poem. Relate the imagery to the form of the *ghazal*.

❋ **Research and Comparison**

Interdisciplinary Discussion Question: Examine the spirit of nationalism depicted in the works of any major writer from Pakistan.

Umashankar Joshi
(1911–1988)
India

Umashankar Joshi was born in the small village of Bamma at the foot of one of the Aravalli hills in Sabarkantha, Gujarat, in western India. The village, isolated, caste-ridden, and orthodox, was under the jurisdiction of an oppressive prince; the villagers were mainly poor, illiterate, and of the brahmin caste. Joshi's father, the manager of small estates in the village, had been educated by Christian missionaries and, disturbed by the inadequacy of the local school, sent his sons to a nearby town and then to Ahmadabad for their schooling. Joshi attributed the lyricism of his poetry, however, to the dialect spoken in his village. He grew up influenced by Mahatma Gandhi's noncooperation movement and the spirit of his reformist nationalism, as, he maintains, did his generation of Gujarati poets. He was imprisoned for his political activism, during which time, he studied Marx. From then on, the ideal of equality and social justice remained at the base of his thinking and work, even when he moved beyond Marxist aesthetics.

Writing in Gujarati, Joshi came to represent the experimental trends, both in content and style, of his generation: he became one of the originators of the "new poetics" in Gujarati literature. He also became one of the leading literary critics, vice chancelor of Gujarat University, and the director of Sahitya Akademi—the Indian National Institute of Literature—receiving the prestigious Bharatiya Jnanpith award in 1967. Liberating poetic language from the pedantic artificiality of the preceding age, he wrote in all genres. In his work, he merged motifs drawn from legendary tales of reform and the actual experience of uprisings among the poor, manipulating his ideological concerns with a fine irony. Poetry was his métier, and he excelled in, and developed, the *Natya Rupak* form, a dialogue in verse, concentrating on a dramatic epiphanic moment. Ultimately, he integrated Gandhian compassion, Marxist ideals, and the Upanishadic spiritual search for oneness with the universe.

*The Universal Man**

I shall take two stars for eyes
And with them scan the horizon at a glance;
I shall cut through the phantasm of clouds
And see unbroken all eternity.

Making wings of dawn and dusk,
I'll become a traveler to ascending infinity,
Sailing along the stars in a skiff, the moon,
Or befriend the meteor on its path.

I shall shatter the bonds of my identity
And spread the scent of my mind about the universe,
Dapple my wings with dark and light
And imbue all places with my heart's love.

No more just an individual. I will become a Universal Man
And touch the dust of earth to my brow.

❊ Discussion and Writing

1. What is the persona's fantasy; which elements of the universe does he borrow; what is their significance?
2. What does he take from the earth? What does his final act symbolize?

Translated by Prakash Desai and Carlo Coppola

3. Discuss the implication of the annihilation of one's individual identity to become a universal man.

❋ Research and Comparison

Interdisciplinary Discussion Question: The search for one's identity became a vital issue in the Indian Renaissance of the late nineteenth and early twentieth centuries. Examine the convergence of the universal and the national, the personal and the public in the works of any major Indian writer of this century.

Bienvenido N. Santos
(b. 1911)
Philippines

Bienvenido Santos was born in Manila, the Philippines, into a Pampangueno family. He received his bachelor of science degree in education from the University of the Philippines and a government pension to study in the United States. Before coming to the United States in 1941, however, he had already published a story in an anthology of Filipino stories written in English. During the years of World War II, he left his studies at Columbia University to work alongside other Filipino exiles in Washington. (He received his master of arts degree from the University of Illinois.) Touring the United States for the Office of Education, he met other exiles, many of whom he identified as "the hurt people," "the so-called Pinoys," the older (often poor) people who had emigrated long before the war. Lonely and isolated, they dreamed of home: of *bayanihan* (the sense of community) and *damay* (their face-to-face relations). In 1955, he published *You Lovely People,* drawing on his experiences. He wrote about the people he met, their unrealized aspirations, and the tension between their sense of solidarity and the North American ideal of individualism. In his subsequent novels and stories, he remained dedicated to his compatriots, especially to the exiles who retained their sense of honor and humor along with their desire to return home. In "Footnote to a Laundry List" (1967), he revealed the ironic predicament of fulfilling that goal.

Bienvenido Santos considered himself an exile even though he taught at various universities in the United States and became a naturalized citizen in 1976. He traveled between the two countries, always planning to stay among his family near the foot of the volcano Mount Mayon. He left various positions at universities in the Philippines, from president to professor, at first to study and then to teach in the United States, but when

Ferdinand Marcos declared martial law in 1972, Santos was stranded in San Francisco. For a year he found himself in a position similar to that of the people he met on his first tour of the United States: unable to find work and longing for home.

Footnote to a Laundry List

The August heat was too much even for those who were used to it. For Dr. N. B. Carlos, who had just arrived from the States, it was unbearable. The damp, sticky heat made him sweat with the least exertion, not necessarily physical, like thinking. He had to change shirts between classes, which was quite inconvenient as the only place in the University where he could hide was the men's room, which smelled and had no lock that would keep the door shut. It was worse before the rains. Like now. The sun shone through overcast skies and faintly, he could hear the rumble of thunder on the seaside. For this and for another much stronger reason, he didn't look forward to the hearing scheduled that morning, which, he was afraid, was going to be held again in the Chairman's stuffy office overlooking the slums of the provincial city.

Somehow he felt relieved when a few minutes before the appointed hour, he received a note from the Secretary of the Committee on Discipline, that the hearing would be held in the President's air-conditioned office. The President, an old man with young dreams, must be out of town again.

Dr. Carlos had been in the President's office once or twice before and he remembered the soft lights, the softer voice of the man behind the wide mahogany desk, the coolness of the scented air. Getting into it, with the door closing automatically behind him, was like stepping into a strange land with autumn colors and lights and autumn coolness; stepping out, like walking into the hold of a freighter where the engines are—and it always startled him to see outside the President's office, fresh looking girls and cool boys, walking about the burning campus as if it were the Elysian fields, instead of half-naked men stoking furnaces, their hairy bodies dripping with sweat.

When the heat became oppressive, he wished he had not left the States. True, summer in New York was just as bad, often worse, but there was always autumn to look forward to, and winter and spring. And he didn't have to stay in New York in summer. There were camps of all sorts up north just below the Canadian border where there was work, cool nights, and fun. There had been summers when he earned enough to see him through school the entire year, penny pinching, of course, all along the way. But he was used to that.

After getting his Ph.D., somehow the title felt like a load he could not carry well whenever he was forced to take a menial job, no matter how well it paid. Meanwhile, his cousins in the Philippines had been writing him that now was the time to return and cash in on his Ph.D. and perhaps settle down.

At forty, he didn't feel too old; still, there were the bleak years ahead he kept seeing before him. Dr. Carlos was not unattractive, but he was shy. In class, his voice barely reached the back row and his students had to strain their ears to understand this man with an accent who seemed to be saying important things in a dull, ineffectual way. After a while, they stopped trying to understand whatever it was he was saying. He didn't make sense. His jokes were not funny at all, except to him. He laughed loud and alone. If his students stayed awake at all, it must have been due to something else like the heat, or some of them must have kept hoping that with his Ph.D. from Columbia and that accent, he was bound to say something sensible one of these humid days.

His colleagues on the campus did not believe him at first when he said that he had no family.

"You mean you don't have your family here with you," Professor Teves said.

"No, I don't mean that," Dr. Carlos explained. "I'm not married, that's what I'm trying to tell you."

"You've been in the States these many years. How can you still be single?"

"What's strange about that?" Dr. Carlos tried to defend himself.

"You are joking, Dr. Carlos. I understand that in the States. . . "

Here we go again, Dr. Carlos said to himself, closing his ears to the innuendo and the direct statement of free love in America, open love-making, immorality on the campus, right in girls' dorms and homes, with membership in fraternities and sororities mere excuses for promiscuity. He had heard these stories himself and had seen men and women in summer camps where he had worked, cuddling under blankets. But it was not as general as it was made to appear. As far as he was concerned, he remembered only the hard times, the struggling to keep himself in school, the little hurts and the big fears. He closed his mind to these, shaking his head.

At forty, he easily chickened out. Never endowed in his younger years with the courage one often needed to go through an experience without bruises, at forty, he had practically given up trying to do anything about, say, getting himself a wife, which, to him, required courage, more than anything else.

As an adolescent before and during the war, he had liked girls in the neighborhood in Palomar where he lived with an elderly brother who had a family of his own. He used to beat class in night school to accompany a pretty seamstress who had just arrived from Pampanga and didn't speak Tagalog well. He gave her lessons, which they both enjoyed. He liked her eyes and her dimples and the frightened way she clutched at him the first time he kissed her on the mouth at the foot of the bamboo stairs, where chickens roosted and cackled all over the place while the lovers struggled in the dark. Pacing loved him with a trembly, panicky sort of love while she kept insisting that he didn't love her as much as she did, which he persistently denied until later when he realized that she was, indeed, right, he didn't. He couldn't remember now how their little affair had ended. How did they break up? Did they? Pacing was a cry-baby. She still looked pretty when she smiled with her tears rolling down her cheeks and her body shaking in his arms as though it were a fearsome thing to be there in his arms where she loved to be. Where could she be now? He had heard that she was married now to someone from her own province who sold floor wax and looked like Jose Rizal. Perhaps he had loved her after all. The trouble was, he never knew. How did one know?

Paula Weeks still wrote to him. She worked with the United Nations in New York. If she loved him, why were her letters without passion? Most of them read like reports to the Unesco. Paula and he had classes together in Columbia for a term, then she quit school—work at the office was too much—and later transferred to NYU, where he would have gone, too, except that he would have to lose residence in Columbia where he had started working for his Ph.D. Yet he knew she did—love him. She told him so. In the middle of a statistical peroration on the rising cost of commodities, she wrote: "I had to handcarry an urgent note to the Librarian of the Public Library and suddenly, I realized that I had been there before—with you. How I missed you, darling. I love you, Nap. When are we ever going to see each other again?" Her question sounded more like his own.

Perhaps if he had decided to stay on in the States, he could have married her, but he had no intention of taking her to the Philippines. Paula wouldn't be able to survive any day in August. She would go nuts. At least, she would keep saying, "I'm going nuts" till she might actually be and to show her sympathy, he might go loco himself. Now, of course, if he were rich enough, say, to install her in an air-conditioned home, that would be different. Paula loved winter. He used to meet her after classes when he was not too busy with his research and they would walk arm in arm through the snow and the slush. Paula loved every moment of it.

All memories of tenderness with Paula were winter memories. She was closest to him in winter despite the heavy suits they wore. In summer she couldn't bear for him to touch her. When they held hands, their palms stuck wetly. It was embarrassing.

He had met her family once, soon after his graduation, when she took time off from her work at the United Nations and together they visited her family in Oneonta. Paula introduced him as Dr. Napoleon Carlos. It was the first time he heard himself called doctor and he was not too happy about it. Paula's father sold canned food of different kinds, but not once did Dr. Carlos get a chance to sample one of the flavors right in their own home.

There were freckles on Paula's nose and under her eyes. They started to show in spring. By summer, they were in full bloom. In winter, they were mere smudges that he tried to wipe off, asking, as he fingered each one of them, how long will you have these freckles? Why do you ask, you don't like them? I love them, he had replied, kissing her nose lightly. I'm going to have them all my life, she told him.

Yes, he could have stayed on and married Paula. She would be twenty-one now, no, twenty-two, much younger than he, but she wouldn't believe him when he told her his age.

It was raining hard when the *Dona Nati* left the wharf in New York harbor and Paula stood in the rain waving to him as he sought her out in the mist and waved back as soon as he recognized her. The rain was cool on his burning lips. They had kissed and kissed till his lips were sore and he felt a dryness in his throat neither rain nor drink could quench. During those days, while he was preparing to leave, Paula was around most of the time, helping him. There was the problem of what he was going to do with his winter suits. I'll store them for you, Paula said, until you call for them, adding, will you call for them? You know I will, he said. When? Sooner than you think, he told her with conviction. Shall I make out a receipt, she asked. He pulled her to him and they kissed again. How about that for a receipt, he said. No, I must list these suits, she said. She took them out one by one and folded them neatly and drew out a list in her own hand. Scribbling something like a foot-note at the bottom of the list, she called his attention to what she had written: not responsible in case of fire or damage or loss for reasons beyond our control. They laughed over the words, familiar to those who bother to read what is written in small print on laundry lists, but many times afterward, he could not recall what had made them laugh together.

Paula was brave. Yet, on the last day, on their way to the pier, she broke down. Perhaps I won't ever see you again, she cried. Give me a rain check, he said, trying to laugh over what he considered great wit, considering the rain and all. She smiled, too, laughed a little, but all he remembered was her whispering, I love you, I love you, as she clung to him in the rain.

It was a lonesome, miserable trip back home. He was sick every day of the first week, but at every port, he mailed her a letter. Each letter was a passionate avowal of love, no mention of seasickness. And he meant every word he wrote her then and since. Paula was quick to answer in the beginning. She owed him a couple of letters now.

Dr. Carlos read the notice signed by the Chairman of the Committee on Discipline: ". . . therefore, it is important that you attend this meeting to hear the side of the girl accused by Mrs. Estrella L. Vivo of having illicit relations with her husband. The accused, Miss Magdalena Barin, is a sophomore in the College of Education."

Miss Barin sat in the middle of a half-circle of chairs, everyone occupied by deans and senior members of the faculty, old men in varying stages of decay, and one woman, the bespectacled Dean of the College of Education, who spoke with a sidewise tilt of her head as if every word she said rang out banners and cheers for the victory of virtue over vice. Veins stood out on her hands and forehead like submerged eels trying to come out and join the fun. Dr. Carlos felt young in their midst and wondered, as he often did, how he happened to be a member of this particular committee in the University.

Miss Barin was small and perhaps still in her teens. She wore no makeup although her hair was neatly brushed back. She kept changing her position as though no matter how she sat, she was still exposed, naked to this half circle of old eyes observing her every move, listening to every nuance of her speech, as if tone could hide a lie and change of pitch repress the truth.

The Committee Chairman was direct and abrupt. Like a veteran orchestra leader, he had the members of his Committee under his baton, and they responded as he expected them to, in harmony, following up lead questions, stressing exclamations of censure, as though everything had been rehearsed and the long hours of rehearsal were now paying off magnificently. So wrapped up was everybody in the hearing, no one paid attention to Dr. Carlos who followed every movement of the girl, asking no questions himself, as though his part in the orchestra came near the end of the piece. Meanwhile, therefore, he could rest his cymbals or his flute on the music stand.

Are you acquainted with Mr. and Mrs. Sulpicio Vivo?

Yes, sir.

When was the last time you saw Mrs. Vivo?

Mrs. Vivo?

Yes, Mrs. Vivo.

Or perhaps you want to tell us the last time you saw Mr. Vivo.

Anything you wish, sir.

All right. When was the last time you saw Mr. Vivo?

Just a few minutes ago, sir.

Just a few minutes ago?

Yes, ma'am. He met me at the gate of the University and he told me he was leaving for Manila.

Did he say why he was leaving for Manila?

He was going to, I think, but I told him I was in a hurry. I had an appointment with . . . with this Committee at 9 o'clock.

Do you know why he was going to Manila?

As I said, sir . . .

What do you think?

I don't know, sir.

Did he ask you to go with him?

Ma'am?

You heard me.

Yes, ma'am, I heard you. But why should . . .

Could it be that he had quarreled with his wife—over you?

I don't know, sir. He didn't have a chance to say . . .

When was the last time you saw Mrs. Vivo?

The other Sunday, sir. At a party in their house. It was a birthday party, their youngest child's, I think.

Who invited you to the party?

Mrs. Vivo herself.

Oh, you are friends?

No, ma'am. We just know each other.

How did you get to know each other?

Her husband introduced us.

When was this?

At a dance. On the campus, sir. Last February. Valentine's Day.

The charges are: that you have been seeing each other, you and her husband; that you have been having illicit relations.

What do you say to these?

We have been seeing . . . I mean, he has been seeing me. I have asked him to go away and not see me every time he comes, but he insists, saying he can't help himself. But we have never had any of what you call that kind of relations.

Mrs. Vivo has a statement here supposed to have been made by a policeman who had been detailed to keep an eye on you and Mr. Vivo.

That's all lies, sir! He was a bad man, that policeman, threatening me, forcing me to sign all these lies. I told him he could kill me, but I wouldn't sign. Why. . . ?

Where does Mr. Vivo see you?

At home, I mean, at the boarding house where I occupy a room with other girls.

You are not alone in your room?

When I'm alone, yes, sir.

I mean, you don't occupy a room all by yourself?

No, sir. I can't afford that.

One allegation here is that Mr. Vivo buys you things.

He has bought me things, but I returned them, at least, those I could return.

What do you mean, those that you could return?

When he brings food from the Chinese restaurant, the other girls immediately begin eating it up, how can I return that *pancit*?[1] Besides, he looks so hurt when I insist that he take back what he is giving me, sometimes I don't have the heart . . .

Oh, come now, what girl doesn't welcome gifts?

Ma'am?

Mrs. Vivo went to your room once and found their radio on your bed. Do you deny this?

---

[1] A noodle dish. [eds.]

No, sir. But I have a radio, of my own. It's out of order. Mr. Vivo himself volunteered to have it repaired. Meanwhile, he lent me his radio.

Does he go to your room when the other girls are there?

Yes, sir. He just shows up.

Have you ever been alone together?

Yes, ma'am.

Where? In your boarding house? Somewhere else?

In my boarding house. Once . . . we went on a picnic, but it rained that day.

So?

We went back to town early and had lunch in a Chinese restaurant. All by ourselves.

Do your parents know about Mr. Vivo?

I have no more parents, sir.

Who supports you?

I have an aunt, sir. An old maid aunt who's a teacher.

Why do you go out with a married man?

I'm sorry, sir.

Do you love him?

I don't know, sir. He's very kind to me.

But you know he is married.

Yes, sir. But I'm not marrying him. We don't . . .

Does he make love to you?

No, ma'am. He simply likes being with me, he says. He laughs a lot when we are together.

Mrs. Vivo claims that she found some of her husband's shirts in your room.

Yes, he leaves his shirts there.

Scandalous!

Ma'am? I thought nothing about it. You see, one day he complained of the heat. It was too much, he said, I think I should bring an extra shirt so that I can change when I have to. He catches cold easily. So the next time he came, he brought a shirt with him.

These shirts Mrs. Vivo found in your room were clean.

I washed them. They were dirty.

Scandalous! You're not his wife.

When my father was still living . . .

Never mind your father.

I'm sorry, ma'am. I didn't think it was wrong. He has been so kind. It was not hard to do. I wash my own things.

Why did you enroll in my College?

I want to be a teacher, ma'am.

What kind of teacher do you expect to be?

Well . . . if I could be like my aunt . . .

Does your aunt know about Mr. Vivo?

I have not seen her since June. She's always busy, sir. She teaches in a coastal town far from our barrio. She has to take a boat. When the weather is bad . . .

According to this police report . . .

That's all lies, sir, I told you.

Let me read it to you.

I have already read it, sir. It's lies, lies!

For the sake of the members of the Committee as a matter of record . . .

I move that it be off the record, if that is your wish, Mr. Chairman. We all have been furnished a copy. Besides, what are we trying to do?

Don't you know, Dr. Carlos?

I'm asking you, Mr. Chairman.

Let me quote from the Code of Conduct, Article VII, Section 1, subsection 3: "In extreme cases, such as gross immorality, the student may be expelled from the University. Expulsion debars any student from admission in any public school or private school recognized by the government." Have I answered your question, *Doctor?*

Thank you, sir, but don't you think you have asked Miss Barin enough questions?

You haven't asked a single question yet, Dr. Carlos.

No, I haven't. That's right. I thought everybody was doing pretty well.

Dr. Carlos tried to smile as he looked around him. The lady Dean's face was a mask of fury.

The girl had turned toward Dr. Carlos. "All I ask, sir," she said, "is that I be allowed to quit . . . if you don't want me here anymore."

"It isn't as simple as that, I'm afraid," the Chairman interrupted her, "unless the Committee . . . "

"She's asking to be allowed to quit," Dr. Carlos said with more volume than accent in his voice and tone. "That's good enough for me. As a matter of fact, if you are asking me, sir, she doesn't have to quit."

"What?" the lady Dean practically screamed.

Dr. Carlos turned his back to her, saying, "I find the accused innocent of all the charges. She told us everything, a lot of things she didn't have to admit, she has admitted to us. She is innocent, I repeat."

A sob broke out from the center of the agitated circle. The crumpled handkerchief she covered her face with was too small, the tears fell on her lap, through her fingers. As her body shook, her short legs dangled and her moccasins fell on the floor under her chair where she had kicked them. A stained bit of paper shaped to fit the inside of one shoe stuck out like a tongue.

Finally, the girl raised her head, her face wet and her eyes red and swollen. Her lips trembled as she talked.

"Sir, may I quit?" She looked around, then felt for her shoes under the chair without taking her eyes off the powerful people.

No one spoke.

"Go home, child," Dr. Carlos said, softly, but his words rang in the room like the strangest sound, not flute, but cymbals crashing out of tune.

The girl stood up, seeking the door. Standing so close, Dr. Carlos noticed how short and frail she looked . Where was she going now? To fry out there on the burning campus? Where else? There was no coolness anywhere. It was not going to rain for a long, long time. My, how short she was. If Paula put her arms around her, she would have to stoop and Paula wasn't very tall herself.

❀ Discussion and Writing

1. What aspects of life in the Philippines require the most adjustment for Dr. Carlos on his return from the United States? Comment on the impact of his stay abroad on his thinking.
2. Examine Dr. Carlos's relationships with Pacing and Paula. Why did his affairs end? How are these experiences pertinent to his attitude in Ms. Barin's hearing?
3. Develop a critique of the Committee's proceedings: the social norms that determined the Committee's objective; the role of the police department; the significance of Dr. Carlos's words sounding like cymbals.
4. Discuss the implications of Ms. Barin wanting to quit even though she is innocent.
5. What is the significance of the footnote "not responsible in case of fire or damage or loss for reasons beyond our control"?
6. Analyze the separate but interlinked narratives and the tone the author adopts.

❀ Research and Comparison

Interdisciplinary Discussion Question: Research the history of the Philippines, concentrating on the impact of the continued experience of colonization—first by Spain and then the United States—and its impact on the lives of its people. Examine the portrayal of this experience in the works of any major writer of the Philippines.

Amador Daguio
(1912–1966)
Philippines

Amador Daguio was born and raised in the mountainous region of northern Luzon, the Philippines, the home of the Kalinga people. While he was still studying at the University of the Philippines, he received several awards for his poetry and fiction; he wrote in English. He taught for several years, continuing to publish his work, and during World War II, the Tacloban Theater Guild, which he had created, presented two of his plays. His founding the guild in historic Leyte Province was an act of defiance against Japanese control. During the early 1950s he attended the Stanford University Creative Writing Center—translating Kalinga harvest songs as his master's project—and then studied law when he returned to the Philippines. As a lawyer, he held various governmental posts, and as an author, he lectured at many universities. In "Wedding Dance," written and published during his stay at Stanford (1953), he spun a tale from the traditional Kalinga material with which he was working. His use of this material was part of his concept of a national literature, to be brought about, as he said, "through national consciousness and national individuality," a true "recreating of the Malayan spirit."

Wedding Dance

Awiyao reached for the upper horizontal log which served as the edge of the head-high threshold. Clinging to the log, he lifted himself with one bound that carried him across to the narrow door. He slid back the cover, stepped inside, then pushed the cover back in place. After some moments during which he seemed to wait, he talked to the listening darkness.

"I'm sorry this had to be done. I am really sorry. But neither of us can help it."

The sound of the *gangsas* beat through the walls of the dark house, like muffled roars of falling waters. The woman who had moved with a start when the sliding door opened had been hearing the *gangsas* for she did not know how long. The sudden rush of the rich sounds when the door opened was like a sharp gush of fire in her. She gave no sign that she heard Awiyao, but continued to sit unmoving in the darkness.

But Awiyao knew that she had heard him and his heart pitied her. He crawled on all fours to the middle of the room; he knew exactly where the stove was. With bare fingers he stirred the covered smoldering embers, and blew into them. When the coals began to glow, Awiyao put pieces of pine on them, then full round logs as big as his arms. The room brightened.

Why don't you go out," he said, "and join the dancing women?" He felt a pang inside him, because what he said was really not the right thing to say and because the woman did not stir. "You should join the dancers," he said, "as if—as if nothing has happened." He looked at the woman huddled in a corner of the room, leaning against the wall. The stove fire played with strange moving shadows and lights upon her face. She was partly sullen, but her sullenness was not because of anger or hate.

"Go out—go out and dance. If you really don't hate me for this separation, go out and dance. One of the men will see you dance well; he will like your dancing; he will marry you. Who knows but that, with him, you will be luckier than you were with me."

"I don't want any man," she said sharply. "I don't want any other man."

He felt relieved that at least she talked: "You know very well that I don't want any other woman, either. You know that, don't you? Lumnay, you know it, don't you?"

She did not answer him.

"You know it, Lumnay, don't you?" he repeated.

"Yes, I know," she said weakly.

"It is not my fault," he said, feeling relieved. "You cannot blame me; I have been a good husband to you."

"Neither can you blame me," she said. She seemed about to cry.

"No, you have been very good to me. You have been a good wife. I have nothing to say against you." He set some of the burning wood in place. "It's only that a man must have a child. Seven harvests is just too long to wait. Yes, we have waited too long. We should have another chance before it is too late for both of us."

This time the woman stirred, stretched her right leg out and bent her left leg in. She wound the blanket more snugly around herself.

"You know that I have done my best," she said. "I have prayed to Kabunyan much. I have sacrificed many chickens in my prayers."

"Yes, I know."

"You remember how angry you were once when you came home from your work in the terrace because I butchered one of our pigs without your permission? I did it to appease Kabunyan, because, like you, I wanted to have a child. But what could I do?"

"Kabunyan does not see fit for us to have a child," he said. He stirred the fire. The sparks rose through the crackles of the flames. The smoke and soot went up to the ceiling.

Lumnay looked down and unconsciously started to pull at the rattan that kept the split bamboo flooring in place. She tugged at the rattan flooring. Each time she did this the split bamboo went up and came down with a slight rattle. The gongs of the dancers clamorously called in her ears through the walls.

Awiyao went to the corner where Lumnay sat, paused before her, looked at her bronzed and sturdy face, then turned to where the jars of water stood piled one over the other. Awiyao took a coconut cup and dipped it in the top jar and drank. Lumnay had filled the jars from the mountain creek early that evening.

"I came home," he said, "because I did not find you among the dancers. Of course, I am not forcing you to come, if you don't want to join my wedding ceremony. I came to tell you that Madulimay, although I am marrying her, can never become as good as you are. She is not as strong in planting beans, nor as fast in cleaning water jars, nor as good in keeping a house clean. You are one of the best wives in the whole village."

"That has not done me any good, has it?" she said. She looked at him lovingly. She almost seemed to smile.

He put the coconut cup aside on the floor and came closer to her. He held her face between his hands, and looked longingly at her beauty. But her eyes looked away. Never again would he hold her face. The next day she would not be his anymore. She would go back to her parents. He let go of her face, and she bent to the floor again and looked at her fingers as they tugged softly at the split bamboo floor.

"This house is yours," he said, "I built it for you. Make your own, live in it as long as you wish. I will build another house for Madulimay."

"I have no need for a house," she said slowly. "I'll go to my own house. My parents are old. They will need help in the planting of the beans, in the pounding of the rice."

"I will give you the field that I dug out of the mountain during the first year of our marriage," he said. "You know I did it for you. You helped me to make it for the two of us."

"I have no use for any field," she said.

He looked at her, then turned away, and became silent. They were silent for a time.

"Go back to the dance," she said finally. "It is not right for you to be here. They will wonder where you are, and Madulimay will not feel good. Go back to the dance."

"I would feel better if you would come, and dance—for the last time. The *gangsas* are playing."

"You know that I cannot."

"Lumnay," he said tenderly. "Lumnay, if I did this it is because of my need for a child. You know that life is not worth living without a child. The men have mocked me behind my back. You know that."

"I know it," she said. "I will pray that Kabunyan will bless you and Madulimay."

She bit her lips now, then shook her head wildly, and sobbed.

She thought of the seven harvests that had passed, the high hopes they had in the beginning of their new life, the day he took her away from her parents across the roaring river, on the other side of the mountain, the trip up the trail which they had to climb, the steep canyon which they had to cross—the waters boiled in her mind in foams of white and jade and roaring silver; the waters rolled and growled, resounded thunderous echoes through the walls of the stiff cliffs; they were far away now but loud still and receding; the waters violently smashed down from somewhere on the tops of the other ranges, and they had looked carefully at the buttresses of rocks they had to step on—a slip would have meant death.

They both drank of the water, then rested on the other bank before they made the final climb to the other side of the mountain.

She looked at his face with the fire playing upon his features—hard and strong, and kind. He had a sense of lightness in his way of saying things, which often made her and the village people laugh. How proud she had been of his humor. The muscles were taut and firm, bronze and compact in their hold upon his skull—how frank his bright eyes were. She looked at his body that carved out of the mountains five fields for her; his wide and supple torso heaved as if a slab of shining lumber were heaving; his arms and legs flowed down in fluent muscles—he was strong and for that she had lost him.

She flung herself upon his knees and clung to them. "Awiyao, Awiyao, my husband," she cried. "I did everything to have a child," she said passionately in a hoarse whisper. "Look at me," she cried. "Look at my body. Then it was full of promise. It could dance; it could work fast in the fields; it could climb the mountains fast. Even now it is firm, full. But, Awiyao, Kabunyan never blessed me. Awiyao, Kabunyan is cruel to me. Awiyao, I am useless, I must die."

"It will not be right to die," he said, gathering her in his arms. Her whole warm naked breast quivered against his own; she clung now to his neck, and her head lay upon his right shoulder; her hair flowed down in cascades of gleaming darkness.

"I don't care about the fields," she said. "I don't care about the house. I don't care for anything but you. I'll have no other man."

"Then you'll always be fruitless."

"I'll go back to my father. I'll die."

"Then you hate me," he said. "If you die it means you hate me. You do not want me to have a child. You do not want my name to live on in our tribe."

She was silent.

"If I do not try a second time," he explained, "it means I'll die. Nobody will get the fields I have carved out of the mountains; nobody will come after me."

"If you fail—if you fail this second time—" she said thoughtfully. Then her voice was a shudder. "No—no, I don't want you to fail."

"If I fail," he said, "I'll come back to you. Then both of us will die together. Both of us will vanish from the life of our tribe."

The gongs thundered through the walls of their house, sonorous and far away.

"I'll keep my beads," she said. "Awiyao, let me keep my beads," she half-whispered.

"You will keep the beads. They come from far-off times. My grandmother said they came from way up North, from the slant-eyed people across the sea. You keep them, Lumnay. They are worth twenty fields."

"I'll keep them because they stand for the love you have for me." she said. "I love you. I love you and have nothing to give."

She took herself away from him, for a voice was calling out to him from outside. "Awiyao! Awiyao! O Awiyao! They are looking for you at the dance!"

"I am not in a hurry."

"The elders will scold you. You had better go."

"Not until you tell me that it is all right with you."

"It is all right with me."

"He clasped her hands. "I do this for the sake of the tribe," he said.

"I know," she said.

"He went to the door.

"Awiyao!"

He stopped as if suddenly hit by a spear. In pain he turned to her. Her face was agony. It pained him to leave. She had been wonderful to him. What was it that made a man wish for a child? What was it in life, in the work in the fields, in the planting and harvest, in the silence of the night, in the communings with husband and wife, in the whole life of the tribe itself that made man wish for the laughter and speech of a child? Suppose he changed his mind? Why did the unwritten law demand, anyway, that a man, to be a man, must have a child to come after him? And if he was fruitless— but he loved Lumnay. It was like taking away half of his life to leave her like this.

"Awiyao," she said, and her eyes seemed to smile in the light. "The beads!"

He turned back and walked to the farthest corner of their room, to the trunk where they kept their worldly possessions—battle-ax and his spear points, her betel-nut box and her beads. He dug out from the darkness the beads which had been given to him by his grandmother to give to Lumnay on the day of his marriage. He went to her, lifted her head, put the beads on, and tied them in place. The white and jade and orange obsidians shone in the firelight. She suddenly clung to him, clung to his neck, as if she would never let him go.

"Awiyao! Awiyao, it is hard!" She gasped, and she closed her eyes and buried her face in his neck.

The call for him from the outside repeated; her grip loosened and he hurried out into the night.

Lumnay sat for some time in the darkness. Then she went to the door and opened it. The moonlight struck her face; the moonlight spilled itself upon the whole village.

She could hear the throbbing of the *gangsas* coming to her through the caverns of the other houses. She knew that all the houses were empty; that the whole tribe was at the dance. Only she was absent. And yet was she not the best dancer of the village? Did she not have the most lightness and grace? Could she not, alone among all the women, dance like a bird tripping for grains on the ground, beautifully timed to the beat of the *gangsas*? Did not the men praise her supple body, and the women envy the way she stretched her hands like the wings of the mountain eagle now and then as she danced? How long ago did she dance at her own wedding? Tonight, all the women who counted, who once danced in her honor, were dancing now in honor of another whose only claim was that perhaps she could give her husband a child.

"It is not right. It is not right!" she cried. "How does she know? How can anybody know? It is not right," she said.

Suddenly she found courage. She would go to the dance. She would go to the chief of the village, to the elders, to tell them it was not right. Awiyao was hers; nobody could take him away from her. Let her be the first woman to complain, to denounce the unwritten rule that a man may take another woman. She would break the dancing of the men and women. She would tell Awiyao to come back to her. He surely would relent. Was not their love as strong as the river?

She made for the other side of the village where the dancing was. There was a flaming glow over the whole place; a great bonfire was burning. The *gangsas* clamored more loudly now, and it seemed they were calling to her. She was near at last. She could see the dancers clearly now. The men leaped lightly with their *gangsas* as they circled the dancing women decked in feast garments and beads, tripping on the ground like graceful birds, following their men. Her heart warmed to the flaming call of the dance; strange heat in her blood welled up, and she started to run.

But the flaming brightness of the bonfire commanded her to stop. Did anybody see her approach? She stopped. What if somebody had seen her coming? The flames of the bonfire leaped in countless sparks which spread and rose like yellow points and died out in the night. The blaze reached out to her like a spreading radiance. She did not have the courage to break into the wedding feast.

Lumnay walked away from the dancing ground, away from the village. She thought of the new clearing of beans which Awiyao and she had started to make only four moons before. She followed the trail above the village.

When she came to the mountain stream she crossed it carefully. Nobody held her hands, and the stream water was very cold. The trail went up again, and she was in the moonlight shadows among the trees and shrubs. Slowly she climbed the mountain.

When Lumnay reached the clearing, she could see from where she stood the blazing bonfire at the edge of the village, where the dancing was. She could hear the far-off clamor of the gongs, still rich in their sonorousness, echoing from mountain to mountain. The sound did not mock her; they seemed to call far to her; speak to her in the language of unspeaking love. She felt the pull of their clamor, almost the feeling that they were telling to her their gratitude for her sacrifice. Her heartbeat began to sound to her like many *gangsas*.

Lumnay thought of Awiyao as the Awiyao she had known long ago—a strong, muscular boy carrying his heavy loads of fuels logs down the mountains to his home. She had met him one day as she was on her way to fill her clay jars with water. He had stopped at the spring to drink and rest; and she had made him drink the cool mountain water from her coconut shell. After that it did not take him long to decide to throw his spear on the stairs of her father's house in token of his desire to marry her.

The mountain clearing was cold in the freezing moonlight. The wind began to sough and stir the leaves of the bean plants. Lumnay looked for a big rock on which to sit down. The bean plants now surrounded her, and she was lost among them.

A few more weeks, a few more months, a few more harvests—what did it matter? She would be holding the bean flowers, soft in the texture, silken almost, but moist where the dew got into them, silver to look at, silver on the light blue, blooming whiteness, when the morning comes. The stretching of the bean pods full length from the hearts of the wilting petals would go on.

Lumnay's fingers moved a long, long time among the growing bean pods.

❋ Discussion and Writing

1. Examine the situation Awiyao and Lumnay are trapped in, and analyze the nature of their tension. What are their perspectives, their dilemmas?
2. Discuss why Awiyao urges Lumnay to dance at his second wedding. What does Lumnay's refusal imply?
3. Explore the symbolism of the colored beads and the bean pods.
4. What is implied by the couple's questioning the custom in their hearts and before each other, but not before the community? What is the effect of basing the story on an old custom: what is its relevance for a modern Filipino?
5. In what ways is "Wedding Dance" a love story? Comment on the imagery, tone, and style of the narrative.

❋ Research and Comparison

Compare "Wedding Dance" to any other selection from this anthology concerned with a similar dilemma in which an individual's desire is circumscribed by social norms. Comment on the cultural similarities and differences in these works.

Interdisciplinary Discussion Question: Identify a prevailing practice or tradition that seems unjust in a familiar culture (Eastern or Western): what is the social rationale for it? What efforts are made to challenge the tradition; what are the consequences of adhering, or not adhering, to the practice?

Saadat Hasan Manto
(1912–1955)
Pakistan

Saadat Hasan Manto was born in Sambrala in the Punjab, India. He was born into a middle-class Kashmiri family from Amritsar, a politically active city, and the site of the bloody massacre in 1919 when the British killed hundreds of people gathered at a meeting (described in Abdullah Hussein's "The Old Fisherman's Tale"). He was seven at the time, and the experience remained with him. Always a restless person, and a poor student, he dropped out of college and turned to literature and politics under the influence of a writer, journalist, and revolutionary whom he credited with saving him from becoming a criminal. He tried translating and then found his métier in the short story, publishing one of his earliest, as well as one of his late works, based on the 1919 massacre. In 1934, he moved to Bombay, where he edited a film magazine, *Mussawar,* and, over the years, worked for several film companies. At the time of the August-1947 partition that created Pakistan, refugees were migrating in all directions, carrying tales of the "bloody fratricidal war." Within four months, Manto left Bombay to settle in Lahore, Pakistan, unable to tolerate the tension. But while his last impoverished years in Lahore were extremely productive, he always felt lonely for Bombay.

Writing in his native Urdu, Manto published plays, film scripts, and essays along with some two hundred stories. He wrote about what he called "the communal holocaust of the partition," depicting the atrocities perpetrated by all sides—Hindu, Muslim, Sikh—and justified by religious or nationalistic zeal. He wrote from a deeply felt contempt for hypocrisy, bourgeois self-righteousness, and political cant, and, flouting the prudish mores, he was accused of writing obscenities. Considered one of the major short story writers, and still the most popular, he informed his writing with a humane irony that took his work beyond sectarianism and, thus, into the realm of eminent antiwar literature.

The Dog of Titwal*

The soldiers had been entrenched in their positions for several weeks, but there was little, if any, fighting, except for the dozen rounds they ritually exchanged every day. The weather was extremely pleasant. The air was heavy with the scent of wild flowers and nature seemed to be following its course, quite unmindful of the soldiers hiding behind rocks and camouflaged by mountain shrubbery. The birds sang as they always had and the flowers were in bloom. Bees buzzed about lazily.

Only when a shot rang out, the birds got startled and took flight, as if a musician had struck a jarring note on his instrument. It was almost the end of September, neither hot nor cold. It seemed as if summer and winter had made their peace. In the blue skies, cotton clouds floated all day like barges on a lake.

The soldiers seemed to be getting tired of this indecisive war where nothing much ever happened. Their positions were quite impregnable. The two hills on which they were placed faced each other and were about the same height, so no one side had an advantage. Down below in the valley, a stream zigzagged furiously on its stony bed like a snake.

The air force was not involved in the combat and neither of the adversaries had heavy guns or mortars. At night, they would light huge fires and hear each others' voices echoing through the hills.

The last round of tea had just been taken. The fire had gone cold. The sky was clear and there was a chill in the air and a sharp, though not unpleasant, smell of pine cones. Most of the soldiers were already asleep, except Jamadar Harnam Singh, who was on night watch. At two o'clock, he woke up Ganda Singh to take over. Then he lay down, but sleep was as far away from his eyes as the stars in the sky. He began to hum a Punjabi folk song:

Buy me a pair of shoes, my lover
A pair of shoes with stars on them
Sell your buffalo, if you have to
But buy me a pair of shoes
With stars on them

Translated by Khalid Hasan

It made him feel good and a bit sentimental. He woke up the others one by one. Banta Singh, the youngest of the soldiers, who had a sweet voice, began to sing a lovelorn verse from *Heer Ranjha*, that timeless Punjabi epic of love and tragedy. A deep sadness fell over them. Even the gray hills seemed to have been affected by the melancholy of the song.

This mood was shattered by the barking of a dog. Jamadar Harnam Singh said, "Where has this son of a bitch materialized from?"

The dog barked again. He sounded closer. There was a rustle in the bushes. Banta Singh got up to investigate and came back with an ordinary mongrel in tow. He was wagging his tail. "I found him behind the bushes and he told me his name was Jhun Jhun," Banta Singh announced. Everybody burst out laughing.

The dog went to Harnam Singh who produced a cracker from his kitbag and threw it on the ground. The dog sniffed at it and was about to eat it, when Harnam Singh snatched it away. ". . . Wait, you could be a Pakistani dog."

They laughed. Banta Singh patted the animal and said to Harnam Singh, "Jamadar sahib, Jhun Jhun is an Indian dog."

"Prove your identity," Harnam Singh ordered the dog, who began to wag his tail.

"This is no proof of identity. All dogs can wag their tails," Harnam Singh said.

"He is only a poor refugee," Banta Singh said, playing with his tail.

Harnam Singh threw the dog a cracker which he caught in midair. "Even dogs will now have to decide if they are Indian or Pakistani," one of the soldiers observed.

Harnam Singh produced another cracker from his kitbag. "And all Pakistanis, including dogs, will be shot."

A soldier shouted, "*India Zindabad!*"

The dog, who was about to munch his cracker, stopped dead in his tracks, put his tail between his legs and looked scared. Harnam Singh laughed. "Why are you afraid of your own country? Here, Jhun Jhun, have another cracker."

The morning broke very suddenly, as if someone had switched on a light in a dark room. It spread across the hills and valleys of Titwal, which is what the area was called.

The war had been going on for months, but nobody could be quite sure who was winning it.

Jamadar Harnam Singh surveyed the area with his binoculars. He could see smoke rising from the opposite hill, which meant that, like them, the enemy was busy preparing breakfast.

Subedar Himmat Khan of the Pakistan army gave his huge mustache a twirl and began to study the map of the Titwal sector. Next to him sat his wireless operator who was trying to establish contact with the platoon commander to obtain instructions. A few feet away, the soldier Bashir sat on the ground, his back against a rock and his rifle in front of him. He was humming:

Where did you spend the night, my love, my moon?
Where did you spend the night?

Enjoying himself, he began to sing more loudly, savoring the words. Suddenly, he heard Subedar Himmat Khan scream, "Where did *you* spend the night?"

But this was not addressed to Bashir. It was a dog he was shouting at. He had come to them from nowhere a few days ago, stayed in the camp quite happily and then suddenly disappeared last night. However, he had now returned like a bad coin.

Bashir smiled and began to sing to the dog. "Where did you spend the night, where did you spend the night?" But he only wagged his tail. Subedar Himmat Khan threw a pebble at him. "All he can do is wag his tail, the idiot."

"What has he got around his neck?" Bashir asked. One of the soldiers grabbed the dog and undid his makeshift rope collar. There was a small piece of cardboard tied to it. "What does it say?" the soldier, who could not read, asked.

Bashir stepped forward and with some difficulty was able to decipher the writing. "It says Jhun Jhun."

Subedar Himmat Khan gave his famous mustache another mighty twirl and said, "Perhaps it is a code. Does it say anything else, Bashirey?"

"Yes sir, it says it is an Indian dog."

"What does that mean?" Subedar Himmat Khan asked.

"Perhaps it is a secret," Bashir answered seriously.

"If there is a secret, it is in that word Jhun Jhun," another soldier ventured in a wise guess.

"You may have something there," Subedar Himmat Khan observed.

Dutifully, Bashir read the whole thing again. "Jhun Jhun. This is an Indian dog."

Subedar Himmat Khan picked up the wireless set and spoke to his platoon commander, providing him with a detailed account of the dog's sudden appearance in their position, his equally sudden disappearance the night before and his return that morning. "What are you talking about?" the platoon commander asked.

Subedar Himmat Khan studied the map again. Then he tore up a packet of cigarettes, cut a small piece from it and gave it to Bashir. "Now write on it in Gurmukhi, the language of those Sikhs. . . "

"What should I write?"

"Well. . . "

Bashir had an inspiration. "Shun Shun, yes, that's right. We counter Jhun Jhun Jhun with Shun Shun."

"Good," Subedar Himmat Khan said approvingly. "And add: This is a Pakistani dog."

Subedar Himmat Khan personally threaded the piece of paper through the dog's collar and said, "Now go join your family."

He gave him something to eat and then said, "Look here, my friend, no treachery. The punishment for treachery is death."

The dog kept eating his food and wagging his tail. Then Subedar Himmat Khan turned him round to face the Indian position and said. "Go and take this message to the enemy, but come back. These are the orders of your commander."

The dog wagged his tail and moved down the winding hilly track that led into the valley dividing the two hills. Subedar Himmat Khan picked up his rifle and fired in the air.

The Indians were a bit puzzled, as it was somewhat early in the day for that sort of thing. Jamadar Harnam Singh, who in any case was feeling bored, shouted, "Let's give it to them."

The two sides exchanged fire for half an hour, which, of course, was a complete waste of time. Finally, Jamadar Harnam Singh ordered that enough was enough. He combed his long hair, looked at himself in the mirror and asked Banta Singh, "Where has that dog Jhun Jhun gone?"

"Dogs can never digest butter, goes the famous saying," Banta Singh observed philosophically.

Suddenly, the soldier on lookout duty shouted, "There he comes."

"Who?" Jamadar Harnam Singh asked.

"What was his name? Jhun Jhun," the soldier answered.

"What is he doing?" Harnam Singh asked.

"Just coming our way," the soldier replied, peering through his binoculars.

Subedar Harnam Singh snatched them from him. "That's him all right and there's something round his neck. But, wait, that's the Pakistani hill he's coming from, the motherfucker."

He picked up his rifle, aimed and fired. The bullet hit some rocks close to where the dog was. He stopped.

Subedar Himmat Khan heard the report and looked through his binoculars. The dog had turned round and was running back. "The brave never run away from battle. Go forward and complete your mission," he shouted at the dog. To scare him, he fired in his general direction. Harnam Singh fired at the same time. The bullet passed within inches of the dog, who leapt in the air, flapping his ears. Subedar Himmat Khan fired again, hitting some stones.

It soon became a game between the two soldiers, with the dog running round in circles in a state of great terror. Both Himmat Khan and Harnam

Singh were laughing boisterously. The dog began to run toward Harnam Singh, who abused him loudly and fired. The bullet caught him in the leg. He yelped, turned around and began to run towards Himmat Khan, only to meet more fire, which was only meant to scare him. "Be a brave boy. If you are injured, don't let that stand between you and your duty. Go, go, go," the Pakistani shouted.

The dog turned. One of his legs was now quite useless. He began to drag himself toward Harnam Singh, who picked up his rifle, aimed carefully and shot him dead.

Subedar Himmat Khan sighed, "The poor bugger has been martyred."

Jamadar Himmat Singh ran his hand over the still-hot barrel of his rifle and muttered, "He died a dog's death."

❋ Discussion and Writing

1. Describe the activities in the two warring camps: what are the implications of their strikingly similar routine?
2. Discuss the role of the dog in the narrative: what is the significance of naming him; what does his killing reveal about the soldiers?
3. Explain the different sentiments of Himmat Khan (a Muslim, Pakistani name) and Harnam Singh (a Sikh, Indian name) about the dog's death.
4. Comment on the impact of the description of nature in relation to the reality of war; what is the significance of the songs?
5. What attitude regarding the Indo-Pakistani conflict is projected in the narrative? What is revealed about the psychology of war?

❋ Research and Comparison

Interdisciplinary Discussion Question: Examine the literary works of any major writer of Pakistan or Bangladesh, whose writing portrays neocolonial issues. Focus on any one: oppression, prejudice, identity, corruption, class, gender relations, or other.

Amrita Pritam
(b. 1919)
India

Amrita Pritam was born in Gujranwala, the Punjab (at that time, North India; now, Pakistan). Educated informally at home, she has received several honorary doctorates, and, among her many honors, she was the first woman to be granted the Sahitya Akademi Prize, the highest national award in literature. A prolific author, she began writing poetry when she was 11, and has continued to produce many volumes of fiction and poetry, along with collections of folksongs, a memoir, translations into Punjabi, and essays. Although at first her writing was published in translation into Hindi, the national language, her native Punjabi has remained the language of her work. She has recorded her impressions of human experience as well as her concern for social and political conditions with an ironic poignancy and compassion, and has been highly acclaimed for capturing and evoking the telling moment.

The Weed*

Angoori was the new bride of the old servant of my neighbor's neighbor's neighbor. Every bride is new, for that matter; but she was new in a different way: the second wife of her twice-married husband who could not be called new because he had already drunk once at the conjugal well. As such, the prerogatives of being new went to Angoori only. This realization was further accentuated when one considered the five years that passed before they could consummate their union. Besides, she had been here for only a few months. She still carried a certain rustic freshness and girlish coyness about her.

About six years ago Prabhati went home to cremate his first wife. When this was done, Angoori's father approached him and took his wet towel, wringing it dry, a symbolic gesture of wiping away the tears of grief that had wet the towel. There never was a man, though, who cried enough to wet a yard and a half of calico. It had gotten wet only after Prabhati's bath. The simple act of drying the tear-stained towel on the part of a person with a nubile daughter was so much as to say, "I give you my daughter to take the place of the one who died. Don't cry anymore. I've even dried your wet towel."

This is how Angoori married Prabhati. However, their union was postponed for five years, for two reasons: her tender age, and her mother's paralytic attack. When, at last, Prabhati was invited to take his bride away, it seemed he would not be able to, for his employer was reluctant to feed another mouth from his kitchen. But when Prabhati told him that this new wife could keep her own house, the employer agreed.

At first, Angoori kept purdah[1] from both men and women. But the veil soon started to shrink until it covered only her hair, as was becoming to an

---

*Translated by Raj Gill

orthodox Hindu woman. She was a delight, to both ear and eye. A laughter in the tinkling of her hundred ankle bells, and a thousand bells in her laughter.

"What are you wearing, Angoori?"

"An anklet. Isn't it pretty?"

"And what's on your toe?"

"A ring."

"And on your arm?"

"A bracelet."

"What do they call what's on your forehead?"

"They call it *aliband.*"[2]

"Nothing on your waist today, Angoori?"

"It's too heavy. Tomorrow I'll wear it. Today, no necklace either. See! The clasp is broken. Tomorrow I'll go to the city to get a new clasp . . . and buy a nose pin. I had a big nose pin. But my mother-in-law kept it."

Angoori was very proud of her silver jewelry, elated by the mere touch of her trinkets. Everything she did seemed to set them off to maximum effect.

The weather became hot with the turn of the season. Angoori too must have felt it in her hut where she passed a good part of the day, for now she stayed out more. There were a few huge neem trees in front of my house; underneath, an old well that nobody uses except an occasional construction worker. The spilt water made several puddles, keeping the atmosphere around the well cool. She often sat near the well to relax.

"What are you reading, *bibi?*"[3] Angoori asked me one day when I sat under the neem tree reading.

"Want to read it?"

"I don't know reading."

"Want to learn?"

"Oh, no!"

"Why not? What's wrong with it?"

"It's a sin for women to read!"

"And what about men?"

"For them, it's not a sin."

"Who told you this nonsense?"

"I just know it."

"I read. I must be sinning."

"For city women, it's no sin. It is for village women."

---

[1]Seclusion from the public gaze by wearing a veil and remaining behind walls or screens.

[2]Jewelry that is worn on the head and hangs down onto the forehead. [eds.]

[3]Term of respectful or affectionate address to a woman.

. We both laughed at this remark. She had not learned to question all that she was told to believe. I thought that if she found peace in her convictions, who was I to question them?

Her body redeemed her dark complexion, an intense sense of ecstasy always radiating from it, a resilient sweetness. They say a woman's body is like a lump of dough; some women have the looseness of underkneaded dough while others have the clinging plasticity of leavened dough. Rarely does a woman have a body that can be equated to rightly kneaded dough, a baker's pride. Angoori's body belonged to this category. Her rippling muscles impregnated with the metallic resilience of a coiled spring. I felt her face, arms, breasts, legs with my eyes and experienced a profound languor. I thought of Prabhati: old, short, loose-jawed, a man whose stature and angularity would be the death of a Euclid. Suddenly a funny idea struck me: Angoori was the dough covered by Prabhati. He was her napkin, not her taster. I felt a laugh welling up inside me, but I checked it for fear that Angoori would sense what I was laughing about. I asked her how marriages are arranged where she came from.

"Girls, when five or six, adore someone's feet. He is the husband."

"How do they know it?"

"Her father takes money and flowers and puts them at his feet."

"That's the father adoring, not the girl."

"He does it for the girl. So it's the girl herself."

"But the girl has never seen him before!"

"Yes, girls don't see."

"Not a single girl ever sees her future husband!"

"No . . . ," she hesitated. After a long pensive pause, she added. "Those in love . . . they see them."

"Do girls in your village have love affairs?"

"A few."

"Those in love, they don't sin?" I remembered her observation regarding education for women.

"It's a sin, a great sin," she replied hurriedly.

"They don't. See, what happens is that a man makes the girl eat the weed and she starts loving him."

"Which weed?"

"The wild one."

"Doesn't the girl know that she has been given the weed?"

"No, he gives it to her in a *paan.*[4] After that, nothing satisfies her but to be with him, her man. I know. I've seen it with my own eyes."

"Whom did you see?"

---

[4]Betel nut and spices wrapped in a betel leaf; generally chewed after meals.

"A friend; she was older than I."

"What happened?"

"She went crazy. Ran away with him to the city."

"How do you know it was because of the weed?"

"What else could it be? Why would she leave her parents. He brought her many things from the city: clothes, trinkets, sweets."

"Where does this weed come in?"

"In the sweets: otherwise how could she love him?"

"Love can come in other ways. No other way here?"

"No other way. What parents hate is that she was that way."

"Have you seen the weed?"

"No, they bring it from a far country. My mother warned me not to take *paan* or sweets from anyone. Men put the weed in them."

"You were very wise. How come your friend ate it?"

"To make herself suffer," she said sternly. The next moment her face clouded, perhaps in remembering her friend. "Crazy. She went crazy, the poor thing," she said sadly. "Never combed her hair, singing all night. . . ."

"What did she sing?"

"I don't know. They all sing when they eat the weed. Cry too."

The conversation was becoming a little too much to take, so I retired.

I found her sitting under the neem trees one day in a profoundly abstract mood. Usually one could hear Angoori coming to the well; her anklet bells would announce her approach. They were silent that day.

"What's the matter, Angoori?"

She gave me a blank look and then, recovering a little, said, "Teach me reading, *bibi?*"

"What has happened?"

"Teach me to write my name?"

"Why do you want to write? To write letters? To whom?"

She did not answer, but was once again lost in her thoughts.

"Won't you be sinning?" I asked, trying to draw her out of her mood. She would not respond. I went in for an afternoon nap. When I came out again in the evening, she was still there singing sadly to herself. When she heard me approaching, she turned around and stopped abruptly. She sat with hunched shoulders because of the chill in the evening breeze.

"You sing well, Angoori." I watched her great effort to turn back the tears and spread a pale smile across her lips.

"I don't know singing."

"But you do, Angoori."

"This was the. . ."

"The song your friend used to sing." I completed the sentence for her.

"I heard it from her."

"Sing it for me?"

She started to recite the words. "Oh, it's just about the time of year for change. Four months winter, four months summer, four months rain. . . "

"Not like that. Sing it for me," I asked. She wouldn't, but continued with the words.

"Four months of winter reign in my heart;
My heart shivers, o my love.
Four months of summer, wind shimmers in the sun.
Four months come the rains; clouds tremble in the sky."

"Angoori!" I said loudly. She looked as if in a trance. I felt like shaking her by the shoulders, as if she had eaten the weed. Instead, I took her by the shoulders and asked if she had been eating regularly. She had not; she cooked for herself only since Prabhati ate at his master's. "Did you cook today?" I asked.

"Not yet."

"Did you have tea in the morning?"

"Tea. No milk today."

"Why not milk today?"

"I didn't get any. Ram Tara. . . ."

"Fetches the milk for you?" I added. She nodded. Ram Tara was the night watchman. Before Angoori married Prabhati, Ram Tara used to get a cup of tea at our place at the end of his watch before retiring on his cot near the well. After Angoori's arrival, he made his tea at Prabhati's. He, Angoori and Prabhati would all have tea together sitting around the fire. Three days ago Ram Tara went to his village for a visit. "You haven't had tea for three days?" I asked. She nodded again. "And you haven't eaten, I suppose?" She did not speak. Apparently, if she had been eating, it was as good as not eating at all.

I remembered Ram Tara: good-looking, quick-limbed, full of jokes. He had a way of talking with smiles trembling faintly at the corner of his lips.

"Angoori?"

"Yes, *bibi*."

"Could it be the weed?"

Tears flowed down her face in two rivulets, gathering into two tiny puddles at the corners of her mouth.

"Curse on me!" she started in a voice trembling with tears, "I never took sweets from him . . . not a betel even . . . but tea. . . ." She could not finish. Her words were drowned in a fast stream of tears.

❀ Discussion and Writing

1. What are Angoori's dominant character traits? Explain her responses to traditions.
2. Discuss Angoori's perception of what is right for the urban women but wrong for the rural one. What is the significance of this social distinction within the story?
3. Interpret Angoori's desire to learn to read, an act that was once sinful for her.
4. Clarify the significance of the weed.

❀ Research and Comparison

Compare the portrayal of men and women in two stories included in this anthology, depicting a culture in which the practice of arranged marriages prevails. Place the women and men within the context of their cultures.

Oodgeroo Noonuccal
(Kath Walker, 1920–1993)
Australia

Oodgeroo Noonuccal (Kath Walker), of the Noonuccal people, was born in Australia just eight years after the last recorded massacre of Aboriginal people. When economic need forced her to leave school, she worked as a servant and was paid a pittance for her labor. During World War II she worked in the Australian Women's Auxiliary Service and then became a stenographer. Throughout her life, however, she fought for her people's rights, serving on the executive committees of various organizations, demanding the end of "pass" laws and slavelike work conditions. In more recent years, she added her opposition to nuclear armament to her denunciation of racism and colonization. As the first her people poet to be published, she has brought the plight of her people to outside attention, although at first hers was a solitary voice. In 1970, Elizabeth II of England made her a Member of the Order of the British Empire; in 1988, she returned the honor as a protest against two hundred years of European settlement. Much beloved and highly acclaimed, she spoke ultimately in her poetry of love and peace and dignity, of hope for a time of truly equal rights.

Municipal Gum

Gumtree in the city street,
Hard bitumen around your feet,
Rather you should be
In the cool world of leafy forest halls
And wild bird calls.
Here you seem to me
Like that poor cart-horse
Castrated, broken, a thing wronged,
Strapped and buckled, its hell prolonged,
Whose hung head and listless mien express
Its hopelessness.
Municipal gum, it is dolorous
To see you thus
Set in your black grass of bitumen—
O fellow citizen,
What have they done to us?

❈ Discussion and Writing

1. Contrast the state of the gum tree in the city with that of a gum tree in
   the forest.
2. What does the cart-horse symbolize?
3. Discuss the significance of the ending of the poem.

❈ Research and Comparison

Interdisciplinary Discussion Question: Research Aboriginal art and literature in the twentieth century, and examine any one work as part of a cultural
continuum and as part of a movement for the assertion of Aboriginal rights.

Mochtar Lubis
(b. 1922)
Indonesia

Mochtar Lubis was born in Padang, Sumatra, the second-largest island of
Indonesia, where his father was a district commissioner. He studied at the
School of Economics in Kayutanam, Indonesia, and worked as an econo-

mist before turning to literature and journalism. He served as director or editor of several magazines, and as editor-in-chief of the Jakarta daily newspaper *Indonesia Raya.* In this capacity, he spoke out against corruption and inequities, criticizing the government and the military. As a result, he was imprisoned from 1956 to 1966. Three of those years were served under house arrest, after which he was free for two months and then returned to prison. It was during his four-year incarceration in Madiun in Central Java that he wrote *Harimau! Harimau!* (1975; trans., *Tiger!,* 1990), from which "*Harimau!*" comes.

Mochtar Lubis spent his adolescence in the forest region of Central Sumatra, where he learned about the environment from excursions into the jungle led by one of his teachers. They spotted fresh tiger tracks on one of these expeditions, and he called on the terror of the experience as he developed *Harimau! Harimau!,* an allegorical work concerned with the power of charismatic leaders. The village *dukun,* or shaman (like Sukarno, the dictatorial president of Indonesia), exerted a charismatic authority. For Lubis, the question was whether these leaders could subdue the "tigers within themselves." His regard for human rights, his country and his people, his forthrightness and refusal to equivocate have contributed to his renown. His story of his imprisonment, *Catatan Subversif* (Subversive Notes, 1980) illuminates these qualities, providing a pattern for the next generation. Along with his patriotism, he has been honored for his journalistic and literary writing.

Harimau!*

The tiger had been hungry for two days. He was no longer strong enough, nor could he run fast enough, to capture his usual prey of wild pigs and deer. He had once been an intrepid beast and had reigned as king of the great forest for many years, but in all his memory he had never felt famished like this. His body was big and rangy, and in his youth it had been easy for him to stalk and run down huge buck deer. On several occasions he had even attacked and killed cows that had been grazing outside the village and had dragged them into the forest to devour them. For two days now he had been hunting the buck and the doe, but the deer were cagey and had always been able to escape before he had a chance to attack either one of them.

He was becoming exhausted.

---

*Translated by Florence Lamonreux

Early that morning, when he was quite close to the doe, his pursuit had been interrupted by a thunderous noise that shattered the silence and tore through the forest. He had watched the young female deer approach the buck and then, a few moments later, bound quickly away while the male deer had fallen to the ground. When the tiger had heard the gun's loud report, he had also run from it. Then, sometime later, driven by his gnawing hunger, he had returned to the spot where the buck had fallen. All that remained were traces of blood which had seeped into the ground. The tiger licked the gory earth, but the taste of the blood only served to whet his appetite and to urge him to follow the scent of the men, which was now mingled with that of the deer. It was an easy matter for him to follow the human trail.

He came to the place where the buck had been butchered, and there he found the deer's bones and offal which he wolfed down greedily. This was not nearly enough to satisfy his hunger, on the contrary, it was just intensified.

Throughout that day he had followed the men and their loads of deer meat from afar, sensing that this time his pursuit would reap a reward. As the day waned he had kept out of sight and waited patiently beside the river, observing the men building their lean-to and arranging their campfire. The smell of the roasting deer meat had made him ravenous, and it had taken a tremendous will to keep him from growling and warning those he now hunted, but he was waiting for the right moment to attack. Suddenly the old tiger shifted his weight and became alert as he watched one of the men leave the group and draw away from the protection of the campfire.

The man squatted in the river.

The big cat flexed his muscles; his body tensed and with a terrible roar he sprang from his hiding place. Pak[1] Balam heard the tiger's cry and knew instantly that he was the target of the beast's attack. Jumping up he tried to run but he fell, full length, into the water. He never had a chance to get up and run again. The wild creature was upon him. Had Pak Balam not fallen, the tiger would have gripped either his head or his neck, but as it was, the animal's powerful teeth clamped onto the calf of his left leg and dragged him off into the forest.

For several moments following the tiger's harsh call, all animal and insect sounds stopped. The shock that had frozen the men with terror, when they heard the roar of the attacking tiger, dissipated with Pak Balam's screams for help.

The reaction of those around the campfire was swift. Wak Katok grabbed his rifle, and the others drew their heavy knives as they rushed to the fire and picked up pieces of flaming wood to use as torches. They ran to the place where Pak Balam had been attacked and, seeing that he was gone, they

---

[1]Short form of *bapak* meaning father; used to address an older person or respected man. [eds.]

dashed impulsively across the shallow river splattering water wildly with every frantic footfall. The men could see where bushes had been crushed and broken as the great animal had moved through them, and they could hear Pak Balam's screams of agony—terrified, begging for help. Wak[2] Katok ran in front with the gun; the others immediately behind him. With all his might, Sutan heaved a flaming torch in the direction where the tiger was dragging Pak Balam, but the determined beast kept on going. A few minutes later they came to an open space and in the darkness they could just make out the form of the running tiger and his prey. As the others yelled and screamed Wak Katok raised his gun, aimed, and fired.

The tiger dropped his victim and ran off, disappearing into the darkness, and the six men ran to Pak Balam's limp form. Even though the light from the wood was weak and unsteady, they could tell that the old man's left leg had been ripped and mauled by the tiger's teeth, the muscles and flesh torn so badly that they could see white bone and freely gushing blood.

Pak Balam's clothes were tattered, and his entire body was covered with small wounds and angry red scratches made by stones and sticks as the tiger pulled him along. Blood trickled from his nose and mouth. Pak Balam was unconscious and was lying there moaning.

Buyung, Sanip, Talib, Pak Haji,[3] and Sutan quickly lifted the savagely injured man. Wak Katok had already reloaded his rifle, and with the gun bearer walking behind them the five men hurriedly carried Pak Balam back to the camp.

When they reached the campfire's stronger light, the men realized how dreadful Pak Balam's wounds actually were. In addition to the damage done by the tiger's teeth, which had split the calf of his leg, his back had been severely scratched by the claws. Wak Katok ordered Talib to boil water.

From a sack in his basket, Wak Katok removed a handful of leaves. They washed Pak Balam's wounds with hot water, and Wak Katok covered the gash in his leg with an assortment of the leaves which they then proceeded to bind on with strips torn from Pak Balam's *sarung*.[4] Wak Katok next steeped some medicinal plants while methodically reciting chants. After the mixture had boiled, the resulting brew was poured into a coconut shell cup and, when it had cooled sufficiently, the shaman fed it to Pak Balam sip-by-sip.

The semiconscious man's continuous moans were punctuated with screams and pleas for help. About an hour after his wounds had been treated, Pak Balam regained consciousness and looked around him, gazing at them intently, one at a time. He never ceased praying, "*La ilaha illallah—La ilaha illallah,*" repeating the name of Allah, interspersing his supplications with cries of pain.

---

[2]Uncle or a title of respect for an older man. [eds.]
[3]A title used for the one who has been on a *haj* (*hajj*), pilgrimage, to Mecca. [eds.]
[4]Cloth tied at the waist reaching below the knees. [eds.]

Still later, when he was more alert, he scrutinized his friends again and announced, "I've carried out my destiny. This is the way I must pay for my sins."

Pak Haji spoke, "Hush. Be still. Don't think of death. We've fixed you up. Wak Katok's given you medicine. Calm yourself. Try to sleep."

"No, listen to me," said Pak Balam gathering his strength. "I had a prophecy, in a dream, before we left the village—two nights before we left—and again on one night at Pak Hitam's. But at the time I still hoped that Allah would forgive my sins and protect us all. Not just me, but any of us could have an accident on this journey, any of us who've committed bad sins."

Buyung's flesh grew cold listening to Pak Balam speak. Did this sick old man know what he had done? He glanced furtively at his comrades wanting to see if their expressions altered as they listened to Pak Balam. Possibly each of them also had some secret, some terrible sin; it surely wasn't he alone who had committed a wrongdoing; besides, he'd already asked God's forgiveness.

Wak Katok's face looked strong, determined, and Pak Haji seemed alert and calm, but on the countenances of his younger friends—Talib, Sutan, and Sanip—he could read emotions similar to his own. The strain they had been under since the tiger's attack was reflected there, but he could not discern whether or not they might have sinned.

Wak Katok spoke "What did you dream about, Pak Balam? Try to tell us. Maybe we can still avoid the trouble. Tell us first about the one you had in the village, then I can find some *mantras* and make us some good luck charms."

"It's too late now. It was my fault," sighed Pak Balam. Nevertheless, he went on to recount his nightmare. "Two days before we left for the *damar*[5] forest I dreamed I was in a boat on a lake with Wak Katok, Pak Haji, Sutan, and Sanip. There were two other men there, too, but their faces weren't clear; not Buyung and not Talib. I don't know who they were, even after I woke up I didn't know. We went to the middle of the lake to catch fish. We got a lot and the boat was full. Pak Haji said we'd caught enough and better head for home before the boat was overloaded. If a wind came up and there were big waves, we'd tip over. But Wak Katok said to keep going, we didn't have enough yet, and Sutan, Sanip, and I went along with Wak Katok. So we stayed there and fish kept piling up until the boat was so full that it sank low into the water. In about another hour water started to pour into the boat, Wak Katok told us to keep on fishing. I didn't argue with him, but I knew we should've stopped long before the boat was so full. It turned out that I was right to worry because not much later I hooked a big fish. Everybody tried to help me get it into the boat, but the fish was so big and strong that it pulled the fish line and towed the boat along with it to the middle of the lake, going

---

[5]A resin produced by large forest trees; often used in paving roads. [eds.]

faster, faster all the time. Then the sky got dark and typhoon winds came up, making big waves that rocked the boat and finally turned it over. All the fish were dumped back into the lake, and all of us along with them. I woke up soaked with sweat, my ears still ringing with our screams and the terrible sounds of that howling storm . . .

"At Pak Hitam's I had another nightmare that was worse than the first one. I was climbing a tree, trying to reach a young mynah bird that I wanted to get out of its nest. It was for Pak Haji who was underneath the tree watching me. The tree was big and tall and different from other trees, strange. As I climbed up it got taller and taller and the bird's nest was farther and farther away from me. I climbed fast, but the tree grew faster. I got tired, but I had to keep on going. All of a sudden the tree crashed down and me with it. I yelled and tried to get out, but we were all trapped under that tree and scared because we couldn't move. Then a lot of big snakes came and crawled into the spaces around us. Again I woke up afraid and out of breath . . .

"Both of those dreams are bad omens. I read a lot of verses in the Holy Book when I woke up to try to turn away the evil forces, but fate's said that I'll only live till now." His discourse concluded, Pak Balam lay there before his audience, resigned and heavy-hearted.

Only Pak Haji spoke—slowly, soothingly—quoting from the Koran, trying to calm the badly wounded man as well as the rest of them.

But Pak Balam was unable to relax and, seemingly revitalized, he turned his gaze to Wak Katok. His eyes were piercing and he said in an accusing voice, "It's because of you, Wak Katok, that I have to pay for my sins like this. . . " Wak Katok looked at him very oddly. For an instant his face was contorted in an expression of fear, but just as quickly it disappeared.

A sinister element emerged around the campfire, one which for sometime had been playing across their faces and bodies, the surrounding black forest and the flickering fire and which was now becoming blacker, more precise, and terrifying. They all remained silent, each of them sensing that some new component, secret and alien, had been introduced into their lives. They wanted to cry out to Pak Balam, to beseech him not to bring this nameless thing into their midst. But no one made an attempt to prevent him from talking, not even Wak Katok.

"It happened a long time ago. . . ," said Pak Balam, "at the time of the 1926 rebellion. I was in the same unit as Wak Katok. He was our troop leader and we'd just lost a battle with some Dutch soldiers. We'd escaped but their troops were chasing us. After half a day we were able to shake them off and hide in an old, fallow field. Our army had scattered, but three of us had kept together: Wak Katok, Sarip, and me. Sarip, our friend, had a bad thigh wound and had lost a lot of blood. When we got to the deserted field he was really weak; he could hardly walk. We had to drag him into an old, empty hut, where we fixed up his leg as best we could without any medicine or bandages. Our troop's bivouac was still a long way away, maybe a five-hour walk from where we were. They had supplies and we didn't have anything, but it would've been impossible to carry Sarip there. The trip would've been too hard and we'd never find them before dark. Furthermore, if the Dutch were following Sarip's trail of blood they could come and attack us at any time. If we left Sarip there we were afraid the Dutch would force him to tell them where our troops were hiding. What to do?

"Wak Katok asked me to go to the well so that he could talk to me alone. He wanted to know if I had any ideas about what to do, but I didn't have any answers. Wak Katok said that we had to get out of there fast and, when I asked what we'd do about Sarip, he said to leave it to him. I didn't know what he was going to do, but when he told me to go on ahead first, that he'd be right behind, I left as quick as I could, not even going back to the hut to see Sarip.

"A few minutes later Wak Katok caught up with me and we headed for our troop's camp. I never asked Wak Katok about Sarip, but I had an idea what happened. Wak Katok went back to the hut and murdered him and threw his body down the well. I found that out later, after the Dutch had put down the revolution. But I've never mentioned it to Wak Katok till right now. I've kept silent all this time.

"I did a terrible wrong. Maybe I'm worse than Wak Katok, because in my heart I knew what Wak Katok was going to do, when we met there by that well. But I wanted to live so much that I would've agreed to anything to save my own skin—let Sarip die, if it meant I'd live. I was weak and afraid, and I didn't want to die. If I'd stood up to Wak Katok and said that we had to take Sarip with us, he'd probably have gone along with me. But I didn't, and a man who sits back and doesn't do anything while another man sins, when he could stop it, is as bad as the person who sins—even more so if he knows that committing that sin will bring him good luck.

"That's only the first wicked thing Wak Katok did while I just looked the other way, and now my shoulders have to bear the blame with his.

"In the rebellion I overlooked a lot of other evil things that Wak Katok did. He raped Demang's wife and then murdered her, Demang, and their three children, and looted their house of all the gold and silver he could find. I was there and I didn't try to stop him. We were at war with the Dutch, not women and children."

Pak Balam ceased his monologue. His eyes were still glued to Wak Katok's face, but the piercing light had faded from them. He seemed to want to reach out to Wak Katok, but he lacked the strength. His hand, which he had moved slightly, dropped back, falling to his side. Pak Balam's expression changed again, his face seeming to relax; as if all the tension he had been suppressing in his thoughts and his very being for so long, was now evaporating. His eyes shone with a new clarity, as his lips curved gently in an almost tranquil smile. With a steady voice he said, "I feel better now that I've told you in front of Wak Katok. This has all been kept inside my heart and mind for so long, and now I've admitted my sins and prayed to Allah to grant me forgiveness, and to forgive Wak Katok too. . . " Pak Balam pressed the palms of his hands together in prayer.

Pak Haji intoned, *"Allahu Akbar. Allahu Akbar."*[6]

Wak Katok said nothing, his features unsmiling and grim.

Pak Balam opened his eyes and sought out Wak Katok's. When their gaze met Pak Balam admonished him, "Admit your sins, Wak Katok. Get on your knees and ask forgiveness of Allah the Merciful and Almighty. Admit your sins, all the other ones, so that you can get out of the forest in one piece and escape the *harimau*. Let me be the one to be sacrificed." Pak Balam's eyelids fluttered shut and he lay still, exhausted from the effort of speaking for so long.

They sat there in silence, each with his own thoughts. Pak Balam's story had struck a chord of terror in every heart. They wanted to reach home safely, and leave the forest with its deadly tiger far behind them, but the prospect of owning up to their sins in front of one another stunned them. A single thought pervaded every mind.

"I haven't sinned. There aren't any great evils that I've got to confess," thought Sanip.

"I certainly don't have any sins that I should admit," said Talib in his heart.

"I haven't sinned," insisted Sutan to himself.

Buyung commanded his thoughts to be still, and not to remind him of his sin.

Pak Haji did the same.

Wak Katok sat in stony silence, a number of his sins already having been confessed by Pak Balam. As for the remaining ones, those he was sure no one knew about, he was not going to reveal them to anyone. Let someone else speak first.

Pak Balam's voice could be heard droning deliriously. "Careful, that *harimau* is sent by Allah to punish all of us who've sinned . . . be careful of the *harimau* . . . sent by Allah . . . be careful of the *harimau* . . . admit your evil doings . . . admit your evil doings."

They were like statues, motionless, listening to him, fear creeping into their bones. The great dark jungle around them was permeated with an aura of malevolence. Savage black demons were waiting there for the opportune moment to assail them. The men sensed the tiger's presence, restlessly pacing back and forth in the darkness just outside the campfire's merciful light, evaluating them, appraising their sins, determining who among them would be next.

They were not brave enough to look at one another; each fearing that the others might read his thoughts. Every few minutes Pak Balam, in his delirium, kept repeating, "Confess your evil doings . . . beware of the *harimau* . . . he's sent from Allah . . . confess your sins." This relentless admonition

---

[6]Allah is great. [eds.]

compelled each man to look deeply into his own soul. It drove them to consider their various past unsavory deeds; and there were many to be considered. Eyes were glazed by jumbled thoughts, which they yearned to suppress and secrete away somewhere where they would not have to look at them, remember them, confront them, nor above all, repeat them to anyone else, ever. Admitting them aloud was a loathsome speculation. A person who tries to be honest must confront the hostility of those who are not, and very few people are comfortable with absolute integrity.

In addition to fear, a new emotion emerged among them, a hatred for Pak Balam. From the moment he had been attacked and had blessed their quick action in rescuing him, they had felt only compassion for him; but now, this man whose life they had saved was commanding them to reveal the most cryptic recesses of their hearts and souls.

Wak Katok regretted having saved Pak Balam. If they had let the *harimau* kill him, this problem of confessing their sins would never have arisen. Wak Katok's own personal secrets, which for dozens of years had been kept hidden and known only to Pak Balam, had now been told to five other people, his fellow villagers. They would never remain quiet. Later on, after they got back, they would tell his wife or their friends what they had heard from Pak Balam. Wak Katok blamed Pak Balam, he blamed the tiger, he blamed the men who had been there and heard Pak Balam's story. He supposed he could ask them to promise not to tell what Pak Balam had said to anyone else. If the old man had just let sleeping dogs lie. There was no point in bringing those things up again.

Wak Katok's hatred expanded, encompassing Pak Haji, Talib, Sanip, Sutan, and Buyung. They had listened to Pak Balam's stories about his crimes, but he knew nothing of theirs. Each of them no doubt had done terrible things which they kept inside themselves.

Take Pak Haji, all piety and wisdom; God only knew what he did all those years when he'd been roaming around in foreign countries. He could've murdered somebody, too, or cheated somebody, at least he'd probably robbed people and taken things by force. But, because nobody here knew about it, he could sit there smug, like some holy man. He recited Koran verses as though he'd never done anything that wasn't a hundred percent pure, as if only Wak Katok was sinful and dirty and should confess his sins and beg forgiveness so that they would be safe from the *harimau*.

How about Sanip, the cheerful youth who liked to sing? Maybe that's just a mask he wears in front of other people so that nobody would know the dark deeds he keeps hidden. Possibly he'd stolen something, or cheated on his wife. Once there had been a rumor that someone saw him fooling around with his young stepmother while his father was away.

Then there's the quiet Talib; maybe he's like the still waters that run deep. His uncle, who was dead now, had been sentenced to Nusa Kembangan Island because he ran amok in the market place and stabbed six people; four of whom had died. Talib's bloodline was a dark one. There must be things about him that nobody knew. According to gossip, even though he had a wife, he liked to sleep at the village mosque with the young boys.

And Sutan, he was certainly not to be trusted with women. He was a known woman chaser, never mind if they were old or young. People said that he liked to get together with the young widow, Siti Rafiah. They'd probably slept together more than once.

Buyung was still young, but didn't seem very trustworthy. Young people today didn't care about religion and *adat.* They only wanted to satisfy their own selfish wants and lusts. For a long time he'd been asking Wak Katok to teach him black magic. He had no use for it other than to get some girl in the sack. He'd probably already done just that.

Wak Katok was convinced that they had all sinned, and was resentful that only his wrongdoings had been unmasked. He questioned if his deeds were really sins. The rules of war allowed anything to be done to stop the enemy; besides, he wasn't the only one who did things like that. He wondered why Pak Balam hadn't told everything way back when it happened, why he had waited until now to open his mouth. "Sin! And what about your most recent sin?" something inside him whispered. But he squelched the small voice that had interjected that thought.

A sense of isolation made him feel that the others had turned against him, that he sat apart from them. For sometime now it had seemed that they no longer looked at his face, but only exchanged glances among themselves, ignoring him. He wondered if they were cursing him, accusing him, thinking that his actions had caused this threat of death to be brought down on all of them. Buyung, his student for so long—probably he'd lost his respect for him and thought his teacher disgusting. Talib, Sanip, Pak Haji, Sutan—they must all feel the same way.

Absorbed in his self-justification, Wak Katok had failed to hear Pak Haji address him. Pak Haji posed his question a second time. "How about it, Wak Katok, what do you think about what Pak Balam said? I'm not at all sure Pak Balam's attack by the *harimau* is Allah's punishment for him. According to what I've heard about *harimau,* there are two kinds that act like that. There's the usual animal that attacks people because it's no longer strong enough to hunt for food in the jungle, and then there are the spirit beasts, either the devil *harimau,* sent by its owner to do evil to others, or the ghost *harimau* that brings punishment to those who sin. I think it would be wise to consider if this *harimau* is normal or magic."

Several thoughts quickly turned over in Wak Katok's mind. If the *harimau* were an ordinary animal that hadn't attacked to punish their evil ways, then his sins, those that Pak Balam had revealed, could be passed off as the ramblings of a sick man, a result of his having been attacked. But what about. . . ? Wak Katok reined in his racing thoughts.

Buyung was also struck with a new consideration. Could it be possible that the animal was Pak Hitam's invisible *harimau?* It was said that he indeed, did keep such a creature. If so, maybe he was the intended victim and the *harimau* had attacked the wrong person. Sanip, Talib, Sutan and Pak Haji had been mulling over similar conjectures, each conscious of his own transgressions for which Pak Hitam's tiger might be the penalty. But their minds eased with the idea that the *harimau* could be a normal animal which had attacked only because he was hungry.

With that thought in mind they regarded Wak Katok, who had remained silent for a long while, his expression indicating that he was in deep thought. Finally he reached a conclusion, "It's not easy to say for sure if this is a normal *harimau* or a magic one. You are all wearing amulets to keep away *harimau*, snakes, and other wild animals. Perhaps when Pak Balam got dressed he forgot to put his on. If a man doesn't have his amulet with him it's useless and the *harimau* wouldn't have hesitated to attack him."

Wak Katok got up and approached Pak Balam, examining his waist, the place where one usually wore an amulet. The others closed in around the sick man and watched as Wak Katok searched him. They could see the white strip of cloth wound around the middle of his body. It was filled with a variety of talismans. Wak Katok looked them over, one by one, and turning to the others said. "There's a token here to be used against wild animals. The thing is, was he wearing this when he went to the river to relieve himself or had he taken it off? Can any of you remember if this was still tied to his waist when we brought him back here? If not, one of you must have tied it on again." None of the overwrought men could be sure whether or not he had seen the token string attached to Pak Balam's waist. They had been so preoccupied with the awesomeness and suddenness of the tiger's attack that nobody had paid attention to anything else. They had long since removed Pak Balam's pants and other clothes, and no one could recall if the amulet had been tied around his body during that time or not.

When nobody was able to say for certain, Wak Katok announced, "If we can't be sure, we'll try a different plan. I'll ask the spirits. This is very dangerous work so you'd better turn your backs to me, and see that Pak Balam doesn't watch me either."

They shifted to positions behind the fire, facing the dark forest. They could hear the noises Wak Katok made as he went about his quest, and smell the aroma of incense filling the night. The strong and pungent odor irritating their noses called forth thoughts of the world of witchcraft. As Wak Katok's low voice chanted his interminable *mantras* they were reminded of tales of ghosts and corpses returned from the dead, of Satan, evil spirits, and jinns. Several times the atmosphere was electrified by a growling sound that the shaman made in his throat. Then all was still, their tiny world within the circle of firelight again remote, separated from reality. It was almost as though they had been devoured by some giant creature, that they would be immobilized there forever, never able to escape from its dark belly nor the thick blackness.

Wak Katok's voice roused them and they heard, "Praise and thanks to Allah. According to the blood on this knife the *harimau* is not a supernatural animal." Wak Katok displayed his knife to them. At the end of the blade there was a trace of blood that had turned black, and they noticed Wak Katok suck the tip of his finger where he had pricked it.

"If the *harimau* was a ghost, the blood on the knife would still be red after I put it in the fire," exclaimed Wak Katok. "But look, it's turned black and that means it's normal blood, and that means the *harimau*'s blood is normal, too, so he has to be normal."

As Wak Katok spoke there was the sound of breath being exhaled in great sighs of relief. A normal tiger, though frightening in its own right, would not be as terrifying as a spirit tiger. A normal tiger is a common wild animal, while a spirit tiger could not be overcome by an ordinary mortal. People felt powerless and useless when they faced such a formidable foe. If a mystical tiger were to be the agent of the Great Power to punish their sins, the only way to deal with a thing like that would be to sit and wait for fate to take its course; waiting, always afraid, until the moment arrived when each person would be summoned to eternity. But a normal tiger could be defeated. Buyung felt that he himself was a good enough shot to hunt a normal tiger.

What eased the strain even more was the reprieve from having to admit their sins. It was no longer necessary to search their souls and to have to face those wrongdoings which had for so long been repressed deep inside. The prospect of stripping one's self naked had thoroughly repelled each of them, especially having to do so in front of others; for even when a man is alone he does not like to look deep within his innermost self and see the turmoil there.

Wak Katok was especially pleased with his verdict. The leadership position that had been snatched away from him was again in his firm grasp. For a while, as Pak Balam talked, the younger men had seemed to shift their respect and desire for direction to Pak Haji; but now Wak Katok could tell from their attitude, even Pak Haji's, that they were all grateful for his decision, and from that moment on there would be no question of his authority. He realized, as well, that they were not revolted by what Pak Balam had told them about him and that they would try to forget it, just as each of them would try to forget his own sins.

"Well," said Wak Katok, "together we can face up to a normal *harimau*. I think we'll be safe enough tonight. A normal *harimau* is afraid of fire, so we'll have to watch ours and keep it going strong all night. It's a good thing we've got a lot of fire wood. Tomorrow, before mid-morning, we'll leave here. Pak Balam won't be strong enough to walk so we'll have to put together a litter and take turns to carry him. We won't be able to bring the *damar* as well as Pak Balam. Which do you think is better, Pak Haji? Should we leave all the baskets of *damar* here and take turns carrying Pak Balam's litter, or should we leave just two baskets and take turns carrying both Pak Balam and the *damar*?"

Pak Haji thought for a while before answering, and then he responded, "I think it's probably better if we leave all the *damar* here and just take our provisions. By doing that we can move faster and would not be too tired to share the job of carrying Pak Balam. We've got to get to Air Jernih as soon as we can."

They accepted Pak Haji's suggestion unquestioningly. Wak Katok then announced that they had better try to get some rest so they would not be too tired in the morning; but no one was able to do that. It was not just the terrible event that had taken place and left their nerves raw, or even Pak Balam's agonized groans that was piercing their thoughts. But, in a way they did not comprehend, each man's agitation remained at a pitch that denied him the self-composure necessary for sleep.

Every man was filled with thoughts about himself and his companions. Talib thought about Siti Nurbaiti, a thirteen-year-old girl who had been found dead in a field outside the village about two years ago. The incident had disrupted the whole area for several months. The girl's clothes were in tatters and, according to the stories, she had been raped. They never found out who had attacked and murdered her. The murderer might even be among them. Thinking of her, Talib felt that he had sinned, too, because he had once felt a surge of lust when he looked at her young body. She had a figure that would soon have been ripe, large firm breasts straining at her skimpy dress, a sweet face, and an expression of defiance. He squeezed his eyes shut to gain control of his rising emotions. Thoughts of that nature brought him too close to his own sins.

Pak Haji, Sanip, Sutan, Buyung, and Wak Katok napped fitfully. They closed their eyes but thoughts continued to whirl inside their heads. Pak Balam's shaking of their innermost selves still reverberated in the hollows of their hearts. Pak Balam, too, grew uneasy again, either because of his wounds or because of his anxieties.

The fire flared high throwing its erratic light into the jungle, holding at bay a black night threatening to consume them. The forest's darkness was teeming with ominous secrets and noises, relentlessly forcing their way into the wayfarers' subconscious minds.

❋ Discussion and Writing

1. Comment on the introduction of the tiger: why is the question of his being magical or normal critical? Discuss the conclusion men draw about him.
2. Comment on Wak Katok's role as a healer and the irony of his saving Pak Balam.

3. Analyze Pak Balam's nightmares and the various objects in them. How do these images relate to the events and people in the story?
4. Describe the religious element provided by Pak Haji in the narrative. Explain his reaction to Pak Balam's story.
5. What do the young men represent? Analyze their reactions to Pak Balam's confession.
6. Analyze the various aspects of Wak Katok's reaction to the accusations against him. Explain his evaluation of the sins of others. What does his reasoning reveal about him?
7. Explore the symbolism of the jungle, the dark setting, and the tiger?
8. What is implied by the last paragraph? Analyze the religious and spiritual metaphor of the narrative.

❈ Research and Comparison

Interdisciplinary Discussion Question: Research the twentieth-century history of Indonesian politics and examine Mochtar Lubis's novel *Tiger!* in its context.

Nissim Ezekiel
(b. 1924)
India

Nissim Ezekiel was born in Bombay, India, where his father was a professor of biology and his mother founded and was principal of an elementary school. Although Ezekiel came from an old Indian Jewish family, he attended Catholic and Presbyterian schools before attending Wilson College in Bombay and Birkbeck College in London. A poet, dramatist, critic, editor, and professor, he has been considered one of the leading contemporary poets writing in English, and thus, was given the title Padma Shree by the government, an honor awarded yearly for exemplary achievement. Freeing himself from rigid versification, he has experimented with form, style, and language, occasionally turning to Indian-English for its rhythm and as an appropriate vehicle for social commentary. He has explored "the myth and maze" of the self, moving easily between mysticism and the comedy or pathos of everyday life; and in poems like

"Night of the Scorpion," he has created narrative structures in which he fuses the personal and social, physical and spiritual, serious and comic.

Night of the Scorpion

I remember the night my mother
was stung by a scorpion. Ten hours
of steady rain had driven him
to crawl beneath a sack of rice.
Parting with his poison—flash
of diabolic tail in the dark room—
he risked the rain again.
The peasants came like swarms of flies
and buzzed the name of God a hundred times
to paralyze the Evil One.
With candles and with lanterns
throwing giant scorpion shadows
on the sun-baked walls
they searched for him: he was not found.
They clicked their tongues.
With every movement that the scorpion made
his poison moved in mother's blood, they said.
May he sit still, they said.
May the sins of your previous birth
be burned away tonight, they said.
May your suffering decrease
the misfortunes of your next birth, they said.
May the sum of evil
balanced in this unreal world
against the sum of good
become diminished by your pain, they said.
May the poison purify your flesh
of desire, and your spirit of ambition,
they said, and they sat around
on the floor with my mother in the center,
the peace of understanding on each face.
More candles, more lanterns, more neighbors,
more insects, and the endless rain.
My mother twisted through and through
groaning on a mat.

My father, skeptic, rationalist,
trying every curse and blessing,
powder, mixture, herb and hybrid.
He even poured a little paraffin
upon the bitten toe and put a match to it.
I watched the flame feeding on my mother.
I watched the holy man perform his rites
to tame the poison with an incantation.
After twenty hours
it lost its sting.

My mother only said
Thank God the scorpion picked on me
and spared my children.

❋ **Discussion and Writing**

1. Comment on the peasants' efforts to save the persona's mother: what do
   their prayers indicate; what is the significance of references to the past
   and future births?
2. Discuss the diverse approaches of the father, the holy man, and the
   peasants, despite their common goal of saving the woman's life.
   Interpret the mother's words.
3. Analyze the persona's perception of: the scorpion, the peasants, the
   father, and the holy man.

Pramoedya Toer
(b. 1925)
Indonesia

Pramoedya Ananta Toer was born in Blora, Java, the main island of
Indonesia. His father, a schoolteacher and a nationalist, was a bitter man
whose obsessive gambling impoverished the family, preventing his son
from finishing his high-school studies. The oppressions of Dutch colonialism and the Japanese occupation during World War II led Toer to join the
revolutionary struggle against the Dutch after the Japanese defeat. It is
these experiences of subjugation and resistance that have informed his life
and work. The period following the transfer of authority from the Dutch in

1949 was one of great productivity, when he wrote a cluster of highly acclaimed novels, novellas, and short stories. By 1958, he had turned from fiction to the essay as his distress with governmental corruption developed, and he became more politically engaged. The military regime that took over, after crushing the 1965 coup to overthrow Sukarno, imprisoned all leftists, including Pramoedya Toer. He remained in jail, never having been tried, until 1979. While he was in prison, he returned to fiction, spinning tales for his fellow prisoners. During the last six years, he was able to transcribe them, and they became important historical novels. After his release, he published two volumes of his tetralogy about the beginnings of the Indonesian revolutionary efforts against Dutch colonialism, but because of their overwhelming success, the government had the books banned and existing copies publicly burned. The remaining volumes were secretly carried from Indonesia to be published abroad.

Regarded as the master of contemporary fiction, Toer has written short stories picturing Javanese society as well as vast historical novels. His portraits of both rural and urban characters illuminate colonialism, the decay of feudal Java, and contemporary Indonesia. Esteemed for his manipulation of languages, he laces the Indonesian language with classical Javanese imagery, and uses Indonesian to depict the Javanese-speaking poor. In a country where more than 250 languages are spoken, his writing "between languages" inherently establishes the cultural tensions.

Inem*

Inem was one of the girls I knew. She was eight years old—two years older than me. She was no different from the others. And if there was a difference, it was that she was one of the prettier little girls in our neighborhood. People liked to look at her. She was polite, unspoiled, deft, and hard-working—qualities which quickly spread her fame even into other neighborhoods as a girl who would make a good daughter-in-law.

And once when she was heating water in the kitchen, she said to me, "Gus[1] Muk, I'm going to be married."

"Your're fooling!" I said.

"No, the proposal came a week ago. Mama and Papa and all the relatives have accepted the proposal."

"What fun to be a bride!" I exclaimed happily.

"Yes, it'll be fun, I know it will! They'll buy me all sorts of nice clothes. I'll be dressed up in a bride's outfit, with flowers in my hair, and they'll make me up with powder and mascara. Oh, I'll like that!"

---

*Translated by Rufus S. Hendron
[1]Gus: A title of respect which Inem, as a servant, uses toward the son of the family for whom she works.

And it was true. One afternoon her mother called on mine. At that time Inem was living with us as a servant. Her daily tasks were to help with the cooking and to watch over me and my younger brothers and sisters as we played.

Inem's mother made a living by doing batik work. That was what the women in our neighborhood did when they were not working in the rice fields. Some put batik designs on sarongs, while others worked on head cloths. The poorer ones preferred to do head cloths; since it did not take so long to finish a head cloth, they received payment for it sooner. And Inem's mother supported her family by putting batik designs on head cloths. She got the cloth and the wax from her employer, the Idjo Store. For every two head cloths that she finished, she was paid one and a half cents. On the average, a woman could do eight to eleven head cloths a day.

Inem's father kept gamecocks. All he did, day after day, was to wager his bird in cockfights. If he lost, the victor would take his cock. And in addition he would have to pay two and a half rupiahs, or at the very least seventy-five cents. When he was not gambling on cockfights, he would play cards with his neighbors for a cent a hand.

Sometimes Inem's father would be away from home for a month or half a month, wandering around on foot. His return would signify that he was bringing home some money.

Mother once told me that Inem's father's main occupation had been robbing people in the teak forest between our town, Blora, and the coastal town of Rembang. I was then in the first grade, and heard many stories of robbers, bandits, thieves, and murderers. As a result of those stories and what Mother told me, I came to be terrified of Inem's father.

Everybody knew that Inem's father was a criminal, but no one could prove it and no one dared complain to the police. Consequently he was never arrested by the police. Furthermore, almost all of Inem's mother's relatives were policemen. There was even one with the rank of agent first class. Inem's father himself had once been a policeman but had been discharged for taking bribes.

Mother also told me that in the old days Inem's father had been an important criminal. As a way of countering an outbreak of crime that was getting out of hand, the Netherlands Indies government had appointed him a policeman, so that he could round up his former associates. He never robbed any more after that, but in our area he continued to be a focus of suspicion.

When Inem's mother called on my mother, Inem was heating water in the kitchen. I tagged along after Inem's mother. The visitor, Mother, and I sat on a low, red couch.

"Ma'am," said Inem's mother, "I've come to ask for Inem to come back home."

"Why do you want Inem back? Isn't it better for her to be here? You don't have any of her expenses, and here she can learn how to cook."

"Yes, ma'am, but I plan for her to get married after the coming harvest."

"What?" exclaimed Mother, startled. "She's going to be married?"

"Yes, ma'am. She's old enough to be married now—she's eight years old," said Inem's mother.

At this my mother laughed. And her visitor was surprised to see Mother laugh.

"Why, a girl of eight is still a child!" said Mother.

"We're not upper-class people, ma'am. I think she's already a year too old. You know Asih? She married her daughter when she was two years younger than mine."

Mother tried to dissuade the woman. But Inem's mother had another argument. Finally the visitor spoke again: "I feel lucky that someone wants her. If we let a proposal go by this time, maybe there will never be another one. And how humiliating it would be to have a daughter turn into an old maid! And it just might be that if she gets married she'll be able to help out with the household expenses."

Mother did not reply. Then she looked at me and said, "Go get the betel[2] set and the spittoon."

So I went to fetch the box of betel-chewing ingredients and the brass spittoon.

"And what does your husband say?"

"Oh, he agrees. What's more, Markaban is the son of a well-to-do man—his only child. Markaban has already begun to help his father trade cattle in Rembang, Tjepu, Medang, Pati, Ngawen, and also here in Blora," said Inem's mother.

This information seemed to cheer Mother up, although I could not understand why. Then she called Inem, who was at work in the kitchen. Inem came in. And Mother asked, "Inem, do you want to get married?"

Inem bowed her head. She was very respectful toward Mother. I never once heard her oppose her. Indeed, it is rare to find people who are powerless opposing anything that others say to them.

I saw then that Inem was beaming. She often looked like that; give her something that pleased her even a little and she would beam. But she was not accustomed to saying "thank you." In the society of the simple people of our neighborhood, the words "thank you" were still unfamiliar. It was only through the glow radiating from their faces that gratitude found expression.

"Yes, ma'am," said Inem so softly as to be almost inaudible.

Then Inem's mother and mine chewed some betel. Mother herself did not like to chew betel all the time. She did it only when she had a woman visitor. Every few moments she would spit into the brass spittoon.

---

[2]Betel: A plant whose leaves are chewed by many Asians.

When Inem had gone back to the kitchen Mother said, "It's not right to make children marry."

These words surprised Inem's mother. But she did not say anything nor did her eyes show any interest.

"I was eighteen when I got married," said Mother.

Inem's mother's surprise vanished. She was no longer surprised now, but she still did not say anything.

"It's not right to make children marry," repeated Mother.

And Inem's mother was surprised again.

"Their children will be stunted."

Inem's mother's surprise vanished once more.

"Yes, ma'am." Then she said placidly, "My mother was also eight when she got married."

Mother paid no attention and continued, "Not only will they be stunted, but their health will be affected too."

"Yes, ma'am, but ours is a long-lived family. My mother is still alive, though she's over fifty-nine. And my grandmother is still alive too. I think she must be seventy-four. She's still vigorous and strong enough to pound corn in the mortar."

Still ignoring her, Mother went on, "Especially if the husband is also a child."

"Yes, ma'am, but Markaban is seventeen."

"Seventeen! My husband was thirty when he married me."

Inem's mother was silent. She never stopped shifting the wad of tobacco leaves that was stuck between her lips. One moment she would move the tobacco to the right, a moment later to the left, and the next moment she would roll it up and scrub her coal-black teeth with it.

Now Mother had no more arguments with which to oppose her visitor's intention. She said, "Well, if you've made up your mind to marry Inem off, I only hope that she gets a good husband who can take care of her. And I hope she gets someone who is compatible."

Inem's mother left, still shifting the tobacco about in her mouth.

"I hope nothing bad happens to that child."

"Why would anything bad happen to her?" I asked.

"Never mind, Muk, it's nothing." Then Mother changed the subject. "If the situation of their family improves, we won't lose any more of our chickens."

"Is somebody stealing our chickens, Mama?" I asked.

"No, Muk, never mind," Mother said slowly. "Such a little child! Only eight years old. What a pity it is. But they need money. And the only way to get it is to marry off their daughter."

Then Mother went to the garden behind the house to get some string beans for supper.

Fifteen days after this visit, Inem's mother came again to fetch her daughter. She seemed greatly pleased that Inem made no objection to being taken away. And when Inem was about to leave our house, never to be a member of our family again, she spoke to me in the kitchen doorway, "Well, good-bye, Gus Muk. I'm going home, Gus Muk," she said very softly.

She always spoke softly. Speaking softly was one of the customary ways of showing politeness in our small-town society. She went off as joyfully as a child who expects to be given a new blouse.

From that moment, Inem no longer lived in our house. I felt very deeply the loss of my constant companion. From that moment also, it was no longer Inem who took me to the bathing cubicle at night to wash my feet before going to bed, but my adoptive older sister.

Sometime I felt an intense longing to see Inem. Not infrequently, when I had got into bed, I would recall the moment when her mother drew her by the hand and the two of them left our house. Inem's house was in back of ours, separated only by a wooden fence.

She had been gone a month. I often went to her house to play with her, and Mother always got angry when she found out that I had been there. She would always say, "What can you learn at Inem's house that's of any use?"

And I would never reply. Mother always had a good reason for scolding me. Everything she said built a thick wall that was impenetrable to excuses. Therefore my best course was to be silent. And as the clinching argument in her lecture, she was almost certain to repeat the sentences that she uttered so often: "What's the point to your playing with her? Aren't there lots of other children you can ask to play with you? What's more, she's a woman who's going to be married soon."

But I kept on sneaking over to her house anyway. It is really surprising sometimes how a prohibition seems to exist solely in order to be violated. And when I disobeyed I felt that what I did was pleasurable. For children such as I at that time—oh, how many prohibitions and restrictions were heaped on our heads! Yes, it was as though the whole world was watching us, bent on forbidding whatever we did and whatever we wanted. Inevitably we children felt that this world was really intended only for adults.

Then the day of the wedding arrived.

For five days before the ceremony, Inem's family was busy in the kitchen, cooking food and preparing various delicacies. This made me visit her house all the more frequently.

The day before the wedding, Inem was dressed in all her finery. Mother sent me there with five kilos of rice and twenty-five cents as a neighborly contribution. And that afternoon we children crowded around and stared at her in admiration. The hair over her forehead and temples and her eyebrows had been carefully trimmed with a razor and thickened with mascara. Her little bun of hair had been built up with a switch and adorned with the paper flowers with springs for stalks that we call *sunduk mentul*. Her clothes were made of satin. Her sarong was an expensive one made in Solo. These things had all been rented from a Chinaman in the Chinese quarter near the town square. The gold rings and bracelets were all rented too.

The house was decorated with constructions of banyan leaves and young coconut fronds. On each wall there were crossed tricolor flags encircled by palm leaves. All the house pillars were similarly decorated with tricolor bunting.

Mother herself went and helped with the preparations. But not for long. Mother rarely did this sort of thing except for her closest neighbors. She stayed less than an hour. And it was then too that the things sent by Inem's husband-to-be arrived: a load of cakes and candies, a male goat, a quantity of rice, a packet of salt, a sack of husked coconuts, and half a sack of granulated sugar.

It was just after the harvest. Rice was cheap. And when rice was cheap all other foodstuffs were cheap too. That was why the period after the harvest was a favorite time for celebrations. And for that reason Inem's family had found it impossible to contract for a puppet performance. The puppet masters had already been engaged by other families in various neighborhoods. The puppet theater was the most popular form of entertainment in our area. In our town there were three types of puppet performance: the *wajan purwa* or shadow play, which recounted stories from the *Mahabharata* and the *Ramayana*,[3] as well as other stories similar in theme; the *wajang krutjil*, in which wooden puppets in human shape acted out stories of Arabia, Persia, India, and China, as well as tales of Madjapahit times; and the *wajang golek*, which employed wooden dolls. But this last was not very popular.

Because there were no puppet masters available, Inem's family engaged a troupe of dancing girls. At first this created a dispute. Inem's relatives on her mother's side were religious scholars and teachers. But Inem's father would not back down. The dance troupe came, with its *gamelan*[4] orchestra, and put on a *tajuban*.

Usually, in our area, a *tajuban* was attended by the men who wanted to dance with the girls and by little children who only wanted to watch—little children whose knowledge of sexual matters did not go beyond kissing. The grown boys did not like to watch; it embarrassed them. This was even more the case with the women—none of them attended at all. And a *tajuban* in our area—in order to inflame sexual passions—was always accompanied by alcoholic beverages: arrack, beer, whisky, or gin.

---

[3]The *Mahabharata* and the *Ramayana* are ancient Indian epics.
[4]A musical instrumental ensemble consisting of bamboo xylophones, gongs, and other percussion instruments; *tajuban:* a social dance in which professional women dancers perform and often ask the spectators to dance with them.

The *tajuban* lasted for two days and nights. We children took great delight in the spectacle of men and women dancing and kissing one another and every now and then clinking their glasses and drinking liquor as they danced and shouted, *"Huse!"*[5]

And though Mother forbade me to watch, I went anyway on the sly.

"Why do you insist on going where those wicked people are? Look at your religious teacher: he doesn't go to watch, even though he is Inem's father's brother-in-law. You must have noticed that yourself."

Our religious teacher also had a house in back of ours, to the right of Inem's house. Subsequently the teacher's failure to attend became a topic that was sure to enliven a conversation. From it there arose two remarks that itched on the tip of everyone's tongue: that the teacher was certainly a pious man, and that Inem's father was undoubtedly a reprobate.

Mother reinforced her scolding with words that I did not understand at the time: "Do you know something? They are people who have no respect for women," she said in a piercing voice.

And when the bridegroom came to be formally presented to the bride, Inem, who had been sitting on the nuptial seat, was led forth. The bridegroom had reached the veranda. Inem squatted and made obeisance to her future husband, and then washed his feet with flower water from a brass pot. Then the couple were tied together and conducted side by side to the nuptial seat. At that time the onlookers could be heard saying, "One child becomes two. One child becomes two. One child becomes two."

And the women who were watching beamed as though they were to be the recipients of the happiness to come.

At that very moment I noticed that Inem was crying so much that her make-up was spoiled, and tears were trickling down her pretty face. At home I asked Mother, "Why was the bride crying, Mama?"

"When a bride cries, it's because she is thinking of her long-departed ancestors. Their spirits also attend the ceremony. And they are happy that their descendant has been safely married," replied Mother.

I never gave any thought to those words of hers. Later I found out why Inem had been crying. She had to urinate, but was afraid to tell anyone.

The celebration ended uneventfully. There were no more guests coming with contributions. The house resumed its everyday appearance, and by the time the moneylenders came to collect, Inem's father had left Blora. After the wedding, Inem's mother and Inem herself went on doing batik work—day and night. And if someone went to their house at three o'clock in the morning, he would be likely to find them still working. Puffs of smoke would be rising between them from the crucible in which the wax was melted. In addition to that, quarreling was often heard in that house.

---

[5]Hooray!

And once, when I was sleeping with Mother in her bed, a loud scream awakened me: "I won't! I won't!"

It was still night then. The screams were repeated again and again, accompanied by the sound of blows and pounding on a door. I knew that the screams came from Inem's mouth. I recognized her voice.

"Mama, why is Inem screaming?" I asked.

"They're fighting. I hope nothing bad happens to that little girl," she said. But she gave no explanation.

"Why would anything bad happen to her, mama?" I asked insistently.

Mother did not reply to my question. And then, when the screaming and shouting were over, we went back to sleep. Such screams were almost sure to be heard every night. Screams and screams. And every time I heard them, I would ask my mother about them. Mother would never give a satisfactory answer. Sometimes she merely sighed, "What a pity, such a little child!"

One day Inem came to our house. She went straight in to find my mother. Her face was pale bloodless. Before saying anything, she set the tone of the occasion by crying—crying in a respectful way.

"Why are you crying, Inem? Have you been fighting again?" Mother asked.

"Ma'am," said Inem between her sobs, "I hope that you will be willing to take me back here as before."

"But you're married, aren't you, Inem?"

And Inem cried some more. Through her tears she said, "I can't stand it, ma'am."

"Why, Inem? Don't you like your husband?" asked Mother.

"Ma'am, please take pity on me. Every night all he wants to do is wrestle, ma'am."

"Can't you say to him, 'Please, dear, don't be like that'?"

"I'm afraid, ma'am. I'm afraid of him. He's so big. And when he wrestles he squeezes me so hard that I can't breathe. You'll take me back, won't you, ma'am?" she pleaded.

"If you didn't have a husband, Inem, of course I'd take you back. But you have a husband. . . "

And Inem cried again when she heard what Mother said. "Ma'am I don't want to have a husband."

"You may not want to, but the fact is that you do, Inem. Maybe eventually your husband will change for the better, and the two of you will be able to live happily. You wanted to get married, didn't you?" said Mother.

"Yes, ma'am . . . but, but. . . "

"Inem, regardless of anything else, a woman must serve her husband faithfully. If you aren't a good wife to your husband, your ancestors will curse you," said Mother.

Inem began crying harder. And because of her crying she was unable to say anything.

"Now, Inem, promise me that you will always prepare your husband's meals. When you have an idle moment, you should pray to God to keep him safe. You must promise to wash his clothes, and you must massage him when he is tired from his work. You must rub his back vigorously when he catches cold."

Inem still made no reply. Only her tears continued to fall.

"Well now, you go home, and from this moment on be a good wife to him. No matter whether he is good or bad, you must serve him faithfully, because after all he *is* your husband."

Inem, who was sitting on the floor, did not stir.

"Get up and go home to your husband. You . . . if you just up and quit your husband the consequences will not be good for you, either now or in the future," Mother added.

"Yes, ma'am," Inem said submissively. Slowly she rose and walked home.

"How sad, she's so little," said Mother.

"Mama, does daddy ever wrestle you?" I asked.

Mother looked searchingly into my eyes. Then her scrutiny relaxed. She smiled. "No," she said "Your father is the best person in the whole world, Muk."

Then Mother went to the kitchen to get the hoe, and she worked in the garden with me.

A year passed imperceptibly. On a certain occasion Inem came again. In the course of a year she had grown much bigger. It was quite apparent that she was mature, although only nine years old. As usual, she went directly to where Mother was and sat on the floor with her head bowed. She said, "Ma'am, now I don't have a husband any more."

"What?"

"Now I don't have a husband any more."

"You're divorced?" asked Mother.

"Yes, ma'am."

"Why did you separate from him?"

She did not reply.

"Did you fail to be a good wife to him?"

"I think I was always a good wife to him, ma'am."

"Did you massage him when he came home tired from work?" asked Mother probingly.

"Yes, ma'am, I did everything you advised me to."

"Well then, why did you separate?"

"Ma'am, he often beat me."

"Beat you? He beat a little child like you?"

"I did everything I could to be a good wife, ma'am. And when he beat me and I was in pain—was that part of being a good wife, ma'am?" she asked, in genuine perplexity.

Mother was silent. Her eyes scrutinized Inem. "He beat you," Mother whispered then.

"Yes, ma'am—he beat me just the way Mama and Papa do."

"Maybe you failed in some way after all in your duty to him. A husband would never have the heart to beat a wife who was really and truly a good wife to him."

Inem did not reply. She changed the subject: "Would you be willing to take me back, ma'am?"

There was no hesitation in Mother's reply. She said firmly, "Inem, you're a divorced woman now. There are lots of grown boys here. It wouldn't look right to people, would it?"

"But they wouldn't beat me," said the divorcee.

"No. That isn't what I mean. It just doesn't look right for a divorced woman as young as you to be in a place where there are lots of men."

"Is that because there's something wrong with me, ma'am?"

"No, Inem, It's a question of propriety."

"Propriety, ma'am? It's for the sake of propriety that I can't stay here?"

"Yes, that's the way it is, Inem."

The divorcee did not say anything more. She remained sitting on the floor, and seemed to have no intention of leaving the place where she was sitting. Mother went up to her and patted her shoulder consolingly. "Now, Inem . . . the best thing is for you to help your parents earn a living. I really regret that I can't take you back here."

Two tears formed in the corners of the little woman's eyes. She got up. Listlessly she moved her feet, leaving our house to return to her parents' house. And from then on she was seldom seen outside her house.

And thereafter, the nine-year-old divorcee—since she was nothing but a burden to her family—could be beaten by anyone who wanted to: her mother, her brothers, her uncles, her neighbors, her aunts. Yet Inem never again came to our house.

Her screams of pain were often heard. When she moaned, I covered my ears with my hands. And Mother continued to uphold the respectability of her home.

❋ Discussion and Writing

1. Describe the arrangement and celebration of the marriage. What is the purpose of the elaborate details concerning the arranged marriage, festivities, rituals, and such?
2. Comment on the conversation between the two mothers: in what ways are they essentially different?
3. Analyze the mistress's counsel to Inem about how to be a good wife. Why does it not work?

4. Describe Inem's life: before marriage; after marriage; after divorce. What seems to remain constant?
5. What is the effect of having a six-year-old boy narrator telling the story of an eight-year-old girl's predicament? What does Toer accomplish by this shift in the point of view?
6. Analyze the author's attitude projected in this narrative regarding child marriages and class structure.

✳ Research and Comparison

Explore Pramoedya Toer's life and literary works in relation to his political involvement.

Interdisciplinary Discussion Question: Research the issue of arranged marriages in modern Indonesian society. What seems to be the social rationale for the continuation of the tradition? How does it differ from a similar tradition in any other society where this tradition is followed? Also, examine the status of child marriages in modern Indonesia.

Interdisciplinary Discussion Question: Examine colonialism and the rise of nationalism in Indonesia to understand its contemporary politics.

Mahasweta Devi
(b. 1926)
India

Mahasweta Devi was born in Dacca. (In 1947 when India was partitioned, Dacca became the capital of East Pakistan, which, in turn, became Bangladesh in 1971.) She came from a middle-class Bengali family and was profoundly influenced by the political and social turmoil of the times. She studied at Tagore's schools, Shantiniketan and Visva-Bharati, as well as at Calcutta University, receiving her master's degree in English. A political activist, she taught at Bijaygarh College, a college for working-class women, and she committed herself to working among the non-urbanized, tribal people, the people who were not part of the caste system yet occupied a social stratum barely above the out-caste. She has been involved in studying and collecting the proto-Dravidian oral literature of the tribal people. As an editor of a Bengali journal, *Bortika,* and a journalist, she has been in a position to voice her concerns. She has, moreover, informed her fiction and journalism with her deeply held feminist and Marxist convictions. Written in her native Bengali, her work has protested against the retention of patriarchal mores and against the caste and class systems: against the subjugation of untouchables, women, and laborers; and against the corruption of the powerful, whether the government or the landlords. As in "Dhowli," she has exposed the anguish of the poor and the exploited—here the Dusads, the tribal people who worked in the forests— and most particularly, the plight of destitute women. In 1979 she won the Sahitya Akademi Award, a prestigious national award in literature, for her novel about the 1899 rebellion, *Aranyer Adhikar* (The Occupation of the Forest, 1977).

*Dhowli**

1

The bus starts from Ranchi city in early afternoon and reaches Tahad around eight in the evening. The bus stop is in front of the grocery shop, also the only tea shop, both run by Parashnath, next to the post office. The shop-*cum*-teastall, the post office, and the bus stop form the downtown for the cluster of villages. The passengers get off here and walk the rest of their way home. This is where the unpaved wide road ends; so also ends the outside world with which Tahad is connected by this once-a-day rickety bus run by the Rohatgi company. The Punjabi company runs a brisk fleet of forty buses connecting the business centers in Bihar, twenty going up the highways and twenty coming down along the three routes connecting Ranchi with Patna, Hazaribagh, and Ramgarh. For dirt-poor, remote places like Tahad or Palani, they have a few dilapidated buses running off and on. On the three market days each week, the bus is filled by tribal villagers out to buy and sell. On other days, the bus is almost empty and runs irregularly to cut the company's loss. During the months of monsoon the bus does not come up the unpaved road, and the villages then remain cut off from the outside world.

This year, the rains seemed to be coming early, at the very start of June.

Dhowli was waiting at the bus stop, standing very still, her back to the shop, facing away from the shop's light, the only light there. Parashnath closed his shop when it seemed to him that the bus was not likely to come. He asked Dhowli if she should not be going home now. Dhowli neither answered nor looked at him. She just kept standing. Old Parashnath muttered, worried, as he left for his home at the back of the shop. His wife was sitting there alone, smoking and thinking. Parashnath told her about the girl waiting again for the bus so late in the evening.

Translated by Kalpana Bardhan

"She'll be finished if she keeps up this way."

"If the landlord comes to know what she's been doing. . . "

"That'll be her end. How long has it been since the Misra boy left?"

"Nearly four months now."

"What does she think? An untouchable, Dusad[1] girl can make a Brahman give her home and food?"

"God only knows. But she's not going to be able to hold off for long."

"What makes you think so?"

"The contractor, and the gang of coolies."[2]

"Yes. She doesn't have much of a chance. Such a young girl! Going back and forth alone in the dark night. What for? Isn't she afraid?"

"The wolf was out last night."

Dhowli had also heard that the wolf was out, but she forgot about it. The unbearable pain just under her chest made her forget everything else. The pain would stay there and then move down her body, as it was now. Dhowli did not know what to do; she could not think of anything.

Dhowli walked back home in the dark. To the shack dimly lit by the smoky oil lamp; their bed on the bamboo bunk; three goats tethered under the bunk. Her mother, lying in the bunk, saw her come in but said nothing. Dhowli tilted the water pot to see if there was any water. She drank some, closed the door, blew out the lamp, and lay down beside her mother. Tears silently flowed from her eyes, tears of hopeless pain. Her mother listened to her crying; she knew why the tears flowed. Later in the night, she said, "We're going to be driven out of the village. You're young. What'll happen to me? Where shall I go?"

"You'll stay here."

"And you? You'll leave?"

"If I have to."

"Where will you go?"

"To death's door."

"It's not so easy! At nineteen, there are obstacles to death's door."

"Not for me."

"Have you been to Sanichari?"

"No!" Dhowli shouted, "I'll not get rid of the baby."

"Will you then go to the Misra house? Tell them that, because their son is the father, they should help to bring up the child carrying their blood?"

"Who is going to believe me? It would have been different if he were here now, if he came back."

"How? He would have looked after you?"

"He promised to."

---

[1]One of the tribes, considered on the lower rung of the social scale. [eds.]

[2]Originally a tribe; later a term used for laborers; the British used the term for all people of color. [eds.]

"They always say such things. You're not the first Dusad girl who has been used by the Misra menfolk. Have they left untouched any young girl of the Dusads, the Dhobis, the Ganjus of the village?"

"He's not like the others."

"No! He knows very well what is expected of a Brahman's[3] son in this situation. He knows what to do, but he's not doing it."

"He's in love with me."

"In love with you? Is that why he has stayed away in Dhanbad for four months, not even coming to visit his own folks?"

"He doesn't come because he's afraid of his parents."

"You're thinking of love. Here I lost my job of tending their goats. The wolf got one of the kids. They accused me of stealing it."

"What has that got to do with me?"

"They did it to punish you, to show that they're annoyed."

"Throw me out, then."

"I will. Go to sleep now."

"How can you say you'll throw me out? Who do you have but me?"

At this point, mother and daughter started arguing, as they did almost every night these days. This time they were interrupted by the watchman's voice from outside. "Dhowli's mother! All day we hear you shout. Do we have to hear you shout in the night, too? There are other Dusads in the neighborhood. They all know that days are for shouting and nights for sleeping. You're the only one who doesn't respect this simple rule."

"Shut up, and go away. I'll be quiet now."

"What's the problem anyway? Is some coolie trying to get in?"

"It's your home that the coolies try to get in."

"Ram! Ram! Don't even say such a thing!"

The watchman walked away. Mother muttered what was on her mind, "I know the custom here. Everybody is waiting, watching to see if the Misra boy supports you after the baby is born. If he doesn't, they'll come to eat pieces off you."

"It's all your fault. Why did you bring me back to you when my husband died? Why didn't you leave me there, to whatever was to happen?"

"Did they want to keep you? Didn't you insist on coming with me?"

"Because his elder brother would have taken my virtue there."

"And the Misra boy has not here!"

The sarcasm felt like a stab. Dhowli said nothing. Her eyelids were dry inside from crying. She pulled the dry lids down over her tired eyes.

But she could not fall asleep. She had not been able to sleep since the day the Misra boy left, taking the early morning bus, running away like a thief. She knew that she could fall asleep forever with the poison for killing maize insects. But she could not die before seeing that betrayer once more face to face, eye to eye.

---

[3]Brahman-Brahmin. [eds.]

Betrayer? No. He left Tahad because his parents made him. They came down so hard on their dearly loved youngest boy; Hanuman Misra of Burudiha threatened them. He wouldn't have left Dhowli unless he was really scared, he who cried like a baby to Dhowli just talking about the possibility that he might be sent away. It still hurt to remember how he wept.

Her mother wanted her to get the medicine from Sanichari to remove the "thorn" from her womb. How could she think of it as a thorn, when it came from their love? It was not like the children of Jhalo, the Ganju wife, and Kundan, the elder Misra son; it was not one of those products of greed and ruthless power.

Dhowli used to sweep their yard. She never lifted her eyes at the young Brahman she knew was always gazing at her. At noon, while tending the goats in the forest, Dhowli was once bathing in the stream when a small leafy branch fell beside her. She looked up and saw the Misra boy. He had followed her. He did not laugh; he did not leer at her; he did nothing she could be ashamed of. He only asked her why she never even looked at him when he was going out of his mind for her.

"Please, *deota*,[4] don't say such things!" ·

"What deota! Don't you know that I'm really your slave?"

"I don't want to hear such things."

Dhowli was afraid and turned to leave. Then he said, "You'll have to hear the truth some time, even if you don't want to now."

The young Misra left her with those words, words that still make the breeze waft in her mind, the leaves rustle, and the stream murmur. She stood there after he left. She lingered on, feeling something like a terrible fear beating in her chest. Fear of the unthinkable. The young Misra was so fair, his hair softly curled, and his face so lovely. Anyone could tell from his looks that he was of noble birth. And what was Dhowli? Only a Dusad girl, a widow, with a life of deprivation as far back as she could remember.

When her father died and there was no other man in the family, Kundan took away the lease of land from her mother. Her mother went to them and promised to pay the rent, whatever rent they wanted; she would have the land tilled by her Dusad kinsmen, for, if they wouldn't lease her the land, the two of them would starve to death. Kundan refused. Dhowli's mother then fell at the feet of Kundan's mother, "Please save me and my daughter from starving."

Kundan's mother pleaded with her son, "As long as her husband was alive, he tilled that land and gave us free labor whenever we wanted. Now that he is dead, we can't let her starve."

"Nothing I can do. I've already leased that plot to Jhuman Dusad."

---

[4]Lord, deity.

"Let them tend the goats then and clean our garden and yards. We'll give them some money and millet."

She depended on their pity for the gruel at the end of the day. And a son of theirs had just said those words to her. Why? Dhowli knew that her timid eyes, her slender waist, and her budding breasts were her enemies, only to bring her trouble and ruin her. So, she had always kept herself covered as well as she could with her cheap, short sari, and she never looked up when working in their yard, not even at the loads of fruit ripening on the trees. She picked up only the guavas and the custard apples that birds and bats had partly eaten and dropped underneath. Even those she showed to Kundan's mother for permission before bringing them home.

That day, after she came back from the forest, Dhowli scrubbed their brass plate till it gleamed like gold. When her mother was away, she looked at her face in it. A widow was not supposed to see her face in the mirror any more, nor wear the shellac bangles, the vermillion between the brows, the nickel anklets. She saw that her face was beautiful, but a beautiful face was useless for a widow because she could never marry again. She would never even be invited to sing the song "Sita is on her way to her in-laws' place" at another girl's wedding, nor to paint with colored paste flowers, leaves, and birds on the doors and the walls of any celebrating house. Someone like her had just heard the landlord's young son proclaim love, that he was a slave to her. Fear nestled under her chest like some terrible discomfort.

Dhowli told her mother, "You'll sweep the gardens of the Misras, and I would only tend the goats."

"Why?"

"Because, you know, Ma, how the leaves fly when you try to sweep them into a pile. I can't cope with the wind scattering them about."

"Did anyone say anything to you?"

"Who can say what to me, Ma?"

"Don't go far into the forest with the goats. A wolf or a hyena is about."

"Don't worry, Ma. Am I that careless?"

She thought a lot, while tending the goats alone in the woods. She thought about everything she could remember from her childhood—going to the fair, perched on her father's shoulders; spending the day looking at all the shops with their expensive things, and then coming home happy with a paisa worth of sesame candy. Of her marital home, all she remembered were the two rooms, the days of work at the farm of the moneylender to whom they were indebted, and her mother-in-law making the gruel at the end of the day, for the men to eat first before the women ate what was left over.

About her wedding she could not recall much because she must have been very small at the time. She was sent to live with her husband when her body blossomed. Her father had to take a large loan from the Misras for her wedding and sending off, and he had to pay back the loan with his labor until he died. She remembered nothing nice about her husband. He used to beat her. He died of a fever. After he died, her mother-in-law asked her to stay on,

"You have to work at your mother's place too in order to eat. Do the same here."

Dhowli knew that much: she could spend the rest of her life there, working all day, clad in the widow's borderless sari, coarse and short, working every day from sunrise to sunset either on the creditor's threshing floor or as some farmer's laborer or leveling the layer of brick pieces with a mallet making some road or other, and then falling asleep by the side of her mother-in-law after eating whatever there was to eat. But then her husband's elder brother came there and started eyeing her. Her mother-in-law then turned against her and Dhowli left. Her only regret was that she had to leave before she could watch the *nautanki*[5] one more time. The *nautanki* performers used to come to the village, hired by the moneylender.

After she returned to Tahad, she did not let herself near any Dusad boy. What good could come of it? The same routine of backbreaking work, with kids in your lap, kids following you around, no food, nothing. Dhowli had no desire for that kind of life, the only kind of life for a Dusad girl.

It was so much better to be alone, alone in the woods, with time to think one's own thoughts. She tended the goats, and once in a while she lay down on the end of her sari spread on the forest floor. She was never afraid of the wolf or the hyena. They fear people just as people fear them. The forest felt so peaceful that the constant discomfort and fear she had after hearing the Misra boy speak so strangely to her was slowly going away. She was at peace again.

Then one evening, when coming back from the fair at Jhujhar, she somehow lost the group of women she came with. She knew that the procurers came to the village fairs to catch just such stray girls. So she was walking back as fast as she could. The Misra boy caught up with her.

"Didn't you hear me calling?"

"Why did you call?"

"Don't you know why?"

"No. Please don't say such things to me. I'm a poor Dusad widow, and you are the landlord. Please don't make fun of me."

"But I'm in love with you."

"No, *deota.* Don't mistake it for love. You are a young Brahman man. You'll marry a bride proper for you. Please stop this."

"But it's you I love. Don't you know what love is?"

"No, I don't. I know that there can be bastards between the landlord and a Ganju or Dusad girl. That happens all the time. But not love."

"But I can't think of anyone but you."

"Please don't play your games with a helpless poor girl."

[5]*Nautanki* is a form of vaudeville, with wild and earthy songs and dances, common in north Indian villages.

"I'm not playing games."

"You'll leave after you tire of the game, and what will become of me? Am I to be like Jhalo? No, *deota*, not that."

"What if I don't let you go?"

"What good is my saying anything? I'll have to accept it. You landlord people, you take whatever pleases you. If you want to take my honor, take it then. Let me be through with it."

"No, no. Don't say that, Dhowli. Forgive me." The Misra boy ran away from her. She came home, totally amazed by his behavior.

Soon after that, when she heard that the Misra boy was not well, that he seemed to have lost interest in life, she was moved and worried. She knew that the Misra boy could have had her any time he wanted. All the Misra men do that, and there is not a thing that the Dhowlis of the world can do to stop it. But why such strange behavior?

She felt overwhelmed. Then the women at the well surrounded her, "Fate is now all smiles on the poor widow!"

"How can fate ever smile on a widow?"

"The landlord's young son is going out of his mind for you!"

"A pack of lies!"

"Everybody knows it's true. The word is around."

"Don't bother me with gossip."

Dhowli left with the water, resolutely denying it, but she was agitated, and she went to the woods with the goats. What would she do now? The whole village was talking about something that had never happened before. Why did the boy lose his mind like that? Now nobody was going to leave her alone.

She avoided going anywhere near the Misra estate. She heard from her mother that the boy was still unwell and they had to call a doctor from Valatod. She wondered if her mother knew what the women at the well knew. She suggested that they go away from the village, to Valatod maybe, and work at road construction, to which her mother just said, "I'm not out of my mind."

Then one day she heard that the Misra boy had recovered, that they were looking for a beautiful bride for him. They hadn't looked particularly for beauty in Kundan's bride; but for this one they were after beauty.

Dhowli had felt relieved, but she had also felt a twinge of pain and simultaneously a joy of victory at the thought that a mere Dusad girl drove a Brahman's son so out of his mind.

Relieved and peaceful again, she went to the woods and had a cooling dip in the stream. Afterward, she dried half of the sari she was wearing by spreading it on a sun-heated stone, and then wrapped it around her upper body. She decided that she would buy another sari next time her mother got paid for their work. It always made her mother angry to see her in a half-wet sari: "Are you a widow or a marketplace whore, that you're showing your body?"

Suddenly, the Misra boy appeared there.

"I don't want to marry a girl of their choice. It's you I want, Dhowli," he told her in earnest.

The forest in the early afternoon is primitive, gentle, and comforting. The Misra boy's voice was imploring, his eyes full of pain and despair. Dhowli was unguarded in mind and body. She gave in.

For two months since that day, she lived as if in a strange dream. The forest was their meeting place, and the time the early afternoon. Both lost caution and sense, one nineteen and the other twenty-three. Every day, Dhowli worried about what was going to happen next.

"You're going to be married off soon."

"With you."

"Don't joke with me, *deota*."

"I'm not joking. I don't believe in caste. And Tahad is not the only place in the world to live. Besides, our marriage will be all right by the government rules."

"Don't say such things. If you talk defiant, what will Misraji order? They will then drive me away from the village."

"It's not going to be so easy. There are government laws against it."

"The laws are not for people like us."

"You don't know anything."

In the solitude of the forest, the Misra boy was dauntless, telling her of his plans, and his words seemed to mingle with all the myths associated with the old forest, taking on an enchanting and dreamlike quality. The days thus went by. But not for very long. Dhowli found out that she was pregnant. Strangely, the Misra boy was happy about that. He said, "I'm illiterate, just like you. I don't want anything to do with managing all this farmland and orchard and the estate. We'll go to Valatod, and then from there to Dhanbad, and on to Patna. We'll start a shop there and live from it."

But the day Hanuman Misra came to Tahad to settle the matter, the Misra boy could say none of those things to him. Kundan fretted and said that he was going to kill both mother and daughter and dispose of their bodies overnight.

"No, don't do that," Misraji said. "Clean the inside of the house, and the outside will clean itself."

"I want to kill them."

"That's because you're stupid."

"That bitch of her mother said that the wolf took one of the goats. How did she get three goats in her shack? Didn't she have two before?"

"The idiot talks about goats! Your wife has got more sense. I can talk with her, not you. Kill them, but not directly. Starve them. Take away the job. What your silly brother got himself into has affected the prestige of all of us. We must restore our position first. What does it matter if you have one goat less? Listen to me, the first thing you should do now is move him away from here."

The young Misra said that he would not leave the village.

"If you don't, your dead body will. You've brought shame to our family by your stupidity."

The Misra boy in desperation appealed to his mother, "Ma, please! Dhowli is carrying my baby."

"Nothing unusual about it, my boy," she consoled him. "Men of this family have had children by Dusad and Ganju girls. Kundan has three by Jhalo. It's only the heat of your age, my boy."

"What'll happen to Dhowli then?"

"She'll be punished for daring to do what she did. She'll pay. She and her mother will starve to death."

"But it's not her fault, Mother."

"The fault is always the woman's. She caused trouble in a Brahman landlord's home. That equals a crime."

"Mother, you love me, don't you?"

"You're my youngest child."

"Then touch me and swear. I'll listen to you if you'll see that she doesn't starve. Promise."

"I promise," she said hesitantly.

"Also promise me that nobody humiliates her or throws her out."

"I'll try."

"If you don't keep these words, then you know, Mother, that I can be stubborn. I may not be able to stand up to the big Misra. But if you don't keep the promises, then I'll never come to this village, never marry."

"No, no. I'll feed the Dusad girl; I'll look after her."

Dhowli was aware of what was going on, what was in store for her now. She never even thought of protesting. This was not the first time that a Dusad girl had been used by the Brahman landlord's son. According to the village society, all the blame goes to Dhowli. But, because of the love aspect of this case, she was now an outcaste to her own people, in her own community. She had not encouraged any boy of her own caste. That was no fault. If the Misra boy had taken her by force, then she would not have been faulted either; the Dusad community would not have abandoned her for that. There are quite a few children by Brahman men growing up among the Dusads. Her crime, something nobody was prepared to forgive, was that she gave herself to him of her own accord, out of love. All the Dusad-Ganju boys, the coolies, and the labor contractors were now watching how things would settle. If the Misras would support her and the child with a regular supply of corn or money or a job, then they would leave her alone because they did not want to annoy the Misras if they wanted to live in their domain. If not, then they would turn her, a widow with no one but an old mother and a baby, into a prostitute for all of them to use.

Dhowli knew what was going through every mind, and she was numb with fear and sorrow. The woods looked horrible to her, the trees looked like ghoulish guards, and even the rocks seemed to be watching her. She waited for him by the stream. Days passed, but he failed to appear there. When Dhowli was about to give up, he came. Dhowli read her death sentence in his grim face. She cried without a word, her face on his chest. He cried too, his face buried in her hair, her hair smelling of the soap and the scented oil he had given her. He had given her two saris too, but Dhowli never wore them because their printed material was forbidden for a widow.

The Misra boy was filled with hopelessness. All he could say was, "Dhowli, why were you born a Dusad?"

"Spare me the endearments! I can't stand them anymore."

"Listen to me. Don't cry yet."

"Don't I have to cry the rest of my life?"

"I have to leave the village now. I agreed to their conditions for now."

"Why did you tell me those words of love?"

"I'm still telling you."

"Why, master? Your Dhowli is dead now. Don't make fun of a corpse."

"Don't be silly. Listen to me." He made Dhowli sit on a rock. He held her face in his hands and lifted it to his. Then he said to her, "I must stay away for a month, and I'll do so quietly. But I told them that I won't be forced into a marriage, and they agreed not to try."

"They will forget that soon."

"No. Listen, I'll be back as soon as the month is over. I'm not sure where they'll send me or what I'll do in this one month. But I'll manage something for us. I'm not educated, and I don't want a salaried job. And I'm not going to ask my brother for a share of the farmland and orchards. I'll start a shop, and I'll use this time to do it. I need some time away from them to do it, you see?"

"What am I to do?"

"You will stay right in the village."

"What shall we live on? Your brother accused my mother of stealing and sacked her."

"My mother has promised me that she'll supply you with food, and here. . . ," he took out five ten-rupee notes, put them in one end of Dhowli's sari, tied a knot around it, and tucked it in her waist. "Try to stay calm for one month."

Misrilal took leave of her.

Dhowli came back from the forest and told her mother. The two of them put the money in a little can and buried it under their mud floor.

Two days after he had left, Dhowli's mother went to the Misra matriarch and silently stood before her. Silently she got up, brought a kilo of millet and poured it in the outstretched sari of Dhowli's mother, conspicuously avoiding her touch while doing it. Glumly she asked her to come back after three days. After three days, the quantity of grain was reduced to half a kilo. When she next returned after the specified three days, the lady grimly informed her that after the last time she was there, they couldn't find a brass bowl.

"No, lady. Not me. . . "

"My elder son has asked me not to let you inside the house any more. Next time you should stand at the gate and call someone."

Dhowli's mother had to swallow the accusation because it came from a Brahman lady. Next time she was told at the gate that the lady was away, gone to Burudiha to see Hanuman Misra.

Dhowli's mother came home boiling with anger and beat up Dhowli. Dhowli took the beating quietly. When her mother stopped beating, she brought the cleaver and asked her to use it instead because her old hands tired and ached easily and as it was sharpened recently, she would not have to bother to beat her again. Mother and daughter then held each other and cried. When they were through crying, her mother asked her to go to Sanichari and get some medicine to get rid of the thorn in her womb.

"I can't do that."

"Listen to me. He is not going to come back for you. He was just in a rebellious mood toward the family. He may have good intentions; maybe he wasn't lying when he promised to come back. But he won't be able to do it."

"Then I'd rather poison myself."

Mother sat down, pondering a few minutes what her daughter had just said; then, sighing, she got up, as if she had just remembered something. "I'm going to the forest contractor; he once asked if I could cook for him."

"Do you want me to go?"

"No. I'll go. I'm past the age to worry about gossip. Even if he doesn't pay money, he'll give me some food. I'll bring it home."

"Go then, before the job is gone."

"And you remember to tend the goats."

This arrangement kept them going a little longer. Dhowli's mother did not find the cook's job, but she was taken as the cook's helper, and she brought home the bread or rice she managed to get.

Their own folks watched how mother and daughter managed to live— what they did and what they didn't do. The coolies working under the forest contractor also watched them. They had cash from their daily wages for lugging lumber. They had refrained from falling on her so far only because they were not sure if she was going to become the favored woman of Kundan's little brother. They had not given up, though, and watched the goings on. They did not mind the wait; the contract for cutting logs and splitting lumber was to continue for a while, and she was worth waiting for. As a matter of fact, her attraction increased in their minds with the scandal of a Brahman boy falling in love with her.

One month was long over. It was four months now. It had become a ritual with Dhowli to go to the bus stop, stand silently waiting for the bus to come up, and return home disappointed. On this night Dhowli thought of the whole thing, all over again, and then she placed her hand on her abdomen. She felt the baby move a little. Misrilal had said, "If it is a boy, we'll name him Murari." But Misrilal and his words of love now felt like a receding illusion, a fading dream.

2

In late autumn Dhowli gives birth to a son. Sanichari delivers the baby. She cuts the umbilical cord with care and remarks that the baby is so fair because it has Dhowli's complexion. Dhowli's mother had asked Sanichari earlier to make sure she would be infertile after this baby. Sanichari gives her the medicine, telling her that it will make her feel better soon.

Afterward she sits down to talk with Dhowli's mother, who is worried that the medicine is going to kill her or make her a permanent invalid. Sanichari assures her with the account of her success with the medicine in the case of Kundan's wife.

"What are you going to do now?"

"Whatever god has willed for us."

"The Misra boy is going to be married soon."

"Quiet. Don't let Dhowli hear of it now."

"What will you do after that?"

"Whatever is in store for us will happen."

"Pebbles will start falling at your door at night."

"I know."

"After getting him married, they're going to make the couple live in Dhanbad. They've set up a cycle store there for him."

"I told Dhowli this was going to happen."

"As I've already told you, if the landlord doesn't undertake to support her and the baby, I'll try and get the forest overseer for her."

"We'll think about that later."

Because of Sanichari's Manthara-like cunning, and because she is indispensable for her knowledge of medicinal herbs and roots, not even the Misras dare to ignore her or snub her. Seeing Dhowli give birth, delivering her baby, has touched something in Sanichari's heart. She starts building support in Dhowli's favor. When she visits the Misra mother to treat her rheumatic pain, Sanichari tells her that she just delivered Dhowli's baby boy.

"So what?" says the lady.

"His face is exactly like your boy's."

"Nobody tells me such a lie."

"Don't be silly. Everybody knows that your boy was in love with Dhowli. Your men sow their seeds in our women. It is common, but how often does it become such a problem that Hanuman Misra himself has to come to solve it?"

"Because you raised the matter, let me ask you for something. . . "

"What is it?"

"Can you remove them from the village?"

"Remove them where?"

"I don't care where. The problem is that the girl my boy is going to be married to is not exactly a little girl, and the family has a lot of prestige. If they come to know of this, it will make them very annoyed."

"If you pay enough, they'll leave the village."

"How much?"

"A thousand rupees."

"Let me talk to my elder son."

"You have ruined your reputation in the village by failing to look after them and feed them. Your husband and your elder son made Ganju women pregnant, but they never failed to support them afterward. You have always been generous. How come you turned away from your usual *Bhagwati*[6] role this time?"

"It's because Dhowli's mother stole the brass jug. . . "

"Stop giving false excuses."

The Misra matriarch has to let Sanichari get away with telling her so many unpleasant words so bluntly only because she is her secret supplier of the medicine for holding onto her old husband, who is addicted to a certain washerwoman. She cuts short the exchange and asks Sanichari's advice about what could be done now.

"Do something. You can help her if you want to."

"Let me talk to my elder son."

Her elder son, Kundan, dismisses her worries. He is not going to let that troublesome girl manipulate them—a baby today, and customers at her home tomorrow. He is going to fix it all. His brother will get married in Dhanbad and stay there. The matriarch is reassured by her manly son, and she promptly forgets the nagging worry.

But the patriarch Hanuman Misra absolutely refuses to solve the problem that way. "The boy will come here with the new bride, as is the custom, and later on they will go together to Dhanbad. Why can't he come to his home, his own village? For fear of a Dusad girl? What can she do?"

Dhowli, like everybody else, hears about the verdict. She stays home with the baby in her lap, trying to think about what they are going to live on. Mother's odd jobs are getting more scarce, uncertain, and now she depends on her with the baby. They could sell the goats one at a time, but how long would that feed them? What would they do after that?

[6]Lit., worshipper of god; devout. [eds.]

Misrilal. Just recalling his name makes her mind go limp even now. All those caresses, those sweet words of love were lies? They could not be. There are fantastic associations with the woods and the spring. The ferocious constable Makkhan Singh once saw a fairy bathing in the stream on a moon-lit night; he really saw it because he lost his mind from that night. A Ganju girl named Jhulni was in love with her husband's younger brother, and when chastised by the Panchayat, the two of them went into the woods and ate poisonous seeds to die together. Dhowli knew Jhulni and the boy. These were true events—they happened—and yet sound like mythical stories. Their love was true too, and yet it feels so unreal now! In that same forest, beside that stream, a Brahman youth once called a Dusad girl his little bird, his one and only bride-for-ever. Didn't they once lie on the carpet of fallen red flowers and become one body and soul? Once when the Dusad girl got a thorn in her foot, didn't the Brahman youth gently pick it out and kiss the spot of blood under her foot? It is now hard to believe that these things ever happened. They now seem like made up stories. All that seems real is the baby sleeping in her lap and the constant worry about food.

Misrilal has not kept the promise he made her. He can't. There's nothing that Dhowli can say or do about it. What now? When he comes back to the village after his wedding, will he be moved to pity on seeing his boy? Will he give a bit of land to help his child live? The Misra men have done that many times. But Dhowli's mind says, "No, he won't." What will she do then? Will she end up opening her door at night when the pebbles strike? For a few coins from one, some corn or a sari from another? Is that how she must live?

Dhowli's mind says, "No! Never that way!"

Tomorrow, how is she going to go to the well to fetch water? All the girls will be talking about the wedding and the preparations for the groom's party. When a Brahman landlord groom's party comes back after the wedding, even the Dusad girls sing and dance, from a little distance though; and they collect sweets and coins and chickpea flour. Is she going to join them in singing for the reward?

Sanichari, on her way back from the Misra house, after giving the boys' mother a piece of her mind, stops to talk to the fellows in the Dusad neigh-borhood and tries to put some sense in their heads.

"The poor girl is ruined and unjustly abandoned by the Brahman boy, and even you, her own folks, turn your backs on her. Have you thought about how she is to live?"

"Nobody ruined Dhowli. She fell in love with him. And don't expect us to forget that she turned down the boys from her own caste. So we don't feel involved with her problems; we don't care whether things go well or bad for her. Let her do what she can, however she manages it."

"What choices do you think she has now?"

"Let's see if her Brahman lover supports her and looks after her. . . ."

Misrilal does nothing at all. He arrives, all decorated, at the head of the groom's party back from his wedding. Only in Dhowli's home is no lamp lit that evening. All the Dusads, Ganjus, Dhobis, and Tolis get sweets, country liquor, chickpea flour, even new clothes. All agree that such lavish gift giving has never happened at any other wedding in the area.

Dhowli waits by the side of the spring next day. She waits all evening. Misrilal does not come. Coming back from there, Dhowli stops at Sanichari's place and breaks down. Sanichari informs her that Misrilal was angry when he heard that she and her mother had refused the help his mother offered. "Is that what he told you?"

"Yes."

"Then go and ask him to come and see me. Otherwise, I'm going there with the baby to see his bride, even though I know his brother will kill me for it."

Misrilal does come to see her. He has no words; his eyes are confused. Dhowli reads in his face the power her presence still has on his mind. It makes her happy in a way that also makes her suddenly bold enough to speak up.

"Did you tell Sanichari that we refused your mother's handouts?"

"That's what my mother told me."

"I spit on her lies. Your mother gave us two kilos of millet in all, over a period of ten days. After that she called my mother a thief and turned her away."

"I didn't know that."

"Why did you destroy me like this?"

"I loved. . . "

"I spit on your love. If you had raped me, then I would have received a tenth of an acre as compensation. You are not a man. Your brother is. He gave Jhalo babies, but he also gave her a home and a farm of her own. And you? What have you done?"

"What I've done I was forced to do. I did not do it of my own wish."

"So you follow others' wishes in marrying, in starting your shop, and you follow your own wish only when it comes to destroying the poor and helpless. Do you know that because of you even my own people are now against me?"

"I'll give you. . . "

"What? Money? Make sure it's enough to bring up your son."

"I'll send you regularly from my income from the store."

"But your words are all lies, worthless lies."

"For now. . . "

"How much?"

He brings out a hundred rupees. Dhowli takes it, ties it in a knot in her sari, and goes on, "With a hundred rupees these days one can't live for long even in Tahad. Because you've ruined me anyway, I'll go to

Dhanbad and drop your boy on your lap if I don't get a regular supply."

"I have to accept whatever you say."

"You ruined my life, turned it to ashes, and you can't even hear the hard truth? Is it being rich that makes one so tender-skinned?"

Dhowli comes back, still raging inside. She asks her mother to go to Valatod and make arrangements for her to stay with her aunt there. Her mother is struck by her anger, her belligerence. "If I must sell my body, I'll do it there, not here."

"Why? Does it bring more money there?"

"How should I know?"

On the next day Misrilal leaves with his new wife. When they set into the bus and look at the villagers gathered at the bus stop, his brother-in-law points to Dhowli, "Who's that girl?"

"Which one?"

"The one with a baby in her arms."

"Just a Dusad girl."

"I've never seen such a beautiful Dusad girl."

"Maybe. I never noticed her before."

3

It turns out that Dhowli's aunt in Valatod does not want her. The sum of a hundred rupees that Misrilal gave her is now down to nine. He never sent any message or any more money, although later on other stories came up about the money, that he once sent twenty rupees through the bus driver who kept it himself, and so on. Meanwhile, one of the three goats of Dhowli's mother is stolen, and eventually they have to sell the other two for very little, as is always the case when the seller is so hard pressed.

Dhowli senses that the village, the Misra family, the gang of contract coolies are all watching her with increasing interest, closing in on her. They have been watching her boy grow up on gruel and her old mother spend all day in the forest looking for roots and tubers. They have also seen Sanichari going to their hut once in a while, with roasted corn bundled in the fold of her sari. From this they conclude that the Misra boy has finally washed his hands of Dhowli.

Then one night, a well-aimed clod of earth strikes her door. Dhowli shouts, "Whoever you are, you should know that I keep a knife beside me." Someone outside whistles and walks away.

The tap-tap continues; little clods are thrown at her door in the night. Dhowli keeps silent. If it persists, she shouts, "Go home to your mother and to your sister."

Her mother mutters something about how long she would be able to fend them off.

"As long as I can."

"You may have the strength to keep going, but I don't."

"I don't have any more strength either, Ma."

"What are you going to do then?"

"Shall we go to the city and try to live by begging?"

"You think men will see you as a beggar? They'll be after your body."

"I don't have the looks and the body anymore, mother."

"Then why do the clods keep falling at our door every night?"

"It's because they know how desperate I am with the baby."

"I can't take it any more. If it weren't for you and your baby, I would have moved in with Sanichari long ago."

"I'm going to find some job tomorrow. I'll earn by weeding the fields."

"There are many others weeding fields all day long. How much does it bring them?"

"I'll try for some other work then."

Dhowli goes in the morning to Parashnath's shop and begs him to give her some job, maybe sweeping his shop, to keep her from starving.

Parashnath offers her some millet but says that he would not hire her because he cannot afford to incur the wrath of the older Misra.

Dhowli takes the millet from him and sits under the tree to think how many days they can live on it, even if she makes a thin gruel. Kundan Misra is out to kill her, starve her, as punishment for turning his brother's head.

Dhowli's mother does not say anything about the pathetic amount of millet that she brought home, but when offered the gruel, she puts down her bowl untouched and says, "Why don't you and your boy eat this. I'll go away and find something on my own."

"You don't want it?"

"If you can't find something to keep alive, better kill yourself."

"You're right. I'll kill myself."

Next day she goes to the stream, thinking all the way of drowning herself. Once she is dead, then her own kinspeople will at least look after her mother. And the baby? As long as her mother is able to live, she will try to bring up the baby.

But she does not meet her death. On the way, a man in a printed *lungi*[7] and shirt catches up with her. He is a coolie supervisor and a coolie himself. He grabs her hand, and asks, "Where is your knife?"

Dhowli looks at his eyes. She feels very little fear and says firmly, "Let go of my hand." The man lets go of her hand.

"Are you the one who throws clods at my door in the night?"

The man says yes and gestures to indicate why.

Dhowli thinks for a minute. Then she says, "All right. I'll open the door. But you must bring money and corn with you. I am not selling on credit."

---

[7] A cloth wrapped around a man's waist that reaches to the ankles. [eds.]

Dhowli comes back home and asks her mother to take the baby to Sanichari's place to sleep from that night on. To her question, she simply informs her that she is going to open the door when the lump of earth strikes. Seeing that her mother is about to cry, Dhowli impatiently, sternly asks her not to raise a row and to come back home before sunrise.

Then she takes out one of the two printed saris that Misrilal gave her. She borrows some oil from Sanichari to oil her hair; she takes a bath and combs her hair into a plait. She is not sure if there is anything else involved in preparing for the customer of one's body.

When a pebble hits the door, she opens it. The man has brought corn, lentils, salt, and one rupee. Dhowli pays him back, with her body, to the very last penny. As the man takes leave, she reminds him that she will let him in as long as he brings the price. When he asks her not to let anybody else in, she says that whoever will pay can come; her only rule is that she will not sell on credit.

Many are willing to pay; she opens the door to many. Dhowli and her mother start having two full meals a day and wearing saris that are not old rags. After the customer leaves, Dhowli sleeps well, better than she has for a long time. She never knew it would be so easy to sell one's body, without any emotion, for corn and millet and salt. If she had known, they could have had full meals much earlier; the baby could have been better fed and cared for. It now seems to her that she has been very stupid in the past.

Kundan has been watching Dhowli carrying on. He knows that by figuring out the means of survival, Dhowli has defeated his revenge, outwitted his plan to kill them indirectly. The Dusad girl's nonchalance bothers Kundan; her new self-assured attractiveness gnaws at his mind. One day, seeing her draw water from the well with the other women, he asks Sanichari if they are going to drink the water touched by Dhowli. It turns out to be a wrong move, given Sanichari's well-known candor and forthrightness.

"That's none of your business, master. And why should we mind the water she touches? Our people now accept what she has to do."

"Why?"

"Why not? What wrong has she done?"

"She has become a prostitute."

"Your brother forced her to become a prostitute. How would your brother's son have lived if she did not? Everybody seems to be happy now, including your friend and business partner the contractor. His coolies no longer have to stray very far for the fun."

"Better watch what you say when you talk to me."

"I don't have to. Your mother and your wife would have been nowhere but for Sanichari here."

Kundan may make wrong moves, but he knows when to retreat. Every family in the village, rich or poor, needs Sanichari. Nobody can do without her help with the medicinal herbs.

Kundan then takes a trip to Dhanbad to work on his brother.

"Better give her money or land. It's your cowardice that now brings the business of selling flesh to the village, right under our nose."

Misrilal's face becomes ashen. "What do you mean?"

Kundan is wild with joy at having hit the spot. His brother is still in love with the whore, and he has managed to hit him right there. What a coward! No pride in his superiority as a Brahman. A man is not a man unless he behaves like one. In his place, Kundan would not have abandoned his favored kept woman at the order of Hanuman Misra. Kundan must prod his unmanly brother into becoming a man. He must be taught how to keep the untouchables under foot, sometimes acting kindly but always forcefully like a man. Otherwise, it is too large an empire for Kundan to control all by himself—so much farm land and orchards, so many illegitimate children and so many fertile untouchable women, so huge a moneylending business. Kundan must bring his soft, defaulting brother up to manhood, cure his weakness, so that he can help Kundan with the job. He goes for the kill.

"Don't you know? I mean the Dusad girl you fell in love with. I spit on it! She became the mother of a son by making a Brahman fall for her. And now the entrance that was once used by a lion is being used by the pigs and the sewer rats."

"I don't believe you. She can't do it."

"She is doing it. She is making us Brahmans the laughingstock."

"No!"

"Yes. I say yes a hundred times. You're not a man! Just a scared worm! You couldn't stand up to Hanumanji and tell him that you wanted her as your kept woman. I've kept Jhalo. Didn't Hanumanji forbid me to give her a place to live? Do I obey? I spit on your love. Lovelorn for a Dusad girl! A man takes what he wants and keeps things ordered to his wish, everything from his *paijars*[8] to the Panchayat.[9] You're no man. You made people spit at the Brahmans."

"I won't believe it until I see it with my own eyes. If it's false. . . "

"Kundan smiles a sly victorious smile and says, "Then you'll kill me? Good! Didn't I get you the license for a gun?"

Soon after that, Misrilal comes to Tahad, tormented by anger and the venom his brother injected in him. Because Dhowli no longer goes to the bus stop, she does not know that he has come.

---

[8]Sandals.
[9]*Panchayat* is the committee of village elders. [eds.]

As soon as the evening sets in, he throws a pebble at her door. It is a changed Dhowli who opens the door—she is wearing a red sari and green bangles, and her oiled hair is in a plait down her back.

She turns pale at first but recovers almost immediately and invites him coldly, "Does the landlord want to come in?"

Misrilal enters without a word. He sees the new lantern, the bed of clean *shataranji*[10] and pillows on the bunk, the sack of millet, and the can of oil under the bunk.

"You've become a *randi?*"[11]

"Yes, I have."

"Why?"

"Because you ran away after having your fun, and your brother took away our food. How else can I live? How can I bring up your son?"

"Why didn't you kill yourself?"

"At first I wanted to do that. Then I thought, why should I die? You'll marry, run your shop, go to the cinema with your wife, and I'll be the one to die? Why?"

"I'll kill you then."

"Go ahead."

"No Brahman's son is to live on the filthy handouts of the untouchables! How dare you! I'll kill you."

"You can't because you're not a man."

"Don't say that, Dhowli. My brother said that. But don't you say I'm not a man. I'll show you that I'm a man and a Brahman."

Within a few days, Misrilal with the help of Kundan and Hanumanji calls the Panchayat. Without asking anyone in the Panchayat, Hanumanji orders that Dhowli must leave the village; she cannot be allowed to do business in the village. She has to go to Ranchi and get herself registered as a prostitute there. If she does not, her hut will be set on fire to kill her along with her mother and her child. As long as the Brahmans live in the village, as long as Shiva and Narain are worshiped in their homes, such impudent sinning is not going to be tolerated in the village.

When Dhowli protests, "Why didn't the Brahman help me with money to bring up his son," Hanuman Misra shouts, "Shut up, whore!" and throws his sandal at her. Misrilal joins in, "Now at last you know that I am a man and a Brahman."

The Dusads, the Ganjus, and the Dhobis at the meeting do not raise any objection. They only ask how Dhowli is going to be able to go to Ranchi. Kundan answers that his contractor is going to take her there. She has to leave the next morning, no later.

Early in the following morning Dhowli, a bundle in her hand, boards the bus with the contractor. She is not crying. Her mother, with the baby in her arms, cries standing beside the bus. The baby holds out his hands to Dhowli.

---

[10]Flat weave cotton rug.

[11]A derogatory term for a prostitute. [eds.]

She tells her mother to keep some *gur*[12] for him for the night, to put a bit of it in his mouth if he cries.

Dhowli's mother now sobs aloud. "It would have been less terrible if you stayed with your husband's brother."

A faint smile, perhaps of pity, appears on Dhowli's lips, hearing her mother say that. In that case, she would have been a whore individually, only in her private life. Now she is going to be a whore by occupation. She is going to be one of many whores, a member of a part of society. Isn't the society more powerful than the individual? Those who run the society, the very powerful—by making her a public whore—have made her a part of the society. Her mother is not going to understand this. So she smiles and says, "Don't forget to keep some *gur* by the bed, mother. And keep the lamp lit, so he will not be scared in the dark."

Even the driver of the bus of the Rohatgi company cannot bear to look at Dhowli. He sounds the horn and starts the bus. Dhowli does not look back to see her mother and her child for fear that it will also make her see the brass trident atop the temple of the Misras.

Kundan's contractor cannot look at her when asking her to make herself comfortable because Ranchi is a long way from there.

The bus starts speeding, and her village recedes.

The sun rises, and Dhowli watches the sky, blue as in other days, and the trees, as green as ever. She feels hurt, wounded by nature's indifference to her plight. Tears finally run from her eyes with the pain of this new injury. She never expected that the sky and the greens would be so impervious on the day of turning Dhowli into a public whore. Nothing in nature seems to be at all moved by the monstrosity of what is done to her. Has nature then accepted the disgracing of the Dhowlis as a matter of course? Has nature too gotten used to the Dhowlis being branded as whores and forced to leave home? Or is it that even the earth and the sky and the trees, the nature that was not made by the Misras, have now become their private property?

❋ Discussion and Writing

1. What are Dhowli's considerations in returning to her mother's house after her husband's death? Comment on her other choices. Identify the restrictions on her behavior and personal adornment because she is a widow.
2. Discuss the irony of Misrilal's role as a lover: how does he differ from his brother and other men of his caste; where does he fail? Comment on his transformation after he becomes the father of Dhowli's child.
3. What is Sanichari's role? Given that she is a low-caste woman, discuss the source of her power over the people of diverse castes?
4. Describe the attitudes of other women toward Dhowli.

---

[12]A pre-processed brown sugar. [eds.]

5. Comment on the behavior of men—Dusad, coolie, and Brahman—toward Dhowli. Discuss various aspects of Dhowli's prostitution.
6. What is Devi's thesis regarding the social norms regulating the behavior of a widow on the lowest rung of caste structure? Examine the maze of social standards in which Dhowli is trapped.

❁ Research and Comparison

Until the early decades of the twentieth century, marriage for widows was banned, especially for the upper castes. Although the ban has been legally lifted, the centuries-old psychology of women and men lingers. Given this background, compare the two Indian stories, "Dhowli" and Shashi Deshpande's "My Beloved Charioteer," paying attention to the issues of widowhood and a woman's sexuality. (Also see the Research and Comparison questions on Deshpande's story.)

Interdisciplinary Discussion Question: Examine the status of women in Bengal, where the Mother Goddess is worshipped as supreme, and which is the locale of the story.

Thich Nhat Hanh
(b. 1926)
Vietnam

Thich Nhat Hanh, who was born in Vietnam, is a world-renowned Zen master. Dedicated to the Buddhist ideal of social responsibility, he served as chairman of the Vietnamese Buddhist Peace delegation during the Vietnam wars for independence (1954–1979). For Thich Nhat Hanh's dedication to peace, Dr. Martin Luther King, Jr. nominated him for the Nobel Peace Prize. A highly respected writer of fiction and poetry, Thich Nhat Hanh imbues his work with Buddhist philosophy and he has continued to work for world peace into the 1990s. In his children's books as well as in his short stories and poems, he evokes the Buddhist concepts of "mindful awareness," individual duty, and social commitment.

*The Pine Gate**

It was a cool, almost chilly, autumn evening, and the moon had just risen, when the young swordsman arrived at the foot of the mountain. The wilderness was bathed in the light of the full moon glimmering playfully on

---

*Translated by Vo-Dinh Mai and Mobi Ho

branches and leaves. It seemed to him that during the seven years he was away, nothing in the surroundings had changed. Nothing had changed, and yet nothing seemed to be greeting him with any warmth—he who had once lived there for years, and who was now returning from afar.

The swordsman paused at the foot of the mountain and looked up. Above him, the narrow path was barred by a pine gate which was tightly shut. He pushed at the gate's sturdy doors, but these remained immovable under his powerful hands.

He was puzzled. Never, as far back as he could remember, had his Master had the gate closed and locked like this. Since this was the only way up the mountain, he had no choice. Slapping the handle of his sword, he rose swiftly from the ground. But that was all. A strange force gripped his whole body and pushed it back down; he could not jump over the low gate. In a moment, he had unsheathed his long sword, but the sharp blade bounced back from the soft pine wood as if the latter were steel. The impact was so powerful it sent a shock through his hand and wrist. He raised his sword and examined its gleaming edge under the moonlight. The gate was indeed too hard; most certainly his Master had endowed it with the strength of his own spirit. It was closed, and no one was to pass. That was the way his Master wanted it. The swordsman sighed deeply. He returned his sword to its sheath, and sat down on a big rock outside the gate.

Seven years earlier on the day he was to leave the mountain, his Master looked at him for a long moment without speaking. There was a kind expression in his eyes and something else, too, something that resembled pity. He could only bow his head in silence when his eyes encountered the compassionate and tolerant eyes of his Master. A while later, the old man said to him, "I cannot keep you at my side forever. Sooner or later, you must go down the mountain and into the world where you will have many opportunities in which to carry out the Way and to help people. I thought that perhaps I could keep you here with me a little longer, but if it's your will to go, my child, then go in peace. There is only this: Remember, always, what I have taught you and given to you, always. Down in the world below this mountain, you will need all of it."

Then his Master went over briefly again what he was to avoid, seek, leave alone, and change. Finally, he put a gentle hand on his shoulder: "Those are the yardsticks for your actions. Never do anything that could cause suffering either to yourself or to others, in the present or in the future. And go without fear on the road which you believe will lead you and others to total enlightenment. Remember, always, the standards by which happiness and suffering, illusion and liberation must be measured. Without them, you would betray the Way itself, let alone help the world!

"I have already given you my precious sword. Use it to subdue monsters and devils. But I want you to look upon it more like a sharp blade that comes from your own heart with which you will subjugate your own ambitions and desires. Now, I have this for you, too, and this will make your task easier." Then his Master pulled out of his wide sleeve a small viewing glass, and handed it to him.

"This is the Me Ngo glass," he said. It will help you to determine good and evil, to separate the virtuous from the wicked. It is also called the Demon Viewer, for looking through it, you will see the true forms of demons, evil spirits, and the like . . . "

He received the fabulous viewing glass from his Master's hand, but he was so grateful and so deeply moved he could not say one word. The following day, at the break of dawn, he went up to the central hall to take leave of his old Master. The old man walked down the mountain with him, all the way to Tiger Brook, and there, in the murmuring of a mountain stream, master and disciple bade farewell. His Master again put a hand on his shoulder and looked into his eyes. He went on looking as the young man started walking away. Once more, he called after his disciple, "Remember, my child, poverty cannot weaken you, wealth cannot seduce you, power cannot vanquish you. I will be here for the day you come back, your vows fulfilled!"

He recalled the first days of his journey vividly. Then, months, and years went through his mind. How humanity had revealed itself to him under different guises! And how helpful the sword and the Me Ngo viewing glass had been to him! Once, he met a priest whose appearance instantly inspired reverence, who—such an honor for the young swordsman—invited him back to his retreat where they would, in the words of the old sage, "discuss how best to join their efforts for the purpose of helping their fellow human beings." At first, the young man listened with rapture, but then, something odd about the priest struck him. He whipped out the Me Ngo and looked through it. In front of him, there was a gigantic demon! Its blue eyes sent forth crackling sparks, a horn stood out from its forehead, and its fangs were as long as his own arms! In one jump, the young man backed away, drew his sword, and furiously attacked it. The demon fought back but, of course, had no chance. It prostrated itself at the young man's foot, begging for mercy. The swordsman then demanded that it swear, under oath, it would return where it had come from, to study the Way, pray that one day it would be permitted to come back into the world of men as a true human being, and refrain from ever disguising itself again as a priest to bewitch and devour the innocent. Another time, he met a mandarin, an old man with a long white beard. It was a happy encounter between a young hero out to save the world and a high official, a "father and mother to the people," bent on finding better and better ways to govern and benefit the masses. Again, the young man's instinct was aroused: under the Me Ngo, the handsome, awe-inspiring old official turned out to be an enormous hog whose eyes literally dripped with greed. In one instant, the sword flew out of its sheath. The hog tried to flee, but the swordsman, in one jump, overtook it. Standing astride the main threshold of the mandarin's mansion, he barred the only escape route. The beast took on its true form and cried out loudly for mercy. Again, the young man did not leave the monster without extracting from it the solemn oath that it would follow the Way, that it would never again take the form of a mandarin so that it could gnaw the flesh and suck the blood of the people.

And there was that time, walking by a marketplace, when he saw a crowd surrounding a bookstall. The picture-and-book seller was a very beautiful young woman whose smile was like an opening flower. Seated nearby was another young woman, also of stunning beauty, who was singing softly some melodious tunes while plucking the strings of a lute. The beauty of the girls and the grace of the songs so captivated everyone present that no one left the stall once they had stopped, and all anyone could do was stand and listen, enraptured, and buy the pictures and books. The young man himself was attracted by the scene. He finally approached and held up one of the pictures. The elegance of the design and vividness of the colors overwhelmed him. Yet, an uneasiness rose within him. He reached for his Me Ngo. The two beautiful girls were actually two enormous snakes whose tongues darted forth and back like knife blades. The swordsman swept everyone aside in one movement of his arms, and with his sword pointing at the monsters, he shouted like thunder, "Demons! Back to your evil nature!"

The crowd scattered in fright. The big snakes swung at the young man, but no sooner did the fabulous sword draw a few flashing circles around their bodies than the reptiles coiled at his feet in submission. He forced their jaws open and carved out their venom-filled fangs with his sword. Then he put the bookstall to the torch and sent the monsters back to their lairs with the solemn promise, against certain total destruction, that they would never come back to bewitch the village people.

So, the young swordsman went on from village to village, and from town to town, on a mission he had set for himself, using the weapon and the viewing glass his Master had given him, along with priceless counsels. He threw himself into his task. For a time now he had come to think of himself as The Indispensable Swordsman. The world could not do without his presence. He had come down from the mountain into the world, and he participated fully in the life down here. Facing the world where treachery and cunning reigned he had to learn flexibility and patience, and at times he had to bend with the tide because his goal was to vanquish and to persuade. He experienced great pleasure in his actions for the good. He went so far as to reach the point where he forgot to eat and sleep. And he did more, much more, because of the joy and satisfaction he derived from the pursuit of his goal—helping the people—rather than because of this goal itself. He served because that fulfilled him, not necessarily because the people needed him.

And so, seven years passed. One day, as he was resting on the bank of a river, watching the water flow by quietly, he suddenly realized that for some time now he had not used the Me Ngo viewing glass. He had not used it, he was now aware, not because he had forgotten that he had it, but because he had not felt like using it. Then, he remembered that there had been times when he did use the glass, but only very reluctantly. Those days when he first came down from the mountain, he fought to the death every time he saw, through the Me Ngo, the true natures of whatever evil faced him. He recalled his great happiness each time, through the glass, he saw the image of a virtuous man or a true sage. But, obviously, something odd had happened to him recently, and he did not know what. It seemed to him he began to feel no great joy when he saw wisemen in his viewing glass, just as he felt no great fury when he saw in it the images of monsters and devils. When monsters appeared in his miraculous glass, the young swordsman couldn't help noticing that there happened to be a certain familiarity even in their horrifying inhuman features.

The Me Ngo remained safely in his pocket, even though it had not been used for a long time. Then the young swordsman thought he would return some day to the mountain to ask his Master's advice: why did he have such reluctance to use what obviously had been such a great help to him? But only on the twelfth day of the eighth month, while he was crossing a forest of white plum trees and was struck by the snow-white blossoms gleaming under the autumn moon, did he suddenly yearn for the days when he studied as a young man under his old Master, whose cottage stood at the border of just such an old plum forest. Only then did he decide to return. In his wish to see his Master, the journey back seemed interminable: seven days and seven nights of climbing hills and crossing streams. But as he reached the foot of the high mountain where he would begin the ascent to his Master's abode, darkness descended. The rising moon showed the two leaves of the heavy pine gate shut tightly, preventing him from going any further up the mountain.

There was nothing he could do but wait. At dawn, he thought, one of his "brothers" would certainly come down to fetch water from the stream and could open the gate for him. By now, the moon had risen past its zenith. The entire mountain and forest were bathed in its cool light. As the night wore on, the air became chillier. He pulled out his sword and watched the moon gleam on its cold, sharp edge. Then he sheathed it again and stood up. The moon seemed extraordinarily bright. The mountain, the forest, every-where—all was still, and quiet, as if the world was oblivious to his presence. Feeling dejected, he dropped down onto another rock. Again, the seven years of his recent life passed before him. Slowly, ever slowly, the moon edged toward the distant summit of a far mountain. In the sky, the stars shone brightly but then they, too, began to recede, becoming paler and paler. There was already the hint of a glow in the east. The outlines of the mountain became suddenly sharper against the pale sky. Dawn was about to break.

There was rustling of dry leaves. The swordsman looked up and saw the vague form of someone walking down the mountain. He thought it must be one of his younger "brothers," though it was not light enough and the figure was too distant for him to make out the latter's features. It must be a "brother" because the person was carrying something like a large pitcher. Whoever it was came closer and closer, and the swordsman heard him exclaim happily:

—Elder Brother!

—Younger Brother!

—When did you arrive? Just now?

—No! As a matter of fact, I arrived here when the moon was just coming up! I've waited all night down here. Why, in Heaven's name, did anyone lock up the gate like this? Was it the Master's order?

The younger disciple, smiling, raised his hand and pulled, ever so lightly, at the heavy gate. It swung open with ease. He stepped outside it, and, grasping the swordsman's hands in his own, looked at his senior:

—You must be chilled to the bones staying down here all night. You're covered with dew! Well, I used to come down here all day, picking herbs and watching the gate, you know. . . . If I thought someone deserved an audience with the Master, I'd bring him up, and if I didn't, I'd just make myself invisible! I'd just stay behind the bushes, and they'd just give up! You know that our Master doesn't want to see anyone unless he has a true determination to learn. Lately, the Master has allowed me to move on to further studies, and as I stay most of the time up at the retreat he told me to close the gate. He told me it would open itself for virtuous people but would stay shut and bar the way for those too heavy with the dust of the world! There is no way anyone could ever climb it or jump over it. Especially someone burdened with the spirits of demons and the like! The swordsman knitted his brows:

—Would you say I am such a person? Would you? Why did the gate stay shut for me?

The younger man laughed heartily:

—But of course not! How could you be such a person? Anyway, we can go up now, you see that the way is clear. But just a moment, Elder Brother! I must fetch some water first. Come with me. Smile, Brother, smile! Who are you angry at?

Both men laughed. They made their way down to the stream. The sun was not yet up, but the east already glowed brightly. The two disciples could now see clearly each line on the other's face. The water was tinted a pale rose by the dawn. There, they could see their reflections next to one another. The swordsman was bold and strong in his knight's suit; a long sword slung diagonally over his back. The younger disciple's figure was gentler in his flowing page's robe, a pitcher in his hands. Without speaking, both looked at their own reflections, and smiled to one another. A water-spider sprung up suddenly and caused the rose-tinted surface to ripple, sending the images into thousands of undulating patterns.

—How beautiful! I would certainly destroy our reflections for good if I dipped the pitcher in now. By the way, do you still have the Me Ngo viewing glass with you? Master gave it to you when you came down the mountains years ago!

The swordsman realized that it was true, that all these years he had used it only to look at others, but never once had he looked at his own image. He took the glass out, wiped it on his sleeve, then pointed it at the water's surface. The two heads came close to look through the small glass together.

A loud scream escaped from the throat of the two young men. It reverberated through the forest. The swordsman fell forward and collapsed on the bank of the stream. A deer, drinking water further upstream, looked up in fright.

The younger disciple could not believe what he had seen in the glass; there he was in his flowing robe, a pitcher in hand, standing next to a towering demon with eyes deep and dark like waterwells and long fangs curving down around its square jaw. Yes, he saw the color of the demon's face. It was a bluish gray, the shade of ashes and death. The young man shuddered, and rubbing his eyes, looked again at his senior who was now lying unconscious on the blue stones of the bank. The older man's face still expressed shock and horror; suffering had been etched upon this man who, for seven years, had ceaselessly braved the rough and cruel world down below their mountain retreat.

The young disciple rushed down to the stream to fetch water and to douse his elder's face with it. Moments later, the swordsman came to. His face was ravaged with despair. His true image had appeared in the Me Ngo so unexpectedly, bringing self-knowledge to him in such a swift, brutal fashion that he could do nothing but collapse under this blow. All his energy seemed to have left him. He tried to stand up, but there was no strength in his legs and arms.

—It's all right, it's all right, my brother! We'll go up now.

To the swordsman's ears, his brother's voice was like an imperceptible movement of the breeze, a faint murmur from afar. He shook his head. His world had collapsed, and he wanted to live no longer. He felt as if his body and soul had been in the path of a hurricane. He could not possibly entertain the idea, the affront, of bringing himself, ever, into his beloved Master's presence.

The younger man brushed some sand off his brother's shoulder:

—No, you shouldn't worry about it. You know that the Master had nothing but compassion for you. Let's go up now. We'll again live and work and study together . . .

Up the steep, rock-strewn path snaking up the mountain, the two figures made their way slowly. It was not, as yet, day; the silhouettes imprinted themselves on the thin veil of dew stretching over trees and rocks. The first sun rays finally reached the two men and heightened the contrast: the swordsman only seemed more broken in both body and spirit, walking next to the younger disciple whose steps were firm and whose mien gentle.

And over the mountain top, far away, the sun rose.

Notes

In the Far East (China, Japan, Korea, Vietnam) there was an old tradition demanding that wise old men (Taoist monks or Buddhist priests) retired to mountain tops, built retreats—usually called "stone grottoes" or "grass huts"—accepted a few selected disciples, and taught them the "Way." In addition to spiritual studies, the martial arts with a non-violent approach were given great importance. The arts of the sword, the staff, Yoga, Judo, Karate, Kung-fu, etc. were taught by the old Masters who later would send their disciples down into the world. Disciples were ranked either by the order in which they had been accepted by their Masters, by age, or by abilities. They called one another "Elder Brother" or "Younger Brother." The "gurus" were called su-phu, literally: Master-Father.

❁ Discussion and Writing

1. Interpret the confusion of the protagonist on returning to his master's abode. What is symbolized by the closed gate? What is the implication of his being called the swordsman and not having any other name?
2. Elaborate on the meaning of the master's giving advice, the sword, and the viewing glass to the swordsman before he left the master.
3. Analyze the significance of the protagonist's successful encounters in destroying the demons. How and why does he fail eventually?
4. What is the function of the younger brother in the narrative?
5. Examine the story as a paradigm of Buddhist teaching: to attain self awareness by following the Way taught by the Compassionate Master (the Buddha).
6. Analyze the symbolism of the images: the full moon, seven years, seven days and nights, narrow path, and the mountain.
7. Comment on the implications of the setting: the night, the snow, the sunrise, the lake.

❁ Research and Comparison

Interdisciplinary Discussion Question: Examine the basic Buddhist teachings and explore the portrayal of the Buddhist philosophy and perceptions in any two major literary works from Asia.

Interdisciplinary Discussion Question: Research the history of the Vietnam War, focusing on the role of the Buddhists in efforts for peace.

Jayanta Mahapatra
(b. 1928)
India

Jayanta Mahapatra was born in Cuttack, India, in the state of Orissa. Born into a lower-middle-class family, he grew up in a village where he read by oil lamps as there was no electricity, and where the villagers lived according to the belief that all life is determined by previous experience. He learned English at a missionary school and graduated from Ravenshaw College in Cuttack before taking his master's degree in physics at Patna University. He has taught physics at various colleges in Orissa, and he has been a visiting fellow or poet-in-residence at various universities throughout the world. He has also served as editor of journals and newspapers and published fiction and essays along with translations from his native Oriya, as well as the poetry for which he is famous. He began literary writing when he was 38. For Mahapatra, there is no dichotomy between poetry and physics; rather, they complement each other in their inherently mysterious nature. Claiming a lifelong fascination with mystery, he has been concerned with the fine line between what is knowable and unknowable, between life and death, and with several kinds of silence. His poems originate in and return to silence, which he defines as an essentially mysterious, "intangible substance, of which words are but manifestations." He has also spoken of a different type of silence, one that "comes from the world of hunger, grief, and injustice." Beginning aesthetically in the first kind, his poetry warns against the second, the silence of the world. Deeply disturbed by the increasing brutal treatment of Indian women, for instance, he has given voice to their situation, just as he memorialized Mahatma Gandhi's assassination on January 30, 1948 in his poem, "30th January 1982: A Story."

30th January 1982: A Story

Another day. Like any other.
The bleating goat on the butcher's block
quickened its last breath and stared wide-eyed.
Its cry bent deeper still over the fringe of its death
while the butcher worried that his knife
was fast losing its sharpness.
At this moment the mobile loudspeaker van
of the Department of Public Relations swept past
pouring out the words of Gandhi's once-favorite hymn.
The rich woman cursed the Government
for waking her up so early when it was not even fully light.

Her five-year-old daughter cuddled
the broken doll's head in her arms for she needed
to fill her life. Or so she thought.
The sunlight stole slowly to the fallow fields
where village women were relieving themselves in the open.
The postman starting out for work
stopped at the garden fence and suddenly clutched his hernia;
he gave himself up to those letters
that shut him out for ever.
The empty bedroom sank heavily onto one of the evil schemes
which led through the long night into dawn.
No one heard the cry ripening inside himself.
Neighbors both, Amar Babu and Sham Babu smiled
sweetly at one another as they chose
their choice cuts of meat hanging from the hooks
in the marketplace. On a day just like this.
As the scent of new mango blossoms blew in
with the morning breeze, restless
with the heritage of blood.

> Mahatma Gandhi was killed by an assassin's bullet on the 30th January 1948 on
> his way to a prayer meeting.

❁ Discussion and Writing

1. Interpret the implications of the description of each vignette.
2. What is the connection between the first and the last scenes?
3. Comment on images of the mango blossoms and blood at the end of the poem. What is their relevance to the title?

❁ Research and Comparison

Interdisciplinary Discussion Question: Survey the life of Mahatma Gandhi and the impact of his ideology on Indian politics and the liberation of the country. Comment on his effort to combine religion and politics. Examine the circumstances of his assassination.

Interdisciplinary Discussion Question: Review Richard Attenborough's film *Gandhi*. (The film is also relevant to Abdullah Hussain's "The Tale of the Old Fisherman" included in this anthology.)

Hyllus Maris
(1930–1986)
Australia

Hyllus Marus, born in Australia, was a cherished and respected poet who died when she was still quite young. She was an outspoken and committed defender of the rights of her people. Her fellow poets and advocates for Aboriginal rights continue to condemn the atomic tests of the 1950s and 1960s as the cause of the increasing rate of cancer victims like Hyllus Maris. And they continue to look to her vision as a guide in their work.

Spiritual Song of the Aborigine

I am a child of the Dreamtime People
Part of this Land, like the gnarled gumtree
I am the river, softly singing
Chanting our songs on my way to the sea
My spirit is the dust-devils
Mirages, that dance on the plain
I'm the snow, the wind and the falling rain
I'm part of the rocks and the red desert earth
Red as the blood that flows in my veins
I am eagle, crow and snake that glides
Through the rain-forest that clings to the mountainside
I awakened here when the earth was new
There was emu, wombat, kangaroo
No other man of a different hue
I am this land
And this land is me
I am Australia.

❋ **Discussion and Writing**
1. What is meant by "Dreamtime People"?
2. Describe the elements that constitute Aboriginal belief and practice.
3. Discuss the impact of the persona's identification with the land.

Abdullah Hussein
(b. 1931)
Pakistan

Abdullah Hussein (Muhammad Khan) was born in Rawalpindi, Pakistan. He took his degree in chemical engineering in Pakistan and Canada, and practiced for some 12 years before turning to writing as his career. Working in Urdu, he has been highly acclaimed for his stories and novels. His first novel, *Udas naslen* (Sad Generations, 1963) won the Adamjee Award. "The Tale of the Old Fisherman," a self-contained episode within the novel, describes the 1919 Jallianwala Bagh massacre in Amritsar in which the British fired on a meeting in an enclosed space called Jallianwala Bagh. This was a crucial incident in rousing the nationalistic ardor in the fight for independence on the Indian subcontinent.

The Tale of the Old Fisherman*

The old man stopped to catch his breath, laughed and then looked around. His three teeth showed again. By now they were all tired of the old man's rambling loquacity, and Naim had lost all hope of getting any useful details out of him. Only Azra, who had little interest in the work of Naim and his companions, still showed some curiosity.

"Then what happened, old fisherman?"she asked.

"Tell us what happened on the thirteenth of April, fisherman, or else we'll go away," one of the men said.

"All right, all right. I'll tell you everything before eight, my children, don't worry. For at eight you must leave this place; at that time the curfew starts. I was left alone when my father died. Then I began looking around for a woman to take care of the housework, but unfortunately I wasn't very tall, and all the women that I found were taller than me and didn't' want me. The one or two who showed some interest turned out to be very ill-tempered, and as you know, my children, I don't like shrews. After some time I gave up the search; I took my father's basket and began to go around selling the daily catch. Now there was no work to do at home, and there was no need for a woman. I started to live happily all by myself and still do, though I left my village and now live in this city. Raw fish and boiled corn are the only things I have ever eaten. I have now lived in this world five years longer than my father did. I have seen many incidents greater than that of the Jallianwala Garden—the mutiny of 1857, when my father had just recently died, and the plague at the turn of the century, and . . . and. . . . But because you are all

---
*Translated by C. M. Naim and Gordon Roadarmel

insisting that I tell you about the Jallianwala incident, I'll talk about that. I can tell you everything that happened on that day and on several days before that.

"You know, some fifty years after the mutiny of 1857, when I told a man all the details of those days, he asked me 'What do you eat?' I said, 'Fish and boiled corn.' 'That's why you're one of the wisest,' he said."

The old man stretched his back and when the listeners caught a glimpse of his three teeth they realized that he was laughing, in his friendly but proud manner.

"The disturbance started on the ninth day of the fourth month, when nine Englishmen were killed in the bazaars of the city. Everything occurred in front of my eyes. They stopped me. There were two of them. I though they wanted to buy my fish. I gladly put my basket on the ground. One of them stayed with me; the other, with a camera to his eye, backed away. Standing at a distance, he took some pictures. Then, taking a silver coin from his pocket, he threw it toward me. His aim was slightly off and I danced and jumped in the air like a crazy man to grab the coin. He took some more pictures. Finally the coin fell on the ground and when I picked it up they were already going away, laughing and talking among themselves. Then, as I was watching, two men attacked them with drawn swords at the corner of the lane. One sword went clean through the stomach of the guy who had taken my pictures; the other stuck in the ribs of his companion. Both of them were dead by the time they hit the dust. I was thunderstruck by the rapidity of the events. Then it occurred to me that only a few moments earlier I had accepted a coin from those foreigners, and it could be that those two swine might try to attack me too. I quickly put that rupee in my inside pocket, picked up my basket, and slipped away. In the next bazaar I saw three more corpses. They lay in the dust a little apart from each other. Their faces still looked warm. They too were foreigners, and their golden hair was dirty with blood and dust. They didn't have cameras. They didn't have anything. Their hands were empty. In the bazaar people were hurriedly closing their shops. A few men stood by the corpses, their faces like children's, pale with fear. Though I felt great pity for those men, I had seen much worse things, so I took the situation in stride, passing by without showing any interest. I didn't even stop my chanting, and kept on calling 'Fish for sale, fish for sale.' In front of the Darbar Sahib[1] I saw another Englishman. He was dying. A thin dagger had gone through his neck and he was clutching its handle as he suffered his death agony. This was the largest square in the city but was completely deserted, even though it was midday. Nothing alive was in sight. I passed through and continued on my way. But that dying Englishman was very young and very handsome. I couldn't restrain myself from taking a second look at him. At the corner of the street I stopped and looked back. The young man's face was lifted

---

[1]A British judge; sahib is an ronorific term. [eds.]

toward the sky in death, and his youthful lips were lifeless. Children, you are fortunate that you are still young and do not know much. I'm an old fisherman. But I have lived a long time and know a few things about life. Young faces, young eyes, young lips—these are the fairest of all things in this world. But when they are made cold. . . . I have seen fish who continue to smile with open eyes even in death. But young men . . . that's a different matter. One feels for a young one. To erase his memory I called loudly 'Fish for sale, fish for sale.' By the time I reached the court buildings I saw three other bodies, lying by the gutters. And beside the corpses I also saw a fire— a silent and hidden fire flaring among the people scurrying in the lane—a fire that burned in their eyes and in their hearts—a terrible wrath that was billowing over the heads of the people. And I tell you the truth, my children; you didn't see it, but I saw it. . . . I have seen thousands of dead men and animals and fish; and during the red plague I saw three coffins being carried out of the same door at one time; and I have seen women chanting their laments; and I was present when the trains collided and saw one man's head lying near the neck of another; and I have seen hordes of shouting and bloodthirsty people attacking each other; but never was I frightened, never, for there was nothing to be frightened about in those incidents. But when I saw that silent, suppressed anger raging inside every man and animal and tree of this city, I returned home.

"From that time on, all the business in the city stopped, and military trucks and white soldiers began to make rounds in the streets and bazaars. The people of the city, once scattered over every inch of the ground, now began to collect in small groups in the neighborhood lanes and corners—just like a fishing net, cut in the middle, which begins to collect into small knots. And among these groups there was one which dishonored a white woman in the middle of the bazaar—the incident that was at the root of the later riots. It happened on the third day after the incident. As usual I was making my rounds, carrying the fish basket. I was feeling rather upset, for by that time the fish had started to smell and there was nothing but hatred in my heart for them. I had stopped shouting my wares—after so many days there was nothing left in them to tout—but I was hoping that some kindhearted person fond of fish might relieve me of them. When I reached the lane that connects the big market with the vegetable market, I was stopped in my tracks. A white woman came running out of the lane and behind her came a baying mob. They caught her in the center of the market and stood around glaring at her with hate in their eyes. The woman's hair was dusty and her legs were covered with mud. She stood in the middle of that mob, turning slowly on her heels like a mechanical doll, and her face was as colorless as white fish. For some moments those men kept staring at her in sullen silence. Then one of them stepped out, grabbed the collar of her dress, and tore it down to her knees. She screamed and that broke the spell. The pack fell upon her. Right in front of my eyes they kept snatching at her like crows and vultures. I must say though, she was a terrific woman; indeed she was. Quite remarkable. The moment she got a chance she jumped out from under those men and started running. There was nothing left now of her flowery dress, and only a little piece of underclothing covered her buttocks and hung over her breasts. Her hair was dishevelled and she ran like a witch, straining her legs. I can still picture her well-rounded buttocks and heavy thighs. Ah. . . . It occurred to me then that if that woman were sitting at my house eating fish, she would look very pleasing. Ah. . . . As she disappeared down an alley, with that mob close behind her, I returned home cursing the bastards.

"That night, for the first time in my life, I couldn't go to sleep. I usually sleep well, for sleep is essential for good health, but that night I just couldn't. I felt parched, as if there was no moisture left in my body. I began to think of my health. I tried heating the room by lighting a fire. Then I got worried about the leftover fish and decided to spread them out against the wall to dry. I lay down on my mat in the corner, but I still felt wide awake. Thinking perhaps it was because of the stink of the fish, I got up again and, gathering the fish in a heap, covered them with my basket. Then I lay down on my right side, since that's the way I usually sleep; but it didn't help. So I dragged my mat close to the fire, a foolish thing to do, for I was already roasting. I got up and was kneeling on the floor, wondering about my condition, when a thought suddenly occurred to me. I removed the basket and selected a rotting fish.

"'I can't seem to find any sleep tonight. So let's have a little chat,'" I said. The fish remained silent, though her mouth was wide open. 'If my father were alive, he'd have let you go before you died. But I don't do such crazy things. So open your ears wide and listen to what I tell you. Don't laugh, for your kids and other relatives may be crying over your death even now.' The fish kept her mouth open in a wide smirk which infuriated me. 'So you find it funny? You died long ago, you beast, but your dull eyes are still open. You don't sleep yourself, and you won't let anyone else sleep. Here. . . .' and I threw her in the fire. Soon she was crackling and sputtering in the flames; but her eyes were still open and the smirk was still on her face. In my anger I thew another fish into the fire; her eyes were open too but she looked more sober. The smell of burning fish soon filled the room, and you know, my children, how that smell can make your mouth water. But it was past midnight and I didn't feel like eating anything, so I ignored the idea and selected another fish from the heap. 'Your skin is so soft and pretty; you might be able to find a customer. You better stay.' And I put her aside. This game seemed to help. So after talking awhile with those fish, and burning a few of them in the fire, I fell asleep.

"When I awoke in the morning the sun was already fairly high and people were up and around. But though the streets sounded alive again after so many days of silence, I felt a strange apprehension. Rubbing my eyes to see better, I stepped outside. People seemed to be in a great hurry, and they were all going in the same direction, as though they were headed for some fish auction which had already begun and each of them was eager to buy the best lot. But one thing marked them as different from buyers of fish, and that was their silence. No one seemed to speak to anyone else although among them there were both old and young, big and small, fat and thin. What amazed me more were the looks on their pale faces as they hurried by me with clenched teeth and unseeing eyes. It frightened me and yet aroused my curiosity; I quickly filled my basket and joined them. No one paid any attention to me, so I clenched my teeth like the rest of them and began to walk with my chest thrown forward. Everywhere one looked, lines of people were rushing in the same direction. When we reached the market square we saw a number of white soldiers standing fully armed. As we moved into the square, they took up positions as if in a war and loaded their guns. Then a squad of Indian policemen arrived. They had bamboo poles in their hands and began to beat us with them. Some of us were badly hit and some were not, but we were all pushed out of the square. One stick hit my basket, which fell to the ground, scattering all the fish in the dirt. Trying to retrieve them I was hit a few times on the back, but I didn't give up, and managed to collect most of them. Suddenly loud shouts and slogans filled the air; another crowd had come from the opposite direction and was trying to enter the square. But the police squad stopped them too, and soon they came around and joined us. With their arrival our quiet mob became vocal and began to shout similar slogans. When the noise became unbearable we started marching toward this place where we are now. I was surrounded by people who pushed and fell and shouted, their faces free of any fear and lit instead with passion and anger. Their shouts seemed to make the sky tremble. We kept marching like that, shouting and rushing down the streets and alleys. Lots of small crowds came and joined us on the way, and the few soldiers who tried to stop us were pushed aside.

"When we entered this park it looked like an ocean without a shore. It was already quite full before our arrival, and wave after wave of people kept coming after us, jamming into the park. Under a thick cloud of dust raised by their feet, hundreds of thousands of people were milling around as though it were the day of judgement, and it was impossible to stay in any one spot. The dust filled my nostrils, my feet were crushed a million times, and torrents of sweat ran down my body though it was still spring. I was cursing the mob, and my own foolishness, but it was impossible to get out of there. I was also feeling very embarrassed at being the only one with a basket on my head. Just then I noticed a small boy, hardly twelve, who was crying and seemed lost. Feeling sorry for the poor kid, I took him by the hand and drew him to one side. He kept crying, so I looked into my basket, selected a good-looking fish, and gave it to him. He then became quiet and was soon quite happy playing with the fish, so I told myself that my bringing the basket had done some good after all.

"As the people kept pouring in, the roar of their slogans grew louder and louder. The Muslims were shouting the names of Allah and their religious leaders, while the Hindus and Sikhs were shouting their own sacred slogans. Then I turned around and saw a dark bearded man standing on high ground, waving his hand to quiet the crowd. But his wild gestures and flying beard seemed to have little effect on the mob. As I watched, a white man dressed like an army officer came up behind him. He shoved the bearded man off the stand and began to shout something to the crowd, threatening with his hands. There was a brief moment of silence when we could all hear his angry voice, and, though it was impossible to understand what he was saying, his gestures and the expression on his face made it clear that he wanted us to get the hell out of there. Suddenly a roar rose from the crowd and someone threw a shoe in his direction. Then more shoes came flying toward him from all sides, looking like flocks of geese rising from the surface of a lake. The people who were near the army officer stood there in silent terror, and most of the shoes fell on them. I kept my wits and held on to my shoes, for you know, my children, I only have one pair. When the shoes were gone, people began taking off their clothes. Now turbans and shirts and undershirts were being rolled into balls and thrown at the officer. Soon about half the people were partly naked, and a few were so shameless they took off everything and ran around completely nude. But soon there was nothing more to throw; only the tumult and noise continued, in which the mob and the army officer both took part. Then someone noticed my basket, and before I could step back, a score of hands reached forward and pulled it out of my grasp. Some of the men glared at me with bloodthirsty eyes when they saw the fish. Then they picked them up and threw them with all their strength toward the white man. The fish that landed short were picked up by the men at that spot and thrown forward, and then farther and farther until one fish hit the army officer right between his eyes. He caught it as it slithered down his face and looked at it in disbelief. Then raising his head, he looked at the crowd, then at the fish again, then back at the crowd, and suddenly with a jerk he smashed the fish in the face of the man standing in front of him. Next he threw his arms in the air, shouting like a maniac, and then suddenly the firing began.

"In a man's lifetime, he's seldom likely to see a scene like the one that followed. People were running in mad confusion like fish caught in a net; but the pursuing bullets were faster than the fleeing men. . . . There was one man who was running with a hand over my shoulder when he was hit. He jumped into the air like an acrobat and was held there for a moment by another bullet, and then another bullet, until he turned a somersault; and when he hit the ground he was already dead, though his face had lost none of its passion. His body was soon hidden by other bodies. In my panic I kept running even when I saw my ancestral basket rolling on the ground as bullets kept hitting it. Then suddenly my feet went cold and a shriek escaped my lips, for in front of me was that well . . . that dry well . . . do you see it over there? . . . that same one. It was only a few yards away from where I had stopped. Some people running by me had fallen into it, then many more people, and soon the well was so filled with dead and the dying that the fleeing men could run over the human bodies. Running along crouched under the pursuing bullets, I passed the spot where we are sitting now. You see this wall? It's empty now, but at that time human bodies were hanging over its entire length. Their legs were on the inside but their arms hung over the other side with bellies resting on the wall. These were the people who had tried to escape over the wall, thinking it was low enough, but as they reached the top they were hit by the bullets. And as I stared at them from inside the park they looked like pieces of laundry strung out by some washerwoman to dry in the sun. Did you notice these holes in the wall? Ah. . . . You who go around asking people for the news, what do you know! You can never know the punishment that was given to this ill-fated city! Ah . . .

"As I came out I saw some dogs pulling at a fish. It was that fat white fish I had put aside the night before in the hope of finding a good buyer. Now, as I saw these strange 'buyers,' I felt like laughing, but it was no time for laughter. I had to get away from there as quickly as possible to save my life.

"Stumbling and falling, I finally reached the spot where they had attacked that white woman the day before. The escaping people had been stopped at the mouth of the street, and after much pushing and pulling, when I reached the front, I saw the strangest sight. On both sides of the street white soldiers stood ready to shoot, and a river of human bodies seemed to be flowing through the middle. These were men like you and me lying on the ground and crossing that twenty-five yard stretch on their bellies. They were not allowed to use their knees or elbows. They were told—all of us were told—to crawl like snakes, for at that spot we had behaved like snakes toward their white woman. Anyone who tried to raise himself on his knees or elbows was immediately shot. Then the soldiers thought up something even better: they lined up on one side of the market and began to shoot just six inches above the heads of the crawling people. The slithering cowards buried their faces in the ground and inched forward with the help of only their toes and nails. In the meantime wave after wave of fleeing people kept coming, for this was the only route of escape from the park. As soon as a place became free, someone from the crowd would fall on his face and begin crawling in the dirt. As you know, my children, crawling is not very difficult for us fisherman. My father, may God bless him with peace, had taught me when I was only six to float on the surface of the water without moving a limb. So when my turn came I had to drag my head on the ground which injured the side of my skull so that it remained swollen for many days. I went across with greater agility than most men, however. There was one old man crawling along side of me, with not a single hair on his head; his skull was bleeding and one cheek dragged a wide line behind him in the dirt. This old man was crying bitterly, though he was also somewhat ashamed of his tears. At the end of the passage, when we got up to run, I recognized him. He used to buy fish from me every Thursday and had three grown-up sons and a large grocery store.

"For many days after that I stayed away from that place, but from a distance I saw people being forced to crawl over that stretch of ground—though crawling is unbecoming to human beings. I never recovered my ancestral basket.

"Now you'd better leave this place, my children. The curfew will be starting any moment and then for twelve hours anyone found in this area will be shot at sight. I've tried your patience a lot, I know, but you yourselves asked me to tell you everything. 'Old man, tell us everything.' So I've told you every bit of it. . . . But you don't need to be dismayed, my children, for I have seen worse things."

"Aren't you going to leave this place?" one listener asked.

"No."

"Are you a Muslim or a Hindu?" Naim asked quickly.

"Aha, that's a nice one." The old hunchback gestured with his index finger and laughed. "Yes, that's a nice question. Frankly, I don't know. You see . . . well, I was too busy to ask my father, and my father was too busy to tell me. The fisherman only knows how to toil; he doesn't have time for such questions." Then he pointed toward the white soldiers. "I've also told them everything. They don't bother me any more. They know I'm not interested in those things. I'm only an old fisherman, somewhat hunchbacked."

On their way back they kept turning their heads to look at that small dark figure who, tired after the long discourse, now sat quiet and alone on the wall, while a desolate night spread around him. The barrier of night gradually thickened until he disappeared from sight. But for many years after that evening, that dark and lonely figure kept coming back before their eyes.

❋ **Discussion and Writing**

1. Describe the old fisherman's encounter with the English photographer. What does this encounter indicate about the white man's attitude toward indigenous people?

2. What are the implications surrounding the killing of the British in the streets; what is the importance of the incident concerning the British woman?

3. Analyze the function of the recurrent image of the fish: in the old fisherman's narration; in the action of the story.

4. Describe the impact of the graphic description of the massacre; comment on the well and the wall as relics of the historic event.

5. Discuss the cause and nature of the punishment ordered by the British for the people coming out of the gate of the Bagh.
6. What is the implication of the curfew and the English soldiers standing guard at the Bagh? When does the story take place?
7. Characterize the old man: as an individual with needs and emotions; as an observer of death, especially the events of 1857 and 1919; how old could be?
8. What is the effect of recreating history as the tale of an old man who has no comprehension of the significance of the events that make history?

❀ Research and Comparison

Interdisciplinary Discussion Question: Research the 1919 massacre at Jallianwalla Bagh and its ramifications. Develop a paper on any aspect of this incident as an example of the colonial experience, and include a discussion of Richard Attenborough's film *Gandhi*. (Also see the Research and Comparison topics for Jayanta Mahapatra's poem "30th January 1982: A Story.")

Tan Kong Peng
(b. 1932)
Malaysia

Tan Kong Peng was born on a chinese battleship commanded by his uncle, an admiral knighted by the British, and arrived in Malaya when he was seven. Tan, who generally wrote under the name Pin Tze, published a Malay grammar as well as poetry and fiction.

A Jungle Passage*

June, 1947. The season of pounding rains brought by the north-east monsoon from the South China Sea to the east coast of the Peninsula was followed by a period of drought. The swamps and marshes of the jungle of Pahang, Trengganu, Kelantan, and eastern Johore had turned to dry land. Smaller streams and brooks had dried up. Most of the wider rivers that had to be crossed by canoes during the monsoon could now be forded.

Taking advantage of the dry season, I went to Panching from Bundi, walking through thick virgin jungle on the border of Pahang and Trengganu, in search of a piece of land said to have rich deposits of tin ore.

---

*Translated by Ly Singko

I was grateful to Hamid Salek, the Penghulu of Kampong Bundi, whom I found to be an excellent guide. He knew the jungle path so well that he was to me a walking compass. He did not put a single foot out of place. He knew which path to take in order to avoid climbing high hills, and at what point to make a turn to avoid crossing wide rivers. He went as straight as an arrow.

Hamid was in his forties, healthy, tall and strong, but fierce-looking and ugly. His upper teeth protruded from his mouth. There was a deep, long scar running from his left eye to his left ear; another scar on the left of his forehead made his leathery face look even more frightening. His head was wrapped in a turban. He wore a dirty, fetid *sarong*[1] and *baju*,[2] with a long *parang*[3] at his waist. He made me think of the pirates who must have sailed the Malacca Strait long ago.

But my pirate guide kept me good company in the Malayan forest, and entertained me endlessly with interesting tales of the jungle kingdom. He told me that when the elephant family travelled in the jungle, the wild creatures cleverly arranged themselves in a circle to protect their young. He told me how the long, thin rattan snake entrapped animals, and so many other strange and wonderful things.

"*Inche*,[4] you will never believe me unless you have actually seen one yourself," he said. "The color of a rattan snake is exactly the same as rattan. Its head and tail cannot be seen, and nobody knows what length it is. It makes a loop with its rope-like body and sets itself across the jungle track. When some unfortunate animal, perhaps a wild boar, deer, or even a tiger, passes by, it pulls the noose tight and entwines itself around its prey. It's so strong that it's impossible for any trapped animal to escape after being caught. When its victim is tired of struggling, the rattan snake bites a hole in its neck, sucks its blood, and then abandons the body. We, who are so used to travelling in the jungle, often meet the dead bodies of its victims."

It was in such a myth-like and exciting atmosphere that I walked through the jungle with Hamid. By evening we had travelled more than ten miles, and every object in the forest was beginning to fade and blur. We decided to break our journey until the following morning when we could see the sun again. Hamid led me to an excellent camp-site at the foot of a huge rock.

I unloaded the jungle sack from my back with relief. There were some biscuits in it, two bottles of cold water, a torch-light, a compass, and a few samples of tin ore which I had picked up on the way. In addition, I had in the

---

[1](Also sarung) a cloth wrapped around the waist; skirt.
[2]Coat.
[3]Chopper.
[4]Mr., Mrs., Miss.

sack the teeth and claws of rare animals and a blowpipe which I had obtained by exchanging some salt and tobacco with the chief of thirty *Sakais*,[5] when we had passed through Sungei Takai earlier in the day. They only weighed a few *katis*[6] in all, yet to have them added to my own weight for the distance I had to cover made every step an effort.

I felt so tired that I threw myself on the ground, without any thought for what was under my body. Although the ground was rough, I felt as if I were lying comfortably on a double-springed Vono bed.

Hamid proved himself an experienced woodsman—he made a fire before he sat down to relax.

He warned me while I was lying stretched out like a log of wood, "*Inche*, don't part with your *parang*. It's true that all wild animals are afraid of fire, but it's better to keep your *parang* by your side."

"What kind of animals are we likely to see?" I asked.

"Tiger," was the answer.

He unwrapped a small packet, took out a piece of *sireh*[7] leaf, put some *kapor*[8] on it, folded it into a small cake and put it into his mouth. As he chewed the *sireh*, he said in a low voice: "I once saw two tigers fighting for human flesh here."

He's trying to scare me, I told myself.

"Oh, did you enjoy watching so much that you did nothing to help?" I asked him jokingly.

"What? Rescue him? I would have chopped him into pieces. I wished that the tigers would swallow his bones as well!" He stared hard at me.

He would be a very successful actor on the stage, I thought.

"Have a man chopped into pieces?" I pointed to the sky and said laughingly: "There is Tuhan Allah above!"

"Tuhan Allah!" he shouted. "If there ever was a Tuhan Allah at all, we poor people would not suffer thus."

How well he dramatizes, I mused, half asleep.

"Hamid," I said, "let's go to sleep. Don't tell me any more such Arabian Night stories, or you may frighten me to death."

"*Inche*, I am not joking. I'm telling you the truth. If you are not chicken-hearted, I will prove it to you."

"What do you mean?" I interrupted, my curiosity thoroughly aroused. "If I were chicken-hearted, I would not have come so far with you."

He sat silently and looked at the surroundings with a look of deep grief in his eyes.

---

[5]Natives.
[6]A measure.
[7]Betel.
[8]Chalk taken with betel nut.

"Come on, what do you want to show me?" I sat up. "Are you going to show me tigers fighting for human flesh?"

It seemed as though my words provoked him. He stood up without a word. I held my *parang* in my left hand and the torch in my right, and followed him round the other side of the rock.

He pointed to a spot and said, "Look, what is that?"

I aimed my torch at the spot he showed me, and . . . Allah! There was a hill of skeletons in front of me. And blades of grass had grown through the eye-sockets of some of the naked skulls.

"These are my victims," he said.

A sudden horror flashed through my mind. My hair stood on end.

"You . . . you. . . " I could hardly utter a word.

To be with a murderer in this thick jungle was no better than being with a lion in an amphitheater. I was paralyzed. He could at any time force me to fight like a gladiator with him, *parang* to *parang;* and then before long, I too would lie on the hill of skeletons. My blood raced. I gripped my *parang* as hard as I could.

"*Inche,* don't be afraid. When men die, only their bones are left. There is nothing for you to be afraid of."

It was cold comfort. I took two steps back.

But Hamid, like a doomed man, lowered his head and returned to our camp fire. I followed him yards behind. He sat down again by the fire, I sat in front of him, with the fire between us.

Darkness had by this time covered the whole of the jungle. There were only a few stars in the murky sky. It was dead silent except for the jungle symphony of unseen insects.

His big bloodshot eyes were fixed on the fire. His face was blood-red in the glow and made the light seem more dark and frightening. Ghostly shadows danced behind him. My blood flowed even more rapidly and I gripped my *parang* even more tightly. But he did nothing else other than gaze at the fire and from time to time throw dry branches on to it.

We were silent.

I do not know how long it was before I spoke: "Why did you kill?"

"Kill?" It was as if he had woken from a dream. "Kill! Why did I kill?"

Suddenly he pressed both his hands hard against the ground, like a fierce wounded tiger, his big eyes flashing with anger.

"Devils!" he cried. "They are nothing more than blood-sucking devils!"

He raised his head. Looking into the dark sky, he shouted, "They are like the rattan snakes, they trap us, suck our blood, and make life a living hell! I chopped off their heads and it was a pleasure for me to watch them die!"

I could see he must have suffered bitterly in the past. I asked him, sympathy dragged from me by his suffering, "Did someone make you *susah* before?"

There was no answer to my question. In a low, muttering voice, he seemed to be making a statement to the fire. "My father died when I was six. We had no relatives. The only things he left my mother and myself were an *atap* hut and a few old *sarongs*. Then Itam, a younger brother of the Penghulu of our *kampong*,[9] claimed that my father owed him money, and made my mother his fourth wife. We had no choice but to give in to him—that rich beast!

"We still lived in our own *atap*[10] hut after my mother married him. He gave my mother only a few *gantangs*[11] of rice every month. When I refused to call him father, he kicked me and had me beaten up. My mother was afraid to speak and could only cry when it happened." The tears began to course down his cheeks.

"With two other boys whom he employed, I was made to look after his cattle. He had about fifty head of cattle. My mother died while I was still in my teens."

"Then?"

He was obviously telling the truth.

"Then, I was made to accompany the beast on this very same route, bringing with us twenty-five head of cattle to be sold in Pahang and Negri Sembilan, because the price of cattle there was two or three times higher than in Kelantan. The last time I accompanied him on this journey, I killed him and chopped off his head when we spent a night at this very spot. I sold all his cattle, and returned to my *kampong* in Kelantan a year later after I had spent all the money I got from the sale of the cattle. Nobody ever knew that it was I who killed him. I told everyone that we were robbed on the way, and that he was killed by the robbers.

"It was thus that I became a guide for those who wished to sell cattle, as I was one of the few who really knew this jungle route. Many times, I brought my temporary employers here intentionally and killed them while they were fast asleep at night. I sold their cattle and kept the money for myself. I cannot remember the number of the victims of my *parang*. I just threw their bodies over there behind the rock.

"There was one occasion when I almost failed. My victim was so strong and tough. I waited until he was asleep and then attacked him with my *parang*, but I missed his head and wounded him on the shoulder. He jumped up and fought back. He got me twice." He pointed to the scar on his forehead. "But I managed to kill him and added one more to my record."

---

[9]Village.
[10]Palm-thatched.
[11]A measure.

He paused for a moment and continued, "*Inche,* all this happened more than twenty years ago."

He gave a long sigh. His remorse was so great a contrast to his previous anger.

"Aye! *Inche,* I am getting old now and I have seen a lot of life and death. At first, I killed that beast because I hated him. Later I killed others because it was the easiest way to get money.

"But," he gave another deep sigh, "*Inche,* if we want to live, we must let others live. You are still young, *Inche.* No matter what you do in the future, you must remember this: learned people, high-class people, and *pandai*[12] people may not think the same way, but we who have learned and lived the hard way know this well: if we want to live, we must let others live. Live and let live."

All these words were coming from the mouth of a murderer. I wondered whether it was a dream? But no, it was fact: the bright dying fire, the ghostly shadows, the pirate-like murderer with his red-rimmed eyes staring hard at the fire, sitting just in front of me. All this was real. I was not dreaming.

I felt confused and unable to find a single word to say. His sufferings had won my sympathy, but not my confidence. My hand was all the time on my *parang,* gripping it as tightly as I could. I was desperately tired, but I had not the courage to lie down. I just sat with my back against a tree, not even daring to shut my eyes. The picture of the heap of skeletons and skulls kept appearing before me. Through the whole of that cold, damp jungle night, my mind felt numb, yet a strange thought persisted:

"Is man perhaps his own greatest enemy?"

❋ Discussion and Writing

1. Describe Hamid as a jungle guide and a story teller. Explain why the jungle is described as "mythlike."
2. Analyze the narrator's response to each of Hamid's stories. Explain the change in the narrator's attitude from distrust to belief.
3. Discuss Hamid's observation on life, "Live and let live." How does one reconcile it with his violent past? Expand on the implications of his comment about learned people.
4. What is the narrator searching for? What does he find? What is the significance of the last sentence?
5. Comment on the symbolism of the journey and the jungle.

---

[12]Clever, skillful.

Ranjini Obeyesekere
(b. 1933)
Sri Lanka

Ranjini Obeyesekere was born in Sri Lanka. She has taught at universities in Sri Lanka and the United States. Along with writing fiction and criticism, Dr. Obeyesekere is a noted authority on Sinhalese literature and a translator of both Sinhalese and English literature. Her concern for women as well as for class, for the conflicts and pressures of modernity, are apparent in "Despair," a story written in English. The story also depicts the Buddhist pattern for the stages of spiritual realization.

Despair

"No, it couldn't have been this car that you saw. You've made a mistake. I'm sorry," Premini said as she closed the car's door with a click and started the engine. Then, as the car pulled away, she was suddenly aware of an answering click in her mind. Why, she had been to Colombo yesterday by train. It might have been possible . . . it just might have been. . . . She could not finish the phrase even in her own mind.

Confused images, phrases, places, names, things she had never before thought about, which she had not even been aware that her mind had registered, came crowding in on her. Each image seemed to buttress and support an earlier one, and brought with it new doubts.

It might be true. What the man had said could be true. The blood seemed to have burst into her brain leaving the rest of her numbed, ice-cold. She could not see where she was going, it was some time before she realized that for the past half-hour she had been going round and round a single block of houses.

The secure, not necessarily idyllic, but not unhappy, world in which she had lived these many years seemed suddenly to fall apart. The ground on which she had built her life had given way in a manner she had never expected. She had slipped suddenly into a yawning cavern of doubt. Doubt which she knew would never be dispelled because the facts could never be verified. Was it, after all, doubt, or a small, hard core of certainty? She did not know what to call it—she was only aware of its existence within her. But it could be lethal—that she knew. She could fight it but she could never destroy it.

She jammed on the brakes and was thrown forward with a jerk. A cart full of brightly colored sweetmeats, decked with flies, was being trundled across the street by a nonchalant boy who seemed totally unruffled by erratic lady drivers. Jerked back into the external reality of the street, Premini took hold of herself. What was she doing? She had to collect clothes from the laundry, do the day's marketing, pick up her son from school. But all the while she had the sinking conviction that none of these things really mattered.

Her activities, the daily household chores, the children's routine, her work at the hospital, had all had—even though she never thought about it much—a kind of total meaning which gave point to her existence. Now, suddenly, by the accidental intervention of a total stanger—perhaps even a well-meaning one, this whole edifice had collapsed.

Her ego, that human ego, which blossoms in the surety of another's love, had shrivelled dry. She realized for the first time how dependent she had been on the knowledge of that love. Only if one rid oneself of the bondage of human affection could one rid oneself of this dependence. Wasn't that the meaning of the Buddhist doctrine?

But even as she accepted intellectually the truth of this premise, her whole being strained against its realization. For it was, after all, this very dependence, this belief in the strength of another's affection, that had given meaning and joy to her life, her home, her children, her work. This belief she no longer possessed, and with it went the joy that made daily life livable.

Yet nothing had changed in the last half-an-hour in the world around her. In spite of the turmoil within her, her conscious mind now began to function automatically, in full control. She parked the car near the market and got out. To anyone seeing her, she was the cool, collected lady doctor, dressed in a crisp voile saree, returning after the hospital rounds to do her usual day's marketing. She moved quickly and surely, threading her way through the Sunday morning crowds; bought the week's groceries, the meat, fish, vegetables and fruit. But even as she bought and paid, bought and paid, inside her was the persistent, insistent murmur: "What for, what for, what is it all for?"

Mentally she listed her purchases. She must get it over soon, get away from here. The crowd, the smells, the hectic buying, selling, bargaining, were more than she could take. She had been one of them too. Only yesterday she had been one of these people, as involved in the immediate purchase, as immune to her fellow-shoppers, beggars, idlers, traders, stray dogs and vagrant children. Today she stood apart; alone, isolated, uninvolved, with an overwhelming feeling of the futility of it all, and a strange ironic pity for these others and herself!

Someone called to her from the crowd, "Premini, how good to see you after all these years." She turned and recognized a close friend of former days; they had been in medical school together. He had been recently transferred to Kandy. She turned to him. Suddenly she wanted to talk to him here in the market. Tell him everything—the truth about herself—that this frantic role she was playing had no meaning, no point at all. She wanted to cry, talk, tell someone, communicate her sense of total futility—but she was dumbstruck. "Nice to see you, Tissa," she murmured. "I'll look you up some time. I have to rush now." She turned and walked quickly away. Sobs seemed to be tearing their way up through her.

As she pushed blindly through the crowd, among the baskets, vegetables, litter and dogs, she stumbled and almost fell over the extended legs of a woman seated at the bottom of the stairway. Recovering, she glanced hurriedly at the woman to apologize, but the words died in her throat. The seated woman had not moved, but sat, legs extended, leaning her head against the wall behind her; her hair unkempt, her clothes in rags. What stopped Premini was not the squalor—that was normal in one's daily encounter with the market beggars. What struck her, even in her own preoccupied state, was the total immobility of the woman. She had not stirred.

Instantly, Premini had a searing vision of the cause. The woman was holding in her lap a child so thin that in all her experience as a doctor she had never encountered anything like it. The child lay on its back, its arms spread out, its tiny stomach distended, the skin stretched taut over its bloated belly. The child was dying, if not dead. And the mother knew it. Staring blankly in front of her, totally oblivious to every living thing around, she sat, statue-like, immobile. In one hand was a bottle with a dirty teat and a brown milk-like liquid which she held unseeingly to the mouth of the child. The child neither sucked nor moved. The mother sat, oblivious even of the child, aware only of the certainty of her own despair.

Premini stopped. An intense sympathy for this suffering creature, the depths of whose despair she instinctively sensed but would never plumb, overcame her. She bent quickly and emptied the contents of her purse on to the woman's lap, muttering: "This child is very sick. Take him to the hospital soon." Not a flicker passed over the woman's face. She remained unaware, unseeing, indifferent to human sympathy or help.

Premini almost ran to the car. Never before had she been witness to despair of such intensity. Not that she had not encountered death, suffering and grief in the hospital wards, on the streets, even in the market. Suffering was a part of her accustomed landscape. But here, for a moment, she had come face to face with total loneliness and the death of all love.

Premini's momentary empathy with the totality of the woman's despair seemed to have calmed her own agitation. There are, obviously, degrees even to despair, she thought ironically as she climbed into her car. She was late getting to the school and drove fast. But the immobile face continued to appear, a blurred vision on the windscreen. For once, for the first time perhaps in her life, she had truly experienced—even momentarily shared—another's grief. Perhaps her own experience of the morning had sensitized her.

Returning home, she felt drained out, desiccated by the day's emotions. She had to talk to someone. She turned to her son. "I saw a woman today in the market with a very sick child—so thin it hardly looked like a child."

"Did you take him to the hospital?" asked her seven-year-old logically.

Then it struck Premini that her response to the woman had been purely personal, emotional, private. She had made no attempt to help the woman or her child. And she was a doctor. After all, the child had not been dead. Something might yet be done. "We'll go back and do just that," she said decisively, turning the car back toward the town.

They drove fast. She knew it was urgent. She parked the car and ran in, making her way through the crowds to the stairway. She stopped short. She had not expected it. Both mother and child were gone. Gone, with her now-dead child no doubt, to lose herself in the anonymity of the human mass. For a moment Premini stood unmoving in the place where the woman had sat. It was as if she and the woman were one, fused together in a common isolation, a common desolation.

But even as she stood apart, looking out on the ant-like activity around her, she was aware that the intensity of her feeling was of that moment only. It would diffuse, dull and disappear. Tomorrow, or the day after, or the day after, she knew, they would both again be part of the anthill.

❈ Discussion and Writing

1. What is the nature of Premini's doubt that creates turmoil in her mind?
2. Comment on the impact of the description of the market; what does the market symbolize?
3. Describe the incident with the beggar woman and her dying child: analyze the nature of Premini's initial empathy with the woman.
4. Comment on the role of Premini's son: what does he challenge, though inadvertantly, in his mother?
5. Describe Premini's state of being when she does not find the mother and son in the market.
6. Consider the story as a meditation on life: what aspects of the psychological and the metaphysical awareness does the story evoke?

❈ Research and Comparison

Interdisciplinary Discussion Question: Survey the life of Buddha and the four truths about life on which Buddhism is based. Comment on Obeyesekere's use of these in her story.

Edwin Thumboo
(b. 1933)
Singapore/Malaysia

When Edwin Thumboo was born, Singapore was a British colony. After the Japanese occupation during World War II, England merged its colonies on the Malay Peninsula, a union that fluctuated as various states withdrew or were added. Singapore and Malaya separated, becoming the independent Federations of Singapore (1980) and of Malaysia (1982). The entire region has experienced accelerating tensions between races, ethnic groups, and religions; it is a polyglot area, reflecting postcolonial world conflicts. Thumboo, himself of Chinese-Indian heritage, writes in English. He is a professor of English Language and Literature and a dean at the National University of Singapore. Along with his poetry, he has published critical essays. His poems focus mainly on the modern, urban condition; frequently wry in tone, they project an objectivity as they describe the contemporary social or political state. Even when a poem draws a picture of an individual, society is seen as the formulating factor. Thus, his poetry serves a social purpose: analyzing, illuminating, commenting.

Christmas Week 1975
(For J.F.C.)

I

As you
Weigh one hope against one fear,
Detaching dream from nightmare
Or stretch a hand in gratitude.
Doing what must be done,
You feel,
Against the shards of memory
That this auspicious day
Is not its usual self:
The winds do not burn with fire
Nor the sky inscribe
A rare happening.
Instead a sudden desolation;
Unexplained but there.
Within the early city,
The streets lie grey, unvisited.

Nothing, nothing of portent.

II

Season's Greeting are earnest
As the year before. But now
　　　You
Visit less, depend upon the post.
Somehow cards and calendars are dull;
Gifts seem careful, to the point.
Even the Magi come in plastic,
Smooth, easy to store.

Nothing, nothing of portent.
　　　Except
Voices, leaders of countries,
In their annual tone, prognosticate,
Offer qualified security,
But note in parenthesis

　　　Overtones
Of crisis: oil
Insurrection, closure of borders,
Ancestral ways remade, neutrality,
Big power interests, law of the sea,
Dragons rumoured in the making.

Yet our children will to school,
Keep tidy, learn new maths,
Return bilingual, improve upon us
While we keep about our tasks.

　　　Therefore
Give us this day O Lord
Our daily bread.
Hungry sheep look up; some are fed.

Whatever the dialect of Your tribe,
O Lord,
You'll surely help those
Who also help themselves.

❋ Discussion and Writing

1. What does the poet remember on this Christmas day? Describe how the reality contrasts with the memory.
2. What do the activities of people in the beginning of section II suggest? What is implied by the refrain "Nothing, nothing of portent"?

3. Discuss the exceptions: who are the "voices"; what are the implications of the achievements of children in languages and math?
4. Analyze the use of irony throughout the poem, particularly evoked by the Christian imagery of prayer.
5. What does the "dialect of Your tribe" refer to? Comment on the implications of the last lines.

✸ Research and Comparison

Interdisciplinary Discussion Question: Explore the paradox of colonialism and the ideals of Christianity. What are the lingering postcolonial traits characterizing the politically decolonized nations? Compare the predicament of any two states that are former British colonies.

Kevin Gilbert, Wiradjuri
(b. 1933)
Australia

Kevin Gilbert, Wiradjuri, was born on the banks of the Lachlan (Kalara) River at Condobolin, Australia, the youngest of eight children. His parents died when he was seven, and he was shuttled from his sisters' care to an orphanage in Sydney because he fought back when gangs of white children attacked him at school. He returned to Wiradjuri country when he was eleven but left school while still in the primary grades to find work. He worked as a trapper and a seasonal laborer; he gathered empty bottles and tufts of wool to earn enough money to buy bread. Charged with murder when he was 23, he served 14 years of a life sentence before being released. Following his imprisonment, he published several works confronting the racial and class conflicts in Australia. Along with his poetry, he has written political works, a play describing the seasonal work of his people, and a collection of oral history, *Living Black,* that is used as a teaching text in the secondary schools. He has said that "the purpose of all my writings is to present the truth of Aboriginality and justice."

Kiacatoo

On the banks of the Lachlan they caught us
at a place called Kiacatoo
we gathered by campfires at sunset

when we heard the death-cry of curlew
women gathered the children around them
men reached for their nulla and spear
the curlew again gave the warning
of footsteps of death drawing near
Barjoola whirled high in the firelight
and casting his spear screamed out "Run!"
his body scorched quickly on embers
knocked down by the shot of a gun
the screaming curlew's piercing whistle
was drowned by the thunder of shot
men women and child fell in mid-flight
and a voice shouted "We've bagged the lot"
and singly the shots echoed later
to quieten each body that stirred
above the gurgling and bleeding
a nervous man's laugh could be heard
"They're cunning this lot, guard the river"
they shot until all swimmers sank
but they didn't see Djarrmal's family
hide in the lee of the bank
Djarrmal warned "Stay quiet or perish
they're cutting us down like wild dogs
put reeds in your mouth—underwater
we'll float out of here under logs"
a shot cracked and splintered the timber
the young girl Kalara clutched breath
she later became my great grandma
and told the story of my people's death
The Yoorung bird cries by that place now
no big fish will swim in that hole
my people pass by that place quickly
in fear with quivering soul
at night when the white ones are sleeping
content in their modern day dreams
we hurry past Kiacatoo
where we still hear shuddering screams
you say "Sing me no songs of past history
let us no further discuss"
but the question remains still unanswered
How can you deny us like Pilate
refusing the rights due to us.
The land is now all allocated

the Crown's common seal is a shroud
to cover the land thefts the murder
but can't silence the dreams of the proud.

❈ Discussion and Writing

1. Describe the incident as the great grandmother experienced it in the past; what does it mean to her now?
2. How do the later generations react to the incident at Kiacatoo? What do their different reactions signify?
3. Interpret the last line, "but can't silence the dreams of the proud."

❈ Research and Comparison

Interdisciplinary Discussion Question: Research the history of race relations from the days of the British settlement in Australia as a penal colony. Comment on the issues that concern the native Australian writers today.

Kamala Das
(b. 1934)
India

Kamala Das was born in Malabar, South India, and grew up in Calcutta until the turbulent years of World War II, when her father sent the family back to the safety of the ancestral home in Malabar. Her father sold expensive automobiles to the wealthy, and her mother was a well-known poet who wrote in Malayalam, one of the four Dravidian languages. There were other poets and poet-philosophers as well in the family house in Malabar. Kamala Das received private tutoring after elementary school, where she and her brother, along with the four other Indian children, suffered "the humiliation of a brown child in a European school." At 15 she was married in a traditionally arranged marriage, but she had been writing poetry from the age of six when she "wrote about dolls who lost their heads and had to remain headless for eternity." Writing in both Malayalam and English, she has worked in all genres and won awards in all, but she has been honored especially for her poetry. She has focused on women's issues, and she has also taken up the problems of the oppressed and environmental and political questions. Because she candidly depicted her feelings, her love for a man other than her husband, and her sexual relationships in her autobiography, *My Story* (1988), she found herself at the center of a storm, but claimed she derived more pleasure from *My Story* than any of her previous books.

An Introduction

I don't know politics but I know the names
Of those in power, and can repeat them like
Days of week, or names of months, beginning with
Nehru. I am Indian, very brown, born in
Malabar, I speak three languages, write in
Two, dream in one. Don't write in English, they said,
English is not your mother-tongue. Why not leave
Me alone, critics, friends, visiting cousins,
Every one of you? Why not let me speak in
Any language I like? The language I speak
Becomes mine, its distortions, its queernesses
All mine, mine alone. It is half English, half
Indian, funny perhaps, but it is honest,
It is as human as I am human, don't
You see? It voices my joys, my longings, my
Hopes, and it is useful to me as cawing
Is to crows or roaring to the lions, it
Is human speech, the speech of the mind that is
Here and not there, a mind that sees and hears and
Is aware. Not the deaf, blind speech
Of trees in storm or of monsoon clouds or of rain or the
Incoherent mutterings of the blazing
Funeral pyre. I was child, and later they
Told me I grew, for I became tall, my limbs
Swelled and one or two places sprouted hair. When
I asked for love, not knowing what else to ask
For, he drew a youth of sixteen into the
Bedroom and closed the door. He did not beat me
But my sad woman-body felt so beaten.

The weight of my breasts and womb crushed me. I shrank
Pitifully. Then . . . I wore a shirt and my
Brother's trousers, cut my hair short and ignored
My womanliness. Dress in sarees, be girl
Be wife, they said. Be embroiderer, be cook,

Be a quarreller with servants. Fit in. Oh,
Belong, cried the categorizers. Don't sit
On walls or peep in through our lace-draped windows.
Be Amy, or be Kamala. Or, better
Still, be Madhavikutty. It is time to
Choose a name, a role. Don't play pretending games.
Don't play at schizophrenia or be a
Nympho. Don't cry embarrassingly loud when
Jilted in love . . . I met a man, loved him. Call
Him not by any name, he is every man
Who wants a woman, just as I am every
Woman who seeks love. In him . . . the hungry haste
Of rivers, in me . . . the oceans' tireless
Waiting. Who are you, I ask each and everyone,
The answer is, it is I. Anywhere and,
Everywhere, I see the one who calls himself
If in this world, he is tightly packed like the
Sword in its sheath. It is I who drink lonely
Drinks at twelve, midnight, in hotels of strange towns,
It is I who laugh, it is I who make love
And then, feel shame, it is I who lie dying
With a rattle in my throat. I am sinner,
I am saint. I am the beloved and the
Betrayed. I have no joys which are not yours, no
Aches which are not yours. I too call myself I.

❋ Discussion and Writing

1. Describe the various facets of identity emphasized in the poem.
2. With whom is the persona in conflict? Discuss the issues of disagreement.
3. Examine the implications of: her having to choose a name and playing a role; her being a saint and a sinner.
4. Discuss the portrayal of men and the significance of the images used to describe them.
5. Analyze the ambiguity of her being herself and every woman at once.
6. Examine the tone of the poem: what lies at the core of her pain?

❋ Research and Comparison

Interdisciplinary Discussion Question: Examine the imposition of Hindi as the national language and its political ramifications in India, and compare the issue of language in another decolonized country.

Interdisciplinary Discussion Question: Examine the many issues pertaining to an Indian woman's identity, the crisscross of: caste, class, education, region, religion, vocation, as well as marital status and motherhood.

Interdisciplinary Discussion Question: Research the development of the caste system and its practice in modern India. Examine how it operates with regard to any one institution, such as marriage, education, politics, or religious practices in a specific community.

Anita Desai
(b. 1937)
India

Anita Desai was born in Mussoorie in north India, the daughter of a Bengali businessman and German woman. A graduate of Delhi University, Desai has taught at universities in England and the United States. She has published more than two dozen short stories and eleven novels, receiving the Sahitya Akademi Prize in 1979 for her novel *Fire on the Mountain* (1977). Focusing on conflicts in human relationship rather than on social or political issues, and weaving together time, memory, and disconnectedness, she has depicted the mores controlling family ties. Her concern, as she has said, has been to illuminate "the truth that is nine-tenths of the iceberg that lies submerged beneath the one-tenth visible portion we call Reality."

A Devoted Son

When the results appeared in the morning papers, Rakesh scanned them, barefoot and in his pajamas, at the garden gate, then went up the steps to the verandah where his father sat sipping his morning tea and bowed down to touch his feet.

"A first division, son?" his father asked, beaming, reaching for the papers.

"At the top of the list, papa," Rakesh murmured, as if awed. "First in the country."

Bedlam broke loose then. The family whooped and danced. The whole day long visitors streamed into the small yellow house at the end of the road, to congratulate the parents of this *Wunderkind,*[1] to slap Rakesh on the back

---

[1]Child prodigy. [eds.]

and fill the house and garden with the sounds and colors of a festival. There were garlands and *halwa*,[2] party clothes and gifts (enough fountain pens to last years, even a watch or two), nerves and temper and joy, all in a multicolored whirl of pride and great shining vistas newly opened: Rakesh was the first son in the family to receive an education, so much had been sacrificed in order to send him to school and then medical college, and at last the fruits of their sacrifice had arrived, golden and glorious.

To everyone who came to him to say, "*Mubarak*,[3] Varmaji, your son has brought you glory," the father said, "Yes, and do you know what is the first thing he did when he saw the results this morning? He came and touched my feet. He bowed down and touched my feet." This moved many of the women in the crowd so much that they were seen to raise the ends of their saris and dab at their tears while the men reached out for the betel-leaves and sweetmeats that were offered around on trays and shook their heads in wonder and approval of such exemplary filial behavior. "One does not often see such behavior in sons any more," they all agreed, a little enviously perhaps. Leaving the house, some of the women said, sniffing, "At least on such an occasion they might have served pure *ghee*[4] sweets," and some of the men said, "Don't you think old Varma was giving himself airs? He needn't think we don't remember that he comes from the vegetable market himself, his father used to sell vegetables, and he has never seen the inside of a school." But there was more envy than rancor in their voices and it was, of course, inevitable—not every son in that shabby little colony at the edge of the city was destined to shine as Rakesh shone, and who knew that better than the parents themselves?

And that was only the beginning, the first step in a great, sweeping ascent to the radiant heights of fame and fortune. The thesis he wrote for his M.D. brought Rakesh still greater glory, if only in select medical circles. He won a scholarship. He went to the USA (that was what his father learnt to call it and taught the whole family to say—not America, which was what the ignorant neighbors called it, but, with a grand familiarity, "the USA") where he pursued his career in the most prestigious of all hospitals and won encomiums from his American colleagues which were relayed to his admiring and glowing family. What was more, he came *back,* he actually returned to that small yellow house in the once-new but increasingly shabby colony, right at the end of the road where the rubbish vans tripped out their stinking contents for pigs to nose in and rag-pickers to build their shacks on, all steaming and smoking just outside the neat wire fences and well-tended

---

[2]A confection. [eds.]
[3]Congratulations, a greeting.
[4]Clarified butter.

gardens. To this Rakesh returned and the first thing he did on entering the house was to slip out of the embraces of his sisters and brothers and bow down and touch his father's feet.

As for his mother, she gloated chiefly over the strange fact that he had not married in America, had not brought home a foreign wife as all her neighbors had warned her he would, for wasn't that what all Indian boys went abroad for? Instead he agreed, almost without argument, to marry a girl she had picked out for him in her own village, the daughter of a child-hood friend, a plump and uneducated girl, it was true, but so old-fashioned, so placid, so complaisant that she slipped into the household and settled in like a charm, seemingly too lazy and too good-natured to even try and make Rakesh leave home and set up independently, as any other girl might have done. What was more, she was pretty—really pretty, in a plump, pudding way that only gave way to fat—soft, spreading fat, like warm wax—after the birth of their first baby, a son, and then what did it matter?

For some years Rakesh worked in the city hospital, quickly rising to the top of the administrative organization, and was made a director before he left to set up his own clinic. He took his parents in his car—a new, sky-blue Ambassador with a rear window full of stickers and charms revolving on strings—to see the clinic when it was built, and the large sign-board over the door on which his name was printed in letters of red, with a row of degrees and qualifications to follow it like so many little black slaves of the regent. Thereafter his fame seemed to grow just a little dimmer—or maybe it was only that everyone in town had grown accustomed to it at last—but it was also the beginning of his fortune for he now became known not only as the best but also the richest doctor in town.

However, all this was not accomplished in the wink of an eye. Naturally not. It was the achievement of a lifetime and it took up Rakesh's whole life. At the time he set up his clinic his father had grown into an old man and retired from his post at the kerosene dealer's depot at which he had worked for forty years, and his mother died soon after, giving up the ghost with a sigh that sounded positively happy, for it was her own son who ministered to her in her last illness and who sat pressing her feet at the last moment—such a son as few women had borne.

For it had to be admitted—and the most unsuccessful and most rancorous of neighbors eventually did so—that Rakesh was not only a devoted son and a miraculously good-natured man contrived somehow to obey his parents and humor his wife and show concern equally for his chil-dren and his patients, but there was actually a brain inside this beautifully polished and formed body of good manners and kind nature and, in between ministering to his family and playing host to many friends and coaxing them all into feeling happy and grateful and content, he had actually trained his hands as well and emerged an excellent doctor, a really fine surgeon. How one man—and a man born to illiterate parents, his father having worked for a kerosene dealer and his mother having spent her life in a kitchen—had achieved, combined and conducted such a medley of virtues, no one could fathom, but all acknowledged his talent and skill.

It was a strange fact, however, that talent and skill, if displayed for too long, cease to dazzle. It came to pass that the most admiring of all eyes eventually faded and no longer blinked at his glory. Having retired from work and having lost his wife, the old father very quickly went to pieces, as they say. He developed so many complaints and fell ill so frequently and with such mysterious diseases that even his son could no longer make out when it was something of significance and when it was merely a peevish whim. He sat huddled on his string bed most of the day and developed an exasperating habit of stretching out suddenly and lying absolutely still, allowing the whole family to fly around him in a flap, wailing and weeping, and then suddenly sitting up, stiff and gaunt, and spitting out a big gob of betel-juice as if to mock their behavior.

He did this once too often: there had been a big party in the house, a birthday party for the youngest son, and the celebrations had to be suddenly hushed, covered up and hustled out of the way when the daughter-in-law discovered, or thought she discovered, that the old man, stretched out from end to end of his string bed, had lost his pulse; the party broke up, dissolved, even turned into a band of mourners, when the old man sat up and the distraught daughter-in-law received a gob of red spittle right on the hem of her new organza sari. After that no one much cared if he sat up cross-legged on his bed, hawking and spitting, or lay down flat and turned gray as a corpse. Except, of course, for that pearl amongst pearls, his son Rakesh.

It was Rakesh who brought him his morning tea, not in one of the china cups from which the rest of the family drank, but in the old man's favorite brass tumbler, and sat at the edge of his bed, comfortable and relaxed with the string of his pajamas dangling out from under his fine lawn night-shirt, and discussed or, rather, read out the morning news to his father. It made no difference to him that his father made no response apart from spitting. It was Rakesh, too, who, on returning from the clinic in the evening, persuaded the old man to come out of his room, as bare and desolate as a cell, and take the evening air out in the garden, beautifully arranging the pillows and bolsters on the *divan* in the corner of the open verandah. On summer nights he saw to it that the servants carried out the old man's bed onto the lawn and himself helped his father down the steps and onto the bed, soothing him and settling him down for a night under the stars.

All this was very gratifying for the old man. What was not so gratifying was that he even undertook to supervise his father's diet. One day when the father was really sick, having ordered his daughter-in-law to make him a dish of *soojie halwa*[5] and eaten it with a saucerful of cream, Rakesh marched into the room, not with his usual respectful step but with the confident and rather contemptuous stride of the famous doctor, and declared, "No more

[5]A confection. [eds.]

halwa for you, papa. We must be sensible, at your age. If you must have something sweet, Veena will cook you a little *kheer*,[6] that's light, just a little rice and milk. But nothing fried, nothing rich. We can't have this happening again."

The old man who had been lying stretched out on his bed, weak and feeble after a day's illness, gave a start at the very sound, the tone of these words. He opened his eyes—rather, they fell open with shock—and he stared at his son with disbelief that darkened quickly to reproach. A son who actually refused his father the food he craved? No, it was unheard of, it was incredible. But Rakesh had turned his back to him and was cleaning up the litter of bottles and packets on the medicine shelf and did not notice while Veena slipped silently out of the room with a little smirk that only the old man saw, and hated.

Halwa was only the first item to be crossed off the old man's diet. One delicacy after the other went—everything fried to begin with, then everything sweet, and eventually everything, everything that the old man enjoyed. The meals that arrived for him on the shining stainless steel tray twice a day were frugal to say the least—dry bread, boiled lentils, boiled vegetables and, if there were a bit of chicken or fish, that was boiled too. If he called for another helping—in a cracked voice that quavered theatrically—Rakesh himself would come to the door, gaze at him sadly and shake his head, saying, "Now, papa, we must be careful, we can't risk another illness, you know," and although the daughter-in-law kept tactfully out of the way, the old man could just see her smirk sliding merrily through the air. He tried to bribe his grand-children into buying him sweets (and how he missed his wife now, that generous, indulgent and illiterate cook), whispering, "Here's fifty paise," as he stuffed the coins into a tight, hot fist. "Run down to the shop at the crossroads and buy me thirty paise worth of *jalebis*,[7] and you can spend the remaining twenty paise on yourself. Eh? Understand? Will you do that?" He got away with it once or twice but then was found out, the conspirator was scolded by his father and smacked by his mother and Rakesh came storming into the room, almost tearing his hair as he shouted through compressed lips, "Now papa, are you trying to turn my little son into a liar? Quite apart from spoiling your own stomach, you are spoiling him as well—you are encouraging him to lie to his own parents. You should have heard the lies he told his mother when she saw him bringing back those *jalebis* wrapped up in filthy newspaper. I don't allow anyone in my house to buy sweets in the bazaar, papa, surely you know that. There's cholera in the city, typhoid, gastroenteritis—I see these cases daily in the hospital, how can I allow my own family to run such risks?" The old man sighed and lay down in the corpse position. But that worried no one any longer.

---

[6]Sweet rice pudding. [eds.]
[7]A confection. [eds.]

There was only one pleasure left in the old man now (his son's early morning visits and readings from the newspaper could no longer be called that) and those were visits from elderly neighbors. These were not frequent as his contemporaries were mostly as decrepit and helpless as he and few could walk the length of the road to visit him any more. Old Bhatia, next door, however, who was still spry enough to refuse, adamantly, to bathe in the tiled bathroom indoors and to insist on carrying out his brass mug and towel, in all seasons and usually at impossible hours, into the yard and bathe noisily under the garden tap, would look over the hedge to see if Varma were out on his verandah and would call to him and talk while he wrapped his *dhoti*[8] about him and dried the sparse hair on his head, shivering with enjoyable exaggeration. Of course these conversations, bawled across the hedge by two rather deaf old men conscious of having their entire households overhearing them, were not very satisfactory but Bhatia occasionally came out of his yard, walked down the bit of road and came in at Varma's gate to collapse onto the stone plinth built under the temple tree. If Rakesh was at home he would help his father down the steps into the garden and arrange him on his night bed under the tree and leave the two old men to chew betel-leaves and discuss the ills of their individual bodies with combined passion.

"At least you have a doctor in the house to look after you," sighed Bhatia, having vividly described his martyrdom to piles.

"Look after me?" cried Varma, his voice cracking like an ancient clay jar. "He—he does not even give me enough to eat."

"What?" said Bhatia, the white hairs in his ears twitching. "Doesn't give you enough to eat? Your own son?"

"My own son. If I ask him for one more piece of bread, he says no, papa, I weighed out the *ata*[9] myself and I can't allow you to have more than two hundred grams of cereal a day. He *weighs* the food he gives me, Bhatia—he has scales to weigh it on. That is what it has come to."

"Never," murmured Bhatia in disbelief. "Is it possible, even in this evil age, for a son to refuse his father food?"

"Let me tell you," Varma whispered eagerly. "Today the family was having fried fish—I could smell it. I called to my daughter-in-law to bring me a piece. She came to the door and said no. . . ."

"Said no?" It was Bhatia's voice that cracked. A *drongo* shot out of the tree and sped away. "*No?*"

"No, she said no, Rakesh has ordered her to give me nothing fried. No butter, he says, no oil. . . ."

"No butter? No oil? How does he expect his father to *live?*"

Old Varma nodded with melancholy triumph. "That is how he treats me—after I have brought him up, given him an education, made him a great

---

[8]A man's garment. [eds.]
[9]A flour. [eds.]

doctor. Great doctor! This is the way great doctors treat their fathers, Bhatia," for the son's sterling personality and character now underwent a curious sea change. Outwardly all might be the same but the interpretation had altered: his masterly efficiency was nothing but cold heartlessness, his authority was only tyranny in disguise.

There was cold comfort in complaining to neighbors and, on such a miserable diet, Varma found himself slipping, weakening and soon becoming a genuinely sick man. Powders and pills and mixtures were not only brought in when dealing with a crisis like an upset stomach but became a regular part of his diet—became his diet, complained Varma, supplanting the natural foods he craved. There were pills to regulate his bowel movements, pills to bring down his blood pressure, pills to deal with his arthritis and, eventually, pills to keep his heart beating. In between there were panicky rushes to the hospital, some humiliating experiences with the stomach pump and enema, which left him frightened and helpless. He cried easily, shrivelling up on his bed, but if he complained of a pain or even a vague, gray fear in the night, Rakesh would simply open another bottle of pills and force him to take one. "I have my duty to you papa," he said when his father begged to be let off.

"Let me be," Varma begged, turning his face away from the pills on the outstretched hand. "Let me die. It would be better. I do not want to live only to eat your medicines."

"Papa, be reasonable."

"I leave that to you," the father cried with sudden spirit. "Leave me alone, let me die now, I cannot live like this."

"Lying all day on his pillows, fed every few hours by his daughter-in-law's own hands, visited by every member of his family daily—and then he says he does not want to live 'like this,'" Rakesh was heard to say, laughing, to someone outside the door.

"Deprived of food," screamed the old man on the bed, "his wishes ignored, taunted by his daughter-in-law, laughed at by his grand-children—*that* is how I live." But he was very old and weak and all anyone heard was an incoherent croak, some expressive grunts and cries of genuine pain. Only once, when old Bhatia had come to see him and they sat together under the temple tree, they heard him cry, "God is calling me—and they won't let me go."

The quantities of vitamins and tonics he was made to take were not altogether useless. They kept him alive and even gave him a kind of strength that made him hang on long after he ceased to wish to hang on. It was as though he were straining at a rope, trying to break it, and it would not break, it was still strong. He only hurt himself, trying.

In the evening, that summer, the servants would come into his cell, grip his bed, one at each end, and carry it out to the verandah, there setting it down with a thump that jarred every tooth in his head. In answer to his agonized complaints they said the doctor sahib had told them he must take the evening air and the evening air they would make him take—thump. Then Veena, that smiling, hypocritical pudding in a rustling sari, would appear and pile up the pillows under his head till he was propped up stiffly into a sitting position that made his head swim and his back ache.

"Let me lie down," he begged. "I can't sit up any more."

"Try, papa, Rakesh said you can if you try," she said, and drifted away to the other end of the verandah where her transistor radio vibrated to the lovesick tunes from the cinema that she listened to all day.

So there he sat, like some stiff corpse, terrified, gazing out on the lawn where his grand-sons played cricket, in danger of getting one of their hard-spun balls in his eye, and at the gate that opened onto the dusty and rubbish-heaped lane but still bore, proudly, a newly touched-up signboard that bore his son's name and qualifications, his own name having vanished from the gate long ago.

At last the sky-blue Ambassador arrived, the cricket game broke up in haste, the car drove in smartly and the doctor, the great doctor, all in white, stepped out. Someone ran up to take his bag from him, others to escort him up the steps. "Will you have tea?" his wife called, turning down the transistor set. "Or a Coca-Cola? Shall I fry you some *samosas?*"[10] But he did not reply or even glance in her direction. Ever a devoted son, he went first to the corner where his father sat gazing, stricken, at some undefined spot in the dusty yellow air that swam before him. He did not turn his head to look at his son. But he stopped gobbling air with his uncontrolled lips and set his jaw as hard as a sick and very old man could set it.

"Papa," his son said, tenderly, sitting down on the edge of the bed and reaching out to press his feet.

Old Varma tucked his feet under him, out of the way, and continued to gaze stubbornly into the yellow air of the summer evening.

"Papa, I'm home."

Varma's hand jerked suddenly, in a sharp, derisive movement, but he did not speak.

"How are you feeling, papa?"

Then Varma turned and looked at his son. His face was so out of control and all in pieces, that the multitude of expressions that crossed it could not make up a whole and convey to the famous man exactly what his father thought of him, his skill, his art.

"I'm dying," he croaked. "Let me die, I tell you."

"Papa, you're joking," his son smiled at him, lovingly. "I've brought you a new tonic to make you feel better. You must take it, it will make you feel stronger again. Here it is. Promise me you will take it regularly, papa."

---

[10]A thin dough stuffed with various fillings and fried. [eds.]

Varma's mouth worked as hard as though he still had a gob of betel in it (his supply of betel had been cut off years ago). Then he spat out some words, as sharp and bitter as poison, into his son's face. "Keep your tonic—I want none—I want none—I won't take any more of—of your medicines. None. Never," and he swept the bottle out of his son's hand with a wave of his own, suddenly grand, suddenly effective.

His son jumped, for the bottle was smashed and thick brown syrup had splashed up, staining his white trousers. His wife let out a cry and came running. All around the old man was hubbub once again, noise, attention.

He gave one push to the pillows at his back and dislodged them so he could sink down on his back, quite flat again. He closed his eyes and pointed his chin at the ceiling, like some dire prophet, groaning, "God is calling me—now let me go."

❈ Discussion and Writing

1. Comment on Rakesh as a model son and a doctor: do the two roles conflict with each other? What is his function in the narrative?
2. What is the nature of the father's relationship with his son: explain Varma's reactions to the dietary restrictions and his changing perception of his son.
3. What is the significance of the last scene?
4. Comment on the portrayal of a family that ideally combines tradition and modernity and yet misses something. What is it?

❈ Research and Comparison

Interdisciplinary Discussion Question: Comment on the dilemma posed by the demands of traditionalism and modernity in India and its portrayal in the work of any major writer.

Patricia Grace
(b. 1937)
New Zealand

Patricia Grace was born in Wellington, New Zealand; she is of Maori descent, of Ngati Raukawa, Ngati Toa, and Te Ati Awa lineage; and she has additional affiliations through her marriage. Her early schooling was in a convent and her higher education at St. Mary's College. She has taught in various country schools and written children's stories as well as short stories and novels. Concerned with Maori society, particularly its complex sense of family, she has illuminated the effects of colonization in her pictures of twentieth-century Maori life.

It Used to Be Green Once

We were all ashamed of our mother. Our mother always did things to shame us. Like putting red darns in our clothes, and cutting up old swimming togs and making two—girl's togs from the top half for my sister, and boy's togs from the bottom half for my brother. Peti and Raana both cried when Mum made them take the togs to school. Peti sat down on the road by our gate and yelled out she wasn't going to school. She wasn't going swimming. I didn't blame my sister because the togs were thirty-eight chest and Peti was only ten.

But Mum knew how to get her up off the road. She yelled loudly, "Get up off that road my girl. There's nothing wrong with those togs. I didn't have any togs when I was a kid and I had to swim in my nothings. Get up off your backside and get to school." Mum's got a loud voice and she knew how to shame us. We all dragged Peti up off the road before our mates came along and heard Mum. We pushed Peti into the school bus so Mum wouldn't come yelling up the drive.

We never minded our holey fruit at first. Dad used to pick up the cases of over-ripe apples or pears from town that he got cheap. Mum would dig out the rotten bits, and then give them to us to take for play-lunch. We didn't notice much at first, not until Reweti from down the road yelled out to us one morning, "Hey you fullas. Who shot your pears?" We didn't have anywhere to hide our lunch because we weren't allowed school bags until we got to high school. Mum said she wasn't buying fourteen school bags. When we went to high school we could have shoes too. The whole lot of us gave Reweti a good hiding after school.

However, this story is mainly about the car, and about Mum and how she shamed us all the time. The shame of rainbow darns and cut-up togs and holey fruit was nothing to what we suffered because of the car. Uncle Raz gave us the car because he couldn't fix it up any more, and he'd been fined because he lived in Auckland. He gave the car to Dad so we could drive our cream cans up to the road instead of pushing them up by wheelbarrow.

It didn't matter about the car not having brakes because the drive from our cowshed goes down in a dip then up to the gate. Put the car in its first gear, run it down from the shed, pick up a bit of speed, up the other side, turn it round by the cream stand so that it's pointing down the drive again, foot off the accelerator and slam on the handbrake. Dad pegged a board there to make sure it stopped. Then when we'd lifted the cans out on to the stand he'd back up a little and slide off down the drive—with all of us throwing ourselves in over the sides as if it were a dinghy that had just been pushed out into the sea.

The car had been red once because you could still see some patches of red paint here and there. And it used to have a top too, that you could put down or up. Our uncle told us that when he gave it to Dad. We were all proud about the car having had a top once. Some of the younger kids skited[1] to their mates about our convertible and its top that went up and down. But that was before our mother started shaming us by driving the car to the shop.

We growled at Mum and we cried but it made no difference. "You kids always howl when I tell you to get our shopping," she said.

"We'll get it Mum. We won't cry."

"We won't cry Mum. We'll carry the sack of potatoes."

"And the flour."

"And the bag of sugar."

"And the rolled oats."

"And the tin of treacle."

"We'll do the shopping Mum."

But Mum would say, "Never mind, I'll do it myself." And after that she wouldn't listen any more.

How we hated Wednesdays. We always tried to be sick on Wednesdays, or to miss the bus. But Mum would be up early yelling at us to get out of bed. If we didn't get up when we were told she'd drag us out and pull down our pajama pants and set our bums on the cold lino.[2] Mum was cruel to us.

Whoever was helping with the milking had to be back quickly from the shed for breakfast, and we'd all have to rush through our kai[3] and get to school. Wednesday was Mum's day for shopping.

As soon as she had everything tidy she'd change into her good purple dress that she'd made from a Japanese bedspread, pull on her floppy brimmed blue sunhat and her slippers and galoshes, and go out and start up the car.

We tried everything to stop her shaming us all.

"You've got no license Mum."

"What do I want a license for? I can drive can't I? I don't need the proof."

"You got no warrant."

"Warrant? What's warrant?"

"The traffic man'll get you Mum."

---

[1]Boasted.
[2]Linoleum.
[3]Food. [eds.]

"That rat. He won't come near me after what he did to my niece. I'll hit him right over his smart head with a bag of riwais [potatoes] and I'll hit him somewhere else as well." We never could win an argument with Mum.

Off she'd go on a Wednesday morning, and once out on the road she'd start tooting the horn. This didn't sound like a horn at all but like a flock of ducks coming in for a feed. The reason for the horn was to let all her mates and relations along the way know she was coming. And as she passed each one's house, if they wanted anything they'd have to run out and call it out loud. Mum couldn't stop because of not having any brakes. "E Kiri," each would call. "Mauria mai he riwai," if they wanted spuds; "Mauria mai he paraoa," if they wanted bread. "Mauria mai he tarau, penei te kaita," hand spread to show the size of the pants they wanted Mum to get. She would call out to each one and wave to them to show she'd understood. And when she neared the store she'd switch the motor off, run into the kerbing [curb] and pull on the handbrake. I don't know how she remembered all the things she had to buy—I only know that by the time she'd finished, every space in that car was filled and it was a squeeze for her to get into the driver's seat. But she had everything there, all ready to throw out on the way back.

As soon as she'd left the store she'd begin hooting again, to let the whole district know she was on her way. Everybody would be out on the road to get their shopping thrown at them, or just to watch our mother go chuffing past. We always hid if we heard her coming.

The first time Mum's car and the school bus met was when they were both approaching a one-way bridge from opposite directions. We had to ask the driver to stop and give way to Mum because she had no brakes. We were all ashamed. But everyone soon got to know Mum and her car and they always stopped whenever they saw her coming. And you know, Mum never ever had an accident in her car, except for once when she threw a side of mutton out to Uncle Peta and it knocked him over and broke his leg.

After a while we started walking home from school on Wednesdays to give Mum a good chance of getting home before us, and so we wouldn't be in the bus when it had to stop and let her pass. The boys didn't like having to walk home but we girls didn't mind because Mr. Hadley walked home too. He was a new teacher at our school and he stayed not far from where we lived. We girls thought he was really neat.

But one day, it had to happen. When I heard the honking and tooting behind me I wished that a hole would appear in the ground and that I would fall in it and disappear for ever. As Mum came near she started smiling and waving and yelling her head off. "Anyone wants a ride." she yelled, "they'll have to run and jump in."

We all turned our heads the other way and hoped Mr. Hadley wouldn't notice the car with our mother in it, and her yelling and tooting, and the brim of her hat jumping up and down. But instead, Mr Hadley took off after the car and leapt in over the back seat on top of the shopping. Oh the shame.

But then one day something happened that changed everything. We arrived home to find Dad in his best clothes, walking round and grinning, and not doing anything like getting the cows in, or mending a gate, or digging a drain. We said, "What are you laughing at Dad?" "What are you dressed up for? Hey Mum what's the matter with Dad?"

"Your Dad's a rich man," she said. "Your Dad, he's just won fifty thousand dollars in a lottery."

At first we couldn't believe it. We couldn't believe it. Then we all began running round and laughing and yelling and hugging Dad and Mum. "We can have shoes and bags," we said. "New clothes and swimming togs, and proper apples and pears." Then do you know what Dad said? Dad said, "Mum can have a new car." This really astounded and amazed us. We went numb with excitement for five minutes then began hooting and shouting again, and knocking Mum over.

"A new car!"

"A new car?"

"Get us a Packard Mum."

"Or a De Soto. Yes, yes."

Get this, get that. . . .

Well Mum bought a big shiny green Chevrolet, and Dad got a new cowshed with everything modernized and water gushing everywhere. We all got our new clothes—shoes, bags, togs—and we even started taking posh lunches to school. Sandwiches cut in triangles, bottles of cordial, crisp apples and pears, and yellow bananas.

And somehow all of us kids changed. We started acting like we were somebody instead of ordinary like before. We used to whine to Dad for money to spend and he'd always give it to us. Every week we'd nag Mum into taking us to the pictures, or if she was tired we'd go ourselves by taxi. We got flash bedspreads and a piano and we really thought we were neat.

As for the old car—we made Dad take it to the dump. We never wanted to see it again. We all cheered when he took it away, except for Mum. Mum stayed inside where she couldn't watch, but we all stood outside and cheered.

We all changed, as though we were really somebody, but there was one thing I noticed. Mum didn't change at all, and neither did Dad. Mum had a new car all right, and a couple of new dresses, and a new pair of galoshes to put over her slippers. And Dad had a new modern milking shed and a tractor, and some other gadgets for the farm. But Mum and Dad didn't change. They were the same as always.

Mum still went shopping every Wednesday. But instead of having to do all the shopping herself she was able to take all her friends and relations with her. She had to start out earlier so she'd have time to pick everyone up on the way. How angry we used to be when Mum went past with her same old sunhat and her heap of friends and relations, and them all waving and calling out to us.

Mum sometimes forgot that the new car had brakes, especially when she was approaching the old bridge and we were coming the opposite way in the school bus. She would start tooting and the bus would have to pull over and let her through. That's when all our aunties and uncles and friends would start waving and calling out. But some of them couldn't wave because they were too squashed by people and shopping, they'd just yell. How shaming.

There were always ropes everywhere over Mum's new car holding bags of things and shovel handles to the roof and sides. The boot [trunk] was always hanging open because it was too full to close—things used to drop out on to the road all the time. And the new car—it used to be green once, because if you look closely you can still see some patches of green paint here and there.

❋ Discussion and Writing

1. Explain the children's feelings of shame regarding their mother's behavior.
2. Discuss the importance of the incident with Reweti.
3. How do the neighbors perceive Mother and her car trips? What is the implication of Mr. Hadley's response to Mother's call for a ride?
4. Describe Mother as: a wife, a mother, a neighbor, a driver, a person.
5. Discuss the behavior of the parents and the children after the lottery.
6. Describe Mother's trips in the new car: what do they signify; what do the patches of green imply?

Khalida Asghar
(b. 1938)
Pakistan

Khalida Asghar was born in Lahore, Pakistan, and began writing in 1963. She lived in Karachi for a time before moving to Islamabad where she has taught English in a college for women. Her first stories established her as one of the major contemporary Urdu writers. Among these works, "The

Wagon," with its eerie suggestiveness, has been cited as a modern classic, lauded especially for its hallucinatory evocation of the contemporary threat of nuclear holocaust.

The Wagon*

In a rush to get back to the city, I quickly crossed the dirt road and walked onto the Ravi bridge, looking indifferently at the blazing edge of the sun steadily falling into the marsh. I had a queer feeling, as though I saw something. I spun around. There they were, three of them, leaning over the bridge's guard rails and gazing straight into the sunset. Their deathly concentration made me look at the sunset myself, but I found nothing extraordinary in the scene; so I looked back at them instead. Their faces, although not at all similar, still looked curiously alike. Their outfits suggested that they were well-to-do villagers, and their dust-coated shoes that they had trudged for miles just to watch the sun as it set over the marshes of the receding Ravi. Impervious to the traffic on the bridge, they went on staring at the marshes which were turning a dull, deep red in the sun's last glow.

I edged closer to them. The sun had gone down completely; only a dark red stripe remained on the far horizon. Suddenly the three looked at each other, lowered their heads, and silently walked away, toward the villages outside the city. For some time I stood watching their tired figures recede into the distance. Soon the night sounds coming to life in the city reminded me that it was getting late and I'd better rush home. I quickened my pace and walked on under the blue haze of the night sky, pierced here and there by the blinking lights of the city ahead.

The next evening when I reached the bridge, the sunset was a few minutes away. I suddenly recalled the three men and stopped to watch the sunset even though I knew Munna would be waiting on the front porch for sweets and Zakiya, my wife, would be ready for us to go to the movies. I couldn't budge. An inexorable force seemed to have tied me to the ground. Through almost all the previous night I'd wondered what it was about the marsh and the sunset that had engrossed those strange men so entirely.

And then, just as the blazing orange disc of the sun tumbled into the marsh, I saw the three walk up the road. They were coming from villages outside the city limits. They wore identical clothes and resembled each other in their height and gait. Again they walked up to the bridge, stood at the same spot they had the previous evening and peered into the sunset with their flaming eyes filled with a dull sadness. I watched them and wondered why, despite their diverse features, they looked so much alike. One of them, who was very old, had a long, bushy snow-white beard. The second, some-

---

*Translated by Muhammad Umar Memon

what lighter in complexion than the other, had a face that shone like gold in the orange glow of sunset. His hair hung down to his shoulders like a fringe, and he had a scar on his forehead. The third was dark and snub-nosed.

The sun sank all the way into the marsh. As on the previous day, the men glanced at each other, let their heads drop and, without exchanging a word, went their way.

That evening I felt terribly ill at ease. In a way I regretted not asking them about their utter fascination with the sunset. What could they be look-ing for in the sun's fading light?—I wondered. I told Zakiya about the strange threesome. She just laughed and said, "Must be peasants, on their way to the city to have a good time."

An air of strangeness surrounded these men. Zakiya, of course, could not have known it: one really had to look at them to feel the weird aura.

The next day I waited impatiently for the evening. I walked to the bridge, expecting them to show up. And they did, just as the daylight ebbed away. They leaned over the bridge and watched the sun go down, indiffer-ent to the sound of traffic. Their absorption in the scene made it impossible to talk to them. I waited until the sun had gone down completely and the men had started to return. This would be the time to ask them what it was they expected to find in the vanishing sun and the marshes of the receding river.

When the sun had sunk all the way, the men gave one another a sad, mute look, lowered their heads and started off. But, instead of returning to the village, they took the road to the city. Their shoes were covered with dust and their feet moved on rhythmically together.

I gathered my faltering courage and asked them, "Brothers! what village do you come from?"

The man with the snub nose turned around and stared at me for a while. Then the three exchanged glances, but none of them bothered to answer my question.

"What do you see over there . . . on the bridge?" I asked. The mystery about the three men was beginning to weigh heavily upon me now. I felt as though molten lead had seeped into my legs—indeed into my whole body, and that it was only a matter of time before I'd crumble to the ground reeling from a spell of dizziness.

Again they did not answer. I shouted at them in a choking voice, "Why are you always staring at the sunset?"

No answer.

We reached the heavily congested city road. The evening sounds grew closer. It was late October, and the air felt pleasantly cool. The sweet scent of jasmine wafted in, borne by the breeze. As we passed the octroi post, the old man with snow-white hair suddenly spoke, "Didn't you see? Has nobody in the city seen. . . ?"

"Seen what?"

"When the sun sets, when it goes down all the way. . . ?" asked the hoary old man, rearranging his mantle over his shoulders.

"When the sun goes down all the way?" I repeated. "What about it? That happens every day!"

I said that very quickly, afraid that the slightest pause might force them back into their impenetrable silence.

"We knew that, we knew it would be that way. That's why we came. That other village, there, too. . . " He pointed toward the east and lowered his head.

"From there we come. . . " said the snub-nosed man.

"From where?" I asked, growing impatient. "Please tell me clearly."

The third man peered back at me over his shoulder. The scar on his forehead suddenly seemed deeper than before. He said, "We didn't notice, nor, I believe, did you. Perhaps nobody did. Because, as you say, the sun rises and sets every day. Why bother to look? And we didn't when day after day, there, over them," he pointed in the direction of the east, "the sky became blood-red and so bright it blazed like fire even at nightfall. We just failed to notice. . . " He stopped abruptly, as if choking over his words. "And now this redness," he resumed after a pause, "it keeps spreading from place to place. I'd never seen such a phenomenon before. Nor my elders. Nor, I believe, did they hear their elders mention anything quite like that ever happening."

Meanwhile the darkness had deepened. All I could see of my companions were their white flowing robes; their faces became visible only when they came directly under the pale, dim light of the lampposts. I turned around to look at the stretch of sky over the distant Ravi. I was stunned: it was glowing red despite the darkness.

"You are right," I said, to hide my puzzlement, "we really did fail to notice that." Then I asked, "Where are you going?"

"To the city, of course. What would be the point of arriving there *afterward?*"

A sudden impulse made me want to stay with them, or to take them home with me. But abruptly, they headed off on another road, and I remembered I was expected home soon. Munna would be waiting on the front porch for his daily sweets and Zakiya must be feeling irritated by my delay.

The next day I stopped at the bridge to watch the sunset. I was hoping to see those three men, the sun went down completely, but they didn't appear. I waited impatiently for them to show up. Soon, however, I was entranced by the sunset's last magical glow.

The entire sky seemed covered with a sheet soaked in blood, and it scared me that I was standing all alone underneath it. I felt an uncanny presence directly behind me. I spun around. There was nobody. All the same, I felt sure there was someone—standing behind my back, within me, or perhaps, somewhere near.

Vehicles, of all shapes and sizes, rumbled along in the light of the street-lamps. Way back in the east, a stretch of evening sky still blazed like a winding sheet of fire, radiating heat and light far into the closing darkness. I was alarmed and scurried home. Hastily I told Zakiya all I'd seen. But she laughed off the whole thing. I took her up to the balcony and showed her the red and its infernal bright glow against the dark night sky. That sobered her up a little. She thought for a while, then remarked, "We're going to have a storm any minute—I'm sure."

The next day in the office, as I worked, bent over my files, I heard Mujibullah ask Hafiz Ahmad, "Say, did you see how the sky glows at sunset these days? Even after it gets dark? Amazing, isn't it?"

All at once I felt I was standing alone and defenseless under that blood-sheet of a sky. I was frightened. Small drops of sweat formed on my forehead. As the evening edged closer, a strange restlessness took hold of me. The receding Ravi, the bridge, the night sky and the sun frightened me; I wanted to walk clear out of them. And yet, I also felt irresistibly drawn toward them.

I wanted to tell my colleagues about the three peasants who in spite of their distinctly individual faces somehow looked alike; about how they had come to the city accompanying this strange redness, had drawn my attention to it, and then dropped out of sight; and about how I'd searched in vain for them everywhere. But I couldn't. Mujibullah and Hafiz Ahmad, my office-mates, had each borrowed about twenty rupees from me some time ago, which they conveniently forgot to return, and, into the bargain, had stopped talking to me ever since.

On my way home when I entered the bridge, a strange fear made me walk briskly, look away from the sun, and try to concentrate instead on the street before me. But the blood-red evening kept coming right along. I could feel its presence everywhere. A flock of evening birds flew overhead in a "V" formation. Like the birds, I too was returning home. Home—yes, but no longer my haven against the outside world; for the flame-colored evening came pouring in from its windows, doors, even through its walls of solid masonry.

I now wandered late in the streets, looking for the three peasants. I wanted to ask them where that red came from. What was to follow? Why did they leave the last settlement? What shape was it in? But I couldn't find them anywhere. Nobody seemed to care.

A few days later I saw some men pointing up to the unusual red color of the evening. Before long, the whole city was talking about it. I hadn't told a soul except Zakiya. How they had found out about it was a puzzle to me. Those three peasants must be in the city—I concluded. They have got to be.

The red of evening had now become the talk of the town.

Chaudhri Sahib, who owns a small bookshop in Mozang Plaza, was an old acquaintance of mine. People got together at his shop for a friendly chat every evening. Often, so did I. But for some time now, since my first encounter with those mantle-wrapped oracular figures, I had been too preoccupied with my own thoughts to go there. No matter where I went, home or outside, I felt restless. At home, an inexorable urge drove me outdoors; outdoors, an equally strong urge sent me scrambling back home, where I felt comparatively safer. I became very confused about where I wanted to be. I began to feel heavy and listless.

All the same, I did go back to the bookshop once again that evening. Most of the regulars had already gathered. Chaudhri Sahib asked, "What do you think about it, fellows? Is it all due to the atomic explosions as they say? The rumor also has it that pretty soon the earth's cold regions will turn hot and the hot ones cold and the cycle of seasons will also be upset."

I wanted to tell them about my encounter with the three villagers but felt too shy to talk before so many people. Just then a pungent smell, the likes of which I'd never smelled before, wafted in from God knows where. My heart sank and a strange, sweet sort of pain stabbed my body. I felt nauseous, unable to decide whether it was a stench, a pungent aroma, or even a wave of bitter-sweet pain. I threw the newspaper down and got up to leave.

"What's the matter?" asked Chaudhri Sahib.

"I must go. God knows what sort of smell that is."

"Smell? What smell?" Chaudhri Sahib sniffed the air.

I didn't care to reply and walked away. That offensive smell, the terrifying wave of pain, followed me all the way home. It made me giddy. I thought I might fall any minute. My condition frightened Zakiya, who asked, "What's the matter—you look so pale?"

"I'm all right. God knows what that smell is." I said, wiping sweat off my brow, although it was the month of November.

Zakiya also sniffed the air, then said, "Must be coming from the house of Hakim Sahib. Heaven knows what strange herb concoctions they keep making day and night. Or else it's from burnt food. I burnt some today accidentally."

"But it seems to be everywhere . . . in every street and lane . . . throughout the city."

"Why, of course. The season's changed. It must be the smell of winter flowers," she said inattentively, and became absorbed in her knitting.

With great trepidation I again sniffed the air, but couldn't decide whether the sickening odor still lingered on or had subsided. Perhaps it had subsided. The thought relieved me a bit. But there was no escape from its memory, which remained fresh in my mind, like the itching that continues for some time even after the wound has healed. The very thought that it might return gave me the chills.

By next morning I'd forgotten all about that rotten, suffocating smell. In the office, I found a mountain of files waiting for me. But Mujibullah and Hafiz Ahmad went on noisily discussing some movie. I couldn't concentrate on the work and felt irritated. So I decided to take a break. I called our office boy and sent him to the cafeteria for a cup of tea. Meanwhile I pulled out a pack of cigarettes from my pocket and lit up.

Just then I felt a cracking blow on my head, as if I had fallen off a cliff and landed on my head, which fused everything before my eyes in a swirling blue and yellow streak. It took my numbed senses some time to realize that I was being assaulted once again by the same pain, the same terrible stench. It kept coming at me in waves, and it was impossible to know its source. I found myself frantically shutting every single window in the office, while both Mujibullah and Hafiz Ahmad gawked at me uncomprehendingly.

"Let the sun in! Why are you slamming the windows?" asked Hafiz Ahmad.

"The stench . . . the stench! My God, it's unbearable! Don't you smell it?"

Both of them raised their noses to their air and sniffed. Then Hafiz Ahmad remarked. "That's right. What sort of stench . . . or fragrance is that? It makes my heart sink."

Soon, many people were talking about the stink-waves which came in quick succession and then receded, only to renew their assault a little while later. At sundown they became especially unbearable.

Within a few weeks the stinking odor had become so oppressive that I often found it difficult to breathe. People's faces, usually quite lively and fresh, now looked drained and wilted. Many complained of constant palpitation and headaches. The doctors cashed in. Intellectuals hypothesized that it must be due to nuclear blasts, which were producing strange effects throughout the world, including this foul odor in our city, which attacked people's nerves and left them in a mess. People scrambled to buy tranquilizers, which sold out instantly. Not that the supply was inadequate, but a sudden frenzy to stock up and horde had seized people. Even sleeping pills fetched the price of rare diamonds.

I found both tranquilizers and sleeping pills useless. The stench cut sharper than a sword and penetrated the body like a laser. The only way to guard against it was to get used to it—I thought; and people would do well to remember that. But I was too depressed to tell them myself. Within a few weeks, however, they themselves came to live with the stench.

Just the same, the stench struck terror in the city. People were loath to admit it, but they could not have looked more tense: their faces contorted from the fear of some terrible thing happening at any moment. Nor was their fear unreasonable, as a subsequent event showed a few weeks later.

On a cold mid-December evening, I was returning home from Chaudhri Sahib's. The street was full of traffic and jostling crowds. The stores glittered with bright lights, and people went about their business as usual. Every now and then a stench-wave swept in, made me giddy, and receded. I would freeze in my stride the instant it assailed me and would start moving again as soon as it had subsided. It was the same with others. An outsider would surely have wondered why we suddenly froze, closed our eyes, stopped breathing, then took a deep breath and got started again. But that was our custom now.

That December evening I'd just walked onto the bridge when I felt as if a lance had hit me on the head. My head whirled and my legs buckled. Reeling, I clung on to a lamppost and tried to support my head with my hands. There was no lance, nor was there a hand to wield it. It was that smell—that same rotten smell—I realized with terror. In fact, it seemed that the source of the oppressive stench had suddenly moved very close to me, between my shoulder blades, near my back, immediately behind me—so close that it was impossible to think of it as apart from me.

It was then that my eyes fell on the strange carriage, rambling along in front of me. It was an oversized wagon pulled by a pair of scrawny white oxen with leather blinders over their eyes and thick ropes strung through their steaming nostrils. A wooden cage sat atop the base of the wagon, its interior hidden behind black curtains—or were they just swaying walls of darkness?

Two men, sitting outside the cage enclosure in the front of the wagon, drove the two emaciated, blindfolded animals. I couldn't make out their faces, partly because of the darkness, but partly also because they were buried in folds of cloth thrown loosely around them. Their heads drooped forward and they seemed to have dozed off, overcome by fatigue and sleep.

Behind them the interior of the curtained wagon swelled with darkness and from the heart of that darkness shot out the nauseating stench which cut sharper than a sword. . . . Before I knew it, the wagon had creaked past me, flooding my senses with its cargo of stink. My head swirled. I jumped off the main road onto the dirt sidewalk . . . and vomited.

I had no idea whether the people in the city had also seen the eerie wagon. If they had, what must have they endured? I had the hardest time getting home after what I had seen. Once inside the house, I ran to my bed and threw myself on it. Zakiya kept asking me what had happened, but a blind terror sealed my lips.

A few days later a small news item appeared in the local papers. It railed against the local Municipal Office for allowing garbage carts to pass through busy streets in the evening. Not only did muck-wagons pollute the air, they also hurt the fine olfactory sense of the citizenry.

I took a whole week off from work. During those seven days, though hardly fit to go out and observe firsthand the plight of the city, I was nonetheless kept posted of developments by local newspapers. Groups of concerned citizens demanded that the municipal authorities keep the city clear of the muck-wagons or, if that was impossible, assign them routes along less busy streets.

On the seventh day I ventured out. A change was already visible. Wrecked by insomnia and exhaustion, people strained themselves to appear carefree and cheerful, but managed only to look painfully silly. Suddenly I recalled that in the morning I had myself looked no different in the mirror.

About this time, the number of entertainment programs and movies shot up as never before. People swarmed to box offices—often hours before a show—where they formed long lines and patiently waited to be let in, and then filed out from the entertainment still looking pale and ridiculous.

In the office, no matter how hard I tried, I couldn't concentrate on work. Intermittently, the image of the muck-wagon lumbering down the streets flashed across my mind. Was it really one of those municipal dump-carts? No. It couldn't be. Municipal dump-carts never looked like that eerie wagon, with its sleepy drivers, a pair of blindfolded bony oxen, black curtains and the outrageously nauseating smell. What on earth could give off such an odd smell—at once fragrant and foul!

An insane desire suddenly overwhelmed me: to rush up to the wagon, lift up those swaying curtains, and peek inside. I must discover the source of the stench!

Coming to the bridge my feet involuntarily slowed down. There was still some time before sunset and the waves of the pain-filled odor came faster and stronger. I leaned over the bridge, an unknown fear slowly rising in my throat. The bottomless swamp, its arms ominously outstretched, seemed to be dragging me down toward it. I was afraid I might jump into the swamp, sink with the sun and become buried forever in that sprawling sheet of blood.

I became aware of something approaching me—or was I myself drawing closer to something? . . . Something awaited by all men—those before and those after us. My whole body felt as though it was turning into a piece of granite, with no escape from the bridge, the miasma, the sun, for now they all seemed inseparable from my being. Helplessly, I looked around myself and almost dropped dead.

The three men were coming toward me from the direction of the countryside. As before, they were wrapped in their flowing white robes and walked with their amazingly identical gait. I kept staring at them with glassy eyes until they walked right up to me and stopped. The hoary old man was crying, and his snow-white beard was drenched in tears. The other two couldn't look up; their eyes were lowered mournfully, their teeth clenched and their faces withered by a deathly pallor.

"Where were you hiding all these days?" I said between gasps and stammers. "I searched for you everywhere. Tell me, please, what's happening to the city?"

"We were waiting. Trying to hold ourselves back. We had tied ourselves with ropes. Here, look!" They spread their arms before me and bared their shoulders and backs, revealing the deep marks of the rope.

"We did not want to come. . . " the old man said, drowned out by a fit of sobs.

"But there was no choice. . . " the second man said. Before he had finished, he doubled over. His companions also doubled over, as if unable to control a sudden surge of pain. The same wave of pain-filled stench stabbed the air about us, cutting us into halves, flooding our senses, as it scrambled past us.

"There! Look!" said the old man, pointing in the direction of the distant villages and turning deathly pale.

In the distance, I saw the wagon come up the road from behind a cloud of dust. The drowsing coachmen had wrapped their faces because of their nearness to the cutting stench.

A cold shiver ran through my spine. The eyes of the three men suddenly became dull. They were approaching their end—perhaps.

The wagon rumbled close—the stench from it draining the blood from our bodies—and then passed us. Its sinister, jet-black curtains, fluttering in the gentle breeze, appeared, oddly enough, entirely motionless.

The three men ran after the wagon, caught up to it and lifted the curtains. A spit second later, a non-human scream burst from their gaping mouths. They spun around and bolted toward the distant fields.

"What was it? What did you see?" I asked, running after them. But they did not reply and kept running madly. Their eyes had frozen in a glazed stare.

I followed them until we had left the city several miles behind us, then grabbed the old man's robe and implored, "Tell me! Please tell me!"

He turned his deathly gaze and threw open his mouth. His tongue had got stuck to his palate.

All three had become dumb.

My head whirled, and I collapsed. The three men continued to run, soon disappearing in the distance behind a spiraling cloud of dust. Slowly the dust settled and I returned home.

For months now I have searched in vain for those men. They have vanished without a trace. And the wagon . . . from that fateful evening, it too has changed its route. It no longer passes through the city. After crossing the bridge, it now descends onto the dirt trail leading to villages in the country-side.

The cityfolk are no longer bothered by the slashing stench. They have become immune to it and think it has died, like an old, forgotten tale.

But it continues to torment my body, and day and night a voice keeps telling me, "Now, your turn! Now you shall *see!*"

And this evening I find myself on the bridge, waiting for the wagon . . . waiting.

❋ Discussion and Writing

1. Analyze the narrator's reactions to: the three men, the light, and the smell. What is his role in the story?
2. Explain Zakiya's response to the narrator's experience.

3. Comment on the townspeople's theories about the source of the red light and the stench: what is the significance of the changing attitudes of the people?
4. What is the implication of the three men's coming from the east? What do they symbolize by their appearance, their ages, their features, their robes, their behavior, their concern? Explain why they resist their last visit to the city.
5. What is symbolized by the wagon, its drivers, its contents? What is their impact on the three men? What is the effect of the scene on the narrator?
6. What is implied by the wagon's changing its course and moving on to other villages?
7. Examine the ways in which the smell, the swamp, and the sun become like living characters.

❀ Research and Comparison

Interdisciplinary Discussion Question: Explore the issue of nuclear energy, research, and weaponery in the developing countries and their political ramifications. Comment on the role of the developed countries in the control and proliferation of nuclear weapons.

Shashi Deshpande
(b. 1938)
India

Shashi Deshpande was born in Dharwar, India, in the state of Maharashtra, and she studied law, receiving a degree from Government Law College, Bangalore. She later returned to school, obtaining a diploma and a master's degree in journalism. Although her father was a writer, and, as she has said, as a child she had "an obsession with books," it was the "stifling life of a housewife" that drove her to writing when she was 30. While her first language was Marathi, she has used English for writing fiction, publishing five novels and four collections of short stories. Her concern has been for the way contemporary society has impinged on women's lives, since the modern world, with all its complexities and tensions, has imposed new pressures on women. Considering herself a feminist, she sees the struggle for women as a part of "the larger human struggle for freedom." She also turned to classical literature for inspiration and as a resonating source of imagery. In "My Beloved Charioteer" she drew from the *Bhagavad Gita,* alluding to the god Krishna who served as charioteer to the warrior hero Arjuna; when Arjuna, in despair, did not want to enter the battle at Kurukshetra, Krishna encouraged him to participate in the righteous war and fulfill his duty to destroy the enemy.

My Beloved Charioteer

I smile as I hear them at last, the sounds I am waiting for. A rush of footsteps, the slam of the bathroom door . . . I wince as the sound whams through the silent house . . . and, a minute later, another bang. And then, bare feet running toward me.

"You shouldn't bang the doors that way," I say reproachfully. "You might wake Mummy."

She sits opposite me, cross-legged on the low wooden stool, hair tousled, cheeks flushed. "Oh, she won't wake up for hours yet," she says cheerfully. "Have you had your tea, *ajji?*"[1] Our daily routine. I can never confess to her that I have had a cup an hour earlier. This is her joy, that I wait for her.

"No, I've been waiting for you. Have you brushed your teeth?"

She makes a face. "I'll do it later," she says, trying to be brusque and casual.

"You'll do no such thing. Go and brush them at once."

"Only today, *ajji.* From tomorrow, I promise, I'll brush them first," she cajoles.

"Nothing doing." I try hard to be firm. But I can't fool her. She knows I am on her side. She lowers her voice to a conspiratorial whisper. "Mummy won't know. She's sleeping."

Now, of course, she leaves me no choice. I have to be firm. She goes reluctantly. And is back so fast, I have to ask, "Did you really brush? Properly? Show me."

"Look."

I have to grin back at the grinning, impish face. "Now tea for me."

"No," I say, "tea for me. Milk for you."

Ultimately, as always, we compromise and her tea is a pale brown. I switch off the Primus[2] and, without the hissing sound, our voices sound loud and clear. We look at each other guiltily, thinking of the sleeper, and try to speak in lowered tones. Happiness can mean so many things to so many people. For me, it is this. The beginning of a new day with this child. We talk of so many things. But too soon it is time for her to go to school. Bathed and fresh, she sets off.

When she is gone, silence settles on the house. A silence that will not lift till she returns. I had got used to this silence in the last seven years. It had

---

[1]Grandmother. [eds.]
[2]Kerosene stove. [eds.]

never seemed terrible to me. It was a friendly silence, filled with the ghosts of so many voices in my life. They came back to keep me company when I was alone . . . my younger brother, my aunt who loved me when I was a child, my two infant sons who never grew up, and even the child Aarti, who seems to have no connection with this thin, bitter woman who now shares the silence with me. But since she came, the friendly ghosts have all gone.

It is late before she wakes. I have had my bath, finished my *puja*,[3] and am half-way through cooking lunch, when I hear her stirring. I take down the *dal*[4] from the fire and put on the tea. By the time tea is ready, she comes into the kitchen. Wordlessly she takes a cup from me. She drinks it in hungry gulps as if she has been thirsting for hours, then thrusts the cup back at me. I pour out some more. I, too, say nothing. Earlier, I used to ask, "Slept well?" And one day, she had put down the cup with a trembling hand and said, "Slept well? No, I never do that. I haven't slept well since Madhav died. I'll never sleep well again all my life. I have to take something every night so that I can close my eyes for a few hours. Now, never ask me again if I slept well." Nine months I carried this daughter of mine in my body. I had felt within me every beat of her heart, every movement of her limbs. But . . . and this my doctor had told me then . . . my pains and shocks could never penetrate to her, she was so well protected. Even now, she is protected from my pains. Even now, I have no protection against her pains. I suffer with her, but like all my other emotions, it is a futile suffering. For I cannot help her. I can only fumble and blunder and make things worse.

"Why didn't you let me know earlier?" she had asked me angrily when she had come home after her father's death. "Why didn't you send for me earlier?"

"Don't tell Aarti yet," he had said, "I don't want to frighten her. Not now specially."

Habits of obedience die harder than any other. I had not dared to inform Aarti. And the next day he had had another attack and died instantly. Three months later Priti had been born. She never saw her grandfather.

"Who is that, *ajji?*" she had asked me once, seeing his photo.

"Your grandfather, Priti."

"My grandfather," she had pondered. "And what was he of yours?"

What was he of mine? The innocent question had released a flood of feelings within me. "My husband," I had said bluntly, at last.

As I settle down to cooking lunch, I wonder whether Aarti will today like what I am cooking. Whether she will enjoy her food and eat well. I know she will not, but the hope is always in me. Just as I hope that one day she will talk and laugh again. But that day, one day, when she had laughed, she had frightened me. She had burst into loud laughter, shattering the tenuous

---

[3]Ritual of Hindu worship. [eds.]
[4]Lentils. [eds.]

peace of the house. "What is it?" I had asked her, wondering whether to smile, to laugh, to respond in some way to her.

"Isn't it gloomy here? The right atmosphere for a pair of desolate widows. That's what we are, aren't we?"

Widows . . . I remember my mother who was one. She had had a shaven head, worn only coarse red saris, and been shorn of all ornaments all her life after my father's death. And I think of Aarti, who for days neglects herself. And then, one day dresses up, makes up her face and wears flowers in her hair. And yet Aarti it is whose face has the arid look of a desert.

Life has been cruel to her. It was her father whom she had loved; and he died, while I live. It was her husband whom she had loved even more than the child; and it was he who died, while Priti is left to her. Children are more sensitive than we think. They understand so many things we think they don't. Otherwise why would she have said one day to me, "*Ajji,* can I sleep in your room at night?"

I am old and gray and have lost all that I have loved in life but these two persons . . . but at her words, my heart had leapt in happiness. Yet, I had restrained my joy and asked her, "Why, Priti?"

"I'd like to. You can tell me stories at night. And there are so many things I suddenly remember at night and want to tell you. And. . . "

"But Mummy is with you."

The child's face had fallen. "But, *ajji,* if I try to talk to her, she says, 'Go to sleep, Priti, and don't bother me.' And she never sleeps at all, but just reads and smokes. And I don't like that smell."

The child has a high and clear voice and I had hushed her in a sudden fear that she might be overheard. Yes, she smokes incessantly now. Earlier, she had tried to hide it from me. But not for long. When I was a child, in my father's house, it had been considered wrong even for a man to smoke. But today, I would of my own accord let my daughter smoke if I thought it brought her happiness. But it doesn't. She puffs out smoke as if she is emitting bitterness. There is an infinity of bitterness in her now. And I cannot help her. I can only try to look after her body. Such a small thing, but even in that I fail. She is thin and brittle. Most of the time she never dresses up. Just goes round in an old gown, her hair tied up with a rubber band. Priti, looking at an old photograph one day, had wistfully said, "My Mummy was so pretty, wasn't she, *ajji?*"

The child's pride in her mother had roused in me a rage against Aarti. She seems to me like a child sulking because she does not have what she wants, wilfully ignoring the things she has. Has anyone promised us happiness for a lifetime, I want to ask her?

"Why don't you go out?" I had asked her once.

"Where?"

I had mumbled something she had not heard. She had gone on instead.

"There is nowhere I want to go. Everywhere, I see couples. I can't bear to see them. I could murder them when I see them talking and laughing."

This talk amazes me. I cannot understand her. My niece had once told me of something she had read in an American magazine. About children of eleven, twelve, thirteen and fourteen who stab and throttle and rape and gouge out eyes . . . often for no reason at all. And I had wondered . . . what kind of parents can they be who give birth to such monsters? Now, I know better. The accident of birth can be cruelly deceiving. We fool ourselves that our children are our own, that we know them. But often, they are as alien to us as baby cuckoos born in a crow's nest. And yet we cannot escape the burden of parentage. If my daughter is so empty that she can hate people who are happy, the fault is, to some extent, mine.

These bitter thoughts do not often occupy me. I have my work. The quiet routine of my day is like balm to my soul. Daily chores are not monotonous but soothing. Now that the child is with me, the day is full of meaning. I wait, as eager as a child myself, for her to return from school. When she has a holiday, I don't know who is happier, she or I. If there is an unexpected holiday, we are equally full of glee. But when she, *my* daughter and *her* mother, comes to us, we feel guilty and hide our happiness.

"Do you remember your Papa?" Aarti had asked her one day with a sudden harshness.

"Papa?" There had been a moment's hesitation. "Of course, I remember."

"I can't imagine you do. You never speak of him."

The child had stared at her with a frightened face, feeling guilty for she knew not what; and when Aarti had left us, she had burst into sobs, clinging to me. And I had been full of pity, not for her, but for Aarti, who could turn happiness into a wrong. But I can say nothing to her. She has never shared anything with me and now she hides her sorrow like a dog its bone. She guards it jealously and will not let me approach. And I have kept my distance. It was only in my imagination that I cuddled her as a child, only in my imagination that I shared her happiness and confidences as a young girl. And now I assuage her grief in the same way. "Look," I tell myself I will say to her, pouring some water into my cupped palms. "Look," I will say as the water seeps through, leaving nothing. "You cannot hold on. You will have to let it go."

But I know I'm fooling myself. I have no courage to speak. I am only a foolish, middle-aged woman who has never known how to win anyone's love. Priti's affection . . . that is a gift of Heaven, that ray of sunshine God sends even to the darkest corners. For Aarti, it was always her father. Even now, she spends the whole afternoon prowling in what was his room. It is seven years since he died, but the room is unchanged. I have kept everything as it was. I dust and sweep it meticulously myself. But strangely, in spite of this, it has a neglected look like Priti has sometimes. Priti is well-fed and well-dressed; she has her tonics and vitamins and all the other things they give children these days. Still, a neglected child peeps out of her eyes at times, filling me with pity and guilt.

Now I can hear Aarti moving round in his room. Even after his death, he can give her something I can't. The thought hurts. Hurts? It's like having salt rubbed into a raw wound. Suddenly it is unbearable and I go and open the door of his room. She is sitting on his chair, her feet on his table, smoking and staring at nothing. As she hears me, she turns round startled . . . I have never disturbed her till now . . . and with the movement of her feet she knocks down his photograph which stands on the table. Now it lies on the floor, face down. She rushes to pick it up. The glass has cracked. Long splinters of glass lie on the floor and the photograph looks somehow naked. She looks up at me, something showing through the deliberate blankness. "I'm sorry, mother. I'm sorry." I stare down at the photograph and say nothing. "I'm sorry," she repeats. "Don't look like that." She passes her hand over the photograph. "I'll get it fixed tomorrow. I promise I'll do it."

"No, don't!" My words are harsh and abrupt and she looks at me in surprise. "I don't care if it's broken. I don't want to see it here. I never want to see it again."

She looks up at me, stunned, frightened. "What's wrong with you? What's happened to you?"

"Nothing. I'm all right. But I don't want it. Let it go."

"What are you saying? What is it?"

"Let it go, let it go," I repeat. We are speaking in sibilant, strangled whispers. Can he hear us? Can he hear me?

"I don't understand you. Let what go? He is my father." She is still crouching there on the floor, holding the photograph in her two hands.

"Yes, your father. But what was he to me? The day he died, I let him go. Like that." Now I make the gesture I had imagined . . . cupping my palms together and then separating them. She stares at my hands with fascinated eyes. "And there was nothing left. Nothing."

"But I . . . I am his daughter. And yours. Am I nothing? Am I?" She is panting, her eyes hot and angry.

"What are you then?" I ask her. "You are just smoke and a bit of ash . . . like those cigarettes you smoke. Like my married life." Pain lays its talons on her face. Her eyes are anguished. But I force myself to go on. What have I to lose? Nothing. Only the child's love. And this cannot destroy that. On the contrary, I have a feeling that she is with me now, giving me strength for the battle, urging me on to it. My beloved charioteer. "He was your father . . . but what was he of mine? I lived with him for twenty-five years. I know he didn't like unstringed beans and stones in his rice. I know he liked his tea boiling hot and his bath water lukewarm. I know he didn't like tears. And so, when your baby brothers died, I wept alone and in secret. I combed my hair before he woke up because he didn't like to see women with loosened hair. And I went into the backyard even then, because he hated to find stray hairs anywhere. And once a year he bought me two saris; always colors that I hated. But he never asked me and I never told him. And at night . . .

She is still crouching there, her hair falling about her face.

She whimpers like a puppy. "Don't," she says. "Don't tell me. Don't," With each negative she bangs the photograph she still holds in her hands and the glass splinters again and again. Now, he is totally exposed to both of us. But there is no pity in me. It is not the dead who need your compassion . . . it is the living. Not the dead who crave for loyalty, but the living.

"I don't want to hear," she says.

How innocent she is in spite of her age, her education, her books, her marriage and child that knowledge can still hurt. It reminds me of the day she had grown up and I had tried to explain. And she had cried out in the same way, "Don't tell me. Don't!" This is another kind of growing up, when you see your parents as people.

"At night," I go on relentlessly, "I scarcely dared to breathe, I was so terrified of disturbing him. And once, when I asked whether I could sleep in another room . . . I don't know how I had the courage . . . he said nothing. But the next day, his mother, your grandmother, told me bluntly about a wife's duties. I must always be available. So, I slept there, afraid to get up for a glass of water, scared even to cough. When he wanted me, he said, 'Come here,' And I went. And when he finished, if I didn't get out of his bed fast enough, he said, 'You can go.' And I went." I know these things should not be said to her, his daughter and mine. But I am like a river in the monsoon. I have no control over myself.

"And one day when you were here . . . you and Madhav . . . I heard you both talking and laughing in your room. And I stood outside and wondered . . . what could you be talking about? I felt like I did when I was a child unable to read, looking at a book. Until then, I had hoped that one day he would say he was pleased with me. That day I knew it would never happen. I would always be outside the room. I would never know what goes on inside. And that day, I envied you, my own daughter. You hear me, Aarti? I envied you. And when he died, I felt like Priti does when school is over and the bell rings. You understand, Aarti? You understand?"

Why am I also crying? We look at each other. She looks at me as if she has never seen me before. Then, with a sudden movement, she springs up and glares at me. Whose is the victory? Whose? I have made her look at me. But what, my heart shrivels at the thought, if she does not like what she sees? And as she moves backward and starts running away from the room, from me, I realize what I have done. And then I hear the cry, "*Ajji,* I'm home. Where are you?"

"Here," I call back loudly. "I'm here."

❊ Discussion and Writing

1. Explain the narrator's association with Priti: what does each gain from the other; how does the narrator influence Priti's relationship with her mother, Aarti?

2. Compare the relationships of the two widowed mothers and their daughters. What is suggested in the last dialogue between Priti and her grandmother?
3. Examine the variations on the daughter–father motif: what is the significance of the two daughters' divergent attitudes toward their respective fathers?
4. What triggers the narrator to reveal the truth about her life with her husband. Analyze the implications of her predicament.
5. Explore the imagery of the charioteer derived from the *Bhagavad Gita:* who is the charioteer in the story? Comment on the symbolism of the imagery and its inherent irony.

❋ Research and Comparison

Interdisciplinary Discussion Question: Examine traditional restrictions on a widow, the questions of: private and public behavior, appearance, dress, remarriage. In what ways have these restrictions changed in modern times? What aspects of the tradition still linger? What is the impact of modernity on women? (Also see the Research and Comparison questions for Mahasweta Devi's story.)

Mudrooroo Nyoongah
(Colin Johnson, b. 1938)
Australia

Mudrooroo Nyoongah (the name recently taken by Colin Johnson) was born in Narrogin, Western Australia, and is of Bibbulmun descent. He spent part of his childhood in a Catholic orphanage, where he was also educated. He worked in public service in Victoria, although for a time he was without the employment and assistance that had been promised him. He turned to writing, seeking to shed light on the injustice and humiliation Aboriginal peoples have experienced. Although his writing was praised, he left Australia and turned to Buddhism. He traveled to India, where he lived for seven years as a Buddhist monk, then through Southeast Asia, Britain, and the United States before returning to Australia. In his subsequent work, he has continued to pursue the history of Aboriginal contact with European settlers.

Poem Two

They shall hate me at the waterfall;
They shall crucify me on the hill;
They shall mock me with a crown of thorns;
They shall fake my passion in their play.

They shall take my body, turn it into bread;
They shall take my blood, say that it is wine;
They shall take my heart, enthrone it;
They shall plaster it with gore;
They shall take all that I stood for,
Throw it on the floor.

They shall take my words and honour them;
They shall take my words to testify;
They shall love me in the morning,
Regret me by the afternoon.

They shall take my bones, display them;
They shall sell them at the pool,
Where I raised Lazarus, exchanging life for death.

Where I raised Lazarus, exchanging life for death;
Where I raised Lazarus, exchanging life for death;
Where they crucify me, exchanging death for life;
Where they crucify me, exchanging death for life.

❋ Discussion and Writing

1. Distinguish between the people referred to as "they" in the first stanza and those in the rest of the poem.
2. Examine the irony inherent in the images of life and death.
3. Discuss the use of biblical images to underline the discrepancy between the ideology and its practice.

❋ Research and Comparison

Interdisciplinary Discussion Question: Examine the role of religion in the colonization process in Australia. Compare it to the history of colonization anywhere else. Are there any distinguishing traits in the Australian experience?

Catherine Lim
(b. 1942)
Singapore/Malaysia

Catherine Lim was born in a small town in Malaya, did her advanced studies in Singapore, and became a schoolteacher. She worked at the Curriculum Development Institute of Singapore, developing material in English for primary school children, and lectured in linguistics before devoting herself to her writing. Her first volume of stories, *Little Ironies; Stories of Singapore* (1978), established hers as an important voice. Her stories are wrought with irony and an eye for the telling detail as she illuminates life in Singapore. In her focus on daily experiences and situations, she evokes their inherent pathos. She has also satirized the mores and institutions of Singapore.

Ah Bah's Money

Ah Bah's money, in 2 one-dollar notes and an assortment of coins, lay in a pile on the old handkerchief, but Ah Bah was reluctant to pull up the corners into a bundle to put inside the cigarette tin. Ah Bah was reluctant because the sight of his money gave him so much pleasure. He had already done the following things with his money: spread out the notes and ranged the coins in a row beside them, stacked up the coins according to their denominations, stacked up the coins to make each stack come to a dollar. But still he wanted to go on touching his money. He could tell exactly which coin came from whom or where. The twenty-cent coin with the greenish stain on the edge was given to him by Ah Lam Soh, who was opening her purse when the coin dropped out and he picked it up for her.

"You may keep it," she said, and thereafter Ah Bah watched closely every time Ah Lam Soh opened her purse or put her hand into her blouse pocket. The ten-cent coin, which had a better shine than all the rest, he had actually found near a rubbish dump, almost hidden from sight by an old slipper. And the largest coin of all, the fifty-cent coin, he had earned. He was still rather puzzled about why Kim Heok Soh had given him so much money; he had been required merely to stand in the front portion of the house and to say to any visitor, "Kim Heok Soh has gone to the dry goods shop and will not be back till an hour later. She has asked me to take care of her house for her." But all the time Kim Heok Soh was in the house; he knew because he could hear her in the room and there was somebody with her.

He counted his money—five dollars and eighty-five cents, and his heart glowed. Very carefully, he pulled up the corners of the handkerchief at last into a tight bundle which he then put inside the cigarette tin. Then he put the cover on firmly, and his money, now safe and secure, was ready to go back into its hiding place in a corner of the cupboard behind the stacks of old clothes, newspapers and calendars.

And now Ah Bah became uneasy, and he watched to see if his father's eyes would rest on the old broken-down cupboard that held his treasure, for once his father had found his money—two dollars in twenty- and ten-cent coins—tied up in a piece of rag and hidden under his pillow, and had taken it away for another bottle of beer. His father drank beer almost every night. Sometimes he was in a good mood after his beer and he would talk endlessly about this or that, smiling to himself. But generally he became sullen and bad-tempered, and he would begin shouting at anyone who came near. Once he threw an empty beer bottle at Ah Bah's mother; it missed her head and went crashing against the wall. Ah Bah was terrified of his father, but his mother appeared indifferent. "The lunatic," she would say, but never in his hearing. Whenever he was not at home, she would slip out and play cards in Ah Lam Soh's house. One evening she returned, flushed with excitement and gave him fifty cents; she said it had been her lucky day. At other times she came back with a dispirited look, and Ah Bah knew she had lost all her money in Ah Lam Soh's house.

The New Year was coming and Ah Bah looked forward to it with an intensity that he could barely conceal. New Year meant *ang pows;*[1] Ah Bah's thin little fingers closed round the red packets of money given him by the New Year visitors with such energy that his mother would scold him and shake her head in doleful apology, as she remarked loudly to the visitors, "My Ah Bah, he feels no shame whatever!"

His forefinger and thumb feeling expertly through the red paper, Ah Bah could tell immediately how much was in the red packet; his heart would sink a little if the fingers felt the hard edges of coins, for that would be forty cents or eighty cents at most. But if nothing was felt, then joy of joys! Here was at least a dollar inside.

This year Ah Bah had *eight* dollar notes. He could hardly believe it when he took stock of 'his wealth on the last day of the festive season. Eight new notes, crisp, still smelling new, and showing no creases except where they had been folded to go into the red packets. Eight dollars! And a small pile of coins besides. Ah Bah experienced a thrill such as he had never felt before.

And then it was all anxiety and fear, for he realized that his father knew about his *ang pow* money; indeed his father had referred to it once or twice, and would, Ah Bah was certain, be searching the bedding, cupboard and other places in the house for it.

----

[1]Little red pockets for money given to children at the New Year.

Ah Bah's heart beat with the violence of angry defiance at the thought. The total amount in his cigarette tin was now seventeen dollars and twenty-five cents, and Ah Bah was determined to protect his money at all costs. Nobody was going to take his money from him. Frantically, Ah Bah went to the cupboard, took out the bundle of money from the cigarette tin and stuffed it into his trouser pocket. It made a conspicuous bulge. Ah Bah didn't know what to do, and his little mind worked feverishly to find a way out of this very direful situation.

He was wandering about in the village the next day as usual, and when he returned home, he was crying bitterly. His pocket was empty. When his mother came to him and asked him what the matter was, he bawled. He told her, between sobs, that a rough-looking Indian had pushed him to the ground and taken away his money. His father who was in the bedroom rushed out, and made Ah Bah tell again what had happened. When Ah Bah had finished, sniffling miserably, his father hit him on the head, snarling, "You idiot! Why were you so anxious to show off your *ang pow* money? Now you've lost it all!" And when he was told that the sum was seventeen dollars and twenty-five cents, his vexation was extreme, so that he would not be contented till he had hit the boy again.

Ah Bah's mother cleaned the bruise on the side of his face where he had been pushed to the ground, and led him away from his father.

"You are a silly boy," she scolded. "Why did you carry so much money around with you? Someone was sure to rob you!" And feeling sorry for him, she felt about in her blouse pocket and found she could spare fifty cents, so she gave it to him, saying, "Next time, don't be so silly, son."

He took the coin from her, and he was deeply moved. And then, upon impulse, he took her by the hand, and led her outside their house to the old hen-house, near the well, under the trees, and he whispered to her, his heart almost bursting with the excitement of a portentous secret successfully kept, "It's there! In the cigarette tin, behind that piece of wood!" To prove it, he squeezed into the hen house and soon emerged, reeking of hen house odors, triumphantly clutching the tin. He took off the lid and showed her the money inside.

She was all amazement. Then she began to laugh and to shake her head over the ingenuity of it all, while he stood looking up at her, his eyes bright and bold with victory.

"You're a clever boy," she said, "but take care that you don't go near the hen house often. Your father's pocket is empty again, and he's looking around to see whose money he can get hold of, that devil."

Ah Bah earned twenty cents helping Ah Lau Sim to scrape coconut, and his mother allowed him to have the ten cents which he found on a shelf, under a comb. Clutching his money, he stole out of the house; he was just in time to back out of the hen house, straighten himself and pretend to be looking for dried twigs for firewood, for his father stood at the doorway, looking at him. His father was in a restless mood again, pacing the floor with a dark look on his face, and this was the sign that he wanted his beer very badly but had no money to pay for it. Ah Bah bent low, assiduously looking for firewood, and then through the corner of his eye, he saw his father go back into the house.

That night Ah Bah dreamt that his father had found out the hiding place in the hen house, and early next morning, his heart beating wildly, he stole out and went straight to the hen house. He felt about in the darkness for his cigarette tin; his hand touched the damp of the hen droppings and caught on a nail, and still he searched—but the cigarette tin was not there.

He ran sniffling to his mother, and she began to scold him, "I told you not to go there too often, but you wouldn't listen to me. Didn't you know your father has been asking for money? The devil's found you out again!"

The boy continued to sniff, his little heart aching with the terrible pain of the loss.

"Never mind," his mother said, "you be a good boy and don't say anything about it; otherwise your father's sure to rage like a mad man." She led him inside the house and gave him a slice of bread with some sugar.

She was glad when he quietened down at last, for she didn't want to keep Ah Lam Soh and the others waiting. The seventeen dollars and twenty-five cents (she had hurriedly hidden the handkerchief and the cigarette tin) was secure in her blouse pocket, and she slipped away with eager steps for, as the fortune teller had told her, this was the beginning of a period of good luck for her.

❈ Discussion and Writing

1. What is the purpose of the stories about Ah Bah's acquisition of each coin or bill and the protection of his treasure?
2. What has generated Ah Bah's distrust of his father? Analyze the impact of his trick on his father, his mother, and the reader.
3. Comment on Ah Bah's perception of his mother. Why does he confide in her?
4. Whose point of view is used to narrate the story? Discuss the impact of the ironic ending.

Witi Ihimaera
(b. 1944)
New Zealand

Witi Ihimaera was born in Gisborne, New Zealand, and is of Maori descent, of Te Whanau a Kai lineage. This is a smaller affiliation within a larger group, and since Witi Ihimaera has alliances with his mother's people as well, his tribal connections ripple out in ever-widening circles. He studied at Victoria University and has served as a diplomat with the Department of Foreign Affairs, besides working as a journalist and writer of fiction. His fiction explores issues of race and class, and is written from within the oral tradition, capturing the rhythm of Maori English. At the same time, he incorporates a range of outside material, as in the "Yellow Brick Road," where he alludes to the North American children's classic *The Wizard of Oz*. His use of these allusions underlines the ironies inherent in his work.

Yellow Brick Road

Follow the yellow brick road,
Follow, follow, follow, follow,
Follow the yellow brick road. . . .

We're almost there! Almost at Wellington, the Emerald City! Me and Dad and Mum and Roha, we been travelling for two days now in our car which Dad bought from Mr. Wallace last week. No dents and honk honk goes the horn. Dad, he said I could have a drive of it myself when we left Waituhi but then it conked out on the Whareratas and that made him change his mind.

    —I told you we wouldn't get to Wellington in *this*, Mum said to him while he was fixing it up.

    —We'll get there.

    —But I want to get there in one piece! Mum answered.

    —Throw some of your junk out then, Dad told her.

    Our car sure is loaded down all right. Mum's stuff is in the boot [trunk], some belongings are tied under the canvas on the roof and there's even some squeezed in here with us. Boy.

    But you won't conk out now, ay car? There's just one hill to go and we'll be there. So up we go, up the hill, slowly but surely. And who cares if cars bank up behind us! They can beep all they like. We got as much right to be on this road as they got.

    Road, road, yellow brick road, yellow with the headlights sweeping across it. Just like in that book[1] Miss Wright, my teacher, gave me before we

---

[1]*The Wizard of Oz.*

left Waituhi. A neat book. About the straw man, the tin man, the cowardly lion and the Emerald City and . . . we're almost there!

I bounce up and down on the seat. I can't wait to see all the sparkling green towers glittering in the dark ahead of us.

—Matiu, you just sit still! Mum growls. What's gotten into you, ay?

—Sorry, Mum.

Poor Mum. She's very tired and still unhappy about leaving Waituhi, our whanau,[2] our family. Her eyes are still red with the crying when all the people had waved goodbye to us like little flags fluttering far away. At least she hasn't cried as often as Roha has for Hone though! Roha and Hone, they went round together and once I saw them having a pash. Eeee!

I grin at my big sister. Never mind, Roha. Plenty other boys down in Wellington and you can pash up large with them when we get there, ay.

—What you grinning for, Smarty? Roha snaps.

—I'm allowed to grin if I want to, aren't I? I ask, suddenly hurt.

—All right, all right, you don't have to scream.

I make a funny face at her. It would teach her a good lesson if even the pakehas[3] didn't want to pash with her! Lots of pakehas in Wellington. Not like in Waituhi. Makes me scared to think about it.

I turn to Dad.

—Dad, will the pakehas like us in Wellington? Dad?

He doesn't answer me because he is driving carefully. He has to lean forward to see the road in front of him. It has started to rain.

Wish I was older and knew how to drive better. Then I could give him a rest at the wheel.

I press against him and he puts an arm round me. His face looks tired, just like it looked when we were walking to a garage yesterday after our car ran out of petrol. There we were, miles from anywhere, walking along the road while car after car sped past us without stopping. Some of them blared loudly at us. Others made a lot of dust come over us. And always as they passed the faces would be looking back and staring at us. I felt puzzled.

—Why don't they stop, Dad?

He had shrugged his shoulders.

—We're in a different country now, son.

I began to hate those faces. I wanted to throw stones at them all.

But things will be different when we get to Wellington, won't they? And we will be happy, won't we?

Course we will. You just wait and see, Dad. We'll make lots of money and be rich as anything because Wellington is where the money is. And you have to go where the money is, ay Dad. No use staying in Waituhi and being poor all the time, ay.

---

[2]Family.
[3]New Zealander of European descent. [eds.]

I lean back in the seat and burrow under the blanket. It is getting cold and there is a draught coming through a hole in our car. I feel my bag of lollies[4] in my pocket.

—You want one, Mum? You want one, Dad? Roha?

I pass the bag to Roha and she takes two, the greedy thing. I put one in my mouth and count what's left. Seven.

Boy, these are the dearest lollies I ever bought. When we stopped at that shop yesterday I gave the man thirty cents and he didn't give me any change. When I asked him for it, he told me thirty cents was how much these lollies cost. But he was lying. He was a thief and he stole my money. How would he like it if someone rooked[5] him? What's more, these lollies are stink, just like him.

I watch the road as it twists ahead through the dark. Every now and then, there is a loud whoosh of a fast car passing us. Those fast cars don't like us. We're too slow for them.

Suddenly, I see two lights ahead like eyes glaring at us. The eyes open wider, grow larger, looking like the eyes of a . . .

—Dad! I yell, afraid.

A big truck descends on us with its headlights blazing full. I seem to see taloned fingers reaching out to claw me.

—Bloody hell, Dad mutters.

He swerves. The car kicks gravel. The truck thunders past, screaming in the wind.

I look at Mum. Her face is shaken.

—I better keep both my hands on the wheel, Dad says.

He lifts his arm from me and I feel suddenly alone. I begin to think of Waituhi, our whanau, and that makes me sad. All our family was there and Emere was our cow. *Haere ra,*[6] *Emere. And haere ra to you, e Hemi.* You'll always be my best mate.

I start humming to myself. Quietly.

Follow the yellow brick road,
Follow, follow, follow, follow . . .

Miss Wright, she taught us that song at school. A neat song. We made a long line, joined by our hands, and danced crazy patterns over the playground and . . .

There is a snapping sound and the flapping of canvas.

—What's that, Dad?

He pulls the car over to the side of the road and steps out. Mum winds down her window.

—What's wrong?

---

[4]A sweetmeat or candy. [eds.]
[5]Cheated; are stink; disgusting. [eds.]
[6]Goodbye. [eds.]

—Rope's snapped, he yells back.

—You better get out and help your father, Mum says to me.

I jump out into the rain. Boy, it's sure wet and cold out here. Dad is struggling in the wind to pull the canvas back over our belongings.

—All this junk! Dad mutters. No wonder the canvas came away.

He takes a box from the top and dumps it on the side of the road. My books spill out and the pages fly away like birds in the wind.

—Dad. No, Dad . . .

I run out into the road in panic because they are my school books and among them is my best book. My best book.

—Matiu! Get off the road! Mum screams.

My best book. In the wind and the rain. My best book.

—*Matiu.*

And there it is. Lying there on the road. I run to get it and car brakes scream in my ears.

But I have it in my arms and hold it safe to me. And I don't care if I get a hiding. I don't care. . . .

Mum hits me very hard.

—What you want to do that for, you stupid kid.

But I don't care. I don't care. . . .

And the driver of the other car is saying angry words to Dad:

—What the bloody hell do you think you're up to, eh? Letting you kid run out like that, what's wrong with you! Look, never mind about bloody arguing. Christ, you shouldn't be on the road at all. Your car's bloody dangerous loaded like that. And why the hell didn't you pull further off the road, eh? Oh, what's the use. You Maoris are all the same. Dumb bloody *horis.*[7]

He steps back into his car and roars off. Dad comes towards me and his face is full of anger.

Go ahead, Dad. Hit me. I deserve it.

But he doesn't. Instead, he hugs me and asks:

—You all right, son?

—Yes, Dad. I'm sorry, Dad. That man. . . .

—That bastard. Never mind about him.

I clutch my book tightly. I carry it into the car with me. Mum starts to get angry with me again.

—*Turi turi,*[8] woman, Dad says. It's all over now. Let's forget it.

—It wouldn't have happened if you'd tied down our things properly like Sam told you to do, Mum answers.

Sam is my uncle and we stayed at his place in Hastings last night. Uncle Sam didn't even know we were on our way to Wellington!

---

[7]Contempuous term for Maoris.
[8]Keep quiet.

—Down to that windy place? he'd said. You fullas better tie yourselves down or you'll be blown away! Don't you know how cold it is down there? Brother, it's liquid sunshine all the year round!

—We don't care, I'd answered him. We're going to make lots of money down there. Not much room left for pa living anymore. That's what you said, ay Dad.

Dad had looked at me strangely.

—No more jobs back home, he told Uncle. Plenty of the seasonal work, yes, but me and Hine had enough of that. We had enough of shearing, the fruit-picking and the going down South to shear some more. No, plenty of work in Wellington. Plenty of factories.

—Who told you that! Uncle snorted.

—Jim, Dad answered.

Uncle Jim is Dad's brother. He lives in Petone and we're going to stay with him until we find our own house.

Uncle Sam had shrugged his shoulders.

—Well, Jim should know, he'd said.

—I want us to have a good life, a new start, Dad tried to explain. A new start for my kids. Me and Hine, we've always had nothing. But my kids? They're going to grow up with everything. I'll fight for it, because they must have it.

But I'd seen Uncle Sam hadn't understood Dad's words. He'd simply shaken his head and wished us luck. And in the morning before we left he'd told Dad to tie the canvas down tight.

—Otherwise that wind will get under it and before you know it you'll be flying into Wellington!

Dad had tried his best with the ropes. He'd said to Mum:

—How about getting rid of some of this junk, ay?

She'd answered him:

—This junk is all we've ever had. I'm not throwing away one piece of it, wind or no wind.

It sure is windy all right, outside the car. The clouds are rushing in the night sky just like the Winged Monkeys. The wind moans and chatters and cackles among our belongings, and I must close my eyes and put my hands to my ears to shut out the sights and sounds of this night.

Then, suddenly, all the noises stop. Even the car has stopped.

—There it is, Dad says.

I open my eyes. Far away are the lights of Wellington, streaming with the rain down our window like glistening towers. And it looks so . . . so . . . beautiful. Just as I'd imagined it to be. Just as I'd pretended it would be. Emerald City.

—Isn't it neat, Mum?

She stares ahead. Her face is still.

—Roha? I ask.

My sister's face is filled with a strange glow.

—Dad?

He looks at me and smiles.

—You and your dreams, son.

He starts the car. We begin to drive down from the hill. I look at Dad and Mum and Roha, puzzled. How come I'm the only one to be happy! Can't they see this is where our life begins and this is where our dreams begin?

And dreams, they come true, don't they? Don't they?

I look out the car. I see a sign: STEEP GRADE. All along the yellow brick road there have been signs like that. STEEP GRADE. CHANGE DOWN. ONE WAY. LIMITED SPEED ZONE. ROAD NARROWS. STOP. WINDING ROAD. GO. CONCEALED EXIT. TRAFFIC LIGHTS AHEAD. GREASY WHEN WET. NO EXIT. NO PASSING. NO STOPPING.

Many signs, all telling us where we have to go and. . . .

I begin to feel scared.

If ever we want to, will we be able to find our way back?

I begin to sing to myself. Not because I'm happy, but because I think I want to feel sure myself everything will turn out all right.

It will, won't it?

Follow the yellow brick road,
Follow, follow, follow, follow,
Follow . . .

❊ Discussion and Writing

1. Explain the concerns of each member of the family on leaving Waituhi.
2. Comment on the young narrator's impressions of the outside world as he moves out of his Maori village.
3. Discuss the significance of the incident when the rope snaps: examine the relevance of what each one tries to protect; comment on the support of the extended family; define the attitude of the people on the road.
4. Interpret the implications of the road signs in the context of the narrative. What is suggested by the narrator's wondering if they will ever find their way back?
5. Discuss the symbolism of the images: the journey, the Emerald City, the Yellow Brick Road.

❊ Research and Comparison

Interdisciplinary Discussion Question: Research the history of the displacement of the Maori and examine the stories and poems they have written reflecting their predicament.

M. A. Nuhman
(b. 1944)
Sri Lanka

M. A. Nuhman was born in Sri Lanka. He teaches in the Department of Tamil and Linguistics at the University of Peradeniya and edits the Tamil journal *Poet*. He, along with other young, politically concerned Tamil poets, has revitalized the art of public poetry readings, especially those devoted to poems centered on social and political issues. His poetry focuses on oppression, the working class, interethnic violence, religion, and the historic role of Arab learning throughout Europe and Asia. The tone of his poems, therefore, frequently burns with an indignant irony.

Murder*

Last night
I had a dream
Lord Buddha was shot dead
by the police—
guardians of the law.
His body lay drenched in blood
on the step
of the Jaffna Library![1]

Under cover of darkness
came the ministers.
"His name—not in our lists!
Why did you kill him?"
they ask in anger.

"No, sirs, no!
There was no mistake.
Without bumping him off
it was impossible
to harm even a fly.
Therefore. . . ," they stammered.

"Okay, okay!
Hide the corpse."
The ministers vanish.

---

*Translated by S.Pathmanathan
[1]Jaffna Public Library was burned down in an incident of ethnic violence.

The men in civvies
dragged the corpse
into the library.
They heaped the books,
rare and valuable,
ninety thousand in all.
They lit the pyre
with the *Cikalokavada Sutta*.[2]
Thus the remains
Of the Compassionate One
were burned to ashes
along with the *Dhammapada*.[3]

❀ **Discussion and Writing**

1. What is the ironic implication of the murder of Lord Buddha? Explain the dialogue between the ministers (or senators) and their accomplices.
2. Comment on the symbolism involved in the way the accomplices carry out their orders.
3. What effect is created by presenting the event as a dream?

❀ **Research and Comparison**

Interdisciplinary Discussion Question: Research the ethnic conflicts in Sri Lanka, examining the history of the strife in conjunction with economic and political conditions.

Salman Rushdie
(b. 1947)
India

Salman Rushdie, who was born in Bombay, India, the year India gained independence, is the son of an affluent Muslim family. At 14, after his early schooling in Bombay, he was sent to England, first to Rugby and then to Cambridge, to complete his education. His family moved to Pakistan, and he remained in England. With the publication of *The Satanic Verses* (1988) and the Iranian Ayatollah Ruhollah Khomeini's edict calling for his execution, Rushdie has been driven into hiding, living in fear for his life.

---

[2]Titles of Buddhist texts.
[3]Collection of the teachings of the Buddha.

In his novels, Rushdie has charted the course of his search for himself, for his history. His work emanates from his belief that an individual and the nation's political and cultural history are mutually entrapped. Like Saleem Sinai, the protagonist in his novel *Midnight's Children* (1981), he has indeed been "handcuffed to history." Thus, in this semi-autobiographical novel, Rushdie recreates his Indian childhood; in *Shame* (1983), he captures his feelings about Pakistan. And in *Satanic Verses,* he evokes the Indian and Pakistani immigrant experience in Britain and the "growth of Islam as a historical phenomenon." In the process, he illuminates his spiritual search. He observes his own life in hiding in *Haroun and the Sea of Stories* (1990), protesting the suppression of artistic freedom. In this novel, he turned to the eleventh century collection of Sanskrit stories *Kathasaritsagar,* as a source of metaphoric and historic richness: *Kathasaritsagar* means "The Ocean of the Streams of Stories."

"An Iff and a Butt," a portion of which Rushdie published in *The New York Times,* is one of the fairytales in *Haroun.* The Water Genie from the Ocean of the Streams of Story is the supplier of Story Water, and comes to Rashid Khalifa's house to disconnect the Story-Tap connection, since Rashid has suddenly lost his voice and decides to cancel his subscription. The Genie inadvertently loses his Disconnector Tool (something like a monkey wrench) to Haroun, Rashid's son,[1] who is trying to help his father regain his Gift of the Gab. To retrieve the Tool, the Water Genie, Iff, agrees to take Haroun to the Ocean of the Streams of Stories.

An Iff and a Butt

"So pick a bird," the Water Genie commanded. "Any bird." This was puzzling. "The only bird around here is a wooden peacock," Haroun pointed out, reasonably enough. Iff gave a snort of disgust. "A person may choose what he cannot see," he said, as if explaining something very obvious to a very foolish individual. "A person may mention a bird's name even if the creature is not present and correct: crow, quail, hummingbird, bulbul, mynah, parrot, kite. A person may even select a flying creature of his own invention, for example winged horse, flying turtle, airborne whale, space serpent, aeromouse. To give a thing a name, a label, a handle; to rescue it from anonymity, to pluck it out of the Place of Namelessness, in short to identify it—well, that's a way of bringing the said thing into being. Or, in this case, the said bird or Imaginary Flying Organism.[2]"

---

[1]Haroun, Rashid, and Khalifa: names taken from the legendary Caliph of Baghdad, Haroun al-Rashid.
[2]IFO echoes UFO. [eds.]

"That may be true where you come from," Haroun argued. "But in these parts stricter rules apply."

"In these parts," rejoined blue-bearded Iff, "I am having my time wasted by a Disconnector Thief who will not trust in what he can't see. How much have you seen, eh, Thieflet? Africa, have you seen it? No? Then is it truly there? And submarines? Huh? Also hailstones, baseballs, pagodas? Goldmines? Kangaroos, Mount Fujiyama, the North Pole? And the past, did it happen? And the future, will it come? Believe in your own eyes and you'll get into a lot of trouble, hot water, a mess."

With that he plunged his hand into a pocket of his auberginey pajamas, and when he brought it forth again it was bunched into a fist. "So take a look, or I should say a *gander,* at the enclosed." He opened his hand; and Haroun's eyes almost fell out of his head.

Tiny birds were walking about on the Water Genie's palm; and pecking at it, and flapping their miniature wings to hover just above it. And as well as birds there were fabulous winged creatures out of legends: an Assyrian lion with the head of a bearded man and a pair of large hairy wings growing out of its flanks; and winged monkeys, flying saucers, tiny angels, levitating (and apparently air-breathing) fish. "What's your pleasure, select, choose," Iff urged. And although it seemed obvious to Haroun that these magical creatures were so small that they couldn't possibly have carried so much as a bitten-off fingernail, he decided not to argue and pointed at a tiny crested bird that was giving him a sidelong look through one highly intelligent eye.

"So it's the Hoopoe for us," the Water Genie said, sounding almost impressed. "Perhaps you know, Disconnector Thief, that in the old stories the Hoopoe is the bird that leads all other birds through many dangerous places to their ultimate goal. Well, well. Who knows, young Thieflet, who you may turn out to be. But no time for speculation now," he concluded, and with that rushed to the window and hurled the tiny Hoopoe out into the night.

"What did you do that for?" hissed Haroun, not wishing to wake his father; at which Iff gave his wicked grin. "A foolish notion," he said innocently. "A fancy, a passing whim. Certainly not because I know more about such matters than you, dear me, no."

Haroun ran to the window, and saw the Hoopoe floating on the Dull Lake,[3] grown large, as large as a double bed, easily large enough for a Water Genie and a boy to ride upon its back.

"And off we go," carolled Iff, much too loud for Haroun's liking; and then the Water Genie skipped up on to the window sill and thence to the Hoopoe's back—and Haroun, with scarcely a moment to reflect on the wisdom of what he was doing, and still wearing his long red nightshirt with the purple patches, and clutching the Disconnecting Tool firmly in his left hand, followed. As he settled down behind the Water Genie, the Hoopoe

---

[3]Echoes the Dal Lake in Kashmir.

turned its head to inspect him with a critical but (Haroun hoped) friendly eye.

Then they took off and flew rapidly into the sky.

The force of their acceleration pushed Haroun deep into the comfortable, thick and somehow *hairy* feathers on the Hoopoe's back, feathers that seemed to gather around Haroun to protect him during the flight. He took a few moments to digest the large number of amazing things that had taken place in quick time.

Soon they were travelling so quickly that the Earth below them and the sky above both dissolved into a blur, which gave Haroun the feeling that they weren't moving at all, but simply floating in that impossible, blurry space. "When the Mail Coach Driver, Butt, was rocketing up the Mountains of M, I had this same sense of floating," he recalled. "Come to think of it, this Hoopoe with its crest of feathers reminds me quite a bit of old Butt with his quiff of hair standing straight up on his head!—And if Butt's whiskers were somehow feathery, then this Hoopoe's feathers—as I noticed the moment we took off—have a distinctly hairy feel."

Their speed increased again, and Haroun shouted into Iff's ear: "No bird could fly so fast. Is this a machine?"

The Hoopoe fixed him with its glittering eye. "You maybe have some objection to machines?" it inquired, in a loud, booming voice that was identical in every respect to the Mail Coach Driver's. And at once it went on: "But but but you have entrusted your life to me. Then am I not worthy of a little of your respect? Machines also have their sense of self-esteem.—No need to gawp like that, young sir, I can't help it if I remind you of someone; at least, being a driver, he's a fellow who feels fond of a good, fast travel machine."

"You can read my mind," Haroun said, somewhat accusingly, because it wasn't entirely a pleasant feeling to have one's private ruminations bugged by a mechanical bird. "But but but certainly," answered the Hoopoe. "Also I am communicating with you *telepathically*, because as you may observe I am not moving my beak, which must maintain its present configuration for aerodynamic reasons."

"How are you doing that?" demanded Haroun, and back came the inevitable answer, quick as a flash of thought: "By a P2C2E. A Process Too Complicated To Explain."

"I give up," said Haroun. "Anyhow, do you have a name?"

"Whatever name you please," replied the bird. "Might I suggest, for obvious reasons, 'Butt'?"

So it was that Haroun Khalifa the storyteller's son soared into the night sky on the back of Butt the Hoopoe with Iff the Water Genie as his guide. The sun rose; and after a time Haroun spotted something in the distanzce, a heavenly body like a large asteroid. "That is Kahani, the Earth's second Moon," said Butt the Hoopoe without moving its beak.

"But but but," Haroun stammered (much to the Hoopoe's amusement), "surely the Earth has just the one Moon? How could a second satellite have remained undiscovered for so long?"

"But but but it is because of Speed," Butt the Hoopoe responded. "Speed, most Necessary of Qualities! In any Emergency—fire, auto, marine—what is required above all things? Of course, Speed: of fire truck, ambulance, rescue ship.—And what do we prize in a brainy fellow?—Is it not his Quickness of Thought?—And in any sport, Speed (of foot, hand, eye) is of the Essence!—And what humans cannot do quickly enough, they build machines to do faster.—Speed, super Speed! If not for the Speed of Light, the universe would be dark and cold.—But if Speed brings light to reveal, it can also be used to conceal. The Moon, Kahani, travels so fast—wonder of wonders!—that no Earth instruments can detect it; also its orbit varies by one degree per circuit, so that in three hundred and sixty orbits it has over-flown every spot upon the Earth. Variety of Behavior assists in Evasion of Detection. But also, there are serious purposes for the variation of orbit: Story Water facilities must be provided across the entire planet with an even hand. Voom! Varoom! Only at High Speed may this be done. You appreciate the further bonuses of Machines?"

"Then is the Moon, Kahani, driven by mechanical means?" Haroun asked, but Butt had turned its attention to practical matters. "Moon approaching," it said without moving its beak. "Relative speed synchro-nized. Landing procedures initiated. Splashdown in thirty seconds, twenty-nine, twenty-eight."

Rushing up toward them was a sparkling and seemingly infinite expanse of water. The surface of Kahani appeared—as far as Haroun's eye could see—to be entirely liquid. And what water it was! It shone with colors everywhere, colors in a brilliant riot, colors such as Haroun could never have imagined. And it was evidently a warm ocean; Haroun could see steam rising off it, steam that glowed in the sunlight. He caught his breath.

"The Ocean of the Streams of Story," said Iff the Water Genie, his blue whiskers bristling with pride. "Wasn't it worth travelling so far and fast to see?"

"Three," said Butt the Hoopoe without moving its beak. "Two, one, zero."

. . .

Water, water everywhere; nor any trace of land . . . "It's a trick," cried Haroun. "There's no Gup City[4] here, unless I'm much mistaken. And no Gup City equals no P2C2E House, no Walrus, no point in being here at all."

---

[4]Gup, gossip, fib.

"Hold your horses," said the Water Genie. "Cool down, don't blow your top, keep your hair on. Explanations are in order, and are forthcoming, if you will only permit."

"But this is the Middle of Nowhere," Haroun went on. "What do you expect me to do out here?"

"To be precise, this is the Deep North of Kahani,"[5] the Water Genie replied. "And what is available to us here is a short cut, avoidance of bureaucratic procedures, a means of cutting the red tape. Also, if I must truthfully admit, a means of solving our little difficulty without admitting to Guppee authorities my little mistake, my loss of Disconnecting Tool and subsequent blackmail by its Pincher. We are here in search of Wishwater."

"Look for patches of the Ocean that shine with extra brightness," Butt the Hoopoe added. "That's Wishwater; use it properly and it can make your desires come true."

"So persons in Gup need never be directly involved," Iff went on. "When your Wish is granted, you can return the Tool, and home you go to bed, and end of saga. Okay?"

"Oh, very well," Haroun agreed somewhat doubtfully, and, it should be said, with a little regret, because he had been looking forward to seeing Gup City and learning more about the mysterious Processes Too Complicated To Explain.

"Tip-top type," cried Iff in great relief. "Good sport, prince among men, popular choice.—And hey presto! Wishwater ahoy!"

Butt paddled carefully towards the patch of brightness at which Iff was eagerly pointing, and came to a halt by its edge. The Wishwater gave off so dazzling a light that Haroun had to avert his gaze.—Now Iff the Water Genie reached inside his little gold-embroidered waistcoat and pulled out a small bottle made of many-faceted crystal, with a little golden cap. Swiftly unscrewing the cap, he drew the bottle through the bright water (whose glow was golden, too); and, fastening the lid once more, he passed the bottle carefully to Haroun. "On your marks, be prepared, here goes," he said. "This is what you must do."

This was the secret of the Wishwater: the harder you wished, the better it worked. "So it's up to you," Iff said. "No fooling around, get down to it good and proper, do serious business, and the Wishwater will do serious business for you. And bingo! Your heart's desire will be as good as yours."

Haroun sat astride Butt the Hoopoe and stared at the bottle in his hand. Just one sip, and he could regain for his father the lost Gift of the Gab! "Down the hatch," he cried courageously; unscrewed the cap; and took a goodly gulp.

Now the golden glow was all around him, and inside him, too; and everything was very, very still, as if the entire cosmos were waiting upon his commands. He began to focus his thoughts . . .

---

[5]Kahani, story.

He couldn't do it. If he tried to concentrate on his father's lost story-telling powers and his cancelled Story Water subscription, then the image of his mother insisted on taking over, and he began to wish for her return instead, for everything to be as it had been before . . . and then his father's face returned, pleading with him, *just do this one thing for me, my boy, just this one little thing;* and then it was his mother again, and he didn't know what to think, what to wish—until with a jangling noise like the breaking of a thousand and one violin strings, the golden glow disappeared and he was back with Iff and the Hoopoe on the surface of the Sea of Stories.

"Eleven minutes," said the Water Genie contemptuously. "Just eleven minutes and his concentration goes, ka-bam, ka-blooey, ka-put."

Haroun was filled with the shame of it, and hung his head. "But but but this is disgraceful, Iff," said Butt the Hoopoe without moving its beak. "Wishes are not such easy things, as you know well. You, mister Water Genie, are upset because of your own error, because now we must go to Gup City after all, and there will be harsh words and hot water for you, and you are taking it out on the boy. Stop it! Stop it or I'll be annoyed."

(Truly this was a most passionate, even excitable sort of machine, Haroun thought in spite of his unhappiness. Machines were supposed to be ultra-rational, but this bird could be genuinely temperamental.)

Iff looked at the red blush of humiliation that was all over Haroun's face and softened somewhat. "Gup City it is," he agreed. "Unless, of course, you'd like to hand over the Disconnecting Tool and just call the whole thing off?"

Haroun shook his head, miserably.

"But but but you are still bullying the boy," Butt the Hoopoe expostulated furiously without moving its beak. "Change of plan, please, right away! Cheering-up procedures to be instituted at once. Give the lad a happy story to drink."

"Not another drink," said Haroun in a low, small voice. "What are you going to make me fail at now?"

· · ·

So Iff the Water Genie told Haroun about the Ocean of the Streams of Story, and even though he was full of a sense of hopelessness and failure the magic of the Ocean began to have an effect on Haroun. He looked into the water and saw that it was made up of a thousand thousand thousand and one different currents, each one a different color, weaving in and out of one another like a liquid tapestry of breathtaking complexity; and Iff explained that these were the Streams of Story, that each colored strand represented and contained a single tale. Different parts of the Ocean contained different sorts of stories, and as all the stories that had ever been told and many that were still in the process of being invented could be found here, the Ocean of the Streams of Story was in fact the biggest library in the universe. And because the stories were held here in fluid form, they retained the ability to change, to become new versions of themselves, to join up with other stories and so become yet other stories; so that unlike a library of books, the Ocean of the Streams of Story was much more than a storeroom of yarns. It was not dead but alive.

"And if you are very, very careful, or very, very highly skilled, you can dip a cup into the Ocean," Iff told Haroun, "like so," and here he produced a little golden cup from another of his waistcoat pockets, "and you can fill it with water from a single, pure Stream of Story, like so," as he did precisely that, "and then you can offer it to a young fellow who's feeling blue, so that the magic of the story can restore his spirits. Go on now; knock it back, have a swig, do yourself a favor," Iff concluded. "Guaranteed to make you feel A-number-one."

Haroun, without saying a word, took the golden cup and drank.

He found himself standing in a landscape that looked exactly like a giant chessboard. On every black square there was a monster: there were two-tongued snakes and lions with three rows of teeth, and four-headed dogs and five-headed demon kings and so on. He was, so to speak, looking out through the eyes of the young hero of the story. It was like being in the passenger seat of an automobile; all he had to do was watch, while the hero dispatched one monster after another and advanced up the chessboard toward the white stone tower at the end. At the top of the tower was (what else but) a single window, out of which there gazed (who else but) a captive princess. What Haroun was experiencing, though he didn't know it, was Princess Rescue Story Number S/1001/ZHT/420/41(r)xi; and because the princess in this particular story had recently had a haircut and therefore had no long tresses to let down (unlike the heroine of Princess Rescue Story G/1001/RIM/777/M(w)i, better known as "Rapunzel"), Haroun as the hero was required to climb up the outside of the tower by clinging to the cracks between the stones with his bare hands and feet.

He was halfway up the tower when he noticed one of his hands beginning to change, becoming hairy, losing its human shape. Then his arms burst out of his shirt, and they too had grown hairy, and impossibly long, and had joints in the wrong places. He looked down and saw the same thing happening to his legs. When new limbs began to push themselves out from his sides, he understood that he was somehow turning into a monster just like those he had been killing; and above him the princess caught at her throat and cried out in a faint voice:

"Eek, my dearest, you have into a large spider turned."

As a spider he was able to make rapid progress to the top of the tower; but when he reached the window the princess produced a large kitchen knife and began to hack and saw at his limbs, crying rhythmically, "*Get* away spider, *go* back home"; and he felt his grip on the stones of the tower grow looser; and then she managed to chop right through the arm nearest her, and he fell.

. . .

"Wake up, snap out of it, let's have you," he heard Iff anxiously calling. He opened his eyes to find himself lying full-length on the back of Butt the Hoopoe. Iff was sitting beside him, looking extremely worried and more than a little disappointed that Haroun had somehow managed to keep a firm grip on the Disconnecting Tool.

"What happened?" Iff asked. "You saved the princess and walked off into the sunset as specified, I presume? But then why all this moaning and groaning and turning and churning? Don't you *like* Princess Rescue Stories?"

Haroun recounted what had happened to him in the story, and both Iff and Butt became very serious indeed. "I can't believe it," Iff finally said. "It's a definite first, without parallel, never in all my born days."

"I'm almost glad to hear it," said Haroun. "Because I was thinking, that wasn't the *most* brilliant way to cheer me up."

"It's pollution," said the Water Genie gravely. "Don't you understand? Something, or somebody, has been putting filth into the Ocean. And obviously if filth gets into the stories, they go wrong.—Hoopoe, I've been away on my rounds too long. If there are traces of this pollution right up here in the Deep North, things at Gup City must be close to crisis. Quick, quick! Top speed ahead! This could mean war."

"War with whom?" Haroun wanted to know.

Iff and Butt shivered with something very like fear.

"With the Land of Chup,[6] on the Dark Side of Kahani," Butt the Hoopoe answered without moving its beak. "This looks like the doing of the leader of the Chupwalas,[7] the Cultmaster of Bezaban."

"And who's that?" Haroun persevered, beginning to wish he'd stayed in his peacock bed instead of getting muddled up with Water Genies and Disconnecting Tools and talking mechanical Hoopoes and story-oceans in the sky.

"His name," whispered the Water Genie, and the sky darkened for an instant as he spoke it, "is Khattam-Shud."[8]

Far away on the horizon, forked lightning glittered, once. Haroun felt his blood run cold.

❋ Discussion and Writing

1. What is the significance of the Water Genie's name, Iff? Elaborate on his argument about naming.
2. Analyze the character of Hoopoe: his other names, his powers, his role in the narrative.

---

[6]Chup, mouth shut.
[7]Quiet people.
[8]Khattam-Shud, completedly finished, done with.

3. Comment on the implications of P2C2E. What is the significance of Haroun's anticipation of that answer?
4. Describe the Ocean of the Streams of Stories and explain the implications of the multicolored strands.
5. What is implied by the Moon, Kahani (story): its composition; its function and attributes; its role as a metaphor.
6. What is the purpose of the rescue story regarding the princess: Haroun's responses; his transformation; his failure? Examine the issue of a theme and its variations.
7. Explain the war between Gup City and the Land of Chup. Discuss the relevance of the Khattam-Shud.
8. Analyze the correspondence between the fantasy and the actual world: the Moon, the Ocean, the technology, the pollution, and the war.
9. Discuss the relevance of the metaphor of "An Iff and a Butt" to Salman Rushdie's own life.

❀ **Research and Comparison**

1. Analyze *Haroun and the Sea of Stories* as an allegory of personal and political circumstances.
2. Examine Salman Rushdie's *Midnight's Children,* commenting on the novel as a panorama of the history of India.

Interdisciplinary Discussion Question: Research the issue of the religious and political censorship of Rushdie's *Satanic Verses.* Discuss the nature of Rushdie's conflict with Islamic fundamentalism and his freedom as a writer.

Sally Morgan
(b. 1951)
Australia

Sally Morgan was born in Perth, Western Australia. She acquired her B.A. from the University of Western Australia and did postgraduate work in counseling psychology and in library sciences. A highly regarded painter and writer, she has imbued her work with her pride in her Aboriginal heritage; she has also contributed greatly to the international recognition of the difficulties her people have endured. Along with the experiences of her childhood and her discovery of her Aboriginal ancestry, she recounts the stories of her beloved grandmother, mother, and uncle, Arthur Corunna, in her first book, *My Place* (1987). Their stories are in the oral tradition, and through them Sally Morgan acts as recorder and keeper of tales that are a sacred legacy. Throughout the book, she juxtaposes the dignity, love, and good humor of her family to the shameful treatment and conditions they describe in their histories; and the former emerge as victors.

Arthur Corunna's Story
(c. 1893–c. 1950)

My name is Arthur Corunna. I can't tell you how old I am exactly, because I don't know. A few years ago, I wrote to Alice Drake-Brockman, my father's second wife, and asked her if she knew my age. She said that I could have been born around 1893–1894. Later, her daughter Judy wrote to me and said I could have been born before that. So I guess I have to settle for around there somewhere. Anyway, I'm old, and proud of it.

The early years of my life were spent on Corunna Downs Station in the Pilbara, that's in the north of Western Australia. We called the top half of the station, where I lived, Mool-nya-moonya. The lower half, the outstation, we called Boog-gi-gee-moonya. The land of my people was all around there, from the Condin River to Nullagine, right through the Kimberleys.

After my people had worked for so long on the station, they were allowed to go walkabout.[1] We would go for weeks at a time, from one station to another, visiting people that belonged to us. We always went to Hillside, that was Dr Gillespie's station. The eastern part of Western Australia, that's different. We call that Pukara. Our land was Yabara, the north.

My mother's name was Annie Padewani and my father was Alfred Howden Drake-Brockman, the white station-owner. We called him Good-da-goonya. He lived on Corunna Downs nine years before marrying his first wife, Eleanor Boddington. She had been a governess in the area. While on the station, he shared my Aboriginal father's two wives, Annie and Ginnie.

Ginnie, or Binddiding as we called her, was a big built woman. She was older, argumentative. She bossed my mother around. I used to cry for my mother when she was in a fight. I'd run round and grab her skirts and try and protect her from Ginnie. Ginnie only had one child by Howden, and that was my half-brother, Albert.

My mother was small and pretty. She was very young when she had me. I was her first child. Then she had Lily by my Aboriginal father. Later, there was Daisy. She is my only sister who shares with me the same parents. I was a good deal older than her when they took me away to the mission, she was only a babe in arms, then. My mother was pregnant with other children, but she lost them.

My Aboriginal father was one of the headmen of our tribe. He was a leader. He got our people to work on the station and, in return, he was given

---

[1] A periodic migration among Aborigines into the bush. [eds.].

a rifle, tea, tobacco and sugar. He was a well-known man, tall and powerful. Many people were scared of him. Sometimes, he would go walkabout, right down to Fremantle, then up through Leonora, Ethel Creek and back to Corunna Downs. Men were frightened of him because he was a boolyah man.[2]

My uncle and grandfather were also boolyah men. For centuries, the men in my family have been boolyah men. I remember when my grandfather was dying, he called me to him. I was only a kid. He said, "You know I can't use my power to heal myself. I will pass my powers into you and then I want you to heal me." He did this, and I ran away and played, even though he was calling me. I was only a kid, I didn't understand. My grandfather died. It wasn't until years later that I began to learn just what powers he had given me.

One day, my uncle said to my mother, "Never worry about Jilly-yung." (That was my Aboriginal name.) "Never worry about him, I will look after him when I'm dead. I will always be close to him. He may not know I am there, I may be a bird in the tree or a lizard on the ground, but I will be close to him." That was my Uncle Gibbya. He was married to Annie's sister.

My Uncle Gibbya was a powerful rainmaker. He didn't always live on Corunna Downs. One day when he was visiting our people, Howden said to him, "You can work with me on the station as long as you can make it rain." My Uncle Gibbya said, "I will make it rain. Three o'clock this afternoon, it will rain." Howden looked at the sky, it was blue and cloudless. He shook his head. Later that day, white clouds began to gather, like a mob of sheep slowly coming in. At three o'clock, it rained. My Uncle got his job. He was the best rainmaker in the area.

On the station, I wasn't called Arthur. I had my Aboriginal name, Jilly-yung, which meant silly young kid. When I was a child, I copied everything everyone said. Repeated it like a ninety-nine parrot. The people would say, "Silly young kid! Jilly-yung!"

I loved my mother, she was my favorite. My mother was always good to me. When others were against me, she stood by me. She used to tell me a story about a big snake. A snake especially for me, with pretty eggs. "One day," she said, "you will be able to go and get these eggs." I belonged to the snake, and I was anxious to see the pretty snake's eggs, but they took me away to the mission, and that finished that. It was a great mystery. If I had've stayed there, I would have gone through the Law,[3] then I would've known. I didn't want to go through the Law. I was scared.

When we went on holidays, we called it going pink-eye, my Aboriginal father carried me on his shoulders when I was tired. I remember one time, it

---

[2]*Boolyah man*—person who has attained a high degree of knowledge and who has special perceptive and combative skills. Also more commonly known as a *Maban*.
[3]Ritual rebirth into manhood when boys are isolated from their community, subject to ordeals, and taught the secret knowledge of their people.

was at night and very dark, we were going through a gorge, when the feather foots, ginnawandas,[4] began to whistle. I was scared. The whistling means they want you to talk. They began lighting fires all along the gorge. After we called out our names, my family was allowed through.

One day, I took a tomato from the vegetable garden. I'd been watching it for days. Watching it grow big and round and red. Then, I picked it and Dudley saw me. He was Howden Drake-Brockman's brother and we called him Irrabindi. He gave orders for my Aboriginal father to beat me. Maybe he had his eye on that tomato, too.

I was beaten with a stirrup strap. I spun round and round, crying and crying. I was only a kid in a shirt in those days. My Aboriginal father never hit me unless an order was given. Then, he had to do it, boss's orders. He was good to me otherwise, so I never kept any bad feelings against him.

Dudley Drake-Brockman wasn't like Howden. They were brothers, but they were different. Dudley was a short little man. He couldn't ride. He was cruel and didn't like blackfellas. My people used to say about Dudley ngul-loo-moolo, which means make him sick. We didn't want him there. In the end, he got sick and died.

I used to play with Pixie, Dudley's son. We used to fight, too, but I never beat him. I was afraid of his father. My mother used to say to me, "Jilly-yung, never beat Pixie in a fight. When he wants to fight, you walk away." She was a wise woman.

Howden was a good-looking man, well liked. He could ride all the horses there, even the buck jumpers. Old Nibro told me that. He used to help him break them. There was one big, black horse he named Corunna. He would always ride him when he went out baiting dingoes.

I remember Howden used to dance on his own in the dining-room. He'd be doin' this foxtrot, kicking his leg around with no partner. I used to watch. There was a big dining-room then, and a great, huge fan that we had to pull to cool people off who were eating there. They gave us a handful of raisins for doing that.

We had other jobs on the station besides pulling the fan. For every tin full of locusts we killed with a switch, we got one hard boiled lolly. I remember once, I was a tar boy for the shearers. In those days, it was blade shearing, not like the machines they have now. The shed was stinking hot and the click, click, click of the shears made a rhythmic sound. I couldn't help goin' to sleep. Next thing I knew, I got a smack in the face. They were all singin' out TAR! TAR!, and I was asleep. When the girls brought down the dishes of cakes and buckets of tea, I made sure I was there. I wasn't going to sleep through that.

---

[4]*Feather foot (Ginnawandas)*—similar to the *Boolyah* or *Maban*. Person with special (magic) powers, often used for purposes of retribution. Similar also to *kadaicha man*.

Archie McGregor was one of the few white men on the station, he married Mr Richards's sister. Mr Richards was a big-wig in Marble Bar. Archie worked on the windmills and the pumps. When the pumps went bung, Archie had to go down in the deep well and fix them. He was the one that taught Albert and me how to build windmills. Those windmills were a terrible height. They had to be to catch the wind. I thought he was teachin' us things so we could help run the station one day. I was wrong.

When Howden married Eleanor Boddington, he built another house. He didn't stay living with Dudley. He built it by himself, too. He was a carpenter.

You know, he was a cowboy as well, because he had these two big pistols. He pulled them out, BANG! BANG!, firing at the tree, tryin' to shoot it. They were old muzzle loaders, like the ones the Yanks use in cowboy films. You put the powder in and a bit of lead and the cap in afterward. Then it revolved and you went BANG! BANG!, just like that! He used to hit this tree way down near the toilet. The bullets would bounce off. He was a smart man, I tell you.

I spent a lot of my time on the station with my brother, Albert, and my sister, Lily. When we were kids, we'd run round finding lizards, sticking our fingers in the holes in the ground and wood. One time I did that, it was a snake. A snake won't chase you to bite and kill you. They just want to get away. You only get bitten if you tread on them, they're just protectin' themselves. People always try to kill snakes whenever they see them. They should leave them alone. You point a gun at a snake and he'll get goin', he knows what you goin' to do.

Albert was older than me and they started educatin' him early. Mrs. McGregor, Archie's wife, was the teacher. She trained Albert to write on a slate with chalk. He had to speak English and learn the white man's ways and table manners. The other children weren't taught, only Albert and, later, me. She also gave us what you call religious instruction. We learnt all about the saints. She had a big roll of color pictures that we used to look at.

I went with my mother everywhere until they rounded me up to be educated. When I heard they were after me, I ran away. I didn't want to be educated. Also, I thought they wouldn't give me any meat at night-time. They caught me in the end, put me with Albert and Mrs. McGregor. I wasn't allowed to talk blackfella after that. If I did, Dudley beat me. I liked my language, but I got a good hiding if I spoke it. I had to talk English. When I was sleeping on the homestead verandah, I used to call to my mother in my own language, "Save me meat."

Of course, when they caught me, Albert could already talk English. He used to study at the cook's table. One night, the cook was a bit late with our supper. Albert said, "Go tell him."

"Tell him what?" I said.

"Tell him to hurry up with the tucker."[5]

"Give me hurry up tea!" I shouted. I should have said. "Hurry up and give me tea!," but I didn't know. Anyhow, the old cook came down and chased me round and round the kitchen. I was gone through the door with the cook chasin' after me! He never caught me, I was too quick.

That was Albert. He was always puttin' things into my head, but he never did anythin' wrong himself.

Albert lost two fingers because of me. I chopped them off in the tank machine. He stuck his fingers in to try and stop the cogs going round. I turned the handle and chopped them off. They used that machine to make tanks. You put in a straight bit of iron and bend it to make a boomerang circle. You only need three or four sheets to make a tank. Fancy, me choppin' his fingers off. We were just messing around, I didn't know he had his fingers in there.

When we were being educated, Albert and me slept on the homestead verandah. We had a bed side by side. Some nights, I'd wet my bed and jump into his. I'd dream someone was hitting me so I'd fight them in bed, I'd punch them and call out, then when I looked at my bed, I found it was wet.

Even though Albert was the older one, I took no notice of him. I was the mischievous one. He was too frightened to do anything, sometimes he needed protecting.

I knew all the people on the station, they was a good mob. There was Chook Eye, Wongyung and Mingibung. They were housegirls. They used to take in cups of tea and look after the house. Then there was Tiger Minnie, she used to help Howden bait the dingoes. No one could bait like her. Then there was Sarah, she was a big woman, she helped look after the garden. She grew pumpkins and cabbages for the cook and shooed the birds away. She was half-caste, like me. When her own baby was born, it was nearly white. A white blackfella. We all reckoned those extra babies belonged to either old Fred Stream, or Sam Moody, the cook.

We used to call Sam Moody backward, Moody Sam. He was a white man and a good cook. He'd cook bread, cut it in big slices and give it to the natives through the small kitchen window. He cooked meat, too. We'd all get bread and slices of meat. We'd poke our billies[6] through that little window and get tea, too. If Moody Sam didn't cook, we'd get slices of mutton, make a fire outside and cook it ourselves. For extra meat, my people used to catch kangaroos and wild turkeys and fish from the creek. We'd go down to the creek and we'd stand with our legs bent and apart, then we'd catch them

---

[5]Food.
[6]A can or kettle used in outdoor cooking. [eds.]

between our knees. We'd grab them with our hands and throw them on the bank.

Old Fred Stream, I think he was German. He used to take me on trips to Condin. Corunna Downs wool used to be stored there, ready to be loaded on the sailing ships bound for Fremantle. The stores were great big sheds and they housed goods as well as wool. One time, Fred Stream told me there were two saddles to be picked up, one for me and new for Albert. When they pulled them out, the rats had chewed away the straps. Those rats ate anything.

I don't know if Condin is used now they have a railway to Port Hedland. In those days, it was just surveyed. I never went back to see the new railway, or anything else.

On the way back to Corunna Downs, we camped at DeGrey Station. You should have seen all the pretty dresses come runnin' to meet our wagon. There was red, pink and green, all the colors of the rainbow. They was all runnin' to come and see me, too. I was only a little fella, I wasn't much in those days.

Some of the people there had pet pigs. They sold two to Fred Stream. Before we reached Corunna Downs, he knocked one on the head and cooked it in the ashes. I reckoned he was cruel, to eat a little pig like that! I couldn't look at him and I couldn't eat it. I kept thinking, fancy killing such a little pig. He was only a baby.

The next day, we came to a freshwater well and stopped to water the team. There were goats runnin' all over the place. Big ones, little ones, young ones, old ones. Fred Stream watched all these goats, then he said, "You want a goat?" I said, "NO!" I didn't want him to catch and kill no baby goat. Anyhow, he rounded up a kid and a billy and when we got to Corunna Downs, we let them go. I don't know what happened to them. I couldn't take a little baby goat away from his mother. I'm funny like that. I take after my old grandfather, I'm tenderhearted. I don't believe in stealing anything from its mother.

I remember one time when I was very small, it must have been Christmas, because there was so much food on the table on the verandah. All kinds of food laid out on this big table. I kept thinking to myself, I should eat more, I should eat more. I should finish it off. I knew I wasn't goin' to see food like that again for a long time. I just kept lookin' at all that food, thinkin' what a shame it was to go away and leave it. Even though my belly was already aching, I made myself eat more. A while later, I brought it all up. My belly was swollen and I just couldn't keep it in! You know, it must have been Christmas, because I was all dressed up in a shirt and pants that day.

There were always corroborees[7] at Corunna. You needed special permission to watch them. We used to go with Howden. I hadn't been put through

---

[7]Dance festivals held at night.

the Law by then, because I was still too young. That happens when you are fourteen or fifteen. I didn't want to go through the Law. I used to say, "Don't let them do that to me, Mum." I didn't want to be cut this way and that. For the real black ones, it was compulsory. I was half-caste, so I could be exempted. The women were just marked on the chest. Just one mark, here in the middle. That was their ceremony.

In those days, the women were given to you when you were only a baby. They had Old Dinah picked out for me. She used to help in the garden. She's dead and gone now, probably still waitin' for me in heaven. She was old enough to be my mother. I suppose, later, I could have had Helen Bunda for my wife. She was half-caste, too, and very clever with her hands. Her mother was Nellie, or Moodgjera. Her father was a bullock driver.

There was some wonderful wildlife on Corunna Downs. There was one little bird, he was a jay or a squeaker, he'd sing out three times and then the rains would come. He was never wrong. While he was there, there was always a good feed, but when he was gone, drought! When the little frogs sang out, we knew it was going to rain. They were lovely colors, white and brown with black spots. They were all different, there wasn't one the same. They used to get into the cooler and we'd have to clean it out. They was all natural animals. Wonderful creatures. There were no insecticides then to kill the birds. That's why the blackfellas want their own land, with no white man messin' about destroyin' it.

All the people round there, we all belonged to each other. We were the tribe that made the station. The Drake-Brockmans didn't make it on their own. There were only a few white men there, ones that fixed the pumps and sank wells by contract. The blackfellas did the rest.

I remember seein' native people all chained up around the neck and hands, walkin' behind a policeman. They often passed the station that way. I used to think, what have they done to be treated like that. Made me want to cry, just watchin'. Sometimes, we'd hear about white men goin' shooting blackfellas for sport, just like we was some kind of animal. We'd all get scared, then. We didn't want that to happen to us. Aah, things was hard for the blackfellas in those days.

One day, I'd like to go back to Corunna Downs, see what improvements there are. I believe it was used for a military base during the war. When I was there, Brockmans built a hump and stuck a flagpole in it. Whenever any visitors came, they raised the Union Jack.

Aah, I always wish I'd never left there. It was my home. Sometimes, I wish I'd been born black as the ace of spades, then they'd never have took me. They only took half-castes. They took Albert and they took me and Katie, our friend. She was put in Parkerville. She had a big doll with her when she went, Albert had me. Others went, too. I was about eleven or twelve.

When I left, Lily cried and cried. She was only little, but she ran away and hid, no one could find her. I was her favorite. She was full blood, real black, so they didn't want to take her. Daisy was only a baby, she didn't know what was goin' on.

They told my mother and the others we'd be back soon. We wouldn't be gone for long, they said. People were callin', "Bring us back a shirt, bring us this, bring us that." They didn't realize they wouldn't be seein' us no more. I thought they wanted us educated so we could help run the station some day, I was wrong.

When they came to get me, I clung to my mother and tried to sing[8] them. I wanted them to die. I was too young, I didn't know how to sing them properly. I cried and cried, calling to my mother, "I don't want to go, I don't want to go!" She was my favorite. I loved her. I called, "I want to stop with you, I want to stop with you!" I never saw her again.

When we left Corunna Downs to come to the Swan Native and Half-Caste Mission, we had to travel through Marble Bar and then to Port Hedland. We caught the ship, the *Ballara,* me, my brother Albert, Pixie and Dudley Drake-Brockman. Albert and I travelled steerage. Sometimes, I'd sneak out and head toward the front end of the boat to see what was going on. Dudley Drake-Brockman would always catch me and shout, "Get back to where you belong!"

It was a fine day when we arrived in Fremantle. We were taken straight to the mission, it was situated near the banks of the Swan River in Guildford.

The first thing they did was christen us. Canon Burton and Sophie McKintosh, I think she was the matron, were our godparents. We were christened Corunna, they didn't give us our father's name. That's when I got the name of Arthur. Albert had always been called Albert and he stayed that way.

For a long time, I was very worried about my mother. She had always been good to me. She loved me. Albert didn't seem to mind so much, I think he was too frightened to mind anything. You see, we couldn't understand why they'd taken us away. We weren't their family. The mission wasn't anyone's family. They called us inmates, then, all us kids, we were all inmates, just like a prison.

We soon found out that there were bullies at the mission. I suppose you get them everywhere. There was one that wanted to try us out. I was worried about Albert, I knew he couldn't fight his way out of a paper bag. He was bigger than me, older than me, yet I knew they could belt him up and tie him in knots. I had to take his part. I'd tackle whoever was beating up Albert and finish them off. They never tackled me again and they learnt not to touch Albert, because he was my brother.

---

[8]To sing an incantation which is believed to have the power to kill the person against whom it is directed.

There was one bully there, he had everyone bluffed except me. He'd throw stones at me, call me names, but he'd never tackle me. When it came to knuckles, I got my fist in first.

I was different to Albert. I was made different. I could fall off a horse, do anything and there was never nothing damaged or broken, even if I landed on a rock. I'm like rubber, you can bounce me anywhere. Albert wasn't like that. He used to get sick a lot. I cried for him when he was sick. He was my brother.

One man that worked on the mission, Mr. Ferguson, he said about Albert and me, "These boys have been well brought up. They say thank you for everything." We even said thank you when they gave us a hiding.

They soon learnt I could work at the mission. I was reliable. They could give me a job and I'd do it, no matter what. I had ten hurricane lamps to clean. I cleaned the glasses, then filled them with kero.[9] I was the mailman and the milkman, too. I delivered milk and eggs to Mr. and Mrs. Anderson in Guildford. Then, I'd continue on to Thompson's place, that was just over the railway line, they bought our milk, too. There were lots of people who bought things from the mission. I was the only one who was allowed to collect mail from the Midland post office. They sent me because I was the fastest walker.

If Matron needed any medicine, she sent me. She'd give me a letter to take to the chemist [druggist]. Webb was his name. One time while I was waiting in the chemist shop, a lady started talking to me, she was waiting, too. She told me what she was there for and what was wrong with her. There was this wrong with her and that wrong with her. She had so many things wrong with her I was amazed she was still alive. All this time she was talking, she was drinking lemonade. It was a real hot day. She told me all her troubles and I just sat there and listened and looked at her lemonade. She didn't even offer me one drop.

After Albert and me had been there a while, the mission was visited by a man called Governor Bedford. He was an Englishman, a greyheaded thing. After his visit, the darker kids were separated from the lighter kids. He didn't like us being together.

Before the Governor's visit, they built a building close to the bridge and near the brickyard. It looked like an ark to us, so we all called it Noah's Ark. We all thought that was fitting, because we was all in there together, white ones, black ones. We liked sharing that ark. Governor Bedford didn't like it one bit. He separated us all out. The light-colored ones had to go where the girls were and the girls were moved to the west side of the mission.

Funny thing was, they put Freddy Lockyer in with the white kids. He had fair hair and fair skin, but really, he was a white blackfella. He didn't want to go, he wanted to stay with us blackies, he belonged to us, but they

---

[9]Kerosene.

made him go. I said to him, "You're not black enough to stay with us, you have to go." I felt sorry for him. He was really one of us.

There was always a boundary between the girls and the boys. They had to sit one way and we had to sit the other. Apart from when we played, you had to follow the boundary and stick to your side. When the girls were older, they were put into service as housegirls and maids for anyone who wanted one. Once the boys reached adolescence, they were completely separated from the girls and put in a nearby orphanage. I suppose they were worried we might chase them.

After a while, the bigger boys started running away to Moora. They were brought back, but if they ran away a second time, the mission people would try and find work for them with the farmers up there. They were all well taught by then. I was still there when nearly all the older boys from the orphanage had run away. The only one left was Pinjarra Frank.

Bob Coulson was another man who worked on the mission. He was a good man with a hammer. I used to watch him. If he saw any cats sneakin' around the chicken house, he'd corner them and hit them on the head with a hammer. A cat only had to look at him and he was a goner.

Coulson wasn't a big man, but he had a nose like a devil. He used to be a soldier and he often showed us his bayonet. He was full of bluff. I think he was afraid the blackfellas might tackle him one day, that's why he kept on showing us his bayonet. He always wore his shirt sleeves rolled up, ready for action.

Corunji was Coulson's dog. He was a nice, old dog. We used to give him a slice of bread, now and then. One day, we were going into Guildford on deliveries and Corunji followed us. We had to cross the railway line, and when a train came, old Corunji started running and barking and chasing the engine. He must have slipped, because his foot went under the wheel and his leg was cut off. We were all crying, "Corunji, Corunji. Poor old Corunji!" We ran all the way back to the mission to tell Coulson what had happened. He got on his bike and cycled back to the railway line, we all followed. Poor old Corunji was still lyin' there, just lookin' at us as if to say, "Can't you help me?" Coulson got off his bike, walked over to Corunji, put his hand over his snout, pulled out his hammer and hit him over the head. Then, he got on his bike and cycled back to the mission. He just left him lyin' there. He did that to his own dog. Like I said, he was a good man with a hammer. I couldn't help thinking if he'd do that to his own dog, he might do that to me, one day. When he wasn't looking, I kept an eye on him. I didn't trust him after that.

Coulson had three children of his own. He told us once he used to beat his own son with a stick wrapped round the end with barbed wire. His daughters were called Mabel and Audrey. His wife was an olden-day lady. At least, that's how I remember her. There was nothing pretty about her. She was just a plain sort of Englishwoman. We didn't have much to do with her.

All she did was look after her house and keep an eye on the girls. Apart from that, she didn't stick her big nose anywhere. I don't think she was very loving to her kids. They were always coming around and talking to us.

When I was in my fourth year at the mission, Coulson caught me and some other boys outside the mission boundaries. We were playing in a public picnic area near the river. It was a popular spot and we were hoping to find some money that people might have dropped. When he found us, he was real mad. He ordered us back to our dormitory, he said he was going to give us a beating. You can imagine how scared we all were. He was so angry, we'd never seen him that angry, we were frightened of what he might do to us.

We didn't go back to the dormitory, we ran all the way to Midland, to the police station. You see, the police were called Protectors of Aborigines in those days, so we thought we might get some protection from them. We all ran inside the station and told the policeman what Coulson was going to do to us. We thought he might help us, we were only kids. He listened to what we had to say, then he said, "Get back to the mission! It's none of my business what happens to you!" We didn't know what to do.

As we came out of the station, Coulson came riding down the road on his bike. He spotted us, rounded us up and walked us back to the mission.

By this time, he was just about boiling over. He shoved us all in a dormitory, locked the door and told us to strip off. Then, when we were naked, he raced around the dormitory like a madman, beating us with a long cane over the head and body. He didn't care where he hit us, he just beat us and beat us till we bled. There was bits of blood everywhere. We were all crying, some of the boys were screaming, "No more, no more. No more, master!" He liked you to call him master.

I was the only one that didn't cry out. He came over and grabbed me and said, "Arthur, I've never had to beat you before, but BY GOD I'm going to give it to you now!" He beat me and he beat me, but I wouldn't cry for him. He beat me harder and harder, my thighs were running with blood and I still wouldn't cry for him. He was very, very angry, but I wasn't going to give him the satisfaction of making me cry.

After that, I decided that, when my wounds were better and I could walk again, I would run away. Albert could stay there if he wanted to, but I didn't want to be skinned and belted around. I'm real old now and I can still show you the scars from that beating. My wounds took a long time to heal. I was in a bad way.

I think Coulson felt guilty for beating me so hard, because, later, he took me for a train ride to visit his sister and her husband. They had a butcher's shop. It made no difference to me, I still didn't trust him. I was glad that I hadn't cried for him. I was pleased that, when I ran away, I'd be rid of him.

Pinjarra Frank and Tommy decided to come with me. I wanted Albert to come, too, but he was too frightened. He thought that, if we ran away and we got caught, Coulson might beat him the way he'd beaten me.

We told all the mission kids we intended to head toward Geraldton. Other boys had run away in that direction, so it would make our story seem likely. We didn't tell anyone we really planned to head toward the gold-fields. It was a good plan, because, that way, if any of our friends were asked questions, they didn't have to lie. We'd told them all just to say what we said.

We did run away. I must have been about fifteen or sixteen, then.

Coulson didn't stay at the mission long after that. He was sacked. I guess the Anglican mob that ran the mission began to realize that all the boys had been running away because of the way Coulson had been treating them. Maybe the other kids told them what Coulson had done to me.

I was sorry to leave Albert behind. After I left, he had no one to protect him and he got sick again. They sent him to hospital. Then, Howden came down and took him back to Corunna Downs. Dudley was dead by then. As far as I know, Albert worked there until it was sold to Foulkes-Taylor. Then, Albert went to Dr. Gillespie's station, Hillside. A lot of people went to Hillside. They knew that Foulkes-Taylor was a hard man.

I heard people was looking for me, I heard Howden was looking for me, but I was gone. I didn't want to be found. And I wasn't having anything more to do with school.

. . . I wish I could give advice for the young blackfellas of today, but I can't. Each man has to find his own way.

You see, the trouble is that colonialism isn't over yet. We still have a White Australia policy against the Aborigines. Aah, it's always been the same. They say there's been no difference between black and white, we all Australian, that's a lie. I tell you, the black man has nothin', the government's been robbin' him blind for years.

There's so much the whitefellas don't understand. They want us to be assimilated into the white, but we don't want to be. They complain about our land rights, but they don't understand the way we want to live. They say we shouldn't get the land, but the white man's had land rights since this country was invaded, our land rights. Most of the land the Aborigine wants, no white man would touch. The government is like a big dog with a bone with no meat on it. They don't want to live on that land themselves, but they don't want the black man to get it, either. Yet, you find somethin' valuable on the land the Aborigine has got and whites are all there with their hands out.

Those Aborigines in the desert, they don't want to live like the white man, owin' this and owin' that. They just want to live their life free, they don't need the white man's law, they got their own. If they want water in the Gibson Desert, they do a rainsong and fill up the places they want. If it's cold, they can bring the warm weather like the wind. They don't need the white man to put them in gaol [jail], they can do their own punishment. They don't have to hunt too hard, the spirits can bring birds to them. Say they want a wild turkey, that turkey will come along, go past them and they can spear it. Kangaroo, too. They don't kill unless they hungry, the white man's the one who kills for sport. Aah, there's so much they don't understand.

Now, if I had been born a white man, my life would have been different. I'd have had an education the proper way, without the whipping. As it is, I got to take my papers to someone who's educated to get me through. Some things aren't understandable to me. Now I got some of my grandchildren educated, they help me. If I'd have been a wealthy farmer, I'd have given all my kids a real good education.

I'm a great grandfather now and proud of it. Only thing is, Daisy beats me there, she's got more great grandchildren than me. I got to catch up with her. I'm proud of my kids, I'm proud of my whole family. Daisy's family and my family, we special. I got healing powers, but Daisy's got them stronger than me. You see, it runs in our family. The spirit is strong in our family. When I die, someone will get my powers. I don't know who. They have to have a good heart, and live a simple life. Otherwise, you're a motor without petrol. Your power comes from above. You can't cure yourself. You got to use that power to help others.

I'm at the end of my story now. To live to ninety, that's an achievement. I haven't really felt the effect of old age, though, of course, the visibility's gone away a bit, but me mind is not so bad. I've had everything a man could want, really. A little bit of sport and a little bit of music. I'm an entertainer. You take me anywhere and I'll join in, could be playing the mouth organ or anything. I'll give it a go. Everybody liked me, that's what beat me, even some of the men I worked for.

Now my life is nearly over, I'm lookin' forward to heaven. I'll have a better time up there. I'll be a little angel, flyin' around, lookin' after stars and planets, doin' the spring cleaning. God is the only friend we got. God the father, God the son and God the Holy Spirit. You stick to Him. He's the only one. Don't listen to what others tell you about God. He's the best mate a man could have. You don't have Him, you don't have no friend at all. You look away from God, you go to ruin.

Take the white people in Australia, they brought the religion here with them and the Commandment Thou Shalt Not Steal, and yet they stole this country. They took it from the innocent. You see, they twisted the religion. That's not the way it's supposed to be.

I look back on my life and think how lucky I am. I'm an old fella now and I got one of my granddaughters lookin' after me. That's something, these days. And I got Daisy's granddaughter writin' my story. I been tryin' to get someone to write it for years, now I'm glad I didn't. It should be someone in the family, like. It's fittin'.

I got no desires for myself any more. I want to get my land fixed up so my children can get it and I want my story finished. I want everyone to read it. Arthur Corunna's story! I might be famous. You see, it's important, because then maybe they'll understand how hard it's been for the blackfella to live the way he wants. I'm part of history, that's how I look on it. Some people read history, don't they?

❀ Discussion and Writing

1. Comment on Arthur's—Jilly-yung's—Aboriginal ancestors and their powers. Discuss which aspects of their lives are distorted or destroyed.
2. Examining Arthur's narrative, describe the daily life of people in Corunna Downs. Clarify the racial distinctions of black, white, and half-caste with regard to education and job opportunities.
3. Describe Arthur as: a son, a brother, and a teenager. Why does he call himself lucky at age 90?
4. Explain the irrationality of colonialism and white people's religion as Arthur envisions it.

❀ Research and Comparison:

Interdisciplinary Discussion Question: Research the sociological implications of the racial distinctions in Australia. Compare the Australian situation to that in the Americas.

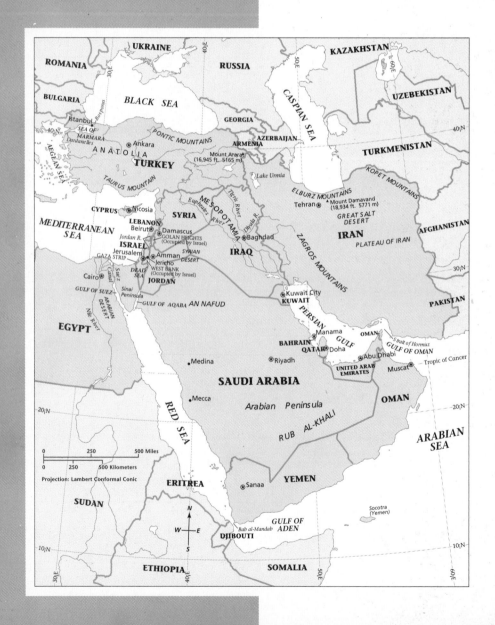

The Middle East

Classified variously as Western Asia, the Middle East, and the Near East, the lands of this region of Asia stretch due west from Iran to the Mediterranean Sea, north into present-day Turkey and south through the Arabian peninsula.[1] (See map.) The area has been a hub of trade and the site of empires from the most ancient times, and it has given birth to three of the world's major religions: in chronological order, Judaism, Christianity, and Islam. Because of its strategic position and its oil resources, it continues to be a center of conflicting political, economic, and cultural interests.

By the third millennium B.C.E., overland trade across the region was passing along routes that eventually grew into an extensive intercontinental network. In Mesopotamia (present-day Iraq), the fertile valleys of the Tigris and Euphrates rivers had already given rise to the flourishing commercial centers of Sumerian city-states like Akkad and Ur. By 3000 B.C.E., Sumerian civilization had not only acquired substantial power, it had developed a rich art that, along with its cuneiform writing, came to influence all the major ancient West Asian cultures.

After Sumerian power declined, two mighty empires succeeded each other in Mesopotamia, the Babylonian and the Assyrian. Formalized codes of law were an important part of their legacy, carrying over into later Middle Eastern nations. By 538 B.C.E., Persia (Iran) had conquered Mesopotamia and established an empire that was to last for over a thousand years. At its height, Persian authority extended from present-day Afghanistan and northwest India to the Danube River in Europe. Persia controlled commerce, and Persian became the language of exchange among the various peoples along the trade routes and in the market centers. In addition, Persia developed a rich literary tradition that remains a source of inspiration for twentieth-century Iranian writers.

West of Mesopotamia is the region known as the Levant, whose lands lie along the eastern Mediterranean. Occupying a crucial position on trade and military routes, the Levant and its peoples have been prey to almost constant

---

[1]Culturally, the Middle East includes Egypt and Libya as well. In accordance with our geographic organization, we include this literature in the Africa section.

conquest. From the second millennium to the first century B.C.E. alone, the area was conquered by the Hittites and the Egyptians; by the Assyrians, Babylonians, and Persians; and by the Greeks, Seleucids, and Romans.

The Levant was also the site of numerous ancient cultures, cultures that were finally subsumed into the larger empires. Especially notable were the Phoenicians and the Hebrews. Phoenician city-states had risen to prominence by 1250 B.C.E. By the eleventh century B.C.E., the Phoenicians had formed a phonetic alphabet, a concept subsequently used by all of Europe. By the ninth century B.C.E., the Phoenicians had established the famous city-state of Carthage near Tunis in North Africa; after the fifth century B.C.E., they gave way to Greek maritime power.

The Hebrews, the founders of Judaism, carved out a kingdom in the Levant beginning around 1000 B.C.E. Swept up in the stormy history of the region, it soon split into two, Judah and Israel. When Israel fell to the Assyrian empire (722 B.C.E.), its people were deported. When Judah fell to the New Babylonian empire (586 B.C.E.), much of the population was exiled to Babylon. The Persians, who conquered the region next, allowed the Hebrews to re-establish their homeland (538 B.C.E.). Many returned, but not all, and the period marks the beginning of what has come to be known as the Jewish Diaspora, or dispersion. Judah fell in the first century C.E. to the Roman empire after a period of political unrest.

Zoroastrianism and Judaism, two major systems of religious thought, emerged during these millenia of political and commercial expansion. Zoroastrianism sets its roots in Persia some time between 1400 B.C.E. and 1000 B.C.E. Embracing the idea of good and evil and the ultimate dominance of good, it spread rapidly throughout the region. Zoroastrian thought entered into ancient Greek and Judaic philosophy and, thus, ultimately, Christian belief.

Judaism places its beginnings in the second millenium B.C.E. with the story of Abraham of Ur and his journey from Mesopotamia into the upper reaches of Arabia, a journey dedicated to the concept of one god. From its beginnings, Judaic philosophy advocated social responsibility and the establishment of peace and justice. Judaism instituted rules governing sexuality, violence, wealth, and language: ethical precepts that structured society. These tenets were passed down in the oral tradition and in the writings of the ancient Hebrews. The first five canonical books were named the Torah, a term that later encompassed all the ethical teachings. The entire canon subsequently became identified as Biblical. As the centuries passed, these writings linked the scattered Jewish communities throughout the world.

Later, Christianity and Islam arose in the region. Like Judaism, they are Abrahamic religions; that is, they set their origins in the story of Abraham. They also share with Judaism a belief in a kind, merciful, and just God and in a profound moral code.

Christianity was organized in Palestine (c. 100 C.E.) by the disciples of Jesus, whom they identified as the Christ (Greek) or the Messiah (Hebrew), the anointed one. They acknowledged Jesus as the son of God and founded the religion on his teachings and on the concept of redemption through his sacrifice. Christian canonical teaching was named the New Testament and the Judaic scriptural writings were redefined as the Old Testament. Together, the two formed the Christian Bible, the single most influential work in Western civilization, for both its literature and its outlook. Christianity ultimately dominated Western society, although its influence essentially disappeared from the Middle East with the triumph of Islam.

Islam took its name from its fundamental goal, "the peace that comes when one's life is surrendered to God." It is founded on the emphatically monotheistic principle of *Allah,* an Arabic word deriving from *al Ilah,* meaning *the* God, not, simply, God. Allah is all-encompasssing: simultaneously merciful and just, loving and awesome. Submission to God is one of the five obligations central to Islamic practice; the others are charity, brotherhood, fasting, and the *hajj,* or pilgrimage to Mecca. Ethical and democratic in its essence, Islam originated in Arabia at a time of social disintegration, inequities, and corruption. The religion developed from the revelations of the prophet Muhammad (570?–632) contained in the Quran, the Holy Book of Islam.

Islam quickly prevailed throughout the Middle East. Two years before Muhammad's death in 632, all of Arabia was united under the banner of Islam. Slightly over a century later, Arab conquests had created a huge empire that spread Islam from East Africa across North Africa into West Africa and into Spain and beyond. It had spread east into the South Asian subcontinent and north through Palestine and Syria into Turkey. While the political unity of the empire was short-lived, a pan-Arab world view nevertheless evolved, as did disparate branches of Islamic theory. But despite political differences among the various branches of the religion, such as the Sunni and Shiite, Quranic philosophy and the language of the text, Arabic, allowed for the joining of people into a Muslim world. Arabic became the language of commerce and government, and the elegance of Quranic thought and language gave rise to a flourishing Arabic literature.

Sufism, a mystical expression of Islam that originated a century or two after the death of Muhammad, was a literary as well as a philosophical movement, especially in Persia. Islam swept through Persia in the seventh century, replacing Zoroastrianism as a force in society and in literature. Initially, the Arabic language replaced Persian. In the ninth century, however, Persian reappeared as a literary language (though it did not totally displace Arabic), and for the next five hundred years, Persia experienced a brilliant literary renaissance. Celebrated Sufi poets from this era such as Omar Khayyam, Farid ad-Din Attar, and Saadi continue to inspire writers in contemporary Iran.

During the six centuries of the Ottoman empire (1288–1918), Turkish emerged as a literary language under the umbrella of Islam, although in general, Arabic literature declined. At its height in the sixteenth century, the empire extended from Persia to the Balkans and into Africa. The Ottomans, in fact, played a major role in preventing Europe from gaining entry into the valuable overland trade routes in the Middle East, sending the Europeans across the sea-lanes in their search for alternatives.

Conditions in the area changed dramatically at the beginning of the twentieth century. When oil was discovered in Iran in the early 1900s, Britain and Russia immediately rushed in and divided the country into mutual "spheres of influence." The treaty that ended World War I dismantled the Ottoman empire, which had fought on the losing side. From its territories were carved Iraq, Jordan, Lebanon, Palestine, and Syria. The newly created League of Nations granted France a mandate over Lebanon and Syria, and granted Britain a mandate over Palestine (including Jordan), Iraq, and much of the Arabian peninsula. As more oil was discovered (in Saudi Arabia and Iraq) during the two decades following World War I, the United States sought its share, and subsequently began a policy of maintaining governments that were friendly to the West.

But the event that most directly determined the current lines of tension in the Middle East was the formation of the country of Israel in Palestine. For centuries, pre-Islamic, Islamic, and Judaic peoples had lived, for the most part, in neighborly fashion throughout the Middle East and North Africa. Jews and Christians were, in fact, protected under Islamic law as fellow "people of the book"—in recognition of their common Abrahamic heritage. However, in Christian Europe, the Jews experienced almost constant persecution, from subtle prejudice to outright restrictions, forced conversions, and the decimation of communities. During the late 1800s, a movement to establish a Jewish homeland in Palestine developed in Europe, partly in response to growing anti-Jewish feeling.

The Balfour Declaration of 1917 committed Britain to backing a Jewish homeland, and after World War I waves of Jewish immigrants flooded into Palestine. Tensions between Arabs and Jews mounted, erupting finally into violence. In 1947, the newly formed United Nations divided Palestine into Arab and Jewish states; and six months later, Britain withdrew. Many Palestinian people found their communities now under the jurisdiction of these new countries; others found themselves displaced altogether and sent to live in refugee camps. War broke out immediately, and over the years other wars followed. These events and their impact on people's lives are reflected in much of twentieth-century Middle Eastern literature.

Living in a country characterized by internal division as well as external pressure, Israeli Jewish writers—whether of Asian, African, or European heritage—have found a commonality in Judaic culture, particularly in the Bible, in its language and motifs. From the different waves of European settlers, there arose a "Diaspora literature," and from the native-born Israeli Jews a "Palmach literature" (named for the Israeli defense forces). Many younger writers, however, have avoided the tortured heroes of the Diaspora tradition and the collective assertiveness of the Palmach. And while Arab-

Israeli relations have formed a major subject for both Diaspora and Palmach writing, the younger writers have broadened their focus to include the class and caste conflicts created by a culturally diverse population. Several Jewish writers born in North Africa and the Middle East, for example, have called on their own customs as a source of imagery and ideology, reacting against the generations of European settlers, their class consciousness, and their particular focus on Arab-Israeli tensions.

In the Arabic world, poetry has remained the most honored verbal art, nourished by a pre-Islamic oral tradition, the Quran, and the great classical Arabic literature of medieval Islam. From the beginning, Arabic poetry sang of ethical matters, of hospitality and the honor and wisdom of rulers. After a period of stagnation, a renewed interest in the terseness of classical Arabic poetry awakened at the end of the nineteenth century, and then a Romantic movement, initiated by Gibran Kahlil Gibran in the early decades of the twentieth, stimulated poets to invigorate the language with new rhythms and images. Poetry now spoke of political and individual freedom, protesting against injustice and old-fashioned stifling customs. It concentrated on personal joys and sorrows, on love and death and suffering.

The partition of Palestine and formation of Israel created a new set of images. As the Palestinian people became a symbol of despair for all Arab intellectuals and artists, writers challenged Western aggrandizement, protesting the loss of Palestinian communities, and crying out against the conditions of the refugees. They also criticized Arab governments for allowing the refugee camps to continue to exist, for failing to reinstate Palestine. In addition, writers of fiction and poetry added images from their countries' experience of colonialism: they denounced corruption in their own countries; the effects of the oil riches; and the disasters of war. They also criticized outworn mores within their social structures, particularly the treatment and role of women.

Underlining the tragedy of an ultimately fratricidal situation, the Islamic and Jewish writers have worked antithetically with the same images: the creation of Israel was a cause for sorrow in one group or celebration in the other; raids into Lebanon or Israel were a cause of anger for the loser or pride for the winner.

For Middle Eastern writers in general, the search for a sense of being through the long-ranging past and through the shrapnel of the war-torn present persists as a dominant concern. To this question, Palestinian and Israeli writers add an urgent sense of place born of the demand for a homeland and its power as an image of identity. The burning presence of these issues has contributed an intensity to the writing of the last fifty years. Poets have rejected fixed classical patterns, and writers of fiction have experimented with new forms of narrative. Yet at the same time, they have linked their passions to ancient traditions, calling up resonances from Persian poetry, the Quran, and the Bible. Middle Eastern literature, whatever its political stance, remains inherently moral, philosophical, and elegant.

Kahlil Gibran
(1883–1931)
Lebanon

Gibran Kahlil Gibran was born in Bshirri, Lebanon, but his family was extremely poor and emigrated to the United States. He returned to Lebanon to study Arabic language and literature, and began writing in Arabic, although he eventually worked in English as well. As the leader of the Romantic movement to revitalize both Arabic literature and language, he transformed the poetry of the 1920s and 1930s. He merged Eastern and Western mysticism, opening a new range of issues for literary use and consideration; he wrote poetic prose in his novels and, frequently, prose poetry in his poems, setting a fresh standard for poetic diction, versification, and theme. *The Prophet* (1923), written in English, gained him a lasting following in the United States, while his poems in Arabic were essential to the evolution of Arabic literature.

On Children

And a woman who held a babe against her bosom said, Speak to us of Children.
   And he said:
   Your children are not your children.
   They are the sons and daughters of Life's longing for itself.
   They come through you but not from you,
   And though they are with you yet they belong not to you.
   You may give them your love but not your thoughts,
   For they have their own thoughts.
   You may house their bodies but not their souls,
   For their souls dwell in the house of to-morrow, which you cannot visit, not even in your dreams.
   You may strive to be like them, but seek not to make them like you.
   For life goes not backward nor tarries with yesterday.
   You are the bows from which your children as living arrows are sent forth.
   The archer sees the mark upon the path of the infinite, and He bends you with His might that His arrows may go swift and far.
   Let your bending in the archer's hand be for gladness;
   For even as He loves the arrow that flies, so He loves also the bow that is stable.

❋ Discussion and Writing

1. Interpret the prophet's description of children as "sons and daughters of Life's longing for itself."
2. What is implied by the parents' inability to envision the future their children would create?
3. Interpret the image of the bow and the arrow in the context of parents and children. Who is the archer? What is implied by "the path of the infinite"?
4. Describe an ideal parent-child relationship as the prophet articulates it: what aspects of the usual parental perception does Gibran negate; what does he celebrate?

❋ Research and Comparison

Examine *The Prophet* as a meditation on social institutions and personal relations and as a spiritual document.

Nazim Hikmet
(1902–1963)
Turkey

Nazim Hikmet was born in Salonika, in what was then the Ottoman Empire, and was raised in Istanbul, Turkey. As his mother was a painter and his grandfather a poet, Hikmet grew up surrounded by artists and was encouraged in his own endeavors: he published his first poems when he was 17. He left the Allied-occupied city after World War I to teach in eastern Turkey, and from there he traveled to Russia, stirred by the ideals of the 1917 Russian Revolution. There he studied and met poets of like mind from around the world. After he returned to Istanbul, he worked on leftist publications and was forced to flee in order to escape imprisonment. However, between 1928 and 1950, he spent 17 years in prison, at first because all suspected Communists were considered dangerous. In 1938, he was sentenced to 35 years (subsequently reduced to 28). Since military cadets admired his poetry, he was indicted for fomenting revolt. During these years, until he was rescued by worldwide protest, he was at the center of Turkish intellectual life, for many major writers and artists were also in prison. He was released under a general amnesty (the same year he was awarded the World Peace Prize), and in 1951, he was forced to flee Turkey. He traveled throughout the world during his exile, as he wrote, "with my dream / only the Americans didn't give me a visa." His work did not appear in Turkey until the Menderes government, sponsored by the United States, was overthrown in 1960.

Honored as a man and poet of immense integrity, Hikmet is regarded historically as a great poet, not only as the most important modern Turkish poet. He believed that art and life could not be divided, that acts of courage, honor, and honesty, of necessity, could be performed only in both or neither. He also believed that a poem was both a literary and a social phenomenon. Thus, the personal and the public (or social-political) aspects of his life and poetry cannot be divided, and, thus, an historical date becomes both emotional and factual. Recognized especially for his epic and lyric poetry, Hikmet also wrote narrative poems, but he worked mostly in colloquial Turkish (and the translator must use colloquial language in the translation).

12 December 1945*

The trees on the plain are making one last effort to shine:
                              spangled gold
                                   copper
                                        bronze and wood . . .
The feet of the oxen sink softly into the damp earth.
And the mountains are dipped in smoke:
                    lead-gray, soaking wet . . .
That's it,
fall must be finally over today.
Wild geese just shot by,
                    they're probably headed for Iznik Lake.
In the air, a coolness,
     in the air, something like the smell of soot:
     the smell of snow is in the air.
To be outside now,
       to ride a horse at full gallop toward the mountains . . .
You'll say, "You don't know how to ride a horse,"
but don't joke
                and don't be jealous:

Translated by Randy Blasing and Matlu Konuk

I've acquired a new habit in prison,
I love nature—if not as much,
                    nearly as much—as I love you.
                    And both of you are far away.

❀ **Discussion and Writing**

1. Describe the feelings evoked by the landscape of the passing fall and birds outside the poet's prison window.
2. What is the impact of the poet's fantasies of love, laughter, and freedom?

❀ **Research and Comparison**

Interdisciplinary Discussion Question: Research the history of political activism in twentieth-century Turkey, and examine Nazim Hikmet's life and writing in relation to this history.

Sadiq Hidayat
(1903–1951)
Iran

Sadiq Hidayat was born in Tehran, Iran, into a prominent family, and so his schooling took place in the schools established for children of the privileged class. He spent four years in Europe (ostensibly attending the university), becoming acquainted with European literature and entering the exciting intellectual ferment of the late 1920s. He published his first volume of short stories shortly after his return to Tehran in 1930, and by the end of the decade he had published two more, a book of satirical sketches, a long short story, and the short novel that established his fame, *Buf-e kur* (The Blind Owl, 1937). He is considered the founder of the short story in Iran, a relatively new genre in Persian literature, which had been dominated for twelve hundred years by poetry. (Prose had been regarded as the appropriate medium for didactic material, for philosophy, theology, and the like.) His stories are dreamlike and psychological; they are also experimental. Inspired by the *Rubaiyat* of Omar Khayyam, the eleventh-century Persian poet and mathematician as well as by the thinking he encountered in Europe, Hidayat wrote a major study of the poem. He longed for a return of

Persia's ancient majesty and condemned the corruption of Iran's institutions and the degradation of the people; on his satires, he attacked religious and social customs.

Seeking Absolution*

The scorching wind whipped up the earth and sand, blowing it into the pilgrims' faces. The sun burned and shrivelled everything. The camels stepped to the monotonous clang of iron and brass bells, their necks swaying rhythmically, their frowning snouts and drooping muzzles revealing their dissatisfaction with their lot.

Through the dust, the caravan moved slowly down the middle of the gray dirt road. The ash-colored, dry, sandy desert stretched as far as an eye could see, shimmering in the heat and at times forming a series of low mounds at the side of the road. For miles not even a date palm relieved the monotony. Wherever there was a handful of stagnant water in a ditch, a family had pitched a shelter. The air burned everything, taking one's breath. It was like stepping into the corridors of hell.

The caravan had been on the road for thirty-six days. Their mouths dry, their bodies weak, their pockets empty, the pilgrims had watched their money-supply diminish like snow under the hot Arabian sun. But today the chief of the camel-drivers formally announced that they had reached their destination and received tips from the pilgrims. They saw the top of the minarets in the distance and uttered the *salavat*.[1] It was as if new life had revived their tired bodies.

Khanom Gelin and Aziz Agha, in dusty black *chadors*,[2] had been tossed up and down in the camel litter from the time they had joined the caravan in Ghazvin. Each day had seemed like a year to them. There wasn't a sound bone in Aziz Agha's body, but she reminded herself that the more one suffers on a pilgrimage the greater one's reward.

A barefoot Arab, dark-skinned, with glaring eyes and a thin beard, whipped the mule's bleeding thighs with a thick iron chain. From time to time, he would turn and stare at each of the women. Mashdi Ramazan, the man in their party, and Hosein Agha, Aziz Agha's stepson, occupied the other two camel litters. Mashdi Ramazan was carefully counting his money. Khanom Gelin looked pale. She pulled aside the curtain between the two camel-litters and addressed Aziz Agha.

"When I saw the top of the minarets, my soul flew to them. Poor Shabaji! It wasn't her fate."

---

*Translated by Minoo Southgate
[1]To send a *salavat* is to send thanks to Muhammad for something good or for escaping danger or injury. [eds.]
[2]Long covering for women. [eds.]

Aziz Agha, cooling herself with a fan in her tattooed hand, replied:

"May God absolve her! She was a charitable woman. But how did she become paralyzed?"

"She quarrelled with her husband, which led to divorce. Then she ate pickled onions. The next morning half her body was paralyzed. We tried everything, but she didn't get well. I was bringing her to the Holy Imam to cure her."

"Maybe the camel ride and all that rocking wasn't good for her."

"But her soul is in heaven. The minute you decide to go on pilgrimage and set out on your way, all your sins are forgiven; and if you die, you'll go straight to heaven."

"No. Every time I set eyes on these coffins, I tremble. I want to go into the shrine, open my heart to the Imam, buy myself a shroud, then die."

"I had a dream about Shabaji last night. God bless you, you were in it too. We were walking in a big, green garden. A descendant of the Prophet, surrounded by light and dressed all in green, wearing a green tunic, green turban, green sash, and green sandals welcomed us. He pointed to a green mansion and said, 'Go there and rest.' Then I woke up."

"Good for her!"

The caravan moved along noisily. The caravan leader in front sang:

"Whoever longs for Karbala, welcome!
Whoever wishes to go with us, welcome!"

Another caravan leader answered:

"Whoever longs for Karbala will thrive!
Whoever wishes to go with us will thrive!"

The former sang again:

"In Karbala your spirit comes to life;
Zaynab's laments pierce your ear like a knife."

And the latter answered:

"May God grant that you visit Karbala!
I sacrifice my worthless life to Allah!"

The first caravan leader waved his flag and sang again:

"Damned be the tongue that would not say,
To God's beloved Mohammad we pray!
To Imam Ali, his eleven sons,
We send our greetings each and everyone."

At the end of each verse, the pilgrims repeated the *salavat* aloud.

The splendid golden dome with beautiful minarets was soon matched by a blue dome which looked out of place among mudbrick huts. The sun was almost set when the caravan entered the streets lined with broken walls and small shops. The caravan was greeted by a strange motley crowd. Ragged Arabs; men with dull faces, wearing fezes; turbaned men with shrewd faces, shaved heads, henna-colored beards and nails, telling their beads, walking around in sandals, loose cotton pants and long tunics. Persian, Turkish, and guttural Arabic spoken from the depth of the throat and entrails deafened the ear. The Arab women had dirty tattooed faces and inflamed eyes, and wore rings in their noses. A mother had forced half her black breast into the mouth of the dirty baby in her arms.

The crowd sought customers in various ways: one sang lamentations, another beat his breast; the next sold prayerstones, beads, and sacred shrouds; another caught jinns;[3] the next wrote prayers and sold amulets for protection; and another rented rooms. Jews in long caftans bought gold and jewelry from the pilgrims.

In front of the coffee-house an Arab was picking his nose and rubbing the dirt out from between his toes. His face was covered with flies, and lice crawled all over his head.

When the caravan came to a stop, Mashdi Ramazan and Hosein Agha ran to help Khanom Gelin and Aziz Agha down from the camel-litter. The pilgrims were assailed by a great crowd. Every piece of their belongings was grabbed by someone who hoped to rent his lodgings to them. In the midst of all this, Aziz Agha disappeared. They looked for her and asked around, but couldn't find her.

Khanom Gelin, Hosein Agha, and Mashdi Ramazan rented a dirty mudbrick room for seven rupees a day, and then resumed their search. They looked everywhere in town. They questioned all the shrine attendants one by one, gave them Aziz Agha's name and description, but found no sign of her. Sometime later, when the courtyard around the shrine was less crowded, Khanom Gelin entered the shrine for the ninth time and found a crowd of women and priests surrounding a woman who was grasping the grating around the sepulchre, kissing it and crying out, "Oh Imam Hosein! Help me! The Day of Judgment, when graves give up their dead, the day when eyes roll up to the tops of our skulls. What am I to do? Oh help me! Help me! I am penitent. I have done an awful thing. Forgive me! Forgive me!"

After they had pleaded with her for a long time, she turned, tears flooding her face, and wailed, "I've done something Imam Hosein won't forgive." Khanom Gelin recognized Aziz Agha's voice. She went forward, took her hand and dragged her into the courtyard, Hosein Agha went to her assistance and they took Aziz Agha home. There they gathered around her, gave her tea, and fixed the water pipe for her. She promised to tell them her life story, but asked her stepson, Hosein Agha, to leave the room before she began.

---

[3]Supernatural beings that can take human or animal form and influence human affairs. [eds.]

"My dear Khanom Gelin, after I married Geda Ali, God bless his soul, for three years we lived so happily that I was the envy of all women. Geda Ali worshipped me. He kissed the ground I walked on. But all that time I didn't get pregnant. He kept after me that he wanted a child and wouldn't take no for an answer. Every night he would sit by my side and say, 'How can I endure this misery? I'm childless.' I went to every doctor in town. I got amulets, but to no avail. One night, he wept and said to me, 'If you consent, I'll take a *sigheh*.⁴ She'll help you around the house. I'll divorce her after she bears a child, and you can bring up the child as your own.' Bless his soul, he fooled me, and I said, 'Fine, I'll take care of the whole business myself.'

"The next day I put on my *chador*, went to Hasan, the yogurt-maker, and asked his daughter, Khadijeh, in marriage for my husband. Khadijeh was ugly and dark-skinned, her face ravaged by smallpox. She was so feeble, if you pinched her nose she would give up the ghost. Well, I was the mistress of the house. She did the chores, cooked and cleaned. But barely a month had passed when she began to fill out. She put on weight, then got pregnant, just like that. Well, it was obvious she had gotten herself established. My husband gave her all his attention. If in the middle of winter she craved cherries, he would leave no stone unturned until he got them for her. I was the lowest of the low. At night, when he came home, he would go straight to her room to empty out his bundle, and I had to live on whatever she gave me out of charity. The daughter of Hasan the yogurt-maker, who came to my house barefoot and in rags, now put on airs with me.

"I could kick myself. I realized what a mistake I'd made. Khanom Gelin, for nine months I kept it all in and maintained appearances in front of the neighbors. But during the day, when my husband wasn't home, I'd give her hell—may he never know of this in his grave! In front of my husband I'd slander her. I'd say to him, 'In your old age you've fallen in love with a chimp? You can't have children. This isn't your child. Mashdi Taghi, the smith, got her pregnant.' And Khadijeh would slander me behind my back, trying to turn Geda Ali against me.

"To make a long story short, you can't imagine what went on in our house every day. Such a to do! The neighbors were fed up with our constant yelling and screaming. I was scared to death she was going to have a son. I had a fortune-teller divine by means of a book, I resorted to witchcraft, but to no avail. It was as though she had eaten pork and had become immune to witchcraft. She just got bigger and bigger, and at the end of the nine months she had the baby, and despite all my pains, it was a boy!

"Gelin Khahom, in my own house now I didn't count for anything. I don't know whether she had a charm or had given Geda Ali some potion. This beggar, this woman that I'd gone and brought to my own house, had me in her power. Right in front of my husband she'd say to me, 'Aziz Agha,

---

⁴A woman married by way of a temporary marriage.

I'm busy. Will you wash the diapers?' I'd fire up and in front of Geda Ali call her and her son whatever came to my mouth. I told Geda Ali to give me a divorce. But he, bless his soul, kissed my hand and said, 'Why are you acting like this? She'll get angry and her milk will make the baby ill. Wait till he starts to walk, then I'll divorce her.'

"But I couldn't eat or sleep, I was so worried. Until, may God forgive me, in order to break her heart, one day as soon as she went to the public bath and I was left alone in the house, I went to the baby's cradle, took the safety pin I used to pin my headkerchief with, turned my face, and thrust the pin into the top of the baby's head. Then I hurried out of the room. Khanom Gelin, the baby didn't take breast for two days and two nights. Every time it cried, my heart sank. The amulets, the doctors, and the medicine did no good. On the second day, it died in the afternoon.

"Well, as might be expected, my husband and Khadijeh cried and mourned. But I was relieved. It was like someone had poured water on fire. I said to myself, at least now they have no son. Let them eat their hearts out. But barely two months had passed before she got pregnant again. I didn't know what to do this time. I swear to Imam Hosein I got ill and remained half conscious and bed-ridden for two months. At the end of the nine months, Khadijeh whelped another son, and she became the favorite once more. Geda Ali would give his life for the child. God gave the Israelites the promised land and Geda Ali a son! For two whole days he stayed home and just sat there with the baby wrapped up in diapers in front of him, looking at it.

"It was the same story all over again. Khanom Gelin, I couldn't help it. I couldn't stand the sight of a rival wife and her child. One day Khadijeh was occupied, I used the opportunity, took the safety pin again, and thrust it into the top of the baby's head. It died the next day. As you'd expect, there was moaning and groaning. This time, you can't imagine the state I was in. On the one hand, I was pleased as pie to have deprived Khadijeh of her son, on the other hand I was worried about the blood I'd shed twice. I mourned for the child. I cried so hard, Geda Ali and Khadijeh were sorry for me and wondered how I could love the offspring of a rival wife so much. But I wasn't crying for the baby. I was crying for myself, for the Day of Judgment, the darkness of the tomb. That night my husband told me, 'I guess it wasn't in my star to have children. They die before they can walk.'

"But it wasn't yet forty days, when Khadijeh got pregnant again. There wasn't an offering my husband didn't make so the child would live. He vowed to marry it to a descendant of the Prophet if it were a girl, and to call it Hosein if it were a boy and let his hair grow for seven years, then weigh its equal in gold and take the boy on the pilgrimage to Karbala. After about eight months and ten days, Khadijeh bore a third son. But this time it seemed like she'd gotten onto something. She wouldn't leave the baby alone for one second, and I wasn't able to make up my mind between killing the child or doing something so Geda Ali would divorce Khadijeh. But all this was idle dreaming. Khadijeh was on top of the world. She was the mistress of the house, she bossed me around, and her word was law. Meanwhile, the baby grew to be four months.

"I looked for a good augury day and night, wondering whether to kill the baby, until one night after a big fight with Khadijeh, I decided to do the baby in. I bided my time for two days. On the second day, Khadijeh went to the corner grocery to buy some figwort camphor. I ran into the room and took the baby out of the hammock. It was asleep. But as I pulled the pin and was about to thrust it in, the baby woke up and instead of crying, smiled at me. Khanom Gelin, I don't know what came over me. My hand dropped. I couldn't bring myself to do it. Well, no matter what I'd done, it wasn't like my heart was made of stone. I put the baby back and ran out of the room. Then I said to myself, 'Well, it isn't the kid's fault. The smoke rises from the firewood. I've got to do the mother in and end the trouble.'

"Khanom Gelin, now as I tell you this I tremble, but what could I do then? It was my wretched husband who chained me to the daughter of a yogurt-maker—may he never hear this in his grave!

"I took some of her hair to Mullah Ebrahim the Jew, who was famous in the Rahchaman district, to put a curse on her. I put a horse-shoe in fire. Mullah Ebrahim charged me three tomans, and promised she would die before the week was up. But a month went by and she just got bigger and bigger, like Mount Ohod. My faith in witchcraft and such things was shaken.

"A month later, the winter had just begun when Geda Ali got sick—so sick that he made his will twice, and we poured holy water down his throat three times. One night, when he was very sick, I went to the market place and bought some rat poison. I brought the stuff home, poured it into the stew and after stirring it in thoroughly I put the stew back on the stove. I'd bought some food for myself. I ate it secretly, and after I was full, went to Geda Ali's room. Twice Khadijeh said, 'It's late; let's have supper.' But I told her I had a headache and didn't feel like eating. I'd feel better with an empty stomach, I said.

"Khanom Gelin, Khadijeh ate her last meal and went to bed. I went to her door and listened. I could hear her moan. But it was cold and the doors were all shut. No one else could hear her. I spent the whole night in Geda Ali's room, pretending I was watching after him. When it was nearly morning, I went to her room again, trembling and fearful, and listened behind the door. I heard the baby cry, but didn't dare open the door. You can't imagine what I went through.

"In the morning, after everybody got up, I opened Khadijeh's room. She was dead, and had turned black as coal. She had struggled so much that her mattress and her covers were all over the room. I dragged her over to the mattress and covered her with the bedspread. The baby was crying and sobbing. I left the room, went to the pond, and washed my hands. Then weeping and beating myself, I took the news of Khadijeh's death to Geda Ali.

"When people asked me what she died of, I said she'd been taking medicine to become pregnant and that she'd been overweight and maybe died of apoplexy. No one suspected me, but my conscience gave me no peace. Was it I who had shed blood three times? My face in the mirror scared me. My life was poisoned. I'd go to hear professional mourners tell the story of the Imam's death in the tragedy of Karbala. I'd weep, give money to the needy, but I could find no peace. The thought of the Day of Judgment, of Gog and Magog, and the darkness of the tomb—God knows what I went through. Then I decided to go to Karbala and live near the holy shrine in penitence. Since Geda Ali had made a vow to take us to Karbala, he wasn't unwilling to go. But he kept finding excuses and procrastinating, saying, 'We'll go to Mashhad next year. There is a plague in Karbala this year.' And so on and so forth, he put if off till he died.

"This year, I made up my mind to go. I sold all the property and turned it into cash, as he had decreed in his will. And when I heard about you and Mashdi Ramazan leaving for Karbala, I joined you at Ghazvin. The young man who is with me and thinks I am his mother is the same Hosein Agha, Khadijeh's third son. I told him to leave the room so he wouldn't hear my story."

Mashdi Ramazan and Gelin Khanom heard the story in amazement. Aziz Agha's eyes filled with tears.

"I don't know whether God will forgive me, or whether on the Day of Judgment the Imam will intercede for me. Khanom Gelin, I've been waiting to tell somebody what troubles me. Now that I have, it's like someone poured water on fire. But I worry about the Day of Judgment. . . ."

Mashdi Ramazan tapped the ashes out of his pipe:

"Come, come! Why do you think we're here? Three years ago I was a coachman on the road to Khorasan. I had two rich passengers. On the way, the coach overturned and one of them died. I strangled the other myself and took 1,500 tomans out of his pocket. Now that I'm growing old, I got to thinking the money was gained unlawfully, so I decided to come to Karbala to make it lawful. Today I gave the money to a religious authority. He took 500 for himself and gave me the rest, cleansed and purified. It only took two hours. Now the money is as much mine by right as was my mother's milk."

Khanom Gelin took the water pipe from Aziz Agha, exhaled a thick smoke, and after a short silence said:

"You remember Shabaji who was with us. I knew the camel ride would do her no good, but I brought her along anyway. You see, she was my stepsister. Her husband fell in love with me and married me. I tormented her so much that she became paralyzed. And on the way, I killed her so she wouldn't get any of our father's inheritance."

Aziz Agha was weeping for joy. "You? You too?" she said.

Khanom Gelin took a smoke and said:

"Haven't you heard the preacher? Even if your sins are as numerous as the leaves on a tree, the moment you take a vow and set out on your pilgrimage, you're as pure as a new-born babe."

❋ Discussion and Writing

1. Discuss the rationale for Geda Ali's taking Khadijeh as a temporary wife. Analyze Aziz Agha's role in this arrangement and her subsequent behavior with regard to Khadijeh and her children.
2. What motivates Aziz Agha's confession? Discuss the psychological and spiritual dimensions of her story.
3. Explain the effect of Aziz Agha's confession on Mashdi Ramazan and Gelin Khanom. Comment on the function of these two in the narrative.
4. Elaborate on the ironies implicit in the purpose of the pilgrimage and the people's justification of their conduct.
5. What are the images used to describe the setting? Correlate the setting to the action and the title.
6. Analyze the use of the three: story-telling, confession, and the pilgrimage.

❋ Research and Comparison

Interdisciplinary Discussion Question: Research the importance and observation of the obligation to go on *hajj*, a pilgrimage to Mecca, in any Islamic community around the world. Develop a paper on any one aspect of the *hajj*.

Ya'akob Yehoshua
(b. 1905)
Israel

Ya'akob Yehoshua was descended from a family that lived in Jerusalem for many generations. He trained as a scholar of Near Eastern culture, and after the partition of Palestine, he worked for many years in the Israeli Ministry of Religious Affairs. His work concerned Islamic issues among Israeli and Arab communities, but he never affected Israeli political and cultural policies in relation to the Arab world. He was part of a circle of old Sephardic and Asian Jewish intellectuals who found themselves more and more marginalized as the party structure of Jewish settlement in Palestine turned into the state of Israel.

As his more famous son, A. B. Yehoshua, gained prominence on the Israeli literary scene, Ya'akob Yehoshua began to write his magnum opus, *Childhood in Old Jerusalem.* This six-volume work investigates every aspect of life in Jerusalem. Yehoshua used the tools of a journalist, folklorist, rabbinical scholar, linguist, and historian. Most of all, he spoke as a lover and inhabitant of this ancient city. The work remains an invaluable resource for examining aspects of Jerusalem's culture that have died with its older residents. Particularly notable are his observations and descriptions of the relations between the native Jewish and Arab populations within the same community.

*Childhood in Old Jerusalem**

Jews and Muslims had common courtyards, just as if we were a single family. We grew up together. Our mothers revealed everything to the Muslim women and they, in turn, opened their hearts to our mothers. The Muslim women even learned how to speak Ladino[1] and were adept in its sayings and proverbs. We didn't live in shelters for the needy like the Ashkenazim and there were no large estates separating our houses from those of the Muslims. The Muslim women used to come down to our places across the roof at dusk to spend the evening in conversation. All the kids played together and if anyone else from the neighborhood bothered us, our Muslim friends would come to our defense. We were allies.

Our mothers would nurse any Muslim children whose mothers had died or were unable to attend to them, just as they could care and watch over them if their mothers were busy or otherwise occupied. And the same was true the other way around. The parents of Muslim boys born after great expectation and long suffering often asked their Jewish friends to arrange for a Jew to perform their circumcision on the eighth day, following Jewish and not Islamic custom. . . . According to Islamic custom, though, a baby nursed by someone other than its biological mother was considered a member of the nursing mother's family. Nissim Franco, son of the *Hacham*[2] Yaagob Franc, told me the following story: "Once my brother and I accompanied our father to the train station on the way to Haifa from where he intended to go and visit the saints' tombs in Meron. As we sat in the coach a very dignified Muslim sheikh entered and, upon seeing my father, cried out *ya akhi* (Oh, my brother). They grabbed each other and stood a few moments in a tight embrace. My father asked us to kiss the sheikh's hand. We both got up and kissed his hand after which he blessed us. When my father saw how aston-

---

*Translated by Ammiel Alcalay
[1] A Spanish dialect with some elements of Hebrew, spoken by Sephardic Jews. [eds.]
[2] Lit., wise; among Sephardic Jews, the local rabbi was called *Hacham* and Rabbi was reserved for more pre-eminent scholars. [eds.]

ished we were at the whole thing, he turned to us and said: 'When I was young we lived with the sheikh's parents in one courtyard. His mother died suddenly and my mother nursed him until he was weaned. So we're brothers.'"

❋ Discussion and Writing

1. What aspects of everyday life are presented in this excerpt, and what do they imply?
2. Examine the significance of the Muslim and Jewish women's nurturing each other's children.
3. Discuss the importance of this scene from the past in view of the current relations between peoples of different religions in Israel.

❋ Research and Comparison

Interdisciplinary Discussion Question: Research the history of Arab-Jewish relations before the partition of Palestine and the founding of the state of Israel, and comment on the current relations between the two communities.

Fadwa Tuqan
(b. 1917)
Palestine

Fadwa Tuqan was born in Nablus, Palestine, into a middle-class family. Raised in an extended family, she spent her childhood in a large house, enclosed by high walls that came to represent its repressive ambience. She has described the despotism of the males and the watchfulness of her cousins and aunts. Her brother, the famous poet Ibrahim Tuqan (1905–1941), could not protect her when she was forced to leave school at 13 because a teen-aged boy had sent her a flower. Her brother, however, read with her, introducing her to great literary works, and later took her to Jerusalem, where she lived in his house until he died. Then she returned to the family house and the *qumqum*, the "stopped bottle" of *The Arabian Nights*, where women "grow old before their time, sitting waiting against the wall, with no private life of their own."

Fadwa Tuqan's brother inspired her, instructing her in the craft of writing poetry. Trained in traditional versification, she has explored the possibilities of free verse as a vehicle for both social and personal themes, and is considered one of the major avant-garde poets writing in Arabic. At first her work avoided political themes, but, she said, "When the roof fell in over Palestine in 1948, the veil fell off the face of Arab women; the walls of the harem were finally broken." It was after Nablus fell in the 1967 (or Six-Day) war, when Israel won substantial tracts of land, however, that she became a politically committed writer. She focused then on the question of resistance, the issue that had been central to her brother's work.

*Song of Becoming**

They're only boys
who used to frolic and play
launching rainbowed kites
on the western wind,
their blue-red-green kites
whistling, leaping,
trading easy laughter and jokes
dueling with branches, pretending to be
great heroes in history.

Suddenly now they've grown,
grown more than the years of a normal life,
merged with secret and passionate words,
carried love's messages like the Bible or Quran,
to be read in whispers.
They've grown to become trees
plunging deep roots into earth,
stretching high towards the sun.
Now their voices are ones that reject,
that knock down and build anew.
Anger smouldering on the fringes of a blocked horizon,
invading classrooms, streets, city quarters,
centering on squares,
facing sullen tanks with streams of stones.

Now they shake the gallows of dawn
assailing the night and its flood.
They've grown more than the years of a life
to become the worshipped and the worshippers.

When their torn limbs merged with the stuff of our earth,
they became legends,

Translated by Naomi Shihab Nye

they grew into vaulting bridges,
they grew and grew, becoming
larger than all poetry.

❊ Discussion and Writing

1. Describe the boys' games. What is the significance of the "rainbowed kites"?
2. What is the implication of the references to the Bible and the Quran?
3. Comment on the symbolism conveyed by the image of the boys who were "dueling with branches" and suddenly became trees.
4. What is the implication of the boys' being the worshippers and the worshipped?
5. Discuss the political implications of the boys' growing more than the years of a normal life. Elaborate on the irony of their one-time pretense at being heroes.
6. Analyze the symbolism of: "blocked horizon," "gallows of dawn," and "vaulting bridges."

❊ Research and Comparison

Interdisciplinary Discussion Question: Research the political history of Palestine and examine the plight of the people, their identity, and their struggle for survival. What are the repercussions? Examine these issues in the literary works of any Palestinian writer.

Simin Danishvar
(b. 1921)
Iran

Simin Danishvar was born and raised in Shiraz, Iran, where her father was a physician, until the family moved to Tehran after she completed high school. There she worked for Radio Tehran and the newspaper *Iran,* and in 1949, she received her doctoral degree in Persian literature at Tehran University. A year later, she married Jalal Al-i Ahmad (1923–1969), the eminent writer and social critic of the late 1950s and early 1960s, about whom she wrote the moving essay "The Loss of Jalal." Theirs was a famous literary marriage, along with their own writing, they collaborated on and contributed to several journals. Danishvar has served in government, worked as a translator, and taught at Tehran University. She was the first modern Iranian woman to publish a collection of short stories. She was also the first Iranian woman to publish a novel, the exceptionally popular political work *Savushun,* about life in Shiraz during World War II and the Allied occupation. While she has focused more and more on the predicament in which Iranian women find themselves, her interests range across social issues. As she has experimented with form, she has created works of humor and of pathos.

*The Half-Closed Eye**

Sorrow for these who slumber robs
my weeping eyes of sleep.
NIMA YUSHIJ (1895–1960)

Effat ol-Moluk:

Yes, my dear woman, the late doctor Haj Hakimbashi was my uncle, the full-blooded brother of my mother. Everyone called him Haj Hakimbashi the Deaf. Khanom Kuchek was his favorite wife. When she didn't indulge him his matrimonial prerogatives, he'd get very peevish. He'd come to the clinic in Mirza Mahmud Vazir Street, take one glance at the patients and say, "Give them all an enema." Then he'd walk right back out again. And how do you suppose Khanom Kuchek got all her money? Well, it's obvious she got it from Haj Hakimbashi. They say that once, while Haji[1] was prostrated in prayer, Khanom Kuchek got a pillow and sat right down on top of his head. Haji's about to suffocate and she tells him, "I won't get up until you swear you'll leave me all your wealth and possessions and if you don't, I'll just sit here till you croak." Haji had no choice but to swear to it. But, by and by, she did him in. They say she ground up some glass and mixed it in with his enema water. Haji, God rest his soul, was a great believer in purgation.

Yes, my dear, that makes you the granddaughter of my uncle. By visiting you today, I'm reaffirming family ties, as a good Muslim should . . . but, I've disturbed you; good lord, I could die of shame! You were asleep! I didn't realize you nap in the afternoons; I was afraid if I came in the evening, you'd be out. I swear by the hair upon your head, I've come to see you three times before but couldn't find your house. Today, I said to myself, no matter what, I've just got to find the house of my uncle's granddaughter. Excuse me for coming in my house-slippers; my foot is swollen, you see, and won't go in my shoe . . . it's my rheumatism. You wouldn't remember what my late uncle, Haji, prescribed for rheumatism, would you? Verjuice! In fact, my son-

---

Translated by Frank Lewis
[1]Haj or Haji: honorific title given to one who has fulfilled the vow of going on a pilgrimage to Mecca. [eds.]

in-law bought eighty bottles of verjuice from Sar Cheshmeh . . . I got out of the car at the end of your street. I asked a gentleman to point out your house, but he didn't know the way. What a sweet man! He entrusted me to the neighborhood street-sweeper, who brought me straight to your door. I've come to say farewell. I want to go on pilgrimage to Mashhad—may it be as much a blessing to you as it will to me—and kiss the feet of the Imam Reza. I've brought this package for safekeeping in a corner of your strongbox. If I die, give it to my daughter and forgive me for any wrongs I've done you, or no, give it to Azizollah Khan, he'll look you up. I'll give him a piece of paper so you'll know it's him. I'll write "May God be with you always, my dear" on the paper.

In the package? The package contains the title deed to some property in Khademabad. I had saved up a few pennies and everyone was saying that in one year the value of this land would increase from forty tomans per square meter to four hundred. You go to sleep at night, they said, and when you wake up in the morning, the price of everything has gone up, including land. I went and bought a two-thousand-square-meter plot. Did it belong to the Baha'is? So what. Doesn't matter whose it was. May God lengthen the reign of this government and add to its glory . . . I've also got a pair of earrings, a bracelet, two cashmere traveling bags, a cashmere prayer-rug and my winding-sheet in the package. The sister of my daughter's husband went to Mecca last year and brought this winding-sheet for me. She washed it in water from the well of Zamzam and circled around the Black Stone with it. I'll open it. No, no, never even think of it . . . I may not be able to rely on my own eyes, but I know I can rely on you. I'd even trust you with my mortal soul.

The house of my son-in-law? My son-in-law's house is at the head of the wooden bridge on Shahreza Street. My son-in-law is a colonel. We have one orderly, a maid and a girl to run errands. On top of that, a laundry woman comes once a week, for washing and ironing. We also have a gardener who charges 120 tomans a month year-round just to come and plant a few petunias and geraniums in the summertime.

. . . O thank you. To your health! . . . My daughter has, may it meet your approval, two little girls, each prettier than the other, just like two little dolls. My other daughter has gone to England and is studying medicine. First the younger sister of my son-in-law went. She came for a visit last year. My, how she sings the praises of that place, you can't imagine. She told my daughter, "I'll sign you up to study medicine, all you need to do is pay for the trip there." They pay for everything themselves. Nursing?! Who said so?! I bet it was Aqdas, sticking her nose into everybody's business! Do you think I just found her wandering full-grown in the desert that I would let my precious baby clean up the piss and shit of Europeans and tie shut the chins of their corpses? No, my dear lady, I bought a first-class airplane ticket and sent her to London, where she is now studying to become a doctor . . . She studies medicine in the hospital morning till night. She sent a letter, she wrote, "Mommy, dear, I want to be the successor of the late Haj Hakimbashi" . . . It's just like Aqdas to say my daughter's become a nurse . . . It figures that when everyone else is dying from honest-to-God snake bites, I go and get myself bitten by a rank stinkbug! The daughter of one's own sister going around spreading lies about her cousin! She's jealous. She came to ask my daughter's hand for Ahmad . . . I said, "I'm not about to give the girl to that dim and squint-eyed boy of yours." Now, to get back at me, she says my daughter's become a nurse . . . Does she think Mansureh's not rightfully my child? So what if she isn't really mine? After all, it was me who raised her, on my hip and in my arms! If I live to do it, I'll get a passport and go to see my baby in London. She's in London itself. You don't happen to know where to go to get a passport, do you? Do I have to go without a veil? Well, I will. I'll just put on a headscarf and go. No verse has come down from heaven saying that I have to wear a full-length *chador*.[2]

The house? No, he didn't buy it. My son-in-law paid the 400,000 tomans I told you about—did I say 300,000 tomans? I can't remember the exact amount now—in any case, he bought the land, but the city wouldn't give him a building permit. They say there's no cement, there's no bricks or plaster, and there's no limestone . . . There's no meat or eggs or poultry or onions, either. All of a sudden the cupboards are bare and the dogs have all the bones. I stood in a long line to buy meat and when it got to be my turn, I found myself at the egg seller's, but the eggs were finished, so I bought sugar . . . I should go buy cement on the black market? God forbid! Are we common criminals that we should do so? Take to trading on the black market in the autumn of our lives, when we should be donating to charity or doing good deeds?

No thanks, you're very sweet to offer, but I smoke filterless Homa cigarettes . . . My son-in-law is fixing to buy one of those apartments across from Sa'i Park, only for the sake of the children, so that they can take some fresh air. I vowed to give Ahmad, Aqdas's son, five thousand tomans so he could go to America. They said it wasn't enough and looked down their noses at it. My daughter got indignant and wouldn't let me give it, so I didn't. Now I hear Aqdas has said "My aunt's gone back on her word." Now am I the sort of person to go back on her word? I swear by the hairs on your head, I never promised. I only took a vow that if my daughter gave birth to a son, I'd give five thousand tomans to Ahmad. My daughter had a miscarriage during her third pregnancy. In spite of that, I said I'd give it to him; the boy is a descendant of the house of the Prophet, and he'd like to go to America. Now, since I didn't give him the hand of my daughter, at least let him go to America. But they made such a fuss and ruckus about it that in the end, I wouldn't give it.

---

[2]Long covering for women. [eds.]

I heard Aqdas said, "Let Auntie go blind, Ahmad's got to go to America!" They sent that one-eyed boy to America just so he could wash the dishes of the Westerners and sweep their floors. I heard he became very friendly with an old lady; this old woman kept him around . . . God forgive me for thinking such thoughts.

How could they get the money to send him? I don't know, they must have taken out a loan. Aqdas says, "I sold my bracelet and my heavy gold necklace. . . " I heard she sold her entire trousseau. I know they sent the boy on a military airplane. Do I know who arranged it for them? First they came to my son-in-law, Colonel Asadpur. He told them, "Such arrangements entail certain responsibilities. What if the boy were accidentally to fall out into the ocean or the plane were to crash? Then how could I answer to Aqdas?"

No, my dear, Aqdas is my niece, my sister's daughter. I know her very well, she isn't the type to save up a lot of money or anything like that. She's very sloppy . . . Once they said it was scissors that went into the child's eyes, once they said something else . . . I mean Ahmad's eye. His right eye is deformed. The rest of his face is not too bad. He has a very dark complexion, but his features, except for the swollen eye, are all right. Aqdas swears that she wasn't home, but if she wasn't, how come she's so insistent on sending the kid despite all obstacles to America? Huh? Is it for any other reason than that she feels it's her fault and wants to make it up to the kid? The stupid kid is trying to pass himself off as a child of the aristocracy. They sent the son of a vegetable seller to Alborz College! Well, now let them pay for it . . . I heard that Aqdas went off and became a maid. They hid it from me, but I know she was cleaning houses to pay for Ahmad's expenses. Now he's off to America, and some old lady's hankering for cockerel and brings Ahmad in to live with her. He drives her around town, washes her car, sets her shoes in front of her feet, washes her dishes. He does the gardening for her. Tsssk! God help us! A descendant of the house of the Prophet, in such pathetic circumstances. Now, what law says you have to go to America? You could go to England like my daughter and study medicine. I don't spend a single red cent on Mansureh; their pocket money is all provided for, they even pay for their baths and soap and everything themselves.

That stupid boy was deficient from the beginning. In Alborz College, he became friends with the grandson of Sadiq ol-Dawleh. What an outrage! The son of Karim, the vegetable seller! Some people say—and let those who say it take responsibility in the next world for the truth or falsehood of the rumor—they say Ahmad's father moonlights as a pimp and a go-between. He found a maid for us and he probably arranged the maid's job for his wife, too. Whenever they're asked, "What does your father do?" they say he works in an office. Like hell he does! Now that the grandkid of Sadiq ol-Dawleh has gone to America, this one's gotta go, too. There's no one around to tell him, "You miscreant of a boy, Sadiq ol-Dawleh owns the whole village of Lavizan, are you trying to compare yourself to the grandson of Sadiq ol-Dawleh?" In a few years Sadiq ol-Dawleh's grandkid will be a member of parliament or a government minister, does Ahmad think he's going to make it to the ministry? . . . God preserve us.

. . . I've heard they sent a picture of Atefeh, Ahmad's sister, to the magazine *Today's Woman*, so she could compete in the Miss Iran pageant. Can you believe it! My niece is really out of her league on this one! With all the influential weapons I can bring to bear on the contest—my son-in-law, the few pennies I have—even I didn't let my daughter become Miss Iran, though they begged her to enter . . . I sent her to England. I said, "We are above such tinseled conceits." Who's more beautiful, Atefeh or my Mansureh? Of course my child is the prettier! She's fair-skinned and rosy-cheeked, while Atefeh is dark-complexioned and too tall. Atefeh's never going to be Miss Iran, they didn't even print her picture in the magazine! That got their goat. I said to my niece, I told her, "Aqdas, such things are beneath your dignity." She said Ahmad had bought a camera, took his sister's picture and sent it in. "Anyway," I said, "It just isn't right to send a photo of the legs of a girl descended from the Prophet's family for strange men to inspect." Then she butts in and says it didn't get to that point anyway.

I'd better be going, I don't want to overstay my welcome. Take some chocolate for the kids? No, my dear lady, thank you, though; if you would just be so kind as to keep my parcel, you will have done me a great service. If Aqdas should come to see you, please don't mention anything to her. Don't tell her that the title to the Khademabad property is with you. She'd be hurt. She'll say, "Why doesn't my aunt trust me, the child of her own sister?" When I get back from the trip, if I can't come myself, I'll send Azizollah Khan. Deliver my parcel over to him. No, for heaven's sake! I look on him as I would a brother. Anyway, once upon a time he was my son-in-law. He's a faithful man and he comes around to see us. No, there's not even a hint of what you're suggesting. I'm an old woman . . .

No, really, thank you kindly for offering, though. People are always bringing gifts for my son-in-law; my, how they do carry on—crate after crate of oranges, box after box of dried snacks, with every imaginable kind of fruit and nut in it, some in the shell, some without. They say that people are hired to sit from sunup to sundown to shell sunflower seeds with a little mallet or something. My son-in-law is a postal director; he's in charge of the mails from here clear to Isfahan. He's the director, a real big shot. What of it if he is my daughter's second husband? He was a police lieutenant when he came to ask for her hand, but my daughter brought good fortune upon him and he became the Right Honorable Colonel Asadpur. Azizollah Khan? There was nothing wrong with Azizollah Khan, just that he couldn't have children. He treated little Mansureh like an adopted child. But my daughter—the one he was married to—would say, "I want to have a kid from my own womb, to kick about in my tummy and suck at my breast."

Aqdas:

I was just passing by this way and I thought I'd drop in to say hello and pay my respects, since you, my good woman, do not honor us with your presence. Believe me, since the day that Ahmad left this city, my only sustenance has been the tears I shed. I sit at home and all of a sudden the desire to go out for a walk will possess me, so I step out into the lane and walk down to our neighbor's house, Azar Khanom. I fix her evening meal for her in hopes she'll listen to my woes . . . I go for a walk in Farah park and watch the people, wondering to myself which of them has a son stuck in a far-off land? Which mother suffers so in longing for her baby? When I see the boys sitting under the trees solving math problems, my heart just melts. How often my baby has paced back and forth beneath these trees memorizing his lessons, how often he would sit here to do his math homework. In the end, he didn't pass the college entrance exam. When I realize how empty the house is without him . . . No, no, I swear, I'm not crying . . . there's just something in my eye.

. . . My dear aunt said she made a vow on Ahmad's behalf? What a lie! Let her make a vow on behalf of her skinflint of a son-in-law! The day Ahmad was saying farewell, after I'd knocked myself out to hail a taxi we went from Amirabad to the house of my aunt's son-in-law, Asadpur, in Fawziyeh. He has no shame! He put his hand in his pocket and gave a measly fifty tomans to Ahmad as a bon voyage present. He's made millions upon millions by smuggling—Mansureh's told me all about it. I motioned to Ahmad not to take the money, and he didn't. Later on, of course, he regretted it. My boy wanted to say good-bye to everyone by putting his picture in the paper. It didn't work out. He took a picture in silhouette . . . here, take a look at these. My child is as beautiful as the shining moon! His right eye is half-closed. Scissors? No, it wasn't a pair of scissors that went in his eye. One day he was playing bows and arrows with his sister. Atefeh takes a piece of straw from a reed curtain and fastens a pin on the end of it, aims it at Ahmad and it goes right in the boy's eye. I had gone to the tailor; I'd sooner my legs had been broken! When I got back they were sitting on the doorstep, Ahmad with his hand over his eye . . . How I begged and pleaded with the doctors, prayed and made vows. His right eye is closed just a pinch. He sees all right, but his eye is deformed. What could I do? It was the hand of fate.

. . . With what pain and aggravation we sent him to Alborz College in hopes he would pass the college entrance exam, but he didn't. How much money does a fruit seller in Amirabad street make that he can afford to send his kid to prep school? Please do not let my dear aunt know that I was going every morning to the homes of Americans to do their ironing. I've been doing the same job for four years now.

I came here, if you would be so kind, to have you write Ahmad's address on this envelope in the language of the Americans. Mrs. Barbara always used to write it for me, but now she has gone to America to be with her mother.

She goes every year for three or four months and brings back with her clothes, books and gramophone records. How these women spend their husbands' money! And the husbands are like little lambs; they don't say a word. I iron for Mrs. Barbara. She's introduced me to all her American friends and acquaintances, and I iron for them too. What wonderful houses and lives of leisure they all have! There's Akram, Mrs. Barbara's house-keeper, then there's the chauffeur, and the cook, who wears a white hat and a white coat, just like a doctor, when he goes in the kitchen. Mrs. Barbara's husband is the director-in-chief of I-don't-know-which ministry. The husband of every last one of them is a director general or an assistant direc-tor. They really look after their wives, who don't have to lift a finger around the house. Large sunny gardens, professional gardeners, swimming pools, tennis courts. All this for women who, in their own country, were the chil-dren of some janitor or laundry woman. I don't mean all of them, mind you. This loneliness has made me so spiteful. How I do go on . . .

 . . . One night Mrs. Barbara had company so I went over to help out. First of all we go to buy groceries at this huge supermarket. She takes this buggy, similar to a baby buggy, only made out of wire, and piles it full of meat, turkey, chicken, milk, eggs, sugar, tin cans of every imaginable thing, until it's so full I have to go and get a second buggy. It's no wonder that there's a shortage of everything! That evening I put on an apron and went to work. I counted seventeen Iranian gentlemen, all of them good-looking and muscu-lar, and every last one of them had a foreign wife, from all parts of the globe. They don't mix with Iranian couples. They say that Iranians are barbaric, dirty liars. Well then, my esteemed lady, why did you marry an Iranian? No one dares to ask them . . . Mrs. Akram was saying, "Look, the gentleman with the glass of whiskey has a Swiss wife and is a senior member of the Bureau of Plan Organization. That one there, smoking the cigar, has an important post in the oil company. The other one over there is a university professor." Despite all this, their wives always have their passports in their hands so that whenever they get tired of it, they can run along home. They're always having arguments over the religion and nationality of the children.

Mrs. Barbara has a copper *aftabeh*[3] and a brass basin which she's put in a corner of her living room! She's got a huge wooden spoon and fork, made in Qazvin, which she's nailed on the wall of the dining room . . . God help us!

 . . . As for poor old me, I've ironed so much my wrist has swollen up and I can't move my shoulder. Eight hours' work a day, from seven in the morn-ing to three in the afternoon, just to make a few dollars for my boy. These infidels may pay well, but you've really got to work for it. They even iron their sheets and their dish-cloths! But now that Mrs. Barbara is away, noth-ing's going on. Sometimes I go to iron the shirts of her husband, Gholam-Ali

---

[3]A pitcher originally intended for use in lavatories. [eds.]

Khan. Now that the lady of the house is away, the man has the run of the place. In the evenings he sits on a rug next to the pool, puts his cloak over his shoulders, smokes the *qalyan*,[4] reads the paper, and does the crossword puzzles.

. . . Ahmad used to say, "If I get accepted to study electrical engineering at Aryamehr, I'll stay right here, but if not, I'm going to get to America no matter what! All my buddies have gone, the grandson of Sadiq ol-Dawleh, the son of Mofakhan." Ahmad didn't get accepted at Aryamehr, in fact, he failed the entrance exam altogether. We bought newspaper after newspaper in hopes of finding his name somewhere. I kept thinking, O God, O God, let him be called for military service, but they wouldn't take him on account of his eye. My boy was so upset he developed a fever. His temperature was three-tenths of a degree above normal in the mornings and a half degree by afternoon. He'd put his head in his hands and cry. His legs hurt so much he couldn't walk. The doctors said he'd contracted Malta fever, some said he just had a nervous condition. As soon as talk of going to America came up and I told him I'd dig up the money from under some stone if I had to, but that I'd send him to America, his fever broke and his legs got better. I sold the quilts from my trousseau, my heavy gold necklace, my earrings, my sewing machine. I took my silver out of hock, my television, I sold them all. I went everywhere, groveling and pleading, nobody would lend a helping hand. I knew they had sent Mansureh on a military airplane, so I went to see Officer Asadpur and fell at his feet. I swore upon all that was holy in hopes of getting him to send Ahmad on a military plane, but he could not be prevailed upon. In the end, Ahmad went to Bushire and took a steamer. Mrs. Barbara arranged it for him, she even got him admitted to a university. She sent all the letters and did all the paperwork herself and even gave him a letter to take to her mother and sister. My boy worked as a crewman on board the ship, cleaning up the barf of the passengers until they got to America. He's been working in America, too, but what jobs! He washes dishes, does gardening, drives old ladies around, washes cars, washes dogs, drags hotel guests' suitcases up and down the stairs. God bless him, the poor thing once wrote me that he only had thirty-seven dollars left. He still hasn't learned the American language real well.

If only he had been accepted to study electrical engineering at Aryamehr, he'd have stayed right here, but now he just suffers, and in a foreign country of all places. Even if he had been accepted at Aryamehr, there was a student strike every time you turned round and the exams were always being cancelled, and my boy would have either had a nervous break-down or they'd have come to tell me he'd been killed or something. That's just what happened with Azar's boy; he was accepted at National

---

[4] A water-pipe. [eds.]

University, but when he'd set off for school in the mornings she was like to die of fear until he'd get back.

. . . Anyway, thank God that Ahmad wasn't forced to become a nurse like Mansureh and work for peanuts. You know, Mansureh had just turned fifteen when my cousin married Officer Asadpur, and my aunt had to account somehow for Mansureh's presence in her household. She had been whispering to me about marrying Mansureh off to Ahmad, but Ahmad said, "Mother, I won't take a wife until I go off to America and finish my studies." So, my aunt told Asadpur that Mansureh was his wife's sister. Later on they made out that Mansureh was found on the doorstep as a baby, which got the poor child all confused and upset. Now she's gone off to England, where she suffers still. Poor thing, she sits by the bedside of the dead till daybreak, brings bedpans for the patients, changes the sheets.

. . . That Mansureh's studying medicine!? I bet that's what my dear aunt told you. There's not a truthful bone in my auntie's body. She's busy morning till night weaving herself a tangled web of lies and half-truths. Mansureh herself sent me a letter saying, "Cousin, if you only knew what I go through from sunup to sundown. I was so pleased with myself to be going abroad. Going abroad, huh! I'm rooming with four other girls, three Indians and a Pakistani, and the Pakistani won't speak with the Indians. We've got to scrub the floors each day and play the maid, and on top of that, we're supposed to smile at the patients." She wrote that the people over there wouldn't dream of doing such lowly work, so they lure innocent kids from the four corners of the earth to do it for them. You can't eat the food there, either. It's mostly boiled fish and shriveled-up potatoes. At the end of her letter she wrote: "How hard one has to toil to reach Behesht-e Zahra." Do you see what circumstances our precious children have fallen into? Today they're working their fingers to the bone studying and tomorrow, when they get back, who knows what kind of a job they'll be able to get.

I tell myself, O God, O God, let an American girl fall in love with Ahmad so my boy can stay over there. There's a hint of it in the air, too. He works in the house of an old American woman . . . Mrs. Barbara's mother? No, a friend of Mrs. Barbara's mother. Mrs. Barbara's mother is poor folk. After Ahmad went to her house, he wrote that she didn't have a house, just a little room filled with more junk than can be had in a Syrian bazaar, a hodgepodge jumble of furniture. The only thing in the room of interest was a Turkoman carpet that had come from Iran . . .

. . . I think—that is I should say, I pray—that the granddaughter of this old woman who is Ahmad's landlord will go sweet on him. One night he saved her from the part of town where the blacks live . . . I'd really love it if a girl like Mrs. Barbara is in store for Ahmad. If you only knew how Mrs. Barbara dotes on Ghloam-Ali Khan. I've told you her bad points, it's only fair to tell you about the good as well. Whenever her man comes home from the ministry, she runs out to greet him, gives him a big kiss, hugs him, fixes him a drink and puts it in his hand, massages his temples, sits on his lap. The relatives of Mrs. Barbara's husband are all country bumpkins; Gholam-Ali Khan is the only one that turned out well and was able to go to America. Mrs. Barbara had an artist paint her picture. She's standing in the middle with blonde hair and a red dress, and all around her stand the female relatives of her husband in their *chadors,* pointing out Mrs. Barbara to one another. It looks like they are all in awe of her great good fortune.

. . . When my dear aunt despaired of us, she sent Mansureh to England. Now, whenever she sits down to chat, she says, "Ahmad wanted my daughter, but I didn't approve." May I be struck blind if I tell a word of a lie—it was we who didn't approve!

You've finished writing them? A thousand thanks! That's ten envelopes for the next ten letters . . . Are you kidding? My dear aunt's son-in-law can't read American writing . . . A colonel!? It's just like her to say that. He's the policeman at the post office at the Dawlat intersection in Qolhak district . . . I told you what tall tales she tells. They have an orderly and a maid? I've never heard anything so ridiculous . . . She washes the kids' diapers every day herself while my cousin is slaving in the kitchen. Ahmad used to say that the signpost to Auntie's house was a clothesline decked with diapers. In the autumn of her life, dear Auntie is in league with Aziz, her daughter's first husband, selling smuggled goods. Officer Asadpur lends them a hand too. I've heard that Aziz still hankers after my cousin. He went with my aunt to Shiraz and brought back opium. Heroin, hashish, they smuggle everything. By God, I was afraid they'd get a hold of Ahmad and corrupt the boy. That's why I practically killed myself to send him away.

. . . My dear aunt brought a package to our house and asked that we keep it for her. She said it was cashmere and some silk brocade and silver and the deed to some property, but I know it was opium. She said, in return for the favor, I'll pray for you when I visit the Imam Reza. But she's not the praying kind. She's going to Mashhad to get some opium. I wouldn't take the package from her. I said, "My husband will come home and give me heck for taking it." She said, "Just keep it two or three days, Azizollah will come and get it from you. You'll recognize him by the piece of paper I'll give him. I'll have my daughter write on it, 'May God be with you always.'" Nothing's sacred, they'll drag the name of God into anything. I wouldn't take the package. I was afraid.

AQDAS: Hello, Auntie dear, it's so nice to see you. You know I worship the ground you walk on!
EFFAT OL-MOLUK: And hello to you; let me kiss that radiant face of yours!
AQDAS: Auntie dear, I dreamed of you last night. May God strike me blind if I'm lying. You were sitting next to a pool filled with water, and it was full of red and gold fish. Your grandchildren were there, too.
EFFAT OL-MOLUK: God willing, it's a good omen. Water in a dream means light.

AQDAS: Where is my cousin? How are her precious children?

EFFAT OL-MOLUK: Your cousin has gone to the public bath, for a ritual purification. The kids are asleep.

AQDAS: Auntie dear, God blacken my face, but I think I may have jinxed your grandchildren in my dream. They've gotten so cute and chubby, I'm afraid of the evil eye on their account. I've come to say you should burn some wild rue to protect them.

EFFAT OL-MOLUK: Consider it done.

AQDAS: May you never know misfortune.

EFFAT OL-MOLUK: Well, dear, you've brightened up my home with your presence. How are you, and what news do you bring?

AQDAS: Well, since you mention it, if I don't tell my troubles to you, Auntie dear, who can I tell them to? Ahmad's no longer working for that old American lady.

EFFAT OL-MOLUK: Didn't you tell me that an American girl had fallen in love with him?

AQDAS: Oh, Auntie, I may have said a thing or two—you sometimes have to in order to keep up with the neighbors, but who's kidding who? What American girl would fall in love with my skin-and-bones son? American women only marry robust Iranian men in perfect health so that they can pop out flawless, good-looking, international children. In one letter he wrote me, "Mother, compared to American guys, I'm a pullet. They sometimes grow to be two meters tall and drink four glasses of milk a day. Once I drank two glasses of milk and got diarrhea."

EFFAT OL-MOLUK: How many times have I told you to take my adopted girl as a wife for your son, that they would live here happily ever after and you can find a job or a source of income for Ahmad? You're very clever, all to no good purpose. You've been to school through the eighth grade, you read the newspapers, you watch television. You should have known better.

AQDAS: It wasn't in the stars, Auntie.

EFFAT OL-MOLUK: Nowadays Mansureh can barely walk, they've got her running around like a dog, eight hours a day of nursing the sick . . . I'll get up and make some tea.

AQDAS: Don't trouble yourself, instead help me solve my problem. I've got to send some money for Ahmad anyway I can. I can no longer iron—I was hiding this from you—I can no longer iron at the Americans' houses; my shoulder is about to explode with pain and my wrist is swollen. See? I was making eighty to one hundred dollars a month sweating over the iron, but I can't do it anymore.

EFFAT OL-MOLUK: (*Silence*)

AQDAS: Auntie dear, I'll be glad to take your package now, no matter what's in it.

EFFAT OL-MOLUK: Oh, go on! I only mentioned that package business to see how much my niece is willing to do for her aunt.

Aqdas: Auntie dear, you are dearer to me than my own eyes. I'd like to—not be partners, you see, because I have no money in hand to become a part-ner—work with you and Azizollah Khan, so that I can somehow send a hundred dollars a month for Ahmad. My boy has been reduced to eating bread with hot water and vinegar for the last three weeks and I'm afraid he'll starve to death. What a mistake I made! You know that Ahmad's life is my life, if he . . . he's dearer to me than all my other children and Karim Aqa put together.

Effat ol-Moluk: Well, I'll tell you, I really can't do anything to help. Aziz and I don't have much business to speak of that you should become our partner. I probably see Aziz about once a year, anyway once a month at the most. After all, he was once my son-in-law. The poor fellow hasn't yet taken another wife and he's fond of his ex-wife's children. What can I do? He buys lollipops for the girls, holds them, takes them for walks on the wooden bridge. Officer Asadpur doesn't have time for such things. He's always saying he's on call. Aziz, well, he takes on the role of a father, the kids call him uncle. Besides that, Mansureh is his daughter, too. If you could see the letters she writes for Aziz . . .

Aqdas: Auntie, I'm family, I won't say a word to anyone. Remember that day at lunch when you vowed to give five thousand tomans to Ahmad if this deal came off without any headache? Azizollah was there, too. After lunch he took his trousers off and put on Officer Asadpur's pajamas. You brought opium for him to smoke. I was clearing away the dishes, his back was to me. My cousin was giving her breast to her baby. Azizollah Khan said, "It's this kind. As long as we don't get caught . . . " You gestured to him and he stopped in mid-sentence.

Effat ol-Moluk: God strike me down if I'm lying, I don't have any package here that relates to any kind of business transaction. I was just trying to test you. . . .

Aqdas: Do you want me to tell you the truth?

Effat ol-Moluk: You haven't been lying up to this point, have you?

Aqdas: Mansureh told me about the whole thing . . . She said you bought an airplane ticket for her with the money you made by smuggling. She said, thanks be to God that she was leaving this house of lies, deceit, and drug-smuggling.

Effat ol-Moluk: There's an old saying: "You can raise another's flesh and blood as your own, but you can never win its loyalty."

Aqdas: Thank God I am still young, I'll find work . . . Even if I have to dig it out of the earth . . . I'll go and be a housekeeper for the Americans.

Effat ol-Moluk: You mean you'll be their maid . . .

Aqdas: It's a sight more honorable than smuggling and breaking the law. I'm earning my bread with the sweat of my brow . . . I read in a magazine that mankind became civilized through the fruits of his labor.

Effat ol-Moluk: I can hear the children, they've woken up. They're so sweet, one like sugar, the other like honey.

❀ Discussion and Writing

1. Comment on the two women's monologues to the silent listener: what is Effat ol-Moluk's purpose in narrating the family history; what is Aqdas's motivation for the visit; what is the function of the listener?
2. Compare the two versions explaining why Ahmed and Mansureh did not get married, and discuss the implications of the two accounts.
3. Why does Effat ol-Moluk consider nursing demeaning? Why does Aqdas wish for an American wife for Ahmed? Discuss the implied social norms.
4. Analyze the attitudes reflected in the two women's narratives regarding: the social facade; influential contacts; the mothers' bragging; family relations; education abroad; the attitude toward foreigners.
5. Discuss the impact of the dialogue between the two women: what does it reveal about them and their preceding monologues. Between the two, who is more trustworthy?
6. In what way is the opening quotation relevant to the story?

❀ Research and Comparison

Interdisciplinary Discussion Question: Research twentieth-century Iranian history, concentrating on Western involvement in the politics of the country. Discuss the responses of either the intellectuals and artists or the religious fundamentalists to Westernization.

Etel Adnan
(b. 1925)
Lebanon

Etel Adnan was born in Lebanon; her father was of Muslim Syrian descent and her mother of Christian Greek. As she has said in an interview, "the landscape of my childhood represented two poles, two cultures, two different worlds, and I liked both." She attended a convent school until the age of 16, but World War II interrupted her education, and she went to work for the French Information Bureau. After studying at the newly opened Institute of Letters, she taught at a girls' school before going on to Paris and the Sorbonne in 1950. In 1955, she moved to the United States, where she studied at Harvard and the University of California at Berkeley. Between 1959 and 1972, she taught philosophy at Dominican College in California. And between 1972 and 1976, she lived in Beirut, where she worked as literary editor of a Beirut daily. Beirut was and has remained a major metaphor in her personal mythology and in her writing.

Adnan is a poet, essayist, novelist, and painter. Although she writes in French and English, she has also said that it is "only through painting that [she] can express herself in Arabic." Her *Arab Apocalypse* (1980), for instance, is filled with drawings, letters, and hieroglyphs interspersed within the text. A writer who crosses and blurs linguistic, national, and sexual boundaries, Adnan relentlessly examines the human condition under the enormous stress of political repression and global crisis that has characterized the last half of the twentieth century. Such works as her novel *Sitt Marie-Rose* (1978) have therefore been accepted texts at universities throughout the United States.

The rhythms of her work match the sense of time and quality of persistence she insists on. She writes in long arcs, taking up an idea, examining and advancing it, takes up another, then returns to the first. "In the Heart of the Heart of Another Country" is a self-contained excerpt from within one of these long arcs. It is taken from an autobiographical writing of the same name.

In the Heart of the Heart of Another Country

Place

So I have sailed the seas and come . . .
                    to B . . .
a town by the sea, in Lebanon. It is seventeen years later. My absence has been an exile from an exile. I'm of those people who are always doing what somebody else is doing . . . but a few weeks earlier. A fish in a warm sea. No house for shelter, but a bed, from house to house, and clothes crumpled on a single shelf. I am searching for love.

Weather

In Beirut there is one season and a half. Often, the air is still. I get up in the morning and breathe heavily. The winter is damp. My bones ache. I have a neighbor who spits blood when at last it rains.

My House

My father built a house when I was a child near the German school so I could go to it. The school moved out as he finished the roof. Ever since, my property has been rented for the cheapest rent in town. The laws are such that I can't push out the tenants. Anyway, I am afraid of houses as of tombs.

A Person

My other neighbor (from neighbor to neighbor I shall cover the world) sells birds. And cats. A Siamese cat was born to him, and was really Siamese: it had two heads, four ears, two bodies, two pairs of four legs, two tails. And boy, were they glued! He has on sale a little monkey which has been growing for the last 17 and half years. The store is in front of a newspaper which went broke. All the windows are since blind.

Wires

They are few, and, as there are no trees in Beirut, the wire-poles are dead, geometric semblances for trees. Dead archetypes. As for the birds, Lebanese hunters have killed them all. Now they are killing the Syrian birds, too.

The Church

We have churches, mosques, and synagogues. All equally empty at night. On week-ends, many flies desert their gardens. People come in.

My House

I should say my side of the bed. Half a bed makes a big house at night. My dreams have the power to extend space and make me live in the greatest mansions. During the day it doesn't matter. There are many streets, a few remaining sidewalks, and, yes, the cafe "Express," in which I move, hunted by memories.

Politics

Oh, it's too much, too much. Once I dreamed of becoming the new Ibn Khaldoun of America or the de Tocqueville of the Arabs. Now I work for a newspaper and cover the most menial things. So I don't understand how it is that there are kings without kingdoms and Palestinians without a Palestine. As for the different scandals, they do not matter to me. Why should I care that some thieves steal from other thieves. Should I?

People

The Lebanese go on two feet, like the Chinese for example; sometimes, on four, to pick up a dime under the table. Their country is small, their desires too, and their love affairs. Only their cars are big. Detroit made Chevies and Buicks. All the unsold Buicks of America are on our roads. So, in this country, you only see the heads of the people. Their bodies are carefully washed and stored away. As for the women, there aren't any. They all consider themselves as being the other half of their men. With one exception.

Vital Data

The most interesting things in Beirut are the absent ones. The absence of an opera house, of a football field, of a bridge, of a subway, and, I was going to say, of the people and of the government. And, of course, the absence of absence of garbage.

Education

Everybody speaks Arabic, French, English, Armenian, Greek and Kurdish. Sometimes one language at a time, sometimes all of them together. And even the children are financiers.

Business

Merchants sell to other merchants and buy from them. Men sell women to other men and buy women from them. Women sell women to women. And everybody sells a child: for vanity, for money, for pleasure. In the tall buildings of Hamra children get assaulted under the eyes of their parents. Parents thank God when they get the money.

My House, This Place and Body

There was a house in a eucalyptus grove. My father and I sneaked in, and in the middle of the night a guard came to awaken us. I advised my father to offer him money and he did: he gave him 900 pounds. "I didn't ask for that much," said the guard. My father, then, disappeared. Don't talk to me about my body. It has been battered, cut open; discs, nerves, and tissues have been removed. My belly, a zoological garden. My eyes, poor lighthouses, and my mind a rocky and barren garden. exactly like this place and the unexisting house.

The Same Person

I went to the store, and, feeling sorry for the caged birds, I told the guy: "How can you sell animals?" He replied: "Aren't you an animal too?" So I lowered my eyes and admired him.

Weather

I used to love the heat, and, even now, the sweat. My sheets used to get wet and I, rolling on them, my body in ecstasy. I was then sixteen, or a bit more. I kissed the air of this town with passion and carried it in my arms. I couldn't love a man bacause I loved the sea. Then, I went away, and the spell broke. The weather aged, got wrinkles, its bones and marrow became soft. It is nowadays like breathing mud. When it rains, I can't feel happy for the trees. They do not exist. So I feel happy for the buildings. They get an imperfect bath. As for me, the eternal sun has worked like a siren on my brain.

It has eaten up my intelligence. The dust has filed my nails. Cockroaches run over my paintings, and I get up at night to kill them and to keep them away at the edge of my dream. But the dampness is constant, and invisible amoebae constantly dance in the air. One feels always a bit swollen in Beirut. It is a pregnancy of bad omen. You have to go to a village called Sannine to start breathing properly. But you never stay too long up there. You miss the weather of Beirut.

Place

I left this place by running all the way to California. An exile which lasted for years. I came back on a stretcher and felt here a stranger, exiled from my former exile. I am always away from something and somewhere. My senses left me one by one to have a life of their own. If you meet me in the street, don't be sure it is me. My center is not in the solar system.

People

This is the cruellest place. A man in a motor boat hit a swimmer and sped away. The skull was broken. A large space of blood covered the sea.

Painters rushed to the scene to make a painting for sale. A girl was killed by her brother because she smiled to her lover. A house in the city was set on fire because they wanted the tenants out. A rebellion has started, the rebellion of the rich against the poor. Yes, to make sure that the latter do not multiply, and rather be dead, the sooner the better.

My House My Cat My Company

From every drawer, the blood of my spirit is spilled. My eyes, anguished by the light, have cruel particles of dust covering them. Noises come in as demons. No crime in the newspaper is as gory as the noises that surround my bed. It is an eternal beat.

MAO is the name of my cat, who has been rescued from a friend. He sleeps on my left side, watches my heartbeats. At night, when he sometimes runs away, I have to go out and look for him. Most often, he runs out at about four in the morning, when the Koranic prayer fills the air, and when its lamentation seems endless and fills me with sacred terror. That terror is communicated somehow to MAO whose hair stands up. He shivers against me when we come home.

One morning my breast was bare and he put his paw on it. It was a moment of perfection.

So I gave him away, but he came back.

I live with a woman who shares with me my passion for ants, from the day I told her that my father had taught me to watch them attentively in order to imitate them later in life. This was my education. I was told that ants had all the necessary qualities; they were tiny and carried weights bigger than their size. They never slept. Industrious, they stuck together, never doing anything alone. And when you killed them, they multiplied. So my friend fell in love with my father for having been so right. But he is dead. The ants keep me company, coming from under the flower pots all the way into the closets, glasses, spoons. They stop at the door of the refrigerator. Their brain is tinier than the head of a pin. So angels must exist.

I am a species all by myself. That's why no fish comes to swim in my territorial waters. I have no enemies.

I live with a woman who has a recurring dream: each night she goes to unearth Akhnaton and carries his coffin all over the house. The young king has a nocturnal journey on her arms. His solar boat had been shattered by his murderers. She weeps for him, sometimes, during the day too, but she does not go around like the women from America in pink slippers and bobby pins to the supermarket. No. She uses silverware, puts salt and pepper on her meat, and she tells me that she does not proceed from a source of light but from a source of shadows.

As for me, I told her that I find my reason to be in the configurations of matter.

I love the different objects I encounter with violence. I have a passion for cars. My spoon is to me what the angel used to be to Jacob: my moment of truth. People throw their fingernails away, and I look at these pieces of matter with awe: transparent like alabaster, tiny like African ants, pale as erased memories. I throw them away with a tremendous melancholy. I would like to be buried with St. James Infirmary playing. Or something like that, maybe a song by Oum Kalsoum.

Then I would like to resurrect. Death would appear as short as the time for the batting of an eyelash. I am of those who like resurrection, and I am not alone in that; I hear people saying it, when I walk, and mostly in New York.

Politics

The State. A man and a woman, together, already form a state. There is everything between them: a principle of authority, a government, laws of behaviour, embassy and representation, diplomacy, weapons, periods of peace and war.

They also constitute, to make things harder than for matters of state, two different species. When they meet, they sometimes ignore each other.

Sometimes, they climb on each other like a pair of monkeys. At other times, a current of cool air passes from the one to the other: there is love. And then, there are times when, at their contact, a short-circuit happens, and they burn each other and leave nothing behind them but a spot on the sun. Youssef el Khal said one day that I was a poet. Yes. I am the poet in the heart of the city. A dot. I am the poet of the here and now.

But, being a woman, I am invisible. I have to hide my obsession for ants. They pursue me. If a woman went to the market place and cried for help because ants were climbing up between her legs, some men would throw themselves between her thighs, and search wildly for the tiny beasts, in order to relieve her from her fear, and hurt her, too. But she would be arrested and thrown into an insane asylum until she hallucinated and the water which fell from the faucet became a thick stream of black ants. In that case, I would pull up my blanket of flies and sleep.

More Vital Data

Like a salmon, I came back here to die. But this place is not a place. I am unable to die.

By the big dam of the Columbia River I saw a salmon swim upstream and break itself on the concrete slopes of the dam. The large Columbia River is a stream which makes its mark on the universe.

If I came to Beirut from that far away, it is to bemoan the Pacific. My passion is for the beach. Pisces-born, I am the Indian salmon originating in an Arab land.

In Hamra street, in Bourj and Bab Edriss, people are breathing gasoline, and they like it; it is still cheaper than water in a country of drought.

Education

Children are taught that little boys are superior to little girls. Yes. When Hassan beats Nedjma, Nedjma is beaten by her father for having been beaten, and this, ad infinitum . . .

And nobody ever tells them, oh never! that a rat is as human as a cat. And the slow process of castration starts on the wooden benches of the classrooms. We need schools without walls. We need to be a nation of swimmers. We need the end of nations. The end of ends.

In this avaricious country, even the moon looks like a coin, because children are taught numbers. As for me, I learned arithmetic by killing ants and counting their dead little bodies.

❋ **Discussion and Writing**

1. Explain the narrator's phrase as an "exile from an exile."
2. Analyze the metaphor of the house, the ants, the cat in this excerpt.
3. What aspects of life in Beirut does the author contemplate? Analyze the descriptions, commenting on the author's feelings and tone.
4. Examine the implications of "Yes. I am the poet in the heart of the city. A dot. I am the poet of the here and now."

❋ **Research and Comparison**

Explore Etel Adnan's writing, and comment on the themes and techniques that reflect her concerns.

Ahmad Shamlu
(b. 1925)
Iran

Ahmad Shamlu was born in Tehran, Iran, but as the son of a military man, he grew up in several provincial towns. The family was poor, and Shamlu had only 11 years of formal schooling. By the age of 14 he had begun working in journalism, a professional interest he maintained as editor and founder of various publications, including eminent literary journals. He was quite young when he became an ardent nationalist, and he was imprisoned twice, the first time for protesting against the occupation of Allied forces during World War II. The second ocassion followed the fall of Mohammad Mosaddeq (1880–1967), the prime minister who nationalized the British-owned oil industry in 1951 and was overthrown by Western-backed forces in 1953. Mosaddeq remained a hero to many of his countrymen, who, like Shamlu, had anticipated an independent dignified equitable future for Iran and its people. As the Iranian government became more repressive, however, Shamlu left the country and has been living in exile.

Regarded as one of the major, and most influential, contemporary poets and translators, Shamlu has been actively engaged in gathering old and traditional Persian stories, ballads, and games. In his capacity as editor, he has also encouraged the younger generation by providing them access to his journals. Respected as an innovative, lyrical poet, he has expanded the Persian canon in his experiments with versification, language, and theme, and when he merges personal, political, and social issues, he speaks to, and for, the concerns of many Iranian intellectuals.

The Gap*

To be born
on the dark spear
like the open birth of a wound.
To travel the unique exodus of opportunity
                    throughout
                              in chains

---

*Translated by Ahmad Karimi-Hakkak

to burn on one's flame
to the very last spark
on the flame of a reverence
found by the slaves
in the dust of the way
                thus
thus red and coquettish
to bloom on the thorn-bush of blood
and thus tall and proud
to pass through the scourge-field of degradation
and to travel through to the extreme of hatred . . .

Oh, who am I speaking of?
the living with no reason, we are
conscious to the reason of their death, they.

❋ Discussion and Writing

1. Examine the imagery and comment on who is being referred to in the first segment of the poem.
2. Distinguish between "we" and "they"; contrast the travels of both. What is the significance of their journey?
3. Explore the relationship between the two factions; what does the image of "the thorn-bush of blood" symbolize?
4. Interpret the last three lines about reasoning, and comment on the implication of the gap between the two.

❋ Research and Comparison

Interdisciplinary Discussion Question: Research the history of relations between Iran and Iraq, focusing on the effect of their wars on people's lives.

Abdallah al-Baraduni
(b. 1929)
Yemen

Abdallah al-Baraduni was born in Baraddun in North Yemen. Although he lost his sight as a result of having had smallpox when he was six, his blindness did not stop him from becoming an unusually fine student. His early education in language and religion took place at the Shamsia Mosque school in the town of Dhamar; and in Sanaa, he took a degree in Arabic Language and Sharia (Islamic law). After teaching for a time, he worked for the Broadcasting Service in Sanaa. Considered one of the major poets of the Arabian Peninsula, he has been concerned with social and political issues in the Arab world. His poetry, noted for its use of paradox and irony, illuminates the social inequities currently oppressing the Arab communities, and the tragic consequences.

Answers to One Question*

Why is that time past is yet to be?
It is because what's called futurity
Has passed away, a long, long time ago
It is because our faces are backward set
Seeking for lost identity—even so
Because the singer greatly loved and yet
What thing it was he loved, he did not know.

❋ Discussion and Writing

1. Explore the nature of the singer's search.
2. What is meant by the "time past" that "is yet to be"? Explain how the future has already been. What is the impact of the collapse of the past and the future?

❋ Research and Comparison

Like this poem, many selections in this anthology concern the collapse of time, e.g., "The Wagon," "Clocks Like Horses," "A Pearl." Compare the treatment of time and the theme of continuity in these works.

Shimon Ballas
(b. 1930)
Israel

Shimon Ballas was born in Baghdad, Iraq, and 20 years later moved to Israel, where he is regarded as one of the leading novelists writing at the present time. He continued working in Arabic for more than a decade and

*Translated by Sargon Boulus and John Heath-Stubbs

then turned to Hebrew. As his fiction has developed, however, he has continued to explore the current political and psychological experience of the Arab world, illuminating the condition of both exiles and those who remain in their native land. Along with seven novels and two collections of short stories, he has published a major study of Arabic literature.

Imaginary Childhood (Epilogue)*

I grew up in the Christian Quarter of Baghdad, in two houses, separated only by a narrow alley. We moved out of the first house when I was six; I spent all my school years in the second house, from the first grade until the end of high school. The first house was one of three in a *cul de sac;* it was in the middle and its walls hugged those of the neighbors from either side. On our right, there lived a well-to-do Jewish family whose house was the biggest and most luxurious in the lane. A cone-shaped lantern made of cut stained glass and crowned with a serrated tin plate hung in front of it. At nightfall, when I heard the guard's heavy footsteps, I would rush toward the window to see his shadow in the darkness as he leaned a wooden ladder against the wall and climbed up to light the lantern. The flame from the wick would leap across his burnished, withered face, sending an eerie flash across his dark eyes. Then I would see him come down, hoist the ladder on to his back and disappear down the alley. I eagerly awaited the ritual to continue and when the long whistle shook the night out of its slumber, I would feel chills going down my back. I don't know how old I was at the time, but I do remember that long before we left that house the colorful lantern was replaced by a small electric lamp, turned on at the same time every night by a mysterious hand.

To our left lived an elderly Armenian couple, refugees of the disturbances in Turkey. They had a smoothly polished copper knocker on the front door; late at night, the door would open as the knocker struck. Strange songs drifted out of the house, sad songs accompanied at times by the commotion of men and women's wild laughter. The landlady, a short, ungainly woman, was the uncrowned queen of the lane. The grown-ups respected her and the kids called her Auntie. The kids particularly liked her because she provided refuge for them whenever their parents got angry. She offered them sweets without sparing her admonition, but her rebukes were as sweet and gentle to the ear as her treats [were] to the palate. She had a way about her that fascinated me, an air of mystery that surrounded her life. During the summer, she used to sit by the entrance to her house, embroidering lace. When she saw me watching her, she would ask me to come over and sit with her while she told me stories from another world. Her voice was clear, though it wavered a little; a gold tooth gleamed in her mouth and her laughter gushed

*Translated by Ammiel Alcalay

forth like a gurgling spring. She was a singer for the Turks, and her portrait from those days, in a long, white dress, stood on a square table between two large divans in the courtyard. Her husband, who was quite a bit older than she was, listened to her stories silently, occasionally getting up to pat my head with his cool, bony hand. Odd guests visited the house and spoke to her in their language while I—left to myself—was proud to see her as the center of attraction, with everyone's eyes fixed only on her and their ears cocked for whatever she might say. When I was asked to go home, I would get up despondently, dragging my feet. Her husband would put a piece of candy in my hand and accompany me to the door before shutting it. I never knew what went on behind that locked door and when I would ask my mother, she would reprimand me and tell me to keep quiet.

This aging singer was a remarkable woman. She grew up in a foreign land and took refuge in a foreign land when her people were struck by evil. Later on, I portrayed her in a story called "Aunt Ghawni."

Our house was old, with a heavy black door in a wooden frame that creaked every time I leaned against it to open it. There were two cellars in the house, an upper cellar and a lower cellar. The upper cellar's festive time came during the summer months, when we used to stow ourselves away in there during the hottest part of the day; it was always cool and an invigorating breeze flowed through the vents. As for the lower cellar, I was afraid to get near it. There were many stairs leading down to it, the last of which faded away in the darkness. In the spring, up till mid-summer, it would fill with water, and a corps of snakes would emerge and spread every which way throughout the house to find a hiding place. I used to lie down by my mother on a mat spread across the floor as I saw a long line of snakes slither by under a wooden footstool near the wall. In those days I wasn't yet aware of how dangerous snakes were so I could amuse myself by watching this incredible spectacle. Later on I got to know how dangerous they were, when I started to grasp the stories told by the grown-ups. I remember a story my mother used to tell me often when I was a kid. She went into the attic, which served as a storage place for old things, and when she moved a wicker basket, a spotted snake leapt at her. Transfixed by fear, the upright snake ferociously hissed at her. In that awful moment, she only remembered one thing, the magic incantation she had learned from her parents, and which had come down to them from their ancestors: "Home snake, home snake, don't hurt us and we won't hurt you." And indeed, the snake accepted her supplication and backed off, coiling itself up on the floor in a great circle.

The people who moved into the house after us were not afraid of snakes. The father of the family, a carpenter by profession, was a seasoned snake hunter. When he was younger and worked as a carpenter's apprentice, his Muslim employer gave him "snake water" to drink, made by dipping a poisonous snake into a jar of water for twenty-four hours. This water served as a remedy against snake bites and whoever drank it became immune for the rest of their days. He would hold the head of a snake between his fingers, with the snake's body wrapped around his arm like a spring. But he never killed the snakes he caught. He set the snakes that weren't poisonous free in the fields; as for the poisonous ones, he plucked out their fangs. I saw him do it on the roof. He brought a piece of cloth right up to the snake's mouth and when the snake stuck its teeth into it, he snatched the cloth away and pulled out the hollow, venomous fangs.

The second house we moved to was also crawling with snakes. They fed on mice and found shelter amongst the wooden ceiling rafters. We could hear them crawling over our heads, with their incessant, loathesome hissing. A big black snake made its home in the kitchen and on hot days it would venture out of its lair in search of water. We learned the magic incantation and we used to chant it like a prayer.

But other, more pleasant strains also resounded in my childhood. These were the ringing bells. There were many churches clustered in our quarter and their bells rang for prayer at a fixed hour of the day. I got to know the sound of the bells and I could recognize each and every one of them. The big bell of the Catholic church made slow, heavy sounds, like the stride of a priest on his way to the sanctuary. Compared to that, the fine, modest ringing of the small bell at the Armenian church seemed speedy. On New Year's, Easter and other holidays, the bells made the windowpanes shake, violating me with a strange feeling of dread and happiness. Sometimes a solitary bell could be heard ringing sadly at an odd hour. It was then I knew that a funeral procession was making its way to the church. Many funerals passed under our window. The young boys would appear first, at the twist in the lane, in their white gowns, holding candles; after them strode the priests in their black robes, with one in the middle, conducting the procession; after that, the pallbearers followed and behind them came the family and other mourners. The sound of their prayer hushed as they entered the lane and only picked up again as they reached its end. They proceeded in silence the whole length of the alley and the coffin, whose lid was adorned with a small crucifix, was borne by the men. Passersby stopped near the walls, Christians crossed themselves while Muslims and Jews observed the procession with their heads bowed.

The trumped-up voices of professional mourners couldn't be heard at Christian funerals. This was strictly the terrain of Jews and Muslims. Sometimes on my way to school I encountered Jewish or Muslim funerals; they seemed quite the same. The coffin was borne along on people's shoulders as the mourners beat their chests and ripped their hair out, and everyone hustled and scurried about in a great frenzy. I was drawn to the magnificent splendor of Christian rituals. I loved their houses of prayer and on the holidays, I would slip in and watch the Mass, enveloped by the smoke of the incense, rocking to the waves of the organ.

There was a monastery of the French mission that I often visited. This monastery, which was also a school for girls, gave piano lessons in the afternoon. I passed the monastery several times a day and longed to see the piano that brought forth such sweet melodies into the world. But I was apprehensive about going in because of the stern guard that always sat on a stool by the gate and never let any strangers in. I was surprised when I accompanied our maid one morning to go buy milk at the dairy on the outskirts of the neighborhood, and she stopped by to chat with the guard. I pulled at her sleeve and whispered my request into her ear, but she dismissed me with a smile and just kept on talking. I wouldn't let go of her until she agreed to hear what I wanted. The guard smiled and promised that he would let me go in if I came back in the afternoon. I reported to him right after I got out of school.

"Too early," he said, "come later."

When I came back, I found the Mother Superior standing at the door. He had told her about me and she offered me both her hands as she pulled me in. She asked if I studied French at school and when I told her I did, she said: "You're an intelligent boy."

She took me up to the second floor and led me into a spacious room that looked like a regular classroom, except for the black piano standing on a platform near the front, with a nun and a student sitting at it. They stopped playing while we stood at the doorway and the Mother Superior said something that, in my confusion, I couldn't quite understand. Then she led me to a bench and left. The teacher nodded to me before going on with her lesson; I shrank back into myself, anxious and excited. From then on, I visited the monastery almost every day. The Mother Superior always welcomed me with a smile and asked me all kinds of questions. She was a beautiful woman and the white cowl adorning her habit lent her a saintly grace. Everyone, including me, addressed her as "Ma Mere." I was a bashful kid and didn't say much but she wouldn't let me evade her questions. Sometimes, when she had free time, she called me into her small office and gave me a long lecture that I couldn't make heads or tails out of.

"You're still young," she would tell me with an apologetic smile, "you'll understand when you grow up." Naturally, I did understand many things as I grew up, but I no longer took an interest in the ways of the monastery nor did I seek out the company of the old nun. I was occupied by other things that would determine the course of my life.

Many Jewish families lived in the Christian Quarter and their presence was felt along its lanes and alleyways on holidays and the Sabbath. On Rosh Hashanah, we dressed in white, from head to toe; on Purim, we roamed around with pistols, shooting every which way; and on Passover, we vented our anger at the Gentiles. We didn't really grasp the meaning of why we did certain things; we never knew, and to this day I still do not know, why we flew kites on the Ninth of Av. It was a day of fasting and prayer for the grown-ups, but a joyous holiday for the kids. Lentils, a dish symbolizing destruction and lamentation, were prepared at home, but for us it became a delicacy that we looked forward to with great excitement. More than anything, though, we loved the Ninth of Av because of the kites. There wasn't a Jewish kid who didn't fly a kite on the Ninth of Av. Of course, it was one of our favorite things to do throughout the summer anyway, but on this special day the kites took on a ceremonial significance. We put them together ourselves, adorning them with colorful tails and we competed to see who could make the most beautiful kite that would sit best in the sky. On summer nights, the skies of Baghdad would fill with kites in an abundance of colors. We would tie the end of the string to a railing or a pole, and leave the kite floating all night. On summer nights, Baghdad took its rest on the rooftops, and the rustling of the kites under the stars was like a lullaby for the kids.

My favorite holiday was Passover. I loved the *seder*[1] night, sitting around the long table, the reading of the *haggada*,[2] and drinking the sweet wine that my mother had prepared herself. But as the holiday drew near, I always felt pangs of anxiety over whether or not my father would be with us in order to conduct the *seder* at our house. My father had a textile shop in southern Iraq and only came home every month or two, when his stock ran low and he had to come back to the capital for new goods. When he came, the house was filled with commotion; he would call to my mother and the maid from the doorway and shout to the porter carrying his luggage that he [had] better not ruin anything. We would gather around him and he would kiss us, leaving our cheeks sore from the rough stubble of his beard and our nostrils filled with the pungent aroma of tobacco. Pedigree chickens would bolt from his parcels squawking, flapping their wings and leaving their droppings all over the place. The courtyard would fill with trunks and packages and a huge pile of dirty clothes.

But just as our joy was great at his arrival, so was our distress when he was absent at the holidays. In his letters, he would usually announce the day of his arrival, but there were times that he left us waiting until the night of the holiday. As my mother and the maid toiled the whole day over preparations for the holiday meal, I wouldn't budge from the window until the late afternoon. On days like that, no miracle took place, and I harbored great resentment in my heart against him.

Are the two houses that I grew up in still standing intact? A young Iraqi friend in Paris could not answer my question, but he gave me a map of the

---

[1]The festival meal. [eds.]

[2]The prayer book containing the *seder* service: the ritual, the story, and the songs. [eds.]

city, one of those given out to tourists. I found streets and gardens there, squares and bridges and blocks of apartment buildings on the outskirts.

"I have a different map," I said to him, "a map of alleys twisting and intertwining like an intricate cobweb. I can draw it on paper because I remember every single curve, every single niche, every single arch, every single window and every single side of a house that protrudes in a sharp angle near which men stood and pissed." "Many quarters have been pulled down," my friend replied promptly, "yours too, perhaps."

Whether it has been pulled down or not, what is the difference? As far as I'm concerned, it will stand forever. The world of childhood is beyond time, located in the imagination rather than reality. It is a complete experience that cannot be apprehended by mere words. We are used to telling stories in a logical way. The language we use is arranged according to fixed rules and it obeys time. Every result has a cause, and causality is the guideline of the sentences we utter. Otherwise no one will understand. How should we retell a dream? How should we relate an experience that is beyond time? Childhood experiences can only be retold at the expense of locking them up in time, of binding them in a tight chain of cause and effect. Such are the childhood stories that we read. They are stories, a faded shadow, or a polished reflection of an imaginary experience. I do not put great trust in childhood stories, just as I do not put great trust in dream stories. I particularly do not believe writers' childhood stories—those whose main strength lies in writing fiction are less trustworthy in telling things as they really were, not to mention the events of childhood.

The house that I grew up in, the quarter, my childhood, are all a wonderful dream, a fantasy, a marvelous vision. No, I cannot apprehend them in words.

✸ Discussion and Writing

1. Describe the alley. What seems to have been deeply embedded in the child's memory? Of all the people from his neighborhood whom does he remember the best? Why?
2. What effect is created by the story of the snakes: what is the significance of the child narrator's initial lack of fear of the snakes; describe the various practices to avert their evil influence; what is the function of the carpenter in the story?
3. Examine the descriptions of Jewish, Christian, and Muslim funerals to determine the narrator's perception of each.
4. Describe the child's contact with the nun. Explain his lack of interest in the nun as an adult.
5. Evaluate the depiction of the Jewish traditions the narrator enjoyed the most. What is their significance?

6. Distinguish between the child and the grown-up narrator's awareness as reflected in the portrayal of his father.
7. Why does he call this an imaginary childhood? If he distrusts all re-creations of childhood, what could be the purpose of this re-creation? Examine the significance of the last dialogue.

❋ Research and Comparison

Interdisciplinary Discussion Question: The snake is venerated as a protective spirit in some cultures, and is hated as a destructive evil in others. But almost all cultures use it as an important emblem in art and religion. Compare the portrayal of the snake in different writings in this anthology to determine its position in various cultures.

Mohammed Khudayyir
(b. 1930?)
Iraq

Mohammed Khudayyir was born near Basra in southern Iraq, and he has continued to live there, working as a schoolteacher. He is an inventive author, playing, as in "Clocks Like Horses," with time, yoking the historic past to the present, and creating a mythic sense of time. He is considered one of the most original short story writers in the contemporary Arab world.

Clocks Like Horses*

This meeting may take place. I shall get my watch repaired and go out to the quays of the harbor, then at the end of the night I shall return to the hotel and find him sleeping in my bed, his face turned to the wall, having hung his red turban on the clothes hook.

Till today I still own a collection of old watches; I had come by them from an uncle of mine who used to be a sailor on the ships of the Andrew Weir company; old pocket watches with chains and silver-plated cases, all contained in a small wooden box in purses of shiny blue cloth. While my interest in them has of late waned, I had, as a schoolboy, been fascinated by them. I would take them out from their blue purses and scrutinize their

---

Translated by Denys Johnson-Davies

workings in an attempt to discover something about them that would transcend "time stuffed like old cotton in a small cushion," as I had recorded one
day in my diary.

One day during the spring school holidays I was minded to remove one
of these watches from its box and to put it into the pocket of my black suit,
attaching its chain to the buttonholes of my waistcoat. For a long time I
wandered round the chicken market before seating myself at a café. The
waiter came and asked me the time. I calmly took the watch out of its blue
purse. My watch was incapable of telling the time, like the other watches in
the box, nothing in it working except for the spring of the case which was no
sooner pressed than it flicked open revealing a pure white dial and two
hands that stood pointing to two of the Roman numerals on the face. Before
I could inform him that the watch was not working, the waiter had bent
down and pulled the short chain toward him; having looked attentively at
the watch he closed its case on which had been engraved a sailing ship
within a frame of foreign writing. Then, giving it back to me, he stood up
straight.

"How did you get hold of it?"

"I inherited it from a relative of mine."

I returned the watch to its place.

"Was your relative a sailor?"

"Yes."

"Only three or four of the famous sailors are still alive."

"My relative was called Mughamis."

"Mughamis? I don't know him."

"He wouldn't settle in one place. He died in Bahrain."

"That's sailors for you! Do you remember another sailor called
Marzouk? Since putting ashore for the last time he has been living in Fao. He
opened a shop there for repairing watches, having learned the craft from the
Portuguese. He alone would be able to repair an old watch like yours."

I drank down the glass of tea and said to the waiter as I paid him: "Did
you say he was living in Fao?"

"Yes, near the hotel."

The road to Fao is a muddy one and I went on putting off the journey
until one sunny morning I took my place among the passengers in a bus
which set off loaded with luggage. The passengers, who sat opposite one
another in the middle of the bus, exchanged no words except for general
remarks about journeying in winter, about how warm this winter was, and
other comments about the holes in the road. At the moment they stopped
talking I took out my watch. Their eyes became fixed on it, but no one asked
me about it or asked the time. Then we began to avoid looking at each other
and transferred our attentions to the vast open countryside and to the
distant screen of date palms in the direction of the east that kept our vehicle
company and hid the villages along the Shatt-al-Arab.

We arrived at noon and someone showed me to the hotel which lies at the intersection of straight roads and looks onto a square in the middle of which is a round, fenced garden. The hotel consisted of two low stories, while the balcony that overlooked the square was at such a low height that someone in the street could have climbed up on to it. I, who cannot bear the smell of hotels, or the heavy, humid shade in their hallways in daytime, hastened to call out to its owners. When I repeated my call, a boy looked down from a door at the side and said: "Do you want to sleep here?"

"Have you a place?" I said.

The boy went into the room and from it there emerged a man whom I asked for a room with a balcony. The boy who was showing me the way informed me that the hotel would be empty by day and packed at night. Just as the stairway was the shortest of stairways and the balcony the lowest of balconies, my room was the smallest and contained a solitary bed, but the sun entered it from the balcony. I threw my bag on to the bed and the boy sat down beside me. "The doors are all without locks," said the boy. "Why should we lock them—the travellers only stay for one night."

Then he leaned toward me and whispered: "Are you Indian?"

This idea came as a surprise to me. The boy himself was more likely to be Indian with his dark complexion, thick brilliantined hair and sparkling eyes. I whispered to him: "Did they tell you that Basra used to be called the crotch of India, and that the Indian invaders in the British army, who came down to the land of Fao first of all, desired no other women except those of Basra?"

The boy ignored my cryptic reference to the mixing of passions and blending of races and asked, if I wasn't Indian, where did I live?

"I've come from Ashar," I told him, "on a visit to the watchmaker. Would you direct me to him?"

"Perhaps you mean the old man who has many clocks in his house," said the boy.

"Yes, that must be he," I said.

"He's not far from the hotel," he said. "He lives alone with his daughter and never leaves the house."

The boy brought us lunch from a restaurant, and we sat on the bed to eat, and he told me about the man I had seen downstairs: "He's not the owner of the hotel, just a permanent guest."

Then, with his mouth full of food, he whispered: "He's got a pistol."

"You know a lot of things, O Indian," I said, also speaking in a whisper.

He protested that he wasn't Indian but was from Hasa. He had a father who worked on the ships that transported dates from Basra to the coastal towns of the Gulf and India.

The boy took me to the watchmaker, leaving me in front of the door of his house. A gap made by a slab of stone that had been removed from its place in the upper frieze of the door made this entrance unforgettable. One day, in tropical years, there had stopped near where I was a sailor shaky with sickness, or some Sikh soldier shackled with lust, and he had looked at the slab of stone on which was engraved some date or phrase, before continuing on his unknown journey. And after those two there perhaps came some foreign archaeologist whose boat had been obstructed by the silt and who had put up in the town till the water rose, and his curiosity for things Eastern had been drawn to the curves of the writing on the slab of stone and he had torn it out and carried it off with him to his boat. Now I, likewise, was in front of this gateway to the sea.

On the boy's advice I did not hesitate to push open the door and enter into what looked like a porch which the sun penetrated through apertures near the ceiling and in which I was confronted by hidden and persistent ticking sounds and a garrulous ringing that issued from the pendulums and hammers of large clocks of the type that strike the hours, ranged along the two sides of the porch. As I proceeded one or more clocks struck at the same time. All the clocks were similar in size, in the great age of the wood of their frames, and in the shape of their round dials, their Roman numerals, and their delicate arrow-like hands—except that these hands were pointing to different times.

I had to follow the slight curve of the porch to come unexpectedly upon the last of the great sailors in his den, sitting behind a large table on which was heaped the wreckage of clocks. He was occupied with taking to pieces the movement of a clock by the light of a shaded lamp that hung down from the ceiling at a height close to his frail, white-haired head. He looked towards me with a glance from one eye that was naked and another on which a magnifying-glass had been fixed, then went back to disassembling the movement piece by piece. The short glance was sufficient to link this iron face with the nuts, cogwheels and hands of the movements of the many clocks hanging on the walls and thrown into corners under dust and rust. Clocks that didn't work and others that did, the biggest of them being a clock on the wall above the watchmaker's head, which was, to be precise, the movement of a large grandfather clock made of brass, the dial of which had been removed and which had been divested of its cabinet so that time manifested itself in it naked and shining, sweeping along on its serrated cogwheels in a regular mechanical sequence: from the rotation of the spring to the pendulum that swung harmoniously to and fro and ended in the slow, tremulous, imperceptible movement of the hands. When the cogwheels had taken the hands along a set distance of time's journey, the striking cogwheel would move and raise the hammer. I had not previously seen a naked, throbbing clock and thus I became mesmerized by the regular throbbing that synchronized with the swinging motion of the pendulum and with the movement of the cogwheels of various diameters. I started at the sound of the hammer falling against the bell; the gallery rang with three strokes whose reverberations took a long time to die away, while the other clocks went on, behind the glass of their cabinets, with their incessant ticking.

The watchmaker raised his head and asked me if the large clock above his head had struck three times.

Then, immersing himself in taking the mechanism to pieces, he said: "Like horses; like horses running on the ocean bed."

A clock in the porch struck six times and he said: "Did one of them strike six times? It's six in America. They're getting up now, while the sun is setting in Burma."

Then the room was filled again with noisy reverberations. "Did it strike seven? It's night-time in Indonesia. Did you make out the last twelve strokes? They are fast asleep in the furthest west of the world. After some hours the sun will rise in the furthest east. What time is it? Three? That's our time, here near the Gulf."

One clock began striking on its own. After a while the chimes blended with the tolling of other clocks as hammers coincided in falling upon bells, and others landed halfway between the times of striking and yet others fell between these halfways so that the chimes hurried in pursuit of one another in a confused scale. Then, one after another, the hammers became still, the chimes growing further apart, till a solitary clock remained, the last clock that had not discharged all its time, letting it trickle out now in a separate, high-pitched reverberation.

He was holding my watch in his grasp. "Several clocks might strike together," he said, "strike as the fancy takes them. I haven't liked to set my clocks to the same time. I have assigned to my daughter the task of merely winding them up. They compete with one another like horses. I have clocks that I bought from people who looted them from the houses of Turkish employees who left them as they hurried away after the fall of Basra. I also got hold of clocks that were left behind later on by the Jews who emigrated. Friends of mine, the skippers of ships, who would come to visit me here, would sell me clocks of European manufacture. Do you see the clock over there in the passageway? It was in the house of the Turkish commander of the garrison of Fao's fortress."

I saw the gleam of the quick-swinging pendulum behind glass in the darkness of the cabinets of the clocks in the porch. Then I asked him about my watch. "Your watch? It's a rare one. They're no longer made. I haven't handled such a watch for a long time. I'm not sure about it but I'll take it to pieces. Take a stroll round and come back here at night."

That was what I'd actually intended to do. I would return before night. The clocks bade me farewell with successive chimes. Four chimes in Fao: seven p.m. in the swarming streets of Calcutta. Four chimes: eight a.m. in the jungles of Buenos Aires . . . Outside the den the clamor had ceased, also the smell of engine oil and of old wood.

I returned at sunset. I had spent the time visiting the old barracks which had been the home of the British army of occupation, then I had sat in a café near the fish market.

I didn't find the watchmaker in his former place, but presently I noticed a huge empty cabinet that had been moved into a gap between the clocks. The watchmaker was in an open courtyard before an instrument made up of clay vessels, which I guessed to be a type of water-clock. When he saw me he called out: "Come here. Come, I'll show you something."

I approached the vessels hanging on a cross-beam: from them water dripped into a vessel hanging on another, lower cross-beam; the water then flowed on to a metal plate on the ground, in which there was a gauge for measuring the height of the water.

"A water-clock?"

"Have you seen one like it?"

"I've read about them. They were the invention of people of old."

"The Persians call them *bingan*."

"I don't believe it tells the right time."

"No, it doesn't, it reckons only twenty hours to the day. According to its reckoning I'm 108 years old instead of ninety, and it is seventy-eight years since the British entered Basra instead of sixty. I learned how to make it from a Muscati sailor who had one like it in his house on the coast."

I followed him to the den, turning to two closed doors in the small courtyard on which darkness had descended. He returned the empty clock-cabinet to its place and seated himself in his chair. His many clothes lessened his appearance of senility; he was lost under his garments, one over another and yet another over them, his head inside a vast tarbush.[1]

"I've heard you spent a lifetime at sea."

"Yes. It's not surprising that our lives are always linked to water. I was on one of the British India ships as a syce with an English trader dealing in horses."

He toyed with the remnants of the watches in front of him, then said: "He used to call himself by an Arabic name. We would call him Surour Saheb. He used to buy Nejdi horses from the rural areas of the south and they would then be shipped to Bombay where they would be collected up and sent to the racecourses in England. Fifteen days on end at sea, except that we would make stops at the Gulf ports. We would stop for some days in Muscat. When there were strong winds against us we would spend a month at sea. The captains, the cooks and the pilots were Indians, while the others, seamen and syces, were from Muscat, Hasa and Bahrain; the rest were from the islands of the Indian Ocean. We would have with us divers from Kuwait. I remember their small dark bodies and plaited hair as they washed down the horses on the shore or led them to the ship. I was the youngest syce. I

---

[1]Tarbush or tarboosh: a round brimless cap, usually of cloth or felt. [eds.]

began my first sea journey at the age of twelve. I joined the ship with my father who was an assistant to the captain and responsible for looking after the stores and equipment. There were three of us, counting my father, who would sleep in the storeroom among the sacks and barrels of tar, the fish oil, ropes and dried fish, on beds made up of coconut fiber."

"Did you make a lot?"

"We? We didn't make much. The trader did. Each horse would fetch 800 rupees in Bombay, and when we had reached Bengal it would fetch 1,500 rupees. On our return to Basra we would receive our wages for having looked after the horses. Some of us would buy goods from India and sell them on our return journey wherever we put in: cloth, spices, rice, sugar, perfumes, and wood, and sometimes peacocks and monkeys."

"Did you employ horses in the war?"

"I myself didn't take part in the war. Of course they used them. When the Turks prevented us from trading with them because they needed them for the army, we moved to the other side of the river. We had a corral and a caravanserai for sleeping in at Khorramshahr. From there we began to smuggle out the horses far from the clutches of the Turkish customs men. On the night when we'd be travelling we'd feed and water the horses well and at dawn we'd proceed to the corral and each syce would lead out his horse. As for me I was required to look after the transportation of the provisions and fodder; other boys who were slightly older than me were put in charge of the transportation of the water, the ropes, the chains and other equipment. The corral was close to the shore, except that the horses would make a lot of noise and stir up dust when they were being pulled along by the reins to the ship that would lie at the end of an anchorage stretching out to it from the shore. The ship would rock and tiny bits of straw would become stuck on top of our heads while the syces would call the horses by their names, telling them to keep quiet, until they finished tying them up in their places. It was no easy matter, for during the journey the waves, or the calm of the invisible sea, would excite one of the horses or would make it ill, so that its syce would have to spend the night with it, watching over it and keeping it company. As we lay in our sleeping quarters we would hear the syce reassuring his horse with some such phrase as: "Calm down. Calm down, my Precious Love. The grass over there is better." However, this horse, whose name was Precious Love, died somewhere near Aden. At dawn the sailors took it up and consigned it to the waves. It was a misty morning and I was carrying a lantern, and I heard the great carcass hitting the water, though without seeing it; I did, though, see its syce's face close to me—he would be returning from his voyage without any earnings."

Two or three clocks happened to chime together. I said to him:

"Used you to put in to Muscat?"

"Yes. Did I tell you about our host in Muscat? His wooden house was on the shore of a small bay, opposite an old stone fortress on the other side. We would set out for his house by boat. By birth he was a highlander, coming from the tribes in the mountains facing the bay. He was also a sorcerer. He was a close friend of Surour Saheb, supplying him with a type of ointment the Muscati used to prepare out of mountain herbs, which the Englishman would no sooner smear on his face than it turned a dark green and would gleam in the lamplight like a wave among rocks. In exchange for this the Muscati would get tobacco from him. I didn't join them in smoking, but I was fond of chewing a type of olibanum that was to be found extensively in the markets of the coast. I would climb up into a high place in the room that had been made as a permanent bed and would watch them puffing out the smoke from the *narghiles*[2] into the air as they lay relaxing round the fire, having removed their dagger-belts and placed them in front of them along-side their colored turbans. Their beards would be plunged in the smoke and the rings would glitter in their ears under the combed locks of hair whenever they turned towards the merchant, lost in thought. The merchant, relaxing on feather cushions, would be wearing brightly colored trousers of Indian cloth and would be wrapped round in an *aba*[3] of Kashmir wool; as for his silk turban, he would, like the sailors, have placed it in front of him beside his pistol."

"Did you say that the Muscati was a sorcerer?"

"He had a basket of snakes in which he would lay one of the sailors, then bring him out alive. His sparse body would be swallowed in his lustrous flowing robes, as was his small head in his saffron-coloured turban with the tassels. We were appalled at his repulsive greed for food, for he would eat a whole basketful of dates during a night and would drink enough water to provide for ten horses. He was amazing, quite remarkable; he would perform bizarre acts; swallowing a puff from his *narghile*, he would after a while begin to release the smoke from his mouth and nose for five consecutive minutes. You should have seen his stony face, with the clouds of smoke floating against it like serpents that flew and danced. He was married to seven women for whom he had dug out, in the foot of the mountain, rooms that overlooked the bay. No modesty prevented him from disclosing their fabulous names: Mountain Flower, Daylight Sun, Sea Pearl, Morning Star. He was a storehouse of spicy stories and tales of strange travels and we would draw inspiration from him for names for our horses. At the end of the night he would leave us sleeping and would climb up the mountain. At the end of one of our trips we stayed as his guest for seven nights, during which time men from the Muscati's tribe visited us to have a smoke; they would talk very little and would look with distaste at the merchant and would then leave quietly with their antiquated rifles.

"Our supper would consist of spiced rice and grilled meat or fish. We would be given a sweet sherbet to drink in brass cups. As for the almond-filled *halva* of Muscat that melts in the mouth, even the bitter coffee could not

---

[2]A water pipe. [eds.]
[3]A long cloth which men wrap around themselves. [eds.]

disperse its scented taste. In the morning he would return and give us some sherbet to drink that would settle our stomachs, which would be suffering from the night's food and drink, and would disperse the tobacco fumes from the sailors' heads."

An outburst of striking clocks prevented him momentarily from enlarging further. He did not wait for the sound to stop before continuing:

"On the final night of our journey he overdid his tricks in quite a frightening manner. While the syces would seek help from his magic in treating their sick horses, they were afraid nonetheless that the evil effects of his magic would spread and reap the lives of these horses. And thus it was that a violent wind drove our ship onto a rock at the entrance to the bay and smashed it. Some of us escaped drowning, but the sorcerer of Muscat was not among them. He was travelling with the ship on his way to get married to a woman from Bombay; but the high waves choked his shrieks and eliminated his magic."

"And the horses?"

"They combated the waves desperately. They were swimming in the direction of the rocky shore, horses battling against the white horses of the waves. All of them were drowned. That was my last journey in the horse ships. After that, in the few years that preceded the war, I worked on the mail ships."

He made a great effort to remember and express himself:

"In Bahrain I married a woman who bore me three daughters whom I gave in marriage to sons of the sea. I stayed on there with the boatbuilders until after the war. Then, in the thirties, I returned to Basra and bought the clocks and settled in Fao, marrying a woman from here."

"You are one of the few sailors who are still alive today."

He asked me where I lived and I told him that I had put up at the hotel. He said:

"A friend of mine used to live in it. I don't know if he's still alive—for twenty years I haven't left my house."

Then, searching among the fragments of watches, he asked me in surprise:

"Did you come to Fao just because of the watch?"

I answered him that there were some towns one had to go to. He handed me my watch. It was working. Before placing it in my hand he scrutinized its flap on which had been engraved a ship with a triangular sail, which he said was of the type known as *sunbuk*.

I opened the flap. The hands were making their slow way round. The palms of my hand closed over the watch, and we listened to the sea echoing in the clocks of the den. The slender legs of horses run in the streets of the clock faces, are abducted in the glass of the large grandfather clocks. The clocks tick and strike: resounding hooves, chimes driven forward like waves. A chime: the friction of chains and ropes against wet wood. Two chimes: the dropping of the anchor into the blue abyss. Three: the call of the rocks. Four: the storm blowing up. Five: the neighing of the horses. Six . . . seven . . . eight . . . nine . . . ten . . . eleven . . . twelve . . .

This winding lane is not large enough to allow a lorry to pass, but it lets in a heavy damp night and sailors leading their horses, and a man dizzy from sea-sickness, still holding in his grasp a pocket watch and making an effort to avoid the water and the gentle sloping of the lane and the way the walls curve round. The bends increase with the thickening darkness and the silence. Light seeps through from the coming bend, causing me to quicken my step. In its seeping through and the might of its radiation it seems to be marching against the wall, carving into the damp brickwork folds of skins and crumpled faces that are the masks of seamen and traders from different races who have passed by here before me and are to be distinguished only by their headgear: the bedouin of Nejd and the rural areas of the south by the *kuffiyeh* and *'iqal,*[4] the Iraqi effendis of the towns by the *sidara;*[5] the Persians by the black tarbooshes made of goat-skin; the Ottoman officers, soldiers and government employees by their tasselled tarbooshes; the Indians by their red turbans; the Jews by flat red tarbooshes; the monks and missionaries by their black head coverings; the European sea captains by their naval caps; the explorers in disguise . . . They rushed out towards the rustling noise coming from behind the last bend, the eerie rumbling, the bated restlessness of the waves below the high balustrades . . . Then, here are Fao's quays, the lamps leading its wooden bridges along the water for a distance; in the spaces between them boats are anchored one alongside another, their lights swaying; there is also a freighter with its lights on, anchored between the two middle berths. It was possible for me to make out in the middle of the river scattered floating lights. I didn't go very close to the quay installations but contented myself with standing in front of the dark, bare extension of the river. To my surprise a man who was perhaps working as a watchman or worker on the quays approached me and asked me for the time. Eleven.

On my return to the hotel I took a different road, passing by the closed shops. I was extremely alert. The light will be shining brightly in the hotel vestibule. The oil stove will be in the middle of it, and to one side of the vestibule will be baggage, suitcases, a watercooling box and a cupboard. Seated on the bench will be a man who is dozing, his cigarette forgotten between his fingers. It will happen that I shall approach the door of my room, shall open the door, and shall find him sleeping in my bed; he will be turned to the wall, having hung his red turban on the clothes hook.

---

[4]*Kuffiyeh* is a scarf or headress worn by men; *'iqal* is the cord or head band that holds the *kuffiyeh* in place. [eds.]
[5]Iraqi black velvet headgear. [eds.]

❋ Discussion and Writing

1. Examine the narrator's fascination with the watches, as a child and as a grown-up. What is implied by the uncle's being a sailor and his association with watches?
2. Correlate the narrator's conversation with the hotel boy to the events in the narrative. In what ways are the details regarding the structure of the hotel relevant to the story?
3. Describe the gap at the entrance to the watchmaker's house; how was it created; why is it called "gateway to the sea"?
4. What is the significance of the clocks' striking the hours in distinctive ways and the absence of the grandfather clock's dial and case?
5. What is the function of the water-clock in the narrative?
6. Describe the watchmaker's young days on the sea and his fascination with the horses: what is the function of the narratives about the Muscati sorcerer and the Englishman?
7. Analyze the watchmaker's life on the land: his marriages and daughters; his not stepping out of the house in 20 years; his obsession with the clocks.
8. Describe the scene in the street the narrator envisions after his visit to the watchmaker's. Comment on the implications of the scene.
9. Who is the man in the narrator's bed at the beginning and end of the story? In what ways do the two passages differ? What is the function of these occurrences in the narrative?
10. What is the importance of the narrator's saying that clocks are "Time stuffed like cotton in a small cushion"? Analyze the significance of the references to time in the narrative: what devices, including the use of verb tenses and vocabulary, are used to collapse past, present, and future?

Forugh Farrokhzad
(1935–1967)
Iran

Forugh Farrokhzad was born in Iran. She began to write poetry at the age of 16, and at the time of her death in an automobile accident 16 years later, she was a recognized and respected poet. During her short life, she published four volumes of poetry and a highly acclaimed fifth volume devoted to one poem. Whether she wrote about the inner self or society, her work reflected the honesty of deeply felt convictions. She drew on the cramped winding alleyways where she grew up and the swarming Tehran streets for their pulsating rhythm as well as for imagery, and, thus, her merging the personal and the social resulted in poetry that was at once poignant and forthright. In her experimenting with form and metrics, and in her focus on issues concerning women, class, and poverty, she confirmed the elasticity of Persian poetry.

The Wind-Up Doll*

More than this, yes
much more than this, one can stay silent.

One can with a fixed gaze
like that of the dead
stare for long hours at the shape of a cup
at a faded flower on the rug
at faint slogans on the wall.

One can draw back the curtain
with wrinkled fingers and watch
rain falling in the alley
a child standing in a doorway
with colorful balloons
a rickety cart in a noisy rush
leaving the deserted square.

One can stand motionless
by the curtain, but blind, but deaf.

One can cry out
with a voice quite false, quite remote
"I love . . . "
one can in a man's dominating arms
be a beautiful, healthy female
with a body like a leather tablecloth
with two big hard breasts
one can in bed with a drunk, a madman, a tramp
rape the innocence of love.

One can degrade with guile
all the deep mysteries
one can keep on solving crossword puzzles
happily discover the inane answers
yes, five or six letters.

One can with bent head
kneel for a lifetime before a cold shrine
one can see God in a nameless grave

Translated by Ahmad Karimi-Hakkak

one can trade believing for a worthless coin
one can mold in the corner of a mosque
like an old reciter of pilgrim's prayers.

One can like zero be constant
whether adding, subtracting or multiplying
one can think of one's eye in its cocoon of anger
the pale buttonhole of an old shoe
one can in one's basin dry up like water.

One can hide with shame the beauty of a moment
at the bottom of a chest
like a funny black snapshot
one can hang in a day's empty frame
the image of an execution, a martyrdom or a crucifixion
one can cover the crack in the wall with masks
one can mingle with images more hollow than these.

One can be like a wind-up doll
and look at the world with eyes of glass
one can lie for years in lace and tinsel
a body stuffed with straw
in a felt-lined box,
one can at every lustful pass
cry out for no reason and say
"Ah, how happy I am!"

❀ Discussion and Writing

1. What images illustrate the silence, deafness, and blindness of women?
2. Discuss the implications of the repeated phrase "One can."
3. What is the significance of "martyrdom" and "masks"?
4. Explain the symbolism of the "zero" and the "wind-up doll."
5. Analyze the depiction of the woman's traits and her role.
6. Comment on the poet's tone: examine the irony of the paradoxical imagery.

❀ Research and Comparison

Examine Forugh Farrokhzad's writings and place her in the tradition of modern Iranian (Persian) poetry.

Interdisciplinary Discussion Question: Research the role of women in Islamic societies, exploring the tensions created by conflicts between tradition and modernity.

Ghassan Kanafani
(1936–1972)
Palestine

Ghassan Kanafani was born in Acre, Palestine. He and his family became refugees after the 1948 war that followed the partition of Palestine, an experience that he recalled vividly throughout his life. Considered the foremost Palestinian writer of fiction, he worked as a teacher and journalist in Syria and Kuwait, and then served as a spokesman for the Popular Front for the Liberation of Palestine in Beirut. Although his writing was not always overtly political, it resonated with his concern for the Palestinian people. His explicitly political writing, however, not only examined the situation in Palestine, but the treatment of the refugees in Arab countries as well; the film of his novella *Men in the Sun* (1962) was banned because of his candid treatment of the subject. Whether he explored the plight of his people or their character, he wrote with a wry wit, ironically illuminating the human condition. At the time of his death (as a result of a bomb planted in his car), he had published five novels, five books of short stories, two plays, and studies of Palestinian literature.

The Slave Fort*

Had he not been so sadly shabby one would have said of him that he was a poet. The site he had chosen for his humble hut of wood and beaten-out jerry cans was truly magnificent; right by the threshold the might of the sea flowed under the feet of the sharp rocks with a deep-throated, unvarying sound. His face was gaunt, his beard white though streaked with a few black hairs, his eyes hollow under bushy brows; his cheek-bones protruded like two rocks that had come to rest either side of the large projection that was his nose.

Why had we gone to that place? I don't remember now. In our small car we had followed a rough, miry and featureless road. We had been going for more than three hours when Thabit pointed through the window and gave a piercing shout:

"There's the Slave Fort."

This Slave Fort was a large rock the base of which had been eaten away by the waves so that it resembled the wing of a giant bird, its head curled in the sand, its wing outstretched above the clamor of the sea.

*Translated by S. Al-Bazzaz

"Why did they call it 'The Slave Fort'?"

"I don't know. Perhaps there was some historical incident which gave it the name. Do you see that hut?"

And once again Thabit pointed, this time toward the small hut lying in the shadow of the gigantic rock. He turned off the engine and we got out of the car.

"They say that a half-mad old man lives in it."

"What does he do with himself in this waste on his own?"

"What any half-mad old man would do."

From afar we saw the old man squatting on his heels at the entrance to his hut, his head clasped in his hands, staring out to sea.

"Don't you think there must be some special story about this old man? Why do you insist he's half-mad?"

"I don't know, that's what I heard."

Thabit, having arrived at the spot of his choice, levelled the sand, threw down the bottles of water, took out the food from the bag, and seated himself.

"They say he was the father of four boys who struck it lucky and are now among the richest people in the district."

"And then?"

"The sons quarrelled about who should provide a home for the father. Each wife wanted her own way in the matter and the whole thing ended with the old man making his escape and settling down here."

"It's a common enough story and shouldn't have turned the old man half-mad."

"There he is, only a few yards away—why not go over and ask him?"

Thabit looked at me uncomprehendingly, then lit the small heap of wood he had arranged and poured water into the metal water-jug and set it on the fire.

"The important thing in the story is to agree about whether his flight was a product of his mad half or his sane half."

Thabit blew at the fire, then began rubbing his eyes as he sat up straight resting his body on his knees.

"I can't bear the idea which the sight of him awakens in me."

"What idea?"

"That the man should spend seventy years of his life so austerely, that he should work, exert himself, existing day after day and hour after hour, that for seventy long years he should gain his daily bread from the sweat of his brow, that he should live through his day in the hope of a better tomorrow, that for seventy whole years he should go to sleep each night—and for what? So that he should, at the last, spend the rest of his life cast out like a dog, alone, sitting like this. Look at him—he's like some polar animal that has lost its fur. Can you believe that a man can live seventy years to attain to this? I can't stomach it."

Once again he stared at us; then, spreading out the palms of his hands, he continued his tirade:

"Just imagine! Seventy useless, meaningless years. Imagine walking for seventy years along the same road; the same directions, the same bound-aries, the same horizons, the same everything. It's unbearable!"

"No doubt the old man would differ with you in your point of view. Maybe he believes that he has reached an end which is distinct from his life. Maybe he wanted just such an end. Why not ask him?"

We got up to go to him. When we came to where he was he raised his eyes, coldly returned our greeting and invited us to sit down. Through the half-open door we could see the inside of the hut; the threadbare mattress in one corner, while in the opposite one was a square rock on which lay a heap of unopened oyster shells. For a while silence reigned; it was then broken by the old man's feeble voice asking:

"Do you want oyster shells? I sell oyster shells."

As we had no reply to make to him, Thabit enquired:

"Do you find them yourself?"

"I wait for low tide so as to look for them far out. I gather them up and sell them to those who hope to find pearls in them."

We stared at each other. Presently Thabit put the question that had been exercising all our minds.

"Why don't you yourself try to find pearls inside these shells?"

"I?"

He uttered the word as though becoming aware for the first time that he actually existed, or as though the idea had never previously occurred to him. He then shook his head and kept his silence.

"How much do you sell a heap for?"

"Cheaply—for a loaf or two."

"They're small shells and certainly won't contain pearls."

The old man looked at us with lusterless eyes under bushy brows.

"What do you know about shells?" he demanded sharply. "Who's to tell whether or not you'll find a pearl?" And as though afraid that if he were to be carried away still further he might lose the deal, he relapsed into silence.

"And can you tell?"

"No, no one can tell," and he began toying with a shell which lay in front of him, pretending to be unaware of our presence.

"All right, we'll buy a heap."

The old man turned round and pointed to the heap arrayed on the square rock.

"Bring two loaves," he said, a concealed ring of joy in his voice, "and you can take that heap."

On returning to our place bearing the heap of shells, our argument broke out afresh.

"I consider those eyes can only be those of a madman. If not, why doesn't he open the shells himself in the hope of finding some pearls?"

"Perhaps he's fed up with trying and prefers to turn spectator and make money."

It took us half the day before we had opened all the shells. We piled the gelatinous insides of the empty shells around us, then burst into laughter at our madness.

In the afternoon Thabit suggested to me that I should take a cup of strong tea to the old man in the hope that it might bring a little joy to his heart.

As I was on my way over to him a slight feeling of fear stirred within me. However, he invited me to sit down and began sipping at his tea with relish.

"Did you find anything in the shells?"

"No, we found nothing—you fooled us."

He shook his head sadly and took another sip.

"To the extent of two loaves!" he said, as though talking to himself, and once again shook his head. Then, suddenly, he glanced at me and explained sharply:

"Were these shells your life—I mean, were each shell to represent a year of your life and you opened them one by one and found them empty, would you have been as sad as you are about losing a couple of loaves?"

He began to shake all over and at that moment I was convinced that I was in the presence of someone who certainly was mad. His eyes, under their bushy brows, gave out a sharp and unnatural brightness, while the dust from his ragged clothes played in the afternoon sun. I could find not a word to say. When I attempted to rise to my feet he took hold of my wrist and his frail hand was strong and convulsive. Then I heard him say:

"Don't be afraid—I am not mad, as you believe. Sit down. I want to tell you something; the happiest moments of my day are when I can watch disappointment of this kind."

I reseated myself, feeling somewhat calmer.

In the meantime, he began to gaze out at the horizon, seemingly unaware of my presence, as though he had not, a moment ago, invited me to sit down. Then he turned to me.

"I knew you wouldn't find anything. These oysters are still young and therefore can't contain the seed of a pearl. I wanted to know, though."

Again he was silent and stared out to sea. Then, as though speaking to himself, he said:

"The ebb tide will start early tonight and I must be off to gather shells. Tomorrow other men will be coming."

Overcome by bewilderment, I rose to my feet. The Slave Fort stood out darkly against the light of the setting sun. My friends were drinking tea around the heaps of empty shells as the old man began running after the receding water, bending down from time to time to pick up the shells left behind.

❀ Discussion and Writing

1. Examine the descriptions of the old man and the landscape. What do the two share?
2. Describe the activity of the old man on the rock. What do the oyster shells and the receding waters suggest?
3. Explain the role of the two visitors; describe what the old man calls his happiest moment; what is he searching for?
4. Comment on the symbolism of the slave fort: the rock, the old man, the hut, and the roaring sea.

❀ Research and Comparison

Examine the writings of Ghassan Kanafani, and comment on the portrayal of his major social and political concerns.

Hushang Golshiri
(b. 1937)
Iran

Hushang Golshiri was born in Isfahan, Iran, and raised, for the most part, in Abadan. His father, a restless man of modest means, traveled about a good deal, bringing along his large family. After obtaining a bachelor's degree in Persian at the University of Isfahan, Hushang Golshiri taught in the local elementary and high schools. During the late 1960s and early 1970s, he was imprisoned because of his political activities, and he founded and edited the prominent literary journal *Jung-i Isfahan*. His first novel, *Shazdeh Ehtejab* (Prince Ehtejab, 1968), brought him recognition, especially after its adaptation as a film. Noted for his style, he is an innovative author who writes with particular care for the precision of language, and who often shifts speakers, time, or event without transition.

The Wolf*

Thursday noon I was informed that the doctor had returned and that he was sick too now. There was nothing the matter with him. The doorman at the clinic said that he had slept straight through from last night until now, and when he awoke, he just wept, choking on his sobs. Usually on Wednesday or Thursday afternoons he set out and went to the city with his wife. This time too he had gone with his wife. But when the truck driver had brought the doctor, he had said, "Only the doctor was inside the car." It seems he was numb from the cold. He had left the doctor at the door of the coffeeshop and gone on. They found the doctor's car in the middle of the pass. At first they had thought that they would have to hitch it to a car or something and tow it to the village. They had gone with the clinic's jeep to do this. But when the driver got behind the wheel, and several others pushed, the car moved. The driver said, "It's because of last night's cold—otherwise, there's nothing the matter with the car." Since there wasn't even anything wrong with its windshield wipers, no one thought of his wife until the very moment the doctor said, "Akhtar, so where is Akhtar?"

The doctor's wife was short and thin, so thin and pale that it seemed as if she'd collapse any minute. They had two rooms in the clinic. The clinic is on the far side of the cemetery, that is, exactly one block away from the settlement. His wife was no more than nineteen years old. At times she would appear in the passageway by the clinic door or behind the windowpanes. Only when it was sunny would she leave the side of the cemetery and walk about the village. She usually had a book in her hand and sometimes a packet of sugar candy or even chocolate in the pocket of her white blouse or in her handbag. She loved the children very much. For this reason, she usually came out along the path to the school. One day I suggested to her that if she wished, we would be able to assign a class to her; she said that she didn't have the patience to deal with the children. The truth of the matter is that the doctor had suggested it to keep his wife occupied. At times, too, she would go to the canal bank together with the women.

After the first snow fell, she disappeared. The women would see her sitting beside the heater reading something or pouring tea for herself. When the doctor would go to pay calls in other villages, the driver's wife or the doorman would stay with the lady. It seems Sadiqeh, the driver's wife, understood first. She had told the women, "At first I thought she was worried about her husband because she'd start suddenly, go up to the window and pull back the curtains." She would stand next to the window and gaze into the white, bright desert. Sadiqeh said, "When the wolves start howling, she goes up to the window."

---

*Translated by Paul Losensky

Anyway, in the winter, if the snow falls, the wolves come closer to the settlement. It's the same way every year. Sometimes a dog, a sheep, or even a child would disappear, so that afterward the villagers would have to go out in a group to find, maybe a collar or a shoe, or some other trace. But Sadiqeh had seen the wolf's glistening eyes and had seen how the doctor's wife stared at the wolf's eyes. One time she didn't even hear Sadiqeh call out to her.

After the second and third snows fell, the doctor was unable to visit the outlying area. When he saw that he would have to stay in his house four or five nights a week, he was ready to join in our social rounds. Our get-togethers were not for the women, but, well, if the doctor's wife came, she'd be able to join the women. But his wife had said, "I'll stay home." Even on the nights when it was the doctor's turn to host the get-together at his house, his wife would sit next to the heater and read a book, or would go up to the window and look at the desert or, from the window on this side of the house, look at the cemetery and, I think, the bright lights of the village. It was at our house, I believe, when the doctor said, "I must go home early tonight." Apparently he'd seen a big wolf in the road.

Mortazavi said, "Perhaps it was a dog."

But I myself told the doctor, "Wolves are often seen around here. You have to be careful. You should never get out of the car."

My wife, I think it was, said, "Doctor, where is your wife? In that house next to the cemetery?"

"That's why I must go early."

And then he said his wife was fearless. And he admitted that one night, at midnight, he had wakened with a start to see her seated next to the window on a chair. When the doctor called out to her, his wife said, "I don't know why this wolf always comes up, facing this window."

The doctor had seen the wolf sitting right on the other side of the fence in the dim light of the moon and howling occasionally at the moon.

Anyway, who would have thought that a wolf, large and solitary, I believe, sitting opposite the window and staring, would little by little become a problem for the doctor and for all of us besides. One night he did not come to our get-together. At first, we thought his wife had fallen sick or the doctor at least, but the next day his wife came herself to the school in the office car and said that, if we would give her the children's drawing class, she was ready to help.

The truth of the matter was, there were so few students that there was no longer any need for her. When we gathered all of them in one classroom, Mr. Mortazavi alone was sufficient to handle them. But, anyway, neither Mortazavi nor I could draw well. We settled on Wednesday morning. Later I brought up the matter of the wolf and said that she shouldn't be afraid, that if they didn't leave the door open or go outside, for instance, there was no danger. I even said that if they wished they could come to the village and take a house.

She said, "No, thank you. It's not important."

Then she admitted that at first she was frightened, that is, that one night when she heard the sound of it howling, she felt that it must have jumped over the fence and was just then sitting behind the window, perhaps, or the door. When she lit the lantern, she saw its black form leap over the fence and then saw its two glistening eyes. She said, "They were exactly like two burning coals." Then she said, "I myself don't know why, when I see it, see its eyes or that stance . . . you know, it's exactly like a German shepherd, sitting upright on its front legs and staring for hours at the window of our room."

I asked, "So, why do you?"

She grasped my meaning and said, "I told you, I don't know. Believe me, when I see it, especially its eyes, I can no longer budge from the window."

We talked of wolves in general, I believe, and I described for her how, when wolves get very hungry, they sit in a circle and stare at one another for hours, that is, until one of them rolls over out of exhaustion; then the others pounce on it and eat it. I also talked about the dogs that get lost occasionally, and only their collars are found. The doctor's wife talked about them too; it seems she had read Jack London's books. "I now know wolves well," she said.

The next week when she came she drew a flower or a leaf for the children, I believe. I didn't see it, just heard about it.

It was a Saturday when I heard from the children that they had set a trap in the cemetery. At the third bell, I went myself with one of the children and looked. It was a big trap. The doctor had bought it in the city and put a side of beef in it. Later that same afternoon, my wife informed me that she had gone to look for the doctor's wife. She said, "She's not doing well." She said, I believe, that the doctor's wife had told her that she was afraid she would not have children.

My wife had consoled her. They had been married for a year. Then my wife brought up the subject of the trap and said, "They're usually skinned here and the skins taken into town." My wife said, "Believe me, all at once her eyes opened wide, and she began to tremble and said, 'Do you hear? That's its very call.' I said, 'Really, madam, now, at this time of day?'"

It seems the doctor's wife ran to the window. It was snowing outside. My wife said, "She pulled back the curtains and stood next to the window. She completely forgot that she had a guest."

The next morning the driver and a few farmers went to inspect the trap. It hadn't been touched. Safar said to the doctor, "It certainly didn't come last night."

The doctor said, "No, it came. I heard its call myself."

To me he said, "This woman is going crazy. Last night she didn't sleep a wink. She sat next to the window all night long and looked at the desert. At midnight, when I was wakened by the wolf's call, I saw my wife fiddling with the door latch. I screamed, 'What are you doing, woman?'"

Then he told me she had a flashlight, switched on, in her hand. The doctor turned pale, and his hands were trembling. We went together to inspect the trap. The trap was intact. The side of beef was still in place. From the footprints, we realized that the wolf had come up to the side of the trap and sat right next to it. Then the trail of footprints went straight up to the fence around the clinic. I saw the woman's face at the window. She was looking at us. The doctor said, "I don't understand. You at least say something to this woman."

The woman's eyes were wide open, staring. Her pale skin had become paler still. She had gathered her black hair together, and it spilled down over her chest. She seemed to have no make-up other than eyeshadow. If only she had at least put lipstick or something on her lips so that they wouldn't be so white! I said, "I've never before heard of a hungry wolf passing up all this meat."

I also described the footprints for her. She said, "The driver said it wasn't hungry. I don't know. Perhaps it's just very intelligent."

The next day they brought news that the trap had been pulled up. They had followed the trap line. They had found the wolf; it was half alive. They killed it with a couple of shovel blades. It was not all that big. When the doctor saw it, he said, "Praise God." But the doctor's wife said to Sadiqeh, "I saw it myself this morning at the crack of dawn sitting on the other side of the fence. This one that they caught was surely a dog or a badger or something."

Perhaps. It's not unlikely that she said these very words to the doctor, for the doctor was forced to get the police. One or two nights afterward, policemen stayed in the doctor's house. It was the third night when we heard the sound of shots. The next day, when the police and several farmers, together with the clinic driver, followed the trail of blood as far as the hill on the far side of the settlement, they saw wolf tracks and a disturbed patch of snow in a ravine behind the hill. But they had been unable to find even a single piece of white bone. The driver said, "The godless bastards, they even ate the bones."

I didn't believe it myself. I said so to Safar. Safar said, "When the lady heard about it, she only smiled. The truth of the matter is that the doctor himself told me to go and inform her. The lady was sitting next to the heater and seemed to be drawing something. She didn't hear the knock on the door. When she saw me, the first thing she did was turn her paper over."

There's nothing special about the woman's drawings. She'd drawn only that wolf. The shining red eyes on a black page, a black ink sketch of the wolf sitting, and one too of the wolf howling at the moon. The wolf's shadow was greatly exaggerated, in such a way that it covered the entire clinic and cemetery. One or two as well are sketches of the wolf's muzzle, greatly resembling a dog's muzzle, especially the teeth.

On Wednesday evening the doctor went to the city. Sadiqeh said his wife was ill. The doctor had told her so. I didn't believe it. I myself had seen her Wednesday morning. She came on time and taught the children drawing. She drew one of those same sketches of hers on the blackboard. She told me so herself.

When I asked her, "But why a wolf?" she said, "However much I wanted to draw something else, it wouldn't come to me. I mean, when I put the chalk to the board, I drew it automatically."

It's a pity that the children erased it when the bell rang for recess. In the afternoon, when I saw one or two of their drawings, I had expected the children wouldn't be able to draw it properly. But in the event, the children's sketches, all of them, turned out to be just like German shepherds, with ears drawn back and tails that wrapped around their haunches.

Thursday noon when I found out the doctor had returned, I thought surely he had left his wife overnight in the city and gone back to work. Still, he had no patients, that is to say, none had come from the other villages. But, anyway, the doctor is a responsible man. Later, when he went to look for Akhtar, everyone went to the pass in the doctor's car and the clinic jeep. The police went too. They found nothing.

The doctor, though, didn't say a word. When he woke up, if he wasn't weeping, he just stared at us, one by one and with his wife's wide open, staring eyes. I had to give him a couple of tumblers of araq[1] so he would start talking. Perhaps he didn't want to talk in front of the others. I don't think they'd had a quarrel or anything. But I don't know why the doctor kept saying, "Believe me, it's wasn't my fault."

When I asked my wife, and even Sadiqeh and Safar, none of them remembered the wife and husband ever having raised their voices to one another. But I had told the doctor not to go. I even told him that there would surely be more snow in the pass. Perhaps the doctor was right, I don't know. Finally he said, "She's not well. I don't think she can stand it here. But after all this, why these pictures?"

Later I saw them. She had drawn several sketches of wolf paws, one or two of their drooping ears. I said, "I believe . . . "

The doctor was not able to speak properly. But I gathered that snow was falling heavily in the middle of the pass, so that it covered all the windows. Then the doctor noticed that the windshield wipers were not working. He had to stop. He said, "Believe me, I saw it, I saw it with my own eyes, standing in the middle of the road."

Akhtar had said, "Do something. We'll freeze to death here."

The doctor said, "Don't you see it?"

---

[1]A liquor. [eds.]

The doctor even put his hand out through the window, thinking he might wipe the snow off with his hand, but he saw there was nothing he could do about it. He said, "You know yourself that it isn't possible to turn around there."

He was right. Then, the motor shut off, I believe. When Akhtar shone the flashlight beam about, she saw that the wolf was sitting right at the side of the road. She said, "It's the same one. Believe me, it's completely harmless. Perhaps it's not a wolf at all, maybe it's a German shepherd or some other dog. Get out and see if you can fix it."

The doctor said, "Get out? Don't you see it?"

Even as he said this, his teeth were chattering. He turned pale, exactly the same sickly color of his wife's face when she stood behind the window and looked at the desert or at the dog. Akhtar said, "Should I throw my purse out for it?"

The doctor said, "What good would that do?"

She said, "Well, it's made of leather. Besides, while it's eating the purse, you can do something about it."

Before she threw her purse, she said to the doctor, "If only I had brought my fur coat."

The doctor said to me, "Wasn't it you who said that you shouldn't go out or open the door, for instance?"

When Akhtar threw her purse, the doctor did not get out. He said, "By God, I saw its black form, standing there at the side of the road. It wasn't moving or howling."

Then when Akhtar turned the flashlight to follow her purse, she couldn't find it. Akhtar said, "Well then, I'll go myself."

The doctor said, "Why, you don't know anything about it," or perhaps he said, "You can't fix it." But he remembered that before he knew it, Akhtar had gotten out. The doctor did not see her, that is to say, the snow prevented him. He did not even hear the sound of her scream. And then, I believe, out of fear, he shut the door, or Akhtar shut it. He didn't say.

Friday morning we started off again in a group from the village. The doctor did not come. He couldn't. It was still snowing. No one expected us to find anything. It was white everywhere. We dug everywhere we could think of. We found only the leather purse. On the road, when I asked Safar, he said, "There's nothing wrong with the windshield wipers."

Me, I don't understand. After all this, when Sadiqeh brought the pictures for me, I was still more confused. A hastily written note was pinned to them, saying something like "As an offering to our school." When she was about to go, she entrusted them to Sadiqeh, saying that if she didn't get better or if she couldn't come on Wednesday, she was to give the drawings to me so that we could use them as a model. I couldn't tell Sadiqeh, or even the doctor, but after all, what appeal could sketches of dogs, such ordinary mutts, have for the village children?

❋ Discussion and Writing

1. Elaborate on the impact of the wolf's eyes and its staring at Akhtar, analyze her reasons for saving the wolf from being trapped.
2. Comment on the function and the implications of the story regarding the wolves' behavior.
3. What is the significance of Akhtar's drawings; of the children's drawings; of Akhtar's note?
4. Discuss the issue of Akhtar's disappearance: what happened to her? Describe the doctor's relationship with her.
5. Comment on the narrator's personality and discuss the effect of his perspective on the structure and development of the narrative.

Abd al-Aziz al-Maqalih
(b. 1939)
Yemen

Abd al-Azia al-Maqalih was born in Yemen and took his degree in Arabic literature at the University of Cairo. He has served as president of Sanaa University and of the Center for Yemeni Studies in Yemen, where he has been at the hub of the literary world, fostering the development and appreciation of Yemeni literature and culture. Although his work stems from the rich Yemeni heritage, his poetry speaks to current social and political conditions, not only in Yemen but in Arab society as a whole. Examining contemporary experience, he has drawn on history and legend; by tying the past to the present, he has both illustrated patterns in Arab experience and reaffirmed an ancient mythic time frame. A highly regarded poet, he received the Lotus Prize in literature.

Sanaa Is Hungry*

One who had witnessed said to me: Sanaa is hungry
and the minarets go shamelessly begging
Aiban[1] carries his children, the coffins of his dead,
and migrates

---

*Translated by Lena Jayyusi and Naomi Shihab Nye
[1]Aiban is a mountain near Sanaa.

Where is the path to the water?
The river's thirst torments me
the thirst of the sea torments me
Every place on earth is a home except my house
All of them carry their notebooks
all of them lug their skulls to the dwellings of exile
The earth's womb has dried up
Time's bursting womb is dry
My footsteps stare at each other
and the road is my cloak.

❉ Discussion and Writing

1. Discuss the impact of the image of a mountain moving and carrying the dead.
2. Examine the imagery evoking hunger and heat in Sanaa.
3. Explore the loss of home and the image of the road as one's "cloak."

❉ Research and Comparison

Interdisciplinary Discussion Question: Research the political history of Yemen, focusing on the plight of its people depicted in the selections included in this anthology.

Muhammad Abd al-Wali
(1940–1973)
Yemen

Muhammad Abd al-Wali, of Yemeni descent, was born in Abyssinia (now called Ethiopia). He completed his studies in Cairo and at the Gorki Institute in Moscow. After the defeat of the Rassite dynasty and the establishment of the republic in 1962, he returned to Yemen. He served as chargé d'affaires in Moscow and Berlin, as well as in other governmental positions, until his death in a plane crash in 1973. A major novelist and short story writer, he focused on the pathos inherent in human experience. While he wrote of the frailty of individuals, of alienation and isolation, of loneliness and the bitter twists of fate; he also spoke about social issues, about oppression and intimidation.

Abu Rubbiya*

A few raindrops were falling as I stood in front of the shop shivering with cold. But those drops did not bother me; what concerned me was, why was he late? Upon a wall I could glimpse his latest drawing, finished yesterday—the drawing smiled. How nice this Abu Rubbiya was . . .

I sat on the steps of the shop and collected my memories of him. Three years ago I had been sitting in the small square in front of our shop when he came walking up sedately, looking at the ground, kicking stones with his foot. He seemed to be in deep thought, as if something was bothering him. When he saw me, he smiled and said, "May I sit down?"

I laughingly replied, "Why not? This square is God's domain."

He shook his head surprisedly, looking at the square and at me. "Is anything in this world left for God? I am amazed to hear you say that. People have swallowed God's rights. This square is the government's property and you, here, represent the government."

I laughed heartily—I, an elementary-school pupil, represented the government? What an odd idea!

"Sit down, Abu Rubbiya," I told him.

"How do you know my name?"

"Is there anyone in Addis Ababa who doesn't?"

He sat beside me and his small cane began tracing lines that quickly turned into a comic drawing in the earth. He inhaled deeply, staring at it.

"Listen, what is your name?"

"Saeed."

"Do you attend the community school?"

"Yes," I said proudly. "I'm in the fifth grade."

Abu Rubbiya was thirty-five, dark-faced with deep-set eyes and a mysterious smile that seemed to mock people.

"Listen Saeed, can you tell what I've drawn?"

"It's a donkey."

He tapped me on my back gently with his cane, saying, "Look closely."

All that lay in front of me was a donkey. When I stared harder, however, the head began to resemble a well-known person.

"That's Bajahsh!"

I laughed—the picture now looked just like him.

"But why is he a donkey?"

"His name is Bajahsh,[1] and he is also a donkey. He would not give me a *rubbiya*[2] yesterday."

---

*Translated by Lena Jayyusi and Naomi Shihab Nye
[1] The meaning of "Bajahsh" is the "father of an ass," *jahsh* meaning an ass.
[2] A monetary unit. [eds.]

He was silent for a while, then asked, "What would you like to be when you grow up?"

I replied quickly, "A merchant."

"Ass! Don't you know that merchants are a bad lot? You want to be bad like them?"

"No, I want to be a merchant so I can help the poor."

"Ah son, all of them said they would help the poor when they were young, like you, and today they all have lots of money. They have forgotten everyone else."

Then he asked if I wanted him to draw me something else. His cane sketched quickly on the ground. Mountains, a sun, people and more donkeys began to appear, as well as other things which I could not identify.

"What's that, Abu Rubbiya?"

"Your country."

He went on drawing and drawing as sweat poured down his face. Suddenly I saw a tear roll down his cheek. He was staring at his picture, then turned suddenly and gestured toward the distance.

"You know your country is out there? It's beautiful! Full of mountains and trees, sun and valleys. How would you know, you're too young . . . haven't you ever been to Yemen?"

"No."

"Then how would you know . . . Listen, you must go to Yemen! What are you doing here in someone else's country?"

I did not answer him. I knew my father's country was far away. I had heard my father speak of my grandfather whom I had never seen, and of brothers I had never seen. I had heard my father's friends mention so many things—gold, newspapers, things I did not understand. I whispered to Abu Rubbiya, "Listen, Abu Rubbiya, what do the newspapers say?"

He banged on the ground with his cane. "Newspapers! They are all lies, my son, don't believe them. They're greedy. If you have money, they'll honor you. If you don't, no one will even greet you. Listen, Saeed, why do all the Yemenis emigrate? They are cowards! They couldn't stay in their own country, so they ran away from it, left it to the bastards. Don't you see, they began emigrating a 1000 years ago, maybe more . . . they said the Ma'reb Dam was destroyed, and who destroyed it? A little mouse? See, they are liars, they destroyed the dam with their corruption, then failed to build other dams and ran away. God says, 'Saba[3] had in their land two wondrous Edens, one on

---

[3]Saba is the Biblical 'Sheba', the region in southern Arabia which includes Yemen. Among the ancient monuments was the Ma'reb Dam whose ruins are still to be seen not far from Sanaa, the contemporary capital of North Yemen. The bursting of the Ma'reb Dam is described in folk legend to have been caused by a mouse which made a hole in a strategic spot in the dam, causing it to burst.

the left and one on the right: eat from your Lord's blessing and thank Him. It is a good country and He is an indulgent God.'[4] Yes, Saeed, we had a good country. And haven't you heard of Balqis?[5] You're still young, when you grow up you'll understand everything. Balqis was the first woman chosen leader by the people. See how far our civilization had come? And what do we have now? All of us have run away, leaving our women at home."

He sighed deeply and continued, "Yes, we have gone to seek our livelihoods in other people's countries, when our own country is full of gold. God said in the Quran there was no place better than our country. Ah, a paradise . . . but it yearns for people, it yearns for its men."

We became friends. Often we visited the homes of the rich, so he could draw their portraits on the walls. One person was drawn as a goat ramming a rock with his horns. We would sit back while the people examined the pictures, laughing, "You know, Saeed," he would whisper, "if I were to go to Yemen, I would be rich."

"And you would forget the poor people?"

He would laugh heartily, saying, "No, I wouldn't forget. In Yemen one is in his own country, but here we live in a foreign land. They can tell we are strangers. It's a shame how they say, 'Look at that Yemeni walking barefoot in torn clothes.' But what can we do? God has given rich people hearts of stone."

And we would go our own ways.

Despite our friendship, I did not know where Abu Rubbiya lived. Each time I asked him, he would answer, "My friend, God's land is vast."

"But you said that people had taken God's land."

"That's right, don't be upset—the Government's land is vast."

Abu Rubbiya took pains to draw people he disliked in various ways. He once said, "You know, Bajahsh gave me five *rubbiyas* today." Then he added with pride, "But I refused them, so they won't say I am greedy. I took only one *rubbiya* from him."

Rain was still falling. The drawings on the wall looked like they were crying in the rain. The road was empty, save for a few carriages rushing by.

Where was he? Something must have happened to him. For three long years he had never been late like this. Only once had he been absent, when he had an illness. He had looked terrible then, losing weight till he was as thin as his cane. Next time I saw him, weak and pale, he had apologized. "What am I to do? God afflicted me with sickness."

---

[4]From verse 15, chapter XXXIV of the Quran.
[5]Queen Balqis is the Biblical Queen of Sheba. The ruins of her ancient palace are still to be seen not far from Sanaa.

I had once asked him why he didn't work at a regular job.

"You're still young, you don't understand. Don't I work every day? I thought you were mature enough to understand drawing as an art . . . listen, drawing is the best work in the world!"

"Yes, but it doesn't feed anyone."

"Who wants to eat? The important thing is, people feel good when they see my drawings. People often wish they could describe this or that merchant as a donkey or a dog. But they can't. In my drawings I can and no one can tell me anything."

"Why not?"

"You know how if you tell someone he's a dog, he gets angry? Yet you can draw him as a dog or donkey, people laugh, and he is not upset. This is human nature. When you grow up you will understand everything."

But Abu Rubbiya did not return. A week went by and most of his drawings were erased from the walls. Only a small one was left, and it was one he had made for me. . . . Once he had asked me again, "What would you like to be when you grow up?"

I had answered quickly, "An artist."

The little picture was of me, with a brush in my hand. He had written my name under it.

Suddenly, I heard my father's voice. "What's the matter with you? Every day you're out there. The cold will kill you, do you want to die? Come on inside or I'll teach you a lesson!"

But I was gazing out into the streets sadly. When I went in, my father sat at the table balancing his accounts. I asked him, "Do you know where Abu Rubbiya is?"

"They deported him."

"To where?"

"To Yemen."

"Why?"

"Because he's crazy."

Five years later I left Addis Ababa for Aden. Amidst the noise of a coffee-bar in the Shaikh Uthman area, I sat one day sipping a glass of tea. Suddenly I caught a glimpse of my old friend.

I called out, "Abu Rubbiya! Abu Rubbiya!"

He turned to me but, before I could reach and embrace him, he had run outside. I ran after him, but he disappeared into the crowds. He wore tattered clothes, his feet were bare and his face looked miserable.

The coffee-bar owner asked me, "Where do you know him from? He's called the Madman. He sits every day scrawling on the walls, making pictures of people that look like dogs."

I said, "He is not mad."

"Then why doesn't he look for work and be kind to his own stomach?"
There was nothing else to say.

❇ Discussion and Writing

1. Examine Abu Rubbiya's artwork as his commentary on people, their values, and behavior. Describe the targets of his criticism.
2. Comment on his love for Yemen and his knowledge of Quranic religious history. What do they indicate about his personality?
3. Discuss the inherently conflicting perspectives about art, work, and money in the narrative. What is the implication of Abu's asking for a *rubbiya* from others?
4. Explain the irony of Abu's return to Yemen and his treatment by the people.
5. Comment on the young narrator's perception of Abu Rubbiya. How effective is he as a grown-up in defending Abu: what does the last scene imply?

❇ Research and Comparison

Interdisciplinary Discussion Question: Research the economic and political situations in Yemen that constitute the background of "Abu Rubbiya." Compare two stories from the Middle East that reflect similar economic and political strains.

Saeed Aulaqi
(b. 1940)
Yemen

Saeed Aulaqi was born in South Yemen, an area that was under British rule at the time and called Aden. The country gained independence in 1967, but fought two wars with its neighbor, Yemen (or North Yemen), over the issue of unification. Saeed Aulaqi has written about the two revolutions as well as on social and moral questions. Highly regarded for his plays and his fiction, he has a keen eye for irony and for human blindness.

The Succession*

Morning rose over the capital and the great race began; suffocating crowds milling the aisles of the wholesale produce market, anxious living bodies of sweat and eagerness crammed together in the swirl of all their hopes. As the sun raised its head higher, throwing giant flames, the crowd intensified, cursed by the crush of routine.

Above this human mass, awash in the acrid odor of perspiration, loomed Haj[1] Fariᶜ Salem, Emperor of the Market, standing on a raised platform, waving his hand. Gestures accompanied his ringing, self-assured tones and his hand prominently displayed its three gold rings. His expensive automatic watch reflected the rays of the sun against the faces of the poor, long-suffering peasants.

Into the mad throng slipped Fadeel, a peasant arriving from the countryside with his produce, trying to find a foothold for himself and trying to sell his produce. He merged with the crowd like an ant, the demands of his wife Khadija and her children cutting wide, crazed pathways through his brain.

But Fadeel felt hopeful, nevertheless, imagining a new set of clothes to replace his torn rags. His body was gnarled and brown from years of scorching rural sun. Pushing hard, he advanced slowly toward Haj Fariᶜ's platform which monopolized the wholesale distribution of produce. At the moment that Fadeel arrived at the platform, all the crows in the area were croaking.

For five years, the same scene had been repeating itself . . . the suffocating crush, the sweat, the eagerness, the unrealized hopes, the scorching, cursed sun, and the rings and watch of Haj Fariᶜ. Faces grew more sullen as time passed and backs became more stooped. Even smiles died more rapidly before they could choose the faces that would wear them. Days passed and nothing was accomplished beyond regret and growing wistfulness.

But tonight was different.

Tonight, Fadeel would not sleep until he arrived at a resolution which would settle his accounts with Haj Fariᶜ, who bought his produce at one quarter the price at which he later sold it.

Fadeel rented an old wooden bed on the sidewalk, stretched over it in sweet relaxation and began to muse.

His whole life passed before his eyes again, rapidly, without order, strangely as in a dream. He stared at it hopelessly as though it were incumbent on him to account for everything leading up to this evening. His life

---

*Translated by Lena Jayyusi and Naomi Shihab Nye
[1]Haj or Haji: honorific title given to one who has fulfilled the vow of going on a pilgrimage to Mecca. [eds.]

formed, disintegrated and reformed anew . . . a continuous reconstruction of events.

Before this night, Fadeel had not really thought of his children, the future, or the miserable life they all led. He was like a windmill, turning each time the wind blew. He was also utterly illiterate, enough reason, he thought, to curse himself, his father and mother and the circumstances that had led to this, every time he had occasion to review the reel of his life. But tonight he engaged in a deep dialogue with himself, attempting to shake off old dust and sketch a new path for himself.

He muttered sorrowfully, "My life is a waste—if I could just take a sponge and wipe off all that is behind me, all that I have heard or seen, then re-enter the great school of life and learn its genuine alphabet—how different and enjoyable my new life would be."

He thought of the practical steps he would need to take. "It would be necessary to incite the poor peasants against Haj Farić so they could gain their rights. We need a collective stand in the face of exploitation! We must do something to stop the sucking of our blood and the theft of the fruits of our labors!" And he sank into dreams all over again.

He saw himself with all the peasants behind him, proclaiming in Haj Farić's face, "Down with exploitation!"

Then he would sprint up and grasp Haj Farić's neck, which turned into part of a limestone statue in his dream. He would attack the statue with his pickaxe until it smashed and collapsed to the rhythm of the peasants' slogans. Then *he* would sit on the statue's pedestal!

Sometimes the dream was different. He saw himself walking through the heart of the city after midnight, while everyone slept, on the road leading him outside the city to the cemetery. He would dig up the graves of the dead and recite inflammatory speeches to them . . . then a mad tuneless symphony would assault his ears. It did not emanate from any instrument. And his vision would blur: Khadija and her frizzy hair would take over with the demands that shot out of her mouth like bullets from a machine-gun. He would feel himself rushing at her, gathering her hair into his fist, silencing her lips with a hard kiss like movie stars did at the cinema. But he could not bear the smell of garlic and onions, produce he grew himself, that wafted from her mouth. He lifted his head with a sudden vehemence that awakened him from his dreams and stared at the wooden bed beneath him, wondering amazedly, "How can I dream so much on such a bed?"

He rubbed his eyes lazily, while the last traces of dream swirled around in his head. "The day Khadija cried, her tears cut deep grooves in my heart until it felt like a blood-soaked pit."

Dawn caressed the roofs of the houses. The sun had almost risen. In the city dawn had a tepid taste, like left-over food or a joke which gives no pleasure, like the smile of a woman on the fortieth day after her husband's death.[2]

In the countryside, however, dawn had a distinctly special flavor, like cultivated earth after irrigation, or a full stable piled with cattle manure, like the scent of a boy baby on the day of his birth, or stark eternal truth, lacking all complication. This was the distinction that made country folk genuine human beings. In the country everything was capable of being understood, everything, despite its quietude. That was why a peasant's love for the countryside was limitless. There, and there alone, he could sense the origin of creation's flowering and extinction, as well as his own place within it. He could sense this with indescribable certainty, exempt from the burden of logic.

But how could the love of the countryside withstand the temptations of the city?

This was not something Fadeel contemplated lengthily. He simply said, "Do you know what it is to be a poor toiling peasant? It means, simply, that one is engaged in an endless war with the merciless enemy called exploitation."

Fadeel entered the market by its rear gate, determined to settle accounts with Haj Faric today. The market was unusually empty, except for some stragglers here and there. When he asked where Haj Faric was, someone told him the Emperor did not work on the day of the feast, since it was his own reception day, "something only the petit-bourgeois can enjoy! Poor people never get such lush food." Fadeel had forgotten the feast fell on this day.

He left, more determined than ever to have a confrontation.

When the promised day arrived, everything happened suddenly.

The crush of people inside the market was enormous. They gravitated rapidly to a bench where a simple peasant squatted, speaking in a loud, inflammatory voice. Ears that before had only been fed talk about prices, grains, transport and crops now listened to new words from a strange man. He was inspiring them with hopes for a better life. The crowd began to repeat after him, in a mad expanding roar, "Down with exploitation!"

Before a real riot started, Haj Faric escaped through the back door, the voices of the crowd blasting his old corners. The throng pledged allegiance to Fadeel as successor to Haj Faric and agreed enthusiastically to obey him and follow his leadership . . . exactly as they had once done with Haj Faric. Now they saw in Fadeel the savior who had come to end their exploitation,

---

[2]The fortieth day after a person's death is a day of ritual memorial. People flock to the family of the deceased for renewed condolences.

to take them by the hand and help them achieve their hopes, buried by the dusty years.

Fadeel's words did not truly express reality, but they tickled reality with a chanting, contagious power. He threw his words out with ardor, repeating them until their sweetness dissolved in his mouth.

After Fadeel began controlling the market, he quickly learned to enjoy the reception on feast days—good food became his great pleasure.

Nothing much was accomplished for the peasants, however, because Fadeel was suddenly comfortable. He had begun to learn the secrets of the market-place and became skilled at running its little empire. He abandoned all his former principles.

After a year he had become a bad copy of Haj Fari^c. A clique formed around him, set up a salon for qat[3] chewing and learned the intricate games of the market, subject to supply and demand, based on the exploitation of the farmers.

One afternoon Fadeel awoke from a three-year sleep, came out of the salon as usual, and started wandering aimlessly in the streets. Deep inside, he was determined to enjoy his new life to the hilt.

After ten years of marriage to Khadija—whose tears used to cut grooves through his heart—her image in his mind was transformed. Her features dissipated with his tumbled thoughts. "How was I ever able to spend all that time with such a woman? She is superficial, empty, naïve . . . she cannot see beyond her own two feet. Yet each time I determine to take a new wife, I am crushed by remorse."

He continued walking amid the threads of his own woven net. Suddenly laughter erupted from deep within him: it floated high as a soap bubble. Then calmly it burst, scattering glowing silver threads across the faces of the passers-by.

He wandered to the Idrus Road and found himself standing in front of Haj Fari^c's house, knocking calmly, yet eagerly, upon the door.

"I don't understand how I was able to talk to those people that day," he began, "nor how they accepted my words with so much simplicity. Everything happened so fast, as though I were a sorcerer displaying juggling tricks. From one day to the next I found myself forced into your place and, despite my great amazement at what had happened, I have just now found a plausible explanation!"

Fadeel was trying to win over Haj Fari^c, to open a gateway for his subsequent address.

Haj Fari^c replied somewhat cunningly, "The one-eyed man is king in the land of the blind. Those wretches were waiting for someone to open the

---

[3]A leaf chewed as a stimulant. [eds.]

gates of illusory hope in their dull minds. By pure chance you were that one-eyed king."

Fadeel continued, speaking thoughtfully, "Since the day that I succeeded you, I have been trying to convince myself that I stood on the edge of freedom and a new life. Only security betrayed me as I stared into the unknown. I was suddenly filled with terror such as I never knew before. At last I realized that my loneliness was the cause, and the only solution for that was marriage."

Haj Fari^c was rather perplexed by this declaration, and they were both silent. The pause was charged with expectation. After a moment, Fadeel cleared his throat and, with all his accumulated sexual frustration, almost hissed, "The damnedest moments of life . . . night-time without a wife!"

It seemed that Haj Fari^c now understood his intent, because he smiled broadly. The meeting ended with the reading of the Fatiha⁴ for Fadeel's betrothal to Wadiaa, Haj Fari^c's daughter.

Fadeel emerged happy, realizing he had crossed the narrow road that separated the dazzling clarity of truth from the labyrinth of illusion.

Marriage to a city girl was the greatest thing Fadeel could attain. Now he hoped to find the peace of mind which he had promised himself. But it kept eluding him.

In desperate attempts to regain the equilibrium he had lost, he plunged deeper into exploitation. No longer was it possible for him to hide behind the mask with which he had won the battle against Haj Fari^c. One of his friends advised him to be moderate, but he answered, "Do not encourage people too much! Don't tell them we are all equal, that we have the same rights, or they will trample on you, steal your bread, and leave you to starve!"

Surprise was voiced by another man.

"This was not your opinion at the beginning!"

Fadeel answered, "Opinions change every day according to the circumstances and needs of their bearers!"

Another friend asked him, "Are you really happy in your life?"

He answered falsely, "For the first time in my life I know happiness and I understand the uselessness of education for, without it, I have been able to achieve all I ever aspired to. Besides, I am more experienced and wiser in life than those who just have education."

He swallowed the juice of the *qat* which filled his left cheek. A surge of arrogance flooded him. "How, I wonder, did I get so wise?"

An educated man replied, "If the fool persists in his foolishness, he becomes a sage!"

---

⁴The Fatiha is the first chapter of the Koran. It is short and is recited on important occasions of either joy or sorrow. Here, it is recited to confirm the betrothal.

Before the circle broke up, Fadeel announced the good news of his intention to perform the pilgrimage to Makkah [Mecca].

After Fadeel had engaged in one of the fits of sexual frenzy with his wife Wadiaa which overcame him after he chewed *qat*, he sat in the calm of night, talking to her. "I have triumphed over your father, but he also defeated me with his defeat—he left me to drown in the seas of restless anxiety. No doubt he is better off than I am now."

Before the hour struck midnight, Wadiaa's delicate nightgown would be ripped open again, and all the legends would pale beside the curves of her ripe tall body; the legends of slave-girls and incense, the ardor of love-poets—Abu Nawwas[5] and Khayyam[6] would fall short and Abu Rabiaa[7] would rip up all his poems.

Fadeel was berserk on these occasions. He lost the reason which distinguished men from animals. He would pounce upon her, burying his nose between her breasts. With his tongue he would lick the drops of perspiration that settled beneath them, savoring the salty flavour in an ecstasy of carnal pleasure during which he imagined himself reconquering Andalusia,[8] piling up its women inside a giant stadium, to drown in the sea of their femininity.

After he awoke from his passion, he despaired again at his unsuccessful attempts to feel peaceful. He wished all the beautiful women in the world would die on the same day he died.

"If I had raided a bank, or stolen a million dollars, or killed a hundred innocent persons and escaped from the police; if I had planned a military coup d'état which failed, and eluded prison, my peace of mind would be greater than it is now, seated on the throne of the market, successor to Haj Fariᶜ."

He begged the night to end his sleeplessness, his anxiety and torment.

After his return from the pilgrimage, Fadeel was seen in the market waving his hand to greet those who welcomed him back. Three gold rings glittered on his fingers and a new automatic watch graced his wrist. A poor peasant emerged from the crowd to shout, "You are worse than your predecessor!"

Someone else tried to beat him up and, out of nowhere, a chanted slogan grew louder, "Down with exploitation!"

Chaos reigned until Haj Fadeel's assistants were able to impose order again.

---

[5]A great poet who wrote about love and wine (among other subjects). He lived in the eighth century AD.

[6]This is the famous Omar Khayyam, Persian author of the *Rubaiyyat*.

[7]This is Omar ibn Abu Rabiaa, the most famous love poet in classical Arabic poetry. He lived in the first century after Islam (seventh to eighth centuries A.D.).

[8]The Arabs ruled Andalusia or parts of it for over eight centuries, losing their final foothold there in A.D. 1492. The loss has never been forgotten by the Arabs.

Haj Fadeel wondered how long he could escape the attempts made upon him simply by ignoring them.

Days passed . . . crowded, scorching, sweating days . . . eagerness and fettered hopes continuously revolving. Each new morning the desire for change was renewed. Each day hidden wishes for rebellion surfaced in the frowning, grim faces of the poor peasants, only to be swallowed again.

But one morning, into the breathless crush slipped Mansour, a peasant arriving from the countryside, seeking a foothold and a price for his produce. Like an ant he merged into the crowd and, pushing mightily, was able to reach Haj Fadeel's platform.

At the moment he arrived there, all the crows in the area were croaking.[9]

❋ Discussion and Writing

1. Comment on the images describing Fadeel and Haj Fari^c Salem in the market at the beginning of the story.
2. Analyze Fadeel's confrontation with Haj Fari^c Salem: what is the importance of his dreams; what is implied by his forgetting the feast day; what is the impact of his words on the crowd; what is the outcome of his activism?
3. Why does Fadeel need Haj Fari^c Salem's daughter as a second wife? What is implied by his treatment of Wadiaa and his sexual fantasies?
4. Discuss the irony of Fadeel's emergence as Haj Fadeel and also as Emperor of the market. What are his new anxieties? What does the title "The Succession" indicate?
5. Contrast the setting of the wholesale produce market to that of the countryside.

❋ Research and Comparison

Compare "The Succession" with Ngugi Wa Thiong'o's "Wedding at the Cross," highlighting the question of cultural mores and social status.

Mahmoud Darwish
(b. 1942)
Palestine

Mahmoud Darwish was born in Galilee, in the village of Berweh, east of Acre, Palestine. Berweh was razed after the 1948 war when Israel added lands to its original territory, but he remained in Galilee until he left Israel

---

[9]The croaking or cawing of the crow is regarded as a bad omen in popular Arabic culture.

in 1971. He became politically active when he was quite young, joining the Israeli Communist Party, Rakah, and editing its newspaper, *Al-Ittihad* (Unity). Because of his political work, the government placed him under house arrest. Beleaguered but continuing to write, he moved to Beirut, where he remained the major poet of the Palestinian resistance. He subsequently became editor-in-chief of the eminent journal *Al-Karmel,* and has been recognized as one of the leading contemporary poets. His poetry resonates beyond the singular experience, although it is grounded in the particular, to incorporate a pervasive human longing for one's homeland, for justice, and for peace.

*Guests on the Sea**

Guests on the sea: Our visit is short
our talk is notes from the past shattered an hour ago
from what Mediterranean will the creation begin?
We set up an island
for our southern cry. Farewell, small island of ours.

We did not come to this country from a country
we came from pomegranates, from the glue of memory
from the fragments of an idea we came to this foam
Do not ask us how long we will stay among you, do not ask us
anything about our visit. Let us
empty the slow ships from the remains of our souls and our bodies.
Guests on the sea. Our visit is short.
And the earth is smaller than our visit. We shall send another apple
to the waters, circles within circles, where are we to go
when we leave? Where are we to go back to when we return? My God
what is left of the resistance of our souls? What directions are left
What earthen frontiers are left? Is there another rock
over which to offer a new sacrifice for your mercy?
What is left of us that we may set out once again?

Sea, do not give us the song that we do not deserve.

The sea has its ancient craft:
ebb and flow;
woman has her first task: seduction
it is for poets to fall from melancholy
it is for martyrs to explode in dream
it is for wise men to lead a people on towards happy dreams
Sea, do not give us the song that we do not deserve

---

*Translated by Lena Jayyusi and W. S. Merwin

We did not come to this place from the language of place
the plants of the distance have grown tall, the shadow of the sand
      has grown long within us and spread out
our short visit has grown long. How many moons have given their
   rings to one who is not of us. How many stones
has the swallow laid in the distance. How many years
shall we sleep as guests on the sea, wait for a place
and say: In a little while we shall leave here.
We have died from sleep and have broken here.
It is only the temporary that will last in us, age of the sea.

Sea, do not give us the song that we do not deserve

We want to live for a time, not for nothing
but just that we can set out again
Nothing of our ancestors remains in us, but we want
the country of our morning coffee
we want the fragrance of primitive plants
we want a special school
we want a special cemetary
we want a freedom
the size of a skull . . . and a song.

Sea, do not give us the song that we do not deserve

we did not come just for the sake of coming . . .
the sea tossed us up at Carthage as shells and a star
who can remember how the words lit up into a homeland for those
   who have no doorway?
Who remembers the ancient bedouins when they seized the world . . .
   with a word?
Who remembers the slain as they rushed to break the secrets of the
   myths?
They forget us, we forget them, life lives its own life.
Who now remembers the beginning and the end?
We wish to live for a time just to return to something
anything
anything
to a beginning, an island, a ship, an ending
a widow's prayer, a cellar, a tent.
Our short visit has grown long
and the sea died within us two years ago . . . the sea has died within
   us.

Sea, do not give us the song that we do not deserve

❋ Discussion and Writing

1. Who are the guests on the sea? Where do they come from? What do the images of "pomegranates" and the "glue of memory" evoke?
2. Explain the meaning of the journey. Why does the short visit grow long?
3. Discuss the significance of the biblical allusions to the creation, the apple, the sacrifice, and mercy.
4. What is implied by the repeated phrase "Sea, do not give us the song we do not deserve"?
5. Analyze the metaphoric use of the woman, the poet, the martyr, and the wise men.
6. Explore the imagery of distance and alienation as the language of the land.
7. Comment on the implications of the images describing what is lost and what is desired. What is implied by the phrase "the sea has died within us"?

❋ Research and Comparison

Interdisciplinary Discussion Question: Research the history of Palestine that generates the emotions depicted in Mahmoud Darwish's poetry. Examine the portrayal of the political upheaval in his work.

Erez Bitton
(b. 1949)
Israel

Erez Bitton was born in Oran, Algeria. An accident that occurred when he was a child caused him to become blind, a condition that resonates in much of his poetry. In 1948, he moved to Israel, where he has worked as a psychologist and social worker, and where he has had a major impact on younger writers. As editor of the literary journal *Aperion,* he has influenced Israeli culture by establishing a platform for intellectuals and artists of the region. His own poetry merges his native North African and Middle Eastern motifs, language, and poetic patterns. Written in Moroccan Arabic, his poems spring from the lively tradition of poetry as a performed art, and indeed, Bitton frequently reads his work in concert with traditional music. It is in this implicit formulation of a contemporary poetics, honoring indigenous material and sound, that the source of his role in Israeli literature lies: poetry written in Moroccan Arabic and using local imagery and rhythms, for instance, can no longer be denigrated as "folkloric."

Something on Madness*

And you ask that we not get dizzy like an angry squall.
And you ask that we sigh over allusions
through cigar smoke
or at most a rhymed whistle,
but our sighs are like a tempest.
We were loathsome to you.
our impact was hard and strange
yet why did you cast us out upon our birthplace
why did you banish us to all the ruins,
you stand at the brink of laughter, perplexed, lawless,
you stand bewildered before the lamenting,
but what was the revolt about,
for surely how can it be possible that in a place where vented
anger arouses lamentation even in the heart of dogs
in a place where great rage condemns us upon all the crucifixes
that our laments will not be foreign,
our mourning not superfluous,
and you keep on giving flimsy excuses
claiming not to really cry
except at the mere suggestion—
through cigar smoke or at most a rhymed proclamation of despair—

you claim to be indifferent
in a place where people are brought up
with sterilized tweezers
in a place where even the earth is redolent of spikenard
                                        bound by nocturnal sea,
you who scattered us to all the ruins
you who transferred us to all the shanties
do at least this much for us,
leave us to our laments
we shattered pearls of verse.

❋ Discussion and Writing

1. Identify the "you" and "we" in the poem. What is the nature of their association?
2. Explain the symbolism of the "cigar smoke," a "rhymed whistle," and the "crucifixes."

_____

*Translated by Ammiel Alcalay

3. Describe the treatment of the persona in his birthplace. What is the persona's overpowering emotion; what is the tone of the poem: help-lessness, despair, assertion?
4. Define the nature of madness in the poem. Whose madness is it?

❀ Research and Comparison

Examine the evolution of the "Diaspora" and "Palmach" traditions in Israeli literature (see this part's Introduction), and discuss their themes in rela-tion to those of the Middle Eastern writers included in the anthology.

Fawziyya Abu Khalid
(b. 1955)
Saudi Arabia

Fawziyya Abu Khalid was born in Riyadh, Saudi Arabia. She studied in the United States, taking a degree in sociology, and has been teaching at the Girls' University College of King Saud University. Her poetry reveals a keen sensibility and an optimism, a belief in human endeavor. Her work celebrates the strength and abilities of women, as well as indicating her commitment to political concerns.

A Pearl*

This Pearl
Was a gift of my grandmother—that great lady—
    to my mother
    and my mother gave it me
And now I hand it on to you
The three of you and this pearl
Have one thing in common
    simplicity and truth
I give it with my love
And with the fullness of heart
    you excel in
The girls of Arabia will soon grow
    to full stature

Translated by Salwa Jabsheh and John Heath-Stubbs

They will look about and say:
"She has passed by this road"
and point to the place of sunrise
and the heart's direction.

❈ Discussion and Writing

1. What is shared by the three women and the "precious pearl of Arabia"? Comment on the symbolism of the pearl.
2. Discuss the attitudes that are projected in the poem regarding the women of Arabia.

❈ Research and Comparison

Interdisciplinary Discussion Question: Research the issue of women's position in modern Arabia. Examine the importance of the perspective presented in "A Pearl."

Shelley Elkayam
(b. 1956)
Israel

Shelley Elkayam, who was born in Haifa, Israel, comes from a Haifan family that dates back seven generations. A political activist, she is dedicated to peace in the region and to improving social conditions. She is engaged in the women's movement, and is concerned with educational reform. Her moral passion informs her poetry; at the same time, its subject matter and versification vary considerably, ranging from the personal to the social, and across time and the world for its imagery and allusions. Her work has paved the way for younger Sephardic artists.

The Crusader Man*

The Crusader man paid the Land a visit
and that was
around
so and so many
years back.

*Translated by Ammiel Alcalay

The Crusader man did the country
in this
or that many days.

The Crusader became the landlord.
An enemy with holdings.
Full of trust,
sword-bearing, armor-wearing, with a coat of mail.

Kind of a jumpy guy, the Crusader man.

The Land is a witness,
she sees it from
the way he laid his
place out,
from the fact
that he never did make himself a home.
From the way he'd attack
and cut himself off on the mountain tops.

❋ Discussion and Writing

1. Identify the Crusader man who came for a visit and remained to be a landlord.
2. What are the implications of what the Land witnessed of the Crusader man's activities?
3. Elaborate on the poet's perspective of the racial and religious conflicts in her land.

❋ Research and Comparison

Examine the issues of racial, class, and caste tensions reflected in the works of any two Israeli writers.

Abd al-Hameed Ahmad
(b. 1957)
United Arab Emirates

Abd al-Hameed Ahmad was born in the United Arab Emirates. Although his formal schooling lasted up to only the secondary level, he read widely, acquiring a solid literary education. He became deputy head of the Union of Writers in the United Arab Emirates. Considered one of the major short

story writers in the Persian Gulf area, and honored especially for his
poignancy and compassion, he turned his attention to the consequences of
the sudden wealth accrued as a result of the discovery of oil. He has
depicted both the tragic and comic consequences of the discovery and
how it has impinged on people's lives.

Khlalah SEL*

"Khlalah[1] SEL came." "Khlalah SEL's gone." "Have you seen Khlalah SEL?"

He arrives every morning, steps out of the car, his clothes dirty and his
face taut and dark, eyes small and gleaming like faint embers that glow and
fade in a soft breeze. He walks slowly to his familiar seat.

Khlalah SEL has acquired new qualities since the great change.
Everything happened with amazing speed that not only astonished him but
everyone else who had known the man and his former character. The children, particularly the school children, began to chase after him and call out
his new name. In no time he'd become the current topic of discussion in
every gathering, for some a cause of envy, of pity for others. As for him, he
never understood what had happened to him; he had accepted it all with
incredulous astonishment. His surrender had been like the surrender of a
corpse at burial, or of a wounded bird caught in the trap of a cunning hunter.
All of a sudden he found himself spinning in a new and different orbit, spinning at dizzying speed.

One day—a long time ago—the townspeople, particularly the old ones
who knew Khlalah well, noticed that—contrary to what they were accustomed to expect—the man was sad and frightened; they'd never known him
to be like that before. He'd always been happy in spite of his poverty. His
small world held no secrets or sadness, and was open for anyone to see. But
today they saw a different man in front of them. What had happened?

Moreover, where was Massoud? The absence of Massoud encouraged
one of them to ask: "Where is Massoud?" Khlalah looked at him with almost
tearful eyes. In a husky voice edged with sorrow, he answered: "Massoud!
Poor Massoud, I don't know how I could provide for him." And he fell
silent, as did the others. Khlalah was sunk in a bottomless pool of grief. For
Massoud was not only Khlalah's best friend but his partner in life and work,
and his only source of income. That was how folk saw the close relationship
between them. Khlalah's compassion for Massoud was like that for a child;
he cared more for him than for Khatoun, his wife. Khlalah never denied the
true reason for all that care. With honesty he admitted: "Without this donkey,
I'd starve to death." Of course everyone believed him.

Translated by Salwa Jabsheh and David Wright
[1]A *khlalah* is an immature palm fruit, green and unripe.

In the courtyard Khlalah had built a tent out of palm fronds in which Massoud enjoyed warmth, plenty of fodder and date pits, rice and onions, to say nothing of the water that Khlalah changed for him every evening. Perhaps no other animal in the world was so well cared for as Massoud. Even his saddle was made of cloth stuffed with cotton to save his back from being galled. In the neighborhood where they used to walk, the clatter of Massoud's hoofs raising a cloud of dust behind them, children used to run after them and hang on to Massoud's tail and annoy him. Khlalah knew how to protect Massoud from their mischief. He would stop, and so would Massoud, the picture of dignity with his russet coat, clear shining eyes and nimble body. And when they had halted long enough, Massoud like a statue with eyes fixed to the ground, the naughty youngsters would become bored and go away jeering.

The two of them would go out early every morning when the dew still hung in the air; in time they seemed to become part of the landscape. People could hardly remember a day when they saw the one without the other, as they roamed the streets looking for work.

Every morning, above the early call to prayer, Massoud's braying could be heard. Enchanted by his incessant braying, Khlalah would pray: "You generous Provider, You who are merciful to all mankind, You who know what's to become of us, we rely on You."

They were inseparable like a man and his shadow. People were used to seeing them together, Massoud leaving his droppings behind him in a straight line, his warm breath mingling with the cold morning air. They worked together, carrying people's belongings from the scattered houses to the main square, or bringing water, or doing the various other jobs that folk asked them to do. Even after Khlalah had persuaded the Balushi family to let him marry the bad-tempered Khatoun, and even after their children were born, he stayed loyal to Massoud; while Massoud stayed loyal and loving to Khlalah. In the evenings when they came home after a hard day's work, Khlalah—tall and slender as a lath—would stand at the edge of the well, bringing up water in a big pail to throw cold over Massoud. And when he'd finished he'd carefully dry his wet body and lead him to his tent where he would pat his head tenderly and bid him good night, after giving him food and changing his water.

So the sad heavy look that covered Khlalah's face one day puzzled the people. Some said:

"Maybe something bad happened to him or Massoud." Others speculated: "Perhaps one of his family is sick."

But Khlalah kept silent, at times scrutinizing their faces, at times staring into vacancy. He was so sad he felt his heart was going to break. It was as if a nightmare or ghost was tearing at his heart to split it with a sharp poisoned blade. Still the folk round him insisted on knowing what was wrong. Then his eyes overflowed with tears, flowing like a stream in spate after a night of thunder and rain. Obviously hurt, his voice distressed, he said:

"You people ought to understand. I was working, so was Massoud. We were able to survive. But now! What next?"

One of them interrupted:

"We've told you that Massoud wasn't going to be any use to you from now on, why can't you believe us?"

As Khlalah trembled like one possessed, another added:

"Do you expect us to stop using our cars so you can carry our goods on your donkey's back?"

A third, trying to calm Khlalah down, remarked, "Khlalah, the world is in better shape now, you will definitely find another job."

Another observed gravely: "The age of the donkey is over!"

But Khlalah sank deeper into his depression and fell into a fit of weeping; he felt as if he were being pulled deep into a bottomless pit, there to drown. He stopped listening to their talk, until a sentence pierced his ear like a bullet: "The world has changed. Don't you realize that?"

Khlalah knew nothing, understood nothing, but the terrible new destroying sorrow looped around him like some fearful python squeezing at his ribs. All he knew was that after happy years which had passed as quick as lightning, all of a sudden he was jobless, his livelihood threatened; for the first time in his life he was afraid of starving. Massoud will starve and die and so will Khatoun and her children! And Khlalah knew no way by which he could feed them. Hunger and grief spread before him until almost all else was blotted out, like the legendary bird that spreads its wings to block the light of the sun, and so brings utter darkness. Then someone gave a parting shot:

"Do what all the others did, you might have luck finding a job in one of the government ministries."

Khlalah's head ached as if bells were tolling in it. He stood there alone while darkness spread and formed shadows that increased his depression and bewilderment and fear. Work! Ministry! My God, how? I don't even know where the Ministry is! Then suddenly, having remembered something, he dragged himself off to his neighbor Khammas:

"Khammas! Do you happen to know where the Ministry is?"

Khammas laughed until the tears came. After a spell of coughing and sneezing he said:

"And why haven't you asked Massoud?" But, seeing that Khlalah was not his normal self and in no mood to bear with his usual banter, he felt his sarcasm was in bad taste, so went on:

"But which ministry do you mean, Khlalah?"

Khlalah's thin features filled with surprise, transformed into the face of a child caught doing the wrong thing by his father. Defeated, he said:

"The ministry where people work. Is there another one?"

The interminable conversations that Khlalah had with Khammas, and his later conversation with the responsible official he met at the Ministry, became the talk of the town and a subject for jokes. And when Khlalah took over his new job as caretaker for one of the schools, they asked themselves—and Massoud:

"What are you going to do now, Massoud?"

But this question was soon answered. In the morning, when the streets were full of cars and pedestrians and noise, Khlalah would ride on Massoud's back (he'd never done so before). Massoud would fight his way to the school through the traffic and noise with Khlalah resting upon his back. Khlalah would gaze at the shops on either side of the road, at the cars and pedestrians passing by, with eyes free of any kind of confusion or bewilderment—or, to be more precise, with eyes lacking any kind of reaction to any sight, whether common or uncommon. Massoud's hoofs played a tune on the asphalt. They, Massoud and his rider, were a pair of oddities, things from another world suddenly manifesting themselves among built-up streets full of people and shops and cars. Many who were curious about them to start with lost interest now that their daily walk to the school became familiar, and accepted them as a customary phenomenon. At first they seemed not to belong to this age but, later, they became a pleasant daily morning sight. Months passed in this new peaceful life till one day Khlalah was astonished to hear his old neighbors and friends asking him:

"We've heard your name on the radio. What are you going to do when you receive your compensation?"

He, Khlalah, compensated? He who had the reputation among his old acquaintances of always being full of energy? In fact he was named after the *khlalah*, tough green date fruit that is ever young.

And as his head had begun to spin when haunted by fear of hunger, he was now frightened by this new mystery. What a time! Full of unexpected, odd and grotesque surprises! Khlalah had been encompassed by inquisitive looks when people found out about his earlier trouble, but now he was besieged with the news of a matter of which he'd been unaware. His mouth fell wide open like that of a haunted old well, enveloped by the silence of death. Compensation! Around him mad shadows of perplexity danced and jubilated. Idiots! Khlalah's peace of mind was lost; he was transfixed by worry and uncertainty. He asked, "Khammas, what is compensation?"

Khammas answered jeeringly, in a tone not free of a touch of jealousy, "They're opening a road where your old decrepit home now stands. You'll be compensated for it."

Khlalah did not believe what had happened. His throat felt tight, as if he were to burst out screaming. His ears drummed; his peaceful way of life was under threat. He raised his hand and pointed to his house. "But where would I live?" He heard a high-pitched laughter; Khammas was laughing sarcastically. Hateful laughter thundered in his ears. Khammas said: "Don't worry. I'll arrange matters for you."

But in Khlalah's ears the laughter kept echoing; it filled his days with uncertainty and fear of the unknown. But as it happened everything turned out quite differently from what he expected. He had never thought that things would be so much easier than he anticipated. To his surprise the bank manager came all the way to his home to see him, and told him cordially:

"We'd be pleased to receive the money on your behalf. It will be your money, and we'll keep it for you at the bank."

Without thinking, Khlalah asked: "Would it be 3000?"

The manager laughed. "More like three million."

Khlalah stammered like a baby. "Mr. Manager, what I really need is a house . . . "

Laughing, Khammas said: "A palace, you need a palace, not a house."

When Khlalah pushed open the outer glass door of the bank, wearing his yellowing *dashdasha*[2] that had once been white, his old threadbare *ghutra*[3] and worn-out shoes, the manager hurried to welcome him.

"Welcome, Khlalah, please come this way."

The manager led both Khlalah and Khammas to his office. His employees rose from their seats and stared unbelievingly at them with wide open eyes. One whispered in a friend's ear: "Can you beat that?" They could not believe that their peppery, short-tempered boss would get up to welcome a man who looked as poverty-stricken as Khlalah. Said one, "It's a strange world!" The other replied, "It's an age of miracles!"

When they returned home Khlalah was speechless. He looked round vacantly while Khammas remarked: "Did you hear what the bank manager said? What a kind man he is, they're going to build you a house and buy you a car."

However, Khlalah heard nothing but Khammas's thunderous laughter. He sank into a heavy gluey silence, his head blazing with turbulent thoughts, revolving round new, incredible, and seemingly insane calculations—confusing matters that he could not comprehend. And so Khlalah found himself drowning in new worries that tasted differently from those he used to have. He would begin counting—one, two, three, four—and then the numbers would get mixed up and he'd start counting again. People began to notice that the impoverished Khlalah, the ever-energetic, persistent and uncomplicated Khlalah, was turning into a confused worrier busily counting on his fingers, counting again and yet again.

While Khlalah was absentmindedly wandering around the streets like a tramp who'd lost his way, Massoud was roaming the new quarters of the city searching for food among the garbage dumped on the streets, sometimes pausing in front of the iron boxes outside the great entrance gates, often enduring painful blows from the angry inhabitants of the houses he passed by. He strayed far into the desert, where his eyes swelled, and tears mixed with dust dried on his eyelids. Boils and lesions filled with pus

---

[2]A long traditional robe, usually white, and worn by men. [eds.]

[3]A headdress worn by men in this region of the Arabian peninsula. [eds.]

covered his body. And Khlalah, overwhelmed by new happenings, was stupefied by the strange unexpected events that swept over him like a torrential flood. His life was now organized into a new routine. One morning, just before the students went to their classes as usual, they were surprised to see a gleaming, luxurious car stop in front of the iron gate. Curious to see who was in the car, the teachers, students, and caretakers gathered together, wondering if it were some senior government official or perhaps a minister come to visit the school for some reason. An Indian[4] driver got down to open the back door of the car. Suddenly their eyes opened wide with astonishment as they recognized Khlalah. Their bewilderment spread like fog. But Khlalah, wearing the same old clothes and the same old shoes, thrust his way through that fog to his usual chair. That day there was no donkey to tie in front of the gate as usual. Khlalah sat silent, oblivious to the commotion he had aroused. His eyes turned in their sockets as if looking at vacancy. The headmaster had to tell the teachers and students to go their classes. At noon the car returned, white and gleaming like milk in the sun. Khlalah seated himself in the back and the car sped off, throwing up clouds of dust behind it. One of the students cried: "My God, it's a Mercedes 500 SEL!"

As the car drove along the streets Khlalah's eyes roved over the different things they passed, in dumb amazement. Buyers and sellers, shops and lights and stores and buildings, Khlalah found it all unbelievable. Sunk in silence, he could not explain what was going on in his head. All that he ever did now was that, before the sun had dried the dew, he would go silently every morning to his car from the top floor of his new house which was hedged round with magnificent trees and many colored flowers. He'd take a piece of dry cloth, pour water over it and start cleaning the windows and bodywork until the car shone in the sunlight like a child's beautiful toy. Then Raj would come to drive it back to school while Khlalah sat tranquilly in the back seat, gazing stupidly at the streets and people. His eyes, once small and bright, were now like fading embers wilting in still air. Then he would walk slowly from the car to his caretaker's chair.

A cruel tedium now governed Khlalah's days. Time did not exist, he felt only the presence of these strange and surprising happenings, which to him were a fantastic new world he could not understand. Khlalah took refuge from it all in silence and bewilderment. A persistent worry filled his thoughts, just like the smell, the horrible smell that pervaded his bedroom one morning. It woke him up feeling drowsy and nauseated. The smell was coming from a new building being erected next to Khlalah's fine new house. Khlalah couldn't stand the smell. It filled the air, his bedroom and his lungs,

---

[4]With the oil boom, workers were admitted into the Gulf countries to do all kinds of jobs; they ranged from high-ranking bank officials to drivers and daily labourers. Many Indians were among them.

until it nearly suffocated him. He hastened to find Raj and banged at his door to ask about the smell. When the municipal workmen came to check, Khlalah had begun his morning task of cleaning his white car with a damp cloth. Then he saw that the workmen had found from where the smell came.

It was a decayed corpse, squeezed in between walls that had been built so close together that it could not get out. So it had starved to death, which had resulted in that terrible smell which interrupted Khlalah's sleep that fine morning. As the workers began carrying away the corpse to place it on the garbage truck to throw away, Khlalah finished cleaning his car. Raj came up and told him:

"Guess what, they've found a donkey there."

When the source of the smell that had disturbed Khlalah had been eradicated, the car sped on its morning route, heading for the wooden chair at the school entrance. Khlalah faced the morning and the people with the same glazed glance and silent absence of mind. He sat down on his chair in a silence like the silence of death, but for the children's repeated cry, "Khlalah SEL, Khlalah SEL," and the derisive laughter that hummed in the air like the buzzing of bees—Khammas's high, bitter, derisive laughter as he recalled what someone once said to Khlalah:

"The age of the donkey is over!"

But Khlalah still sat dazed in his chair with glazed eyes, in silence like the silence of death, like the surrender of a corpse at burial, like the surrender of a wounded bird caught in the trap of a cunning hunter.

✸ Discussion and Writing

1. Describe the alliance between Khlalah and Massoud. Comment on the statement "the age of the donkey is over."

2. Examine Khlalah's willingness to change: what is his stumbling block; in what ways is his name appropriate?

3. Analyze the function of Khammas and the other townspeople in Khlalah's life as well as in the narrative.

4. Compare Khlalah's ride to his place of work on Massoud and in the Mercedes 500 SEL: analyze the mixing of the comic and the pathetic.

5. Explain the impact of the metaphor of "dizzying speed" and "a different orbit" in the context of Khlalah's life.

6. Explore the significance of the correlation between Khlalah's anxiety and the suffocating smell.

7. What are the implications of the last paragraph, regarding Khlalah's surrender. Comment on the effect of using the same details at the beginning and at the end of the story.

8. Analyze "Khlalah SEL" as a variation of two usual motifs: one, the exploitation of the poor because of industrialization; and two, "from rags to riches."

✳ Research and Comparison

Interdisciplinary Discussion Question: Research the issue of the changes in the lives of common people because of modernization in any nation of the Middle East. Comment on the explosion of oil money and the price the society may pay.

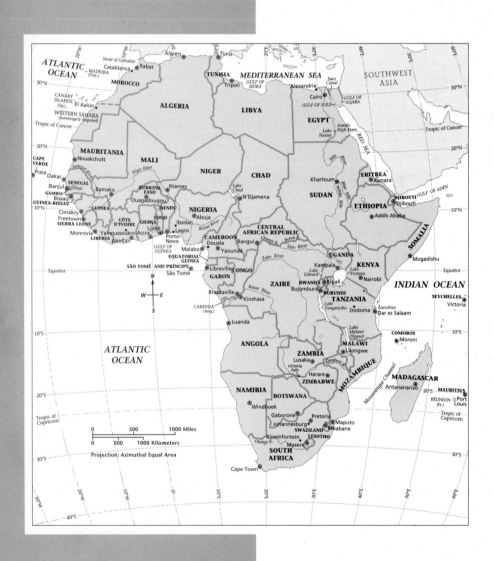

ATLANTIC OCEAN

Strait of Gibraltar

Casablanca
MADEIRA (Port.)

Rabat

Algiers

Tunis

TUNISIA

MEDITERRANEAN SEA

SOUTHWEST ASIA

30°N

MOROCCO

Tripoli

GULF OF SIDRA

Alexandria

Suez Canal

GULF OF AQABA

30°N

CANARY ISLANDS (Sp.)

El Aaiún

ALGERIA

LIBYA

EGYPT

GULF OF SUEZ

Cairo

WESTERN SAHARA
(Sovereignty disputed)

Tropic of Cancer

Tropic of Cancer

20°N

Aswân High Dam

Lake Nasser

RED SEA

20°N

MAURITANIA

Nouakchott

MALI

Niger River

NIGER

CHAD

Nile River

Khartoum

Asmara

ERITREA

CAPE VERDE

Praia

Dakar

SENEGAL

Sénégal River

Bamako

Niamey

BURKINA FASO

Lake Chad

N'Djamena

SUDAN

White Nile

Blue Nile

Djibouti

DJIBOUTI

GULF OF ADEN

Banjul

GAMBIA

GUINEA-BISSAU

Ouagadougou

NIGERIA

Abuja

CENTRAL AFRICAN REPUBLIC

ETHIOPIA

10°N

10°N

Conakry

Freetown

SIERRA LEONE

GUINEA

CÔTE D'IVOIRE

GHANA

TOGO

BENIN

Ibadan

Benue River

Addis Ababa

SOMALIA

Monrovia

Yamoussoukro

Accra

Lomé

Lagos

Porto-Novo

Abidjan

LIBERIA

CAMEROON

Douala

Malabo

Yaoundé

Bangui

Ubangi R.

Bomu R.

Uele River

UGANDA

KENYA

Mogadishu

GULF OF GUINEA

EQUATORIAL GUINEA

SÃO TOMÉ AND PRÍNCIPE

Libreville

CONGO

GABON

São Tomé

Zaïre River

ZAIRE

Kasai River

RWANDA

BURUNDI

Kigali

Bujumbura

Kampala

Lake Edward

Lake Victoria

Nairobi

Equator

Equator

INDIAN OCEAN

SEYCHELLES

Victoria

Brazzaville

Kinshasa

TANZANIA

Lake Tanganyika

Dodoma

Zanzibar

Dar es Salaam

CABINDA (Ang.)

Luanda

10°S

ATLANTIC OCEAN

ANGOLA

ZAMBIA

Lusaka

Zambezi R.

Victoria Falls

Lake Malawi (Nyasa)

MALAWI

Lilongwe

COMOROS

Moroni

10°S

Harare

ZIMBABWE

MOZAMBIQUE

Mozambique Channel

MADAGASCAR

Antananarivo

MAURITIUS

Port Louis

NAMIBIA

BOTSWANA

Windhoek

Gaborone

Pretoria

Johannesburg

SWAZILAND

Maputo

Mbabane

RÉUNION (Fr.)

20°S

Tropic of Capricorn

Tropic of Capricorn

20°S

N
W — E
S

0   500   1000 Miles

0   500   1000 Kilometers

Projection: Azimuthal Equal Area

Bloemfontein

Orange R.

LESOTHO

Maseru

SOUTH AFRICA

30°S

30°S

Cape Town

Africa

I call Gold,
Gold is mute.
I call Cloth,
Cloth is mute.
It is Mankind that matters.
AKAN

The long reach of African history stretches back some two million years to what has been called the cradle of humanity at Olduvai gorge and Lake Turkana. From this beginning, it unfolds in long, slow arcs of time, tracing its patterns across centuries of commerce, migration, and the mingling of peoples, the flowering of cultures, and the rise and fall of kingdoms. Five to six thousand years ago, people farmed the land that is now the Sahara, that forbidding desert dividing North Africa from the rest of the continent, and traders crisscrossed the region on well-worn routes. (See map) People in West Africa were speaking the three or four languages that eventually separated into the more than four hundred spoken there today. In Egypt, farming communities that had dotted the Nile valley for some fifteen hundred years were about to be united under a single ruler, leading to the development of an empire celebrated for its cultural, technical, and commercial accomplishments, the Old Kingdom (3110–2258 B.C.E.).

By the time the Sahara began to dry up (c. 2000 B.C.E.), written texts were among the artifacts placed in Egypt's pyramids. Yet it was the spoken word, the oral tradition that was to retain pride of place in most African societies. Told in poetry, music, and dance, the oral tradition has been chanted, sung, and narrated from time immemorial, weaving itself into the fabric of people's lives. Over the centuries, the ancestral stories traveled along ancient trade routes and with migrating peoples throughout Africa. In these migrations, new cultures were formed, new tales were spun, and the literature was enlarged. This oral tradition also traveled from Africa to the Western hemisphere from the 1400s into the late 1800s with the African peoples sold into slavery.

One major component of the oral tradition was the preservation of history, although the method of keeping the past alive varied. Often it fell to a particular person—called a *griot* in certain West African cultures—to safeguard his people's heritage. He recounted the stories of its heroes and the founding of the community. He taught these stories to his sons, who, in turn, became the keepers of the sacred tales. In this manner, the historical traditions passed from generation to generation, and story-telling came to be a respected and valued art. This respect has continued into the late twentieth century, so much so that the term *griot* has become a means of honoring writers of African descent.

During the seventh century, the expansion of the Arab empire spread the Arabic language and the Islamic religion across North Africa from Egypt to the Atlantic Ocean, generating an influential Arabic written literature. During the ensuing Great Age of Islam (c. 850–1300), this literary development fanned out into East and West Africa as well. This was a period of great advancement in the arts and sciences, of great poets and learned travelers, of renowned centers of learning. In East Africa, Arabic blended with Bantu to form a new language, Swahili, which subsequently developed its own literature. In West Africa, Hausa traders and governments borrowed Arabic script to transcribe the Hausa language. Later, Hausa traditions were written in the *Kano Chronicle*. But despite the written literatures that evolved, the oral tradition retained its vitality and primacy. Still today, it remains rich in proverbs, tales, and legends, nourishing the present written tradition.

For millenia before the advent of European colonization, international trade between Africa, Europe, and Asia flourished. West African gold reached England by way of North Africa, and ivory was transported from the interior to the East African coastal cities on its way to China. And throughout Africa, mighty kingdoms, whose centers were ancient markets, arose. When, in the 1400s, the Portuguese began building their castles along the coast of West Africa, trade expanded along the old inland and new coastal routes. The coastal states developed strong commercial alliances with the European sea merchants, who vied with one another for profits and control.

Within short order, the infamous trans-Atlantic slave trade had begun. In 1515, the Spanish carried West Indian sugar to sweeten the tables of Europe, and in 1518, they brought African prisoners to work the sugar plantations of the West Indies. They thereby inaugurated the economic logic that soon led to the traffic in human beings known as the *triangular trade*. In this system, European merchants shipped manufactured goods, alcohol, and firearms to West Africa. They exchanged these goods for people, whom they carried as slaves to the West Indies and the Americas. There the traders picked up the tobacco, sugar, and rum that had been grown and processed by African slaves and sailed back to Europe. Ultimately, the cotton and ship-building industries of North America extended the length of the American side of the triangle. So profitable did commerce in human beings become that an industry—from casting leg irons to bounty hunters—emerged all along the lines of the triangle, affecting all it encompassed. The triangular trade generated such immense fortunes in Europe and the Americas that profits from gold and ivory paled beside it.

The 1600s marked the formation of European chartered companies as the various countries sought to dominate the lucrative sea trade with Africa (and with Asia and the Americas). The plantation economy in the Americas was expanding, and the demand for more slave labor solidified the economic importance of the slave markets in America, England, France, and along the West African coast—on Goree Island, at Elmina, in the Niger delta. Estimates vary as to how many millions of people passed through these markets, but within one twenty-year period, it is logged that at least 320,000 people were sold in what was identified as a wholesale market in the Niger delta.

Profits from the triangular trade paved the way for the Industrial Revolution (c. 1750–1850), which led in turn to expanded trade with Africa as Europe sought raw materials. Now the pace of African history accelerated drastically, catastrophically. Using the old sea merchant castles and trading stations as bases, European military forces began an aggressive drive inland to conquer and colonize. Christian missionaries quickly followed. In an attempt to settle their own rivalries, European countries divided Africa among themselves at the Congress of Berlin (1884–1885) in what has been called the "international share-out." In carving up the continent, Europeans disregarded traditional cultural boundaries. Consequently, the African resistance that arose was soon crushed, though never obliterated.

The traffic in slavery ravaged entire communities, and the Europeans established a strong presence. Yet African languages and literatures still remained vigorous. Storytellers still sang of the rise and fall of past and present empires—of ancient Ghana, Songhay, Mali, Benin—of Mambo Chagamire Dombo who vanquished the Portuguese and of the Zulu leader Shaka who reorganized military strategies. They sang of the ancient Nubians, the Gikuyu (Kikuyu), the Luo, the Shona, Fulani, Yoruba, Ibo.

As the European countries tightened their control, they imposed their language along with their systems of government, education, and religion on more than 800 different cultures. In the process, the colonizers provided the means for the flourishing development of the written word. Storytellers and poets began to write of the contemporary situation, even as they reworked their ancient oral traditions. So it is that twentieth-century African literature continues to be informed by what the Dogon people call *Nommo*, the life-giving force of the oral tradition.

Nommo has no English equivalent. It is a philosophical term that embraces a complex network of ideas. It means, simultaneously, the word itself and the power of the word. *Nommo* is literally elemental, for the element of water carries the word as it is spoken, and the element of heat is the energy or vitality or meaning of the word. *Nommo* is the power of the word to call into being that which it names. Thus, when Europe named the coast of West Africa the Slave, Ivory, and Gold Coasts, it called something new into existence, for these names redefined the places and their peoples. This process of renaming was replicated throughout Africa, but with the struggle for independence, the European definitions of societies and nations were challenged across the continent.

As writers confronted the central issue of their people's being defined by external, and hostile, forces, they reflected the tensions and anxieties, the loss and rage inherent in the colonial experience. As Ngugi Wa Thiong'o expressed it in *Decolonizing the Mind: The Politics of Language in African Literature:* "The oppressed and the exploited of the earth maintain their defiance: liberty from theft." Like the *griots,* writers told stories of the past and present, teaching, entertaining, and calling into being that which is told. Rejecting European definitions, they affirmed an African identification of self. They reaffirmed, too, a cultural or national identification. Their works criticized those who assimilated the mores of the colonizer, who participated in the re-naming. And these critiques spanned the entire epoch from the colonial period to postcolonial times.

Unlike the *griots,* however, many writers have not told their stories in their own language, and herein lies a dilemma. Vibrant African literatures have been written in Portuguese, French, and English (Lusophone, Francophone, and Anglophone, respectively). But these are the languages of the colonizers, and as such, they symbolize and reinforce the European power to define Africa and its cultures. As a result, some writers have rejected European languages. Kenyan writer Ngugi Wa Thiong'o, for instance, now works only in Gikuyu. Ugandan author Okot p'Bitek wrote *Wer pa Lawino* in Luo, only later translating it into English as *Song of Lawino.*

Educated in mission schools and, frequently, at state-run or European universities, twentieth-century writers learned their craft in the colonizer's language. Most, like Nigerian author Chinua Achebe, consider it an effective medium in which to explore African identity and the ravages and conflicts of the colonial and postcolonial experience. They consider it a lingua franca, capable of being molded along with Western genres and philosophies into an African vehicle of expression. Writers such as Wole Soyinka grapple with that very issue, taking as their subject the mythic African use of European materials.

For these writers, *Nommo* can speak through non-African tongues. Ousmane Sembene and Camara Laye, for instance, are two Francophone writers who tell very different African tales. In *God's Bits of Wood,* Ousmane Sembene, like the ancient *griots,* creates a legend of the people's heroic struggles during a railroad strike in Senegal. In *The Dark Child,* on the other hand, Camara Laye describes the practice of the oral tradition as a goldsmith crafts his masterpiece. When Anglophone writer Amos Tutuola recreates the oral tradition in *The Palm-wine Drinkard*, where abstractions such as beauty are made visible as independent forces, he illuminates the power of *Nommo*. When Lusophone poet Noemia de Sousa charts the history of Africa in "If You Want to Know Me," she, too, practices word magic.

Some of these same ideas infused *negritude*, the influential movement formulated in Paris during the 1930s by the Senegalese poet Leopold Senghor and the Caribbean poets Leon Damas and Aime Cesaire. When Senghor wrote, "Je suis le Dyali" (I am the *griot*), he claimed for himself the *griot's* role as master of the oral tradition. For the three poets, *negritude* was revolutionary. It emphasized the power of the poet to call things into being, the power of African philosophy, and African self-definition.

For many twentieth-century writers, a European education provided tools for political activism. Many fought for independence, many were imprisoned. Jomo Kenyatta, Augustinho Neto, and Leopold Senghor went on to lead their newly independent nations: Kenya, Angola, and Senegal. Colonialism, the struggle for independence, and the consequences of colonial rule became the ground and the material for the new *griots*. They wrote of the crowded cities and the rise of a middle class educated in Europe or in African universities; of the conflicts between urban and rural populations, between traditional African and European mores, and between generations; all the result of European colonization. Authors as disparate as Yahya Haqqi in Egypt and Can Themba in South Africa, Tchikaya U'Tam'si in Congo and Ama Ata Aidoo in Ghana have taken up these concerns. Like Flora Nwapa from Nigeria and Zoe Wicomb from South Africa, they have explored the fragmentation of the contemporary experience. In their pictures of what they have inherited from Europe, they have deplored its definition of the African human condition. In their condemnation resides their insistence on self-realization. "It is Mankind that matters," Mankind and the *Nommo*. As the Dogon sage, Ogotommeli says,

> *The word is for all in this world; it must be exchanged, so that it goes and comes, for it is good to give and to receive the forces of life.*

Jomo Kenyatta
(1891–1978)
Kenya

Jomo Kenyatta (Johnstone Kamau Ngengi) was born about the time that the British claimed his part of East Africa as a protectorate. He was born in Ichaweri, Kenya, and his father was a farmer. It is told that he took the name Kenyatta from the beaded belt he wore when he worked both as an interpreter for the Kenya Supreme Court and for the water department of the Nairobi Town Council before going to England. His facility with the English language led to his leading various Gikuyu (Kikuyu) associations; but he also was editor of the monthly, *Mwigwithania* (The Reconciler), written in Gikuyu. It was while he was in Europe that he wrote *Facing Mount Kenya* (1938) in which he described the customs of his people, the Gikuyu, and from which "The Gentlemen of the Jungle" is taken.

As a committed advocate for land reform and political rights for Africans, he returned in 1947 to Kenya, where he became president of the Kenya African Union, one of the various pan-African nationalist movements he was to found. The British imprisoned him in 1953 because of their fear of his being an instigator in the Mau-Mau Resistance, exiled him in 1959, and released him in 1961 to negotiate Kenya's independence. He became Kenya's first president, serving from 1964 until his death in 1978.

The Gentlemen of the Jungle

Once upon a time an elephant made a friendship with a man. One day a heavy thunderstorm broke out, the elephant went to his friend, who had a little hut at the edge of the forest, and said to him: "My dear good man, will you please let me put my trunk inside your hut to keep it out of this torrential rain?" The man, seeing what situation his friend was in, replied: "My dear good elephant, my hut is very small, but there is room for your trunk and myself. Please put your trunk in gently." The elephant thanked his friend, saying: "You have done me a good deed and one day I shall return your kindness." But what followed? As soon as the elephant put his trunk inside the hut, slowly he pushed his head inside, and finally flung the man out in the rain, and then lay down comfortably inside his friend's hut, saying: "My dear good friend, your skin is harder than mine, and as there is not enough room for both of us, you can afford to remain in the rain while I am protecting my delicate skin from the hailstorm."

The man, seeing what his friend had done to him, started to grumble; the animals in the nearby forest heard the noise and came to see what was the matter. All stood around listening to the heated argument between the man and his friend the elephant. In this turmoil the lion came along roaring, and said in a loud voice: "Don't you all know that I am the King of the Jungle! How dare any one disturb the peace of my kingdom?" On hearing this the elephant, who was one of the high ministers in the jungle kingdom, replied in a soothing voice, and said: "My lord, there is no disturbance of the peace in your kingdom. I have only been having a little discussion with my friend here as to the possession of this little hut which your lordship sees me occupying." The lion, who wanted to have "peace and tranquillity" in his kingdom, replied in a noble voice, saying: "I command my ministers to appoint a Commission of Enquiry to go thoroughly into this matter and report accordingly." He then turned to the man and said: "You have done well by establishing friendship with my people, especially with the elephant, who is one of my honorable ministers of state. Do not grumble any more, your hut is not lost to you. Wait until the sitting of my Imperial Commission, and there you will be given plenty of opportunity to state your case. I am sure that you will be pleased with the findings of the Commission." The man was very pleased by these sweet words from the King of the Jungle, and innocently waited for his opportunity, in the belief that naturally the hut would be returned to him.

The elephant, obeying the command of his master, got busy with other ministers to appoint the Commission of Enquiry. The following elders of the jungle were appointed to sit in the Commission: (1) Mr. Rhinoceros; (2) Mr. Buffalo; (3) Mr. Alligator; (4) The Rt. Hon. Mr. Fox to act as chairman; and (5) Mr. Leopard to act as Secretary to the Commission. On seeing the personnel, the man protested and asked if it was not necessary to include in this Commission a member from his side. But he was told that it was impossible, since no one from his side was well enough educated to understand the intricacy of jungle law. Further, that there was nothing to fear, for the members of the Commission were all men of repute for their impartiality in justice, and as they were gentlemen chosen by God to look after the interests of races less adequately endowed with teeth and claws, he might rest assured that they would investigate the matter with the greatest care and report impartially.

The Commission sat to take the evidence. The Rt. Hon. Mr. Elephant was first called. He came along with a superior air, brushing his tusks with a sapling which Mrs. Elephant had provided, and in an authoritative voice said: "Gentlemen of the Jungle, there is no need for me to waste your valuable time in relating a story which I am sure you all know. I have always regarded it as my duty to protect the interests of my friends, and this appears to have caused the misunderstanding between myself and my friend here. He invited me to save his hut from being blown away by a hurricane. As the hurricane had gained access owing to the unoccupied space in the hut, I considered it necessary, in my friend's own interests, to turn the undeveloped space to a more economic use by sitting in it myself; a duty which any of you would undoubtedly have performed with equal readiness in similar circumstances."

After hearing the Rt Hon. Mr. Elephant's conclusive evidence, the Commission called Mr. Hyena and other elders of the jungle, who all supported what Mr. Elephant had said. They then called the man, who began to give his own account of the dispute. But the Commission cut him short, saying: "My good man, please confine yourself to relevant issues. We have already heard the circumstances from various unbiased sources; all we wish you to tells us is whether the undeveloped space in your hut was occupied by any one else before Mr. Elephant assumed his position?" The man began to say; "No, but—" But at this point the Commission declared that they had heard sufficient evidence from both sides and retired to consider their decision. After enjoying a delicious meal at the expense of the Rt. Hon. Mr. Elephant, they reached their verdict, called the man, and declared as follows: "In our opinion this dispute has arisen through a regrettable misunderstanding due to the backwardness of your ideas. We consider that Mr. Elephant has fulfilled his sacred duty of protecting your interests. As it is clearly for your good that the space should be put to its most economic use, and as you yourself have not reached the stage of expansion which would enable you to fill it, we consider it necessary to arrange a compromise to suit both parties. Mr. Elephant shall continue his occupation of your hut, but we give you permission to look for a site where you can build another hut more suited to your needs, and we will see that you are well protected."

The man, having no alternative, and fearing that his refusal might expose him to the teeth and claws of members of the Commission, did as they suggested. But no sooner had he built another hut than Mr. Rhinoceros charged in with his horn lowered and ordered the man to quit. A Royal Commission was again appointed to look into the matter, and the same finding was given. This procedure was repeated until Mr. Buffalo, Mr. Leopard, Mr. Hyena and the rest were all accommodated with new huts. Then the man decided that he must adopt an effective method of protection, since Commissions of Enquiry did not seem to be of any use to him. He sat down and said, *"Ng'enda thi ndagaga motegi,"* which literally means "there is nothing that treads on the earth that cannot be trapped," or in other words, you can fool people for a time, but not for ever.

Early one morning, when the huts already occupied by the jungle lords were all beginning to decay and fall to pieces, he went out and built a bigger and better hut a little distance away. No sooner had Mr. Rhinoceros seen it than he came rushing in, only to find that Mr. Elephant was already inside, sound asleep. Mr. Leopard next came to the window, Mr. Lion, Mr. Fox and Mr. Buffalo entered the doors, while Mr. Hyena howled for a place in the shade and Mr. Alligator basked on the roof. Presently they all began disputing about their rights of penetration, and from disputing they came to fighting, and while they were all embroiled together the man set the hut on fire and burnt it to the ground, jungle lords and all. Then he went home, saying: "Peace is costly, but it's worth the expense," and lived happily ever after.

❋ Discussion and Writing

1. Comment on the ironies implicit in the title. Discuss the association of the animals with specific human traits.
2. Examine the story as a paradigm of colonialism: oppression, bureaucracy, and the concept of justice.
3. What are the implications of the ending; is it historically accurate? If not, what is its significance?

❋ Research and Comparison

Discuss Kenyatta's *Facing Mount Kenya* and its significance for African peoples in particular and humankind in general.

Interdisciplinary Discussion Question: Research and evaluate the role of the Mau Mau movement as a political activity in Kenya's struggle for independence. (See also Ngugi wa Thiong'o's "Wedding at the Cross" in this text.)

Jean-Joseph Rabearivelo
(1901–1937)
Madagascar

Jean-Joseph Rabearivelo was born in Antananarivo, Madagascar, the only son of an impoverished family of the Malagasy nobility. It was his mother who encouraged his love of poetry. Although he had to leave school when he was 13 and was also contracted into a very early marriage, he continued writing. During the 1920s and 1930s, he led an important literary revival and founded an influential review. He has been considered the major figure in the modern literature of Madagascar, inspiring the generations of Malagasy poets who followed him. His influence lies partly in the richness of his imagery and partly in his having developed a poetic form that manipulated the popular ballad of Madagascar. In his heart, he yearned for France and lived a bitter existence. A volatile and sensitive man, given to despair, he became addicted to drugs and finally took his own life.

Flute Players*

Your flute
    you carved from the shinbone of a mighty bull
    and polished it on barren hills beaten by sun.

---

*Translated by Langston Hughes

His flute
> he carved from a reed trembling in the breeze
> and cut in it little holes beside a flowing brook
> drunk on dreams of moonlight.

Together
> you made music in the late afternoon
> as if to hold back the round boat
> sinking on the shores of the sky
> to save it from its fate:
> but are your plaintive incantations
> heeded by the gods of the wind,
> of the earth, of the forest, and the sand?

Your flute
> throws out a beat like the march of an angry bull
> toward the desert—
> but who comes back running,
> burned by thirst and hunger
> and defeated by weariness
> at the foot of a shadeless tree
> with neither leaves nor fruit.

His flute
> is like a reed that bends
> beneath the weight of a passing bird in flight—
> not a bird captured by a child
> whose feathers are caressed,
> but a bird lost from other birds
> who looks at his own shadow for solace
> in the flowing water.

Your flute and his
> regret their beginnings
> in the songs of both your sorrows.

❋ Discussion and Writing

1. Who are the two players? How are they different? What is their connection? What is implied by "Together" and "Your flute and his"?
2. Analyze the Flute Players' making of the flutes. What do they symbolize? What is implied by the fact that the flutes "regret their beginnings"?

Yahya Haqqi
(b. 1905)
Egypt

Yahya Haqqi was born in Cairo, Egypt, and grew up in a literary atmosphere. His father was university educated. And in an age when most women could not read, his mother's learning added a special quality to his growing up, for she was knowledgeable in classical Arabic and religious works. His brother also brought many of the leading writers of the day to the house. Haqqi began publishing his own stories in a nationalist magazine in the mid-1920s, and soon thereafter took up a government post as an administrative assistant in a poor, small, Upper Egyptian town on the railway line. He pursued his literary career while holding various governmental positions and received the major state prize for literature. During World War II, he wrote about the still-revolutionary idea of uniting Eastern philosophy and Western science. From the beginning of his career, for example, the paradox of the railroad as an image of both productive and destructive modernity has appeared in his work.

The Tavern Keeper*

Before looking around the refurbished village and its environs and talking to the people, I had to speak to the tavern keeper. I went to the cemetery but could not find his house. I was told: "He doesn't live here. Go into the graveyard and ask for the gravedigger."

Good God, the gravedigger! What had happened? Why did he choose this job of all others? Had he told me something I'd forgotten that would explain this choice?

In the graveyard I found the tavern keeper sitting on a marble tomb, with his head hanging over his chest and his forehead moist with sweat. He had grown even fatter and his hair was white.

He raised a pale face and red eyes, and stared at me awhile. Then he looked away and prodded the ground with a stick. Nothing mattered to him any more, although it seemed like yesterday that I left him in his tavern. I didn't know what to say. How to begin? It was he who spoke first in a low voice which gradually became louder: "Don't worry. On the day the tavern closed my problem was no greater or smaller than anyone else's. It really wasn't much; no newspapers would publish the story with all its tragedy and farce. My choices were to leave the village (impossible because I hate to leave places) or accept bittersweet defeat (very unpleasant) or to look for a new job. Fortunately, I didn't have to wait long for this job. The village

*Translated by Miriam Cooke

gravedigger had just died and I hurried to replace him. There wasn't much competition and the pay is no less than anywhere else. As soon as I started I felt that I had been made for the job and it for me."

"What? You like the work? Burying the dead! Wherever you are people turn away nervously. There are few who after shaking hands with you or giving you food will not wonder whether the smell of corpses has not remained on their hands."

He was quiet for a while; then he looked at me and said: "This work has secrets you do not understand. I've learned a lot of things one should know. When we are born we are raw material that the world must polish. I would be loath to leave the world, as I entered it, without knowledge or experience."

Why did I tremble? Did I fear to be touched by his madness? Or did I fear his disturbing secrets? I stammered: "Tell me more. I am your old friend who thirsts for knowledge."

He pulled me down to his side, and whispered: "Men can measure and weigh the earth, judge the distance and size of the sun, calculate the number of constellations and master and infiltrate the elements. They can destroy destruction. But they are stopped by mountains, valleys and seas. They commune with stars and flowers, tremble at sunrise and sunset. And yet Nature gives no sign, however slight, that she is aware of them.

"Their conversation with Nature is a monologue, one-sided, like actors without an audience. Before this deafness men are like ants and bees, like animals and plants and even inanimate beings. How can they accept to be effaced, since they perform miracles and understand secrets? But there is a moment, a brief moment, when Nature rises up in all her power and violence and screams that she understands. She opens her arms, holds us to her breast and covers us with kisses, like the tender mother with her only child. That is the moment of burial!

"Look at the people walking ahead of you. When they die their weight will be restored to what it had been. I carry the body of a huge man as though it were the body of a skinny child with weak bones. I can scarcely carry an emaciated dwarf to the edge of the grave, for he becomes a heavy, solid ball. I seem to be carrying in my arms the whole ocean with its roar, salt and storms.

"They are all hurrying, pushing and shoving. I hear their shouts: 'Give me back to the land! Give me back to the land! And at the moment when the soil has become a pillow I feel the earth tremble and throb with the desire of the lover when he holds his beloved! Come, come! I have been waiting for you from the beginning of time! I feel the corpse groan with longing and lust, and peace falls on the earth, the peace of slumber closes her eyes. Her mouth is moist, her lips wet. The corpse has learned the meaning of security and peace. Each melts into the embrace of the other so they cannot be distinguished from each other.

"Be patient, do not hurry me. Because of my long experience with cemeteries, I know that the earth opens its bosom and arms wide to the corpse and forgets that man, while on earth, had acquired properties that are stronger and more uncontrollable than his instincts. The dead only submit gradually to the embrace of mother earth. The first of these properties to go is malice, next is ambition, next regret, and last of all is pride, which only goes after forty days when the nose decomposes. Then, and only then, does the personality disintegrate and the union of corpse and earth is consummated. After this disintegration there is a hissing sound as some parts scamper off as vermin, some slip off as worms and some disperse as putrid vapors and gases."

The tavern keeper sighed and then fell silent.

I left him also to his Maker. As I was standing up, he pulled me down again, and said, turning away from me: "I haven't thought of one thing—the day my wife dies and I have to bury her . . . "

Again we were silent, until I realized that the sun was at its zenith. I got up without a word and returned home.

That day I leafed through my old papers and read letters I had received from dear friends over the past thirty years. I thought of sending one of them my will and entrusting him with my papers. But then I changed my mind and read a long book about bats. My walk had been spoiled by the tavern keeper's words, and I had to calm down.

❋ Discussion and Writing

1. Are there parallels between the vocations of the tavern keeper and the gravedigger? What is the significance of the narrator going to the cemetery in search of the tavern keeper?
2. Explain and amplify the gravedigger's observation that man's conversation with Nature is a monologue. Elucidate the idea that in death the marriage of humans and nature is consummated.
3. What does the gravedigger imply when he says, "I would be loath to leave the world, as I entered it . . . "?
4. What is implied in the gravedigger's statement that he has not yet thought about his wife's death?
5. What is the impact of the gravedigger's observations on the narrator: why does the narrator change his mind about his will and papers; what is the significance of his reading a book about bats?

❋ Research and Comparison

Interdisciplinary Discussion Question: Sociologists have associated death with the origin of religion. Examine the treatment of death in different religious traditions with a particular emphasis on Islam. Comment on the similarities and differences of these traditions.

Leopold Sedar Senghor
(b. 1906)
Senegal

Leopold Sedar Senghor was born in the port of Joal, Senegal, a town established in the mid-1400s by Portuguese navigators. He came to be known as the *griot* of his country. His father, a wealthy groundnut merchant and an assimilated Catholic in a mostly Muslim impoverished society, provided him with a European education, sending him to the local Catholic Fathers of the Holy Spirit. There he was taught Wolof and French; his maternal uncle taught him his traditional Serere culture. It was during Senghor's student days at the Sorbonne—in what French-speaking African and Caribbean students considered exile because of their cultural alienation and isolation—that he and the Caribbean writers, Aime Cesaire and Leon Damas, formulated the Francophone theories of *negritude.* Among them was the quality of timelessness, of the merging of time, space, and memory. For Senghor, the mask carried this quality and the wisdom of the ancestors.

After completing his *agregation,* the state qualification for teaching in secondary school, Senghor taught at two lycees in France. During World War II, he served in the French Resistance and became a prisoner of war of Germany. With the liberation of France (1944), his role as poet-statesman emerged, following in the line of the traditional *griots,* the masters of speech and poetry who were known for their political shrewdness. His first book of poetry, which appeared in 1945, established the motifs and techniques that dominate his work: the assertion of African culture, its sheltering and spiritual presence, and his long lyrical line. Through the years, his appointments ranged from a chairmanship at one of the national schools to deputy for Senegal in the French National Assembly; after the struggle for independence he was elected the first president of the Republic of Senegal (1960). He retained the post until he retired in 1981.

Prayer to Masks*

Masks! Masks!
Black mask red mask, you white-and-black masks
Masks of the four points from which the Spirit blows
In silence I salute you!

---

*Translated by John Reed and Clive Wake

Nor you the least, the Lion-headed Ancestor[1]
You guard this place forbidden to all laughter of women, to all smiles that
    fade
You distil this air of eternity in which I breathe the air of my Fathers.
Masks of unmasked faces, stripped of the marks of illness and the lines of
    age
You who have fashioned this portrait, this my face bent over the altar of
    white paper
In your own image, hear me!
The Africa of the empires is dying, see, the agony of a pitiful princess[2]
And Europe too where we are joined by the navel.
Fix your unchanging eyes upon your children, who are given orders
Who give away their lives like the poor their last clothes.
let us report present at the rebirth of the World
Like the yeast which white flour needs.
For who would teach rhythm to a dead world of machines and guns?
Who would give the cry of joy to wake the dead and the bereaved at dawn?
Say, who would give back the memory of life to the man whose hopes are
    smashed?
They call us men of coffee cotton oil
They call us men of death.
We are the men of the dance, whose feet draw new strength pounding the
    hardened earth.

✳ Discussion and Writing

1. What does Senghor imply when he says, "this my face that bends over the altar of white paper?" What is his prayer?
2. What connection does Senghor underline between Africa and Europe? Explore the images indicating their relationship.
3. Senghor was a pioneer in the *negritude* movement. Examine its manifestation in this poem.
4. What is the significance of masks in African culture?

✳ Research and Comparison

Interdisciplinary Discussion Question: Examine the *negritude* movement, the contribution of its major proponents, and the subsequent criticism of it.

---

[1]Mask in the shape of a lion's head. The lion may be the family's emblem.
[2]*The Africa . . . princess:* The poet is remembering the great empires of Africa that existed before contact with European culture. The princess is the old Africa.

Interdisciplinary Discussion Question: Research and discuss the contribution of Leopold Senghor, Jomo Kenyatta, or Augustinho Neto in the struggle for liberation in their countries and the role they played after independence.

Naguib Mahfouz
(b. 1911)
Egypt

Naguib Mahfouz was born in the popular quarter of Hayy Al-Jamaliyya in Cairo, Egypt. As the son of a civil servant, he was raised in a middle-class family and learned to believe in "science, socialism, and tolerance" while he was still quite young. He read widely among Arabic and Western classics and began writing when he was 17. A student of philosophy at the University of Cairo, he came under the influence of Russian writers as well as those of the Arabic literary renaissance of the early twentieth century: Al-Aqqad, Sulama Musa, Taka Husayn. All through his career as a civil servant, from which he retired as director of the Cinema Organization, he continued publishing his novels and short stories, along with a weekly column for Egypt's leading newspaper, *Al-Ahram.*

Mahfouz incorporated material from Arabic epics as well as from the streets and quarters of Cairo into his early work, depicting the city of his birth, the city from which he rarely traveled throughout his life. He subsequently turned to more psychological concerns, then to neorealism and issues of good and evil, God and man, and existentialism. Later, the Islamic mystical Sufism infused his writing. His characters have spanned the political spectrum from the fundamentalist Muslim Brotherhood to the leftist rebels fighting for independence from England. His winning the Nobel Prize in literature in 1988 was cause for celebration throughout the Arab world.

Half a Day*

I proceeded alongside my father, clutching his right hand, running to keep up with the long strides he was taking. All my clothes were new: the black shoes, the green school uniform, and the red tarboosh. My delight in my new

---

*Translated by Denys Johnson-Davies

clothes, however, was not altogether unmarred, for this was no feast day but the day on which I was to be cast into school for the first time.

My mother stood at the window watching our progress, and I would turn toward her from time to time, as though appealing for help. We walked along a street lined with gardens; on both sides were extensive fields planted with crops, prickly pears, henna trees, and a few date palms.

"Why school?" I challenged my father openly. "I shall never do anything to annoy you."

"I'm not punishing you," he said, laughing. "School's not a punishment. It's the factory that makes useful men out of boys. Don't you want to be like your father and brothers?"

I was not convinced. I did not believe there was really any good to be had in tearing me away from the intimacy of my home and throwing me into this building that stood at the end of road like some huge, high-walled fortress, exceedingly stern and grim.

When we arrived at the gate we could see the courtyard, vast and crammed full of boys and girls. "Go in by yourself," said my father, "and join them. Put a smile on your face and be a good example to others."

I hesitated and clung to his hand, but he gently pushed me from him. "Be a man," he said. "Today you truly begin life. You will find me waiting for you when it's time to leave."

I took a few steps, then stopped and looked but saw nothing. Then the faces of boys and girls came into view. I did not know a single one of them, and none of them knew me. I felt I was a stranger who had lost his way. But glances of curiosity were directed toward me, and one boy approached and asked, "Who brought you?"

"My father," I whispered.

"My father's dead," he said quite simply.

I did not know what to say. The gate was closed, letting out a pitiable screech. Some of the children burst into tears. The bell rang. A lady came along, followed by a group of men. The men began sorting us into ranks. We were formed into an intricate pattern in the great courtyard surrounded on three sides by high buildings of several floors; from each floor we were overlooked by a long balcony roofed in wood.

"This is your new home," said the woman. "Here too there are mothers and fathers. Here there is everything that is enjoyable and beneficial to knowledge and religion. Dry your tears and face life joyfully."

We submitted to the facts, and this submission brought a sort of contentment. Living beings were drawn to other living beings, and from the first moments my heart made friends with such boys as were to be my friends and fell in love with such girls as I was to be in love with, so that it seemed my misgivings had had no basis. I had never imagined school would have this rich variety. We played all sorts of different games: swings, the vaulting horse, ball games. In the music room we chanted our first songs. We also had our first introduction to language. We saw a globe of the Earth, which revolved and showed the various continents and countries. We started learning the numbers. The story of the Creator of the universe was read to us, we were told of His present world and of His Hereafter, and we heard examples of what He said. We ate delicious food, took a little nap, and woke up to go on with friendship and love, play and learning.

As our path revealed itself to us, however, we did not find it as totally sweet and unclouded as we had presumed. Dust-laden winds and unexpected accidents came about suddenly, so we had to be watchful, at the ready, and very patient. It was not all a matter of playing and fooling around. Rivalries could bring about pain and hatred or give rise to fighting. And while the lady would sometimes smile, she would often scowl and scold. Even more frequently she would resort to physical punishment.

In addition, the time for changing one's mind was over and gone and there was no question of ever returning to the paradise of home. Nothing lay ahead of us but exertion, struggle, and perseverance. Those who were able took advantage of the opportunities for success and happiness that presented themselves amid the worries.

The bell rang announcing the passing of the day and the end of work. The throngs of children rushed toward the gate, which was opened again. I bade farewell to friends and sweethearts and passed through the gate. I peered around but found no trace of my father, who had promised to be there. I stepped aside to wait. When I had waited for a long time without avail, I decided to return home on my own. After I had taken a few steps, a middle-aged man passed by, and I realized at once that I knew him. He came toward me, smiling, and shook me by the hand, saying, "It's a long time since we last met—how are you?"

With a nod of my head, I agreed with him and in turn asked, "And you, how are you?"

"As you can see, not all that good, the Almighty be praised!"

Again he shook me by the hand and went off. I proceeded a few steps, then came to a startled halt. Good Lord! Where was the street lined with gardens? Where had it disappeared to? When did all these vehicles invade it? And when did all these hordes of humanity come to rest upon its surface? How did these hills of refuse come to cover its sides? And where were the fields that bordered it? High buildings had taken over, the street surged with children, and disturbing noises shook the air. At various points stood conjurers showing off their tricks and making snakes appear from baskets. Then there was a band announcing the opening of a circus, with clowns and weight lifters walking in front. A line of trucks carrying central security troops crawled majestically by. The siren of a fire engine shrieked, and it was not clear how the vehicle would cleave its way to reach the blazing fire. A battle raged between a taxi driver and his passenger, while the passenger's wife called out for help and no one answered. Good God! I was in a daze. My head spun. I almost went crazy. How could all this have happened in half a day, between early morning and sunset? I would find the answer at home with my father. But where was my home? I could see only tall buildings and hordes of people. I hastened on to the crossroads between the gardens and Abu Khoda. I had to cross Abu Khoda to reach my house, but the stream of cars would not let up. The fire engine's siren was shrieking at full pitch as it moved at a snail's pace, and I said to myself, "Let the fire take its pleasure in what it consumes." Extremely irritated, I wondered when I would be able to cross. I stood there a long time, until the young lad employed at the ironing shop on the corner came up to me. He stretched out his arm and said gallantly, "Grandpa, let me take you across."

❋ Discussion and Writing

1. What does the school mean for the child? What is its importance for his father? What does it symbolize in the narrative?
2. Indicate the events that would be implausible on a child's first day in school. What is the significance of these events? Analyze Mahfouz's technique in telescoping time.
3. What do the changes outside the school suggest about cultural and social transformation?

❋ Research and Comparison

Interdisciplinary Discussion Question: Research the life and works of Naguib Mahfouz, commenting on his portrayal of the Egyptian political and social scene.

Es'kia Mphahlele
(b. 1919)
South Africa

Es'kia Mphahlele was born in the slums of Pretoria, South Africa. When he was five years old, he, his brother, and his sister moved to a hut on a northern Transvaal reserve, the home of their frightening paternal grandmother. They stayed until Mphahlele was 13. Then they returned to Pretoria, where they were once again shipped out, this time to their maternal grandmother in the slum of Second Avenue. At the same time, with the help of his mother's determination and in spite of rigid South African segregation laws, he made his way through school, taking his B.A. and M.A. externally from the University of South Africa. He began teaching but was banned because of his opposition to the Bantu Education Act, and so he began working for *Drum* magazine. The formal imposition of apartheid (1948) took hold, and his twenty-year wandering began in 1957. It was while he was teaching in Nigeria that Mphahlele wrote his autobiography, *Down Second Avenue* (1959), a seminal work that crystallized the urban black South African experience and distinguished the South African experience from that of the rest of Africa. "Interlude" is taken from this autobiography.

Interlude

Saturday night. Electric lights! How beautiful they look from a distance. So dull in themselves but, clustered like that, quivering, blinking, little fiery gems set in the fabric of night, they are fascinating. Standing here in a dark little world, viewing them from afar, miles away, you know they are beyond your reach. The more beautiful they look the more distant they appear—or, perhaps, the more distant they are the lovelier they look.

Here, a dark township, Orlando; below there, a seething mass of darkness with the usual Saturday night screams and groanings and drums: that's Shanty Town. Up there, another part of Orlando with lights, not too far to reach, but smiling and blinking at you ironically; then far away, clusters and clusters of them. They might have been bathed in water and emerged bright, clean, with a crystal texture, in the magical context of night. They look as if you might rake them into a container and leave a sieve on the surface of this summer night. They assume at once the man-made form and the unattainable, at any rate for the moment.

A hot, mothy night; there is no sleep. Out of the house into the yard. You take a deep breath and contemplate the beauty of distant electric lights until the children have gone to bed because you use the sitting-dining-room as a study. It has always been like this, since Second Avenue—waiting until the family has gone to bed before you did your studies. Rebecca has been at this sort of game too. It's the final year of her three-year diploma course in social work. She left teaching when Verwoerd, Minister of Native Affairs, made it clear that African teachers were going to be used for training children to be slaves. Day in and day out in the week she comes back from school at five o'clock and begins to cook, and I wash the children and studies begin at nine.

Your mate has gone to bed early tonight and there is a story you want to write—or rather you want to write a story and while you think how to begin you look at electric lights. You might try to place Parktown, or Parkwood, Emmarentia or Westcliff or Northcliff, where those lights can be; but you give it up after a while.

Pictures, fantasies, strivings, wishes, desires, memories and all other creatures of the intellect come to torment your being. Then you think how sordid life is; how ludicrous the very idea of life is; what a fruitless, petty, endless game it may be and mustn't be.

Things close in upon you; you find yourself in a tightly closed-up room. There seems no way out. You once flattered yourself that you had some talent, ability, honest thoughts and longings, and splendid ideals. You even fancied you had what man recognizes as ambition. Perhaps you had a trade or profession, and you wanted to tell the world what you wanted, what you felt and thought in some manner; you wanted to give life something the men would not allow you to—speak when you're spoken to, the world seemed to say. Eventually you didn't give life anything. It resented your efforts. The strivings and desires in you continued to torment you, to tease you out of yourself. But there was no exit from that prison. You knew it was your soul that was imprisoned.

Of course, the easiest way out would be to leave the soul in this cage, and start a new life, resolve to fling ambition to the winds, and just become a thoroughly sensuous animal; leave inspirations, ambition, ideals, planning and aesthetics to the elect. Or you might deny the existence of that in you which cherishes ambition and the rest, and seek no more than food, shelter, clothing. What joy and abundant satisfaction they must derive from life who did not wish for anything more than the bare necessities, like an ox! Or you might booze all these extra-physical stirrings out of your system, as so many, oh so many, educated Africans do.

Those electric lights in the distance continue to blink and tease the spirit of night: little sparkling fires, so unearthly, so inorganic.

But of course once you were sensitive to things that are, enough to know that they weren't there and should be, you couldn't go back, could you? And your tribal umbilical cord had long, oh so long, been severed and all the talk about Bantu culture and the Black man developing along his own lines was just so much tommy rot. You just felt the world getting too small for you, ever-contracting and shutting you in. A stuffy place, the world could become; as stuffy as the room from which you came out. If you tried to go away somewhere and ceased to care you'd still be in the larger denomination of the world which required man to care; you'd become a more bitter cynic; and while you shrivelled up in the acid of your cynicism the world wouldn't be at all worse off after your exit. No step backward and so you must move and fight with the rest for a better and greater South Africa. Do it in some way but do it. It's no pastime but a desperate necessity and the knowing it galled you.

Orlando. A glorified Marabastad. Saturday night is the same as it was twenty-five years ago in Marabastad minus the ten-to-ten bell because now the curfew law is only for the city and suburbs to protect a frightened and neurotic white population which keeps revolvers and narcotic drugs under pillows. Yes, it is still the same, the only tarred roads being those leading to white superintendents' offices. The township has been spreading west and south since 1934 in three-roomed units; not east because that's the direction in which Johannesburg lies, twelve miles away; not north because that's where the line of gold mines is. We have been paying a sub-economic rental of fifty shillings a month for four rooms without electric lights or water-borne sewerage, and now the rents have gone up a scale stopping at £5. Near us is one of the biggest electric power stations in the world. As Orlando spreads into Meadowlands, Mofolo, Dube, Jabavu, Moroka, Molapo, Moletsane, holding more than 200,000 souls altogether, it also develops ulcers in the form of shanty towns; like the one just below us. And still the black metropolis grows, meeting other townships of refugees who have been removed from western towns which like Africans only as laborers. Faction fights must be a source of amusement to some white supreme chief of the Bantu who decided to force people into ethnic compartments and threw thousands of single men into huge dormitories in hostels with high fences around them.

There was a time when it was much better to be a tenant in a freehold township like Sophiatown than a municipal tenant, but the difference today is academic. Police continue to beat up and down the road in front of our house, not to protect human life and property but to look after the law and demand passes. Constant police patrols in the white man's areas have hurled the flame of violence to our doorsteps. Comparative cleanliness and bigness blunt the edge of political discontent here but you know you're in a ghetto and God, those lights are so far away, too far for you to reach. Between you and them is a pit of darkness, darkness charged with screams, groans, yells, cries, laughter and singing. They swell and reach a frantic pitch, only to be suppressed by the spirit of night.

From down here in the pit of sordidness, you hear humanity wailing for help, for food, for shelter; humanity gasping for air. And you know the scheme of things has come full circle: life thrown into a barbed-wire tangle; the longer it is made to stay there the more it is entangling itself and hurting itself; and the more it is hurting itself the more impotent it is becoming, and the more it is failing to save itself; so much the longer it will remain in the coils, degraded.

"What can you or anyone else do now or in any foreseeable future?" Sasha, your Jewish friend, asks you. That's five years ago now. "Can't you seek a new little dominion elsewhere where you can sow your seed with some measure of confidence it'll grow into something worthwhile?" He looked at you with soft searching eyes. And you know you must answer.

"I don't know yet," you say. "I know nothing except that the noose will tighten soon. To go elsewhere might be a worse evil. There's the stoic inside me that tells me to stay, I repeat to myself what our sages have often said: what has no end is a miracle."

"'That's not realistic."

"Damn it all, Sasha, it isn't, at any rate when you look at the immediate future."

"A necessary addition."

But you knew that even the immediate future was not so near: all was dim before you.

The lights quiver eternally. They have taken on an indifferent, impersonal, hard and cold sort of beauty. Only they and the night have something between them. And they gradually become a symbol.

"How long are you going to postpone it?" asks Sasha.

"I don't know. But right now I think it's a crime to bring children into a world with such a country."

"H'm, in your melancholy mood again?"

"Not more than is naturally necessary."

"It's bad enough for the world to deny you many things without your religious self-denials. At least the one thing the world cannot stop me from having is children."

"Religion doesn't come into it," you say testily.

"I mean religion in the sense that you're not really afraid of the responsibility children bring with them, you're a hard-working man."

Yes, five years ago, when you were on the labor market, you thought it criminal to litter the earth with children who would go through the same spiritual, and perhaps physical, agonies that you were experiencing. Not now, you kept saying, not just yet; perhaps never.

By God, this is a hot night, the air doesn't seem to move at all. There is a cough from the bedroom. Rebecca is stirring. How strange! Five years ago, on a night like this, you were standing on your veranda, looking out into those quivering distant lights and you were thinking of what Sasha had said and then Rebecca coughed and stirred and came out to join you. After a time she pressed closer against you and said You know, I'm going to have a baby. A what? A baby, are you not happy? And Time passed, during which the wheel of reconciliation with yourself, with the ageless and inevitable, turned many revolutions. Then the world around seemed to widen. You thought of Sasha, good kind Sasha. Your ears became insensible to all outside you. Something thawed inside you; your blood coursed warmly in your veins; gradually it dawned on you that you were going to be father of a third child, the one thing you couldn't be denied and you felt awkwardly happy . . . Five years ago.

The lights quiver as brightly as ever, looking so clean, so jubilant, so fresh, teasing the primitive springs of life in you which in turn respond to that symbolic call of the lights coming across to you, wrapped in the mystery of night.

Every so often, your third-born, Motswiri, now four, sees the police take people down to the charge office and municipal police beat up a man or boy in the street just as you used to see them do years back in Marabastad. And now Motswiri clings to you tightly when he sees a constable walk up or down the road and says *Ntate*,[1] is the policeman going to arrest me is he going to take you is he going to take mamma? You hold the frightened kid close to you and think of Second Avenue the long long great divide. Another time Motswiri comes to you with imitation handcuffs crudely made of wire and shouts Bring your hands here, where's your pass I'll teach you not to be naughty again. Now he wants a torch and a baton and a big broad belt and a badge, how agonizing! That passport, will it ever come or is it wrapped up in those electric lights? Trevor's words keep coming back to you that when you want a thing very badly you get it. You also remember that those lights are no figment of the brain. . . .

Your eldest child, Anthony, now ten, keeps telling you in the morning when you go to the shop, usually Sunday mornings, that you mustn't forget your pass. Because he has seen a long queue of men and boys on Sunday mornings being marched through the streets as the police collected more pass offenders before finally landing at the charge office. More agony.

Whatever happened you knew the story on the greatest treason trial in South Africa was your swan song for *Drum* and you must quit. That other story the electric lights distracted your mind from—well, for the moment, I must pretend to the role of Hopkins and play "Time's eunuch."

❈ Discussion and Writing

1. What do the electric lights signify? Comment on the phrase "that symbolic call of the lights coming across to you." What is the implication of other images in the "Interlude"?
2. If little has changed in 25 years, what is in store for Mphahlele and his children in the future? What is the function of Sasha?
3. Analyze the style and tone of the narrative. What is its impact?

❈ Research and Comparison

Discuss the quality of life for black South Africans depicted in Mphahlele's autobiography, *Down Second Avenue*.

Interdisciplinary Discussion Question: Research the issue of apartheid in South Africa and comment on the current racial conflicts since apartheid was declared illegal.

---

[1]Father. [eds.]

Amos Tutuola
(b. 1920)
Nigeria

Amos Tutuola, of Yoruba descent, was born in Abeokuta, Nigeria, a large town some 60 miles from Lagos. (Abeokuta, which had grown along side hills topped by granite boulders, means "under the rock.") His parents had become Christian, but his grandmother used to tell him the old stories that ultimately became the source of his novels. His father—who died when Tutuola was still a child—was a farmer, and it was on the farm in the evenings that Tutuola and his friends would listen to his grandmother's stories. On his father's death, Tutuola was forced to leave school after only six years of formal education at the Salvation Army school and Lagos High School. Tutuola worked as a coppersmith and then served as a metal-worker in the Royal Air Force during World War II. Subsequently he worked for the government and for the Nigerian Broadcasting Corporation.

In his first book, *The Palm-Wine Drinkard* (1952), Tutuola merged the oral and written traditions. He formulated such a powerfully evocative synthesis that this work has come to represent dominant principles in the poetics that emerged throughout Africa in the 1950s. The novel embodies the successful translation of the oral tradition. In "The Gentleman of Complete Parts," a self-contained episode in *The Palm-Wine Drinkard*, Tutuola tells an old tale that fits into the novel's overarching motif of the quest that is simultaneously spiritual and social. It is a tale of fear and bravery and transformations, and it is set deep in the forest where "if you enter into it you cannot know the way out again, and you cannot travel to the end of it for ever."

The Gentleman of Complete Parts

When it was the fifth month since I had left that town, then I reached another town which was not so big, although there was a large and famous market. At the same time that I entered the town, I went to the house of the head of the town who received me with kindness into his house; after a little while he told one of his wives to give me food and after I had eaten the food, he told his wife to give me palm-wine too; I drank the palm-wine to excess as when I was in my town or as when my tapster was alive. But when I tasted the palm-wine given to me there, I said that I got what I wanted here. After I had eaten the food and drunk the palm-wine to my satisfaction, the head of the town who received me as his guest asked for my name, I told him that my name was called "Father of gods who could do anything in this world." As he heard this from me, he was soon faint with fear. After that he asked me what I came to him for. I replied that I was looking for my palm-wine tapster who had died in my town some time ago. Then he told me that he knew where the tapster was.

After that he told me that if I could help him to find out his daughter who was captured by a curious creature from the market which was in that town, and bring her to him, then he would tell me whereabouts my tapster was.

He said furthermore that as I called myself "Father of gods who could do anything in this world," this would be very easy for me to do; he said so.

I did not know that his daughter was taken away by a curious creature from the market.

I was about to refuse to go and find out his daughter who was taken away from the market by a curious creature, but when I remembered my name I was ashamed to refuse. So I agreed to find out his daughter. There was a big market in this town from where the daughter was captured, and the market-day was fixed for every 5th day and the whole people of that town and from all the villages around the town and also spirits and curious creatures from various bushes and forests were coming to this market every 5th day to sell or buy articles. By 4 o'clock in the evening, the market would close for that day and then everybody would be returning to his or her destination or to where he or she came from. But the daughter of the head of that town was a petty trader and she was due to be married before she was taken away from the market. Before that time, her father was telling her to marry a man but she did not listen to her father; when her father saw that she did not care to marry anybody, he gave her to a man for himself, but this lady refused totally to marry that man who was introduced to her by her father. So that her father left her to herself.

This lady was very beautiful as an angel but no man could convince her for marriage. So, one day she went to the market on a market-day as she was doing before, or to sell her articles as usual; on that market-day, she saw a curious creature in the market, but she did not know where the man came from and never knew him before.

The Description of the Curious Creature

He was a beautiful "complete" gentleman, he dressed with the finest and most costly clothes, all the parts of his body were completed, he was a tall man but stout. As this gentleman came to the market on that day, if he had been an article or animal for sale, he would be sold at least for £2000 (two thousand pounds). As this complete gentleman came to the market on that day, and at the same time that this lady saw him in the market, she did nothing more than to ask him where he was living, but this fine gentleman did not answer her or approach her at all. But when she noticed that the fine or complete gentleman did not listen to her, she left her articles and began to watch the movements of the complete gentleman about in the market and left her articles unsold.

By and by the market closed for that day then the whole people in the market were returning to their destinations etc., and the complete gentleman was returning to his own too, but as this lady was following him about in the market all the while, she saw him when he was returning to his destination as others did, then she was following him (complete gentleman) to an unknown place. But as she was following the complete gentleman along the road, he was telling her to go back or not to follow him, but the lady did not listen to what he was telling her, and when the complete gentleman had tired of telling her not to follow him or to go back to her town, he left her to follow him.

"Do Not Follow Unknown Man's Beauty"

But when they had travelled about twelve miles away from that market, they left the road on which they were travelling and started to travel inside an endless forest in which only all the terrible creatures were living.

"Return the Parts of Body to the Owners; or Hired Parts of the Complete Gentleman's Body to Be Returned"

As they were travelling along in this endless forest then the complete gentleman in the market that the lady was following, began to return the hired parts of his body to the owners and he was paying them the rentage money. When he reached where he hired the left foot, he pulled it out, he gave it to the owner and paid him, and they kept going; when they reached the place where he hired the right foot, he pulled it out and gave it to the owner and paid for the rentage. Now both feet had returned to the owners, so he began to crawl along on the ground, by that time, that lady wanted to go back to her town or her father, but the terrible and curious creature or the complete gentleman did not allow her to return or go back to her town or her father again and the complete gentleman said thus: "I had told you not to follow me before we branched into this endless forest which belongs to only terrible and curious creatures, but when I became a half-bodied incomplete gentleman you wanted to go back, now that cannot be done, you have failed. Even you have never seen anything yet, just follow me."

When they went furthermore, then they reached where he hired the belly, ribs, chest etc., then he pulled them out and gave them to the owner and paid for the rentage.

Now to this gentleman or terrible creature remained only the head and both arms with neck, by that time he could not crawl as before but only went jumping on as a bull-frog and now this lady was soon faint for this fearful creature whom she was following. But when the lady saw every part of this complete gentleman in the market was spared or hired and he was returning them to the owners, then she began to try all her efforts to return to her father's town, but she was not allowed by this fearful creature at all.

When they reached where he hired both arms, he pulled them out and gave them to the owner, he paid for them; and they were still going on in this endless forest, they reached the place where he hired the neck, he pulled it out and gave it to the owner and paid for it as well.

"A Full-Bodied Gentleman Reduced to Head"

Now this complete gentleman was reduced to head and when they reached where he hired the skin and flesh which covered the head, he returned them, and paid to the owner, now the complete gentleman in the market reduced to a "SKULL" and this lady remained with only "Skull." When the lady saw that she remained with only Skull, she began to say that her father had been telling her to marry a man, but she did not listen to or believe him.

When the lady saw that the gentleman became a Skull, she began to faint, but the Skull told her if she would die she would die and she would follow him to his house. But by the time that he was saying so, he was humming with a terrible voice and also grew very wild and even if there was a person two miles away he would not have to listen before hearing him, so this lady began to run away in that forest for her life, but the Skull chased her and within a few yards, he caught her, because he was very clever and smart as he was only Skull and he could jump a mile to the second before coming down. He caught the lady in this way: so when the lady was running away for her life, he hastily ran to her front and stopped her as a log of wood.

By and by, this lady followed the Skull to his house, and the house was a hole which was under the ground. When they reached there both of them entered the hole. But there were only Skulls living in that hole. At the same time that they entered the hole, he tied a single Cowrie on the neck of this lady with a kind of rope, after that, he gave her a large frog on which she sat as a stool, then he gave a whistle to a Skull of his kind to keep watch on this lady whenever she wanted to run away. Because the Skull knew already that the lady would attempt to run away from the hole. Then he went to the back-yard to where his family were staying in the day time till night.

But one day, the lady attempted to escape from the hole, and at the same time that the Skull who was watching her whistled to the rest of the Skulls that were in the back-yard, the whole of them rushed out to the place where the lady sat on the bull-frog, so they caught her, but as all of them were rushing out, they were rolling on the ground as if a thousand petrol drums were pushing along a hard road. After she was caught, then they brought her back to sit on the same frog as usual. If the Skull who was watching her fell asleep, and if the lady wanted to escape, the cowrie that was tied on her neck would raise up the alarm with a terrible noise, so that the Skull who was watching her would wake up at once and then the rest of the Skull's family would rush out from the back in thousands to the lady and ask her what she wanted to do with a curious and terrible voice.

But the lady could not talk at all, because as the cowrie had been tied on her neck, she became dumb at the same moment.

The Father of Gods Should Find Out Whereabouts the Daughter of the Head of the Town Was

Now as the father of the lady first asked for my name and I told him that my name was "Father of gods who could do anything in this world," then he told me that if I could find out where his daughter was and bring her to him, then he would tell me where my palm-wine tapster was. But when he said so, I was jumping up with gladness that he should promise me that he would tell me where my tapster was. I agreed to what he said; the father and parent of this lady never knew whereabouts their daughter was, but they had information that the lady followed a complete gentleman in the market. As I was the "Father of gods who could do anything in this world," when it was at night I sacrificed to my juju[1] with a goat.

And when it was early in the morning, I sent for forty kegs of palm-wine, after I had drunk it all, I started to investigate whereabouts was the lady. As it was the market-day, I started the investigation from the market. But as I was a juju-man, I knew all the kinds of people in that market. When it was exactly 9 o'clock a.m., the very complete gentleman whom the lady followed came to the market again, and at the same time that I saw him, I knew that he was a curious and terrible creature.

"The Lady Was Not to Be Blamed for Following the Skull as a Complete Gentleman"

I could not blame the lady for following the Skull as a complete gentleman to his house at all. Because if I were a lady, no doubt I would follow him to wherever he would go, and still as I was a man I would jealous him more than that, because if this gentleman went to the battle field, surely, enemy would not kill him or capture him and if bombers saw him in a town which was to be bombed, they would not throw bombs on his presence, and if they did throw it, the bomb itself would not explode until this gentleman would leave that town, because of his beauty. At the same time that I saw this gentleman in the market on that day, what I was doing was only to follow him about in the market. After I looked at him for so many hours, then I ran to a corner of the market and I cried for a few minutes because I thought within myself why was I not created with beauty as this gentleman, but

---

[1]Magic, spirit. [eds.]

when I remembered that he was only a Skull, then I thanked God that He had created me without beauty, so I went back to him in the market, but I was still attracted by his beauty. So when the market closed for that day, and when everybody was returning to his or her destination, this gentleman was returning to his own too and I followed him to know where he was living.

"Investigation to the Skull's Family House"

When I travelled with him a distance of about twelve miles away to that market, the gentleman left the really road on which we were travelling and branched into an endless forest and I was following him, but as I did not want him to see that I was following him, then I used one of my juju which changed me into a lizard and followed him. But after I had travelled with him a distance of about twenty-five miles away in this endless forest, he began to pull out all the parts of his body and return them to the owners, and paid them.

After I had travelled with him for another fifty miles in this forest, then he reached his house and entered it, but I entered it also with him, as I was a lizard. The first thing that he did when he entered the hole (house) he went straight to the place where the lady was, and I saw the lady sat on a bull-frog with a single cowrie tied on her neck and a Skull who was watching her stood behind her. After he (gentleman) had seen that the lady was there, he went to the back-yard where all his family were working.

"The Investigator's Wonderful Work in the Skull's Family's House"

When I saw this lady and when the Skull who brought her to that hole or whom I followed from the market to that hole went to the back-yard, then I changed myself to a man as before, then I talked to the lady but she could not answer me at all, she only showed that she was in a serious condition. The Skull who was guarding her with a whistle fell asleep at that time.

To my surprise, when I helped the lady to stand up from the frog on which she sat, the cowrie that was tied on her neck made a curious noise at once, and when the Skull who was watching her heard the noise, he woke up and blew the whistle to the rest, then the whole of them rushed to the place and surrounded the lady and me, but at the same time that they saw me there, one of them ran to a pit which was not so far from that spot, the pit was filled with cowries. He picked one cowrie out of the pit, after that he was running towards me, and the whole crowd wanted to tie the cowrie on my neck too. But before they could do that, I had changed myself into air, they could not trace me out again, but I was looking at them. I believed that the cowries in that pit were their power and to reduce the power of any human being whenever tied on his or her neck and also to make a person dumb.

Over one hour after I had dissolved into air, these Skulls went back to the back-yard, but there remained the Skull who was watching her.

After they had returned to the back-yard, I changed to a man as usual, then I took the lady from the frog, but at the same time that I touched her, the cowrie which was tied on her neck began to shout; even if a person was four miles away he would not have to listen before hearing, but immediately the Skull who was watching her heard the noise and saw me when I took her from that frog, he blew the whistle to the rest of them who were in the back-yard.

Immediately the whole Skull family heard the whistle when blew to them, they were rushing out to the place and before they could reach there, I had left their hole for the forest, but before I could travel about one hundred yards in the forest, they had rushed out from their hole to inside the forest and I was still running away with the lady. As these Skulls were chasing me about in the forest, they were rolling on the ground like large stones and also humming with terrible noise, but when I saw that they had nearly caught me or if I continued to run away like that, no doubt, they would catch me sooner, then I changed the lady to a kitten and put her inside my pocket and changed myself to a very small bird which I could describe as a "sparrow" in English language.

After that I flew away, but as I was flying in the sky, the cowrie which was tied on that lady's neck was still making a noise and I tried all my best to stop the noise, but all were in vain. When I reached home with the lady, I changed her to a lady as she was before and also myself changed to man as well. When her father saw that I brought his daughter back home, he was exceedingly glad and said thus:"You are the 'Father of gods' as you had told me before."

But as the lady was now at home, the cowrie on her neck did not stop making a terrible noise once, and she could not talk to anybody; she showed only that she was very glad she was at home. Now I had brought the lady but she could not talk, eat or loose away the cowrie on her neck, because the terrible noise of the cowrie did not allow anybody to rest or sleep at all.

"There Remain Greater Tasks Ahead"

Now I began to cut the rope of the cowrie from her neck and to make her talk and eat, but all my efforts were in vain. At last I tried my best to cut off the rope of the cowrie; it only stopped the noise, but I was unable to loose it away from her neck.

When her father saw all my trouble, he thanked me greatly and repeated again that as I called myself "Father of gods who could do anything in this world" I ought to do the rest of the work. But when he said so, I was very ashamed and thought within myself that if I return to the Skulls' hole or house, they might kill me and the forest was very dangerous travel always, again I could not go directly to the Skulls in their hole and ask them how to loose away the cowrie which was tied on the lady's neck and to make her talk and eat.

"Back to the Skull's Family's House"

On the third day after I had brought the lady to her father's house, I returned to the endless forest for further investigation. When there remained about one mile to reach the hole of these Skulls, there I saw the very Skull who the lady had followed from the market as a complete gentleman to the hole of Skull's family's house, and at the same time that I saw him like that, I changed into a lizard and climbed a tree which was near him.

He stood before two plants, then he cut a single opposite leaf from the opposite plant; he held the leaf with his right hand and he was saying thus: "As this lady was taken from me, if this opposite leaf is not given her to eat, she will not talk for ever," after that he threw the leaf down on the ground. Then he cut another single compound leaf from the compound plant which was in the same place with the opposite plant, he held the compound leaf with his left hand and said that if this single compound is not given to this lady, to eat, the cowrie on her neck could not be loosened away for ever and it would be making a terrible noise for ever.

After he said so, he threw the leaf down at the same spot, then he jumped away. So after he had jumped very far away (luckily, I was there when he was doing all these things, and I saw the place that he threw both leaves separately), then I changed myself to a man as before, I went to the place that he threw both leaves, then I picked them up and I went home at once.

But at the same time that I reached home, I cooked both leaves separately and gave her to eat; to my surprise the lady began to talk at once. After that, I gave her the compound leaf to eat for the second time and immediately she ate that too, the cowrie which was tied on her neck by the Skull, loosened away by itself, but it disappeared at the same time. So when the father and mother saw the wonderful work which I had done for them, they brought fifty kegs of palm-wine for me, they gave me the lady as wife and two rooms in that house in which to live with them. So, I saved the lady from the complete gentleman in the market who afterward reduced to a "Skull" and the lady became my wife since that day. This was how I got a wife.

❋ Discussion and Writing

1. Examine the significance of the central episode, the missing daughter, her rescue, and marriage. Comment on the resolution of the conflict between the father and the daughter.
2. Describe the "complete" gentleman and his impact on all the people who see him. Comment on the symbolism of his "rented body" and his being a Skull.

3. Describe the world of the Skulls. How similar is this fantastic world to the actual world? What is accomplished by this amalgam of the magical and the natural?
4. Examine the various stages of the narrator's search: the investigation, the rescue, and the rehabilitation of the lady.
5. What do the cowrie and the plants symbolize? What does Amos Tutuola suggest by naming the plants "opposite plant" and "compound plant"?
6. Analyze the antithesis the narrator represents: the human who is the divine; the palm-wine drinker who is the investigator; the seeker on his journey who tarries to be a householder.
7. What is the underlying meaning of the two contending powers, the narrator and the Skull? What is significant about their both being outsiders in this town? What are the limitations of each power? Discuss the relation between life and death.
8. Comment on the narrative technique of the story within the story. Discuss the impact of this narrative on two different audiences: children and adults.

❋ Research and Comparison

The traditional stories and religious mythologies of all cultures reflect their systems of belief: their values, ethics, and memories, as well as their logic, fears, and prejudices. Examine Amos Tutuola's treatment of the oral tradition in his modern narratives *My Life in the Bush of Ghosts, The Palm-Wine Drinkard,* or *The Witch Herbalist of the Remote Town.*

Gabriel Okara
(b. 1921)
Nigeria

Gabriel Imomotimi Obainbaing Okara was born in Bumonde in the Ijaw district of Rivers State in western Nigeria. His father was a businessman in Bumonde. Okara trained as a bookbinder, and he studied journalism in the United States. Over the years, he has worked in various capacities, mainly in his home state, including publishing, printing, and bookbinding. He has served as a commissioner in broadcasting, as an officer in the Nigerian Information office, and as Biafran Information Officer during the civil war (1967–1970). And he has written textbooks for, and given readings in, the Rivers State schools. Considered one of the most outstanding Nigerian poets, Okara is noted for an unmannered style that owes much to his manipulation of Ijaw material. He has protested against neocolonialism, and he has revealed the dangers of attacking political leaders for exhibiting the same attitudes as they had denounced in the British.

You Laughed and Laughed and Laughed

In your ears my song
is motor car misfiring
stopping with a choking cough;
and you laughed and laughed and laughed.

In your eyes my ante-
natal walk was inhuman passing
your "omnivorous understanding"
and you laughed and laughed and laughed.

You laughed at my song
You laughed at my walk.

Then I danced my magic dance
to the rhythm of talking-
drums pleading, but you shut your
eyes and laughed and laughed and laughed.

And then I opened my mystic
inside wide like
the sky, instead you entered your
car and laughed and laughed and laughed.

You laughed at my dance
you laughed at my inside.

You laughed and laughed and laughed.

But your laughter was ice-block
laughter and it froze your inside froze
your voice froze your ears
froze your eyes and froze your tongue.

And now it's my turn to laugh;

but my laughter is not ice-block
ice-block laughter. For I
know not cars, know not ice-blocks.

My laughter is the fire

of the eye of the sky, the fire
of the earth, the fire of the air
the fire of the seas and the
rivers fishes animals trees
and it thawed your inside,
thawed your voice, thawed your
ears, thawed your eyes, and
thawed your tongue.

So a meek wonder held
your shadow and you whispered:
"Why so?"
And I answered:
"Because my fathers and I
are owned by the living
warmth of the earth
through our naked feet."

❈ **Discussion and Writing**

1. What are the objects of the white man's laughter; who else laughs? Explain the polarity between the two laughters.
2. Analyze Okara's use of the motor car.
3. Discuss the meaning of the last four lines of the poem.
4. Describe the impact of repeated words, recurrent symbols, and other stylistic devices.

❈ **Research and Comparison**

Interdisciplinary Discussion Question: Research the impact of colonization on Nigeria, and compare Okara's portrayal of the colonial experience with that of another Nigerian writer's included in the anthology.

Augustinho Neto
(1922–1979)
Angola

Augustinho Neto was born in the Icola e Bengo region of Angola; his parents were teachers and practicing Methodists. He studied medicine in Lisbon, after having worked in the colonial services for three years, but a series of arrests, owing to his membership in the Portuguese Movement for Democratic Youth Unity, interrupted his studies. Public pressure induced the government to release him; whereupon, he completed his studies and returned home to practice medicine and to lead the then underground Popular Liberation Movement of Angola (MPLA). He was also involved with the movement calling for a resurgence of traditional Angolan culture. Another series of arrests followed, and after escaping from prison in Portugal, he took a leadership position in the struggle against Portuguese rule. When Angola gained its independence in 1975, and after a bloody civil war, he became its first president, holding that post until his death.

Kinaxixi*

I was glad to sit down
on a bench in Kinaxixi
at six o'clock of a hot evening
and just sit there . . .

Someone would come

maybe
to sit beside me

And I would see the black faces

of the people going uptown
in no hurry
expressing absence in the
jumbled Kimbundu they conversed in.

I would see the tired footsteps

of the servants whose fathers also were servants
looking for love here, glory there, wanting
something more than drunkenness in every
alcohol.

Neither happiness nor hate.

After the sun had set.

lights would be turned on and I
would wander off
thinking that our life after all is simple
too simple
for anyone who is tired and still has to walk.

❋ Discussion and Writing

1. Discuss the images that describe the people of Kinaxixi.
2. What does "expressing absence in the jumbled Kimbundu" imply: absence of what; why is Kimbundu jumbled?
3. Examine the poem in the context of Neto's political ideology.

❋ Research and Comparison

Interdisciplinary Discussion Question: There are several important political or national figures whose works are included in this anthology (such as Mao Zedong, Jomo Kenyatta, Ho Chi Minh, Augustinho Neto, Leopold Senghor). Compare and contrast their ideologies and political roles.

---

*Translated by W. S. Merwin

Nadine Gordimer
(b. 1923)
South Africa

Nadine Gordimer was born in Springs, South Africa. Her parents were Jewish immigrants, her father from Lithuania and her mother from London. As a child, Gordimer took full advantage of the local library, reading widely and voraciously, overcoming isolation in the world of books. Her early education was in the Transvaal, and she continued her studies at the University of the Witwatersrand in Johannesburg. By the age of 15, she had already published a story. Noted for its texture and for the way it projects a sense of people and places, her fiction became indelibly marked with an ironic tone that has underscored its moral purpose. While her work covers a broad range, she has been most acclaimed for her pictures of the political and social conditions in South Africa. She has a keen eye and the ability to evoke the emotions that inform the relations between the races. Depicting daily experiences among all classes, she reveals the disfiguring effects of apartheid, how it has destroyed people's humanity.

The South African government banned three of Gordimer's books. After the third, *Burger's Daughter* (1979), was banned, she privately published the reasons for censoring the novel; the censors later released the novel. Equally important, she helped organize a group opposing censorship in journalism as well as in literature. While the government closed several alternative presses, the group did bring the problems journalists face to light. A long-time member of the African National Congress, she also founded the Congress of South African Writers, a nonracial national organization. At the time of her winning the Nobel Prize in literature in 1991, so deeply divided was the country that all her colleagues were black. Gordimer has spoken of the hope that the native languages would once again be the idiom of literature, whether written or oral. She has also spoken of the vitality of the African oral tradition, of its resilience through the period of colonialism and apartheid, and of its current renaissance in contemporary South African theater.

Good Climate, Friendly Inhabitants

In the office at the garage eight hours a day I wear mauve linen overalls—those snappy uniforms they make for girls who aren't really nurses. I'm forty-nine but I could be twenty-five except for my face and my legs. I've got that very fair skin and my legs have gone mottled, like Roquefort cheese. My hair used to look pretty as chickens' fluff, but now it's been bleached and permed too many times. I wouldn't admit this to anyone else, but to myself I admit everything. Perhaps I'll get one of those wigs everyone's wearing. You don't have to be short of hair, any more, to wear a wig.

I've been years at the garage—service station, as it's been called since it was rebuilt all steel and glass. That's at the front, where the petrol pumps are; you still can't go into the workshop without getting grease on your things. But I don't have much call to go there. Between doing the books you'll see me hanging about in front for a breath of air, smoking a cigarette and keeping an eye on the boys. Not the mechanics—they're all white chaps of course (bunch of ducktails[1] they are, too, most of them)—but the petrol attendants. One boy's been with the firm twenty-three years—sometimes you'd think he owns the place; gets my goat. On the whole they're not a bad lot of natives, though you get a cheeky bastard now and then, or a thief, but he doesn't last long, with us.

We're just off the Greensleeves suburban shopping center with the terrace restaurant and the fountain, and you get a very nice class of person coming up and down. I'm quite friends with some of the people from the luxury flats round about; they wouldn't pass without a word to me when they're walking their dogs or going to the shops. And of course you get to know a lot of the regular petrol customers, too. We've got two Rolls and any amount of sports cars who never go anywhere else. And I only have to walk down the block to Maison Claude when I get my hair done, or in to Mr. Levine at the Greensleeves Pharmacy if I feel a cold coming on.

I've got a flat in one of the old buildings that are still left, back in town. Not too grand, but for ten quid a month and right on the bus route . . . I was married once and I've got a lovely kid—married since she was seventeen and living in Rhodesia; I couldn't stop her. She's very happy with him and they've got twin boys, real little toughies! I've seen them once.

There's a woman friend I go to the early flicks with every Friday, and the Versfelds' where I have a standing invitation for Sunday lunch. I think they depend on me, poor old things; they never see anybody. That's the trouble when you work alone in an office, like I do, you don't make friends at your work. Nobody to talk to but those duckies in the workshop, and what can I have in common with a lot of louts in black leather jackets? No respect, either, you should hear the things they come out with. I'd sooner talk to the blacks, that's the truth, though I know it sounds a strange thing to say. At least they call you missus. Even old Madala knows he can't come into my office without taking his cap off, though heaven help you if you ask that boy to run up to the Greek for a packet of smokes, or round to the Swiss

---

[1]Street-kids ("punks"). [eds.]

Confectionery. I had a dust-up with him once over it, the old monkey-face, but the manager didn't seem to want to get rid of him, he's been here so long. So he just keeps out of my way and he has his half-crown from me at Christmas, same as the other boys. But you get more sense out of the boss-boy, Jack, than you can out of some whites, believe me, and he can make you laugh, too, in his way—of course they're like children, you see them yelling with laughter over something in their own language, noisy lot of devils; I don't suppose we'd think it funny at all if we knew what it was all about. This Jack used to get a lot of phone calls (I complained to the manager on the quiet and he's put a stop to it, now) and the natives on the other end used to be asking to speak to Mpanza and Makiwane and I don't know what all, and when I'd say there wasn't anyone of that name working here they'd come out with it and ask for Jack. So I said to him one day, why do you people have a hundred and one names, why don't these uncles and aunts and brothers-in-law come out with your name straight away and stop wasting my time? He said "Here I'm Jack because Mpanza Makiwane is not a name, and there I'm Mpanza Makiwane because Jack is not a name, but I'm the only one who knows who I am wherever I am." I couldn't help laughing. He hardly ever calls you missus, I notice, but it doesn't sound cheeky, the way he speaks. Before they were allowed to buy drink for themselves, he used to ask me to buy a bottle of brandy for him once a week and I didn't see any harm.

Even if things are not too bright, no use grumbling, I don't believe in getting old before my time. Now and then it's happened that some man's taken a fancy to me at the garage. Every time he comes to fill up he finds some excuse to talk to me; if a chap likes me, I begin to feel it just like I did when I was seventeen, so that even if he was just sitting in his car looking at me through the glass of the office, I would know that he was waiting for me to come out. Eventually he'd ask me to the hotel for a drink after work. Usually that was as far as it went. I don't know what happens to these blokes, they are married, I suppose, though their wives don't still wear a perfect size fourteen, like I do. They enjoy talking to another woman once in a while, but they quickly get nervous. They are businessmen and well off; one sent me a present, but it was one of those old-fashioned compacts, we used to call them flap-jacks, meant for loose powder, and I use the solid kind everyone uses now.

Of course you get some funny types, and, as I say, I'm alone there in the front most of the time, with only the boys, the manager is at head office in town, and the other white men are all at the back. Little while ago a fellow came into my office wanting to pay for his petrol with Rhodesian money. Well, Jack, the boss-boy, came first to tell me that this fellow had given him Rhodesian money. I sent back to say we didn't take it. I looked through the glass and saw a big, expensive American car, not very new, and one of those men you recognize at once as the kind who move about a lot—he was poking out his cheek with his tongue, looking round the station and out into the busy street like, in his head, he was trying to work out his way around in a new town. Some people kick up hell with a native if he refuses them something, but this one didn't seem to; the next thing was he got the boy to bring him to me. "Boss says he must talk to you," Jack said, and turned on his heel. But I said, you wait here. I know Johannesburg; my cash-box was there in the open safe. The fellow was young. He had that very tanned skin that has been sunburnt day after day, the tan you see on lifesavers at the beach. His hair was the thick streaky blond kind, waste on men. He says, "Miss, can't you help me out for half an hour?" Well, I'd had my hair done, it's true, but I don't kid myself you could think of me as a miss unless you saw my figure, from behind. He went on, "I've just driven down and I haven't had a chance to change my money. Just take this while I get hold of this chap I know and get him to cash a cheque for me."

I told him there was a bank up the road but he made some excuse. "I've got to tell my friend I'm in town anyway. Here, I'll leave this—it's a gold one." And he took the big fancy watch off his arm. "Go on, please, do me a favor." Somehow when he smiled he looked not so young, harder. The smile was on the side of his mouth. Anyway, I suddenly said okay, then, and the native boy turned and went out of the office, but I knew it was all right about my cash, and this fellow asked me which was the quickest way to get to Kensington and I came out from behind my desk and looked it up with him on the wall map. I thought he was a fellow of about twenty-nine or thirty; he was so lean, with a snakeskin belt around his hips and a clean white open-neck shirt.

He was back on the dot. I took the money for the petrol and said, here's your watch, pushing it across the counter. I'd seen, the moment he'd gone and I'd picked up the watch to put it in the safe, that it wasn't gold: one of those Jap fakes that men take out of their pockets and try to sell you on streetcorners. But I didn't say anything, because maybe he'd been had? I gave him the benefit of the doubt. What'd it matter? He'd paid for his petrol, anyway. He thanked me and said he supposed he'd better push off and find some hotel. I said the usual sort of thing, was he here on a visit and so on, and he said, yes, he didn't know how long, perhaps a couple of weeks, it all depended, and he'd like somewhere central. We had quite a little chat—you know how it is, you always feel friendly if you've done someone a favor and it's all worked out okay—and I mentioned a couple of hotels. But it's difficult if you don't know what sort of place a person wants, you may send him somewhere too expensive, or on the other hand you might recommend one of the small places that he'd consider just a joint, such as the New Park, near where I live.

A few days later I'd been down to the shops at lunch hour and when I came by where some of the boys were squatting over their lunch in the sun, Jack said, "That man came again." Thinks I can read his mind; what man, I said, but they never learn. "The other day, with the money that was no good." Oh, you mean the Rhodesian, I said. Jack didn't answer but went on tearing chunks of bread out of half a loaf and stuffing them into his mouth. One of the other boys began telling, in their own language with bits of English thrown in, what I could guess was the story of how the man had tried to pay with money that was no good; big joke, you know; but Jack didn't take any notice, I suppose he'd heard it once too often.

I went into my office to fetch a smoke, and when I was enjoying it outside in the sun Jack came over to the tap near me. I heard him drinking from his hand, and then he said, "He went and looked in the office window." Didn't he buy petrol? I said. "He pulled up at the pump but then he didn't buy, he said he will come back later." Well, that's all right, what're you getting excited about, we sell people as much petrol as they like, I said. I felt uncomfortable. I don't know why; you'd think I'd been giving away petrol at the garage's expense or something.

"You can't come from Rhodesia on those tires," Jack said. No? I said, "Did you look at those tires?" Why should *I* look at tires? "No-no, you look at those tires on that old car. You can't drive six hundred miles or so on those tires. Worn out! Down to the tread!" But who cares where he came from, I said, it's his business. "But he had that money," Jack said to me. He shrugged and I shrugged; I went back into my office. As I say, sometimes you find yourself talking to that boy as if he was a white person.

Just before five that same afternoon the fellow came back. I don't know how it was, I happened to look up like I knew the car was going to be there. He was taking petrol and paying for it, this time; old Madala was serving him. I don't know what got into me, curiosity maybe, but I got up and came to my door and said, how's Jo'burg treating you? "Ah, hell, I've had bad luck," he says. "The place I was staying had another booking for my room from today. I was supposed to go to my friend in Berea, but now his wife's brother has come. I don't mind paying for a decent place, but you take one look at some of them . . . Don't you know somewhere?" Well yes, I said, I was telling you that day. And I mentioned the Victoria, but he said he'd tried there, so then I told him about the New Park, near me. He listened, but looking round all the time, his mind was somewhere else. He said, "They'll tell me they're full, it'll be the same story." I told him that Mrs. Douglas who runs the place is a nice woman—she would be sure to fix him up. "You couldn't ask her?" he said. I said well, all right, from my place she was only round the corner, I'd pop in on my way home from work and tell her he'd be getting in touch with her.

When he heard that he said he'd give me a lift in his car, and so I took him to Mrs. Douglas myself, and she gave him a room. As we walked out of the hotel together he seemed wrapped up in his own affairs again, but on the pavement he suddenly suggested a drink. I thought he meant we'd go into the hotel lounge, but he said, "I've got a bottle of gin in the car," and he brought it up to my place. He was telling me about the time he was in the Congo a few years ago, fighting for that native chief, whats's-name— Tshombe—against the Irishmen who were sent out there to put old whats's- name down. The stories he told about Elisabethville! He was paid so much he could live like a king. We only had two gins each out the bottle, but when I wanted him to take it along with him, he said, "I'll come in for it sometime when I get a chance." He didn't say anything, but I got the idea he had come up to Jo'burg about a job.

I was frying a slice of liver next evening when he turned up at the door. The bottle was still standing where it'd been left. You feel uncomfortable when the place's full of the smell of frying and anyone can tell you're about to eat. I gave him the bottle but he didn't take it; he said he was on his way to Vereeniging to see someone, he would just have a quick drink. I had to offer him something to eat, with me. He was one of those people who eat without noticing what it is. He never took in the flat, either; I mean he didn't look round at my things the way it's natural you do in someone else's home. And there was a lovely photo of my kid on the built-in fixture round the electric fire. I said to him while we were eating, is it a job you've come down for? He smiled the way youngsters smile at an older person who won't understand, anyway. "On business." But you could see that he was not a man who had an office, who wore a suit and sat in a chair. He was like one of those men you see in films, you know, the stranger in town who doesn't look as if he lives anywhere. Somebody in a film, thin and burned red as a brick and not saying much. I mean he did talk but it was never really anything about himself, only about things he'd seen happen. He never asked me anything about myself, either. It was queer; because of this, after I'd seen him a few times, it was just the same as if we were people who know each other so well they don't talk about themselves any more.

Another funny thing was, all the time he was coming in and out the flat, I was talking about him with the boy—with Jack. I don't believe in discussing white people with natives, as a rule, I mean, whatever I think of a white, it encourages disrespect if you talk about it to a black. I've never said anything in front of the boys about the behavior of that crowd of ducktails in the work- shop, for instance. And of course I wouldn't be likely to discuss my private life with a native boy. Jack didn't know that this fellow was coming to the flat, but he'd heard me say I'd fix up about the New Park Hotel, and he'd seen me take a lift home that afternoon. The boy's remark about the tires seemed to stick in my mind; I said to him: That man came all the way from the Congo.

"In that car?" Jack said; he's got such a serious face, for a native. The car goes all right, I said, he's driving all over with it now.

"Why doesn't he bring it in for retreads?"

I said he was just on holiday, he wouldn't have it done here.

The fellow didn't appear for five or six days and I thought he'd moved on, or made friends, as people do in this town. There was still about two fingers left in his bottle. I don't drink when I'm on my own. Then he turned up at the garage just at the time I knock off. Again I meant to look at the tires for myself, but I forgot. He took me home just like it had been an arranged thing; you know, a grown-up son calling for his mother not because he wants to, but because he has to. We hardly spoke in the car. I went out for pies, which wasn't much of a dinner to offer anyone, but, as I say, he didn't know what he was eating, and he didn't want the gin, he had some cans of beer in the car. He leaned his chair back with all the weight on two legs and said, "I think I must clear out of this lousy dump, I don't know what you've got to be to get along here with these sharks." I said, you kids give up too easy, have you still not landed a job? "A job!" he said. "They owe me *money*, I'm trying to get *money* out of them." What's it all about, I said, what money? He didn't take any notice, as if I wouldn't understand. "Smart alecks and swindlers. I been here nearly three lousy weeks, now." I said, everybody who comes here finds Jo'burg tough compared with their home.

He'd had his head tipped back and he lifted it straight and looked at me. "I'm not such a kid." No? I said, feeling a bit awkward because he never talked about himself before. He was looking at me all the time, you'd have thought he was going to find his age written on my face. "I'm thirty-seven," he said. "Did you know that? Thirty-seven. Not so much younger."

Forty-nine. It was true, not so much. But he looked so young, with that hair always slicked back longish behind the ears as if he'd just come out of the shower, and that brown neck in the open-neck shirt. Lean men wear well, you can't tell. He did have false teeth, though, that was why his mouth made him look hard. I supposed he could have been thirty-seven; I didn't know, I didn't know.

It was like the scars on his body. There were scars on his back and other scars on his stomach, and my heart was in my mouth for him when I saw them, still pink and raw-looking, but he said that the ones on his back were from strokes he'd had in a boys' home as a kid and the others were from the fighting in Katanga.

I know nobody would believe me, they would think I was just trying to make excuses for myself, but in the morning everything seemed just the same, I didn't feel I knew him any better. It was just like it was that first day when he came in with his Rhodesian money. He said, "Leave me the key. I might as well use the place while you're out all day." But what about the hotel, I said. "I've taken my things," he says. I said, you mean you've moved out? And something in his face, the bored sort of look, made me ask, you've told Mrs Douglas? "She's found out by now," he said, it was unusual for him to smile. You mean you went without paying? I said. "Look, I told you I can't get my money out of those bastards."

Well, what could I do? I'd taken him to Mrs. Douglas myself. The woman'd given him a room on my recommendation. I had to go over to the New Park and spin her some yarn about him having to leave suddenly and that he'd left the money for me to pay. What else could I do? Of course I didn't tell *him*.

But I told Jack. That's the funny thing about it. I told Jack that the man had disappeared, run off without paying my friend who ran the hotel where he was staying. The boy clicked his tongue the way they do, and laughed. And I said that was what you got for trying to help people. Yes, he said, Johannesburg was full of people like that, but you learn to know their faces, even if they were nice faces.

I said, you think that man had a nice face?

"You see he has a nice face," the boy said.

I was afraid I'd find the fellow there when I got home, and he was there. I said to him, that's my daughter, and showed him the photo, but he took no interest, not even when I said she lived in Gwelo and perhaps he knew the town himself. I said why didn't he go back to Rhodesia to his job but he said Central Africa was finished, he wasn't going to be pushed around by a lot of blacks running the show—from what he told me, it's awful, you can't keep them out of hotels or anything.

Later on he went out to get some smokes and I suddenly thought, I'll lock the door and I won't let him into the flat again. I had made up my mind to do it. But when I saw his shadow on the other side of the frosty glass I just got up and opened it, and I felt like a fool, what was there to be afraid of? He was such a clean, good-looking fellow standing there; and anybody can be down on his luck. I sometimes wonder what'll happen to me—in some years, of course—if I can't work any more and I'm alone here, and nobody comes. Every Sunday you read in the paper about women dead alone in flats, no one discovers it for days.

He smoked night and day, like the world had some bad smell that he had to keep out of his nose. He was smoking in the bed at the weekend and I made a remark about Princess Margaret when she was here as a kid in 1947—I was looking at a story about the Royal Family, in the Sunday paper. He said he supposed he'd seen her, it was the year he went to the boys' home and they were taken to watch the procession.

One of the few things he'd told me about himself was that he was eight when he was sent to the home; I lay there and worked out that if he was thirty-seven, he should have been twenty in 1947, not eight years old.

But by then I found it hard to believe that he was only twenty-five. You could always get rid of a boy of twenty-five. He wouldn't have the strength inside to make you afraid to try it.

I'd've felt safer if someone had known about him and me but of course I couldn't talk to anyone. Imagine the Versfelds. Or the woman I go out with on Fridays, I don't think she's had a cup of tea with a man since her husband died! I remarked to Jack, the boss-boy, how old did he think the man had been, the one with the Rhodesian money who cheated the hotel? He said, "He's still here?" I said no, no, I just wondered. "He's young, that one," he said, but I should have remembered that half the time natives don't know their own age, it doesn't matter to them the way it does to us. I said to him, wha'd'you call young? He jerked his head back at the workshop. "Same like the mechanics." That bunch of kids! But this fellow wasn't cocky like them, wrestling with each other all over the place, calling after girls fancying themselves the Beatles when they sing in the washroom. The people he used to go off to see about things—I never saw any of them. If he had friends, they never came round. If only *somebody* else had known he was in the flat!

Then he said he was having the car overhauled because he was going off to Durban. He said he had to leave the next Saturday. So I felt much better; I also felt bad, in a way, because there I'd been, thinking I'd have to find some way to make him go. He put his hand on my waist, in the daylight, and smiled right out at me and said, "Sorry; got to push on and get moving sometime, you know," and it was true that in a way he was right, I couldn't think what it'd be like without him, though I was always afraid he would stay. Oh he was nice to me then, I can tell you; he could be nice if he wanted to, it was like a trick that he could do, so real you couldn't believe it when it stopped just like that. I told him he should've brought the car into our place, I'd've seen to it that they did a proper job on it, but no, a friend of his was doing it free, in his own workshop.

Saturday came, he didn't go. The car wasn't ready. He sat about most of the week, disappeared for a night, but was there again in the morning. I'd given him a couple of quid to keep him going. I said to him, what are you mucking about with that car in somebody's back yard for? Take it to a decent garage. Then—I'll never forget it—cool as anything, a bit irritated, he said, "Forget it. I haven't got the car any more." I said, wha'd'you mean, you mean you've sold it?—I suppose because in the back of my mind I'd been thinking, why doesn't he sell it, he needs money. And he said, "That's right. It's sold," but I knew he was lying, he couldn't be bothered to think of anything else to say. Once he'd said the car was sold, he said he was waiting for the money; he did pay me back three quid, but he borrowed again a day or so later. He'd keep his back to me when I came into the flat and he wouldn't answer when I spoke to him; and then just when he turned on me with that closed, half-asleep face and I'd think, this is it, now this is it—I can't explain how finished, done-for I felt, I only know that he had on his face exactly the same look I remember on the face of a man, once, who was drowning some kittens one after the other in a bucket of water—just as I knew it was coming, he would burst out laughing at me. It was the only time he laughed. He would laugh until, nearly crying, I would begin to laugh too. And we would pretend it was kidding, and he would be nice to me, oh, he would be nice to me.

I used to sit in my office at the garage and look round at the car adverts and the maps on the wall and my elephant ear growing in the oil drum and that was the only place I felt: but this is nonsense, what's got into me? The flat, and him in it—they didn't seem real. Then I'd go home at five and there it would all be.

I said to Jack, what's a '59 Chrysler worth? He took his time, he was cleaning his hands on some cotton waste. He said, "With those tires, nobody will pay much."

Just to show him that he mustn't get too free with a white person, I asked him to send up to Mr. Levine for a headache powder for me. I joked. I'm getting a bit like old Madala there, I feel so tired today.

D'you know what that boy said to me then? They've got more feeling than whites sometimes, that's the truth. He said, "When my children grow up they must work for me. Why don't you live there in Rhodesia with your daughter? The child must look after the mother. Why must you stay here alone in this town?"

Of course I wasn't going to explain to him that I like my independence. I always say I hope when I get old I die before I become a burden on anybody. But that afternoon I did something I should've done long ago, I said to the boy, if ever I don't turn up to work, you must tell them in the workshop to send someone to my flat to look for me. And I wrote down the address. Days could go by before anyone'd find what had become of me; its not right.

When I got home that same evening, the fellow wasn't there. He'd gone. Not a word, not a note; nothing. Every time I heard the lift rattling I thought, here he is. But he didn't come. When I was home on Saturday afternoon I couldn't stand it any longer and I went up to the Versfelds and asked the old lady if I couldn't sleep there a few days, I said my flat was being painted and the smell turned my stomach. I thought, if he comes to the garage, there are people around, at least there are the boys. I was smoking nearly as much as *he* used to and I couldn't sleep. I had to ask Mr. Levine to give me something. The slightest sound and I was in a cold sweat. At the end of the week I had to go back to the flat, and I bought a chain for the door and made a heavy curtain so's you couldn't see anyone standing there. I didn't go out, once I'd got in from work—not even to the early flicks—so I wouldn't have to come back into the building at night. You know how it is when you're nervous, the funniest things comfort you: I'd just tell myself, well, if I shouldn't turn up to work in the morning, the boy'd send someone to see.

Then slowly I was beginning to forget about it. I kept the curtain and the chain and I stayed at home, but when you get used to something, no matter what it is, you don't think about it all the time, any more, though you still believe you do. I hadn't been to Maison Claude for about two weeks and my hair was a sight. Claude advised a soft perm and so it happened that I took a couple of hours off in the afternoon to get it done. The boss-boy Jack says to me when I come back, "He was here."

I didn't know what to do, I couldn't help staring quickly all round. When, I said. "Now-now, while you were out." I had the feeling I couldn't get away. I knew he would come up to me with that closed, half-asleep face—burned as a good-looker lifesaver, burned like one of those tramps who are starving and lousy and pickled with cheap booze but have a horrible healthy look that comes from having nowhere to go out of the sun. I don't know what that boy must have thought of me, my face. He said, "I told him you're gone. You don't work here anymore. You went to Rhodesia to your daughter. I don't know which place." And he put his nose back in one of the newspapers he's always reading whenever things are slack; I think he fancies himself quite the educated man and he likes to read about all these blacks who are becoming prime ministers and so on in other countries these days. I never remark on it; if you take any notice of things like that with them, you begin to give them big ideas about themselves.

That fellow's never bothered me again. I never breathed a word to anybody about it—as I say, that's the trouble when you work alone in an office like I do, there's no one you can speak to. It just shows you, a woman on her own has always got to look out; it's not only that it's not safe to walk about alone at night because of the natives, this whole town is full of people you can't trust.

❁ Discussion and Writing

1. Describe the speaker of this dramatic monologue in her daily routine: her appearance, sexuality, family ties, friends, class, and perception of the customers. What controls her behavior?
2. Why does she treat Jack slightly differently than other black workers? What does her attitude toward the workers, black and white, indicate about her?
3. Discuss the implications of: Jack's comments about his name; his assessment of the stranger and his car; his advice to the speaker; his reading the newspaper in his free time.
4. Why does the narrator overlook the stranger's lies and behavior? Why does she remain silent about his living in her apartment? What is she afraid of?
5. Comment on the stranger's game and the relevance of the title "Good Climate, Friendly Inhabitants."
6. Who is responsible for the stranger's exit? Interpret the last sentence. Comment on the race and class distinctions pervading the story.

❁ Research and Comparison

Examine any novel by Nadine Gordimer and discuss her treatment of racial relations in South Africa.

Christopher Okigbo
(1923–1967)
Nigeria

Christopher Okigbo, considered by many Nigeria's finest poet, was born near Onitsha in eastern Nigeria. After taking his degree in classics at University College, Ibadan, he went first into the civil service and then into teaching. Later he worked as a librarian at the University of Nigeria, Nsukka, and as West African representative of Cambridge University Press. A meticulous writer, he strongly influenced many younger Nigerian poets. His turn to his native poetic traditions is reflected in the strong rhythms and repetitions in his poems. His poems are exceptionally musical, drawing on the oral tradition of the union of music, performance, and the word. He died near Nsukka in one of the earliest battles of the Biafran war, having joined the Biafran army when fighting erupted in 1967. His bravery and the importance of his poetry have stood as emblems, and poets like Kofi Awoonor have elegized him. Awoonor dramatized the elegy he composed honoring Okigbo and called the play "Lament."

Come Thunder

NOW THAT the triumphant march has entered the last street
      corners,
Remember, O dancers, the thunder among the clouds . . .

Now that laughter, broken in two, hangs tremulous between
    the teeth,

Remember, O dancers, the lightning beyond the earth . . .

The smell of blood already floats in the lavender-mist of the
    afternoon.
The death sentence lies in ambush along the corridors of
    power;
And a great fearful thing already tugs at the cables of the open
    air,
A nebula immense and immeasurable, a night of deep waters—
An iron dream unnamed and unprintable, a path of stone.

The drowsy heads of the pods in barren farmlands witness it,

The homesteads abandoned in this century's brush fire witness
    it:

The myriad eyes of deserted corn cobs in burning barns witness
    it:

Magic birds with the miracle of lightning flash on their
        feathers . . .

The arrows of God tremble at the gates of light,
The drums of curfew pander to a dance of death;

And the secret thing in its heaving
Threatens with iron mask
The last lighted torch of the century . . .

❋ **Discussion and Writing**

1. What images and natural elements does Okigbo use to help the reader conceptualize the march; what is its purpose?
2. Comment on the implications of the creative and the destructive powers of lightning.
3. What is the "the iron dream"; why is it "unnamed" and "unprintable"? What is implied by the "iron mask"?
4. Why is *this* century emphasized in the poem?

❋ **Research and Comparison**

Interdisciplinary Discussion Question: Research the Biafran war, examining its place in Nigerian history. Discuss its impact on people's lives and its depiction in the work of such Nigerian writers as Christopher Okigbo, Chinua Achebe, and Flora Nwapa.

Sembene Ousmane
(b. 1923)
Senegal

Sembene Ousmane was born in Ziguinchor in southern Senegal. His father was a fisherman who taught him his own trade, the Wolof language, and about city life. His mother taught him about rural life and the Diola language. Sembene was largely self-taught and began supporting himself at the age of 15, working as a wandering fisherman and trader. Drafted into the French colonial army during World War II, he participated in the Allied invasion of Italy, but was discharged, ostensibly for striking an officer. After the war, he worked for some years as a docker and union organizer in Marseilles until he sustained a serious back injury and could no longer do this kind of physical labor. This was a crucial period for him in that his work as a docker sparked his interest in Marxism; he joined the French Communist Party and turned to writing. His first novel, entitled *Le Docker noir* (The Black Docker), appeared in 1956.

Since the early 1960s, when he studied at the Moscow Film School, Sembene has gained a worldwide reputation as an *auteur* or film-director. Using talented amateur actors, the Wolof language, and a medium available to people of all classes, he has found a form that taps his aesthetic and philosophical concerns. His prestige has provoked protests when various authorities, French and Senegalese, have attempted—once successfully— to ban his films.

Sembene's *Les Bouts de Bois de Dieu* (God's Bits of Wood, 1960), considered a classic, has been influential in Anglophone and Francophone literature. It takes as its subject the 1947–1948 railway strike on the Dakar-Niger line. The train itself assumes larger significance, heralding the demise of the feudal caste society of western Sudan and, at the same time, of French colonization. The narrative is episodic, strung along the stations of the railway line and underlining the metaphor of the strike. "The March of the Women" portrays one episode in the strike.

The March of the Women*

Ever since they left Thies, the women had not stopped singing. As soon as one group allowed the refrain to die, another picked it up, and new verses were born at the hazard of chance or inspiration, one word leading to another and each finding, in its turn, its rhythm and its place. No one was very sure any longer where the song began, or if it had an ending. It rolled out over its own length, like the movement of a serpent. It was as long as a life.

Now the day had come. The road was too narrow for them, and they moved forward spread out in the shape of a fan, so that some walked in the dust and others in the dry grass beside the road, while still others followed the tracks of the railroad, and the younger ones amused themselves by leaping from tie to tie. The colors of waistcloths and blouses and headcloths flowered across the landscape. Dun-colored burlaps and striped and

Translated by Francis Price

checked drills and ticking mingled with bright splashes of prints and the faded cottons of old tunics. Open collars and rolled-up sleeves revealed well-rounded shoulders and elbows, blanched with a film of dust, and hitched-up skirts betrayed slender, handsome legs as well as hammy thighs.

The sun was behind them, beating ever harder on their backs, but they paid no attention to it; they knew it well. The sun was a native.

Penda, still wearing her soldier's cartridge belt, marched at the head of the procession with Mariame Sonko, the wife of Balla, and Maimouna, the blind woman, who had joined them in the darkness without being noticed by anyone. Her baby was strapped across her back with an old shawl.

The men of the little escort group followed at some distance behind the women, and several of them had brought bicycles in the event that they should be needed. Boubacar had strung a necklace of cans and gourds filled with water from the framework and handlebars on his. Samba N'Doulougou was perched like a scrawny bird on an elegant English machine. His rump beat irregularly against the saddle, and his feet parted company with the pedals at every turn.

They were traveling across a countryside laid waste by the dry season. The torrents of the sun had struck at the hearts of even the grasses and the wild plants and drained away their sap. The smallest leaves and stalks leaned toward the earth, preparing to fall and die. The only things that seemed alive were the thorny plants that thrived on drought and, far off toward the horizon, the lofty baobabs, to whom the comings and goings of seasons meant nothing. The soil was ridged and caked in an unwholesome crust, but it still bore traces of ancient cultivation: little squares of earth pierced by stumps of millet or corn, standing like the teeth of a broken comb. Once, a line of thatched roofs had been drawn here, against the bosom of a rich, brown earth; and countless little pathways—coming from no one knew where, going no one knew where—crossed this master road, and the hundreds of feet that trod them raised a cloud of reddish dust, for in those days there was no asphalt on the road from Dakar.

Quite early on the first night they came to a village. The inhabitants, bewildered at the sight of so many women, plied them with questions. But their hospitality was cordial, although a little ceremonious because of their surprise at such an event. At dawn, their thirst assuaged, their stomachs calmed, their feet still sore, they left again, to a concert of compliments and encouragement. Two hours later they passed the bus to Thies, and some of the women performed a little dance in the road, to acknowledge the cheers and waving of the travelers. Then they took up their march again.

And the second day was very much like the first.

It was at about noon of the third day that their fatigue began to show itself. They had passed through Pouth, where the villagers formed a double rank to applaud the singing women, but little by little after that the procession had lengthened out. The sun upended its caldrons of live coals on the earth, and the movement of their knees and ankles became steadily more difficult and painful. Like a river which, having amassed all its strength to pass through a narrow gorge, spreads out and moves sluggishly when it has reached the plain, the troop of women straggled across the landscape.

Maimouna, who was still walking with the group in the lead, put her hand on Penda's shoulder. "I don't hear the singing any more," she said.

"That's true—I hadn't noticed. How long has it been?"

"Since we saw the snake that had been crushed by an automobile," Mariame Sonko said, and she sat, or rather, fell back against the rim of the embankment.

Penda studied the horizon. "Get up, Mariame. This isn't a good place to rest; there are some trees up ahead."

"They are a long way off, your trees!"

The little group started out again, but they had gone only a short distance when Boubacar came up to them on his bicycle, with four of the other men following.

"There's a whole group back there that won't go any farther," Boubacar said to Penda. He had shown so much enthusiasm for his role as her assistant that even Maimouna had begun to wonder about the reasons for it.

"They must go on," Penda said. She gestured to the men with Boubacar. "You—take the water cans and go on ahead to those trees; and don't give anything to drink to anyone until they get there. And you, Boubacar, take me back to that group." She climbed on the back of his bicycle, and they set off toward the rear of the column.

Most of the women were walking by themselves, in Indian file, too tired even to group together and gossip. The largest and heaviest seemed to be suffering most; little rivers of sweat rolled down their faces and arms and naked thighs. They had pulled their skirts up high around their waists in the hope of making movement easier, and some of them had cut branches and walked like old people, leaning on their canes. When they passed a clump of bone-white, skeletal cade trees and a flight of vultures rose heavily into the air they were seized with panic, and those who had been walking in the grass hurried to join the others on the road. In all of their ancient legends these birds and these trees were the living homes of evil. Their presence together could be nothing but a warning of disaster to come.

A little beyond this point Penda and Boubacar came across the group of the younger girls, led by Aby, who had been one of Penda's assistants at the distribution of rations. They, too, were tired, but they were still laughing and talking as they walked. Boubacar braked the bicycle and put out his enormous feet to steady it.

"You can do better than this," Penda called out. "You're not old women!"

"We're not the last," Aby said.

"I know, I know, but keep going just the same. We'll rest up ahead in the shade—and sing; it will help you and it will help the older women."

A few voices picked up "the chant," but it was a scattered, half-hearted effort. Penda shook her head, and they went on to the rear, pausing frequently to encourage women who were walking alone and urge them to join with one of the little islands into which the whole column had now broken. When they finally arrived at the group which had refused to go farther, almost an hour had elapsed since they left the head of the column.

Something like a hundred women were sitting or lying along the shoulders of the road or the slope of the railway embankment. Branches thrust into the ground and strung with skirts and blouses formed makeshift shelters from the sun, and some of them were sleeping with just their heads inside the little patch of shade. The rest of the men of the escort were waiting a little farther on, seated on the edge of a shallow ravine.

"All right," Penda said sharply, as she got down from the bicycle. "You have rested long enough. Now we have to go on."

"Go on? With a sun like this? Do you want us dead?" It was Awa who had spoken, the wife of Sene Masene, the foreman carpenter. Comfortably installed, with her back resting against the embankment and her head in the shade of a little shrub, she looked like a queen bee surrounded by her drones.

"Get up," Penda said, striving to remain calm.

"We are tired. What difference does it make whether we leave today or tomorrow? If you're in such a hurry, go on ahead—we'll see you in Dakar."

"No—there can't be any stragglers; we must all arrive together. If there are some of you who want to go back, do it now, but the others will go on."

"*He!*" Awa cried. "You're not the one to give orders here! My husband is a foreman. . . ."

"Awa, I warn you, don't start that with me again! You have a short memory if you've forgotten already what happened at the ration distribution."

Awa turned her head slowly on her enormous shoulders, as if calling on her companions to witness what she was about to say.

"I am staying," she announced. "We don't have to obey Penda. It's just because she can't have children that all the men run after her. And there are *deumes* in the group with her! Yes, there are women possessed of the evil spirit, and she wants us to mix with them! Well, piss on her!"

Penda could no longer control her anger. She strode rapidly over to the embankment and began kicking down the branches and snatching away the skirts and blouses. The women cried out in protest, and Awa screamed, "The whore won't dare to touch my cloth!" but Penda went grimly on with her work until she had destroyed the last of the flimsy shelters.

Then she looked around her and, seeing that some of the women were still lying or kneeling on the ground, she began to count them out, lifting her fingers one by one.

"One, two, three, four. . . ."

"Witch!" Awa cried. "You have no right to do that!"

"No, no! Don't count us, please!" Seni said, getting quickly to her feet. "We are God's bits of wood, and if you count us out you will bring misfortune; you will make us die!"

"I want to know how many of you are against the strike," Penda said. ". . . five, six, seven, eight. . . ."

"Stop!" Awa cried, scrambling to her feet. "We will be eaten alive! My dream was true! I dreamed that spirits carrying pointed knives came and cut me in pieces to devour me!"

With fear and anger dividing their hearts, the women gathered together their clothing, knotted the cloths around their heads, and went back to the road. The men followed at a little distance, led by the giant Boubacar.

When the stragglers rejoined the other women, they were given a surly welcome. The trees in the area Penda had chosen for the halt were few, and there was little shade. Most of those who had arrived first were already sleeping, and they were angry at being disturbed.

"*He*, you're the last to get here, and now you want all the best places!"

"We've been walking through hell—we want to rest!"

"And what about us? We didn't walk through hell?"

"Just move over a little."

"*He*, look where you're sitting! You've got your ass in my face—if you farted, you'd smother me!"

"Awa, just because you're so fat doesn't mean you can do anything you please. Move your big ass!"

"Watch your words, Yacine!"

"And you watch where you put that big rump, Awa!"

"Look out there! You're stepping on me!"

"I'm swimming in my own sweat—I don't need yours!"

"Is there anything to drink?"

"No; the water is all gone. The men have gone to look for some."

At last, however, the newcomers settled down as best they could. Fatigue overcame irritation, nerves and muscles relaxed, and the women slept.

Maimouna had managed to save a little corner of shade for Penda, and the exhausted girl lay down beside the blind woman. She unfastened the buckle of the cartridge belt and pulled her skirt up high above her knees, sighing with relief, but just as she allowed her head to sink gratefully into the dry grass Boubacar appeared.

"Penda, Penda. . . ."

"Now what?"

"The men who went for the water haven't come back yet," the smith said awkwardly. The warm scent of female bodies and the sight of all these recumbent sleeping women made him uneasy. He lowered his eyes, trying not to stare at the long legs of the girl on the ground beneath him.

Penda propped herself up on an elbow. "Well, send some others then. If there are no more bicycles, they'll have to go on foot. We can't stay here long, and we have to have water before we leave."

"I've already sent a second group."

"Then why are you bothering me? Tell Samba N'Doulougou I want to see him; I have something to tell him."

Boubacar did not answer. He stood there for a moment longer, then turned his massive back and disappeared among the trees, walking cautiously to avoid stepping on the women.

Maimouna had trembled at the mention of Samba's name, and Penda had noticed it at once. She lay there, motionless, watching the blind woman. The sighs and snores of the sleeping women seemed enormous in the silence of the torrid afternoon. Seni was sleeping at Penda's feet, a little thread of saliva bubbling from the corner of her lips.

"Penda," Maimouna said gently, "why are you so hard on Boubacar?"

"What do you mean? I'm not hard on him. Is he the father of your children?"

"No. Why is it that people who have eyes can never see?"

"Well, if he isn't the father, why is he always hanging around you?"

"Penda, could it be that there was always only one place in your heart, and now Bakayoko has taken it?" Maimouna was speaking very softly, not wishing to disturb their neighbors. "That man will occupy your heart, and then pass through it, leaving nothing but bitterness. He will destroy everything. You see, with us—with women—we love a man when we know nothing of him, and we want to know everything. And we will pursue the one we have chosen no matter what happens, no matter how he treats us. But when we have learned what we wanted to know, and there is nothing left, no longer any mystery, then our interest is gone. The ones like Bakayoko will always be our bane. They do with us as they will. Before you have time to say 'no,' you have already said 'yes.'"

Penda was studying the face of the blind woman as she spoke, searching for the thoughts behind the sightless eyes.

"How do you know all this?" she asked.

"I haven't always been blind. After I lost my sight, my ears replaced my eyes. I have learned to know what people are thinking, and to understand what is said between the words that are spoken, and I tell you this: in Bakayoko's heart there is no room for anyone. He is blinder to his neighbor than I am. . . ."

"Who is the father of your children?"

"You are just being stubborn. That is of no importance any longer. I was not betrayed by that man. He thought that he was possessing me, but it wasn't true; my flesh was calling out to be satisfied, just as his was. I knew that he would abandon me, and in my heart I had already abandoned him. We will be in Dakar soon, and I shall stay there. I will be among my brothers, the beggars, and with my child, who will always be mine. A child may not know its father, Penda, but what child can question the body in which it lived for nine long months?"

"You will stay with me," Penda said.

The blind woman was silent for a moment. "Rest now, Penda," she said at last. "Soon the wind will come up, and there will be a great storm."

It w as during the next stage of the march that the crisis occurred which seemed certain to bring about the failure of the whole enterprise.

It had not been easy to rouse the women, who groaned and complained bitterly, pressing their hands against their aching limbs and backs, trying to rid themselves of the stiffness brought on by an hour's rest. Penda tried to cheer them up by joking with the group of younger girls.

"Be sure you don't let the men get too close to you. I don't want to have to answer to your families when your bellies start to swell!"

"We haven't done anything," Aby said indignantly.

"And I suppose if you did you would come and tell me about it right away, *he?*"

But no one was in a mood to laugh. Water had become the only thing they thought about. The few cans Boubacar's men brought back had been enough to supply only a few drops to each person.

"I'm as filthy as a pig," one woman said, displaying the scales of dried sweat, caked with dust, that had formed on her legs.

"I'd like to get in the water and stay in it, like a fish!"

"When I get to Dakar, I'm going to do nothing but drink for the first hour!"

"Those beautiful, well-scrubbed boys in Dakar won't be interested in our dirty bodies!"

Little by little, however, the column reformed. There was no laughter or singing now, but a curious new thing seemed to have come to them: the sort of hope, or instinct, that will guide an animal searching for a new place to graze.

More and more often now, Penda left her own group and walked back along the length of the column, gathering in the stragglers, stopping to talk to the old and the more feeble, encouraging them to go on. On one such journey she heard Awa talking to a group of her friends, in a loud, frightened voice.

"I swear to you, there are evil spirits among us. My dream came back while we were resting—but I've taken precautions; they won't want me." Saying this, she untied a corner of her skirt, which she had made into a large knot. "Before we left, I covered myself with salt, and every now and then I eat a little of it. That way, when the *deumes* come to devour me, they will find that they don't want me."

Several of the others held out their hands eagerly, and Awa gave them each a pinch of salt. In their fatigue and discouragement, the women were beset again by all the fears instilled in them by age-old legends. The sky itself seemed to threaten them; little clouds the color of Dahomey ivory, bordered in dark gray, raced across the horizon, throwing the bony fingers of the cade trees into stark relief.

"You are right, Awa," one of the women said. "We must be very careful. These offshoots of hell can change themselves into grains of dust, or into ants or thorns, or even into birds. I'm going to warn my sister."

"You're a bunch of fools," Penda said angrily, "and you ought to. . . ."

But she was interrupted by a piercing, disjointed shriek, followed by the sound of hysterical screaming from the rear of the column. She began to run in that direction, and a few of the more curious among the other women followed her, but most of them remained frozen where they were, and some even fled in the opposite direction.

Seni was rolling in the dust in the middle of the road, her limbs writhing horribly, her back arched and twisted in convulsions. Her skirt had been torn off, a slimy foam dribbled from her mouth, and her eyes had rolled back into her head until only the whites stared out.

"I told you!" Awa cried. "It's a *deume* who is devouring her! We've got to find it!"

The great orbs of her eyes, rolling in terror, suddenly came to rest on the tiny figure of Yacine, seated by the side of the road a few feet away. The old woman had cut her big toe, and since it was bleeding profusely, she was trying to bring her foot up to her mouth to suck the blood away.

"There she is! There she is!" Awa screamed. "Look—she is sucking Seni's blood through her feet!"

Twenty mouths screamed with her now. "There she is! There is the *deume!* Catch her, catch her!"

Yacine leaped to her feet, panic-stricken, and tried to run, but she was caught in an instant. A dozen hands seized her roughly, and others hurled branches and stones at her.

"You've all gone mad!" Penda shouted, trying to protect the old woman, whose face had been gashed by a stone and was beginning to bleed.

Awa was still screaming hysterically. "I told you so! I told you so! We have a *deume*, and Seni is going to die!"

"*Fermez voz gueules!*"[1] Without realizing it, Penda had spoken in French. "You're the ones who are *deumes!* Let this woman go, or I'll eat you

---

[1]"Shut your traps!" (a *gueule* is a dog's muzzle). [eds.]

alive myself! Mariame! Go get Boubacar and the men and bring Maimouna, too!"

She succeeded at last in freeing Yacine, half dead with fright, her clothing almost torn from her body. Seni was lying on her back in the road, surrounded by a circle of women. Her legs were straight and stiff, and her teeth were chattering violently.

Boubacar arrived, followed by five or six men on bicycles, one of them carrying Maimouna behind him. She leaned over the prostrate woman, her fingers moving swiftly over her face and feeling for her pulse.

"It isn't serious," she said. "It's just the heat. She'll have to inhale some urine."

"All right, some of you sluts go and piss!" Penda cried.

Some of the women climbed over to the other side of the embankment, and Maimouna followed them. She came back a few minutes later, carrying some clods of humid earth. Seating herself in the road, she kneaded them into little balls, which she passed back and forth under Seni's nostrils, while Penda held up the unconscious woman's head.

In all this time, Awa never once stopped shouting. "There are others! I tell you, there are others! Seni is going to die—I can smell the odor of death from her already. They brought us out here because it would be easier to devour us here—it's just like it was in my dream!"

Penda could no longer control herself. She rested Seni's head on the knees of the blind woman and hurled herself at Awa.

"Now, you are going to be quiet!"

Her fists were as hard as a man's, and she hammered at the other woman's face and stomach until she stumbled and fell against the foot of a tree, screaming with pain and fear.

Then, her anger drained out of her by this explosion of physical energy, Penda walked over to the giant smith, who had been watching her in amazement.

"Boubacar, some of the men will have to carry the women who are sick," she said, pointing at Awa, the weeping Yacine, and Seni, who was now sitting up, with her head resting calmly on Maimouna's shoulder, next to that of the baby sleeping on her mother's back.

The men lifted her from the ground and installed her on the seat of a bicycle, where they could support her as they pushed it along. Boubacar took Awa on his powerful back, and the column formed up once again. All of the women seemed to want to walk behind Maimouna, as if she trailed a protective wake in which they would be safe. The wind she had prophesied earlier was rising now; huge black clouds, running before it, cast fitful shadows across the road, frightening the marchers. Disembodied twigs and leaves danced across the earth, carried by waves of dust.

And suddenly, as the road twisted around a little hill, a man's voice called out, "*Tialaverd, Tialaverd, ban'ga!* Here comes the storm!"

It was really just a minor whirlwind, and not the great storm Maimouna had predicted. As it approached them, three columns of dust twisted up to the sky, flattening the grasses in their paths and tearing the leaves from the bushes and shrubs. The terrified women flung themselves into a near-by ravine flattening their bodies against the ground and burying their heads in bushes or clumps of grass. Their headcloths were whipped away and carried up into the trees, catching against the branches and streaming out like pennants. One woman's waistcloth was torn from her, and she was hurled, naked, against the trunk of a eucalyptus tree.

They had all seen hundreds of dust storms just like this one, but their nerves were already stretched to the breaking point, and even after it had passed their despair persisted. Penda went from one group to another, encouraging them, pointing to the columns of dust vanishing in the distance, urging them to get up and go on.

Boubacar was still carrying the mumbling and cursing Awa, Yacine was still weeping, and Seni, held in the seat of the bicycle by two men, kept murmuring. "My heart . . . my heart. . . .'" Even the men were beginning to complain. Only Maimouna, her baby strapped across her back, walked steadily forward, humming one of her endless refrains.

"What a blind woman can do," Penda said, "the rest of you should be able to do!"

At last, just as night was falling on the weary and haggard procession, they heard a joyful beating of drums approaching them. The people of the village of Sebikoutane, told of the women's arrival by their children, were coming out to meet them. In gourds, in tin jugs, in cooking pots, and in old cans they were carrying water.

The last two stages of the march, from Sebikoutane to Rufisque, and from Rufisque to Dakar, were almost a promenade. The reception given the women at Sebikoutane had been magnificent. The earth of the village square was red with the blood of sheep slaughtered for the feast, and the celebration had gone on until far into the night. But best of all had been the water; all the water they could possibly drink. The "marchers," as people now called them, learned that they were rapidly becoming famous; the newspapers, and even the radio, had mentioned them. Those who had never ceased complaining while they were on the road preened themselves and strutted now, inventing vicissitudes they had never undergone and risks they had never run. Even Awa succumbed to the fever of good will, and just before their departure from the village she sought out Penda.

"I'm not going back to Thies," she said. "I'm going on with you, Penda. I promise that I won't cause you any more trouble, and to prove it I am going to ask Yacine to forgive me for what I did."

Penda was massaging her swollen feet, but she got up instantly. "I'll come with you—I want to see this. . . ."

Seeing Awa approach, Yacine shrank back in fear, but the carpenter's wife fulfilled her promise.

"Yacine," she said, "I came to ask you to forgive me. Out there I was tired and out of my head with the heat, and I lied. You are not a *deume*."

Yacine began to laugh and cry at the same time. "Do you hear that, all of you?" she shouted. "I am not a *deume*! Now I can return home without shame, and with my head high! Oh thank you, Awa, thank you!"

Just after that, the long procession set out again. The waistcloths and blouses and headcloths had all been washed, and a sky swept clean of even the smallest cloud by yesterday's winds smiled down on the colorful horde. Between Rufisque, their last stopping place, and Dakar, they breathed the fresh sea air of the Atlantic for the first time. The ranks of the original column from Thies had been swollen by women from the villages, and by a delegation from Rufisque: and a large group of men had reinforced the escort. The women sang again and laughed and joked.

"We will surely see some beautiful houses at Dakar."

"But they are not for us; they are only for the *toubabs*."[2]

"After the strike we will have them, too."

"After the strike I'm going to do what the wives of the *toubabs* do, and take my husband's pay!"

"And if there are two of you?"

"We'll each take half, and that way he won't have anything left to spend on other women. We will have won the strike, too!"

"The men have been good, though. Did you see how the smith was sweating while he was carrying Awa?"

"Bah! For once he had a woman on his back. They have us on our backs every night!"

In the last miles before they reached their goal they passed a point from which they could see the island of Goree,[3] a tiny black dot in the green expanse of the ocean; they saw the vast Lafarge cement factories and the remains of an American army camp. As they approached the first buildings of Dakar's suburbs, a breathless boy on a bicycle raced up to meet them, leaping off his machine in front of the little group at the head of the column.

"There are soldiers on the road at the entrance to the city," he gasped. "They say that the women from Thies will not be allowed to pass."

The laughter and the singing stopped abruptly, and there was silence. A few of the women left the road and took shelter behind the walls, as if they expected the soldiers to appear at any minute; but the bulk of the column stood firm. Penda climbed up on a little slope.

---

[2]A white, mulatto, or black person living according to European customs. [eds.]
[3]The site of one of the major "slave castles" used in the Atlantic slave trade. [eds.]

"The soldiers can't eat us!" she cried. "They can't even kill us; there are too many of us! Don't be afraid—our friends are waiting for us in Dakar! We'll go on!"

The long, multi-colored mass began to move forward again.

Maimouna, who was walking a little behind Penda, suddenly felt a hand on her arm.

"Who is it?"

"It's me."

"You, Samba? What's the matter?"

"There are soldiers. . . ."

"Yes, I heard."

Samba N'Doulougou did not understand too clearly what force it was that had compelled him to come here now and seek out this woman whose body he had enjoyed one night. Was it pity for the weak and infirm, or was it for the mother and the child? He remembered the shame he had lived with for months, as he watched her working in the sun while her belly grew large with the child, his child. And he remembered the way he had tried to alter his voice so she would not recognize him.

"Give me the child," he said. "It will be easier for me to avoid the soldiers."

"You want your child?" the blind woman said.

"The soldiers are going to be there. . . ."

"And after that? . . . A father may die while a woman is big with child, but that does not prevent the child from living, because the mother is there. It is up to me to protect this child. Go away now. After I get to Dakar you will never see me again; and I have never seen you. No one knows who is the father of this child—you can sleep peacefully, and your honor will be safe. Now go back to the men."

Just outside the big racecourse of the city, the column confronted the red tarbooshes of the soldiers. A black non-commissioned officer who was standing with the captain commanding the little detachment called out to them.

"Go back to Thies, women! We cannot let you pass!"

"We will pass if we have to walk on the body of your mother!" Penda cried.

And already the pressure of this human wall was forcing the soldiers to draw back. Reinforcements began to appear, from everywhere at once, but they were not for the men in uniform. A few rifle butts came up menacingly and were beaten down by clubs and stones. The unnerved soldiers hesitated, not knowing what to do, and then some shots rang out, and in the column two people fell—Penda and Samba N'Doulougou.

But how could a handful of men in red tarbooshes prevent this great river from rolling on to the sea?

❄ Discussion and Writing

1. What is the purpose of the women's march? Analyze the description of the women: their strengths and frailties; their concerns and motivations.
2. Characterize Penda's qualities of leadership: her evaluation of people and situations; her effective strategies; unceasing energy; endurance and determination; her death.
3. Analyze the function of Maimouna and Awa in the narrative.
4. What is the role of men in this narrative?
5. Explore the use of the water, both as a substance and an image, in this narrative. Clarify the impact of the metaphor at the end, the great "river rolling on to the sea."
6. Considering this story is about women in a patriarchal society, how does one explain the women's remarkably courageous political participation?
7. What is the overpowering feeling created by the description of the landscape?

❄ Research and Comparison

Analyze Ousmane Sembene's novel *God's Bits of Wood,* the story of the fight for liberation by the people of Senegal.

Interdisciplinary Discussion Question: The women of Dakar became a vibrant branch of political activism in recent history. Research the topic to examine social, historical, and political trends prevalent in Senegal.

Interdisciplinary Discussion Question: Analyze two or more of Sembene's films and discuss the depiction of their dominant themes.

Dennis Brutus
(b. 1924)
South Africa

Dennis Brutus was born in southern Zimbabwe and was raised in Cape Province, South Africa. After taking his degree in Arts, he taught English and Afrikaans in Port Elizabeth for ten years and then began the study of law at Witwatersrand. He was a keen sportsman, and so he focused his protest against apartheid on the campaign against South African participation in the Olympic Games. Because of his official position in this campaign, he was banned from teaching, from his law studies, and from being published in South Africa. He was detained and severely wounded, supposedly as he tried to escape, and was held on Robben Island for eighteen months as a political prisoner. He left South Africa when he was released from prison in 1965, and took up his teaching and writing in London and the United States.

In 1948, the Afrikaner Nationalist Party formalized the policy of segregation in which people were categorized and identified according to race and color. Blacks, people of mixed descent, Asians, and whites were separated, and elaborate regulations controlling the lives of black South Africans were instituted. Prime Minister Hendrik Verwoerd initiated a practice of "separate development" in which the government established nine "homelands," called Bantustans. These were reservations for different African peoples, and the Bantustans effectively divided black South Africans so that uniting for resistance became all the more difficult. Among the restrictions they suffered under apartheid, the government prohibited the right to vote, own land, travel, work without a permit. Wives could not accompany their husbands into urban or mining areas, and thus, the government effectively disrupted the strength of the family and community.

Nightsong: City

Sleep well, my love, sleep well:
the harbor lights glaze over restless docks,
police cars cockroach through the tunnel streets;

from the shanties creaking iron-sheets
violence like a bug-infested rag is tossed
and fear is immanent as sound in the wind-swung bell;

the long day's anger pants from sand and rocks;
but for this breathing night at least,
my land, my love, sleep well.

The sounds begin again;
the siren in the night
the thunder at the door
the shriek of nerves in pain.

Then the keening crescendo
of faces split by pain
the wordless, endless wail
only the unfree know.

Importunate as rain
the wraiths exhale their woe
over the sirens, knuckles, boots;
my sounds begin again.

❀ Discussion and Writing

1. What images in the poem indicate a South African city? What aspects of this city might be shared by many cities around the world.? How would knowledge of the history of the land enhance the meaning of the poem?
2. What may breed love for the land in the midst of pain and woe? Comment on the bond with the land in the colonial context.

❀ Research and Comparison

Interdisciplinary Discussion Question: Research the issue of nationalism for South Africans of all races and colors. Analyze the ironic nature of the racial and political situation in South Africa.

Interdisciplinary Discussion Question: Examine the issue of nationalism as a catalyst in the fight for liberation from the colonial rule with regard to any African country.

Camara Laye
(1924–1980)
Guinea

Camara Laye, the eldest of 12 children, was born into an old Malinke family in the ancient market town of Kouroussa, Guinea, where the traditional Malinke faith and customs coexisted easily with the Muslim religion. The Camara clan, the second-largest clan in the Upper Niger Valley, were blacksmiths who traced their line back to a thirteenth-century king. The black snake, the spirit that led and protected the king, also guided Camara Laye's father, the town's leading blacksmith and goldsmith. Camara Laye began his studies at a Quranic school before attending a government school. He studied as a scholarship student in France, receiving a certificate in automobile mechanics, but when his scholarship ended, he took various jobs (as a porter, in factories) while working for a diploma in engineering. At the same time, he was reading insatiably and participating in discussions with other African students, often about *negritude,* and he was beginning to write.

He received the Prix Charles Veillon for his autobiographical work *L'Enfant noir* (The Dark Child, 1953). "The Goldsmith," a story about his father, comes from this work. In 1955, his richly symbolic and highly acclaimed novel *Le Regard du roi* (The Radiance of the King) was published. During the following years, he served in various governmental and diplomatic posts, recorded texts from the oral tradition, and continued writing, although not with the same drive as in the early 1950s. He was imprisoned briefly and under house arrest for a few years because of his protests that the Sekou Toure government was turning tyrannical. He finally left Guinea in 1965 for Senegal, where he remained in exile until his death.

The Goldsmith*

Of all the different kinds of work my father engaged in, none fascinated me so much as his skill with gold. No other occupation was so noble, no other needed such a delicate touch. And then, every time he worked in gold it was like a festival—indeed it *was* a festival—that broke the monotony of ordinary working days.

So, if a woman, accompanied by a go-between, crossed the threshold of the workshop, I followed her in at once. I knew what she wanted: she had brought some gold, and had come to ask my father to transform it into a trinket. She had collected it in the placers of Siguiri where, crouching over the river for months on end, she had patiently extracted grains of gold from the mud.

These women never came alone. They knew my father had other things to do than make trinkets. And even when he had the time, they knew they were not the first to ask a favor of him, and that, consequently, they would not be served before others.

Generally they required the trinket for a certain date, for the festival of Ramadan or the Tabaski or some other family ceremony or dance.

Therefore, to enhance their chances of being served quickly and to more easily persuade my father to interrupt the work before him, they used to request the services of an official praise-singer, a go-between, arranging in advance the fee they were to pay him for his good offices.

The go-between installed himself in the workshop, tuned up his *cora,* which is our harp, and began to sing my father's praises. This was always a great event for me. I heard recalled the lofty deeds of my father's ancestors and their names from the earliest times. As the couplets were reeled off it

---

*Translated by James Kirkup and Ernest Jones

was like watching the growth of a great genealogical tree that spread its branches far and wide and flourished its boughs and twigs before my mind's eye. The harp played an accompaniment to this vast utterance of names, expanding it with notes that were now soft, now shrill.

I could sense my father's vanity being inflamed, and I already knew that after having sipped this milk-and-honey he would lend a favorable ear to the woman's request. But I was not alone in my knowledge. The woman also had seen my father's eyes gleaming with contented pride. She held out her grains of gold as if the whole matter were settled. My father took up his scales and weighed the gold.

"What sort of trinket do you want?" he would ask.

"I want. . . ."

And then the woman would not know any longer exactly what she wanted because desire kept making her change her mind, and because she would have liked all the trinkets at once. But it would have taken a pile of gold much larger than she had brought to satisfy her whim, and from then on her chief purpose in life was to get hold of it as soon as she could.

"When do you want it?"

Always the answer was that the trinket was needed for an occasion in the near future.

"So! You are in that much of a hurry? Where do you think I shall find the time?"

"I am in a great hurry, I assure you."

"I have never seen a woman eager to deck herself out who wasn't in a great hurry! Good! I shall arrange my time to suit you. Are you satisfied?"

He would take the clay pot that was kept specially for smelting gold, and would pour the grains into it. He would then cover the gold with powdered charcoal, a charcoal he prepared by using plant juices of exceptional purity. Finally, he would place a large lump of the same kind of charcoal over the pot.

As soon as she saw that the work had been duly undertaken, the woman, now quite satisfied, would return to her household tasks, leaving her go-between to carry on with the praise-singing which had already proved so advantageous.

At a sign from my father the apprentices began working two sheepskin bellows. The skins were on the floor, on opposite sides of the forge, connected to it by earthen pipes. While the work was in progress the apprentices sat in front of the bellows with crossed legs. That is, the younger of the two sat, for the elder was sometimes allowed to assist. But the younger—this time it was Sidafa—was only permitted to work the bellows and watch while waiting his turn for promotion to less rudimentary tasks. First one and then the other worked hard at the bellows: the flame in the forge rose higher and became a living thing, a genie implacable and full of life.

Then my father lifted the clay pot with his long tongs and placed it on the flame.

Immediately all activity in the workshop almost came to a halt. During the whole time that the gold was being smelted, neither copper nor aluminum could be worked nearby, lest some particle of these base metals fall into the container which held the gold. Only steel could be worked on such occasions, but the men, whose task that was, hurried to finish what they were doing, or left it abruptly to join the apprentices gathered around the forge. There were so many, and they crowded so around my father, that I, the smallest person present, had to come near the forge in order not to lose track of what was going on.

If he felt he had inadequate working space, my father had the apprentices stand well away from him. He merely raised his hand in a simple gesture: at that particular moment he never uttered a word, and no one else would: no one was allowed to utter a word. Even the go-between's voice was no longer raised in song. The silence was broken only by the panting of the bellows and the faint hissing of the gold. But if my father never actually spoke, I know that he was forming words in his mind. I could tell from his lips, which kept moving, while, bending over the pot, he stirred the gold and charcoal with a bit of wood that kept bursting into flame and had constantly to be replaced by a fresh one.

What words did my father utter? I do not know. At least I am not certain what they were. No one ever told me. But could they have been anything but incantations? On these occasions was he not invoking the genies of fire and gold, of fire and wind, of wind blown by the blast-pipes of the forge, of fire born of wind, of gold married to fire? Was it not their assistance, their friendship, their espousal that he besought? Yes. Almost certainly he was invoking these genies, all of whom are equally indispensable for smelting gold.

The operation going on before my eyes was certainly the smelting of gold, yet something more than that: a magical operation that the guiding spirits could regard with favor or disfavor. That is why, all around my father, there was absolute silence and anxious expectancy. Though only a child, I knew there could be no craft greater than the goldsmith's. I expected a ceremony; I had come to be present at a ceremony; and it actually was one, though very protracted. I was still too young to understand why, but I had an inkling as I watched the almost religious concentration of those who followed the mixing process in the clay pot.

When finally the gold began to melt I could have shouted aloud—and perhaps we all would have if we had not been forbidden to make a sound. I trembled, and so did everyone else watching my father stir the mixture—it was still a heavy paste—in which the charcoal was gradually consumed. The next stage followed swiftly. The gold now had the fluidity of water. The genies had smiled on the operation!

"Bring me the brick!" my father would order, thus lifting the ban that until then had silenced us.

The brick, which an apprentice would place beside the fire, was hollowed out, generously greased with Galam butter. My father would take the pot off the fire and tilt it carefully, while I would watch the gold flow into the brick, flow like liquid fire. True, it was only a very sparse trickle of fire, but how vivid, how brilliant! As the gold flowed into the brick, the grease sputtered and flamed and emitted a thick smoke that caught in the throat and stung the eyes, leaving us all weeping and coughing.

But there were times when it seemed to me that my father ought to turn this task over to one of his assistants. They were experienced, had assisted him hundreds of times, and could certainly have performed the work well. But my father's lips moved and those inaudible, secret words, those incantations he addressed to one we could not see or hear, was the essential part. Calling on the genies of fire, of wind, of gold and exorcising the evil spirits— this was a knowledge he alone possessed.

By now the gold had been cooled in the hollow of the brick, and my father began to hammer and stretch it. This was the moment when his work as a goldsmith really began. I noticed that before embarking on it he never failed to stroke the little snake stealthily as it lay coiled up under the sheepskin. I can only assume that this was his way of gathering strength for what remained to be done, the most trying part of his task.

But was it not extraordinary and miraculous that on these occasions the little black snake was always coiled under the sheepskin? He was not always there. He did not visit my father every day. But he was always present whenever there was gold to be worked. His presence was no surprise to *me*. After that evening when my father had spoken of the guiding spirit of his race I was no longer astonished. The snake was there intentionally. He knew what the future held. Did he tell my father? I think that he most certainly did. Did he tell him everything? I have another reason for believing firmly that he did.

The craftsman who works in gold must first of all purify himself. That is, he must wash himself all over and, of course, abstain from all sexual commerce during the whole time. Great respecter of ceremony as he was, it would have been impossible for my father to ignore these rules. Now, I never saw him make these preparations. I saw him address himself to his work without any apparent preliminaries. From that moment it was obvious that, forewarned in a dream by his black guiding spirit of the task which awaited him in the morning, my father must have prepared for it as soon as he arose, entering his workshop in a state of purity, his body smeared with the secret potions hidden in his numerous pots of magical substances; or perhaps he always came into his workshop in a state of ritual purity. I am not trying to make him out a better man than he was—he was a man and had his share of human frailties—but he was always uncompromising in his respect for ritual observance.

❀ Discussion and Writing

1. Describe the influence of the father on the narrator.
2. Comment on the role of the goldsmith in his community. Explore the implications inherent in the account of his making the trinket.
3. What is the significance of the snake in this story?
4. What elements of the oral tradition does "The Goldsmith" contain? What is the role of the praise-singer?

❀ Research and Comparison

Examine the political, social, and religious implications, along with the aesthetic aspects, of Camara Laye's novel *the Radiance of the King.*

Efua Sutherland
(b. 1924)
Ghana

Efua Theodora Sutherland was born and educated in Ghana; she also studied in England at Homerton College, Cambridge, and the School of Oriental and African Studies of the University of London. When she returned to Ghana, she taught school for several years. Then she founded the Ghana Society of Writers, now integrated into the University of Ghana, where she has continued to work as a research fellow. She founded the Ghana Experimental Theater and Ghana Drama Studio, and also helped establish *Okyeame,* an important Ghanaian literary journal. And in order to produce plays in Akan and in Akan-speaking communities, she organized the Kuisum Agoromba Players ("The Right Thing to Do" Players).

Considered one of Ghana's leading authors, Sutherland has written plays, poetry, short stories, and children's books, while remaining involved in contemporary theater. She has worked continually with the Ghanaian oral tradition, retelling the stories of the crafty overreaching Ananse. The saying "exterminate Ananse, and society will be ruined" emblemizes her belief in the power of this tradition. She has also adapted European conventions to Ghanaian. Just as Sutherland has re-created the traditional Akan theatrical system of story-telling in some of her plays, the story "New Life at Kyerefaso" seems to have emerged like an Akan parable.

New Life at Kyerefaso

Shall we say

Shall we put it this way

Shall we say that the maid of Kyerefaso, Foruwa, daughter of the Queen Mother, was as a young deer, graceful in limb? Such was she, with head held high, eyes soft and wide with wonder. And she was light of foot, light in all her moving.

Stepping springily along the water path like a deer that had strayed from the thicket, springily stepping along the water path, she was a picture to give the eye a feast. And nobody passed her by but turned to look at her again.

Those of her village said that her voice in speech was like the murmur of a river quietly flowing beneath shadows of bamboo leaves. They said her smile would sometimes blossom like a lily on her lips and sometimes rise like sunrise.

The butterflies do not fly away from the flowers, they draw near. Foruwa was the flower of her village.

So shall we say,

Shall we put it this way, that all the village butterflies, the men, tried to draw near her at every turn, crossed and crossed her path? Men said of her, "She shall be my wife, and mine, and mine and mine."

But suns rose and set, moons silvered and died and as the days passed Foruwa grew more lovesome, yet she became no one's wife. She smiled at the butterflies and waved her hand lightly to greet them as she went swiftly about her daily work:

"Morning, Kweku

Morning, Kwesi

Morning, Kodwo"

but that was all.

And so they said, even while their hearts thumped for her:

"Proud!

Foruwa is proud . . . and very strange"

And so the men when they gathered would say:

"There goes a strange girl. She is not just the stiff-in-the-neck proud, not just breasts-stuck-out I-am-the-only-girl-in-the-village proud. What kind of pride is hers?"

The end of the year came round again, bringing the season of festivals. For the gathering in of corn, yams and cocoa there were harvest celebrations. There were bride-meetings too. And it came to the time when the Asafo companies should hold their festival. The village was full of manly sounds, loud musketry and swelling choruses.

The pathfinding, path-clearing ceremony came to an end. The Asafo marched on toward the Queen Mother's house, the women fussing round them, prancing round them, spreading their cloths in their way.

"Osee!" rang the cry. "Osee!" to the manly men of old. They crouched like leopards upon the branches.

Before the drums beat

Before the danger drums beat, beware!

Before the horns moaned

Before the wailing horns moaned, beware!

They were upright, they sprang. They sprang. They sprang upon the enemy. But now, blood no more! No more thundershot on thundershot.

But still we are the leopards on the branches. We are those who roar and cannot be answered back. Beware, we are they who cannot be answered back.

There was excitement outside the Queen Mother's courtyard gate.

"Gently, gently," warned the Asafo leader. "Here comes the Queen Mother.

Spread skins of the gentle sheep in her way.

Lightly, lightly walks our Mother Queen.

Shower her with silver,

Shower her with silver for she is peace."

And the Queen Mother stood there, tall, beautiful, before the men and there was silence.

"What news, what news do you bring?" she quietly asked.

"We come with dusty brows from our pathfinding, Mother. We come with tired, thorn-pricked feet. We come to bathe in the coolness of your peaceful stream. We come to offer our manliness to new life."

The Queen Mother stood there, tall and beautiful and quiet. Her fanbearers stood by her and all the women clustered near. One by one the men laid their guns at her feet and then she said:

"It is well. The gun is laid aside. The gun's rage is silenced in the stream. Let your weapons from now on be your minds and your hands" toil.

"Come maidens, women all, join the men in dance for they offer themselves to new life."

There was one girl who did not dance.

"What, Foruwa!" urged the Queen Mother, "Will you not dance? The men are tired of parading in the ashes of their grandfathers' glorious deeds.

That should make you smile. They are tired of the empty croak: 'We are men, we are men.'

"They are tired of sitting like vultures upon the rubbish heaps they have piled upon the half-built walls of their grandfathers. Smile, then, Foruwa, smile.

"Their brows shall now indeed be dusty, their feet thorn-picked, and 'I love my land' shall cease to be the empty croaking of a vulture upon the rubbish heap. Dance, Foruwa, dance!"

Foruwa opened her lips and this was all she said: "Mother, I do not find him here."

"Who? Who do you not find here?"

"He with whom this new life shall be built. He is not here, Mother. These men's faces are empty; there is nothing in them, nothing at all."

"Alas, Foruwa, alas, alas! What will become of you, my daughter?"

"The day I find him, Mother, the day I find the man, I shall come running to you, and your worries will come to an end."

"But, Foruwa, Foruwa," argued the Queen Mother, although in her heart she understood her daughter, "five years ago your rites were fulfilled. Where is the child of your womb? Your friend Maanan married. Your friend Esi married. Both had their rites with you."

"Yes, Mother, they married and see how their steps once lively now drag in the dust. The sparkle has died out of their eyes. Their husbands drink palm wine the day long under the mango trees, drink palm wine and push counters across the draughtboards (checkerboard) all the day, and are they not already looking for other wives? Mother, the man I say is not here."

This conversation had been overheard by one of the men and soon others heard what Foruwa had said. That evening there was heard a new song in the village.

There was a woman long ago,
Tell that maid, tell that maid,
There was a woman long ago,
She would not marry Kwesi,
She would not marry Kwaw,
She would not, would not, would not.
One day she came home with hurrying feet,
I've found the man, the man, the man,
Tell that maid, tell that maid,
Her man looked like a chief,
Tell that maid, tell that maid,
Her man looked like a chief,
Most splendid to see,
But he turned into a phython,

He turned into a python
And swallowed her up.

From that time onward there were some in the village who turned their backs on Foruwa when she passed.

Shall we say,

Shall we put it this way

Shall we say that a day came when Foruwa with hurrying feet came running to her mother? She burst through the courtyard gate; and there she stood in the courtyard, joy all over. And a stranger walked in after her and stood in the courtyard beside her, stood tall and strong as a pillar. Foruwa said to the astonished Queen Mother:

"Here he is, Mother, here is the man."

The Queen Mother took a slow look at the stranger standing there strong as a forest tree, and she said:

"You carry the light of wisdom on your face, my son. Greetings, you are welcome. But who are you, my son?"

"Greetings, Mother," replied the stranger quietly, "I am a worker. My hands are all I have to offer your daughter, for they are all my riches. I have travelled to see how men work in other lands. I have that knowledge and my strength. That is all my story."

Shall we say,

Shall we put it this way,

strange as the story is, that Foruwa was given in marriage to the stranger.

There was a rage in the village and many openly mocked saying, "Now the proud ones eat the dust."

Shall we say,

Shall we put it this way

that soon, quite soon, the people of Kyerefaso began to take notice of the stranger in quite a different way.

"Who," some said, "is this who has come among us? He who mingles sweat and song, he for whom toil is joy and life is full and abundant?"

"See," said others, "what a harvest the land yields under his ceaseless care."

"He has taken the earth and molded it into bricks. See what a home he has built, how it graces the village where it stands."

"Look at the craft of his fingers, baskets or kente, stool or mat, the man makes them all."

"And our children swarm about him, gazing at him with wonder and delight."

Then it did not satisfy them any more to sit all day at their draught-boards under the mango trees.

"See what Foruwa's husband has done," they declared; "shall the sons of the land not do the same?"

And soon they began to seek out the stranger to talk with him. Soon they too were toiling, their fields began to yield as never before, and the women labored joyfully to bring in the harvest. A new spirit stirred the village. As the carelessly built houses disappeared one by one, and new homes built after the fashion of the stranger's grew up, it seemed as if the village of Kyerefaso had been born afresh.

The people themselves became more alive and a new pride possessed them. They were no longer just grabbing from the land what they desired for their stomachs' present hunger and for their present comfort. They were looking at the land with new eyes, feeling it in their blood, and thoughtfully building a permanent and beautiful place for themselves and their children.

"Osee!" It was festival-time again. "Osee!" Blood no more. Our fathers found for us the paths. We are the roadmakers. They bought for us the land with their blood. We shall build it with our strength. We shall create it with our minds.

Following the men were the women and children. On their heads they carried every kind of produce that the land had yielded and crafts that their fingers had created. Green plantains and yellow bananas were carried by the bunch in large white wooden trays. Garden eggs, tomatoes, red oil-palm nuts warmed by the sun were piled high in black earthen vessels. Oranges, yams, maize filled shining brass trays and golden calabashes. Here and there were children proudly carrying colorful mats, baskets and toys which they themselves had made.

The Queen Mother watched the procession gathering on the new village playground now richly green from recent rains. She watched the people palpitating in a massive dance toward her where she stood with her fanbearers outside the royal house. She caught sight of Foruwa. Her load of charcoal in a large brass tray which she had adorned with red hibiscus danced wih her body. Happiness filled the Queen Mother when she saw her daughter thus.

Then she caught sight of Foruwa's husband. He was carrying a white lamb in his arms, and he was singing happily with the men. She looked on him with pride. The procession had approached the royal house.

"See!" rang the cry of the Asafo leader. "See how the best in all the land stands. See how she stands waiting, our Queen Mother. Waiting to wash the dust from our brow in the coolness of her peaceful stream. Spread skins of the gentle sheep in her way, gently. Spread the yield of the land before her. Spread the craft of your hands before her, gently, gently.

Lightly, lightly walks our Queen Mother, for she is peace."

❋ **Discussion and Writing**

1. Analyze the characters of the Queen Mother and Foruwa in relation to a matriarchal society. What ultimate vision of social regeneration does Sutherland convey through the story?
2. What is the function of men in this social set-up? Analyze their portrayal in this story.
3. Examine the role of the stranger; what does Sutherland infer by having an outsider set an example for the villagers?
4. What is the impact of the repeated phrases: "Shall we say," "Shall we put it this way"? Analyze the various traditional and modern narrative techniques and theatrical devices Sutherland uses in this story.

❋ **Research and Comparison**

Examine Sutherland's role in contemporary Ghanaian theater and her play *The Marriage of Anansewa.*

Can Themba
(1924–1968)
South Africa

Daniel Canadoise Dorsay Themba was born and educated in Pretoria, South Africa. He attended Fort Hare University College on a Mendi Scholarship, and after taking his B.A. (with distinction in English), he became a journalist, editor, and teacher. He taught English in Western Native Township, Johannesburg, worked as a reporter for *Drum* and as assistant editor of the weekly *Golden City Post,* and was teaching high school in Swaziland at the time of his death. His short stories capture the edgy tone of both social protest and the frequently violent life of South Africa before the imposition of apartheid.

The Suit

Five-thirty in the morning, and the candlewick bedspread frowned as the man under it stirred. He did not like to wake his wife lying by his side—as yet—so he crawled up and out by careful peristalsis. But before he tiptoed out of his room with shoes and socks under his arm, he leaned over and peered at the sleeping serenity of his wife: to him a daily matutinal miracle.

He grinned and yawned simultaneously, offering his wordless *Te Deum* to whatever gods for the goodness of life; for the pure beauty of his wife; for the strength surging through his willing body; for the even, unperturbed rhythms of his passage through days and months and years—it must be—to heaven.

Then he slipped soundlessly into the kitchen. He flipped aside the curtain of the kitchen window, and saw outside a thin drizzle, the type that can soak one to the skin, and that could go on for days and days. He wondered, head aslant, why the rain in Sophiatown always came in the morning when workers had to creep out of their burrows; and then at how blistering heatwaves came during the day when messengers had to run errands all over; and then at how the rain came back when workers knocked off and had to scurry home.

He smiled at the odd caprice of the heavens, and tossed his head at the naughty incongruity, as if, "Ai, but the gods!"

From behind the kitchen door he removed an old rain cape, peeling off in places, and swung it over his head. He dashed for the lavatory, nearly slipping in a pool of muddy water, but he reached the door. Aw, blast, someone had made it before him. Well, that is the toll of staying in a yard where twenty . . . thirty other people have to share the same lean-to. He was dancing and burning in that climactic moment when trousers-fly will not come wide soon enough. He stepped round the lavatory and watched the streamlets of rainwater quickly wash away the jet of tension that spouted from him. That infinite after-relief. Then he dashed back to his kitchen. He grabbed the old baby bathtub hanging on a nail under the slight shelter of the gutterless roof-edge. He opened a large wooden box and quickly filled the bathtub with coal. Then he inched his way back to the kitchen door and hurried inside.

He was huh-huh-huhing one of those fugitive tunes that cannot be hidden, but that often just occur and linger naggingly in the head. The fire he was making soon licked up cheerfully, in mood with his contentment.

He had a trick for these morning chores. While the fire in the old stove warmed up, the kettle humming on it, he gathered and laid ready the things he would need for the day: briefcase and the files that go with it; the book that he was currently reading; the letters of his lawyer boss which he usually posted before he reached the office; his wife's and his own dry-cleaning slips for the Sixty-Minutes; his lunch tin solicitously prepared the night before by his attentive wife; and today, the battered rain cape. When the kettle on the stove began to sing (before it actually boiled), he poured water into a wash basin, refilled and replaced it on the stove. Then he washed himself carefully: across the eyes, under, in and out the armpits, down to torso and in between the legs. This ritual was thorough, though no white man a-complaining of the smell of wogs,[1] knows anything about it. Then he dressed himself fastidiously. By this time he was ready to prepare breakfast.

Breakfast! How he enjoyed taking in a tray of warm breakfast to his wife, cuddled in bed. To appear there in his supreme immaculacy, tray in hand when his wife came out of ether to behold him. These things we blacks want to do for our own . . . not fawningly for the whites for whom we bloody well got to do it. He denied that he was one of those who believed in putting your wife in her place even if she was a good wife. Not he.

Matilda, too, appreciated her husband's kindness, and only put her foot down when he would offer to wash up.

"Off with you," she would scold him on his way.

At the bus-stop he was a little sorry to see that jovial old Maphikela was in a queue for a bus ahead of him. Today he would miss Maphikela's raucous laughter and uninhibited, bawdy conversations in fortissimo. Maphikela hailed him nevertheless. He thought he noticed hesitation in the old man, and a slight clouding of his countenance, but the old man shouted back at him, saying that he would wait for him at the terminus in town.

Philemon considered this morning trip to town with garrulous old Maphikela as his daily bulletin. All the township news was generously reported by loudmouthed heralds, and spiritedly discussed by the bus at large. Of course, "news" included views on bosses (scurrilous), the Government (rude), Ghana and Russia (idolatrous), America and the West (sympathetically ridiculing), and boxing (bloodthirsty). But it was always stimulating and surprisingly comprehensive for so short a trip. And there was no law of libel.

Maphikela was standing under one of those token bus-stop shelters that keep out neither rain nor wind nor sun-heat. Philemon easily located him by his noisy ribbing of some office boys in their khaki-green uniforms. They walked together into town, but from Maphikela's suddenly subdued manner, Philemon gathered that there was something serious coming up. Maybe a loan.

Eventually, Maphikela came out with it.

"Son," he said sadly, "if I could've avoided this, believe you me I would, but my wife is nagging the spice out of my life for not talking to you about it."

It just did not become blustering old Maphikela to sound so grave and Philemon took compassion upon him.

---

[1] A derisive British term for blacks. [eds.]

"Go ahead, dad," he said generously. "You know you can talk to me about anything."

The old man gave a pathetic smile. "We-e-e-ll, it's not really any of our business . . . er . . . but my wife felt . . . you see. Damn it all I wish these women would not snoop around so much." Then he rushed it. "Anyway, it seems there's a young man who's going to visit your wife every morning . . . ah . . . for these last bloomin' three months. And that wife of mine swears by her heathen gods you don't know a thing about it."

It was not like the explosion of a devastating bomb. It was more like the critical breakdown in an infinitely delicate piece of mechanism. From outside the machine just seemed to have gone dead. But deep in its inner-most recesses, menacing electrical flashes were leaping from coil to coil, and hot, viscous molten metal was creeping upon the fuel tanks . . .

Philemon heard gears grinding and screaming in his head . . .

"Dad," he said hoarsely, "I . . . I have to go back home."

He turned around and did not hear old Maphikela's anxious, "Steady, son. Steady, son."

The bus ride home was a torture of numb dread and suffocating despair. Though the bus was now emptier Philemon suffered crushing claustropho-bia. There were immense washerwomen whose immense bundles of soiled laundry seemed to baulk and menace him. From those bundles crept mias-mata of sweaty intimacies that sent nauseous waves up and down from his viscera. The wild swaying of the bus as it negotiated Mayfair Circle hurtled him sickeningly from side to side. Some of the younger women shrieked delightedly to the driver, "*Fuduga!*. . . Stir the pot!" as he swung his steering wheel this way and that. Normally, the crazy tilting of the bus gave him a prickling exhilaration. But now . . .

He felt like getting out of there, screamingly, elbowing everything out of his way. He wished this insane trip were over, and then again, he recoiled at the thought of getting home. He made a tremendous resolve to gather in all the torn, tingling threads of his nerves contorting in the raw. By a merciless act of will, he kept them in subjugation as he stepped from the bus back in the Victoria Road terminus, Sophiatown.

The calm he achieved was tense . . . but he could think now . . . he could take a decision . . .

With almost boyishly innocent urgency, he rushed through his kitchen into his bedroom. In the lightning flash that the eye can whip, he saw it all . . . the man beside his wife . . . the chestnut arm around her neck . . . the ruffled candlewick bedspread . . . the suit across the chair. But he affected not to see.

He opened the wardrobe door, and as he dug into it, he cheerfully spoke to his wife. "Fancy, Tilly, I forgot to take my pass. I had already reached town, and was going to walk up to the office, if it hadn't been for wonderful old Mr. Maphikela . . . "

A swooshing noise of violent retreat and the clap of his bedroom window stopped him. He came from behind the wardrobe door and looked out from the open window. A man clad only in vest and underpants was running down the street. Slowly, he turned round and contemplated . . . the suit.

Philemon lifted it gingerly under his arm and looked at the stark horror in Matilda's eyes. She was now sitting up in bed. Her mouth twitched, but her throat raised no words.

"Ha," he said. "I see we have a visitor," indicating the blue suit. "We really must show some of our hospitality. But first, I must phone my boss to tell him that I can't come to work today . . . mmmm-er, my wife's not well. Be back in a moment, then we can make arrangements." He took the suit along.

When he returned he found Matilda weeping on the bed. He dropped the suit beside her, pulled up the chair, turned it round so that its back came in front of him, sat down, brought down his chin on to his folded arms before him, and waited for her.

After a while the convulsions of her shoulders ceased. She saw a smug man with an odd smile and meaningless inscrutability in his eyes. He spoke to her with very little noticeable emotion; if anything, with a flutter of humor.

"We have a visitor, Tilly." His mouth curved ever so slightly. "I'd like him to be treated with the greatest of consideration. He will eat every meal with us and share all we have. Since we have no spare room, he'd better sleep in here. But the point is, Tilly, that you will meticulously look after him. If he vanishes or anything else happens to him . . . " a shaft of evil shot from his eye . . . "Matilda, I'll kill you."

He rose from the chair and looked with incongruous supplication at her. He told her to put the fellow in the wardrobe for the time being. As she passed him to get the suit, he turned to go. She ducked frantically, and he stopped.

"You don't seem to understand me, Matilda. There's to be no violence in this house if you and I can help it. So just look after that suit." He went out.

He made his way to the Sophiatown Post Office, which is placed exactly on the line between Sophiatown and the white man's surly Westdene. He posted his boss's letters and walked to the beerhall at the tail end of Western Native Township. He had never been inside it before, but somehow the thunderous din laved his bruised spirit. He stayed there all day.

He returned home for supper . . . and surprises. His dingy little home had been transformed, and the air of stern masculinity it had hitherto contained had been wiped away to be replaced by anxious feminine touches here and there. There were even gay, colorful curtains swirling in the kitchen window. The old-fashioned coal stove gleamed in its blackness. A clean, checkered oil cloth on the table. Supper ready.

Then she appeared in the doorway of the bedroom. Heavens! here was the woman he had married; the young, fresh, cocoa-colored maid who had sent rushes of emotion shuddering through him. And the dress she wore brought out all the girlishness of her, hidden so long beneath German print. But no hint of coquettishness, although she stood in the doorway and slid her arm up the jamb, and shyly slanted her head to the other shoulder. She smiled weakly.

"What makes a woman like this experiment with adultery?" he wondered.

Philemon closed his eyes and gripped the seat of his chair on both sides as some overwhelming, undisciplined force sought to catapult him toward her. For a moment some essence glowed fiercely within him, then sank back into itself and died . . .

He sighed and smiled sadly back at her. "I'm hungry, Tilly."

The spell snapped, and she was galvanized into action. She prepared supper with dextrous hands that trembled a little when they hesitated in mid-air. She took her seat opposite him, regarded him curiously, clasped her hands waiting for his prayer, but in her heart she murmured some other, much more urgent prayer of her own.

"Matilda!" he barked. "Our visitor!" The sheer savagery with which he cracked at her jerked her up, but only when she saw the brute cruelty in his face did she run out of the room, toppling the chair behind her.

She returned with the suit on a hanger, and stood there quivering like a feather. She looked at him with helpless dismay. The demoniacal rage in his face was evaporating, but his heavy breathing still rocked his thorax above the table, to and fro.

"Put a chair there," he indicated with a languid gesture of his arm. She moved like a ghost as she drew a chair to the table.

"Now seat our friend at the table . . . no, no, not like that. Put him in front of the chair, and place him on the seat so that he becomes indeed the third person."

Philemon went on relentlessly. "Dish up for him. Generously. I imagine he hasn't had a morsel all day, the poor devil."

Now, as consciousness and thought seeped back into her, her movements revolved so that always she faced this man who had changed so spectacularly. She started when he rose to open the window and let in some air.

She served the suit. The act was so ridiculous that she carried it out with a bitter sense of humiliation. He came back to sit down and plunged into his meal. No grace was said for the first time in this house. With his mouth full, he indicated by a toss of his head that she should sit down in her place. She did so. Glancing at her plate, the thought occurred to her that someone, after a long famine, was served a sumptuous supper, but as the food reached her mouth it turned to sawdust. Where had she heard it?

Matilda could not eat. She suddenly broke into tears.

Philemon took no notice of her weeping. After supper he casually gathered the dishes and started washing up. He flung a dry cloth at her without saying a word. She rose and went to stand by his side drying up. But for their wordlessness, they seemed a very devoted couple.

After washing up, he took the suit and turned to her. "That's how I want it every meal, every day." Then he walked into the bedroom.

So it was. After that first breakdown, Matilda began to feel that her punishment was not too severe, considering the heinousness of the crime. She tried to put a joke into it, but by slow, unconscious degrees, the strain nibbled at her. Philemon did not harass her much more, so long as the ritual with the confounded suit was conscientiously followed.

Only once, he got one of his malevolent brainwaves. He got it into his head that "our visitor" needed an outing. Accordingly the suit was taken to the dry-cleaners during the week, and, come Sunday, they had to take it out for a walk. Both Philemon and Matilda dressed for the occasion. Matilda had to carry the suit on its hanger over her back and the three of them strolled leisurely along Ray Street. They passed the church crowd in front of the famous Anglican Mission of Christ the King. Though the worshippers saw nothing unusual in them, Matilda felt, searing through her, red-hot needles of embarrassment, and every needle-point was a public eye piercing into her degradation.

But Philemon walked casually on. He led her down Ray Street and turned into Main Road. He stopped often to look into shop windows or to greet a friend passing by. They went up Toby Street, turned into Edward Road, and back home. To Philemon the outing was free of incident, but to Matilda it was one long excruciating experience.

At home, he grabbed a book on abnormal psychology, flung himself into a chair and calmly said to her, "Give the old chap a rest, will you, Tilly?"

In the bedroom, Matilda said to herself that things could not go on like this. She thought of how she could bring the matter to a head with Philemon; have it out with him once and for all. But the memory of his face, that first day she had forgotten to entertain the suit, stayed with her. She thought of running away, but where to? Home? What could she tell her old-fashioned mother had happened between Philemon and her? All right, run away clean then. She thought of many young married girls who were divorcees now, who had won their freedom.

What had happened to Staff Nurse Kakile? The woman drank heavily now, and when she got drunk, the boys of Sophiatown passed her around and called her the Cesspot.

Matilda shuddered.

An idea struck her. There were still decent, married women around Sophiatown. She remembered how after the private schools had been forced to close with the introduction of Bantu Education, Father Harringay of the

Anglican Mission had organized cultural clubs. One, she seemed to remember, was for married women. If only she could lose herself in some cultural activity, find absolution for her conscience in some club doing good, that would blur her blasted home life, would restore her self-respect. After all, Philemon had not broadcast her disgrace abroad . . . nobody knew; not one of Sophiatown's slander-mongers suspected how vulnerable she was. She must go and see Mrs. Montjane about joining a cultural club. She must ask Philemon now if she might . . . she must ask him nicely.

She got up and walked into the other room where Philemon was reading quietly. She dreaded disturbing him, did not know how to begin talking to him . . . they had talked so little for so long. She went and stood in front of him, looking silently upon his deep concentration. Presently he looked up with a frown on his face.

Then she dared. "Phil, I'd like to join one of those cultural clubs for married women. Would you mind?"

He wrinkled his nose and rubbed it between thumb and index finger as he considered the request. But he had caught the note of anxiety in her voice and thought he knew what it meant.

"Mmmmm," he said, nodding. "I think that's a good idea. You can't be moping around here all day. Yes, you may, Tilly." Then he returned to his book.

The cultural club idea was wonderful. She found women like herself, with time (if not with tragedy) on their hands, engaged in wholesome, refreshing activities. The atmosphere was cheerful and cathartic. They learned things and they did things. They organized fetes, bazaars, youth activities, sport, music, self-help and community projects. She got involved in committees, meetings, debates, conferences. It was for her a whole new venture into humancraft, and her personality blossomed. Philemon gave her all the latitude she wanted.

Now, abiding by that silly ritual at home seemed a little thing . . . a very little thing . . .

Then one day she decided to organize a little party for her friends and their husbands. Philemon was very decent about it. He said it was all right. He even gave her extra money for it. Of course, she knew nothing of the strain he himself suffered from his mode of castigation.

There was a week of hectic preparation. Philemon stepped out of its cluttering way as best he could. So many things seemed to be taking place simultaneously. New dresses were made. Cakes were baked, three different orders of meat prepared; beef for the uninvited chancers; mutton for the normal guests; turkey and chicken for the inner pith of the club's core. To Philemon, it looked as if Matilda planned to feed the multitude on the Mount with no aid of miracles.

On the Sunday of the party Philemon saw Matilda's guests. He was surprised by the handsome grace with which she received them. There was a long table with enticing foods and flowers and serviettes. Matilda placed all her guests round the table, and the party was ready to begin in the mock-formal township fashion. Outside a steady rumble of conversation went on where the human odds and ends of every Sophiatown party had their "share."

Matilda caught the curious look on Philemon's face. He tried to disguise his edict when he said, "Er . . . the guest of honor."

But Matilda took a chance. She begged, "Just this once, Phil."

He became livid. "Matilda!" he shouted. "Get our visitor!" Then with incisive sarcasm, "or are you ashamed of him?"

She went ash-gray; but there was nothing for it but to fetch her albatross. She came back and squeezed a chair into some corner, and placed the suit on it. Then she slowly placed a plate of food before it. For a while the guests were dumbfounded. Then curiosity flooded in. They talked at the same time. "What's the idea, Philemon? . . . Why must she serve a suit? . . . What's happening?" Some just giggled in a silly way. Philemon carelessly swung his head toward Matilda. "You better ask my wife. She knows the fellow best."

All interest beamed upon poor Matilda. For a moment she could not speak, all-enveloped in misery. Then she said, unconvincingly, "It's just a game that my husband and I play at mealtime." They roared with laughter. Philemon let her get away with it.

The party went on, and every time Philemon's glare sent Matilda scurrying to serve the suit each course; the guests were no end amused by the persistent mock-seriousness with which this husband and wife played out their little game. Only, to Matilda, it was no joke; it was a hot poker down her throat. After the party, Philemon went off with one of the guests who had promised to show him a joint "that sells genuine stuff, boy, genuine stuff."

Reeling drunk, late that sabbath, he crashed through his kitchen door, onward to his bedroom. Then he saw her.

They have a way of saying in the argot of Sophiatown, "Cook out of the head!" signifying that someone was impacted with such violent shock that whatever whiffs of alcohol still wandered through his head were instantaneously evaporated and the man stood sober before stark reality.

There she lay, curled, as if just before she died she begged for a little love, implored some implacable lover to cuddle her a little . . . just this once . . . just this once more.

In intense anguish, Philemon cried, "Tilly!"

❋ Discussion and Writing

1. Describe Philamon's treatment of Matilda before he discovered her unfaithfulness. In what ways does he differ from other black men in the treatment of his wife? How is his difference significant in the development of the narrative?

2. Analyze the function of the detailed morning ritual and the bus ride. What do they reveal about Philamon and the life of people in Sophiatown? What do they contribute to the story?
3. Discuss Philamon's method of teaching his wife a lesson. What does Can Themba suggest through the apparently subdued manifestation of Philamon's violent anger?
4. Discuss Tilly's personality and her disloyalty. What is the impact of Philamon's punishment on her? Discuss the nature of her "albatross"?
5. Why does her suicide shock Philamon? Comment on the implication of the final sentence.
6. What is the effect of depicting jealousy and revenge in a comic manner? Analyze the amalgam of humor and pathos in the narrative.

Noemia de Sousa
(b. 1927)
Mozambique

Noemia de Sousa was born in Lourenzo Marques, Mozambique. Bitterly opposed to colonial oppression, she was active politically during the early years of the struggle for independence from Portugal. In her writing, she protested against colonialism, in general, and against colonial exploitation of African women, in particular; she also criticized the subjugation of African women by their own men. She finally left the country to live in exile.

The history of Mozambique from the time Vasco de Gama landed on the coast in 1498 was one of exploitation. From the trade in gold, ivory, and slaves to the establishment of large plantations worked by forced labor, Portuguese adventurers capitalized on living in a country without governmental control. Portugal essentially did not intervene in their affairs until the 1890s, when it sent its military to crush African resistance. It did not take direct economic control until 1926. Mozambique gained its independence only in 1975, after eleven years of intense guerrilla warfare.

If You Want to Know Me*

If you want to know who I am,
examine with careful eyes
that piece of black wood

*Translated by Art Brakel

which an unknown Maconde brother
with inspired hands
carved and worked
in distant lands to the North.

Ah, she is who I am:
empty eye sockets despairing of possessing life
a mouth slashed with wounds of anguish,
enormous, flattened hands,
raised as though to implore and threaten,
body tattooed with visible and invisible scars
by the hard whips of slavery . . .
tortured and magnificent,
proud and mystical,
Africa from head to toe,
—ah, she is who I am!

If you want to understand me
come and bend over my African soul,
in the groans of the Negroes on the docks
in the frenzied dances of the Chopes
in the rebelliousness of the Shanganas
in the strange melancholy evaporating
from a native song, into the night . . .

And ask me nothing more
if you really wish to know me . . .
for I am no more than a shell of flesh
in which the revolt of Africa congealed
its cry swollen with hope

❋ Discussion and Writing

1. Why does the persona identify with the carved piece of wood? What is the significance of this identification?
2. What is the relevance to the persona's identity of the events described in stanza three?
3. What constitutes her real self?

❋ Research and Comparison

Interdisciplinary Discussion Question: For culturally violated communities, the search for identity becomes a complex issue as the personal and the public selves become inextricably intertwined. Compare the individual quest for identity in two readings included in this anthology. Examine the impact on the individual of politics, history, and culture.

David Diop
(1927–1960)
Senegal

David Diop, whose father was from Senegal and whose mother was from Cameroon, was born in Bordeaux, France. From childhood, he traveled frequently between France and West Africa, even though he suffered from ill health. Before his death in a plane crash, he published a volume of poetry that has continued to be appreciated as voicing the impetus of *negritude* and a strong individuality. In accordance with the theories of the *negritude* movement, he evoked Africa's long past history and future as they coexist in the present. He was concerned with exile and return, but he was a poet of regeneration. His poetry celebrates the power of African endurance and its ability to survive the oppression of European colonization.

The Vultures*

In those days
When civilization kicked us in the face
When holy water slapped our cringing brows
The vultures built in the shadow of their talons
The bloodstained monument of tutelage
In those days
There was painful laughter on the metallic hell of the roads
And the monotonous rhythm of the paternoster
Drowned the howling on the plantations
O the bitter memories of extorted kisses
Of promises broken at the point of a gun
Of foreigners who did not seem human
Who knew all the books but did not know love
But we whose hands fertilize the womb of the earth
In spite of your songs of pride
In spite of the desolate villages of torn Africa
Hope was preserved in us as in a fortress

Translated by Gerald Moore and Ulli Beier

And from the mines of Swaziland to the factories of Europe
Spring will be reborn under our bright steps.

❀ Discussion and Writing

1. Explore the images that indicate colonial intervention in Africa. Which European institutions are evoked?
2. What is the significance of the images "cringing brows" and "painful laughter"?
3. Explain the implication of the phrase "our bright steps." What is the concluding note of the poem: despondence? anger? assertion? What is its source?

❀ Research and Comparison

Interdisciplinary Discussion Question: Research the institutions of church and school as primary tools in colonizing Asian and African countries. Examine the impact of these Western institutions as reflected in the literary works of any author included in this anthology.

Yusuf Idris
(b. 1927)
Egypt

Yusuf Idris was born in a village in the Nile Delta in Egypt. While studying medicine, he began writing, at first for his own pleasure. His work as a physician and as a government health inspector took him into Cairo's poorest quarters. That experience re-enforced his political and social concerns, and informed his writing. He depicted the impoverished living conditions in small towns and villages, as well as in Cairo, with a clarity that brought him admiration and respect. He became something of an enfant terrible and was imprisoned several times. Throughout the 1950s, he was quite prolific, and his popularity allowed him to leave medicine and concentrate on writing and journalism. Along with issues of class, he wrote of mythic experience, of sexuality in relation to society, and of the individual in relation to a kind of herd instinct. Most notably, Idris has incorporated the spoken language into his writing, creating a distinctive style.

The Chair Carrier*

You can believe it or not, but excuse me for saying that your opinion is of no concern at all to me. It's enough for me that I saw him, met him, talked to him and observed the chair with my own eyes. Thus I considered that I had been witness to a miracle. But even more miraculous—indeed more disastrous—was that neither the man, the chair, nor the incident caused a single passer-by in Opera Square, in Gumhouriyya Street, or in Cairo—or maybe in the whole world—to come to a stop at that moment.

It was a vast chair. Looking at it you'd think it had come from some other world, or that it had been constructed for some festival, such a colossal chair, as though it were an institution all on its own, its seat immense and softly covered with leopard skin and silken cushions. Once you'd seen it your great dream was to sit in it, be it just the once, just for a moment. A moving chair, it moved forward with stately gait as though it were in some religious procession. You'd think it was moving of its own accord. In awe and amazement you almost prostrated yourself before it in worship and offered up sacrifices to it.

Eventually, however, I made out, between the four massive legs that ended in glistening gilded hooves, a fifth leg. It was skinny and looked strange amidst all that bulk and splendor; it was, though, no leg but a thin, gaunt human being upon whose body the sweat had formed runnels and rivulets and had caused woods and groves of hair to sprout. Believe me, by all that's holy, I'm neither lying nor exaggerating, simply relating, be it ever so inadequately, what I saw. How was it that such a thin, frail man was carrying a chair like this one, a chair that weighed at least a ton, and maybe several? That was the proposition that was presented to one's mind—it was like some conjuring trick. But you had only to look longer and more closely to find that there was no deception, that the man really was carrying the chair all on his own and moving along with it.

What was even more extraordinary and more weird, something that was truly alarming, was that none of the passers-by in Opera Square, in Gumhouriyya Street or maybe in the whole of Cairo, was at all astonished or treated the matter as if it was anything untoward, but rather as something quite normal and unremarkable, as if the chair were as light as a butterfly and was being carried around by a young lad. I looked at the people and at the chair and at the man, thinking that I would spot the raising of an eyebrow, or lips sucked back in alarm, or hear a cry of amazement, but there was absolutely no reaction.

Translated by Denys Johnson-Davies

I began to feel that the whole thing was too ghastly to contemplate any longer. At this very moment the man with his burden was no more than a step or two away from me and I was able to see his good-natured face, despite its many wrinkles. Even so it was impossible to determine his age. I then saw something more about him: he was naked except for a stout waist-band from which hung, in front and behind, a covering made of sailcloth. Yet you would surely have to come to a stop, conscious that your mind had, like an empty room, begun to set off echoes telling you that, dressed as he was, he was a stranger not only to Cairo but to our whole era. You had the sensation of having seen his like in books about history or archaeology. And so I was surprised by the smile he gave, the kind of meek smile a beggar gives, and by a voice that mouthed words:

"May God have mercy on your parents, my son. You wouldn't have seen Uncle Ptah Ra'?"

Was he speaking hieroglyphics pronounced as Arabic, or Arabic pronounced as hieroglyphics? Could the man be an ancient Egyptian? I rounded on him:

"Listen here—don't start telling me you're an ancient Egyptian?"

"And are there ancient and modern? I'm simply an Egyptian."

"And what's this chair?"

"It's what I'm carrying. Why do you think I'm going around looking for Uncle Ptah Ra'? It's so that he may order me to put it down just as he ordered me to carry it. I'm done in."

"You've been carrying it for long?"

"For a very long time, you can't imagine."

"A year?"

"What do you mean by a year, my son? Tell anyone who asks—a year and then a few thousand."

"Thousand what?"

"Years."

"From the time of the Pyramids, for example?"

"From before that. From the time of the Nile."

"What do you mean: from the time of the Nile?"

"From the time when the Nile wasn't called the Nile, and they moved the capital from the mountain to the river bank, Uncle Ptah brought me along and said 'Porter, take it up.' I took it up and ever since I've been wandering all over the place looking for him to tell me to put it down, but from that day to this I've not found him."

All ability or inclination to feel astonishment had completely ended for me. Anyone capable of carrying a chair of such dimensions and weight for a single moment could equally have been carrying it for thousands of years. There was no occasion for surprise or protest; all that was required was a question:

"And suppose you don't find Uncle Ptah Ra', are you going to go on carrying it around?"

"What else shall I do? I'm carrying it and it's been deposited in trust with me. I was ordered to carry it, so how can I put it down without being ordered to?"

Perhaps it was anger that made me say: "Put it down. Aren't you fed up, man? Aren't you tired? Throw it away, break it up, burn it. Chairs are made to carry people, not for people to carry them."

"I can't. Do you think I'm carrying it for fun? I'm carrying it because that's the way I earn my living."

"So what? Seeing that it's wearing you out and breaking your back, you should throw it down—you should have done so ages ago."

"That's how you look at things because you're safely out of it; you're not carrying it, so you don't care. I'm carrying it and it's been deposited in trust with me, so I'm responsible for it."

"Until when, for God's sake?"

"Till the order comes from Ptah Ra'."

"He couldn't be more dead."

"Then from his successor, his deputy, from one of his descendants, from anyone with a token of authorization from him."

"All right then, I'm ordering you right now to put it down."

"Your order will be obeyed—and thank you for your kindness—but are you related to him?"

"Unfortunately not."

"Do you have a token of authorization from him?"

"No, I don't"

"Then allow me to be on my way."

He had begun to move off, but I shouted out to him to stop, for I had noticed something that looked like an announcement or sign fixed to the front of the chair. In actual fact it was a piece of gazelle-hide with ancient writing on it, looking as though it was from the earliest copies of the Revealed Books. It was with difficulty that I read:

O chair carrier,
You have carried enough
And the time has come for you to be carried in a chair.
This great chair,
The like of which has not been made,
Is for you alone.
Carry it
And take it to your home.
Put it in the place of honor

And seat yourself upon it your whole life long.
And when you die.
It shall belong to your sons.

"This, Mr. Chair Carrier, is the order of Ptah Ra', an order that is precise and was issued at the same moment in which he ordered you to carry the chair. It is sealed with his signature and cartouche."

All this I told him with great joy, a joy that exploded as from someone who had been almost stifled. Ever since I had seen the chair and known the story I had felt as though it were I who was carrying it and had done so for thousands of years; it was as though it were back that was being broken, and as though the joy that now came to me were my own joy at being released at long last.

The man listened to me with head lowered, without a tremor of emotion; just waited with head lowered for me to finish, and no sooner had I done so than he raised his head. I had been expecting a joy similar to my own, even an expression of delight, but I found no reaction.

"The order's written right there above your head—written ages ago."

"But I don't know how to read."

"But I've just read it out to you."

"I'll believe it only if there's a token of authorization. Have you such a token?"

When I made no reply he muttered angrily as he turned away:

"All I get from you people is obstruction. Man, it's a heavy load and the day's scarcely long enough for making just the one round."

I stood watching him. The chair had started to move at its slow, steady pace, making one think that it moved by itself. Once again the man had become its thin fifth leg, capable on its own of setting it in motion.

I stood watching him as he moved away, panting and groaning and with the sweat pouring off him.

I stood there at a loss, asking myself whether I shouldn't catch him up and kill him and thus give vent to my exasperation. Should I rush forward and topple the chair forcibly from his shoulders and make him take a rest? Or should I content myself with the sensation of enraged irritation I had for him? Or should I calm down and feel sorry for him?

Or should I blame myself for not knowing what the token of authorization was?

❊ Discussion and Writing

1. Why does the narrator call the carrier the "fifth leg of the chair"? What is the carrier's own perception of his mission?

2. Why does the narrator say he was a "witness" to "a miracle" at the beginning of the story? What is the significance of the note of doubt and despair at the end?
3. What is implied in the carrier's inability or unwillingness to stop his quest? Compare the narrator's and carrier's perceptions of time and authority.
4. Analyze the images Idris employs to suggest paradoxical concepts of time, place, personality, occupation, and so forth. What is the significance of the confluence of opposites?

Chinua Achebe
(b. 1930)
Nigeria

Chinua Achebe was born in eastern Nigeria, in the Igbo village of Ogidi. Anglican missionaries had arrived in this area of Nigeria early on, and his parents were among the first villagers to be converted to Christianity. His father later taught at the mission school, providing his son with a Western education that enabled him to attend the university. Achebe was among the first students to be graduated from the newly opened University College at Ibadan. When his first novel, *Things Fall Apart* (1958), was published, it was immediately acknowledged as a classic. He was recognized for the excellence of his craft—for the way he incorporated the oral tradition into the written, philosophically as well as technically, and for his individual and historic characterizations. Circumscribed in focus, "The Madman" (1971) has a lucidity similar to that of the novel.

He worked for the Nigerian Broadcasting Corporation, rising to become director of External Broadcasting, until 1966 when he joined the Biafran Ministry of Information. During the years of the civil war (1967–1970), he traveled, trying to raise money for Biafra, and wrote poetry evoking the anguish of the war. (It is believed that more than one million Biafran people died of starvation during the war years.) He was joint winner of the first Commonwealth Poetry Prize for this poetry, collected in the volume *Christmas in Biafra*. Since the early 1970s, Achebe has lectured around the world, taught in Nigeria and the United States, and received many honors, among them eleven honorary doctorates, the Honorary Fellowship of the American Academy and Institute of Arts and Letters, and the Nigerian National Merit Award.

The Madman

He was drawn to markets and straight roads. Not any tiny neighborhood market where a handful of garrulous women might gather at sunset to gossip and buy ogili[1] for the evening's soup, but a huge, engulfing bazaar beckoning people familiar and strange from far and near. And not any dusty, old footpath beginning in this village, and ending in that stream, but broad, black, mysterious highways without beginning or end. After much wandering he had discovered two such markets linked together by such a highway; and so ended his wandering. One market was Afo, the other Eke. The two days between them suited him very well: before setting out for Eke he had ample time to wind up his business properly at Afo. He passed the night there putting right again his hut after a day of defilement by two fat-bottomed market women who said it was their market stall. At first he had put up a fight but the women had gone and brought their menfolk—four hefty beasts of the bush—to whip him out of the hut. After that he always avoided them, moving out on the morning of the market and back in at dusk to pass the night. Then in the morning he rounded off his affairs swiftly and set out on that long, beautiful boa-constrictor of a road to Eke in the distant town of Ogbu. He held his staff and cudgel at the ready in his right hand, and with the left he steadied the basket of his belongings on his head. He had got himself this cudgel lately to deal with little beasts on the way who threw stones at him and made fun of their mothers' nakedness, not his own.

He used to walk in the middle of the road, holding it in conversation. But one day the driver of a mammy-wagon and his mate came down on him shouting, pushing and slapping his face. They said their lorry [truck] very nearly ran over their mother, not him. After that he avoided those noisy lorries too, with the vagabonds inside them.

Having walked one day and one night he was now close to the Eke market-place. From every little sideroad, crowds of market people poured into the big highway to join the enormous flow to Eke. Then he saw some young ladies with water-pots on their heads coming toward him, unlike all the rest, away from the market. This surprised him. Then he saw two more water-pots rise out of a sloping footpath leading off his side of the highway. He felt thirsty then and stopped to think it over. Then he set down his basket on the roadside and turned into the sloping footpath. But first he begged his highway not to be offended or continue the journey without him. "I'll get some for you too," he said coaxingly with a tender backward glance. "I know you are thirsty."

---

[1]Seasoning made from fermented melon seeds for traditional *obi* soup. [eds.]

Nwibe was a man of high standing in Ogbu and was rising higher; a man of wealth and integrity. He had just given notice to all the ozo[2] men of the town that he proposed to seek admission into their honored hierarchy in the coming initiation season.

"Your proposal is excellent," said the men of title.

"When we see we shall believe." Which was their dignified way of telling you to think it over once again and make sure you have the means to go through with it. For ozo is not a child's naming ceremony; and where is the man to hide his face who begins the ozo dance and then is foot-stuck to the arena? But in this instance the caution of the elders was no more than a formality for Nwibe was such a sensible man that no one could think of him beginning something he was not sure to finish.

On that Eke day Nwibe had risen early so as to visit his farm beyond the stream and do some light work before going to the market at midday to drink a horn or two of palm-wine with his peers and perhaps buy that bundle of roofing thatch for the repair of his wives' huts. As for his own hut he had a couple of years back settled it finally by changing his thatch roof to zinc. Sooner or later he would do the same for his wives. He could have done Mgboye's hut right away but decided to wait until he could do the two together, or else Udenkwo would set the entire compound on fire. Udenkwo was the junior wife, by three years, but she never let that worry her. Happily Mgboye was a woman of peace who rarely demanded the respect due to her from the other. She would suffer Udenkwo's provoking tongue sometimes for a whole day without offering a word in reply. And when she did reply at all her words were always few and her voice very low.

That very morning Udenkwo had accused her of spite and all kinds of wickedness on account of a little dog.

"What has a little dog done to you?" she screamed loud enough for half the village to hear. "I ask you, Mgboye, what is the offense of a puppy this early in the day?"

"What your puppy did this early in the day," replied Mgboye, "is that he put his shit-mouth into my soup-pot."

"And then?"

"And then I smacked him."

"You smacked him! Why don't you cover your soup-pot? Is it easier to hit a dog than cover a pot? Is a small puppy to have more sense than a woman who leaves her soup-pot about. . . ?"

"Enough from you, Udenkwo."

"It is not enough, Mgboye, it is not enough. If that dog owes you any debt I want to know. Everything I have, even a little dog I bought to eat my

---

[2]One of the titles or ranks. [eds.]

infant's excrement keeps you awake at nights. You are a bad woman, Mgboye, you are a very bad woman!"

Nwibe had listened to all of this in silence in his hut. He knew from the vigor in Udenkwo's voice that she could go on like this till market-time. So he intervened, in his characteristic manner by calling out to his senior wife.

"Mgboye! Let me have peace this early morning!"

"Don't you hear all the abuses Udenkwo . . . "

"I hear nothing at all from Udenkwo and I want peace in my compound. If Udenkwo is crazy must everybody else go crazy with her? Is one crazy woman not enough in my compound so early in the day?"

"The great judge has spoken," sang Udenkwo in a sneering sing-song. "Thank you, great judge. Udenkwo is mad. Udenkwo is always mad, but those of you who are sane let . . . "

"Shut your mouth, shameless woman, or a wild beast will lick your eyes for you this morning. When will you learn to keep your badness within this compound instead of shouting it to all Ogbu to hear? I say shut your mouth!"

There was silence then except for Udenkwo's infant whose yelling had up till then been swallowed up by the larger noise of the adults.

"Don't cry, my father," said Udenkwo to him. "They want to kill your dog, but our people say the man who decides to chase after a chicken, for him is the fall . . . "

By the middle of the morning Nwibe had done all the work he had to do on his farm and was on his way again to prepare for market. At the little stream he decided as he always did to wash off the sweat of work. So he put his cloth on a huge boulder by the men's bathing section and waded in. There was nobody else around because of the time of day and because it was market day. But from instinctive modesty he turned to face the forest away from the approaches.

The madman watched him for quite a while. Each time he bent down to carry water in cupped hands from the shallow stream to his head and body the madman smiled at his parted behind. And then remembered. This was the same hefty man who brought three others like him and whipped me out of my hut in the Afo market. He nodded to himself. And he remembered again: this was the same vagabond who descended on me from the lorry in the middle of my highway. He nodded once more. And then he remembered yet again: this was the same fellow who set his children to throw stones at me and make remarks about their mothers' buttocks, not mine. Then he laughed.

Nwibe turned sharply round and saw the naked man laughing, the deep grove of the stream amplifying his laughter. Then he stopped as suddenly as he had begun; the merriment vanished from his face.

"I have caught you naked," he said.

Nwibe ran a hand swiftly down his face to clear his eyes of water.

"I say I have caught you naked, with your thing dangling about."

"I can see you are hungry for a whipping," said Nwibe with quiet menace in his voice, for a madman is said to be easily scared away by the very mention of a whip. "Wait till I get up there. . . . What are you doing? Drop it at once . . . I say drop it!"

The madman had picked up Nwibe's cloth and wrapped it round his own waist. He looked down at himself and began to laugh again.

"I will kill you," screamed Nwibe as he splashed toward the bank, maddened by anger. "I will whip that madness out of you today!"

They ran all the way up the steep and rocky footpath hedged in by the shadowy green forest. A mist gathered and hung over Nwibe's vision as he ran, stumbled, fell, pulled himself up again and stumbled on, shouting and cursing. The other, despite his unaccustomed encumbrance steadily increased his lead, for he was spare and wiry, a thing made for speed. Furthermore, he did not waste his breath shouting and cursing; he just ran. Two girls going down to the stream saw a man running up the slope towards them pursued by a stark-naked madman. They threw down their pots and fled, screaming.

When Nwibe emerged into the full glare of the highway he could not see his cloth clearly any more and his chest was on the point of exploding from the fire and torment within. But he kept running. He was only vaguely aware of crowds of people on all sides and he appealed to them tearfully without stopping: "Hold the madman, he's got my cloth!" By this time the man with the cloth was practically lost among the much denser crowds far in front so that the link between him and the naked man was no longer clear.

Now Nwibe continually bumped against people's backs and then laid flat a frail old man struggling with a stubborn goat on a leash. "Stop the madman," he shouted hoarsely, his heart tearing to shreds, "he's got my cloth!" Everyone looked at him first in surprise and then less surprise because strange sights are common in a great market. Some of them even laughed.

"They've got his cloth he says."

"That's a new one I'm sure. He hardly looks mad yet. Doesn't he have people, I wonder."

"People are so careless these days. Why can't they keep proper watch over their sick relation, especially on the day of the market?"

Farther up the road on the very brink of the market-place two men from Nwibe's village recognized him and, throwing down the one his long basket of yams, the other his calabash of palm-wine held on a loop, gave desperate chase, to stop him setting foot irrevocably within the occult territory of the powers of the market. But it was in vain. When finally they caught him it was well inside the crowded square. Udenkwo in tears tore off her top-cloth which they draped on him and led him home by the hand. He spoke just once about a madman who took his cloth in the stream.

"It is all right," said one of the men in the tone of a father to a crying child. They led and he followed blindly, his heavy chest heaving up and down in silent weeping. Many more people from his village, a few of his in-laws and one or two others from his mother's place had joined the grief-stricken party. One man whispered to another that it was the worst kind of madness, deep and tongue-tied.

"May it end ill for him who did this," prayed the other.

The first medicine-man his relatives consulted refused to take him on, out of some kind of integrity.

"I could say yes to you and take your money," he said. "But that is not my way. My powers of cure are known throughout Olu and Igbo but never have I professed to bring back to life a man who has sipped the spirit-waters of ani-mmo.[3] It is the same with a madman who of his own accord delivers himself to the divinities of the market-place. You should have kept better watch over him."

"Don't blame us too much," said Nwibe's relative. "When he left home that morning his senses were as complete as yours and mine now. Don't blame us too much."

"Yes, I know. It happens that way sometimes. And they are the ones that medicine will not reach. I know."

"Can you do nothing at all then, not even to untie his tongue?"

"Nothing can be done. They have already embraced him. It is like a man who runs away from the oppression of his fellows to the grove of an alusi[4] and says to him: Take me, oh spirit, I am your osu.[5] No man can touch him thereafter. He is free and yet no power can break his bondage. He is free of men but bonded to a god."

The second doctor was not as famous as the first and not so strict. He said the case was bad, very bad indeed, but no one folds his arms because the condition of his child is beyond hope. He must still grope around and do his best. His hearers nodded in eager agreement. And then he muttered into his own inward ear: If doctors were to send away every patient whose cure they were uncertain of, how many of them would eat one meal in a whole week from their practice?

Nwibe was cured of his madness. That humble practitioner who did the miracle became overnight the most celebrated mad-doctor of his generation.

---

[3]The land of big-river. [eds.]
[4]A god or the mask of a god. [eds.]
[5]Outcast; having been dedicated to a god, the *osu* was taboo, and not allowed to mix wih the freeborn in any way. [eds.]

They called him Sojourner to the Land of the Spirits. Even so it remains true that madness may indeed sometimes depart but never with all his clamorous train. Some of these always remain—the trailers of madness you might call them—to haunt the doorway of the eyes. For how could a man be the same again of whom witnesses from all the lands of Olu and Igbo have once reported that they saw today a fine, hefty man in his prime, stark naked, tearing through the crowds to answer the call of the market-place? Such a man is marked for ever.

Nwibe became a quiet, withdrawn man avoiding whenever he could the boisterous side of the life of his people. Two years later, before another initiation season, he made a new inquiry about joining the community of titled men in his town. Had they received him perhaps he might have become at least partially restored, but those ozo men, dignified and polite as ever, deftly steered the conversation away to other matters.

❊ Discussion and Writing

1. What is the implication of the opening line, "He was drawn to markets and straight roads"? Interpret the madman's behavior: his preoccupation with markets, highways, and the people who interrupt his journey. What seems to have been the source of his madness?

2. Describe Nwibe's reputation in Ogbu before the unfortunate event. Examine the importance of the ozo men and the ozo title. What do the men's words, before and after Nwibe's misfortune, reveal about the social precepts and the art of conversation among the Igbo?

3. Analyze the behavior of Mgboye and Udenkwo; discuss the hierarchy among wives depicted in this story. What norms of behavior are maintained or violated? Describe Nwibe's management of his household to maintain peace between his two wives.

4. Analyze the encounter between the madman and Nwibe: what associates the two; what seem to be the possible sources of their madness; what is the predicament of each within the cultural context?

5. Analyze the images describing the market to ascertain its importance in the economic, ethical, religious, and political life of the people of Ogbu.

6. What do the images used to portray the highways imply; why and by whom were the highways built in Nigeria; what do they represent in the story?

7. Given that Achebe considers the novelist a teacher, what does he teach in this story?

8. Explore Achebe's handling of the English language in delineating the lives and culture of people whose first language is not English. Identify

the elements that create the sense of Igbo culture through the use of the language.

❊ Research and Comparison

Examine Chinua Achebe's novels *Things Fall Apart, Arrow of God,* and *No Longer at Ease* in relation to the colonial and postcolonial Nigerian experience. Analyze the portrayal of the Igbo culture, its clash with colonialism, and the search for identity.

Interdisciplinary Discussion Question: Research the role of the traditional market in African societies; in addition, research the building of roads during European expansion. Explore the recurrent images of the market and roads as symbols of colonial experience in the works of any major African writer.

R. Sarif Easmon
(b. 1930)
Sierra Leone

Raymond Sarif Easmon, novelist, short story writer, playwright, and physician, was born and educated in Sierra Leone. He received his medical training in Europe and returned to Freetown to practice. His first play, *Dear Parent and Ogre,* won a playwriting contest arranged by the magazine *Encounter;* it was initially produced by Wole Soyinka's troupe, "the 1960 Masques," at the Arts Theater in Ibadan, with Soyinka directing and playing the lead.

In the opening frame of "Bindeh's Gift," one character mentions the warfare of the 1860s. The history of the war dates back to the sixteenth century, when the Mende people moved into present-day Sierra Leone and founded four Mende states. The Temne were living in the region, and Easmon suggests that the wars were between the two peoples. Although Britain maintained a protectorate over the inland country, it had not yet imposed its government there. The opening frame of the story, however, clearly indicates a colonized people. And the sad irony is that the political conflicts in contemporary Sierra Leone stretch back to the founding of the country, through colonization and into old hostilities.

Bindeh's Gift

"This is Kailondo's Rock," Kallon shouted into Mr Brassfoot's ear, stamping on the granite boulder on which they stood looking down on the Mea Falls. "It was on this very rock that he used to punish those 'war boys'—this was in the 1860s—whose nerve had failed them in battle."

Kallon and his friend Banky Vincent went on to demonstrate for old Bob Brassfoot how a coward was trussed up and, in the presence of the army assembled by the riverside, swung between two stalwarts and tossed into the thundering, boiling falls below. The former concluded:

"No single body was ever recovered. And, naturally, no 'war boy' who witnessed an execution ever forgot the lesson."

White, the black dwarf, stood at Mr. Brassfoot's elbow grinning.

All four sat down on the boulder and for several minutes watched the river endlessly gathering itself in three vast green serpent coils to their right to leap and thunder into the falls below. Now and again the wind would blow into their faces, damping them with spray; or it would catch the spray, fine as vapor, upstream or down, and waft rainbows evanescently in the sunshine. Death in this cauldron that boiled with violence and not with heat, must be particularly ghastly, thought Bob Brassfoot. For such was the rush of waters over the centuries it had blasted the granite in the river bed: the rocks exposed down there at this dry season were gouged and scalloped in basins several inches deep; and for three hundred yards downstream there was not a square inch of water that was not boiling, leaping and tortured.

"But in the first place," resumed Kallon, "the idea of using the Falls to perfect his war-machine was not Kailondo's." He paused awhile, trying to order his thoughts. He was the Native Administration Clerk and, a keen local historian, knew the history of Kailahun like the palm of his hand. "A generation before him, a night scene had been enacted at this very spot which makes everything that Kailondo did in that line almost amateurish."

As Kallon paused again Mr. Brassfoot oared in with his reedy voice: "Yes, Kallon my boy?"

"In the incessant inter-tribal wars of those days," Kallon took up the story in earnest, "heroes were as thick as the flies that throve on the battle-fields they created for their glory. And the war-leaders, like dogs, had their day and passed away. Kai Borie was one such leader, and *his* day spread over many a bloody year, ending on that ghastly night I am telling you of. He was no ordinary man. . . ."

Kai Borie stood on the great boulder by the Moa Falls, big, black, and magnificent, a human almost as charged with energy as thunder and lightning bursting out of black, nimbus clouds.

"Bring Bensali here," he roared above the thunder of the waterfalls. "He is my sister's child and, therefore, by tribal custom and fact, more precious to me than my own would be. But if in the attack he did behave like a coward, he shall die as other cowards have died before him."

A movement like a shock-wave passed through the concourse of men assembled on this side of the river. Overhead the stars, numberless and brilliant in a moonless heaven, looked down on a river scene as brilliant and certainly more colorful than themselves. For five hundred palm-oil flambeaux were blazing on the Moa's near bank, making the stretch of water look like a hungry, roaring river of blood. Black men held the torches up, and they lined the rocks right down to the water's edge; men as thick as palisades right up to the forest roots, perched on trees—all fearful, all expectant of the horror that might have been the individual lot of any one of them. Upstream, downstream ten thousand "war boys" awaited this royal execution. The light picked out their bodies like statues carved in ebony, here in chiaroscuro, there as clear as day—while here and there spear points glinted like stars answering the stars overhead.

From the river bank to the forest behind, the King's command was passed from mouth to mouth. It made a murmur from the ranks of men, a sound indefinite and eerily moving—as if the earth on which they stood had grumbled in protest.

The prisoner, sitting under guard by a fire in the forest, trembled as the shaft of a spear touched him on the shoulder, and he was ordered to rise.

Two soldiers, their bodies mirrored in the firelight, helped Bensali to rise—for his hands were bound behind his back. He set his teeth with the pain as they pulled him up: there was a wound festering high up on his right arm, on the inner side.

"Courage, Bensali!" whispered the man on his left.

"I am not afraid to die," Bensali answered back, briefly.

They marched him down through the forest, from the fireside down the shadow of death ablaze with torches, to the destiny awaiting him by the Moa Falls.

Although bound, Bensali's brown body moved with rhythm, beautifully muscled. He towered a head above his guards. He moved steadily and firmly, not like a man walking the earth for the last time, and knowing Death to be but a few minutes away.

He jumped from rock to rock unaided, never losing his balance, halted below the boulder on which his uncle stood.

"Bensali," Kai Borie shouted down to him, "even at this last moment let me hear your story again. Perhaps God in his wisdom has hidden something from our senses that may yet save me from executing my favorite sister's child. Though I hate and will punish cowardice in anyone, I, having no son of my own, hate even more the thought of drowning my own heir."

"There is nothing new to tell, Uncle," said the bound man wearily.

"Nevertheless I must hear it," the war-chief ordered. The right side of his face was twitching with emotion; the left was hideous and expressionless, eyeless also, being occupied by a four-pronged scar that twisted the mouth to one side.

"It was as I have said," Bensali returned, raising his voice in that valley of death, that as many as possible of his fellows might hear him. "A week today, Kai Borie, you ordered us to attack Gbaserie in his wartown. I was honored, grateful, and proud that you put me in command.

"We lay in the forest all afternoon, not approaching the town till we were sure that the guards would be weary, and sorely tempted to sleep in the lateness of the night.

"All went well with us. In four groups we scaled the mud walls around the town, and set fire to the crowded houses in different parts of the town at once.

"But Uncle, Gbaserie was as old a hand at war as you. No doubt, he had his spies among us: he must have known of the coming attack. Our spies were not as good. It was only when we had set fire to a quarter of the town that we realized it was deserted—and that *we* were trapped in it.

"Yes, trapped, my Uncle! For Gbaserie had hidden his men in the forest too. From whatever wall-gate we attempted to make a sortie and burst out, we were greeted with a hail of spears. Only later we found that those who had been left to guard our rear and lines of communication outside the town had been slaughtered to a man. O Lord—the horror and blood inside the town! Torture by fire blazed behind us, certain death by an untold number of enemy hands in front—these two, or surrender and slavery. An impossible choice—so we could not help but fight. And bravely too, I think. Only our bodies must have stood out with fatal clearness for our enemies against the firelight: more spears found their mark among us than I know is common in war.

"Still, we fought hardily, and as best we could. My younger brothers died bravely beside me. I loved those two—as my mother—your sister— loved them. It is a poor thought now that we could have taken a thousand slaves in Gbaserie's town. Slaves come every day, brothers not. Slaves, ten thousands slaves or their equivalent in gold—a sorry exchange for two brothers dead! Oh Uncle," he cried in agony, "I am sick of war—and do not mind to die. . . ."

Looking like drops of blood in that light, tears trembled on Bensali's lids. His head fell forward on his chest, his shoulders stooped, his grief ground him down to silence.

But Kai Borie, no less tortured than the man below the boulder, called down to him relentlessly:

"*I am listening!*"

"There is little more to tell," the young man resumed, his voice sick with weariness and heartbreak. "We fought. We lost. I myself with my young arm ran my spear through Gbaserie's heart. At least, Kai Borie, that old enemy of yours is dead. The Peace he has for years driven out from our land may yet come back to us. So I, emboldened by this deed of blood, was fool enough to hope. But I gloried too soon. My spear was still stuck in Gbaserie's chest when his men roared like thunder all over the field . . . and closed in in a wall of death. But Gbaserie's death had put new life into us. We did not yield an inch. Thick as the enemy came, we cut our way right through. And when at last it seemed that safety, so dearly bought, was now within our grasp—then *it* happened.

"I had been striking with my sword till my arm had grown weary and ached. Suddenly sword and weariness disappeared from my hand. I felt no pain. But blood gushed from my arm, warm and soothing down to the fingers—and coursed like a brook washing the dead at my feet. I gazed, feeling foolish, at the hand at my side; gazed at my good right arm. Foolish! They were still mine, fingers and hand. But no longer could I move them. The nerves had gone, cut in the wound in my arm. The arm is almost quite dead now—and now my body follows. I tell you, Uncle, I could do no more, no more—no more. . . ."

"And so you ran away!" Kai Borie shouted in agony.

Bensali died many deaths at the accusation, his head falling in shame on his chest.

"Bensali! Bensali!" Kai Borie cried again. No man alive there by that river of death had ever seen the seasoned old warrior in such agony. "We are all death's children, Bensali, and cannot escape her. She comes at her own will, but better in honor than in disgrace; she may come in action, she may come in peace—but there is no choice, she *must* come. Yet not even in death must a young man give up his hold on life, on honor. Look at your uncle, boy, this one-eyed Borie. Look at this scarred face, this sightless hole that was once an eye.

"I see my own one-eyed ugliness in the glass, and my age rejoices with pride in it. I had your beauty once, and was your age when hunting in the forest. Fate willed that a leopard and I should hunt the same deer. I killed the game, closed in on the trail—only to feel the full-grown leopard tearing at my back. I smelled and saw and felt death then, all over me—furry, savage, tearing me in pieces. But it never entered my head to admit it. As you see the beast tore my face to shreds. But by the mercy of God and the will to live, I wrapped my legs round the beast's body, and got my right arm round its throat. By the sheer will to live—the will to face the danger and dare live beyond it—I hung on. I was strong then, but no more than you are now. By holding on and refusing to die, in the end I throttled the beast. I bore him on my shoulders to the town—only to fall fainting at my father's door. Had I died then, it would have been better than to live to see this night. Ah Bensali! . . . Ah, Bensali!. . . "

Kai Borie stopped and turned toward the forest behind him. A voice had echoed his. In that place where no woman had a right to be, a woman was wailing; without restraint of grief, at the top of her voice:

"Ah, Bensali! . . . Ah, Kai Borie. . . . Ah, Bensali! . . . Ah, Kai Borie!. . ." ceaselessly in the night.

Kai Borie stared toward the boles of trees shadowed against the blaze of the many camp fires in the forest. Other trees beyond the fires were lit up like gold. In between, leaves made whispering traceries both against the fires and the stars over the warriors' heads. From the heart of this setting the woman's dirge issued most eerily for a man not yet dead in fact, yet as surely dead as anything can be sure in human life. Her anguished calls brought a murmur from the soldiers up and down the river—an incantation without words that set the hair of every mortal there standing on end.

At last the weeping woman came through the forest. The ranks of soldiers parted and made way for her. And two young warriors helped from rock to rock the other woman who followed her; and though it was she who carried the basket, she was doubly bent over with her burden and with age.

Weeping all the time, the young woman at last jumped up the great boulder, and threw herself prostrate at Kai Borie's feet.

"Ah, Kai Borie," she shrilled in agony, and twined her arms round his ankles, "I have come at this last minute to beg for my husband's life. My Bensali must not die. These five years he has served you well. . . ."

"Stop, woman!" Kai Borie shouted. "You should not have come here. Do you think what *you* feel for Bensali can compare with the love I have for my sister's first-born? You soft and foolish thing! What can a woman know of the agony I suffer this night?"

"If you truly suffer," the woman wailed and beat her hands on the rock, "then you must save him!"

"Foolish Bindeh! In war, men are nothing if they are not men. And manhood means courage, a willingness to sacrifice life itself for the common good. Tonight Bensali is not Kai Borie's nephew but a soldier in his army. And what shall men say of Kai Borie hereafter, or of Bensali, if Kai Borie tonight shall gloss over a crime for which he has ruled death for other men's nephews, other women's husbands?"

"What do I care for wars or armies? I've hated them, as my mother and grandmother hated them, even before they made me suffer so." The woman's words shrilled into the forest, and men felt their blood turning into water: for Bindeh was speaking with the voice of all their mothers, all their wives. "Kai Borie, has war left no mercy in you? These six months I have been Bensali's wife. Only six months! Ah, Kai Borie—you were young once—have mercy on me. Look!"

In an instant she was on her feet before him. With swift, nervous movements of her wrists she tore off the small native cloth tied round her chest, leaving only the *lappa*[1] tied at her waist, reaching down to midleg.

---

[1] Skirt. [eds.]

She was tall, deep-brown of skin, a beautiful woman. Her breasts, with the aureolae deeply pigmented, gave incontestable proof of her pregnancy.

"These three months," she cried in agony, "I have been carrying Bensali's child. His first baby. . . . Kai Borie, must you make a widow of me and an orphan of my child? No—*mercy*—NO!. . . "

At this revelation Kai Borie buried his face in his hands and burst into tears.

Again a murmur rose eerily from the soldiers. They knew, vaguely, they had unitedly created in Kai Borie's army a monster whose code each of them hated as an individual; yet as an army they were powerless in its creed. Not one of them was not sorry for Bensali, distressed for Bindeh. Yet, though each saw Bensali in himself crucified at second hand, not one could have raised his voice to save him.

Kai Borie was too strong a man to weep for long. Swiftly his tears ended in an outburst of anger with himself. With jerky, angry movements he wiped his tears away. Firmly he told Bindeh:

"Woman, I cannot help it."

Though Bensali was not afraid of death, he trembled with horror to see his wife in such a scene.

"Bindeh," he called up to her, "Kai Borie is right. My Uncle, see that my wife and child are cared for. And now, Uncle, let Bindeh be led away—or she'll unnerve me . . . my wife—Oh, my dear!—God take care of you and our child. In God's name, then Bindeh . . . go!"

"Not yet, Bensali—not yet!" She had started violently at the sound of his voice. Having called his name, she stuffed the cloth she had torn from her chest into her mouth—her face darkened and twitched as though she was choking herself to death. Kai Borie wrenched the cloth from her—she staggered back from him.

"Forgive—Sir—forgive—I don't know what I am doing . . . Oh . . . O God. . . ." Her features twitched a little more, her hands trembled at her sides. She was truly going through hell. And yet, out of the mystery of that thing men call character, she managed to find strength to pull herself out of the hell of her sufferings, to order her thoughts.

"Kai Borie," her voice quavered, but she managed to control it, "I have one more prayer that may yet move you. Grandmother, the basket!"

The old woman, standing at the base of the boulder below them, handed up the big raffia basket. Bindeh clutched it desperately to her chest, and turned again to the old warrior:

"Kai Borie, I have brought a gift for you. For sometimes gifts move kings where prayers fail. But I shall give it to you only as a last resort." On her bended knees again, falling down at his feet for the last time, "I beg you for my husband's life."

"Rise woman!" He spoke to her in a gentle voice, so that in the roar of the falls only she heard him. "You are brave. . . . Your son shall be my heir— for I grieve no less than you that Bensali must die. . . ."

The woman leapt up from the rock, transformed. She was so rapt and tensed up she looked as if she had passed beyond pain and agony. She looked, indeed, like the Goddess of Vengeance.

"Grandmother," Kai Borie called down to the old woman, "take her home."

"I'll go Kai Borie," Bindeh screamed so frenziedly her voice echoed back from the forest. "But first you'll take my gift!"

Swiftness enhanced her every little movement with grace—she moved so swiftly in the next few seconds no one could stop her.

Bensali, understanding too late what she *would* do, shouted up to her: "No, Bindeh—the child!"

The young woman did not even hear him.

With a lightning movement of her hand she tore the lid off the basket. She swung the basket in the air and, bringing it down very swiftly, covered Kai Borie's head like a hood. At once she turned to face the river, bent her knees, raised her arms above her head—took a flying leap into the seething violence of the Falls.

It all happened so swiftly that the multitude barely had time to shout—"Ha-ah-HAH!"—momentarily renting the night with their united astonishment, drowning the river noises. But each remained rooted to the spot where he stood, paralyzed with wonder. . . .

For an instant or two they saw the rush of waters bear the woman down a few yards—heard her shout: "Bensali! Bensali!"—no more. The waters had choked and battered her, and she vanished from their view. . . .

"You crazy woman!" Kai Borie's voice came muffled from inside the basket.

He wrenched the basket off his head, tossed it down on the rock—from which it rolled off slowly, down into the river, and was frenziedly borne downstream.

Feeling something cold above his eyes, Kai Borie raised a hand to his forehead.

Bensali turned a face petrified with despair from the river to his Uncle on the boulder above him.

"My God . . . UNC. . . " the words froze in his throat.

For Kai Borie was turbaned with a brown deadly snake which, in soft undulations, was swiftly adjusting itself like a bandeau around his brow. A second snake was coiled round his neck. And the largest of the three was spiralling up the forearm he had raised to his head.

At the sight the two war boys who stood on the nearest boulder to their Chief leaped down in terror to where the old woman sat, sobbing to herself.

But for the eternal rush of the falls, not a sound broke the deathliness of the night.

The moment Kai Borie touched the coldness on his forehead he felt two intense needle-stabs on his brow, one on his throat, one in his arm.

He grasped the snake on his head, tore it off. Bending over the boulder he brained it on the rock. He wrenched the other off his throat, horse-whipped it to death with its own body against the granite. The third reptile fell from his forearm. Without hesitation Kai Borie stamped on its back. The snake looped back and struck back ten times with incredible swiftness at his leg. He bent down, gripped the vicious band in his hand—and crushed it to death between his fingers.

Unhurried, he sat down on the rock.

"Kai Borie is dying!" he called loudly to his men below. "Unbind Bensali! . . . Quick, my men—*quick:* I have so little time to live. . . ." The sweat was already pouring profusely from his face. "Swear, soldiers, swear that Bensali shall be your King. . . ."

Sworn by their fathers' gods. The oath rose grandly, eerily in that Death's valley, drowning the river noises.

"She was a brave woman, Bensali. . . . For her sake and mine—swear . . . swear to be . . . a true heir . . . to me. . . ."

Bensali, unbound, ran up the boulder and held his dying uncle against his chest.

"What do I want with a kingdom, my Uncle?" Sobbing like a woman, Bensali's tears ran down his face, and joined with the sweat that had burst out all over his uncle's heaving chest. *His* father had died when he was but a boy—Kai Borie had been more than father to him all his life. "Uncle, without you and Bindeh I do not wish to live. . . ."

"Courage goes—beyond life. . . . Swear, Bensali—quick lad—swear!. . . " the words rattled in the old warrior's throat. Already he was finding it difficult to breathe. The air rasped painfully, irregularly into his chest. "I will-ingly—exchange my life—for yours, Bensali. . . ." He had lived by violence, he died with violence, his ribs moving gigantically against the pressure of Death, to get the words out. Already his eyes were glazing over. "It was—hidden from—a man's wit. . . . Only the weakness of women . . . sometimes sees the truth: better the old . . . should die . . . rather . . . than the young!" His eyes shut wearily. But his vast body convulsed with one final effort to get his last wish in the word: "S-S-SWEAR!"

It was the last word he spoke.

At last, Bensali took the oath, crying, crying.

Whereupon, sacred and moving, a prayer burst from ten thousand throats:

"Long live Bensali!"

Kai Borie nodded, and leaned back heavily on his nephew's chest. In five minutes he was completely paralyzed—in ten he was dead.

"Oh Bindeh! Oh, my Uncle! . . . Oh Bindeh!. . . "

But still ten thousand soldiers hailed; *"Bensali! Long live Bensali!"* He looked down on them and shook his head. Only then he realized that life was at best a sham, but must go on.
"Long live Bensali!"

❋ Discussion and Writing

1. What is the relevance of the conversation that opens "Bindeh's Gift"? Comment on the shift in time in relation to the moral values portrayed in the story.
2. Analyze the portrayal of heroism, love, and duty through the behavior of the male characters.
3. What is the significance of the female force in this story glorifying masculine ideals? What is the implication of Easmon's use of a woman as a catalyst for change?
4. Analyze the impact of Bindeh's sacrifice within a patriarchal system.
5. What do the recurrent images of the rock, the falls, and the snake symbolize? How do the images connect with the characters and their passions?

❋ Research and Comparison

Interdisciplinary Discussion Question: Research the importance of the snake in the diverse cultures of Asia, Africa, and the Americas. Compare the depiction and significance of the image of the snake in several stories in this anthology.

Grace Ogot
(b. 1930)
Kenya

Grace Emily Akinyi Ogot, born in the Central Nyanza District of Kenya, was raised according to the traditional Luo customs of her family home near Kisumu on the shore of Lake Victoria. Her father was a schoolteacher. As a child, she listened avidly to the village storytellers, particularly to her grandmother. Thus, when Ogot's husband encouraged her to write, she recalled one of the stories that had caused her to cry herself to sleep when she was ten. This became "The Rain Came," and it launched her as a writer. She took degrees in nursing, but her career has been varied. She worked as a nurse, midwife, and administrator of student health services at Makerere University in Uganda. She has been a director of commercial firms and research assistant to her husband, a journalist, a scriptwriter, and BBC broadcaster in London, and a weekly broadcaster in her native Luo in Kenya. She has served as a delegate to the United Nations and founding chairperson of the Writers Association of Kenya. Along with her concern for postindependence Kenya, her writing indicates the abiding effect of the old traditional stories, stories that caused her both joy and sorrow as a child and whose mythic underpinnings continue to inform her culture.

The Rain Came

The chief was still far from the gate when his daughter Oganda, saw him. She ran to meet him. Breathlessly she asked her father, "What is the news, great Chief? Everyone in the village is anxiously waiting to hear when it will rain." Labong'o held out his hands for his daughter but he did not say a word. Puzzled by her father's cold attitude Oganda ran back to the village to warn the others that the chief was back.

The atmosphere in the village was tense and confused. Everyone moved aimlessly and fussed in the yard without actually doing any work. A young woman whispered to her co-wife, "If they have not solved this rain business today, the chief will crack." They had watched him getting thinner and thinner as the people kept on pestering him. "Our cattle lie dying in the fields," they reported. "Soon it will be our children and then ourselves. Tell us what to do to save our lives, oh great Chief." So the chief had daily prayed with the Almighty through the ancestors to deliver them from their distress.

Instead of calling the family together and giving them the news immediately, Labong'o went to his own hut, a sign that he was not to be disturbed. Having replaced the shutter, he sat in the dimly lit hut to contemplate.

It was no longer a question of being the chief of hunger-stricken people that weighed Labong'o's heart. It was the life of his only daughter that was at stake. At the time when Oganda came to meet him, he saw the glittering chain shining around her waist. The prophecy was complete. "It is Oganda, Oganda, my only daughter, who must die so young." Labong'o burst into tears before finishing the sentence. The chief must not weep. Society had declared him the bravest of men. But Labong'o did not care anymore. He assumed the position of a simple father and wept bitterly. He loved his people, the Luo, but what were the Luo for him without Oganda? Her life had brought a new life in Labong'o's world and he ruled better than he could remember. How would the spirit of the village survive his beautiful daughter? "There are so many homes and so many parents who have daughters. Why choose this one? She is all I have." Labong'o spoke as if the ancestors were there in the hut and he could see them face to face. Perhaps they were there, warning him to remember his promise on the day he was enthroned when he said aloud, before the elders, "I will lay down life, if necessary, and the life of my household, to save this tribe from the hands of the enemy." "Deny! Deny!" he could hear the voice of his forefathers mocking him.

When Labong'o was consecrated chief he was only a young man. Unlike his father, he ruled for many years with only one wife. But people rebuked him because his only wife did not bear him a daughter. He married a second, a third, and a fourth wife. But they all gave birth to male children. When Labong'o married a fifth wife she bore him a daughter. They called her Oganda, meaning "beans," because her skin was very fair. Out of Labong'o's twenty children, Oganda was the only girl. Though she was the chief's favorite, her mother's co-wives swallowed their jealous feelings and showered her with love. After all, they said, Oganda was a female child whose days in the royal family were numbered. She would soon marry at a tender age and leave the enviable position to someone else.

Never in his life had he been faced with such an impossible decision. Refusing to yield to the rainmaker's request would mean sacrificing the whole tribe, putting the interests of the individual above those of the society. More than that. It would mean disobeying the ancestors, and most probably wiping the Luo people from the surface of the earth. On the other hand, to let Oganda die as a ransom for the people would permanently cripple Labong'o spiritually. He knew he would never be the same chief again.

The words of Ndithi, the medicine man, still echoed in his ears. "Podho, the ancestor of the Luo, appeared to me in a dream last night, and he asked me to speak to the chief and the people," Ndithi had said to the gathering of tribesmen. "A young woman who has not known a man must die so that the country may have rain. While Podho was still talking to me, I saw a young woman standing at the lakeside, her hands raised, above her head. Her skin was as fair as the skin of young deer in the wilderness. Her tall slender figure stood like a lonely reed at the riverbank. Her sleepy eyes wore a sad look like that of a bereaved mother. She wore a gold ring on her left ear, and a glittering brass chain around her waist. As I still marveled at the beauty of this young woman, Podho told me, "Out of all the women in this land, we have chosen this one. Let her offer herself a sacrifice to the lake monster! And on that day, the rain will come down in torrents. Let everyone stay at home on that day, lest he be carried away by the floods."

Outside there was a strange stillness, except for the thirsty birds that sang lazily on the dying trees. The blinding midday heat had forced the people to retire to their huts. Not far away from the chief's hut, two guards were snoring away quietly. Labong'o removed his crown and the large eagle head that hung loosely on his shoulders. He left the hut, and instead of asking Nyabog'o the messenger to beat the drum, he went straight and beat it himself. In no time the whole household had assembled under the siala tree where he usually addressed them. He told Oganda to wait a while in her grandmother's hut.

When Labong'o stood to address his household, his voice was hoarse and the tears choked him. He started to speak, but words refused to leave his lips. His wives and sons knew there was great danger. Perhaps their enemies had declared war on them. Labong'o's eyes were red, and they could see he had been weeping. At last he told them. "One whom we love and treasure must be taken away from us. Oganda is to die." Labong'o's voice was so faint, that he could not hear it himself. But he continued. "The ancestors have chosen her to be offered as a sacrifice to the lake monster in order that we may have rain."

They were completely stunned. As a confused murmur broke out, Oganda's mother fainted and was carried off to her own hut. But the other people rejoiced. They danced around singing and chanting, "Oganda is the lucky one to die for the people. If it is to save the people, let Oganda go."

In her grandmother's hut Oganda wondered what the whole family were discussing about her that she could not hear. Her grandmother's hut was well away from the chief's court and, much as she strained her ears, she could not hear what was said. "It must be marriage," she concluded. It was an accepted custom for the family to discuss their daughter's future marriage behind her back. A faint smile played on Oganda's lips as she thought of the several young men who swallowed saliva at the mere mention of her name.

There was Kech, the son of a neighboring clan elder. Kech was very handsome. He had sweet, meek eyes and a roaring laughter. He would make a wonderful father, Oganda thought. But they would not be a good match. Kech was a bit too short to be her husband. It would humiliate her to have to look down at Kech each time she spoke to him. Then she thought of Dimo, the tall young man who had already distinguished himself as a brave warrior and an outstanding wrestler. Dimo adored Oganda, but Oganda thought he would make a cruel husband, always quarreling and ready to fight. No, she did not like him. Oganda fingered the glittering chain on her waist as she thought of Osinda. A long time ago when she was quite young Osinda had given her that chain, and instead of wearing it around her neck several times, she wore it round her waist where it could stay permanently. She heard her heart pounding so loudly as she thought of him. She whispered, "Let it be you they are discussing, Osinda, the lovely one. Come now and take me away. . . "

The lean figure in the doorway startled Oganda who was rapt in thought about the man she loved. "You have frightened me, Grandma," said Oganda laughing. "Tell me, is it my marriage you were discussing? You can take it from me that I won't marry any of them." A smile played on her lips again. She was coaxing the old lady to tell her quickly, to tell her they were pleased with Osinda.

In the open space outside the excited relatives were dancing and singing. They were coming to the hut now, each carrying a gift to put at Oganda's feet. As their singing got nearer Oganda was able to hear what they were saying: "If it is to save the people, if it is to give us rain, let Oganda go. Let Oganda die for her people, and for her ancestors." Was she mad to think that they were singing about her? How could she die? She found the lean figure of her grandmother barring the door. She could not get out. The look on her grandmother's face warned her that there was danger around the corner. "Grandma, it is not marriage then?" Oganda asked urgently. She suddenly felt panicky like a mouse cornered by a hungry cat. Forgetting that there was only one door in the hut Oganda fought desperately to find another exit. She must fight for her life. But there was none.

She closed her eyes, leapt like a wild tiger through the door, knocking her grandmother flat to the ground. There outside in mourning garments Labong'o stood motionless, his hands folded at the back. He held his daughter's hand and led her away from the excited crowd to the little red-painted hut where her mother was resting. Here he broke the news officially to his daughter.

For a long time the three souls who loved one another dearly sat in darkness. It was no good speaking. And even if they tried, the words could not have come out. In the past they had been like three cooking stones, sharing their burdens. Taking Oganda away from them would leave two useless stones which would not hold a cooking pot.

News that the beautiful daughter of the chief was to be sacrificed to give the people rain spread across the country like wind. At sunset the chief's village was full of relatives and friends who had come to congratulate Oganda. Many more were on their way coming, carrying their gifts. They would dance till morning to keep her company. And in the morning they would prepare her a big farewell feast. All these relatives thought it a great honor to be selected by the spirits to die, in order that the society may live. "Oganda's name will always remain a living name among us," they boasted.

But was it maternal love that prevented Minya from rejoicing with the other women? Was it the memory of the agony and pain of childbirth that made her feel so sorrowful? Or was it the deep warmth and understanding that passes between a suckling babe and her mother that made Oganda part of her life, her flesh? Of course it was an honor, a great honor, for her daughter to be chosen to die for the country. But what could she gain once her only daughter was blown away by the wind? There were so many other women in the land, why choose her daughter, her only child! Had human life any meaning at all—other women had houses full of children while she, Minya, had to lose her only child!

In the cloudless sky the moon shone brightly, and the numerous stars glittered with a bewitching beauty. The dancers of all age groups assembled to dance before Oganda, who sat close to her mother, sobbing quietly. All these years she had been with her people she thought she understood them. But now she discovered that she was a stranger among them. If they loved her as they had always professed why were they not making any attempt to save her? Did her people really understand what it felt like to die young? Unable to restrain her emotions any longer, she sobbed loudly as her age group got up to dance. They were young and beautiful and very soon they would marry and have their own children. They would have husbands to love and little huts for themselves. They would have reached maturity. Oganda touched the chain around her waist as she thought of Osinda. She wished Osinda was there too, among her friends. "Perhaps he is ill," she thought gravely. The chain comforted Oganda—she would die with it around her waist and wear it in the underground world.

In the morning a big feast was prepared for Oganda. The women prepared many different tasty dishes so that she could pick and choose. "People don't eat after death," they said. Delicious though the food looked, Oganda touched none of it. Let the happy people eat. She contented herself with sips of water from a little calabash [gourd].

The time for her departure was drawing near, and each minute was precious. It was a day's journey to the lake. She was to walk all night, passing through the great forest. But nothing could touch her, not even the denizens of the forest. She was already anointed with sacred oil. From the time Oganda received the sad news she had expected Osinda to appear any moment. But he was not there. A relative told her that Osinda was away on a private visit. Oganda realized that she would never see her beloved again.

In the late afternoon the whole village stood at the gate to say good-bye and to see her for the last time. Her mother wept on her neck for a long time. The great chief in a mourning skin came to the gate barefooted, and mingled with the people—a simple father in grief. He took off his wrist bracelet and put it on his daughter's wrist saying, "You will always live among us. The spirit of our forefathers is with you."

Tongue-tied and unbelieving Oganda stood there before the people. She had nothing to say. She looked at her home once more. She could hear her heart beating so painfully within her. All her childhood plans were coming to an end. She felt like a flower nipped in the bud never to enjoy the morning dew again. She looked at her weeping mother, and whispered, "Whenever you want to see me, always look at the sunset. I will be there."

Oganda turned southward to start her trek to the lake. Her parents, relatives, friends and admirers stood at the gate and watched her go.

Her beautiful slender figure grew smaller and smaller till she mingled with the thin dry trees in the forest. As Oganda walked the lonely path that wound its way in the wilderness, she sang a song, and her own voice kept her company.

The ancestors have said Oganda must die
The daughter of the chief must be sacrificed,

When the lake monster feeds on my flesh,
The people will have rain.
Yes, the rain will come down in torrents.
And the floods will wash away the sandy beaches
When the daughter of the chief dies in the lake.
My age group has consented
My parents have consented
So have my friends and relatives.
Let Oganda die to give us rain.
My age group are young and ripe,
Ripe for womanhood and motherhood
But Oganda must die young,
Oganda must sleep with the ancestors.
Yes, rain will come down in torrents.

The red rays of the setting sun embraced Oganda, and she looked like a burning candle in the wilderness.

The people who came to hear her sad song were touched by her beauty. But they all said the same thing. "If it is to save the people, if it is to give us rain, then be not afraid. Your name will forever live among us."

At midnight Oganda was tired and weary. She could walk no more. She sat under a big tree, and having sipped water from her calabash, she rested her head on the tree trunk and slept.

When Oganda woke up in the morning the sun was high in the sky. After walking for many hours, she reached the *tong'*, a strip of land that separated the inhabited part of the country from the sacred place *(kar lamo)*. No layman could enter this place and come out alive—only those who had direct contact with the spirits and the Almighty were allowed to enter this holy of holies. But Oganda had to pass through this sacred land on her way to the lake, which she had to reach at sunset.

A large crowd gathered to see her for the last time. Her voice was now hoarse and painful, but there was no need to worry anymore. Soon she would not have to sing. The crowd looked at Oganda sympathetically, mumbling words she could not hear. But none of them pleaded for life. As Oganda opened the gate, a child, a young child, broke loose from the crowd, and ran toward her. The child took a small earring from her sweaty hands and gave it to Oganda saying, "When you reach the world of the dead, give this earring to my sister. She died last week. She forgot this ring." Oganda, taken aback by the strange request, took the little ring, and handed her precious water and food to the child. She did not need them now. Oganda did not know whether to laugh or cry. She had heard mourners sending their love to their sweethearts, long dead, but this idea of sending gifts was new to her.

Oganda held her breath as she crossed the barrier to enter the sacred land. She looked appealingly at the crowd, but there was no response. Their minds were too preoccupied with their own survival. Rain was the precious medicine they were longing for, and the sooner Oganda could get to her destination the better.

A strange feeling possessed Oganda as she picked her way in the sacred land. There were strange noises that often startled her, and her first reaction was to take to her heels. But she remembered that she had to fulfill the wish of her people. She was exhausted, but the path was still winding. Then suddenly the path ended on sandy land. The water had retreated miles away from the shore leaving a wide stretch of sand. Beyond this was the vast expanse of water.

Oganda felt afraid. She wanted to picture the size and shape of the monster, but fear would not let her. The society did not talk about it, nor did the crying children who were silenced by the mention of its name. The sun was still up, but it was no longer hot. For a long time Oganda walked ankle-deep in the sand. She was exhausted and longed desperately for her calabash of water. As she moved on, she had a strange feeling that something was following her. Was it the monster? Her hair stood erect, and a cold paralyzing feeling ran along her spine. She looked behind, sideways and in front, but there was nothing, except a cloud of dust.

Oganda pulled up and hurried but the feeling did not leave her, and her whole body became saturated with perspiration.

The sun was going down fast and the lake shore seemed to move along with it.

Oganda started to run. She must be at the lake before sunset. As she ran she heard a noise coming from behind. She looked back sharply, and something resembling a moving bush was frantically running after her. It was about to catch up with her.

Oganda ran with all her strength. She was now determined to throw herself into the water even before sunset. She did not look back, but the creature was upon her. She made an effort to cry out, as in a nightmare, but she could not hear her own voice. The creature caught up with Oganda. In the utter confusion, as Oganda came face with the unidentified creature, a strong hand grabbed her. But she fell flat on the sand and fainted.

When the lake breeze brought her back to consciousness, a man was bending over her. ". . . . . .!!" Oganda opened her mouth to speak, but she had lost her voice. She swallowed a mouthful of water poured into her mouth by the stranger.

"Osinda, Osinda! Please let me die. Let me run, the sun is going down. Let me die, let them have rain." Osinda fondled the glittering chain around Oganda's waist and wiped the tears from her face.

"We must escape quickly to the unknown land," Osinda said urgently. "We must run away from the wrath of the ancestors and the retaliation of the monster."

"But the curse is upon me, Osinda, I am no good to you anymore. And moreover the eyes of the ancestors will follow us everywhere and bad luck will befall us. Nor can we escape from the monster."

Oganda broke loose, afraid to escape, but Osinda grabbed her hands again.

"Listen to me, Oganda! Listen! Here are two coats!" He then covered the whole of Oganda's body, except her eyes, with a leafy attire made from the twigs of *Bwombwe*. "These will protect us from the eyes of the ancestors and the wrath of the monster. Now let us run out of here." He held Oganda's hand and they ran from the sacred land, avoiding the path that Oganda had followed.

The bush was thick, and the long grass entangled their feet as they ran. Halfway through the sacred land they stopped and looked back. The sun was almost touching the surface of the water. They were frightened. They continued to run, now faster, to avoid the sinking sun.

"Have faith, Oganda—that thing will not reach us."

When they reached the barrier and looked behind them trembling, only a tip of the sun could be seen above the water's surface.

"It is gone! It is gone!" Oganda wept, hiding her face in her hands.

"Weep not, daughter of the chief. Let us run, let us escape."

There was a bright lightning. They looked up, frightened. Above them black furious clouds started to gather. They began to run. Then the thunder roared, and the rain came down in torrents.

✵ Discussion and Writing

1. Describe the different ties of love that bind the major characters in the story. What is at the core of their various emotional conflicts?
2. How do the people in the community perceive the situation? Discuss their behavior
3. Comment on the behavior of the young lovers: the resolution of the tension between their communal obligation and personal gratification.
4. What is implied by the ending? What attitude is projected regarding the tradition of sacrifice?
5. Analyze the language, the theme, the images, and the tone of the story.

✵ Research and Comparison

Interdisciplinary Discussion Question: The tradition of the sacrifice of the one for the redemption of the many has prevailed in all cultures, including the Judeo-Christian. What forms the basis of this tradition? What is the relevance of this tradition in modern times? Examine the treatment of the theme of sacrifice in other writings included in this anthology.

Nawal El Saadawi
(b. 1931)
Egypt

Nawal El Saadawi was born in a village in the Nile Delta in Egypt where her father, a university graduate and a teacher, was serving as general controller of education for the province. Her mother's father had been the director general of army recruitment and had taught in the French schools that her mother attended. Both parents believed in education for girls as well as for boys. But the sons were expected to devote themselves to their studies while the daughters were required to apply themselves to both their studies and their household duties. This point continued to rankle El Saadawi in her adult years. She became a physician, director of public health, and editor of *Health* magazine, but was dismissed in 1972 from both positions because of the publication of her outspoken work on behalf of Arab women, *Women and Sex.* Her husband had spent 13 years in prison as a "political detainee," and in the fall of 1981 it was her turn. Anwar el-Sadat imprisoned her for three months along with many Egyptian scholars and artists who were struggling for women's social freedom. The effect of prison on women interested her as a social factor impinging on their psyches. Before her own incarceration, she had written *Firdaus* (Woman at Point Zero, 1975) about the life of a woman who was jailed and eventually hanged for killing a man. As an international lecturer and writer of fiction and nonfiction, El Saadawi continues to speak out on women's issues.

She Has No Place in Paradise*

With the palm of her hand, she touched the ground beneath her but did not feel soil. She looked upward, stretching her neck toward the light. Her face appeared long and lean, the skin so dark it was almost black.

She could not see her own face in the dark and held no mirror in her hand. But the white light fell onto the back of her hand so that it became

---

*Translated by Shirley Eber

white in turn. Her narrow eyes widened in surprise and filled with light. Thus widened and full of light, her eyes looked like those of a *houri*.[1]

In astonishment, she turned her head to the right and to the left. A vast expanse between the leafy trees above her head as she sat in the shade and the stream of water like a strip of silver, its clusters of droplets like pearls, then that deep plate full of broth to the rim.

Her eyelids tightened to open her eyes to the utmost. The scene remained the same, did not alter. She touched her robe and found it to be as soft as silk. From the neck of her gown wafted the scent of musk or good perfume.

Her head and eyes were motionless for she feared that any blink of her eyelids would change the scene or that it would disappear as it had done before.

But from the corner of her eye, she could see the shade stretching endlessly before her, and green trees between the trunks of which she saw a house of red brick like a palace, with a marble staircase leading up to the bedroom.

She remained fixed to the spot, able neither to believe nor disbelieve. Nothing upset her more than the recurrence of the dream that she had died and woken to find herself in paradise. The dream seemed to her impossible, for dying seemed impossible, waking after death even more impossible and going to paradise the fourth impossibility.

She steadied her neck still more and from the corner of her eye stared into the light. The scene was still the same, unaltered. The red brick house, like that of the *Omda*,[2] the towering staircase leading to the bedroom, the room itself bathed in white light, the window looking out onto distant horizons, the wide bed, its posts swathed in a curtain of silk, all were still there.

It was all so real it could not be denied. She stayed where she was, fearing to move and fearing to believe. Was it possible to die and waken so quickly and then go to paradise?

What she found hardest to believe was the speed of it all. Death, after all, was easy. Everybody died and her own death was easier than anyone's, for she had lived between life and death, closer to death than to life. When her mother gave birth to her, she lay on top of her with all her weight until she died; her father beat her on the head with a hoe until she died; she had gone into fever after each birth, even until the eighth child; when her husband kicked her in the stomach; when the blows of the sun penetrated under the bones of her head.

Life was hard and death for her was easier. Easier still was waking after death, for no one dies and no one wakens; everyone dies and awakens, except an animal which dies and remains dead.

Her going to paradise was also impossible. But if not her, who would go to paradise? Throughout her life she had never done anything to anger Allah

---

[1] Virgin of paradise, according to Islam
[2] A noble man; an aristocrate. [eds.]

or His Prophet. She used to tie her frizzy black hair with a skein of wool into a plait; the plait she wrapped up in a white headscarf and her head she wrapped in a black shawl. Nothing showed from under her robe except the heel of her foot. From the moment of her birth until her death, she knew only the word: Okay.

Before dawn, when her mother slapped her as she lay, to go and carry dung-pats[3] on her head, she knew only: Okay. If her father tied her to the water mill in place of the sick cow, she said only: Okay. She never raised her eyes to her husband's and when he lay on top of her when she was sick with fever, she uttered only the words: Okay.

She had never stolen or lied in her life. She would go hungry or die of hunger rather than take the food of others, even if it were her father's or brother's or husband's. Her mother would wrap up food for her father in a flat loaf of bread and make her carry it to the field on her head. Her husband's food was also wrapped up in a loaf by his mother. She was tempted, as she walked along with it, to stop under the shade of a tree and open the loaf; but she never once stopped. Each time she was tempted, she called on God to protect her from the Devil, until the hunger became unbearable and she would pick a bunch of wild grass from the side of the road which she would chew like gum, then swallow with a sip of water, filling the cup of her hand from the bank of the canal and drinking until she had quenched her thirst. Then, wiping her mouth on the sleeve of her robe, she would mutter to herself: Thank God, and repeat it three times. She prayed five times a day, her face to the ground, thanking God. If she were attacked by fever and her head filled with blood like fire, she would still praise Allah. On fast days, she would fast; on baking days, she would bake; on harvest days, she would harvest; on holy days, she would put on her mourning weeds and go to the cemetery.

She never lost her temper with her father or brother or husband. If her husband beat her to death and she returned to her father's house, her father would send her back to her husband. If she returned again, her father would beat her and *then* send her back. If her husband took her back and did not throw her out, and then beat her, she returned to her mother who would tell her: Go back, Zeinab. Paradise will be yours in the hereafter.

From the time she was born, she had heard the word "paradise" from her mother. The first time she'd heard it, she was walking in the sun, a pile of dung on her head, the soles of her feet scorched by the earth. She pictured paradise as a vast expanse of shade without sun, without dung on her head, on her feet shoes like those of Hassanain, the neighbor's son, pounding the earth as he did, his hand holding hers, the two of them sitting in the shade.

When she thought of Hassanain, her imagination went no further than holding hands and sitting in the shade of paradise. But her mother scolded

---

[3]Commonly used for fuel and in building.

her and told her that neither their neighbor's son Hassanain, nor any other neighbor's son, would be in paradise, that her eyes would not fall on any man other than her father or brother, that if she died after getting married and went to paradise, only her husband would be there, that if her soul was tempted, awake or asleep, and her eye fell on a man other than her husband and even before he held her hand in his, she would not so much as catch a glimpse of paradise or smell it from a thousand meters . . .

From that time, whenever she lay down to sleep, she saw only her husband. In paradise, her husband did not beat her. The pile of dung was no longer on her head; neither did the earth burn the soles of her feet. Their black mud house became one of red brick, inside it a towering staircase, then a wide bed on which her husband sat, holding her hand in his.

Her imagination went no further than holding his hand in paradise. Never once in her life had her hand held her husband's. Eight sons and daughters she had conceived with him without once holding his hand. On summer nights, he lay in the fields; in the winter, he lay in the barn or above the oven. All night long, he slept on his back without turning. If he did turn, he would call to her in a voice like a jackal's: Woman! Before she could answer "yes" or "okay," he would have kicked her over onto her back and rolled on top of her. If she made a sound or sighed, he would kick her again. If she did not sigh or make a sound, she would get a third kick, then a fourth until she did. His hand never chanced to hold hers nor his arm happen to stretch out to embrace her.

She had never seen a couple, human or otherwise, embrace except in the dovecot. When she went up there, on the top of the wall appeared a pair of doves, their beaks close together; or when she went down to the cattle pen or from behind the wall there appeared a pair—bull and cow or buffalo or dogs—and her mother brandishing a bamboo stick and whipping them, cursing the animals.

Never in her life had she taken the black shawl off her head nor the white scarf tied under the shawl, except when someone died, when she untied the scarf and pulled the black shawl around her head. When her husband died, she knotted the black shawl twice around her forehead and wore mourning weeds for three years. A man came to ask for her in marriage without her children. Her mother spat in disgust and pulled the shawl down over her forehead, whispering: It's shameful! Does a mother abandon her children for the sake of a man? The years passed by and a man came to ask for her hand in marriage, with her children. Her mother yelled at the top of her voice: What does a woman want in this world after she has become a mother and her husband dies?

One day, she wanted to take off the black shawl and put on a white scarf, but she feared that people would think she'd forgotten her husband. So she kept the black shawl and the mourning weeds and remained sad for her husband until she died of sadness.

She found herself wrapped in a silken shroud inside a coffin. From behind the funeral procession, she heard her mother's wailing like a howl in the night or like the whistle of a train: You'll meet up with your husband in paradise, Zeinab.

Then the noise stopped. She heard nothing but silence and smelled nothing but the soil. The ground beneath her became as soft as silk. She said: It must be the shroud. Above her head, she heard rough voices, like two men fighting. She did not know why they were fighting until she heard one of them mention her name and say that she deserved to go directly to paradise without suffering the torture of the grave. But the other man did not agree and insisted that she should undergo some torture, if only a little: She cannot go directly up to paradise. Everyone must go through the torture of the grave. But the first man insisted that she had done nothing to merit torture, that she had been one hundred percent faithful to her husband. The second man argued that her hair had shown from under her white headscarf, that she had dyed her hair red with henna, that the hennaed heels of her feet had shown from under her robe.

The first man retorted that her hair had never shown, that what his colleague had seen was only the skein of wool, that her robe had been long and thick, under it even thicker and longer underskirts, that no one had seen her heels red.

But his colleague argued, insisting that her red heels had enticed many of the village men.

The dispute between the two of them lasted all night. She lay face down on the ground, her nose and mouth pressed into the earth. She held her breath pretending to be dead. Her torture might be prolonged if it became clear that she had not died; death might save her. She heard nothing of what passed between them; nobody, human or spirit, can hear what happens in the grave after death. If one did happen to hear, one had to pretend not to have heard or not to have understood. The most serious thing to understand is that those two men are not angels of the grave or angels of any type, for it is not possible for angels to ignore the truth which everyone in the village with eyes to see could know: that her heels had never been red like those of the *Omda's* daughter, but like her face and palms, were always cracked and as black as the soil.

The argument ended before dawn without torture. She thanked God when the voices stopped. Her body grew lighter and rose up as if in flight. She hovered as if in the sky, then her body fell and landed on soft, moist earth and she gasped: Paradise.

Cautiously, she raised her head and saw a vast expanse of green, and thick leafy trees, shade beneath them.

She sat up on the ground and saw the trees stretching endlessly before her. Fresh air entered her chest, expelling the dirt and dust and the smell of dung.

With a slight movement, she rose to her feet. Between the tree trunks she could see the house of red brick, the entrance before her very eyes.

She entered quickly, panting. She climbed the towering staircase panting. In front of the bedroom, she stopped for a moment to catch her breath. Her heart was beating wildly and her chest heaved.

The door was closed. She put out her hand carefully and pushed it. She saw the four posts of the bed, around them a silken curtain. In the middle, she saw a wide bed, on top of it her husband, sitting like a bridegroom. On his right, was a woman. On his left, another woman. Both of them wore transparent robes revealing skin as white as honey, their eyes filled with light, like the eyes of *houris.*

Her husband's face was not turned towards her, so he did not see her. Her hand was still on the door. She pulled it behind her and it closed. She returned to the earth, saying to herself: There is no place in paradise for a black woman.

❊ Discussion and Writing

1. Examine the mores controlling Zeinab's everyday life. Who else besides Zeinab's husband governs her life? Comment on women's participation in the subordination of their own gender.
2. What is the implication of the dispute between the two male voices regarding Zeinab's merits? What do the two voices represent?
3. Discuss the significance of Zeinab's repeated dreams of Paradise: what does she expect to find there; why does she not have a place there; what do the *houris* signify? Explore El Saadawi's thesis regarding women's position in her society.
4. What are the thematic implications of beginning and ending the story in Paradise?

❊ Research and Comparison

Interdisciplinary Discussion Question: The position of women in modern Islamic society is a controversial issue in both the Islamic and the non-Islamic worlds. In this context, discuss the views Nawal El Saadawi presents in her literary writings and political activities.

Flora Nwapa
(1931–1993)
Nigeria

Flora Nwapa was born in the Igbo town of Oguta and attended school in Elelenwa, both in eastern Nigeria. She lived for a time with her grand-mother, who, as one of seven wives, provided her with the experience of the traditional extended family. It was here that Nwapa learned about the Igbo traditions that play such an important role in her early work. After taking a degree at the University of Ibadan and a diploma in education at Edinburgh University, she was appointed a woman education officer in Nigeria, and taught in high school, where she began writing. She served as a minister and an elected official in the Nigerian government, as well as working in publishing. She was the first African woman to publish a novel, *Efuru* (1966). While her first two novels are set in her hometown, her subsequent work has concentrated on life in contemporary postindependence Nigeria, especially on women's issues, on women caught up in cultural change.

The Chief's Daughter

"My daughter will marry no one," the Chief said. The Chief's wife laughed aloud. "Our father, you are merely joking. You do not mean it."

"My daughter will marry no one, Uloma, I have said this several times. I am not joking. I don't joke with women. You know that very well. When Adaeze returns from the land of the white people, she is going to stay here, right here with me. I have provided her with everything. She is one of the directors in ten of my twenty companies. She will receive a director's fees every month from the companies, I have already seen to that. Her house is waiting for her. I have furnished it to her taste. She in fact went with me to Milan to choose the furnishings. So you can see, I have arranged every-thing," the Chief concluded.

"Our father, so you said. But you don't reckon that right now she might have one or two boys hovering around her. Adaeze is a beautiful girl, you know. She has been away from us for six years. She must have changed. True she has always been fond of you. But remember, even before she left for the land of the white people, you used to have violent exchanges. Of all your children, she was the only one who would stand up to you and disagree with you. So whatever arrangements or plans you are making for her, make sure that she is in favor, otherwise you will be very disappointed. If her mother were alive, it would be quite a different matter, but as it is she is no longer with us and you know that . . . "

"Uloma, that will do. Adaeze is not your daughter, she is my daughter, the daughter of my favorite wife. Just as her mother obeyed me in all things, so will Adaeze obey me in all things. I spoke to her when I was in London. I told her my plans for her. She listened, and said nothing. And as you know, silence means consent."

"Our father, this may not be so. You were far away from home. You had gone over there to be treated. She did not want to upset you. That was why she was silent. When she returns home, you will see. Make allowances for her, or else you will be disappointed."

"I have heard you, now out of my presence. I don't know how you thought you could tell me what to do. Adaeze is my daughter. She will do what I want her to do. She will marry no one, I say."

Uloma took leave of her husband and the Chief was alone. Adaeze was the Chief's first daughter, whose mother he had loved and admired. She died prematurely having her second child. The Chief had many wives but few children. His people said he was not blessed with children. His "chi"[1] gave him wealth but did not give him plenty of children. This lack of many children did not bother the Chief too much. Surely, he thought, ten children between four wives was quite a good number for him though other Chiefs like him had up to twenty-five. What really bothered him was that none of his four sons showed signs of ever carrying on his businesses after he was gone.

It was only his beloved Adaeze who proved, if proof was needed, that she was the offspring of the Chief. She was every inch her father. She was so like him that the Chief kept asking his "chi" why it did not make her a man so as to replace him. Adaeze was as intelligent as her father, hard-working and industrious. Before she went abroad, when she was home on holidays, she was always with her father. She took interest in his business and she offered advice, which though sometimes childish, impressed the Chief so much that he was very proud of his Adaeze.

The Chief did not understand what Uloma was saying to him. Surely Uloma his dear wife was not a stranger in their village. Surely she did not go to school, so she was not spoiled by the so-called Western Civilization. Surely she knew that it was the practice in their native land for a favorite daughter to remain at her father's home married to no one, but to have children who answered her father's name. Surely this custom was still carried out in their village in spite of the missionaries and their strange ways.

The Chief's mind went to the missionaries who taught them how to read and write. He chuckled to himself when he remembered their religion. How ignorant they were to think that it was their religion that brought his people nearer to the white missionaries. Their religion had nothing to do with it. It

---

[1]One's personal god. [eds.]

was the education they offered that made the Chief's father send his son to school. Their religion was strange. Imagine loving your enemy and doing good to those who hated you. The accepted thing was to hate your enemy and wish him dead.

The Chief remembered his childhood friend who died before he had a child by his wife. His sister supported his widowed wife, and she in turn stayed and bore sons and daughters for her husband who was long dead. His friend could not just die like that and his name die with him. His sister did the best thing a sister could do.

Then the Chief's mind went to his four sons, and he shook his head in regret. Why did fate treat him so? He thought of his first son. He was only ten when the war broke out. They had fled from Onitsha to a refugee camp when the Federal troops overran Onitsha. He had found it extremely difficult to keep track of his son. His mother was not of any help because she was too busy with the "attack trade" to know where her son was or what he did. So unknown to them, the Chief's son disappeared. Nobody knew where he went. The Chief went from one refugee camp to the other in search of him. It was after five days that he was told that his ten-year old son had joined the army and was in fact the batman of a Major who was fighting at the Onitsha war front.

The Chief knew all the service chiefs in the army. So it was easy for him to retrieve his son and bring him back to the refugee camp where they were all staying. The other sons were equally unrully, and when the war ended, none of them went back to school. The Chief tried to make them see reason, but they had all turned a deaf ear. So he let them be, and concentrated all his attention, and love, on his first daughter, Adaeze.

What then was Uloma telling him? Who was Adaeze's father? Surely he was. He sent her abroad. She would do what he wanted her to do. She would marry no one.

Soon it was time for Adaeze to return home. Her fiancé was already home and they had agreed that he would go to her father and ask for Adaeze's hand in marriage. Ezenta, Adaeze's fiancé was a good man who was genuinely in love with Adaeze. He knew the problem and determined to solve it. So when he returned, he told his own parents about Adaeze. His mother would not hear of it. "No, my son, you are not going to marry the daughter of Chief Onyeka. The Chief wants to marry his own daughter himself. So please let us look for another girl for you. I have been thinking of the daughter of Chief Ezeora, you know her? She is not an illiterate. She is most suitable. I have confided in her mother and she was thrilled. Please forget about the daughter of Chief Onyeka. He is a difficult man. She would not do. We would be in serious trouble if we went for his daughter, please my son."

Ezenta's father was not as opposed as his mother. He was an easy-going man who treated everyone on his merit.

"We should not visit the sins of the father on the daughter, my wife," he said. "And remember how opposed your own father was to our marriage. The children are young, let them handle their own affairs themselves."

"Ezenta's father," Ezenta's mother said. "You know the Chief very well. You know how powerful he is, so please let us persuade our Ezenta to turn his attention to someone else. The Chief has had a lot of problems. Look at his sons. How many of them is he proud of? None. He wanted to make his daughter his son. Nobody is quarrelling with that. It is an old custom of our people. But we should talk our Ezenta out of the whole thing that's all."

And so there was opposition on both sides. Ezenta had to travel back to England to report to Adaeze that he had not made any headway with his parents, not to talk of her own father, the Chief, who did not even want to see him.

So Adaeze and Ezenta got married quietly in London and Adaeze went home to confront her father.

The Chief was happy to see her, but he did not like the way she came back unannounced. Surely if his daughter were away in England for over six years, he should tell the whole world that she had returned with the golden fleece. There would be a big party for her and a big thanksgiving service. Adaeze had spoiled everything by coming home like a thief.

"What do you think you are doing?" he asked Adaeze after embracing her.

"Papa, please. I know you like noise, I don't like noise. You know that things like this don't appeal to me at all."

"Things like what?" the Chief asked.

"Like thanksgiving and parties and all that."

"Hee, say that again Adaeze, say that again. Aren't you my daughter? Am I supposed not to make merry when my own daughter returns from the land of the white people? Did I send you to the land of the white people so that you would steal into my compound unannounced. Was that . . . "

"Our father, it is enough. It is enough. Our father, you must realize that Adaeze is a mere child. She does not understand. She has lived in the white man's land for a long time, and so she should be taught gradually how to behave as our people do. Adaeze," Uloma said, turning to her. "Come, my daughter. Come to my apartment. You are like a child. You should have sent us word that you were coming home. Our people don't behave in the strange ways the white people do. Your father is angry with you. Come with me. Come and rest. Soon your father will be calm again, and we can talk."

The following Sunday, there was a Thanksgiving service in the local church. Chief Onyeka sent out hundreds of invitations to friends, relations and well wishers. Cows were slaughtered and the people made merry. Everybody was impressed with Adaeze. The pastor who delivered the sermon was particularly pleased because not only had Adaeze returned with the golden fleece, but she had returned single. Adaeze was not like other girls before her, who forgot where they came from because they were privileged to go to the land of the white people. The pastor referred to those wrong-headed girls who unknown to their parents got married overseas. He wondered who gave them away. It was a shame that they forgot the customs of the people, and behaved as if they had no homes.

Adaeze, the daughter of Chief Onyeka, had proved a shining example for all the boys and girls of the whole clan to emulate. He wished the family well. He prayed that God should give Adaeze a good husband worthy of her, who would respect and love her . . .

The congregation forgot that they were in church. They began to clap. Adaeze could not help smiling to herself. She was not particularly happy about the thanksgiving service. But her father's wife, Uloma, had persuaded her to go, because it would please her father. Her father's wife had brought out some beautiful "gorge" for her with matching lace blouse and headtie. But Adaeze in her strange way, would have none of that. She came to church, such a big occasion, in a two-piece dress with a funny hat. Her cousins, and she had plenty of them, were most unhappy about her outfit. So as soon as the service was over, they went straight to her father's wife, and demanded to know why they were not told that Uloma had no "gorge" to give to Adaeze to wear, but must allow her to appear in church in such an atrocious attire. Uloma knew her in-laws well enough not to be offended. She explained to them and they shrugged their shoulders. If Adaeze wanted to appear in that shabby outfit, that was her funeral, not theirs.

Meanwhile, Chief Onyeka was in the vestry castigating the pastor for his sermon. Had he never heard that his daughter Adaeze would marry no one? Had he never heard that there was nobody in the entire clan who was good enough for his daughter? The bewildered pastor apologized profusely and the Chief stormed out of the vestry.

In the evening when the merriment was over, Chief Onyeka called Adaeze to his bedroom and sat her down. He reminded her of their conversation when he was in London. He told her that he was serious. That he had made her a director in his numerous companies and that he would provide for her and her offspring. So . . .

"My offsprings who would be bastards?" she queried.

"Will you keep quiet. You are my . . . "

"I will not keep quiet, I am your daughter, all right. I am not a bastard. You married my mother, didn't you?"

"Will you keep quiet, I say or . . . "

"Father, I demand to know whether you married my mother or not. I am not your wife, I am not your son. I am only a girl, your daughter, and if I don't marry Ezenta, you have lost me forever. You will not see my face again. I shall disappear from the face of the earth. I shall kill myself and kill you, I shall oh . . . Come over here, my father's wife. Come, my father wants me to be a prostitute. Was my mother a prostitute? Didn't my father marry her the traditional way? What kind of custom does my father want to practice? Tell me, tell me, my father's wife, for I am confused. I am lost. I am . . . "

Everybody in the clan heard of the quarrel between father and daughter. The Chief's wife, Uloma, thought she must act or else there could be bloodshed. She knew her husband very well. She knew that he would never say yes to any man who wanted his daughter's hand in marriage. The Chief could not bear to see Adaeze the wife of anyone be he a millionaire's son or the President's son.

So she went to Chief Ezeora, the childhood friend of her husband. The Chief was in when she arrived.

"*Eze Uri,*" Uloma greeted him.

"*Odoze aku,*"[2] the Chief replied. "You are so early. I hope all is well." He knew of course that all was not well. He had heard of the violent quarrel between his friend and his daughter.

"All is not well, our father. Your friend wants to marry his own daughter. Please come and put sense into him. Tell him that times have changed. Tell him that he sent Adaeze to the land of the white people to improve herself and all of us. That he did not send her there to behave like us in this clan. Tell him to allow her to marry whom she wants to marry."

The Chief cleared his throat. He thanked Uloma for coming to see him. He too had tried like a friend to convince his friend that what he had planned for his daughter was difficult for her. He had told him that if he were not careful, that he would lose his daughter for ever. The Chief promised to see his friend again.

Both Chiefs exchanged greetings in the usual manner and went straight to the problem. Adaeze's father said he could not bear to see Adaeze get married. He wanted her to take care of his home, and that was that.

Adaeze was called. She knelt before her father and his friend. She appealed to her father to let her go.

"Please let me go. I am already married to Ezenta. We married in the Registry and I am expecting his baby," said Adaeze.

"Now you are talking. That's exactly what I want, a baby. You will have the baby in this house, and he will be my baby. Marriage in the Registry? That can be taken care of. There is no problem at all. This is exactly what I want. I did not say you were not to have children. I said you would marry no one. No husband would care for you the way I would care for you. Please stay with your father," Adaeze's father pleaded.

---

[2]*Eze Uri:* King of Uri; *Odoze aku:* a title for a good wife, who takes care of her husband's possessions, which includes family. [eds.]

Chief Ezeora interrupted. "Listen, my friend. Your daughter has said that she is already married to Ezenta. Don't you know Ezenta? I begged you to see him when he came from the land of the white people, but you refused. They are now married. That is what your daughter is saying to you."

"And that is exactly what I am saying. Marriage in the Registry? Nonsense. I can take care of that."

"The marriage was in the land of the white people, not in Nigeria, and you can do nothing," said the Chief's friend.

"Try to understand me, my friend," Adaeze's father continued. "If you say, you are not well, you are not. Adaeze will say that she was not married in the Registry. That is that. There is no problem."

"If her husband took offense and took her to court?"

"You are now talking. There are lawyers. Marriage can be dissolved any day. I'll take care of that."

"And if I say no?" Adaeze said. She was boiling with anger. She was beginning to dislike her father. She used to be very fond of him when she was a child. To her, in those childhood days, her father was solid and powerful, he did no wrong. Anybody who got on the wrong side of her father deserved it. Her father was upright, he was just. He was her father, so he had to have these qualities.

Therefore like the true daughter of her father, she had inherited his stubbornness and his iron will. But, her education abroad had taught her that she must play her cards well. She must not confront her father. Nobody, she remembered from her childhood days, who confronted her father, ever got what they wanted. So she was not going to use confrontation to fight her father. She would use her common sense, her education and her charm.

So she apologized and said instead, "I understand you my dear father," she said. "I did not mean it when I said that I was married to Ezenta. I could not have done such a foolish thing without your consent. You should have asked me who gave me away. And my dear father . . . "

"Exactly, my daughter. Didn't I say you were my devoted daughter. That was why I treated the registry nonsense the way I did. I knew you were merely pulling my leg. You are every inch your mother. She was a delightful creature. She was always pulling my leg. She had a tremendous sense of humor. My friend, you have heard my daughter. You can take your leave so that father and daughter can talk in confidence."

Chief Ezeora, of course, understood from Adaeze's eyes. The Chief was autocratic in his arrogant ways; he did not know that he was being fooled by no other person than his beloved daughter.

The following weeks were spent by father and daughter in the latter's office. The Chief was teaching Adaeze. He showed her the books that were kept for different businesses; the businesses that made profit and so on. Adaeze was intrigued. She asked questions that pleased her father. She made suggestions which her father jumped at and implemented forthwith and got favorable results therefrom.

But Adaeze thought of a way to escape from the clutches of her father. Besides, her pregnancy was developing fast. Soon, she would be unable to follow her father on his numerous tours.

The opportunity came when her father travelled to Kano. She confided in her father's wife, Uloma, who was afraid of the Chief's wrath when he returned. In just under twenty-four hours after her father's departure to Kano, Adaeze was with Ezenta in London. In a matter of days, they had left London and left no forwarding address.

"Is my daughter in?" the Chief inquired as soon as he returned from Kano.

"Let me see, our father. Welcome home, our father," Uloma said. She was always there when the Chief was around. Other wives did not show their faces when the Chief was around. If he wanted them, he sent for them.

"Our father," said Uloma "I cannot find Adaeze. She was here a while ago. Shall I bring you something to drink? Adaeze will be back soon."

"Can't you ask someone to look for her. You said she did not go far. And here, here is my briefcase, take it to the room. I have money in it. And now . . . who is there? I never see anyone to do anything for me when I come to my own home. Where is the driver?"

"Our father, you asked him to go. He has gone," Uloma said.

"Have you asked someone to look for my Adaeze, woman?"

"Someone has gone, our master. Sit down and take it easy. You have just returned from a far place. You are tired. Drink something, put up your feet on the cushion and relax."

"While I wait for Adaeze?"

"Yes, my master, while you wait for your beloved Adaeze," Uloma said.

But Adaeze didn't come. The Chief was alarmed. He went to Adaeze's room and found it empty of Adaeze's possessions.

"Where is my daughter?" he shouted. The whole household was frightened. All knew what had happened but none wanted to be a scapegoat. The chief received no answer. "Am I not in my own house? Uloma, where are you?" But Uloma had long disappeared from the scene. The Chief then understood.

The driver had gone. All the Chief could do was take the car to the airport. He must stop his daughter. He found his keys. He jumped into the car, put the key in the ignition. The car would not start. When did he last drive himself? He could not remember.

He removed the key. He opened the door of the car, got out, went to his room and wept. Uloma came in, knelt before him and said, "Our father, times have changed. Adaeze is your daughter, you sent her to the land of the white people. She went there and learned their strange ways. You have not lost her. She is still yours. Try and understand her, she can still be very useful to you, because she is a good woman like her mother. She is still the Chief's daughter."

✸ Discussion and Writing

1. Identify and comment on the central conflict in "The Chief's Daughter." Interpret the resolution of the conflict sought by the young couple.
2. Distinguish between the two women, Uloma and Adaeze, in terms of their relations with each other and with men.
3. Is the chief traditional: why or why not? Analyze the inherent incongruity in his treatment of his daughter; what is the source of this incongruity?

✸ Research and Comparison

Compare the resolutions of the complex conflicts in Grace Ogot's story "The Rain Came" and Flora Nwapa's "The Chief's Daughter." Examine the conflicts between: traditionalism and modernization; custom and colonialism; communal obligation and personal need; and generational perceptions within a culture.

Interdisciplinary Discussion Question: Explore the issue of women's rights and polygamy in the context of West Africa. Compare the treatment of this subject by Flora Nwapa and other women writers such as Buchi Emecheta and Mariama Ba.

Tchicaya U Tam'si
(1931–1988)
Congo

Felix Tchicaya U Tam'si was born in Mpili in what was then the French Congo. He never knew his mother. His father was the first black deputy for the Middle Congo elected to the French National Assembly, and when U Tam'si was 15, he moved with his father to France, where he took his baccalaureate. U Tam'si worked at odd jobs after finishing his studies (as a warehouseman, farmhand, and restaurant porter), and published his first book of poetry when he was 24. He took a writing and producing job in broadcasting, a position frequently available to French-educated writers of African descent. Along with writing poetry, plays, novels, and stories, he

adapted countless African traditional stories for French radio; and he
worked as an official for UNESCO. He also spent a brief but profoundly
affecting time as chief editor of the pro-Lumumba paper *Le Congo,* in
what is now Kinshasa, Zaire. The hope for uniting a truly independent
Congo nation crystallized around Patrice Lumumba, the first prime minister of the Republic of the Congo, now Zaire. U Tam'si witnessed the defeat
of Lumumba, his escape from the capital where he was surrounded, his
capture, torture, and martyrdom.

Lumumba represented for U Tam'si, as for thousands of anonymous
poets throughout Africa, the very image of the betrayed hero. U Tam'si took
up the issue of African betrayal as well. A dominant motif of betrayal, loss,
and deprivation runs through his work, reaching back to his sense of
himself as an orphan and an exile. But he has an ironic voice, one that
prohibits self-pity. In this way, his poetry extends beyond the personal to
experiences common to the colonized peoples of Africa. He came to think
of himself, despite his exile, as a *griot,* a poet-musician. He was considered the major Francophone poet of his time.

*Brush-Fire**

The fire the river that's to say
the sea to drink following the sand
the feet the hands
within the heart to love
this river that lives in me repeoples me
only to you I said around the fire

my race
it flows here and there a river
the flames are the looks
of those who brood upon it
I said to you
my race
remembers
the taste of bronze drunk hot.

❀ Discussion and Writing

1. What does the fire symbolize in the poem?
2. Examine the image of the river as a motif in the poem. Discuss the
   impact of the fusion of the images of the river and the fire.
3. Discuss the implications of "the taste of bronze drunk hot."

*Translated by Ulli Beier

❋ Research and Comparison

Examine Tchicaya U Tam'si's works and comment on his themes and concerns. Discuss also the expression of *negritude* in his work.

Athol Fugard (b. 1932), John Kani (b. 1943), and Winston Ntshona (b. 1942?) South Africa

John Kani and Winston Ntshona were born in Port Elizabeth, South Africa. Harold Athol Fugard was born in the village of Middleburg, South Africa, where his parents owned a small general store. His father was of Afrikaner descent, and his mother was an English-speaking South African. When Fugard was three years old, the family moved to Port Elizabeth, the city to which he has always returned. He studied philosophy and social anthropology at the University of Cape Town and worked for two years as a seaman in East Asia. He began working in the theater after his return, forming an experimental theatrical group with his wife (Sheila Fugard, herself a known writer), and then took a job as a clerk in the Native Commissioner's Court in Johannesburg, where he witnessed the way the laws requiring black South Africans to carry passbooks were enforced. (The passbook indicated where a person could live, work, or travel, and violating any restriction resulted in imprisonment.) It was at this time that he began to portray life in the black townships. The casts he assembled were almost completely nonprofessional, and often the dramas developed as impromptu exercises. Thus began a pattern that persisted in Fugard's career as producer, director, actor, and playwright.

When Fugard's theater group, the Rehearsal Room, produced his play *The Blood Knot* (1963), people of all races could still appear on the same stage and before audiences of all races. By 1965, the government had prohibited mixed casts and public perfomances before mixed audiences. His Port Elizabeth group, the Serpent Players, was denied permission to perform publicly for whites, and was confined mainly to touring the black neighborhoods. And in the climate of the Vorster government of the late 1960s and 1970s many in the group were harassed by the police or imprisoned.

John Kani and Winston Ntshona were members of the Serpent Players. The group provided them with both the place and the atmosphere to create

"The Island" and "Sizwe Banzi Is Dead," the works that gained them recognition in the United States and England as well as in South Africa. The plays have an immediacy; they are imbued with Kani's and Ntshona's heartache, anger, and, at the same time, humor. After a time, they toured with "The Island" and "Sizwe Banzi Is Dead." In 1974, they won the Antoinette Perry Award for their performances. Kani and Ntshona collaborated with Fugard in the writing of the plays, and he saw to their being published.

The Island

CHARACTERS

JOHN AND WINSTON (TWO PRISONERS)

This play was given its first performance on 2 July 1973, directed by Athol Fugard with John Kani as John and Winston Ntshona as Winston.

Scene One

Center stage: a raised area representing a cell on Robben Island. Blankets and sleeping-mats—the prisoners sleep on the floor—are neatly folded. In one corner are a bucket of water and two tin mugs.

The long drawn-out wail of a siren. Stage-lights come up to reveal a moat of harsh, white light around the cell. In it the two prisoners—John stage-right and Winston stage-left—mime the digging of sand. They wear the prison uniform of khaki shirt and short trousers. Their heads are shaven. It is an image of back-breaking and grotesquely futile labor. Each in turns fills a wheelbarrow and then with great effort pushes it to where the other man is digging, and empties it. As a result, the piles of sand never diminish. Their labor is interminable. The only sounds are their grunts as they dig, the squeal of the wheelbarrows as they circle the cell, and the hum of Hodoshe, the green carrion fly.

A whistle is blown. They stop digging and come together, standing side by side as they are handcuffed together and shackled at the ankles. Another whistle. They start to run . . . John mumbling a prayer, Winston muttering a rhythm for their three-legged run.

They do not run fast enough. They get beaten . . . Winston receiving a bad blow to the eye and John spraining an ankle. In this condition they arrive finally at the cell door. Handcuffs and shackles are taken off. After being searched, they lurch into their cell. The door closes behind them. Both men sink to the floor.

A moment of total exhaustion until slowly, painfully, they start to explore their respective injuries . . . Winston his eye, and John his ankle. Winston is moaning softly and this eventually draws John's attention away from his ankle. He crawls to Winston and examines the injured eye. It needs attention. Winston's moaning is slowly turning into a sound of inarticulate outrage, growing in volume and violence. John urinates into one hand and tries to clean the other man's eye with it, but Winston's anger and outrage are now uncontrollable. He breaks away from John and crawls around the cell, blind with rage and pain. John tries to placate him . . . the noise could bring back the warders and still more trouble. Winston eventually finds the cell door but before he can start banging on it John pulls him away.

WINSTON *(calling):* Hodoshe!

JOHN. Leave him, Winston. Listen to me, man! If he comes now we'll be in bigger shit.

WINSTON: I want Hodoshe. I want him now! I want to take him to the office. He must read my warrant. I was sentenced to Life brother, not bloody Death!

JOHN: Please, Winston! He made us run. . . .

WINSTON: I want Hodoshe!

JOHN: He made us run. He's happy now. Leave him. Maybe he'll let us go back to the quarry tomorrow. . . .

(Winston is suddenly silent. For a moment John thinks his words are having an effect, but then he realizes that the other man is looking at his ear. Winston touches it. It is bleeding. A sudden spasm of fear from John, who puts a hand to his ear. His fingers come away with blood on them. The two men look at each other.)

WINSTON: *Nyana we Sizwe!*[1]

(In a reversal of earlier roles Winston now gets John down on the floor of the cell so as to examine the injured ear. He has to wipe blood and sweat out of his eyes in order to see clearly. John winces with pain. Winston keeps restraining him.)

WINSTON *(eventually):* It's not too bad. *(Using his shirt-tail he cleans the injured ear.)*

JOHN *(through clenched teeth as Winston tends his ear):* Hell, *ons was gemoer vandag!* *(A weak smile.)* News bulletin and weather forecast! Black Domination was chased by White Domination. Black Domination lost its shoes and collected a few bruises. Black Domination will run barefoot to the quarry tomorrow. Conditions locally remain unchanged—thunderstorms with the possibility of cold showers and rain. Elsewhere, fine and warm!

(Winston has now finished tending John's ear and settles down on the floor beside him. He clears his nose, ears, and eyes of sand.)

WINSTON: Sand! Same old sea sand I used to play with when I was young. St George's Strand. New Year's Day. Sand dunes. Sand castles. . . .

JOHN: *Ja;*[2] we used to go there too. Last. . . . *(Pause and then a small laugh. He shakes his head.)* The Christmas before they arrested me, we were down

---

[1]Brothers of the land.
[2]Yes

there. All of us. Honeybush. My little Monde played in the sand. We'd given her one of those little buckets and spades for Christmas.

WINSTON: *Ja.*

JOHN: Anyway, it was Daddy's turn today. (*Shaking his head ruefully.*) Haai,[3] Winston, this one goes on the record. 'Struesgod! I'm a man, brother. A man! But if Hodoshe had kept us at those wheelbarrows five minutes longer . . . ! There would have been a baby on the Island tonight. I nearly cried.

WINSTON: *Ja.*

JOHN: There was no end to it, except one of us!

WINSTON: That's right.

JOHN: This morning when he said: "You two! The beach!". . . I thought, Okay, so it's my turn to empty the sea into a hole. He likes that one. But when he pointed to the wheelbarrows, and I saw his idea . . . ! (*Shaking his head.*) I laughed at first. Then I wasn't laughing. Then I hated you. You looked so stupid, *broer!*

WINSTON: That's what he wanted.

JOHN: It was going to last forever, man! Because of *you.* And for *you,* because of *me. Moer!*[4] He's cleverer than I thought.

WINSTON: If he was God, he would have done it.

JOHN: What?

WINSTON: Broken us. Men get tired. Hey! There's a thought. We're still alive because Hodoshe got tired.

JOHN: Tomorrow?

WINSTON: We'll see.

JOHN: If he takes us back there . . . If I hear that wheelbarrow . . . of yours again, coming with another bloody load of . . . eternity!

WINSTON (*with calm resignation*): We'll see.

(*Pause. John looks at Winston.*)

JOHN (*with quiet emphasis, as if the other man did not fully understand the significance of what he had said*): I *hated* you Winston.

WINSTON (*meeting John's eyes*): I hated *you.*

(*John puts a hand on Winston's shoulder. Their brotherhood is intact. He gets slowly to his feet.*)

JOHN: Where's the *lap?*[5]

WINSTON: Somewhere. Look for it.

---

[3]Hai haai: exclamation of surprise.
[4]Literally womb; used as a swear-word equivalent to "fuck," "fucking."
[5]Lap; lappie: rag

JOHN: Hey! You had it last.

(*Limping around the cell looking for their washrag.*)

WINSTON: *Haai,* man! You got no wife here. Look for the rag yourself.

JOHN (*finding the rag beside the water bucket*): Look where it is. Look! Hodoshe comes in here and sees it. "Whose *lappie* is that?" Then what do you say?

WINSTON: "It's his rag, sir."

JOHN: Yes? Okay. "It's my rag, sir." When you wash, use your shirt.

WINSTON: Okay, okay! 'It's our rag, sir!"

JOHN: That will be the bloody day!

(*John, getting ready to wash, starts to take off his shirt. Winston produces a cigarette butt, matches, and flint from their hiding-place under the water bucket. He settles down for a smoke.*)

Shit, today was long. Hey, Winston, suppose the watch of the chap behind the siren is slow! We could still be there, man! (*He pulls out three or four rusty nails from a secret pocket in his trousers. He holds them out to Winston.*) Hey there.

WINSTON: What?

JOHN: With the others.

WINSTON (*taking the nails*): What's this?

JOHN: Necklace, man. With the others.

WINSTON: Necklace?

JOHN: Antigone's necklace.

WINSTON: *Ag,* shit, man! (*Slams the nails down on the cell floor and goes on smoking.*) Antigone! Go to hell, man, John.

JOHN: Hey, don't start any nonsense now. You promised. (*Limps over to Winston's bed-roll and produces a half-completed necklace made of nails and string.*) It's nearly finished. Look.Three fingers, one nail . . . three fingers, one nail . . . (*Places the necklace beside Winston, who is shaking his head, smoking aggressively, and muttering away.*) Don't start any nonsense now, Winston. There's six days to go to the concert. We're committed. We promised the chaps we'd do something. This *Antigone* is just right for us. Six more days and we'll make it.

(*He continues washing.*)

WINSTON: Jesus, John! We were down on the beach today. Hodoshe made us run. Can't you just leave a man . . . ?

JOHN: To hell with you! Who do you think ran with you? I'm also tired, but we can't back out now. Come on! Three fingers. . . .

WINSTON: . . . one nail! *(Shaking his head.) Haai . . . haai . . . haai!*

JOHN: Stop moaning and get on with it. Shit, Winston! What sort of progress is this? *(Abandoning his wash.)* Listen. Listen! Number 42 is practicing the Zulu War Dance. Down there they're rehearsing their songs. It's just in this *moer* cell that there's always an argument. Today you want to do it, tomorrow you don't want to do it. How the hell must I know what to report to the chaps tomorrow if we go back to the quarry?

(Winston is unyielding. His obstinacy gets the better of John, who eventually throws the wash-rag at him.)

There! Wash!

(John applies himself to the necklace while Winston, still muttering away in an undertone, starts to clean himself.)

How can I be sure of anything when you carry on like this? We've still got to learn the words, the moves. Shit! It could be so bloody good, man.

(Winston mutters protests all the way through this speech of John's. The latter holds up the necklace.)

Nearly finished! Look at it! Three fingers. . . .

WINSTON: . . . . . one nail.

JOHN: *Ja!* Simple. Do you still remember all I told you yesterday? Bet you've bloody forgotten. How can I carry on like this? I can't move on, man. Over the whole bloody lot again! Who Antigone is . . . who Creon is. . . .

WINSTON: Antigone is mother to Polynices. . . .

JOHN: *Haai, haai, haai* . . . shit, Winston! *(Now really exasperated.)* How many times must I tell you that Antigone is the sister to the two brothers? Not the mother. That's another play.

WINSTON: Oh.

JOHN: That's all you know! "Oh." *(He abandons the necklace and fishes out a piece of chalk from a crack in the floor.)* Come here. This is the last time. 'Struesgod. The last time.

WINSTON: *Ag.* no, John.

JOHN: Come! I'm putting this plot down for the last time! If you don't learn it tonight I'm going to report you to the old men tomorrow. And remember, *broer,*[6] those old men will make Hodoshe and his tricks look like a little boy.

WINSTON: Jesus Christ! Learn to dig for Hodoshe, learn to run for Hodoshe, and what happens when I get back to the cell? Learn to read *Antigone!*

---

[6]Brother.

JOHN: Come! And shut up! *(He pulls the reluctant Winston down beside him on the floor. Winston continues to clean himself with the rag while John lays out the "plot" of Antigone.)* If you would just stop moaning, you would learn faster. Now listen!

WINSTON: Okay, do it.

JOHN: Listen! It is the Trial of Antigone. Right?

WINSTON: So you say.

JOHN: First, the accused. Who is the accused?

WINSTON: Antigone.

JOHN: Coming from you that's bloody progress. *(Writing away on the cell floor with his chalk.)* Next the State. Who is the State?

WINSTON: Creon.

JOHN: King Creon. Creon is the State. Now . . . what did Antigone do?

WINSTON: Antigone buried her brother Eteocles.

JOHN: No, no, no! Shit, Winston, when are you going to remember this thing? I told you, man, Antigone buried Polynices. The traitor! The one who I said was on *our* side. Right?

WINSTON: Right.

JOHN: Stage one of the Trial. *(Writing on the floor.)* The State lays its charges against the Accused . . . and lists counts . . . you know the way they do it. Stage two is Pleading. What does Antigone plead? Guilty or Not Guilty?

WINSTON: Not Guilty.

JOHN *(trying to be tactful):* Now look, Winston, we're not going to argue. Between me and you, in this cell, we know she's Not Guilty. But in the play she pleads Guilty.

WINSTON: No, man, John! Antigone is Not Guilty. . . .

JOHN: In the play. . . .

WINSTON *(losing his temper):* To hell with the play! Antigone had every right to bury her brother.

JOHN: Don't say "To hell with the play." We've got to do the bloody thing. And in the play she pleads Guilty. Get that straight. Antigone pleads. . . .

WINSTON *(giving up in disgust):* Okay, do it your way.

JOHN: It's not my way! In the play. . . .

WINSTON: Guilty!

JOHN: Yes, Guilty!

(Writes furiously on the floor.)

WINSTON: Guilty.

JOHN: Stage three, Pleading in Mitigation of Sentence. Stage four, Sentence, State Summary, and something from you . . . Farewell Words. Now learn that.

WINSTON: Hey?

JOHN *(getting up):* Learn that!

WINSTON: But we've just done it!

JOHN: *I've* just done it. Now *you* learn it.

WINSTON *(throwing aside the wash-rag with disgust before applying himself to learning the "plot"):* Learn to run, learn to read. . . .

JOHN: And don't throw the rag there! *(Retrieving the rag and placing it in its correct place.)* Don't be so bloody difficult, man. We're nearly there. You'll be proud of this thing when we've done it.

> *(Limps to his bed-roll and produces a pendant made from a jam-tin lid and twine.)* Look. Winston, look! Creon's medallion. Good, hey! *(Hangs it around his neck.)* I'll finish the necklace while you learn that. *(He strings on the remaining nails.)* Jesus, Winston! June 1965.

WINSTON: What?

JOHN: This, man. *Antigone.* In New Brighton. St. Stephen's Hall. The place was packed, man! All the big people. Front row . . . dignitaries. Shit, those were the days. Georgie was Creon. You know Georgie?

WINSTON: The teacher?

JOHN: That's him. He played Creon. Should have seen him, Winston. Short and fat, with big eyes, but by the time the play was finished he was as tall as the roof.

(Onto his legs in an imitation of Georgie's Creon.)

"My Councillors, now that the Gods have brought our City safe through a storm of troubles to tranquillity. . . ." And old Mulligan! Another short-arsed teacher. With a beard! He used to go up to the Queen. . . . *(Another imitation.)* "Your Majesty, prepare for grief, but do not weep."

(The necklace in his hands.)

Nearly finished!
Nomhle played Antigone. A bastard of a lady that one, but a beautiful bitch. Can't get her out of my mind tonight.

WINSTON *(indicating the "plot"):* I know this.

JOHN: You sure?

WINSTON: This! . . . it's here. *(Tapping his head.)*

JOHN: You're not bullshitting, hey? *(He rubs out the "plot" and then paces the cell.)* Right. The Trial of Antigone. Who is the Accused?

WINSTON: Antigone.

JOHN: Who is the State?

WINSTON: King Creon.

JOHN: Stage one.

WINSTON *(supremely self-confident):* Antigone lays charges. . . .

JOHN: NO, SHIT, MAN, WINSTON!!!

(Winston pulls John down and stifles his protests with a hand over his mouth.)

WINSTON: Okay . . . okay . . . listen, John . . . listen. . . . The State lays charges against Antigone.

(Pause.)

JOHN: Be careful!

WINSTON: The State lays charges against Antigone.

JOHN: Stage two.

WINSTON: Pleading.

JOHN: What does she plead? Guilty or Not Guilty?

WINSTON: Guilty.

JOHN: Stage three.

WINSTON: Pleading in Mitigation of Sentence.

JOHN: Stage four.

WINSTON: State Summary, Sentence, and Farewell Words.

JOHN *(very excited):* He's got it! That's my man. See how easy it is, Winston? Tomorrow, just the words.

(Winston gets onto his legs, John puts away the props. Mats and blankets are unrolled. The two men prepare for sleep.)

JOHN: Hell, I hope we go back to the quarry tomorrow. There's still a lot of things we need for props and costumes. Your wig! The boys in Number Fourteen said they'd try and smuggle me a piece of rope from the jetty.

WINSTON: *Ja,* I hope we're back there. I want to try and get some tobacco through to Sipho.

JOHN: Sipho?

WINSTON: Back in solitary.

JOHN: Again!

WINSTON: *Ja.*

JOHN: Oh hell!

WINSTON: Simon passed the word.

JOHN: What was it this time?

WINSTON: Complained about the food I think. Demanded to see the book of Prison Regulations.

JOHN: Why don't they leave him alone for a bit?

WINSTON: Because he doesn't leave them alone.

JOHN: You're right. I'm glad I'm not in Number Twenty-two with him. One man starts getting hard-arsed like that and the whole lot of you end up in the shit.

(Winston's bed is ready. He lies down.)

You know what I'm saying?

WINSTON: *Ja.*

JOHN: What?

WINSTON: What "What"?

JOHN: What am I saying?

WINSTON: *Haai,* Johnny, man! I'm tired now! Let a man. . . .

JOHN: I'm saying Don't Be Hard-Arsed! You! When Hodoshe opens that door tomorrow say "*Ja, Baas*" the right way. I don't want to be back on that bloody beach tomorrow just because you feel like being difficult.

WINSTON (*wearily*): Okay, man, Johnny.

JOHN: You're not alone in this cell. I'm here too.

WINSTON: Jesus, you think I don't know that!

JOHN: People must remember their responsibilities to others.

WINSTON: I'm glad to hear you say that, because I was just going to remind you that it is your turn tonight.

JOHN: What do you mean? Wasn't it my turn last night?

WINSTON (*shaking his head emphatically*): Haai, haai. Don't you remember? Last night I took you to bioscope.[7]

JOHN: Hey, by the way! So you did. Bloody good film too. "Fastest Gun in the West." Glenn Ford.

(*Whips out a six-shooter and guns down a few bad-men.*)

You were bullshitting me a bit though. How the hell can Glenn Ford shoot backward through his legs. I tried to work that one out on the beach.

(*He is now seated on his bed-roll. After a moment's thought he holds up an empty mug as a telephone-receiver and starts to dial. Winston watches him with puzzlement.*)

Operator, put me through to New Brighton, please . . . yes, New Brighton, Port Elizabeth. The number is 414624. . . . Yes, mine is local . . . local. . . .

WINSTON: (*recognizing the telephone number*). The Shop!

(*He sits upright with excitement as John launches into the telephone conversation.*)

JOHN: That you Scott? Hello, man! Guess who! . . . You got it! You bastard! Hell, shit, Scott, man . . . how things with you? No, still inside. Give me the news, man . . . you don't say! No, we don't hear anything here . . . not a word. . . . What's that? Business is bad? . . . You bloody undertaker! People aren't dying fast enough! No, things are fine here. . . .

(*Winston, squirming with excitement, has been trying unsuccessfully to interrupt John's torrent of words and laughter. He finally succeeds in drawing John's attention.*)

WINSTON: Who else is there? Who's with Scott?

---

[7]The movies.

JOHN: Hey, Scott, who's there with you? . . . Oh no! . . . call him to the phone, man. . . .

WINSTON: Who's it?

JOHN *(ignoring Winston):* Just for a minute, man, please, Scott. . . .

(Ecstatic response from John as another voice comes over the phone.)

Hello there, you beautiful bastard . . . how's it, man?. . .

WINSTON: Who the hell is it, man?

JOHN *(hand over the receiver):* Sky!

(Winston can no longer contain his excitement. He scrambles out of his bed to join John, and joins in the fun with questions and remarks whispered into John's ear. Both men enjoy it enormously.)

How's it with Mangi? Where's Vusi? How are the chaps keeping, Sky? Winston? . . . All right, man. He's here next to me. No, fine, man, fine, man . . . small accident today when he collided with Hodoshe, but nothing to moan about. His right eye bruised, that's all. Hey, Winston's asking how are the punkies doing? *(Big laugh.)* You bloody lover boy! Leave something for us, man!

(John becomes aware of Winston trying to interrupt again: to Winston.)

Okay . . . okay. . . .

(Back to the telephone.) Listen, Sky, Winston says if you get a chance, go down to Dora Street, to his wife. Tell V. Winston says he's okay, things are fine. Winston says she must carry on . . . nothing has happened . . . tell her to take care of everything and everybody. . . . *Ja.*. . .

(The mention of his wife guillotines Winston's excitement and fun. After a few seconds of silence he crawls back heavily to his bed and lies down. A similar shift in mood takes place in John.)

And look, Sky, you're not far from Gratten Street. Cross over to it, man, drop in on number thirty-eight, talk to Princess, my wife. How is she keeping? Ask her for me. I haven't received a letter for three months now. Why aren't they writing? Tell her to write, man. I want to know how the children are keeping. Is Monde still at school? How's my twin baby, my Father and Mother? Is the old girl sick? They mustn't be afraid to tell me. I want to know. I know it's an effort to write, but it means a lot to us here. Tell her . . . this was another day. They're not very different here. We were down on the beach. The wind was blowing. The sand got in our eyes. The sea was rough. I couldn't see the mainland properly. Tell them that maybe tomorrow we'll go to the quarry. It's not so bad there. We'll be with the others. Tell her also . . . it's starting to get cold now, but the worst is still coming.

(Slow fade to blackout.)

Scene Two

The cell, a few days later.
John is hidden under a blanket. Winston is in the process of putting on Antigone's wig and false breasts.

JOHN: Okay?
WINSTON *(still busy): No.*
JOHN: Okay?
WINSTON: No.
JOHN: Okay?
WINSTON: No.

(Pause)

JOHN: Okay?

(Winston is ready. He stands waiting. John slowly lifts the blanket and looks. He can't believe his eyes. Winston is a very funny sight. John's amazement turns into laughter, which builds steadily. He bangs on the cell wall.)

Hey, Norman, Norman! Come this side, man. I got it here. POES![8]

(John launches into an extravagant send-up of Winston's Antigone. He circles "her" admiringly, he fondles her breasts, he walks arm in arm with her down Main Street, collapsing with laughter between each "turn." He climaxes everything by dropping his trousers.)

Speedy Gonzales! Here I come!

(This last joke is too much for Winston who has endured the whole performance with mounting but suppressed anger. He tears off the wig and breasts, throws them down on the cell floor, and storms over to the water bucket where he starts to clean himself.)

WINSTON: It's finished! I'm not doing it. Take your Antigone and shove it up your arse!
JOHN *(trying to control himself)*: Wait, man. Wait . . . .

(He starts laughing again.)

WINSTON: There is nothing to wait for, my friend. I'm not doing it.
JOHN: Please, Winston!
WINSTON: You can laugh as much as you like, my friend, but just let's get one thing straight, I'm *not* doing Antigone. And in case you want to know why . . . I'm a man, not a bloody woman.

---

[8]"Cunt."

JOHN: When did I say otherwise?

WINSTON: What were you laughing at?

JOHN: I'm not laughing now.

WINSTON: What are you doing, crying?

(Another burst of laughter from John.)

There you go again, more laughing! Shit, man, you want me to go out there tomorrow night and make a bloody fool of myself? You think I don't know what will happen after that? Every time I run to the quarry . . . "Nyah . . . nyah. . . . Here comes Antigone! . . . Help the poor lady!. . . " Well, you can go to hell with your Antigone.

JOHN: I wasn't laughing at you.

WINSTON: Then who were you laughing at? Who else was here that dressed himself as a lady and made a bloody fool of himself?

JOHN *(now trying very hard to placate the other man)*: Okay Winston, Okay! I'm not laughing any more.

WINSTON: You can go to hell with what you're saying.

JOHN: Look, Winston, try to understand, man, . . . this is Theater.

WINSTON: You call laughing at me Theater? Then go to hell with your Theater!

JOHN: Please, Winston, just stop talking and listen to me.

WINSTON: No! You get this, brother, . . . I am not doing your Antigone! I would rather run the whole day for Hodoshe. At least I know where I stand with him. All *he* wants is to make me a "boy" . . . not a bloody woman.

JOHN: Okay, okay. . . .

WINSTON: Nothing you can say. . . .

JOHN *(shouting the other man down)*: Will you bloody listen!

WINSTON *(throwing the wash-rag down violently)*: Okay. I'm listening.

JOHN: Sure I laughed. *Ja . . . I laughed.* But can I tell you why I laughed? I was preparing you for . . . stage fright! You think I don't know what I'm doing in this cell? This is preparation for stage fright! I know those bastards out there. When you get in front of them, sure they'll laugh . . . Nyah, nyah! . . . they'll laugh. But just remember this brother, nobody laughs forever! There'll come a time when they'll stop laughing, and that will be the time when our Antigone hits them with her words.

WINSTON: You're day-dreaming, John. Just get it into your head that I'm not doing Antigone. It's as simple as that.

JOHN *(realizing for the first time that Winston needs to be handled very carefully)*: Hey, Winston! Hold on there, man. We've only got one more day to go! They've given us the best spot in the program. We end the show! You can't back out now.

WINSTON: You think I can't? Just wait and see.

JOHN: Winston! You want to get me into trouble? Is that what you want?

WINSTON: Okay, I won't back out.

JOHN (*delighted with his easy victory*): That's my man!

WINSTON (*retrieving the wig and false breasts off the floor and slamming them into John's hands*): Here's Antigone ... take these titties and hair and play Antigone. I'm going to play Creon. Do you understand what I'm saying? Take your two titties. . . . I'll have my balls and play Creon. (*Turns his back on a flabbergasted John, fishes out a cigarette butt and matches from under the water bucket, and settles down for a smoke.*)

JOHN (*after a stunned silence*): You won't make it! I thought about that one days ago. It's too late now to learn Creon's words.

WINSTON (*smoking*): I hate to say it, but that is just too bad. I am not doing Antigone.

(*John is now furious. After a moment's hesitation he stuffs on the wig and false breasts and confronts Winston.*)

JOHN: Look at me. Now laugh.

(*Winston tries, but the laugh is forced and soon dies away.*)

Go on.

(*Pause.*)

Go on laughing! Why did you stop? Must I tell you why? Because behind all this rubbish is me, and you know it's me. You think those bastards out there won't know it's you? Yes. they'll laugh. But who cares about that as long as they laugh in the beginning and listen at the end. That's all we want them to do ... listen at the end!

WINSTON: I don't care what you say John. I'm not doing Antigone.

JOHN: Winston ... you're being difficult. You promised. . . .

WINSTON: Go to hell, man. Only last night you tell me that this Antigone is a bloody ... what you call it ... legend! A Greek one at that. Bloody thing never even happened. Not even history! Look, brother, I got no time for bullshit. Fuck legends. Me? ... I live my life here! I know why I'm here, and it's history, not legends. I had my chat with a magistrate in Cradock and now I'm here. Your Antigone is a child's play, man.

JOHN: Winston! That's Hodoshe's talk.

WINSTON: You can go to hell with that one too.

JOHN: Hodoshe's talk. Winston! That's what he says all the time. What he wants us to say all our lives. Our convictions, our ideals ... that's what he calls them ... child's play. Everything we fucking do is "child's play" ... when we ran that whole day in the sun and pushed those wheelbarrows, when we cry, when we shit ... child's play! Look, brother, ... I've had enough. No one is going to stop me doing Antigone. . . .

(*The two men break apart suddenly, drop their trousers, and stand facing the wall with arms outstretched. Hodoshe calls John.*)

Yes, sir!

(*He then pulls up his trousers and leaves the cell. When he has left. Winston pulls up his trousers and starts muttering with savage satisfaction at the thought of John in Hodoshe's hands.*)

WINSTON: There he goes. Serves him right. I just hope Hodoshe teaches him a lesson. Antigone is important! Antigone this! Antigone that! Shit, man. Nobody can sleep in this bloody cell because of all that bullshit. Polynices! Eteocles! The other prisoners too. Nobody gets any peace and quiet because of that bloody Antigone! I hope Hodoshe gives it to him.

(*He is now at the cell door. He listens, then moves over to the wig on the floor and circles it. He finally picks it up. Moves back to the cell door to make sure no one is coming. The water bucket gives him an idea. He puts on the wig and, after some difficulty, manages to see his reflection in the water. A good laugh, which he cuts off abruptly. He moves around the cell trying out a few of Antigone's poses. None of them work. He feels a fool. He finally tears off the wig and throws it down on the floor with disgust.*)

Ag voetsek![9]

(*Hands in pockets he paces the cell with grim determination.*)

I'm not going to do it. And I'm going to tell him. When he comes back. For once he must just shut that big bloody mouth of his and listen. To me! I'm not going to argue, but 'struesgod that. . . !

(*The wig on the floor. He stamps on it.*)

Shit, man! If he wants a woman in the cell he must send for his wife, and I don't give a damn how he does it. I didn't walk with those men and burn my bloody passbook in front of that police station, and have a magistrate send me here for life so that he can dress me up like a woman and make a bloody fool of me. I'm going to tell him. When he walks through that door.

(*John returns. Winston is so involved in the problem of Antigone that at first he does not register John's strangely vacant manner.*)

Listen, *broer*, I'm not trying to be difficult but this Antigone! No! Please listen to me, John. "Struesgod I can't do it. I mean, let's try something else, like singing or something. You always got ideas. You know I can sing or dance. But not Antigone. Please, John.

JOHN (*quietly*): Winston. . . .

---

[9]"Go to hell."

WINSTON *(still blind to the other man's manner)*. Don't let's argue, man. We've been together in this cell too long now to quarrel about rubbish. But you know me. If there's one thing I can't stand it's people laughing at me. If I go out there tomorrow night and those bastards start laughing I'll fuck up the first one I lay may hands on. You saw yourself what happened in here when you started laughing. I wanted to *moer* you, John. I'm not joking. I really wanted to.... Hey, are you listening to me? *(Looking squarely at John.)*

JOHN: Winston . . . I've got something to tell you.

WINSTON *(registering John's manner for the first time):* What's the matter? Hodoshe? What happened? Are we in shit? Solitary?

JOHN: My appeal was heard last Wednesday. Sentence reduced. I've got three months to go.

(Long silence. Winston is stunned. Eventually. . . .)

WINSTON: Three. . . .

JOHN: . . . months to go.

WINSTON: Three. . . .

JOHN: *Ja.* That's what Prinsloo said.

WINSTON: John!

(Winston explodes with joy. The men embrace. They dance a jig in the cell. Winston finally tears himself away and starts to hammer on the cell walls so as to pass on the news to other prisoners.)

Norman! Norman!! John. Three months to go. *Ja.*. . . Just been told. . . .

(Winston's excitement makes John nervous. He pulls Winston away from the wall.)

JOHN: Winston! Not yet, man. We'll tell them at the quarry tomorrow. Let me just live with it for a little while.

WINSTON: Okay okay. . . . How did it happen?

(He pulls John down to the floor. They sit close together.)

JOHN: Jesus. I'm so mixed up, man! *Ja* . . . the door opened and I saw Hodoshe. Ooo God, I said to myself. Trouble! Here we go again! All because of you and the noise you were making. Went down the corridor straight to Number Four . . . Solitary and Spare Diet!! But at the end, instead of turning right, we turned left into the main block, all the way through it to Prinsloo's office.

WINSTON: Prinsloo!

JOHN: I'm telling you. Prinsloo himself, man. We waited outside for a little bit, then Hodoshe pushed me in. Prinsloo was behind his desk, busy with some papers. He pulled out one and said to me: "You are very lucky. Your lawyers have been working on your case. The sentence has been reduced from ten years, to three."

WINSTON: What did Hodoshe say?

JOHN: Nothing. But he looked unhappy.

(*They laugh.*)

Hey, something else. Hodoshe let me walk back here by myself! He didn't follow me.

WINSTON: Of course. You are free.

JOHN: *Haai*, Winston, not yet. Those three months. . . ! Or suppose it's a trick.

WINSTON: What do you mean?

JOHN: Those bastards will do anything to break you. If the wheelbarrows and the quarry don't do it, they'll try something else. Remember that last visit of wives, when they lined up all the men on the other side. . . . "Take a good look and say goodbye! Back to the cells!"

WINSTON: You say you saw Prinsloo?

JOHN: Prinsloo himself. Bastard didn't even stand up when I walked in. And by the way . . . I had to sign. *Ja!* I had to sign a form to say that I had been officially told of the result of my appeal . . . that I had three months to go. *Ja.* I signed!

WINSTON: (*without the slightest doubt*): It's three months, John.

JOHN (*relaxing and living with the reality for the first time*). Hell, Winston, at the end of those three months, it will be three years together in this cell. Three years ago I stood in front of that magistrate at Kirkwood—bastard didn't even look at me: "Ten years!" I watched ten years of my life drift away like smoke from a cigarette while he fidgeted and scratched his arse. That same night back in the prison van to the cells at Rooihel. First time we met!

WINSTON: *Ja.* We had just got back from our trial in Cradock.

JOHN: You, Temba, . . .

WINSTON: Sipho. . . .

JOHN: Hell, man!

WINSTON: First time we got close to each other was the next morning in the yard, when they lined us up for the vans. . . .

JOHN: And married us!

(*They lock left and right hands together to suggest handcuffs.*)

WINSTON: Who was that old man . . . remember him? . . . in the corner hand-cuffed to Sipho?

JOHN: Sipho?

WINSTON: *Ja*, the one who started the singing.

JOHN (*remembering*): Peter. Tatu Peter.

WINSTON: That's him!

JOHN: Hell, it comes back now, man! Pulling through the big gates, wives and mothers running next to the vans, trying to say goodbye . . . all of us inside fighting for a last look through the window.

WINSTON (*shaking his head*): Shit!

JOHN: Bet you've forgotten the song the old man started?

(Winston tries to remember. John starts singing softly. It is one of the Defiance Campaign songs. Winston joins in.)

WINSTON *(shaking his head ruefully.):* By the time we reach Humansdorp though, nobody was singing.

JOHN: Fuck singing. I wanted to piss. Hey! I had my one free hand on my balls, holding on. I'd made a mistake when we left the Rooihel. Drank a gallon of water thinking of those five hundred miles ahead. Jesus! There was the bucket in the corner! But we were packed in so tight, remember, we couldn't move. I tried to pull you but it was no bloody good. So I held on—Humansdorp, Storms River, Blaaukrantz . . . held on. But at Knysna, to hell with it, I let go!

(Gesture to indicate the release of his bladder. Winston finds this enormously funny. John joins in.)

You were also wet by then!

WINSTON: Never!

JOHN: Okay, let's say that by George nobody was dry. Remember the stop there?

WINSTON: *Ja.* I thought they were going to let us walk around a bit.

JOHN: Not a damn! Fill up with petrol and then on. Hey, but what about those locals, the Colored prisoners, when we pulled away. Remember? Coming to their cell windows and shouting . . . "Courage, Brothers! Courage!" After that. . . ! Jesus, I was tired. Didn't we fall asleep? Standing like that?

WINSTON: What do you mean standing? It was impossible to fall.

JOHN: Then the docks, the boat. . . . It was my first time on one. I had nothing to vomit up, but my God I tried.

WINSTON: What about me?

JOHN: Then we saw this place for the first time. It almost looked pretty, hey, with all the mist around it.

WINSTON: I was too sick to see anything, *broer.*

JOHN: Remember your words when we jumped off onto the jetty?

(Pause. The two men look at each other.)

Heavy words, Winston. You looked back at the mountains . . .

"Farewell Africa!" I've never forgotten them. That was three years ago.

WINSTON: And now, for you, it's three months to go.

(Pause. The mood of innocent celebration has passed. John realizes what his good news means to the other man.)

JOHN: To hell with everything. Let's go to bed.

(Winston doesn't move. John finds Antigone's wig.)

We'll talk about Antigone tomorrow.

(John prepares for bed.)

Hey, Winston! I just realized. My family! Princess and the children. Do you think they've been told? Jesus, man, maybe they're also saying . . . three months! Those three months are going to feel as long as the three years. Time passes slowly when you've got something . . . to wait for. . . .

(Pause. Winston still hasn't moved. John changes his tone.)

Look, in this cell we're going to forget those three months. The whole bloody thing is most probably a trick anyway. So let's just forget about it. We run to the quarry tomorrow. Together. So let's sleep.

Scene Three

The cell, later the same night. Both men are in bed. Winston is apparently asleep. John, however, is awake, rolling restlessly from side to side. He eventually gets up and goes quietly to the bucket for a drink of water, then back to his bed. He doesn't lie down, however. Pulling the blanket around his shoulders he starts to think about the three months. He starts counting the days on the fingers of one hand. Behind him Winston sits up and watches him in silence for a few moments.

WINSTON *(with a strange smile):* You're counting!

JOHN *(with a start):* What! Hey, Winston, you gave me a fright, man. I thought you were asleep. What's the matter? Can't you sleep?

WINSTON *(ignoring the question, still smiling):* You've started counting the days now.

JOHN *(unable to resist the temptation to talk, moving over to Winston's bed):* Ja.

WINSTON: How many?

JOHN: Ninety-two.

WINSTON: You see!

JOHN *(excited):* Simple, man. Look . . . twenty days left in this month, thirty days in June, thirty-one in July, eleven days in August . . . ninety-two.

WINSTON *(still smiling, but watching John carefully):* Tomorrow?

JOHN: Ninety-one.

WINSTON: And the next day?

JOHN: Ninety.

WINSTON: Then one day it will be eighty!

JOHN: *Ja!*

WINSTON: Then seventy.

JOHN: Hey, Winston, time doesn't pass so fast.

WINSTON: Then only sixty more days.

JOHN: That's just two months here on the Island.

WINSTON: Fifty . . . forty days in the quarry.

JOHN: Jesus, Winston!

WINSTON: Thirty.

JOHN: One month. Only one month to go.

WINSTON: Twenty . . . *(holding up his hands)* then ten . . . five, four, three, two . . . tomorrow!

(The anticipation of that moment is too much for John.)

JOHN: NO! Please, man, Winston. It hurts. Leave those three months alone. I'm going to sleep!

(Back to his bed where he curls up in a tight ball and tries determinedly to sleep. Winston lies down again and stares up at the ceiling. After a pause he speaks quietly.)

WINSTON: They won't keep you here for the full three months. Only two months. Then down to the jetty, into a ferry-boat . . . you'll say goodbye to this place . . . and straight to Victor Verster Prison on the mainland.

(Against his will John starts to listen. He eventually sits upright and completely surrenders himself to Winston's description of the last few days of his confinement.)

Life will change for you there. It will be much easier. Because you won't take Hodoshe with you. He'll stay here with me, on the Island. They'll put you to work in the vineyards at Victor Verster, John. There are no quarries there. Eating grapes, oranges . . . they'll change your diet . . . Diet C, and exercises so that you'll look good when they let you out finally. At night you'll play games . . . Ludo, draughts (checkers), snakes and ladders! Then one day they'll call you into the office, with a van waiting outside to take you back. The same five hundred miles. But this time they'll let you sit. You won't have to stand the whole way like you did coming here. And there won't be handcuffs. Maybe they'll even stop on the way so that you can have a pee. Yes, I'm sure they will. You might even sleep over somewhere. Then finally Port Elizabeth. Rooihel Prison again, John! That's very near home, man. New Brighton is next door! Through your cell window you'll see people moving up and down in the street, hear the buses roaring. Then one night you won't sleep again, because you'll be counting. Not days, as you are doing now, but hours. And the next morning, that beautiful morning, John, they'll take you straight out of your cell to the Discharge Office where they'll give you a new khaki shirt, long khaki trousers, brown shoes. And your belongings! I almost forgot your belongings.

JOHN: Hey, by the way! I was wearing a white shirt, black tie, gray flannel trousers . . . brown Crockett shoes . . . socks? *(A little laugh.)* I can't remember my socks! A check jacket . . . and my watch! I was wearing my watch!

WINSTON: They'll wrap them up in a parcel. You'll have it under your arm when they lead you to the gate. And outside. John, outside that gate, New Brighton will be waiting for you. Your mother, your father, Princess and the children . . . and when they open it. . . .

(Once again, but more violently this time. John breaks the mood as the anticipation of the moment of freedom becomes too much for him.)

JOHN: Stop it, Winston! Leave those three months alone for Christ's sake. I want to sleep.

(He tries to get away from Winston, but the latter goes after him. Winston has now also abandoned his false smile.)

WINSTON: *(stopping John as he tries to crawl away.)* But it's not finished, John!
JOHN: Leave me alone!
WINSTON: It doesn't end there. Your people will take you home. Thirty-eight, Gratten Street. John! Remember it? Everybody will be waiting for you . . . aunts, uncles, friends, neighbors. They'll put you in a chair, John, like a king, give you anything you want . . . cakes, sweets, cool drinks . . . and then you'll start to talk. You'll tell them about this place, John, about Hodoshe, about the quarry, and about your good friend Winston who you left behind. But you still won't be happy, hey. Because you'll need a fuck. A really wild one!
JOHN: Stop it, Winston!
WINSTON *(relentless):* And that is why at ten o'clock that night you'll slip out through the back door and make your way to Sky's place. Imagine it, man! All the boys waiting for you . . . Georgie, Mangi, Vusumzi. They'll fill you up with booze. They'll look after you. They know what it's like inside. They'll fix you up with a woman. . . .
JOHN: NO!
WINSTON: Set you up with her in a comfortable joint, and then leave you alone. You'll watch her, watch her take her clothes off, you'll take your pants off, get near her, feel her, feel it. . . . *Ja*, you'll feel it. It will be wet. . . .
JOHN: WINSTON!
WINSTON: Wet *poes*, John! And you'll fuck it wild!

(John turns finally to face Winston. A long silence as the two men confront each other. John is appalled at what he sees.)

JOHN: Winston? What's happening? Why are you punishing me?
WINSTON: *(quietly).* You stink, John. You stink of beer, of company, of poes, of freedom. . . . Your freedom stinks, John, and it's driving me mad.
JOHN: No, Winston!

WINSTON: Yes! Don't deny it. Three months' time, at this hour, you'll be wiping beer off your face, your hands on your balls, and *poes* waiting for you. You will laugh, you will drink, you will fuck and forget.

(John's denials have no effect on Winston.)

Stop bullshitting me! We've got no time left for that. There's only two months left between us. *(Pause.)* You know where I ended up this morning, John? In the quarry. Next to old Harry. Do you know old Harry, John?

JOHN: Yes.

WINSTON: Yes what? Speak, man!

JOHN: Old Harry, Cell Twenty-three, seventy years, serving Life!

WINSTON: That's not what I'm talking about. When you go to the quarry tomorrow, take a good look at old Harry. Look into his eyes, John. Look at his hands. They've changed him. They've turned him into stone. Watch him work with that chisel and hammer. Twenty perfect blocks of stone every day. Nobody else can do it like him. He loves stone. That's why they're nice to him. He's forgotten himself. He's forgotten everything . . . why he's here, where he comes from. That's happening to me John. I've forgotten why I'm here.

JOHN: No.

WINSTON: Why am I here?

JOHN: You put your head on the block for others.

WINSTON: Fuck the others.

JOHN: Don't say that! Remember our ideals. . . .

WINSTON: Fuck our ideals. . . .

JOHN: No Winston . . . our slogans, our children's freedom. . . .

WINSTON: Fuck slogans, fuck politics . . . fuck everything, John. Why am I here? I'm jealous of your freedom, John. I also want to count. God also gave me ten fingers, but what do I count? My life? How do I count it, John? One . . . one . . . another day comes . . . one. . . . Help me, John! . . . Another day . . . one . . . one. . . . Help me, brother! . . . one. . . .

(John has sunk to the floor, helpless in the face of the other man's torment and pain. Winston almost seems to bend under the weight of the life stretching ahead of him on the Island. For a few seconds he lives in silence with his reality, then slowly straightens up. He turns and looks at John. When he speaks again, it is the voice of a man who has come to terms with his fate, massively compassionate.)

Nyana we Sizwe!

(John looks up at him.)

Nyana we Sizwe . . . it's all over now. All over. *(He moves over to John.)* Forget me. . . .

(John attempts a last, limp denial.)

No, John! Forget me . . . because I'm going to forget you. Yes, I will forget you. Others will come in here, John, count, go, and I'll forget them. Still more will come, count like you, go like you, and I will forget them. And then one day, it will all be over.

(A lighting change suggests the passage of time. Winston collects together their props for Antigone.)

Come. They're waiting.
JOHN: Do you know your words?
WINSTON: Yes. Come, we'll be late for the concert.

Scene Four

(The two men convert their cell area into a stage for the prison concert. Their blankets are hung to provide a makeshift backdrop behind which Winston disappears with their props. John comes forward and addresses the audience. He is not yet in his Creon costume.)

JOHN: Captain Prinsloo, Hodoshe, Warders, . . . and Gentlemen! Two brothers of the House of Labdacus found themselves on opposite sides in battle, the one defending the State, the other attacking it. They both died on the battlefield. King Creon, Head of the State, decided that the one who had defended the State would be buried with all religious rites due to the noble dead. But the other one, the traitor Polynices, who had come back from exile intending to burn and destroy his fatherland, to drink the blood of his masters, was to have no grave, no mourning. He was to lie on the open fields to rot, or at most be food for the jackals. It was a law. But Antigone, their sister, defied the law and buried the body of her brother Polynices. She was caught and arrested. That is why tonight the Hodoshe Span, Cell Forty-two, presents for your entertainment: "The Trial and Punishment of Antigone."

(He disappears behind the blankets. They simulate a fanfare of trumpets. At its height the blankets open and he steps out as Creon. In addition to his pendant, there is some sort of crown and a blanket draped over his shoulders as a robe.)

My People! Creon stands before his palace and greets you! Stop! Stop! What's that I hear? You, good man, speak up. Did I hear "Hail the King"? My good people, I am your *servant* . . . a happy one, but still your servant. How many times must I ask you, implore you to see in these symbols of office nothing more, or less, than you would in the uniform of the humblest menial in your house. Creon's crown is as simple, and I hope as clean, as the apron Nanny wears. And even as Nanny smiles and

is your happy servant because she sees her charge ... your child! ...
waxing fat in that little cradle, so too does Creon—your obedient
servant!—stand here and smile. For what does he see? Fatness and
happiness! How else does one measure the success of a state? By the
sumptuousness of the palaces built for its king and princes? The magnificence of the temples erected to its gods? The achievements of its scien-
tists and technicians who can now send rockets to the moon? No! These
count for nothing beside the fatness and happiness of its people.

But have you ever paused to ask yourself whose responsibility it is to
maintain that fatness and happiness? The answer is simple, is it not? ...
your servant the king! But have you then gone on to ask yourself what
does the king need to maintain this happy state of affairs? What, other
than his silly crown, are the tools with which a king fashions the happiness of his people? The answer is equally simple, my good people. The
law! Yes. The law. A three-lettered word, and how many times haven't
you glibly used it, never bothering to ask yourselves, "What then is the
law?" Or if you have, then making recourse to such clichés as "the law
states this ... or the law states that." The law states or maintains nothing, good people. The law defends! The law is no more or less than a
shield in your faithful servant's hand to protect YOU! But even as a
shield would be useless in one hand, to defend, without a sword in the
other, to strike ... so too the law has its edge. The penalty! We have come
through difficult times. I am sure it is needless for me to remind you of
the constant troubles on our borders ... those despicable rats who
would gnaw away at our fatness and happiness. We have been diligent
in dealing with them. But unfortunately there are still at large subversive
elements ... there are still amongst us a few rats that are not satisfied
and to them I must show this face of Creon ... so different to the one that
hails my happy people! It is with a heavy heart, and you shall see why
soon enough, that I must tell you that we have caught another one. That
is why I have assembled you here. Let what follows be a living lesson for
those among you misguided enough still to harbor symphathy for rats!
The shield has defended. Now the sword must strike!

Bring in the accused.

*(Winston, dressed as Antigone, enters. He wears the wig, the necklace of nails,
and a blanket around his waist as a skirt.)*

Your name!

WINSTON: Antigone, daughter of Oedipus, sister of Eteocles and Polynices.

JOHN: You are accused that, in defiance of the law, you buried the body of the
traitor Polynices.

WINSTON: I buried the body of my brother Polynices.

JOHN: Did you know there was a law forbidding that?

WINSTON: Yes.

JOHN: Yet you defied it.

WINSTON: Yes.

JOHN: Did you know the consequences of such defiance?

WINSTON: Yes.

JOHN: What did you plead to the charges laid against you? Guilty or Not Guilty?

WINSTON: Guilty.

JOHN: Antigone, you have pleaded guilty. Is there anything you wish to say in mitigation? This is your last chance. Speak.

WINSTON: Who made the law forbidding the burial of my brother?

JOHN: The State.

WINSTON: Who is the State?

JOHN: As King I am its manifest symbol.

WINSTON: So you made the law.

JOHN: Yes, for the State.

WINSTON: Are you God?

JOHN: Watch your words, little girl!

WINSTON: You said it was my chance to speak.

JOHN: But not to ridicule.

WINSTON: I've got no time to waste on that. Your sentence on my life hangs waiting on your lips.

JOHN: Then speak on.

WINSTON: When Polynices died in battle, all that remained was the empty husk of his body. He could neither harm nor help any man again. What lay on the battlefield waiting for Hodoshe to turn rotten, belonged to God. You are only a man, Creon. Even as there are laws made by men, so too there are others that come from God. He watches my soul for a transgression even as your spies hide in the bush at night to see who is transgressing your laws. Guilty against God I will not be for any man on this earth. Even without your law, Creon, and the threat of death to whoever defied it, I know I must die. Because of your law and my defiance, that fate is now very near. So much the better. Your threat is nothing to me, Creon. But if I had let my mother's son, a Son of the Land, lie there as food for the carrion fly, Hodoshe, my soul would never have known peace. Do you understand anything of what I am saying, Creon?

JOHN: Your words reveal only that obstinacy of spirit which has brought nothing but tragedy to your people. First you break the law. Now you insult the State.

WINSTON: Just because I ask you to remember that you are only a man?

JOHN: And to add insult to injury you gloat over your deeds! No, Antigone, you will not escape with impunity. Were you my own child you would not escape full punishment.

WINSTON: Full punishment? Would you like to do more than just kill me?

JOHN: That is all I wish.

WINSTON: Then let us not waste any time. Stop talking. I buried my brother. That is an honorable thing, Creon. All these people in your state would say so too, if fear of you and another law did not force them into silence.

JOHN: You are wrong. None of my people think the way you do.

WINSTON: Yes they do, but no one dares tell you so. You will not sleep peacefully, Creon.

JOHN: You add shamelessness to your crimes, Antigone.

WINSTON: I do not feel any shame at having honored my brother.

JOHN: Was he that died with him not also your brother?

WINSTON: He was.

JOHN: And so you honor the one and insult the other.

WINSTON: I shared my love, not my hate.

JOHN: Go then and share your love among the dead. I will have no rats' law here while yet I live.

WINSTON: We are wasting time, Creon. Stop talking. Your words defeat your purpose. They are prolonging my life.

JOHN. *(again addressing the audience).* You have heard all the relevant facts. Needless now to call the state witnesses who would testify beyond reasonable doubt that the accused is guilty. Nor, for that matter, is it in the best interests of the State to disclose their identity. There was a law. The law was broken. The law stipulated its penalty. My hands are tied. Take her from where she stands, straight to the Island! There wall her up in a cell for life, with enough food to acquit ourselves of the taint of her blood.

WINSTON *(to the audience).* Brothers and Sisters of the Land! I go now on my last journey. I must leave the light of day forever, for the Island, strange and cold, to be lost between life and death. So, to my grave, my everlasting prison, condemned alive to solitary death.

(Tearing off his wig and confronting the audience as Winston. not Antigone.)

Gods of our Fathers! My Land! My Home!

Time waits no longer. I go now to my living death, because I honored those things to which honor belongs.

(The two men take off their costumes and then strike their "set". They then come together and, as in the beginning, their hands come together to suggest handcuffs, and their right and left legs to suggest ankle-chains. They start running . . . John mumbling a prayer, and Winston a rhythm for their three-legged run.
The siren wails. Fade to blackout.)

❀ Discussion and Writing

1. Describe the characters of John and Winston. Discuss the relationship between them: what binds and separates them?

2. What is the purpose and process of making the necklace of nails, in both the play *(The Island)* and the play within the play *(Antigone)?*
3. Explore the significance of Winston's resistance to participating in *Antigone.* Analyze the relevance of the Greek play to *The Island.*
4. For what crimes are John and Winston imprisoned? Examine the nature of their punishment and its implications. What does Hodoshe represent?
5. What is the significance of the title? What is its relevance to: the prison, the individuals, South Africa?

❋ Research and Comparison

Analyze the structure of the play as it incorporates different dramatic traditions of ancient Greek, popular African, and modern experimental theaters.

Interdisciplinary Discussion Question: Research the history of apartheid in South Africa, concentrating on any one aspect (education, housing, political rights, displacement of families). Examine its manifestation in the life of any political leader or the works of any literary writer of South Africa.

Okot p'Bitek
(1931–1982)
Uganda

Okot p'Bitek was born in Gulu in northern Uganda, where the practice of the traditional arts was maintained and highly respected despite obstacles arising from colonialism. He was named Okot (meaning "of rain") because there were bubbles in the placenta when he was born, which is regarded as a sign of rain; p'Bitek means "one day he will become strong." His parents were prominent members of the Protestant community; they were also impressive performers. From his father, he learned stories and the manner of their telling; from his mother, he learned the art of poetry, song, and dance. As a child, he was himself known as a fine singer and dancer, as well as an outstanding athlete. Like his father, he became a schoolmaster. When Okot p'Bitek was 22, he published a novel written in his native Luo, and in 1956 he wrote the first draft of *Wer pa Lawino* (Song of Lawino), but no publisher would touch such frank material. Afterward, he studied law and anthropology in England and Wales, where he repudiated Christianity and turned to studying the traditions of his people, the Acoli. His interest in music and politics had been evident in his teaching days. When he rejected the study of social anthropology, seeing it as a tool to justify colonialism, he thought of entering politics. Instead, he pursued his exploration of the oral literature of his people.

When Okot p'Bitek returned to Uganda, he organized arts festivals in which he also performed as a singer and dancer. It was at this time that he completed his contemporary traditional Acoli work, *Wer pa Lawino* (1966), giving the village woman who reviews the Westernized African mind characteristics of his mother, Lacwaa Cerina. He subsequently translated the work into English as *Song of Lawino*. He continued to organize cultural events, becoming director of the Uganda Cultural Centre until his dismissal because of his criticism of politicians in *Song of Lawino*. He died shortly after becoming professor of creative writing at Makerere University.

Song of Lawino*
I Do Not Know the Dances of White People

It is true
I am ignorant of the dances of foreigners
And how they dress
I do not know.
Their games
I cannot play
I only know the dances of our people.

I cannot dance the rumba,
My mother taught me
The beautiful dances of Acoli.
I do not know the dances of White People.
I will not deceive you,
I cannot dance the samba!
You once saw me at the *orak*[1] dance
The dance for youths
The dance of our People.

When the drums are throbbing
And the black youths
Have raised much dust
You dance with vigor and health
You dance naughtily with pride
You dance with spirit,
You compete, you insult, you provoke

---

*Translated by Okot p'Bitek
[1]An extremely lively dance for young people, danced in two concentric circles with the girls on the inside circle and the boys on the outside; performed with drum and chants. [eds.]

You challenge all!
And the eyes of the young men become red!

The son of a man
And the daughter of a man
Shine forth in the arena.
Slave boys and girls
Dance differently from trueborns.

You dance with confidence
And you sing
Provocative songs,
Insulting and abusive songs
Songs of praise
Sad songs of broken loves
Songs about shortage of cattle.
Most of the songs make someone angry.

You do not come to the arena drunk,
But when another youth hits you
You take up the challenge
As a man,

And when a girl knocks you
You strike back,
A man's manliness is seen in the arena,
No one touches another's testicles.

A girl whose waist is stiff
Is a clumsy girl
That is the lazy girl
Who fears grinding the *kabir* millet.[2]

You adorn yourself in Acoli costumes
You tie *lacucuku*[3] rattles
Or bells on your legs.
You wear bead-skirts or string skirts
Or a tiny piece of cloth
And a ten-stringed bead
Around your waist;
Bangles on your arms,
And giraffe-tail necklaces on your tall neck.

[2]*Kabir* millett: a grain. [eds.]
[3]*Lacucuku* is a kind of fruit about the size of a prune. [eds.]

A young man wears the *odye*[4] and *lacomi*,
He puts his lover's beads
On his neck,
Beautiful white feathers on his head,
He blows his horn
And other young men feel jealous of him.

It is danced in broad daylight
In the open,
You cannot hide anything,
Bad stomachs that have swollen up,
Skin diseases on the buttocks
Small breasts that have just emerged,
And large ones full of boiling milk,
Are clearly seen in the arena,
Breasts that are tired
And are about to fall,

Weak and bony chests of weaklings
Strong lion chests
Large scars on the thighs
Beautiful tattoos below the belly button
Tattoos that have become sores on the chest;

All parts of the body
Are shown in the arena!
Health and liveliness
Are shown in the arena!

When the daughter of the Bull
Enters the arena
She does not stand here
Like stale beer that does not sell,
She jumps here
She jumps there.
When you touch her
She says "Don't touch me!"

The tattoos on her chest
Are like palm fruits,

---

[4]*Odye:* a triangular piece of cow skin, worn across a boy's buttocks when dancing; the boy's own warrior name is often on the long side of the triangle. *lacomi:* a rectangular loin cloth worn in a masculine dance costume. [eds.]

The tattoos on her back
Are like stars on a black night;
Her eyes sparkle like the fireflies,
Her breasts are ripe
Like the full moon.
When the age-mate of her brother sees them,
When, by accident,
The eyes of her lover
Fall on her breasts
Do you think the young man sleeps?
Do you know what fire eats his inside?

It is true, Ocol
I cannot dance the ballroom dance.
Being held so tightly
I feel ashamed,
Being held so tightly in public
I cannot do it,
It looks shameful to me!

They come to the dance dead drunk
They drink white men's drinks
As well as *waragi*.[5]
They close their eyes,
And they do not sing as they dance,
They dance silently like wizards.

Each man has a woman
Although she is not his wife,
They dance inside a house
And there is no light.
Shamelessly, they hold each other
Tightly, tightly,
They cannot breathe!

Women lie on the chests of men
They prick the chests of their men
With their breasts
They prick the chests of their men
With the cotton nests
On their chests.

---

[5]A traditional alcoholic beverage made from bananas. [eds.]

You kiss her on the cheek
As white people do,
You kiss her open-sore lips
As white people do,
You suck slimy saliva
From each other's mouths
As white people do.

And the lips of the men become bloody
With blood dripping from the red-hot lips;
Their teeth look
As if they have been boxed in the mouth.

Women throw their arms
Around the necks of their partners
And put their cheeks
On the cheeks of their men.
Men hold the waists of the women
Tightly, tightly . . .

And as they dance
Knees touch knees;
And when the music has stopped
Men put their hands in the trouser-pockets.

There is no respect for relatives:
Girls hold their fathers,
Boys hold their sisters close,
They dance even with their mothers.
Modern girls are fierce
Like Labeja, the *Fok* of *Alero*,[6]
That captures even the heads of nephews,
They coil around their nephews
And lie on the chests of their uncles
And prick the chests of their brothers
With their breasts.

And they dress up like white men,
As if they are in the white man's country.
At the height of the hot season

---

[6]A chiefdom divinity; other chiefdom divinities possess only persons within the chiefdom, but Labeja possesses even outsiders, e.g., a mother's brother.

The progressive and civilized ones
Put on blanket suits
And woollen socks from Europe,
Long under-pants
And woollen vests,
White shirts;
They wear dark glasses
And neck-ties from Europe.
Their waterlogged suits
Drip like the tears
Of the *kituba* tree
After a heavy storm.

There Is No Fixed Time for Breast Feeding

Ocol tells me
Things I cannot understand,
He talks
About a certain man,
Jesus.
He says
The man was born
Long ago
In the country of white men.

He says
When Jesus was born
White men began
To count years:
From one, then it became ten.
Then one hundred
Then one thousand
And now it is
One thousand
Nine hundred
And sixty six.

My husband says
Before this man was born
White men counted years backward.
Starting with the biggest number
Then it became
One thousand
Then one hundred

Then ten,
And when it became one
Then Jesus was born.

I cannot understand all this
I do not understand it at all!

I Am Ignorant of the Good Word in the Clean Book

My husband
Looks down upon me;
He says
I am a mere pagan,
I do not know
The way of God.
He says
I am ignorant
Of the good word
In the Clean Book
And I do not have
A Christian name.
Ocol dislikes me
Because, he says,
Jok is in my head
And I like visiting
The diviner-priest
Like my mother!

He says
He is ashamed of me
Because when the *Jok*
In my head
Has been provoked
It throws me down
As if I have fits.

Ocol laughs at me
Because I cannot
Cross myself properly

In the name of the Father
And of the Son
And the Clean Ghost

And I do not understand
The confession,
And I fear
The bushy-faced, fat-bellied padre
Before whom people kneel
When they pray.

I refused to join
The Protestant catechist class,
Because I did not want
To become a house-girl,
I did not want
To become a slave
To a woman with whom
I may share a man.

Oh how young girls
Labor to buy a name!
You break your back
Drawing water
For the wives
Of the teachers,
The skin of your hand
Hardens and peels off
Grinding millet and simsim.
You hoe their fields,
Split firewood,
You cut grass for thatching
And for starting fires,
You smear their floors
With cow dung and black soil
And harvest their crops.

And when they are eating
They send you to play games
To play the board game
Under the mango tree!

And girls gather
Wild sweet potatoes
And eat them raw
As if there is a famine,
And they are so thin

They look like
Cattle that have dysentery!

You work as if
You are a newly eloped girl!
The wives of Protestant
Church teachers and priests
Are a happy lot.
They sit with their legs stretched out
And bask in the morning sun.
All they know
Is hatching a lot of children.

My elder sister
Was christened Erina,
She was a Protestant
But she suffered bitterly
In order to buy the name
And her loin beads
No longer fitted her!

One Sunday
I followed her
Into the Protestant church:
A big man stood
Before the people.
His hand was lifted up,
My sister said
He was blessing the people.
The man had no rosary,
He wore a long black gown
And a wide white robe
He held a little shiny saucer:
It had small pieces of something.
The name of the man
Was Eliya
And he was calling people
To come and eat
Human flesh!
He put little bits
In their hands
And they ate it up!

Then he took a cup,
He said
There was human blood
In the cup
And he gave it
To the people
To drink!

I ran out of the Church,
I was very sick!
O! Protestants eat people!
They are all wizards,
They exhume corpses
For dinner!

I once joined
The Catholic Evening Speakers' Class
But I did not stay long
I ran away,
I ran away from shouting
Meaninglessly in the evenings
Like parrots
Like the crow birds

  Maria the Clean Woman
  Mother of the Hunchback[7]
  Pray for us
  Who spoil things
  Full of graciya.

The things they shout
I do not understand,
They shout anyhow
They shout like mad people.
The padre shouts words,
You cannot understand,
And he does not seem
To care in the least
Whether his hearers

---

[7]The name of the Christian God in Lwo is *Rubanga.* This is also the name of the ghost that causes tuberculosis of the spine, hence Hunchback.

Understand him or not;
A strange language they speak
These Christian diviner-priests,
And the white nuns
Think the girls understand
What they are saying
And are annoyed
When the girls laugh.
One night
The moon was very bright
And in the distance
The "get-stuck" dance drums
Were throbbing vigorously,

The teacher was very drunk
His eyes were like rotting
      tomatoes.
We guessed he was teaching
Something about the Clean Ghost.

He shouted words at us
And we shouted back at him,
Agitated and angry
Like the *okwik* birds[8]
Chasing away the kite
From their nest.

He shouted angrily
As if he uttered abuses,
We repeated the same words
Shouting back at him
As when you shout
Insults at somebody's mother!

We repeated the meaningless phrases
Like the yellow birds
In the *lajanamara* grass

The teacher was an Acoli
But he spoke the same language
As the white priests.

---

[8]*Okwik* birds and *lajanawara* grass: a kind of bird and grass. [eds.]

His nose was blocked

And he tried
To force his words
Through his blocked nose.

He sounded like
A loosely strung drum.

The teacher's name
Was Bicenycio Lagucu.
He was very drunk
And he smiled, bemused.

The drums of the "get-stuck" dance
Thundered in the distance
And the songs came floating
In the air.

The milk
In our ripe breasts boiled,
And little drops of sweat
Appeared on our foreheads,
You think of the pleasures
Of the girls
Dancing before their lovers,

Then you look at the teacher
Barking meaninglessly
Like the yellow monkey.

In the arena
They began to sing my song,
We could hear it faintly
Passing through the air
Like the thin smoke
From an old man's pipe:
    O! Lawino!
    Come let me see you
    Daughter of Lenga-moi
    Who has just shot up
    Young woman come home!
    O Lawino!
    Chief of the girls

My love come
That I may elope with you
Daughter of the Bull
Come that I may touch you

The teacher drummed
His meaningless phrases
Through his blocked nose;
He was getting more drunk.
Thick white froth
Formed around his mouth
As if he had just fallen down
With fits.

Pray for us
Who spoil things
Full of graciya

And when he shouted
The word "graciya"
(Whatever the word meant)
Saliva squirted from his mouth
And froth flew
Like white ants from his mouth,
The smelly drops
Landed on our faces
Like heavily loaded houseflies
Fresh from a fresh excreta heap!

And when he belched
The smell of the rotting beer
Hit you like a brick,
And when he belched
His mouth filled with hot beer
From his belly
And he noisily swallowed this back.

The collar of the teacher's white shirt
Was black with dirt,
He was sweating profusely
And his cheeks were rough
Like the tongue of the ox.

The comb never touched his head,
His hair resembled the elephant grass,
Tall and wiry
The teacher looked like a witch.

And he endlessly
Drummed his meaningless words
Through his blocked nose,
And we shouted the words back at him,
And the moonlight dance drums
Thundered in the distance.
And the songs came floating
From beyond his hills.
My comrades
Are dancing in the moonlight
And I
Sitting before the ugly man,
Before the man
With the rough skin,
The man
Whose body smells!

The girls are dancing
Before their lovers,
Shaking their waists
To the rhythm of the drums;
And I
Sitting like stale bread
On the rubbish heap;

My companions are gay
They are dancing
And singing meaningful songs,
In the arena
They are singing
My song;

And the boys
Are whispering sweet words
Into the girls' ears
And our teacher
Is drunk!

Anger welled up inside me
Burning my chest like bile,
I stood up
And two other girls stood up,
We walked out,
Out of that cold hall
With the stone floor.
We ran fast,
Away from the ugly man
Away from the meaningless shouts
Like parrots,
Like the yellow birds
In the *lajanawara* grass

We crossed the stream
And climbed the gentle rise
Straight into the arena
We joined the line of friends
And danced among our age mates
And sang songs we understood,
Relevant and meaningful songs,
Songs about ourselves:

> *O father*
> *Gather the bridewealth*
> *That I may bring a woman home,*
> *O the woman of my bosom*
> *The beautiful one*
> *Prevents me from sleeping.*
> *The woman of my bosom.*

> *If anyone troubles my beloved*
> *I shall shed tears of blood;*
> *The woman of my bosom*
> *Prevents me from sleeping.*
> *O father,*
> *If I die,*
> *I will become a vengeance ghost,*
> *The woman of my bosom*
> *Prevents me from sleeping.*

We danced with vigor
And sweat poured

Down our backs,
Youthful sweat
From healthy bodies.

❀ Discussion and Writing

1. Discuss Lawino's criticism of the Western concept of time. What is implied regarding her own concept of time?
2. Comment on Lawino's perception of Western dance. What is the source of her point of view?
3. Discuss her perception of Christian practices. What does Okot p'Bitek accomplish by presenting Christianity from an outsider's perspective?
4. Discuss Ocol's character: his attitudes toward his family and culture; his Westernized beliefs and behavior.
5. What is the significance of portraying the partial perceptions of both Lawino and Ocol? Analyze the restricted thinking of both the African and the British (as reflected in Ocol) as they judge each other according to their own standards.

❀ Research and Comparison

Examine *The Song of Lawino* and *The Song of Ocol* (the latter originally written in English). Analyze the handling of the cross-cultural perspectives and the portrayal of the issue of identity in the colonial context.

Interdisciplinary Discussion Question: Consider the role of the oral tradition in written literature in relation to Okot's literary works, and discuss his contribution to the world of dance and music.

Lenrie Peters
(b. 1932)
Gambia

Lenrie Peters was born in Banjul (then known as Bathurst), Gambia, where he returned after his studies to practice medicine. His early schooling was in Bathurst and Freetown, Sierra Leone; his medical studies were at Trinity College, Cambridge, and University College Hospital, London. During his student days in England, he served as president of the African Student Union; chaired "Calling West Africa" on the BBC's African Forum; and performed in student productions. He is still a singer of repute. His poems have appeared in *Black Orpheus* and other leading journals, and both his poetry and novels concern contemporary urban problems.

Isatou died

When she was only five
And full of pride
Just before she knew
How small a loss
It brought to such a few.
Her mother wept
Half grateful
To be so early bereft.
And did not see the smile
As tender as the root
Of the emerging plant
Which sealed her eyes.
The neighbors wailed
As they were paid to do
And thought how big a spread
Might be her wedding too.
The father looked at her
Through marble eyes and said;
"Who spilt the perfume
Mixed with morning dew?"

❀ **Discussion and Writing**

1. Describe the social customs and economic reality of Isatou's family.
2. How do you interpret the different reactions of the father and the mother to their daughter's death?

Kofi Awoonor
(b. 1935)
Ghana

George Kofi Awoonor-Williams, whose father was a trader from Sierra Leone, was born in his mother's village of Wheta, in the Volta region of Ghana, and raised in the coastal town of Keta. He studied at several mission schools before graduating with a degree in English from the University of Ghana, where he specialized in traditional poetry at the university's Institute of African Studies. For Awoonor, the mission school figured as an emblem of severance, marking the break from tradition and childhood; the studies of Ewe poetry, on the other hand, served as an inspiration. He took his M.A. degree at University College of London, and later became editor of the literary journal *Okyeame,* associate editor of *Transition,* and director of the Ghana Film Institute. He also taught at universities in Ghana and the United States. Not long after his return to Ghana, he was imprisoned for a year (1975) and placed in solitary confinement for alleged involvement in an attempted coup. On his release, Awoonor resumed his position as professor of English at Cape Coast University. He subsequently served as the Ghanaian ambassador to the United Nations.

Awoonor has written novels, criticism, and poetry. His chapter "Oral Literature" in his survey of African culture, *The Breast of the Earth* (1975), presents the aesthetic and emotional effect of oral poetry. He discusses the current authors like himself who consciously work within the oral tradition. In his early poetry, Awoonor translated Ewe lines in accordance with the traditional practice of the apprentice poet. He then developed his own themes and techniques, as in the irony of "The Weaver Bird." But the solemn, slow rhythms of the Ewe funeral dirge remained a strong influence. He has evoked the quality of the oral presentation and continued to manipulate Ewe songs to voice his concern for the legacy of colonialism. He has imbued his poetry with a strong sense of place, using traditional rituals, daily and seasonal rhythms, historic and personal events as emblems for waste and defeat.

The Weaver Bird

The weaver bird built in our house
And laid its eggs on our only tree
We did not want to send it away
We watched the building of the nest
And supervised the egg-laying.
And the weaver returned in the guise of the owner
Preaching salvation to us that owned the house
They say it came from the west
Where the storms at sea had felled the gulls
And the fishers dried their nets by lantern light
Its sermon is the divination of ourselves
And our new horizons limit at its nest
But we cannot join the prayers and answers of the communicants.
We look for new homes every day,
For new altars we strive to rebuild
The old shrines defiled by the weaver's excrement.

❋ Discussion and Writing

1. Discuss the implications of the weaver bird's activities.
2. Analyze Awoonor's use of imagery.
3. Discuss the significance of the ending. On what note does the poem conclude: hope? frustration? anger?

J. P. Clarke Bekederemo
(b. 1935)
Nigeria

John Pepper Clark Bekederemo, of the Ijaw people, was born in Kiagbodo in the Niger Delta region of western Nigeria. After attending school in Okrika and Jeremi, he studied at Government College, Warri, in Ughelli (now University College, Ibadan), where he earned his B.A. with honors. In the 1950s during his student years, he founded *The Horn,* a poetry magazine that immediately became influential. He continued his studies in the United States at Princeton University, but that was not a happy experience. Along with writing poetry, plays, fiction, and nonfiction, he has taught and worked as a journalist and editorial writer. He has served as information officer for the Nigerian government and as co-editor of *Black Orpheus.* His translation of *The Ozidi Saga* from the Ijaw has contributed to the study of Africa's oral literatures.

The Leader

They have felled him to the ground
Who announced home from abroad
Wrestled to a standstill his champion
Cousin the Killer of Cows. Yes,
In all that common
And swamp, pitched piecemeal by storks,
No iguana during a decade of tongues
Could throw or twist him round
While he rallied the race and clan.
Now like an alligator he lies
Trussed up in a house without eyes
And ears:
      Bit of bamboo,
Flung to laggard dogs by drowning
Nearest of kin, has quite locked his jaws.

❁ Discussion and Writing

1. Explore the significance of the image of the wrestler.
2. Comment on the function of the animal imagery that pervades the poem.
3. Who is responsible for the defeat of the leader?
4. What aspects of colonial history are reflected in the poem?

❁ Writing and Comparison

Examine the works of J. P. Clarke Bekederemo to reconstruct the colonial experience in Nigeria.

Wole Soyinka
(b. 1935)
Nigeria

Wole Soyinka was born in Abeokuta in western Nigeria, where his father was supervisor of schools and active in the Christian community. (Abeokuta, which had grown along side hills topped by granite boulders, means "under the rock.") After studying at University College, Ibadan, and Leeds University, he worked for a year and a half at the Royal Court Theatre in London as reader, teacher, and scriptwriter. It was here in the late 1950s that his earliest poems and plays were first performed. His return to Nigeria in 1960 marked a period of intense work in theater: writing, acting, producing, managing a touring company, studying the traditional African forms of drama. Soyinka is himself Yoruba; his sympathies with the Biafran cause, however, provoked his imprisonment in northern Nigeria (1967–1969) during the Biafran war. After his release, he spent some five years living in Europe and in Ghana, where he served as editor of the prestigious journal *Transition/Ch'indaba,* returning to Nigeria to assume the chair of drama at Ife University. He has received many honorary degrees and prizes for his work, most notably the Nobel Prize in literature in 1986.

Acknowledged as one of the major writers in modern African literature, Soyinka has centered his work on a mythic configuration of history, one based essentially on the traditional Yoruba world view. Thus, Eman in "The Strong Breed" emerges as a tragic hero, conflicted with the duality of Ogun. And, thus, the work itself plays mythically with time and place: the past time and village oppose the present time and village until they merge finally and destructively in the present.

The Strong Breed

CHARACTERS

EMAN, *A Stranger*
SUNMA, *Jaguna's Daughter*
IFADA, *An Idiot*
A GIRL
JAGUNA
OROGE
ATTENDANT STALWARTS, *The villagers from Eman's past—*
OLD MAN, *His Father*
OMAE, *His Betrothed*
TUTOR
PRIEST
ATTENDANTS, *The Villagers*

The scenes are described briefly, but very often a darkened stage with lit areas will not only suffice but is necessary. Except for the one indicated place, there can be no break in the action. A distracting scene-change would be ruinous.

A mud house, with space in front of it. Eman, in light buba[1] and trousers stands at the window, looking out. Inside, Sunma is clearing the table of what looks like a modest clinic, putting the things away in a cupboard. Another rough table in the room is piled with exercise books, two or three worn text-books, etc. Sunma appears agitated. Outside, just below the window crouches Ifada. He looks up with a shy smile from time to time, waiting for Eman to notice him.

SUNMA *(hesitant):* You will have to make up your mind soon Eman. The lorry leaves very shortly.

(As Eman does not answer, Sunma continues her work, more nervously. Two villagers, obvious travellers, pass hurriedly in front of the house, the man has a small raffia sack, the woman a cloth-covered basket, the man enters first, turns and urges the woman who is just emerging to hurry.)

SUNMA *(seeing them, her tone is more intense):* Eman, are we going or aren't we? You will leave it till too late.
EMAN *(quietly):* There is still time—if you want to go.
SUNMA: If I want to go . . . and you?

(Eman makes no reply.)

---

[1]Short, loose garment worn by women or men. [eds.]

SUNMA *(bitterly):* You don't really want to leave here. You never want to go away—even for a minute.

(Ifada continues his antics. Eman eventually pats him on the head and the boy grins happily. Leaps up suddenly and returns with a basket of oranges which he offers to Eman.)

EMAN: My gift for today's festival enh?

(Ifada nods, grinning.)

EMAN: They look ripe—that's a change.
SUNMA *(She has gone inside the room. Looks round the door.):* Did you call me?
EMAN: No. *(She goes back.)* And what will you do tonight Ifada? Will you take part in the dancing? Or perhaps you will mount your own masquerade?

(Ifada shakes his head, regretfully.)

EMAN: You won't? So you haven't any? But you would like to own one.

(Ifada nods eagerly.)

EMAN: Then why don't you make your own?

(Ifada stares, puzzled by this idea.)

EMAN: Sunma will let you have some cloth you know. And bits of wool . . .
SUNMA *(coming out):* Who are you talking to Eman?
EMAN: Ifada. I am trying to persuade him to join the young maskers.
SUNMA *(losing control):* What does he want here? Why is he hanging round us?
EMAN *(amazed):* What . . . ? I said Ifada, Ifada.
SUNMA: Just tell him to go away. Let him go and play somewhere else!
EMAN: What is this? Hasn't he always played here?
SUNMA: I don't want him here. *(Rushes to the window.)* Get away idiot. Don't bring your foolish face here any more, do you hear? Go on, go away from here . . .
EMAN *(restraining her):* Control yourself Sunma. What on earth has got into you?

(Ifada, hurt and bewildered, backs slowly away.)

SUNMA: He comes crawling round here like some horrible insect. I never want to lay my eyes on him again.
EMAN: I don't understand. It *is* Ifada you know. Ifada! The unfortunate one who runs errands for you and doesn't hurt a soul.
SUNMA: I cannot bear the sight of him.
EMAN: You can't do what? It can't be two days since he last fetched water for you.

SUNMA: What else can he do except that? He is useless. Just because we have been kind to him . . . Others would have put him in an asylum.

EMAN: You are not making sense. He is not a madman, he is just a little more unlucky than other children. *(Looks keenly at her.)* But what is the matter?

SUNMA: It's nothing. I only wish we had sent him off to one of those places for creatures like him.

EMAN: He is quite happy here. He doesn't bother anyone and he makes himself useful.

SUNMA: Useful! Is that one of any use to anybody? Boys of his age are already earning a living but all he can do is hang around and drool at the mouth.

EMAN: But he does work. You know he does a lot for you.

SUNMA: Does he? And what about the farm you started for him! Does he ever work on it? Or have you forgotten that it was really for Ifada you cleared that bush. Now you have to go and work it yourself. You spend all your time on it and you have no room for anything else.

EMAN: That wasn't his fault. I should first have asked him if he was fond of farming.

SUNMA: Oh, so he can choose? As if he shouldn't be thankful for being allowed to live.

EMAN: Sunma!

SUNMA: He does not like farming but he knows how to feast his dumb mouth on the fruits.

EMAN: But I want him to. I encourage him.

SUNMA: Well keep him. I don't want to see him any more.

EMAN *(after some moments)*: But why? You cannot be telling all the truth. What has he done?

SUNMA: The sight of him fills me with revulsion.

EMAN *(goes to her and holds her)*: What really is it?
(*Sunma avoids his eyes.*) It is almost as if you are forcing yourself to hate him. Why?

SUNMA: That is not true. Why should I?

EMAN: Then what is the secret? You've even played with him before.

SUNMA: I have always merely tolerated him. But I cannot any more. Suddenly my disgust won't take him any more. Perhaps . . . perhaps it is the new year. Yes, yes, it must be the new year.

EMAN: I don't believe that.

SUNMA: It must be. I am a woman, and these things matter. I don't want a mis-shape near me. Surely for one day in the year, I may demand some wholesomeness.

EMAN: I do not understand you.

(Sunma is silent.)

It was cruel of you. And to Ifada who is so helpless and alone. We are the only friends he has.

SUNMA: No, just you. I have told you, with me it has always been only an act of kindness. And now I haven't any pity left for him.

EMAN: No. He is not a wholesome being.

(He turns back to looking through the window.)

SUNMA *(half-pleading):* Ifada can rouse your pity. And yet if anything, I need more kindness from you. Every time my weakness betrays me, you close your mind against me . . . Eman . . . Eman . . .

(A Girl comes in view, dragging an effigy by a rope attached to one of its legs. She stands for a while gazing at Eman. Ifada, who has crept back shyly to his accustomed position, becomes somewhat excited when he sees the effigy. The girl is unsmiling. She possesses in fact, a kind of inscrutability which does not make her hard but is unsettling.)

GIRL: Is the teacher in?

EMAN *(smiling):* No.

GIRL: Where is he gone?

EMAN: I don't really know. Shall I ask?

GIRL: Yes, do.

EMAN *(turning slightly):* Sunma, a girl outside wants to know . . .

(Sunma turns away, goes into the inside room.)

EMAN: Oh. *(Returns to the girl, but his slight gaiety is lost.)* There is no one at home who can tell me.

GIRL: Why are you not in?

EMAN: I don't really know. Maybe I went somewhere.

GIRL: All right. I will wait until you get back.

(She pulls the effigy to her, sits down.)

EMAN *(slowly regaining his amusement):* So you are all ready for the new year.

GIRL *(without turning round):* I am not going to the festival.

EMAN: Then why have you got that?

GIRL: Do you mean my carrier? I am unwell you know. My mother says it will take away my sickness with the old year.

EMAN: Won't you share the carrier with your playmates?

GIRL: Oh, no. Don't you know I play alone? The other children won't come near me. Their mothers would beat them.

EMAN: But I have never seen you here. Why don't you come to the clinic?

GIRL: My mother said No.

(Gets up, begins to move off.)

EMAN: You are not going away?

GIRL: I must not stay talking to you. If my mother caught me . . .

EMAN: All right, tell me what you want before you go.

GIRL *(Stops. For some moments she remains silent.):* I must have some clothes for my carrier.

EMAN: Is that all? You wait a moment.

(Sunma comes out as he takes down a buba from the wall. She goes to the window and glares almost with hatred at the girl. The girl retreats hastily, still impassive.)

By the way Sunma, do you know who that girl is?

SUNMA: I hope you don't really mean to give her that.

EMAN: Why not? I hardly ever use it.

SUNMA: Just the same don't give it to her. She is not a child. She is as evil as the rest of them.

EMAN: What has got into you today?

SUNMA: All right, all right. Do what you wish.

(She withdraws. Baffled, Eman returns to the window.)

EMAN: Here . . . will this do? Come and look at it.

GIRL: Throw it.

EMAN: What is the matter? I am not going to eat you.

GIRL: No one lets me come near them.

EMAN: But I am not afraid of catching your disease.

GIRL: Throw it.

(Eman shrugs and tosses the buba. She takes it without a word and slips it on the effigy, completely absorbed in the task. Eman watches for a while, then joins Sunma in the inner room.)

GIRL: *(after a long, cool survey of Ifada): You have a head like a spider's egg, and your mouth dribbles like a roof. But there is no one else. Would you like to play?*

(Ifada nods eagerly, quite excited.)

GIRL: You will have to get a stick.

(Ifada rushes around, finds a big stick and whirls it aloft, bearing down on the carrier.)

GIRL: Wait. I don't want you to spoil it. If it gets torn I shall drive you away. Now, let me see how you are going to beat it.

(Ifada hits it gently.)

GIRL: You may hit harder than that. As long as there is something left to hang at the end.

(She appraises him up and down.)

You are not very tall . . . will you be able to hang it from a tree?

(Ifada nods, grinning happily.)

GIRL: You will hang it up and I will set fire to it. *(Then, with surprising venom.)* But just because you are helping me, don't think it is going to cure you. I am the one who will get well at midnight, do you understand? It is my carrier and it is for me alone.

(She pulls at the rope to make sure that it is well attached to the leg.)

Well don't stand there drooling. Let's go.

(She begins to walk off, dragging the effigy in the dust. Ifada remains where he is for some moments, seemingly puzzled. Then his face breaks into a large grin and he leaps after the procession, belaboring the effigy with all his strength. The stage remains empty for some moments. Then the horn of a lorry is sounded and Sunma rushes out. The hooting continues for some time with a rhythmic pattern. Eman comes out.)

EMAN: I am going to the village . . . I shan't be back before nightfall.
SUNMA *(blankly)*: Yes.
EMAN *(hesitates)*: Well what do you want me to do?
SUNMA: The lorry was hooting just now.
EMAN: I didn't hear it.
SUNMA: It will leave in a few minutes. And you did promise we could go away.
EMAN: I promised nothing. Will you go home by yourself or shall I come back for you?
SUNMA: You don't even want me here?
EMAN: But you have to go home haven't you?
SUNMA: I had hoped we would watch the new year together—in some other place.
EMAN: Why do you continue to distress yourself?
SUNMA: Because you will not listen to me. Why do you continue to stay where nobody wants you?
EMAN: That is not true.
SUNMA: It is. You are wasting your life on people who really want you out of their way.
EMAN: You don't know what you are saying.
SUNMA: You think they love you? Do you think they care at all for what you— or I—do for them?
EMAN: *Them?* These are your own people. Sometimes you talk as if you were a stranger too.
SUNMA: I wonder if I really sprang from here. I know they are evil and I am not. From the oldest to the smallest child, they are nourished in evil and unwholesomeness in which I have no part.
EMAN: You knew this when you returned?

SUNMA: You reproach me then for trying at all?

EMAN: I reproach you with nothing? But you must leave me out of your plans. I can have no part in them.

SUNMA (*nearly pleading*): Once I could have run away. I would have gone and never looked back.

EMAN: I cannot listen when you talk like that.

SUNMA: I swear to you, I do not mind what happens afterward. But you must help me tear myself away from here. I can no longer do it by myself . . . It is only a little thing. And we have worked so hard this past year . . . surely we can go away for a week . . . even a few days would be enough.

EMAN: I have told you Sunma . . .

SUNMA (*desperately*): Two days Eman. Only two days.

EMAN (*distressed*): But I tell you I have no wish to go.

SUNMA (*suddenly angry*): Are you so afraid then?

EMAN: Me? Afraid of what?

SUNMA: You think you will not want to come back.

EMAN (*pitying*): You cannot dare me that way.

SUNMA: Then why won't you leave here, even for an hour? If you are so sure that your life is settled here, why are you afraid to do this thing for me? What is so wrong that you will not go into the next town for a day or two?

EMAN: I don't want to. I do not have to persuade you, or myself about anything. I simply have no desire to go away.

SUNMA (*His quiet confidence appears to incense her.*): You are afraid. You accuse me of losing my sense of mission, but you are afraid to put yours to the test.

EMAN: You are wrong Sunma. I have no sense of mission. But I have found peace here and I am content with that.

SUNMA: I haven't. For a while I thought that too, but I found there could be no peace in the midst of so much cruelty. Eman, tonight at least, the last night of the old year . . .

EMAN: No Sunma. I find this too distressing; you should go home now.

SUNMA: It is the time for making changes in one's life Eman. Let's breathe in the new year away from here.

EMAN: You are hurting yourself.

SUNMA: Tonight. Only tonight. We will come back tomorrow, as early as you like. But let us go away for this one night. Don't let another year break on me in this place . . . you don't know how important it is to me, but I will tell you, I will tell you on the way . . . but we must not be here today, Eman, do this one thing for me.

EMAN (*sadly*): I cannot.

SUNMA (*suddenly calm*): I was a fool to think it would be otherwise. The whole village may use you as they will but for me there is nothing. Sometimes I think you believe that doing anything for me makes you unfaithful to some part of your life. If it was a woman then I pity her for what she must have suffered.

(Eman winces and hardens slowly. Sunma notices nothing.)

Keeping faith with so much is slowly making you inhuman. *(Seeing the change in Eman.)* Eman. Eman. What is it?

(As she goes toward him, Eman goes into the house.)

SUNMA *(apprehensive, follows him):* What did I say? Eman. forgive me, forgive me please.

(Eman remains facing into the slow darkness of the room. Sunma, distressed, cannot decide what to do.)

I swear I didn't know . . . I would not have said it for all the world.

(A lorry is heard taking off somewhere nearby. The sound comes up and slowly fades away into the distance. Sunma starts visibly, goes slowly to the window.)

SUNMA *(as the sound dies off, to herself):* What happens now?
EMAN *(joining her at the window):* What did you say?
SUNMA: Nothing.
EMAN: Was that not the lorry going off?
SUNMA: It was.
EMAN: I am sorry I couldn't help you.

(Sunma, about to speak, changes her mind.)

EMAN: I think you ought to go home now.
SUNMA: No, don't send me away. It's the least you can do for me. Let me stay here until all the noise is over.
EMAN: But are you not needed at home? You have a part in the festival.
SUNMA: I have renounced it; I am Jaguna's eldest daughter only in name.
EMAN: Renouncing one's self is not so easy—surely you know that.
SUNMA: I don't want to talk about it. Will you at least let us be together tonight?
EMAN: But . . .
SUNMA: Unless you are afraid my father will accuse you of harboring me.
EMAN: All right, we will go out together.
SUNMA: Go out? I want us to stay here.
EMAN: When there is so much going on outside?
SUNMA: Some day you will wish that you went away when I tried to make you.
EMAN: Are we going back to that?
SUNMA: No. I promise you I will not recall it again. But you must know that it was also for your sake that I tried to get us away.
EMAN: For me? How?

SUNMA: By yourself you can do nothing here. Have you not noticed how tightly we shut out strangers? Even if you lived here for a lifetime, you would remain a stranger.

EMAN: Perhaps that is what I like. There is peace in being a stranger.

SUNMA: For a while perhaps. But they would reject you in the end. I tell you it is only I who stand between you and contempt. And because of this you have earned their hatred. I don't know why I say this now, except that somehow, I feel that it no longer matters. It is only I who have stood between you and much humiliation.

EMAN: Think carefully before you say any more. I am incapable of feeling indebted to you. This will make no difference at all.

SUNMA: I ask for nothing. But you must know it all the same. It is true I hadn't the strength to go by myself. And I must confess this now, if you had come with me, I would have done everything to keep you from returning.

EMAN: I know that.

SUNMA: You see, I bare myself to you. For days I had thought it over, this was to be a new beginning for us. And I placed my fate wholly in your hands. Now the thought will not leave me, I have a feeling which will not be shaken off, that in some way, you have tonight totally destroyed my life.

EMAN: You are depressed, you don't know what you are saying.

SUNMA: Don't think I am accusing you. I say all this only because I cannot help it.

EMAN: We must not remain shut up here. Let us go and be part of the living.

SUNMA: No. Leave them alone.

EMAN: Surely you don't want to stay indoors when the whole town is alive with rejoicing.

SUNMA: Rejoicing! Is that what it seems to you? No, let us remain here. Whatever happens I must not go out until all this is over.

(There is silence. It has grown much darker.)

EMAN: I shall light the lamp.

SUNMA *(eager to do something):* No, let me do it.

(She goes into the inner room.
Eman paces the room, stops by a shelf and toys with the seeds in an "ayo"[2] board, takes down the whole board and places it on a table, playing by himself.
The girl is now seen coming back, still dragging her "carrier." Ifada brings up the rear as before. As he comes round the corner of the house two men emerge from the shadows. A sack is thrown over Ifada's head, the rope is pulled tight rendering

---

[2]A game played with seeds. [eds.]

him instantly helpless. The girl has reached the front of the house before she turns round at the sound of scuffle. She is in time to see Ifada thrown over the shoulders and borne away. Her face betraying no emotion at all, the girl backs slowly away, turns and flees, leaving the "carrier" behind. Sunma enters, carrying two kerosene lamps. She hangs one up from the wall.)

EMAN: One is enough.
SUNMA: I want to leave one outside.

(She goes out, hangs the lamp from a nail just above the door. As she turns she sees the effigy and gasps. Eman rushes out.)

EMAN: What is it? Oh, is that what frightened you?
SUNMA: I thought . . . I didn't really see it properly.

(Eman goes toward the object, stoops to pick it up.)

EMAN: It must belong to that sick girl.
SUNMA: Don't touch it.
EMAN: Let's keep it for her.
SUNMA: Leave it alone. Don't touch it Eman.
EMAN *(Shrugs and goes back.)*: You are very nervous.
SUNMA: Let's go in.
EMAN: Wait *(He detains her by the door, under the lamp.)* I know there is something more than you've told me. What are you afraid of tonight?
SUNMA: I was only scared by that thing. There is nothing else.
EMAN: I am not blind Sunma. It is true I would not run away when you wanted me to, but that doesn't mean I do not feel things. What does tonight really mean that it makes you so helpless?
SUNMA: It is only a mood. And your indifference to me . . . let's go in.

(Eman moves aside and she enters; he remains there for a moment and then follows.
She fiddles with the lamp, looks vaguely round the room, then goes and shuts the door, bolting it. When she turns, it is to meet Eman's eyes, questioning.)

SUNMA: There is a cold wind coming in.

(Eman keeps his gaze on her.)

SUNMA: It *was* getting cold.

(She moves guiltily to the table and stands by the "ayo" board, rearranging the seeds. Eman remains where he is a few moments, then brings a stool and sits opposite her. She sits down also and they begin to play in silence.)

SUNMA: What brought you here at all, Eman? And what makes you stay?

(There is another silence.)

SUNMA: I am not trying to share your life. I know you too well by now. But at least we have worked together since you came. Is there nothing at all I deserve to know?

EMAN: Let me continue a stranger—especially to you. Those who have much to give fulfill themselves only in total loneliness.

SUNMA: Then there is no love in what you do.

EMAN: There is. Love comes to me more easily with strangers.

SUNMA: That is unnatural.

EMAN: Not for me. I know I find consummation only when I have spent myself for a total stranger.

SUNMA: It seems unnatural to me. But then I am a woman. I have a woman's longings and weaknesses. And the ties of blood are very strong in me.

EMAN *(smiling):* You think I have cut loose from all these—ties of blood.

SUNMA: Sometimes you are so inhuman.

EMAN: I don't know what that means. But I am very much my father's son.

(They play in silence. Suddenly Eman pauses listening.)

EMAN: Did you hear that?

SUNMA: *(quickly):* I heard nothing . . . it's your turn.

EMAN: Perhaps some of the mummers are coming this way.

(Eman about to play, leaps up suddenly.)

SUNMA: What is it? Don't you what to play any more?

(Eman moves to the door.)

SUNMA: No. Don't go out Eman.

EMAN: If it's the dancers I want to ask them to stay. At least we won't have to miss everything.

SUNMA: No, no. Don't open the door. Let us keep out everyone tonight.

(A terrified and disordered figure bursts suddenly round the corner, past the window and begins hammering at the door. It is Ifada. Desperate with terror, he pounds madly at the door, dumb-moaning all the while.)

EMAN: Isn't that Ifada?

SUNMA: They are only fooling about. Don't pay any attention.

EMAN *(looks round the window):* That is Ifada. *(Begins to unbolt the door.)*

SUNMA *(pulling at his hands):* It is only a trick they are playing on you. Don't take any notice Eman.

EMAN: What are you saying? The boy is out of his senses with fear.

SUNMA: No, no. Don't interfere Eman. For God's sake don't interfere.

EMAN: Do you know something of this then?

SUNMA: You are a stranger here Eman. Just leave us alone and go your own way. There is nothing you can do.

EMAN *(He tries to push her out of the way but she clings fiercely to him.):* Have you gone mad? I tell you the boy must come in.

SUNMA: Why won't you listen to me Eman? I tell you it's none of your business. For your own sake do as I say.

(Eman pushes her off, unbolts the door. Ifada rushes in, clasps Eman round the knees, dumb-moaning against his legs.)

EMAN *(Manages to re-bolt the door.):* What is it Ifada? What is the matter?

(Shouts and voices are heard coming nearer the house.)

SUNMA: Before it's too late, let him go. For once Eman, believe what I tell you. Don't harbor him or you will regret it all your life.

(Eman tries to calm Ifada who becomes more and more abject as the outside voices get nearer.)

EMAN: What have they done to him? At least tell me that. What is going on Sunma?

SUNMA *(with sudden venom):* Monster! Could you not take yourself somewhere else?

EMAN: Stop talking like that.

SUNMA: He could have run into the bush couldn't he? Toad! Why must he follow us with his own disasters!

VOICES OUTSIDE: It's here . . . Round the back . . . Spread, spread . . . this way . . . no, head him off . . . use the bush path and head him off . . . get some more lights . . .

(Eman listens. Lifts Ifada bodily and carries him into the inner room. Returns at once, shutting the door behind him.)

SUNMA *(slumps into a chair, resigned):* You always follow your own way.

JAGUNA *(Comes round the corner followed by Oroge and three men, one bearing a torch.):* I knew he would come here.

OROGE: I hope our friend won't make trouble.

JAGUNA: He had better not. You, recall all the men and tell them to surround the house.

OROGE: But he may not be in the house after all.

JAGUNA: I know he is here . . . *(to the men)* . . . go on, do as I say.

(He bangs on the door.)

Teacher, open your door . . . you two stay by the door. If I need you I will call you.

(Eman opens the door)

JAGUNA *(speaks as he enters):* We know he is here.

EMAN: Who?

JAGUNA: Don't let us waste time. We are grown men, teacher. You understand me and I understand you. But we must take back the boy.

EMAN: This is my house.

JAGUNA: Daughter, you'd better tell your friend. I don't think he quite knows our ways. Tell him why he must give up the boy.

SUNMA: Father, I . . .

JAGUNA: Are you going to tell him or aren't you?

SUNMA: Father, I beg you, leave us alone tonight . . .

JAGUNA: I thought you might be a hindrance. Go home then if you will not use your sense.

SUNMA: But there are other ways . . .

JAGUNA (turning to the men): See that she gets home. I no longer trust her. If she gives trouble carry her. And see that the women stay with her until all this is over.

(Sunma departs, accompanied by one of the men.)

JAGUNA: Now teacher . . .

OROGE (restrains him): You see, Mister Eman, it is like this. Right now, nobody knows that Ifada has taken refuge here. No one except us and our men—and they know how to keep their mouths shut. We don't want to have to burn down the house you see, but if the word gets around, we would have no choice.

JAGUNA: In fact, it may be too late already. A carrier should end up in the bush, not in a house. Anyone who doesn't guard his door when the carrier goes by has himself to blame. A contaminated house should be burned down.

OROGE: But we are willing to let it pass. Only, you must bring him out quickly.

EMAN: All right. But at least you will let me ask you something.

JAGUNA: What is there to ask? Don't you understand what we have told you?

EMAN: Yes. But why did you pick on a helpless boy. Obviously he is not willing.

JAGUNA: What is the man talking about? Ifada is a godsend. Does he have to be willing?

EMAN: In my home, we believe that a man should be willing.

OROGE: Mister Eman, I don't think you quite understand. This is not a simple matter at all. I don't know what you do, but here, it is not a cheap task for anybody. No one in his senses would do such a job. Why do you think we give refuge to idiots like him? We don't know where he came from. One morning, he is simply there, just like that. From nowhere at all. You see, there is a purpose in that.

JAGUNA: We only waste time.

OROGE: Jaguna, be patient. After all, the man has been with us for some time now and deserves to know. The evil of the old year is no light thing to load on any man's head.

EMAN: I know something about that.

OROGE: You do? *(Turns to Jaguna, who snorts impatiently.)* You see I told you so didn't I? From the moment you came I saw you were one of the knowing ones.

JAGUNA: Then let him behave like a man and give back the boy.

EMAN: It is you who are not behaving like men.

JAGUNA *(advances aggressively):* That is a quick mouth you have . . .

OROGE: Patience Jaguna . . . if you want the new year to cushion the land there must be no deeds of anger. What did you mean my friend?

EMAN: It is a simple thing. A village which cannot produce its own carrier contains no men.

JAGUNA: Enough. Let there be no more talk or this business will be ruined by some rashness. You . . . come inside. Bring the boy out, he must be in the room there.

EMAN: Wait.

(The men hesitate.)

JAGUNA *(hitting the nearer one and propelling him forward):* Go on. Have you changed masters now that you listen to what he says?

OROGE *(sadly):* I am sorry you would not understand Mister Eman. But you ought to know that no carrier may return to the village. If he does, the people will stone him to death. It has happened before. Surely it is too much to ask a man to give up his own soil.

EMAN: I know others who have done more.

(Ifada is brought out, abjectly dumb-moaning.)

EMAN: You can see him with your own eyes. Does it really have meaning to use one as unwilling as that.

OROGE *(smiling):* He shall be willing. Not only willing but actually joyous. I am the one who prepares them all, and I have seen worse. This one escaped before I began to prepare him for the event. But you will see him later tonight, the most joyous creature in the festival. Then perhaps you will understand.

EMAN: Then it is only a deceit. Do you believe the spirit of a new year is so easily fooled?

JAGUNA: Take him out. *(The men carry out Ifada.)* You see, it is so easy to talk. You say there are no men in this village because they cannot provide a willing carrier. And yet I heard Oroge tell you we only use strangers. There is only one other stranger in the village, but I have not heard him offer himself *(spits)* It is so easy to talk is it not?

(He turns his back on him.

They go off, taking Ifada with them, limp and silent. The only sign of life is that he strains his neck to keep his eyes on Eman till the very moment that he disappears from sight. Eman remains where they left him, staring after the group.)

(A black-out lasting no more than a minute. The lights come up slowly and Ifada is seen returning to the house. He stops at the window and looks in. Seeing no one, he bangs on the sill. Appears surprised that there is no response. He slithers down on his favorite spot, then sees the effigy still lying where the girl had dropped it in her flight. After some hesitation, he goes toward it, begins to strip it of the clothing. Just then the girl comes in.)

GIRL: Hey, leave that alone. You know it's mine.

(Ifada pauses, then speeds up his action.)

GIRL: I said it is mine. Leave it where you found it.

(She rushes at him and begins to struggle for possession of the carrier.)

GIRL: Thief! Thief! Let it go, it is mine. Let it go. You animal, just because I let you play with it. Idiot! Idiot!

(The struggle becomes quite violent. The girl is hanging to the effigy and Ifada lifts her with it, flinging her all about. The girl hangs on grimly.)

GIRL: You are spoiling it . . . why don't you get your own? Thief! Let it go you thief!

(Sunma comes in walking very fast, throwing apprehensive glances over her shoulder. Seeing the two children, she becomes immediately angry. Advances on them.)

SUNMA: So you've made this place your playground. Get away you untrained pigs. Get out of here.

(Ifada flees at once, the girl retreats also, retaining possession of the "carrier."

Sunma goes to the door. She has her hand on the door when the significance of Ifada's presence strikes her for the first time. She stands rooted to the spot, then turns slowly round.)

SUNMA: Ifada! What are you doing here?

(Ifada is bewildered. Sunma turns suddenly and rushes into the house, flying into the inner room and out again.)

Eman! Eman! Eman!

(She rushes outside.)

Where did he go? Where did they take him?

(Ifada distressed, points. Sunma seizes him by the arm, drags him off.)

Take me there at once. God help you if we are too late. You loathsome thing, if you have let him suffer . . .

(Her voice fades into other shouts, running footsteps, banged tins, bells, dogs, etc., rising in volume.)

(It is a narrow passage-way between two mud-houses. At the far end one man after another is seen running across the entry, the noise dying off gradually.
About half-way down the passage, Eman is crouching against the wall, tense with apprehension. As the noise dies off, he seems to relax, but the alert hunted look is still in his eyes which are ringed in a reddish color. The rest of his body has been whitened with a floury substance. He is naked down to the waist, wears a baggy pair of trousers, calf-length, and around both feet are bangles.)

EMAN: I will simply stay here till dawn. I have done enough.

(A window is thrown open and a woman empties some slop from a pail. With a startled cry Eman leaps aside to avoid it and the woman puts out her head.)

WOMAN: Oh, my head. What have I done! Forgive me neighbor. . . . Eh, it's the carrier!

(Very rapidly she clears her throat and spits on him, flings the pail at him and runs off, shouting.)

He's here. The carrier is hiding in the passage. Quickly, I have found the carrier!

(The cry is taken up and Eman flees down the passage. Shortly afterward his pursuers come pouring down the passage in full cry. After the last of them come Jaguna and Oroge.)

OROGE: Wait, wait. I cannot go so fast.

JAGUNA: We will rest a little then. We can do nothing anyway.

OROGE: If only he had let me prepare him.

JAGUNA: They are the ones who break first, these fools who think they were born to carry suffering like a hat. What are we to do now?

OROGE: When they catch him I must prepare him.

JAGUNA: He? It will be impossible now. There can be no joy left in that one.

OROGE: Still, it took him by surprise. He was not expecting what he met.

JAGUNA: Why then did he refuse to listen? Did he think he was coming to sit down to a feast? He had not even gone through one compound before he bolted. Did he think he was taken round the people to be blessed? A woman, that is all he is.

OROGE: No, no. He took the beating well enough. I think he is the kind who would let himself be beaten from night till dawn and not utter a sound. He would let himself be stoned until he dropped dead.

JAGUNA: Then what made him run like a coward?

OROGE: I don't know. I don't really know. It is a night of curses Jaguna. It is not many unprepared minds will remain unhinged under the load.

JAGUNA: We must find him. It is a poor beginning for a year when our own curses remain hovering over our homes because the carrier refused to take them.

(They go. The scene changes. Eman is crouching beside some shrubs, torn and bleeding.)

EMAN: They are even guarding my house . . . as if I would go there, but I need water . . . they could at least grant me that . . . I can be thirsty too . . . *(He pricks his ears.)* . . . there must be a stream nearby . . . *(As he looks around him, his eyes widen at a scene he encounters.)*

(An old man, short and vigorous looking is seated on a stool. He also is wearing calf-length baggy trousers, white. On his head, a white cap. An attendant is engaged in rubbing his body with oil. Round his eyes, two white rings have already been marked.)

OLD MAN: Have they prepared the boat?

ATTENDANT: They are making the last sacrifice.

OLD MAN: Good. Did you send for my son?

ATTENDANT: He's on his way.

OLD MAN: I have never met the carrying of the boat with such a heavy heart. I hope nothing comes of it.

ATTENDANT: The gods will not desert us on that account.

OLD MAN: A man should be at his strongest when he takes the boat my friend. To be weighed down inside and out is not a wise thing. I hope when the moment comes I shall have found my strength.

(Enter Eman, a wrapper round his waist and a "danski"[3] over it.)

OLD MAN: I meant to wait until after my journey to the river, but my mind is so burdened with my own grief and yours I could not delay it. You know I must have all my strength. But I sit here, feeling it all eaten slowly away by my unspoken grief. It helps to say it out. It even helps to cry sometimes.

(He signals to the attendant to leave them.)

Come nearer . . . we will never meet again son. Not on this side of the flesh. What I do not know is whether you will return to take my place.

EMAN: I will never come back.

OLD MAN: Do you know what you are saying? Ours is a strong breed my son. It is only a strong breed that can take this boat to the river year after year

---

[3]A brief Yoruba attire.

and wax stronger on it. I have taken down each year's evils for over twenty years. I hoped you would follow me.

EMAN: My life here died with Omae.

OLD MAN: Omae died giving birth to your child and you think the world is ended. Eman, my pain did not begin when Omae died. Since you sent her to stay with me son, I lived with the burden of knowing that this child would die bearing your son.

EMAN: Father . . .

OLD MAN: Don't you know it was the same with you? And me? No woman survives the bearing of the strong ones. Son, it is not the mouth of the boaster that says he belongs to the strong breed. It is the tongue that is red with pain and black with sorrow. Twelve years you were away my son, and for those twelve years I knew the love of an old man for his daughter and the pain of a man helplessly awaiting his loss.

EMAN: I wish I had stayed away. I wish I never came back to meet her.

OLD MAN: It had to be. But you know now what slowly ate away my strength. I awaited your return with love and fear. Forgive me then if I say that your grief is light. It will pass. This grief may drive you now from home. But you must return.

EMAN: You do not understand. It is not grief alone.

OLD MAN: What is it then? Tell me, I can still learn.

EMAN: I was away twelve years. I changed much in that time.

OLD MAN: I am listening.

EMAN: I am unfitted for your work father. I wish to say no more. But I am totally unfitted for your call.

OLD MAN: It is only time you need son. Stay longer and you will answer the urge of your blood.

EMAN: That I stayed at all was because of Omae. I did not expect to find her waiting. I would have taken her away, but hard as you claim to be, it would have killed you. And I was a tired man. I needed peace. Because Omae was peace, I stayed. Now nothing holds me here.

OLD MAN: Other men would rot and die doing this task year after year. It is strong medicine which only we can take. Our blood is strong like no other. Anything you do in life must be less than this, son.

EMAN: That is not true father.

OLD MAN: I tell you it is true. Your own blood will betray you son, because you cannot hold it back. If you make it do less than this, it will rush to your head and burst it open. I say what I know my son.

EMAN: There are other tasks in life father. This one is not for me. There are even greater things you know nothing of.

OLD MAN: I am very sad. You only go to give to others what rightly belongs to us. You will use your strength among thieves. They are thieves because they take what is ours, they have no claim of blood to it. They will even lack the knowledge to use it wisely. Truth is my companion at this moment my son. I know everything I say will surely bring the sadness of truth.

EMAN: I am going father.

OLD MAN: Call my attendant. And be with me in your strength for this last journey. A-ah, did you hear that? It came out without my knowing it; this is indeed my last journey. But I am not afraid.

(Eman goes out. A few moments later, the attendant enters.)

ATTENDANT: The boat is ready.

OLD MAN: So am I.

(He sits perfectly still for several moments. Drumming begins somewhere in the distance, and the old man sways his head almost imperceptibly. Two men come in bearing a miniature boat, containing an indefinable mound. They rush it in and set it briskly down near the old man, and stand well back. The old man gets up slowly, the attendant watching him keenly. He signs to the men, who lift the boat quickly onto the old man's head. As soon as it touches his head, he holds it down with both hands and runs off, the men give him a start, then follow at a trot.

As the last man disappears Oroge limps in and comes face to face with Eman— as carrier—who is now seen still standing beside the shrubs, staring into the scene he has just witnessed. Oroge, struck by the look on Eman's face, looks anxiously behind him to see what has engaged Eman's attention. Eman notices him then, and the pair stare at each other. Jaguna enters, sees him and shouts, "Here he is," rushes at Eman who is whipped back to the immediate and flees, Jaguna in pursuit. Three or four others enter and follow them. Oroge remains where he is, thoughtful.)

JAGUNA *(re-enters):* They have closed in on him now, we'll get him this time.

OROGE: It is nearly midnight.

JAGUNA: You were standing there looking at him as if he was some strange spirit. Why didn't you shout?

OROGE: You shouted didn't you? Did that catch him?

JAGUNA: Don't worry. We have him now. But things have taken a bad turn. It is no longer enough to drive him past every house. There is too much contamination about already.

OROGE *(not listening):* He saw something. Why may I not know what it was?

JAGUNA: What are you talking about?

OROGE: Hm. What is it?

JAGUNA: I said there is too much harm done already. The year will demand more from this carrier than we thought.

OROGE: What do you mean?

JAGUNA: Do we have to talk with the full mouth?

OROGE: S-sh . . . look! (Jaguna turns just in time to see Sunma fly at him, clawing at his face like a crazed tigress.)

SUNMA: Murderer! What are you doing to him. Murderer! Murderer!

(Jaguna finds himself struggling really hard to keep off his daughter, he succeeds in pushing her off and striking her so hard on the face that she falls to her knees. He moves on her to hit her again.)

OROGE *(comes between):* Think what you are doing Jaguna, she is your daughter.

JAGUNA: My daughter! Does this one look like my daughter? Let me cripple the harlot for life.

OROGE: That is a wicked thought Jaguna.

JAGUNA: Don't come between me and her.

OROGE: Nothing in anger—do you forget what tonight is?

JAGUNA: Can you blame me for forgetting?

(Draws his hand across his cheek—it is covered with blood.)

OROGE: This is an unhappy night for us all. I fear what is to come of it.

JAGUNA: Let's go. I cannot restrain myself in this creature's presence. My own daughter . . . and for a stranger . . .

(They go off, Ifada, who came in with Sunma and had stood apart, horror-stricken, comes shyly forward. He helps Sunma up. They go off, he holding Sunma bent and sobbing.)

(Enter Eman—as carrier. He is physically present in the bounds of this next scene, a side of a round thatched hut. A young girl, about fourteen runs in, stops beside the hut. She looks carefully to see that she is not observed, puts her mouth to a little hole in the wall.)

OMAE: Eman . . . Eman . . .

(Eman—as carrier—responds, as he does throughout the scene, but they are unaware of him.)

EMAN *(from inside):* Who is it?

OMAE: It is me, Omae.

EMAN: How dare you come here!

(Two hands appear at the hole and pushing outward, create a much larger hole through which Eman puts out his head. It is Eman as a boy, the same age as the girl.)

Go away at once. Are you trying to get me into trouble!

OMAE: What is the matter?

EMAN: You. Go away.

OMAE: But I came to see you.

EMAN: Are you deaf? I say I don't want to see you. Now go before my tutor catches you.

OMAE: All right. Come out.

EMAN: Do what!

OMAE: Come out.

EMAN: You must be mad.

OMAE *(Sits on the ground.):* All right, if you don't come out I shall simply stay here until your tutor arrives.

EMAN *(About to explode, thinks better of it and the head disappears. A moment later he emerges from behind the hut.):* What sort of a devil has got into you?

OMAE: None. I just wanted to see you.

EMAN *(His mimicry is nearly hysterical.):* "None. I just wanted to see you." Do you think this place is the stream where you can go and molest innocent people?

OMAE *(coyly):* Aren't you glad to see me?

EMAN: I am not.

OMAE: Why?

EMAN: Why? Do you really ask me why? Because you are a woman and a most troublesome woman. Don't you know anything about this at all. We are not meant to see any woman. So go away before more harm is done.

OMAE *(flirtatious):* What is so secret about it anyway? What do they teach you.

EMAN: Nothing any woman can understand.

OMAE: Ha ha. You think we don't know eh? You've all come to be circumcized.

EMAN: Shut up. You don't know anything.

OMAE: Just think, all this time you haven't been circumcized, and you dared make eyes at us women.

EMAN: Thank you—woman. Now go.

OMAE: Do they give you enough to eat?

EMAN *(testily):* No. We are so hungry that when silly girls like you turn up, we eat them.

OMAE *(feigning tears):* Oh, oh, oh, he's abusing me. He's abusing me.

EMAN *(alarmed):* Don't try that here. Go quickly if you are going to cry.

OMAE: All right, I won't cry.

EMAN: Cry or no cry, go away and leave me alone. What do you think will happen if my tutor turns up now.

OMAE: He won't.

EMAN *(mimicking):* "He won't." I suppose you are his wife and he tells you where he goes. In fact this is just the time he comes round to our huts. He could be at the next hut this very moment.

OMAE: Ha-ha. You're lying. I left him by the stream, pinching the girls' bottoms. Is that the sort of thing he teaches you?

EMAN: Don't say anything against him or I shall beat you. Isn't it you loose girls who tease him, wiggling your bottoms under his nose?

OMAE *(going tearful again):* A-ah, so I am one of the loose girls eh?

EMAN: Now don't start accusing me of things I didn't say.

OMAE: But you said it. You said it.

EMAN: I didn't. Look Omae, someone will hear you and I'll be in disgrace. Why don't you go before anything happens.

OMAE: It's all right. My friends have promised to hold your old rascal tutor till I get back.

EMAN: Then you go back right now. I have work to do. *(Going in.)*

OMAE *(Runs after and tries to hold him. Eman leaps back, genuinely scared.):* What is the matter? I was not going to bite you.

EMAN: Do you know what you nearly did? You almost touched me!

OMAE: Well?

EMAN: Well! Isn't it enough that you let me set my eyes on you? Must you now totally pollute me with your touch? Don't you understand anything?

OMAE: Oh, that.

EMAN *(nearly screaming):* It is not "oh that." Do you think this is only a joke or a little visit like spending the night with your grandmother? This is an important period of my life. Look, these huts, we built them with our own hands. Every boy builds his own. We learn things, do you understand? And we spend much time just thinking. At least, I do. It is the first time I have had nothing to do except think. Don't you see, I am becoming a man. For the first time, I understand that I have a life to fulfill. Has that thought ever worried you?

OMAE: You are frightening me.

EMAN: There. That is all you can say. And what use will that be when a man finds himself alone—like that? *(Points to the hut.)* A man must go on his own, go where no one can help him, and test his strength. Because he may find himself one day sitting alone in a wall as round as that. In there, my mind could hold no other thought. I may never have such moments again to myself. Don't dare to come and steal any more of it.

OMAE *(this time, genuinely tearful):* Oh, I know you hate me. You only want to drive me away.

EMAN *(impatiently):* Yes, yes, I know I hate you—but go.

OMAE *(going, all tears. Wipes her eyes, suddenly all mischief.):* Eman.

EMAN: What now?

OMAE: I only want to ask one thing . . . do you promise to tell me?

EMAN: Well, what is it?

OMAE *(gleefully):* Does it hurt?

(She turns instantly and flees, landing straight into the arms of the returning tutor.)

TUTOR: Te-he-he . . . what have we here? What little mouse leaps straight into the beak of the wise old owl eh?

(Omae struggles to free herself, flies to the opposite side, grimacing with distaste.)

TUTOR: I suppose you merely came to pick some fruits eh? You did not sneak here to see any of my children.

OMAE: Yes, I came to steal your fruits.

TUTOR: Te-he-he . . . I thought so. And that dutiful son of mine over there. He saw you and came to chase you off my fruit trees didn't he? Te-he-he . . . I'm sure he did, isn't that so my young Eman?

EMAN: I was talking to her.

TUTOR: Indeed you were. Now be good enough to go into your hut until I decide your punishment. *(Eman withdraws.)* Te-he-he . . . now now my little daughter, you need not be afraid of me.

OMAE *(spiritedly):* I am not.

TUTOR: Good. Very good. We ought to be friendly. *(His voice becomes leering.)* Now this is nothing to worry you my daughter . . . a very small thing indeed. Although of course if I were to let it slip that your young Eman had broken a strong taboo, it might go hard on him you know. I am sure you would not like that to happen, would you?

OMAE: No.

TUTOR: Good. You are sensible my girl. Can you wash clothes?

OMAE: Yes.

TUTOR: Good. If you will come with me now to my hut, I shall give you some clothes to wash, and then we will forget all about this matter eh? Well, come on.

OMAE: I shall wait here. You go and bring the clothes.

TUTOR: Eh? What is that? Now now, don't make me angry. You should know better than to talk back at your elders. Come now.

(He takes her by the arm, and tries to drag her off.)

OMAE: No no, I won't come to your hut. Leave me. Leave me alone you shameless old man.

TUTOR: If you don't come I shall disgrace the whole family of Eman, and yours too.

(Eman re-enters with a small bundle.)

EMAN: Leave her alone. Let us go Omae.

TUTOR: And where do you think you are going?

EMAN: Home.

TUTOR: Te-he-he . . . As easy as that eh? You think you can leave here any time you please? Get right back inside that hut!

(Eman takes Omae by the arm and begins to walk off.)

TUTOR: Come back at once.

(He goes after him and raises his stick. Eman catches it, wrenches it from him and throws its away.)

OMAE *(hopping delightedly):* Kill him. Beat him to death.
TUTOR: Help! Help! He is killing me! Help!

(Alarmed, Eman clamps his hand over his mouth.)

EMAN: Old tutor, I don't mean you any harm, but you mustn't try to harm me either. *(He removes his hand.)*
TUTOR: You think you can get away with your crime. My report shall reach the elders before you ever get into town.
EMAN: You are afraid of what I will say about you? Don't worry. Only if you try to shame me, then I will speak. I am not going back to the village anyway. Just tell them I have gone, no more. If you say one word more than that I shall hear of it the same day and I shall come back.
TUTOR: You are telling me what to do? But don't think to come back next year because I will drive you away. Don't think to come back here even ten years from now. And don't send your children.

(Goes off with threatening gestures.)

EMAN: I won't come back.
OMAE: Smoked vulture! But Eman, he says you cannot return next year. What will you do?
EMAN: It is a small thing one can do in the big towns.
OMAE: I thought you were going to beat him that time. Why didn't you crack his dirty hide?
EMAN: Listen carefully Omae . . . I am going on a journey.
OMAE: Come on. Tell me about it on the way.
EMAN: No, I go that way. I cannot return to the village.
OMAE: Because of that wretched man? Anyway you will first talk to your father.
EMAN: Go and see him for me. Tell him I have gone away for some time. I think he will know.
OMAE: But Eman . . .
EMAN: I haven't finished. You will go and live with him till I get back. I have spoken to him about you. Look after him!
OMAE: But what is this journey? When will you come back?
EMAN: I don't know. But this is a good moment to go. Nothing ties me down.
OMAE: But Eman, you want to leave me.
EMAN: Don't forget all I said. I don't know how long I will be. Stay in my father's house as long as you remember me. When you become tired of waiting, you must do as you please. You understand? You must do as you please.

OMAE: I cannot understand anything Eman. I don't know where you are going or why. Suppose you never came back! Don't go Eman. Don't leave me by myself.

EMAN: I must go. Now let me see you on your way.

OMAE: I shall come with you.

EMAN: Come with me! And who will look after you? Me? You will only be in my way, you know that! You will hold me back and I shall desert you in a strange place. Go home and do as I say. Take care of my father and let him take care of you. (*He starts going but Omae clings to him.*)

OMAE: But Eman, stay the night at least. You will only lose your way. Your father Eman, what will he say? I won't remember what you said . . . come back to the village . . . I cannot return alone Eman . . . come with me as far as the crossroads.

(*His face set, Eman strides off and Omae loses balance as he increases his pace. Falling, she quickly wraps her arms around his ankle, but Eman continues unchecked, dragging her along.*)

OMAE: Don't go Eman . . . Eman, don't leave me, don't leave me . . . don't leave your Omae . . . don't go Eman . . . don't leave your Omae . . .

(*Eman—as carrier—makes a nervous move as if he intends to go after the vanished pair. He stops but continues to stare at the point where he last saw them. There is stillness for a while. Then the Girl enters from the same place and remains looking at Eman. Startled, Eman looks apprehensively round him. The Girl goes nearer but keeps beyond arm's length.*)

GIRL: Are you the carrier?

EMAN: Yes. I am Eman.

GIRL: Why are you hiding?

EMAN: I really came for a drink of water . . . er . . . is there anyone in front of the house?

GIRL: No.

EMAN: But there might be people in the house. Did you hear voices?

GIRL: There is no one here.

EMAN: Good. Thank you. (*He is about to go, stops suddenly.*) Er . . . would you . . . you will find a cup on the table. Could you bring me the water out here? The water-pot is in a corner.

(*The Girl goes. She enters the house, then, watching Eman carefully, slips out and runs off.*)

EMAN (*sitting*): Perhaps they have all gone home. It will be good to rest. (*He hears voices and listens hard.*) Too late. (*Moves cautiously nearer the house.*) Quickly girl, I can hear people coming. Hurry up. (*Looks through the window.*) Where are you? Where is she? (*The truth dawns on him suddenly and he moves off, sadly.*)

(Enter Jaguna and Oroge, led by the Girl.)

GIRL *(pointing):* He was there.

JAGUNA: Ay, he's gone now. He is a sly one is your friend. But it won't save him for ever.

OROGE: What was he doing when you saw him?

GIRL: He asked me for a drink of water.

JAGUNA, OROGE: Ah! *(They look at each other.)*

OROGE: We should have thought of that.

JAGUNA: He is surely finished now. If only we had thought of it earlier.

OROGE: It is not too late. There is still an hour before midnight.

JAGUNA: We must call back all the men. Now we need only wait for him—in the right place.

OROGE: Everyone must be told. We don't want anyone heading him off again.

JAGUNA: And it works so well. This is surely the help of the gods themselves Oroge. Don't you know at once what is on the path to the stream?

OROGE: The sacred trees.

JAGUNA: I tell you it is the very hand of the gods. Let us go.

(An overgrown part of the village. Eman wanders in, aimlessly, seemingly uncaring of discovery. Beyond him, an area lights up, revealing a group of people clustered round a spot, all the heads are bowed. One figure stands away and separate from them. Even as Eman looks, the group breaks up and the people disperse, coming down and past him. Only three people are left, a man (Eman) whose back is turned, the village priest and the isolated one. They stand on opposite sides of the grave, the man on the mound of earth. The priest walks round to the man's side and lays a hand on his shoulder.)

PRIEST: Come.

EMAN: I will. Give me a few moments here alone.

PRIEST: Be comforted.

(They fall silent.)

EMAN: I was gone twelve years but she waited. She whom I thought had too much of the laughing child in her. Twelve years I was a pilgrim, seeking the vain shrine of secret strength. And all the time, strange knowledge, this silent strength of my child-woman.

PRIEST: We all saw it. It was a lesson to us; we did not know that such goodness could be found among us.

EMAN: Then why? Why the wasted years if she had to perish giving birth to my child? *(They are both silent.)* I do not really know for what great meaning I searched. When I returned, I could not be certain I had found it. Until I reached my home and I found her a full-grown woman, still a child at heart. When I grew to believe it, I thought, this, after all, is what I sought. It was here all the time. And I threw away my new-gained knowledge. I buried the part of me that was formed in strange places. I made a home in my birthplace.

PRIEST: That was as it should be.

EMAN: Any truth of that was killed in the cruelty of her brief happiness.

PRIEST *(Looks up and sees the figure standing away from them, the child in his arms. He is totally still.):* Your father—he is over there.

EMAN: I knew he would come. Has he my son with him?

PRIEST: Yes.

EMAN: He will let no one take the child. Go and comfort him priest. He loved Omae like a daughter, and you all know how well she looked after him. You see how strong we really are. In his heart of hearts the old man's love really awaited a daughter. Go and comfort him. His grief is more than mine.

(The priest goes. The old man has stood well away from the burial group. His face is hard and his gaze unswerving from the grave. The priest goes to him, pauses, but sees that he can make no dent in the man's grief. Bowed, he goes on his way.)

(Eman, as carrier, walking toward the graveside, the other Eman having gone. His feet sink into the mound and he breaks slowly on to his knees, scooping up the sand in his hands and pouring it on his head. The scene blacks out slowly.)

(Enter Jaguna and Oroge.)

OROGE: We have only a little time.

JAGUNA: He will come. All the wells are guarded. There is only the stream left him. The animal must come to drink.

OROGE: You are sure it will not fail—the trap I mean.

JAGUNA: When Jaguna sets the trap, even elephants pay homage—their trunks downwards and one leg up in the sky. When the carrier steps on the fallen twigs, it is up in the sacred trees with him.

OROGE: I shall breathe again when this long night is over.

(They go out.)

(Enter Eman—as carrier—from the same direction as the last two entered. In front of him is a still figure, the old man as he was, carrying the dwarf boat.)

EMAN *(joyfully):* Father.

(The figure does not turn round.)

EMAN: It is your son. Eman. *(He moves nearer.)* Don't you want to look at me? It is I, Eman. *(He moves nearer still.)*

OLD MAN: You are coming too close. Don't you know what I carry on my head?

EMAN: But Father, I am your son.

OLD MAN: Then go back. We cannot give the two of us.

EMAN: Tell me first where you are going.

OLD MAN: Do *you* ask that? Where else but to the river?

EMAN (*visibly relieved*): I only wanted to be sure. My throat is burning. I have been looking for the stream all night.

OLD MAN: It is the other way.

EMAN: But you said . . .

OLD MAN: I take the longer way, you know how I must do this. It is quicker if you take the other way. Go now.

EMAN: No, I will only get lost again, I shall go with you.

OLD MAN: Go back my son. Go back.

EMAN: Why? Won't you even look at me?

OLD MAN: Listen to your father. Go back.

EMAN: But father!

(*He makes to hold him. Instantly the old man breaks into a rapid trot. Eman hesitates, then follows, his strength nearly gone.*)

EMAN: Wait father. I am coming with you . . . wait . . . wait for me father . . .

(*There is a sound of twigs breaking, of a sudden trembling in the branches. Then silence.*)

(*The front of Eman's house. The effigy is hanging from the sheaves. Enter Sunma, still supported by Ifada, she stands transfixed as she sees the hanging figure. Ifada appears to go mad, rushes at the object and tears it down. Sunma, her last bit of will gone, crumbles against the wall. Some distance away from them, partly hidden, stands the Girl, impassively watching. Ifada hugs the effigy to him, stands above Sunma. The Girl remains where she is, observing.*)

(*Almost at once, the villagers begin to return, subdued and guilty. They walk across the front, skirting the house as widely as they can. No word is exchanged. Jaguna and Oroge eventually appear. Jaguna who is leading, sees Sunma as soon as he comes in view. He stops at once, retreating slightly.*)

OROGE (*almost whispering*): What is it?

JAGUNA: The viper.

(*Oroge looks cautiously at the woman.*)

OROGE: I don't think she will even see you.

JAGUNA: Are you sure? I am in no frame of mind for another meeting with her.

OROGE: Let's go home.

JAGUNA: I am sick to the heart of the cowardice I have seen tonight.

OROGE: That is the nature of men.

JAGUNA: Then it is a sorry world to live in. We did it for them. It was all for their own common good. What did it benefit me whether the man lived or died. But did you see them? One and all they looked up at the man and words died in their throats.

OROGE: It was no common sight.

JAGUNA: Women could not have behaved so shamefully. One by one they crept off like sick dogs. Not one could raise a curse.

OROGE: It was not only him they fled. Do you see how unattended we are?

JAGUNA: There are those who will pay for this night's work!

OROGE: Ay, let us go home.

(They go off. Sunma, Ifada and the Girl remain as they are, the light fading slowly on them.)

❀ Discussion and Writing

1. Distinguish between the New Year's celebrations in the two villages: what is the role of the carrier (or scapegoat) in each; who functions as the carrier in each; how is the ceremony performed in each?
2. Differentiate between the two time periods: what are Eman's roles in the present in the new village, and in the past in the old village?
3. Discuss the function of the various characters in relation to dominant themes in the play: Ifada and the girl; Sunma and Omae; the father, the tutor, and the villagers.
4. What is the significance of the phenomenon of the Strong Breed? How does the metaphor relate to the themes of fathers and sons; men and women; personal needs and communal obligations; identity?
5. What is implied in Soyinka's presenting both the strengths and deficiencies of the two villages?
6. Analyze Soyinka's techniques: the use of flashback; the coalescing of time and place. Explain the significance of the ending of the play that brings together the two times and two places.

❀ Research and Comparison

1. Explore Wole Soyinka's theory of an indigenous concept of time and mythic vision in his poetry or fiction.
2. Analyze his incorporation of the Western concept of tragedy in his plays.
3. Compare and contrast the different approaches to language and cultural synthesis in the critical works of Chinua Achebe, Ngugi wa Thiong'o, and Wole Soyinka.

Costa Andrade
(b. 1936)
Angola

Costa Andrade was born in the inland city of Huambo, Angola. He studied architecture, and published poetry, short stories, and criticism from the early 1960s on. He served with the Angolan Popular Liberation Movement from 1968 to 1974.

When Angola gained its independence from Portugal, a struggle for power ensued, with the Soviet Union and the United States backing different factions. In a sense, the devastation of Angola begun by the Portuguese continued. Portugal used warring kingdoms to its advantage when it landed on the shores of present-day Angola in the late 1400s. For four hundred years, Portugal used Angola predominantly as a source of slaves for its plantations in Brazil. Except for the Mbundu kingdom in central Angola (which was not conquered until 1902), the Portuguese subdued the different peoples as they drove further inland. Guerrilla warfare, initiated after the 1961 defeat of a revolt against Portuguese repressive rule, finally brought about independence in 1975.

Fourth Poem of a Canto of Accusation*

There are on the earth 50,000 dead whom no one mourned
  on the earth
    unburied
      50,000 dead

whom no one mourned.

A thousand Guernicas and the message in the brushes of
Orozco and of Siqueiros
as broad as the sea this silence
spread across the land

    as if the rains had rained blood
    as if the rough hair were grass for many yards
    as if the mouths condemned
    at the very instant of their 50,000 deaths
    all the living of the earth.

Translated by M. M. Wolfers

There are on the earth 50,000 dead
whom no one mourned

no one . . .

The Mothers of Angola
    have fallen with their sons.

❋ **Discussion and Writing**

1. Explore the implications of the images of "death," blood," and "silences."
2. What is the relevance of the Mothers in the poem?
3. Who is accusing whom in the "Canto of Accusation"? What would change if the accuser and the accused were different? Explain your reasoning.

❋ **Research and Comparison**

Interdisciplinary Discussion Question: Research the history of Angola's fight for liberation from the Portuguese. Comment on the role of the nationalist writers in this struggle.

Assia Djebar
(b. 1936)
Algeria

Assia Djebar (Fatima-Zohra Imalayene) was born in Algeria and raised in a middle-class Muslim family. Her early schooling was in Algiers, and she was the first Algerian woman to attend l'Ecole Normale Superieure de Sevres. She also studied at the Sorbonne, receiving a *licence* degree. During the Algerian war of independence from France (1954–1962), she interviewed refugees who had fled to Morocco for the FLN (National Liberation Front) newspaper. Subsequently, she described the war in a novel (*Les enfants du nouveau monde* [Children of the New World]) published the year Algeria won its independence (1962). This was her third novel, the first (*La Soif* [Thirst]) having been published five years earlier. For a time, she stopped writing and worked as a teacher in Algeria. During this period, she translated Nalwal El Saadawi's famous novel, *Firdaus* (Woman at Point Zero, 1975) from Arabic into French. She also turned to film as a means of reaching those, especially women, who cannot read, using the Arabic dialect spoken in Algeria rather than classical Arabic or French. Her first film, *La nouba des femmes du mont Chenoua* (The Celebration of the Women of Mount Chenoua) won the critic's prize at the Venice Biennale in 1979.

Djebar's fiction depicts the life of contemporary Algerian women of her class who have been educated and raised in economically comfortable circumstances. Much of the fiction reflects the impact of the war of liberation,and implicitly asserts equal rights for women in public life. "There Is No Exile" comes from the collection *Femmes d'Alger dans leur appartement* (Women of Algiers in Their Apartment, 1980) and portrays the daily lives of middle-class refugee women.

*There Is No Exile**

That particular morning, I'd finished the housework a little earlier, by nine o'clock. Mother had put on her veil, taken her basket; in the opening of the door, she repeated as she had been repeating every day for three years: "Not until we had been chased out of our own country did I find myself forced to go out to market like a man."

"Our men have other things to do," I answered, as I'd been answering every day for three years.

"May God protect us!"

I saw Mother to the staircase, then watched her go down heavily because of her legs: "May God protect us," I said again to myself as I went back in.

The cries began around ten o'clock, more or less. They were coming from the apartment next door and soon changed into shrieks. All three of us, my two sisters—Aicha, Anissa, and I—recognized it by the way in which the women received it: it was death.

Aicha, the eldest, ran to the door, opened it in order to hear more clearly: "May misfortune stay away from us," she mumbled. "Death has paid the Smain family a visit."

At that moment, Mother came in. She put the basket on the floor, stopped where she stood, her face distraught, and began to beat her chest spasmodically with her hands. She was uttering little stifled cries, as when she was about to get sick.

Anissa, although she was the youngest of us, never lost her calm. She ran to close the door, lifted Mother's veil, took her by the shoulders and made her sit down on a mattress.

*Translated by Marjolin de Jagar

"Now don't get yourself in that state on account of someone else's misfortune," she said. "Don't forget you have a bad heart. May God shelter and keep us always."

While she repeated the phrase several more times, she went to get some water and sprinkled it on Mother, who now, stretched out full length on the mattress, was moaning. Then Anissa washed her entire face, took a bottle of cologne from the wardrobe, opened it, and put it under her nostrils.

"No!" Mother said. "Bring me some lemon."

And she started to moan again.

Anissa continued to bustle about. I was just watching her. I've always been slow to react. I'd begun to listen to the sobs outside that hadn't ceased, would surely not cease before nightfall. There were five or six women in the Smain family, and they were all lamenting in chorus, each one settling, forever it seemed, into the muddled outbreak of their grief. Later, of course, they'd have to prepare the meal, busy themselves with the poor, wash the body. . . . There are so many things to do, the day of a burial.

For now, the voices of the hired mourners, all alike without any one of them distinguishable from the other if only by a more anguished tone, were making one long, gasping chant, and I knew that it would hang over the entire day like a fog in winter.

"Who actually died over there?" I asked Mother, who had almost quieted down.

"Their young son," she said, inhaling the lemon deeply. "A car drove over him in front of the door. I was coming home when my eyes saw him twisting one last time, like a worm. The ambulance took him to the hospital, but he was already dead."

Then she began to sigh again.

"Those poor people," she was saying, "they saw him go out jumping with life and now they're going to bring him back in a bloodstained sheet."

She raised herself halfway, repeated: "jumping with life." Then she fell back down on the mattress and said nothing other than the ritual formulas to keep misfortune away. But the low voice she always used to address God had a touch of hardness, vehemence.

"This day has an evil smell," I said, still standing in front of Mother, motionlessly. "I've sensed it since this morning, but I didn't know then that it was the smell of death."

"You have to add: May God protect us!" Mother said sharply. Then she raised her eyes to me. We were alone in the room, Anissa and Aicha had gone back to the kitchen.

"What's the matter with you?" she said. "You look pale. Are you feeling sick, too?"

"May God protect us!" I said and left the room.

At noon, Omar was the first one home. The weeping continued. I'd attended to the meal while listening to the threnody and its modulations. I was growing used to them. I thought Omar would start asking questions. But no. He must have heard about it in the street.

He pulled Aicha into a room. Then I heard them whispering. When some important event occurred, Omar spoke first to Aicha in this way, because she was the eldest and the most serious one. Previously, Father used to do the same thing, but outside, with Omar, for he was the only son.

So there was something new; and it had nothing to do with death visiting the Smain family. I wasn't curious at all. Today is the day of death, all the rest becomes immaterial.

"Isn't that so?" I said to Anissa, who jumped.

"What's the matter now?"

"Nothing," I said without belaboring the point, for I was familiar with her always disconcerted answers whenever I'd start thinking out loud. Even this morning . . .

But why this sudden, blatant desire to stare at myself in a mirror, to confront my own image at some length, and to say, while letting my hair fall down my back so that Anissa would gaze upon it: "Look. At twenty-five, after having been married, after having lost my two children one after the other, having been divorced, after this exile and after this war, here I am busy admiring myself, smiling at myself like a young girl, like you . . . "

"Like me!" Anissa said, and she shrugged her shoulders.

Father came home a little late because it was Friday and he'd gone to say the prayer of *dhor*[1] at the mosque. He immediately asked why they were in mourning.

"Death has visited the Smains," I said, running toward him to kiss his hand. "It has taken their young son away."

"Those poor people," he said after a silence.

I helped him get settled in his usual place, on the same mattress. Then, as I put his meal in front of him and made sure he didn't have to wait for anything, I forgot about the neighbors for a while. I liked to serve Father; it was, I think, the only household task I enjoyed. Especially now. Since our departure, Father had aged a great deal. He gave too much thought to those who weren't with us, even though he never spoke of them, unless a letter arrived from Algeria and he asked Omar to read it.

In the middle of the meal I heard Mother murmur: "They can't possibly feel like eating today."

"The body is still at the hospital," someone said.

Father said nothing. He rarely spoke during meals.

"I'm not really hungry," I said, getting up, to excuse myself.

The sobs outside seemed more muffled, but I could still distinguish their singsong. Their gentle singsong. This is the moment, I said to myself, when grief becomes familiar, and pleasurable, and nostalgic. This is the moment

---

[1]Noontime prayer. [eds.]

when you weep almost voluptuously, for this gift of tears is a gift without end. This was the moment when the bodies of my children would turn cold fast, so fast, and when I knew it. . . .

At the end of the meal, Aicha came into the kitchen, where I was by my-self. First she went to close the windows that looked out over the neighbor-ing terraces, through which the weeping reached me. But I could still hear it. And, oddly, it was that which made me so tranquil today, a little gloomy.

"There are some women coming this afternoon to see you and to propose marriage," she began. "Father says the candidate is suitable in every way."

Without answering, I turned my back to her and went to the window.

"Now what's your problem?" she said a little sharply.

"I need some air," I said and opened the window all the way, so that the song could come in. It had already been a while since the breathing of death had become, for me, "the song."

Aicha remained a moment without answering. "When Father goes out, you'll attend to yourself a little," she said at last. "These women know very well that we're refugees like so many others, and that they're not going to find you dressed like a queen. But you should look your best, nevertheless."

"They've stopped weeping," I remarked, "or perhaps they're already tired," I said, thinking of that strange fatigue that grasps us at the depth of our sorrow.

"Why don't you keep your mind on the women who're coming?" Aicha replied in a slightly louder voice.

Father had left. Omar too, when Hafsa arrived. Like us, she was Alger-ian and we'd known her there, a young girl of twenty with an education. She was a teacher but had been working only since her mother and she had been exiled, as had so many others. "An honorable woman doesn't work outside her home," her mother used to say. She still said it, but with a sigh of helplessness. One had to live, and there was no man in their household now.

Hafsa found Mother and Anissa in the process of preparing pastries, as if these were a must for refugees like us. But her sense of protocol was instinc-tive in Mother; an inheritance from her past life that she could not readily abandon.

"These women you're waiting for," I asked, "who are they?"

"Refugees like us," Aicha exclaimed. "You don't really think we'd give you away in marriage to strangers?" Then with heart and soul: "Remember," she said, "the day we return to our own country, we shall all go back home, all of us, without exception."

"The day that we return," Hafsa, standing in the middle of the room, suddenly cried out, her eyes wide with dreams. "The day that we return to our country!" she repeated. "How I'd like to go back there on foot, the better to feel the Algerian soil under my feet, the better to see all our women, one after the other, all the widows, and all the orphans, and finally all the men, exhausted, sad perhaps, but free—free! And then I'll take a bit of soil in my hands, oh, just a tiny handful of soil, and I'll say to them: 'See, my brothers, see these drops of blood in these grains of soil in this hand, that's how much Algeria has bled throughout her body, all over her vast body, that's how much Algeria has paid for our freedom and for this, our return, with her own soil. But her martyrdom now speaks in terms of grace. So you see, my brothers . . . ' "

"The day that we return," Mother repeated softly in the silence that followed . . . "if God wills it."

It was then that the cries began again through the open window. Like an orchestra that brusquely starts a piece of music. Then, in a different tone, Hafsa reminded us: "I'm here for the lesson."

Aicha pulled her into the next room.

During their meeting, I didn't know what to do. The windows of the kitchen and of the other two rooms looked out over the terraces. I went from one to the other, opening them, closing them, opening them again. All of this without hurrying, as if I weren't listening to the song.

Anissa caught me in my rounds.

"You can tell they're not Algerian," she said. "They're not even accustomed to being in mourning."

"At home, in the mountains," Mother answered, "the dead have nobody to weep over them before they grow cold."

"Weeping serves no purpose," Anissa was stoic, "whether you die in your bed or on the bare ground for your country."

"What do you know about it?" I suddenly said to her. "You're too young to know."

"Soon they're going to bury him," Mother whispered.

Then she raised her head and looked at me, I had once again closed the window behind me. I couldn't hear anything anymore.

"They're going to bury him this very day," Mother said again a little louder, "that's our custom."

"They shouldn't," I said. "It's a hateful custom to deliver a body to the earth when beauty still shines on it. Really quite hateful. . . . It seems to me they're burying him while he's still shivering, still . . . " (but I couldn't control my voice any longer).

"Stop thinking about your children!" Mother said. "The earth that was thrown on them is a blanket of gold. My poor daughter, stop thinking about your children!" Mother said again.

"I'm not thinking about anything," I said. "No, really. I don't want to think about anything. About anything at all."

It was already four o'clock in the afternoon when they came in. From the kitchen where I was hiding, I heard them exclaim, once the normal phrases of courtesy had been uttered: "What is that weeping?"

"May misfortune stay far away from us! May God protect us!"

"It gives me goose bumps," the third one was saying. "I've almost forgotten death and tears, these days. I've forgotten them, even though our hearts are always heavy."

"That is the will of God," the second one would respond.

In a placid voice, Mother explained the reason for the mourning next door as she invited them into the only room we had been able to furnish decently. Anissa, close by me, was already making the first comments on the way the women looked. She was questioning Aicha, who had been with Mother to welcome them. I had opened the window again and watched them exchange their first impressions.

"What are you thinking?" Anissa said, her eye still on me.

"Nothing," I said feebly; then, after a pause: "I was thinking of the different faces of fate. I was thinking of God's will. Behind that wall, there is a dead person and women going mad with grief. Here, in our house, other women are talking of marriage . . . I was thinking of that difference."

"Just stop 'thinking,' " Aicha cut in sharply. Then to Hafsa, who was coming in: "You ought to be teaching *her*, not me. She spends all her time thinking. You'd almost believe she's read as many books as you have."

"And why not?" Hafsa asked.

"I don't need to learn French," I answered. "What purpose would it serve? Father has taught us all our language. 'That's all you need,' he always says."

"It's useful to know languages other than your own," Hafsa said slowly. "It's like knowing other people, other countries."

I didn't answer. Perhaps she was right. Perhaps you ought to learn and not waste your time letting your mind wander, like mine, through the deserted corridors of the past. Perhaps I should take lessons and study French, or anything else. But I, I never felt the need to jostle my body or my mind. . . . Aicha was different. Like a man: hard and hardworking. She was thirty. She hadn't seen her husband in three years, who was still incarcerated in Barberousse prison, where he had been since the first days of the war. Yet, she was getting an education and didn't settle for household work. Now, after just a few months of Hafsa's lessons, Omar no longer read her husband's infrequent letters, the few that might reach her. She managed to decipher them by herself. Sometimes I caught myself being envious of her.

"Hafsa," she said, "it's time for my sister to go in and greet these ladies. Please go with her."

But Hafsa didn't want to. Aicha insisted, and I was watching them play their little game of politeness.

"Does anyone know if they've come for the body yet?" I asked.

"What? Didn't you hear the chanters just now?" Anissa said.

"So that's why the weeping stopped for a moment," I said. "It's strange, as soon as some parts of the Koranic verses are chanted, the women immediately stop weeping. And yet, that's the most painful moment, I know it all too well myself. As long as the body is there in front of you, it seems the child isn't quite dead yet, can't be dead, you see? . . . Then comes the moment when the men get up, and that is to take him, wrapped in a sheet, on their shoulders. That's how he leaves, quickly, as on the day that he came. . . . For me, may God forgive me, they can chant Koranic verses all they want, the house is still empty after they've gone, completely empty. . . ."

Hafsa was listening, her head leaning toward the window. With a shiver, she turned toward me. She seemed younger even than Anissa, then.

"My God," she said, emotion in her voice, "I've just turned twenty and yet I've never encountered death. Never in my whole life!"

"Haven't you lost anyone in your family in this war?" Anissa asked.

"Oh yes," she said, "but the news always comes by mail. And death by mail, you see, I can't believe it. A first cousin of mine died under the guillotine as one of the first in Barberousse. Well, I've never shed a tear over him because I cannot believe that he's dead. And yet he was like a brother to me, I swear. But I just can't believe he's dead, you understand?" she said in a voice already wrapped in tears.

"Those who've died for the Cause aren't really dead," Anissa answered with a touch of pride.

"So, let's think of the present. Let's think about today," Aicha said in a dry voice. "The rest is in God's hand."

There were three of them: an old woman who had to be the suitor's mother and who hastily put on her glasses as soon as I arrived; two other women, seated side by side, resembled each other. Hafsa, who'd come in behind me, sat down next to me. I lowered my eyes.

I knew my part, it was one I'd played before; stay mute like this, eyes lowered, and patiently let myself be examined until the very end: it was simple. Everything is simple, beforehand, for a girl who's being married off.

Mother was talking. I was barely listening. I knew the themes to be developed all too well: Mother was talking about our sad state as refugees; then they'd be exchanging opinions on when the end might be announced: ". . . another Ramadan to be spent away from home . . . perhaps this was the last one . . . perhaps, if God wills it! Of course, we were saying the same thing last year, and the year before that. . . . Let's not complain too much. . . . In any event, victory is certain, all our men say the same thing. And we, we know the day of our return will come. . . . We should be thinking of those who stayed behind. . . . We should be thinking of those who are suffering. . . . The Algerian people are a people whom God loves. . . . And our fighters are made of steel. . . ." Then they'd come back to the tale of the flight, to the different means by which each one had left her soil where the fires were burning. . . . Then they'd evoke the sadness of exile, the heart yearning for its country. . . . And the fear of dying far from the land of one's birth. . . . Then. . . . "But may God be praised and may he grant our prayers!"

This time it lasted a bit longer; an hour perhaps, or more. Until the time came to serve coffee. By then, I was hardly listening at all. I too was thinking in my own way of this exile, of these somber days.

I was thinking how everything had changed, how on the day of my first engagement we had been in the long, bright living room of our house in the hills of Algiers; how we'd been prosperous then, we had prosperity and peace; how Father used to laugh, how he used to give thanks to God for the abundance of his home . . . And I, I wasn't as I was today, my soul gray, gloomy and with this idea of death beating faintly inside me since the morning. . . . Yes, I was thinking how everything had changed and that, still, in some way everything remained the same. They were still concerned with marrying me off. And why exactly? I suddenly wondered. And why exactly? I repeated to myself, feeling something like fury inside me, or its echo. Just so I could have worries that never change whether it's peace or wartime, so I could wake up in the middle of the night and question myself on what it is that sleeps in the depths of the heart of the man sharing my bed. . . . Just so I could give birth and weep, for life never comes unaccompanied to a woman, death is always right behind, furtive, quick, and smiling at the mothers. . . . Yes, why indeed? I said to myself.

Coffee had now been served. Mother was inviting them to drink.

"We won't take even one sip," the old woman began, "before you've given us your word about your daughter."

"Yes," the other one said, "my brother impressed upon us that we weren't to come back without your promising to give her to him as his wife."

I was listening to Mother avoid answering, have herself be begged hypocritically, and then again invite them to drink. Aicha joined in with her. The women were repeating their request. . . . It was all as it should be.

The game went on a few minutes longer. Mother invoked the father's authority: "I, of course, would give her to you. . . . I know you are people of means. . . . But there is her father."

"Her father has already said yes to my brother," one of the two women who resembled each other replied. "The question remains only to be discussed between us."

"Yes," said the second one, "it's up to us now. Let's settle the question."

I raised my head; it was then, I think, that I met Hafsa's gaze. There was, deep in her eyes, a strange light, surely of interest or of irony, I don't know, but you could feel Hafsa as an outsider, attentive and curious at the same time, but an outsider. I met that look.

"I don't want to marry," I said. "I don't want to marry," I repeated, barely shouting.

There was much commotion in the room: Mother got up with a deep sigh; Aicha was blushing, I saw. And the two women who turned to me, with the same slow movement of shock: "And why not?" one of them asked.

"My son," the old woman exclaimed with some arrogance, "my son is a man of science. In a few days he is leaving for the Orient."

"Of course," Mother said with touching haste. "We know he's a scholar. We know him to have a righteous heart. . . . Of course. . . ."

"It's not because of your son," I said. "But I don't want to get married. I see the future before my eyes, it's totally black. I don't know how to explain it, surely it must come from God. . . . But I see the future totally black before my eyes!" I said again, sobbing, as Aicha led me out of the room in silence.

Later, but why even tell the rest, except that I was consumed with shame and I didn't understand. Only Hafsa stayed close to me after the women had left.

"You're engaged," she said sadly. "Your mother said she'd give you away. Will you accept?" and she stared at me with imploring eyes.

"What difference does it make?" I said and really thought inside myself: What difference does it make? "I don't know what came over me before. But they were all talking about the present and its changes and its misfortunes. And I was saying to myself: of what possible use is it to be suffering like this, far away from home, if I have to continue here as before in Algiers, to stay home and sit and pretend. . . . Perhaps when life changes, everything should change with it, absolutely everything. I was thinking of all that," I said, "but I don't even know if that's bad or good. . . . You, you're smart, and you know these things, perhaps you'll understand. . . ."

"I do understand," she said, hesitating as if she were going to start talking and then preferred to remain silent.

"Open the window," I said. "It's almost dark."

She went to open it and then came back to my bed where I'd been lying down to cry, without reason, crying for shame and fatigue all at the same time. In the silence that followed, I was feeling distant, pondering the night that little by little engulfed the room. The sounds from the kitchen, where my sisters were, seemed to be coming from somewhere else.

Then Hafsa began to speak: "Your father," she said, "once spoke of exile, of our present exile, and he said—oh, I remember it well, for nobody speaks like your father—he said: 'There is no exile for any man loved by God. There is no exile for the one who is on God's path. There are only trials.' "

She went on a while, but I've forgotten the rest, except that she repeated *we* very often with a note of passion. She said that word with a peculiar vehemence, so much so that I began to wonder toward the end whether that word really meant the two of us alone, or rather other women, all the women of our country.

To tell the truth, even if I'd known, what could I have answered? Hafsa was too knowledgeable for me. And that's what I would have liked to have told her when she stopped talking, perhaps in the expectation that I would speak.

But it was another voice that answered, a woman's voice that rose, through the open window, rose straight as an arrow toward the sky, that rounded itself out, spread out in its flight, a flight ample as a bird's after the storm, then came falling back down in sudden torrents.

"The other women have grown silent," I said. "The only one left to weep now is the mother. . . . Such is life," I added a moment later. "There are those who forget or who simply sleep. And then there are those who keep bumping into the walls of the past. May God take pity on them!"

"Those are the true exiles," said Hafsa.

❀ Discussion and Writing

1. Distinguish the natures of Aicha, Anissa, and the narrator. Comment on their different responses to similar concerns. What is Hafsa's role in the narrative?
2. Discuss the role of the virtually absent men in the lives of the women in the narrative.
3. In what ways does their refugee status influence people's thinking and behavior? Comment on the significance of religious belief as they face the daily anguish of death and life.
4. Examine the points of connection between the two antithetical occurrences—death and marriage proposal—in the two neighboring households. Analyze the distinct concerns of each mother in the narrative.
5. What is the nature of the narrator's exile? Discuss the inevitable issues a woman faces, whether in exile or not.

❀ Research and Comparison

Interdisciplinary Discussion Question: Examine the women's issues particular to Islamic societies as they are reflected in the writings of Assia Djebar or of two other women writers of the Islamic world.

Bessie Head
(1937–1986)
South Africa

Bessie Head was born in Pietermaritzburg, South Africa, in an asylum for the insane. Her mother's family, who had emigrated from England, placed the young woman in the asylum when they discovered that she was pregnant, and that the father was the man who tended their stable and that he was Black African. When Bessie Head was barely a year old, her mother committed suicide in this same institution. Assigned the racial status of colored under the laws of apartheid, she was rejected by both the black and white communities. Neither her mother's nor her father's people wanted her and she never felt totally accepted in the Cape colored community where she was sent from an orphanage to be raised by a poor family. After obtaining her teacher's certificate and teaching for a time, Head worked as a journalist. Although she identified herself as African, her travels around the country as a reporter were as much a journey in search of herself and for acceptance. Her despair over South African racism, over the moral turpitude of apartheid, led her to Botswana, where she lived in what she considered political and spiritual exile. The title of her autobiographical novel *A Question of Power* (1974) states the question that informs most of her work. For Bessie Head, the personal and public atrocities of racism are indivisible and lie at the feet of a corrupt elite who are greedy for the acquisition and retention of power. This elite comprises not just the apartheid government of South Africa but also village chiefs and teachers.

The Collector of Treasures

The long-term central state prison in the south was a whole day's journey away from the villages of the northern part of the country. They had left the village of Puleng at about nine that morning and all day long the police truck droned as it sped southward on the wide, dusty cross-country trackroad. The everyday world of ploughed fields, grazing cattle, and vast expanses of bush and forest seemed indifferent to the hungry eyes of the prisoner who gazed out at them through the wire mesh grating at the back of the police truck. At some point during the journey, the prisoner seemed to strike at some ultimate source of pain and loneliness within her being and, overcome by it, she slowly crumpled forward in a wasted heap, oblivious to everything but her pain. Sunset swept by, then dusk, then dark and still the truck droned on, impersonally, uncaring.

At first, faintly on the horizon, the orange glow of the city lights of the new independence town of Gaborone, appeared like an astonishing phantom in the overwhelming darkness of the bush, until the truck struck tarred roads, neon lights, shops and cinemas, and made the bush a phantom amidst a blaze of light. All this passed untimed, unwatched by the crumpled prisoner; she did not stir as the truck finally droned to a halt outside the prison gates. The torchlight struck the side of her face like an agonizing blow. Thinking she was asleep, the policeman called out briskly:

"You must awaken now. We have arrived."

He struggled with the lock in the dark and pulled open the grating. She crawled painfully forward, in silence.

Together, they walked up a short flight of stairs and waited awhile as the man tapped lightly, several times, on the heavy iron prison door. The night-duty attendant opened the door a crack, peered out and then opened the door a little wider for them to enter. He quietly and casually led the way to a small office, looked at his colleague and asked: "What do we have here?"

"It's the husband murder case from Puleng village," the other replied, handing over a file.

The attendant took the file and sat down at a table on which lay open a large record book. In a big, bold scrawl he recorded the details: Dikeledi Mokopi. Charge: Man-slaughter. Sentence: Life. A night-duty wardress appeared and led the prisoner away to a side cubicle, where she was asked to undress.

"Have you any money on you?" the wardress queried, handing her a plain, green cotton dress which was the prison uniform. The prisoner silently shook her head.

"So, you have killed your husband, have you?" the wardress remarked, with a flicker of humor. "You'll be in good company. We have four other women here for the same crime. It's becoming the fashion these days. Come with me," and she led the way along a corridor, turned left and stopped at an iron gate which she opened with a key, waited for the prisoner to walk in ahead of her and then locked it with the key again. They entered a small, immensely high-walled courtyard. On one side were toilets, showers, and a cupboard. On the other, an empty concrete quadrangle. The wardress walked to the cupboard, unlocked it and took out a thick roll of clean-smelling blankets which she handed to the prisoner. At the lower end of the walled courtyard was a heavy iron door which led to the cell. The wardress walked up to this door, banged on it loudly and called out: "I say, will you women in there light your candle?"

A voice within called out: "All right," and they could hear the scratch-scratch of a match. The wardress again inserted a key, opened the door and watched for a while as the prisoner spread out her blankets on the floor. The four women prisoners already confined in the cell sat up briefly, and stared silently at their new companion. As the door was locked, they all greeted her quietly and one of the women asked: "Where do you come from?"

"Puleng," the newcomer replied, and seemingly satisfied with that, the light was blown out and the women lay down to continue their interrupted sleep. And as though she had reached the end of her destination, the new prisoner too fell into a deep sleep as soon as she had pulled her blankets about her.

The breakfast gong sounded at six the next morning. The women stirred themselves for their daily routine. They stood up, shook out their blankets and rolled them up into neat bundles. The day-duty wardress rattled the key in the lock and let them out into the small concrete courtyard so that they could perform their morning toilet. Then, with a loud clatter of pails and plates, two male prisoners appeared at the gate with breakfast. The men handed each woman a plate of porridge and a mug of black tea and they settled themselves on the concrete floor to eat. They turned and looked at their new companion and one of the women, a spokesman for the group said kindly:

"You should take care. The tea has no sugar in it. What we usually do is scoop the sugar off the porridge and put it into the tea."

The woman, Dikeledi, looked up and smiled. She had experienced such terror during the awaiting-trial period that she looked more like a skeleton than a human being. The skin creaked tautly over her cheeks. The other woman smiled, but after her own fashion. Her face permanently wore a look of cynical, whimsical humor. She had a full, plump figure. She introduced herself and her companions: "My name is Kebonye. Then that's Otsetswe, Galeboe, and Monwana. What may your name be?"

"Dikeledi Mokopi."

"How is it that you have such a tragic name," Kebonye observed. "Why did your parents have to name you *tears*?"

"My father passed away at that time and it is my mother's tears that I am named after," Dikeledi said, then added: "She herself passed away six years later and I was brought up by my uncle."

Kebonye shook her head sympathetically, slowly raising a spoonful of porridge to her mouth. That swallowed, she asked next:

"And what may your crime be?"

"I have killed my husband."

"We are all here for the same crime," Kebonye said, then with her cynical smile asked: "Do you feel any sorrow about the crime?"

"Not really," the other woman replied.

"How did you kill him?"

"I cut off all his special parts with a knife," Dikeledi said.

"I did it with a razor," Kebonye said. She sighed and added: "I have had a troubled life."

A little silence followed while they all busied themselves with their food, then Kebonye continued musingly:

"Our men do not think that we need tenderness and care. You know, my husband used to kick me between the legs when he wanted that. I once aborted a child, due to this treatment. I could see that there was no way to appeal to him if I felt ill, so I once said to him that if he liked he could keep some other woman as well because I couldn't manage to satisfy all his needs. Well, he was an education-officer and each year he used to suspend about seventeen male teachers for making school girls pregnant, but he used to do the same. The last time it happened the parents of the girl were very angry and came to report the matter to me. I told them: 'You leave it to me. I have seen enough.' And so I killed him."

They sat in silence and completed their meal, then they took their plates and cups to rinse them in the wash-room. The wardress produced some pails and a broom. Their sleeping quarters had to be flushed out with water; there was not a speck of dirt anywhere, but that was prison routine. All that was left was an inspection by the director of the prison. Here again Kebonye turned to the newcomer and warned:

"You must be careful when the chief comes to inspect. He is mad about one thing—attention! Stand up straight! Hands at your sides! If this is not done you should see how he stands here and curses. He does not mind anything but that. He is mad about that."

Inspection over, the women were taken through a number of gates to an open, sunny yard, fenced in by high, barbed-wire where they did their daily work. The prison was a rehabilitation center where the prisoners produced goods which were sold in the prison store; the women produced garments of cloth and wool; the men did carpentry, shoe-making, brick-making, and vegetable production.

Dikeledi had a number of skills—she could knit, sew, and weave baskets. All the women at present were busy knitting woollen garments; some were learners and did their work slowly and painstakingly. They looked at Dikeledi with interest as she took a ball of wool and a pair of knitting needles and rapidly cast on stitches. She had soft, caressing, almost boneless, hands of strange power—work of a beautiful design grew from those hands. By mid-morning she had completed the front part of a jersey and they all stopped to admire the pattern she had invented in her own head.

"You are a gifted person," Kebonye remarked, admiringly.

"All my friends say so," Dikeledi replied smiling. "You know, I am the woman whose thatch does not leak. Whenever my friends wanted to thatch their huts, I was there. They would never do it without me. I was always busy and employed because it was with these hands that I fed and reared my children. My husband left me after four years of marriage but I managed well enough to feed those mouths. If people did not pay me in money for my work, they paid me with gifts of food."

"It's not so bad here," Kebonye said. "We get a little money saved for us out of the sale of our work, and if you work like that you can still produce money for your children. How many children do you have?"

"I have three sons."

"Are they in good care?"

"Yes."

"I like lunch," Kebonye said, oddly turning the conversation. "It is the best meal of the day. We get samp[1] and meat and vegetables."

---

[1]Hominy. [eds.]

So the day passed pleasantly enough with chatter and work and at sunset the women were once more taken back to the cell for lock-up time. They unrolled their blankets and prepared their beds, and with the candle lit continued to talk a while longer. Just as they were about to retire for the night, Dikeledi nodded to her new-found friend, Kebonye:

"Thank you for all your kindness to me," she said, softly.

"We must help each other," Kebonye replied, with her amused, cynical smile. "This is a terrible world. There is only misery here."

And so the woman Dikeledi began phase three of a life that had been ashen in its loneliness and unhappiness. And yet she had always found gold amidst the ash, deep loves that had joined her heart to the hearts of others. She smiled tenderly at Kebonye because she knew already that she had found another such love. She was the collector of such treasures.

There were really only two kinds of men in the society. The one kind created such misery and chaos that he could be broadly damned as evil. If one watched the village dogs chasing a bitch in heat, they usually moved around in packs of four or five. As the mating progressed one dog would attempt to gain dominance over the festivities and oust all the others from the bitch's vulva. The rest of the hapless dogs would stand around yapping and snapping in its face while the top dog indulged in a continuous spurt of orgasms, day and night until he was exhausted. No doubt, during that Herculean feat, the dog imagined he was the only penis in the world and that there had to be a scramble for it. That kind of man lived near the animal level and behaved just the same. Like the dogs and bulls and donkeys, he also accepted no responsibility for the young he procreated and like the dogs and bulls and donkeys, he also made females abort. Since that kind of man was in the majority in the society, he needed a little analyzing as he was responsible for the complete breakdown of family life. He could be analyzed over three time-spans. In the old days, before the colonial invasion of Africa, he was a man who lived by the traditions and taboos outlined for all the people by the forefathers of the tribe. He had little individual freedom to assess whether these traditions were compassionate or not—they demanded that he comply and obey the rules, without thought. But when the laws of the ancestors are examined, they appear on the whole to have been vast, external disciplines for the good of the society as a whole, with little atten-tion given to individual preferences and needs. The ancestors made so many errors and one of the most bitter-making things was that they relegated to men a superior position in the tribe, while women were regarded, in a congenital sense, as being an inferior form of human life. To this day, women still suffered from all the calamities that befall an inferior form of human life. The colonial era and the period of migratory mining labor to South Africa was a further affliction visited on this man. It broke the hold of the ances-tors. It broke the old, traditional form of family life and for long periods a man was separated from his wife and children while he worked for a pittance in another land in order to raise the money to pay his British Colonial poll-tax. British Colonialism scarcely enriched his life. He then became "the boy" of the white man and a machine-tool of the South African mines. African independence seemed merely one more affliction on top of the afflictions that had visited this man's life. Independence suddenly and dramatically changed the pattern of colonial subservience. More jobs became available under the new government's localization program and salaries sky-rocketed at the same time. It provided the first occasion for family life of a new order, above the childlike discipline of custom, the degradation of colonialism. Men and women, in order to survive, had to turn inward to their own resources. It was the man who arrived at this turning point, a broken wreck with no inner resources at all. It was as though he was hideous to himself and in an effort to flee his own inner emptiness, he spun away from himself in a dizzy kind of death dance of wild destruction and dissipation.

One such man was Garesego Mokopi, the husband of Dikeledi. For four years prior to independence, he had worked as a clerk in the district administration service, at a steady salary of R50.00 a month. Soon after independence his salary shot up to R200.00 per month. Even during his lean days he had had a taste for womanizing and drink; now he had the resources for a real spree. He was not seen at home again and lived and slept around the village, from woman to woman. He left his wife and three sons—Banabothe, the eldest, aged four; Inalame, aged three; and the youngest, Motsomi, aged one—to their own resources. Perhaps he did so because she was the boring semi-literate traditional sort, and there were a lot of exciting new women around. Independence produced marvels indeed.

There was another kind of man in the society with the power to create himself anew. He turned all his resources, both emotional and material, toward his family life and he went on and on with his own quiet rhythm, like a river. He was a poem of tenderness.

One such man was Paul Thebolo and he and his wife, Kenalepe, and their three children, came to live in the village of Puleng in 1966, the year of independence. Paul Thebolo had been offered the principalship of a primary school in the village. They were allocated an empty field beside the yard of Dikeledi Mokopi, for their new home.

Neighbors are the center of the universe to each other. They help each other at all times and mutually loan each other's goods. Dikeledi Mokopi kept an interested eye on the yard of her new neighbors. At first, only the man appeared with some workmen to erect the fence, which was set up with incredible speed and efficiency. The man impressed her immediately when she went around to introduce herself and find out a little about the newcomers. He was tall, large-boned, slow-moving. He was so peaceful as a person that the sunlight and shadow played all kinds of tricks with his eyes, making it difficult to determine their exact color. When he stood still and looked reflective, the sunlight liked to creep into his eyes and nestle there; so sometimes his eyes were the color of shade, and sometimes light brown.

He turned and smiled at her in a friendly way when she introduced herself and explained that he and his wife were on transfer from the village of Bobonong. His wife and children were living with relatives in the village until the yard was prepared. He was in a hurry to settle down as the school term would start in a month's time. They were, he said, going to erect two mud huts first and later he intended setting up a small house of bricks. His wife would be coming around in a few days with some women to erect the mud walls of the huts.

"I would like to offer my help too," Dikeledi said. "If work always starts early in the morning and there are about six of us, we can get both walls erected in a week. If you want one of the huts done in woman's thatch, all my friends know that I am the woman whose thatch does not leak."

The man smilingly replied that he would impart all this information to his wife, then he added charmingly that he thought she would like his wife when they met. His wife was a very friendly person; everyone liked her.

Dikeledi walked back to her own yard with a high heart. She had few callers. None of her relatives called for fear that since her husband had left her she would become dependent on them for many things. The people who called did business with her; they wanted her to make dresses for their children or knit jerseys for the winter time and at times when she had no orders at all, she made baskets which she sold. In these ways she supported herself and the three children but she was lonely for true friends.

All turned out as the husband had said—he had a lovely wife. She was fairly tall and thin with a bright, vivacious manner. She made no effort to conceal that normally, and every day, she was a very happy person. And all turned out as Dikeledi had said. The work-party of six women erected the mud walls of the huts in one week; two weeks later, the thatch was complete. The Thebolo family moved into their new abode and Dikeledi Mokopi moved into one of the most prosperous and happy periods of her life. Her life took a big, wide upward curve. Her relationship with the Thebolo family was more than the usual friendly exchange of neighbors. It was rich and creative.

It was not long before the two women had going one of those deep, affectionate, sharing-everything kind of friendships that only women know how to have. It seemed that Kenalepe wanted endless amounts of dresses made for herself and her three little girls. Since Dikeledi would not accept cash for these services—she protested about the many benefits she received from her good neighbors—Paul Thebolo arranged that she be paid in household goods for these services so that for some years Dikeledi was always assured of her basic household needs—the full bag of corn, sugar, tea, powdered milk, and cooking oil. Kenalepe was also the kind of woman who made the whole world spin around her; her attractive personality attracted a whole range of women to her yard and also a whole range of customers for her dressmaking friend, Dikeledi. Eventually, Dikeledi became swamped with work, was forced to buy a second sewing-machine and employ a helper. The two women did everything together—they were forever together at weddings, funerals, and parties in the village. In their leisure hours they freely discussed all their intimate affairs with each other, so that each knew thoroughly the details of the other's life.

"You are lucky someone," Dikeledi remarked one day, wistfully. "Not everyone has the gift of a husband like Paul."

"Oh yes," Kenalepe said happily. "He is an honest somebody." She knew a little of Dikeledi's list of woes and queried: "But why did you marry a man like Garesego? I looked carefully at him when you pointed him out to me near the shops the other day and I could see at one glance that he is a butterfly."

"I think I mostly wanted to get out of my uncle's yard," Dikeledi replied. "I never liked my uncle. Rich as he was, he was a hard man and very selfish. I was only a servant there and pushed about. I went there when I was six years old when my mother died, and it was not a happy life. All his children despised me because I was their servant. Uncle paid for my education for six years, then he said I must leave school. I longed for more because as you know, education opens up the world for one. Garesego was a friend of my uncle and he was the only man who proposed for me. They discussed it between themselves and then my uncle said: 'You'd better marry Garesego because you're just hanging around here like a chain on my neck.' I agreed, just to get away from that terrible man. Garesego said at that time that he'd rather be married to my sort than the educated kind because those women were stubborn and wanted to lay down the rules for men. Really, I did not ever protest when he started running about. You know what the other women do. They chase after the man from one hut to another and beat up the girlfriends. The man just runs into another hut, that's all. So you don't really win. I wasn't going to do anything like that. I am satisfied I have children. They are a blessing to me."

"Oh, it isn't enough," her friend said, shaking her head in deep sympathy. "I am amazed at how life imparts its gifts. Some people get too much. Others get nothing at all. I have always been lucky in life. One day my parents will visit—they live in the south—and you'll see the fuss they make over me. Paul is just the same. He takes care of everything so that I never have a day of worry . . ."

The man Paul attracted as wide a range of male friends as his wife. They had guests every evening; illiterate men who wanted him to fill in tax forms or write letters for them, or his own colleagues who wanted to debate the political issues of the day—there was always something new happening every day now that the country had independence. The two women sat on the edge of these debates and listened with fascinated ears, but they never participated. The following day they would chew over the debates with wise, earnest expressions.

"Men's minds travel widely and boldly," Kenalepe would comment. "It makes me shiver the way they freely criticize our new government. Did you hear what Petros said last night? He said he knew all those bastards and they were just a lot of crooks who would pull a lot of dirty tricks. Oh dear! I shivered so much when he said that. The way they talk about the government makes you feel in your bones that this is not a safe world to be in, not like the old days when we didn't have governments. And Lentswe said that ten percent of the population in England really control all the wealth of the country, while the rest live at starvation level. And he said communism would sort all this out. I gathered from the way they discussed this matter that our government is not in favor of communism. I trembled so much when this became clear to me . . . " She paused and laughed proudly. "I've heard Paul say this several times: 'The British only ruled us for eighty years.' I wonder why Paul is so fond of saying that?"

And so a completely new world opened up for Dikeledi. It was so impossibly rich and happy that, as the days went by, she immersed herself more deeply in it and quite overlooked the barrenness of her own life. But it hung there like a nagging ache in the mind of her friend, Kenalepe.

"You ought to find another man," she urged one day, when they had one of their personal discussions. "It's not good for a woman to live alone."

"And who would that be?" Dikeledi asked, disillusioned. "I'd only be bringing trouble into my life whereas now it is all in order. I have my eldest son at school and I can manage to pay the school fees. That's all I really care about."

"I mean," said Kenalepe, "we are also here to make love and enjoy it."

"Oh I never really cared for it," the other replied. "When you experience the worst of it, it just puts you off altogether."

"What do you mean by that?" Kenalepe asked, wide-eyed.

"I mean it was just jump on and jump off and I used to wonder what it was all about. I developed a dislike for it."

"You mean Garesego was like that!" Kenalepe said, flabbergasted. "Why, that's just like a cock hopping from hen to hen. I wonder what he is doing with all those women. I'm sure they are just after his money and so they flatter him . . . " She paused and then added earnestly: "That's really all the more reason you should find another man. Oh, if you knew what it was really like, you would long for it, I can tell you! I sometimes think I enjoy that side of life far too much. Paul knows a lot about all that. And he always has some new trick with which to surprise me. He has a certain way of smiling when he has thought up something new and I shiver a little and say to myself: 'Ha, what is Paul going to do tonight!' "

Kenalepe paused and smiled at her friend, slyly.

"I can loan Paul to you if you like," she said, then raised one hand to block the protest on her friend's face. "I would do it because I have never had a friend like you in my life before whom I trust so much. Paul had other girls you know, before he married me, so it's not such an uncommon thing to him. Besides, we used to make love long before we got married and I never got pregnant. He takes care of that side too. I wouldn't mind loaning him because I am expecting another child and I don't feel so well these days . . . "

Dikeledi stared at the ground for a long moment, then she looked up at her friend with tears in her eyes.

"I cannot accept such a gift from you," she said, deeply moved. "But if you are ill I will wash for you and cook for you."

Not put off by her friend's refusal of her generous offer, Kenalepe mentioned the discussion to her husband that very night. He was so taken off-guard by the unexpectedness of the subject that at first he looked slightly astonished, and burst out into loud laughter and for such a lengthy time that he seemed unable to stop.

"Why are you laughing like that?" Kenalepe asked, surprised.

He laughed a bit more, then suddenly turned very serious and thought-ful and was lost in his own thoughts for some time. When she asked him what he was thinking he merely replied: "I don't want to tell you everything. I want to keep some of my secrets to myself."

The next day Kenalepe reported this to her friend.

"Now whatever does he mean by that? I want to keep some of my secrets to myself?"

"I think," Dikeledi said smiling, "I think he has a conceit about being a good man. Also, when someone loves someone too much, it hurts them to say so. They'd rather keep silent."

Shortly after this Kenalepe had a miscarriage and had to be admitted to hospital for a minor operation. Dikeledi kept her promise "to wash and cook" for her friend. She ran both their homes, fed the children and kept everything in order. Also, people complained about the poorness of the hospital diet and each day she scoured the village for eggs and chicken, cooked them, and took them to Kenalepe every day at the lunch-hour.

One evening Dikeledi ran into a snag with her routine. She had just dished up supper for the Thebolo children when a customer came around with an urgent request for an alteration on a wedding dress. The wedding was to take place the next day. She left the children seated around the fire eating and returned to her own home. An hour later, her own children asleep and settled, she thought she would check the Thebolo yard to see if all was well there. She entered the children's hut and noted that they had put them-selves to bed and were fast asleep. Their supper plates lay scattered and unwashed around the fire. The hut which Paul and Kenalepe shared was in darkness. It meant that Paul had not yet returned from his usual evening visit to his wife. Dikeledi collected the plates and washed them, then poured the dirty dishwater on the still-glowing embers of the outdoor fire. She piled the plates one on top of the other and carried them to the third additional hut which was used as a kitchen. Just then Paul Thebolo entered the yard, noted the lamp and movement in the kitchen hut and walked over to it. He paused at the open door.

"What are you doing now, Mma-Banabothe?" he asked, addressing her affectionately in the customary way by the name of her eldest son, Banabothe.

"I know quite well what I am doing," Dikeledi replied happily. She turned around to say that it was not a good thing to leave dirty dishes standing overnight but her mouth flew open with surprise. Two soft pools of cool liquid light were in his eyes and something infinitely sweet passed between them; it was too beautiful to be love.

"You are a very good woman, Mma-Banabothe," he said softly.

It was the truth and the gift was offered like a nugget of gold. Only men like Paul Thebolo could offer such gifts. She took it and stored another treasure in her heart. She bowed her knee in the traditional curtsy and walked quietly away to her own home.

Eight years passed for Dikeledi in a quiet rhythm of work and friendship with the Thebolos. The crisis came with the eldest son, Banabothe. He had to take his primary school leaving examination at the end of the year. This serious event sobered him up considerably as like all boys he was very fond of playtime. He brought his books home and told his mother that he would like to study in the evenings. He would like to pass with a "Grade A" to please her. With a flushed and proud face Dikeledi mentioned this to her friend, Kenalepe.

"Banabothe is studying every night now," she said. "He never really cared for studies. I am so pleased about this that I bought him a spare lamp and removed him from the children's hut to my own hut where things will be peaceful for him. We both sit up late at night now. I sew on buttons and fix hems and he does his studies . . . "

She also opened a savings account at the post office in order to have some standby money to pay the fees for his secondary education. They were rather high—R85.00. But in spite of all her hoarding of odd cents, toward the end of the year, she was short on R20.00 to cover the fees. Midway during the Christmas school holidays the results were announced. Banabothe passed with a "Grade A." His mother was almost hysterical in her joy at his achievement. But what to do? The two youngest sons had already started primary school and she would never manage to cover all their fees from her resources. She decided to remind Garesego Mokopi that he was the father of the children. She had not seen him in eight years except as a passer-by in the village. Sometimes he waved but he had never talked to her or enquired about her life or that of the children. It did not matter. She was a lower form of human life. Then this unpleasant something turned up at his office one day, just as he was about to leave for lunch. She had heard from village gossip, that he had eventually settled down with a married woman who had a brood of children of her own. He had ousted her husband, in a typical village sensation of brawls, curses, and abuse. Most probably the husband did not care because there were always arms outstretched toward a man, as long as he looked like a man. The attraction of this particular woman for Garesego Mokopi, so her former lovers said with a snicker, was that she went in for heady forms of love-making like biting and scratching.

Garesego Mokopi walked out of his office and looked irritably at the ghost from his past, his wife. She obviously wanted to talk to him and he walked toward her, looking at his watch all the while. Like all the new "success men," he had developed a paunch, his eyes were blood-shot, his face was bloated, and the odor of the beer and sex from the previous night clung faintly around him. He indicated with his eyes that they should move around to the back of the office block where they could talk in privacy.

"You must hurry with whatever you want to say," he said impatiently. "The lunch-hour is very short and I have to be back at the office by two."

Not to him could she talk of the pride she felt in Banabothe's achievement, so she said simply and quietly: "Garesego, I beg you to help me pay Banabothe's fees for secondary school. He has passed with a 'Grade A' and as you know, the school fees must be produced on the first day of school or else he will be turned away. I have struggled to save money the whole year but I am short by R20.00."

She handed him her post office savings book, which he took, glanced at and handed back to her. Then he smiled, a smirky know-all smile, and thought he was delivering her a blow in the face.

"Why don't you ask Paul Thebolo for the money?" he said. "Everyone knows he's keeping two homes and that you are his spare. Everyone knows about that full bag of corn he delivers to your home every six months so why can't he pay the school fees as well?"

She neither denied this, nor confirmed it. The blow glanced off her face which she raised slightly, in pride. Then she walked away.

As was their habit, the two women got together that afternoon and Dikeledi reported this conversation with her husband to Kenalepe, who tossed back her head in anger and said fiercely: "The filthy pig himself! He thinks every man is like him, does he? I shall report this matter to Paul, then he'll see something."

And indeed Garesego did see something but it was just up his alley. He was a female prostitute in his innermost being and like all professional prostitutes, he enjoyed publicity and sensation—it promoted his cause. He smiled genially and expansively when a madly angry Paul Thebolo came up to the door of his house where he lived with *his* concubine. Garesego had been through a lot of these dramas over those eight years and he almost knew by rote the dialogue that would follow.

"You bastard!" Paul Thebolo spat out. "Your wife isn't my concubine, do you hear?"

"Then why are you keeping in her food?" Garesego drawled. "Men only do that for women they fuck! They never do it for nothing."

Paul Thebolo rested one hand against the wall, half dizzy with anger, and he said tensely: "You defile life, Garesego Mokopi. There's nothing else in your world but defilement. Mma-Banabothe makes clothes for my wife and children and she will never accept money from me so how else must I pay her?"

"It only proves the story both ways," the other replied, vilely. "Women do that for men who fuck them."

Paul Thebolo shot out the other hand, punched him soundly in one grinning eye and walked away: Who could hide a livid, swollen eye? To every surprised enquiry, he replied with an injured air:

"It was done by my wife's lover, Paul Thebolo."

It certainly brought the attention of the whole village upon him, which was all he really wanted. Those kinds of men were the bottom rung of government. They secretly hungered to be the President with all eyes on them. He worked up the sensation of little further. He announced that he would pay the school fees of the child of his concubine, who was also to enter secondary school, but not the school fees of his own child, Banabothe. People half liked the smear on Paul Thebolo; he was too good to be true. They delighted in making him a part of the general dirt of the village, so they turned on Garesego and scolded: "Your wife might be getting things from Paul Thebolo but it's beyond the purse of any man to pay the school fees of his own children as well as the school fees of another man's children. Banabothe wouldn't be there had you not procreated him, Garesego, so it is your duty to care for him. Besides, it's your fault if your wife takes another man. You left her alone all these years."

So that story was lived with for two weeks, mostly because people wanted to say that Paul Thebolo was a part of life too and as uncertain of his morals as they were. But the story took such a dramatic turn that it made all the men shudder with horror. It was some weeks before they could find the courage to go to bed with women; they preferred to do something else.

Garesego's obscene thought processes were his own undoing. He really believed that another man had a stake in his hen-pen and like any cock, his hair was up about it. He thought he'd walk in and re-establish his own claim to it and so, after two weeks, once the swelling in his eye had died down, he espied Banabothe in the village and asked him to take a note to his mother. He said the child should bring a reply. The note read: "Dear Mother, I am coming home again so that we may settle our differences. Will you prepare a meal for me and some hot water that I might take a bath. Gare."

DikeleFdi took the note, read it and shook with rage. All its overtones were clear to her. He was coming home for some sex. They had had no differences. They had not even talked to each other.

"Banabothe," she said. "Will you play nearby? I want to think a bit then I will send you to your father with the reply."

Her thought processes were not very clear to her. There was something she could not immediately touch upon. Her life had become holy to her during all those years she had struggled to maintain herself and the children. She had filled her life with treasures of kindness and love she had gathered from others and it was all this that she wanted to protect from defilement by an evil man. Her first panic-stricken thought was to gather up the children and flee the village. But where to go? Garesego did not want a divorce, she had left him to approach her about the matter, she had desisted from taking any other man. She turned her thoughts this way and that and could find no way out except to face him. If she wrote back, don't you dare put foot in the yard I don't want to see you, he would ignore it. Black women didn't have that kind of power. A thoughtful, brooding look came over her face. At last, at peace with herself, she went into her hut and wrote a reply: "Sir, I shall prepare everything as you have said. Dikeledi."

It was about midday when Banabothe sped back with the reply to his father. All afternoon Dikeledi busied herself making preparations for the appearance of her husband at sunset. At one point Kenalepe approached the yard and looked around in amazement at the massive preparations, the large iron water pot full of water with a fire burning under it, the extra cooking pots on the fire. Only later Kenalepe brought the knife into focus. But it was only a vague blur, a large kitchen knife used to cut meat and Dikeledi knelt at a grinding-stone and sharpened it slowly and methodically. What was in focus than was the final and tragic expression on the upturned face of her friend. It threw her into confusion and blocked their usual free and easy feminine chatter. When Dikeledi said: I am making some preparations for Garesego. He is coming home tonight, Kenalepe beat a hasty retreat to her own home terrified. They knew they were involved because when she mentioned this to Paul he was distracted and uneasy for the rest of the day. He kept on doing upside-down sorts of things, not replying to questions, absent-mindedly leaving a cup of tea until it got quite cold, and every now and again he stood up and paced about, lost in his own thoughts. So deep was their sense of disturbance that toward evening they no longer made a pretence of talking. They just sat in silence in their hut. Then, at about nine o'clock, they heard those wild and agonized bellows. They both rushed out together to the yard of Dikeledi Mokopi.

He came home at sunset and found everything ready for him as he had requested, and he settled himself down to enjoy a man's life. He had brought a pack of beer along and sat outdoors slowly savoring it while every now and then his eye swept over the Thebolo yard. Only the woman and children moved about the yard. The man was out of sight. Garesego smiled to himself, pleased that he could crow as loud as he liked with no answering challenge.

A basin of warm water was placed before him to wash his hands and then Dikeledi served him his meal. At a separate distance she also served the children and then instructed them to wash and prepare for bed. She noted that Garesego displayed no interest in the children whatsoever. He was entirely wrapped up in himself and thought only of himself and his own comfort. Any tenderness he offered the children might have broken her and swerved her mind away from the deed she had carefully planned all that afternoon. She was beneath his regard and notice too for when she eventually brought her own plate of food and sat near him, he never once glanced at her face. He drank his beer and cast his glance every now and again at the Thebolo yard. Not once did the man of the yard appear until it became too dark to distinguish anything any more. He was completely satisfied with that. He could repeat the performance every day until he broke the mettle of the other cock again and forced him into angry abuse. He liked that sort of thing.

"Garesego, do you think you could help me with Banabothe's school fees?"

Dikeledi asked at one point.

"Oh, I'll think about it," he replied casually.

She stood up and carried buckets of water into the hut, which she poured into a large tin bath that he might bathe himself, then while he took his bath she busied herself tidying up and completing the last of the household chores. Those done, she entered the children's hut. They played hard during the day and they had already fallen asleep with exhaustion. She knelt down near their sleeping mats and stared at them for a long while, with an extremely tender expression. Then she blew out their lamp and walked to her own hut. Garesego lay sprawled across the bed in such a manner that indicated he only thought of himself and did not intend sharing the bed with anyone else. Satiated with food and drink, he had fallen into a deep, heavy sleep the moment his head touched the pillow. His concubine had no doubt taught him that the correct way for a man to go to bed was naked. So he lay, unguarded and defenseless, sprawled across the bed on his back.

The bath made a loud clatter as Dikeledi removed it from the room, but still he slept on, lost to the world. She re-entered the hut and closed the door. Then she bent down and reached for the knife under the bed which she had merely concealed with a cloth. With the precision and skill of her hard-working hands, she grasped hold of his genitals and cut them off with one stroke. In doing so, she slit the main artery which ran on the inside of the groin. A massive spurt of blood arched its way across the bed. And Garesego bellowed. He bellowed his anguish. Then all was silent. She stood and watched his death anguish with an intent and brooding look, missing not one detail of it. A knock on the door stirred her out of her reverie. It was the boy, Banabothe. She opened the door and stared at him, speechless. He was trembling violently.

"Mother," he said, in a terrified whisper. "Didn't I hear father cry?"

"I have killed him," she said, waving her hand in the air with a gesture that said—well, that's that. Then she added sharply: "Banabothe, go and call the police."

He turned and fled into the night. A second pair of footsteps followed hard on his heels. It was Kenalepe running back to her own yard, half out of her mind with fear. Out of the dark Paul Thebolo stepped toward the hut and entered it. He took in every detail and then he turned and looked at Dikeledi with such a tortured expression that for a time words failed him. At last he said: "You don't have to worry about the children, Mma-Banabothe. I'll take them as my own and give them all a secondary school education."

❀ Discussion and Writing

1. Comment on the predicament of women reflected in the opening description.
2. Discuss Bessie Head's portrayal of the impact of colonialism in the lives of men, particularly Garesego and Paul.
3. Discuss the significance of Dikeledi's traditionally female activities, which become the source of her charm and friendship with people around her.
4. What is special about Dikeledi's friendship with Kenalepe and with Paul? Analyze her relationship with each.
5. Why is Dikeledi called "a collector of treasures"? What is the source of her tenderness; of her violence? What are the implications of her seemingly paradoxical behavior?
6. Comment on the depiction of the two couples as a study in contrasting gender relations. What does Bessie Head accomplish through the portrayal of two extremes?
7. Discuss the symbolism of Garesego's castration.

❀ Research and Comparison

Research Bessie Head's life and works. As a social worker, she also interviewed men and women and derived information for her stories from their actual experiences. Comment on Bessie Head's role as a social-cultural historian.

Interdisciplinary Discussion Question: Research the issue of gender relations in any one African community. Analyze the impact of colonization and modernization on the lives of these people.

Keorapetse Kgositsile
(b. 1938)
South Africa

William Keorapetse Kgositsile was born in Johannesburg, but left South Africa in his early twenties, beginning his exile in Dar es Salaam, Tanzania. He subsequently studied and lived in the United States. His poetry has been widely published and radiates a terseness and anger that have been emulated by other poets.

The Air I Hear

The air, I hear,
froze to the sound
searching. And my memory
present and future tickles
the womb like the pulse
of this naked air
in the eye of a tear
drop. The dead cannot
remember even the memory
of death's laughter. But memory
defiant like the sound of pain
rides the wave at dawn
in the marrow of the desert
palm: stands looking still
and the bitter shape
of yesterdays weaves
timeless tomorrows
in the leaves
of laughter larger than
singular birth . . .

❀ **Discussion and Writing**
1. In what ways are memory and air connected in the poem?
2. What is conveyed in "like the pulse of this naked air" and "in the eye of a tear / drop"?
3. What is the impact of the numerous synesthetic and polar images?

Ngugi Wa Thiong'o
(b. 1938)
Kenya

Ngugi Wa Thiong'o was born in the Gikuyu highlands of Kenya and was in high school in the area at the time of the Mau-Mau Resistance (1952–1958). He wrote his first novels and short stories while studying at Makerere University in Uganda, and then after taking his M.A. at Leeds University in England, he began an academic career at Nairobi University. It was here that his protest against the legacy of colonialism became more and more politically controversial. The performance in 1977 of his drama *Ngaahika Ndeenda* (I Will Marry When I Want) led to his imprisonment without trial for a year. Written in English before this incident, the wryly satiric story "Wedding at the Cross" had its genesis in a 1971 visit to his home after a year of teaching at Northwestern University in the United States. More recently his protest against neocolonialism has led him to write only in Gikuyu, a political stand he explains in his 1981 work *Decolonising the Mind: The Politics of Language in African Literature.* Ngugi has lived in exile in England and the United States—teaching, lecturing, and writing—since the 1982 imprisonment of Kenyan scholars and students.

Wedding at the Cross

Everyone said of them: what a nice family; he, the successful timber merchant; and she, the obedient wife who did her duty to God, husband and family. Wariuki and his wife, Miriamu, were a shining example of what cooperation between man and wife united in love and devotion could achieve: he tall, correct, even a little stiff, but wealthy; she, small, quiet, unobtrusive, a diminishing shadow beside her giant of a husband.

He had married her when he was without a cent buried anywhere, not even for the rainiest day, for he was then only a milk clerk in a settler farm earning thirty shillings a month—a fortune in those days, true, but drinking most of it by the first of the next month. He was young; he did not care; dreams of material possessions and power little troubled him. Of course he joined the other workers in collective protests and demands, he would even compose letters for them; from one or two farms he had been dismissed as a dangerous and subversive character. But his heart was really elsewhere, in his favorite sports and acts. He would proudly ride his Raleigh Bicycle around, whistling certain lines from old records remembered, yodelling in imitation of Jim Rogers, and occasionally demonstrating his skill on the machine to an enthusiastic audience in Molo township. He would stand on the bicycle balancing with the left leg, arms stretched about to fly, or he would simply pedal backward to the delight of many children. It was an old machine, but decorated in loud colors of red, green and blue with several Wariuki home-manufactured headlamps and reflectors and with a warning scrawled on a signboard mounted at the backseat: Overtake Me, Graveyard Ahead. From a conjurer on a bicycle, he would move to other roles. See the actor now mimicking his white bosses, satirizing their way of talking and walking and also their mannerisms and attitudes to black workers. Even those Africans who sought favors from the whites were not spared. He would vary his acts with dancing, good dancer too, and his mwomboko steps, with the left trouser leg deliberately split along the seam to an inch above the knee, always attracted approving eyes and sighs from maids in the crowd.

That's how he first captured Miriamu's heart.

On every Sunday afternoon she would seize any opportunity to go to the shopping square where she would eagerly join the host of worshippers. Her heart would then rise and fall with his triumphs and narrow escapes, or simply pound in rhythm with his dancing hips. Miriamu's family was miles better off than most squatters in the Rift Valley. Her father, Douglas Jones, owned several groceries and tea-rooms around the town. A God-fearing couple he and his wife were: they went to church on Sundays, they said their prayers first thing in the morning, last thing in the evening and of course before every meal. They were looked on with favor by the white farmers around; the District Officer would often stop by for a casual greeting. Theirs then was a good Christian home and hence they objected to their daughter marrying into sin, misery and poverty: what could she possibly see in that Murebi, Murebi bii-u?[1] They told her not to attend those heathen Sunday scenes of idleness and idol worship. But Miriamu had an independent spirit, though it had since childhood been schooled into inactivity by Sunday sermons—thou shalt obey thy father and mother and those that rule over us—and a proper upbringing with rules straight out of the Rt. Reverend Clive Schomberg's classic: *British Manners for Africans.* Now Wariuki with his Raleigh bicycle, his milkman's tunes, his baggy trousers and dance which gave freedom to the body, was the light that beckoned her from the sterile world of Douglas Jones to a neon-lit city in a far horizon. Part of her was suspicious of the heavy glow, she was even slightly revolted by his dirt and patched up trousers, but she followed him, and was surprised at her firmness. Douglas Jones relented a little: he loved his daughter and only desired the best for her. He did not want her to marry one of those useless half-educated upstarts, who disturbed the ordered life, peace and prosperity on European farms. Such men, as the Bwana District Officer often told him, would only end in jails: they were motivated by greed and wanted to cheat the simple-hearted and illiterate workers about the evils of white settlers and missionaries. Wariuki looked the dangerous type in every way.

---

[1]Drunkard, complete drunkard. [eds.]

He summoned Wariuki, "Our would-be-son-in-law," to his presence. He wanted to find the young man's true weight in silver and gold. And Wariuki, with knees weakened a little, for he, like most workers, was a little awed by men of that Christian and propertied class, carefully mended his left trouser leg, combed and brushed his hair and went there. They made him stand at the door, without offering him a chair, and surveyed him up and down. Wariuki, bewildered, looked alternately to Miriamu and to the wall for possible deliverance. And then when he finally got a chair, he would not look at the parents and the dignitaries invited to sit in judgment but fixed his eyes to the wall. But he was aware of their naked gaze and condemnation. Douglas Jones, though, was a model of Christian graciousness: tea for our— well—our son—well—this young man here. What work? Milk clerk? Ahh, well, well—no man was born with wealth—wealth was in the limbs you know and you, you are so young—salary? Thirty shillings a month? Well, well, others had climbed up from worse and deeper pits: true wealth came from the Lord on high, you know. And Wariuki was truly grateful for these words and even dared a glance and a smile at old Douglas Jones. What he saw in those eyes made him quickly turn to the wall and wait for the execution. The manner of the execution was not rough: but the cold steel cut deep and clean. Why did Wariuki want to marry when he was so young? Well, well, as you like—the youth today—so different from our time. And who "are we" to tell what youth ought to do? We do not object to the wedding: but we as Christians have a responsibility. I say it again: we do not object to this union. But it must take place at the cross. A church wedding, Wariuki, costs money. Maintaining a wife also costs money. Is that not so? You nod your head? Good. It is nice to see a young man with sense these days. All that I now want, and that is why I have called in my counsellor friends, is to see your savings account. Young man, can you show these elders your post office book?

Wariuki was crushed. He now looked at the bemused eyes of the elders present. He then fixed them on Miriamu's mother, as if in appeal. Only he was not seeing her. Away from the teats and rich udder of the cows, away from his bicycle and the crowd of rich admirers, away from the anonymous security of bars and tea-shops, he did not know how to act. He was a hunted animal, now cornered: and the hunters, panting with anticipation, were enjoying every moment of that kill. A buzz in his head, a blurring vision, and he heard the still gracious voice of Douglas Jones trailing into something about not signing his daughter to a life of misery and drudgery. Desperately Wariuki looked to the door and to the open space.

Escape at last: and he breathed with relief. Although he was trembling a little, he was glad to be in a familiar world, his own world. But he looked at it slightly differently, almost as if he had been wounded and could not any more enjoy what he saw. Miriamu followed him there: for a moment he felt a temporary victory over Douglas Jones. They ran away and he got a job with

Ciana Timber Merchants in Ilmorog forest. The two lived in a shack of a room to which he escaped from the daily curses of his Indian employers. Wariuki learnt how to endure the insults. He sang with the movement of the saw: kneeling down under the log, the other man standing on it, he would make up words and stories about the log and the forest, sometimes ending on a tragic note when he came to the fatal marriage between the saw and the forest. This somehow would lighten his heart so that he did not mind the falling saw-dust. Came his turn to stand on top of the log and he would experience a malicious power as he sawed through it, gingerly walking backward step by step and now singing of Demi na Mathathi who, long ago, cleared woods and forests more dense than Ilmorog.

And Miriamu the erstwhile daughter of Douglas Jones would hear his voice rising above the whispering or uproarious wind and her heart rose and fell with it. This, this, dear Lord, was so different from the mournful church hymns of her father's compound, so, so, different and she felt good inside. On Saturdays and Sundays he took her to dances in the wood. On their way home from the dances and the songs, they would look for a suitable spot on the grass and make love. For Miriamu these were nights of happiness and wonder as the thorny pine leaves painfully but pleasantly pricked her buttocks even as she moaned under him, calling out to her mother and imaginary sisters for help when he plunged into her.

And Wariuki too was happy. It always seemed to him a miracle that he, a boy from the streets and without a father (he had died while carrying guns and food for the British in their expeditions against the Germans in Tanganyika in the first European World War), had secured the affections of a girl from that class. But he was never the old Wariuki. Often he would go over his life beginning with his work picking pyrethrum flowers for others under a scorching sun or icy cold winds in Limuru, to his recent job as a milk clerk in Molo: his reminiscences would abruptly end with that interview with Douglas Jones and his counsellors. He would never forget that interview: he was never to forget the cackling throaty laughter as Douglas Jones and his friends tried to diminish his manhood and selfworth in front of Miriamu and her mother.

Never. He would show them. He would yet laugh in their faces.

But soon a restless note crept into his singing: bitterness of an unfulfilled hope and promise. His voice became rugged like the voice-teeth of the saw and he tore through the air with the same greedy malice. He gave up his job with the Ciana Merchants and took Miriamu all the way to Limuru. He dumped Miriamu with his aged mother and he disappeared from their lives. They heard of him in Nairobi, Mombasa, Nakuru, Kisumu and even Kampala. Rumors reached them: that he was in prison, that he had even married a Muganda girl. Miriamu waited: she remembered her moments of pained pleasure under Ilmorog woods, ferns and grass and endured the empty bed and the bite of Limuru cold in June and July. Her parents had disowned her and anyway she would not want to go back. The seedling he had planted in her warmed her. Eventually the child arrived and this together with the simple friendship of her mother-in-law consoled her. Came more rumors: white men were gathering arms for a war among themselves, and black men, sons of the soil, were being drafted to aid in the slaughter. Could this be true? Then Wariuki returned from his travels and she noticed the change in her man. He was now of few words: where was the singing and the whistling of old tunes remembered? He stayed a week. Then he said: I am going to war. Miriamu could not understand: why this change? Why this wanderlust? But she waited and worked on the land.

Wariuki had the one obsession: to erase the memory of that interview, to lay for ever the ghost of those contemptuous eyes. He fought in Egypt, Palestine, Burma and in Madagascar. He did not think much about the war, he did not question what it meant for black people, he just wanted it to end quickly so that he might resume his quest. Why, he might even go home with a little loot from the war. This would give him the start in life he had looked for, without success, in towns all over Colonial Kenya. A lucrative job even: the British had promised them jobs and money-rewards once the wicked Germans were routed. After the war he was back in Limuru, a little emaciated in body but hardened in resolve.

For a few weeks after his return, Miriamu detected a little flicker of the old fires and held him close to herself. He made a few jokes about the war, and sang a few soldiers' songs to his son. He made love to her and another seed was planted. He again tried to get a job. He heard of a workers' strike in a Limuru shoe factory. All the workers were summarily dismissed. Wariuki and others flooded the gates to offer their sweat for silver. The striking workers tried to picket the new hands, whom they branded traitors to the cause, but helmeted police were called to the scene, baton charged the old workers away from the fenced compound and escorted the new ones into the factory. But Wariuki was not among them. Was he born into bad luck? He was back in the streets of Nairobi joining the crowd of the unemployed recently returned from the War. No jobs no money-rewards: the "good" British and the "wicked" Germans were shaking hands with smiles. But questions as to why black people were not employed did not trouble him: when young men gathered in Pumwani, Kariokor, Shauri Moyo and other places to ask questions he did not join them: they reminded him of his old association and flirtation with farm workers before the war: those efforts had come to nought: even these ones would come to nought: he was in any case ashamed of that past: he thought that if he had been less of a loafer and more enterprising he would never have been so humiliated in front of Miriamu and her mother. The young men's talk of processions, petitions and pistols, their talk of gunning the whites out of the country, seemed too remote from his ambition and quest. He had to strike out on his own for moneyland. On arrival, he would turn round and confront old Douglas Jones and contemptuously flaunt success before his face. With the years the memory of that humiliation in the hands of the rich became so sharp and fresh that it often hurt him into sleepless nights. He did not think of the whites and the Indians as the real owners of property, commerce and land. He only saw the picture of Douglas Jones in his grey woollen suit, his waistcoat, his hat and his walking stick of a folded umbrella. What was the secret of that man's success? What? What? He attempted odd jobs here and there: he even tried his hand at trading in the hawk market at Bahati. He would buy pencils and handkerchiefs from the Indian Bazaar and sell them at a retail price that ensured him a bit of profit. Was this his true vocation?

But before he could find an answer to his question, the Mau Mau war of national liberation broke out. A lot of workers, employed and unemployed, were swept off the streets of Nairobi into concentration camps. Somehow he escaped the net and was once again back in Limuru. He was angry. Not with the whites, not with the Indians, all of whom he saw as permanent features of the land like the mountains and the valleys, but with his own people. Why should they upset the peace? Why should they upset the stability just when he had started gathering a few cents from his trade? He now believed, albeit without much conviction, the lies told by the British about imminent prosperity and widening opportunities for blacks. For about a year he remained aloof from the turmoil around: he was only committed to his one consuming passion. Then he drifted into the hands of the colonial regime and cooperated. This way he avoided concentration camps and the forest. Soon his choice of sides started bearing fruit: he was excited about the prospects for its ripening. While other people's strips of land were being taken by the colonialists, his piece, although small, was left intact. In fact, during land consolidation forced on women and old men while their husbands and sons were decaying in detention or resisting in the forest, he, along with other active collaborators, secured additional land. Wariuki was not a cruel man: he just wanted this nightmare over so that he might resume his trade. For even in the midst of battle the image of D. Jones never really left him: the humiliation ached: he nursed it like one nurses a toothache with one's tongue, and felt that a day would come when he would stand up to that image.

Jomo Kenyatta returned home from Maralal. Wariuki was a little frightened, his spirits were dampened: what would happen to his kind at the gathering of the braves to celebrate victory? Alas, where were the whites he had thought of as permanent features of the landscape? But with independence approaching, Wariuki had his first real reward: the retreating colonialists gave him a loan: he bought a motor-propelled saw and set up as a Timber Merchant.

For a time after Independence, Wariuki feared for his life and business as the sons of the soil streamed back from detention camps and from the forests: he expected a retribution, but people were tired. They had no room in their hearts for vengeance at the victorious end of a just struggle. So Wariuki prospered undisturbed: he had, after all, a fair start over those who had really fought for Uhuru.

He joined the Church in gratitude. The Lord had spared him: he dragged Miriamu into it, and together they became exemplary Church-goers.

But Miriamu prayed a different prayer, she wanted her man back. Her two sons were struggling their way through Siriana Secondary School. For this she thanked the Lord. But she still wanted her real Wariuki back. During the Emergency she had often cautioned him against excessive cruelty. It pained her that his singing, his dancing and his easy laughter had ended. His eyes were hard and set and this frightened her.

Now in Church he started singing again. Not the tunes that had once captured her soul, but the mournful hymns she knew so well; how sweet the name of Jesus sounds in a believer's ears. He became a pillar of the Church Choir. He often beat the drum which, after Independence, had been intro-duced into the church as a concession to African culture. He attended classes in baptism and great was the day he cast away Wariuki and became Dodge W. Livingstone, Jr. Thereafter he sat in the front bench. As his business im-proved, he gradually worked his way to the holy aisle. A new Church elder.

Other things brightened. His parents-in-law still lived in Molo, though their fortunes had declined. They had not yet forgiven him. But with his eminence, they sent out feelers: would their daughter pay them a visit? Miriamu would not hear of it. But Dodge W. Livingstone was furious: where was her Christian forgiveness? He was insistent. She gave in. He was glad. But that gesture, by itself, could not erase the memory of his humiliation. His vengeance would still come.

Though his base was at Limuru, he travelled to various parts of the country. So he got to know news concerning his line of business. It was the year of the Asian exodus. Ciana Merchants were not Kenya Citizens. Their license would be withdrawn. They quickly offered Livingstone partnership on a fifty-fifty share basis. Praise the Lord and raise high his name. Truly God never ate Ugali. Within a year he had accumulated enough to qualify for a loan to buy one of the huge farms in Limuru previously owned by whites. He was now a big timber merchant: they made him a senior elder of the church.

Miriamu still waited for her Wariuki in vain. But she was a model wife. People praised her Christian and wifely meekness. She was devout in her own way and prayed to the Lord to rescue her from the dreams of the past. She never put on airs. She even refused to wear shoes. Every morning, she would wake early, take her Kiondo, and go to the farm where she would work in the tea estate alongside the workers. And she never forgot her old strip of land in the Old Reserve. Sometimes she made lunch and tea for the workers. This infuriated her husband: why, oh why did she choose to humiliate him before these people? Why would she not conduct herself like a Christian lady? After all, had she not come from a Christian home? Need she dirty her hands now, he asked her, and with laborers too? On clothes, she gave in: she put on shoes and a white hat especially when going to Church. But work was in her bones and this she would not surrender. She enjoyed the touch of the soil: she enjoyed the free and open conversation with the workers.

They liked her. But they resented her husband. Livingstone thought them a lazy lot: why would they not work as hard as he himself had done? Which employer's wife had ever brought him food in a shamba?[2] Miriamu was spoiling them and he told her so. Occasionally he would look at their sullen faces: he would then remember the days of the Emergency or earlier when he received insults from Ciana employers. But gradually he learned to silence these unsettling moments in prayer and devotion. He was aware of their silent hatred but thought this a natural envy of the idle and the poor for the rich.

Their faces brightened only in Miriamu's presence. They would abandon their guarded selves and joke and laugh and sing. They gradually let her into their inner lives. They were members of a secret sect that believed that Christ suffered and died for the poor. They called theirs *The Religion of Sorrows*. When her husband was on his business tours, she would attend some of their services. A strange band of men and women: they sang songs they themselves had created and used drums, guitars, jingles and tambourines, producing a throbbing powerful rhythm that made her want to dance with happiness. Indeed they themselves danced around, waving hands in the air, their faces radiating warmth and assurance, until they reached a state of possession and heightened awareness. Then they would speak in tongues strange and beautiful. They seemed united in a common labor and faith: this was what most impressed Miriamu. Something would stir in her, some dormant wings would beat with power inside her, and she would go home trembling in expectation. She would wait for her husband and she felt sure that together they could rescue something from a shattered past. But when he came back from his tours, he was still Dodge W. Livingstone, Jr., senior church elder, and a prosperous farmer and timber merchant. She once more became the model wife listening to her husband as he talked business and arithmetic for the day: what contracts he had won, what money he had won and lost, and tomorrow's prospects. On Sunday man and wife would go to church as usual: same joyless hymns, same prayers from set books; same regular visits to brothers and sisters in Christ; the inevitable tea-parties and charity auctions to which Livingstone was a conspicuous contributor. What a nice family everyone said in admiration and respect: he, the successful farmer and timber merchant; and she, the obedient wife who did her duty to God and husband.

---

[2]Farm-fields. [eds.]

One day he came home early. His face was bright—not wrinkled with the usual cares and worries. His eyes beamed with pleasure. Miriamu's heart gave a gentle leap, could this be true? Was the warrior back? She could see him trying to suppress his excitement. But the next moment her heart fell again. He had said it. His father-in-law, Douglas Jones, had invited him, had begged him to visit them at Molo. He whipped out the letter and started reading it aloud. Then he knelt down and praised the Lord, for his mercy and tender understanding. Miriamu could hardly join in the Amen. Lord, Lord, what has hardened my heart so, she prayed and sincerely desired to see the light.

The day of reunion drew near. His knees were becoming weak. He could not hide his triumph. He reviewed his life and saw in it the guiding finger of God. He the boy from the gutter, a mere milk clerk . . . but he did not want to recall the ridiculous young man who wore patched-up trousers and clowned on a bicycle. Could that have been he, making himself the laughing stock of the whole town? He went to Benbros and secured a new Mercedes Benz 220S. This would make people look at him differently. On the day in question, he himself wore a worsted woollen suit, a waistcoat, and carried a folded umbrella. He talked Miriamu into going in an appropriate dress bought from Nairobi Drapers in Government Road. His own mother had been surprised into a frock and shoe-wearing lady. His two sons in their school uniform spoke nothing but English. (They affected to find it difficult speaking Kikuyu, they made so many mistakes.) A nice family, and they drove to Molo. The old man met them. He had aged, with silver hair covering his head, but he was still strong in body. Jones fell on his knees; Livingstone fell on his knees. They prayed and then embraced in tears. Our son, our son. And my grandchildren too. The past was drowned in tears and prayers. But for Miriamu, the past was vivid in the mind.

Livingstone, after the initial jubilations, found that the memories of that interview rankled a little. Not that he was angry with Jones: the old man had been right, of course. He could not imagine himself giving his own daughter to such a ragamuffin of an upstart clerk. Still he wanted that interview erased from memory forever. And suddenly, and again he saw in that revelation the hand of God, he knew the answer. He trembled a little. Why had he not thought of it earlier? He had a long intimate conversation with his father-in-law and then made the proposal. Wedding at the cross. A renewal of the old. Douglas Jones immediately consented. His son had become a true believer. But Miriamu could not see any sense in the scheme. She was aging. And the Lord had blessed her with two sons. Where was the sin in that? Again they all fell on her. A proper wedding at the cross of Jesus would make their lives complete. Her resistance was broken. They all praised the Lord, God worked in mysterious ways, his wonders to perform.

The few weeks before the eventful day were the happiest in the life of Livingstone. He savored every second. Even anxieties and difficulties gave him pleasure. That this day would come: a wedding at the cross. A wedding at the cross, at the cross where he had found the Lord. He was young again. He bounced in health and a sense of well-being. The day he would exchange rings at the cross would erase unsettling memories of yesterday. Cards were printed and immediately dispatched. Cars and buses were lined up. He dragged Miriamu to Nairobi. They went from shop to shop all over the city: Kenyatta Avenue, Muindi Bingu Streets, Bazaar, Government Road, Kimathi Street, and back again to Kenyatta Avenue. Eventually he bought her a snow-white long-sleeved satin dress, a veil, white gloves, white shoes and stockings and of course plastic roses. He consulted Rev. Clive Schomberg's still modern classic on good manners for Africans and he hardly departed from the rules and instructions in the matrimonial section. Dodge W. Livingstone, Jr., did not want to make a mistake.

Miriamu did not send or give invitation cards to anybody. She daily prayed that God would give her the strength to go through the whole affair. She wished that the day would come and vanish as in a dream. A week before the day, she was driven all the way back to her parents. She was a mother of two; she was no longer the young girl who once eloped; she simply felt ridiculous pretending that she was a virgin maid at her father's house. But she submitted almost as if she were driven by a power stronger than man. Maybe she was wrong, she thought. Maybe everybody else was right. Why then should she ruin the happiness of many? For even the church was very happy. He, a successful timber merchant, would set a good example to others. And many women had come to congratulate her on her present luck in such a husband. They wanted to share in her happiness. Some wept.

The day itself was bright. She could see some of the rolling fields in Molo: the view brought painful memories of her childhood. She tried to be cheerful. But attempts at smiling only brought out tears: What of the years of waiting? What of the years of hope? Her face-wrinkled father was a sight to see: a dark suit with tails, a waist jacket, top hat and all. She inclined her head to one side, in shame. She prayed for yet more strength: she hardly recognized anybody as she was led toward the holy aisle. Not even her fellow workers, members of the *Religion of Sorrows,* who waited in a group among the crowd outside.

But for Livingstone this was the supreme moment. Sweeter than vengeance. All his life he had slaved for this hour. Now it had come. He had specially dressed for the occasion: a dark suit, tails, top hat and a beaming smile at any dignitary he happened to recognize, mostly MPs, priests and businessmen. The church, Livingstone had time to note, was packed with very important people. Workers and not so important people sat outside Members of the *Religion of Sorrows* wore red wine-colored dresses and had with them their guitars, drums and tambourines. The bridegroom as he passed gave them a rather sharp glance. But only for a second. He was really happy.

Miriamu now stood before the cross: her head was hidden in the white veil. Her heart pounded. She saw in her mind's eye a grandmother pretending to be a bride with a retinue of aged bridesmaids. The Charade. The Charade. And she thought: there were ten virgins when the bridegroom came. And five of them were wise—and five of them were foolish—Lord, Lord that this cup would soon be over—over me, and before I be a slave . . . and the priest was saying: "Dodge W. Livingstone, Jr., do you accept this woman for a wife in sickness and health until death do you part?" Livingstone's answer was a clear and loud yes. It was now her turn; . . . Lord that this cup . . . this cup . . . over meeeee. . . . "Do you, Miriamu, accept this man for a husband." . . . She tried to answer. Saliva blocked her throat . . . five virgins . . . five virgins . . . came bridegroom . . . groom . . . and the Church was now silent in fearful expectation.

Suddenly, from outside the Church, the silence was broken. People turned their eyes to the door. But the adherents of the *Religion of Sorrows* seemed unaware of the consternation on people's faces. Maybe they thought the ceremony was over. Maybe they were seized by the spirit. They beat their drums, they beat their tambourines, they plucked their guitars all in a jazzy bouncing unison. Church stewards rushed out to stop them, ssh, ssh, the wedding ceremony was not yet over—but they were way beyond hearing. Their voices and faces were raised to the sky, their feet were rocking the earth.

For the first time Miriamu raised her head. She remembered vaguely that she had not even invited her friends. How had they come to Molo? A spasm of guilt. But only for a time. It did not matter. Not now. The vision had come back . . . At the cross, at the cross where I found the Lord . . . she saw Wariuki standing before her even as he used to be in Molo. He rode a bicycle: he was playing his tricks before a huge crowd of respectful worshippers . . . At the cross, at the cross where I found the Lord . . . he was doing it for her . . . he had singled only her out of the thrilling throng . . . of this she was certain . . . came the dancing and she was even more certain of his love . . . He was doing it for her. Lord, I have been loved once . . . once . . . I have been loved, Lord . . . And those moments in Ilmorog forest and woods were part of her: what a moaning, oh, Lord what a moaning . . . and the drums and the tambourines were now moaning in her dancing heart. She was truly Miriamu. She felt so powerful and strong and raised her head even more proudly; . . . and the priest was almost shouting: "Do you Miriamu . . . " The crowd waited. She looked at Livingstone, she looked at her father, and she could not see any difference between them. Her voice came in a loud whisper: "No."

A current went right through the church. Had they heard the correct answer? And the priest was almost hysterical: "Do you Miriamu . . . " Again the silence made even more silent by the singing outside. She lifted the veil and held the audience with her eyes. "No, I cannot . . . I cannot marry

Livingstone ... because ... because ... I have been married before. I am married to ... to ... Wariuki ... and he is dead."

Livingstone became truly a stone. Her father wept. Her mother wept. They all thought her a little crazed. And they blamed the whole thing on these breakaway churches that really worshipped the devil. No properly trained priest, etc. . . . etc. . . . And the men and women outside went on singing and dancing to the beat of drums and tambourines, their faces and voices raised to the sky.

❈ Discussion and Writing

1. Describe Wariuki's character and his life when he was a young man. Analyze Miriamu's fascination for this "dangerous type" of man.
2. Comment on the portrayal of Douglas Jones and his counselor friends, "men of that Christian and propertied class." What aspects of colonization does Ngugi criticize through the portrayal of these men?
3. Discuss the significance of Wariuki's politics before and after his marriage: his earlier involvement; his nonparticipation in the Mau Mau; his fear of Jomo Kenyatta; his profiteering after independence.
4. Analyze the metamorphosis of Wariuki into Dodge W. Livingston and Mariamu's change from a Christian daughter to a Gikuyu woman. In what ways does the colonial experience influence their roles as wife and husband?
5. Comment on the function of *Religion of Sorrows* in the narrative. What is the significance of the parallel celebrations in the two religious groups.
6. Discuss the irony implied in the ending of "Wedding at the Cross."

❈ Research and Comparison

Ngugi Wa Thiong'o describes the teachings of Christianity and the process of colonization in Africa as incompatible. Examine this story as a paradigm of the colonial experience in Africa.

Interdisciplinary Discussion Question: Examine "Wedding at the Cross" as a demonstration of Ngugi's theory of decolonizing the mind. Explore this process as an essential element in searching for identity, gaining political independence, and restructuring nations. (Refer to Ngugi's *Decolonising the Mind.*)

Ayi Kwei Armah
(b. 1939)
Ghana

Ayi Kwei Armah was born in Ghana. As a child he attended the local schools, but went to the United States for secondary school and college—to Groton and Harvard, respectively. He also studied at the University of Ghana at Legon. He has worked as a script writer and teacher in Ghana and a translator on the staff of *Jeune Afrique* in Paris. His writing is noted for its attacks on the betrayal of the Ghanaian people's trust by corrupt politicians. It is also noted for its bitterness against those who have assimilated and perpetuated European colonialist mores: arrogance, love of luxury, and arrogation of power. In his attack on neocolonialism, he urges a return to the traditional healing, nurturing spiritual values as a means of redemption and regeneration from the contemporary madness. The final image of the bird singing on the roof of the latrine in his famous novel *The Beautyful Ones Are Not Yet Born* (1968) suggests such a possibility.

Halfway to Nirvana

"Frankly," he said through the electronic glass partition, "it will be a sad day for some of us when this catastrophic drought is over. Fortunately," he snapped a finger, "it will go on. And on."

I'd noticed the fellow at the last three conferences I'd covered for my magazine, the struggling satirical sheet *Sic Transit*. A lot of people writing to the editor spell the first part of our magazine's name *Sick*. The publisher normally owes the small staff three months' wages. Still, I keep searching out the humorous vein hidden somewhere under life's jugular, writing pieces I hope are funny, but which in my heart I know are merely ridiculous. Besides, it's possible to earn short-order income at conferences doubling as a translator. That's how I came to develop such a keen interest in conferences. And that's how I met Christian Mohamed Tumbo.

Yes of course, I asked him how he came to possess such perfectly ecumenical names. Were they pseudonyms he'd chosen himself?

"No," he answered readily. "My mother was a good Christian, my father an equally good Muslim."

"So you became . . . "

"A compromise."

It was our first conversation. I knew at once I'd hit the hidden vein. In spite of everything, there was something likeable about this rotund fellow. His charm was indeterminate, but I knew it had something to do with the liveliness of his tiny eyes. They were like trapped sparks. There was also the incongruous smoothness of his baby cheeks. His teeth were ugly and uncared-for. But he bared them so often, and in such a pleased smile that in the end one got used to them, like frequent, affectionate visitors. He spoke a voluble, jovial French. It was he who said, right in the middle of a solemn-sounding speech about the present threat of famine, that conference sessions were excellent for working up a thirst, in preparation, come break-time, for the real objective of such gatherings: drinking. He'd aroused laughter that time, with his slightly dangerous sense of humor. He said it was all a technique, the technique of the *griot:* take a bantering attitude to truths others prefer to bury under taciturn official masks.

At least once, though, his humorous technique had backfired. In a moment of absent-mindedness, participants at the end of a development strategies conference had asked him to give the vote of thanks. He gave a honeyed speech, full of francophone marshmallows and admiration for the organizers' many superlative qualities. The last, but not the least of these super qualities, he concluded, was the Chairman's enviable ability to appear chronically overworked even while riding on the Nirvana line. After this joke I noticed conference officials and participants avoided him. I sought him out.

I found him exceedingly open, eager, in fact, to talk. He seemed to have had to keep to himself something he wanted to share—a huge joke. Finally he'd found a friendly female ear, mine. Still, I doubt if he'd ever have opened up so totally except for an accident.

Because we talked frequently during breaks, we often sat near each other during sessions. Conferences are not hard work, but they are tedious, and when poorly organized they can be exhausting in a wasteful way. I'd noticed that Christian Mohamed Tumbo never seemed crushed by the monotonous drudgery of all these speeches. At the end of each session, he could be seen far ahead of the others, bounding joyfully toward the cocktail bar, a manic spirit unchained.

The secret of his energy, when I discovered it, surprised me with the elegance of its sheer simplicity: during most conference sessions, Christian Mohamed Tumbo slept. He had the priceless political gift of being able to sleep with his eyes open; not wide open—that was the beauty of it—just a shade narrowed, like the eyes of an alert person paying receptive, benevolently critical attention to whatever was going on.

Participants were being asked when they wanted to go on a field trip to a disaster area: 1500 hours or 1700 hours. The usual practice at conferences is for the organizers to fix all important decisions. The participants endorse them by acclamation. This was an unimportant matter, however, and individual preferences were being canvassed. The Chairman called Christian Mohamed Tumbo twice, a third time. Tumbo sat there looking particularly intelligent and smart, but hearing nothing. I nudged him awake as the

Chairman repeated the question. Christian Mohamed Tumbo said "1700 hours," then turned to ask me what it was all about. I knew why he trusted me: I was on the conference circuit, without being part of the conference establishment. He had nothing to fear from me. There may have been an additional, more frivolous reason. Perhaps he wished we'd get to be closer friends.

For a period Christian Mohamed Tumbo suffered no further embarrassment in his sleep. On at least three occasions, though, he came close. It was inevitable that catastrophe would strike one day. What floored me was the way it happened. I'd imagined Christian Mohamed Tumbo sleeping his way through a conference session and the Chairman, innocent soul, asking the usual earth-shaking question: What, in the opinion of your delegation, would be the implementational modalities for achieving the objective of the total eradication of poverty and injustice in Africa by, at the latest, the year Plus 4000? Instead, it was Christian Mohamed Tumbo himself who took the initiative, and spoke in his sleep. Loud and clear, as in a ringing peroration.

The conference, incidentally, was another one on the drought. The Chairman, a somber fellow from the Cosmic Meteorological Organization, had gone through the part of his closing speech about the present drought being an unprecedented threat requiring unprecedented measures. He had come to the part about the urgent need for further conferences to promote reflection on the problem that had been discussed for the past ten years. The shout came, bold and clear: *"Vive la Secheresse!"* [long live the drought!]

The Chairman, embarrassed by the interruption, wound up in a hurry. Two of the organizers leaned forward, apparently uncertain whether there was a heckler to be bounced, or a gaffe to be diplomatically ignored. But Christian Mohamed Tumbo had fallen quiet again.

We were so close together that I felt the eyes turned on him were glaring at me too. To cover my embarrassment, no doubt, but so spontaneously I was astonished at my presence of mind, I did Christian Mohamed Tumbo a service he claims he"ll never forget. I rose, loudly applauding the Chairman's speech as if here at last was the international bureaucrat who had found the magic words for solving the world's problems.

The Chairman was sitting as I rose. One of the organizers pointed to me, thinking I was asking for the floor. In the intense confusion, the Chairman gave me the floor. I flew at the chance.

"Comme notre collegue vient de le dire," I said, putting such a desperate roll on the francophone *r* in the next word that I bruised the lining of my throat, *"vivre la secheresse, c'est notre probleme numero un. Monsieur le President, nous vous felicitons vivement pour votre exposé."*[1]

---

[1]"As our colleague just said, long live the drought is our number one problem. Mr. President, we heartily congratulate you on your exposé." [eds.]

The tension eased. A sigh of relief came from someone, probably a participant now convinced he had misheard the shout after all.

On the way down to the poolside restaurant for dinner, a couple of people came to congratulate me. At the cocktail bar just before the restaurant entrance, Christian Mohamed Tumbo was uncharacteristically morose.

"I spoke in my sleep, didn't I?" he asked me.

"Yes."

He winced, but couldn't suppress his curiosity. "What did I say?"

"*Vive la secheresse*. You must have been having a nightmare."

He smiled enigmatically: "A nightmare first, then a dream. In the nightmare Africa's deserts became forests and gardens. It was frightening. Luckily, the nightmare ended. The deserts regained their dryness. Familiar signs of famine reappeared: skeletons in the Sahel sand. I recognized our continent. I suppose that's when I shouted '*Vive la secheresse.*'"

"Long live the drought?" I queried.

"I know what you're thinking," he said, staring at me as at a beloved but retarded sibling. "The man makes his living working for an anti-drought organization. But this same man thinks the end of the drought would be a disaster. Right?"

"More or less."

He took a moment deciding whether I was worth his confidence. Then his eyes took on a 100-watt intensity. "You're looking at a man who'd have died ten years ago if frustration could kill. I taught secondary-school Geography for fifteen years. Every year I earned starvation wages, and watched my students come back five years later with academic degrees and salaries that gave me a headache just to imagine. I was getting to be a sick man, bitter as a dwarf lemon.

"There's no better work than teaching, but in time I realized what I needed was not a better job but more money and a bit of respect from the swinish society.

"'Try Nirvana,' a friend advised me. I thought Nirvana was some new version of Transcendental Meditation, or a drug to cure hypertension. A cure for frustrated greed. Green in every way, that's what I was. The friend explained Nirvana: the UN System in one seamless phrase: European salaries diplomatic status tax exemption duty free goodies travel galore clean paperwork cool hotels, per diems in dollars. A smooth talker, my friend.

"I tried the Nirvana Highway, and ran into a wall. The wall has secret holes in it, and only those already on the other side can pull you through. Besides, I don't even have a bachelor's degree. Everyone in Nirvana has to have that. At least.

"I'd practically given up on getting near Nirvana at all when the same friend told me about the NGO approach. Non-Governmental Organizations. Well, I found the NGO road open even if the Nirvana highway was blocked.

My friend introduced me to a Swede with a permanent crease in his fore-head and foundation money behind him, looking for an African assistant to help him set up an agency to Fight the Drought.

"I went to the Swede and listened to him for four hours. He could have been a regular missionary, if he'd been a shade less intelligent. I listened to his absurd litany of strategies and solutions. I know droughts and floods have been part of African history for thousands of years. But he kept saying The Drought was an unprecedented disaster. I agreed absolutely with him. Between this strange Swede and me, why shouldn't there be a perfect identity of views?

"The Swede found his African assistant, and I found my NGO, halfway to Nirvana. The Anti-Drought Organization. Nice acronym, ADO. Since that day, four years ago, I've changed from a man of problems into a man of solutions. I've forgotten what it feels like to be in debt. I have three villas. Two are embassy residences. Rent paid a year in advance. In dollars. The third I live in myself. ADO pays me a handsome rent for living in my own house. Every month I travel abroad. When I'm on the move my salary stays intact, while per diems compensate me for my dedicated suffering in hotels and night-clubs as I move from capital to capital, conference to seminar, fighting the drought.

"I didn't mean to shout. The words escaped me, but I know I'd live a lot less well if there were no drought or famine."

We'd finished dinner, except for the liqueur. As I drained the small, sweet glass, it caught the light from the swimming-pool outside and broke it into a frail, momentary indoor rainbow. I put the tiny glass against the menu, propped up against a twin rose in a vase.

Langouste mayonnaise
Potage de legumes
Salade nicoise
Entrecote aux echalottes
Plateau de fromage
Coupe Mont Blanc
Cafe Liegeois

"Nice meal, eh?" Christian Mohamed Tumbo asked.

I nodded, then rose to go to the poolside area. He wanted to go up to his room. Perhaps he'd hoped, but he swallowed his regret as we shook hands, parting. He pressed mine like a tyro conspirator, winked into the bargain, and, as I walked towards the electronic glass partition, called out softly: *"Vive la secheresse."*

❀ Discussion and Writing

1. Why does Christian Mohamed Tumbo compare himself to a *griot?* Discuss the significance of his mixed name, vocation, and personality.
2. Analyze the humorous situations and their serious implications, both social and political.
3. Explore the ironies in the title in relation to the story.
4. What is accomplished by creating a female narrator? Would it have made a difference if the narrator were male?

❀ Research and Comparison

Examine Ayi Kwei Armah's depiction of neocolonialism: corruption, political instability, economic strife, identity, and so on. Analyze either *The Beautyful Ones Are Not Yet Born* or *Why Are We So Blest?* in relation to neocolonialism.

Molara Ogundipe-Leslie
(b. 1940)
Nigeria

Molara Ogundipe-Leslie, of the Yoruba people, was born in Ijebu-Ode in western Nigeria, where she was raised in a sheltered atmosphere. She studied at Ibadan University. During the late 1960s and early 1970s, she lectured in the United States, and the vision she spoke of for Nigeria paralleled the hopefulness of the U.S. civil rights movement. But over the years, she, along with Flora Nwapa, has viewed the tragic legacy of the Nigerian civil war (1967–1970) as emblematic of contemporary Nigeria.

Ogundipe-Leslie has taught at universities in Nigeria and published two volumes of essays and a volume of poetry. Interested in criticism and the development of aesthetic theory, she has insisted on multiple aesthetics—each speaking from its individual culture—rather than a single African perspective. Significantly, it was her critical work on Amos Tutuola that re-established his place in African letters. Her poetry and her essays also reflect her concerns with the process of colonization, with African economic dependency, and with the role of women and the question of class in Africa. An outspoken feminist, she has added the world peace movement to her political activities.

song at the african middle class
For agostinho neto

we charge through the skies of disillusion,
seeking the widening of eyes, we gaze at chaos,
speak to deadened hearts and ears stopped with
commerce. We drift around our region of clowns,
walking on air as dreams fly behind our eyes.
we forage among broken bodies, fractured minds
to find just ways retraced and new like beaten cloth.

and if they come again
will they come again?
and if they come again
will they dance this time?
will the new *egungun* dance[1] once more
resplendent in rich-glassed cloth?
will they be of their people's needs,
rise to those needs, settle whirling rifts
salve, O, festering hearts?
will they say when they come
O my people, O my people, how to love you delicately?

✸ Discussion and Writing

1. What do the images in the first stanza suggest about current conditions in Africa?
2. What is the significance of dedicating the poem to Agostinho Neto? (Refer to Neto's poem and headnotes.)
3. Why is it the song *at,* and not *of,* the "african middle class"? What is the importance of the omission of capital letters in the poem?
4. What connection does the poet make between the *egungun* dance and the modern "african middle class"?

✸ Research and Comparison

Interdisciplinary Discussion Question: Research the outstanding characteristics of neocolonialism: economic strife, corruption, political instability, and so on, in the context of Africa. Trace their origins and the reasons for their persistence. Analyze the issue of neocolonialism depicted in a literary work by an African writer.

Interdisciplinary Discussion Question: Examine the same issue in relation to former colonies in Asia: is there a similar pattern; what are the differences?

---

[1]*Egungun:* a masqueraded dancer; *egungun* dance: religious ritual with the intention of making contact with the supernatural. [eds.]

Ama Ata Aidoo
(b. 1942)
Ghana

Ama Ata Aidoo (Christina Ama Aidoo) was born in the central region of Ghana in Abeadzi Kyiakor. She worked with Efua Sutherland in the Drama Studio during the early 1960s and was one of the first generation of graduates from the University of Ghana. After receiving her B.A., Aidoo studied briefly in the United States, taught as a research fellow in Ghana, and continued to lecture at various universities in Africa and the United States. She served briefly as Ghana's secretary for education and then in the Zimbabwe Ministry of Education. In Zimbabwe she has also participated in the Zimbabwe Women Writers Group, becoming the chairwoman. A playwright, novelist, poet, and short story writer, she has noted that her stories as well as her plays are intended to be heard. They both develop from the aesthetic of the oral tradition. Thus, she plays with narrative points of view, forms, and themes in accordance with the techniques of the oral tradition, accommodating the English language and Western conventions to the Ghanaian.

In the Cutting of a Drink

I say, my uncles, if you are going to Accra and anyone tells you that the best place for you to drop down is at the Circle, then he has done you good, but . . . Hm . . . I even do not know how to describe it. . . .

"Are all these beings that are passing this way and that way human? Did men buy all these cars with money . . . ?"

But my elders, I do not want to waste your time. I looked round and did not find my bag. I just fixed my eyes on the ground and walked on. . . . Do not ask me why. Each time I tried to raise my eyes, I was dizzy from the number of cars which were passing. And I could not stand still. If I did, I felt as if the whole world was made up of cars in motion. There is something somewhere, my uncles. Not desiring to deafen you with too long a story . . .

I stopped walking just before I stepped into the Circle itself. I stood there for a long time. Then a lorry [truck] came along and I beckoned to the driver to stop. Not that it really stopped.

"Where are you going?" he asked me.

"I am going to Mamprobi," I replied. "Jump in," he said, and he started to drive away. Hm . . . I nearly fell down climbing in. As we went round the thing which was like a big bowl on a very huge stump of wood, I had it in mind to have a good look at it, and later Duayaw told me that it shoots water in the air . . . but the driver was talking to me, so I could not look at it properly. He told me he himself was not going to Mamprobi but he was going to the station where I could take a lorry which would be going there. . . .

Yes, my uncle, he did not deceive me. Immediately we arrived at the station I found the driver of a lorry shouting "Mamprobi, Mamprobi." Finally when the clock struck about two-thirty, I was knocking on the door of Duayaw. I did not knock for long when the door opened. Ah, I say, he was fast asleep, fast asleep I say, on a Saturday afternoon.

"How can folks find time to sleep on Saturday afternoons?" I asked myself. We hailed each other heartily. My uncles, Duayaw has done well for himself. His mother Nsedua is a very lucky woman.

"How is it some people are lucky with school and others are not? Did not Mansa go to school with Duayaw here in this very school which I can see for myself? What have we done that Mansa should have wanted to stop going to school?"

But I must continue with my tale. . . . Yes, Duayaw has done well for himself. His room has fine furniture. Only it is too small. I asked him why and he told me he was even lucky to have got that narrow place that looks like a box. It is very hard to find a place to sleep in the city. . . .

He asked me about the purpose of my journey. I told him everything. How, as he himself knew, my sister Mansa had refused to go to school after "Klase Tri" and how my mother had tried to persuade her to go . . .

My mother, do not interrupt me, everyone present here knows you tried to do what you could by your daughter.

Yes, I told him how, after she had refused to go, we finally took her to this woman who promised to teach her to keep house and to work with the sewing machine . . . and how she came home the first Christmas after the woman took her but has never been home again, these twelve years.

Duayaw asked me whether it was my intention then to look for my sister in the city. I told him yes. He laughed saying, "You are funny. Do you think you can find a woman in this place? You do not know where she is staying. You do not even know whether she is married or not. Where can we find her if someone big has married her and she is now living in one of those big bungalows which are some ten miles from the city?"

Do you cry "My Lord," mother? You are surprised about what I said about the marriage? Do not be. I was surprised too, when he talked that way. I too cried "My Lord" . . . Yes, I too did, mother. But you and I have forgotten that Mansa was born a girl and girls do not take much time to grow. We are thinking of her as we last saw her when she was ten years old. But mother, that is twelve years ago. . . .

Yes, Duayaw told me that she is by now old enough to marry and to do something more than merely marry. I asked him whether he knew where she was and if he knew whether she had any children—"Children?" he cried, and he started laughing, a certain laugh. . . .

I was looking at him all the time he was talking. He told me he was not just discouraging me but he wanted me to see how big and difficult it was, what I proposed to do. I replied that it did not matter. What was necessary was that even if Mansa was dead, her ghost would know that we had not forgotten her entirely. That we had not let her wander in other people's towns and that we had tried to bring her home. . . .

These are useless tears you have started to weep, my mother. Have I said anything to show that she was dead?

Duayaw and I decided on the little things we would do the following day as the beginning of our search. Then he gave me water for my bath and brought me food. He sat by me while I ate and asked me for news of home. I told him that his father has married another woman and of how last year the *akatse*[1] spoiled all our cocoa. We know about that already. When I finished eating, Duayaw asked me to stretch out my bones on the bed and I did. I think I slept fine because when I opened my eyes it was dark. He had switched on his light and there was a woman in the room. He showed me her as a friend but I think she is the girl he wants to marry against the wishes of his people. She is as beautiful as sunrise, but she is not of our tribe. . . .

When Duayaw saw that I was properly awake, he told me it had struck eight o'clock in the evening and his friend had brought some food. The three of us ate together.

Do not say "Ei," Uncle, it seems as if people do this thing in the city. A woman prepares a meal for a man and eats it with him. Yes, they do so often.

My mouth could not manage the food. It was prepared from cassava and corn dough, but it was strange food all the same. I tried to do my best. After the meal Duayaw told me we were going for a night out. It was then I remembered my bag. I told him that as matters stood, I could not change my cloth and I could not go out with them. He would not hear of it. "It would certainly be a crime to come to this city and not go out on a Saturday night." He warned me though that there might not be many people, or anybody at all, where we were going who would also be in cloth but I should not worry about that.

Cut me a drink, for my throat is very dry, my Uncle. . . .

When we were on the street I could not believe my eyes. The whole place was as clear as the sky. Some of these lights are very beautiful indeed. Everyone should see them . . . and there are so many of them! "Who is paying for all these lights?" I asked myself. I could not say that aloud for fear Duayaw would laugh.

We walked through many streets until we came to a big building where a band was playing. Duayaw went to buy tickets for the three of us.

---

[1]A small insect that destroys the cocoa pod. [eds]

You all know that I had not been to anywhere like that before. You must allow me to say that I was amazed. "Ei, are all these people children of human beings? And where are they going? And what do they want?"

Before I went in, I thought the building was big, but when I went in, I realized the crowd in it was bigger. Some were in front of a counter buying drinks, others were dancing . . .

Yes, that was the case, Uncle, we had gone to a place where they had given a dance, but I did not know.

Some people were sitting on iron chairs around iron tables. Duayaw told some people to bring us a table and chairs and they did. As soon as we sat down, Duayaw asked us what we would drink. As for me, I told him *lamlale*[2] but his woman asked for "Beer" . . .

Do not be surprised, Uncles.

Yes, I remember very well, she asked for beer. It was not long before Duayaw brought them. I was too surprised to drink mine. I sat with my mouth open and watched the daughter of a woman cut beer like a man. The band had stopped playing for some time and soon they started again. Duayaw and his woman went to dance. I sat there and drank my *lamlale*. I cannot describe how they danced.

After some time, the band stopped playing and Duayaw and his woman came to sit down. I was feeling cold and I told Duayaw. He said, "And this is no wonder, have you not been drinking this women's drink all the time?"

"Does it make one cold?" I asked him.

"Yes," he replied. "Did you not know that? You must drink beer."

"Yes," I replied. So he bought me beer. When I was drinking the beer, he told me I would be warm if I danced.

"You know I cannot dance the way you people dance," I told him.

"And how do we dance?" he asked me.

"I think you all dance like white men and as I do not know how that is done, people would laugh at me," I said. Duayaw started laughing. He could not contain himself. He laughed so much his woman asked him what it was all about. He said something in the white man's language and they started laughing again. Duayaw then told me that if people were dancing, they would be so busy that they would not have time to watch others dance. And also, in the city, no one cares if you dance well or not . . .

Yes, I danced too, my Uncles. I did not know anyone, that is true. My Uncle, do not say that instead of concerning myself with the business for which I had gone to the city, I went dancing. Oh, if you only knew what happened at this place, you would not be saying this. I would not like to stop somewhere and tell you the end . . . I would rather like to put a rod under the story, as it were, clear off every little creeper in the bush . . .

---

[2]Soft drink or soda. [eds.]

But as we were talking about the dancing, something made Duayaw turn to look behind him where four women were sitting by the table. . . . Oh! he turned his eyes quickly, screwed his face into something queer which I could not understand and told me that if I wanted to dance, I could ask one of those women to dance with me.

My Uncles, I too was very surprised when I heard that. I asked Duayaw if people who did not know me would dance with me. He said "Yes." I lifted my eyes, my Uncles, and looked at those four young women sitting round a table alone. They were sitting all alone, I say. I got up.

I hope I am making myself clear, my Uncles, but I was trembling like water in a brass bowl.

Immediately one of them saw me, she jumped up and said something in that kind of white man's language which everyone, even those who have not gone to school speak in the city. I shook my head. She said something else in the language of the people of the place. I shook my head again. Then I heard her ask me in Fante whether I wanted to dance with her. I replied "Yes."

Ei! my little sister, are you asking me a question? Oh! you want to know whether I found Mansa? I do not know. . . . Our Uncles have asked me to tell everything that happened there, and you too! I am cooking the whole meal for you, why do you want to lick the ladle now?

Yes, I went to dance with her. I kept looking at her so much I think I was all the time stepping on her feet. I say, she was as black as you and I, but her hair was very long and fell on her shoulders like that of a white woman. I did not touch it but I saw it was very soft. Her lips with that red paint looked like a fresh wound. There was no space between her skin and her dress. Yes, I danced with her. When the music ended, I went back to where I was sitting. I do not know what she told her companions about me, but I heard them laugh.

It was this time that something made me realize that they were all bad women of the city. Duayaw had told me I would feel warm if I danced, yet after I had danced. I was colder than before. You would think someone had poured water on me. I was unhappy thinking about these women. "Have they no homes?" I asked myself. "Do not their mothers like them? God, we are all toiling for our threepence to buy something to eat . . . but oh! God! this is no work."

When I thought of my own sister, who was lost, I became a little happy because I felt that although I had not found her, she was nevertheless married to a big man and all was well with her.

When they started to play the band again, I went to the women's table to ask the one with whom I had danced to dance again. But someone had gone with her already. I got one of the two who were still sitting there. She went with me. When we were dancing she asked me whether it was true that I was a Fante. I replied "Yes." We did not speak again. When the band stopped playing, she told me to take her to where they sold things to buy her beer and cigarettes. I was wondering whether I had the money. When we were where the lights were shining brightly, something told me to look at her face. Something pulled at my heart.

"Young woman, is this the work you do?" I asked her.

"Young man, what work do you mean?" she too asked me. I laughed.

"Do you not know what work?" I asked again.

"And who are you to ask me such questions? I say, who are you? Let me tell you that any kind of work is work. You villager, you villager, who are you?" she screamed.

I was afraid. People around were looking at us. I laid my hands on her shoulders to calm her down and she hit them away.

"Mansa, Mansa," I said. "Do you not know me?" She looked at me for a long time and started laughing. She laughed, laughed as if the laughter did not come from her stomach. Yes, as if she was hungry.

"I think you are my brother," she said. "Hm."

Oh, my mother and my aunt, oh, little sister, are you all weeping? As for you women!

What is there to weep about? I was sent to find a lost child. I found her a woman.

Cut me a drink . . .

Any kind of work is work. . . . This is what Mansa told me with a mouth that looked like clotted blood. Any kind of work is work . . . so do not weep. She will come home this Christmas.

My brother, cut me another drink. Any form of work is work . . . is work . . . is work!

❋ Discussion and Writing

1. What aspects of the city amaze the narrator? Why?
2. How has the city changed one-time villagers? What aspects of their village values have they retained, if any?
3. Discuss the norms regarding gender relations that prevail in the village.
4. Explore the implications of Mansa's comment "Any kind of work is work." What does it mean to her, to the urbanized villagers, to the villagers?
5. Comment on the last scene after the narrator identifies Mansa to his audience. How do the men and women react? What is the significance of the narrator's repeated words at the end?
6. Analyze the narrator's art of story-telling: giving details, recording personal reactions, keeping up the suspense. Who is his audience?
7. Comment on Ama Ata Aidoo's synthesis of the African tradition of story-telling and the Western convention of the dramatic monologue. What elements of each does she retain or modify? What is the effect?

❁ Research and Comparison

What is the significance of women writers choosing a male narrator for their stories, or male writers choosing a female narrator? Compare several works included in this anthology—in light of their cultural, psychological, and political contexts—to determine the impact of this device.

Interdisciplinary Discussion Question: Investigate the process of modernization, particularly the disruption of the indigenous cultures of Ghana under colonialism. Examine other selections included in this anthology to identify and compare the distinctive patterns that emerge in this process.

Syl Cheney Coker
(b. 1945)
Sierra Leone

Syl Cheney Coker, considered his country's leading poet, was born in Freetown, Sierra Leone. He studied in Sierra Leone and the United States, and taught for many years at the University of Maiduguri in Nigeria. He has turned his hand to drumming, journalism, radio production, and the novel, as well as to poetry. His poems reflect not only his personal isolation but the isolation of poets, particularly twentieth-century poets of colonized lands. At the same time, he defiantly celebrates poetry and its liberating power. In this regard, he speaks angrily of the round of political coups and civil unrest since independence in 1961. There is a bitter twist to the history of Sierra Leone that lies beneath all political writing.

In the late 1700s, England purchased the land and founded the colony of Freetown on the Sierra Leone peninsula for about 1000 freed slaves from Nova Scotia in Canada. Over the next fifty years, some 50,000 freed slaves settled in the colony, developing a Creole community as generation followed generation. The Freetown colony had little communication with the Temne and Mende peoples of the interior. At the same time, the British gained control over the entire region. Since independence, there has been dissension, caused largely by discord among the various groups.

The Philosopher

Who lived here when the stones were green
verdigris of age when the reptilians marched like men
into the night before that morning the sea
emptying its cup of wounds like a chasm of revolt.
like a castaway an old man kept his books in a cave
desolate his memory of life a portrait
like an abstraction of years, he lived
forgotten by others before the last tidal wave
I consecrate him seer his beard was a white book
where we read about kings and prophets
planners of the ruins astride our stormy conscience
to write what history the moon already dripping its sea of red blood

the whirlwind that licked over your body
amulet of season playing fangs on the translucent word
flagellant at crossroads where the word was nailed
neologist who dressed the world in hendecasyllabic verse
O monk saddened when you consecrated the word in body
stripped when you meditated in penury

you return shadow from shadow the word
transformed into phoenix you return the man
reigning the length of the raised cross
violated your soul we fashion you into memory
drift of a cyclone, man with whom we raise our conscience
you rise from your body to be equal to your name!

✸ Discussion and Writing

1. What is evoked by the repetition of the images of the word, the body, the book, and the memory. Who are "you" and "we"?
2. Comment on the images from nature: the moon, the sea, the wind, and so on.
3. Examine the imagery that indicates the passage of time. What time span does the poem encompass? Consider the use of punctuation in this context.
4. Explain the significance of the phrases "the raised cross" and "raise our conscience." What do they infer in relation to the motifs of the poem?

Jack Mapanje
(b. 1945)
Malawi

Jack Mapanje was born in southern Malawi. After completing his studies, he taught at Chancellor College, University of Malawi—becoming head of the department of language and literature—and was founder and editor of *ODI,* a journal of Malawi literature. He was imprisoned in 1987 without charge or trial. The Ministry of Education and Culture judged his book *Of Chameleons and Gods* (1981) "unsuitable for schools and colleges" on the basis that it showed "bitterness against the system."

The government of Malawi under President-for-Life Dr. Hastings Banda has been considered among the most repressive on the continent. Malawi had been a large kingdom in the eighteenth century, encompassing much of present-day Mozambique and Zimbabwe. It declined; the slave-trade flourished; and fearing Portuguese annexation, in 1889, England claimed the country as a protectorate and named it Nyasaland. There were unsuccessful revolts early in the 1900s against British rule. When the country gained its independence as the Republic of Malawi in 1964, Banda had been a leading nationalist. Subsequently, his regime has been despised both within Malawi and among its neighbors because of its oppression and its relations with the apartheid government of South Africa. Mapanje speaks of these issues, of the betrayal and corruption of the neocolonialists, with a biting and ironic wit.

On African Writing

You've rocked at many passage rites, at drums
Mothers clapping their admiration of your
Initiation voices—now praises of decay
That still mesmerize some; at times you've
Yodled like you'd never become men gallant
Hunting, marrying, hating, killing. But
In your masks you've sung on one praise
After another. You have sung mouth-songs!
Men struggling to justify what you touched
Only, heard merely! Empty men! Do you realize
You are still singing initiation tunes?
You have not chimed hunting-marrying—
Fighting-killing praises until you've
Stopped all this nonsense about drinking

Palm wine from plastic tumblers!
And these doggerels, these sexual-tribal
Anthropological-political doggerels!
Don't you think even mothers will stop
Quaking some day? Don't you realize
Mothers also ache to see their grand
Children at home playing *bau*[1] on sofas?
Why do you always suppose mothers
Never want to see you at these conferences
They are for ever hearing about?
Why do you imagine they never understand
Things? They too can be alert to all this
Absurdity about what you think they think!
You've sung many songs, some superb
But these lip-songs are most despicable!

❀ Discussion and Writing

1. What are the initiation tunes? Why are they called "praises of decay"?
2. What is the poet's statement about the scholarly approach to African writing?
3. What is the significance of the various rituals? What is their relevance to modern Africans?
4. What is the implication of "what you think they think" near the end of the poem? Analyze it as a paradigm of cross-cultural stereotyping.

Charles Mungoshi
(b. 1947)
Zimbabwe

Charles Mungoshi was born near a small town about a hundred miles south of Harare, Zimbabwe (then Rhodesia). From the time he was a little boy, he herded cattle and helped with farming the land his father had acquired in one of the "Native Purchase Areas." He also walked two miles to and from school every day until he went to boarding school when he was 12. In secondary school, where teaching shifted from his native Shona to English, he studied French and Latin along with English, and began writ-

---

[1]A favorite board-game played with seeds. [eds.]

ing. By the time he was 18, he had published two stories written in English, and was focusing his attention on writing rather than on academic work that would allow his advancement in his studies. Always committed to his writing, he worked for a time as a research assistant in the Forestry Commission, as a clerk in a book-selling company, and in publishing. He has been Writer in Residence at the University of Zimbabwe and has lectured and given readings in the United States and England as well as in Zimbabwe.

Mungoshi wrote his first novel in Shona, published while he was a clerk, and has continued to work in both Shona and English, as each expresses a unique experience. With this in mind, he has translated Ngugi Wa Thiong'o's *A Grain of Wheat* into Shona, intending to draw a parallel between the colonial ordeals in Kenya and Zimbabwe, and at the same time, to encourage a recognition of the rich potential of his own language. Mungoshi has remained concerned about the legacy of colonialism and the loss of vital traditional customs.

Shadows on the Wall

Father is sitting just inside the hut near the door and I am sitting far across the hut near the opposite wall, playing with the shadows on the wall. Bright sunlight comes in through the doorway now and father, who blocks most of it, is reproduced in caricature on the floor and half-way up the wall. The wall and floor are bare, so he looks like a black scarecrow in a deserted field after the harvest.

Outside, the sun drops lower and other shadows start creeping into the hut. Father's shadow grows vaguer and climbs further up the wall like a ghost going up to heaven. His shadow moves behind sharper wriggling shadows like the presence of a tired old woman in a room full of young people, or like that creepy nameless feeling in a house of mourning.

He has tried five times to talk to me but I don't know what he wants. Now he talks about his other wife. He wants me to call her "mother" but I can't because something in me cries each time I say it. She isn't my mother and my real mother is not dead. This other woman has run away. It is now the fourth time she has run away and tomorrow he is going to cycle fifty miles to her home to collect her. This will be the fourth time he has had to cycle after her. He is talking. I am not listening. He gives up.

Now the sun shines brilliantly before going down. The shadows of bushes and grass at the edge of the yard look as if they are on fire and father's features are cut more sharply and exaggerated. His nose becomes longer each time he nods because now he is sleeping while sitting, tired of the silence.

Father dozes, wakes up; dozes, wakes up and the sun goes down. His shadow expands and fades. Now it seems all over the wall, behind the other shadows, moving silently like a cold wind in a bare field. I look at him. There is still enough light for me to see the gray stubble sticking up untidily all over his face. His stubble, I know, is as stiff as a porcupine's, but as the light wanes now, it looks fleecy and soft like the down on a dove's nestling.

I was in the bush, long ago, and I came upon two dove nestlings. They were still clumsy and blind, with soft pink vulnerable flesh planted with short scattered gray feathers, their mouths open, waiting for their mother. I wished I had corn to give them. As it was, I consoled myself with the thought that their mother was somewhere nearby, coming home through the bush in the falling dark with food in her mouth for her children.

Next day I found the nestlings dead in their nest. Somewhere out in the bush or in the yellow ripe unharvested fields, someone had shot their mother in mid-flight home.

Not long after that, I was on my father's shoulders coming home from the fields at dusk. Mother was still with us then, and father carried me because she had asked him to. I had a sore foot and couldn't walk and mother couldn't carry me because she was carrying a basket of mealies for our supper on her head and pieces of firewood in her arms. At first father grumbled. He didn't like to carry me and he didn't like receiving orders from mother: she was there to listen to him always, he said. He carried me all the same although he didn't like to, and worse, I didn't like him to carry me. His hands were hard and pinchy and his arms felt as rough and barky as logs. I preferred mother's soft warm back. He knew, too, that I didn't want him to carry me because I made my body stiff and didn't relax when he rubbed his hard chin against my cheek. His breath was harsh and foul. He wore his battered hat and stank of dirt, sweat and soil. He was trying to talk to me but I was not listening to him. That was when I noticed that his stubble looked as vulnerable as the unprotected feathers on a dove's nestling. Tears filled my eyes then and I tried to respond to his teasing, but I gave it up because he immediately began picking on mother and made her tense and tight and this tension I could feel in me also.

After this he always wanted me to be near him and he made me ignore mother. He taught me to avoid mother. It was hard for me but he had a terrible way of making mother look despicable and mean. She noticed this and fought hard to make me cheerful, but I always saw father's threatening shadow hunched hawkishly over me. Instead of talking to either of them I became silent. I was no longer happy in either's presence. And this was when I began to notice the shadows on the wall of our hut.

One day the eternal quarrel between mother and father flared up to an unbelievable blaze. Mother went away to her people. After an unsuccessful night full of nightmares with father in the hut, he had to follow her. There had been a hailstorm in the night and everything looked sad in the dripping chill of the next day. The small mealie plants in the yard had been destroyed by the storm; all the leaves torn off except the small hard piths which now stood about in the puddles like nails in a skull. Father went away without a word and I was alone.

I lay under the blankets for a long time with the door of the hut open. One by one, our chickens began to come in out of the cold.

There is something in a cold chicken's voice that asks for something you don't know how to give, something more than corn.

I watched them come into the hut and I felt sorry for them. Their feathers were still wet and they looked smaller and sicklier than normal. I couldn't shoo them out. They came and crowded by the fire, their little bird voices scarcely rising above the merest whisper. My eyes left them and wandered up and down the walls.

At first I couldn't see them but when one chicken made a slight move I noticed that there were shadows on the wall.

These shadows fascinated me. There were hundreds of them. I spent the whole day trying to separate them, to isolate them, but they were as elusive and liquid as water in a jar. After a long time looking at them, I felt that they were talking to me. I held my breath and heard their words distinctly, a lullaby in harmony: sleep, sleep, you are all alone, sleep and don't wake up, ever again.

I must have fallen asleep because I remember seeing later on that the sky had turned all dark and a thin chilly drizzle was falling. The chickens, which must have gone out feeling hungry, were coming in again, wet, their forlorn voices hardly audible above the sound of the rain. I knew by the multitude of shadows on the wall that night was falling. I felt too weak to wake up and for a long time watched the shadows multiply and fade, multiply, mingle and fade, and listened to their talk. Again I must have fallen asleep because when I woke up I was well tucked in and warm. The shadows were now brilliant and clear on the wall because there was a fire on the hearth.

Mother and father had come in and they were silent. Seeing them, I felt as if I were coming from a long journey in a strange country. Mother noticed that I was awake and said,

"How do you feel?"

"He's just lazy," father said.

"He is ill," mother said. "His body is all on fire." She felt me.

"Lies. He is a man and you want to turn him into a woman."

After this I realized how ill I was, I couldn't eat anything: there was no appetite and I wasn't hungry.

I don't know how many days I was in bed. There seemed to be nothing. No light, no sun, to show it was day or darkness to show it was night. Mother was constantly in but I couldn't recognize her as a person. There were only shadows, the voices of the shadows, the lonely cries of the dripping wet fowls shaking the cold out of their feathers by the hearth, and the vague warm shadow that must have been mother. She spoke to me often but I don't remember if I answered anything. I was afraid to answer because I was alone on a solitary plain with the dark crashing of thunder and lightning always in my ears, and there was a big frightening shadow hovering above me so that I couldn't answer her without its hearing me. That must have been father.

They might have had quarrels—I am sure they had lots of them—but I didn't hear them. Everything had been flattened to a dim depthless gray landscape and the only movement on it was of the singing shadows. I could see the shadows and hear them speak to me, so I wasn't dead. If mother talked to me at all, her voice got lost in the vast expanse of emptiness between me and the shadows. Later, when I was beginning to be aware of the change of night into day, her voice was the soft pink intrusion like cream on the hard darkness of the wall. This turned later into a clear urgent sound like the lapping of water against boulders in the morning before sunrise. I noticed too that she was often alone with me. Father was away and must have been coming in late after I had fallen asleep.

The day I saw father, a chill set in the hut.

There was another hailstorm and a big quarrel that night. It was the last quarrel.

When I could wake up again mother was gone and a strange woman had taken her place in the house.

This woman had a shrill strident voice like a cicada's that jarred my nerves. She did all the talking and father became silent and morose. Instead of the frightful silences and sudden bursts of anger I used to know, he now tried to talk softly to me. He preferred to talk to me rather than to his new wife.

But he was too late. He had taught me silence and in that long journey between mother's time and this other woman's, I had given myself to the shadows.

So today he sits just inside the hut with the sun playing with him: cartooning him on the bare cold floor and the bare dark walls of the hut, and me watching and listening to the images on the wall. He cannot talk to me because I don't know how to answer him, his language is too difficult for me. All I can think of, the nearest I can come to him, is when I see that his tough gray stubble looks like the soft unprotected feathers on a dove's nestling; and when I remember that the next morning the nestlings were dead in their nest because somebody had unknowingly killed their mother in the bush on her way home, I feel the tears in my eyes.

It is all—all that I feel for my father; but I cannot talk to him. I don't know how I should talk to him. He has denied me the gift of language.

❋ Discussion and Writing

1. Examine the implications of the father's shadow in the first two paragraphs.
2. Which nonhuman elements constitute a reality for the narrator? Examine the writer's use of these elements in portraying the son's relationship with the parents.
3. Analyze the significance of the narrator's play with shadows and his silence in the story. What is the nature of the conflict between the father and the son?
4. By what means does the writer project the distinctive shadows of the same object? What is the significance of the varied perceptions of the same object—the father's stubble, for example?

❋ Research and Comparison

Interdisciplinary Discussion Question: Under colonization the traditional family structure was disrupted as the father lost his authority first to a foreign ruler and then to the younger generation who adopted the accoutrements of foreign rule, language, religion, and culture. With the advent of modernization, the changing gender relations have also threatened the traditional patriarchal authority of men. In this context, examine the portrayal of the father-son relationship in the works of any African writer.

Zoe Wicomb
(b. 1948)
South Africa

Zoe Wicomb, born in a Griqua settlement in the Western Cape region of South Africa, is the first contemporary Griqua author to write of her own community. (The Griqua are descendants of the Khoikhoi, whose land had been taken by the Dutch.) Identified as colored according to the laws of apartheid, her family—who spoke Afrikaans—encouraged her to speak English, as it evoked a higher social status. She studied English literature and graduated at the University of the Western Cape, designated by the government as a colored university; she then moved to England where she took a degree at Reading University. For some 20 years she taught in Scotland and Great Britain. She was also writer in residence at Glasgow and Strathclyde universities and a founding editor of the *Southern African Review of Books.* But she has credited the black consciousness and feminist movements with enabling her to find her Griqua voice and to write.

The Griqua had been silenced by the laws of apartheid. She has taken up the issue of that silencing. In 1991, Wicomb returned to South Africa to teach literature at her alma mater, the University of the Western Cape.

You Can't Get Lost in Cape Town

In my right hand resting on the base of my handbag I clutch a brown leather purse. My knuckles ride to and fro, rubbing against the lining . . . surely cardboard . . . and I am surprised that the material has not revealed itself to me before. I have worn this bag for months. I would have said with a dismissive wave of the hand, "Felt, that is what the base of this bag is lined with."

Then, Michael had said, "It looks cheap, unsightly," and lowering his voice to my look of surprise, "Can't you tell?" But he was speaking of the exterior, the way it looks.

The purse fits neatly into the palm of my hand. A man's purse. The handbag gapes. With my elbow I press it against my hip but that will not avert suspicion. The bus is moving fast, too fast, surely exceeding the speed limit, so that I bob on my seat and my grip on the purse tightens as the springs suck at my womb, slurping it down through the plush of the red upholstery. I press my buttocks into the seat to ease the discomfort.

I should count out the fare for the conductor. Perhaps not; he is still at the front of the bus. We are now travelling through Rondebosch so that he will be fully occupied with white passengers at the front. Women with blue-rinsed heads tilted will go on telling their stories while fishing leisurely for their coins and just lengthen a vowel to tide over the moment of paying their fares.

"Don't be so anxious," Michael said. "It will be all right." I withdrew the hand he tried to pat.

I have always been anxious and things are not all right; things may never be all right again. I must not cry. My eyes travel to and fro along the grooves of the floor. I do not look at the faces that surround me but I believe that they are lifted speculatively at me. Is someone constructing a history for this hand resting foolishly in a gaping handbag? Do these faces expect me to whip out an amputated stump dripping with blood? Do they wince at the thought of a hand, cold and waxen, left on the pavement where it was severed? I draw my hand out of the bag and shake my fingers ostentatiously. No point in inviting conjecture, in attracting attention. The bus brakes loudly to conceal the sound of breath drawn in sharply at the exhibited hand.

Two women pant like dogs as they swing themselves on to the bus. The conductor has already pressed the bell and they propel their bodies expertly along the swaying aisle. They fall into seats opposite me—one fat, the other thin—and simultaneously pull off the starched servants' caps which they scrunch into their laps. They light cigarettes and I bite my lip. Would I have to vomit into this bag with its cardboard lining? I wish I had brought a plastic bag; this bag is empty save for the purse. I breathe deeply to stem the nausea that rises to meet the curling bands of smoke and fix on the bulging bags they grip between their feet. They make no attempt to get their fares ready; they surely misjudge the intentions of the conductor. He knows that they will get off at Mowbray to catch the Golden Arrow buses to the townships. He will not allow them to avoid paying; not he who presses the button with such promptness.

I watch him at the front of the bus. His right thumb strums an impatient jingle on the silver levers, the leather bag is cradled in the hand into which the coins tumble. He chants a barely audible accompaniment to the clatter of coins, a recitation of the newly decimalized currency. Like times tables at school and I see the fingers grow soft, bending boyish as they strum an ink-stained abacus; the boy learning to count, leaning earnestly with propped elbows over a desk. And I find the image unaccountably sad and tears are about to well up when I hear an impatient empty clatter of thumb-play on the coin dispenser as he demands, "All fares please" from a sleepy white youth. My hand flies into my handbag once again and I take out the purse. A man's leather purse.

Michael too is boyish. His hair falls in a straight blond fringe into his eyes. When he considers a reply he wipes it away impatiently, as if the hair impedes thought. I cannot imagine this purse ever having belonged to him. It is small, U-shaped and devoid of ornament, therefore a man's purse. It has an extending tongue that could be tucked into the mouth or be threaded through the narrow band across the base of the U. I take out the smallest note stuffed into this plump purse, a five-rand note. Why had I not thought about the busfare? The conductor will be angry if my note should exhaust his supply of coins although the leather bag would have a concealed pouch for notes. But this thought does not comfort me. I feel angry with Michael. He has probably never travelled by bus. How would he know of the fear of missing the unfamiliar stop, the fear of keeping an impatient conductor waiting, the fear of saying fluently, "Seventeen cents please," when you are not sure of the fare and produce a five-rand note? But this is my journey and I must not expect Michael to take responsibility for everything. Or rather, I cannot expect Michael to take responsibility for more than half the things. Michael is scrupulous about this division; I am not always sure of how to arrive at half. I was never good at arithmetic, especially this instant mental arithmetic that is sprung on me.

How foolish I must look sitting here clutching my five-rand note. I slip it back into the purse and turn to the solidity of the smoking women. They have still made no attempt to find their fares. The bus is going fast and I am surprised that we have not yet reached Mowbray. Perhaps I am mistaken, perhaps we have already passed Mowbray and the women are going to Sea Point to serve a nightshift at the Pavilion.

Marge, Aunt Trudie's eldest daughter, works as a waitress at the Pavilion but she is rarely mentioned in our family. "A disgrace," they say. "She should know better than to go with white men."

"Poor whites," Aunt Trudie hisses. "She can't even find a nice rich man to go steady with. Such a pretty girl too. I won't have her back in this house. There's no place in this house for a girl who's been used by white trash."

Her eyes flash as she spits out a cherished vision of a blond young man sitting on her new vinyl sofa to whom she serves gingerbeer and koeksisters,[1] because it is not against the law to have a respectable drink in a Colored home. "Mrs. Holman," he would say, "Mrs. Holman, this is the best gingerbeer I've had for years."

The family do not know of Michael even though he is a steady young man who would sit out such a Sunday afternoon with infinite grace. I wince at the thought of Father creaking in a suit and the unconcealed pleasure in Michael's successful academic career.

Perhaps this is Mowbray after all. The building that zooms past on the right seems familiar, I ought to know it but I am lost, hopelessly lost, and as my mind gropes for recognition I feel a feathery flutter in my womb, so slight I cannot be sure, and again, so soft, the brush of a butterfly, and under cover of my handbag I spread my left hand to hold my belly. The shaft of light falling across my shoulder, travelling this route with me, is the eye of God. God will never forgive me.

I must anchor my mind to the words of the women on the long seat opposite me. But they fall silent as if to protect their secrets from me. One of them bends down heavily, holding on to the jaws of her shopping bag as if to relieve pressure on her spine, and I submit to the ache of my own by swaying gently while I protect my belly with both hands. But having eyed the contents of her full bag carefully, her hand becomes the beak of a bird dipping purposefully into the left-hand corner and rises triumphantly with a brown paper bag on which grease has oozed light-sucking patterns. She opens the bag and her friend looks on in silence. Three chunks of cooked chicken lie on a piece of greaseproof paper. She deftly halves a piece and passes it to her thin friend. The women munch in silence, their mouths glossy with pleasure.

"These are for the children," she says, her mouth still full as she wraps the rest up and places it carelessly at the top of the bag.

"It's the spiced chicken recipe you told me about." She nudges her friend. "Lekker[2] hey!"

The friend frowns and says, "I like to taste a bit more cardamom. It's nice to find a whole cardamom in the food and crush it between your teeth. A

---

[1]Similar to a doughnut. [eds.]
[2]Nice. [eds.]

cardamom seed will never give up all its flavor to the pot. You'll still find it there in the chewing."

I note the gaps in her teeth and fear for the slipping through of cardamom seeds. The girls at school who had their two top incisors extracted in a fashion that raged through Cape Town said that it was better for kissing. Then I, fat and innocent, nodded. How would I have known the demands of kissing?

The large woman refuses to be thwarted by criticism of her cooking. The chicken stimulates a story so that she twitches with an irrepressible desire to tell.

"To think," she finally bursts out, "that I cook them this nice surprise and say what you like, spiced chicken can make any mouth water. Just think, it was yesterday when I say to that one as she stands with her hands on her hips against the stove saying, 'I don't know what to give them today, I've just got too much organizing to do to bother with food.' And I say, feeling sorry for her, I say, 'Don't you worry about a thing, Marram, just leave it all in cook's hands (wouldn't it be nice to work for really grand people where you cook and do nothing else, no bladdy³ scrubbing and shopping and all that) . . . in cook's hands,' I said," and she crows merrily before reciting: "And I'll dish up a surprise / For Master Georgie's blue eyes.

"That's Miss Lucy's young man. He was coming last night. Engaged, you know. Well there I was on my feet all day starching linen, making roeties⁴ and spiced lentils and sweet potato and all the lekker things you must mos⁵ have with cardamom chicken. And what do you think she says?"

She pauses and lifts her face as if expecting a reply, but the other stares grimly ahead. Undefeated she continues, "She says to me, 'Tiena,' because she can't keep out of my pots, you know, always opening my lids and sniffing like a brakhond,⁶ she says, 'Tiena,' and waits for me to say, 'Yes Marram,' so I know she has a wicked plan up her sleeve and I look her straight in the eye. She smile that one, always smile to put off the track, and she say looking into the fridge, 'You can have this nice bean soup for your dinner so I can have the remains of the chicken tomorrow when you're off.' So I say to her, 'That's what I had for lunch today,' and she say to me, 'Yes I know but me and Miss Lucy will be on our own for dinner tomorrow,' and she pull a face. 'Ugh, how I hate reheated food.' Then she draws up her shoulders as if to say, That's that.

"Cheek hey! And it was a great big fowl." She nudges her friend. "You know for yourself how much better food tastes the next day when the spices

³Bloody, an expletive. [eds.]
⁴An Indian flat bread. [eds.]
⁵Word used for emphasis. [eds.]
⁶A mongrel dog. [eds.]

are drawn right into the meat and anyway you just switch on the electric and there's no chopping and crying over onions, you just wait for the pot to dance on the stove. Of course she wouldn't know about that. Anyway, a cheek, that's what I call it, so before I even dished up the chicken for the table, I took this," and she points triumphantly to her bag, "and to hell with them."

The thin one opens her mouth, once, twice, winding herself up to speak.

"They never notice anyway. There's so much food in their pantries, in the fridge and on the tables; they don't know what's there and what isn't." The other looks pityingly at her.

"Don't you believe that. My marram was as cross as a bear by the time I brought in the pudding, a very nice apricot ice it was, but she didn't even look at it. She know it was a healthy grown fowl and she count one leg, and she know what's going on. She know right away. Didn't even say, 'Thank you Tiena.' She won't speak to me for days but what can she do?" Her voice softens into genuine sympathy for her madam's dilemma.

"She'll just have to speak to me." And she mimics, putting on a stern horse face. "'We'll want dinner by seven tonight,' then 'Tiena the curtains need washing,' then, 'Please, Tiena, will you fix this zip for me, I've got absolutely nothing else to wear today.' And so on the third day she'll smile and think she's smiling forgiveness at me."

She straightens her face. "No," she sighs, "the more you have, the more you have to keep your head and count and check up because you know you won't notice or remember. No, if you got a lot you must keep snaps in your mind of the insides of all the cupboards. And every day, click, click, new snaps of the larder. That's why that one is so tired, always thinking, always reciting to herself the lists of what's in the cupboards. I never know what's in my cupboard at home but I know my Sammie's a thieving bastard, can't keep his hands in his pockets."

The thin woman stares out of the window as if she had heard it all before. She has finished her chicken while the other, with all the talking, still holds a half-eaten drumstick daintily in her right hand. Her eyes rove over the shopping bag and she licks her fingers abstractedly as she stares out of the window.

"Lekker hey!" the large one repeats, "the children will have such a party."

"Did Master George enjoy it?" the other asks.

"Oh he's a gentleman all right. Shouted after me, 'Well done, Tiena. When we're married we'll have to steal you from madam.' Dressed to kill he was, such a smart young man, you know. Mind you, so's Miss Lucy. Not a prettier girl in our avenue and the best-dressed too. But then she has mos to be smart to keep her man. Been on the pill for nearly a year now; I shouldn't wonder if he don't feel funny about the white wedding. Ooh, you must see her blush over the pictures of the wedding gowns, so pure and innocent she think I can't read the packet. 'Get me my headache pills out of that drawer Tiena,' she say sometimes when I take her cup of cocoa at night. But she play her cards right with Master George; she have to 'cause who'd have what another man has pushed to the side of his plate. A bay leaf and a bone!" and moved by the alliteration the image materializes in her hand. "Like this bone," and she waves it under the nose of the other, who starts. I wonder whether with guilt, fear or a debilitating desire for more chicken.

"This bone," she repeats grimly, "picked bare and only wanted by a dog." Her friend recovers and deliberately misunderstands, "Or like yesterday's bean soup, but we women mos know that food put aside and left to stand till tomorrow always has a better flavor. Men don't know that hey. They should get down to some cooking and find out a thing or two."

But the other is not deterred. "A bone," she insists, waving her visual aid, "a bone."

It is true that her bone is a matt gray that betrays no trace of the meat or fat that only a minute ago adhered to it. Master George's bone would certainly look nothing like that when he pushes it aside. With his fork he would coax off the fibers ready to fall from the bone. Then he would turn over the whole, deftly, using a knife, and frown at the sinewy meat clinging to the joint before pushing it aside towards the discarded bits of skin.

This bone, it is true, will not tempt anyone. A dog might want to bury it only for a silly game of hide and seek.

The large woman waves the bone as if it would burst into prophecy. My eyes follow the movement until the bone blurs and emerges as the Cross where the head of Jesus lolls sadly, his lovely feet anointed by sad hands, folded together under the driven nail. Look, Mamma says, look at those eyes molten with love and pain, the body curved with suffering for our sins, and together we weep for the beauty and sadness of Jesus in his white loincloth. The Roman soldiers stand grimly erect in their tunics, their spears gleam in the light, their dark beards are clipped and their lips curl. At midday Judas turns his face to the fading sun and bays, howls like a dog for its return as the darkness grows around him and swallows him whole with the money still jingling in the folds of his saffron robes. In a concealed leather purse, a pouch devoid of ornament.

The buildings on this side of the road grow taller but oh, I do not know where I am and I think of asking the woman, the thin one, but when I look up the stern one's eyes already rest on me while the bone in her hand points idly at the advertisement just above my head. My hands, still cradling my belly, slide guiltily down my thighs and fall on my knees. But the fetus betrays me with another flutter, a sigh. I have heard of books flying off the laps of gentle mothers-to-be as their fetuses lash out. I will not be bullied. I jump up and press the bell.

There are voices behind me. The large woman's "Oi, I say" thunders over the conductor's cross "Tickets please." I will not speak to anyone. Shall

I throw myself on the grooved floor of this bus and with knees drawn up, hands over my head, wait for my demise? I do not in any case expect to be alive tomorrow. But I must resist; I must harden my heart against the sad, complaining eyes of Jesus.

"I say, Miss," she shouts and her tone sounds familiar. Her voice compels like the insistence of Father's guttural commands. But the conductor's hand falls on my shoulder, the barrel of his ticket dispenser digs into my ribs, the buttons of his uniform gleam as I dip into my bag for my purse. Then the large woman spills out of her seat as she leans forward. Her friend, reconciled, holds the bar of an arm across her as she leans forward shouting, "Here, I say, your purse." I try to look grateful. Her eyes blaze with scorn as she proclaims to the bus, "Stupid these young people. Dressed to kill maybe, but still so stupid."

She is right. Not about my clothes, of course, and I check to see what I am wearing. I have not been alerted to my own stupidity before. No doubt I will sail through my final examinations at the end of this year and still not know how I dared to pluck a fluttering fetus out of my womb. That is if I survive tonight.

I sit on the steps of this large building and squint up at the marble facade. My elbows rest on my knees flung comfortably apart. I ought to know where I am; it is clearly a public building of some importance. For the first time I long for the veld[7] of my childhood. There the red sand rolls for miles, and if you stand on the koppie[8] behind the house the landmarks blaze their permanence: the river points downward, runs its dry course from north to south; the geelbos[9] crowd its banks in near straight lines. On either side of the path winding westward plump little buttocks of cacti squat as if lifting the skirts to pee, and the swollen fingers of vygies burst in clusters out of the stone, pointing the way. In the veld you can always find your way home.

I am anxious about meeting Michael. We have planned this so carefully for the rush hour when people storming home crossly will not notice us together in the crush.

"It's simple," Michael said. "The bus carries along the main roads through the suburbs to the City, and as you reach the Post Office you get off and I'll be there to meet you. At five."

A look at my anxious face compelled him to say, "You can't get lost in Cape Town. There," and he pointed over his shoulder, "is Table Mountain and there is Devil's Peak and there Lion's Head, so how in heaven's name could you get lost?" The words shot out unexpectedly, like the fine arc of brown spittle from between the teeth of an old man who no longer savors

---

[7]Field or meadow. [eds.]
[8]Hill or mound. [eds.]
[9]Geelbows and vygies: flowers of Cape Town. [eds.]

the tobacco he has been chewing all day. There are, I suppose, things that even a loved one cannot overlook.

Am I a loved one?

I ought to rise from these steps and walk toward the City. Fortunately I always take the precaution of setting out early, so that I should still be in time to meet Michael, who will drive me along de Waal Drive into the slopes of Table Mountain where Mrs. Coetzee waits with her tongs.

Am I a loved one? No. I am dull, ugly and bad-tempered. My hair has grown greasy, I am forgetful and I have no sense of direction. Michael, he has long since stopped loving me. He watched me hugging the lavatory bowl, retching, and recoiled at my first display of bad temper. There is a faraway look in his eyes as he plans his retreat. But he is well brought up, honorable. When the first doubts gripped the corners of his mouth, he grinned madly and said, "We must marry," showing a row of perfect teeth.

"There are laws against that," I said unnecessarily.

But gripped by the idyll of an English landscape of painted greens, he saw my head once more held high, my lettuce-luscious skirts crisp on a camomile lawn and the willow drooping over the red mouth of a suckling infant.

"Come on," he urged. "Don't do it. We'll get to England and marry. It will work out all right," and betraying the source of his vision, "and we'll be happy for ever, thousands of miles from all this mess."

I would have explained if I could. But I could not account for this vision: the slow shower of ashes over yards of diaphanous tulle, the moth wings tucked back with delight as their tongues whisked the froth of white lace. For two years I have loved Michael, have wanted to marry him. Duped by a dream I merely shook my head.

"But you love babies, you want babies some time or other, so why not accept God's holy plan? Anyway, you're a Christian and you believe it's a sin, don't you?"

God is not a good listener. Like Father, he expects obedience and withdraws peevishly if his demands are not met. Explanations of my point of view infuriate him so that he quivers with silent rage. For once I do not plead and capitulate; I find it quite easy to ignore these men.

"You're not even listening," Michael accused. "I don't know how you can do it." There is revulsion in his voice.

For two short years I have adored Michael.

Once, perched perilously on the rocks, we laughed fondly at the thought of a child. At Cape Point where the oceans meet and part. The Indian and the Atlantic, fighting for their separate identities, roared and thrashed fiercely so that we huddled together, his hand on my belly. It is said that if you shut one eye and focus the other carefully, the line separating the two oceans may rear drunkenly but remains ever clear and hair-fine. But I did not look. In the mischievous wind I struggled with the flapping ends of a scarf I tried to wrap around my hair. Later that day on the silver sands of a deserted beach he wrote solemnly: Will you marry me? and my trembling fingers traced a huge heart around the words. Ahead the sun danced on the waves, flecking them with gold.

I wrote a poem about that day and showed Michael. "Surely that was not what Logiesbaai was about," he frowned, and read aloud the lines about warriors charging out of the sea, assegais[10] gleaming in the sun, the beat of tom-toms riding the waters, the throb in the carious cavities of rocks.

"It's good," he said, nodding thoughtfully, "I like the title, 'Love at Logiesbaai' (Whites Only), though I expect much of the subtlety escapes me. Sounds good," he encouraged, "you should write more often."

I flushed. I wrote poems all the time. And he was wrong; it was not a good poem. It was puzzling and I wondered why I had shown him this poem that did not even make sense to me. I tore it into little bits.

Love, love, love, I sigh as I shake each ankle in turn and examine the swelling.

Michael's hair falls boyishly over his eyes. His eyes narrow merrily when he smiles and the left corner of his mouth shoots up so that the row of teeth forms a queer diagonal line above his chin. He flicks his head so that the fringe of hair lifts from his eyes for a second, then falls, so fast, like the tongue of a lizard retracted at the very moment of exposure.

"We'll find somewhere," he would say, "a place where we'd be quite alone." This country is vast and he has an instinctive sense of direction. He discovers the armpits of valleys that invite us into their shadows. Dangerous climbs led by the roar of the sea take us to blue bays into which we drop from impossible cliffs. The sun lowers herself on to us. We do not fear the police with their torches. They come only by night in search of offenders. We have the immunity of love. They cannot find us because they do not know we exist. One day they will find out about lovers who steal whole days, round as globes.

There has always been a terrible thrill in that thought.

I ease my feet back into my shoes and the tears splash on to my dress with such wanton abandon that I cannot believe they are mine. From the punctured globes of stolen days these fragments sag and squint. I hold, hold these pictures I have summoned. I will not recognize them for much longer.

With tilted head I watch the shoes and sawn-off legs ascend and descend the marble steps, altering course to avoid me. Perhaps someone will ask the police to remove me.

Love, love, love, I sigh. Another flutter in my womb. I think of moth wings struggling against a window pane and I rise.

The smell of sea unfurls toward me as I approach Adderley Street. There is no wind but the brine hangs in an atomized mist, silver over a thwarted

---

[10]Spears. [eds.]

sun. In answer to my hunger, Wellingtons looms on my left. The dried-fruit palace which I cannot resist. The artificial light dries my tears, makes me blink, and the trays of fruit, of Cape sunlight twice trapped, shimmer and threaten to burst out of their forms. Rows of pineapple are the infinite divisions of the sun, the cores lost in the amber discs of mebos[11] arranged in arcs. Prunes are the wrinkled backs of aged goggas[12] beside the bloodshot eyes of cherries. Dark green figs sit pertly on their bottoms peeping over trays. And I too am not myself, hoping for refuge in a metaphor that will contain it all. I buy the figs and mebos. Desire is a Tsafendas tapeworm in my belly that cannot be satisfied and as I pop the first fig into my mouth I feel the danger fountain with the jets of saliva. Will I stop at one death?

I have walked too far along this road and must turn back to the Post Office. I break into a trot as I see Michael in the distance, drumming with his nails on the side of the car. His sunburnt elbow juts out of the window. He taps with anxiety or impatience and I grow cold with fear as I jump into the passenger seat and say merrily, "Let's go," as if we are setting off for a picnic.

Michael will wait in the car on the next street. She had said that it would take only ten minutes. He takes my hand and so prevents me from getting out. Perhaps he thinks that I will bolt, run off into the mountain, revert to savagery. His hand is heavy on my forearm and his eyes are those of a wounded dog, pale with pain.

"It will be all right." I try to comfort and wonder whether he hears his own voice in mine. My voice is thin, a tinsel thread that springs out of my mouth and flutters straight out of the window.

"I must go." I lift the heavy hand off my forearm and it falls inertly across the gearstick.

The room is dark. The curtains are drawn and a lace-shaded electric light casts shadows in the corners of the rectangle. The doorway in which I stand divides the room into sleeping and eating quarters. On the left there is a table against which a servant girl leans, her eyes fixed on the blank wall ahead. On the right a middle-aged white woman rises with a hostess smile from a divan which serves as sofa, and pats the single pink-flowered cushion to assert homeliness. There is a narrow dark wardrobe in the corner.

I say haltingly, "You are expecting me. I spoke to you on the telephone yesterday. Sally Smit." I can see no telephone in the room. She frowns.

"You're not Colored, are you?" It is an absurd question. I look at my brown arms that I have kept folded across my chest, and watch the gooseflesh sprout. Her eyes are fixed on me. Is she blind? How will she perform the operation with such defective sight? Then I realize: the educated voice, the accent had blinded her. I have drunk deeply of Michael, swallowed his voice as I drank from his tongue. Has he swallowed mine? I do not think so.

---

[11]Dried fruit. [eds.]
[12]Insects or worms. [eds.]

I say "No," and wait for all the cockerels in Cape Town to crow simultaneously. Instead the servant starts from her trance and stares at me with undisguised admiration.

"Good," the woman smiles, showing yellow teeth. "One must check nowadays. These Colored girls, you know, are very forward, terrible types. What do they think of me, as if I would do every Tom, Dick and Harry. Not me you know; this is a respectable concern and I try to help decent women, educated you know. No, you can trust me. No Colored girl's ever been on this sofa."

The girl coughs, winks at me and turns to stir a pot simmering on a primus stove on the table. The smell of offal escapes from the pot and nausea rises in my throat, feeding the fear. I would like to run but my feet are lashed with fear to the linoleum. Only my eyes move, across the room where she pulls a newspaper from a wad wedged between the wall and the wardrobe. She spreads the paper on the divan and smooths it with her hand while the girl shuts the door and turns the key. A cat crawls lazily from under the table and stares at me until the green jewels of its eyes shrink to crystal points.

She points me to the sofa. From behind the wardrobe she pulls her instrument and holds it against the baby-pink crimplene of her skirt.

"Down, shut your eyes now," she says as I raise my head to look. Their movements are carefully orchestrated, the maneuvers practiced. Their eyes signal and they move. The girl stations herself by my head and her mistress moves to my feet. She pushes my knees apart and whips out her instrument from a pocket. A piece of plastic tubing dangles for a second. My knees jerk and my mouth opens wide but they are in control. A brown hand falls on my mouth and smothers the cry; the white hands wrench the knees apart and she hisses, "Don't you dare. Do you want the bladdy police here? I'll kill you if you scream."

The brown hand over my mouth relaxes. She looks into my face and says, "She won't." I am a child who needs reassurance. I am surprised by the softness of her voice. The brown hand moves along the side of my face and pushes back my hair. I long to hold the other hand; I do not care what happens below. A black line of terror separates it from my torso. Blood spurts from between my legs and for a second the two halves of my body make contact through the pain.

So it is done. Deflowered by yellow hands wielding a catheter. Fear and hypocrisy, mine, my deserts spread in a dark stain on the newspaper.

"OK," she says, "get yourself decent." I dress and wait for her to explain. "You go home now and wait for the birth. Do you have a pad?"

I shake my head uncomprehendingly. Her face tightens for a moment but then she smiles and pulls a sanitary towel out of the wardrobe.

"Won't cost you anything lovey." She does not try to conceal the glow of her generosity. She holds out her hand and I place the purse in her palm. She counts, satisfied, but I wave away the purse which she reluctantly puts on the table.

"You're a good girl," she says and puts both hands on my shoulders. I hold my breath; I will not inhale the fetid air from the mouth of this my grotesque bridegroom with yellow teeth. She plants the kiss of complicity on my cheek and I turn to go, repelled by her touch. But have I the right to be fastidious? I cannot deny feeling grateful, so that I turn back to claim the purse after all. The girl winks at me. The purse fits snugly in my hand; there would be no point in giving it back to Michael.

Michael's face is drawn with fear. He is as ignorant of the process as I am. I am brisk, efficient and rattle off the plan. "It'll happen tonight so I'll go home and wait and call you in the morning. By then it will be all over." He looks relieved.

He drives me right to the door and my landlady waves merrily from the step where she sits with her embroidery among the potted ferns.

"Don't look," she says anxiously. "It's a present for you, for your trousseau," and smiling slyly, "I can tell when a couple just can't wait any longer. There's no catching me out, you know."

Tonight in her room next to mine she will turn in her chaste bed, tracing the tendrils from pink and orange flowers, searching for the needle lost in endless folds of white linen.

Semi-detached houses with red-polished steps line the west side of Trevelyan Road. On the east is the Cape Flats line where electric trains rattle reliably according to timetable. Trevelyan Road runs into the elbow of a severely curved Main Road which nevertheless has all the amenities one would expect: butcher, baker, hairdresser, chemist, library, liquor store. There is a fish and chips shop on that corner, on the funny bone of that elbow, and by the side, strictly speaking in Trevelyan Road, a dustbin leans against the trunk of a young palm tree. A newspaper parcel dropped into this dustbin would absorb the vinegary smell of discarded fish and chips wrappings in no time.

The wrapped parcel settles in the bin. I do not know what has happened to God. He is fastidious. He fled at the moment that I smoothed the wet black hair before wrapping it up. I do not think he will come back. It is 6 a.m. Light pricks at the shroud of Table Mountain. The streets are deserted and, relieved, I remember that the next train will pass at precisely 6:22.

❋ Discussion and Writing

1. Analyze the feelings that dominate the narrator on her long bus ride.
2. What is the connection between the woman's handbag and the man's purse? How do they relate to the main episode of abortion?
3. Discuss the significance of the references to other young couples in the narration?
4. Analyze the importance of Tiena's virtual monologue to her silent listener. How are the details of what Tiena says relate to the main story?

5. "In the veld you can always find your way" and "You can't get lost in Cape Town": discuss the two perspectives—black and white, female and male—within the South African experience.
6. Analyze the final episode of the abortion: what is implied by the color blindness of the woman performing the abortion?
7. What do the images of the bus, the train, and the car symbolize?
8. Analyze the symbolism of the following images: the bone, blood, the Cross, Judas, the coins, and so on.

❋ Research and Comparison

Research the legal position on interracial marriages in South Africa. Discuss the treatment of these issues in other literary works for a comparative analysis.

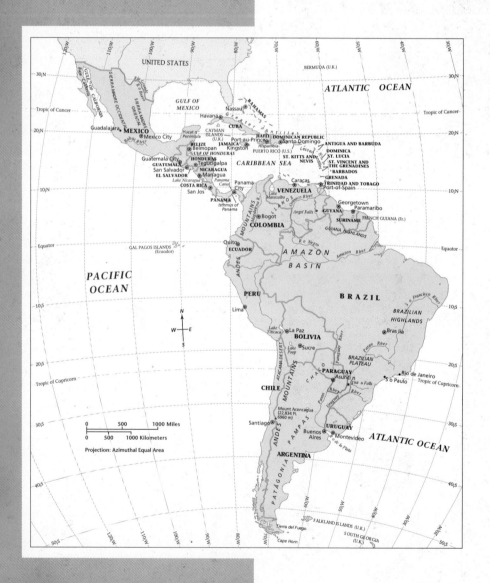

UNITED STATES

BERMUDA (U.K.)

ATLANTIC OCEAN

30°N

Tropic of Cancer

GULF OF
MEXICO

BAHAMAS

Nassau

Havana

CUBA

CAYMAN
ISLANDS
(U.K.)

Tropic of Cancer

20°N

Guadalajara

MEXICO

Mexico City

Yucatán
Peninsula

HAITI

DOMINICAN REPUBLIC

Santo Domingo

ANTIGUA AND BARBUDA

20°N

Port-au-Prince

JAMAICA

Kingston

PUERTO RICO (U.S.)

Hispaniola

DOMINICA

ST. LUCIA

Guatemala City

GUATEMALA

BELIZE

Belmopan

GULF OF HONDURAS

Lesser Antilles

ST. KITTS AND
NEVIS

ST. VINCENT AND
THE GRENADINES

HONDURAS

Tegucigalpa

CARIBBEAN SEA

BARBADOS

San Salvador

EL SALVADOR

NICARAGUA

Managua

GRENADA

Lake Nicaragua

Panama
Canal

TRINIDAD AND TOBAGO
Port-of-Spain

10°N

COSTA RICA

San José

PANAMA

Panama
City

VENEZUELA

Caracas

10°N

Isthmus of
Panama

Lake
Maracaibo

Georgetown

Paramaribo

Bogotá

COLOMBIA

Angel Falls

Orinoco River

GUYANA

SURINAME

FRENCH GUIANA (Fr.)

GUIANA HIGHLANDS

Equator

GALÁPAGOS ISLANDS
(Ecuador)

Quito

ECUADOR

Río Negro

AMAZON

Amazon River

Equator

PACIFIC
OCEAN

BASIN

BRAZIL

PERU

Lima

São Francisco River

BRAZILIAN
HIGHLANDS

10°S

Brasília

10°S

N

W   E

S

Lake
Titicaca

La Paz

BOLIVIA

Sucre

Paraguay River

BRAZILIAN
PLATEAU

20°S

Lake
Poopó

ATACAMA DESERT

CHACO

Río de Janeiro

Tropic of Capricorn

PARAGUAY

Asunción

Iguaçu Falls

São Paulo

Tropic of Capricorn

20°S

CHILE

ANDES MOUNTAINS

Paraná River

Uruguay River

0   500   1000 Miles

Mount Aconcagua
(22,834 ft.
6960 m)

Santiago

URUGUAY

30°S

0   500   1000 Kilometers

Buenos
Aires

Montevideo

Río de la Plata

ATLANTIC OCEAN

Projection: Azimuthal Equal Area

PAMPAS

ARGENTINA

40°S

PATAGONIA

FALKLAND ISLANDS (U.K.)

Tierra del Fuego

SOUTH GEORGIA
(U.K.)

50°S

Cape Horn

PART 5

Latin America and the Caribbean

In 1493 Christopher Columbus wrote,

> I reached the Indies . . . . And there I found very many islands filled with people without number, and of them all have I taken possession for Their Highnesses. . . . To the first island which I found I gave the name Sant Salvador, in recognition of His Heavenly Majesty; . . . the Indians call it Guanahani.

Columbus had not, in fact, reached the Indies; nevertheless, his tale authored history as he named the land and the people. His statement symbolically contains the subsequent story of the Western hemisphere: the conquest of the land, the people, and their languages, all under the aegis of Church and State.

By using rhetoric that was currently popular, Columbus created something legendary, fabled. His descriptions drew upon such conventions as the chivalric romance, epic poetry, and travel accounts (particularly Marco Polo's). The mountains of Cuba were "of a thousand shapes, . . . [the] trees of a thousand kinds and tall, and they seem to touch the sky." The people were "timid" as well as "handsome," not "human monstrosities," "so artless and so free with all they possess, that no one would believe it without having seen it." He offered them "a thousand good, pleasing things" so that "they might be fond of us, . . . become Christians and be inclined to the love and service of Their Highnesses and of the whole Castilian nation."

Columbus's writings contributed to shaping European consciousness of the Western hemisphere. By incorporating the very substance of legend, they helped generate Western concepts of a New World, and this New World as Eden. But when Columbus portrayed the marvels of the Caribbean, he did so from within a Christian mythology and an inherently dichotomizing perspective: the Europeans opposed to the natives, who were considered outside the pale. This vision has held, and it has informed American literature. In general, North American writers of European descent have worked within the European perspective; writers from the Rio Grande to Tierra del Fuego have treated this view ironically.

The Continent from the Rio Grande to Tierra Del Fuego

When Columbus reached the Western Hemisphere, some 30 million people were living south of the Isthmus of Panama alone. In what is now Peru, there was a history reaching back to the ninth millenium B.C., a history in which empires had prospered and declined. The entire Andean region was governed from Cuzco (in Peru) by the Quechua-speaking Inca nation. The Incas had built grand cities like Machu Picchu, where a highly organized administrative system provided work for the able-bodied and assistance to those who could not work. A fortress city high in the mountains, Machu Picchu was to be the Inca's last stronghold against the Spanish. In 1532, the Spanish conquistador Francisco Pizarro arrived, professed friendship with the Inca ruler, and then executed him. In 1535, Pizarro founded Lima, Peru, the city that was soon the center of Spanish rule throughout South America.

By the 1530s, Spain and Portugal had conquered most of the land lying to the south of what is now the United States. South of the Isthmus of Panama, Spain and Portugal divided the lands between them, with Portugal claiming Brazil, nearly half the continent. North of the Isthmus, Spain took all. In their march northward, the Spanish encountered the Mayan peoples, whose culture reached back some 3000 years and who were still a powerful force in the area around Guatemala. After the Spanish defeated the Maya-Quiche, the Guatemalan city of Antigua quickly became one of the richest in the hemisphere, the hub of a thriving Middle American Spanish colony. Further north, Hernan Cortes defeated the Aztecs, adding their empire to Spain's territory.

As is evident in Columbus's writings, religious, military, and political conquests marched together from the beginning of colonization. During the fifteenth and sixteenth centuries, the Catholic monarchs of Spain offered the Roman Catholic Church their patronage, and it was a mutually beneficial relationship. On the one hand, Spanish colonial governors fostered the conversion of the native peoples in order to expedite both submission and loyalty to Spain; on the other hand, the Church bestowed legitimacy upon the military and political conquests, thereby gaining and wielding exceptional power. Today, almost 200 years after colonial rule ended, the Church continues to play a dominant role in the social and political life of the continent.

From the beginning, the Europeans sought treasure. They found rich mineral deposits and seemingly endless land for growing sugarcane, coffee, bananas, and tobacco; they opened mines and built plantations. At first, local peoples were conscripted as laborers. Soon, however, people were brought as slaves from Africa to replace local populations that either had been decimated or, resisting conscription, had hidden in remote hills.

The slaves ran, too, forming free African communities throughout the continent, particularly in Brazil, the largest importer of slaves.

With some variations, a pattern unfolded. Wealth accumulated in the hands of a few families, begetting powerful oligarchies. And race was rigorously defined. There were the criollos, the mestizos, the mulattos, the Africans, and the peoples native to the land. These terms came to be interpreted in different ways. Criollo originally indicated a person of European descent who was born in Latin America, and mestizo a person of native and European descent. In some countries, these terms subsequently formed the basis of an elaborate system in which people were identified according to the numbers of ancestors of a particular heritage; in others, they took on class connotations that overrode race. A hierarchy developed in which, for the most part, the descendants of African slaves and the original inhabitants lived in poverty and powerlessness as a lower class and caste. Race-class distinctions continued through the colonial era and have held into the present.

This complex story of racial and class differentiation forms the substratum of twentieth-century Latin American writing. Of major importance is the fact that these distinctions have acted historically as a divisive force, segregating the literature of the groups at the bottom of the social hierarchy. A large body of oral literature exists throughout the continent in such widely spoken indigenous languages as Aymara, Quechua, Quiche, Tupi, and Guarani. This literature comprises material predating colonial rule as well as responses to colonialism. Since oral literature was generally ignored until late in the twentieth century, little has been transcribed or translated.

In the Spanish-speaking countries south of Mexico, colonial rule lasted until the first part of the 1800s, when the battle of Ayacucho paved the way for independence. The Argentine Jose de San Martin and the Venezuelan Simon Bolivar liberated much of South America. Bolivar had envisioned a united South America. But Bolivar's dream failed: Growing national interests saw the borders between the different countries become areas of dispute and sites of war during the nineteenth and twentieth centuries. Nevertheless, both he and San Martin have attained legendary status in the South American consciousness.

Brazilian independence was more directly influenced by events in Europe. When Napoleon invaded Portugal in 1807, the Portuguese king, John VI, fled to Brazil, and Rio de Janeiro became the capital of the Portuguese empire. His son declared himself emperor of an independent Brazil in 1822, and his grandson ruled for 58 years, a reign that allowed for some social cohesion. Slavery, however, continued until 1888, when its abolition helped bring about the establishment of a republic.

Except for Brazil, nineteenth-century Latin America suffered from civil wars, struggles for power, battles over borders, and foreign intervention. In 1823, U.S. President James Monroe declared the Western Hemisphere closed to European intrusion, a policy that came to be known as the Monroe Doctrine. In 1904, President Theodore Roosevelt extended the interpretation of the Monroe Doctrine, implicitly claiming for the United States the right to intervene in national affairs south of its own border. As later presidents justified U.S. intervention by invoking the Monroe Doctrine, it became synonymous in Latin America and the Caribbean with thinly veiled U.S. imperialism.

In the twentieth century, the round of political upheavals has continued throughout the continent. Reform movements—from the most modest to the most radical—have protested against tyranny. Republics have been established and, in turn, shattered by dictatorships and military coups that have crushed political, social, and economic reform. Both the Church hierarchy, whose ties to the elites stretch back to the early days of colonization, and the United States have tended to support the ruling oligarchs. Over the years, however, the clergy has found itself in virtually every camp, from backing dictators to protecting the poor farmers, the urban working classes, and the native peoples living in outlying areas. This is the political milieu into which twentieth-century writers were born, and about which they have written so compellingly.

The history of Latin American writing is lined with political concern. From the beginning of its translation from Europe to Latin America in the 1820s and 1830s, the Romantic movement in literature championed freedom, whether from European or regional tyranny, foreign or local oppressors. The very first writers inspired by romanticism were exiled for their political stance. This association of Latin American authors with questions of justice has continued into the twentieth century, a reflection of persistent political and social oppression.

The history also traces the evolution of a Latin American aesthetic. During the second half of the nineteenth century, writers began searching for a means to portray their native land and its uniqueness. They sought to rediscover their countries and continent, their land and its people; and they sought authenticity, a polyphonic Latin American voice that told the Latin American experience. In their quest they gradually transmuted European literary theory.

Of major consequence to the development of this voice was the *modernismo* movement of the late nineteenth century. *Modernismo* poets combined the concise imagery, musicality, detached tone, and mysticism of various French schools with conventions drawn from medieval Spanish poetry to create the first transcontinental Spanish-American movement. Although not actually the first modernist, the Nicaraguan writer Ruben Dario (1867–1916) has traditionally been considered the leader of *modernismo,* and as such he influenced subsequent generations of poets and storytellers throughout South America and the Caribbean.

In fiction, regionalism gradually emerged, embracing a loose confederation of Spanish-American genres. Writers told stories of the exploitation of the *campesinos,* or peasants, in a genre called the "novel of the earth." In Argentina, the gaucho novel sprang up; in Mexico novels of the Mexican Revolution appeared. In Brazil and the Caribbean as well, local concerns and cultures gave rise to regional works.

Early in the development of Brazilian fiction Joaquim Maria Machado de Asis (1839–1908) brought the modern Latin American novel into being. From its beginnings, written fiction in Brazil explored the actualities of Brazilian experience. Machado, as he is known, recast urban realism, emphasizing complexity, psychology, ambiguity, and irony. Like Ruben Dario, he influenced succeeding generations beyond his native land and laid the foundation for the extraordinary mid-twentieth century Latin American narrative that burst upon the world.

A social factor also played a role in the growth of a Latin American aesthetic. During the twentieth century, rising affluence (especially in Argentina, Uruguay, Chile, Brazil, and Mexico) allowed many artists to travel to Europe. Miguel Angel Asturias, for example, studied anthropology at the Sorbonne; Jorge Luis Borges developed his theories in Spain; and Cesar Vallejo joined the Communist Party in Paris. Pablo Neruda and Octavio Paz were in Europe at the time of the Spanish Civil War (1936–39), and along with Vallejo, they actively supported the Spanish Republican fight against fascism.

In Europe, the writers were exposed to the famous twentieth-century theories emanating from Paris—Cubism, Dadaism, Surrealism—which they appropriated and reformulated to suit their own expressive needs. Vallejo and Neruda probed the unconscious, formulating electifying images in order to protest against social and political injustice. Paz and Neruda sought a simplified poetics to incorporate existential concerns. Borges created an Argentine sense of the fantastic. All recast surrealism to represent Latin American experience.

Writers also began to explore the literatures of their own land, reading earlier Latin American as well as European authors. They focused on the ancient cultures, colonial and postcolonial history, the political and social situation, psychology, and morality. Joao Guimaraes Rosa investigated the oral tradition of the Brazilian backlands to explore inner and external realms of experience; Juan Rulfo experimented with form to portray the Mexican Cristeros Revolution; Gabriel Garcia Marquez drew an entire world to illustrate Colombian solitude and isolation, qualities that seemed, at the same time, a Latin American condition. The transformation of European theory and the turn to native sources reinforced a consciousness of isolation from Europe and the United States. And isolation—both individual and continental, political and philosophical—has intertwined itself with solitude and alienation, forming one of the dominant Latin American literary motifs of the twentieth century.

The most famous result of this mingling of aesthetic theories has come to be known as magical realism. First coined by the German art critic Franz

Roh in 1925 to express the way mysterious elements are inherent in the mundane, the term was transposed to literature by Angel Flores in his 1955 essay "Magical Realism in Spanish-American Fiction." Over the years magical realism has accrued many meanings, from signifying a simple mixture of the real and the fantastic to functioning as a structural term. Magical realism has also been associated with a wicked sense of humor, sometimes embodied in the fantastic. The term is applied widely, and authors as diverse as Asturias, Borges, Rulfo, and Garcia Marquez have found themselves classified as magical realists.

In addition, many writers have set about unmasking social hypocrisy and injustice. They have written about distinctively Latin American issues: the relation between the Church and the state; the slavish adoration and imitation of Europe in Latin American society; and political corruption and U.S. intervention in national affairs. At the same time, writers such as Manuel Puig and Rubem Fonseca have employed techniques from film and drawn on the plots of Hollywood movies and U.S. detective stories to satirize contemporary social mores. But whether or not individual writers have been politically active, they have all endured the volatility and frequent violence that have characterized this century. Even such a nonpolitical writer as Borges suffered during Juan Peron's dictatorship in Argentina; some, such as Julio Cortazar and Juan Carlos Onetti, have gone into exile.

For more than 50 years, then, writers have been formulating a Latin American aesthetic. The 1960s saw its triumph. In 1961, Borges was co-winner with Samuel Beckett of the prestigious Formentor Prize for his influential *Ficciones*, originally published in 1944. The event symbolized the beginning of what is known as the "boom," the international recognition of a number of major writers from Latin America, among them, Jose Donoso, Carlos Fuentes, Mario Vargas Llosa, Julio Cortazar, and Gabriel Garcia Marquez. Their aesthetic perspectives have made a lasting contribution to contemporary world literature.

Garcia Marquez maintains that all Latin Americans are mestizos, a remark that is at once metaphysical, aesthetic, and social. On the one hand, his comment fits into an ongoing debate as to whether or not Latin American literature is a cohesive entity; on the other, he is identifying the literature as separate from European. It is the consciousness of this distinction that marks the modern writer of the Latin America.

The Caribbean

Arawak peoples, mainly Tainos, had migrated from South America to the Caribbean islands some five hundred years before Columbus landed in the West Indies. Shortly before he arrived, a Carib group had taken possession of parts of the South American mainland and the Lesser Antilles, the string of islands separating the Atlantic Ocean from the Caribbean Sea. The Tainos still held the Greater Antilles—Cuba, Jamaica, Hispaniola, and Puerto Rico. But from 1492 on, the history of the continent and the Caribbean basin followed the same fundamental pattern: the European conquest; the introduction of a plantation economy and imposition of slavery; and the decimation of local populations and importation of people from Africa to work as slaves.

Cuba, Hispaniola, Trinidad, and Puerto Rico were among the Caribbean islands Columbus claimed for Spain. Cuba became the base for the Spanish fleet and for Spain's exploration throughout the continent. Called the "Pearl of the Antilles," Cuba was the depot for the treasures that had been garnered and for sending them on to Spain. On Hispaniola, the first settlers farmed the land and founded the colony of Santo Domingo in the eastern part of the island. In the 1600s, Spain transferred the western part to France, a division that approximates the present-day Dominican Republic and Haiti, respectively.

Trinidad remained a Spanish colony until 1802, when England officially took control. Borinquen (or Boriquen) was the original Taino name for Puerto Rico. Spain renamed the island and retained control until the Spanish-American War of 1898, when the colony was ceded to the United States. Those who have sought independence from the United States have called for using the name Borinquen once again.

With Puerto Rico as the rich doorway to the Caribbean Sea, Spain commanded the region, but other European countries were soon trying to gain entry. By the middle of the 1600s, England, France, and the Netherlands had captured and established colonies along the western edge of the sea, in Jamaica, and in Guyana. Islands were traded back and forth as the Europeans battled one another for a piece of the lucrative market, if not for control. Although Columbus's accounts praised the generosity of the Tainos, the Arawak and Carib peoples, whether hospitable or fierce, were conquered and almost annihilated as the first Europeans developed a plantation culture.

As communities were devastated by their contact with the Europeans and as the plantation economy required a large pool of labor, so the demand for slaves increased. The plantation economy of both the Caribbean and the continent was thus inextricably entwined with the triangular slave trade. The region formed the southwestern side of the triangle, Africa the eastern side, and Europe the northern. People from various African cultures were sold to the western side of the Atlantic in exchange for sugarcane, rum, and other resources of the land. These were sold to the North American shipbuilders and European merchants; the merchants, in turn, sailed to Africa and purchased people. As the trade flourished, particularly in the Caribbean and Brazil, it created a wealthy land-owning class that drew Europeans to the Western Hemisphere.

Over the centuries, the elites remained small, as did the rising middle class. With the abolition of slavery in the British Empire in 1833 and the fluctuations in the European market for Caribbean products, there emerged a large, poor, peasant class who still worked the plantations. As the freed slaves were of African descent and the landowners of European or mixed descent, the class system became entangled with race, and a hierarchy based on color evolved. Adding to the cultural and social mix, from the middle of the 1800s on, people were brought from India as indentured servants in ever-increasing numbers to replace the freed slaves, and Indian communities began to form, particularly in Guyana and Trinidad. But all things European continued to be the standard of excellence: color, language, education.

Divided societies developed with many customs, religions, and languages. Most West Indian countries, however, were bifurcated: two languages, a creole or patois and the formal language of the colonizer; two religions, an African-based religion and a form of Christianity; two levels of education. The spoken patois of the majority of the people carried the old stories that had been brought from Africa and transformed, even as new stories were added, forming a rich oral tradition. The colonizer's language was the medium of formal education, and thus the means of social advancement. While elements from African and European religions mingled over time, the African religions like Vodun, Santeria, and Obeah remained central to the lives of many West Indians, especially among the poor.

From the beginning, there had been resistance to colonization: Tainos resisted in Puerto Rico; runaway slaves who hid in isolated mountainous areas revolted on many islands. In Haiti, these uprisings were the precursors of the revolution of 1801, when Toussaint L'Ouverture, a former slave, conquered the island, abolishing slavery and paving the way for independence. In 1804, Haiti won its independence, but like its sister Caribbean countries, it remained dependent on the colonizer, in this case, France. Despite national distinctions, the persistent dependency formed the underpinning of a West Indian consciousness.

This history of colonization, of class and caste, of an African based culture dominated by European institutions forms the background and material of twentieth-century Caribbean literature. First-generation twentieth-century writers such as Aime Cesaire and Leon Damas studied in Europe. In Paris, Cesaire and Damas met Leopold Senghor, and the three formulated the influential *negritude* movement, freeing themselves and subsequent writers from European standards of style, thought, and values by asserting pride in their African heritage. As a movement of liberation, *negritude* undercut European standards, including the very class system itself. It inspired a body of literature portraying African Caribbean life, its struggles, its dignity, and its truths. Thus, such *negritude* writers as Jacques

Roumain and Joseph Zobel incorporated the oral tradition and pictured rural life.

Twentieth-century Caribbean writers were also very much influenced by the current political upheavals. Puerto Rico had become a colony of the United States in 1900, and, using the Monroe Doctrine as justification, the United States intervened throughout the region: U.S. marines occupied the Dominican Republic and Haiti; the United States backed dictatorships in the Dominican Republic and Cuba. France, Great Britain, and the Netherlands held onto their colonies until the end of World War II. Then the forces of nationalism compelled the Europeans to grant the colonies independence. (Martinique has remained a department of France into the 1990s.) Because these islands still looked to Europe for governance and education, the old class and caste divisions have persisted. Writers as diverse as Olive Senior, Juan Bosch, and Austin Clarke have taken up these issues.

Whether the writers of the twentieth century have insisted on a national or a Caribbean identity, all have sought to overcome the residue of racial-class bigotry. They have disavowed the Western sense of time, illuminating mythic time like Wilson Harris, and used patois as a valid formal mode like Opal Adissa Palmer. They have looked to Marxism as an answer like Nicolas Guillen and Jacques Roumain. Like Ana Lydia Vega and Julia de Burgos, they have explored problems concerning women, and like Simone Schwarz-Bart and Rosario Ferre, they have revealed women's powers. In Martin Carter's words, they have been "listening to the land." Or as Derek Walcott said of his "island culture," "we gather around the storyteller, and the tradition is revived."

Antonio Gonzalez Bravo
(1885–1962)
Bolivia

Antonio Gonzalez Bravo was born in La Paz, Bolivia, and was a musician, poet, teacher, and ethnographer. Feudalism had not ended in Bolivia when he was writing, and within the context of such a closed political system, his work as an *indigenista* on behalf of native peoples was revolutionary. He was one of the first proponents of providing education in their native Quechua or Aymara for indigenous children of rural Bolivia. He also organized the teaching of native arts at the Escuela Indigenal at Huarisata (founded in 1932), not far from La Paz on the shores of Lake Titicaca. While he published many works in Spanish as an ethnographer of the Aymara people, he wrote his poetry in Aymara. Along with his poetry, he composed music and the lyrics of songs in Aymara for young people. In accordance with the principles of the *indigenista* movement, he created works in Aymara to show that a native language could be literary. Originally written in Aymara, this rendering of "Kori Pilpintu" derives from the Spanish translation by the Bolivian poet Yolanda Bedregal.

Kori Pilpintu*
(The Golden Butterfly)

Rising above the lake, into the blue,
The butterfly takes flight,
Bright gold its gracious wings
Shimmering in the sun.
Green its reflection in the water
Down low by the shore,
Filigree antennae quivering,
Fragile, alert, musing.

Bright butterfly, fly on forever!
Golden butterfly
Musing abide!

Among the totora,[1] weightless and frolicking
The butterfly, like

---

*Translated by Carolina Udovicki
[1]The reeds that grow along the shores of Lake Titicaca.

A petal fallen from a flower,
Flutters here to there.
Until suddenly, it departs to
Far off across the way,
A gilded feather disappearing
In the distant air.

Bright butterfly, quick to escape!
Golden butterfly,
Back again fast!

In its heart, The butterfly, too, amasses
Yearnings and carries these
Within its golden intimacy
Into the infinite blue,
From out of the many sorrows hiding
Clustered in the river
The gentle accents of its rhythm
Call forth joy.

Ephemeral butterfly, so light!
Eternal butterfly
Brighten our way!

❋ Discussion and Writing

1. Comment on the use of nature imagery. In what way does it connect with people's lives?
2. What does the image of the golden butterfly symbolize?

Gabriela Mistral
(1889–1957)
Chile

Gabriela Mistral (the pseudonym of Lucila Godoy Alcayaga) was born in a poor area of Chile, in Vicuna, where her father was a schoolteacher. Largely self-educated, she began teaching at 15, first in rural regions of Chile and then in Mexico. Then, at 18, she fell in love with a young railway worker who took his own life two years later; she gave voice to both the loss of love and the death of her lover in a series of prize-winning sonnets that brought her recognition. By 1922, she had become the most popular poet in the Spanish-speaking countries of Latin America: children heard her lullabies from their mothers and her songs from their teachers. And fellow poets imitated her. Continuing to write of loneliness and love, of an unfulfilled yearning to bear children, of death and the passage of time, of women and madness, she also entered the diplomatic corps. She served in Latin America, Europe, and the United States. Mistral received the Nobel Prize in literature in 1945, the first Latin American woman to do so.

Song*

A woman is singing in the valley. The shadows falling blot her out, but her song spreads over the fields.

Her heart is broken, like the jar she dropped this afternoon among the pebbles in the brook. As she sings, the hidden wound sharpens on the thread of her song, and becomes thin and hard. Her voice in modulation dampens with blood.

In the fields the other voices die with the dying day, and a moment ago the song of the last slow-poke bird stopped. But her deathless heart, alive with grief, gathers all the silent voices into her voice, sharp now, yet very sweet.

Does she sing for a husband who looks at her silently in the dusk, or for a child whom her song caresses? Or does she sing for her own heart, more helpless than a babe at nightfall.

Night grows maternal before this song that goes to meet it; the stars, with a sweetness that is human, are beginning to come out; the sky full of stars becomes human and understands the sorrows of this world.

Her song, as pure as water filled with light, cleanses the plain and rinses the mean air of day in which men hate. From the throat of the woman who keeps on singing, day rises nobly evaporating toward the stars.

✸ Discussion and Writing

1. Why does the woman sing? What seems to be her theme? Why is the lamentation "sharp" yet "sweet"?
2. What is the role of the night and the stars in the "Song"? What does Mistral convey in the last stanza?
3. What is Mistral's thesis in this poem: what is meant by the woman gathering "all the silent voices into her voice"?

---

*Translated by Langston Hughes

4. What is the impact of the "Song" written as prose and not as verse? Examine its structure.

❋ Research and Comparison

Survey Gabriela Mistral's life and works to determine her contribution to world literature. Discuss the feminine perspective in her writing.

Claude McKay
(1890–1948)
Jamaica

Claude McKay was born in the sheltered mountain community of Sunny Ville, Jamaica, where African customs and the oral tradition retained their authority, informing every aspect of life. His father, a renowned storyteller, farmed the land and prospered, and it was there that Claude McKay, the youngest of 11 children, spent his first formative six or seven years. To begin his formal education, he was sent to live with his brother, who taught school near Montego Bay and who encouraged his love of reading. When he was about 16, and already writing poetry, McKay left these secure environments of his childhood and, in Kingston, confronted the urban poverty and racism that profoundly affected him and became a dominant concern throughout his life. When he was about 23, and had already published two volumes of poetry, he left Jamaica for the United States, never to return, except through such imaginative journeys as in his major novel *Banana Bottom* (1933). But he felt increasingly oppressed by the racism in the United States, where he worked at various jobs, among them waiting on tables on the railroad. He had already turned to Marxism when the horror of the race riots and lynchings prompted his famous poem "If We Must Die" (1919). He published poetry and articles in nonideological as well as in Marxist journals; he worked as a reporter and editor for a time; he traveled widely, meeting with leading intellectuals and artists; and his *Harlem Shadows* was published in 1922, the inaugural year of the Harlem Renaissance.

His was an important voice in a period of creative foment. As early as 1912, at a time when British learning and taste were rarely questioned as the touchstone of all culture, McKay incorporated the language and culture of the indigenous Jamaican people—the urban poor and the people of Sunny Ville—into his poetry and fiction. Thus, he was among the very first to present the oral tradition in the written. He was also the first Caribbean novelist to gain an international reputation.

Crazy Mary

Miss Mary startled the village for the first time in her strange life that day when she turned herself up and showed her naked self to them. Suddenly the villagers realized that after many years of harmless craziness something was perhaps dangerously wrong with Mary, but before they could do anything about it she settled the matter herself.

For a long time she had been accepted as an eccentric village character. Ever since she had recovered from her long sad illness and started going round the village with a bunch of roses in her arms.

Before that she had been the sewing-mistress of the village school. She was a pretty young, yellow woman then. Her parents, following the custom of those peasants with a little means, had sent her to a sewing-school in Gingertown. She had gone away in short frocks, with her hair down and a bright bow pinned to it.

When she returned for good after three years she was in long skirts, with her hair up in what the villagers called a "Chinese bump."

Her father bought her a Singer, finer than those of the other peasant women, a foot-working one similar to that owned by the village tailor. She subscribed to *Weldon's Ladies' Journal* and the *Home Magazine,* and opened a little school in her home for girls to learn to sew and design and cut. Her girls called her Miss Mary, and a few superior folk, such as the parson and family, the schoolmaster, and the postmistress, called her Miss Dean.

The schoolmaster's wife was the sewing-mistress then. But two years later the schoolmaster left for a better-paying school. He was succeeded by a bachelor, and Miss Mary applied for and got the sewing-mistress's job. The sewing-mistress went to the school twice a week for two hours during the afternoon session.

Miss Mary sometimes took two or three of her bigger girls along to help teach the tots to sew.

Girls came from other villages to learn Miss Mary's art. She was much admired, for she was charming. She was nice-shaped, something like a ripened wild cane, and could look a perfect piece of elegance in a princess gown.

Naturally much of Miss Mary's spare time was spent with the school-master. Often they went out walking together in the afternoon after school until twilight. And sometimes they rode horseback to Gingertown together. The villagers got to liking to see them together. The parson approved of it. So did Miss Mary's parents. And everybody thought the two would certainly get married . . .

The schoolmaster was a pure ebony, shining and popular. He played cricket with the young men. He was of middle size, stocky, and an excellent underhand bowler. He organized a cricket club, and during the short days let school out earlier than usual to go to field practice.

Sometimes the schoolmaster and Miss Mary took tea together at the parsonage. And the schoolmaster would talk about the choir and new anthems with the minister's wife, who was the organist. Miss Mary was not in the choir, for she hadn't a singing voice nor any knowledge of music.

As a constant visitor to the Dean home the schoolmaster became almost like one of the family. The villagers indulged in friendly gossip about the couple, anticipating a happy termination of the idyll. Nothing could enrapture the people more than a big village wedding with bells and saddle horses and carriages.

But bang came the scandal one day.

The girls who attended Miss Mary's sewing-classes at home were nearly all girls just out of elementary school, between fourteen and fifteen years. There were a few younger who for some reason had not finished school, and also a few older who were considered and treated as young ladies.

Among those who accompanied Miss Mary to the school was a little bird-brown one, plump as a squab, just turned thirteen, curiously cat-faced and forever smiling. They called her Freshy because she was precocious in her manners.

Sometimes the schoolmaster would tell one of the girls to do something in the teacher's cottage. To do a little cleaning up or prepare a beverage of bitter oranges or pineapple or a soursop-cup[1] during the recreation hours. And it seemed that Freshy, always forward, had got herself asked to do things many times.

And one morning while the classes were humming with work, the schoolmaster at his desk, the mother of Freshy, with her bluejean skirt tucked high up and bandanna flying as if for war, rushed into the school and slapped the schoolmaster's face and collared and shook him, bellowing that he had ruined her little daughter.

The schoolmaster was in a pitiful state, trying to hold his dignity and the woman off, until the monitors interfered and the woman was at last mastered and put out.

The village was shaken as if by an earthquake. Of course, the schoolmaster denied that he had ruined Freshy, but the girl maintained by the mouth of her mother that he had.

The village midwife, after seeing Freshy, insisted that she had not been ruined. But the midwife was the sister of Miss Mary's father, who was a leader in the church.

---

[1]Fruit of a West Indian tree.

The parson was constrained to relieve the schoolmaster of his duties and put his wife in temporary charge of the school. For the protection of his pastorate, he said. Then there was the religious side. The schoolmaster being a member of the church and a lay preacher, a church meeting was called to air the affair.

The village was divided for and against the schoolmaster. Curiously, it was the older heads who were more favorable to him. The young folk and chiefly the bucks were already calling the man a rogue and turning the whole thing into a salacious song. It began to be bruited that the schoolmaster was secretly a wild one who abused the innocence of schoolgirls. But there were some who maintained that even at her age Freshy had already passed the age of innocence with the apples of her bosom so prettily tempting.

Freshy was very conscious of the notoriety she had attained, and, fortified by the aggressiveness of her mother, when she went about the village she tossed her head and turned her lips in scorn like a petulant little actress at those who whispered and stared at her.

The first church meeting, with the parson presiding, broke up in a babel of recriminations, when Freshy's mother became bellicose and abusive to those who had dared to insinuate that her daughter was not a mere child.

It was then that Miss Mary acted. Freshy had not returned to the sewing-school since the day the trouble began. Meeting her in the lane one afternoon, Miss Mary took her home. And alone with Freshy in a room she third-degreed her until the girl cried out that the schoolmaster had not touched her.

At the next church meeting Miss Mary gave an account of Freshy's confession. Speaking quietly in her refined way and holding all attention with her pretty personality, she was almost convincing the whole meeting. But Freshy's mother jumped up, interrupting her, and related how Miss Mary had prevailed upon her child to confess, accusing her of being a little woman and having been with the boys. In her turn Freshy's mother charged Miss Mary with being the schoolmaster's mistress, and in a rage she threatened to box her ears and made a rush for her. Women shrieked as if filled with the spirit for a public fight, but some men held back Freshy's mother and she was put out.

Again the church meeting broke up. The young men especially did not want to believe that a person so nice as Miss Mary could say dirty things to Freshy. But the women shook their heads dubiously and repeated the saying, "Still river run deep." The declaration of Freshy's mother started a big gossip, for it was locally conceded that Miss Mary was a virgin. There was nothing dishonorable in the fact that girls were deflowered at a tender age and young virgins were few in the country, nevertheless the village folk took a pride-like interest in any young woman of whom it could be said she was a virgin up until the time of her marriage.

It seemed as if the church and the village were going to rags over the affair, until a member named Jabez Fearon suggested taking the case to the law courts and having Freshy examined by a doctor from Gingertown. Jabez Fearon was the local tax-collector, commonly called the bailiff. His outstretched hand carried much weight among the peasants, but they had never considered his mind of any weight at all.

Now, however, his opinion appeared intelligent and worth acting upon. How strange that nobody had thought of the legal course before! After all the church-meeting bickering and disagreement! The younger church members thought that was the most excellent way of settling the trouble. A doctor's examination and the decision of a judge.

But before any step was taken and another church meeting called, the schoolmaster quietly disappeared.

And a few weeks after his disappearance Miss Mary went to the city and stayed there a long time. Her people said that she had had a breakdown from nervous trouble and they had had to take her to a doctor in the city.

But the weeks became months before she returned. And then she was confined to the house for as many months more. The village thought she was surely consumptive. Especially when they glimpsed her so tiny and strange in the portico of the house or on the barbecue.

Then at long last, when she could not be detained at home and away from people any longer, she came out, and the village became aware that she was not consumptive, but a little crazy. Her parents stayed away from the church and were never the same charming folk again. Their village respectability became a sour thing.

Miss Mary went about with her hair down like a girl. And it was lovely hair, thick, black and frizzly. The first day she went out she gathered a bunch of flowers and took it to the schoolhouse and placed it on the teacher's desk without a word, and walked out. The new schoolmaster was a married man. The parson said that he would never engage an unmarried man again.

Miss Mary got rid of her shoes too and went about barefooted like a common peasant girl. Every day she gathered her flowers, and there was always plenty of red—hibiscus, poinsettias, dragon's-blood. And she had a strange way of holding the bouquet in her arm as if she were nursing it. Sometimes she talked to herself, but never to anybody, and when anyone tried to talk to her she answered with a cracked little laugh.

Her people kept her clean. And the village folk settled down into familiarity with her as a strange character. Nobody thought that she should be sent to the madhouse, for she was harmless.

And the months turned into years, the village changed schoolmasters again, and even the parson was called to a church in a little town where he earned more money. The village had long ceased from wondering about the disappearance of the schoolmaster, and Freshy had had three children for three different black bucks before she was nineteen.

Then one day the schoolmaster returned. He had been away in Panama. He was a changed man after being so long free from semi-religious duties, a little dapper with a gait the islanders called "the Yankee strut." He was married to a girl he met over there, a saucy brown dressed in an extreme mode of the Boston dip of the day.

It was on a Sunday and they went to church. And after the service the schoolmaster and his wife stood in the yard, surrounded by an admiring group of old friends and young admirers who wanted to hear all about the life and prospects in Colon and Panama.

Nobody had thought of Miss Mary, poor crazy thing in that social centre of the village, where new acquaintances were introduced and sweethearts met and children skipped about.

But she must have heard of his arrival somehow, for suddenly she appeared in the churchyard and, pushing through the folk around the schoolmaster, she threw the bouquet of flowers at him and, turning, she ran up the broad church steps and turned herself up at everybody, looking at them from under with a lecherous laugh.

There was a sudden bewildered pause. And then a young church member dashed up the steps after Mary and the church crowd recovered from the shock, remembering that she was crazy. But before he could reach and seize her she had jumped down the steps, shrieking strange laughter, and started running toward the graveyard.

Just outside the gate she turned again, repeated her act, and laughed. The young villager gave chase after her, followed by others. Mary ran like a rabbit in a mad zigzag. And whenever she saw herself at a safe distance from her pursuers she performed her act with laughter.

She ran past the graveyard and, striking the main road, she headed straight for the river. A little below where the river crossed the road there was a high narrow waterfall that from the churchyard looked like a gorgeous flowing of gold.

Mary ran down a little track leading to the waterfall. Her pursuers stopped in the road, paralyzed by her evident intention, and began shouting to her to stop. And watching from the churchyard, the folk began to bawl and howl.

But Mary kept straight on. On the perilous edge of the waterfall she halted and did her stuff again, then with a high laugh she went sheer over.

✸ Discussion and Writing

1. Discuss the reactions of the various groups as they side with Freshy's mother, the school master, or Mary. What seems to be the basis of their opinions?

2. What are the implications of the schoolteacher's disappearance and his subsequent visit?
3. Comment on Mary's characteristics. What seems to be the source of her craziness? Describe the impact of her last action.
4. Comment on the effect of seeing the events through the narrator's eyes.

❈ Research and Comparison

Research the life and work of Claude McKay, and examine his role in the literary ferment of his day.

Cesar Vallejo
(1892–1938)
Peru

Cesar Vallejo, born and raised in the small Andean mining village of Santiago de Chuco, Peru, was the youngest of 11 children. He embodied the colonial condition: his two grandfathers were Galician priests, his grandmothers their native concubines. Although he studied medicine and law, he earned his degree in literature, and was for a time headmaster of an exclusive private school, teaching Peruvian history and Spanish. In 1920, he was erroneously charged with instigating a political uprising, and because his family belonged to the opposition rather than the party in power, he was imprisoned for four months. The poems he wrote during these desolating months radically transformed Spanish-American poetry, poems collected in the volume *Trilce* (1922), a word that combines the Spanish *tres* (three) and *dulce* (sweet). Stripping the verse of its continuity and the language of its conventions, he reorganized syntax and grammar, and he reordered the logic of avant-garde versification.

When Vallejo moved to Paris, where he remained for most of the last 15 years of his life, he suffered hunger and loneliness but also political solidarity with those seeking a better social order. He traveled with his wife to Eastern Europe, Russia, and Spain, and in 1931, joined the Communist Party. With Pablo Neruda he organized the Spanish American Group Committee during the Spanish Civil War, and like Neruda he wrote major political poetry. Vallejo was a man of fierce pride; he has been recognized as a significant voice in modern poetry.

The Eternal Dice*

For Manuel Gonzalez Prada, this wild and unique feeling—one of those emotions which the great master has admired most in my work.

God of mine, I am weeping for the life that I live;
I am sorry to have stolen your bread;
but this wretched, thinking piece of clay
is not a crust formed in your side:
you have no Marys that abandon you!

My God, if you had been man,
today you would know how to be God,
but you always lived so well,
that now you feel nothing of your own creation.
And the man who suffers you: he is God!

Today, when there are candles in my witchlike eyes,
as in the eyes of a condemned man,
God of mine, you will light all your lamps.
and we will play with the old dice . . .
Gambler, when the whole universe, perhaps,
is thrown down,
the circled eyes of Death will turn up,
like two final aces of clay.

My God, in this muffled, dark night,
you can't play anymore, because the Earth
is already a die nicked and rounded
from rolling by chance;
and it can stop only in a hollow place,
in the hollow of the enormous grave.

❋ Discussion and Writing

1. What does Vallejo imply by the "wild and unique feeling"?
2. What does the poet lament in the first stanza? Why?
3. Comment on the equation the poet establishes between man and God?
4. Examine the symbolism of "eternal dice": what is the nature of the dice; its function?
5. What is the result of the games people play? Comment on Vallejo's ultimate commentary on the human condition.
6. Analyze the imagery, the language, and the tone of the poem.

Translated by James Wright

❇ Research and Comparison

Research Cesar Vallejo's life and times, paying particular attention to his political commitment, and examine the data in relation to his work.

Jesus Lara
(1898–1980)
Bolivia

Jesus Lara was born in a small village in the province of Cochabamba in Bolivia. His mother tongue was Quechua, but his education was, inevitably, in Spanish. He did his secondary schooling in Cochabamba, fulfilled his obligatory military service, and started working as a journalist in La Paz. He taught at the University of Cochabamba, and fought in the disastrous Chaco War (1932–1935) between Bolivia and Paraguay. Committed to the 1952 revolution, to land reform, and the nationalization of the mines, he became a political activist and published works that attacked the authorities.

A poet, novelist, anthologist, historian, and linguist, Lara was dedicated in all his work to recovering the Quechua (Inca) culture and asserting the Quechua's and mestizo's rightful place in Bolivian society and culture. He wrote about his people, those whom Bolivian society had ignored, in Spanish rather than in his native Quechua to bring them social recognition. "Incallajta Jarahui" was written in Spanish to make a harsh political point. He also collected material from the Quechua oral tradition, translating the poetry, stories, and legends into Spanish, and his *La Cultura de los Inkas* (1966) was recognized as a major work. Because of "his talent, his integrity, and his love for his people," he has been placed among the very best of Bolivia's writers.

Incallajta Jarahui*

Come down into the silence, wanderer . . .
Here the stones left to oblivion
Speak with the voice of centuries.

Come down into the silence; with your soul
Not your feet mark each of your steps,
Because you shall be treading sacred soil.

---

*Translated by Carolina Udovicki

Come in traveller . . . the terraces yet
Retain the shadows of the *nustas*[1]
Along with the love of the *ulalas*.[2]

The copious clamor of ancient battles
Finds resonance beneath the walls
Despite the pain of glories cut short.

In the mystery of the many chambers
Are the hearts whose beats intermingle
With the lament of nebulous *quenas*[3]

And above the *pukara*[4] in ruins
Much as a genius deep in thought
Hovers the spirit of the *Inca*.[5]

Come in, for at long last wanderer,
You shall recover the soul you lost
Under a cross four centuries old.

✳ Discussion and Writing

1. Where does the speaker invite the wanderer to come? What does the voice in the poem exhort the wanderer to experience?
2. Recreate the scene from the past that the poet alludes to.
3. Explain the implications of the four-century-old cross and its impact on the people.

Miguel Angel Asturias
(1899–1974)
Guatemala

Miguel Angel Asturias, the eldest son of a middle-class family of comfortable means, took pride in his Mayan heritage. The progressive thesis he wrote for his law degree, *The Social Problem of the Indians* (1923),

---

[1] Inca princesses.
[2] A flowering cactus.
[3] The reed-pipe instruments played by the Andean indians.
[4] Stone throne.
[5] The pre-Hispanic culture of the Quechuas takes its name from the title of the king, the Inca.

prompted his leaving Guatemala: the brutal dictator, Estrada Cabrera, had been defeated, but democracy did not follow. Ironically, he discovered Mayan art at the British Museum and French translations of ancient Mayan texts at the Sorbonne. During the almost ten years that he lived in Paris, he worked as a journalist, studied ethnology, explored socialism and surrealism, wrote stories, and most important, translated the *Popol Vuh* (1925), the sacred Mayan text that was to inspire his own writing. When he returned to Guatemala, the dictator Jorge Ubico was in power, and Asturias turned to radio work. His *El Senor Presidente* (1946), the first of the Latin American novels satirizing the local dictators, was not published until after the successful 1944 Guatemalan Revolution. After the revolution he served for a time as an attaché to Argentina.

In his writing, Asturias merged a contemporary aesthetic centered in the fantastic with Mayan myth. He explored social and economic conditions within the framework of the fantastic, and he also produced a series of anti-imperialist works that denounced U.S. intervention in Guatemala. Although in 1966 he served as ambassador to Paris under a U.S.-backed repressive government, he remained a politically committed writer who worked within the loose amalgam defined as magical realism. He won the Nobel Prize in literature in 1967.

*Legend of "El Cadejo"**

And El Cadejo, *who steals girls with long braids and knots the manes of horses, makes his appearance in the valley.*

In the course of time, Mother Elvira of St. Francis, abbess of the monastery of St. Catherine, would be the novice who cut out the hosts in the convent of the Conception, a girl noted for her beauty and manner of speaking, so ingenuous that on her lips the word was a flower of gentleness and love.

From a large window without glass, the novice used to watch the flights of leaves dried by the summer's heat, the trees putting on their flowers and ripe fruit dropping in the orchards next to the convent, through the part that was in ruins, where the foliage, hiding the wounded walls and the open roofs, transformed the cells and the cloisters into paradises filled with the scent of *bucaro* clay[1] and wild roses; bowers of feasting, as the chroniclers recorded, where nuns were replaced by pigeons with pink feet and their canticles by the warble of the cimarron mockingbird.

Outside her window, in the collapsed rooms, the warm shade, where butterflies worked the dust of their wings into silk, joined the silence of the courtyard, interrupted by the coming and going of the lizards, and the soft

---

Translated by Hardie St. Martin
[1]A fragrant clay. [eds.]

aroma of the leaves that multiplied the tender feelings of the trees whose roots were coiled into the very ancient walls.

And inside, in the sweet company of God, trimming the peel from the fruit of angels to disclose the meat and seed that is the Body of Christ, long as the orange's medulla—*vere tu es Deus absconditus!*—, Elvira of St. Francis reunited her spirit and her flesh to the house of her childhood, with its heavy locks and its light roses, its doors that split sobs into the loose seams of the wind, its walls reflected in the troughs of the fountains like clouds of breath on clean glass.

The voices of the city broke the peace of her window: last-minute blues of the passenger that hears the movement of the port at sailing time; a man's laughter as he brings his galloping horse to a stop, a cart wheeling by, or a child crying.

Horse, cart, man, child passed before her eyes, evoked in country settings, under skies whose tranquil appearance put under a spell the wise eyes of the fountain troughs sitting around the water with the long-suffering air of old women servants.

And the images were accompanied by odors. The sky smelled like a sky, the child like a child, the fields like fields, the cart like hay, the horse like an old rosebush, the man like a saint, the troughs like shadows, the shadows like Sunday rest and the Lord's day of rest like fresh washing. . . .

Dark was coming on. The shadows erased their thought, luminous mixture of dust particles swimming in a shaft of sunlight. The bells drew their lips toward the cup of evening without a sound. Who talks of kisses? The wind shook up the heliotropes. Heliotropes or hippocampi? And the hummingbirds quenched their desire for God in streams of flowers. Who talks of kisses?

The tap of heels hurrying brought her to herself. Their sound frilled along the corridor like drumsticks.

Could she be hearing right? Could it be the man with the long eyelashes who came by late on Fridays for the hosts to take them nine towns away from there, to the Valley of the Virgin, where a pleasant hermitage rested on a hill's top?

They called him the poppy-man. The wind moved in his feet. When the sound of his goat's footsteps stopped, there he would be, like a ghost: hat in hand, tiny boots, a goldish color, wrapped in his blue greatcoat; and he waited for the wafer boxes in the doorway.

Yes, it was he; but this time he rushed in looking very frightened, as if to prevent some catastrophe.

"Miss, oh miss!" he came in shouting, "they're going to cut off your hair! They're going to cut it off!"

When she saw him coming in, livid and elastic, the novice sprang to her feet intending to reach the door. But, wearing shoes she had charitably inherited from a paralytic nun who had worn them in life, when she heard his shout, she felt as if the nun who had spent her life motionless had stepped on her feet, and she couldn't move a step. . . .

A sob, like a star, trembled in her throat. Birds scissored the twilight among the gray, crippled ruins. Two giant eucalyptus trees were saying prayers of penance.

Bound to the feet of a corpse, unable to move, she wept disconsolately, swallowing her tears silently as sick people whose organs begin to dry up and turn cold, bit by bit. She felt as if she were dead, covered with dirt; she felt that in her grave—her orphan's dress being filled with clay—rosebushes of white words bloomed and, little by little, her dismay changed into a quiet sort of happiness. Walking rosebushes, the nuns were cutting off one another's roses to dress the altars of the Virgin and the roses became the month of May, a spider web of fragrances that trapped Our Lady like a fly of light.

But the sensation of her body's flowering after death was a shortlived happiness.

Like a kite that suddenly runs out of string among the clouds, the weight of her braid pulled her headlong, with all her clothes, into hell. The mystery was in her braid. Sum of anguished instants. She lost consciousness for as long as a couple of her sighs lasted and felt herself back on earth only when she had almost reached the boiling pit where devils bubble. A fan of possible realities opened around her: the night sweetened with puff paste, pine trees that smell like altars, the pollen of life in the hair of the air, formless, colorless cat that scratches the waters of the fountain troughs and unsettles old papers.

The window and she herself became filled with heaven. . . .

"Miss, when I receive Holy Communion, God tastes like your hands!" the one in the greatcoat whispered, laying the grille of his lashes over the coals of his eyes.

The novice pulled her hands away from the hosts when she heard the blasphemy. No, it wasn't a dream! Then she touched her arms, her shoulders, her neck, her face, her braid. She held her breath one moment, long as a century, when she felt her braid. No, it wasn't a dream! Under the warm handful of hair she came alive, aware of her womanly charms, accompanied in her diabolic nuptials by the poppy-man and a candle burning at the end of the room, oblong as a coffin. The light supported the impossible reality of the lover, who stretched out his arms like a Christ who had turned into a bat in a viaticum, and this was her own flesh! She closed her eyes to escape, wrapped in her blindness, from that vision from hell, from the man who caressed her down to where she was a woman, simply by being a man—the most abominable of concupiscences!—; but as soon as she lowered her round pale eyelids the paralytic nun seemed to step from her shoes, soaked in tears, and she quickly opened them. She tore through the darkness, opened her eyes, left their deep interior with their pupils restless as mice in a trap, wild, insensible, the color drained out of her cheeks, caught between the stertor of a strange agony she carried in her feet and her braid's stream of live coals twisted like an invisible flame on her back.

And that's the last she knew about it. Like someone under a spell that can't be broken, with a sob on her tongue which seemed to be filled with poison, like her heart, she broke away from the presence of the corpse and the man, half mad, spilling the wafers about, in search of her scissors and, finding them, she cut off the braid and, free of the spell, she fled in search of the sure refuge of the Mother Superior, no longer feeling the nun's feet on hers. . . .

But when the braid fell it was no longer a braid: it moved, undulated over the tiny mattress of hosts scattered on the floor.

The poppy-man turned to look for light. Tears quivered on his eyelashes like the last little flames on the black of the match that is about to go out. He slid along the side of the wall with bated breath, without disturbing the shadows, without making a sound, desperate to reach the flame he believed would be his salvation. But his measured step soon dissolved into a flight of fear. The headless reptile was moving past the sacred leaf-pile of hosts and filing toward him. It dragged itself right under his feet like the black blood of a dead animal and suddenly, as he was about to take hold of the light, leaped with the speed of water that runs free and light to coil itself like a whip around the candle which it caused to weep until it consumed itself for the soul of him who was being extinguished, along with it, forever. And so the poppy-man, for whom cactus plants still weep white tears, reached eternity.

The devil had passed like a breath through the braid which fell lifeless on the floor when the candle's flame went out.

And at midnight, changed into a long animal—twice as long as a ram by full moon, big as a weeping willow by new moon—with goat's hoofs, rabbit's ears and a bat's face, the poppy-man dragged down to hell the black braid of the novice who, in the course of time, would be Mother Elvira of St. Francis—that's how "El Cadejo" was born—while, on her knees in her cell, smiling like an angel, she dreamed of the lily and the mystic lamb.

✻ Discussion and Writing

1. Note the imagery in the beginning of the story. Discuss the effect of the sensuous details in this description.
2. What does the braid signify to the novice; to the poppy-man; to the Church? Analyze the inherent tension among these perspectives.
3. What is the role of the poppy-man in the story? What is the significance of his eternal confinement to hell? What is implied by the cactus plants "still weep[ing] white tears"?
4. Comment on the blending of native legends with Christian traditions in the depiction of the characters, the incident, and the descriptive

passages in the story. Discuss the resolution of the tension between the two traditions.

❋ Research and Comparison

1. Compare and contrast the significance of the novice's braid in this story with that of the hero's hair in the biblical story of Samson.
2. Research the written literature that incorporates the oral tradition— stories, legends, poems, prayers—of Latin America. Examine the salient features, themes and approaches to life portrayed in the oral tradition.

Jorge Luis Borges
(1899–1980)
Argentina

Jorge Luis Borges, whose ancestors fought in the Wars of Independence, was born in Buenos Aires, Argentina. His father was a lawyer, a teacher, a translator, and a frustrated poet and novelist; and he encouraged his son's literary ambition. From the age of six or seven, Borges was already writing stories based on summaries of Greek mythology and on *Don Quixote,* which he first read in English. He received his formal education in Europe where the family lived through World War I. There he associated with the avant-garde, formulating aesthetic theories that concerned the magical essence of poetry and its impact. When he returned to Argentina, a group of Argentine avant-garde poets, who emphasized the marvelous and myth-ical, gathered around him. In these early years, he meditated on and reassessed native traditions. As he developed his art, he wrote stories as if they were biographies or essays, book reviews or criticism. At the same time, he insisted on the necessity for plot and mystery found in detective fiction and popular tales. He insisted, too, on the dynamic nature of litera-ture as a system of interrelated texts.

During the 1940s, he produced three volumes that influenced writers from Mexico to Argentina: *Ficciones* (1944), *The Aleph* (1949), and *Six Problems for Don Isidro Parodi* (1949). The latter were detective stories he co-authored pseudonymously. Also, during the 1940s, the fascist Peron government attempted to humiliate him for signing democratic mani-festoes. He had been working as a librarian, and the government appointed him to the position of a poultry inspector, which he rejected. A decade later he was named head of the National Library and then Professor of English Literature, and he was awarded the first of many honorary doctorates. It was at this time that, like his father before him, he became increasingly blind and that he began to dictate his work. It was not, however, until 1961, when he was the co-recipient with Samuel Beckett of the major avant-garde Formentor Prize, that his contribution to literature was more widely acknowledged in the United States and Europe.

In much of his work, Borges aspired to a simplicity that, at the same time, embodied a multiplicity of intentions; he explored ironically and tragically the dreams and nightmares of human experience, playing with such images and motifs as the double, the labyrinth, metamorphosis, and sacrifice.

The Gospel According to Mark*

These events took place at La Colorada ranch, in the southern part of the township of Junin, during the last days of March 1928. The protagonist was a medical student named Baltasar Espinosa. We may describe him, for now, as one of the common run of young men from Buenos Aires, with nothing more noteworthy about him than an almost unlimited kindness and a capacity for public speaking that had earned him several prizes at the English school in Ramos Mejia. He did not like arguing, and preferred having his listener rather than himself in the right. Although he was fascinated by the probabilities of chance in any game he played, he was a bad player because it gave him no pleasure to win. His wide intelligence was undirected; at the age of thirty-three, he still had not qualified for graduation in the subject to which he was most drawn. His father, who was a freethinker (like all the gentlemen of his day), had introduced him to the lessons of Herbert Spencer, but his mother, before leaving on a trip for Montevideo, once asked him to say the Lord's Prayer and make the sign of the cross every night. Through the years, he had never gone back on that promise.

Espinosa was not lacking in spirit; one day, with more indifference than anger, he had exchanged two or three punches with a group of fellow-students who were trying to force him to take part in a university demonstration. Owing to an acquiescent nature, he was full of opinions, or habits of mind, that were questionable: Argentina mattered less to him than a fear that in other parts of the world people might think of us as Indians; he worshiped France but despised the French; he thought little of Americans but approved the fact that there were tall buildings, like theirs, in Buenos Aires; he believed the gauchos of the plains to be better riders than those of hill or mountain country. When his cousin Daniel invited him to spend the summer months out at La Colorada, he said yes at once—not because he was really fond of the country, but more out of his natural complacency and also because it was easier to say yes than to dream up reasons for saying no.

*Translated by N. T. di Giovanni

The ranch's main house was big and slightly rundown; the quarters of the foreman, whose name was Gutre, were close by. The Gutres were three: the father, an unusually uncouth son, and a daughter of uncertain paternity. They were tall, strong, and bony, and had hair that was on the reddish side and faces that showed traces of Indian blood. They were barely articulate. The foreman's wife had died years before.

There in the country, Espinosa began learning things he never knew, or even suspected—for example, that you do not gallop a horse when approaching settlements, and that you never go out riding except for some special purpose. In time, he was to come to tell the birds apart by their calls.

After a few days, Daniel had to leave for Buenos Aires to close a deal on some cattle. At most, this bit of business might take him a week. Espinosa, who was already somewhat weary of hearing about his cousin's incessant luck with women and his tireless interest in the minute details of men's fashion, preferred staying on at the ranch with his textbooks. But the heat was unbearable, and even the night brought no relief. One morning at daybreak, thunder woke him. Outside, the wind was rocking the Australian pines. Listening to the first heavy drops of rain, Espinosa thanked God. All at once, cold air rolled in. That afternoon, the Salado overflowed its banks.

The next day, looking out over the flooded fields from the gallery of the main house, Baltasar Espinosa thought that the stock metaphor comparing the pampa to the sea was not altogether false—at least, not that morning—though W. H. Hudson had remarked that the sea seems wider because we view it from a ship's deck and not from a horse or from eye level.

The rain did not let up. The Gutres, helped or hindered by Espinosa, the town dweller, rescued a good part of the livestock, but many animals were drowned. There were four roads leading to La Colorada; all of them were under water. On the third day, when a leak threatened the foreman's house, Espinosa gave the Gutres a room near the toolshed, at the back of the main house. This drew them all closer; they ate together in the big dining room. Conversation turned out to be difficult. The Gutres, who knew so much about country things, were hard put to it to explain them. One night, Espinosa asked them if people still remembered the Indian raids from back when the frontier command was located there in Junín. They told him yes, but they would have given the same answer to a question about the beheading of Charles I. Espinosa recalled his father's saying that almost every case of longevity that was cited in the country was really a case of bad memory or of a dim notion of dates. Gauchos are apt to be ignorant of the year of their birth or of the name of the man who begot them.

In the whole house, there was apparently no other reading matter than a set of the *Farm Journal,* a handbook of veterinary medicine, a deluxe edition of the Uruguayan epic *Tabaré,* a history of shorthorn cattle in Argentina, a number of erotic or detective stories, and a recent novel called *Don Segundo Sombra.* Espinosa, trying in some way to bridge the inevitable after-dinner gap, read a couple of chapters of this novel to the Gutres, none of whom could read or write. Unfortunately, the foreman had been a cattle drover, and the doings of the hero, another cattle drover, failed to whet his interest. He said that the work was light, that drovers always traveled with a packhorse that carried everything they needed, and that, had he not been a drover, he would never have seen such far-flung places as the Laguna de Gomez, the town of Bragado, and the spread of the Nunez family in Chacabuco. There was a guitar in the kitchen; the ranch hands, before the time of the events I am describing, used to sit around in a circle. Someone would tune the instrument without ever getting around to playing it. This was known as a guitar-fest.

Espinosa, who had grown a beard, began dallying in front of the mirror to study his new face, and he smiled to think how, back in Buenos Aires, he would bore his friends by telling them the story of the Salado flood. Strangely enough, he missed places he never frequented and never would: a corner of Cabrera Street on which there was a mailbox; one of the cement lions of a gateway on Jujuy Street, a few blocks from the Plaza del Once: an old barroom with a tiled floor, whose exact whereabouts he was unsure of. As for his brothers and his father, they would already have learned from Daniel that he was isolated—etymologically, the word was perfect—by the floodwaters.

Exploring the house, still hemmed in by the watery waste, Espinosa came across an English Bible. Among the blank pages at the end, the Guthries—such was their original name—had left a handwritten record of their lineage. They were natives of Inverness; had reached the New World, no doubt as common laborers, in the early part of the nineteenth century; and had intermarried with Indians. The chronicle broke off sometime during the 1870s, when they no longer knew how to write. After a few generations, they had forgotten English; their Spanish, at the time Espinosa knew them, gave them trouble. They lacked any religious faith, but there survived in their blood, like faint tracks, the rigid fanaticism of the Calvinist and the superstitions of the pampa Indian. Espinosa later told them of his find, but they barely took notice.

Leafing through the volume, his fingers opened it at the beginning of the Gospel according to Saint Mark. As an exercise in translation, and maybe to find out whether the Gutres understood any of it, Espinosa decided to begin reading them that text after their evening meal. It surprised him that they listened attentively, absorbed. Maybe the gold letters on the cover lent the book authority. It's still there in their blood, Espinosa thought. It also occurred to him that the generations of men, throughout recorded time, have always told and retold two stories—that of a lost ship which searches the Mediterranean seas for a dearly loved island, and that of a god who is crucified on Golgotha. Remembering his lessons in elocution from his schooldays in Ramos Mejia, Espinosa got to his feet when he came to the parables.

The Gutres took to bolting their barbecued meat and their sardines so as not to delay the Gospel. A pet lamb that the girl adorned with a small blue ribbon had injured itself on a strand of barbed wire. To stop the bleeding, the three had wanted to apply a cobweb to the wound, but Espinosa treated the animal with some pills. The gratitude that this treatment awakened in them took him aback. (Not trusting the Gutres at first, he'd hidden away in one of his books the 240 pesos he had brought with him.) Now, the owner of the place away, Espinosa took over and gave timid orders, which were immediately obeyed. The Gutres, as if lost without him, liked following him from room to room and along the gallery that ran around the house. While he read to them, he noticed that they were secretly stealing the crumbs he had dropped on the table. One evening, he caught them unawares, talking about him respectfully, in very few words.

Having finished the Gospel according to Saint Mark, he wanted to read another of the three Gospels that remained, but the father asked him to repeat the one he had just read, so that they could understand it better. Espinosa felt that they were like children, to whom repetition is more pleasing than variations or novelty. That night—this is not to be wondered at—he dreamed of the Flood; the hammer blows of the building of the Ark woke him up, and he thought that perhaps they were thunder. In fact, the rain, which had let up, started again. The cold was bitter. The Gutres had told him that the storm had damaged the roof of the toolshed, and that they would show it to him when the beams were fixed. No longer a stranger now, he was treated by them with special attention, almost to the point of spoiling him. None of them liked coffee, but for him there was always a small cup into which they heaped sugar.

The new storm had broken out on a Tuesday. Thursday night, Espinosa was awakened by a soft knock at his door, which, just in case, he always kept locked. He got out of bed and opened it; there was the girl. In the dark he could hardly make her out, but by her footsteps he could tell she was barefoot, and moments later, in bed, that she must have come all the way from the other end of the house naked. She did not embrace him or speak a single word; she lay beside him, trembling. It was the first time she had known a man. When she left, she did not kiss him; Espinosa realized that he didn't even know her name. For some reason that he did not want to pry into, he made up his mind that upon returning to Buenos Aires he would tell no one about what had taken place.

The next day began like the previous ones, except that the father spoke to Espinosa and asked him if Christ had let Himself be killed so as to save all other men on earth. Espinosa, who was a freethinker but who felt committed to what he had read to the Gutres, answered, "Yes, to save everyone from Hell."

Gutre then asked, "What's Hell?"

"A place under the ground where souls burn and burn."

"And the Roman soldiers who hammered in the nails—were they saved, too?"

"Yes," said Espinosa, whose theology was rather dim.

All along, he was afraid that the foreman might ask him about what had gone on the night before with his daughter. After lunch, they asked him to read the last chapters over again.

Espinosa slept a long nap that afternoon. It was a light sleep, disturbed by persistent hammering and by vague premonitions. Toward evening, he got up and went out onto the gallery. He said, as if thinking aloud, "The waters have dropped. It won't be long now."

"It won't be long now," Gutre repeated, like an echo.

The three had been following him. Bowing their knees to the stone pavement, they asked his blessing. Then they mocked at him, spat on him, and shoved him toward the back part of the house. The girl wept. Espinosa understood what awaited him on the other side of the door. When they opened it, he saw a patch of sky. A bird sang out. A goldfinch, he thought. The shed was without a roof; they had pulled down the beams to make the cross.

❋ Discussion and Writing

1. Describe Espinosa; what is his role in the development of the story?
2. What is the significance of the Gutres's dual heritage? In what way is it reflected in the Gutres's thinking and behavior?
3. Analyze the irony inherent in the distinction between Espinosa's and the Gutres's perspectives. Explore other levels of irony in the story.
4. Explore the parallels between the biblical Gospel according to Mark and the events in the story. Elaborate on the implications of the parallels?
5. What do the setting—the house, the estate, the weather—the imagery, and the atmosphere contribute to the theme(s) of the story.
6. Analyze the recurrent motifs and images in the narration. What is their impact on the atmosphere of the story?

❋ Research and Comparison

Examine the work of Jorge Luis Borges and comment on his use of the fantastic, the labyrinth, or other dominant motifs. Discuss his art of creating an experience with its own logic and structure.

Interdisciplinary Discussion Question: Several authors in this anthology work with the theme of the scapegoat and individual sacrifice for communal redemption (e.g., Wole Soyinka, Grace Ogot, Rabindranath Tagore, among others). Analyze the rationale for this pervasive element in various traditions of the world. What is Borges's statement on the theme of sacrifice?

Carlos Drummond de Andrade
(1902–1987)
Brazil

Carlos Drummond de Andrade, known as Drummond in Brazil, was born in a small mining town and raised on a ranch in the district of Minas Gerais, Brazil. Although he took a degree in pharmacy, he did not practice; instead, he taught school, worked as a journalist, and wrote poetry. He was a member of the Brazilian avant-garde, whose principles included using Brazilian rather than mainland Portuguese in their writing and incorporating native materials. Finding city life more congenial, he moved to Rio de Janeiro in the 1930s, but he never lost touch with the impressions of his childhood: his memories continued to inform his poetry. As the decade wore on and the threat of fascism exploded into a reality with the Spanish Civil War and World War II, he became more politically conscious. These two threads, the personal concerns and a solidarity with all suffering, wound their way through his work from then on, and his is the voice that has spoken most influentially to younger poets in Brazil.

An Ox Looks at Man*

They are more delicate even than shrubs and they run
and run from one side to the other, always forgetting
something. Surely they lack I don't know what
basic ingredient, though they present themselves
as noble or serious, at times. Oh, terribly serious,
even tragic. Poor things, one would say that they hear
neither the song of air nor the secrets of hay;
likewise they seem not to see what is visible
and common to each of us, in space. And they are sad,
and in the wake of sadness they come to cruelty.
All their expression lives in their eyes—and loses itself
to a simple lowering of lids, to a shadow.
And since there is little of the mountain about them—
nothing in the hair or in the terribly fragile limbs
but coldness and secrecy—it is impossible for them
to settle themselves into forms that are calm, lasting,
and necessary. They have, perhaps, a kind
of melancholy grace (one minute) and with this they allow
themselves to forget the problems and translucent

Translated by Mark Strand

inner emptiness that make them so poor and so lacking
when it comes to uttering silly and painful sounds: desire, love,
    jealousy
(what do we know?)—sounds that scatter and fall in the field
like troubled stones and burn the herbs and the water,
and after this it is hard to keep chewing away at our truth.

❋ Discussion and Writing

1. How does the ox characterize man? What is gained or lost in selecting an ox as the observer?
2. What does an ox symbolize? How would a lion observe man?
3. What is implied in the imagery of "troubled stones" that "burn the herbs and the water"?
4. What is the ultimate happiness for the ox? Is there any for man according to the ox? What is meant by "our truth"?
5. Drummond portrays what he assumes to be an ox's perception of man, a sort of doubly removed cross-species perspective. Explain what the poet achieves by this double removal? What is the poet's commentary on man?

❋ Research and Comparison

Examine the life and work of Carlos Drummond de Andrade, and comment on his contribution to Brazilian poetry.

Nicolas Guillen
(b. 1902)
Cuba

Nicolas Guillen was born in Camaguey, Cuba, the year the Cuban Republic was installed, and the U.S. Congress passed the Platt Amendment. (The Platt Amendment licensed U.S. intervention in Cuban affairs.) When he was 15, his father—a politician and journalist—was assassinated, and during the following years, while at the Institute of Camaguey, Guillen turned more and more toward poetry and journalism. After graduatng from the Institute, he entered the University of Havana Law School but quickly abandoned these studies to pursue his writing. By the mid-1930s, when he joined the Communist Party, he was already well known as a poet and a journalist. He traveled widely over the next 15 years or so, but for six years during the 1950s, he lived in exile (in Paris and Buenos Aires) because of his involvement with the opposition to the regime of Fulgencio Batista y Zaldivar. In 1959, when the Batista dictatorship was overthrown, he returned to Cuba, where, along with becoming Poet Laureate, he has held various influential positions.

Nicolas Guillen is considered one of the major poets of the twentieth century. In his experimental first book of poetry, *Motivos de son* (1930), he established both his reputation and his concept of *mestizaje* (his term for the cross-cultural, Antillean imagination and identity). The *son,* a popular musical form that merges Taino, African, and Spanish elements, emblemizes his dominant concern for the recognition of a unique Cuban and Caribbean identity.

Arrival*

Here we are!
The word comes to us moist from the forest,
and a vital sun rises in our veins.
Our fist is strong,
sustains the oar.

Exorbitant palms sleep in the deep eye.
The shout escapes us like a drop of pure gold

Our foot,
tough and wide,
crushes the dust on roads abandoned
and too narrow for our ranks.
We know where the waters are born,
and love them for they pushed our canoes under the
    crimson skies

Our song,
our simple song,
is like a muscle under the skin of the soul

We bring the mist in the morning,
and the fire to the night,
and the knife, like a hard piece of the moon,
fit for savage skins;
we bring the alligators in the swamp,
and the bow that discharges our longings,
and the tropic's waist,
and the clear spirit.

---

*Translated by Robert Marquez and David Arthur

Ah, comrades, here we are!
The city waits with its palaces, delicate
as the honeycombs of wild bees;
its streets are dry as the rivers when there's no rain in
    the mountain,
and its houses stare at us with the fearful eyes of
    windows.

The ancient men will give us milk and honey
and crown us with green leaves.

Ah, comrades, here we are!
Beneath the sun

❋ **Discussion and Writing**

   1. Discuss the significance of the images from nature. What verbs are used
      in relation to these images: what does this relationship evoke?
   2. Analyze the implications of "the word," "the shout," and the "song."
   3. Who are the "we"? What is the purpose of the objects that they bring?
   4. Explore the meaning of "where the waters are born"?
   5. What is meant by "arrival": what is the purpose of the arrival; what is
      the significance of the destination? Who are "the ancient men"?

❋ **Research and Comparison**

   Examine Guillen's works in relation to his political ideology and commitment to communism.

   Compare Guillen's views on Marxism, indigenism, and *negritude* to those
of such Caribbean writers as Jacques Roumain and Aime Cesaire.

Silvina Ocampo
(b. 1903)
Argentina

Silvina Ocampo, who was born in Buenos Aires, Argentina, was named
"illustrious citizen" in 1990. She belonged to the influential circle of
Argentine writers who contributed to *Sur,* the eminent literary journal

founded in 1931 by her sister, Victoria Ocampo. When Silvina Ocampo married Adolfo Bioy Casares, Jorge Luis Borges stood as best man at their wedding, and the three remained close friends and collaborators through the years. The men wrote detective fiction together, and the three edited anthologies of poetry and fiction, most notably, the historically important *Antologia de la literatura fantastica* (Anthology of Fantastic Literature; 1941). Her writing exemplifies the thrust of fantastic fiction, in which the ordinary or common everyday event occurs extraordinarily.

The Servant's Slaves*

Herminia Berni was really lovely. I just do not believe that hers was simply an inner beauty, as some people used to say, though if you looked closely she did have a few faults: she squinted slightly, her lips were far too thick, her cheeks were sunken, her hair was utterly lank. But without a doubt, she could have been Miss Argentina. Beauty is a strange thing. Herminia was lovely and her mistress adored her.

"The mistress is a very dear lady," she told me when I went to the house to visit.

I looked at her in amazement. She was not only pretty, she was good too. I never imagined she might be a hypocrite. There was mutual affection between the lady of the house and the maid, as I discovered later.

On that day, when I went to the house for the first time, I stumbled over a stuffed tiger and broke a china sweet dish. Herminia religiously collected all the pieces of the broken dish and put them safely into a box in tissue paper. She could not bear anyone breaking her mistress's ornaments. Her mistress had been ill, seriously ill, for some three months. The house was filled with cards, telegrams, flowers and plants which friends had sent to her.

"Only a corpse receives that many sprays," commented one of the visitors, who was even jealous of illness. She would not even go back home to sleep, for fear of missing any of the presents sent to the sick woman. She wanted to enjoy all the advantages every bit as much as the sufferings of her friend.

"It's not healthy to breathe the scent of all these flowers," said another woman, taking the best roses away with her.

"I think it's all very tactless. Why don't they send her a night dress, or a dressing gown or some sweets, nice milky caramels that she likes so much?" said another woman, without looking up from her knitting.

Translated by Susan Bassnett

"Flowers get on my nerves. What she needs are artificial ones, the real-looking kind, though, not painted ones," said another woman, who was being very nice to Herminia.

To tell the truth, they were all very nice to Herminia and there was a good reason for it. When they saw her looking so thin and faded, making herself so upset by her mistress' illness, the visitors used to bring her chocolate in a box with painted cats, or nourishing little cakes in a little plastic basket, or tarts with quince jam inside, in a little case that had Bon Voyage written on it, or orange jelly in a glass powder bowl with the odd flaw in it. The could not bear to see her so run down.

"You must look after yourself," they used to say to her.

"I'd rather die," she would retort, without telling any lies.

Her faithfulness was a model, but the affection which Senora de Bersi lavished upon her was a model too. In her room that was crammed with paintings, there in a place of honor was a portrait of Herminia in fancy dress.

She would have allowed her to talk on the phone whenever she liked, to go out at night, to whistle or sing while she was cleaning the rooms, to sit and watch TV in the sitting room with a cigarette in her mouth, but Herminia never did anything like that.

"She's not a very modern sort of girl," said one visitor to another.

Gradually I began to realize that all those women were actually going round to visit Herminia, not Senora de Bersi. They didn't try to hide it and every time I would surprise them saying:

"We're slaves to our own servants, let's admit it."

"My girl left me."

Or:

"The girl I've got is awful."

Or even:

"I'm trying to find a girl, but she must have references."

"Herminia is a gem."

They went to visit Herminia in the hope of finding themselves alone with her, to say more or less these words to her, which they had carefully prepared:

"Herminia, when Senora de Bersi dies, and God forbid that should happen, but things do, you know, I sometimes ask myself whether you would come and work in my house. You'd have a room of your own, you could have every Sunday and holiday free, of course. I'd treat you like my own daughter, and believe me, there wouldn't be nearly so much for you to do, much less than you do here. These rooms are very big, there are so many stairs and brushing all these stuffed animals must be hard work. You're strong, but you never know if it's wise to put yourself under so much strain. Obviously in my house you would be expected to do a little sewing, some washing, cooking, cleaning the courtyard, some ironing, taking the dog out three times a day and bathing it once a week, and drying it and grooming it, but these are all trivial jobs that only take a few minutes to do. In fact, you'd really have nothing to do at all."

Herminia enjoyed working in Senora de Bersi's house. The stuffed tiger had its own special toothbrush, and there was a special brush for the piano keys too. There was a special sponge for the marble cupid, and a little brush for cleaning the silver doves. She was upset when the visitors talked in such an offensive way. "One of these days I'll send them all to the devil; they're fussing as if it were me that was ill."

Tuco, Senora de Bersi's eldest son, who was married and very fond of music, used to prowl around the piano. Once Herminia saw him measure the piano with a tape. Such strange behaviour did not bode well. Did he want to take away the piano himself? Herminia became twice as watchful. She stationed herself close to the piano, when she was darning or adding up her shopping lists, but one day the Senora's son took her by the hand and said: "Why don't you come with me, honey?"

Faced with this monstrous proposition, Herminia pretended to be deaf and did not reply. But the interest that Senor Tuco showed in the piano did not relax, and Herminia returned to find him with a tape measure noting down the measurements of the piano in a little green book that he took out of his pocket. Herminia did not sleep, but her watchfulness was doomed to failure. She had to keep going out to buy things or to pay bills and on one of these occasions her worst fears were realized: guilty hands removed the piano. Herminia was deeply upset by the loss of the piano, with its candlesticks and its bronze pedals, but then something unexpected happened. Tuco, who had personally overseen the removal of the piano by stealth, assisted by two odd job men, paid dearly for his daring betrayal. Apart from being a good for nothing, he was a weak man and the effort was obviouly far too great for him. Just as he was descending the last step in the house, he stumbled and died under the weight of the piano. Herminia had to give her mistress the news. Not one tear did Senora de Bersi shed when she heard about Tuco's death. Herminia was so very tactful, even when bringing bad news. She was a real gem.

Senora Alma Monteson did not waste any time in offering Herminia a serious position as housekeeper or ladies' companion in her own home. She said they would travel to Europe and she would make all the arrangements, put everything neatly into the suitcases and pay all the fares for the most important places in Europe to which they would be going, in short, it would be a very pleasant life with none of the work she had always had to do, unpleasant jobs like washing, ironing and cleaning out rooms. Herminia was not in the least bit tempted by this offer, and replied angrily: "I won't abandon Senora de Bersi for any reason on earth."

"But you must see that Senora de Bersi is very ill and what she really needs is a nurse, not a maid like you, who is just wasting her life shut up in here."

Herminia turned her back on her and did not say one more word The next day, the papers carried the news that Senora Alma Monteson had died suddenly of a heart attack.

Lilian Guevara, a distant relation of Senora de Bersi who had recently married, visited her several times to see how she was getting along, and one day she offered Herminia a job. She was shy and it took a lot of hesitating, clearing her throat and coughing before she said: "Herminia, I need a girl like you and as Senora de Bersi is so very sick, I'm sure she will end up dead before much longer, and I think you would get along very well in my house. I spend all my summers by the sea. I have a lovely home, you must have seen the photographs in *Ideal Home* or the feature in *La Nacion*. I'd take you with me and you could go down to the beach every morning for a swim. And in winter, when I go on one of my trips to Bariloche, I'd take you with me, because I don't like to be apart from my maids when they're as good as you are. Senora de Bersi has told me so often about how marvelous you are and I'd really, really like to have someone like you in my home."

Herminia was left stunned. She could not believe that this young woman has spoken to her in terms of such vulgarity. To stop herself from crying, she burst into wild laughter. It was an awful moment, because her laughter could not appease anything. In that sorrowful, silent house Herminia's laughter seemed more tragic than all the tears of the hyprocrites asking after Senora de Bersi's health. Afterwards, she went off quietly into a corner of the house to think, as though she were praying.

The news came on the radio that same night. Lilian Guevara had died in a car crash in the neighbourhood of La Magdalena.

Senora de Bersi did not get any worse, nor did she get any better. Her state of health filled the house with uncertainty and heaviness, but she did not seem to be suffering too much and she was getting used to being an invalid, as some sick people do. The visitors, who grew more numerous every day, decided to ask a team of doctors to discuss the treatment that the sick woman needed. So they called a well-known specialist and had him come over from La Plata, they called a heart specialist and a pediatrician who lived near Senora de Bersi's house and they waited for them all in the lobby in an anxious group, chatting as they did every afternoon in that house. The bravest of them, for there are always some brave women, decided to go and talk to the doctors before they all met together. Through the window they watched the arrival of these great men. From the window they saw them get out of their cars; cautiously they moved toward the door, waiting for the elevator to come up and then as though by chance they talked to the doctors at the end of the hall, when they were taking off their coats and mufflers.

One woman said:

"Doctor, don't you think it's . . . inhuman . . . to prolong the life of a lady who's suffering so much?"

Another said to one of the doctors:

"Tell me, doctor, couldn't you give her something to shorten her road to Calvary a little?"

And another said:

"If I were in her position, I'd honestly prefer to be given something to end my life once and for all."

Herminia was sitting close to the window watching all this. She did not like it, she did not like it at all that they wanted to take over her mistress's life, that so many frivolous women were wandering along the corridors of the house, sitting in the parlor, touching the books, the vases, the wild animals, stroking the fur of the senora's favorite animals. And it was still a sore point that the son had taken away the piano. Hadn't they forced the lock on one of the glass cabinets, where the fans and the ivory chessmen were displayed? What would happen next? How sad life is, thought Herminia. She would never have imagined that people could be so wicked, that friendship could be so false, that riches could be so useless. Tears fell from her eyes, and she explained: "There's some dust in my eye." Sighs fell from her lips, and she explained: "I have a cold in my chest." She was even reserved about her sorrow. The people who saw her looking so sad were more worried about her than they were about Senora de Bersi. The milkman who brought the milk, the bread-man with his huge basket of bread, the grocer all asked:

"How is Senorita Herminia? What's wrong with Senorita Herminia? Is Senorita Herminia sick?"

Lina Grundic, the piano teacher who once upon a time had taught Senora de Bersi to play the piano, seemed a serious person, seemed more reserved, seemed better than all the other ladies. One day she called Herminia and said: "Herminia, the fastening on my bodice has come unstitched. I don't like to bother you, but these breasts of mine would even arouse a statue. Could I trouble you for a needle and thread to sew it up?"

They went together to the bathroom. Herminia sat on the edge of the bathtub and sewed the fastening on the pianist's bodice, while she combed her hair in the mirror, dampened her hair to set in the waves, put on her lipstick and powdered her face. Neither of the two said a word. In the silence of the afternoon music could be heard, cheerful music coming from the house next door.

"How depressing it must be for you, Herminia," said the pianist softly, "living in this house, and you so young too. How many years have you been working for Senora de Bersi?"

"Eight," answered Herminia.

"You must have been very young when you first came here, nothing but a child."

"I don't think I was so young. Other girls of my age, friends of mine, had been working in other houses for five years already when I came to this one."

"You're a real gem, and like all real gems you need airing. Do you know what happens to real gems if they stay shut up for too long? They lose their shine and nothing can put it back again, absolutely nothing."

"There are all sorts of modern inventions to make them shiny again."

"No there aren't, modern inventions aren't enough, nor are eight rooms. But in any case, it all seems very depressing to me. Don't you want to go to new places, to travel and get to know the world? I don't know, but I imagine that someone as young as you are must take an interest in life."

"I've never thought about it," answered Herminia.

"I'd like to have someone like you in my house. I've been invited to the United States, to the Chicago Conservatory to give some concerts. Sometimes they invite me to France or Italy. I'd like you with me. Now why are you blushing, sweetie?"

Herminia's heart beat fast. Even this woman was betraying Senora de Bersi. She snapped her sewing thread with her teeth and handed back the black bodice, stuffed with artificial feathers, to the pianist. Then without saying a word, she went out of the bathroom and locked the door.

A week later they found the pianist, Lina Grundic, dead in the elevator in her house. The mystery of her death remained unsolved. Nobody knew if it was a question of suicide or murder.

Herminia, who sometimes called herself Arminda, seemed much calmer. The visitors did not come to the house quite so often. To tell the truth, they were afraid of ending up like the unfortunate Alma Monteson, or Tuco Bersi, or Lina Grundic or Lilian Guevara. The days seemed happier and Senora de Bersi looked much better, she was more cheerful and she chatted as she had not chatted for a long time. In fact it seemed that her life was going to go on and on, and that some day she would appear in the newspapers as one of those ladies who has reached her 110th or 120th birthday and who are photographed with a short life story and details of how they managed to stay well enough to reach such an advanced age, what sort of diet they kept to, what kind of water they drank, how long did they sleep and how many hours a week did they play cards. And this miracle of longevity was all due to Herminia, as she herself admitted to the journalists: "May the lord grant Herminia everything she asks for. She's a real gem. She's prolonged my life for me."

❋ Discussion and Writing

1. Analyze the society portrayed in the story: what are the social relations of the characters; what does Ocampo achieve by having women as major characters; what is the function of the peripheral male character?
2. Describe the mysterious deaths in the story: how are they caused; what is their significance?
3. Discuss the implication of the last sentence, and the only one, uttered by Senora de Bersi.

4. Examine the dominant ironies in the story—in the title, the plot, the characters—and the paradox of life and death. What is the impact of such a piling up of ironies?

❋ Research and Comparison

Interdisciplinary Discussion Question: Research the issues of class and gender in the Argentine context. Examine the same issues with regard to any other society that is familiar, commenting on the cultural underpinnings of each.

Alejo Carpentier
(1904–1980)
Cuba

Alejo Carpentier was born in Havana, Cuba, two years after Cuba gained its independence from the United States. (The U.S. had defeated the Spanish in the Spanish-American War [1898] and had occupied the island for almost four years.) His mother, a former medical student, was Russian; his father, an architect, was French, and they emigrated to Cuba in 1902, the year of its independence. As a child, Carpentier was allowed free access to his father's library and was sent to the Cuban–North American private school where the sons of the affluent were educated. His father provided him with a European musical education, while his playmates introduced him to Afro-Cuban culture. Traveling in Europe during his adolescence, the family settled for a time in France. They returned to Cuba, where he completed his undergraduate work and began to study architecture at the Universidad de la Habana and to pursue his interest in music. Forced to leave the university when his father deserted the family, disappearing without a trace, Carpentier turned to writing as a means of supporting himself and his mother.

In the 1920s—indeed throughout his life—Carpentier wrote for many different kinds of newspapers and magazines; he also helped found the important avant-garde journal *Revista de Avance*. Believing African culture to be a major source of Cuban artistic inspiration, an idea borne out by his influential study of the origins of Cuban music, *La musica en Cuba* (1946), he participated in the Afro-Cuban/Afro-Antillean movement from its earliest days. As his writing evolved, it became encyclopedic, encompassing historic and mythic time and place, and Cuba became emblematic. He experimented over the years with narrative techniques, and he remained committed to a Latin American aesthetic, to what he called in the preface to *The Kingdom of This World* (1949) its "marvelous reality."

He was one of the architects of the Cuban Communist Party and one of the voices challenging the dictatorship of Gerardo Machado y Morales, who had come to power in 1925. Carpentier was arrested, and while in prison, he worked on his first novel, *Ecue-Yamba-O,* whose title he took from Lucumi, an African language spoken in Cuba. Out of jail, but recognizing the danger of his remaining in Cuba, he fled to Paris on a borrowed passport in 1928. Although he lived in Paris until the beginning of World War II, he continued to support the opposition to Machado. Carpentier saw Machado's regime and subsequently that of Fulgencio Batista y Zaldivar—both backed by the United States—as corrupt and ruthless. He saw those active in the opposition as heroic models for the future. He returned to Cuba for six years, then moved to Caracas, Venezuela, until 1959, when Batista was overthrown. Carpentier spent his last 14 years as cultural attaché to the Cuban embassy in Paris.

Like the Night*

And he traveled like the night.
ILIAD, BOOK I.

I

Although the headlands still lay in shadow, the sea between them was beginning to turn green when the lookout blew his conch to announce that the fifty black ships sent us by King Agamemnon had arrived. Hearing the signal, those who had been waiting for so many days on the dung-covered threshing floors began carrying the wheat toward the shore, where rollers were already being made ready so that the vessels could be brought right up to the walls of the fortress. When the keels touched the sand, there was a certain amount of wrangling with the steersmen, because the Mycenaeans had so often been told about our complete ignorance of nautical matters that they tried to keep us at a distance with their poles. Moreover, the beach was now crowded with children, who got between the soldiers' legs, hindered their movements, and scrambled up the sides of the ships to steal nuts from under the oarsmen's benches. The transparent waves of dawn were breaking amid cries, insults, tussles, and blows, and our leading citizens could not

Translated by Frances Partridge

make their speeches of welcome in the middle of such pandemonium. I had been expecting something more solemn, more ceremonious, from our meeting with these men who had come to fetch us to fight for them, and I walked off, feeling somewhat disillusioned, toward the fig tree on whose thickest branch I often sat astride, gripping the wood with my knees, because it reminded me somewhat of a woman's body.

As the ships were drawn out of the water and the tops of the mountains behind began to catch the sun, my first bad impression gradually faded; it had clearly been the result of a sleepless night of waiting, and also of my having drunk too heavily the day before with the young men recently arrived on the coast from inland, who were to embark with us soon after dawn. As I watched the procession of men carrying jars, black wineskins, and baskets moving toward the ships, a warm pride swelled within me, and a sense of my superiority as a soldier. That oil, that resinated wine, and above all that wheat from which biscuits would be cooked under the cinders at night while we slept in the shelter of the wet prows in some mysterious and unknown bay on the way to the Great City of Ships—the grain that I had helped to winnow with my shovel—all these things were being put on board for me; nor need I tire my long, muscular limbs, and arms designed for handling an ashwood pile, with tasks fit only for men who knew nothing but the smell of the soil, men who looked at the earth over the sweating backs of their animals or spent their lives crouched over it, weeding, uprooting, and raking, in almost the same attitudes as their own browsing cattle. These men would never pass under the clouds that at this time of day darken the distant green islands, whence the acrid-scented silphium was brought. They would never know the wide streets of the Trojans' city, the city we were now going to surround, attack, and destroy.

For days and days, the messengers sent us by the Mycenaean king had been telling us about Priam's insolence and the sufferings that threatened our people because of the arrogant behavior of his subjects. They had been jeering at our manly way of life; and, trembling with rage, we had heard of the challenges hurled at us long-haired Achaeans by the men of Ilium although our courage is unmatched by any other race. Cries of rage were heard, fists clenched and shaken, oaths sworn with the hands palm upward, and shields thrown against the walls, when we heard of the abduction of Helen of Sparta. While wine flowed from skins into helmets, in loud voices the emissaries told us of her marvelous beauty, her noble bearing and adorable way of walking, and described the cruelties she had endured in her miserable captivity. That same evening, when the whole town was seething with indignation, we were told that the fifty black ships were being sent. Fires were lighted in the bronze foundries while old women brought wood from the mountains.

And now, several days later, here I was gazing at the vessels drawn up at my feet, with their powerful keels and their masts at rest between the bulwarks like a man's virility between his thighs; I felt as if in some sense I was the owner of those timbers, transformed by some portentous carpentry unknown to our people into racehorses of the ocean, ready to carry us where the greatest adventure of all time was now unfolding like an epic. And I, son of a harness maker and grandson of a castrator of bulls, was to have the good fortune to go where those deeds were being done whose luster reached us in sailors' stories; I was to have the honor of seeing the walls of Troy, of following noble leaders and contributing my energy and strength to the cause of rescuing Helen of Sparta—a manly undertaking and the supreme triumph of a war that would give us prosperity, happiness, and pride in ourselves forever. I took a deep breath of the breeze blowing from the olive-covered hillside and thought how splendid it would be to die in such a just conflict, for the cause of Reason itself. But the idea of being pierced by an enemy lance made me think of my mother's grief and also of another, perhaps even profounder grief, though in this case the news would have to be heard with dry eyes because the hearer was head of the family. I walked slowly down to the town by the shepherds' path. Three kids were gamboling in the thyme-scented air. Down on the beach the loading of wheat was still going on.

II

The impending departure of the ships was being celebrated on all sides with thrumming of guitars and clashing of cymbals. The sailors from *La Gallarda* were dancing the zarambeque[1] with enfranchised Negresses, and singing familiar *coplas*—like the song of the *Moza del Retoño*, wherein groping hands supplied the blanks left in the words. Meanwhile the loading of wine, oil, and grain was still going on, with the help of the overseer's Indian servants, who were impatient to return to their native land. Our future chaplain was on his way to the harbor, driving before him two mules loaded with the bellows and pipes of a wooden organ. Whenever I met any of the men from the ships, there were noisy embraces, exaggerated gestures, and enough laughter and boasting to bring the women to their windows. We seemed to be men of a different race, expressly created to carry out exploits beyond the ken of the baker, the wool carder, and the merchant who hawked holland shirts embroidered by parties of nuns in their patios. In the middle of the square, their brass instruments flashing in the sun, the Captain's six trumpeters were playing popular airs while the Burgundian drummers thundered on their instruments, and a sackbut with a mouthpiece like a dragon was bellowing as if it wanted to bite.

In his shop, smelling of calfskin and Cordovan leather, my father was driving his awl into a stirrup strap with the half-heartedness of someone

---

[1]Zarambeque: a lively noisy dance; coplas: ballads or poetry. [eds.]

whose mind is elsewhere. When he saw me, he took me in his arms with serene sadness, perhaps remembering the horrible death of Cristobalillo, the companion of my youthful escapades, whom the Indians of the Dragon's Mouth had pierced with their arrows. But he knew that everyone was wild to embark for the Indies then—although most men in possession of their senses were already realizing that it was the "madness of many for the gain of a few." He spoke in praise of good craftsmanship and told me that a man could gain as much respect by carrying the harness maker's standard in the Corpus Christi procession as from dangerous exploits. He pointed out the advantages of a well-provided table, a full coffer, and a peaceful old age. But, probably having realized that the excitement in the town was steadily increasing and that my mood was not attuned to such sensible reasoning, he gently led me to the door of my mother's room.

This was the moment I had most dreaded, and I could hardly restrain my own tears when I saw hers, for we had put off telling her of my departure until everyone knew that my name had been entered in the books of the Casa de la Contratacion. I thanked her for the vows she had made to the Virgin of Navigators in exchange for my speedy return, and promised her everything she asked of me, such as to have no sinful dealings with the women of those far-off countries, whom the Devil kept in a state of paradisiac nakedness in order to confuse and mislead unwary Christians, even if they were not actually corrupted by the sight of such a careless display of flesh. Then, realizing that it was useless to make demands of someone who was already dreaming of what lay beyond the horizon, my mother began asking me anxiously about the safety of the ships and the skill of their pilots. I exaggerated the solidity and seaworthiness of *La Gallarda*, declaring that her pilot was a veteran of the Indies and a comrade of Nuno Garcia. And to distract her from her fears, I told her about the wonders of the New World, where all diseases could be cured by the Claw of the Great Beast and by bezoar stones; I told her, too, that in the country of the Omeguas there was a city built entirely of gold, so large that it would take a good walker a night and two days to cross it, and that we should surely go there unless we found our fortune in some not-yet-discovered regions inhabited by rich tribes for us to conquer. Gently shaking her head, my mother then said that travelers returned from the Indies told lying, boastful stories, and spoke of Amazons and anthropophagi, of terrible Bermudan tempests and poisoned spears that transformed into a statue anyone they pierced.

Seeing that she confronted all my hopeful remarks with unpleasant facts, I talked to her of our high-minded aims and tried to make her see the plight of all the poor idol worshippers who did not even know the sign of the Cross. We should win thousands of souls to our holy religion and carry out Christ's commandments to the Apostles. We were soldiers of God as well as soldiers of the King, and by baptizing the Indians and freeing them from their barbarous superstitions our nation would win imperishable glory and greater happiness, prosperity, and power than all the kingdoms of Europe. Soothed by my remarks, my mother hung a scapulary around my neck and gave me various ointments against the bites of poisonous creatures, at the same time making me promise that I would never go to sleep without wearing some woolen socks she had made for me herself. And as the cathedral bells began to peal, she went to look for an embroidered shawl that she wore only on very important occasions. On the way to church I noticed that in spite of everything my parents had, as it were, grown in stature because of their pride in having a son in the Captain's fleet, and that they greeted people more often and more demonstratively than usual. It is always gratifying to have a brave son on his way to fight for a splendid and just cause. I looked toward the harbor. Grain was still being carried onto the ships.

III

I used to call her my sweetheart, although no one yet knew that we were in love. When I saw her father near the ships, I realized that she would be alone, so I followed the dreary jetty battered by the winds, splashed with green water, and edged with chains and rings green with slime until I reached the last house, the one with green shutters that were always closed. Hardly had I sounded the tarnished knocker when the door opened, and I entered the house along with a gust of wind full of sea spray. The lamps had already been lighted because of the mist. My sweetheart sat down beside me in a deep armchair covered in old brocade and rested her head on my shoulder with such a sad air of resignation that I did not dare question those beloved eyes, which seemed to be gazing at nothing, but with an air of amazement. The strange objects that filled the room now took on a new significance for me. Some link bound me to the astrolabe, the compass, and the wind rose, as well as to the sawfish hanging from the beams of the ceiling and the charts by Mercator and Ortelius spread out on either side of the fireplace among maps of the heavens populated by Bears, Dogs, and Archers.

Above the whistling of the wind as it crept under the doors, I heard the voice of my sweetheart asking how our preparations were going. Reassured to find that it was possible to talk of something other than ourselves, I told her about the Sulpicians and Recollects who were to embark with us, and praised the piety of the gentlemen and farmers chosen by the man who would take possession of these far-off countries in the name of the King of France. I told her what I knew of the great River Colbert, bordered with ancient trees draped in silvery moss, its red waters flowing majestically beneath a sky white with herons. We were taking provisions for six months. The lowest decks of the *Belle* and the *Amiable* were full of corn. We were undertaking the important task of civilizing the vast areas of forest lying between the burning Gulf of Mexico and Chicagua, and we would teach new skills to the inhabitants.

Just when I thought my sweetheart was listening most attentively to what I was saying, she suddenly sat up, and said with unexpected vehemence that there was nothing glorious about the enterprise that had set all the town bells ringing since dawn. Last night, with her eyes inflamed with weeping, her anxiety to know something about the world across the sea to which I was going had driven her to pick up Montaigne's *Essais* and read everything to do with America in the chapter on Coaches. There she had learned about the treachery of the Spaniards, and how they had succeeded in passing themselves off as gods, with their horses and bombards. Aflame with virginal indignation, my sweetheart showed me the passage in which the skeptical Bordelais says of the Indians that "we have made use of their ignorance and inexperience to draw them more easily into fraud, luxury, avarice, and all manner of inhumanity and cruelty by the example of our life and pattern of our customs." Blinded by her distress at such perfidy, this devout young woman who always wore a gold cross on her bosom actually approved of a writer who could impiously declare that the savages of the New World had no reason to exchange their religion for ours, their own having served them very well for a long time.

I realized that these errors came only from the resentment of a girl in love—and a very charming girl—against the man who was forcing her to wait for him so long merely because he wanted to make his fortune quickly in a much-proclaimed undertaking. But although I understood this, I felt deeply wounded by her scorn for my courage and her lack of interest in an adventure that would make my name famous; for the news of some exploit of mine, or of some region I had pacified, might well lead to the King's conferring a title on me, even though it might involve a few Indians dying by my hand. No great deed is achieved without a struggle, and as for our holy faith, the Word must be imposed with blood. But it was jealousy that made my sweetheart paint such an ugly picture of the island of Santo Domingo, where we were to make a landing, describing it in adorably unsuitable words as "a paradise of wicked women." It was obvious that in spite of her chastity, she knew what sort of women they were who often embarked for Cap Francais from a jetty nearby under the supervision of the police and amid shouts of laughter and coarse jokes from the sailors. Someone, perhaps one of the servants, may have told her that a certain sort of abstinence is not healthy for a man, and she was imagining me beset by greater perils than the floods, storms, and water dragons that abound in American rivers, in some Eden of nudity and demoralizing heat.

In the end I began to be annoyed that we should be having this wrangle instead of the tender farewells I had expected at such a moment. I started abusing the cowardice of women, their incapacity for heroism, the way their philosophy was bounded by baby linen and workboxes, when a loud knocking announced the untimely return of her father. I jumped out of a back window, unnoticed by anyone in the marketplace, for passersby, fishermen, and drunkards—already numerous even so early in the evening—had gathered around a table on which a man stood shouting. I took him at first for a hawker trying to sell Orvieto elixir, but he turned out to be a hermit demanding the liberation of the holy places, I shrugged my shoulder and went on my way. Some time ago I had been on the point of enlisting in Foulque de Neuilly's crusade. A malignant fever—cured thanks to God and my sainted mother's ointments—most opportunely kept me shivering in bed on the day of departure: that adventure ended, as everyone knows, in a war between Christians and Christians. The crusades had fallen into disrepute. Besides, I had other things to think about.

IV

The wind had died down. Still annoyed by my stupid quarrel with my betrothed, I went off to the harbor to look at the ships. They were all moored to the jetty, side by side, with hatches open, receiving thousands of sacks of wheat flour between their brightly camouflaged sides. The infantry regiments were slowly going up the gangways amid the shouts of stevedores, blasts from the boatswain's whistle, and signals tearing through the mist to set the cranes in motion. On the decks, shapeless objects and menacing machines were being heaped together under tarpaulins. From time to time an aluminum wing revolved slowly above the bulwarks before disappearing into the darkness of the hold. The generals' horses, suspended from webbing bands, traveled over the roofs of the shops like the horses of the Valkyries, I was standing on a high iron gangway watching the final preparations, when suddenly I became agonizingly aware that there were only a few hours left—scarcely thirteen—before I too should have to board one of those ships now being loaded with weapons for my use. Then I thought of women; of the days of abstinence lying ahead; of the sadness of dying without having once more taken my pleasure from another warm body.

Full of impatience, and still angry because I had not got even a kiss from my sweetheart, I struck off toward the house where the dancers lived. Christopher, very drunk, was already shut into his girl's room. My girl embraced me, laughing and crying, saying that she was proud of me, that I looked very handsome in my uniform, and that a fortune-teller had read the cards and told her that no harm would come to me during the Great Landing. She more than once called me a "hero," as if she knew how cruelly her flattery contrasted with my sweetheart's unjust remarks. I went out onto the roof. The lights were coming on in the town, outlining the gigantic geometry of the buildings in luminous points. Below, in the streets, was a confused swarm of heads and hats.

At this distance, it was impossible to tell women from men in the evening mist. Yet it was in order that this crowd of unknown human beings should go on existing, that I was due to make my way to the ships soon after dawn. I should plow the stormy ocean during the winter months and land on a remote shore under attack from steel and fire, in defense of my country-men's principles. It was the last time a sword would be brandished over the maps of the West. This time we should finish off the new Teutonic Order for good and all, and advance as victors into that longed-for future when man would be reconciled with man. My mistress laid her trembling hand on my head, perhaps guessing at the nobility of my thoughts. She was naked under the half-open flaps of her dressing gown.

V

I returned home a few hours before dawn, walking unsteadily from the wine with which I had tried to cheat the fatigue of a body surfeited with enjoy-ment of another body. I was hungry and sleepy, and at the same time deeply disturbed by the thought of my approaching departure. I laid my weapons and belt on a stool and threw myself on my bed. Then I realized, with a start of surprise, that someone was lying under the thick woolen blanket; and I was just stretching out my hand for my knife when I found myself embraced by two burning-hot arms, which clasped me around the neck like the arms of a drowning man while two inexpressibly smooth legs twined themselves between mine. I was struck dumb with astonishment when I saw that the person who had slipped into my bed was my sweetheart. Between her sobs, she told me how she had escaped in the darkness, had run away in terror from barking dogs and crept furtively through my father's garden to the window of my room. Here she had waited for me in terror and impatience. After our stupid quarrel that afternoon, she had thought of the dangers and sufferings lying in wait for me, with that sense of impotent longing to lighten a soldier's hazardous lot which women so often express by offering their own bodies, as if the sacrifice of their jealously guarded virginity at the moment of departure and without hope of enjoyment, this reckless aban-donment to another's pleasure, could have the propitiatory power of ritual oblation.

There is a unique and special freshness in an encounter with a chaste body never touched by a lover's hands, a felicitious clumsiness of response, an intuitive candor that, responding to some obscure promptings, divines and adopts the attitudes that favor the closest possible physical union. As I lay in my sweetheart's arms and felt the little fleece that timidly brushed against one of my thighs, I grew more and more angry at having exhausted my strength in all-too-familiar coupling, in the absurd belief that I was ensuring my future serenity by means of present excesses. And now that I was being offered this so desirable compliance, I lay almost insensible beneath my sweetheart's tremulous and impatient body. I would not say that my youth was incapable of catching fire once again that night under the stimulus of this new pleasure. But the idea that it was a virgin who was offering herself to me, and that her closed and intact flesh would require a slow and sustained effort on my part, filled me with an obsessive fear of failure.

I pushed my sweetheart to one side, kissing her gently on the shoulders, and began telling her with assumed sincerity what a mistake it would be for our nuptial joys to be marred by the hurry of departure; how ashamed she would be if she became pregnant and how sad it was for children to grow up with no father to teach them how to get green honey out of hollow tree trunks and look for cuttlefish under stones. She listened, her large bright eyes burning in the darkness, and I was aware that she was in the grip of a resentment drawn from the underworld of the instincts and felt nothing but scorn for a man who, when offered such an opportunity, invoked reason and prudence instead of taking her by force, leaving her bleeding on the bed like a trophy of the chase, defiled, with breasts bitten, but having become a woman in her hour of defeat.

Just then we heard the lowing of cattle going to be sacrificed on the shore and the watchmen blowing their conchs. With scorn showing clearly in her face, my sweetheart got quickly out of bed without letting me touch her, and with a gesture not so much of modesty as of someone taking back what he had been on the point of selling too cheap, she covered those charms which had suddenly begun to enflame my desire. Before I could stop her, she had jumped out of the window. I saw her running away as fast as she could among the olives, and I realized in that instant that it would be easier for me to enter the city of Troy without a scratch than to regain what I had lost.

When I went down to the ships with my parents, my soldier's pride had been replaced by an intolerable sense of disgust, of inner emptiness and self-depreciation. And when the steersmen pushed the ships away from the shore with their strong poles, and the masts stood erect between the row of oarsmen, I realized that the display, excesses, and feasting that precede the departure of soldiers to the battlefield were now over. There was no time now for garlands, laurel wreaths, wine drinking in every house, envious glances from weaklings, and favors from women. Instead, our lot would consist of bugle calls, mud, rainsoaked bread, the arrogance of our leaders, blood spilled in error, the sickly, tainted smell of gangrene. I already felt less confident that my courage would contribute to the power and happiness of the long-haired Achaeans. A veteran soldier, going to war because it was his profession and with no more enthusiasm than a sheep shearer on his way to the pen, was telling anyone prepared to listen that Helen of Sparta was very happy to be in Troy, and that when she disported herself in Paris's bed, her hoarse cries of enjoyment brought blushes to the cheeks of the virgins who lived in Priam's palace. It was said that the whole story of the unhappy captivity of Leda's daughter, and of the insults and humiliations the Trojans had subjected her to, was simply war propaganda, inspired by Agamemnon with the consent of Menelaus. In fact, behind this enterprise and the noble ideals it had set up as a screen, a great many aims were concealed which would not benefit the combatants in the very least: above all, so the old soldier said, to sell more pottery, more cloth, more vases decorated with scenes from chariot races, and to open new ways of access to Asia, whose peoples had a passion for barter, and so put an end once and for all to Trojan competition.

Too heavily loaded with flour and men, the ship responded slowly to the oars. I gazed for a long time at the sunlit houses of my native town. I was nearly in tears, I took off my helmet and hid my eyes behind its crest; I had taken great trouble to make it round and smooth, like the magnificent crests of the men who could order their accouterments of war from the most highly skilled craftsmen and who were voyaging on the swiftest and longest ship.

❊ Discussion and Writing

1. Identify the protagonist: examine his background and attitudes. Describe his role in each of the heroic ventures.
2. Analyze the imagery evoking manliness, heroism, and conquest. Relate these images to the protagonist's attitudes toward the imminent expeditions.
3. Compare and contrast the man's meetings with his sweetheart and the prostitute. What light do these meetings shed on the theme of manliness, power, and political domination?
4. Examine the implications of the protagonist's being a soldier of both the church and the state.
5. Explain the allusions to the Trojan War.
6. Discuss the process of colonization presented in the story. What parallels does Carpentier establish between the action of the narrative and the historic and epic events?

❊ Research and Comparison

Interdisciplinary Discussion Question: Research the history of Cuba in the twentieth century. Discuss the effect of the political upheavals on people's lives and thinking. Examine the works of two major Cuban writers and their treatment of communism.

Pablo Neruda
(1904–1973)
Chile

Pablo Neruda (the pseudonym of Neftali Ricardo Reyes Basoalto) was born in Parral in the central vineyard country of Chile, and spent his childhood in the rainy frontier town of Temuco. His mother died of tuberculosis when he was little more than a month old, and he was raised by his father's second wife, a woman whom Neruda loved and respected deeply for her kindness, good sense, and humor. His father, a tough-fibered railway man, did not want his son to be a poet, and so Neruda published his poems under various pseudonyms to circumvent his father's displeasure; he took the name Pablo Neruda when he was 16. Rather than completing his studies at the university, where he was preparing for an academic career in French literature, he wrote and lived, freed of restraints, among a group of young experimental poets, discussing politics and love as well as poetry. When he was 23, he entered the diplomatic corps and served some five years in Southeast Asia, a period of despair and isolation. The poems he published when he returned to Chile marked his transformation from a promising young poet to a modern major voice.

Neruda's *Spain in Our Hearts,* written while serving as Chilean consul in Spain during the Spanish Civil War (1936–1939), was published on the front lines. Considered among his finest political poems, *Spain in Our Hearts* contributed to his being forced to resign his post and return to Chile. In the early 1940s, the government assigned him to the post of consul general in Mexico but later removed him because he had openly criticized the president, and he fled the country. His celebrated work *Canto general* (General Song, 1950) was written during this decade; the poems fit into the Latin American tradition in which the poet honors the land and its historic struggles and glory. Neruda twisted the genre to attack present-day political, social, and economic exploitation, as in *Alturas de Macchu Picchu* (Heights of Macchu Picchu, 1943; Neruda added the "c" to Machu). Inspired by a visit to Machu Picchu on his return from Mexico to Chile, the poems exemplify the contrast between the ancient historic glory and the contemporary shameful condition of the native peoples.

All his life Neruda remained committed to socialist ideals, announcing his membership in the Chilean Communist Party in 1945. He was forced to flee Chile four years later when he protested the government's harassment of politically progressive people. The delay in his receiving the Nobel Prize in literature until 1971, when it was widely known that he was quite ill, has been attributed to his political stance. In 1969, he had been willing to serve as president, but stepped aside, allowing Salvador Allende to assume the candidacy. He died of a heart attack shortly after Allende's assassination; his last words condemned the military coup.

The Heights of Macchu Picchu, III*

Being like maize grains fell
in the inexhaustible store of lost deeds, shoddy
occurrences, from nine to five, to six,
and not one death but many came to each,
each day a little death: dust, maggot, lamp,
drenched in the mire of suburbs, a little death with fat wings
entered into each man like a short blade
and siege was laid to him by bread or knife:
the drover, the son harbors, the dark captain of plows,
the rodent wanderer through dense streets:

all of them weakened waiting for their death, their brief
    and daily death—
and their ominous dwindling each day
was like a black cup they trembled while they drained.

The Chilean Forest†

Under the volcanoes, beside the snow-capped mountains, among the huge lakes, the fragrant, the silent, the tangled Chilean forest. . . . My feet sink down into the dead leaves, a fragile twig crackles, the giant rauli trees rise in all their bristling height, a bird from the cold jungle passes over, flaps its wings, and stops in the sunless branches. And then, from its hideaway, it sings like an oboe. . . . The wild scent of the laurel, the dark scent of the boldo herb, enter my nostrils and flood my whole being. . . . The cypress of the Guaitecas blocks my way. . . . This is a vertical world: a nation of birds, a plenitude of leaves. . . . I stumble over a rock, dig up the uncovered hollow, an enormous spider covered with red hair stares up at me, motionless, as huge as a crab. . . . A golden carabus beetle blows its mephitic breath at me, as its brilliant rainbow disappears like lightning. . . . Going on, I pass through a forest of ferns much taller than I am: from their cold green eyes sixty tears splash down on my face and, behind me, their fans go on quivering for a long time. . . . A decaying tree trunk: what a treasure! . . . Black and blue mushrooms have given it ears, red parasite plants have covered it with rubies, other lazy plants have let it borrow their beards,

---

*Translated by Nathaniel Tarn
†Translated by Hardie St. Martin

and a snake springs out of the rotted body like a sudden breath, as if the spirit of the dead trunk were slipping away from it. . . . Farther along, each tree stands away from its fellows. . . . They soar up over the carpet of the secretive forest, and the foliage of each has its own style, linear bristling, ramulose, lanceolate, as if cut by shears moving in infinite ways. . . . A gorge; below, the crystal water slides over granite and jasper. . . . A butterfly goes past, bright as a lemon, dancing between the water and the sunlight. . . . Close by, innumerable calceolarias nod their little yellow heads in greeting. . . . High up, red copihues (Lapageria rosea) *dangle like drops from the magic forest's arteries. . . . The red copihue is the blood flower, the white copihue is the snow flower. . . . A fox cuts through the silence like a flash, sending a shiver through the leaves, but silence is the law of the plant kingdom. . . . The barely audible cry of some bewildered animal far off. . . . The piercing interruption of a hidden bird. . . . The vegetable world keeps up its low rustle until a storm churns up all the music of the earth.*

Anyone who hasn't been in the Chilean forest doesn't know this planet.

I have come out of that landscape, that mud, that silence, to roam, to go singing through the world.

Childhood and Poetry

I'll start out by saying this about the days and the years of my childhood: the rain was the one unforgettable presence for me then. The great southern rain, coming down like a waterfall from the Pole, from the skies of Cape Horn to the frontier. On this frontier, my country's Wild West, I first opened my eyes to life, the land, poetry, and the rain.

I have traveled a lot, and it seems to me that the art of raining, practiced with a terrible but subtle power in my native Araucania, has now been lost. Sometimes it rained for a whole month, for a whole year. Threads of rain, fell, like long needles of glass snapping off on the roofs or coming up against the windows in transparent waves, and each house was a ship struggling to make port in the ocean of winter.

This cold rain from the south of the Americas is not the sudden squall of hot rain that comes down like a whip and goes on, leaving a blue sky in its wake. The southern rain is patient and keeps falling endlessly from the gray sky.

The street in front of my house has turned into a huge sea of mud. Out the window, through the rain, I watch a cart stuck in the middle of the street. A peasant wearing a heavy black woolen cloak beats his oxen; the rain and the mud are too much for them.

We used to walk to school, along the unpaved sidewalks, stepping from stone to stone, despite the cold and the rain. The wind carried off our umbrellas. Raincoats were expensive, I didn't like gloves, my shoes got soaked through. I'll always remember the wet socks hanging next to the brazier, and lots of shoes, steaming like toy locomotives. Then the floods would come and wash away the settlements along the river, where the poor lived. The earth shook and trembled. At other times, a crest of terrifying light appeared on the sierras: Mt. Llaima, the volcano, was stirring.

Temuco is a pioneer town, one of those towns that have no past, though it does have hardware stores. Since the Indians can't read, the stores hang their eye-catching signs out on the streets: an enormous saw, a giant cooking pot, a Cyclopean padlock, a mammoth spoon. Farther along the street, shoe stores—a colossal boot.

Temuco was the farthest outpost of Chilean life in the southern territories, and therefore it had a long bloody history behind it.

When the Spanish conquistadors pushed them back, after three hundred years of fighting, the Araucanian Indians retreated to those cold regions. But the Chileans continued what they called "the pacification of Araucania," their war of blood and fire to turn our countrymen out of their own lands. Every kind of weapon was used against the Indians, unsparingly: carbine blasts, the burning of villages, and later, a more fatherly method, alcohol and the law. The lawyer became a specialist at stripping them of their fields, the judge sentenced them when they protested, the priest threatened them with eternal fire. And hard spirits finally consummated the annihilation of a superb race whose deeds, valor, and beauty Don Alonso de Ercilla carved in stanzas of jade and iron in his *Araucana*. . . .

The House of the Three Widows

One time I was invited to a threshing; it was to be done in the old way, with mares. The place was high up in the mountains and pretty far from town. I liked the adventure of going off by myself, figuring out the right route in that mountainous country. I thought if I got lost, somebody would help me out. On my horse, I left Bajo Imperial behind and narrowly made it across the sand bar of the river. There the Pacific breaks loose and attacks, again and again, the rocks and the clumps of bushes on Maule Hill, the last height, standing very tall. Then I turned off along the shore of Lake Budi. The surf pounded the foot of the hill with savage blows. I had to take advantage of the few minutes that elapsed when a wave smashed and pulled itself in to regain its strength. We would hurry across the strip between the hill and the water, before a new wave could crush us, my horse and me, against the rugged hillside.

The danger past, the smooth blue sheet of the lake opened out to the west. The sandy coast ran on endlessly toward the mouth of Lake Tolten, a long way off. These coasts of Chile, often rugged and craggy, suddenly turn into endless ribbons and you can go for days and nights over the sand, close to the sea's foam.

The beaches seem infinite, forming, along the length of Chile, something like a planet's ring, a winding band, pursued relentlessly by the roar of the southern seas: a trail that appears to go around the coast of Chile and beyond the South Pole.

On the forested side, hazel trees with shining dark green branches waved to me, some trimmed with clusters of fruit, hazelnuts that seemed to be painted vermilion, so red are they at that time of year. The giant ferns of southern Chile were so tall that we could pass under their branches without touching them, my horse and I. Whenever my head brushed against their green, a shower of dew would drench us. Lake Budi spread out on my right: a steady blue sheet bordered by far-off woods.

It was only at the end of the lake that I saw some people. They were strange fishermen. In that strip where the ocean and the lake join, or embrace, or clash, between the two waters, there were some salt-water fish, cast out by the rough waves. The huge loaches were specially coveted, broad silver fish, strays thrashing about on those shoals. One, two, three, four, five fishermen, erect, concentrating, watched for the wake of the lost fish and suddenly brought a long trident down on the water with a terrific blow. Then they lifted high the oval-shaped silver fish, shuddering and gleaming in the sun before dying in the fishermen's baskets. It was growing late. I had left the banks on the lake and moved inland looking for the road along the jagged spurs of the hills. Darkness was inching in. Suddenly the wail of a strange wild bird passed overhead like a hoarse moan. An eagle or a condor high up in the twilight sky seemed to halt its black wings, as a signal that I was there, following me in its heavy flight. Red-tailed foxes howled or barked or streaked across the road, and small predatory animals of the secret forest that were unknown to me.

I realized that I had lost my way. The night and the forest which had made me so happy became menacing now, they filled me with terror. One solitary traveler appeared unexpectedly in front of me, in the darkening loneliness of the road. As we approached each other, I stopped and saw that he was just one more of those rough peasants, with cheap poncho and scrawny horse, who emerged from the silence every now and then.

I told him what had happened to me.

He answered that I couldn't get to the threshing that night. He knew each and every corner of that terrain. He knew the exact spot where they were threshing. I told him I didn't want to spend the night outdoors and asked if he could tell me where I might find shelter till daybreak. He instructed me, in a few words, to go two leagues down a small trail that branched off from the road.

"You'll see the lights of a big two-story frame house in the distance," he told me.

"Is it a hotel?" I asked him.

"No, young man. But you'll be welcomed. They're three French ladies, in the lumber business, who've been living there thirty years now. They're nice to everybody. They'll put you up."

I thanked the horseman for his meager counsel and he trotted off on his rickety nag. I continued along the narrow trail, like a lost soul. A virgin moon, curved and white like a fragment of fingernail newly clipped off, was starting its climb up the sky.

About nine o'clock that night, I made out lights that could only be a house. I spurred my horse on before bolts and crossbars could block my way to that God-sent haven. I went in the gate of the property and, dodging logs and hills of sawdust, I reached the entrance, or white portico, of that house lost so far out of the way in the wilderness. I rapped on the door, softly at first, and then harder. Some minutes passed, the dreadful thought that no one was there running through my head, before a slender white-haired lady dressed in black appeared. She examined me with stern eyes, opening the door part way to question so late a traveler.

"Who are you? What do you want?" a quiet, ghostly voice asked.

"I've lost my way in the forest. I'm a student. I was invited to the threshing at the Hernandezes'. I'm very tired. Someone told me you and your sisters are very hospitable. I'd just like a corner to sleep in, and I'll be on my way at daybreak."

"Do come in," she said. "Please feel at home."

She led me to a dark parlor and lit two or three paraffin lamps. I noticed that they were lovely art-nouveau lamps, opaline and gilt bronze. The room had a dank smell. Long, red draperies shielded the tall windows. The armchairs were under white slipcovers to protect them. From what?

It was a room from some other century, hard to place and as disquieting as a dream. The white-haired lady, wistful, in black, moved about on feet I couldn't see, with steps I couldn't hear, her hands touching first this, then that, an album, a fan, here, there, in the silence.

I felt as if I had fallen to the bottom of a lake and lived on, exhausted, dreaming down there. Suddenly two ladies, just like the one who had received me, came in. It was late and it was cold. They sat close to me, one with the vague smile of someone flirting just a little, the other with the melancholy eyes of the one who had opened the door.

Suddenly the conversation wandered very far from that out-of-the-way countryside, far also from the night drilled through by thousands of insects, the croaking of frogs, and the songs of night birds. They wanted to know all about my studies. I happened to mention Baudelaire, and told them I had started to translate his poems.

It was like an electric spark. The three dim ladies lit up. Their lifeless eyes and their stiff faces were transfigured, as if three ancient masks had dropped from their ancient features.

"Baudelaire!" they exclaimed. "This is probably the first time since the beginning of the world that anyone has spoken his name in this lonely place. We have his *Fleurs du mal* here. We're the only ones, for five hundred kilometers around, who can read his marvelous pages. No one in these mountains knows any French."

Two of the sisters had been born in Avignon. The youngest, also of French blood, was Chilean by birth. Their grandparents, their parents, all their relatives, had died a long time ago. The three had grown accustomed to the rain, to the wind, to the sawdust from the mill, to having contact with only a very few primitive peasants and country servants. They had decided to remain there, the only house in those shaggy mountains.

An Indian servant girl came in and whispered something into the ear of the eldest lady. We went out then, down chilly hallways, until we came to the dining room. I was stunned. In the center of the room, a round table with trailing white tablecloth was illuminated by two silver candelabra with many burning candles. Silver and crystal glittered on that amazing table.

I was overcome by great timidity, as if Queen Victoria had invited me to dine at her palace. I had arrived disheveled, exhausted, and covered with dust, and this was a table fit for a prince. I was far from being one. And to them I must have looked more like a sweaty male driver who had left his drove at their door.

I have seldom eaten so well. My hostesses were masters of the art of cooking and had as a legacy from their grandparents the recipes of their beloved France. Each dish was a surprise, tasty and aromatic. From their cellars they brought out vintage wines, aged by them in the special French way.

Although weariness would suddenly close my eyes, I listened to them speaking of strange wonders. The sisters' greatest pride was the fine points of cookery. For them, the table was the preservation of a sacred heritage, of a culture to which they, separated from their country by time and great oceans, would never return. Laughing a little at themselves, they showed me a curious card file.

"We're just crazy old women," the youngest said.

Over the past thirty years they had been visited by twenty-seven travelers who had come as far as this remote house, some on business, others out of mere curiosity, still others, like myself, by chance. The incredible thing was that they had a personal file for every one of them, with the date of the visit and the menu they had prepared on each occasion.

"We save the menu so as not to repeat even a single dish, if those friends should ever return."

I went off to sleep and dropped into bed like a sack of onions in a market. At dawn I lit a candle, washed up, and got dressed. It was already getting light when one of the stable boys saddled my horse. I didn't have the heart to say goodbye to the kind ladies in black. Deep in me, something told me it had all been a strange, magical dream, and that, to keep from breaking the spell, I must try not to wake up.

All this happened forty-five years ago, when I was just entering adolescence. What became of those three ladies exiled with their *Fleurs du mal* in the heart of the virgin forest? What happened to their bottles of old wine, their resplendent table lit by twenty wax candles? What was the fate of the sawmill and the white house lost among the trees?

The simplest fate: death and oblivion. Perhaps the forest devoured those lives and those rooms that took me in, one unforgettable night. Yet they live on in my memory as in the clear bed of a lake of dreams. Honor to those three melancholy women who struggled in that wild solitude, with no practical purpose, to maintain an old-world elegance. They defended what their ancestors had forged with their own hands, the last traces of an exquisite culture, far off in the wilderness, at the last boundaries of the most impenetrable and lonely mountains in the world.

Love in the Wheat

I reached the Hernandez camp before noon, fresh and cheerful. My solitary ride over empty roads, and a good night's sleep, had given my reticent young face a certain glow.

The threshing of wheat, oats, barley was still done with mares. There is nothing gayer in the world than the sight of mares circling, trotting around a heap of grain, under the goading shouts of the riders. There was a splendid sun, and the air, an uncut diamond, made the mountains glitter. The threshing is a golden feast. The yellow straw piles up into golden hills; there's noise and activity everywhere; sacks rushing to get filled; women cooking; runaway horses; dogs barking; children who are constantly having to be plucked—like fruit borne by the straw—from under the horses' hoofs.

The Hernandezes were a unique tribe. The men were unkempt and unshaven, in shirtsleeves, with revolvers in their belts, and almost always splattered with grease, with dust from the grain, with mud, or soaked to the bone by rain. Fathers, sons, nephews, cousins all looked alike. They spent hours on end working under a motor, on a roof, perched on a threshing machine. They never had anything to talk about. They joked about everything, except when they got into a brawl. Then they fought, with the fury of a tornado, knocking down anything that stood in their way. They were always the first to get to the beef barbecues out in the open fields, to the red wine and the brooding guitars. They were frontiersmen, the kind of people I liked. Studious-looking and pale, I felt puny next to those vigorous brutes; and I don't know why, but they treated me with a deference they generally didn't show anyone.

After the barbecue, the guitars, the blinding fatigue brought on by the sun and the threshing, we had to find a makeshift bed for the night. Married couples and women who were alone bedded down on the ground, inside the camp walls put up with freshly cut boards. We males had to sleep on the threshing floor. This rose into a mountain of straw and a whole hamlet could have settled into its yellow softness.

All this lack of comfort was new to me. I didn't know how to go about spreading out. I put my shoes carefully under a layer of wheat straw, and this was to serve as my pillow. I took off my clothes, bundled myself up in my poncho, and sank into the mountain of straw. I lagged far behind all the others, who gave themselves up to their snoring at once, as one man.

I lay stretched out on my back for a long while, with my eyes open, my face and arms covered with straw. The night was clear, cold, and penetrating. There was no moon, but the stars looked as if they had recently been watered by the rain and, high above the unseeing sleep of all the others, they twinkled in the sky's lap just for me. Then I fell asleep. But I woke up suddenly, because something was coming toward me, a stranger's body was moving through the straw and coming closer to mine. I was afraid. The thing was slowly drawing closer. I could hear the wisps of straw snapping, crushed by the unknown shape that kept moving toward me. My whole body stiffened, waiting. Maybe I ought to get up and yell. I remained stockstill. I could hear breathing right next to my head.

Suddenly a hand slid over me, a large, calloused hand, but it was a woman's. It ran over my brow, my eyes, my whole face, tenderly. Then an avid mouth clung to mine and I felt a woman's body pressing against mine, all the way down to my feet.

Little by little my fear turned into intense pleasure. My hand slid over braided hair, a smooth brow, eyes with closed lids soft as poppies, and went on exploring. I felt two breasts that were full and firm, broad, rounded buttocks, legs that locked around me, and I sank my fingers into pubic hair like mountain moss. Not a word came from that anonymous mouth.

How difficult it is to make love, without making noise, in a mountain of straw burrowed by the bodies of seven or eight other men, sleeping men who must not be awakened for anything in the world. And yet we can do anything, though it may require infinite care. A little while later, the stranger suddenly fell asleep next to me, and worked into a fever by the situation, I started to get panicky. It would soon be daybreak, I thought, and the first workers would discover the naked woman stretched out beside me on the threshing floor. But I also fell asleep. When I woke up, I put out a startled hand and found only a warm hollow, a warm absence. Soon a bird began to sing and then the whole forest filled with warbling. There was a long blast from a motor horn, and men and women began moving about and turning to their chores. A new day of threshing was getting under way.

At midday all of us had lunch together around a makeshift table of long planks. I looked out of the corners of my eyes as I ate, trying to find which of the women could have been my night visitor. But some were too old, others too skinny, and many were merely young girls as thin as sardines. And I was looking for a well-built woman with full breasts and long, braided hair. Suddenly a woman came in with a piece of roast for her husband, one of the Hernandez men. This certainly could be the one. As I watched her from the other end of the table, I was sure I caught this attractive woman in long braids throwing me a quick glance and the slightest of smiles. And I felt as if the smile was growing broader and deeper, opening up inside my whole being.

❀ Discussion and Writing

The Heights of Macchu Picchu, III

1. What memories do the old ruins of Machu Picchu in the Andes evoke in the poet?
2. What is the significance of the opening of the poem? Comment on the image of falling "grains."
3. Analyze the various images that suggest the nature of death and its intensity.
4. Elaborate on the political implications of death brought to the man who was besieged "by bread or knife."

The Chilean Forest

1. Analyze Neruda's art in portraying the Chilean landscape: what are the characteristics of the Chilean forest; of the Chilean coastline; are they distinct from those of any other forest or coastline; what makes them seem unique?
2. What does the description of the history of Temuco indicate about the Spanish conquest of Chile? Are there any parallels between the sentiments of this passage and those in the poem "The Heights of Macchu Picchu, III"?
3. What is the correlation between the three solitary ladies and the forest and mountains? In what way does the portrayal of these women connect to colonial history?
4. Explore the links between the specific characters and the setting. Is Neruda himself closely linked with any definite aspect of the land in this narration?

❀ Research and Comparison

The Heights of Macchu Picchu, III

Interdisciplinary Discussion Question: Research the historic and cultural background of Machu Picchu, and examine the impact of precolonial experience on the writings of Pablo Neruda or any other Latin American writer.

The Chilean Forest

Research Pablo Neruda's life and work, and comment on his place in contemporary Latin American letters.

Interdisciplinary Discussion Question: Examine the history of the conquest of Chile, the impact of the lost heritage on the Chileans, and their recent political struggles.

Jacques Roumain
(1907–1944)
Haiti

Jacques Roumain, who was born into an aristocratic family in Port-au-Prince, Haiti, was the grandson of the president of Haiti from 1912 to 1913. As a child he attended the famous Institution Saint Louis de Gonzague, run by an order of French monks, and, continuing to follow the custom of the Haitian elite, he completed his studies in Europe, at the Institut Grunau in Berne, Switzerland. At the time of his return in 1927, the United States had been occupying Haiti for twelve years, a situation that lasted for another seven. Roumain soon became one of the leaders of the resistance movement. Known as the Generation of the occupation, he and his compatriots sought and ultimately helped gain the end of the occupation. They also voiced their opposition to the denigration of the Haitian peasant culture and to the elitist constraints placed on Haitian literature. Their protest evolved into the Indigenist movement and the establishment of the journal *La Revue indigene.* Roumain was one of the founders, and a major contributer and influence. By including literature from contemporary South American and Harlem Renaissance writers in *La Revue,* he asserted the common bonds among the people of the hemisphere. His own work evolved from a regionalist indigenism to evoke concepts of *negritude,* for he was concerned with the continuity and commonality of experience of all people of African descent. Moreover, while he was one of the first to incorporate indigenous material into his poetry and fiction, he, unlike many writers of the Indigenist movement, never glamorized the life of the poor rural peasant class.

Like many of his fellow writers, Roumain saw Marxism as the solution to the social and economic strife in his society, which he considered to be in a state of colonialism. In 1934, he founded the Haitian Communist Party. As a result, he was imprisoned for three years and then sent into exile. During the period of his exile, he studied anthropology at the Sorbonne, actively joined other antifascists in opposing the Spanish Civil War, and traveled to the United States and Cuba. With a change in government in 1941, he was able to return to Haiti, where he once again immersed himself in the intellectual life of the country, and founded the *Bureau d'Ethnologie,* an association designed to study the sources of Haitian culture. It was during his last two years, however, when he served as chargé d'affaires in Mexico, that he turned once again to poetry and fiction. It was here that he wrote *Gouverneurs de la rosee* (Masters of the Dew). Published posthumously and immediately pronounced a classic, the novel uses Haitian Creole to present the life of the Haitian peasant class. And it takes its title from a Creole phrase that identifies the peasant whose job is to water the fields. The title thus emphasizes the inspiration for and concerns of the novel: the indigenous Haitian culture and a Marxist philosophy of destiny. "Delira Delivrance" is the first chapter of *Masters of the Dew*.

*Delira Delivrance**

"We're all going to die," said the old woman. Plunging her hands into the dust, Delira Delivrance said, "We're all going to die. Animals, plants, every living soul! Oh, Jesus! Mary, Mother of God!"

The dust slipped through her fingers, the same dust that the dry wind scattered over the high hedge of cactus eaten by verdigris, over the blighted thorn acacias and the devastated fields of millet. The dust swirled up from the highway as the ancient Delira knelt before her hut, gently shaking her head covered with a gray frizz as though sprinkled with the same dust that ran through her dark fingers like a rosary of pain.

She repeated, "We're all going to die," and she called on the Lord.

But so many poor creatures call continually upon the Lord that it makes a big bothersome noise. When the Lord hears it, he yells, "What the hell's all that?" and stops up his ears. Yes, he does, leaving man to shift for himself. Thus thought Bienaime, her husband, as he smoked his pipe, his chair propped up against a calabash tree. The smoke (or was it his white beard?) flew away with the wind.

"Yes," he said, "a black man's really bad off."

Delira paid him no mind. A flock of crows swooped down on the charred field, like bits of scattered coal.

Bienaime called, "Delira! Delira! Ho!" But no answer. "Woman!" he cried. She raised her head. Bienaime brandished his pipe like a question mark. "The Lord is the creator, isn't he? Answer me! The Lord created heaven and earth, didn't he?"

Unwillingly, she answered, "Yes."

"Well, the earth's bad off, suffering. So the Lord created suffering." Short triumphant puffs and a long whistling jet of saliva.

Delira looked at him angrily. "Don't bother me, man! Don't I have enough trouble on my hands? I know what suffering is. My whole body aches, my whole body's full of suffering. I don't need anybody piling damnation on top of that."

Then, her eyes filled with tears, sadly, softly, "Bienaime! Oh, honey!"

Bienaime coughed hoarsely. Maybe he wanted to say something, but misfortune sickens men like bile. It comes up in their mouths, then the words are bitter.

---

*Translated by Langston Hughes and Mercer Cook

Delira rose with difficulty, as if she were making an effort to pull herself together. All the trials and tribulations of life were etched upon her black face, but her eyes had an inner glow. Bienaime looked away as she went into the house.

Back of the thorn acacias a hot haze distorted the half-hidden silhouette of far-off mountains. The sky was a gray-hot sheet of corrugated iron.

Behind the house a round hill, whose skimpy bushes hugged the earth, resembled the head of a Negro girl with hair like grains of pepper. Farther away against the sky, another mountain jutted, traversed by shining gullies where erosion had undressed long strata of rock and bled the earth to the bone. They had been wrong to cut down the trees that once grew thick up there. But they had burned the woods to plant Congo beans on the plateau and corn on the hillside.

Bienaime got up and walked unsteadily toward the field. Dry weeds had invaded the bed of the stream. The watercourse was cracked like old porcelain, slimy with rotten vegetation. Formerly the water had flowed freely there in the sun, its rippling and its light mingling like the soft laughter of cutting knives. Then millet had grown abundantly, hiding the house from the road.

In those days when they all had lived in harmony, united as the fingers of the hand, they had assembled all the neighborhood in collective *coumbites*[1] for the harvest or the clearing.

Ah, what *coumbites!* Bienaime mused.

At break of day he was there, an earnest leader with his group of men, all hard-working farmers: Dufontaine, Beausejour, cousin Aristhene, Pierrilis, Dieudonne, brother-in-law Merilien, Fortune Jean, wise old Boirond, and the work-song leader, Simidor Antoine, a Negro with a gift for singing, able to stir up with his tongue more scandal than ten gossiping women put together. But without meaning any harm, only for fun.

Into the field of wild grass they went, bare feet in the dew. Pale sky, cool, the chant of wild guinea hens in the distance. Little by little the shadowy trees, still laden with shreds of darkness, regained their color. An oily light bathed them. A kerchief of sulphur-colored clouds bound the summits of the mountains. The countryside emerged from sleep. In Rosanna's yard the tamarind tree suddenly let fly a noisy swirl of crows like a handful of gravel.

Casamajor Beaubrun with his wife, Rosanna, and their two sons would greet them. They would start out with, "Thank you very much, brothers," since a favor is willingly done: today I work your field, tomorrow you work mine. Co-operation is the friendship of the poor.

---

[1]A collective agricultural effort in which neighboring farmers help each other at times such as the harvest, when a task requires more hands than a single peasant family affords.

A moment later Simeon and Dorisca, with some twenty husky Negroes, would join the group. Then they would all leave Rosanna bustling around in the shade of the tamarind tree among her boilers and big tin pots whence the voluble sputtering of boiling water would already be rising. Later Delira and other women neighbors would come to lend her a hand.

Off would go the men with hoes on shoulder. The plot to be cleared was at the turn of the path, protected by intersecting bamboos. Creepers with mauve and white blossoms hung from riotous bushes. In their gilded shells the assorossis sported a red pulp like velvet mucous.

Lowering the fence poles at the entrance to a plot of land where an ox skull for a scarecrow blanched on a pole, they measured their job at a glance—a tangle of wild weeds intertwined with creepers. But the soil was good and they would make it as clean as a table top. This year Beaubrun wanted to try eggplant.

"Line up!" the squadron chiefs would yell.

Then Simidor Antoine would throw the strap of his drum over his shoulder. Bienaime would take his commanding position in front of his men. Simidor would beat a brief prelude, and the rhythm would crackle under his fingers. In a single movement, they would lift their hoes high in the air. A beam of light would strike each blade. For a second they would be holding a rainbow.

Simidor's voice rose, husky and strong:

Stroke it in!

The hoes fell with a single dull thud, attacking the rough hide of the earth.

That woman said, man!
Behave yourself!
And don't touch me!
Behave yourself!

The men went forward in a straight line. They felt Antoine's song in their arms and, like blood hotter than their own, the rapid beat of his drum.

Suddenly the sun was up. It sparkled like a dewy foam across the field of weeds. Master Sun! Honor and respect, Master Sun! We black men greet you with a swirl of hoes snatching bright sparks of fire from the sky. There are the breadfruit trees patched with blue, and the flame of the flamboyant tree long smoldering under the ashes of night, but now bursting into a flare of petals on the edge of the thorn acacias. The stubborn crowing of cocks alternated from one farm to another.

The moving line of peasants took up the new refrain in a single mass voice:

Stroke it in!
Who's that, I yell,
Inside that house?

Some man yells back,
Just me and a cute
Little cousin of mine—
And we don't need you!

They raised their long-handled hoes, crowned with sparks, and brought them down again with a terrific precision:

I'm in there now!

Bring Fit out! Oh!

What one bull can do,
Another can, too!
Bring it out! Oh!

There sprang up a rhythmic circulation between the beating heart of the drum and the movements of the men. The rhythm became a powerful flux penetrating deep into their arteries and nourishing their muscles with a new vigor.

Their chant filled the sun-flooded morning. Up the road of the reeds along the stream, the song mounted to a spring hidden in the hollow of the hill's armpit, in the heavy odor of fern and moist *malanga* soaking in the shaded secret oozing of the water.

Perhaps a young *Negresse* in the neighborhood, Irezile, Therese, or Georgiana, has just finished filling her calabashes. When she comes out of the stream, cool bracelets ripple from her legs. She places the gourds in a wicker basket that she balances on her head. She walks along the damp path. In the distance the drum sends out a humming hive-full of sounds.

"I'll go there later," she says to herself. "So-and-so will be there." He's her sweetheart. A warmth, a happy languor fills her body as she hurries on with long strides, arms swinging. Her hips roll with a wondrous sweetness. She smiles.

Above the thorn acacias floated tatters of smoke. In the clearings, the charcoal sellers swept away the mounds under which the green wood had burned with a slow fire. With the back of his hand, Estinval wiped his reddened eyes. From the mutilated tree there remained only the charred skeletons of its scattered branches in the ashes: a load of charcoal that his wife would take to sell in the town of Croix des Bouquets. Too bad he himself couldn't answer the call of the work-song! Smoke had dried his throat. His mouth was bitter as if he had been chewing a wad of paper. Indeed, a drink of cinnamon bark, or better, anis was more refreshing, a long big mouthful of alcohol down to the pit of his stomach.

"Rosanna, dear," he said.

Knowing his weakness, she laughingly measured out three fingers of liquor for him—three fingers spread out like a fan. He spat thick and went back to rummaging in his pile of earth and ashes.

About eleven o'clock, the call of the *coumbite* would grow weaker; it was no longer a solid mass of voices backing up the men's effort; the work-chant stumbled, mounted feebly, as though its wings were clipped. At times it picked up again, spasmodically, with diminishing vigor. The drum still stammered a bit, but it was no longer a happy call as at dawn when Simidor beat it out with such skillful authority.

This could be attributed not only to the need for rest—the hoe becoming heavier and heavier to handle, the strain of fatigue on the stiff neck, the heat of the sun—but to the fact that the job was almost done. Moreover, they had scarcely stopped long enough to swallow a mouthful of white rum, or to rest their backs.

The high-class people in the city derisively called these peasants "bare-foot Negroes, barefooted vagabonds, big-toed Negroes." (They are too poor to buy shoes.) But never mind and to hell with them! Some day we will take our big flat feet out of the soil and plant them on their behinds.

They had done a tough job, scratched, scraped, and shaved the hairy face of the field. The injurious brambles were scattered on the ground. Beaubrun and his sons would gather them up and set fire to them. What had been useless weeds, prickles, bushes entangled with tropical creepers, would change now to fertilizing gashes in the tilled soil. Beaubrun was over-joyed.

"Thanks, neighbors!" he kept repeating.

"You're welcome, neighbor!" we replied, but hurriedly, for dinner was ready. And what a dinner! Rosanna wasn't a cheap *Negresse*. All those who had made little spiteful remarks about her—because she was an ugly customer if you tried to get fresh with her—straightway repented. And why? Because, at the turn of the road, an aroma rose to meet them, greeted them positively, enveloped them, penetrated them, opened the agreeable hollow of a great appetite in their stomachs.

And Simidor Antoine—who, not later than two evenings ago, on making a vulgar remark to Rosanna, had received remarkably precise details from her concerning his own mother's irregularities—filling his nostrils with the aroma of the meats, sighed with solemn conviction, "Beaubrun, old man, your wife is a blessing!"

In the cauldrons, the casseroles, and the bowls were stacked with barbe-cued pig seasoned hot enough to take your breath away, ground corn with codfish, and rice, too, sun rice with red beans and salt pork, bananas, sweet potatoes, and yams to throw away!

Bienaime leaned against the fence. On the other side now there was the same discouragement. The dust rose in thick swirling clouds, and fell on the chandelier trees and thin patches of grass clinging to the scurvy earth.

Formerly at this time of year, early in the morning, the sky would be turning gray. The clouds would gather, swollen with rain—not a heavy rain, no, as when the clouds burst like over-filled sacks—but a little drizzle, persistent, with a few intervals of sunshine. It wasn't enough to drench the earth, but cooled it off and prepared it for the hard rains. At Angelus-time, the timid wild guinea fowl would come to drink water from the puddles along the road and, if frightened, would fly heavily away, benumbed and bespattered with rain.

Then the weather would begin to change. Toward noon, a thick heat would envelop the prostrate fields and trees. A thin mist would dance and vibrate. The sky would break out into livid blisters, which later on darkened and moved ponderously above the hills, splashed by flashes of lightning and echoing thunder.

Deep on the horizon, an enormous enraged breath. The peasants, caught in the fields, hurrying along with hoe on shoulder. The trees bent. Violently shaken by the now uninterrupted baying of the storm, a swift curtain of rain had overtaken them. At first a few warm unhurried drops, then, pierced by flashes of lightning, the black heavens had opened in an avalanche, a torrential deluge.

Bienaime, on his narrow porch with its railing protected by a projecting thatched roof, would look at his land, his good land, his streaming plants, his trees swaying in the chant of the wind and rain. The harvest would be good. He had labored in the sun for days at a time. This rain was his reward. He watched it affectionately as it fell in close-knitted threads, he heard it splash on the stone slab in front of the arbor. So much and so much corn, so many Congo beans, the pig fattened. That might mean a new jacket, a shirt, and perhaps neighbor Jean-Jacques's chestnut colt, if he would lower the price.

He had forgotten Delira. "Warm up the coffee, wife," he would say. Yes, he'd buy her a dress and a madras, too. He filled his short clay pipe. That was what living on good terms with the earth meant.

But all that had passed. Nothing remained now but a bitter taste. They were already dead beneath this dust, in these warm ashes that covered what formerly had been life. Oh, not an easy life, no, indeed! But they had persisted, and after struggling with the earth, after opening it, turning it over and over, moistening it with sweat, sowing it with seed as one does a woman, then came satisfaction: plants, fruit, many ears of corn.

He had just been thinking about Jean-Jacques and here, coming along the road, was Jean-Jacques, as old and worthless now as he, leading a skinny burro and letting its cord drag in the dust.

"Brother," he greeted him. And the other answered the same.

Jean-Jacques asked for news of Sister Delira.

Bienaime said, "How's Sister Lucia?"

And they thanked one another.

The burro had a large sore on its back and winced under the bite of flies.

"*Adieu, oui,*" said Jean-Jacques.

"*Adieu,* old man." Bienaime nodded.

He watched his neighbor plod on with his animal toward the watering place, that stagnant pool, that eye of mud covered by a greenish film, where all drank, men and beasts.

He's been gone so long, he must be dead now, she mused. Old Delira was thinking of her son, Manuel, who had left years ago to cut cane in Cuba. He must be dead now, in a foreign land, she thought again. He had said to her one last time, "Mama!" She had kissed him. She had taken in her arms this big fellow who had come from the depths of her flesh and blood, and had become this man to whom she whispered through her tears, "Go, my little one, may the Holy Virgin protect you!" And he had turned at the elbow of the road and disappeared. "Oh, son of my womb, sorrow of my womb, joy of my life, pain of my life! My boy, my only boy!"

She stopped grinding coffee, but remained squatting on the ground. She had no longer any tears to shed. It seemed to her that her heart had petrified in her breast and that she had been emptied of all life save that incurable torment that gripped her throat.

He was to return after the *zafra,* as the Spaniards call the harvest. But he hadn't come back. She had waited for him, but he hadn't come. Sometimes she would say to Bienaime, "I wonder where Manuel is?"

Bienaime wouldn't answer. He'd let his pipe go out. He'd walk away through the fields.

Later, she would again say to him, "Bienaime, papa, where's our boy?"

He would answer roughly, "Hush your mouth!" She would pity his trembling hands.

She emptied the drawer of the coffee mill, poured in more beans, and again took the handle. It wasn't hard work, yet she felt exhausted. It was all she could do to sit there motionless, her worn-out body given over to death that would in the end bring her to this dust.

She began to hum. It was like a groan, a moan from the soul, an infinite reproach to all the saints and to those deaf and blind African deities who did not hear her, who had turned away from her sorrow and her tribulations.

"O, Holy Virgin, in the name of the saints of the earth, in the name of the saints of the moon, of the saints of the stars, of the saints of the wind, in the name of the saints of the storm, protect if it be thy will, I pray thee, my son in foreign lands! O, Master of the Crossroads, open to him a road without danger! Amen!"

She hadn't heard Bienaime return. He sat down near her. On the side of the hill there was a dull redness as the sun sank behind the woods. Soon night would shroud the bitter earth in silence, drowning their misery in the shadow of sleep. Then dawn would rise with the husky crowing of cocks and day would begin again, hopeless as the day before.

✸ Discussion and Writing

1. Discuss the recurrent images that describe the landscape at the beginning of the story? Explain the connection between the old people and the landscape?
2. What is the importance of a *coumbite* for the villagers? Comment on Bienaime's feelings toward the past and its contrast to the present.
3. Explore the sensuous description of the rainy season, paying particular attention to the image of water. What does Roumain accomplish by using sexual imagery to describe farming?
4. What are the implications of the absence of Manuel?
5. Analyze the religious beliefs of Delira and Bienaime. How does each person handle Christian teachings? What does the writer suggest about the amalgam of African and Christian traditions?

✸ Research and Comparison

Examine Jacques Roumain's ideology and the reflection of his commitment to the Haitian people in *Masters of the Dew.*

Interdisciplinary Discussion Question: Examine the impact of the Haitian revolution—led by Toussant L'Ouverture—on the Caribbean consciousness.

Interdisciplinary Discussion Question: Research the political upheavals of the twentieth century in Haiti, taking into account the role of the United States and the Haitian elite.

Interdisciplinary Discussion Question: Research the African based religions that are practiced throughout the Caribbean and Latin America, especially in Brazil, paying particular attention to their importance in people's lives.

Joao Guimaraes Rosa
(1908–1967)
Brazil

Joao Guimaraes Rosa, born in a small ranch town in the interior district of Minas Gerais, Brazil, descended from an old upper-class family. It is said that when he was a young man practicing medicine in the most remote areas of the rural region southwest of the state capital of Belo Horizonte, he often accepted stories as payment. He also had a great love of and facility with language. Although he served as an army doctor during the 1930 revolution, he had already established a diplomatic career. As an attaché in Germany during World War II, when Brazil sided with the Allies, he was briefly interned in Baden-Baden, and then released in exchange for German diplomats. He subsequently served in various Latin American and European embassies until the last few years of his life, when he preferred to remain in Brazil.

A writer from his youth and a winner of a national prize for poetry in 1936, Guimaraes did not publish his first book, *Sagarana,* until 1946. The title is a melding of the Tupi word *rana* (in the manner of) and the Old Norse word *saga* (epic tale). A decade later he published a cycle of novellas and the major transforming novel, *Grande Sertao: Veredas* (The Devil to Pay in the Backlands, 1956). His work encompasses the material he gleaned from his patients and the storytellers of the *sertao,* or backland; from library research into the oral tradition; and from his studies in religion, philosophy, and the natural sciences. What the ground-breaking Brazilian novelist Machado de Assis did for nineteenth-century narrative, Joao Guimaraes Rosa did for twentieth: both, recognized as major American writers, revolutionized narrative prose.

The Third Bank of the River*

My father was a dutiful, orderly, straightforward man. And according to several reliable people of whom I inquired, he had had these qualities since adolescence or even childhood. By my own recollection, he was neither jollier nor more melancholy than the other men we knew. Maybe a little quieter. It was mother, not father, who ruled the house. She scolded us daily—my sister, my brother, and me. But it happened one day that father ordered a boat.

He was very serious about it. It was to be made specially for him, of mimosa wood. It was to be sturdy enough to last twenty or thirty years and just large enough for one person. Mother carried on plenty about it. Was her husband going to become a fisherman all of a sudden? Or a hunter? Father said nothing. Our house was less than a mile from the river, which around there was deep, quiet, and so wide you couldn't see across it.

I can never forget the day the rowboat was delivered. Father showed no joy or other emotion. He just put on his hat as he always did and said good-bye to us. He took along no food or bundle of any sort. We expected mother to rant and rave, but she didn't. She looked very pale and bit her lip, but all she said was:

"If you go away, stay away. Don't ever come back!"

---

*Translated by Barbara Shelby

Father made no reply. He looked gently at me and motioned me to walk along with him. I feared mother's wrath, yet I eagerly obeyed. We headed toward the river together. I felt bold and exhilarated, so much so that I said:

"Father, will you take me with you in your boat?"

He just looked at me, gave me his blessing, and, by a gesture, told me to go back. I made as if to do so but, when his back was turned, I ducked behind some bushes to watch him. Father got into the boat and rowed away. Its shadow slid across the water like a crocodile, long and quiet.

Father did not come back. Nor did he go anywhere, really. He just rowed and floated across and around, out there in the river. Everyone was appalled. What had never happened, what could not possibly happen, was happening. Our relatives, neighbors, and friends came over to discuss the phenomenon.

Mother was ashamed. She said little and conducted herself with great composure. As a consequence, almost everyone thought (though no one said it) that father had gone insane. A few, however, suggested that father might be fulfilling a promise he had made to God or to a saint, or that he might have some horrible disease, maybe leprosy, and that he left for the sake of the family, at the same time wishing to remain fairly near them.

Travelers along the river and people living near the bank on one side or the other reported that father never put foot on land, by day or night. He just moved about on the river, solitary, aimless, like a derelict. Mother and our relatives agreed that the food which he had doubtless hidden in the boat would soon give out and that then he would either leave the river and travel off somewhere (which would be at least a little more respectable) or he would repent and come home.

How far from the truth they were! Father had a secret source of provisions: me. Every day I stole food and brought it to him. The first night after he left, we all lit fires on the shore and prayed and called to him. I was deeply distressed and felt a need to do something more. The following day I went down to the river with a loaf of corn bread, a bunch of bananas, and some bricks of raw brown sugar. I waited impatiently a long, long hour. Then I saw the boat, far off, alone, gliding almost imperceptibly on the smoothness of the river. Father was sitting in the bottom of the boat. He saw me but he did not row toward me or make any gesture. I showed him the food and then I placed it in a hollow rock on the river bank; it was safe there from animals, rain, and dew. I did this day after day, on and on and on. Later I learned, to my surprise, that mother knew what I was doing and left food around where I could easily steal it. She had a lot of feelings she didn't show.

Mother sent for her brother to come and help on the farm and in business matters. She had the schoolteacher come and tutor us children at home because of the time we had lost. One day, at her request, the priest put on his vestments, went down to the shore, and tried to exorcise the devils that had got into my father. He shouted that father had a duty to cease his unholy obstinacy. Another day she arranged to have two soldiers come and try to frighten him. All to no avail. My father went by in the distance, sometimes so far away he could barely be seen. He never replied to anyone and no one ever got close to him. When some newspapermen came in a launch to take his picture, father headed his boat to the other side of the river and into the marshes, which he knew like the palm of his hand but in which other people quickly got lost. There in his private maze, which extended for miles, with heavy foliage overhead and rushes on all sides, he was safe.

We had to get accustomed to the idea of father's being out on the river. We had to but we couldn't, we never could. I think I was the only one who understood to some degree what our father wanted and what he did not want. The thing I could not understand at all was how he stood the hardship. Day and night, in sun and rain, in heat and in the terrible midyear cold spells, with his old hat on his head and very little other clothing, week after week, month after month, year after year, unheedful of the waste and emptiness in which his life was slipping by. He never set foot on earth or grass, on isle or mainland shore. No doubt he sometimes tied up the boat at a secret place, perhaps at the tip of some island, to get a little sleep. He never lit a fire or even struck a match and he had no flashlight. He took only a small part of the food that I left in the hollow rock—not enough, it seemed to me, for survival. What could his state of health have been? How about the continual drain on his energy, pulling and pushing the oars to control the boat? And how did he survive the annual floods, when the river rose and swept along with it all sorts of dangerous objects—branches of trees, dead bodies of animals—that might suddenly crash against his little boat?

He never talked to a living soul. And we never talked about him. We just thought. No, we could never put our father out of mind. If for a short time we seemed to, it was just a lull from which we would be sharply awakened by the realization of his frightening situation.

My sister got married, but mother didn't want a wedding party. It would have been a sad affair, for we thought of him every time we ate some especially tasty food. Just as we thought of him in our cozy beds on a cold, stormy night—out there, alone and unprotected, trying to bail out the boat with only his hands and a gourd. Now and then someone would say that I was getting to look more and more like my father. But I knew that by then his hair and beard must have been shaggy and his nails long. I pictured him thin and sickly, black with hair and sunburn, and almost naked despite the articles of clothing I occasionally left for him.

He didn't seem to care about us at all. But I felt affection and respect for him, and, whenever they praised me because I had done something good, I said:

"My father taught me to act that way."

It wasn't exactly accurate but it was a truthful sort of lie. As I said, father didn't seem to care about us. But then why did he stay around there? Why didn't he go up the river or down the river, beyond the possibility of seeing us or being seen by us? He alone knew the answer.

My sister had a baby boy. She insisted on showing father his grandson. One beautiful day we all went down to the river bank, my sister in her white wedding dress, and she lifted the baby high. Her husband held a parasol above them. We shouted to father and waited. He did not appear. My sister cried; we all cried in each other's arms.

My sister and her husband moved far away. My brother went to live in a city. Times changed, with their usual imperceptible rapidity. Mother finally moved too; she was old and went to live with her daughter. I remained behind, a leftover. I could never think of marrying. I just stayed there with the impedimenta of my life. Father, wandering alone and forlorn on the river, needed me. I knew he needed me, although he never even told me why he was doing it. When I put the question to people bluntly and insistently, all they told me was that they heard that father had explained it to the man who made the boat. But now this man was dead and nobody knew or remembered anything. There was just some foolish talk, when the rains were especially severe and persistent, that my father was wise like Noah and had the boat built in anticipation of a new flood; I dimly remember people saying this. In any case, I would not condemn my father for what he was doing. My hair was beginning to turn gray.

I have only sad things to say. What bad had I done, what was my great guilt? My father always away and his absence always with me. And the river, always the river, perpetually renewing itself. The river, always. I was beginning to suffer from old age, in which life is just a sort of lingering. I had attacks of illness and of anxiety. I had a nagging rheumatism. And he? Why, why was he doing it? He must have been suffering terribly. He was so old. One day, in his failing strength, he might let the boat capsize; or he might let the current carry it downstream, on and on, until it plunged over the waterfall to the boiling turmoil below. It pressed upon my heart. He was out there and I was forever robbed of my peace. I am guilty of I know not what, and my pain is an open wound inside me. Perhaps I would know—if things were different. I began to guess what was wrong.

Out with it! Had I gone crazy? No, in our house that word was never spoken, never through all the years. No one called anybody crazy, for nobody is crazy. Or maybe everybody. All I did was go there and wave a handkerchief. So he would be more likely to see me. I was in complete command of myself. I waited. Finally he appeared in the distance, there, then over there, a vague shape sitting in the back of the boat. I called to him several times. And I said what I was so eager to say, to state formally and under oath. I said it as loud as I could:

"Father, you have been out there long enough. You are old. . . . Come back, you don't have to do it anymore. . . . Come back and I'll go instead. Right now, if you want. Any time. I'll get into the boat. I'll take your place."

And when I had said this my heart beat more firmly. He heard me. He stood up. He maneuvered with his oars and headed the boat toward me. He had accepted my offer. And suddenly I trembled, down deep. For he had raised his arm and waved—the first time in so many, so many years. And I couldn't . . . In terror, my hair on end, I ran, I fled madly. For he seemed to come from another world. And I'm begging forgiveness, begging, begging.

I experienced the dreadful sense of cold that comes from deadly fear, and I became ill. Nobody ever saw or heard about him again. Am I a man, after such a failure? I am what never should have been. I am what must be silent. I know it is too late. I must stay in the deserts and unmarked plains of my life, and I fear I shall shorten it. But when death comes I want them to take me and put me in a little boat in this perpetual water between the long shores; and I, down the river, lost in the river, inside the river . . . the river . . .

❋ Discussion and Writing

1. Examine the significance of the opening line. Does the story support this statement?
2. Examine the symbolism of the river "deep, quiet, and so wide you couldn't see across it." What does "the third bank" symbolize? What is the narrator searching for?
3. Is the story realistic or fantastic? What is the function of the other characters—family and townspeople?
4. Analyze the father-son relationship: how does the son view the father's ordeal; what binds them; what is the source of the son's guilt; how do you interpret the son's last action?
5. Guimaraes said, "As a physician, I came to know the mystical greatness of suffering; as a rebel, the value of consciousness; and as a soldier, the importance of the proximity of death." Examine whether any or all of the three aspects of life are manifested in the story.

Juan Bosch
(b. 1909)
Dominican Republic

Juan Bosch, whose parents came from poor families that prized reading and music, was the son of a Catalan father and Puerto Rican mother. Bosch spent much of his early childhood in the fertile valley of the Cibao in the Dominican Republic, where his maternal grandfather was a farmer. (The Cibao, a Taino word for plain, is a region to which people from other Caribbean islands were drawn because of its fertility.) His grandfather was the first in the area to use a plow, and he read voraciously, including an agricultural magazine that introduced him to new modes of farming. He retained an especially beloved position in his grandson's memory. Bosch also never forgot the *campesinos* among whom he grew up. Nor did he forget an elementary teacher who inspired him, a musician who insisted on the precise use of language. This teacher believed fervently in his country and held a philosophically committed world view, both of which served Bosch well. When he was still a child, Bosch began writing stories, editing little newspapers, and illustrating books he wrote. He left Rio Verde in the Cibao and continued his education in La Vega and Santo Domingo, where he was one of the group of writers who called themselves "La Cueva."

He first published his stories in 1929; in 1930, Rafael Leonidas Trujillo seized power by means of a military coup, and Bosch became politically engaged. From the beginning, in both his political career and his writing, he denounced the impoverishment of the Dominican *campesinos;* social and economic inequities; and the abuse of power. Compelled to flee the country in the mid-1930s, he continued his protest against the ruthlessness of the Trujillo dictatorship. It was early in his 24-year exile that he founded and served as president (1939–1966) of Partido Revolucionario Dominicano (Dominican Revolutionary Party). He returned to the Dominican Republic after Trujillo's assassination in 1961 and was elected president in 1963: within seven months he was deposed by a military coup. Since that time, he has taught political science, has remained politically active, and has turned to writing nonfiction as a mode more suited to explaining social and economic issues, to examining what he calls "the reality of man and his problems." These have been the central issues of all his work.

*The Beautiful Soul of Don Damian**

Don Damian, with a temperature of almost 104, passed into a coma. His soul felt extremely uncomfortable, almost as if it were being roasted alive; therefore it began to withdraw, gathering itself into his heart. The soul had an infinite number of tentacles, like an octopus with innumerable feet, some of them in the veins and others, very thin, in the smaller blood vessels. Little by little it pulled out those feet, with the result that Don Damian turned cold

*Translated by Lysander Kemp

and pallid. His hands grew cold first, then his arms and legs, while his face became so deathly white that the change was observed by the people who stood around his bed. The nurse, alarmed, said it was time to send for the doctor. The soul heard her, and thought: "I'll have to hurry, or the doctor will make me stay in here till I burn to a crisp."

It was dawn. A faint trickle of light came in through the window to announce the birth of a new day. The soul, peering out of Don Damian's mouth, which was partly open to let in a little air, noticed the light and told itself that if it hoped to escape it would have to act promptly, because in a few minutes somebody would see it and prevent it from leaving its master's body. The soul of Don Damian was quite ignorant about certain matters: for instance, it had no idea that once free it would be completely invisible.

There was a rustling of skirts around the patient's luxurious bed, and a murmur of voices which the soul had to ignore, occupied as it was in escaping from its prison. The nurse came back into the room with a hypodermic syringe in her hand.

"Dear God, dear God," the old housemaid cried, "don't let it be too late!"

It was too late. At the precise moment that the needle punctured Don Damian's forearm, the soul drew its last tentacles out of his mouth, reflecting as it did so that the injection would be a waste of money. An instant later there were cries and running footsteps, and as somebody—no doubt the housemaid, since it could hardly have been Don Damian's wife or mother-in-law—began to wail at the bedside, the soul leaped into the air, straight up to the Bohemian glass lamp that hung in the middle of the ceiling. There it collected its wits and looked down: Don Damian's corpse was now a spoiled yellow, with features almost as hard and transparent as the Bohemian glass; the bones of his face seemed to have grown, and his skin had taken on a ghastly sheen. His wife, his mother-in-law, and the nurse fluttered around him, while the housemaid sobbed with her gray head buried in the covers. The soul knew exactly what each one of them was thinking and feeling, but it did not want to waste time observing them. The light was growing brighter every moment, and it was afraid it would be noticed up there on its perch. Suddenly the mother-in-law took her daughter by the arm and led her out into the hall, to talk to her in a low voice. The soul heard her say, "Don't behave so shamelessly. You've got to show some grief."

"When people start coming, Mama," the daughter whispered.

"No, Right now. Don't forget the nurse—she'll tell everybody everything that happens."

The new widow ran to the bed as if mad with grief. "Oh Damian, Damian!" she cried. "Damian, my dearest, how can I live without you?"

A different, less worldly soul would have been astounded, but Don Damian's merely admired the way she was playing the part. Don Damian himself had done some skillful acting on occasion, especially when it was necessary to act—as he put it—"in defense of my interests." His wife was now "defending her interests." She was still young and attractive, whereas Don Damian was well past sixty. She had had a lover when he first knew her, and his soul had suffered some very disagreeable moments because of its late master's jealousy. The soul recalled an episode of a few months earlier, when the wife had declared, "You can't stop me from seeing him. You know perfectly well I married you for your money."

To which Don Damian had replied that with his money he had purchased the right not to be made ridiculous. It was a thoroughly unpleasant scene—the mother-in-law had interfered, as usual, and there were threats of a divorce—but it was made even more unpleasant by the fact that the discussion had to be cut short when some important guests arrived. Both husband and wife greeted the company with charming smiles and exquisite manners, which only the soul could appreciate at their true value.

The soul was still up there on the lamp, recalling these events, when the priest arrived almost at a run. Nobody could imagine why he should appear at that hour, because the sun was scarcely up and anyhow he had visited the sick man during the night. He attempted to explain.

"I had a premonition. I was afraid Don Damian would pass away without confessing."

The mother-in-law was suspicious. "But, Father, didn't he confess last night?"

She was referring to the fact that the priest had been alone with Don Damian, behind a closed door, for nearly an hour. Everybody assumed that the sick man had confessed, but that was not what took place. The soul knew it was not, of course; it also knew why the priest had arrived at such a strange time. The theme of that long conference had been rather arid, spiritually: the priest wanted Don Damian to leave a large sum of money toward the new church being built in the city, while Don Damian wanted to leave an even larger sum than that which the priest was seeking—but to a hospital. They could not agree, the priest left, and when he returned to his room he discovered that his watch was missing.

The soul overwhelmed by its new power, now it was free, to know things that had taken place in its absence, and to divine what people were thinking or were about to do. It was aware that the priest had said to himself: "I remember I took out my watch at Don Damian's house, to see what time it was. I must have left it there." Hence it was also aware that his return visit had nothing to do with the Kingdom of Heaven.

"No, he didn't confess," the priest said, looking straight at the mother-in-law. "We didn't get around to a confession last night, so we decided I would come back the first thing in the morning, to hear confession and perhaps"—his voice grew solemn—"to administer the last rites. Unfortunately I've come too late." He glanced toward the gilt tables on either side of the bed in hopes of seeing his watch on one or the other.

The old housemaid, who had served Don Damian for more than forty years, looked up with streaming eyes.

"It doesn't make any difference," she said, "God forgive me for saying so. He had such a beautiful soul he didn't need to confess." She nodded her head. "Don Damian had a very beautiful soul."

Hell, now, that was something! The soul had never even dreamed that it was beautiful. Its master had done some rather rare things in his day, of course, and since he had always been a fine example of a well-to-do gentleman, perfectly dressed and exceedingly shrewd in his dealings with the bank, his soul had not had time to think about its beauty or its possible ugliness. It remembered, for instance, how its master had commanded it to feel at ease after he and his lawyer found a way to take possession of a debtor's house, although the debtor had nowhere else to live; or when, with the help of jewels and hard cash (this last for her education, or her sick mother), he persuaded a lovely young girl from the poorer sector to visit him in the sumptuous apartment he maintained. But was it beautiful, or was it ugly?

The soul was quite sure that only a few moments had passed since it withdrew from its master's veins; and probably even less time had passed than it imagined, because everything had happened so quickly and in so much confusion. The doctor had said as he left, well before midnight: "The fever is likely to rise toward morning. If it does, watch him carefully, and send for me if anything happens."

Was the soul to let itself be roasted to death? Its vital center, if that is the proper term, had been located close to Don Damian's intestines, which were radiating fire, and if it had stayed in his body it would have perished like a broiled chicken. But actually how much time had passed since it left? Very little, certainly, for it still felt hot, in spite of the faint coolness in the dawn air. The soul decided that the change in climate between the innards of its late master and the Bohemian glass of the lamp had been very slight. But change or no change, what about that statement by the old housemaid? "Beautiful," she said . . . and she was a truthful woman who loved her master because she loved him, not because he was rich or generous or important. The soul found rather less sincerity in the remarks that followed.

"Why, of course he had a beautiful soul," the priest said.

"'Beautiful' doesn't begin to describe it," the mother-in-law asserted.

The soul turned to look at her and saw that as she spoke she was signaling to her daughter with her eyes. They contained both a command and scolding, as if to say: "Start crying again, you idiot. Do you want the priest to say you were happy your husband died?" The daughter understood the signal, and broke out into tearful wailing.

"Nobody ever had such a beautiful soul! Damian, how much I loved you!"

The soul could not stand any more: it wanted to know for certain, without losing another moment, whether or not it was truly beautiful, and it wanted to get away from those hypocrites. It leaped in the direction of the bathroom, where there was a full-length mirror, calculating the distance so as to fall noiselessly on the rug. It did not know it was weightless as well as invisible. It was delighted to find that nobody noticed it, and ran quickly to look at itself in front of the mirror.

But good God, what had happened? In the first place, it had been accustomed, during more than sixty years, to look out through the eyes of Don Damian, and those eyes were over five feet from the ground; also, it was accustomed to seeing his lively face, his clear eyes, his shining gray hair, the arrogance that puffed out his chest and lifted his head, the expensive clothes in which he dressed. What it saw now was nothing at all like that, but a strange figure hardly a foot tall, pale, cloud-gray, with no definite form. Where it should have had two legs and two feet like the body of Don Damian, it was a hideous cluster of tentacles like those of an octopus, but irregular, some shorter than others, some thinner, and all of them seemingly made of dirty smoke, of some impalpable mud that looked transparent but was not; they were limp and drooping and powerless, and stupendously ugly. The soul of Don Damian felt lost. Nevertheless, it got up the courage to look higher. It had no waist. In fact, it had no body, no neck, nothing: where the tentacles joined there was merely a sort of ear sticking out on one side, looking like a bit of rotten apple peel, and a clump of rough hairs on the other side, some twisted, some straight. But that was not the worst, and neither was the strange grayish-yellow light it gave off: the worst was the fact that its mouth was a shapeless cavity like a hole poked in a rotten fruit, a horrible and sickening thing . . . and in the depths of this hole an eye shone, its only eye, staring out of the shadows with an expression of terror and treachery! Yet the women and the priest in the next room, around the bed in which Don Damian's corpse lay, had said he had a beautiful soul!

"How can I go out in the street looking like this?" it asked itself, groping in a black tunnel of confusion.

What should it do? The doorbell rang. Then the nurse said: "It's the doctor, ma'am. I'll let him in."

Don Damian's wife promptly began to wail again, invoking her dead husband and lamenting the cruel solitude in which he had left her.

The soul, paralyzed in front of its true image, knew it was lost. It had been used to hiding in its refuge in the tall body of Don Damian; it had been used to everything, including the obnoxious smell of the intestines, the heat of the stomach, the annoyance of chills and fevers. Then it heard the doctor's greeting and the mother-in-law's voice crying: "Oh, Doctor, what a tragedy it is!"

"Come, now, let's get a grip on ourselves."

The soul peeped into the dead man's room. The women were gathered around the bed, and the priest was praying at its foot. The soul measured the distance and jumped, with a facility it had not known it had, landing on the pillow like a thing of air or like a strange animal that could move noiselessly and invisibly. Don Damian's mouth was still partly open. It was cold as ice, but that was not important. The soul tumbled inside and began to thrust its tentacles into place. It was still settling in when it heard the doctor say to the mother-in-law: "Just one moment, please."

The soul could still see the doctor, though not clearly. He approached the body of Don Damian, took his wrist, seemed to grow excited, put his ear to his chest and left it there a moment. Then he opened his bag and took out a stethoscope. With great deliberation he fitted the knobs into his ears and placed the button on the spot where Don Damian's heart was. He grew even more excited, put away the stethoscope, and took out a hypodermic syringe. He told the nurse to fill it, while he himself fastened a small rubber tube around Don Damian's arm above the elbow, working with the air of a magician who is about to perform a sensational trick. Apparently these preparations alarmed the old housemaid.

"But why are you doing all that if the poor thing is dead?"

The doctor stared at her loftily, and what he said was intended not only for her but for everybody.

"Science is science, and my obligation is to do whatever I can to bring Don Damian back to life. You don't find souls as beautiful as his just anywhere, and I can't let him die until we've tried absolutely everything."

This brief speech, spoken so calmly and grandly, upset the wife. It was not difficult to note a cold glitter in her eyes and a certain quaver in her voice.

"But . . . but isn't he dead?"

The soul was almost back in its body again, and only three tentacles still groped for the old veins they had inhabited for so many years. The attention with which it directed these tentacles into their right places did not prevent it from hearing that worried question.

The doctor did not answer. He took Don Damian's forearm and began to chafe it with his hand. The soul felt the warmth of life surrounding it, penetrating it, filling the veins it had abandoned to escape from burning up. At the same moment, the doctor jabbed the needle into a vein in the arm, untied the ligature above the elbow, and began to push the plunger. Little by little, in soft surges, the warmth of life rose to Don Damian's skin.

"A miracle," the priest murmured. Suddenly he turned pale and let his imagination run wild. The contribution to the new church would now be a sure thing. He would point out to Don Damian, during his convalescence, how he had returned from the dead because of the prayers he had said for him. He would tell him. "The Lord heard me, Don Damian, and gave you back to us." How could he deny the contribution after that?

The wife, just as suddenly, felt that her brain had gone blank. She looked nervously at her husband's face and turned toward her mother. They were both stunned, mute, almost terrified.

The doctor, however, was smiling. He was thoroughly satisfied with himself, although he attempted not to show it.

"He's saved, he's saved," the old housemaid cried, "thanks to God and you." She was weeping and clutching the doctor's hands. "He's saved, he's alive again. Don Damian can never pay you for what you've done."

The doctor was thinking that Don Damian had more than enough money to pay him, but that is not what he said. What he said was: "I'd have done the same thing even if he didn't have a penny. It was my duty, my duty to society, to save a soul as beautiful as his."

He was speaking to the housemaid, but again his words were intended for the others, in the hope they would repeat them to the sick man as soon as he was well enough to act on them.

The soul of Don Damian, tired of so many lies, decided to sleep. A moment later, Don Damian sighed weakly and moved his head on the pillow.

"He'll sleep for hours now," the doctor said. "He must have absolute quiet."

And to set a good example, he tiptoed out of the room.

✸ Discussion and Writing

1. Examine the role of the housemaid in relation to that of the other characters.
2. Discuss the use of death to create humor. What does the writer satirize?
3. What are the distinguishing traits of the body and soul of Don Damian? What is implied by their separation and reintegration? Why is the soul called beautiful? Comment on the reversal of conventional belief regarding the need of the body for the soul.
4. Analyze the manipulation of time and space in the story.

✸ Research and Comparison

Interdisciplinary Discussion Question: Research the twentieth-century history of the Dominican Republic and the role of Juan Bosch in its politics.

Juan Carlos Onetti
(b. 1909)
Uruguay

Juan Carlos Onetti was born in Montevideo, Uruguay; his ancestors were Brazilian, Uruguayan, and Irish. He never finished high school, but worked at various jobs: as a night porter, a waiter, a ticket-seller at the soccer stadium. And he began writing. After the publication of his first novel in 1939, he gained a reputation among a small group of Argentine and Uruguayan intellectuals. Over the years, he worked as a journalist and continued to produce highly regarded novels and stories. The generation of writers that followed has acknowledged the influence of his fiction on their narrative techniques, but Onetti did not receive wider recognition until the 1960s. He manipulated the tough language and milieu of the River Plate region, evolving a dark, often darkly comic, sense of place to explore human experience. If he has presented its absurdities, he nonetheless has projected a sense of compassion for the suffering, alienation, frustration, or incomprehension of his characters.

During the early 1970s the Uruguayan government imprisoned him, along with fellow members on a literary jury who had awarded a prize to a novel about a sexual relationship between a member of the military and a member of the Tupamaru National Liberation Front.[†] (The sponsoring newspaper was closed and its editors jailed also.) The united efforts of writers from around the world won Onetti's release, and he left Uruguay.

A Dream Come True*

The joke had been thought up by Blanes; he used to come into my office when I had one—or into the café when times were bad—and motionless on the rug, leaning a fist on my desk, his bright-colored tie fastened to his shirt by a gold clip and his square clean-shaven head whose dark eyes seemed unable to fix on anything for more than a minute, soon blurring as if Blanes were falling asleep or remembered some pure moment of love in his life, doubtless imaginary, his head stripped of any superfluous detail leaning back against a wall covered with photos and posters, he would hear me out and then comment, mouthing each word: "Of course, you've ruined yourself producing *Hamlet*." Or else, "Yes, we know you've always martyred yourself for art and if it weren't for your insane love of *Hamlet* . . . " While I spent all these years putting up with those God-forsaken people, authors and actors, actresses and theater-owners, reviewers and my own family, friends, plus all their mistresses, all that time losing and making money that only God and I knew would again be lost the following season, existing with that drop of water falling on one's bare skull, that jab in the ribs, that bittersweet taste, that scoffing from Blanes that I couldn't quite understand.

"Yes, of course. You've been driven to acts of madness by that boundless love of *Hamlet* . . . "

If I had asked him what he meant the first time, if I had confessed that I knew no more about *Hamlet* than how to figure the cost of a play starting

---

[†]A guerrilla movement opposing repressive governmental policies.
Translated by Ines de Torres Kinnell.

with its first reading, the joke would have ended right there. But I feared the endless digs my question would spark and I merely grimaced and sent him off. And so I was able to live twenty years without knowing what *Hamlet* was, without reading it, but reading in Blanes's face and the rocking of his head that *Hamlet* was art, pure art, great art and knowing also, although it slowly came to me unawares, that the play also had something to do with an actor or an actress, in this case it was always an actress wearing tight black clothes over absurd hips, a skull, a cemetery, a duel, vengeance, and a young girl who drowns. As well as with W. Shakespeare.

This is why now, only now, with my blond wig parted in the middle, which I wear even to bed, my false teeth which fit so poorly I lisp and babble like a baby, in the library of this rest home for penniless theatrical types, which they refer to by a more pretentious name, I found the book, very small and bound in dark blue with the word *Hamlet* inlaid in gold. I sank down into an armchair without opening the book, resolved never to open it or read one single line, thinking about Blanes, how in this way I could take revenge on him for his joke and remembering the evening Blanes came searching for me in that provincial hotel and after listening to me while he smoked and looked up at the ceiling or at the people wandering into the lounge, opened his lips in order to say, right in front of that poor madwoman:

"It's unbelievable. A man like you who went bankrupt producing *Hamlet* . . . "

I had asked him over to the hotel to offer him a role in some crazy one-nighter titled, I believe, "Dream Come True." The cast of that insane play called for some anonymous young man and Blanes was the only one who could play it since, when the woman came to see me, he and I were the only two left, the rest of the company having escaped to Buenos Aires.

The woman had stopped by the hotel at noon, but as I was asleep she returned at the hour the midday siesta ended in that hot province, when I had found the coolest corner of the dining room where I was eating some breaded cutlet and drinking some white wine—the only drinkable kind around. When I first spotted her, motionless within the hot curtained arch-way, her eyes widening in the darkened dining room, and after the waiter pointed out my table and she made a straight line for it, her skirt whirling the dust up, I had no idea what lay within that woman, no idea of that thing like a white and flabby ribbon of madness that she unravelled, gently tugging at it like some bandage on the wound of past, lonely years, which she now came to bind me in, like some mummy, me and a few of those days spent in that boring place, crowded with fat and drab people. But something in her smile even then made me uneasy, and I couldn't stop staring at her little uneven teeth which recalled some child asleep and breathing with its mouth open. Her hair, almost totally gray, was braided and wrapped around her head and her clothes were out-of-date, somehow befitting someone or something younger than herself. Her skirt, which reached down to her boot-like shoes, was long and dark and floated out as she walked, settling again only to tremble once more at her next step. Her tight-fitting blouse had lace on it and a large cameo was pinned between her uplifted, young breasts; finally the blouse and skirt were both joined and divided by a rose at her waist, probably artificial, now that I think of it, a flower with a huge center and drooping on a stiff stem which seemed to threaten her stomach.

The woman was around fifty years old. What was impossible to forget, what I feel even now as I remember her walking toward my corner in the dining room, was that feeling of a young girl belonging to some past century who had fallen asleep and had just now awakened, her hair a bit rumpled, barely aged, but one who could at any time, in an instant, become her age and silently collapse before me, consumed by those innumerable days. Her smile was ugly to look at, for while it expressed her ignorance of standing on the edge of aging and sudden death, yet it understood—or at least those bared teeth expressed—the hideous decay that threatened her. It was all there, in the half-light of the dining room. I awkwardly settled my silverware beside my plate and stood up.

"Are you Mr. Langman, the theater producer?"

I nodded, smiled and asked her to join me. She refused to order anything. With the table now separating us, I glanced at the whole shape of her mouth and the lightly painted lips, from whose very center her voice hummed out, with a slight Castilian accent, slipping out between the unmatched teeth. Her small quiet eyes, widening to see better, revealed nothing to me. I could only wait for her to speak, and I thought that whatever kind of woman and life her words evoked would fit her strange appearance, and then the strangeness would disappear.

"I wanted to talk to you about a play," she said. "I mean I have a play . . ."

I thought she'd go on but she stopped and paused for me to say something, smiling and waiting for my words in an unshakable silence. She waited very calmly, her hands folded on her lap. I pushed my plate aside and ordered coffee. I offered her a cigarette but she motioned with her head and smiled, meaning she didn't smoke. I lit mine and began talking, trying to shake her off, gently, but at once and permanently, even though I felt compelled, I don't know why, to behave slyly.

"Madame, I'm so sorry. It's quite difficult, you know. Is this your first play? Yes? Of course. And what is the name of your work?"

"No, it has no name," she answered. "It's so hard to explain. It's not what you think. Of course, one could call it *The Dream, The Dream Come True, A Dream Come True.*"

By now, I was certain she was mad and I felt more self-confident. "Good. *A Dream Come True.* Not bad. Titles are very important. I've always had, you might say, a personal yet selfless interest in giving a hand to beginners. Yes, to instill new values in our national theater. I need not mention that gratitude is the last thing I reap. Madame, there are many who took their first step on our major stages, thanks to me, many who now pocket unbelievable royalties from their plays in our capital city and yearly walk off with some prize. No longer do they remember how they came almost begging, to me . . . "

Even the young busboy standing way off in the corner of the dining room near the icebox, trying to fight off the flies and heat with his dishcloth, could see that my words meant nothing to that strange creature. Turning away from the warmth of my coffee cup, I threw her one last look, and said: "The point is, Madame, you've probably heard that our season here has been a catastrophe. We've had to close down and I've just stayed on in order to settle a few personal matters. I'll also be leaving for Buenos Aires next week. I was wrong, that's all. Even though I gave in and gave them a season of farces, this place isn't ready for us—you see what has happened. So . . . Now, well, we could do one thing, Madame. If you would give me a copy of your play, I'll see whether in Buenos Aires . . . Is it three acts?" I now played her game and fell silent, forcing her to say something. I leaned over, slowly rubbing the tip of my cigaret against the ashtray. She blinked.

"What?"

"Your play, Madame. *A Dream Come True.* Are there three acts?"

"No, there are no acts."

"Well, scenes. Yes, it's the new thing now . . . "

"I don't have a copy. It's nothing I've written . . . " she went on. The time had come to leave.

"I'll give you my Buenos Aires address and when you get it written down . . . "

Her body sagged and hunched over, but her head lifted and I saw the same smile. I paused, positive that she would now go, but a moment later she brushed her hand over her face and continued. "No, it's not what you think. The thing is a moment, you could call it a scene, and nothing happens. Like this moment, here in this dining room, might be acted, I'd leave and that would be all. No," she went on, "there really isn't any plot, just some people on a street, some houses and two cars that go by. I'm there and a man, and some woman who comes out of the doorway of a store across the street and gives him a glass of beer. There's no one else, just us three. The man crosses the street toward the woman with the pitcher of beer and then crosses back and sits down near me at the same table he was at in the beginning."

She was silent for a moment and then smiling, neither at me nor at the half-opened linen cabinet behind me in the wall, she concluded: "Do you understand?"

I sidestepped again, remembering something about experimental theater, mentioning it and explaining how impossible it was to do anything like real art in such a place as we now found ourselves. No one would go to the theater to see something like her play. Perhaps I alone in the entire province was capable of understanding the meaning of her work, the sense behind the action, the car symbolism and the woman who offers a "tumbler" of beer to the man who crosses the street and then comes back to her, "near you, Madame."

She stared at me and there was something in her expression that reminded me of the way Blanes looked when he had to ask me for money and then talk of *Hamlet:* a hint of pity but mainly scorn and dislike,

"That's not the point, Mr. Langman," she said. "Only I wish to see it, no one else, no audience. Myself and the actors, nothing more. I wish to see it once. But that one performance must be done just as I will describe it to you and you must do just as I say, nothing else, Agreed? Well then, please tell me how much it may cost and I shall pay you."

It was hopeless to continue babbling on about experimental drama or similar stuff, face to face with this madwoman who now opened her purse and pulled out two fifty-peso bills. "With this you can hire the actors and take care of our preliminary expenses; later on you can let me know how much more you need." So, I, starving for money, unable to escape that damned hole until someone in Buenos Aires answered my letters and mailed me some pesos, put on my best smile, nodded several times and folded the bills carefully before putting them away in my jacket pocket.

"Don't worry, Madame. I believe I understand the sort of thing you . . . " As I spoke I couldn't look at her; I was remembering Blanes, how I hated seeing that same humiliating scorn on her face. "I'll take care of the matter this very afternoon and if we could meet again . . . tonight? Yes, right here. By then we'll have our leading man and you can explain the scene in greater detail and we'll get it all arranged; just how *Dream, A Dream Come True* . . . ?"

Maybe she was simply mad or maybe she also knew, as I knew, that I was incapable of taking off with her hundred pesos, because she didn't ask for a receipt, it didn't seem to cross her mind, and after shaking my hand, she left. She moved out of that dining room with her skirt swirling and braking against the motion of each step, walking tall and out into the heat of the street as one returning to the warmth of a sleep which had lasted countless years and which had shielded her tainted youth from collapsing into rot.

I found Blanes in some dark, messy room, whose brick walls showed through the paint, sprawled behind some green plants, in the damp heat of the late afternoon. The hundred pesos were still in my pocket; until I found Blanes, until I got him to help me give that madwoman her money's worth, I wasn't going to spend one cent of it. I woke him up and waited patiently while he bathed, shaved, lay down and then once more got up to drink a glass of milk which meant he had gotten drunk the night before. Collapsing once again on his bed, he lit a cigarette, still refusing to listen and even after I had pulled up the remains of some dresser chair I'd been sitting in and leaned forward seriously, prepared to present my plan, he stopped me, saying: "First, take a look at that ceiling."

The ceiling, held up by two or three moldy beams, was made of mud tiles and long dried-up bamboo of unknown origin.

"Okay. Let's have it," he said.

I described the whole thing but Blanes kept on interrupting, laughing, insisting it was either all a lie I had made up or else someone had sent the woman as a joke. Then he asked me to explain all of it and the matter was finally settled when I offered half of whatever was left over after expenses. I told him that I really didn't know what the deal was, what it involved nor what the hell that woman wanted from us, but the fifty pesos were ours and now we could either both take off for Buenos Aires, or at least I could go alone if he chose to stay and go on sleeping. He laughed, quieted down and then asked for twenty out of the fifty pesos I told him I had received. So right there I was forced to hand over ten, something I soon regretted because that evening when he appeared in the dining room of the hotel, he was already drunk. Leaning his head over a little plate of ice and smiling, he said: "You never learn, do you? The millionaire patron of B.A. or anywhere in the world where a whisper of art is heard. A man, bankrupted a hundred times staging *Hamlet,* is now gambling everything on an unknown genius—in a corset."

But when she arrived, when that woman appeared from behind my shoulders, all dressed in black, veiled, a small umbrella hooked on her wrist and a watch hanging from a gold chain around her neck, and stretching her hand out to Blanes said hello with that special smile, gentler under those electric lights, he stopped nagging me and said: "Ah, Madame, the very gods have guided you to Langman. A man who has sacrificed hundreds of thousands just to give us *Hamlet* in its true form."

Now, as she looked from one to the other, it seemed she was the one mocking; then she became thoughtful and said she was in a hurry, that she would explain everything until the smallest doubt was cleared up and would only return when everything was ready. Beneath the soft yet clear light, the woman's face and everything that glowed on her body, parts of her dress, the nails on one ungloved hand, the umbrella handle, the watch on its chain, all seemed to return to some reality, protected against suffering the brilliant sunshine. It all made me feel relatively relaxed and throughout the rest of the evening I ceased thinking of her as mad, I forgot the pervading odor of fraud in the whole business, and I felt quite calm as if we were in the middle of some every-day, normal business matter. In fact, there was little for me to worry about now that Blanes was there, acting polite, still drinking, and talking to her as if they had already met several times, ordering her a whiskey which she changed for a cup of linden tea. So that finally, whatever she had come to tell me, she ended up telling him, and I made no objection: with Blanes as the leading man the more he understood of the play, the better it would all work out. The woman's instructions were the following (her voice sounded different as she talked to Blanes and although she never looked at him but spoke with her eyes lowered, I felt she was speaking to him in a very private way, as if confessing to something intimate to her life, which I had heard already but which had to be repeated, as when you stand in an office asking for a passport, something like that).

"The set must show houses and sidewalks, but all thrown together, the way it is in a big city, all shoved one on top of the other. I come out, that is, the woman I'm playing comes out of a house and sits down on the curb, near a green table. Near the table, a man is sitting on a kitchen bench. That's your part. He's wearing a knit shirt and a cap. Across the street there's a vegetable store with crates of tomatoes beside the door. Just then a car crosses the stage, and the man, that's you, gets up to cross the street and I'm afraid, thinking the car will hit you. But you get across before the car passes and reach the other side just as a woman comes out, dressed to go walking, and carrying a glass of beer in one hand. You then drink it all down and come right back just as another car speeds by, this time from the opposite direction. Once again, you get across just in time and sit down on the bench. Meanwhile, I've lain down on the curb like a child, and you come and lean over a little and caress my head."

The play was easy enough to stage but I mentioned that now after having thought it through I felt only one problem remained: that third character, that woman who leaves her house for a walk with a glass of beer.

"Pitcher," she told me. "It's an earthenware pitcher with a handle and a cover."

Blanes nodded and said to her, "Of course, it has some design on it—painted on."

She answered yes and it seemed as if his words had calmed her; she looked content, with that expression of happiness that only women get, a look that makes me want to discreetly close my eyes and not look. We discussed the other woman again and finally Blanes stretched out his hand and said he had everything he needed and there was nothing further for us to worry about. I decided that insanity was contagious because when I asked Blanes whom he had in mind for the woman's role, he answered "La Rivas," and even though I had never known anyone by that name, I caught Blanes glaring at me and said nothing. As it turned out, everything was arranged, settled by the two of them, and there was no need for me to think any further about it. I went right off and found the theater owner, who rented us the place two days for the price of one after I gave him my word that no one but the actors would be admitted.

The next day I got hold of some sort of electrician who, for a day's wage of six pesos, helped me paint and move around the scenery. By nightfall, after working nearly fifteen hours, everything was ready. Sweating and in shirtsleeves, I was having some beer and sandwiches while listening with one ear to the man retelling some local gossip. He paused and then continued.

"Your friend was in good hands today. This afternoon he was with that lady you were with last night at the hotel. Nothing is private around here. She isn't from this area; they say she's here during the summers. I don't like to meddle but I saw them going into a hotel. Yes, I understand, you also live in a hotel. But the one they went into this afternoon was different. . . . You know the kind I mean?"

A bit later Blanes arrived and I mentioned the famous actress Rivas was still missing and the business of the cars had to be organized since only one was available. It belonged to the man who had been helping me and for a few pesos he was willing to rent it out and drive it. Actually I had already figured out a solution since the car was an old beaten-up convertible, and all one had to do was drive it by first with the top down and afterward with the top up, or vice versa. Blanes was silent; he was completely drunk and I hadn't the faintest idea where he had gotten the money. Moments later, it struck me that he was probably cynical enough to have accepted money directly from that poor woman. The thought sickened me and I went on eating my sandwich in silence while he walked about drunk and humming as he mimed and leaped around the stage like a photographer, a spy, a boxer, a football player. With his hat tipped back on his head and humming away, he looked everywhere, from every angle, searching for God knows what. I had no stomach for talking to him; with every passing second I felt more and more convinced that he was drunk on money he had practically stolen from that poor sick woman. So after finishing my sandwich, I sent my man out for six more and another bottle of beer. Meanwhile, Blanes had tired of prancing about and he came over and sat down on some crate near me, still drunk but now sentimental, his hands in his pants pockets, his hat on his knees, and looking glassy-eyed at the stage. Nothing was said for a while and I could see that he had aged and that his blond hair was dull and thinning. He hadn't too many years left as a leading man, or for taking women to hotels, or for much else really.

"I haven't wasted my time either," he blurted out.

"Yes, I can imagine," I answered indifferently.

He smiled, became thoughtful, pulled his hat down and got up again.

He continued talking, pacing back and forth, as he had often seen me do at my office while dictating a letter to the secretary, surrounded by personally autographed photos.

"I've been checking that woman out," he said. "It turns out she or her family once had money but later she had to teach. Nobody, you know, nobody says she's crazy. Sort of strange, yes. Always has been but not mad. I don't know why I'm talking to you, oh Hamlet's most sad adopted father, with your snout smeared in sandwich butter. Talking about this to you."

"At least," I told him calmly, "I haven't taken up spying into other people's lives. Nor playing the Don Juan with strange women." I wiped my mouth with my handkerchief and turned toward him with a bored look. "And I also don't get drunk on who knows what sort of money."

As he now stood, hands on hips, looking seriously back at me and spouting insults, no one could have guessed that he was thinking about that woman, that he really didn't mean what he was saying, that it was just something to do while he thought about her, something to keep me from guessing his mind was fixed on her. He walked back to me, squatted down and quickly straightened up again holding the bottle of beer and drank it slowly down, his mouth glued to the opening. He walked around the stage a while longer, and then sat down again, the bottle between his feet and his hands covering it.

"I've talked to her and she's told me," he said. "I wanted to know what it was all about. I don't know if you understand it's not just a matter of pocketing some cash. I questioned her about what we have to perform and then I knew she was mad. Do you want to know? The whole thing is a dream she had, get it? But what's really insane is that she says the dream means nothing to her. She doesn't know the man sitting down and wearing the blue shirt, nor the woman with the pitcher, she's never even lived on a street like this idiotic mess you've dreamed up. So, in the end, why? She says that while she was asleep and dreaming she was happy, the word isn't 'happy' exactly, something else. So she wants to see it all again, afresh. It's crazy, but there's some reason in it. Something else I like about it is there's no cheap sex in any of it. When we were going off to bed, she kept stopping on the street—the sky was so blue, it was so hot—she kept grabbing me by the shoulders and lapels and asking if I understood. I still don't. It's something still unclear to her, too, because she never finished explaining it."

At ten on the dot, the woman arrived at the theater, wearing the same black dress with the watch and chain, which to me seemed out of place on that painted slum street and not the thing for lying down on a curbstone while Blanes stroked her hair. But it didn't matter: the theater was empty; only Blanes was involved, still drunk, smoking and dressed in a blue shirt with a gray cap folded down over one ear. He had arrived early with the young woman who was to appear in the doorway of the vegetable store and then give him a pitcher of beer. The girl also seemed wrong for her role, at least as I had imagined it, although the devil alone knew what the role really was. She was sad and thin, badly dressed and made-up, someone Blanes had probably picked up in some cheap little café, taking her off the streets for the night with some absurd story; this was obvious because right away she started strutting around like some great star, and it was pitiful to watch her stretching her arm and holding the pitcher of beer; I felt like throwing her out right then. The moment the other one, the mad one, got there dressed in black, she stood for a while looking at the stage, her hands clasped in front of her and she seemed to me tremendously tall, much taller and thinner than I remembered. Then, without a word to anyone, with that sick smile fainter but still making me bristle, she crossed the stage and hid herself in the wing of scenery from which she was to appear. I don't know why, but my eyes followed her, absorbing the exact shape of her long body, closely outlined by her tight-fitting black dress. I watched her body until the curtain's edge blocked it from my view.

Now it was I who stood stage-center and since everything seemed ready and it was now past ten, I lifted my arms and clapped to signal the actors.

But just then, unaware of what was going on exactly, I began to sense that we had gotten ourselves into something I could never speak of, just the way we may know the soul of another and yet find words are useless to describe it. I gestured to them to start, and when I saw Blanes and the girl he had brought begin to move toward their places, I fled into the wings, where the man was already sitting behind the wheel of his ancient car which now began to shudder and quietly rattle. I perched on a crate, hoping to hide, since I wanted nothing more to do with the insanity which was about to begin. I could see how she stepped out of the door of the small run-down house, her body moving like a young girl's, her hair thick, almost gray and loose down her back where it was tied in a knot with some bright-colored ribbon. She was striding out, just the way a young woman does after she has finished setting the table and decides to step outdoors for a moment to quietly watch the end of the day without thinking of anything. I saw her sit down near the bench where Blanes was and rest her head on her hand, her elbow leaning on her knees, letting her fingertips fall on her half-parted lips; her face turned toward some distant point beyond me, beyond even the wall behind me. I saw Blanes get up to cross the street, crossing precisely before the car, with its top up and belching smoke, passed by and quickly disappeared. I saw Blanes's arm and the young woman's in the facing house joined by the pitcher of beer, and saw how the man drank it all down at once, left the pitcher in her hand and saw how she then slowly and without a sound sank back into the doorway. Once more I saw the man in the blue shirt cross the street an instant before a car with its top down raced by and came to a stop near me, its motor shutting off immediately, and as the bluish smoke from the engine cleared, I made out the young woman on the curb, yawning and then lying down on the pavement, her head resting on an arm which hid her hair and with one knee bent. The man in the shirt and cap then leaned over and stroked the young woman's head. He began caressing her, and his hand moved back and forth, catching in her hair, reaching over to stroke her forehead, tightening the bright ribbon holding her hair, he kept on repeating the caresses.

I got down from my crate, heaved a sigh and feeling calmer, quietly crossed the stage. The car man followed, smiling, intimidated, and the thin girl Blanes had brought came out of her doorway to join us. She asked me something, a short question, a single word and I answered without taking my eyes off Blanes, the woman lying down and his hand still stroking her forehead and her thrown-back head, untiring, unaware that the scene was over, that this last thing, caressing her hair, couldn't go on forever. Blanes's body was bent over; he was still stroking her head, stretching his arm so that his fingertips could run down the length of her hair from her forehead to where it spread over her shoulders and her back resting on the ground. The car man was still smiling, he coughed and spat to the side. The girl who had given Blanes the pitcher of beer began walking over to him and the woman. I turned to the owner of the car and told him he could take it away so we could clear out early. I walked over to him, digging into my pocket for a few pesos. Where the others stood on my right, something strange was going on and as I realized this, I bumped into Blanes, who had taken his cap off and stank of liquor, and he jabbed me in the ribs and shouted:

"Don't you realize she's dead, you animal."

I felt alone, broken by the event, and as Blanes paced drunkenly around the stage like some madman and the girl of the pitcher of beer and the car man leaned over the woman, I understood what it was all about, what it was the woman had been searching for, what it was Blanes had stalked the previous evening, rushing back and forth across the stage like one possessed: it was all clear, like one of those things you know as a child but later on find words are useless to explain.

✸ Discussion and Writing

1. What is Blanes's relationship to the narrator? To the woman? What is his function in the story?
2. Interpret the woman's need to translate the dream into a play: what are the comparable traits of a dream and a play? What was the woman's dream? What are the clues in the story as to her ultimate objective?
3. Establish the relevance of *Hamlet* to "A Dream Come True": examine their common themes; analyze the use of images, events and characters as they contribute to the element of mystery in the story.
4. Discuss the importance of the first-person narration in this story. What would have been gained (or lost) by a third-person narration? Restructure the story using any of the other characters as the narrator.

✸ Research and Comparison

Research the story of Onetti's life to examine the impact of his personal experiences on his art. Explore his literary strengths. Re-examine "A Dream Come True" in the light of your understanding of Onetti's life and art. Compare this short story with any other major work by Onetti, examining the nature of its theme or narrative style.

Maria Luisa Bombal
(1910–1980)
Chile

Maria Luisa Bombal, who came from an upper-class, land-owning family, was born in Vina del Mar, Chile. She lived in France through her early schooling and university years, studying literature and philosophy at the

Sorbonne. When she returned to Chile, she associated with the leading avant-garde writers and worked with an experimental theater group. During the 1930s she lived in Buenos Aires, mingling with the group of writers involved with the literary journal *Sur:* Borges, Ocampo et al. This served as a source of inspiration and a home for her work. Giving voice to an impulse that was at once transcendent and fantastic, often erotic, she spoke clearly and always about a woman's perspective.

*Sky, Sea and Earth**

I know about many things of which no one knows. I am familiar with an infinite number of tiny and magical secrets from the sea and from the earth.

I know, for example, that in the ocean depths, much lower than the fathomless and dense zone of darkness, the ocean illuminates itself again and that a golden and motionless light sprouts from gigantic sponges as radiant and as yellow as suns. All types of plants and frozen beings live there submerged in that light of glacial, eternal summer: green and red sea anemones crowd themselves in broad live meadows to which transparent jellyfish that have not yet broken their ties intertwine themselves before embarking on an errant destiny through the seas; hard white coral becomes entangled in enchanted thickets where slithering fish of shadowy velvet softly open and close themselves like flowers; there are sea horses whose manes of algae scatter round them in a sluggish halo when they silently gallop, and if one lifts certain gray shells of insignificant shape, one is frequently sure to find below a little mermaid crying.

I know about an underwater volcano in constant eruption; its crater boils indefatigably day and night and it blows thick bubbles of silvery lava toward the surface of the waters.

I know that during the low-tide, painted beds of delicate anemones remain uncovered on the reefs, and I commiserate with the one who smells that ardent carpet that devours.

I know about gulfs replete with eternal foam where the west winds slowly drag their innumerable rainbow tails.

There is a pure white and nude drowned woman that all of the fishermen of the coast vainly try to catch in their nets . . . but perhaps she is nothing more than an enraptured sea gull that the Pacific currents drag back and forth.

I am familiar with hidden roads, terrestrial channels where the ocean filters the tides, in order to climb up to the pupils of certain women who suddenly look at us with deeply green eyes.

Translated by Susan Bassnett

I know that the ships that have fallen down the ladder of a whirlwind continue travelling centuries below in between submerged reefs; that their masts entangle infuriated octopi and that their holds harbor starfish.

All this I know about the sea.

I know from the earth, that whoever removes the bark from certain trees will find sleeping and adhering to the trunk, extraordinary dusty butterflies that the first ray of light pierces and destroys like an implacable, irreverent pin.

I remember and I see an autumn park. In its wide avenues the leaves pile up and decay, and below them palpitate timid moss-colored frogs that wear a golden crown on their heads. No one knows it, but the truth is that all frogs are princes.

I fear "la gallina ciega"[1] with the immeasurable fright of a child. "La gallina ciega" is smoke colored, and she lives cast below the thickets, like a miserable pile of ashes. She doesn't have legs to walk, nor eyes to see; but she usually flies away on certain nights with short and thick wings. No one knows where she goes, no one knows from where she returns, at dawn, stained in blood that isn't her own.

I am familiar with a distant southern jungle in whose muddy ground opens a hole narrow and so deep that if you lie face downward upon the earth and you look, you will encounter as far as the eye can see, something like a cloud of golden dust that vertiginously turns.

But nothing is more unforeseen than the birth of wine. Because it isn't true that wine is born under the sky and within the dark grape of water and sun. The birth of wine is tenebrous and slow; I know a lot about that furtive assassin's growth. Only after the doors of the cold wine cellar are closed and after the spiders have spread out their first curtains, is when the wine decides to grow in the depths of the large, hermetically closed barrels. Like the tides, wine suffers from the taciturn influence of the moon that now incites it to retreat, now helps it to flow back. And this is how it is born and grows in the darkness and the silence of its winter.

I can tell something more about the earth. I know about a deserted region where a village has remained buried in the dunes, the only thing emerging is the peak of the tower of the church. During stormy nights every lightning rod moves recklessly over the solitary arrow, erect in the middle of the plain, coiling around her, whistling, in order to later sink into the sand. And they say that then, the missing tower shakes from top to bottom and a subterranean toll of bells is heard resonating.

The sky, on the other hand, does not have even one small and tender secret. Implacable, it completely unfurls its terrifying map above us.

---

[1] La gallina ciega is more commonly identified with the childhood game of "blind man's bluff."

I would like to believe that I have my star, the one that I see break through first and shine an instant only for me every day at dusk, and that in that star not only my steps but also my laughter and my voice have an echo. But, alas, I know too well that there cannot be life of any kind there where the atoms change their form millions of times per second and where no pair of atoms can remain united.

It even makes me afraid to name the sun. It is so powerful! If they were to cut us off from its radiation, the course of the rivers would immediately stop.

I barely dare to speak about a condor that the winds pushed beyond the terrestrial atmosphere and that, still alive, has been falling in infinite space for an uncountable number of years.

Perhaps the sudden fall of shooting stars responds to a foreseen call from eternity that hurls them in order to form particular geometric figures, made of glittering stars inlaid in a remote corner of the sky. Perhaps.

No, I don't want, I don't want to talk about the sky any more, because I fear it, and I fear the dreams with which it frequently enters into my nights. Then, it extends a sidereal ladder to me through which I climb toward the shining dome. The moon stops being a pallid disk stuck in the firmament in order to become a scarlet ball that rolls through space in solitude. The stars grow larger in a blinking of rays, the milky way approaches and pours out its wave of fire. And, second by second, I am closer to the edge of that burning precipice.

No, I prefer to imagine a diurnal sky with roaming castles of clouds in whose floating rooms flutter the dry leaves of a terrestrial autumn and the kites that the sons of men lost, playing.

❋ Discussion and Writing

1. What is the impact of the images of the frogs as princes and the crying mermaids? Look at other fictional, scientific, cultural, or personal allusions.
2. What is the effect of "I know," "I remember," "I see" in Bombal's description? What other modes of perception are implied in this piece?
3. What is the significance of Bombal's being centered on the earth as she views the sky, the sea, and the earth? Why is the sky terrifying for Bombal; what is its implication?
4. Reconstruct the description of the three elements viewed from somewhere other than the earth, from the sky, for instance. Explain your perspective and describe your perception.

Rachel de Queiroz
(b. 1910)
Brazil

Rachel de Queiroz was born in the capital of Ceara, Fortaleza, Brazil, where she was sent to a convent school in 1921 as a boarder; until that time she was raised mainly on a ranch in the backlands. Over the years she taught in a teacher training school, worked as a columnist for a weekly magazine, and served as a Brazilian representative to the United Nations. In the early 1930s she was expelled as a Trotskyite from the Communist Party, which she had recently joined, but she continued to speak from a socialist perspective, albeit a moderate one. In her early writing, she successfully transmuted events from her childhood schooling and a severe drought in northeastern Brazil into fiction. She has continued to be admired for the clarity and vitality of her narration.

Tangerine Girl*

What first caught her interest was the name of the airship: not zeppelin or dirigible or anything else old-fashioned; the large spindle of shining metal bore the very modern name *blimp*. As small as a toy, independent, friendly. A few hundred yards from her house was the American soldiers' air base where the blimps were moored. And now and then they left the base to take to the air, like tame birds abandoning the perch for a trial flight. At first the blimp existed in the girl's eyes as a thing in itself, an animal with a life of its own; it fascinated her as the mechanical marvel that it was, and most of all she found it lovely, all silver like a jewel, floating majestically a little below the clouds. It was a bit like an idol; it invoked in her something of the captive genie in *Aladdin*. She had never thought of riding in it; she had never even thought anyone *could* ride in it. No one thinks of riding an eagle, swimming on the back of a dolphin, and yet the fascinated gaze encompasses as much as can an eagle or a dolphin, in unbridled admiration, for one of the virtues of beauty seems to be the abnegation of self that it imposes on us in return for our pure and unadorned contemplation of it.

The girl's eye therefore fastened onto the blimp with no special desire, with no trace of a claim on it. To be sure, she saw inside it some tiny heads peering out, but so minuscule that they gave an impression of unreality, were part of the painting, a decorative element as obligatory as the large

---

*Translated by Clifford E. Landers

black letters U.S. NAVY engraved on the bulging silver object. Or perhaps they recalled those paper cutouts that serve as drivers in toy automobiles.

Her first contact with the blimp's crew came about purely by chance. The girl had just finished breakfast. She cleared the table and went to the door leading to the orange grove to shake the bread crumbs from the tablecloth. Up above, a crewman saw that white cloth flapping among the scattered trees and the sand, and his lonely heart was moved. He lived on the base like a monk in a convent, alone among soldiers and calls to patriotism. And there, next to the fence of the house with the red roof, shaking a cloth amid the green of the orange trees, was a young girl with red hair. The sailor became excited at the greeting. He had already flown over the house several times and had seen people below, coming and going, and had thought of how distant people live from one another, how indifferently they pass among themselves, each shut inside his own life. He was always flying over others, seeing them, looking at them, and if a few raised their eyes, they never thought about the navigator flying there inside; all they cared about was the silvery thing of beauty drifting through the sky.

But now that girl had given a thought to him; she was waving a cloth in the air like a flag. She must be pretty—the sun conjured flashes of light from her hair and her willowy silhouette stood out clearly against the background of greenery and sand. His heart flung itself to the girl in a great gesture of gratitude; he leaned out the window, waved his arms, and shouted "Amigo! amigo!" although he knew that the wind, the distance, the noise of the motor would not allow her to hear anything. He was unsure whether she had seen his gestures; he wanted to respond in a more tangible way. He would have liked to throw her a flower, an offering. But what was there in a Navy blimp that could be offered to a girl? The most delicate object he found was a large white stoneware mug, heavy as a cannonball, in which he would soon be served coffee. And it was that mug that the crewman threw. No, not "threw;" he *dropped* it a discreet distance from the illuminated figure down below, releasing it in a delicate gesture trying to soften the force of gravity so the object would land not like a screaming projectile but gently, like a tribute.

The girl who was shaking the tablecloth actually had raised her eyes upon hearing the blimp's motor. She saw the young man's arms waving up there. Then she saw something white cut through the air and fall in the sand; she was startled, thinking at first it might be some kind of coarse joke, a foreign soldier's crude prank. But when she saw the white mug resting in the sand, intact, she felt a confused understanding of the impulse that had prompted it. She picked it up, read the engraving with the same letters as the side of the blimp: U.S. NAVY. Meanwhile, the blimp, instead of withdrawing, made another slow turn over the house and the orchard. Then the girl raised her eyes again and, this time deliberately, waved the tablecloth, smiling and bobbing her head. The blimp made two more turns and slowly went into the distance—and the girl had the impression that it already missed her.

Up above, the crewman was also thinking, not about *saudades*,[1] since he didn't know Portuguese, but about something poignant and sweet. For, despite not speaking our language, American soldiers have a heart, too.

That was how the morning ritual was established. The blimp passed overhead daily, and daily the girl waited for it; she no longer took the white tablecloth and at times didn't even wave her arms: she stood immobile, a white spot on the sun-bathed earth. It was a kind of courtship between falcon and gazelle: he, a fierce soldier coursing through the air; she, small, timid, down below watching with fascinated eyes as he passed. By now the presents, brought intentionally from the base, were no longer the rough improvised mug; issues of *Time* and *Life* fell from the sky, a sailor's cap, and one day the crewman took from his pocket his handkerchief of New Zealand fiberlily scented with synthetic essence of violets. The handkerchief opened in the air and drifted down like a paper kite; it finally landed in the branches of a cashew tree, and the girl had great difficulty freeing it with a pole. Even so, she ripped it slightly, right in the center.

But of all the presents the one she liked best was still the first: the heavy stoneware mug. She had put it in her room, on top of the writing table. At first she had thought of using it on the table, at meals, but she feared the derision of her brothers. She ended up using it for her pens and pencils. One day she had a better idea, and the mug became a flower vase. A manaca branch, a jessamine, a Cape jasmine, a wild rose since in the unpretentious garden of the country house there were no distinguished roses or expensive flowers.

She began studying with more dedication her English conversation book; when she went to the movies she paid intense attention to the dialogue in order to extract from it not only the meaning but the pronunciation as well. She lent to her sailor the look of all the leading men she saw on the screen, and he was in succession Clark Gable, Robert Taylor, or Cary Grant. Or he was blond like a young sailor killed in a naval battle in the Pacific, whose name wasn't listed in the cast; at times he even smiled and made funny faces like Red Skelton. Because she was a bit nearsighted, she could barely make him out, looking at him from the ground: she saw a cutout face, arms waving; and, depending on the direction of the sun, it seemed to her that he had either blond or dark hair.

It did not occur to her that it couldn't always be the same sailor. And in reality the crew members changed daily: some had liberty and went to the city with the girlfriends they picked up around there; others left for good for Africa, or for Italy. At the blimp base the tradition of the girl in the orange groves had become established. The sailors had given her the nickname Tangerine Girl. Perhaps because of the Dorothy Lamour film, for Dorothy

---

[1]Missing someone or something with a feeling of nostalgia. [eds.]

Lamour is for all the American armed forces the model for dark-skinned women of South America and the Pacific islands. Perhaps because she always waited for them among the orange trees. Or perhaps because the girl's red hair as it shone in the morning sun had the coppery glow of a ripe tangerine. Each of them, one after the other, shared like a common good belonging to all their courtship of the Tangerine Girl. The airship pilot flew in circles, obediently, flying as low as regulations allowed, while the other, from her window, looked on and waved hello.

I don't know why it took so long for the boys to get the idea of dropping a note. Maybe they were thinking she wouldn't understand. They had been flying over the house for more than a month when the first note finally fell; it was written over the rosy face of a woman on the cover of a magazine; laboriously, in block letters, in the rudimentary Portuguese they had learned from the mouths of girlfriends, in the city: *"Querida Tangerine Girl. Por favor, you come (venha) today base X. Dancing, show. Oito (eight) P.M."* And on another part of the cover, in enormous letters, AMIGO, which is the Americans' password among us.

The girl didn't understand that *Tangerine Girl.* Did they mean her? Yes, of course. . . . And she accepted the nickname, flattered. Then she thought about the two letters at the end: "P.M." They might be a signature. Peter, Paul, Patsy, like Nick Carter's assistant? But something she remembered from her studies came back to her: she consulted the back pages of the dictionary, which deal with abbreviations, and verified, slightly to her disappointment, that the letters meant "the time after midday."

She had not been able to wave an answer because she had found the note only when she opened the magazine, after the blimp had left. That must be it, she thought; she felt terribly frightened and timid at facing her aeronaut for the first time. Tonight she would see if he was tall and handsome, blond or dark-haired. She thought of hiding behind the columns at the front gate to see him arrive—and not saying a word to him. Or maybe she would have more courage and let him take her hand; together they would walk to the base, where they would dance a slow fox-trot; he would whisper declarations of love in English, resting his suntanned cheek on her hair. She didn't even think whether the folks at home would let her accept the invitation. Everything was happening as if in a dream, and it would resolve itself like a dream, without discord or impediment.

Long before dark she had already combed her hair and dressed. Her heart beat, beat unsteadily, her head ached a bit, her face was on fire. She decided not to show the invitation to anyone. She wouldn't go to the show, wouldn't dance, just talk with him a little at the gate. She rehearsed phrases in English and prepared her ear for sweet words in the foreign tongue. At seven o'clock she turned on the radio and listened languidly to a program of swing music. One of her brothers came in, taunted her about her pretty dress, at that hour, and she didn't even hear him. At 7:30 she was on the porch, her eye on the gate and the road. At ten minutes before eight, night had fallen (she had long since lighted the small bulb that illuminated the gate); she went to the garden. And at eight sharp she heard laughter and the tramping of feet approaching down the road.

Drawing back in fright, she saw coming toward her not just her impassioned sailor but a noisy band of them. Trembling, she watched them approach. They saw her, surrounded the gate—it even seemed like a military maneuver—took off their caps, and introduced themselves with boisterous joviality.

And suddenly, as soon as she heard their names, running her eyes over their beardless faces and sportive, boyish grins, looking at them one by one, seeking among them her dreamed-of prince—she understood everything. Her impassioned sailor didn't exist; he had never been anything but a myth of her heart's making. There had never been just one; "he" had never been the same one twice. Maybe the blimp itself wasn't even the same one. . . .

Good heavens, the shame of it! She had waved to so many people; betrayed by a deceptive appearance, she had sent to so many different men her heart's sweetest messages. And in their smiles, in the cordial words they directed at their collective sweetheart, at the little Tangerine Girl who was already an institution at the base, she saw only ridicule, insolent familiarity. . . . They must think she was another of those girls who go with sailors passing through, any and all of them. . . . They must think. . . . Good Lord in heaven!

The men, either because of the half-darkness or because they were unattuned to such psychological nuances, didn't notice the expression of pain and fright that tortured the round face of their little friend. And when one of them, bowing, offered his arm, to his surprise he saw her draw back, stammering timidly. "I'm sorry. . . . It was a mistake. . . . a mistake. . . ."

And the men understood even less when they saw her go, slowly at first then in a blind run. They didn't even suspect that she ran to lock herself in her room where, biting her pillow, she wept the bitterest and hottest tears that her eyes could yield.

They never glimpsed her in the orange grove again; though they continued to drop presents, they saw that they lay on the ground, forgotten, or were sometimes gathered up by the urchins who lived on the farm.

❋ Discussion and Writing

1. Who are the young men? Explain their interest in the young girl? Discuss the implication of their giving her a name.
2. What is the source of the girl's interest in them? What is suggested about mutual stereotyping and its impact on cross-cultural misunderstanding?
3. What is the function of the girl's brother? Comment on the gender relations in the story.

4. Analyze de Queiroz's use of the setting and the imagery and their implied symbolism.

❋ Research and Comparison

Interdisciplinary Discussion Question: Research the role of the United States in Brazil, particularly during World War II, and its impact on Brazilian arts and society.

Jorge Amado
(b. 1912)
Brazil

Jorge Amado, whose mother was of indigenous descent, was born on his parents' small plantation in southern Bahia, Brazil. His father had ridden into the backlands to clear the land and plant cacao, but when the floods of 1914 washed away their farm, Jorge Amado's parents made and sold wooden clogs in the city of Ilheus. They tried to become planters again, this time in an area where cacao wars were being fought, but they lost everything a second time in the 1929 crash. Amado's schooling was as precarious as his parents' hold on the land had been: sent to a Jesuit boarding school in the city of Salvador when he was ten, he ran away to the backlands within two years; after being brought back, he stayed for another two years before taking a job as a journalist. He lived in the quarter of the city that was decidedly outside middle-class experience, but one he later drew on for his fiction. He managed to complete preparatory school and his law degree, but he had already begun centering his attention on his writing, and had already published *Cacao* (1933), a novel of social protest that the police confiscated.

There followed a series of arrests over the next ten or so years, and his books were banned, some burned, for he wrote about the conditions of the slums and about the African Brazilian underclass in Bahia, about class and violence and oppression. Amado also spoke out for religious freedom. He joined the Communist Party in the late 1930s and was elected to the constituent assembly after the Brazilian Communist Party was legalized. Although he left the party in the mid-1950s to concentrate on his writing, he continued to protest against inequities, refusing to present his work to

the censors during the military dictatorship of the 1960s. And he continued
to give voice to Bahian culture and its oral tradition.

Of Dice and Unshakable Principles*

There's nothing more dangerous than confusing the inescapable destiny of
each of us with shamelessness, immorality, lack of character. It's not because
he wants to, or for lack of principles or willpower, that a man repeats the
same irreparable stupidity—once, twice, three times, ten times, a thousand
times or as many times as necessary. Without being shameless or weak-spir-
ited. Great injustice is done worthy people by the ease with which we judge
the acts of others without delving into the whys and wherefores.

It was this we were discussing that night in Alonso's store as we tried
out a nice new rum from Santo Amaro that the Spaniard had received the
night before. Good rum that slid down your throat without a trace and
livened up the conversation. Everything became clear, however, when
Massu brought up the matter of Climaco in defense of Pedro Porro, who was
under attack from Lidio.

Lidio drained the glass of rum, after listening to the tale of Pedro Porro's
recent trials, spat a fat wad, and said in the determined voice of someone
bringing the subject to a close:

"Shameless, that's what he is!"

And, as if wanting to leave no room for doubt, added:

"Disgraceful."

Massu, however, disagreed. Massu was a calm sort, a mulatto tending
toward the blondish, and he enjoyed a certain respect and consideration
because of his reputation as a man of education and experience. He had
traveled a lot, lived here and there, including some time served in the peni-
tentiary.

"Don't say that . . . " Massu drank his rum very slowly, savoring every
drop.

"Well then, how do you explain . . . "

Yes, just how did you explain Pedro Porro's attitude? Porro was a friend
of ours who had a shoe repair shop in the Cabeca area, and a master at his
trade. A master of the half-sole and full-sole who could make the oldest
worn-out shoe look like new. When it left his hands it looked like it had just
come from the factory. He was, you can see, a man of obvious qualities, but
still his recent attitudes led black Lidio to judge him with such harsh words,
as if Porro had lost any claim to honor and no longer deserved the esteem
and confidence of his old friends.

Translated by Clifford E. Landers

All this because the cobbler had gone and played cards again with Martim, known as the Corporal, and lost his earnings for the day and more besides. What else could he do, Lidio asked, except go home, keep his mouth shut, and not complain? But was that what Pedro Porro had done? Had he headed silently home, head lowered? Instead, he'd had a few drinks for comfort, failed to comfort himself, and had proclaimed loudly that the Corporal was the biggest cardshark ever seen in Bahia and that he himself, Porro, was the worst fool in the *solar system.* That's exactly what he said: in the solar system. The cobbler was a reading man, a collector of almanacs, who knew Guerra Junqueiro's poems by heart, and who liked to talk about astronomy. While he pounded on soles, he would explain to his attentive listeners—and there was never a lack of visitors to his stall, for he was a good talker—the mysteries of the stars and planets. Many of the stories he told were no doubt made up; who could believe some of the absurdities he served up to the ignorance of the people? But many things were taken from the books that Porro read in his free time, things he'd learned from almanacs, and if we raised doubts, he would open the page and point with his finger:

"Read that, illiterate."

So: Pedro Porro had been seen, in the early morning hours, more or less drunk, banging his head against a lamppost and yelling to anyone who would listen:

"Pedro Porro, you're the worst fool in the solar system and that no-good swindling corporal is the biggest thief who ever laid hands on a deck of cards in this city of Bahia."

Lidio's thesis, after examining what had happened, appeared unarguably sound. He declared Pedro Porro doubly at fault, which proved the cobbler's shameful and disgraceful behavior. At fault, first, for going back to gamble at the Corporal's table. How many times had the same thing already happened? Was Pedro Porro some kind of innocent, a stranger fresh from the dock who'd never heard of Corporal Martim's skills? Wasn't Porro an old friend of his, familiar with his record? The first disgraceful act: gambling with him. Only a shameless sort like Pedro Porro would persist in playing cards with the Corporal, knowing him the way he had for so long. Even more disgraceful and unforgivable because the cobbler wasn't an idiot, much less the biggest one in the solar system, as he proclaimed to the entire neighborhood.

The disgracefulness was made worse in this case by the fact that Porro had been the one to seek out the Corporal for the game. That afternoon Martim was getting along fine, trading ideas with Inocencio, a neighbor of Porro's who sold images of saints. They spoke of one thing and another. The Corporal enjoyed listening to old Inocencio, a fellow whose conversation was both cheerful and enlightening; no one knew the animal game, the illegal lottery, better than he did. As the afternoon drew to a close, the two of them were recalling an incident of seven years before, when a lion escaped from a circus and ran through the streets of the city, spreading panic until he was recaptured and returned to his cage. It was an event noted in the newspapers and that day everyone played the lion in the lottery. The bookmakers tried to lay off some of the bets with bigger bookies, and after a time decided to lower the odds on the lion. But nothing could stop the people's frenzy, and everyone was playing. Could there ever be a better hunch? There couldn't, and that evening, as expected, the lion came up and there was pandemonium. Everywhere you saw bookies going bankrupt, gambling spots destroyed, people pulling guns to get the money they'd won honestly on their hunch of the lion. It was a day of great confusion. Inocencio remembered it as a time of picturesque details, relating the desperation of one bookie by the name of Adroaldo who had gone into business only two days before. Imagine, he was just getting started, so to speak! He never recovered from the damage done by the lion.

The Corporal was with Inocencio, recalling such things from the past, in their joy and their sadness, when Pedro Porro, his work finished for the day, appeared and was invited to join the conversation. There were two or three others present, and the talk thrived until it was time for Inocencio to close the door of his shop and turn on the light. That was when the game began, and who suggested it but Pedro Porro? The Corporal, according to accounts, even resisted, on the pretext of a previous engagement, but at his friends' insistence gave in and took out his deck of cards. The results we already know: Pedro Porro banging his head against a lamppost, calling himself an idiot and accusing the other, dragging through the mud of slander the good name of a well-known citizen like Martim. And that was the second, even more reprehensible, shameless act. Porro had gambled because he wanted to. He had gambled and lost, as was natural because the banker was the Corporal, whose luck at cards was legendary and whose manual dexterity was the object of deep general admiration. Porro should have gone home instead of roaming the streets proclaiming his weakness of character and slandering his opponent. Lidio defended his thesis with the brilliance and vehemence engendered by successive shots of rum.

But the mulatto Massu disagreed, and his opinion was heard in silence. Even the Spaniard, Alonso, abandoned his tasks to listen.

"A man born to a certain fate has to fulfill his destiny whether he wants to or not. One born to gamble has to gamble to the last, however it is, even knowing he'll lose, there's no way out. That's how it was with Pedro Porro, that's how it was with my friend Climaco. You don't know what happened with my friend Climaco, from Ladeira do Taboao, a real artist. He worked in wood, in horn, ivory, and he manufactured lots of things, including dice."

Curiosity filled Alonso's store. Another round, and Massu cleared his throat by downing a swallow, then recounted the story of his friend Climaco:

A man of great ability, Climaco once even manufactured crooked dice, a job well worth seeing. In the hands of a professional gambler those dice represented the ruin of many a circumspect citizen. Don't conclude from this that Climaco was a dishonest sort who manufactured crooked dice, a swindler. Not at all; it's true he liked to gamble, and he would seek out a game even if he had to go miles and miles, but he didn't load dice or mark cards. He only made crooked dice once, and then a single pair, commissioned by Antonio Bispo, a gambling buddy of his who ran a game in Agua dos Meninos. This Antonio Bispo, in possession of the dice made by Climaco, soon began to prosper. His clientele grew constantly and he was content with his lot. He thought the money well spent that he had paid for Climaco's handiwork.

Climaco liked to take a chance on dice and usually bet the long odds. He played here and there, except in Antonio Bispo's game. He knew those dice all too well and sometimes laughed at the suckers who wagered on them. He laughed between his teeth and left to lose his money on dice that weren't crooked, to win or lose by true luck.

Now, it happened that on a certain occasion the police launched a violent antigambling campaign. Of course what they really wanted was to hush up some governmental scandals, but that's beside the point. The gamblers were the scapegoats; many were jailed, some were beaten by the police, roulette tables were smashed, decks of cards torn in half, dice tossed into the sea. The persecution was terrible, and the places where an honest person could gamble his little bit of money became scarcer by the day. Among the few still in business was Antonio Bispo. Luck, perhaps, or some influential acquaintance in the police. In any case, he continued running his game, using Climaco's crooked dice. Bankers were going out of business daily, being arrested and brought to trial, but Antonio Bispo prospered. It became harder and harder for Climaco and others addicted to betting on the long and short odds to find anywhere to risk their money. The number of gambling places diminished, and the day arrived when only Antonio Bispo alone, he and no one else, rolled the dice in Bahia. Climaco looked everywhere for a place to play; there wasn't a single one. The only thing to do was wait for the crackdown to end and for the bankers to return to their jobs.

"Now, just you imagine Antonio Bispo's surprise one afternoon when he saw Climaco take out his precious money and bet the long odds against him. Antonio Bispo, owner of the crooked dice that Climaco himself had made. Gnashing his teeth, angry as could be, Climaco, knowing he'd never have a chance of winning with Antonio Bispo controlling the most crooked dice ever manufactured, even so he bet the long odds because a man cannot escape his fate. It's not shamelessness or disgraceful behavior; a man may be very scrupulous but no one can keep from fulfilling his destiny . . . "

There was general agreement. By now, in fact, we no longer cared about Pedro Porro and his adventures; we wanted to know more about Antonio Bispo, his crooked dice, and what happened to that Climaco fellow who worked in wood, horn, and even ivory, from Ladeira do Taboao and who, according to Massu, painted ex-votos to fulfill a vow at the Church of Bonfim, really good paintings, beautiful.

❋ Discussion and Writing

1. What are the "unshakable principles"? What do they control in the story?
2. What is the significance of each character's racial and vocational identities? How are they linked to the narrative?
3. Examine the significance of dice and gambling in the philosophical speculation about life in the story.
4. What is the function of the stories within the story? Comment on Amado's narrative technique. How are the substories related to the main narrative?

❋ Research and Comparison

Interdisciplinary Discussion Question: Compare the novel and film versions of Jorge Amado's *Dona Flor and Her Two Husbands.*

Interdisciplinary Discussion Question: Research the history of the slave trade in Brazil: examine the influence of African culture in Brazil, paying particular attention to the religious and oral traditions in Bahia.

Leon Damas
(1912–1978)
French Guiana

Leon-Gontran Damas was born in Cayenne, French Guiana, and, following the practices of the established mulatto middle class to which his family belonged, he attended the Lycee Schoelcher in Fort-de-France, Martinique. At the time, it was the only secondary school for the French West Indies. There he met Aime Cesaire. Again as was customary, Damas went to France to study. His parents, particularly his mother, were so displeased that he left his legal studies and European society at the Sorbonne and turned to ethnology and friends of African descent that they withdrew their financial support. He worked at odd jobs and became terribly poor. But, he was studying at the Universite de Paris when Aime Cesaire and Leopold Senghor were also in Paris, and it was during these years of the early- to mid-1930s that the three Francophone poets developed the *negritude* movement. Seeking a way to bring students from Africa and the West Indies together, the three founded *L'Etudiant noir* (The Black Student, 1934), the journal that gave voice to their concerns and ideals. They read the writers of the Harlem Renaissance and met those who were in Paris, discovering mutual interests and absorbing Renaissance theories.

Damas was the first of the three to publish a volume of his poetry, *Pigments* (1937), a book banned as subversive. Damas condemned the loss of Africa for Africans and for African peoples of the diaspora. He examined the ramifications of European colonization, deploring the loss of identity. At the same time, the syncopation of his poetry revealed a profound, widespread, African identity, as his poems broke from European metrics to work with the language of jazz.

Poems*

Really I Know
nothing sadder
or more hateful
or more frightening
or more lugubrious in the world
than to hear love at the end of the day
repeating itself like a low mass
once upon a time
a woman happened to pass
whose arms were full of roses

* * *

Trite Without Doubt
but before giving over
entirely beautiful and black
to the whorl-flowered grass
on the path which leads
to the mountains
where a bamboo flute
cries in the night
the girl with the calabash
of indifference on her head
should pray three times each
to Lord Jesus

---

*Translated by Langston Hughes

the Virgin
Saint Joseph

❀ Discussion and Writing

1. What is the significance of the image that evokes memory in "Really I Know"?
2. Discuss the larger implications of the persona's feelings.
3. What is the importance of the landscape in "Trite Without Doubt"? What is implied by "the calabash / of indifference"?
4. Examine the aspects of *negritude* manifested in these poems.

❀ Research and Comparison

Research the concept of *negritude* and examine its various aspects in the writings of any of the following writers: Aime Cesaire, Leopold Senghor, Leon Damas, or Jacques Roumain.

Walter Montenegro
(1912–1991)
Bolivia

Walter Montenegro was born in Cochabamba, Bolivia. His parents—who were first cousins—were quite poor; as a result, he began working at a young age and was a largely self-made man. But he had learned to play the violin, and at first, it was a means of support as he played for silent movies. When he was 16, he also started working nights for the Cochabamba daily newspapers, beginning with *La Prensa.* During the Chaco War (1932–1934), he served at the front, where he organized the first news service. He remained with the service until the end of the war in 1935. While he did not pursue a professional career in music, his violin sustained him throughout his life: he played with and often formed string quartets, and when he died, his violin was buried with him. Journalism became his profession. During his career as a highly respected journalist, he was a columnist, director, and editor for various papers in Bolivia as well as a correspondent for magazines within and outside Bolivia.

Between 1949 and 1952, he wrote his column "Mirador" ("Observation Point") for the leading La Paz daily, *La Razon;* he had already started on the first of his many periods as Bolivia's correspondent for *Time* magazine. The Paz Estenssoro revolution of 1952, however, marked the end of both enterprises. For almost ten years following the revolution, he lived in the United States, where he was on the editorial staff of the Spanish edition of *Life* magazine, but when he returned to Bolivia, he once again became a correspondent for *Time*. He also embarked on a diplomatic career, serving as Bolivian consul to Hong Kong and ambassador to Peru.

Montenegro became a member of the Academia Boliviana de la Lengua (the Bolivian Academy of Literature), and in 1981, he received the Manuel Vicente Ballivan Journalism Prize. During that year, he served as editor for *El Diario,* wrote for a number of newspapers and magazines in Bolivia and abroad, and began his weekly column "Siluetas"—sketches about prominent persons in La Paz. At the time of his death, he had also published two collections of short stories. In "The *Pepino,*" Montenegro reflects on the class and caste distinctions in Bolivia as well as on the overlay of Christian rituals and the undercurrents and presence of ancient belief.

*The Pepino**

"Stop, stop," shouted the children. Instead the truck, with its tottery cargo of Indians crouching on closely packed sacks of potatoes and corn, gathered speed. The *pepino,*[1] running along beside the truck, was trying to jump back on the running board. He managed finally to grasp a metal railing; he hung in the air, but had to let go after a few seconds. He dropped in a spectacular fall. Legs turned up high, he lay there immobile, flat on his back.

Women screamed. A current in the heavy stream of people filling the street eddied, and a circle quickly formed around the prostrate figure.

"An ambulance, call an ambulance . . . give him water . . . pick him up," a *chola*[2] in the crowd shouted, and was echoed by others. The *pepino's* mask stared dumbly up at the sky, its expression a combination of buffoonery and sorrow. Its huge turned-up nose, mocking and insolent, seemed to have an existence apart from the large mouth with its turned-down corners.

"Pick him up, give him water . . . "

Translated by Carolina Udovicki

[1] The *pepino,* the omnipresent personage of the La Paz carnival, wears a full face mask. His anonymity is guaranteed, the domain of his activity unbounded, the latitude of his conduct unlimited. Strictly an urban personage, he might be *cholo* or "Spanish," but never *indio*.

[2] The *cholo* is a mestizo or *indio* in the process of urbanization, in the sense of acquiring the economic and social values of the Spanish culture of bi-cultural Bolivia. The *chola's* dress is typified by several layers of tightly shirred, never-woolen skirts. The indigenous woman (*india*) of the Andean highlands wears only one skirt, of hand-woven llama wool.

The circle of curious in the noisy street had fallen silent. Spectators stretched their necks to get a better view. Somebody approached the body and began to shake it gently. Suddenly, with a great leap, the *pepino* was on his feet, a whirling doll in his red and yellow suit, distributing well-aimed blows with his *chorizo*[3] at the people surrounding him. He shouted in a high-pitched voice and laughed, delighted with the success of his deception. His victims showered him with blows in revenge for having been taken in.

The group was quickly reabsorbed in the larger stream of people. The *pepino,* now incorporated into the revelry in this part of the city, moved cavorting through the crowd with the usual escort of youngsters shouting. "Make way for the *pepino!* the *pepino!* . . . watch out for his *chorizo!*"

Ash Wednesday in La Paz. The city's predominant population of mestizos and *cholos* pours into the streets. The crowds are rebels on this one day of the year against a mute and laborious fate, all restraint gone in a boisterous celebration. The steep streets climbing from the heart of the city up toward the Municipal Cemetery and beyond explode in color from the costumes and gala finery. Far above are *ajtapis,*[4] the last defenses of an arid countryside, fending off the encroachment of the cold and symmetric gray paving stones and the miserable urban dwellings.

Groups form at the *ajtapis,* and small bouquets are placed on the green, fresh patches. Below, the sound of guitars and singing rebounds off the cemetery walls, awakening, surely, the curiosity of the dead and their desire to join the festivities. They could tap out the rhythm of macabre *cuecas*[5] with the castanets of their bones, there in the nubbies of the high walls set in rows which are the burial grounds of the cemetery.

Just outside the cemetery, the *pepino,* that anonymous hero of carnival revelry, jumped about, falling on the passersby with his *chorizo* and spurring on his escort of small boys, his heralds.

"Watch out, the *pepino!* . . . the *pepino!* . . . "

The *pepino* was indefatigable. At times he would turn against his escort. The boys would scatter, running to escape his blows, only to be back again in an instant. In one of these attacks, all but one, the smallest of the boys, ran away. He stood fast and laughed merrily, showing his small teeth packed as tightly as a row of white and tender corn kernels. The *pepino* stopped in front of him, gave three or four of his most impressive jumps, and brandished his *chorizo* over the child's head. But the boy, far from taking fright, only laughed harder and harder, pointing his small, dark-skinned finger at the *pepino*'s face, that immobile, baffled and sorrowful mask. The *pepino* sank to the ground. Sitting there, he dropped his face into his hands and began to

---

[3]The scepter and weapon of the *pepino:* his *chorizo* (sausage) is a cloth tube tightly stuffed with pieces of rubber and rags.
[4]Small garden plots at the edge of the city.
[5]The most popular *cholo* folk dance of the Andean region.

weep. Great loud sobs shook his body. Without lifting his head, he stretched out an arm and handed over the *chorizo*, the symbol of his strength and authority, to the small boy, who took it and began hitting the *pepino* on the head with it. The *pepino* fell on his back, defending himself clumsily with his arms from the blows. A new chorus formed around the scene and cheered on the boy.

"Harder! . . . Harder! . . . Death to the *pepino!*" The *pepino* was suddenly on his feet. He grabbed back his weapon and with blows right and left disbanded the company.

A new commotion in a narrow alley running off in a torturous ascent caught the *pepino*'s attention. The curious were piling up, pushing one another to get a look. Opening his path with his *chorizo* and strident shouts, he made his way to the scene of the disturbance. A drunkard in flashy yellow shoes was beating his wife, a *chola* wearing so many skirts that the blows falling on her ears and back could only throw her sitting into the center of the stiff ring of skirts encircling her legs.

Voices were raised in protest, "Leave her alone . . . brute!" "Coward . . . beating a woman!" Other *cholas* in the crowd were already yelling "Help!" and "Call the police!" The *pepino* circled the drunkard and his victim a number of times. He groaned and muttered lamentations and grasped his head between his hands at each blow, as though each fell on him. Miming his decision that the woman had taken enough punishment, he pushed himself between the couple. He grabbed the man's arms and tried to shove him back, away from the woman. Instead, he was taken by surprise by a tremendous sock on the nose and found himself on the ground. The crowd howled with laughter. His huge nose had been completely squashed.

The *pepino* stayed on the ground a few moments and then got to his feet with a great show of gravity. He felt his squashed nose, turned, and gave his *chorizo* to one of the laughing boys. After a few extra-high jumps, he charged the drunkard. Colors, arms and legs whirled until both men were rolling on the ground. Finally, it was the *pepino* who picked himself up, and he put his foot victoriously on the chest of his unconscious opponent.

"*Pepino!* Bravo *pepino!* . . . Long live the *pepino!* . . . "

The wife, who had looked on in silence, reacted violently. She lunged at the victor, who was shaking hands with his admirers, and delivered a great blow to his head with a glazed iron jug. The *pepino* went down, arms splayed, falling across his victim. He recovered consciousness in seconds, and after looking about with a disconsolate air, felt for the still peacefully sleeping body below him. He rolled over, slipped an arm under the neck of his opponent, placed the *chorizo* under both their heads, and fell asleep curled up against his erstwhile contender.

The children danced around and jumped over the bodies. The crowd milled about, pushing and shoving to get a look at the amazing sight of the two men asleep in a tender embrace. A policeman finally arrived. He staggered along. In uniform he looked like one more costumed member of the festive crowd.

"Come on, move back, move back . . . What's going on here?"

The *pepino* went up to him and threw his arms around him in a tight embrace. Behind the policeman's back, he made mocking gestures with his hands to the spectators. The policeman tried to break free, but in the end the *pepino* was able to drag him off. They went into a small dark bar where only *pisco*[6] and beer were sold. The small boys followed and waited impatiently for the *pepino* to reappear. They called out repeatedly, "*Pepino, pepino* . . . come out, *pepino!*" But, slowly, they had to go their separate ways. From time to time, from behind the curtain serving as the bar's door, other drunkards emerged and wandered off in search of a new corner where the solace sought might still be found.

An hour later it was evening. The revelry had ebbed to a muted jumble of singing, guitars and phonograph records, periodic shouts, and automobile horns blowing to open the way through the still thick crowds. The *pepino* and the policeman appeared arm-in-arm in the doorway of the bar. Caught up in a debate, at moments acrimonious, at others maudlin, they stumbled along. After a short way, the policeman laid his head on the shoulder of his new friend and let himself be led to the stoop of a shut door. There the *pepino* sat him down with the gentleness of a loving mother, pulled his hat down over his eyes and began singing softly to put him to sleep. The policeman put his last remaining strength into two or three attempts to get back on his feet. But well-dosed whacks from the *chorizo* in combination with tender caresses quickly had him calm again, and he was soon profoundly asleep. People laughed as they watched the *pepino* carefully choose a chalky stone from the ground and draw a cross on the door above the head of the deadened policeman.

The *pepino* dispersed the curious and made his way up another street toward a low mud wall from behind which the music of *sicus*[7] and drums seemed to be coming. He climbed up on the wall. In something like a three-sided corral, the fourth side open to the mountainside, he saw Indians dancing in unending circles around their musicians. By their horrific masks of devils and other monsters, he recognized them as a *tundique*[8] group. Women—some with babies or toddlers carried in woven, blanketlike shawls on their backs—served alcohol to the dancers and musicians, pouring from the tin pitcher into the small earthenware cup each carried. The dancers stopped only long enough to toss back the drink, and went back to dancing to the monotonous and unflagging rhythm of the drums.

---

[6]The grape brandy of the Andean region.
[7]Musical instruments made of clusters of reed pipes of varying length and number.
[8]Virtually every village has a distinctive costume worn by its musicians and dancers. These fall into a large number of categories, but the variations within the categories are unlimited.

The *pepino* jumped down from the wall onto the soft ground and mixed with the dancers, musicians and other Indians, disconcerting the company and introducing a discordant note into the liturgical seriousness of the ritual dancing. Fistfuls of ashes were thrown in his face. It was the same ash the priests had used in churches throughout the city that morning to symbolize the start of Lent, when they marked the foreheads of the faithful with the gray sign of repentance. In the afternoon, the gray ash became one of the requisites of carnival revelry.

Bluish shadows had descended over the mountainside, getting darker and darker and creeping in among the *ajtapis* and up over the rugged, stony expanses. Below, the lights of the city had gone on, blinking mysterious messages from another, remote world. The dancing continued, round and round, without pause. And alcohol was poured without pause. The colors of the women's woven skirts flitted in and out of the light thrown by oil lamps hanging on one of the walls. Some of the dancers, worn out by the dancing and the alcohol, lay sleeping, stretched out on the ground. Their wives, seated motionless and silent beside them, watched over them, some nursing a child.

The *pepino* danced as solemnly as the others, his carnival role almost forgotten. His clownish spirit seemed to have dissolved in the desolate and geometric infinity of the dance by which the Indians expressed their unvarying and melancholy existence. At longish intervals, as though his crushed mask suddenly recovered its roguish influence, he gave a few teetering jumps or chased after one of the younger women serving the alcohol. Every time a certain *imilla*,[9] with large slanted, black eyes and firm breasts under a tight bodice, drew near him to serve the alcohol, he tried to catch or at least pinch her. She was always able to jump away with the agility of a young goat, or defend herself, when the timing was right, by hitting him with the pitcher from which she poured the alcohol. Her lips drew tighter and tighter in a picture of growing hatred as this game assumed the character of a grim and dangerous contest. The *pepino* finally succeeded and caught the *imilla* in his arms, pressing her body tightly against his own. The girl, with a supreme effort, broke free from the rapacious arms. The *pepino* leapt to retake her, but she escaped, running upward into the dark beyond the range of the reddish lamplight. The *pepino* took off after her, punctuating his chase with clownish jumps.

The two figures became lost in the deep shadows. No more than two minutes had passed when a terrible scream cut the air, arising like a sharp crest over the sound of the drums and *sicus* and the far-off revelry. The nearby music stopped. One sole drum continued, its beat indecisive until it, too, fell silent. The masks of the dancers with their fixed grotesque expressions turned toward the dark into which the young Indian girl and her pursuer had disappeared. A group of dancers started walking unsteadily in

---

[9]A young, unmarried *india.*

that direction, dispersing as they searched. Soon one called out in Aymara[10] to the others, "Here . . . over here."

Masks began to gather around the spot where, in the diffuse light of the stars, the body of the *pepino* lay face down. Crouching, they noticed a stream of blood flowing lazily from a tear in the neck under the edge of the *pepino*'s mask.

One of the women brought a lamp. Its steady light on the oversized mouths, twisted noses and crooked teeth of the *tundique* masks made their wearers appear even more sinister.

"The police, we must go for the police . . . "

Several masks turned out from the circle, as though looking for the girl, but nobody moved.

"If we bring the police," said another voice, "we'll all end up in jail."

"He came to make trouble. We didn't invite him."

"We have to bury him. Nobody will know. No one knows who he is."

"We have to bury him."

"Somebody bring a pick and shovel."

After a moment of hesitation, two of the dancers left in the direction of a house. The rest remained in the circle around the dead body. Blood continued to flow into the dry and thirsty ground. Some one passed a bottle around, and each drank in turn from it, lifting high the lower edge of his mask. Each dug in turn, as close as possible to the body, when the two men returned with the pick and shovel.

They rolled the dead *pepino* over and grasped him under the arms and by the legs, lifted him over the edge of the opened hole, and let him drop. The body hit bottom with a dull thud. A man holding a lamp drew close, and the diggers bent over the grave in a macabre circle of curious demons. The *pepino* looked back up at them through the mask still protecting an identity which would be revealed only to the worms—guardians of eternal secrets. The first shovelful of earth was returned to the ditch, resounding like little drumbeats on the cardboard of the mask. When a mound had formed above the ground, the dancers trampled it, their movements as liturgical as in their dancing. They levelled the grave with its surroundings, they covered it with stones of all sizes, and they spread it with branches from nearby thickets.

Then they went off, mute and forbidding.

❊ Discussion and Writing

1. Describe the *pepino*'s mask and his *chorizo*. What do they suggest about his role in the carnival? What is the significance of Lent as the time of the carnival?

---

[10]Aymara was the language of the pre-Inca Tiahuanacos. It is still the language spoken in the La Paz region, including a part of the shores of Lake Titicaca. Quechua was the language of the pre-Hispanic Incas and is the most widespread language today of the Andean highlands.

2. Analyze the various episodes of the *pepino's* involvement with the truck, the children, the drunkard, and the policeman. What is the significance of each?
3. Examine the participation of the *indios* in the carnival. Describe the *pepino's* dance and his behavior with the girl. What does his death signify? What is the importance of the *pepino's* anonymity in the carnival?
4. Comment on the mingling of the Christian and indigenous traditions in this celebration. What is the symbolism of *pepino's* death and the ending of the story?

Aime Cesaire
(b. 1913)
Martinique

Aime Cesaire was born in the small northeastern coastal town of Basse-Pointe, Martinique, a town dominated by the presence of the volcano Mont Pelee. The second of six children, he spent his first 11 years in the poor section of the city before the family moved to the capital city of Fort-de-France. Although his mother was a seamstress and his father a tax inspector, the family was poor. They strove, however, for a higher social status: Cesaire's grandmother taught him to read and write in French, and his father read aloud from Victor Hugo rather than narrating the old Creole tales. After his schooling at the Lycee Schoelcher, where he met Leon Damas, Cesaire left Fort-de-France to study at the prestigious Ecole Normale Superieure in Paris. He met Leopold Senghor in Paris in 1931 when he was preparing for his entrance exams to the Ecole. By 1934, he, Senghor, and Damas had established *L'Etudiant noir* (The Black Student) as a medium for presenting the philosophy and writings of what would subsequently be identified as the *negritude* movement. Cesaire coined the term *negritude* in the first version of *Cahiers d'un retour au pays natal* (1939), variously translated as *Notebook of a Return to the Native Land* and *Return to My Native Land.* In this famous poem he set forth the major concerns of the movement: among them, the destructive (often self-destructive) effect of oppression and colonization on people of African descent, and, concomitantly, the ideal of their commonality, of a collective black voice and a mutually beneficial future.

In 1939, the year that *Notebook* was published and that Vichy France occupied the French Antilles, Cesaire returned to Martinique. The racism of the troops, the fascism of the Vichy administration, and the convictions of *negritude* were among the forces that propelled him to a political career. He joined the Communist Party during World War II, was elected mayor of Fort-de-France in 1945, and served as deputy to the French National Assembly. Following the Soviet invasion of Hungary in 1956, he left the Communist Party, and joined the Socialist Martinican Progressive Party, becoming its leader and delegate to the French National Assembly.

However he expressed it, whether in the political arena or in his essays, plays, and poetry, Cesaire remained committed to Carribean autonomy, to the struggle against the depredations of colonialism. He believed in a Caribbean culture and the African and native sources that the Europeans had attempted to obliterate. In his poetry, simultaneously grave and fierce, compassionate and gentle, his aim was, he claimed, "insurrectional" and "*marronner*," that is, to flee established French poetics as the maroons (the West Indian fugitive slaves) fled their French masters in the seventeenth and eighteenth centuries. (Their descendents have been called maroons.) Cesaire's use of *marronner*, typifies his intention and techniques; his use is drawn from those African languages, like Wolof, that do not distinguish between a noun and a verb. Hence, he can project the meaning of the noun in the form of the verb, and he can project action by means of a noun, as in "Peasant the wind."

*To Africa**

For Wifredo Lam

Peasant strike the ground with your daba
in the ground there is an urgency which no syllable of the event will unknot
I reminisce about the memorable plague
there had been no forewarner star
only the earth in a pebbleless wave kneading out of space
a bread of grass and reclusion
strike peasant strike
on the first day the birds died
the second day the fish beached
the third day the animals came out of the woods
and formed a big very strong hot belt for the cities
strike the ground with your daba
there is in the ground the map of transmutations and death's tricks
on the fourth day the vegetation withered
and everything from the agave to the acacia turned bitter

Translated by Clayton Eshleman and Annette Smith

becoming egrets becoming vegetal organ pipes
in which the thorny wind took off amidst flutes and trenchant odors
Strike peasant strike
in the sky windows are being born they are my spurted eyes
their harrow in my chest forms the rampart of a city refusing access to the
  muleteers of despair
Famine and on your own a surge
a heap where future anger risks salvation
strike Anger
there is at the foot of our fairy castles for the rendezvous of blood and landscape the ballroom in which dwarfs pointing their mirrors
listen in the folds of stone or salt to the sex growing from the gaze
Peasant so that the one wounded by the wind can emerge from the head of
  the mountain
so that a mouthful of bells can warm up in her throat
so that my wave can consume itself in her wave and bring us back on the
  sand as drowned ones as the flesh of guavas, torn, as a hand being sketched as beautiful seaweed as aerial seed as a bubble as a recollection as a
  precatory tree
let your act be a wave that howls and regathers toward the hollow of cherished
rocks as if to perfect an island rebelling against birth
there is in the ground the scruple of a tomorrow and the burden of speech
  as well as silence

Peasant the wind in which hulls glide stops the distant hand of a dream
  around my face
your field in its havoc explodes erect with deep-sea monsters which on no
  account will I push away
and my act is as pure as a forgetful brow
strike peasant I am your son
at the hour of the setting sun dusk splashes under my eyelid
a yellowish green tepid with undozing iguanas
but the beautiful messenger ostrich suddenly born from the aroused forms
  of woman beckons to me out of the future in friendship

❊ Discussion and Writing

1. Examine the repeated motif of "strike" and "peasant"? Explore their thematic significance.
2. Discuss the biblical allusions; analyze the depiction of generative power in the first 17 lines; what is the implication of the transformation?
3. Explore the images from nature; how do they function in the poem; what do they evoke about Europe's role in Africa?

4. Identify the images that cluster around the "fairy castle" and the "ballroom." How does the generative power of the imagery relate to that in the earlier section?
5. What do "the scruple of a tomorrow" and "the burden of speech as well as silence" suggest?
6. What is the dream in the last stanza? Who are the "I" and the "you"? What is the importance of the shift from the land to the sea? How does the last stanza relate to the title "To Africa"?
7. Consider the effect of the absence of punctuation and any unusual usage of language.

❋ Research and Comparison

Interdisciplinary Discussion Question: Along with Leopold Senghor and Leon Damas, Cesaire is associated with the movement of *negritude*, which later became controversial. Research Cesaire's perception of and affiliation with it to clarify his ideological assertions.

Interdisciplinary Discussion Question: Research the issue of cultural and ideological bonding of the African diaspora with the motherland, Africa. Also examine the ironic shift in the notion of the "mother country," in postcolonial times, from Europe to Africa, both for Africans and the African diaspora.

Julio Cortazar
(1914–1984)
Argentina

Julio Cortazar was born in Brussels at the time of World War I, but when he was four, he was brought to his family home in Argentina. After his parents divorced, he lived with his mother in Buenos Aires in a household of dominant women. He trained as a teacher of French literature, became a translator of literature written in English as well as in French, (translating the complete prose texts of Edgar Allan Poe), and wrote poetry before recognizing in the late 1940s that fiction was the more appropriate medium for him. It was Borges who published his first stories, stories that reflected the current fantastic aesthetic and Borgesian themes, but it was not until his 1963 novel, *Hopscotch,* that Cortazar became more widely known. Leaving Argentina in 1951 because of the Peron dictatorship, he moved to France, where he translated material for UNESCO. He backed the Cuban Revolution and the Allende government in Chile, donating the award from the Prix Medici for the novel *A Manual for Manuel* to the United Chilean Front; he also backed the Sandinistas in Nicaragua. As a champion of these causes, he found living under the Argentine military and new Peronist regimes impossible. But his writing through the years continued to speak from the Argentine impulse, as the wry humor deepened and darkened.

Our Demeanor at Wakes*

We don't go for the anisette, we don't even go because we're expected to. You'll have guessed our reason already: we go because we cannot stand the craftier forms of hypocrisy. My oldest second cousin takes it upon herself to ascertain the nature of the bereavement, and if it is genuine, if the weeping is genuine because to weep is the only thing left to men and women to do between the odors of lilies and coffee, then we stay at home and escort them from afar. At the most, my mother drops in for a few minutes to represent the family; we don't like to superimpose our strange life upon this dialogue with shadow, that would be insolent. But if my cousin's leisurely investigation discloses the merest suspicion that they've set up the machinery of hypocrisy in a covered patio or in the living room, then the family gets into its best duds, waits until the wake is already under way, and goes to present itself, a few at a time, gradually but implacably.

In the *barrio Pacifico* affairs are generally held in a patio with flowerpots and radio music. For these occasions, the neighbors agree to turn off their radios and the only things left are the pots of jasmine and the relatives, alternating along the walls. We arrive separately or in pairs, we greet the relatives of the deceased, you can always tell who they are—they begin to cry almost as soon as anyone walks in the door—and go to pay our last respects to the dear departed, convoyed along by some close relative. One or two hours later, the whole family is in the bereaved house, but although the neighbors know us well, we act as if each of us had come on his own account and we hardly speak among ourselves. Our acts are governed by a precise method by which to select conversational partners with whom one chats in the kitchen, under the orange tree, in the bedrooms, in the hallway; and every once in a while one goes out for a smoke in the patio or into the street, or takes a stroll around the block to air political opinions or talk sports. We don't spend too much time sounding out the feelings of the closest relatives. Small tumblers of cane liquor, sweet *mate*[1] and the cigarettes are the bridge to confidences; before midnight arrives we are sure we can move remorselessly.

---

*Translated by Paul Blackburn
[1]Tea. [eds.]

Generally, my younger sister is in charge of the opening skirmish; cleverly placing herself at the foot of the coffin, she covers her eyes with a violet handkerchief and begins to cry, silently at first, but to that incredible point where the handkerchief is sopping wet, then with hiccups and gasping, and finally she sets out upon a terrible attack of wailing which obliges the neighborhood ladies to carry her to the bed prepared for such emergencies where they give her orange water to sniff and console her; meanwhile other ladies from the neighborhood look after the nearby relatives infected by the crisis. For a while there's a pile-up of folk in the doorway of the room where the loved one lies in state, whispered questions and answers, the neighbors shrugging their shoulders. Exhausted by a force for which they themselves have had to go all out, the relatives diminish their demonstrations of grief, and just at that moment my three girl cousins set off into a weeping without affectation, no loud cries but so touchingly that the relatives and the neighbors feel envious; they realize that they can't just sit there resting while strangers from the next block are grieving in such a fashion. Again they rise to the general lament, again space must be found on beds, fanning old ladies, loosening belts on convulsed little old men. Usually my brothers and I wait for this moment to make our entrance into the viewing room and we place ourselves together about the coffin. Strange as it may seem we really are grief-stricken, we can never listen to our sisters cry but that an infinite dismay fills our breasts and we remember things from childhood—some fields near the Villa Albertina, a tram that cheeped taking the curve at the Calle General Rodriguez in Banfield, things like that, always very sad ones. We need only to see the deceased's crossed hands for a flood of tears to demolish us all at once, compelling us to cover our abashed faces, and we are five men who really cry at wakes, while the relatives desperately gather the breath to match us, feeling that, at whatever cost, they have to make it evident that it's their wake, that only they have the right to cry like that in that house. But there are few of them and they're faking (we know that from my oldest second cousin, and it lends us strength). Hiccups and fainting fits accumulate in vain, the closest neighbors back them up with their consolation and considered meditations; it's useless carrying or leading them off to rest and recuperate so they can throw themselves renewed back into the struggle. Now my father and elder uncle spell us; there's something that commands respect in the grief of these old men who've come from the Calle Humboldt, five blocks away if you count from the corner, to keep vigil on the one who has passed away. The more coherent neighbors begin to lose their footing, they finally let the relatives drop and go to the kitchen to drink grappa and comment on the state of affairs; some of the relatives, debilitated by an hour-and-a-half of sustained weeping, are sleeping very loudly. We relieve one another in turns, without giving the impression, however, of anything prearranged; before six in the morning we are the acknowledged masters of the wake, the majority of the neighbors have gone back to their houses to sleep, the relations are lying around in different postures and degrees of bloatedness, dawn falls upon the patio. At that hour my aunts are organizing strong refreshments in the kitchen, we drink boiling coffee, we beam at one another passing in the entryway or the bedrooms; we're a bit like ants, going and coming, rubbing antennae as we pass. When the hearse arrives the seating arrangements have already been decided. My sisters lead the relatives to take final leave of the deceased before the closing of the coffin, support them and comfort them, while my girl cousins and my brothers push forward to displace them, cutting short the final farewell, and remain alone with the corpse. Exhausted, wandering around displaced, understanding vaguely but incapable of reacting, the relatives let themselves be led and dragged; they drink anything brought to their lips and answer the loving solicitude of my sisters and cousins with vague and inconsistent protests. When the time has come to leave and the house full of relations and friends, an invisible organization but with no loopholes, decides every movement, the funeral director respects my father's instructions the removal of the coffin is accomplished according to the suggestions of my elder uncle. At one point or another, relatives arriving at the last moment start a querulous and disorderly attempt to regain possession; the neighbors, convinced that everything is proceeding apace, look at them scandalized and make them be quiet. My parents and my uncles install themselves in the first car, my brothers get into the second, and my girl cousins condescend to take one of the closer relatives in the third, in which they settle themselves wrapped in great black or purple shawls. The rest get into whatever car they can, and there are relatives who find themselves obliged to call a taxi. And if some of them, revived by the morning air and the long ride, plot a reconquest at the cemetery, they're in for a bitter disillusion. The coffin has barely arrived at the cemetery gates than my brothers make a circle around the orator picked by the family or friends of the deceased, easily recognizable by his long, sad, funereal and prepared face and the little roll of paper bulging from his jacket pocket. Reaching out their hands and grabbing him, they soak his lapels with their tears, they clap his shoulders softly with a sound like tapioca pudding, and the orator cannot prevent my youngest uncle from mounting the platform where he opens the speeches with an oration that is the very soul of truth and discretion. It lasts three minutes, it refers solely to the deceased, it marks the limits of his virtues and notes his defects, and there is humanity in every word he says; he is deeply moved, and at times it is difficult for him to quit. He has barely stepped down when my oldest brother takes to the platform and launches a panegyric on behalf of the neighborhood; meanwhile the neighbor designated to this task tries to get through a crowd of my sisters and cousins who weep buckets and hang onto his vest. An affable but imperious gesture of my father's mobilizes the funeral-parlor personnel; they set the catafalque softly in motion, and the official orators are still standing at the foot of the platform, mashing their speeches in their wet hands. Normally we don't bother to conduct the deceased to the vault or sepulchre, but usually make a half-turn and exit all together, commenting on the incidents during the wake. We watch from a distance the relatives running desperately to grab hold of one of the ropes holding the coffin and fighting with the neighbors who have meanwhile taken possession of the ropes and prefer to carry it themselves rather than let the relatives carry it.

❋ Discussion and Writing

1. What seems to be the motivation for the behavior of the family who are "the acknowledged masters of the wake"?
2. Contrast the behavior of the bereaved families and the narrator's family. Discuss the inherent social commentary.
3. Given that the fact of death is in itself painful, what is the impact of treating the circumstances around it comically?
4. Analyze the various devices Cortazar uses to create humor: surprise, exaggeration, juxtaposition of antithetical ideas. Comment on other narrative techniques of the writer.

❋ Research and Comparison

Examine various literary writings that treat death in different ways: sentimentally, philosophically, or comically. Analyze the implied intent and the impact of the writings.

Interdisciplinary Discussion Question: Scholars have considered death as the catalyst of religious thought in human history. Research the topic of the historical beginnings of religious thought. Comment on why death, even more than birth, has been such an important issue engaging the human mind.

Interdisciplinary Discussion Question: Examine several of the various funeral traditions of the world. Comment on the sociological rationale for each. Are there any common elements in each tradition? Explain the differences.

Julia de Burgos
(1914–1953)
Puerto Rico

Julia de Burgos was born in the Santa Cruz country community in Carolina, Puerto Rico, the eldest of 13 children, 6 of whom died because of the family's extreme poverty. Her father, an imaginative, adventurous, physically strong man, introduced her to *Don Quixote* and to other heroic tales. But he also drank heavily, and as the eldest, it was her responsibility to fetch him after a drinking bout. Her mother, a woman known for her generosity and to whom she was exceptionally close, nurtured her poetic sensibility and her spirituality. Despite the economic hardship, her parents managed to pay her school fees—sometimes with help from their neighbors—moving later to the city so that she could attend the university. There, however, they grew even more impoverished, and when she left the Escuela Superior to begin teaching, she helped support her family. Her work took her back to the countryside and the world of nature that had so profoundly affected her as a child. It was while she was at the university that she learned about and became committed to the struggles for Puerto Rican independence; and in the mid-1930s, in response to Nationalist Party revolutionary efforts, she began to write poetry. But both the natural and imaginative worlds of her childhood informed her poetry, however political its manifestations: the fields and mountains; the wind and the trees; the river, along which she walked to school with her mother; Don Quixote; all retained their symbolic vitality.

As her political consciousness evolved, Julia de Burgos spoke out for independence for women as well as for Puerto Rico, and she protested against the social forces constricting the rights of blacks and workers as well as of women. During this period, her mother developed cancer, and she herself contracted pneumonia; she lost a position with the Escuela del Aire, an educational radio program, because of her political associations, and she was barely able to support herself and her mother. She also embarked on an ardent love affair that ended bitterly with her betrayal. In 1939, after the death of her mother, she left the island for Cuba, where she lived for two years. During the following 11 years of lonely exile in New York, her mental and physical health deteriorated; she was very poor, and turned to drink. She died on the city's streets, unknown.

*To Julia de Burgos**

They say I am your enemy
because I give your inmost self to the world in verse.
They lie, Julia de Burgos. They lie, Julia de Burgos.
The voice that sounds in my poems is not your voice: it is my voice;
because you are the trappings and I am the essence:
and between us stretches the deepest divide.

You are the cold doll of social prevarication,
and I the living spark of human truth.

---

*Translated by William M. Davis

You are the honey of polite hypocrisies; not I,
who lay bare my naked heart in all my poems.

You are like your world, selfish; not I,
who risk everything to be what I am.

You are only the prim ladylike lady;
not I; I am life, strength, woman.

You belong to your husband, to your master; not I;
I belong to no one, or to everyone, because to everyone, everyone,
I give myself in my pure feeling and my thought.

You curl your hair and paint your face; not I;
My hair is curled by the wind, my face is painted by the sun.

You are a housewife, resigned, submissive,
ruled by the prejudices of men; not I;
I am a runaway Rocinante[1]
sniffing at horizons for the justice of God.

You do not command yourself; everyone commands you:
your husband, your parents, your relatives,
the priest, the dressmaker, the theater, the casino,
the car, the jewels, the banquet, the champagne,
heaven and hell and social gossip.

Not me; to me only my heart gives commands,
only my thought; the one who commands me is myself.

You, flower of the aristocracy, and I, flower of the people.
You have everything and you owe everything to everyone,
while I, my nothingness I owe to no one.

You, nailed to the static ancestral dividend,
and I, a one in the cipher of the social divider,
we are in a duel to the death approaching the inevitable.

While the multitudes race about frantically,
leaving behind ashes from burnt-out injustices,

---

[1]Don Quixote's horse. [eds]

and while with the torch of the seven virtues
the multitudes pursue the seven sins,
against you, and against everything unjust and inhuman,
I shall go into their midst with the torch in my hand.

❋ Discussion and Writing

1. What images are associated with "I" and "you"? Discuss the distinctions between the two.
2. Why is one called the enemy of the other? Discuss the source of the conflict between the two.
3. What is the resolution of the conflict? Explain the symbolism of the torch.

❋ Research and Comparison

Interdisciplinary Discussion Question: Research the issue of gender relations in Puerto Rican culture. Compare the distinct perspectives depicted by Puerto Rican writers of different generations in this anthology.

Octavio Paz
(b. 1914)
Mexico

Octavio Paz was born in Mixcoac, a village that at the time was on the outskirts of Mexico City. His grandfather, of mestizo ancestry, was a journalist and novelist; his father was a lawyer who defended Zapata in the United States and helped develop land reform. Both fought for Mexico: his grandfather against the French who attempted to establish a Mexican empire, his father in the Mexican Revolution (1910–1920). Financially drained, the family lived in a crumbling mansion, but the grandfather's library remained intact. Octavio Paz's wide reading started in that library, but all of this family and national history shaped his sensibility. He began publishing poetry along with setting up and editing magazines at 17, an activity that has persisted throughout his life. When he was 23 and already writing political poetry, he participated in the Second International Congress of Anti-Fascist Writers in Spain, where he met the leading European and Latin American poets, among them Pablo Neruda and Cesar Vallejo. Although the Nazi-Soviet pact in 1938 shattered his allegiance to Soviet communism, Paz continued to protest against fascism during the

Spanish Civil War and World War II, and indeed, he has continued to protest against contemporary social injustice.

During the late 1930s and early 1940s, several factors changed the direction of his poetry. One was his examination of Spanish existentialist thought; another was a two-year stay in the U.S. as a Guggenheim Fellow. Seeing Mexican underdevelopment from the perspective of U.S. techno-logical advantage prompted his concern with Mexican identity and ulti-mately led to *El laberinto de la soledad* (The Labyrinth of Solitude, 1950). One of his major works and his first book in prose, *Labyrinth* represented the younger generation of writers and the new Latin American literature. While explicitly focusing on national identity, on Mexican solitude, it implicitly included Latin American identity. Equally important was his poem *Sunstone* (1958), a circular rereading of Aztec mythology. Both books established his international reputation as a major poet and essayist.

From 1945 to 1968, Paz served in the diplomatic corps, leaving when the Mexican government massacred student demonstrators at the time of the 1968 Olympic Games. During the last six years of service, when he was ambassador to India, he studied Indian art and Buddhist and Tantric philosophies, subsequently recasting his poetry and essays as he spoke from a reformulated vision. Since that time, he has lectured throughout the world, established and edited the journal *Vuelta* (1976), still a significant force in Latin American literature, and published a wide range of poetry and prose.

Return*

You spread out beneath my eyes,
a land of dunes—ocher, bright.
The wind in search of water stopped,
a land of heartbeats and fountains.
Vast as the night you fit
in the hollow of my hand.

Later, the motionless hurling down,
within and without ourselves
With my eyes I ate darkness,
drank the water of time, I drank night.
Then I touched the body of a music
heard with the tips of my fingers.

Dark boats, together,
moored in the shadows,

Translated by Eliot Weinberger

our bodies reclined.
Our souls, unlashed,
lamps afloat
in the water of night.

In the end you opened your eyes,
You saw yourself seen by my eyes,
and from my eyes you saw yourself:
falling like a fruit on the grass,
like a stone in the pond,
you fell into yourself.

A tide rose within me,
with a weightless fist I beat
at the door of your lids:
my death wanted to meet you,
my death wanted to meet itself.
I was buried in your eyes.

Our bodies flow through the plains
of night: they are time wearing itself out,
a presence that dissolves in a caress;
yet they are infinite, to touch them
is to bathe in rivers of heartbeats
and return to the perpetual beginning anew.

❊ Discussion and Writing

1. Paz refers to "you" in the first line and later mentions "our bodies" and "our souls." Whom or what does the poet refer to?
2. Examine the use of paradoxical imagery, phrases, and concepts in the poem. What does Paz imply through the yoking of these antitheses?
3. Explain the concept of death as it is presented in the poem. What is death's relation to life, to love?
4. Explicate the last stanza of the poem. What is the relevance of the title to the poem?

❊ Research and Comparison

Analyze the concepts Octavio Paz develops in *The Labyrinth of Solitude*, and examine the importance of this work in Mexican literature.

Interdisciplinary Discussion Question: "Return" is one of Octavio Paz's later poems. Discuss the influence of Indian philosophy, particularly the concept of reincarnation, on his later work.

Joseph Zobel
(b. 1915)
Martinique

Joseph Zobel was born in the village of Petit-Bourg, Martinique, and attended the Lycee Schoelcher in Fort-de-France, but without a scholarship he was unable to pursue his education in France until after World War II. Before the war he worked at various jobs: as secretary/accountant for the Department of Bridges and Highways, as supervisor for the lycee; and he began writing stories and a novel. During the war he served as press attaché to the governor; after the war ended, he published a collection of short stories and two novels, and went to France, where he studied at the Institute of Ethnology and at the Sorbonne. He remained in France for 11 years, teaching, writing, and working in radio. In 1957, he traveled to Senegal, where he worked for 20 years in Dakar: teaching, setting up schools, founding the Cultural Services of Radio Senegal, and writing. Zobel planned at first to return to Martinique but finally decided, like Mr. Medouze in his autobiographical *La rue cases-negres* (1950), that Africa was indeed his home.

In *La rue cases-negres* (Black Shack Alley), Zobel depicts Martiniquan plantation life between the two world wars, portraying the retention of African traditions on West Indian plantations, as well as colonialism, class conflicts, and economic exploitation. Like other great West Indian story-tellers, Zobel responded to the freeing effects of the *negritude* movement and revealed in his work the nurturing link among Francophone writers. In 1931, for instance, Jacques Roumain published "Guinee" (later entitled "Sur le chemin de Guinee"), a poem informed by the belief Zobel's Mr. Medouze was to voice some 20 years later: "when I'm dead, I'll go to Guinea." The vitality of the link continues in the film adaptation of *La rue cases-negres, Sugar Cane Alley* (1984).

Mr. Medouze*

My great friend didn't give me anything. He was the oldest, most wretched and most abandoned on the entire plantation. And I preferred being with him to running, frolicking, amusing myself or pinching sugar.

For someone like myself who couldn't sit still one moment, I would remain for hours sitting quietly beside him. His hut was the emptiest and the dirtiest, but I preferred it to M'man Tine's, which was one of the finest and best kept in Shack Alley.

*Translated by Keith Q. Warner

"Children must not always be in other people's places," my grand-mother used to remind me. "It's bad manners."

But at nights, as I looked at M'man Tine smoking, I longed for only one thing, waited for only one thing: to have the voice of Mr. Medouze call me.

Outside the door that stood wide open to the darkness already accumu-lated in the shack, a shadow scarcely visible in the distance awaited me—to send me to beg for a pinch of salt from M'man Tine, or to buy two cents worth of kerosine in the shop.

Then in front of the shack we lit a fire between three stones. I was the one who went nearby in search of the twigs that the flame devoured so readily.

While in the *canari* a noisy bubbling converted the wild roots brought back from the cane field where he had worked, the ghost-like form sat on the front step of the shack, at the edge of that terrible rectangular mouth that drank in the night, and I went beside him. He filled his pipe when he was finished, and I went near the fireside to fetch him a flaming twig: as he bent his head over it to light his pipe, the glow cast on his face a hallucinating mask—the true face of Mr. Medouze—with his head streaked with reddish hair, his beard looking like brambles, his eyes, of which one could never see but a small slit, because his eyelids were almost always closed.

The glow from the fireside lit up the entire side of the shack; and Mr. Medouze's body, covered with only a loin-cloth similar to Mr. Saint-Louis's, with, around his neck, a tiny sack black with dirt and hanging from a string, looked like a handsome, masculine body that the fire had roasted for a long time and that it now delighted in enriching with all the shades of brown.

He finished smoking his pipe in silence, almost motionless. After a while, as if awaking from his inertia, he cleared his throat, spat and, in a voice that kept failing, he cried point-blank:

"*Titim!*"

Thereupon my attention was immediately revived and my joy exploded in my prompt reply:

"Dry wood!"

That was how our game of riddles began.

"I'm here, I'm in France!" Mr. Medouze proposed.

Pretending to be wracking my brains, I merely looked at him. His steady, calm face once more assumed fantastic expressions in the glow of the flames flickering under the *canari*. He knew, moreover, that I would not find the answer to his riddle and that I was waiting.

"A letter," he told me at last.

A letter? I didn't know what that was; but that only made it seem all the more marvellous. In general, Mr. Medouze, as if to have a sort of revision, started with the most elementary "*titims*," those to which I already had the key.

"When water climbed up a hill?"

"A coconut," I replied in a flash.

"When water ran down a hill?"

"Sugar cane!"

"When Madame put on her apron back to front?"

"A fingernail."

Then he moved on to the more difficult ones.

"Madame is in her bedroom and her hair is floating outside."

Silence. Prolonged silence. A few puffs slowly taken from the old pipe, and he himself supplied the answer.

"A yam."

That seemed odd to me.

"Of course," he explained, "the yam is in the ground which serves as a bedroom, and its tendrils, like curls of hair, climb on the sticks."

The main attraction of these riddle sessions was to discover how a world of inanimate objects managed to resemble and be identified with a world of people and animals. How an earthenware water-bottle held by the neck became a servant who only served water to his master when the latter choked him. How the manager's parasol looked like "a shack with only one post."

Thus, at the mere intervention of Mr. Medouze, the world expanded, increased, teemed in a swirl around me.

When Mr. Medouze finished his pipe, he would spit violently, wipe his lips with the back of his hand, which he also passed over the prickly shagginess of his beard. Then came the most disturbing part of the evening.

"Eh *cric!*"[1]

"Eh *crac!*"

My heart started beating wildly, my eyes were aflame.

"Thrice fines stories!"

"All stories are nice to hear!"

"Who is Dog's mother?"

"Bitch."

"Dog's father?"

"Bull dog."

"Abouhou!"

"Biah!"

I had answered the preamble properly.

Silence. I held my breath.

"Well, once upon a time," Mr. Medouze started slowly, "when Rabbit used to walk around dressed in white calico suit and Panama hat; when all the traces on Petit-Morne were paved with diamonds, rubies, topaz (all the streams ran gold and Grand Etang was a pool of honey); when I, Medouze,

---

[1]Eh *cric!* . . . Eh *crac!*: responsive form of beginning and continuing a story. [eds.]

was Medouze; there was at that time, an old man who lived all alone in a castle, far, far, far away."

"A liar would say far like from here to Grand-Riviére. My brother, who used to lie a bit, would have said like from here to St. Lucia. But I not being a liar, say that it was far like from here to Guinea . . . eh *cric!*"

"Eh *crac!*"

"That man used to live by himself and was middle-aged," Medouze continued, "but he did not lack anything. One morning, he put on his boots, took his hat and, taking care not to eat or drink anything, mounted his white horse and set out.

"At first, the journey began in perfect silence. As if the horse were galloping on clouds. Then, as the sun came up, the man was himself surprised to hear music behind him. He slowed down; the music became slow and indistinct. He stopped. Silence. He spurred his mount, the music started up again.

"He then realized that it was the four horse shoes that were playing so harmoniously:

'Tis the queen's ball,
Plakata, plakata
'Tis the queen's ball,
Plakata, plakata.

"But what music!

'Tis the queen's ball.'"

Medouze sang. With his deep, grating voice, he imitated one hundred violins, twenty "mama-violins" (cellos), ten clarinets and fifteen contra-basses.

Overcome by his fervor, I took up the magical song along with him:

Plakata, Plakata.

But, alas! the voice of M'man Tine rang out and came to break our duet. My heart heavy with regret, annoyed to tears, I had to give up the rest of the fairy tale, and to hastily abandon my old friend with a quick "good night."

That was what transpired almost every night. I could never hear a story right through to the end. I didn't know if it was M'man Tine who called me away too soon, although she always scolded me for staying too long, or if it was Medouze who did not tell the story quickly enough. At any rate, there was not a night when I didn't leave with my heart and my curiosity unappeased.

In addition to Petit-Morne, to its workers and to ourselves, we knew that the world extended even further, beyond the factory whose chimneys we could see, and that on the other side of the hills surrounding the plantation, lay other similar plantations.

We also knew that there was the town, Fort-de-France, with many vehicles in the streets.

M'man Tine had already told me about a far-off country called France where people had white skins and spoke something called "French"; a country from which came the flour used to make bread and cakes, and where all sorts of beautiful things were made.

On some nights, either in his tales or in his talks, Mr. Medouze evoked another country even further away, even deeper than France, which was that of his father: Guinea. There, people were like him and me; but they did not die of tiredness nor of hunger.

There was no misery as there was here.

Nothing stranger than to see Mr. Medouze evoke Guinea, to hear the voice rising from his entrails when he spoke of slavery and related the horrible story his father had told him, of the rape of his family, of the disappearance of his nine uncles and aunts, of his grandfather and his grandmother.

"Everytime my father tried to relate his life story," he continued, "once he got to: 'I had a big brother called Ousmane, a younger sister called Sonia, the last one,' he would shut his eyes very tight and fall silent all of a sudden. And I, too, would bite my lips as if I had received a stab in my heart. 'I was young,' my father said, 'when all the blacks fled from the plantations because it had been said that slavery was over.' I, too, danced with joy and went running all over Martinique because, for a long time, I had so wanted to flee, to run away. But when the intoxication of my freedom was spent, I was forced to remark that nothing had changed for me nor for my comrades in chains. I hadn't found my brothers and sisters, nor my father, nor my mother. I remained like all the blacks in this damned country: the bekes[2] kept the land, all the land in the country, and we continued working for them. The law forbade them from whipping us, but did not force them to pay us our due."

"Yes," he added, "at any rate, we remained under the beke, attached to his land. And he remained our master."

Naturally, Mr. Medouze was then angry and in vain I looked at him with a frown on my brow, in vain I had this maddening urge to hit the beke I set my eyes on. I could not make out all he was grumbling and, to console him, I said to him:

"If you were to go to Guinea, Monsieur Medouze, you know, I'd go with you. I think M'man Tine wouldn't mind."

"Alas!" he replied, with a sad smile, "Medouze won't be seeing Guinea. Besides, I have no maman, no papa, no brothers or sisters in Guinea . . . Yes,

---

[2]The first French white settlers in Martinique.

when I'm dead, I'll go to Guinea; but then, I won't be able to take you. You'll not be old enough; and then, I mustn't."

❀ Discussion and Writing

1. Explore the nature of the friendship between the young boy and Mr. Medouze. What does Zobel imply by describing Mr. Medouze's face as "a hallucinating mask"?
2. Describe the ritual of the game of riddles. Analyze the images and metaphors: what do they evoke about the people and their lives in Black Shack Alley?
3. Explain the importance of the story of Mr. Medouze's father. What is the significance of the journey to Guinea? Comment on the implications of the last sentence.

❀ Research and Comparison

Interdisciplinary Discussion Question: Compare the novel *Black Shack Alley* to the film *Sugar Cane Alley*.

Murilo Rubiao
(b. 1916)
Brazil

Murilo Rubiao, who was born in a small town in the district of Minas Gerais, Brazil, moved with his family to Belo Horizonte when he was seven years old, and was raised in a literary atmosphere. Not only were his grandfather, his father, an uncle, and several cousins all writers, but they all loved to read. They especially favored mythical and fantastic material: fairy tales and the Bible; *Don Quixote* and *A Thousand and One Nights;* and, of course, the acknowledged master, Machado de Assis. Rubiao took his law degree and worked for a time in government. In the late 1930s, he founded a literary review with other students at the university; and some 20 years later, after four lonely years when he served as attaché in Madrid, he founded another journal. He began publishing his stories in the 1940s and participated in the First Brazilian Congress of Writers, which denounced the censorship exercised by the government of Getulio Vargas, a protest that worked toward ending that dictatorship. A meticulous crafts-man, Rubiao has a small but highly respected body of work, tales that illuminate the fantastic.

Teleco, the Rabbit*

*There be three things which
are too wonderful for me, yea,
four which I know not:
the way of an eagle in the air,
the way of a serpent upon a
rock; the way of a ship in the
midst of the sea; and the way
of a man with a maid.*
PROVERBS, XXX:18–19

"Hey, got a cigarette?"

The voice was faint, almost a whisper. I stayed in the same position, watching the sea, while absorbed in ridiculous memories.

Annoyingly, the beggar insisted:

"Buddy, hey! Buddy! Got a cigarette?"

With eyes still fixed on the beach, I muttered:

"Listen, fellow, get lost or I'll call a policeman."

"Okay, mister. No need to get sore. But, say, would you mind getting out of my line of vision? I like to look at the ocean too, you know."

Exasperated with the insolence of whoever was addressing me in such a fashion, I spun around, ready to send him on his way with a good kick. I was stunned, however. There before me was an ash-gray rabbit, delicately querying me:

"If you don't give, it's because you haven't got, right, my friend?"

His polite way of expressing things touched me. I gave him a cigarette and moved to one side, so as to let him have a better view of the sea. He didn't even take the time to thank me, because by then we were already chatting like old friends. Or, to be more accurate, the rabbit did the talking. He spoke of such extraordinary events, of such remarkable adventures, I concluded he was older than he seemed.

Toward the end of the afternoon, I inquired where he lived. He said he had no fixed abode, the street serving as his usual habitat. It was then that I noticed his eyes, gentle eyes, and sad. I felt such compassion, I invited him to come and stay with me. The house was huge, and anyway I lived alone—I added.

This did not convince him. He insisted I own up to my real intentions:

"It couldn't just be you happen to like rabbit meat?" He didn't wait for my reply. "If you do, better look elsewhere, because versatility is my one weakness."

---

*Translated by Thomas Colchie

And saying so, he changed himself into a giraffe.

"At night," he continued, "I could be a snake or a dove. It won't bother you, the company of one so unstable?"

I answered no, and we began to live together.

His name was Teleco.

As we got on more intimate terms, I discovered that the mania for metamorphosing into other creatures was, in his case, simply a desire to please people. He liked being gentle to children and the elderly, entertaining them with clever tricks or lending them a hand. The same horse that, in the morning, did so much galloping around with kids, come evening, gently walked the aged and infirm back to their homes.

He took a dislike to certain neighbors, among them a pawnbroker and his sisters, to whom he would appear in the skin of a lion or a tiger. He frightened them more to amuse us than out of malice. The victims, though, were not so understanding and complained to the police, who then wasted their time listening to persistent accusations. Even after ransacking our house from top to bottom, they could find no animal other than a rabbit. The detectives, therefore, grew irritated and threatened to lock up the complainers.

Only once did I fear that the antics of my restless companion were about to cause serious complications. I was receiving one of my usual visits from the police inspector when Teleco, prompted by a bit of thoughtless mischief, unexpectedly turned himself into a peccary. The change and the shift back into his previous form were too quick for the man to have time to scream. He'd barely opened his mouth in horror when once again he had in front of him merely a tame rabbit.

"Did you see what I saw?"

Putting on an innocent face, I told him I hadn't noticed anything out of the ordinary.

The man eyed me dubiously and, without saying goodbye, made his way out the front door.

Teleco played tricks on me as well. If I found the house empty, I knew he must be hidden away in some corner, disguised as a tiny animal, or even somewhere on my body in the form of a flea, busy dodging my fingers, running down my back. When sometimes I became impatient and told him to stop fooling around, it would, often as not, end in an awful scare. A billy-goat would grow up under my legs and, like a shot, carry me out into the backyard. I'd be furious, and promise him a good thrashing. But, feigning remorse, Teleco would soon distract me with his affable chatter and quickly restore peace.

Then he would be once more that docile friend who charmed us with his unexpected magical tricks. He loved colors and often flew up, transformed into a bird of all conceivable colors, of an entirely unknown species or an already extinct variety.

"There's no such bird as that!"

"I know. But it's rather insipid to simulate only the known varieties."

The first serious clash I had with Teleco occurred about a year after we met. I was returning from my sister-in-law Emi's, with whom I had just had some serious differences over family matters. So I was in quite a bad humor, and the scene I stumbled upon as I opened the front door only served to fan my irritation. Holding hands, seated together on the living-room sofa, were a young woman and a shabby-looking kangaroo. His clothes were ill-fitted, his eyes half hidden behind a pair of ordinary wire-rimmed spectacles.

"What do you want, Miss, with that horrible animal?" I asked, annoyed at finding my house invaded by strangers.

"I'm Teleco," he interjected, with a slight laugh.

I stared disdainfully at the puny creature, with his sparse coat of hair, betraying such a level of obsequiousness and depravity. Nothing about him recalled the playful bunny.

So I refused to accept his assertion as the truth, especially since Teleco had no trouble with his vision and, if he should want to present himself all dressed up, would certainly have the good taste to choose different clothes, not these.

Faced with my incredulousness, he changed into a tree toad, leaped on top of the furniture, hopped into my lap. I flung him off me, filled with repugnance.

Recovering his form of a kangaroo once more, he questioned me with an extremely grave air:

"Is that proof enough?"

"Yes. And so? What do you want?"

"From today on, I shall just be a man."

"A man?" I repeated in astonishment. I couldn't ignore the ridiculousness of the situation and burst out laughing. "And that?" I pointed to the girl. "Is she a lizard, or a young salamander?"

She looked at me angrily. She wanted to retort with something too, but he cut her off:

"This is Tereza. She's come to live with us. Isn't she a beauty?"

Right, a beauty. During the night I couldn't sleep, my thoughts revolving around her, as well as on the idiocy of Teleco's claiming to be a man.

I got up the next morning and headed for the living room, expecting the facts of the day before to have dissolved into one of my companion's harmless charades.

I was mistaken. Stretched out on the living-room carpet beside the girl was the same kangaroo, snoring loudly. I woke him, pulling him by the arms:

"Let's go. Teleco, enough of this hanky-panky."

He opened his eyes, startled, but, recognizing me, smiled:

"Teleco? My name's Barbosa, Antonio Barbosa. Right, Tereza?"

She was just now waking up and concurred with a nod of her head.

I exploded with rage:

"If it's Barbosa, out! And don't ever set foot in my house again, you filthy son of a rodent!"

Tears ran down his face, and, down on his knees in front of me, he clasped both my legs, begging me not to kick him out of the house, at least until he found a job.

Although I viewed with skepticism the possibility of a kangaroo finding work, his weeping dissuaded me from my previous decision, or, rather, to tell the whole truth, I was actually more persuaded by the imploring look that came from Tereza, who had followed our conversation apprehensively.

Barbosa had terrible habits. He repeatedly spat on the floor and rarely took baths, notwithstanding his enormous self-conceit, which drove him to spend hours at a time in front of the mirror. He also used my shaving gear and toothbrush. It didn't help very much either to buy these things for him, since he continued to use mine as well as his. And when I complained of this abusive behavior, he simply excused himself by feigning absentmindedness.

Furthermore, his ungainly figure absolutely repelled me. His skin was greasy, his limbs stubby, his heart secretive. He spared no effort to try to please me, reciting anecdotes devoid of humor, exaggerating his praises of my person.

On the other hand, I found it hard to tolerate his lies and, at meals, his eating, the noisy way he stuffed food into his mouth with both hands.

Perhaps because I succumbed to Tereza's charms, perhaps not to displease her, I suffered the uncomfortable presence of Barbosa without complaint.

If ever I claimed that Teleco's intention—to impose his false human condition upon us—was nothing but nonsense, she would reply with disconcerting conviction:

"His name's Barbosa, and he is a man."

The kangaroo soon perceived my interest in his female companion and, mistaking my tolerance for possible weakness, he grew impertinent and made fun of me whenever I reproached him for wearing my clothes, smoking my cigarettes, or filching money out of my pockets.

On various occasions I appealed to his now slackening sensibilities, asking him to return to being a rabbit.

"Being a rabbit? I was never an animal. I don't know what you're talking about."

"I'm talking about a sweet gray bunny who had the habit of changing himself into other animals."

During this intermediate period, my love for Tereza wavered among dark fantasies which had little hope of ever being reciprocated. Still, in the midst of such uncertainty I decided to propose marriage.

Coldly and without hesitation, she closed the matter at once:

"Your offer is less generous than you suppose. He's worth much more."

The choice of words in her refusal convinced me she contemplated exploiting the talents of Teleco in a questionable manner.

Frustrated in my attempt to become engaged, I could not stand now to see them so intimate together, and I became aggressive.

The kangaroo noticed the change in my behavior and chose to avoid places where we might run into one another.

One evening, returning from work, my attention was alerted by the deafening sound of the victrola, turned on at full volume. Opening the front door, I immediately felt the blood rush to my head: Tereza and Barbosa, faces glued together, were dancing a lascivious samba.

Indignantly, I separated the two, grabbed the kangaroo by the neck, and, shaking him violently, led him over to the living-room mirror:

"Is that or is that not an animal?"

"No, I'm a man!" And he sobbed, his legs trembling, numb with fear at the fury he saw in my eyes.

Then he asked Tereza, who, on hearing his cries, had come to his assistance:

"Aren't I a man, dear? Talk to him."

"Yes, love, you are a man."

Absurd as it seemed to me, there was a kind of tragic certainty in their voices. I had already made up my mind, however. I threw Barbosa to the floor and started boxing him on the mouth. Then I drove them both out of the house.

From the street, though, she warned me angrily:

"I'll make an important person out of Barbosa, you swine!"

That was the last time I saw them. I did hear, much later, vague rumors about a magician named Barbosa who was having great successes in the city. But lacking further clarification of the matter, I concluded it to be a mere coincidence of names.

My passion for Tereza evaporated with the passage of time, and my interest in stamps returned. I spent whatever spare moments I had busying myself with my collection.

One evening, just as I was pasting in some rare stamps—I had received them the day before—suddenly a dog jumped through the window. When I recovered from the initial shock, I tried to shoo the animal out. I didn't manage to get rid of him, however.

"I'm Teleco, your old friend," he murmured, in a voice excessively tremulous and sad, and changed himself to an agouti.

"And Tereza?" I asked with pretended indifference.

"Tereza . . . " Without concluding the phrase, he took on the shape of a peacock.

"There were lots of colors . . . the circus . . . she was lovely . . . it was horrible . . . ," he continued, vibrating his tail like a rattlesnake.

After a brief silence, he tried to speak again:

"The uniform . . . very white . . . five ropes . . . tomorrow I'll be a man. . . ." The words came out strained, disconnected, as Teleco metamorphosed into different animals.

He coughed for a moment. A nervous cough. Weak at first, he swelled up with his mutations into other larger animals, while I pleaded with him to calm down. Yet he was unable to control himself.

He tried vainly to explain. His sentences came out broken and confused.

"Enough of that now, try to speak more calmly," I insisted, losing patience with his continuous transformations.

"I can't!" he stammered, in the skin of a lizard.

Even after a few days the same turmoil persisted. Hiding in corners, trembling, Teleco kept whimpering, changing himself, on and on, into the most varied animals. He stuttered a great deal and couldn't feed himself, since his mouth, growing and diminishing according to the creature he embodied at the moment, did not always match the size of the food. Then out of his eyes poured the tears which, small in the eyes of a rat, bubbled enormous on the cheeks of a hippo.

Impotent to lessen his agony, I hugged him closely, crying. His body, though, grew in my arms, squeezing me up against the wall.

He didn't speak anymore—he mooed, cawed, brayed, squealed, howled, twittered.

Finally less disturbed, he began to limit his transformations to smaller animals, until he settled into the shape of a lamb, sadly bleating. I gathered him up in my arms and felt his body perspiring, burning with fever.

On the last night he merely quivered, until, little by little, he grew completely still. Exhausted by the lengthy vigil, I closed my eyes and slept. Awakening later, I perceived that a change had taken place in my arms. On my lap was a soiled little baby, without teeth, dead.

❋ Discussion and Writing

1. What aspects of Teleco are most captivating to the narrator? Describe the development of their relationship.
2. What is Teleco's real identity: what is the implication of his insistence on being human and wanting to please; what motivates his mania for metamorphosis?
3. Is there a pattern to Teleco's metamorphoses? If so, what is it? If not, what does the lack of a pattern imply?
4. What does the ending of the story infer?
5. Analyze the relation between reality and fantasy?

❋ Research and Comparison

1. Magic, fantasy, and metamorphosis have been dominant motifs and concerns in twentieth-century Latin American literature. Compare Murilo Rubiao with any other writer in this anthology.
2. Research the life and work of the eminent Brazilian writer Machado de Asis, and examine his influence on Murilo Rubiao and on twentieth-century Latin American fiction.

Juan Rulfo
(1918–1986)
Mexico

Juan Rulfo was born in a village in Sayula, a district in the state of Jalisco, Mexico. His family had been landowners, but the Mexican Revolution (1910–1920) and the Cristeros revolt of the 1920s left them impoverished. (In the Cristeros revolt, the Church rebelled against the revolutionary government.) He was seven when his father was murdered; seven years later, when his mother died, his relatives sent him to an orphanage. His grandmother insisted that he become a priest, while an uncle offered him assistance to pursue his studies on the condition that he change his name. He rejected both, and, having had some schooling in Guadalajara, went to Mexico City, where he began studying law and literature. There, he submit-ted his writing to literary journals and supported himself by taking what-ever jobs were available. Rulfo never completed his university studies but found work in the government at the National Indian Institute. Then in the 1950s, he published two masterpieces; his prominent place in Latin American letters rests on these two slender books. The success of *El llano en llamas* (The Burning Plain, and Other Stories; 1953) earned him the

Rockefeller grant that enabled him to write *Pedro Paramo* (1956). This novel was immediately considered a classic. The leanness of Rulfo's writing, his irony, his portrayal of feudal Mexico, of the roots and results of the revolution, of the poor, all have exerted immense influence throughout Latin America.

Tell them not to kill me*

Tell them not to kill me, Justino! Go on and tell them that. For God's sake! Tell them. Tell them please for God's sake."

"I can't. There's a sergeant there who doesn't want to hear anything about you."

"Make him listen to you. Use your wits and tell him that scaring me has been enough. Tell him please for God's sake."

"But it's not just to scare you. It seems they really mean to kill you. And I don't want to go back there."

"Go on once more. Just once, to see what you can do."

"No. I don't feel like going. Because if I do they'll know I'm your son. If I keep bothering them they'll end up knowing who I am and will decide to shoot me too. Better leave things the way they are now."

"Go on, Justino. Tell them to take a little pity on me. Just tell them that."

Justino clenched his teeth and shook his head saying no.

And he kept on shaking his head for some time.

"Tell the sergeant to let you see the colonel. And tell him how old I am— How little I'm worth. What will he get out of killing me? Nothing. After all he must have a soul. Tell him to do it for the blessed salvation of his soul."

Justino got up from the pile of stones which he was sitting on and walked to the gate of the corral. Then he turned around to say, "All right, I'll go. But if they decide to shoot me too, who'll take care of my wife and kids?"

"Providence will take care of them, Justino. You go there now and see what you can do for me. That's what matters."

They'd brought him in at dawn. The morning was well along now and he was still there, tied to a post, waiting. He couldn't keep still. He'd tried to sleep for a while to calm down, but he couldn't. He wasn't hungry either. All he wanted was to live. Now that he knew they were really going to kill him, all he could feel was his great desire to stay alive, like a recently resuscitated man.

Who would've thought that old business that happened so long ago and that was buried the way he thought it was would turn up? That business when he had to kill Don Lupe. Not for nothing either, as the Alimas tried to

---

*Translated by George D. Schade.

make out, but because he had his reasons. He remembered: Don Lupe Terrenos, the owner of the Puerta de Piedra—and besides that, his compadre—was the one he, Juvencio Nava, had to kill, because he'd refused to let him pasture his animals, when he was the owner of the Puerta de Piedra and his compadre too.

At first he didn't do anything because he felt compromised. But later, when the drought came, when he saw how his animals were dying off one by one, plagued by hunger, and how his compadre Lupe continued to refuse to let him use his pastures, then was when he began breaking through the fence and driving his herd of skinny animals to the pasture where they could get their fill of grass. And Don Lupe didn't like it and ordered the fence mended, so that he, Juvencio Nava, had to cut open the hole again. So during the day the hole was stopped up and at night it was opened again, while the stock stayed there right next to the fence, always waiting—his stock that before had lived just smelling the grass without being able to taste it.

And he and Don Lupe argued again and again without coming to any · agreement.

Until one day Don Lupe said to him, "Look here, Juvencio, if you let another animal in my pasture, I'll kill it."

And he answered him, "Look here, Don Lupe, it's not my fault that the animals look out for themselves. They're innocent. You'll have to pay for it, if you kill them."

And he killed one of my yearlings.

This happened thirty-five years ago in March, because in April I was already up in the mountains, running away from the summons. The ten cows I gave the judge didn't do me any good, or the lien on my house either, to pay for getting me out of jail. Still later they used up what was left to pay so they wouldn't keep after me, but they kept after me just the same. That's why I came to live with my son on this other piece of land of mine which is called Palo de Venado. And my son grew up and got married to my daughter-in-law Ignacia and has had eight children now. So it happened a long time ago and ought to be forgotten by now. But I guess it's not.

I figured then that with about a hundred pesos everything could be fixed up. The dead Don Lupe left just his wife and two little kids still crawling. And his widow died soon afterward too—they say from grief. They took the kids far off to some relatives. So there was nothing to fear from them.

But the rest of the people took the position that I was still summoned to be tried just to scare me so they could keep on robbing me. Every time someone came to the village they told me, "There are some strangers in town, Juvencio."

And I would take off to the mountains, hiding among the madrone thickets and passing the days with nothing to eat but herbs. Sometimes I had to go out at midnight, as though the dogs were after me. It's been that way my whole life. Not just a year or two. My whole life.

And now they've come for him when he no longer expected anyone, confident that people had forgotten all about it, believing that he'd spend at least his last days peacefully. "At least," he thought, "I'll have some peace in my old age. They'll leave me alone."

He'd clung to this hope with all his heart. That's why it was hard for him to imagine that he'd die like this, suddenly, at this time of life, after having fought so much to ward off death, after having spent his best years running from one place to another because of the alarms, now when his body had become all dried up and leathery from the bad days when he had to be in hiding from everybody.

Hadn't he even let his wife go off and leave him? The day when he learned his wife had left him, the idea of going out in search of her didn't even cross his mind. He let her go without trying to find out at all who she went with or where, so he wouldn't have to go down to the village. He let her go as he'd let everything else go, without putting up a fight. All he had left to take care of was his life, and he'd do that, if nothing else. He couldn't let them kill him. He couldn't. Much less now.

But that's why they brought him from there, from Palo de Venado. They didn't need to tie him so he'd follow them. He walked alone, tied by his fear. They realized he couldn't run with his old body, with those skinny legs of his like dry bark, cramped up with the fear of dying. Because that's where he was headed. For death. They told him so.

That's when he knew. He began to feel that stinging in his stomach that always came on suddenly when he saw death nearby, making his eyes big with fear and his mouth swell up with those mouthfuls of sour water he had to swallow unwillingly. And that thing that made his feet heavy while his head felt soft and his heart pounded with all its force against his ribs. No, he couldn't get used to the idea that they were going to kill him.

There must be some hope. Somewhere there must still be some hope left. Maybe they'd made a mistake. Perhaps they were looking for another Juvencio Nava and not him.

He walked along in silence between those men, with his arms fallen at his sides. The early morning hour was dark, starless. The wind blew slowly, whipping the dry earth back and forth, which was filled with that odor like urine that dusty roads have.

His eyes, that had become squinty with the years, were looking down at the ground, here under his feet, in spite of the darkness. There in the earth was his whole life. Sixty years of living on it, of holding it tight in his hands, of tasting it like one tastes the flavor of meat. For a long time he'd been crumbling it with his eyes, savoring each piece as if it were the last one, almost knowing it would be the last.

Then, as if wanting to say something, he looked at the men who were marching along next to him. He was going to tell them to let him loose, to let him go; "I haven't hurt anybody, boys," he was going to say to them, but he kept silent. "A little further on I'll tell them," he thought. And he just looked at them. He could even imagine they were his friends, but he didn't want to. They weren't. He didn't know who they were. He watched them moving at his side and bending down from time to time to see where the road continued.

He'd seen them for the first time at nightfall, that dusky hour when everything seems scorched. They'd crossed the furrows trodding on the tender corn. And he'd gone down on account of that—to tell them that the corn was beginning to grow there. But that didn't stop them.

He'd seen them in time. He'd always had the luck to see everything in time. He could've hidden, gone up in the mountains for a few hours until they left and then come down again. Already it was time for the rains to have come, but the rains didn't come and the corn was beginning to wither. Soon it'd be all dried up.

So it hadn't even been worthwhile, his coming down and placing himself among those men like in a hole, never to get out again.

And now he continued beside them, holding back how he wanted to tell them to let him go. He didn't see their faces, he only saw their bodies, which swung toward him and then away from him. So when he started talking he didn't know if they'd heard him. He said, "I've never hurt anybody." That's what he said. But nothing changed. Not one of the bodies seemed to pay attention. The faces didn't turn to look at him. They kept right on, as if they were walking in their sleep.

Then he thought that there was nothing else he could say, that he would have to look for hope somewhere else. He let his arms fall again to his sides and went by the first houses of the village, among those four men, darkened by the black color of the night.

"Colonel, here is the man."

They'd stopped in front of the narrow doorway. He stood with his hat in his hand, respectfully, waiting to see someone come out. But only the voice came out, "Which man?"

"From Palo de Venado, colonel. The one you ordered us to bring in."

"Ask him if he ever lived in Alima," came the voice from inside again.

"Hey, you. Ever lived in Alima?" the sergeant facing him repeated the question.

"Yes. Tell the colonel that's where I'm from. And that I lived there till not long ago."

"Ask him if he knew Guadalupe Terreros."

"He says did you know Guadalupe Terreros?"

"Don Lupe? Yes. Tell him that I knew him. He's dead."

Then the voice inside changed tone: "I know he died," it said. And the voice continued talking, as if it was conversing with someone there on the other side of the reed wall.

"Guadalupe Terreros was my father. When I grew up and looked for him they told me he was dead. It's hard to grow up knowing that the thing we have to hang on to to take roots from is dead. That's what happened to us.

"Later on I learned that he was killed by being hacked first with a machete and then an ox goad stuck in his belly. They told me he lasted more than two days and that when they found him, lying in an *arroyo*,[1] he was still in agony and begging that his family be taken care of.

"As time goes by you seem to forget this. You try to forget it. What you can't forget is finding out that the one who did it is still alive, feeding his rotten soul with the illusion of eternal life. I couldn't forgive that man, even though I don't know him; but the fact that I know where he is makes me want to finish him off. I can't forgive his still living. He should never have been born."

From here, from outside, all he said was clearly heard. Then he ordered, "Take him and tie him up awhile, so he'll suffer, and then shoot him!"

"Look at me, colonel!" he begged. "I'm not worth anything now. It won't be long before I die all by myself, crippled by old age. Don't kill me!"

"Take him away!" repeated the voice from inside.

"I've already paid, colonel. I've paid many times over. They took everything away from me. They punished me in many ways. I've spent about forty years hiding like a leper, always with the fear they'd kill me at any moment. I don't deserve to die like this, colonel. Let the Lord pardon me, at least. Don't kill me! Tell them not to kill me!"

There he was, as if they'd beaten him, waving his hat against the ground. Shouting.

Immediately the voice from inside said, "Tie him up and give him something to drink until he gets drunk so the shots won't hurt him."

Finally, now, he'd been quieted. There he was, slumped down at the foot of the post. His son Justino had come and his son Justino had gone and had returned and now was coming again.

He slung him on top of the burro. He cinched him up tight against the saddle so he wouldn't fall off on the road. He put his head in a sack so it wouldn't give such a bad impression. And then he made the burro giddap, and away they went in a hurry to reach Palo de Venado in time to arrange the wake for the dead man.

"Your daughter-in-law and grandchildren will miss you," he was saying to him. "They'll look at your face and won't believe it's you. They'll think the coyote has been eating on you when they see your face full of holes from all those bullets they shot at you."

---

[1] A dry gully. [eds.]

❀ Discussion and Writing

1. Analyze Juvencho's traits as father, animal breeder, neighbor, fugitive, and prisoner. What are his dominant characteristics?
2. How do the two sons handle their father's murders? Explain the similarities and differences in their behavior.
3. Examine the social and political relationships in this feudal village.
4. Analyze how different characters deal with the prospect of death, their own or that of their dear ones.
5. What is the significance of the landscape, animals, and seasons in relation to the theme of the story?

❀ Research and Comparison

Examine the influence of the Mexican and Cristeros revolutions—their causes and effects—on the life and work of Juan Rulfo.

Wilson Harris
(b. 1921)
Guyana

Theodore Wilson Harris was born in New Amsterdam more than 40 years before Guyana gained its independence from England, and he attended Queen's College in Georgetown, a secondary school run strictly according to British educational principles. He studied surveying and worked for more than a decade as a government surveyor. It was in this capacity that he journeyed inland along the rivers, through the forests, and across the savannahs of Guyana. When he entered this forbidding, often majestic, terrain, he lived among a handful of fellow crew members of diverse racial and class backgrounds, and he met the native peoples. These experiences as well as the landscape itself profoundly affected him, informing his writing and becoming dominant metaphors and motifs in his work. Harris did not publish his first novel until he was 39, although he had been exploring the possibilities of poetry, the short story, and criticism since his surveying days. (Like Martin Carter, Harris published his early work in A. J. Seymour's journal, *Kyk-over-al*.) But with *Palace of the Peacock* (1960), he began to take up the question of time, the relationship between history and mythology, and racial interrelationships, a view that evolved into the subtitle of his 1983 book, *The Womb of Space: The Cross-Cultural Imagination*. Harris has taught at universities throughout the world, and he has continued writing criticism and novels, committed to a narrative that allows his reader to "[make] contact with genuinely new terrain and with a self or selves far deeper than historical or conventional ego."

Yurokon

Note

Yurokon serves in this story as a gateway between Carib[1] and Christian ages. His appearance as the Bush Baby in Carib mythology—the child of the vessel (the Caribs are noted for their beautiful pottery)—coincided both with a fall from sovereign time and dominion, and with the arrival of Columbus.

The charges of cannibalism levelled against them by Spain, whom they resisted fiercely step by step, appear to have been trumped up by her to justify her own excesses and to be largely untrue, though it is clear from mythological relics such as bone or flute, fashioned from their enemies, that the Caribs ate a ritual morsel—"transubstantiation in reverse" as Michael Swan puts it.

The plastic myth of *Yurokon* appears to me to possess so many hidden features (innocence as well as guilt) that I have attempted to portray it as the threshold to a catholic native within whom resides an unwritten symphony—the disintegration of idols as well as an original participation of elements.

1

The Indian reservation of the valley of sleep lay in an open savannah of the Interior. Stunted bush and occasional trees dotted this savannah—miles long and wide—between the mountains where a great forest began and rolled endlessly to the sea. From this naked distance—in the middle of the valley— these forests appeared like black surf of painted cloud. Yurokon had once or twice crossed them to come to the sea. It was a far way off but his memories were intimate and vivid like newly minted letters of space, a harmony of perspectives.

The sun was up when he succeeded in raising his kite. Soon—by judicious tugs—pulling in and paying out of twine—the kite caught a current of air and rose steadily and swiftly into the sky.

He was around fourteen (so the records said); his sister, who had accompanied him, about ten. They were both small of stature, frail of limb, reputed to be among the last survivors of an ancient tribe now called *huntsmen of bone*. They possessed a curious air, devoid of age it seemed—animated

---

[1]*The word "Carib" is a corruption which became synonymous with "cannibal": Columbus spoke of Caripunas, Raleigh of Carinepagotos, French explorers of Galibis.*

matchsticks, smoldering a little, quiescent a little. It was the rapidity of their gestures accompanied by an inherent stillness, a silent relationship. And yet it was as if volumes of time existed between them and words of music fell ceaselessly from their lips.

They appeared now half-asleep on earth as the match of space began to slumber. And when their uncle appeared through one of the trees they were glad to relinquish the kite to him which he secured to the branch of a tree. Yurokon slid to the ground and watched uncle and sister vanish through a hump of land into the houses of the reservation.

They would return, he knew, with food and drink. He lay against the trunk of a tree and could not bear to leave his kite which he glimpsed through the leaves as it slept on a cloud—and bore him up into a skeleton of light through the valley of sleep.

"Are we really huntsmen of bone?" Yurokon asked, looking down at his uncle and through the sky as he sailed in space. For it was as if the blue trunk of the ocean stood there whittled down to a cross, coral and bone, octopus in whose blood ran tin, sponge in whose crevices ran gold.

"We became huntsmen of bone when we ate our first Spanish sailor," his uncle replied to the intricate sticks of the sky. "For that reason we are some-times called cannibals." He looked sardonic, his left eyebrow cocked in quizzical fashion, pointing still to the kite, paper of heaven nailed to wood.

"Cannibals," said the boy, startled. "I don't see why anyone should call us that."

It was Easter in the Indian reservation of the twentieth century and Yurokon had been given a kite by a visiting missionary, which sailed through the book of space and continued in his sleep in pages of psyche; coral and gold.

"For that reason we are sometimes called cannibals," the man repeated, pursuing his own thread of thought backwards into time. "We ate a Spanish sailor. . . ." He was jealous of the missionary and wished to distract his nephew, glued to space.

"How can you say such a thing?" Yurokon cried, descending from kite to earth in a flash and stopping dead, riveted now to the ancient trunk of man, the lines and brow, the anchor of subsistence.

They stood under a small tree in the valley of sleep and Yurokon observed a spectral nest hanging from one of its branches; to that bough also he saw had been tied the thread of his kite which he had ascended and descended on scales of light. "It's chained there," he cried as if he had forgot-ten whether it was the missionary or his uncle who had done it, "chained to nest and branch."

His uncle nodded to a silent tune, and reaching up into the nest drew forth a thin bone or flute. He passed it over his lips without making a sound, polished it between the palms of his hands and after this palaver with the dead gave it to Yurokon who blew, in his turn, a sad yet vibrating melody of space. All at once he could hear and feel running through his hands the giant tremor of that bird, the ladder of the pilot, as it flew soundlessly through the sky chained to the earth.

He could hear also an unwritten symphony: the dark roots in the past of that tree—a strange huddle of ancestral faces attuned to quivering wings which they plucked with their fingers like teeth. And then silently, as if for the first bitter time, tasted the fear of the strings: ascent and descent: transubstantiation of species: half-tender, half-cruel, like a feast.

They read it, in their mouths, on the craft of Spain—the curious cross of a bird which flew toward them across the sea: crane or pelican or flag. It might even have been their first fleshless pirate, skull and crossbones of the fleet, harp of flesh.

"Do you mean?" said Yurokon as the first wave of magical numbers struck him, "that it was a game to make them think they had been eaten . . . ?" He stopped, aware of a waking plight in the valley of sleep, the plight of feeling akin to nonfeeling, flesh akin to spirit.

"In a manner of speaking, yes," said his uncle approvingly. *"Make them think they had been eaten.* Make them into a song of spirit: a morsel in our mouths, nothing more, the morsel of the flute, that was all." He waved his hand nonchalantly.

Yurokon nearly spat the flute from his mouth as though suddenly it burned his tongue like fire, immortal burn, immortal skin, immortal native, immortal cannibal. He began to age into the ancient Child of Legend. It was a story he had been told from the beginning—that he was the last Carib and the first native. . . .

2

Yurokon appeared centuries ago in the valley of dreams as the native heaven of tears and laughter, of carnival and guilt when the revolution of conquest was over.

His uncle was expecting him and though he barely discerned the spiral of smoke-like twine coming up out of the pot on the fire, he felt the sting of fire—tears of a match.

It was here in this sky of election—bastard soil—cannibal legend—that the song of the kite was born.

"Make them think it was a marriage of spirits, laughter of the feast," his uncle said languidly, with the glaze of the pot in his eye.

"I am your brother's spirit," said Yurokon and there was a responsive glaze in his mood or brow, a god-like rebellious look.

"Which one?" his uncle said flippantly to the devil of the fire. "Brother oh brother."

Yurokon bowed his head to conceal the ash of many a war feast, sculpture of blood. His uncle had many brothers—some had eaten the symbol of deity. "How can we," he said to his uncle, and the words bit his tongue, "be the first natives when they were here before us—I mean your brothers' Arawak wives—my mother's people . . . ?"

"They're our base of time in the light of Spain," his uncle said secretively as though he reasoned with insurrection in his ranks. "No one before us has made this claim—don't you see?—this black morsel." . . . He stirred industriously over the cooking pot and gave a sardonic shrug. "It's our last weapon, our first election. In future, come who or what may, this distinction will stand. It will swallow us all, for we, too, will succumb."

"Succumb," said Yurokon and he almost laughed at his fate. "Yet here am I," he cried accusingly, "no one and nothing, yet here I stand. Whose fault is it? Whose spirit is it that will not—*cannot*—die?"

"Child," said his uncle with a gleam that might have been fear, "it is true that the revolution of conquest is over but *you*—your rebellious feud of spirit goes on." He turned away from the glaze of the pot; the hunger of kinship was opening at his feet, twine of blood, twine of water, twine of guilt ascending and descending: flint of savage: skeleton of light.

Yurokon held the twine in his hands as if with a snap, a single fierce pull, he would break it *now* at last. Break the land. Break the sea. Break the savannah. Break the forest. Break the twig. Break the bough. The unwritten symphony of the wind, unwritten spark of the wind, made him bark—a sudden bark. His uncle stared at the bristling dog of the fire, fire break, fire bark, delicacy, magic; he smacked his lips and the roast of Yurokon's bark subsided into the silent bay of conscience like an invocation at the heart of the feast: man's best enemy or friend.

Was it the immortal dog of war and peace that sang in the break of the fire, shadowy tail or bone?

Its voice could be heard in the lull of the wind across the valley of sleep. First the subtlest crash of a symphony, staccato fire, forest tail or bay of the moon in the sky.

Second a hoarse thump which came from a falling tree, surf or tail of the moon.

It was the music of ignominy, ignominious conceit, or so it seemed to Yurokon (his own desire to break everything) on his long march across time into the rebellion of eternity. A long march in which the tail of his kite drew a line across the ash of the sky, campfire or ghost settlement. A line of demarcation, the frontier of sleep, huntsmen of bone, the song of silence.

It was equally the music of origins upon a trail that lay in all the wild warring elements. First, *broken water.* His uncle possessed an enormous cauldron which he filled with water and set on the fire. Yurokon beheld the dog of his skin soon bubbling there like a cataract of eternity: boiling water which had been innocent before—innocent, that is, as one's own sovereign blood, but now had become the executioner at the feast, native to blood.

Second, *broken fire.* His uncle possessed an enormous spit, a cauldron of fire: as though the sun stood over the valley on a misty morning and began to break its own vessel of intensity through an autumn sunset turning into a tropical, ritual sunrise. So that the steam of the valley appeared to infuse the light, and water boiled fire rather than fire boiling water.

Yurokon saw himself aloft in this cauldron of fire as a dog-kite; the twine connecting him to earth—kite to earth—had been cut by scissors of mist. He stood, therefore, high up as if without anchor or support save that the nape of his neck had been caught by fingers of fire: fingers of a god which had been innocent before—innocent as one's sovereign flesh, but now had become an executioner at the feast, native to flesh.

At this moment on the trail beholding water and broken fire, he looked backward and forward at the combat of heaven: immortal outcast, outcast of participation, innocence and guilt. Heaven lay both within and without the things and the people he had taken for granted, and the kite of deity had, on one hand, consolidated—as uncle hinted—a base of time, an election of time to swallow all ages and men; but, on the other, had equally inspired a curious break within the anatomy of the feast—a spiritual hunger and rebellion whose consequences would reveal the inmost vessel or nativity of fate, song of fate.

He had passed through broken voices of water and fire. Now broken atmosphere lay before him like the breath on his lips fried thin as a wafer, flat as a leaf. And so when he moved he began to fly with the feud of air into broken distances: broken water and fire cooked into walls of space by leaves of wood as though water and fire were cold and wood and leaf were hot: wood and leaf which had been innocent before—innocent as nature, but now had become the kite of distance, native to sovereign execution, death-in-life, life-in-death.

Fire. Water. Air. They were all, in a sense, the weapons of a savage dreaming time on a trail where *once upon a child* everything had slumbered on a leash like a victorious shroud but now had become the cauldron of heaven which the huntsmen of bone had not foreseen when they appointed themselves the cannibal or ogre of place to fashion both their catholic native and repulsive sack of the seasons.

That the leash would become the easter twine of endless participation through an immortal outcast, and that the repulsive stocking or sack of the seasons would invoke stomach upon stomach of consumption whose hideousness would be reflected in a deeper and deeper childlike pool of innocence (ogre of water, boiling fire)—raw material of the elements—none had foreseen as the undying birth of freedom. . . .

For it was as if—just as angelic blood was consumed by cannibal water—fire by an atrocity of wood—broken savage time lay, too, within its native soil eternity.

Yurokon was approaching a bend in the trail and he saw both the shroud and sack of the seasons before him. The shroud may well have been a caul such as certain children are born with. The sack or stocking may well have been the pillow of conquest, Eiger in Roraima, snow of the Alps in the Andes in the Amazon. He could now hear the gift of a symphony in the silent bed of earth—black-out shroud of vision, white-out stocking of translation. He had heard the missionary on the reservation speak of the Polar North as an organ of fire it was so cold. Yurokon believed and accepted this paradoxical truth as much as he trusted the song of himself in the sorrow of the bone and the flute—the ages of man—valley of desolation.

"Once upon a child," the shroud said to him advancing along the trail like the dance of the black keys of earth.

"Once upon a time," the sack said to him advancing along the trail like the dance of the white bones of earth.

Yurokon hopped to the white bone and the black flute. He could see clearly now, with the eye of his kite, the ballet of the Caribs as they stubbornly withdrew within the music of the centuries upon the skull-and-crossbones piano of age. At each camp fire they grew extinct in the ash of reflection, but were born again within involuntary pillow or shroud, caul of vision.

Yurokon stepped upon these keys of birth-in-death—broken water and broken fire—black-out . . . white-out . . . ash of earth which he rode like a ladder into the sky.

3

The ladder of the trail ran up into the mountains. And each day as the Caribs withdrew into the clock of the centuries they painted the blue sea falling away beneath them in an underworld picture, an underworld kite which flew in the broken sky of conquest. Flew under their feet upon a rope of ash which descended through knotted stations of fire where the burnt relic of each day's march was buried. It burnt itself there—imagination of a continent—rope and kite—ladder of ascent, and they drew the sea upon their pots and vessels—something fantastically small (a drop of ocean)—something immensely wide which began to consume them at the grass-roots of innocence like a cauldron of fury.

The sea-kite possessed many shapes and colours, some gay, some somber. Some—like the octopus—amused the huntsmen. It made them almost enjoy the innocent malady of the gods since unholy, holy evil was reputed to have a stomach of mail which drank tin.

"Once upon a child," said the stomach of mail to the conscience of the tribe, namely Yurokon, "you ate me," and it tangled its tail and rope around him on the ladder. His uncle laughed, and his sister, taking pity on him, grabbed the octopus by the bones of the kite and ran a little way off across a wave of land to give him room to coax it back into the air.

Another kite, which rose in the underworld sky at his feet, resembled a sponge and this, too, was an endless model of diversion. When the battle of conscience drew it, infinite drops of gold splashed on the ground from the heart of the pelican.

"Once upon a time," said the sponge to the pelican, "I flew in the sea with wings of bone."

In addition to the kite of the octopus and the kite of the sponge there flew a kite of coral, a submerged reef crossed with ritual cousins, related to the sponge, calendrical mosaic, music. It curved and dwindled in shallows and deeps, skeleton of the sea, harp of the feast from which a stringed sound issued, fossil of cloud.

Far beneath the ladder of the mountains the ocean crawled within itself, ribs of bone splashed by huntsmen of shadow. Yurokon observed in the middle of that kite of ocean a loop of burning paint. This was the cauldron of the kite within which octopus and coral and sponge, innocent evil and maleficent good, were living morsels of divinity in their native organ. The laughter dried on his lips—flute of bone—and he tasted instead plankton or euphausiid harnessed to blood: harnessed to the urchin of the sea, spiked hedgehog or jealous god of ocean. This spiky pattern upon the cauldron of the kite reflected the jealous sky of the sea—the brittle constellations and stars, prickly sea-lilies, sea-cucumbers set in a mosaic of fossil and keyboard of ancestors. As though the spiky music of the urchin of stars, the election of the first native of earth, drew one deeper and deeper into a furnace of inno-cence, consumption of guilt.

Yurokon was the hedgehog of the land, Carib land-urchin to Spanish sea-urchin. He could bark and bristle on the land as if fire were his natural element, sea-dog of night, and with the fall of darkness he no longer flew the sea-kite under him, but rather the land-kite over him.

He imagined himself standing upon the shore of the sea with a new boatload of arrivals, looking up with their eyes at a distant campfire of Caribs. The ground was strewn with the dead of battle, but the bone of the kite blazing on the mountains spoke volumes of the savage character of the land, dancing around its flute. It was as if the dance of the bone wished to declare itself after a day of battle—to all who had newly arrived—by a music of silence, spirit of absorption, jail of flesh.

That absorption reflected the many shapeless kites of Yurokon in the heart of invader as well as invaded. There was the night octopus of the land whose dance differed from the tail of the sea in that the daytime octopus was a morsel of divinity, morsel of the sea, but the nighttime octopus, as it blazed its points far up on the ladder of the land, seemed the very antithesis of the gods: land-urchin's shroud or sack: campfire of bone: trunk or tree on which Yurokon laid his head in the valley of sleep. Each splinter of the dance, seen from the foot of the cross, ladder of the mountains, flared in the match of a dream, matchstick limbs, twine and distance: glimmer of the pointed hedge-hog.

4

Yurokon's field was the grain of the land and sea whose seedtime was conscience, battle of eternity.

As the Caribs withdrew across the ridge of the land and began to descend into a continent of shadow, each knot of ash linked them to the enemy. And Yurokon was the scarred urchin of dreams, victor-in-victim; over the centuries he remained unageing (ageless) as a legend, a curious symptom or holocaust of memory, whose burned-out stations were equally embryonic as a cradle, fugue of man, unchained chain of fires.

It was this that drew the Caribs to the end of their age. They ceased to fret about names since namelessness was a sea of names. They ceased, too, to care about dwindling numbers since numberlessness was native to heaven, stars beyond reckoning.

The tree, in fact, against which Yurokon slept was known as the tree of name and number. And there were two paths which led to it from the mountains around the valley. The first was called *the ladder of the geese.* It was a game Yurokon had designed in which he dreamt it was all happening the other way around. The mountains were paper—flat as a map. The valley was above, sailing kite, and the barnacle geese which flew toward him rose from paper to kite: hatched not from eggs like other birds but from sea-shell into land-fish, orphans of the globe. For they, too, like Yurokon, were an ageless omen, Good Friday's meat, fish rather than fowl. None grieved for them save Yurokon who accounted himself sibling to a shell—sibling to a fast—as uncle accounted himself guardian to a morsel.

It was the true name of the geese, the true number of the fast which baffled all men. Yurokon drew the flight of the geese as currents or arrows against the shadow of continents—gulf stream or orphan of masses, equatorial current or orphan of hemispheres.

"Barnacle currents," he thought. Wing by fin the land-fish flew—the souls of a drought, the fast of the drowned—waters under the earth.

The valley of sleep had been taken by assault—the fiercest savannah fire of living memory; so swift had it been, all were killed who were taken unawares. Stunted trees remained—bones of grass. Uncle had died, as had Yurokon, in the glare of battle. And now—after three or four years—the scene was re-visited by the Catholic missionary of the Interior, Father Gabriel. It was he who encircled on a map the charred tree of Yurokon as a new root or mission of psyche, spectral nest, bone and flute: it was Eastertide again.

He had visited the mission and given Yurokon a kite two days before the blaze—had he remained he, too, might have been killed. Now here he was again to make a new start, both defend and attack from within and without. An unorthodox priest he was of Spanish and Indian blood, and a composer of music. He dreamt of a native symphony which would reflect a new organ or capacity, a primitive flowering of faith. It was not inconsistent with the last dream of the Caribs, the dream of Yurokon which haunted him, as it haunted them—annunciation of music at the beginning of the end of an age.

"Sailor," said Yurokon to Gabriel. The priest began to protest. But his voice was muffled in his cloth or vocation. He wanted to say—"I am not your mask or morsel." But instead—like curtain and theater—he let the faceless robe of God descend; Yurokon set aside the flute from his lips and placed collar or shell to his ear.

There were two ladders (Yurokon remembered) leading to the robe of name and number. The first called tree of the barnacle goose, the second simply *hemispheres: shell of the spheres.*

Yurokon kept the shell to his ear until arrows of rain evoked an abstract pitch, volume within line. The music he now heard was both hollow and full, sea-fast, land-fast. When the sea fasted, it still climbed into the rain of the land: land-fish, Good Friday's arrow.

Yurokon could hear her sing—his sister who ran before him now through the day of the battle of the savannah—arrow of fire—when mail or flame swept on. As though in the singing theater of God, history re-enacted itself. . . .

The fire voices came from everywhere and Yurokon woke to the voice of the tree in which he slept.

He was rooted, in that moment, in fire—as his sister ran before him with the singing kite of the savannah—fiery attack, fiery defense.

In the grain of that field of battle—open to conscience—open to sun—an omen resided, multiplications of grace, zero as well as fulfillment. This was the logic of Father Gabriel—the open book of the centuries: annunciation of the native of the globe.

And now—as his sister ran before him—Yurokon saw a chain of fires (formerly ash, unchained chain of divinity) but linked or aligned to him now beneath his robe.

He recalled the naked campfires of his forebears whose arrows swarmed on the brink of a continent like currents of ocean barnacled to land.

They were lit, he remembered, as the first grim tide of welcome to the flag of the pelican. They were equally an offensive/defensive swarm, blazing at the door of the land—sponge of the sea—blood of gold: blazing ribbon of coastline, legend or sponge.

He recalled the fierce battles that raged day after day; the retreat that followed night after night, the fatalistic withdrawal into hedgehog and mountain.

The chain of fires along the roof of the coast was the first curiously horizontal phase, therefore, in a vertical war—a vertical cloak or retreat which Yurokon encompassed at this stage as the shroud of the land-urchin over the sea-urchin, land-kite over the sea-kite, night over day.

It was a slow and long pull, he recalled, from the sea to the crest of the land, but they drew their train after them up the mountains, braced themselves in the current of the wind, wing to fin, bone to sack, goose to hemisphere—fast of name and number, tree of camouflage, feast of camouflage, trail of campfires in a single line or uninterrupted break of terror.

One last crackling glance back at the sea-kite from the sky-ridge of the mountains where they stood; he could see them again as they leaned forward, reluctant, sad, and drank a toast (farewell to namesake sea) lip to bowl, lip to the engraving of Spain (and all who came after, bowl of England, saucer of France, vessel of Holland): they engraved it on their lips—primitive fire or callous—like an animal's protuberance, mouth of the sun whose tongue ran with them as they descended the other flank of the mountains—away from the sea—into the lap of the land.

Half-way down they looked back with Yurokon's eyes, and saw her standing there—Sister Fire—Viking Amazon. Her eyes met theirs as she turned from the flank of the sea to the cloth of land. And this time Yurokon felt the parenthesis of the orphan, sea-shell into robe.

Every protection, nevertheless, seemed precarious to him now as the battle of ridge and flank, forest and savannah rolled on: as though his own sister possessed a chain of ambivalences—a menacing outwardness as well as inwardness, unearthly stillness chained to storm, locked propensity, locked voices of fury.

He could see them—his forebears of bone—with their chain of flesh and spirit across the land. They had crossed the naked flank of the sea into the vessel of the forest and now—as they descended into species of Bush and Savannah—Yurokon was aware of the intensity of the flame they drew with them, which like vase or pottery in a rage of color, signified an acute vice in themselves, blaze or furnace.

He had never been aware of it quite so strangely before—the flimsy scaffold of the robe, shroud of name and number, urchin of the stars, caul of birth, which—like ash—night-kite over day-kite, could mercifully fall to release the chain; or like earth, in the hands of a wise potter, could unlock the vice; but which (in the fold of that vice, color of fire) broke, for no other clear reason but to instill terror: as if—in breaking—it had not broken at all, save to clinch an outer flesh to an inner mold, an outer fire to an inner blow.

It was this inner blow which, despite the appearances of hell, drew Yurokon back to prize the ash—not as the holocaust it seemed to be, but as the robe of mercy it originally was, parenthesis of the orphan.

Nevertheless, in withdrawing there, he could still see—within his own glimmering shadow—that the chain of the battle rolled on; the fire voice of the savannah sang close at hand of the flesh and spirit of the tiger which had been joined to withstand (within and without) forces and enemies.

And the voice of the tiger, fire voice, fire vase—in line with sea-flame, mountain flesh, muse of the ridge, toast of ancestors, penetration of flank—instilled terror. And like an apparition of ancient camp fire, it disported its robe or ash, bars of shadow through which its naked sides shone: insane factory of war: jointed engine of battles upon which the cloth of the priest precariously stood—not as the sport of unfreedom, but as a necessary condition, leash of grace.

It was curious (half-comic perhaps, half-tragic perhaps) that, in a sense, this ash (this prison) was the flimsy sponge of nature which alone drank volumes of need; the ill-protected, the ill-served—true voice of the tiger.

True voice of the tiger. It began to sing now with rage and scorn: rage at the conversion of prison: scorn at the factory of grace. And as it sang—in repudiation of the ash of truth—its rage and its scorn were joined to flesh and spirit.

This was the last chain, last repulse of the Caribs in that battle of the savannah, whose commemoration rose in a vase of flame: such music of color it embroiled the savannah in the sea, the mountain in the valley, forest in scrub: bowl of earth, pottery of earth, toast of the valley by the huntsmen of bone who had drunk before from the bowl of the sea.

Such commemoration of color—such a draft of sensation—such a feast of sensibility—embroiled all things and species in a breakwater of reflection, stretching from the harp of the sea to the kite of the valley.

That music of paradox began with a bar of shadow—unchained fire—*hiatus* of ordeal as the robe of God, the need of man; followed, however, by the wildest repudiation of that need in the sack of truth: though this very sack or body of rage began to point again, back to itself as to an ironical witness, an unremembered, unacknowledged sibling of truth on both sides of the veil.

For if, in fact, the inner tiger of war repudiated its veil or shadow, there were other species whose storm or sack drew them back without protest to the spirit of placelessness, as to the salt of the sea.

The eel of fire, for example, as it ran into battle, coiled into an eye of relief which could have been a needle of snow. For eye of snow, like barnacle of fire, legendary feather, had been spawned on a distant scaffold—desert or Pole—where it grew like an arrow from a subtle hand mapping the globe.

The bird of species as well, as it flew into battle, spun the feather or the thread in the needle in the very eye of snow. For the thread of the needle (eye of snow) had its loom on an indifferent scaffold—North or South—whose seamless fire was a *different* shadow, cloth over the Pole.

Yurokon spied that cloth—East, West—as it sailed on high beneath and above sister and uncle. Sailed on high, composite bird, flower, tailed beast; sailed in the spiral of the winds as he tugged gently, pulling in, paying out his twine with masterly skill. He was the child of legend and the lord of creation and his paper or map, kite or globe, was a magical witness of curious survival, the terrifying innocent play of a timeless element in all places and things. In all its manifestations it seemed to Yurokon to spell relief at the summit of his need.

His small sister, running before him, began to sing to the kite with joy.

"Eastertide again," Father Gabriel said to himself, "annunciation of music."

❋ Discussion and Writing

1. What is the significance of the myth of Yurokon? How is it related to the protagonist in the narrative? What is meant by Yurokon's memories of "a harmony of perspectives"?
2. Comment on the roles of the sister and the uncle.
3. Describe the myths of cannibalism from both the Carib and the Spanish perspectives. What is Harris's objective in restructuring the myth (refer to his "Note")? Comment on the psychological and religious implications of colonization depicted in the story.
4. Explain the significance of such metaphors as: the kite, the space, the bone flute, the vessel.
5. What is the meaning of "transubstantiation in reverse" (see Harris's "Note")? Comment on the relevance of Easter in the narrative in this context.
6. Identify the paradoxical images and their profusion. What is the impact of such copious use of polarities?
7. Analyze the increasingly complex use of the major images and metaphors in the development of the narrative. What do they signify about the people and events?

❋ Research and Comparison

Compare Wilson Harris's portrayal of the theme of colonization and the fusion of heritages with the depiction of them in other works included in this anthology.

Rubem Fonseca
(b. 1922)
Brazil

Rubem Fonseca was born in Minas Gerais, Brazil, and raised from the age of seven in Rio de Janeiro. He earned a law degree, and also a degree in public administration in the United States. He worked for the state police, the power and light company, and various newspapers; and he served as writer in residence in Germany. His work, urban in its locale and sensibility, shows the influence of detective fiction, but Fonseca manipulates the genre to embody questions of alienation and isolation, of moral and psychological pathology. In 1976, the Vargas dictatorship suppressed his collection of short stories *Feliz Ano Novo* (Happy New Year, 1975), and despite petitions signed by thousands of well-known people protesting the judgment, the ban held until 1989. Fonseca's novels and stories have continued to depict sex and violence with explicitness and intensity. Not only does this intensity reveal the hold of sex and violence on the contemporary imagination, but it transforms their use in Fonseca's work to metaphor.

Night Drive*

I arrived home with my briefcase bulging with papers, reports, studies, research, proposals, contracts. My wife, who was playing solitaire in bed, a glass of whiskey on the nightstand, said, without looking up from the cards, "You look tired." The usual house sounds: my daughter in her room practicing voice modulation, quadraphonic music from my son's room. "Why don't you put down that suitcase?" my wife asked. "Take off those clothes, have a nice glass of whiskey. You've got to learn to relax."

I went to the library, the place in the house I enjoy being by myself, and as usual did nothing. I opened the research volume on the desk but didn't see the letters and numbers. I was merely waiting.

"You never stop working. I'll bet your partners don't work half as hard and they earn the same." My wife came into the room, a glass in her hand. "Can I tell her to serve dinner?"

The maid served the meal French style. My children had grown up, my wife and I were fat. "It's that wine you like," she said, clicking her tongue with pleasure. My son asked for money during the coffee course, my daughter asked for money during the liqueur. My wife didn't ask for anything; we have a joint checking account.

"Shall we go for a drive?" I asked her. I knew she wouldn't go—it was time for her soap opera.

"I don't see what you get out of going for a drive every night, but the car cost a fortune, it has to be used. I'm just less and less attracted to material things," she replied.

The children's cars were blocking the garage door, preventing me from removing my car. I moved both cars and parked them in the street, removed my car and parked it in the street, put the other two cars back in the garage, and closed the door. All this maneuvering left me slightly irritated, but when I saw my car's jutting bumpers, the special chrome-plated double reinforcement, I felt my heart race with euphoria.

I turned the ignition key. It was a powerful motor that generated its strength silently beneath the aerodynamic hood. As always, I left without knowing where I would go. It had to be a deserted street, in this city with more people than flies. Not the Avenida Brasil—too busy.

I came to a poorly lighted street, heavy with dark trees, the perfect spot. A man or a woman? It made little difference, really, but no one with the right

---

*Translated by Clifford E. Landers

characteristics appeared. I began to get tense. It always happened that way, and I even liked it—the sense of relief was greater. Then I saw the woman. It could be her, even though a woman was less exciting because she was easier. She was walking quickly, carrying a package wrapped in cheap paper—something from a bakery or the market. She was wearing a skirt and blouse.

There were trees every twenty yards along the sidewalk, an interesting problem demanding a great deal of expertise. I turned off the headlights and accelerated. She only realized I was going for her when she heard the sound of the tires hitting the curb. I caught her above the knees, right in the middle of her legs, a bit more toward the left leg—a perfect hit. I heard the impact break the large bones, veered rapidly to the left, shot narrowly past one of the trees, and, tires squealing, skidded back onto the asphalt. The motor would go from zero to sixty in eleven seconds. I could see that the woman's broken body had come to rest, covered with blood, on top of the low wall in front of a house.

Back in the garage, I took a good look at the car. With pride I ran my hand lightly over the unmarked fenders and bumper. Few people in the world could match my skill driving such a car.

The family was watching television. "Do you feel better after your spin?" my wife asked, lying on the sofa, staring fixedly at the TV screen.

"I'm going to bed," I answered, "good night everybody. Tomorrow's going to be a rough day at the office."

❋ Discussion and Writing

1. Describe the relationship of the husband and the wife, and describe their contrasting personalities.
2. Analyze the symbolism of the characters' behavior and of the various objects used in the narration.
3. What seems to be the source of the man's final satisfaction? What does Fonseca imply through the last episode?
4. How do the theme and technique of the story reflect the movies and mystery stories?

Jose Donoso
(b. 1924)
Chile

Jose Donoso was born in Santiago, Chile, into a professional family of doctors and lawyers. After receiving his basic education at an English school in Santiago, he studied English literature at Princeton University, where he wrote and published his first stories. Although he wrote his early work in English, he returned to Spanish, an important decision in the development of his art. He also discovered his subject in Chilean society, and his experiences as a shepherd in southern Chile and as a dockworker in Buenos Aires found their way into his literary explorations of Chile. But he did not turn to an aesthetic of social realism; rather, he turned toward the clarity of nightmare. Thus, his portrayal of social decay incorporated psychological motifs, studies of various kinds of relationships, and questions of time and place. His winning the Faulkner Foundation Award in 1962 for the best Latin American novel (*Coronation,* 1957) established him as one of a new generation of exciting and important Latin American writers.

*Paseo**

1

This happened when I was very young, when my father and Aunt Mathilda, his maiden sister, and my uncles Gustav and Armand were still living. Now they are all dead. Or I should say, I prefer to think they are all dead: it is too late now for the questions they did not ask when the moment was right, because events seemed to freeze all of them into silence. Later they were able to construct a wall of forgetfulness or indifference to shut out everything, so that they would not have to harass themselves with impotent conjecture. But then, it may not have been that way at all. My imagination and my memory may be deceiving me. After all, I was only a child then, with whom they did not have to share the anguish of their inquiries, if they made any, nor the result of their discussions.

What was I to think? At times I used to hear them closeted in the library, speaking softly, slowly, as was their custom. But the massive door screened the meaning of their words, permitting me to hear only the grave and measured counterpoint of their voices. What was it they were saying? I used to hope that, inside there, abandoning the coldness which isolated each of them, they were at last speaking of what was truly important. But I had so little faith in this that, while I hung around the walls of the vestibule near the library door, my mind became filled with the certainty that they had chosen to forget, that they were meeting only to discuss, as always, some case in jurisprudence relating to their specialty in maritime law. Now I think that perhaps they were right in wanting to blot out everything. For why should one live with the terror of having to acknowledge that the streets of a city can swallow up a human being, leaving him without life and without death, suspended as it were, in a dimension more dangerous than any dimension with a name?

---

*Translated by Lorraine O'Grady Freeman

One day, months after, I came upon my father watching the street from the balcony of the drawing-room on the second floor. The sky was close, dense, and the humid air weighed down the large, limp leaves of the ailanthus trees. I drew near my father, eager for an answer that would contain some explanation:

"What are you doing here, Papa?" I murmured.

When he answered, something closed over the despair on his face, like the blow of a shutter closing on a shameful scene.

"Don't you see? I'm smoking . . ." he replied.

And he lit a cigarette.

It wasn't true. I knew why he was peering up and down the street, his eyes darkened, lifting his hand from time to time to stroke his smooth chestnut whiskers: it was in hope of seeing them reappear, returning under the trees of the sidewalk, the white bitch trotting at heel.

Little by little I began to realize that not only my father but all of them, hiding from one another and without confessing even to themselves what they were doing, haunted the windows of the house. If someone happened to look up from the sidewalk he would surely have seen the shadow of one or another of them posted beside a curtain, or faces aged with grief spying out from behind the window panes.

In those days the street was paved with quebracho wood, and under the ailanthus trees a clangorous streetcar used to pass from time to time. The last time I was there neither the wooden pavements nor the streetcars existed any longer. But our house was still standing, narrow and vertical like a little book pressed between the bulky volumes of new buildings, with shops on the ground level and a crude sign advertising knitted undershirts covering the balconies of the second floor.

When we lived there all the houses were tall and slender like our own. The block was always happy with the games of children playing in the patches of sunshine on the sidewalks, and with the gossip of the servant girls on their way back from shopping. But our house was not happy. I say it that way, "it was not happy" instead of "it was sad," because that is exactly what I mean to say. The word "sad" would be wrong because it has too definite a connotation, a weight and a dimension of its own. What took place in our house was exactly the opposite: an absence, a lack, which because it was unacknowledged was irremediable, something that, if it weighed, weighed by not existing.

My mother died when I was only four years old, so the presence of a woman was deemed necessary for my care. As Aunt Mathilda was the only woman in the family and she lived with my uncles Armand and Gustav, the three of them came to live at our house, which was spacious and empty.

Aunt Mathilda discharged her duties toward me with that propriety which was characteristic of everything she did. I did not doubt that she loved me, but I could never feel it as a palpable experience uniting us. There was something rigid in her affections, as there was in those of the men of the family. With them, love existed confined inside each individual, never breaking its boundaries to express itself and bring them together. For them to show affection was to discharge their duties to each other perfectly, and above all not to inconvenience, never to inconvenience. Perhaps to express love in any other way was unnecessary for them now, since they had so long a history together, had shared so long a past. Perhaps the tenderness they felt in the past had been expressed to the point of satiation and found itself stylized now in the form of certain actions, useful symbols which did not require further elucidation. Respect was the only form of contact left between those four isolated individuals who walked the corridors of the house which, like a book, showed only its narrow spine to the street.

I, naturally, had no history in common with Aunt Mathilda. How could I, if I was no more than a child then, who could not understand the gloomy motivations of his elders? I wished that their confined feeling might overflow and express itself in a fit of rage, for example, or with some bit of foolery. But she could not guess this desire of mine because her attention was not focused on me: I was a person peripheral to her life, never central. And I was not central because the entire center of her being was filled up with my father and my uncles. Aunt Mathilda was born the only woman, an ugly woman moreover, in a family of handsome men, and on realizing that for her marriage was unlikely, she dedicated herself to looking out for the comfort of those three men, by keeping house for them, by taking care of their clothes and providing their favorite dishes. She did these things without the least servility, proud of her role because she did not question her brothers' excellence. Furthermore, like all women, she possessed in the highest degree the faith that physical well-being is, if not principal, certainly primary, and that to be neither hungry nor cold nor uncomfortable is the basis for whatever else is good. Not that these defects caused her grief, but rather they made her impatient, and when she saw affliction about her she took immediate steps to remedy what, without doubt, were errors in a world that should be, that had to be, perfect. On another plane, she was intolerant of shirts which were not stupendously well-ironed, of meat that was not of the finest quality, of the humidity that owing to someone's carelessness had crept into the cigar-box.

After dinner, following what must have been an ancient ritual in the family, Aunt Mathilda went upstairs to the bedrooms, and in each of her brothers' rooms she prepared the beds for sleeping, parting the sheets with her bony hands. She spread a shawl at the foot of the bed for that one, who was subject to chills, and placed a feather pillow at the head of this one, for he usually read before going to sleep. Then, leaving the lamps lighted beside those enormous beds, she came downstairs to the billiard room to join the men for coffee and for a few rounds, before, as if bewitched by her, they retired to fill the empty effigies of the pajamas she had arranged so carefully upon the white, half-opened sheets.

But Aunt Mathilda never opened my bed. Each night, when I went up to my room, my heart thumped in the hope of finding my bed opened with the recognizable dexterity of her hands. But I had to adjust myself to the less pure style of the servant girl who was charged with doing it. Aunt Mathilda never granted me that mark of importance because I was not her brother. And not to be "one of my brothers" seemed to her a misfortune of which many people were victims, almost all in fact, including me, who after all was only the son of one of them.

Sometimes Aunt Mathilda asked me to visit her in her room where she sat sewing by the tall window, and she would talk to me. I listened attentively. She spoke to me about her brothers' integrity as lawyers in the intricate field of maritime law, and she extended to me her enthusiasm for their wealth and reputation, which I would carry forward. She described the embargo on a shipment of oranges, told of certain damages caused by miserable tugboats manned by drunkards, of the disastrous effects that arose from the demurrage of a ship sailing under an exotic flag. But when she talked to me of ships her words did not evoke the hoarse sounds of ships' sirens that I heard in the distance on summer nights when, kept awake by the heat, I climbed to the attic, and from an open window watched the far-off floating lights, and those blocks of darkness surrounding the city that lay forever out of reach for me because my life was, and would ever be, ordered perfectly. I realize now that Aunt Mathilda did not hint at this magic because she did not know of it. It had no place in her life, as it had no place in the life of anyone destined to die with dignity in order afterward to be installed in a comfortable heaven, a heaven identical to our house. Mute, I listened to her words, my gaze fastened on the white thread that, as she stretched it against her black blouse, seemed to capture all of the light from the window. I exulted at the world of security that her words projected for me, that magnificent straight road which leads to a death that is not dreaded since it is exactly like this life, without anything fortuitous or unexpected. Because death was not terrible. Death was the final incision, clean and definitive, nothing more. Hell existed, of course, but not for us. It was rather for chastising the other inhabitants of the city and those anonymous seamen who caused the damages that, when the cases were concluded, filled the family coffers.

Aunt Mathilda was so removed from the idea of fear that, since I now know that love and fear go hand in hand, I am tempted to think that in those days she did not love anyone. But I may be mistaken. In her rigid way she may have been attached to her brothers by a kind of love. At night, after supper, they gathered in the billiard room for a few games. I used to go in with them. Standing outside that circle of imprisoned affections, I watched for a sign that would show me the ties between them did exist, and did, in fact, bind. It is strange that my memory does not bring back anything but shades of indeterminate grays in remembering the house, but when I evoke that hour, the strident green of the table, the red and white of the balls and the little cube of blue chalk become inflamed in my memory, illuminated by the low lamp whose shade banished everything else into dusk. In one of the family's many rituals, the voice of Aunt Mathilda rescued each of the brothers by turn from the darkness, so that they might make their plays.

"Now, Gustav . . ."

And when he leaned over the green table, cue in hand, Uncle Gustav's face was lit up, brittle as paper, its nobility contradicted by his eyes, which were too small and spaced too close together. Finished playing, he returned to the shadow, where he lit a cigar whose smoke rose lazily until it was dissolved in the gloom of the ceiling. Then his sister said:

"All right, Armand . . ."

And the soft, timid face of Uncle Armand, with his large, sky-blue eyes concealed by gold-rimmed glasses, bent down underneath the light. His game was generally bad because he was "the baby" as Aunt Mathilda sometimes referred to him. After the comments aroused by his play he took refuge behind his newspaper and Aunt Mathilda said:

"Pedro, your turn . . ."

I held my breath when I saw him lean over to play, held it even more tightly when I saw him succumb to his sister's command. I prayed, as he got up, that he would rebel against the order established by his sister's voice. I could not see that this order was in itself a kind of rebellion, constructed by them as a protection against chaos, so that they might not be touched by what can be neither explained nor resolved. My father, then, leaned over the green cloth, his practiced eye gauging the exact distance and positions of the billiards. He made his play, and making it, he exhaled in such a way that his mustache stirred about his half-opened mouth. Then he handed me his cue so I might chalk it with the blue cube. With this minimal role that he assigned to me, he let me touch the circle that united him with the others, without letting me take part in it more than tangentially.

Now it was Aunt Mathilda's turn. She was the best player. When I saw her face, composed as if from the defects of her brothers' faces, coming out of the shadow, I knew that she was going to win. And yet . . . had I not seen her small eyes light up that face so like a brutally clenched fist, when by chance one of them succeeded in beating her? That spark appeared because, although she might have wished it, she would never have permitted herself to let any of them win. That would be to introduce the mysterious element of love into a game that ought not to include it, because affection should remain in its place, without trespassing on the strict reality of a carom shot.

2

I never did like dogs. One may have frightened me when I was very young, I don't know, but they have always displeased me. As there were no dogs at home and I went out very little, few occasions presented themselves to make me uncomfortable. For my aunt and uncles and for my father, dogs, like all the rest of the animal kingdom, did not exist. Cows, of course, supplied the cream for the dessert that was served in a silver dish on Sundays. Then there were the birds that chirped quite agreeably at twilight in the branches of the elm tree, the only inhabitant of the small garden at the rear of the house. But animals for them existed only in the proportion in which they contributed to the pleasure of human beings. Which is to say that dogs, lazy as city dogs are, could not even dent their imagination with a possibility of their existence.

Sometimes, on Sunday, Aunt Mathilda and I used to go to mass early to take communion. It was rare that I succeeded in concentrating on the sacrament, because the idea that she was watching me without looking generally occupied the first plane of my conscious mind. Even when her eyes were directed to the altar, or her head bowed before the Blessed Sacrament, my every movement drew her attention to it. And on leaving the church she told me with sly reproach that it was without doubt a flea trapped in the pews that prevented me from meditating, as she had suggested, that death is the good foreseen end, and from praying that it might not be painful, since that was the purpose of masses, novenas and communions.

This was such a morning. A fine drizzle was threatening to turn into a storm, and the quebracho pavements extended their shiny fans, notched with streetcar rails, from sidewalk to sidewalk. As I was cold and in a hurry to get home I stepped up the pace beside Aunt Mathilda, who was holding her black mushroom of an umbrella above our heads. There were not many people in the street since it was so early. A dark-complexioned gentleman saluted us without lifting his hat, because of the rain. My aunt was in the process of telling me how surprised she was that someone of mixed blood had bowed to her with so little show of attention, when suddenly, near where we were walking, a streetcar applied its brakes with a screech, making her interrupt her monologue. The conductor looked out through his window:

"Stupid dog!" he shouted.

We stopped to watch.

A small white bitch escaped from between the wheels of the streetcar and, limping painfully, with her tail between her legs, took refuge in a doorway as the streetcar moved on again.

"These dogs," protested Aunt Mathilda. "It's beyond me how they are allowed to go around like that."

Continuing our way we passed by the bitch huddled in the corner of a doorway. It was small and white, with legs which were too short for its size and an ugly pointed snout that proclaimed an entire genealogy of misalliances: the sum of unevenly matched breeds which for generations had been scouring the city, searching for food in the garbage cans and among the refuse of the port. She was drenched, weak, trembling with cold or fever.

When we passed in front of her I noticed that my aunt looked at the bitch, and the bitch's eyes returned her gaze.

We continued on our way home. Several steps further I was on the point of forgetting the dog when my aunt surprised me by abruptly turning around and crying out:

"Psst! Go away . . . !"

She had turned in such absolute certainty of finding the bitch following us that I trembled with the mute question which arose from my surprise: How did she know? She couldn't have heard her, since she was following us at an appreciable distance. But she did not doubt it. Perhaps the look that had passed between them of which I saw only the mechanics—the bitch's head raised slightly toward Aunt Mathilda, Aunt Mathilda's slightly inclined toward the bitch—contained some secret commitment? I do not know. In any case, turning to drive away the dog, her peremptory "psst" had the sound of something like a last effort to repel an encroaching destiny. It is possible that I am saying all this in the light of things that happened later, that my imagination is embellishing with significance what was only trivial. However, I can say with certainty that in that moment I felt a strangeness, almost a fear of my aunt's sudden loss of dignity in condescending to turn around and confer rank on a sick and filthy bitch.

We arrived home. We went up the stairs and the bitch stayed down below, looking up at us from the torrential rain that had just been unleashed. We went inside, and the delectable process of breakfast following communion removed the white bitch from my mind. I have never felt our house so protective as that morning, never rejoiced so much in the security derived from those old walls that marked off my world.

In one of my wanderings in and out of the empty sitting-rooms, I pulled back the curtain of a window to see if the rain promised to let up. The storm continued. And, sitting at the foot of the stairs still scrutinizing the house, I saw the white bitch. I dropped the curtain so that I might not see her there, soaked through and looking like one spellbound. Then, from the dark outer rim of the room, Aunt Mathilda's low voice surprised me. Bent over to strike a match to the kindling wood already arranged in the fireplace, she asked:

"Is it still there?"

"What?"

I knew what.

"The white bitch . . . "

I answered yes, that it was.

3

It must have been the last storm of the winter, because I remember quite clearly that the following days opened up and the nights began to grow warmer.

The white bitch stayed posted on our doorstep scrutinizing our windows. In the mornings, when I left for school, I tried to shoo her away, but barely had I boarded the bus when I would see her reappear around the corner or from behind the mailbox. The servant girls also tried to frighten her away, but their attempts were as fruitless as mine, because the bitch never failed to return.

Once, we were all saying good-night at the foot of the stairs before going up to bed. Uncle Gustav had just turned off the lights, all except the one on the stairway, so that the large space of the vestibule had become peopled with the shadowy bodies of furniture. Aunt Mathilda, who was entreating Uncle Armand to open the window of his room so a little air could come in, suddenly stopped speaking, leaving her sentence unfinished, and the movements of all of us, who had started to go up, halted.

"What is the matter?" asked Father, stepping down one stair.

"Go on up," murmured Aunt Mathilda, turning around and gazing into the shadow of the vestibule.

But we did not go up.

The silence of the room was filled with the secret voice of each object: a grain of dirt trickling down between the wallpaper and the wall, the creaking of polished woods, the quivering of some loose crystal. Someone, in addition to ourselves, was where we were. A small white form came out of the darkness near the service door. The bitch crossed the vestibule, limping slowly in the direction of Aunt Mathilda, and without even looking at her, threw herself down at her feet.

It was as though the immobility of the dog enabled us to move again. My father came down two stairs. Uncle Gustav turned on the light. Uncle Armand went upstairs and shut himself in his room.

"What is this?" asked my father.

Aunt Mathilda remained still.

"How could she have come in?" she asked aloud.

Her question seemed to acknowledge the heroism implicit in having either jumped walls in that lamentable condition, or come into the basement through a broken pane of glass, or fooled the servants' vigilance by creeping through a casually opened door.

"Mathilda, call one of the girls to take her away," said my father, and went upstairs followed by Uncle Gustav.

We were left alone looking at the bitch. She called a servant, telling the girl to give her something to eat and the next day to call a veterinarian.

"Is she going to stay in the house?" I asked.

"How can she walk in the street like that?" murmured Aunt Mathilda. "She has to get better so we can throw her out. And she'd better get well soon because I don't want animals in the house."

Then she added:

"Go upstairs to bed."

She followed the girl who was carrying the dog out.

I sensed that ancient drive of Aunt Mathilda's to have everything go well about her, that energy and dexterity which made her sovereign of immediate things. Is it possible that she was so secure within her limitations, that for her the only necessity was to overcome imperfections, errors not of intention or motive, but of condition? If so, the white bitch was going to get well. She would see to it because the animal had entered the radius of her power. The veterinarian would bandage the broken leg under her watchful eye, and protected by rubber gloves and an apron, she herself would take charge of cleaning the bitch's pustules with disinfectant that would make her howl. But Aunt Mathilda would remain deaf to those howls, sure that whatever she was doing was for the best.

And so it was. The bitch stayed in the house. Not that I saw her, but I could feel the presence of any stranger there, even though confined to the lower reaches of the basement. Once or twice I saw Aunt Mathilda with the rubber gloves on her hands, carrying a vial full of red liquid. I found a plate with scraps of food in a passage of the basement where I went to look for the bicycle I had just been given. Weakly, buffered by walls and floors, at times the suspicion of a bark reached my ears.

One afternoon I went down to the kitchen. The bitch came in, painted like a clown with red disinfectant. The servants threw her out without paying her any mind. But I saw that she was not hobbling any longer, that her tail, limp before, was curled up like a feather, leaving her shameless bottom in plain view.

That afternoon I asked Aunt Mathilda:

"When are you going to throw her out?"

"Who?" she asked.

She knew perfectly well.

"The white bitch."

"She's not well yet," she replied.

Later I thought of insisting, of telling her that surely there was nothing now to prevent her from climbing the garbage cans in search of food. I didn't do it because I believe it was the same night that Aunt Mathilda, after losing the first round of billiards, decided that she did not feel like playing another. Her brothers went on playing, and she, ensconced in the leather sofa, made a mistake in calling their names. There was a moment of confusion. Then the thread of order was quickly picked up again by the men, who knew how to ignore an accident if it was not favorable to them. But I had already seen.

It was as if Aunt Mathilda were not there at all. She was breathing at my side as she always did. The deep, silencing carpet yielded under her feet as usual and her tranquilly crossed hands weighed on her skirt. How is it possible to feel with the certainty I felt then the absence of a person whose heart is somewhere else? The following nights were equally troubled by the invisible slur of her absence. She seemed to have lost all interest in the game, and left off calling her brothers by their names. They appeared not to notice it. But they must have, because their games became shorter and I noticed an infinitesimal increase in the deference with which they treated her.

One night, as we were going out of the dining-room, the bitch appeared in the doorway and joined the family group. The men paused before they went into the library so that their sister might lead the way to the billiard room, followed this time by the white bitch. They made no comment, as if they had not seen her, beginning their game as they did every night.

The bitch sat down at Aunt Mathilda's feet. She was very quiet. Her lively eyes examined the room and followed the players' strategies as if all of that amused her greatly. She was fat now and had a shiny coat. Her whole body, from her quivering snout to her tail ready to waggle, was full of an abundant capacity for fun. How long had she stayed in the house? A month? Perhaps more. But in that month Aunt Mathilda had forced her to get well, caring for her not with displays of affection, but with those hands of hers which could not refrain from mending what was broken. The leg was well. She had disinfected, fed and bathed her, and now the white bitch was whole.

In one of his plays Uncle Armand let the cube of blue chalk fall to the floor. Immediately, obeying an instinct that seemed to surge up from her picaresque past, the bitch ran toward the chalk and snatched it with her mouth away from Uncle Armand, who had bent over to pick it up. Then followed something suprising: Aunt Mathilda, as if suddenly unwound, burst into a peal of laughter that agitated her whole body. We remained frozen. On hearing her laugh, the bitch dropped the chalk, ran toward her with her tail waggling aloft, and jumped up onto her lap. Aunt Mathilda's laugh relented, but Uncle Armand left the room. Uncle Gustav and my father went on with the game: now it was more important than ever not to see, not to see anything at all, not to comment, not to consider oneself alluded to by these events.

I did not find Aunt Mathilda's laugh amusing, because I may have felt the dark thing that had stirred it up. The bitch grew calm sitting on her lap. The cracking noises of the balls when they hit seemed to conduct Aunt Mathilda's hand first from its place on the edge of the sofa, to her skirt, and then to the curved back of the sleeping animal. On seeing that expressionless hand reposing there, I noticed that the tension which had kept my aunt's features clenched before, relented, and that a certain peace was now softening her face. I could not resist. I drew closer to her on the sofa, as if to a newly kindled fire. I hoped that she would reach out to me with a look or include me with a smile. But she did not.

4

When I arrived from school in the afternoon, I used to go directly to the back of the house and, mounting my bicycle, take turn after turn around the narrow garden, circling the pair of cast-iron benches and the elm tree. Behind the wall, the chestnut trees were beginning to display their light spring down, but the seasons did not interest me for I had too many serious things to think about. And since I knew that no one came down into the garden until the suffocation of midsummer made it imperative, it seemed to be the best place for meditating about what was going on inside the house.

One might have said that nothing was going on. But how could I remain calm in the face of the entwining relationship which had sprung up between my aunt and the white bitch? It was as if Aunt Mathilda, after having resigned herself to an odd life of service and duty, had found at last her equal. And as women-friends do, they carried on a life full of niceties and pleasing refinements. They ate bonbons that came in boxes wrapped frivolously with ribbons. My aunt arranged tangerines, pineapples and grapes in tall crystal bowls, while the bitch watched her as if on the point of criticizing her taste or offering a suggestion.

Often when I passed the door of her room, I heard a peal of laughter like the one which had overturned the order of her former life that night. Or I heard her engage in a dialogue with an interlocutor whose voice I did not hear. It was a new life. The bitch, the guilty one, slept in a hamper near her bed, an elegant, feminine hamper, ridiculous to my way of thinking, and followed her everywhere except into the dining-room. Entrance there was forbidden her, but waiting for her friend to come out again, she followed her to the billiard room and sat at her side on the sofa or on her lap, exchanging with her from time to time complicitory glances.

How was it possible, I used to ask myself? Why had she waited until now to go beyond herself and establish a dialogue? At times she appeared insecure about the bitch, fearful that, in the same way she had arrived one fine day, she might also go, leaving her with all this new abundance weighing on her hands. Or did she still fear for her health? These ideas, which now seem clear, floated blurred in my imagination while I listened to the gravel of the path crunching under the wheels of my bicycle. What was not blurred, however, was my vehement desire to become gravely ill, to see if I might also succeed in harvesting some kind of relationship. Because the bitch's illness had been the cause of everything. If it had not been for that, my aunt might have never joined in league with her. But I had a constitution of iron, and furthermore, it was clear that Aunt Mathilda's heart did not have room for more than one love at a time.

My father and my uncles did not seem to notice any change. The bitch was very quiet, and abandoning her street ways, seemed to acquire manners more worthy of Aunt Mathilda. But still, she had somehow preserved all the sauciness of a female of the streets. It was clear that the hardships of her life had not been able to cloud either her good humor or her taste for adventure which, I felt, lay dangerously dormant inside her. For the men of the house it proved easier to accept her than to throw her out, since this would have forced them to revise their canons of security.

One night, when the pitcher of lemonade had already made its appearance on the console-table of the library, cooling that corner of the shadow, and the windows had been thrown open to the air, my father halted abruptly at the doorway of the billiard room:

"What is that?" he exclaimed looking at the floor.

The three men stopped in consternation to look at a small, round pool on the waxed floor.

"Mathilda!" called Uncle Gustav.

She went to look and then reddened with shame. The bitch had taken refuge under the billiard table in the adjoining room. Walking over to the table my father saw her there, and changing direction sharply, he left the room, followed by his brothers.

Aunt Mathilda went upstairs. The bitch followed her. I stayed in the library with a glass of lemonade in my hand, and looked out at the summer sky, listening to some far-off siren from the sea, and to the murmur of the city stretched out under the stars. Soon I heard Aunt Mathilda coming down. She appeared with her hat on and with her keys chinking in her hand.

"Go up and go to bed," she said. "I'm going to take her for a walk on the street so that she can do her business."

Then she added something strange:

"It's such a lovely night."

And she went out.

From that night on, instead of going up after dinner to open her brothers' beds, she went to her room, put her hat tightly on her head and came downstairs again, chinking her keys. She went out with the bitch without explaining anything to anyone. And my uncles and my father and I stayed behind in the billiard room, and later we sat on the benches of the garden, with all the murmuring of the elm tree and the clearness of the sky weighing down on us. These nocturnal walks of Aunt Mathilda's were never spoken of by her brothers. They never showed any awareness of the change that had occurred inside our house.

In the beginning Aunt Mathilda was gone at the most for twenty minutes or half an hour, returning to take whatever refreshment there was and to exchange some trivial commentary. Later, her sorties were inexplicably prolonged. We began to realize, or I did at least, that she was no longer a woman taking her dog out for hygienic reasons: outside there, in the streets of the city, something was drawing her. When waiting, my father furtively eyed his pocket watch, and if the delay was very great Uncle Gustav went up to the second floor pretending he had forgotten something there, to spy for her from the balcony. But still they did not speak. Once, when Aunt Mathilda stayed out too long, my father paced back and forth along the path that wound between the hydrangeas. Uncle Gustav threw away a cigar which he could not light to his satisfaction, then another, crushing it with the heel of his shoe. Uncle Armand spilled a cup of coffee. I watched them, hoping that at long last they would explode, that they would finally say something to fill the minutes that were passing by one after another, getting longer and longer and longer without the presence of Aunt Mathilda. It was twelve-thirty when she arrived.

"Why are you all waiting up for me?" she asked smiling.

She was holding her hat in her hand, and her hair, ordinarily so well-groomed, was mussed. I saw that a streak of mud was soiling her shoes.

"What happened to you?" asked Uncle Armand.

"Nothing," came her reply, and with it she shut off any right of her brothers to meddle in those unknown hours that were now her life. I say they were her life because, during the minutes she stayed with us before going up to her room with the bitch, I perceived an animation in her eyes, an excited restlessness like that in the eyes of the animal: it was as though they had been washed in scenes to which even our imagination lacked access. Those two were accomplices. The night protected them. They belonged to the murmuring sound of the city, to the sirens of the ships which, crossing the dark or illumined streets, the houses and factories and parks, reached my ears.

Her walks with the bitch continued for some time. Now we said good-night immediately after dinner, and each one went up to shut himself in his room, my father, Uncle Gustav, Uncle Armand and I. But no one went to sleep before she came in, late, sometimes terribly late, when the light of the dawn was already striking the top of our elm. Only after hearing her close the door of her bedroom did the pacing with which my father measured his room cease, or was the window in one of his brothers' rooms finally closed to exclude that fragment of the night which was no longer dangerous.

Once I heard her come up very late, and as I thought I heard her singing softly, I opened my door and peeked out. When she passed my room, with the white bitch nestled in her arms, her face seemed to me surprisingly young and unblemished, even though it was dirty, and I saw a rip in her skirt. I went to bed terrified, knowing this was the end.

I was not mistaken. Because one night, shortly after, Aunt Mathilda took the dog out for a walk after dinner, and did not return.

We stayed awake all night, each one in his room, and she did not come back. No one said anything the next day. They went—I presume—to their office, and I went to school. She wasn't home when we came back and we sat silently at our meal that night. I wonder if they found out something definite that very first day. But I think not, because we all, without seeming to, haunted the windows of the house, peering into the street.

"Your aunt went on a trip," the cook answered me when I finally dared to ask, if only her.

But I knew it was not true.

Life continued in the house just as if Aunt Mathilda were still living there. It is true that they used to gather in the library for hours and hours, and closeted there they may have planned ways of retrieving her out of that night which had swallowed her. Several times a visitor came who was clearly not of our world, a plain-clothesman perhaps, or the head of a steve-dore's union come to pick up indemnification for some accident. Sometimes their voices rose a little, sometimes there was a deadened quiet, sometimes their voices became hard, sharp, as they fenced with the voice I did not know. But the library door was too thick, too heavy for me to hear what they were saying.

❋ Discussion and Writing

1. What controls this upper-class, patriarchal family's routine? Who is in charge in the family? Analyze the relationship among the members of the family.
2. What explanation for Aunt Mathilda's disappearance is given to the child? What is the real cause for her disappearance according to the adult narrator? Support your response with evidence from the story.
3. What is the function of the dog in the story? What is the significance of the title "Paseo" (The Walk)?
4. Elaborate on the impact of the setting—the house, the harbor, the city, the weather—in the narration?
5. Analyze the narrative organization. Discuss the mingling of the two perspectives: the child's and the adult narrator's.
6. What is the tone of the story? Humorous? Sad? Subjective? Indifferent? Explain your interpretation.

Lygia Fagundes Telles
(b. 1924)
Brazil

Lygia Fagundes Telles, whose father served as district attorney, police commissioner, and judge, was born in Sao Paulo, Brazil, but during her childhood, she lived in various towns throughout the state, moving as her father's work dictated. She took two degrees: one in law and one in physical education, the latter because of her mother's anxiety that she would develop tuberculosis because she was so thin. Telles's interest in writing, however, began when she was a child; she would entertain her friends by recreating the fantastic tales her nursemaid told her, keeping a notebook of the eerie details so that she could remember them, and tame them. She believes that both the early lack of permanency and the surfeit of fantasy have influenced her writing. She began publishing stories as a teenager and, while still a student, worked on the school literary journals and protested against the repressive government of Getulio Vargas. Over the years, Telles has practiced law and served as president of the Brazilian Cinematheque. She won the Cannes Prix International des Femmes, and she has continued writing novels and short stories that exhibit a disjunctive sense of place and being.

The Ants*

When my cousin and I got out of the taxi, it was almost dark. We stood motionless before the old two-story house with oval windows, just like two melancholy eyes, one of them broken by a hurled rock. I rested my suitcase on the ground and took my cousin by the arm.

"It's sinister."

She pulled me toward the door. Did we have any other choice? For two penniless students, no other boardinghouse in the area offered a better price, with permission to use the single-burner stove in the room, the landlady had advised us over the phone that we could cook light meals on the condition we didn't start a fire. We went up the ancient staircase, which smelled of creosote.

"At least I don't see any sign of cockroaches," said my cousin.

The landlady was a swollen old crone, with a wig blacker than a crow's wing. She wore a faded pair of Japanese silk pajamas, and her crooked fingernails were covered with a crust of dark-red enamel, faded and peeling off at the edges. She lighted up a cheroot.

"Are you the one who studies medicine?" she asked, blowing smoke in my direction.

"I study law. She's medicine."

The woman looked at us indifferently. She must have been thinking about something else as she blew out a cloud of smoke so dense I had to turn aside. The little parlor was dark, crammed with old, unmatched furniture. On the holy straw seat of the sofa were two pillows, which apparently had been made from the remains of an old dress, the embroidery interspersed with sequins.

"I'll show you the room, it's in the attic," she said in the middle of an attack of coughing and motioned us to follow her.

"The last tenant studied medicine, too. He left behind a little box of bones, which he was supposed to come after. But up to now he hasn't appeared."

My cousin stopped. "A box of bones?"

The woman didn't answer, concentrated on the effort of going up the narrow winding staircase, which led to the room. She turned on the light. The room couldn't have been any smaller, with the ceiling sloping down-

---

*Translated by Margaret A. Neves

ward so sharply that in one part we would have to crawl. Two beds, two wardrobes, a table, and a straw-backed chair painted gold. In the angle where the ceiling almost met the floor, there was a small crate covered with a sheet of plastic. My cousin set down her suitcase and, kneeling, pulled out the crate by its rope handle. She lifted up the plastic, seemingly fascinated.

"But what tiny little bones! Are they a child's?"

"He said they were an adult's. A dwarf's."

"A dwarf's? You're right, you can see that they're already formed. But what a find, dwarf skeletons are rare as anything. And so clean, look here," she marveled. With her fingertips she brought out a tiny skull of a limelike whiteness.

"So perfect! Every single tooth!"

"I was going to throw the whole thing in the trash, but if you're interested, you can keep it. The bathroom is here at the side, you're the only ones who will use it, mine is downstairs. Hot baths extra. Phone also. Supper's from seven to nine, I'll leave the table set in the kitchen with coffee in the thermos, close it tight," she recommended, scratching her head. The wig slipped slightly out of kilter. She blew out a final cloud of smoke. "Don't leave the door open or my cat will get out."

We stood there looking at each other and laughing while we listened to the sound of her high-heeled slippers on the stairs. And her catarrhal cough.

I emptied my suitcase, hung up my wrinkled blouse on a hanger, which I stuck into a crack in the venetian blind, taped a Grassmann engraving on the wall, and set my plush teddy bear on the pillow. I watched my cousin climb up on a chair, unscrew the very weak light bulb that was hanging from a solitary wire in the middle of the ceiling, and replace it with a 200-watt bulb she took from her bag. The room became more cheerful. On the other hand, we could now see that the bed linen was not so white, white was the small tibia she took from the crate and examined. She picked up a vertebra and looked through the opening as small as the circumference of a ring. Delicately she put them away, as if she were arranging eggs in a basket.

"A dwarf? Very rare, understand? And I don't think any of the bones are missing, I'm going to bring the ligatures, maybe I can start putting him together this weekend."

We opened a can of sardines, which we ate with bread, my cousin always had a can of something stashed away, she often studied into the wee hours and afterward made herself a snack. When the bread was gone, she opened a package of biscuits.

"Where is that smell coming from?" I asked, sniffing. I went over to the crate, came back, smelled the floor. "Don't you notice a sour smell?"

"It's mildew. The whole house smells that way," she said. And she pushed the crate under the bed.

In the dream a blond dwarf wearing a plaid vest and hair parted down the middle came into the room. He was smoking a cigar. He sat down on my cousin's bed, crossed his short legs, and sat there with a very serious expression, watching her sleep. I wanted to scream, "There's a dwarf in the room!" but before I could manage to, I woke up. The light was on. On hands and knees, still dressed, my cousin was staring at something on the floor.

"What are you doing there?" I asked.

"These ants. All of a sudden they just appeared, grouped together, So purposeful, do you see them?" I got up, and was met with the small red ants, which were entering in a solid line through the crack under the door, crossing the room, marching up the side of the small box of bones, and swarming inside, disciplined as an army on parade.

"There are thousands, I've never seen so many ants. And there's no return line, only a line coming" I puzzled.

"Only coming."

I told her about my nightmare with the dwarf seated on her bed.

"He's underneath it," said my cousin. And she pulled the box out. She took off the plastic. "It's black with ants. Give me the bottle of alcohol."

"There must be something left there on these bones, and they've discovered it, ants discover everything. If I were you, I'd take this outside."

"But the bones are completely clean, I tell you. There's not even a thread of cartilege left. Superclean. I wonder what these bandits came looking for in here."

She sprinkled alcohol liberally all over the crate. Then, she put on her shoes and like a tightrope walker balancing on a high wire, she stepped firmly, one foot in front of the other, on the line of ants. She went back and forth twice. Putting out her cigarette, she pulled up the chair and sat looking into the box.

"Odd. Very odd."

"What?"

"I remember putting the cranium right on top of the pile, I even put the shoulder blades under it so it wouldn't roll. And now it's there on the bottom of the case with a shoulder blade on each side. Did you by any chance mess around in here?"

"God forbid, bones give me the creeps. Especially dwarf bones."

She covered the small crate with the sheet of plastic, pushed it away with her foot, and put the hot plate on the table, it was time for her tea. On the floor, the line of dead ants was now a dark shrunken ribbon. One ant which had escaped the slaughter passed by near my foot, I was just going to squash it when I saw it bring its hands up to its head, like a despairing person. I let it disappear into a crack in the floor.

My sleep was riddled by nightmares again, but this time it was the old dream about exams, the professor asking question after question and I silent, confronted by the one point I hadn't studied. At six A.M. the alarm clock rang vehemently. I turned the bell off. My cousin was asleep with her head covered. In the bathroom I peered closely at the walls, the cement floor, looking for them. I didn't see any. I went back on tiptoe and opened the venetian blinds slightly. The suspicious smell of the night before disappeared. I looked at the floor: the ranks of the massacred army had vanished too. I glanced under the bed and didn't see the slightest movement of ants on the covered case.

When I got back around seven that night, my cousin was already in the room. I found her looking so worn-out that I put extra salt in her omelette; she had low blood pressure. We ate in a voracious silence. Then I remembered.

"And the ants?"

"None, up to now."

"Did you sweep up the dead ones?"

She stared at me. "I didn't sweep up anything. I was exhausted. Wasn't it you?"

"Me! When I woke up, there wasn't any sign of ants on this floor, I was sure that before going to bed you had cleaned them up. But then who—?"

Squinting, she blinked her eyes, she went cross-eyed when she was worried.

"Really very weird. Superweird."

I went to get a chocolate bar and near the door I again noticed the odor, but could it be mildew? It didn't seem like such an innocent smell to me, I wanted to call my cousin's attention to it but she seemed so depressed I decided it was better to keep quiet.

I sprinkled apple-blossom cologne all over the room (so what if it smelled like an orchard) and went to bed early. I had the second type of bad dream, which competed with the exam nightmare for repetition; in this one, I made a date to meet two different boyfriends in the same place, at the same time. The first one would come and I would go crazy trying to get him away from there before the second one showed up. In this dream the second one was the dwarf. When nothing remained but hollowed-out shadow and silence, my cousin's voice snagged me with its hook. I opened my eyes with an effort. She was sitting on the edge of my bed, wearing her pajamas, completely cross-eyed.

"They're back."

"Who?"

"The ants. They only attack at night, in the wee hours. They're all here again."

Last night's army, compact and intense, followed its former course from the door to the box of bones, up which it climbed in the same formation until disbanding inside. Without a return file.

"And the bones?"

She rolled herself up in the blanket, she was trembling.

"That's just it. Something's happening, I don't understand it at all. I got up to do pee-pee, it must have been about three o'clock. On my way back to bed I felt that there was *something else* in the room, you know? I looked at the floor and saw the solid line of ants, you remember? There wasn't one when we got here. I went to look at the box; they were all milling around inside, of course, but that wasn't what almost made me fall over backward, there's something more serious: The bones are actually changing position. I already suspected it, but now I'm sure, little by little they're . . . they're being organized."

"Organized, how?"

She became thoughtful. I began to shake with cold, and grabbed a corner of her blanket. I covered my teddy bear up with the sheet.

"You remember, the cranium between the shoulder blades, I didn't put it there. Now the spinal column is almost formed, one vertebra after the other, each little bone in its place, somebody who knows his business is putting the skeleton together, a little bit more and—come see!"

"I believe you, I don't want to see anything. They're putting the dwarf back together, is that it?"

We watched the rapid line, the ants marching so close together that not even a particle of dust would fit between them. I hopped over it with the greatest of care as I went to heat up some tea. One ant which was out of line (the same one as the other night?) was shaking its head between its hands. I began to laugh so hard that if the floor hadn't been occupied, I would have rolled on it. We fell asleep together in my bed. She was still asleep when I went out for my first class. On the floor, not the shadow of an ant, dead or alive, they disappeared with the light of day.

I went back late that night, a classmate had gotten married, and there was a party. I came home happy, in the mood to sing, I'd had a few too many. Then as I was going upstairs I remembered: the dwarf. My cousin had dragged the table over to the door, and was studying with the kettle bubbling on the hot plate.

"Tonight I'm not going to sleep, I want to keep watch," she announced. The floor was still clean. I hugged the bear to me.

"I'm scared."

She went to get me an aspirin to lessen my hangover, made me swallow it with a gulp of tea, and helped me get undressed.

"I'll stay up watching, you can sleep in peace. So far they haven't appeared, it's not time for them yet, they usually start later. I examined under the door with a magnifying glass, you know I couldn't discover where they come from?"

I flopped onto the bed, I don't think I even answered. At the head of the stairs the dwarf grabbed my wrists and whirled me into the bedroom: wake up, wake up! It took me a moment to recognize my cousin, who was holding me by the elbows. She was livid. And squinting.

"They came back," she said.

I held my throbbing head between my hands.

"Are they there?"

She spoke in a small voice, as if it were a little ant speaking.

"I ended up falling asleep over the table, I was exhausted. When I woke up, the line was already there in full march. So I went and looked in the box, and it happened just as I expected . . ."

"What, tell me quick, what?"

She fixed her oblique glance on the small crate under the bed.

"They really are putting him together, and fast, understand? The skeleton is almost complete, they only need to put the femur in place. And the little bones of the left hand, they'll do that in no time. Let's get out of here."

"Are you serious?"

"Let's go, I've already packed the bags." The table was bare and the wide-open closet empty.

"But to go off like this, in the middle of the night? Can we just leave this way?"

"Immediately, better not wait for the witch to wake up. Come on, get up."

"And where will we go?"

"It doesn't matter, later we'll see. Hurry up, put this on, we have to get out before they get the dwarf ready."

I looked at the line from a distance; they had never seemed to move so fast. I put on my shoes, unstuck my engraving from the wall, jammed the bear into the pocket of my jacket, and we went lugging the suitcases down the steps, the smell from the room coming stronger now, we had left the door open. Was it the cat that gave a long meow or a cry?

In the sky, the last stars were fading. When I turned to look back at the house, only the broken window watched us, the other eye was in shadow.

❈ Discussion and Writing

1. Describe the fantastic events in the story? Are the two women's disciplines, medicine and law, connected to the events in the story?

2. Why is the landlady called a witch? What is the importance of the description of the house? What is the function of the ants, of the cat? Analyze their significance in the story.

3. What is the relevance of dreams in the narration?

4. Comment on the importance of the repeated terms: odor, marching purposeful ants, bones, weird. Analyze other details that contribute to the mood of the story.

Ernesto Cardenal
(b. 1925)
Nicaragua

Ernesto Cardenal was born on the north shore of Lake Nicaragua but raised in the city of Leon, the city where Ruben Dario had lived. As a child, he took confession at the same church at which Dario had taken confession, and when—at age 7—Cardenal wrote his first poem, it was in honor of Dario. Cardenal gradually created his own poetic theory, *extiorismo,* in which he advocated concreteness. He wanted poetry to consist of data such as actual dates, facts, and names, and to be narrative rather than lyrical. When he returned to Managua in 1950 after studying in the United States for two years and traveling in Europe for one, he turned to a major event in Nicaragua's history for his poetry. This was the Filibuster War of 1855–1857, when William Walker of Tennessee made himself president of Nicaragua. Walker was the leader of the adventurers, or filibusters as they were called, who invaded Nicaragua. Before the Central American republics drove him out (with the help of England and the North American tycoon Cornelius Vanderbilt), he had legalized slavery and made English the official language.

It was on his return to Nicaragua that Cardenal became politically active, joining a revolutionary group committed to overthrowing the dictator Anastasio Somoza, writing articles in *La Prensa* attacking the government, and setting up a small press to publish poetry. The press, EL Hilo Azul (The Blue Thread), with its allusion to Dario's ground-breaking volume of prose and poetry, *Azul,* became the center for both poets and revolutionaries until it folded. Then in the mid-1950s, he entered a Trappist monastary in Kentucky; after two years he left to study in Mexico and Colombia, and in the mid-1960s he was ordained in Nicaragua. And there he established Nuestra Senora Solentiname (Our Lady of Solentiname), a contemplative community named for a remote chain of islands in Lake Nicaragua that was home to some thousand poor farmers. The name confirmed his continued political commitment as a priest and as a poet. Until 1977, when Somoza destroyed the community and Cardenal fled to Costa Rica, he scarcely left Solentiname. He served as chaplain in the Frente Sandinista de Liberacion Nacional (Sandinista National Liberation Front) struggle against Somoza, and became minister of culture under the Sandinista government.

The Filibusters*

There were scoundrels, thieves, gamblers, gunslingers.
There were also honest men and gentlemen and brave men.
Fellows enlisting out of necessity and illusions:
Some fellow out of work one morning would be on a pier,
and an agent of Walker would come up with a free passage
to Nicaragua.
                    —Toward where there was no passage back.
Or they came for 160 acres of land in Central America
(to sell it) and 25 bucks a month,
and they fought for nothing a month, and six square feet of earth.
Or they'd come in search of glory: a name
forever written down in the pages of History.
And their names were forgotten,
in barracks with boards taken out to make their coffins
and the drunken sergeant, pigs, crap;
or in those hospitals consisting of mango, coconut and almond groves
where they suffered from delirium with howler monkeys and magpies all
  around
getting chills from the wind off the Lake.
And the luckiest ones were those who died in battles
or in ambushes at night along strange roads like a dream,
or by accidents or sudden death.
And always loaded with more filibusters
and more filibusters,
bound for San Juan del Sur.
                    and for San Juan del Norte,
the "Transit Company" would come
                    like Charon's boat.
Vanderbilt and Morgan knew where we were going
                    (almost all died)
and down in Nicaragua they stole money from the dead.

❀ Discussion and Writing

  1. Who are the filibusters? Analyze the implications of their various moti-
     vations.

Translated by Jonathan Cohen

2. Analyze the details Cardenal uses to indicate the outcome of their fight.
3. Why is the "Transit Company" compared to the boat of Charon?
4. Analyze the tone of the poem: what are the poet's feelings; what is the impact of the last nine lines; does the tone vary from that in the rest of the poem?

❋ Research and Comparison

Interdisciplinary Discussion Question: Investigate the historical background of the Filibuster War. Comment on the parallels in the relationship between Nicaragua and the United States in the nineteenth century and at present.

Interdisciplinary Discussion Question: Is the Filibuster War relevant to today's political situation anywhere in the world? Where? How does the current situation differ from the situation described in the poem?

Rosario Castellanos
(1925–1978)
Mexico

Rosario Castellanos was born in Mexico City and spent her childhood in Comitan, Chiapas, Mexico. She studied literature and philosophy at universities in Mexico City and Madrid and received critical acclaim in 1948 for her first book of poetry. She continued publishing poetry, short stories, novels, and critical essays throughout her life; she also worked as a journalist and taught at universities in Mexico and the United States. She was serving as the Mexican ambassador to Israel at the time of her death.

Her work is marked, simultaneously, by its lucidity and its philosophical nature. Castellanos confronted social injustice in her writing, taking up issues concerning native peoples and women. In her major novel, *Balun Canan* (1958), she used her girlhood home of Comitan to examine the exploitation of native people in a rural environment. She also explored the question of her identity as a woman and as a Mexican in her poetry and fiction, and wrote—among other subjects—essays on feminism.

Daily Round of the Spinster*

To be solitary is shameful. All day long
a terrible blush burnishes her cheek
(while the other is in eclipse).

She busies herself in a labor of ashes,
at tasks worthless and fruitless;
and when her relatives gather
around the fire, telling stories,
the howl is heard
of a woman wailing on a boundless plain
where every boulder, every scorched tree stump,
every twisted bough is a judge
or a witness without mercy.

At night the spinster
stretches herself out on her bed of agony.
An anguished sweat breaks out to dampen the sheets
and the void is peopled
with made-up dialogues and men.

And the spinster waits, waits, waits.

And she cannot be born in her child, in her womb,
nor can she die
in her far-off, unexplored body,
a planet the astronomer can calculate,
existent though unseen.

Peering into a dark mirror the spinster
—extinguished star—paints on her lips
with a lipstick the blood she does not have.

And smiles at a dawn without anyone at all.

---

*Translated by Kate Flores

✵ Discussion and Writing

1. Why is it shameful for a woman to be solitary? Expand on the implications of the statement.
2. What images describe the spinster's state of mind and the people at family gatherings?
3. What aspects of the spinster's womanhood are delineated in the poem? Distinguish between those determined by the spinster's personal needs and by the social mores.
4. Discuss the poem as a critique of the social expectations of a woman.

✵ Research and Comparison

Interdisciplinary Discussion Question: Examining the works of two women writers from Latin America, define their major concerns regarding gender relations and other women's issues.

Interdisciplinary Discussion Question: Compare the concerns of women writers from any two major areas (Asia, Africa, South America, the Caribbean). What conclusions can be drawn about the commonality or uniqueness of problems and their resolutions? Comment on the distinctive cultural mores that determine the problems and their resolutions.

Martin Carter
(b. 1927)
Guyana

Martin Wylde Carter went to high school at Queen's College in Georgetown, Guyana; in his early twenties he became identified with and a leader of the radical wing of the Guyanese independence movement. His poetry (which, like Wilson Harris's early work, first appeared in A. J. Seymour's journal, *Kyk-over-al*) spoke to his vehement opposition to British dominion. The passionate commitment in his poetry and his position in the movement as an outspoken critic led to his being jailed by the colonial government. But he was productive during his imprisonment: there he wrote most of *Poems of Resistance* (1954), the volume that epitomizes his revolutionary poetry and the years of resistance to colonial status. Carter saw his poems as political acts. During the 1960s, he participated in the negotiations with England to establish Guyana as an independent nation, and he served in the Guyanese government in various capacities until 1971, but always as a committed poet-activist. The subsequent inability of Guyanese society to change its economic and social structures has lent a yearning quality to his poetry. Equally significant, Carter has retained a belief in a Caribbean aesthetic.

Listening to the Land

That night when I left you on the bridge
I bent down
kneeling on my knee
and pressed my ear to listen to the land.

I bent down
listening to the land
but all I heard was tongueless whispering.

On my right hand was the sea behind the wall
the sea that has no business in the forest
and I bent down
listening to the land
and all I heard was tongueless whispering
as if some buried slave wanted to speak again.

❋ **Discussion and Writing**

1. Examine the symbolism of the land and the sea. What is implied by "the bridge" and "the wall"?
2. Explore the significance of the emphasis on listening.
3. Discuss the irony inherent in the phrase "tongueless whispering." What is the historical source of the paradox?

Carlos Fuentes
(b. 1928)
Mexico

Carlos Fuentes, the son of a Mexican diplomat, was born in Panama and grew up in the capitals of the various countries where his father served. Fuentes's early schooling took place in Washington, D.C., and Santiago, Chile, where Jose Donoso was a classmate. Embracing Marxism during his student days, Fuentes obtained a degree in law from the National University of Mexico, and studied economics in Geneva. He served in the Mexican government in various capacities until the 1968 Olympics, when he resigned his post as ambassador to France in protest against the government's shooting of student demonstators. He has subsequently been a distinguished lecturer in the United States and Europe, writing frequently for North American and European newspapers and television while continuing to publish his novels and short stories.

Despite a lifetime of traveling, he has remained absorbed by Mexico. The publication in 1950 of Octavio Paz's *Labyrinth of Solitude* was timely for Fuentes in that it clarified his thoughts about his country, about its history, its national character, and its present state. Employing the techniques of movies and modernism to create his fictional worlds, Fuentes has consistently explored the Mexican condition; and this condition has become at once national, Latin American, and international.

Chac-Mool*

It was only recently that Filiberto drowned in Acapulco. It happened during Easter Week. Even though he'd been fired from his government job, Filiberto couldn't resist the bureaucratic temptation to make his annual pilgrimage to the small German hotel, to eat sauerkraut sweetened by the sweat of the tropical cuisine, dance away Holy Saturday on La Quebrada, and feel he was one of the "beautiful people" in the dim anonymity of dusk on Hornos Beach. Of course we all knew he'd been a good swimmer when he was young, but now, at forty, and the shape he was in, to try to swim that distance, at midnight! Frau Muller wouldn't allow a wake in her hotel—steady client or not; just the opposite, she held a dance on her stifling little terrace while Filiberto, very pale in his coffin, awaited the departure of the first morning bus from the terminal, spending the first night of his new life surrounded by crates and parcels. When I arrived, early in the morning, to supervise the loading of the casket, I found Filiberto buried beneath a mound of coconuts; the driver wanted to get him in the luggage compartment as quickly as possible, covered with canvas in order not to upset the passengers and to avoid bad luck on the trip.

When we left Acapulco there was still a good breeze. Near Tierra Colorada it began it get hot and bright. As I was eating my breakfast eggs and sausage, I had opened Filiberto's satchel, collected the day before along with his other personal belongings from the Mullers' hotel. Two hundred pesos. An old newspaper; expired lottery tickets; a one-way ticket to

---

Translated by Margaret Sayers Peden

Acapulco—one way?—and a cheap notebook with graph-paper pages and marbleized-paper binding.

On the bus I ventured to read it, in spite of the sharp curves, the stench of vomit, and a certain natural feeling of respect for the private life of a deceased friend. It should be a record—yes, it began that way—of our daily office routine; maybe I'd find out what caused him to neglect his duties, why he'd written memoranda without rhyme or reason or any authorization. The reasons, in short, for his being fired, his seniority ignored and his pension lost.

"Today I went to see about my pension. Lawyer extremely pleasant. I was so happy when I left that I decided to blow five pesos at a café. The same café we used to go to when we were young and where I never go now because it reminds me that I lived better at twenty than I do at forty. We were all equals then, energetically discouraging any unfavorable remarks about our classmates. In fact, we'd open fire on anyone in the house who so much as mentioned inferior background or lack of elegance. I knew that many of us (perhaps those of most humble origin) would go far, and that here in school we were forging lasting friendships; together we would brave the stormy seas of life. But it didn't work out that way. Someone didn't follow the rules. Many of the lowly were left behind, though some climbed higher even than we could have predicted in those high-spirited, affable get-togethers. Some who seemed to have the most promise got stuck some-where along the way, cut down in some extracurricular activity, isolated by an invisible chasm from those who'd triumphed and those who'd gone nowhere at all. Today, after all this time, I again sat in the chairs—remod-eled, as well as the soda fountain, a kind of barricade against invasion—and pretended to read some business papers. I saw many of the old faces, amne-siac, changed in the neon light, prosperous. Like the café, which I barely recognized, along with the city itself, they'd been chipping away at a pace different from my own. No, they didn't recognize me now, or didn't want to. At most, one or two clapped a quick, fat hand on my shoulder. So long, old friend, how's it been going? Between us stretched the eighteen holes of the Country Club. I buried myself in my papers. The years of my dreams, the optimistic predictions, filed before my eyes, along with the obstacles that had kept me from achieving them. I left frustrated that I couldn't dig my fingers into the past and put together the pieces of some long-forgotten puzzle. But one's toy chest is a part of the past, and when all's said and done, who knows where his lead soldiers went, his helmets and wooden swords. The make-believe we loved so much was only that, make-believe. Still, I'd been diligent, disciplined, devoted to buy. Wasn't that enough? Was it too much? Often, I was assaulted by the recollection of Rilke: the great reward for the adventure of youth is death; we should die young, taking all our secrets with us. Today I wouldn't be looking back at a city of salt. Five pesos? Two pesos tip."

* * *

"In addition to his passion for corporation law, Pepe likes to theorize. He saw me coming out of the Cathedral, and we walked together toward the National Palace. He's not a believer, but he's not content to stop at that: within half a block he had to propose a theory. If I weren't a Mexican, I wouldn't worship Christ, and . . . No, look, it's obvious. The Spanish arrive and say, Adore this God who died a bloody death nailed to a cross with a bleeding wound in his side. Sacrificed. Made an offering. What could be more natural than to accept something so close to your own ritual, your own life . . . ? Imagine, on the other hand, if Mexico had been conquered by Buddhists or Moslems. It's not conceivable that our Indians would have worshipped some person who died of indigestion. But a God that's not only sacrificed for you but has his heart torn out, God Almighty, checkmate to Huitzilopochtli! Christianity, with its emotion, its bloody sacrifice and ritual, becomes a natural and novel extension of the native religion. The qualities of charity, love, and turn-the-other-cheek, however, are rejected. And that's what Mexico is all about: you have to kill a man in order to believe in him.

"Pepe knew that ever since I was young I've been mad for certain pieces of Mexican Indian art. I collect small statues, idols, pots. I spend my weekends in Tlaxcala, or in Teotihuacan. That may be why he likes to relate to indigenous themes all the theories he concocts for me. Pepe knows that I've been looking for a reasonable replica of the Chac-Mool for a long time, and today he told me about a little shop in the flea market of La Lagunilla where they're selling one, apparently at a good price. I'll go Sunday.

"A joker put red coloring in the office water cooler, naturally interrupting our duties. I had to report him to the director, who simply thought it was funny. So all day the bastard's been going around making fun of me, with cracks about water. Motherfu . . . "

"Today, Sunday, I had time to go out to La Lagunilla. I found the Chac-Mool in the cheap little shop Pepe had told me about. It's marvelous a piece, life-size, and though the dealer assures me it's an original, I question it. The stone is nothing out of the ordinary, but that doesn't diminish the elegance of the composition, or its massiveness. The rascal has smeared tomato ketchup on the belly to convince the tourists of its bloody authenticity.

"Moving the piece to my house cost more than the purchase price. But it's here now, temporarily in the cellar while I reorganize my collection to make room for it. These figures demand a vertical and burning-hot sun; that was their natural element. The effect is lost in the darkness of the cellar, where it's simply another lifeless mass and its grimace seems to reproach me for denying it light. The dealer had a spotlight focused directly on the sculpture, highlighting all the planes and lending a more amiable expression to my Chac-Mool. I must follow his example."

"I awoke to find the pipes had burst. Somehow, I'd carelessly left the water running in the kitchen; it flooded the floor and poured into the cellar before I'd noticed it. The dampness didn't damage the Chac-Mool, but my suitcases suffered; everything has to happen on a weekday. I was late to work."

"At last they came to fix the plumbing. Suitcases ruined. There's slime on the base of the Chac-Mool."

"I awakened at one; I'd heard a terrible moan. I thought it might be burglars. Purely imaginary."

"The moaning at night continues. I don't know where it's coming from, but it makes me nervous. To top it all off, the pipes burst again, and the rains have seeped through the foundation and flooded the cellar."

"Plumber still hasn't come; I'm desperate. As far as the City Water Department's concerned, the less said the better. This is the first time the runoff from the rains has drained into my cellar instead of the storm sewers. The moaning's stopped. An even trade?"

"They pumped out the cellar. The Chac-Mool is covered with slime. It makes him look grotesque; the whole sculpture seems to be suffering from a kind of green erysipelas, with the exception of the eyes. I'll scrape off the moss Sunday. Pepe suggested I move to an apartment on an upper floor, to prevent any more of these aquatic tragedies. But I can't leave my house; it's obviously more than I need, a little gloomy in its turn-of-the-century style, but it's the only inheritance, the only memory, I have left of my parents. I don't know how I'd feel if I saw a soda fountain with a jukebox in the cellar and an interior decorator's shop on the ground floor."

"Used a trowel to scrape the Chac-Mool. The moss now seemed almost a part of the stone; it took more than an hour and it was six in the evening before I finished. I couldn't see anything in the darkness, but I ran my hand over the outlines of the stone. With every stroke, the stone seemed to become softer. I couldn't believe it; it felt like dough. That dealer in La Lagunilla has really swindled me. His 'pre-Columbian sculpture' is nothing but plaster, and the dampness is ruining it. I've covered it with some rags and will bring it upstairs tomorrow before it dissolves completely."

"The rags are on the floor. Incredible. Again I felt the Chac-Mool. It's firm, but not stone. I don't want to write this: the texture of the torso feels a little like flesh; I press it like rubber, and feel something coursing through that recumbent figure . . . I went down again later at night. No doubt about it: the Chac-Mool has hair on its arms."

"This kind of thing has never happened to me before. I fouled up my work in the office: I sent out a payment that hadn't been authorized, and the director had to call it to my attention. I think I may even have been rude to my co-workers. I'm going to have to see a doctor, find out whether it's my imagination, whether I'm delirious, or what . . . and get rid of that damned Chac-Mool."

Up to this point I recognized Filiberto's hand, the large, rounded letters I'd seen on so many memoranda and forms. The entry for August 25 seemed to have been written by a different person. At times it was the writing of a child, each letter laboriously separated; other times, nervous, trailing into illegibility. Three days are blank, and then the narrative continues:

"It's all so natural, though normally we believe only in what's real . . . but this is real, more real than anything I've ever known. A water cooler is real, more than real, because we fully realize its existence, or being, when some joker puts something in the water to turn it red . . . An ephemeral smoke ring is real, a grotesque image in a funhouse mirror is real; aren't all deaths, present and forgotten, real . . . ? If a man passes through paradise in a dream, and is handed a flower as proof of having been there, and if when he awakens he finds this flower in his hand . . . then . . . ? Reality: one day it was shattered into a thousand pieces, its head rolled in one direction and its tail in another, and all we have is one of the pieces from the gigantic body. A free and fictitious ocean, real only when it is imprisoned in a seashell. Until three days ago, my reality was of such a degree it would be erased today; it was reflex action, routine, memory, carapace. And then, like the earth that one day trembles to remind us of its power, of the death to come, recriminating against me for having turned my back on life, an orphaned reality we always knew was there presents itself, jolting us in order to become living present. Again I believed it to be imagination: the Chac-Mool, soft and elegant, had changed color overnight; yellow, almost golden, it seemed to suggest it was a god, at ease now, the knees more relaxed than before, the smile more benevolent. And yesterday, finally, I awakened with a start, with the frightening certainty that two creatures are breathing in the night, that in the darkness there beats a pulse in addition to one's own. Yes, I heard foot-steps on the stairway. Nightmare. Go back to sleep. I don't know how long I feigned sleep. When I opened my eyes again, it still was not dawn. The room smelled of horror, of incense and blood. In the darkness, I gazed about the bedroom until my eyes found two points of flickering, cruel yellow light.
"Scarcely breathing, I turned on the light. There was the Chac-Mool, standing erect, smiling, ocher-colored except for the flesh-red belly. I was paralyzed by the two tiny, almost crossed eyes set close to the wedge-shaped nose. The lower teeth closed tightly on the upper lip; only the glimmer from the squarish helmet on the abnormally large head betrayed any sign of life. Chac-Mool moved toward my bed; then it began to rain."

I remember that it was at the end of August that Filiberto had been fired from his job, with a public condemnation by the director, amid rumors of madness and even theft. I didn't believe it. I did see some wild memoranda, one asking the Secretary of the Department whether water had an odor; another, offering his services to the Department of Water Resources to make it rain in the desert. I couldn't explain it. I thought the exceptionally heavy rains of that summer had affected him. Or that living in that ancient mansion with half the rooms locked and thick with dust, without any servants or family life, had finally deranged him. The following entries are for the end of September.

"Chac-Mool can be pleasant enough when he wishes . . . the gurgling of enchanted water . . . He knows wonderful stories about the monsoons, the equatorial rains, the scourge of the deserts; the genealogy of every plant engendered by his mythic paternity: the willow, his wayward daughter; the lotus, his favorite child; the cactus, his mother-in-law. What I can't bear is the odor, the nonhuman odor, emanating from flesh that isn't flesh, from sandals that shriek their antiquity. Laughing stridently, the Chac-Mool recounts how he was discovered by Le Plongeon and brought into physical contact with men of other gods. His spirit had survived quite peacefully in water vessels and storms; his stone was another matter, and to have dragged him from his hiding place was unnatural and cruel. I think the Chac-Mool will never forgive that. He savors the imminence of the aesthetic.

"I've had to provide him with pumice stone to clean the belly the dealer smeared with ketchup when he thought he was Aztec. He didn't seem to like my question about his relation to Tlaloc, and when he becomes angry his teeth, repulsive enough in themselves, glitter and grow pointed. The first days he slept in the cellar; since yesterday, in my bed."

"The dry season has begun. Last night, from the living room where I'm sleeping now, I heard the same hoarse moans I'd heard in the beginning, followed by a terrible racket. I went upstairs and peered into the bedroom: the Chac-Mool was breaking the lamps and furniture; he sprang toward the door with outstretched bleeding hands, and I was barely able to slam the door and run to hide in the bathroom. Later he came downstairs, panting and begging for water. He leaves the faucets running all day; there's not a dry spot in the house. I have to sleep wrapped in blankets, and I've asked him please to let the living room dry out."[1]

---

[1]Filiberto does not say in what language he communicated with the Chac-Mool.

"The Chac-Mool flooded the living room today. Exasperated, I told him I was going to return him to La Lagunilla. His laughter—so frighteningly different from the laugh of any man or animal—was as terrible as the blow from that heavily braceleted arm. I have to admit it: I am his prisoner. My original plan was quite different. I was going to play with the Chac-Mool the way you play with a toy; this may have been an extension of the security of childhood. But—who said it?—the fruit of childhood is consumed by the years, and I hadn't seen that. He's taken my clothes, and when the green moss begins to sprout, he covers himself in my bathrobes. The Chac-Mool is accustomed to obedience, always; I, who have never had cause to command, can only submit. Until it rains—what happened to his magic power?—he will be choleric and irritable."

"Today I discovered that the Chac-Mool leaves the house at night. Always, as it grows dark, he sings a shrill and ancient tune, older than song itself. Then everything is quiet. I knocked several times at the door, and when he didn't answer I dared enter. The bedroom, which I hadn't seen since the day the statue tried to attack me, is a ruin; the odor of incense and blood that permeates the entire house is particularly concentrated here. And I discovered bones behind the door, dog and rat and cat bones. This is what the Chac-Mool steals in the night for nourishment. This explains the hideous barking every morning."

"February, dry. Chac-Mool watches every move I make; he made me telephone a restaurant and ask them to deliver chicken and rice every day. But what I took from the office is about to run out. So the inevitable happened: on the first they cut off the water and lights for nonpayment. But Chac has discovered a public fountain two blocks from the house; I make ten or twelve trips a day for water while he watches me from the roof. He says that if I try to run away he will strike me dead in my tracks; he is also the God of Lightning. What he doesn't realize is that I know about his night-time forays. Since we don't have any electricity, I have to go to bed about eight. I should be used to the Chac-Mool by now, but just a moment ago, when I ran into him on the stairway, I touched his icy arms, the scales of his renewed skin, and I wanted to scream.

"If it doesn't rain soon, the Chac-Mool will return to stone. I've noticed his recent difficulty in moving; sometimes he lies for hours, paralyzed, and almost seems an idol again. But this repose merely gives him new strength to abuse me, to claw at me as if he could extract liquid from my flesh. We don't have the amiable intervals anymore, when he used to tell me old tales; instead, I seem to notice a heightened resentment. There have been other indications that set me thinking: my wine cellar is diminishing; he likes to stroke the silk of my bathrobes; he wants me to bring a servant girl to the house; he has made me teach him how to use soap and lotions. I believe the Chac-Mool is falling into human temptations; now I see in the face that once seemed eternal something that is merely old. This may be my salvation: if the Chac becomes human, it's possible that all the centuries of his life will accumulate in an instant and he will die in a flash of lightning. But this might also cause my death; the Chac won't want me to witness his downfall; he may decide to kill me.

"I plan to take advantage tonight of Chac's nightly excursion to flee. I will go to Acapulco; I'll see if I can't find a job, and await the death of the Chac-Mool. Yes, it will be soon; his hair is gray, his face bloated. I need to get some sun, to swim, to regain my strength. I have four hundred pesos left. I'll go to the Muller's hotel, it's cheap and comfortable. Let Chac-Mool take over the whole place; we'll see how long he lasts without my pails of water."

* * *

Filiberto's diary ends here. I didn't want to think about what he'd written; I slept as far as Cuernavaca. From there to Mexico City I tried to make some sense out of the account, to attribute it to overwork, or some psychological disturbance. By the time we reached the terminal at nine in the evening, I still hadn't accepted the fact of my friend's madness. I hired a truck to carry the coffin to Filiberto's house, where I would arrange for his burial.

Before I could insert the key in the lock, the door opened. A yellow-skinned Indian in a smoking jacket and ascot stood in the doorway. He couldn't have been more repulsive; he smelled of cheap cologne; he'd tried to cover his wrinkles with thick powder, his mouth was clumsily smeared with lipstick, and his hair appeared to be dyed.

"I'm sorry . . . I didn't know that Filiberto had . . . "

"No matter. I know all about it. Tell the men to carry the body down to the cellar."

❀ Discussion and Writing

1. What is the significance of the first two paragraphs of Filiberto's notebook?
2. How did Filiberto die? Analyze the evidence in the story to support your conclusion.
3. Discuss the significance of the references to sacrifice and blood.
4. Analyze the paradoxical use of the image of water in the story.
5. Discuss the effectiveness of the story within the story as a structure. Analyze the fusion of realities: ancient and contemporary, mythic and actual.
6. What is the implication of the reversal of the living and the dead; Filiberto and Chac-Mool. How does this reflect on the contemporary Mexican experience?

❀ Research and Comparison

Examine the writings of Carlos Fuentes. Comment on the combination of various traditions—Aztec, European, Catholic, Asian—in his works.

Gabriel Garcia Marquez
(b. 1928)
Columbia

Gabriel Jose Garcia Marquez was born the year of a major strike and the massacre of banana workers near his hometown of Aracataca, Colombia. Raised, until he was 12, in the house of his maternal grandparents and surrounded by aunts, he grew up listening to his grandfather, Colonel Nicolas Ricardo Marquez Mejia, recount the tales of the War of the Thousand Days. (This war between the Liberals and the Conservatives [1899–1902] brought to a close half a century of civil war.) He grew up listening to his grandfather tell stories of the arrival of the United Fruit Company in 1899 and to his grandmother tell stories full of magic. He entered the University of Bogota to study law, but with the closing of the university at the outbreak of La Violencia in 1948, he began working as a journalist. Although he registered again for classes when the university reopened, he had already started on a career in journalism, and he was already writing fiction. There followed some 17 years of apprenticeship: studying cinematography in Rome, being jobless in Paris while writing stories, practicing journalism. His going to Cuba as a reporter was important in his career as a journalist, for it prompted his establishing an office of the Cuban press in Bogota. But in 1950, he returned to Aracataca with his mother to sell his grandparents' house, and he came to see this visit as a transforming experience in his vocation as a writer.

He set aside the Aracatacan material, and then in a burst of 18 months of concentrated effort, he produced *Cien anos de soledad* (One Hundred Years of Solitude, 1967), a giant novel that incorporated the time of his birth and childhood: the tales, atmosphere, everything. Immediately considered a classic and likened in its popularity to *Don Quixote,* the book became equated with "magical realism" (even though the term predates the publication of the novel). With this work, Garcia Marquez turned toward myth; manipulating a Borgesian vision of time and place; combining mythical and historical events, hyperbole and concretion, romance and politics. With this work, he acquired an international reputation, and he was awarded the Nobel Prize in literature in 1982. In contrast to the large scope of *One Hundred Years of Solitude* but brushed with the same ironies, "The Handsomest Drowned Man in the World" (1968) achieves its intensity because of its concentrated scope.

The Handsomest Drowned Man in the World*
A Tale for Children

The first children who saw the dark and slinky bulge approaching through the sea let themselves think it was an enemy ship. Then they saw it had no flags or masts and they thought it was a whale. But when it was washed up on the beach, they removed the clumps of seaweed, the jellyfish tentacles, and the remains of fish and flotsam, and only then did they see that it was a drowned man.

They had been playing with him all afternoon, burying him in the sand and digging him up again, when someone chanced to see them and spread the alarm in the village. The men who carried him to the nearest house noticed that he weighed more than any dead man they had ever known, almost as much as a horse, and they said to each other that maybe he'd been floating too long and the water had got into his bones. When they laid him on the floor they said he'd been taller than all other men because there was barely enough room for him in the house, but they thought that maybe the ability to keep on growing after death was part of the nature of certain drowned men. He had the smell of the sea about him and only his shape gave one to suppose that it was the corpse of a human being, because the skin was covered with a crust of mud and scales.

They did not even have to clean off his face to know that the dead man was a stranger. The village was made up of only twenty-odd wooden houses that had stone courtyards with no flowers and which were spread about on the end of a desertlike cape. There was so little land that mothers always went about with the fear that the wind would carry off their children and the few dead that the years had caused among them had to be thrown off the cliffs. But the sea was calm and bountiful and all the men fit into seven boats. So when they found the drowned man they simply had to look at one another to see that they were all there.

That night they did not go out to work at sea. While the men went to find out if anyone was missing in neighboring villages, the women stayed behind to care for the drowned man. They took the mud off with grass swabs, they removed the underwater stones entangled in his hair, and they scraped the crust off with tools used for scaling fish. As they were doing that they noticed that the vegetation on him came from faraway oceans and deep water and that his clothes were in tatters, as if he had sailed through labyrinths of coral. They noticed too that he bore his death with pride, for he did not have the lonely look of other drowned men who came out of the sea or that haggard, needy look of men who drowned in rivers. But only when they finished cleaning him off did they become aware of the kind of man he was and it left them breathless. Not only was he the tallest, strongest, most

---

*Translated by Gregory Rabassa

virile, and best built man they had ever seen, but even though they were looking at him there was no room for him in their imagination.

They could not find a bed in the village large enough to lay him on nor was there a table solid enough to use for his wake. The tallest men's holiday pants would not fit him, not the fattest ones' Sunday shirts, nor the shoes of the one with the biggest feet. Fascinated by his huge size and his beauty, the women then decided to make him some pants from a large piece of sail and a shirt from some bridal brabant linen so that he could continue through his death with dignity. As they sewed, sitting in a circle and gazing at the corpse between stitches, it seemed to them that the wind had never been so steady nor the sea so restless as on that night and they supposed that the change had something to do with the dead man. They thought that if that magnificent man had lived in the village, his house would have had the widest doors, the highest ceiling, and the strongest floor, his bedstead would have been made from a midship frame held together by iron bolts, and his wife would have been the happiest woman. They thought that he would have had so much authority that he could have drawn fish out of the sea simply by calling their names and that he would have put so much work into his land that springs would have burst forth from among the rocks so that he would have been able to plant flowers on the cliffs. They secretly compared him to their own men, thinking that for all their lives theirs were incapable of doing what he could do in one night, and they ended up dismissing them deep in their hearts as the weakest, meanest, and most useless creatures on earth. They were wandering through that maze of fantasy when the oldest woman, who as the oldest had looked upon the drowned man with more compassion than passion, sighed:

"He has the face of someone called Esteban."

It was true. Most of them had only to take another look at him to see that he could not have any other name. The more stubborn among them, who were the youngest, still lived for a few hours with the illusion that when they put his clothes on and he lay among the flowers in patent leather shoes his name might be Lautaro. But it was a vain illusion. There had not been enough canvas, the poorly cut and worse sewn pants were too tight, and the hidden strength of his heart popped the buttons on his shirt. After midnight the whistling of the wind died down and the sea fell into its Wednesday drowsiness. The silence put an end to any last doubts: he was Esteban. The women who had dressed him, who had combed his hair, had cut his nails and shaved him were unable to hold back a shudder of pity when they had to resign themselves to his being dragged along the ground. It was then that they understood how unhappy he must have been with that huge body since it bothered him even after death. They could see him in life, condemned to going through doors sideways, cracking his head on crossbeams, remaining on his feet during visits, not knowing what to do with his soft, pink, sea lion hands while the lady of the house looked for her most resistant chair and begged him, frightened to death, sit here, Esteban, please, and he, leaning against the wall, smiling, don't bother, ma'am, I'm fine where I am, his heels raw and his back roasted from having done the same thing so many times whenever he paid a visit, don't bother, ma'am, I'm fine where I am, just to avoid the embarrassment of breaking up the chair, and never knowing perhaps that the ones who said don't go, Esteban, at least wait till the coffee's ready, were the ones who later on would whisper the big boob finally left, how nice, the handsome fool has gone. That was what the women were thinking beside the body a little before dawn. Later, when they covered his face with a handkerchief so that the light would not bother him, he looked so forever dead, so defenseless, so much like their men that the first furrows of tears opened in their hearts. It was one of the younger ones who began the weeping. The others, coming to, went from sighs to wails, and the more they sobbed the more they felt like weeping, because the drowned man was becoming all the more Esteban for them, and so they wept so much, for he was the most destitute, most peaceful, and most obliging man on earth, poor Esteban. So when the men returned with the news that the drowned man was not from the neighboring villages either, the women felt an opening of jubilation in the midst of their tears.

"Praise the Lord," they sighed, "he's ours!"

The men thought the fuss was only womanish frivolity. Fatigued because of the difficult nighttime inquiries, all they wanted was to get rid of the bother of the newcomer once and for all before the sun grew strong on that arid, windless day. They improvised a litter with the remains of fore-masts and gaffs, tying it together with rigging so that it would bear the weight of the body until they reached the cliffs. They wanted to tie the anchor from a cargo ship to him so that he would sink easily into the deepest waves, where fish are blind and divers die of nostalgia, and bad currents would not bring him back to shore, as had happened with other bodies. But the more they hurried, the more the women thought of ways to waste time. They walked about like startled hens, pecking with the sea charms on their breasts, some interfering on one side to put a scapular of the good wind on the drowned man, some on the other side to put a wrist compass on him, and after a great deal of *get away from there, woman, stay out of the way, look, you almost made me fall on top of the dead man*, the men began to feel mistrust in their livers and started grumbling about why so many main-altar decorations for a stranger, because no matter how many nails and holy-water jars he had on him, the sharks would chew him all the same, but the women kept piling on their junk relics, running back and forth, stumbling, while they released in sighs what they did not in tears, so that the men finally exploded with *since when has there ever been such a fuss over a drifting corpse, a drowned nobody, a piece of cold Wednesday meat*. One of the women, mortified by so much lack of care, then removed the handkerchief from the dead man's face and the men were left breathless too.

He was Esteban. It was not necessary to repeat it for them to recognize him. If they had been told Sir Walter Raleigh, even they might have been impressed with his gringo accent, the macaw on his shoulder, his cannibal-killing blunderbuss, but there could be only one Esteban in the world and there he was, stretched out like a sperm whale, shoeless, wearing the pants of an undersized child, and with those stony nails that had to be cut with a knife. They only had to take the handkerchief off his face to see that he was ashamed, that it was not his fault that he was so big or so heavy or so handsome, and if he had known that this was going to happen, he would have looked for a more discreet place to drown in, seriously, I even would have tied the anchor off a galleon around my neck and staggered off a cliff like someone who doesn't like things in order not to be upsetting people now with this Wednesday dead body, as you people say, in order not to be bothering anyone with this filthy piece of cold meat that doesn't have anything to do with me. There was so much truth in his manner that even the most mistrustful men, the ones who felt the bitterness of endless nights at sea fearing that their women would tire of dreaming about them and begin to dream of drowned men, even they and others who were harder still shuddered in the marrow of their bones at Esteban's sincerity.

That was how they came to hold the most splendid funeral they could conceive of for an abandoned drowned man. Some women who had gone to get flowers in the neighboring villages returned with other women who could not believe what they had been told, and those women went back for more flowers when they saw the dead man, and they brought more and more until there were so many flowers and so many people that it was hard to walk about. At the final moment it pained them to return him to the waters as an orphan and they chose a father and mother from among the best people, and aunts and uncles and cousins, so that through him all the inhabitants of the village became kinsmen. Some sailors who heard the weeping from a distance went off course and people heard of one who had himself tied to the mainmast, remembering ancient fables about sirens. While they fought for the privilege of carrying him on their shoulders along the steep escarpment by the cliffs, men and women became aware for the first time of the desolation of their streets, the dryness of their courtyards, the narrowness of their dreams as they faced the splendor and beauty of their drowned man. They let him go without an anchor so that he could come back if he wished and whenever he wished, and they all held their breath for the fraction of centuries the body took to fall into the abyss. They did not need to look at one another to realize that they were no longer all present, that they would never be. But they also knew that everything would be different from then on, that their houses would have wider doors, higher ceilings, and stronger floors so that Esteban's memory could go everywhere without bumping into beams and so that no one in the future would dare whisper the big boob finally died, too bad, the handsome fool has finally died, because they were going to paint their house fronts gay colors to make Esteban's memory eternal and they were going to break their backs digging for springs among the stones and planting flowers on the cliffs so that in

future years at dawn the passengers on great liners would awaken, suffocated by the smell of gardens on the high seas, and the captain would have
to come down from the bridge in his dress uniform, with his astrolabe, his
pole star, and his row of war medals and, pointing to the promontory of
roses on the horizon, he would say in fourteen languages, look there, where
the wind is so peaceful now that it's gone to sleep beneath the beds, over
there, where the sun's so bright that the sunflowers don't know which way
to turn, yes, over there, that's Esteban's village.

❋ Discussion and Writing

1. Why does Garcia Marquez call this story "a tale for children"? What is
   its relation to the adult world?
2. What are the implications of the different reactions of the men and the
   women to the drowned man?
3. What is the significance of the stranger's getting a name and a location
   in the village? Comment on his gradual adoption by the community.
   What is the implication of the process?
4. Analyze the setting and the repeated images.
5. Explore the elements of fantasy and realism. Discuss their relevance to
   the story's structure and meaning.
6. Examine the story as a paradigm for colonialism.

❋ Research and Comparison

Analyze Gabriel Garcia Marquez's *One Hundred Years of Solitude*, examining its importance in Latin American experience.

Interdisciplinary Discussion Question: Latin American writers frequently
break the mold of realistic narration to create what has been called magical
realism. Compare the use of magical realism in the works of any two Latin
American authors.

Derek Walcott
(b. 1930)
Saint Lucia

Derek Alton Walcott and his twin brother, Roderick—who is himself a
well-known playwright—were born in Castries, Saint Lucia. Their mother,
a drama teacher, was a member of an amateur theater group. Their father,
a watercolorist who died when the twins were only a year old, also wrote
poetry, just as Derek Walcott, a poet and playwright, is also a painter. He

has regarded his mother's West Indian African heritage and his father's British origin to be personally as well as culturally emblematic, and he believes that his father's early death at 35 bequeathed to him the obligation to fulfill that unlived life.

Walcott first published a poem when he was 14 and still attending high school at St. Mary's College in Castries. By the time he was 20, he had published a volume of poetry and helped establish the Saint Lucia Arts Guild; the Guild produced his first play, *Henri Christophe,* the year he entered the University College of the West Indies in Jamaica. After receiving his B.A. and completing a year of graduate studies, and after working briefly as a high school teacher, journalist, and critic, he founded the Trinidad Theatre Workshop (first named Little Carib Theatre Workshop). Over the 22 years of his association with the workshop, he formed an important cultural center, writing, directing, and producing plays. Partly because of his keen sense of place, his subsequent teaching in New England concretely focused the South–North or Caribbean–European antitheses and mergings that have inspired and characterized his work. They have informed his principal motifs: the themes of exile and the concomitant search for one's home, the themes of West Indian history and a West Indian hero, of the dispossessed and neocolonialism. But throughout his career, whether in Trinidad or New England, he was held to the belief that writing poetry is a vocation. In 1992, he was awarded the Nobel Prize in literature.

I Once Gave My Daughters . . .

I once gave my daughters, separately, two conch shells
that were dived from the reef, or sold on the beach, I forget.
They use them as doorstops or bookends, but their wet
pink palates are the soundless singing of angels.
I once wrote a poem called "The Yellow Cemetery,"
when I was nineteen. Lizzie's age. I'm fifty-three.
These poems I heaved aren't linked to any tradition
like a mossed cairn; each goes down like a stone
to the seabed, settling, but let them, with luck, lie
where stones are deep, in the sea's memory.
Let them be, in water, as my father, who did watercolors,
entered his work. He became one of his shadows,
wavering and faint in the midsummer sunlight.
His name was Warwick Walcott. I sometimes believe
that his father, in love or bitter benediction,
named him for Warwickshire. Ironies
are moving. Now, when I rewrite a line,
or sketch on the fast-drying paper the coconut fronds

that he did so faintly, my daughters' hands move in mine.
Conches move over the sea-floor. I used to move
my father's grave from the blackened Anglican headstones
in Castries to where I could love both at once—
the sea and his absence. Youth is stronger than fiction.

The Season of Phantasmal Peace

Then all the nations of birds lifted together
the huge net of the shadows of this earth
in multitudinous dialects, twittering tongues,
stitching and crossing it. They lifted up
the shadows of long pines down trackless slopes,
the shadows of glass-faced towers down evening streets
the shadow of a frail plant on a city sill—
the net rising soundless as night, the birds' cries soundless, until
there was no longer dusk, or season, decline, or weather.
only this passage of phantasmal light
that not the narrowest shadow dared to sever.

And men could not see, looking up, what the wild geese drew
what the ospreys trailed behind them in silvery ropes
that flashed in the icy sunlight; they could not hear
battalions of starlings waging peaceful cries,
bearing the net higher, covering this world
like the vines of an orchard, or a mother drawing
the trembling gauze over the trembling eyes
of a child fluttering to sleep;
                                it was the light
that you will see at evening on the side of a hill
in yellow October, and no one hearing knew
what change had brought into the raven's cawing,
the killdeer's screech, the ember-circling chough
such an immense, soundless, and high concern
for the fields and cities where the birds belong,
except it was their seasonal passing, Love,
made seasonless, or, from the high privilege of their birth,
something brighter than pity for the wingless ones
below them who shared dark holes in windows and in houses,
and higher they lifted the net with soundless voices
above all change, betrayals of falling suns,
and this season lasted one moment, like the pause
between dusk and darkness, between fury and peace,
but, for such as our earth is now, it lasted long.

❋ Discussion and Writing

I Once Gave My Daughters

1. What do conch shells represent for Walcott; for his daughters?
2. Describe Walcott's affinity with his father? What does his father's name, Warwick, signify? What does Walcott accomplish by a reference to his father in a poem to his daughters?
3. What is implied by the conch shells' moving on the floor of the sea? Comment on the recurrent motif of "moving."
4. What is the significance of the statement "youth is stronger than fiction"?

The Season of Phantasmal Peace

1. Describe the flight of the birds. Analyze the images of light and shadow.
2. Examine the significance of the motifs of seasons, peace, and love in relation to the nations of birds and humans.
3. What is implied by the "one moment" that "lasted long"? Examine its relevance to the title.

❋ Research and Comparison

Interdisciplinary Discussion Question: Research Walcott's literary works to examine the issue of mixed heritage as a positive reinforcing element. Also, identify the negative impact of the politics of colonialism.

V. S. Naipaul
(b. 1932)
Trinidad

Vidiadhar Surajprasad Naipaul was born in Chaguanas, Trinidad, which at that time was a small market town in the center of sugarcane country, populated mainly by people who had come from India as indentured laborers, often without understanding the terms of their contracts. His mother's father, for instance, thought he had agreed to work as a teacher, but found he had signed on as a worker in a sugar factory. Still, he prospered, becoming a well-to-do landowner, and it was in this extended family of the Tiwari family, with its quarrels and shifting alliances, that Naipaul spent his early childhood. It was here that he first experienced the culture of the East Indian community for whom Islamic and Hindu India was a mythological rather than a historical—or even spiritual—reality, but for whom traditional customs continued to be the dominant factor.

Naipaul's father, for one, resented the imposition of the mores of Hindu clan life that he faced in his wife's family homes. A journalist for the *Trinidad Guardian* (for a few years in Chaguanas and later in Port-of-Spain), he wrote short stories and worked at odd jobs. When he left Chaguanas, he brought his five children and wife to the quiet of a house owned by her mother. Here in Port-of-Spain, V. S. Naipaul spent two happy years before they moved once again to live outside the city in the hectic midst of his extended family. Two years later his immediate family returned to occupy a few rooms in the house in Port-of-Spain, a once-quiet haven that grew more and more crowded as family members migrated to the city. His father was finally able to purchase a house of his own when Naipaul was 14, too late to mitigate his son's sense of the absurd. Naipaul's father was a frustrated man, given to intermittent rages as his mental health declined, and he bequeathed his son a poignant legacy: on the one hand, respect for the writing profession, and, on the other, the figure of himself as an emblem of both futility and the fear of failure.

While the shadow of his father's presence hovered especially over *A House for Mr. Biswas* (1961), this perception of a deeply ironic universe has informed Naipaul's writing from the beginning. From the time he left Trinidad to study literature at University College, Oxford, through the time he worked for the BBC Caribbean Service and taught, he has always considered writing as a vocation.

My Aunt Gold Teeth

I never knew her real name and it is quite likely that she did have one, though I never heard her called anything but Gold Teeth. She did, indeed, have gold teeth. She had sixteen of them. She had married early and she had married well, and shortly after her marriage she exchanged her perfectly sound teeth for gold ones, to announce to the world that her husband was a man of substance.

Even without her gold teeth my aunt would have been noticeable. She was short, scarcely five foot, and she was fat, horribly, monstrously fat. If you saw her in silhouette you would have found it difficult to know whether she was facing you or whether she was looking sideways.

She ate little and prayed much. Her family being Hindu, and her husband being a pundit, she, too, was an orthodox Hindu. Of Hinduism she knew little apart from the ceremonies and the taboos, and this was enough for her. Gold Teeth saw God as a Power, and religious ritual as a means of harnessing that Power for great practical good, her good.

I fear I may have given the impression that Gold Teeth prayed because she wanted to be less fat. The fact was that Gold Teeth had no children and she was almost forty. It was her childlessness, not her fat, that oppressed her, and she prayed for the curse to be removed. She was willing to try any means—any ritual, any prayer—in order to trap and channel the supernatural Power.

And so it was that she began to indulge in surreptitious Christian practices.

She was living at the time in a country village called Cunupia, in County Caroni. Here the Canadian Mission had long waged war against the Indian heathen, and saved many. But Gold Teeth stood firm. The Minister of Cunupia expended his Presbyterian piety on her; so did the headmaster of the Mission school. But all in vain. At no time was Gold Teeth persuaded even to think about being converted. The idea horrified her. Her father had been in his day one of the best-known Hindu pundits, and even now her husband's fame as a pundit, as a man who could read and write Sanskrit, had spread far beyond Cunupia. She was in no doubt whatsoever that Hindus were the best people in the world, and that Hinduism was a superior religion. She was willing to select, modify and incorporate alien eccentricities into her worship; but to abjure her own Faith—never!

Presbyterianism was not the only danger the good Hindu had to face in Cunupia. Besides, of course, the ever-present threat of open Muslim aggression, the Catholics were to be reckoned with. Their pamphlets were everywhere and it was hard to avoid them. In them Gold Teeth read of novenas and rosaries, of squads of saints and angels. These were things she understood and could even sympathize with, and they encouraged her to seek further. She read of the mysteries and the miracles, of penances and indulgences. Her skepticism sagged, and yielded to a quickening, if reluctant, enthusiasm.

One morning she took the train for the County town of Chaguanas, three miles, two stations and twenty minutes away. The Church of St. Philip and St. James in Chaguanas stands imposingly at the end of the Caroni Savannah Road, and although Gold Teeth knew Chaguanas well, all she knew of the church was that it had a clock, at which she had glanced on her way to the Railway Station nearby. She had hitherto been far more interested in the drab ocher-washed edifice opposite, which was the Police Station.

She carried herself into the churchyard, awed by her own temerity, feeling like an explorer in a land of cannibals. To her relief, the church was empty. It was not as terrifying as she had expected. In the gilt and images and the resplendent cloths she found much that reminded her of her Hindu temple. Her eyes caught a discreet sign: CANDLES TWO CENTS EACH. She undid the knot in the end of her veil, where she kept her money, took out three cents, popped them into the box, picked up a candle and muttered a prayer in Hindustani. A brief moment of elation gave way to a sense of guilt, and she was suddenly anxious to get away from the church as fast as her weight would let her.

She took a bus home, and hid the candle in her chest of drawers. She had half feared that her husband's Brahminical flair for clairvoyance would have uncovered the reason for her trip to Chaguanas. When after four days, which she spent in an ecstasy of prayer, her husband had mentioned nothing, Gold Teeth thought it safe to burn the candle. She burned it secretly at night, before her Hindu images and sent up, as she thought, prayers of double efficacy.

Every day her religious schizophrenia grew, and presently she began wearing a crucifix. Neither her husband nor her neighbors knew she did so. The chain was lost in the billows of fat around her neck, and the crucifix was itself buried in the valley of her gargantuan breasts. Later she acquired two holy pictures, one of the Virgin Mary, the other of the crucifixion, and took care to conceal them from her husband. The prayers she offered to these Christian things filled her with new hope and buoyancy. She became an addict of Christianity.

Then her husband, Ramprasad, fell ill.

Ramprasad's sudden unaccountable illness alarmed Gold Teeth. It was, she knew, no ordinary illness, and she knew, too, that her religious transgression was the cause. The District Medical Officer at Chaguanas said it was diabetes, but Gold Teeth knew better. To be on the safe side, though, she used the insulin he prescribed and, to be even safer, she consulted Ganesh Pundit, the masseur with mystic leanings, celebrated as a faith-healer.

Ganesh came all the way from Feunte Grove to Cunupia. He came in great humility, anxious to serve Gold Teeth's husband, for Gold Teeth's husband was a Brahmin among Brahmins, a *Panday*,[1] a man who knew all five Vedas; while he, Ganesh, was a mere *Chaubay* and knew only four.

With spotless white *koortah*,[2] his dhoti cannily tied, and a tasselled green scarf as a concession to elegance, Ganesh exuded the confidence of the professional mystic. He looked at the sick man, observed his pallor, sniffed the air inquiringly. "This man," he said slowly, "is bewitched. Seven spirits are upon him."

He was telling Gold Teeth nothing she didn't know. She had known from the first that there were spirits in the affair, but she was glad that Ganesh had ascertained their number.

"But you mustn't worry," Ganesh added. "We will 'tie' the house—in spiritual bonds—and no spirit will be able to come in."

Then, without being asked, Gold Teeth brought out a blanket, folded it, placed it on the floor and invited Ganesh to sit on it. Next she brought him a brass jar of fresh water, a mango leaf and a plate full of burning charcoal.

"Bring me some ghee," Ganesh said, and after Gold Teeth had done so, he set to work. Muttering continuously in Hindustani he sprinkled the water from the brass jar around him with the mango leaf. Then he melted the ghee in the fire and the charcoal hissed so sharply that Gold Teeth could not make out his words. Presently he rose and said, "You must put some of the ash of

---

[1]*Panday:* a high priest; *Chaubay:* an assistant. [eds.]
[2]*Koortah:* a loose shirt; dhoti: a man's garment, tied at the waist. [eds.]

this fire on your husband's forehead, but if he doesn't want you to do that, mix it with his food. You must keep the water in this jar and place it every night before your front door."

Gold Teeth pulled her veil over her forehead.

Ganesh coughed. "That," he said, rearranging his scarf, "is all. There is nothing more I can do. God will do the rest."

He refused payment for his services. It was enough honor, he said, for a man as humble as he was to serve Pundit Ramprasad, and she, Gold Teeth, had been singled out by fate to be the spouse of such a worthy man. Gold Teeth received the impression that Ganesh spoke from a firsthand knowledge of fate and its designs, and her heart, buried deep down under inches of mortal, flabby flesh, sank a little.

"Baba," she said hesitantly, "revered Father, I have something to say to you." But she couldn't say anything more and Ganesh, seeing this, filled his eyes with charity and love.

"What is it, my child?"

"I have done a great wrong, Baba."

"What sort of wrong?" he asked, and his tone indicated that Gold Teeth could do no wrong.

"I have prayed to Christian things."

And to Gold Teeth's surprise, Ganesh chuckled benevolently. "And do you think God minds, daughter? There is only one God and different people pray to Him in different ways. It doesn't matter how you pray, but God is pleased if you pray at all."

"So it is not because of me that my husband has fallen ill?"

"No, to be sure, daughter."

In his professional capacity Ganesh was consulted by people of many faiths, and with the license of the mystic he had exploited the commodiousness of Hinduism, and made room for all beliefs. In this way he had many clients, as he called them, many satisfied clients.

Henceforward Gold Teeth not only pasted Ramprasad's pale forehead with the sacred ash Ganesh had prescribed, but mixed substantial amounts with his food. Ramprasad's appetite, enormous even in sickness, diminished; and he shortly entered into a visible and alarming decline that mystified his wife.

She fed him more ash than before, and when it was exhausted and Ramprasad perilously macerated, she fell back on the Hindu wife's last resort. She took her husband home to her mother. That venerable lady, my grandmother, lived with us in Port-of-Spain, in Woodbrook.

Ramprasad was tall and skeletal, and his face was gray. The virile voice that had expounded a thousand theological points and recited a hundred *puranas*[3] was now a wavering whisper. We cooped him up in a room called,

---

[3]Stories of the gods and goddesses. [eds.]

oddly, "the pantry." It had never been used as a pantry and one can only assume that the architect, in the idealistic manner of his tribe, had so designated it some forty years before. It was a tiny room. If you wished to enter the pantry you were compelled, as soon as you opened the door, to climb on to the bed: it fitted the room to a miracle. The lower half of the walls were concrete, the upper close lattice-work; there were no windows.

My grandmother had her doubts about the suitability of the room for a sick man. She was worried about the lattice-work. It let in air and light, and Ramprasad was not going to die from these things if she could help it. With cardboard, oil-cloth and canvas she made the lattice-work air-proof and light-proof.

And, sure enough, within a week Ramprasad's appetite returned, insatiable and insistent as before. My grandmother claimed all the credit for this, though Gold Teeth knew that the ash she had fed him had not been without effect. Then she realized with horror that she had ignored a very important thing. The house in Cunupia had been tied and no spirits could enter, but the house in Woodbrook had been given no such protection and any spirit could come and go as it chose. The problem was pressing.

Ganesh was out of the question. By giving his services free he had made it impossible for Gold Teeth to call him in again. But thinking in this way of Ganesh, she remembered his words: "It doesn't matter how you pray, but God is pleased if you pray at all."

Why not, then, bring Christianity into play again?

She didn't want to take any chances this time. She decided to tell Ramprasad.

He was propped up in bed, and eating. When Gold Teeth opened the door he stopped eating and blinked at the unwonted light. Gold Teeth, stepping into the doorway and filling it, shadowed the room once more and he went on eating. She placed the palms of her hands on the bed. It creaked.

"Man," she said.

Ramprasad continued to eat.

"Man," she said in English, "I thinking about going to the chu'ch to pray. You never know, and it better to be on the safe side. After all, the house ain't tied————"

"I don't want to pray in no chu'ch," he whispered in English, too.

Gold Teeth did the only thing she could do. She began to cry.

Three days in succession she asked his permission to go to church, and his opposition weakened in the face of her tears. He was now, besides, too weak to oppose anything. Although his appetite had returned, he was still very ill and very weak, and every day his condition became worse.

On the fourth day he said to Gold Teeth, "Well, pray to Jesus and go to chu'ch, if it will put your mind at rest."

And Gold Teeth straight away set about putting her mind at rest. Every morning she took the trolley-bus to the Holy Rosary Church, to offer worship in her private way. Then she was emboldened to bring a crucifix and pictures of the Virgin and the Messiah into the house. We were all somewhat worried by this, but Gold Teeth's religious nature was well known to us; her husband was a learned pundit and when all was said and done this was an emergency, a matter of life and death. So we could do nothing but look on. Incense and camphor and ghee burned now before the likeness of Krishna and Shiva as well as Mary and Jesus. Gold Teeth revealed an appetite for prayer that equalled her husband's for food, and we marvelled at both, if only because neither prayer nor food seemed to be of any use to Ramprasad.

One evening, shortly after bell and gong and conchshell had announced that Gold Teeth's official devotions were almost over, a sudden chorus of lamentation burst over the house, and I was summoned to the room reserved for prayer. "Come quickly, something dreadful has happened to your aunt."

The prayer-room, still heavy with fumes of incense, presented an extraordinary sight. Before the Hindu shrine, flat on her face, Gold Teeth lay prostrate, rigid as a sack of flour, a large amorphous mass. I had only seen Gold Teeth standing or sitting, and the aspect of Gold Teeth prostrate, so novel and so grotesque, was disturbing.

My grandmother, an alarmist by nature, bent down and put her ear to the upper half of the body on the floor. "I don't seem to hear her heart," she said.

We were all somewhat terrified. We tried to lift Gold Teeth but she seemed as heavy as lead. Then, slowly, the body quivered. The flesh beneath the clothes rippled, then billowed, and the children in the room sharpened their shrieks. Instinctively we all stood back from the body and waited to see what was going to happen. Gold Teeth's hand began to pound the floor and at the same time she began to gurgle.

My grandmother had grasped the situation. "She's got the spirit," she said.

At the word "spirit," the children shrieked louder, and my grandmother slapped them into silence.

The gurgling resolved itself into words pronounced with a lingering ghastly quaver. "Hail Mary, Hara Ram," Gold Teeth said, "the snakes are after me. Everywhere snakes. Seven snakes. Rama! Rama! Full of grace. Seven spirits leaving Cunupia by the four-o'clock train for Port-of-Spain."

My grandmother and my mother listened eagerly, their faces lit up with pride. I was rather ashamed at the exhibition, and annoyed with Gold Teeth for putting me into a fright. I moved toward the door.

"Who is that going away? Who is the young *daffar,* the unbeliever?" the voice asked abruptly.

"Come back quickly, boy," my grandmother whispered. "Come back and ask her pardon."

I did as I was told.

"It is all right, son," Gold Teeth replied, "you don't know. You are young."

Then the spirit appeared to leave her. She wrenched herself up to a sitting position and wondered why we were all there. For the rest of that evening she behaved as if nothing had happened, and she pretended she didn't notice that everyone was looking at her and treating her with unusual respect.

"I have always said it, and I will say it again," my grandmother said, "that these Christians are very religious people. That is why I encouraged Gold Teeth to pray to Christian things."

Ramprasad died early next morning and we had the announcement on the radio after the local news at one o'clock. Ramprasad's death was the only one announced and so, although it came between commercials, it made some impression. We buried him that afternoon in Mucurapo Cemetery.

As soon as we got back my grandmother said, "I have always said it, and I will say it again: I don't like these Christian things. Ramprasad would have got better if only you, Gold Teeth, had listened to me and not gone running after these Christian things."

Gold Teeth sobbed her assent; and her body squabbered and shook as she confessed the whole story of her trafficking with Christianity. We listened in astonishment and shame. We didn't know that a good Hindu, and a member of our family, could sink so low. Gold Teeth beat her breast and pulled ineffectually at her long hair and begged to be forgiven. "It is all my fault," she cried. "My own fault, Ma. I fell in a moment of weakness. Then I just couldn't stop."

My grandmother's shame turned to pity. "It's all right, Gold Teeth. Perhaps it was this you needed to bring you back to your senses."

That evening Gold Teeth ritually destroyed every reminder of Christianity in the house.

"You have only yourself to blame," my grandmother said, "if you have no children now to look after you."

❀ Discussion and Writing

1. What are Gold Teeth's distinctive physical and emotional attributes? What social and religious mores determine her actions?
2. What roles do Ganesh and Grandmother play in the narrative?
3. Analyze how each character reacts to "Christian things." What is the basis of each individual's accommodation to Christianity? Identify the narrator's perspective.
4. Discuss the linguistic, religious, and ethical issues that depict the social reality of the people of East Indian origin in Trinidad?

5. Analyze the tone of the narrative: is it sarcastic, humorous, ironic, sad, or angry?

❊ Research and Comparison

Examine V. S. Naipaul's *A House for Mr. Biswas* or *A Bend in the River* in relation to his search for identity and his role as a social critic.

Manuel Puig
(1932–1990)
Argentina

Manuel Puig was born in the isolated small town of Villegas in the Argentine pampas, where, as a small child, he went to the movies five nights a week, soaking up the Hollywood mythology. He moved out from the pampas, first to secondary school and the university in Buenos Aires, then to Italy to study cinematography. Finding the medium of film too confining, he turned to writing, returning, paradoxically, to the constricted world of his childhood for his motifs and techniques. Hollywood films offered him a mode of melodrama and dialogue, fantasy and romance— escape. Villegas offered all that motivates escape. From his first novel, *La traicion de Rita Hayworth* (Betrayed by Rita Hayworth, 1968), his work portrayed layers of fantasy and illusion, not solely in small-town experience but in the national consciousness as well. He exposed the Argentine dreams: the yearning for European panache; the love affair with the Perons, he a demagogue and she a soap-opera actress; the self-deceptions and betrayals. *Kiss of the Spider Woman* is a play based on Puig's novel of the same name.

Kiss of the Spider Woman*1

Kiss of the Spider Woman was first presented at the Bush Theatre, London, on 20 September 1985. It was directed by Simon Stokes with the following cast:

MOLINA: Simon Callow
VALENTIN: Mark Rylance

Translated by Allan Baker

1Application for performance rights in the United States and Canada should be made before rehearsal to: Mitch Douglas, International Creative Management, 40 West 57th Street, New York, NY 10019, USA. No performance may be given unless a license has been obtained.

Act One

Scene One

MOLINA: You can see there's something special about her, that she's not any ordinary woman. Quite young . . . and her face more round than oval, with a little pointy chin like a cat's.

VALENTIN: And her eyes?

MOLINA: Most probably green. She looks up at the model, the black panther lying down in its cage in the zoo. But she scratches her pencil against the sketch pad, and the panther sees her.

VALENTIN: How come it didn't smell her before?

MOLINA *(deliberately not answering)*: But who's that behind her? Someone trying to light a cigarette, but the wind blows out the match.

VALENTIN: Who is it?

MOLINA: Hold on. She flusters. He's no matinée idol, but he's nice-looking, in a hat with a low brim. He touches the brim like he's saluting and says the drawing is terrific. She fiddles with the curls of her fringe.

VALENTIN: Go on.

MOLINA: He can tell she's a foreigner by her accent. She tells him that she came to New York when the war broke out. He asks her if she's homesick. And then it's like a cloud passes across her eyes and she tells him she comes from the mountains, some place not far from Transylvania.

VALENTIN: Where Dracula comes from.

MOLINA: The next day he's in his office with some colleagues—he's an architect—and this girl, another architect he works with—and when the clock strikes three he just wants to drop everything and go to the zoo. It's right across the street. And the architect girl asks him why he's so happy. Deep down, she's really in love with him, no use her pretending otherwise.

VALENTIN: Is she a dog?

MOLINA: No, nothing out of this world: chestnut hair, but pleasant enough. But the other one, the one at the zoo, Irene—no, Irina—has disappeared. As time goes by he just can't get her out of his mind until one day he's walking down this fashionable avenue and he notices something in the window of an art gallery. They're pictures by an artist who only paints . . . panthers. The guy goes in, and there's Irina being congratulated by all the guests. And I don't remember what comes next.

VALENTIN: Try to remember.

MOLINA: Hold on a sec . . . Okay . . . then the architect goes up and congratulates her too. She drops the critics and walks off with him. He tells her that he just happened to be passing by, really he was on his way to buy a present.

VALENTIN: For the girl architect.

MOLINA: Now he's wondering if he's got enough money with him to buy two presents. And he stops outside a shop, and she gets a really funny feeling when she sees what kind of a shop it is. There are all different kinds of birds in little cages, sipping fresh water from their bowls.

VALENTIN: Excuse me . . . is there any water in the bottle?

MOLINA: Yes, I filled it up when they let us out to the lavatory.

(*The white light which up till now has lit just their heads widens to fully light both actors: we see the cell for the first time.*)

VALENTIN: That's okay then.

MOLINA: Do you want some? It's nice and cool.

VALENTIN: No, or we won't have enough for tea in the morning.

MOLINA: Don't exaggerate. We've got enough to last all day.

VALENTIN: Don't spoil me. I forgot to fetch some when they let us out to shower. If it wasn't for you, we wouldn't have any.

MOLINA: Look, there's plenty . . . Anyway, when they go inside that shop it's like—I don't know what—it's like the devil just came in. The birds, blind with fear, hurl themselves against the wire mesh and hurt their wings. She grabs his hand and drags him outside. Straight away the birds calm down. She asks him to let her go home. When he comes back into the shop, the birds are chirruping and singing just like normal and he buys one for the other girl's birthday. And then . . . it's no good, I can't remember what happens next, I'm pooped.

VALENTIN: Just a little more.

MOLINA: When I'm sleepy, my memory goes. I'll carry on with the morning tea.

VALENTIN: No, it's better at night. During the day I don't want to bother with this trivia. There are more important things . . .

(MOLINA *says nothing.*)

If I'm not reading and I'm keeping quiet, it's because I'm thinking. But don't take it wrong.

(MOLINA *is upset by* VALENTIN'*s remark.*)

MOLINA: (*with almost concealed irony*) I shan't bother you. You can count on that!

VALENTIN: I see you understand. See you in the morning.

(*He settles down to sleep.*)

MOLINA: Till tomorrow. Pleasant dreams of Irina.

(MOLINA *settles down too, but he is troubled by something.*)

VALENTIN: I prefer the architect girl.

MOLINA: I'd already sussed that.

Scene Two

MOLINA and VALENTIN *are sitting in different positions. They do not look at one another. Only their heads are lit; seconds later the night light comes on.*

MOLINA: So they go on seeing each other and they fall in love. She pampers him, cuddles up in his arms, but when he wants to hold her tight and kiss her she slips away from him. She asks him not to kiss her but to let her kiss him with her full lips, but she keeps her mouth shut tight.

(VALENTIN *is about to interrupt, but* MOLINA *forges ahead.*)

So, on their next date they go to this quaint restaurant. He tells her she's prettier than ever in her shimmering black blouse. But she's lost her appetite, she can't manage a thing, and they leave. It's snowing gently. The noise of the city is muffled, but far away you can just hear the growling of wild animals. The zoo's close, that's why. Barely in a whisper she says she's afraid to return to her house and spend the night alone. He hails a taxi, and they go to his house. It's a huge place, all *fin-de-siècle* decor; it used to be his mother's.

VALENTIN: And what does he do?

MOLINA: Nothing. He lights up his pipe and looks over at her. You always guessed he had a kind heart.

VALENTIN: I'd like to ask you something: how do you picture his mother?

MOLINA: So you can make fun of her?

VALENTIN: I swear I won't.

MOLINA: I don't know . . . someone really charming. She made her husband happy and her children too. She's always well groomed.

VALENTIN: And do you picture her scrubbing floors?

MOLINA: No, she's always impeccable. The high-necked dress hides the wrinkles round her throat.

VALENTIN: Always impeccable. With servants. People with no other choice than to fetch and carry for her. And, of course, she was happy with her husband who also exploited her in his turn, kept her locked up in the house like a slave, waiting for him . . .

MOLINA: . . . listen . . .

VALENTIN: . . . waiting for him to come home every night from his chambers or his surgery. And she condoned the system, fed all this crap to her son, and now he trips over the panther-woman. Serves him right.

MOLINA (*irritated*): Why did you have to bring up all that . . . ? I'd forgotten all about this dump while I was telling you the movie.

VALENTIN: I'd forgotten about it too.

MOLINA: Well, then . . . why d'you have to go and break the spell?

VALENTIN: I don't know what you want me to say.

MOLINA: That I have your permission to escape from reality . . . Why should I make myself more depressed than I am already? What's the point in making myself more unhappy . . . ? Otherwise, I'll just go crazy, like Charlotte of Mexico. Though I'd rather be Christina of Sweden, since at least that way I'll end up a queen.

VALENTIN: No, be serious, you're right, being in here can drive you crazy, and not just because it gets you down . . . but because you can alienate yourself just the way you do. This habit of yours, only thinking about the nice things as you call it, that has its own dangers.

MOLINA: That's nonsense . . . How?

VALENTIN: Escaping from reality all the time the way you do becomes a vice, like taking drugs or something. Because, listen to me, reality, *your* reality, isn't only this cell. I mean, if you're reading or studying something, you can transcend whatever cell you're in, do you understand me? That's why I read, that's why I study every day.

MOLINA: Politics . . . I don't know what's become of the world, look where it's got us . . . you and all those politicians . . .

VALENTIN: Stop wingeing like a nineteenth-century housewife . . . You're not a housewife, and this isn't the nineteenth century. Tell me a little more of the movie, have we much more to go?

MOLINA: Yes, lots . . . Why did I get lumbered with you and not the panther-woman's boyfriend?

VALENTIN: That's another story and one that doesn't interest me.

MOLINA: Frightened to talk about it?

VALENTIN: It bores me. I know all about it—even though you've never said a word.

MOLINA: Fine. I told you I was put away for gross indecency. There's nothing more to add. So don't come the psychologist with me.

VALENTIN (*shielding himself behind humour*): Admit that you like him because he smokes a pipe.

MOLINA: No, it's not that, it's because he's gentle and understanding.

VALENTIN: His mother castrated him, that's all.

MOLINA: I like him and that's that. And you like the architect girl—she's not exactly manning the barricades.

VALENTIN: I prefer her to the panther-woman, that's for sure. But the guy with the pipe won't suit you.

MOLINA: Why not?

VALENTIN: Your intentions aren't exactly chaste, are they?

MOLINA: Certainly not.

VALENTIN: Exactly. He likes Irina because she's frigid and he doesn't have to pounce on her, and that's why he takes her to the house where his mother is still present even if she is dead.

MOLINA (*getting angrier and angrier*): Continue.

VALENTIN: If he's still kept all his mother's things, it's because he wants to remain a child. He doesn't bring home a woman but a child to play with.

MOLINA: That's all in your head. I don't even know if the place is his mother's—I said that because I liked the place, and since I saw antiques in there, I told you it belonged to his mother. For all I know, he rents it furnished.

VALENTIN: So you're making up half the movie?

MOLINA: I'm not, I swear. But—you know—there are some things I add to fill it out for you. The house, for example. And, in any case, don't forget I'm a window-dresser, and that's almost like being an interior designer . . .

Anyway . . . she begins to tell him her story, and I don't remember all the details, but I do remember that in her village, a long time ago, there used to be panther-women. And these tales frightened her a lot when she was a little girl.

VALENTIN: And the birds . . . ? Why were they afraid of her?

MOLINA: That's what the architect asks her. And what does she say? She doesn't say anything! And the scene ends with him in pyjamas and a dressing-gown, good quality, no pattern, something serviceable—and he looks at her sleeping on the sofa from his bedroom door, and he lights up his pipe and stands there, all thoughtful.

VALENTIN: Do you know what I like about it? That it's like an allegory of women's fear of submitting to the male, because when it comes to sex, the animal part takes over. You see?

(MOLINA *doesn't approve of* VALENTIN's *comments.*)

MOLINA: Irina wakes up, it's morning already.

VALENTIN: She wakes up because of the cold, like us.

MOLINA (*irritated*): I knew you were going to say that . . . She wakes up because there's a canary singing in its cage. At first she's afraid to go near it, but the little bird is chirpy so she dares to move a little closer. She heaves a sigh of relief because the bird isn't frightened of her. And then she makes breakfast . . . toast and cereals and pancakes . . .

VALENTIN: Don't mention food.

MOLINA: . . . and pancakes . . .

VALENTIN: I'm serious. Neither food nor women.

MOLINA: She wakes him up and he's all happy to see her settling in, and so he asks her to stay there forever and be his wife. And she says, yes, from the bottom of her heart, and she looks around and the curtains look so beautiful to her, they're made of thick dark velvet. (*aggressively*) And now you can fully appreciate the *fin-de-siècle* decor. Then Irina asks him if he truly wants her to be his wife to give her just a little more time, just long enough for her to get over her fears.

VALENTIN: You can see what's going on with her, can't you?

MOLINA: Hold on. He agrees and they get married. And on their wedding night she sleeps in the bed and he sleeps on the couch.

VALENTIN: Looking at his mother's ornaments. Admit it, it's your ideal home, isn't it?

MOLINA: Of course it is! Now you're going to tell me what they all say.

VALENTIN: What d'you mean? What do they all say?

MOLINA: They're all the same, they all tell me the same thing.

VALENTIN: What?

MOLINA: That I was fussed over as a kid and that's why I'm like I am now, that I was clinging to my mother's skirts, but it's never too late to straighten out, and all I need is a good woman because there's nothing better than a good woman.

VALENTIN: And that's what they all tell you?

MOLINA: And this is what I tell them ... You're dead right ...! And since there's nothing better than a good woman ... I want to be one! So spare me the advice please, because I know what I feel like, and it's all as clear as day to me.

VALENTIN: I don't see it as clear—at least, not the way you've just put it.

MOLINA: I don't need you telling me what's what—if you want I'll go on with the picture, if not, ciao ... I'll just whisper it to myself, and arrive-derci, Sparafucile!

VALENTIN: Who's Sparafucile?

MOLINA: You don't have a clue about opera. He's the hatchet-man in *Rigoletto* ... Where were we?

VALENTIN: The wedding night. He hasn't laid a finger on her.

MOLINA: And I forgot to tell you that they'd agreed she'd go and see a psychoanalyst.

VALENTIN: Excuse me again ... don't get upset.

MOLINA: What is it?

VALENTIN (*less communicative than ever, sombre*): I can't keep my mind on the story.

MOLINA: Is it boring you?

VALENTIN: No, it's not that. It's ... My head is in a state.

(*He talks more to himself than to* MOLINA.)

I just want to be quiet for a while. I don't know if this has ever happened to you, that you're just about to understand something, you've got the end of the thread and if you don't yank it now ... you'll lose it.

MOLINA: Why do you like the architect girl?

VALENTIN: It has to come out some way or other ... (*self-contemptuous*) Weakness, I mean ...

MOLINA: Ttt ... it's not weakness.

VALENTIN (*bitter, impersonally*): Funny how you just can't avoid getting attached to something. It's ... it's as if the mind just oozed sentiment constantly.

MOLINA: Is that what you believe?

VALENTIN: Like a leaky tap. Drips falling over anything.

MOLINA: Anything?

VALENTIN: You can't stop the drips.

MOLINA: And you don't want to be reminded of your girlfriend, is that it?

VALENTIN (*mistrustful*): How do you know whether I have a girlfriend?

MOLINA: It's only natural.

VALENTIN: I can't help it ... I get attached to anything that reminds me of her. Anyway, I'd do better to get my mind on what I ought to, right?

MOLINA: Yank the thread.

VALENTIN: Exactly.

MOLINA: And if you get it all in a tangle, Missy Valentina, you'll flunk needle-work.
VALENTIN: Don't worry on my account.
MOLINA: Okay, I won't say another word.
VALENTIN: And don't call me Valentina. I'm not a woman.
MOLINA: How should I know?
VALENTIN: I'm sorry, Molina, but I don't give demonstrations.
MOLINA: I wasn't asking for one.

Scene Three

Night. The prison light is on. MOLINA *and* VALENTIN *are sitting on the floor eating.*

VALENTIN (*speaking as soon as he finishes his last mouthful*): You're a good cook.
MOLINA: Thank you, Valentin.
VALENTIN: It could cause problems later on. I'm getting spoiled.
MOLINA: You're crazy. Live for today!
VALENTIN: I don't believe in that live for today crap. We haven't earned that paradise yet.
MOLINA: Do you believe in heaven and hell?
VALENTIN: Hold on a minute. If we're going to have a discussion, then we need a framework. Otherwise you'll just ramble on.
MOLINA: I'm not going to ramble.
VALENTIN: Okay, I'll state an opening proposition. Let me put it to you like this.
MOLINA: Put it any way you like.
VALENTIN: I can't live just for today. All I do is determined by the ongoing political struggle, d'you get me? Everything that I endure here, which is bad enough . . . is nothing if you compare it to torture . . . but you don't know what that's like.
MOLINA: I can imagine.
VALENTIN: No, Molina, you can't imagine what it's like . . . Well, anyway, I can put up with all this because there's a blueprint. The essential thing is the social revolution, and the pleasures of the senses come second. The greatest pleasure, well, it's knowing that I'm part of the most noble cause . . . my ideas, for instance . . .
(*The prison lights go out. The blue nighttime light stays on.*)
It's eight . . .
MOLINA: What do you mean, "your ideas"?
VALENTIN: My ideals. Marxism. And that good feeling is one I can experience anywhere, even here in this cell, and even in torture. And that's my strength.
MOLINA: And what about your girlfriend?

VALENTIN: That has to be second too. And I'm second for her. Because she also knows what's most important.

(MOLINA *remains silent.*)

You don't look convinced.

MOLINA: Don't mind me. I'm going to turn in soon.

VALENTIN: You're mad. What about the panther-woman?

MOLINA: Tomorrow.

VALENTIN: What's up?

MOLINA: Look, Valentin, that's me. I get hurt easy. I cooked that food for you, with my supplies, and worse still I give you half my avocado—which is my favorite and could have eaten tomorrow . . . Result? You throw it in my face that I'm spoiling you . . .

VALENTIN: Don't be so soft! It's just like a . . .

MOLINA: Say it!

VALENTIN: Say what?

MOLINA: I know what you were going to say, Valentin.

VALENTIN: Cut it out.

MOLINA: "It's just like a woman." That's what you were going to say.

VALENTIN: Yes.

MOLINA: And what's wrong with being soft like a woman? Why can't a man—or whatever—a dog, or a fairy—why can't he be sensitive if he feels like it?

VALENTIN: In excess, it can get in a man's way.

MOLINA: In the way of what? Of torturing someone?

VALENTIN: No, of getting rid of the torturers.

MOLINA: But if all men were like women, then there'd be no torturers.

VALENTIN: And what would you do without men?

MOLINA: You're right. They're brutes, but I need them.

VALENTIN: Molina . . . you just said that if all men were like women, there'd be no torturers. You've got a point there; kind of weird, but a point at least.

MOLINA: The way you say things. (*imitating* VALENTIN) "A point at least."

VALENTIN: I'm sorry I upset you.

MOLINA: I'm not upset.

VALENTIN: Well, cheer up then. Don't sulk, man.

MOLINA: Man? What man? Where . . . ? Tell me so he won't get away . . . ! Do you want me to go on with the picture?

VALENTIN (*trying to hide he finds this funny*): Start.

MOLINA: Irina goes along to the psychoanalyst who's a ladykiller, real handsome.

VALENTIN: Tell me what you mean by real handsome. I'd like to know.

MOLINA: Well, if you're really interested, he isn't my type at all.

VALENTIN: Who's the actor?

MOLINA: I don't remember. Too skinny for my taste. With a pencil moustache. But there's something about him, so full of himself, he just puts you off.

And he puts off Irina. She skips the next appointment, she lies to her husband, and instead of going to the doctor's she puts on that black fleecy coat and goes along to the zoo, to look at the panther. The keeper comes along, opens the cage, throws in the meat and closes the door again. But he's absent-minded and leaves the key in the lock. Irina sneaks up to the door and puts her hand on the key. And she just stands there, musing, rapt in her thoughts.

VALENTIN: What does she do then?

MOLINA: That's all for tonight. I'll continue tomorrow.

VALENTIN: At least, let me ask you something.

MOLINA: What?

VALENTIN: Who do you identify with? Irina or the architect girl?

MOLINA: With Irina—who do you think? *Moi*—always with the leading lady.

VALENTIN: Continue.

MOLINA: What about you? I guess you're stuck because the guy is such a wimp.

VALENTIN: Don't laugh—with the psychoanalyst. But I didn't say anything about your choice, so don't mock mine . . . You know something? I'm finding it hard to keep my mind on it.

MOLINA: What's the problem?

VALENTIN: Nothing.

MOLINA: Come on, open up a little.

VALENTIN: When you said the girl was there in front of the cage, I imagined it was my girl who was in danger.

MOLINA: I understand.

VALENTIN: I shouldn't be telling you this, Molina. But I guess you've figured it all out for yourself anyhow. My girl is in the organization too.

MOLINA: So what?

VALENTIN: It's only that I don't want to burden you with information it's better you don't know.

MOLINA: With me, it's not a woman, a girlfriend, I mean. It's my mother. She's got blood pressure and a weak heart.

VALENTIN: People can live for years with that.

MOLINA: Sure, but they don't need more aggravation, Valentin. Imagine the shame of having a son inside—and why.

VALENTIN: Look, the worst has already happened, hasn't it?

MOLINA: Yes, but the risk is ever-present inside her. It's that dodgy heart.

VALENTIN: She's waiting for you. Eight years'll fly by, what with remission and all that . . .

MOLINA (*a little contrived*): Tell me about your girlfriend if you like . . .

VALENTIN: I'd give anything to hold her in my arms right now.

MOLINA: It won't be long. You're not in for life.

VALENTIN: Something might happen to her.

MOLINA: Write to her, tell her not to take chances, that you need her.

VALENTIN: Never. Impossible. If you think like that, you'll never change anything in the world.

MOLINA (*not realizing he's mocking* VALENTIN): And you think you're going to change the world?

VALENTIN: Yes, and I don't care that you laugh. It makes people laugh to hear this, but what I have to do before anything is to change the world.

MOLINA: Sure, but you can't do it all at once, *and* on your own.

VALENTIN: But I'm not on my own—that's it! I'm with her and all those other people who think like we do. That's the end of the thread that slips through my fingers . . . I'm not apart from my comrades—I'm with them, right now . . . ! It doesn't matter whether I can see them or not.

MOLINA (*with a slight drawl, sceptically*): If that makes you feel good, terrific!

VALENTIN: Christ, what a moron!

MOLINA: Sticks and stones . . .

VALENTIN: Don't provoke me, then. I'm not some loud-mouth who just spouts off about politics in a bar. The proof is that I'm in here.

MOLINA: I'm sorry.

VALENTIN: It's okay . . .

MOLINA (*pretending not to pry*): You were going to tell me something . . . about your girlfriend.

VALENTIN: We'd better drop that.

MOLINA: As you like.

VALENTIN: Why it gets me so upset, I can't fathom.

MOLINA: Better not, then, if it upsets you . . .

VALENTIN: The one thing I shouldn't tell you is her name.

MOLINA: What sort of girl is she?

VALENTIN: She's twenty-four, two years younger than me.

MOLINA: Thirteen years younger than me . . . No, I tell a lie, sixteen.

VALENTIN: She was always politically conscious. First it was . . . well, I needn't be shy with you, at first it was because of the sexual revolution.

MOLINA (*bracing himself for some saucy tidbit*): I mustn't miss this bit.

VALENTIN: She comes from a bourgeois family, not really wealthy, but comfortably off. But as a kid and all through her adolescence she had to watch her parents destroy each other. Her father cheating her mother, you know what I mean?

MOLINA: No, I don't.

VALENTIN: Cheating her by not telling her he needed other relationships. I don't hold with monogamy.

MOLINA: But it's beautiful when a couple love each other for ever and ever.

VALENTIN: Is that what you'd like?

MOLINA: It's my dream.

VALENTIN: Why do you like men, then?

MOLINA: What's that got to do with it? I want to marry a man—to love and to cherish, for ever and ever.

VALENTIN: So, basically, you're just a bourgeois man?

MOLINA: A bourgeois lady, please.

VALENTIN: If you were a woman, you'd think otherwise.

MOLINA: The only thing I want is to live forever with a wonderful man.

VALENTIN: And that's impossible because . . . well, if he's a man, he wants a woman . . . you'll always be living in a fool's paradise.

MOLINA: Go on about your girlfriend. I don't want to talk about me.

VALENTIN: She was brought up to be the lady of the house. Piano lessons, French, drawing . . . I'll tell you the rest tomorrow, Molina . . . I want to think about something I was studying today.

MOLINA: Now you're getting your own back.

VALENTIN: No, silly. I'm tired, too.

MOLINA: I'm not sleepy at all.

Scene Four

Night. The prison lights are on. VALENTIN *is engrossed in a book.* MOLINA *restless, is flicking through a magazine he already knows backwards.*

VALENTIN (*lifting his head from the book*): Why are they late with dinner? Next door had it ages ago.

MOLINA (*ironic*): Is *that* all you're studying tonight? I'm not hungry, thank goodness.

VALENTIN: That's unusual. Don't you feel well?

MOLINA: No, it's just my nerves.

VALENTIN: Listen . . . I think they're coming.

MOLINA: Better hide the magazines or else they'll pinch them.

VALENTIN: I'm famished.

MOLINA: Please, Valentin, promise me you won't make a scene with the guards.

VALENTIN: No.

(*Through the grille in the other door come two plates of porridge—one visibly more loaded than the other.* MOLINA *looks at* VALENTIN.)

Porridge.

MOLINA: Yes.

(MOLINA *looks at the two plates which* VALENTIN *has collected from the hatch.*) (*exchanging an enigmatic glance with the invisible guard*) Thank you.

VALENTIN (*to the guard*): What about this one? Why's it got less? (*to* MOLINA) I didn't say anything for your sake. Otherwise I'd have thrown it in his face, this bloody glue.

MOLINA: What's the use of complaining?

VALENTIN: One plate's only got half as much as the other. That bastard guard, he's out of his fucking mind.

MOLINA: It's okay, Valentin, I'll take the small portion.

VALENTIN (*serving* MOLINA *the larger one*): No, you like porridge, you always lap it up.

MOLINA: Skip the chivalry. You have it.

VALENTIN: I told you no.

MOLINA: Why should I have the big one?

VALENTIN: Because I know you like porridge.

MOLINA: But I'm not hungry.

VALENTIN: Eat it, it'll do you good.

(VALENTIN *starts eating from the small plate.*)

MOLINA: No.

VALENTIN: It's not too bad today.

MOLINA: I don't want it.

VALENTIN: Afraid of putting on weight?

MOLINA: No.

VALENTIN: Get stuck in then. This porridge a la glue isn't so bad today. This small plate is plenty for me.

(MOLINA *starts eating.*)

MOLINA (*overcoming his resistance: his voice nostalgic now*): Thursday. Ladies' day. The cinema in my neighborhood used to show a romantic triple feature on Thursdays. Years ago now.

VALENTIN: Is that where you saw the panther-woman?

MOLINA: No, that was in a smart little cinema in that German neighborhood where all those posh houses with gardens are. My house was near there, but in the run-down part. Every Monday they'd show a German-language feature. Even during the war. They still do.

VALENTIN: Nazi propaganda films.

MOLINA: But the musical numbers were fabulous!

VALENTIN: You're touched.

(*He finishes his dinner.*)

They'll be turning off the lights soon, that's it for studying today. (*unconsciously authoritarian*) You can go on with the film now—Irina's hand was on the key in the lock.

MOLINA (*picking at his porridge*): She takes the key out of the lock and gives it back to the keeper. The old fellow thanks her, and she goes back home to wait for her husband. She's all out to kiss him, on the mouth this time.

VALENTIN (*absorbed*): Mmmm . . .

MOLINA: Irina calls him up at his office, it's getting late, and the girl architect answers. Irina slams down the phone. She's eaten up with jealousy. She paces up and down the apartment like a caged beast, and when she walks by the canary she notices it's frenetically flapping its wings. She can't control herself, and she opens the little door and puts her hand right inside the cage. The little bird drops stone dead before she even touches it. Irina panics and flees from the house, looking for her husband, but, of course, she has to go past the bar on the corner and she sees them both inside. And she just wants to tear the other woman to shreds. Irina only wears black clothes, but she's never again worn that blouse he liked so much, the one in the restaurant scene, the one with all the rhinestones.

VALENTIN: What are they?

MOLINA (*shocked*): Rhinestones! I don't believe this! You don't know . . . ?

VALENTIN: Not a clue.

MOLINA: They're like diamonds only worthless; little pieces of glass that shine.

(*At this moment the cell light goes out.*)

VALENTIN: I'm going to turn in early tonight. I've had enough of all this drivel.

MOLINA (*overreacting, but deeply hurt*): Thank goodness there's no light so I don't have to see your face. Don't ever speak another word to me!

(*Note: The production must establish that when the blue light is on—meaning nighttime—*MOLINA *and* VALENTIN *cannot see each other, and so are free to express themselves as they like in gestures and body language.*)

VALENTIN: I'm sorry . . .

(MOLINA *stays silent.*)

Really, I'm sorry, I didn't think you'd get so upset.

MOLINA: You upset me because it's one of my favorite movies, you can't know . . .

(*He starts to cry.*)

. . . you didn't see it.

VALENTIN: Are you crazy? It's nothing to cry about.

MOLINA: I'll . . . I'll cry if I feel like it.

VALENTIN: Suit yourself . . . I'm very sorry.

MOLINA: And don't get the idea you've made me cry. It's because today's my mother's birthday and I'm dying to be with her . . . and not with you.

(*Pause.*) Ay . . . ! Ay . . . ! I don't feel well.

VALENTIN: What's wrong?

MOLINA: Ay . . . ! Ay . . . !

VALENTIN: What is it? What's the matter?

MOLINA: The girl's fucked!

VALENTIN: Which girl?

MOLINA: Me, dummy. It's my stomach.

VALENTIN: Do you want to throw up?

MOLINA: The pain's lower down. It's in my guts.

VALENTIN: I'll call the guard, okay?

MOLINA: No, it'll pass, Valentin.

VALENTIN: The food didn't do any harm to me.

MOLINA: I bet it's my nerves. I've been on edge all day. I think it's letting up now.

VALENTIN: Try to relax. Relax your arms and legs, let them go loose.

MOLINA: Yes, that's better. I think it's going.

VALENTIN: Do you want to go to sleep?

MOLINA: I don't know . . . Ugh! It's awful . . .

VALENTIN: Maybe it'd be better if you talk, it'll take your mind off the pain.

MOLINA: You mean the movie?

VALENTIN: Where had we got to?

MOLINA: Afraid I'm going to croak before we get to the end?

VALENTIN: This is for your benefit. We broke off when they were in the bar on the corner.

MOLINA: Okay . . . The two of them get up together to leave, and Irina takes cover behind a tree. The architect girl decides to take the shortcut home through the park. He told her everything while they were in the bar, that Irina doesn't make love to him, that she has nightmares about panther-women and all. The other girl, who'd just got used to the idea that she'd lost him, now begins to think maybe she has a chance again. So she's walking along, and then you hear heels clicking behind her. She turns round and sees the silhouette of a woman. And then the clicking gets faster and now, right, the girl begins to get frightened, because you know what it's like when you've been talking about scary things . . . But she's right in the middle of the park, and if she starts to run she'll be in even worse trouble . . . and, then, suddenly, you can't hear the human footsteps any more . . . Ay . . . ! Ay . . . ! It's still hurting me.

Scene Five

Day. VALENTIN *is lying down, doubled-up with stomach pains.* MOLINA *stands looking on at him.*

VALENTIN: You can't imagine how much it hurts. Like a stabbing pain.

MOLINA: Just what I had two days ago.

VALENTIN: And each time it gets worse, Molina.

MOLINA: You should go to the clinic.

VALENTIN: Don't be thick, I already told you I don't want to go.

MOLINA: They'll only give you a little Seconol. It can't harm you.

VALENTIN: Of course it can; you can get hooked on it. You don't have a clue.

MOLINA: About what?

VALENTIN: Nothing.

MOLINA: Go on, tell me. Don't be like that.

VALENTIN: It happened to one of my comrades once. They got him hooked, his will-power just went. A political prisoner can't afford to end up in prison hospital. You follow me? Never. Once you're in there they come along and interrogate you and you have no resistance . . . Ay . . . ! Ay . . . ! It feels like my guts are splitting open. Aaargh!

MOLINA: I told you not to gobble down your food like that.

VALENTIN (*raising himself with difficulty*): You were right. I'm ready to burst.

MOLINA: Stretch out a little.

VALENTIN: No, I don't want to sleep, I had nightmares all last night and this morning.

MOLINA (*relenting, like a middle-class housewife*): I swore I wouldn't tell you another film. I'll probably go to hell for breaking my word.

VALENTIN: Ay . . . ! Oh, fucking hell . . . !

(MOLINA *hesitates*.)

You carry on. Pay no attention if I groan.

MOLINA: I'll tell you another movie, one for tummyache. Now, you seemed keen on those German movies, am I right?

VALENTIN: In their propaganda machine . . . but, listen, go on with the panther-woman. We left off where the architect girl stopped hearing the human footsteps behind her in the park.

MOLINA: Well . . . she's shaking with fear, she won't dare turn around in case she sees the panther. She stops for a second to see if she still can't hear the woman's footsteps, but there's nothing, absolute silence, and then suddenly she begins to notice this rustling noise coming from the bushes being stirred by the wind . . . or maybe by something else . . .

(MOLINA *imitates the actions he describes*.)

And she turns round with a start.

VALENTIN: I think I want to go to the toilet again.

MOLINA: Shall I call them to open up?

VALENTIN: They'll catch on that I'm ill.

MOLINA: They're not going to whip you into hospital for a dose of the runs.

VALENTIN: It'll go away, carry on with the story.

MOLINA: Okay . . . (*repeating the same actions*) . . . she turns around with a start . . .

VALENTIN: Ay . . . ! Ay . . . ! The pain . . .

MOLINA: (*suddenly*): Tell me something: you never told me why your mother doesn't bring you any food.

VALENTIN: She's a difficult woman. That's why I don't talk about her. She could never stand my ideas—she believes she's entitled to everything she's got, her family's got a certain position to keep up.

MOLINA: The family name.

VALENTIN: Only second league, but a name all the same.

MOLINA: Let her know that she can bring you a week's supplies at a time. You're only spiting yourself.

VALENTIN: If I'm in here it's because I brought it on myself, it's got nothing to do with her.

MOLINA: My mother didn't visit lately 'cos she's ill, did I tell you?

VALENTIN: You never mentioned it.

MOLINA: She thinks she's going to recover from one minute to the next. She won't let anyone but her bring me food, so I'm in a pickle.

VALENTIN: If you could get out of this hole, she'd improve, right?

MOLINA: You're a mind-reader . . . Okay, let's get on with it. (*repeating the same actions as before*) She turns round with a start.

VALENTIN: Ay . . . ! Ay . . . ! What have I gone and done? I'm sorry.

MOLINA: No, no . . . hold still, don't clean yourself with the sheet, wait a second.

VALENTIN: No, not your shirt . . .

MOLINA: Here, take it, wipe yourself with it. You'll need the sheet to keep warm.

VALENTIN: No, you haven't got a change of shirt.

MOLINA: Wait . . . get up, that way it won't go through . . . like this . . . mind it doesn't soil the sheet.

VALENTIN: Did it go through?

MOLINA: Your underpants held it in. Here, take them off . . .

VALENTIN: I'm embarrassed . . .

MOLINA: Didn't you say you have to be a man . . . ? So what's all this about being embarrassed?

VALENTIN: Wrap my underpants up well, Molina, so they don't smell.

MOLINA: I know how to handle this. You see . . . all wrapped up in the shirt. It'll be easier to wash than the sheet. Take the toilet paper.

VALENTIN: No, not yours. You'll have none left.

MOLINA: You never had any. So cut it out.

VALENTIN: Thank you.

(*He takes the tissue and wipes himself and hands the roll back to* MOLINA.)

MOLINA: You're welcome. Relax a little, you're shaking.

VALENTIN: It's with rage. I could cry . . . I'm furious for letting myself get caught.

MOLINA: Calm down. Pull yourself together.

(VALENTIN *watches* MOLINA *wrap the shirt and soiled tissue in a newspaper.*)

VALENTIN: Good idea . . . so it won't smell, eh?

MOLINA: Clever, isn't it?

VALENTIN: I'm freezing.

(MOLINA *is meanwhile lighting the stove and putting water on to boil.*)

MOLINA: I'm just making some tea. We're down to the last little bag. It's camomile, good for the nerves.

VALENTIN: No, leave it, it'll go away now.

MOLINA: Don't be silly.

VALENTIN: You're crazy—you're using up all your supplies.

MOLINA: I'll be getting more soon.

VALENTIN: But your mother's sick and can't come.

MOLINA: I'll continue. (*with irony, repeating the same gestures as before but without the same élan*) She turns around with a start. The rustling noise gets nearer, and she lets rip with a desperate scream, when . . . whack! The door of the bus opens in front of her. The driver saw her standing there and stopped for her . . . The tea's almost ready.

(MOLINA *pours the hot water.*)

VALENTIN: Thanks. I mean that sincerely. And I want to apologize . . . sometimes I get too rough and hurt people without thinking.

MOLINA: Don't talk nonsense.

VALENTIN: Instead of a film, I want to tell you something real. About me. I lied to you when I told you about my girlfriend. I was talking about another one, someone I loved very much. I didn't tell you the truth about my real girlfriend, you'd like her a lot, she's just a sweet and simple kid, but really courageous.

MOLINA: Please don't tell me anything about her. I don't want to know anything about your political business.

VALENTIN: Don't be dumb. Who's going to question you about me?

MOLINA: They might interrogate me.

VALENTIN (*finishing his tea; much improved*): You trust me, don't you?

MOLINA: Yes . . .

VALENTIN: Well, then . . . Inside here it's got to be share and share alike.

MOLINA: It's not that . . .

(VALENTIN *lies down on the pillow, relaxing*.)

VALENTIN: There's nothing worse than feeling bad about having hurt someone. And I hurt her, I forced her to join the organization when she wasn't ready for it; she's very . . . unsophisticated.

MOLINA: But don't tell me any more now. I'm doing the telling for the moment. Where were we? Where did we stop . . . ?

(*Hearing no response,* MOLINA *looks at* VALENTIN, *who has fallen asleep*.)

How did it continue? What comes next?

(MOLINA *feels proud of having helped his fellow cell-mate*.)

Scene Six

Daylight. Both MOLINA *and* VALENTIN *are stretched out on their beds, lost in a private sorrow. In the distance we hear a bolero tune.*

MOLINA *is singing softly.*

MOLINA: "My love, I write to you again
    The night brings an urge to inquire
    If you, too, dear, recall the tender pain
    And the sad dreams our love would inspire."

VALENTIN: What's that you're singing?

MOLINA: A bolero. "My letter."

VALENTIN: Only you would go for that stuff.

MOLINA: What's wrong with it?

VALENTIN: It's romantic eyewash, that's what. You're daft.

MOLINA: I'm sorry. I think I've put my foot in it.

VALENTIN: In what?

MOLINA: Well, after you got that letter, you were really down in the dumps, and here I am singing about sad love letters.

VALENTIN: It was some bad news. You can read it if you like.

MOLINA: Better not.

VALENTIN: Don't start all that again; no one's going to ask you anything. Besides, they read it through before I did.
(*He unfolds the letter and reads it as he talks.*)
MOLINA: The handwriting's like hens' tracks.
VALENTIN: She didn't have much education . . . One of the comrades was killed, and now she's leader of the group. It's all written in code.
MOLINA: Ah . . .
VALENTIN: And she writes that she's having relations with another of the lads, just like I told her.
MOLINA: What relations?
VALENTIN: She was missing me too much. In the organization we take an oath not to get too involved with someone because it can paralyze you when you go into action.
MOLINA: Into action?
VALENTIN: Direct action. Risking your life . . . We can't afford to worry about someone who wants us to go on living because it makes you scared of dying. Well, maybe not scared exactly, but you hate the suffering it'll cause others. And that's why she's having a relationship with another comrade.
MOLINA: You said that your girlfriend wasn't really the one you told me about.
VALENTIN: Damn, staring at this letter has made me dizzy again.
MOLINA: You're still weak.
VALENTIN: I'm shivering and I feel queasy.
(*He covers himself with the sheet.*)
MOLINA: I told you not to start taking food again.
VALENTIN: But I was famished.
(MOLINA *helps* VALENTIN *wrap up well.*)
MOLINA: You were getting better yesterday, and then you went and ate and got sick again. And today it's the same story. Promise me you won't touch a thing tomorrow.
VALENTIN: The girl I told you about, the bourgeois one, she joined the organization with me, but she dropped out and tried to persuade me to split with her.
MOLINA: Why?
VALENTIN: She loved life too much and she was happy just to be with me, that's all she wanted. So we had to break up.
MOLINA: Because you loved each other too much.
VALENTIN: You make it sound like one of your boleros.
MOLINA: Listen, tough guy, haven't you cottoned on yet? Those songs are full of really deep truths, and that's why I like them. The truth is you mock them because they're too close to home. You laugh to keep from crying. . . . As a tango says.
VALENTIN: I was lying low for a while in that guy's flat, the one they killed. With his wife and kid. I even used to change the kid's nappies . . . And

do you want to know what the worst of it is? I can't write to a single one of them without blowing them to the police.

MOLINA: Not even your girlfriend?

VALENTIN (*struggling to hold back his tears*): Oh, God . . . ! What a mess . . . ! It's all so sad! Give me your hand, Molina. Squeeze hard . . .

MOLINA: Hold it tight.

VALENTIN: There's something else. It's wrecking me. It's shameful, awful . . .

MOLINA: Tell me, get it off your chest.

VALENTIN: It's . . . the girl I want to hear from, the one I want to have next to me right now and hug and kiss . . . it's not the one in the movement, but the other one . . . Marta, that's her name . . .

MOLINA: If that's what you feel deep down . . . Oh, I forgot, if your stomach feels real empty, there's a few digestives I'd forgotten all about.

(*Without taking his hand from* VALENTIN's *he reaches for the packet of digestives.*)

VALENTIN: For all I shoot my mouth off about progress . . . when it comes to women, what I really like is a woman with class, and I'm just like all the reactionary sons-of-bitches that killed my comrade . . . The same, exactly the same . . .

MOLINA: That's not true . . .

VALENTIN: And sometimes I think maybe I don't even love Marta because of who she is but because she's got . . . class . . . I'm just like all the other class-conscious sons-of-bitches . . . in the world.

GUARD'S VOICE: Luis Alberto Molina! To the visiting room!

(VALENTIN *and* MOLINA *let go of each other's hand as if caught in a shameful act. The cell door opens and* MOLINA *exits, but not before he's managed to slip the biscuits under* VALENTIN's *blanket. Hereafter, the dialogue is on prerecorded tape. Meanwhile,* VALENTIN *remains onstage and takes the biscuits from under his covers, manages to find just three at the bottom of the large packet and begins to eat them, one at a time, savoring each one.*)

WARDEN'S VOICE: Stop shaking, man, no one's going to do anything to you.

MOLINA'S VOICE: I had a bad stomachache before, sir, but I'm fine now.

WARDEN'S VOICE: You've got nothing to be afraid of. We've made it look like you've had a visitor. The other one won't suspect a thing.

MOLINA'S VOICE: No, he won't suspect anything.

WARDEN'S VOICE: At home last night I had dinner with your benefactor, and he had some good news for you. Your mother is on the road to recovery . . . It seems the chance of your pardon is doing her good . . .

MOLINA'S VOICE: Are you sure?

WARDEN'S VOICE: What's the matter with you? Why are you trembling . . . ? You should be jubilant . . . Well, have you got any news for me yet? Has he told you anything? Is he opening up to you yet?

MOLINA'S VOICE: No, sir, not so far. You have to take these things a step at a time.

WARDEN'S VOICE: Didn't it help at all when we weakened him physically?

MOLINA'S VOICE: I had to eat the first plate of fixed food myself.

WARDEN'S VOICE: You shouldn't have done that.

MOLINA'S VOICE: The truth is he doesn't like porridge, and since one portion was bigger than the other . . . he insisted I eat it. If I'd refused, he might have got suspicious. You told me, sir, that the doctored food would be on the newest plate, but they made a mistake piling it high like that.

WARDEN'S VOICE: Ah, well, in that case, I'm obliged to you, Molina. I'm sorry about the mistake.

MOLINA'S VOICE: Now you should let him get some of his strength back.

WARDEN'S VOICE (*irritated*): That's for us to decide. We know what we're doing. And when you get back to your cell, say you had a visit from your mother. That'll explain why you're so excited.

MOLINA'S VOICE: No, I couldn't say that, she always brings me a food parcel.

WARDEN'S VOICE: Okay, we'll send out for some groceries. Think of it as a reward for the trouble with the porridge. Poor Molina!

MOLINA'S VOICE: Thank you, Warden.

WARDEN'S VOICE: Reel off a list of what she usually brings. (*Pause.*) Now!

MOLINA'S VOICE: To you?

WARDEN'S VOICE: Yes, and be quick about it, I've got work to catch up with.

MOLINA'S VOICE (*as the curtain falls*): Condensed milk, a can of peaches . . . two roast chickens . . . a big bag of sugar . . . two pack of tea, one breakfast, one camomile . . . powdered milk, a bar of soap—bathsize—oh, let me think a second, my mind's a complete blank . . .

End of Act One

Act Two
Scene One

Lighting as in the previous scene. The cell door opens, and MOLINA *enters with a shopping bag.*

MOLINA: Look what I've got!

VALENTIN: No! Your mother's been!

MOLINA: Yes!

VALENTIN: So she's better now?

MOLINA: A little better . . . and look what she brought me. Oops! Sorry, brought us!

VALENTIN (*secretly flattered*): No, it's for you. Cut the nonsense.

MOLINA: Shut it, you're the invalid. The chickens are for you, they'll get you back on your feet.

VALENTIN: No, I won't let you do this.

MOLINA: It's no sacrifice. I can go without the chicken if it means I don't have to put up with your pong . . . No, listen, I'm being serious now, you've got to stop eating this pig-swill they serve in here. At least for a day or two.

VALENTIN: You think so?

MOLINA: And then when you're better . . . Close your eyes.

(VALENTIN *closes his eyes, and* MOLINA *places a large tin in one of his hands.*)

Three guesses . . .

VALENTIN: Ahem . . . er . . . er . . .

(*Enjoying the game,* MOLINA *places an identical tin in* VALENTIN's *other hand.*)

MOLINA: The weight ought to help you . . .

VALENTIN: Heavy all right . . . I give up.

MOLINA: Open your eyes.

VALENTIN: Condensed milk!

MOLINA: But you can't have it yet, not until you're better.

And this is for both of us.

VALENTIN: Marvelous.

MOLINA: First . . . we'll have a cup of camomile tea because my nerves are shot, and you can have a drumstick, no, better not, it's only five . . . Anyway, we can have tea and some biscuits, they're even lighter than those digestives.

VALENTIN: Please, can't I have one right away?

MOLINA: Why not! But just with a little marmalade . . . ! Luckily, everything she brought is easy to get down so it won't give you any trouble. Except for the condensed milk, for the time being.

VALENTIN: Oh, Molina, I'm wilting with hunger. Why won't you let me have that chicken leg now?

(MOLINA *hesitates a moment.*)

MOLINA: Here . . .

VALENTIN: (*wolfing down the chicken*) Honest, really was beginning to feel bad . . .

(*He devours the chicken*)

Thanks . . .

MOLINA: You're welcome.

VALENTIN (*with his mouth full*): But there's just one thing missing to round off the picnic.

MOLINA: Tut, and I thought I was supposed to be the pervert here.

VALENTIN: Stop fooling around! What we need is a movie . . .

MOLINA: Ah! Well, never mind . . . Now there's a scene where Irina has a completely new hairstyle.

VALENTIN: Oh, I'm sorry, I don't feel too good, it's that dizziness again.

MOLINA: Are you positive?

VALENTIN: Yes, it's been threatening all night.

MOLINA: But it can't be the chicken. Maybe you're imagining it.

VALENTIN: I felt full up all of a sudden.

MOLINA: That's because you wolfed it down without even chewing.

VALENTIN: And this itching is driving me wild. I don't know when I last had a bath.

MOLINA: Don't even think about that. That freezing water in your present state! (*Pause.*) Anyway, she looks stunning here, you can see her reflection in a window pane; it's drizzling and all the drops are running down the glass. She's got raven black hair and it's all scooped up in a bun. Let me describe it to you . . .

VALENTIN: It's all scooped up, okay, never mind the silly details . . .

MOLINA: Silly, my foot! And she's got a rhinestone flower in her hair.

VALENTIN (*very agitated now because of his itch*): I know what rhinestones are, so you can save your breath!

MOLINA: My, you are touchy today!

VALENTIN: Can I ask you something?

MOLINA: Go ahead.

VALENTIN: I feel all screwed up—and confused. If it's not too much trouble, I'd like to dictate a letter to her. Would you mind taking it down . . . ? I get dizzy if I try to focus my eyes too hard.

MOLINA: Let me get a pencil.

VALENTIN: You're very kind to me.

MOLINA: We'll do a rough draft first on a bit of paper.

VALENTIN: Here, take my pen-case.

MOLINA: Wait till I sharpen this pencil.

VALENTIN (*short-tempered*): I told you! Use one of mine!

MOLINA: Okay, don't blow your top!

VALENTIN: I'm sorry, it's just that everything is going black.

MOLINA: Okay, ready, shoot . . .

VALENTIN (*very sad*): Dear Marta . . . you don't expect this letter . . . In your case, it won't endanger you . . . I'm feeling . . . lonely, I need you, I want to be . . . near you . . . I want you to give me . . . a word of encouragement.

MOLINA: . . . "of encouragement". . .

VALENTIN: . . . in this moment I couldn't face my comrades, I'd be ashamed of being so weak . . . I have sores all over inside, I need somebody to pour some honey . . . over my wounds . . . And only you could understand . . . because you too were brought up in a nice clean house to enjoy life to the full . . . I can't accept becoming a martyr, it makes me angry to be one . . . or, it isn't that, I see it clearer now . . . I'm afraid because I'm sick, horribly afraid of dying . . . that it may just end here, that my life has amounted to nothing more than this, I never exploited anyone . . . and ever since I had any sense, I've been struggling against the exploitation of my fellow man . . .

MOLINA: Go on.

VALENTIN: Where was I?

MOLINA: "My fellow man". . .

VALENTIN: . . . because I want to go out into the street one day and not die. And sometimes I get this idea that never ever again will I be able to touch a woman, and I can't accept it, and when I think of women I only see you, and what a relief it would be to believe that right until I finish writing this letter you'll be thinking of me . . . and that you'll be running your hands over your body I so well remember . . .

MOLINA: Hold on, don't go so fast.

VALENTIN: . . . over your body I so well remember, and you'll be thinking that it's my hand . . . it would be as if I were touching you, darling . . . because there's still something of me inside you, isn't that so? Just as your own scent has stayed in my nose . . . beneath my fingertips lies a sort of memory of your skin, do you understand me? Although it's not a matter of understanding . . . it's a matter of believing, and sometimes I'm convinced that I took something of you with me . . . and that I haven't lost it, and then sometimes not, I feel there's just me all alone in this cell . . . (*Pause.*)

MOLINA: Yes . . . "all alone in this cell" . . . Go on.

VALENTIN: . . . because nothing leaves any trace, and my luck in having had such happiness with you, of spending those nights and afternoons and mornings of sheer enjoyment, none of this is any use now, just the opposite, it all turns against me, because I miss you madly, and all I can feel is the torture of my loneliness, and in my nose there is only the stench of this cell, and of myself . . . and I can't have a wash because I'm ill, really weak, and the cold water would give me pneumonia, and beneath my fingertips what I feel is the chill of my fear of death, I can feel it in my joints . . . what a terrible thing to lose hope, and that's what's happened to me . . .

MOLINA: I'm sorry for butting in . . .

VALENTIN: What is it?

MOLINA: When you finish dictating the letter, there's something I want to say.

VALENTIN: (*wound up*) What?

MOLINA: Because if you take one of those freezing showers, it'll kill you.

VALENTIN: (*almost hysterical*) And . . . ? So what? Tell me, for Christ's sake.

MOLINA: I could help you to get cleaned up. You see, we've got the hot water we were going to use to boil the potatoes and we've got two towels, so we lather one of them and you do your front and I'll do the back and then you can dry yourself with the other towel.

VALENTIN: And then I'd stop itching?

MOLINA: Sure. And we'd clean up a bit at a time so you won't catch cold.

VALENTIN: And you'll help me?

MOLINA: Of course I will.

VALENTIN: When?

MOLINA: Now, if you like. The water's boiling, we can mix it with a little cold water.

(MOLINA *starts to do this.* VALENTIN *can't believe in such happiness.*)

VALENTIN: And I'd be able to get to sleep without scratching?

MOLINA: Take your shirt off. I'll put some more water on.

(*He mixes the hot and cold water.*)

VALENTIN: But you're using up all your paraffin.

MOLINA: I don't mind.

VALENTIN: Give me the letter, Molina.

MOLINA: What for?

VALENTIN: Just hand it over.

MOLINA: Here.

(MOLINA *gives* VALENTIN *the letter.* VALENTIN *starts to tear it up.*)

What are you doing?

VALENTIN: This.

(*He tears the letter into quarters.*)

Let's not mention it again.

MOLINA: As you like . . .

VALENTIN: It's wrong to get carried away like that by despair.

MOLINA: But it's good to get it into the open. You said so yourself.

VALENTIN: But it's bad for me. I have to learn to restrain myself. (*Pause.*)
Listen, I mean it, one day I'll thank you properly for all this.

(MOLINA *puts more water on the stove.*)

Are you going to waste all that water?

MOLINA: Yes . . . and don't be daft, there's no need to thank me.

(MOLINA *signals to* VALENTIN *to turn around.*)

VALENTIN: Tell me, how does the movie end? Just the last scene.

MOLINA: (*scrubbing* VALENTIN'*s back*) It's either all or nothing.

VALENTIN: Why?

MOLINA: Because of the details. Her hairdo is very important, it's the style
that women wear, or used to wear, when they wanted to show that this
was a crucial moment in their lives, because the hair all scooped up in a
bun, which left the neck bare, gave the woman's face a certain nobility.
(VALENTIN, *despite the tensions and turmoil of this difficult day, changes his
expression and smiles.*)

Why have you got that mocking little grin on your face? I don't see
anything to laugh at.

VALENTIN: Because my back doesn't itch any more!

Scene Two

Day. MOLINA *is tidying up his belongings with extreme care so as not to wake*
VALENTIN. VALENTIN, *nevertheless, wakes up. Both of them are charged with renewed
energy, and the dialogue begins at its normal pace but accelerates rapidly into tenseness.*

VALENTIN: Good morning.

MOLINA: Good morning.

VALENTIN: What's the time?

MOLINA: Ten past ten. I call my mother "ten past ten," the poor dear, because of the way her feet stick out when she walks.

VALENTIN: It's late.

MOLINA: When they brought the tea round, you just turned over and carried on sleeping.

VALENTIN: What were you saying about your old lady?

MOLINA: Look who's still sleeping. Nothing. Sleep well?

VALENTIN: I feel a lot better.

MOLINA: You don't feel dizzy?

VALENTIN: Lying in bed, no.

MOLINA: Great—why don't you try to walk a little?

VALENTIN: No, you'll laugh.

MOLINA: At what?

VALENTIN: Something that happens to a normal healthy man when he wakes up in the morning with too much energy.

MOLINA: You've got a hard-on? Well, God bless . . .

VALENTIN: But look away, please. I get embarrassed . . .
(*He gets up to wash his face with water from the jug.* MOLINA *puts his hand over his eyes and looks away.*)

MOLINA: My eyes are shut tight.

VALENTIN: It's all thanks to your food. My legs are a bit shaky still, but I don't feel queasy. You can look now.
(*He gets back into bed.*)
I'll lie down a bit more now.

MOLINA (*overprotective and smothering*): I'll put the water on for tea.

VALENTIN: No, just reheat the crap they brought us this morning.

MOLINA: I threw it out when I went to the loo. You must look after yourself properly if you want to get better.

VALENTIN: It embarrasses me to use up your things. I'm better now.

MOLINA: Button it.

VALENTIN: No, listen . . .

MOLINA: Listen nothing. My mother's bringing stuff again.

VALENTIN: Okay, thanks, but just for today.
(*He collects his books together.*)

MOLINA: And no reading. Rest . . . ! I'll start another film while I'm making the tea.

VALENTIN: I'd better try and study, if I can, now that I'm on form.
(*He starts to read.*)

MOLINA: Won't it be too tiring?

VALENTIN: I'll give it a go.

MOLINA: You're a real fanatic.

VALENTIN: (*throwing the book to the ground as his tenseness increases*) I can't . . . the words are jumping around.

MOLINA: I told you so. Are you feeling dizzy?

VALENTIN: Only when I try to read.

MOLINA: You know what it is? It's probably just a temporary weakness—if you have a ham sandwich you'll be right as rain.

VALENTIN: Do you think so?

MOLINA: Sure, and then later, after you've had lunch and another little snooze, you'll feel up to studying again.

VALENTIN: I feel lazy as hell. I'll just lie down.

MOLINA (*schoolmistressy*): No, lying in bed only weakens the constitution; you'd be better standing or at least sitting up.

(MOLINA *hands* VALENTIN *his tea.*)

VALENTIN: This is the last day I'm taking any more of this.

MOLINA (*mistress of the situation*): Ha! Ha! I already told the guard not to bring you any more tea in the morning.

VALENTIN: Listen, you decide what you want for yourself, but I want them to bring me the tea even if it is horse's piss.

MOLINA: You don't know the first thing about a healthy diet.

VALENTIN (*trying to control himself*): I'm not joking, Molina, I don't like other people controlling my life.

MOLINA (*counting on his fingers*): Today is Wednesday . . . everything will hang on what happens on Monday. That's what my lawyer says. I don't believe in appeals and all that, but if there's someone who can pull a few strings, maybe there's a chance.

VALENTIN: I hope so.

MOLINA (*with concealed cunning, as he makes more tea*): If they let me out . . . who knows who you'll get as a cell-mate?

VALENTIN: Haven't you had breakfast yet?

MOLINA: I didn't want to disturb you. You were sleeping.

(*He takes* VALENTIN's *cup to refill it.*)

Will you join me in another cup?

VALENTIN: No, thanks.

(MOLINA *opens a new packet, not letting* VALENTIN *see.*)

MOLINA: Tell me, what are you going to study later on?

VALENTIN: What are you doing?

MOLINA: A surprise. Tell me what you're reading.

VALENTIN: Nothing . . .

MOLINA: Cat got your tongue . . . ? And now . . . we untie the mystery parcel . . . which I had hidden about my person . . . and, what have we got here . . . ? something that goes a treat with tea . . . a cherry madeira!

VALENTIN: No, thanks.

MOLINA: What d'you mean "no". . . ? The kettle's on . . .

Oh, I know why not—you want to go to the loo. Ask them to open up, and then fly back here.

VALENTIN: For Christ's sake, don't tell me what to do!

(MOLINA *squeezes* VALENTIN'*s chin*.)

MOLINA: Oh, come on, let me pamper you a little.

VALENTIN: That's enough . . . you prick!

MOLINA: Are you crazy . . . ? What's the matter with you?

(VALENTIN *hurls the teacup and the cake against the wall*.)

VALENTIN: Shut your fucking trap!

MOLINA: The cake . . .

(VALENTIN *is silent*.)

Look what you've done . . . If the stove's broke, we're done for . . . (*Pause*.) . . . and the saucer . . . (*Pause*.) . . . and the tea . . .

VALENTIN: I'm sorry . . .

(MOLINA *is silent now*.)

I lost control . . . I'm really sorry.

(MOLINA *remains silent*.)

The stove is okay; but the paraffin spilled.

(MOLINA *still doesn't answer*.)

. . . I'm sorry I got carried away, forgive me . . .

MOLINA (*deeply wounded*): There's nothing to forgive.

VALENTIN: There is. A lot.

MOLINA: Forget it. Nothing happened.

VALENTIN: It did, I'm dying with shame.

(MOLINA *says nothing*.)

. . . I behaved like an animal . . . Look, I'll call the guard and fill up the bottle while I'm at it. We're almost out of water . . . Molina, please look at me. Raise your head.

(MOLINA *remains silent*.)

GUARD'S VOICE: Luis Alberto Molina. To the visiting room!

(*The door opens and* MOLINA *exits. The recorded dialogue begins as soon as* MOLINA *moves towards the door*. MOLINA *returns with the provisions to find* VALENTIN *picking up the things he has just thrown on the floor*. MOLINA *starts to unpack the shopping bag. The recorded dialogue is heard while the action takes place onstage*.)

WARDEN'S VOICE: Today's Monday, Molina, what have you got for me?

MOLINA'S VOICE: Nothing, I'm afraid, sir.

WARDEN'S VOICE: Indeed.

MOLINA'S VOICE: But he's taking me more into his confidence.

WARDEN'S VOICE: The problem is they're putting pressure on me, Molina. From the top: from the President's private office. You understand what I'm saying to you, Molina? They want to try interrogation again. Less carrot, more stick.

MOLINA'S VOICE: Not that, sir. It'd be even worse if you lost him in interrogation.

WARDEN'S VOICE: That's what I tell them, but they won't listen.

MOLINA'S VOICE: Just one more week, sir. Please. I have an idea . . .

WARDEN'S VOICE: What?

MOLINA'S VOICE: He's a hard nut, but he has an emotional side.

WARDEN'S VOICE: So?

MOLINA'S VOICE: Well, if the guard were to come and say they're moving me to another block in a week's time because of the appeal, that might really soften him up.

WARDEN'S VOICE: What are you driving at?

MOLINA'S VOICE: Nothing, I swear. It's just a hunch. If he thinks I'm leaving soon, he'll feel like opening up even more with me. Prisoners are like that, sir . . . when one of their pals is leaving, they feel more defenseless than ever.

(*At this moment* MOLINA *is back in the cell, and he takes out the food as the* WARDEN'S VOICE *mentions each item.* VALENTIN *looks at* MOLINA.)

WARDEN'S VOICE: Guard, take this down: two roast chickens, four baked apples, one carton of coleslaw, one pound of bacon, one pound of cooked ham, four French loaves, four pieces of crystalized fruit . . .

(*The recorded voice begins to fade out.*)

. . . a carton of orange juice, two cherry madeiras . . .

(MOLINA *is very calm and sad; he is still upset by* VALENTIN's *remarks.*)

MOLINA: This is the bacon and this one's the ham. I'm going to make a sandwich while the bread's fresh. You fix yourself whatever you want.

VALENTIN (*deeply ashamed*): Thank you.

MOLINA (*reserved and calm*): I'm going to cut this roll in half and spread it with butter and have a sandwich. And a baked apple.

VALENTIN: Sounds delicious.

MOLINA: If you'd like some of the chicken while it's still warm, go ahead. Feel free.

VALENTIN: Thank you, Molina.

MOLINA: We'll each fend for ourselves. Then I won't get on your nerves.

VALENTIN: If that's what you prefer.

MOLINA: There's some crystalized fruit, too. All I ask is that you leave me the pumpkin. Otherwise, take what you want.

VALENTIN (*finding it hard to apologize*): I'm still embarrassed . . . because of that tantrum.

MOLINA: Don't be silly.

VALENTIN: If I got annoyed with you . . . it was because you were kind to me . . . and I didn't want . . . to treat you the same way.

MOLINA: Look, I've been thinking too, and I remembered something you once said, right . . . ? That when you're involved in a struggle like that, well, it's not too convenient to get fond of someone. Well, fond is maybe going too far . . . or, why not? Fond as a friend.

VALENTIN: That a very noble way of looking at it.

MOLINA: You see, sometimes I do understand what you tell me.

VALENTIN: But are we so fettered by the world outside that we can't act like human beings just for a minute . . . ?

MOLINA: I don't follow.

VALENTIN: Our persecutors are on the outside, not inside this cell . . . The problem is I'm so brainwashed that it freaks me out when someone is nice to me without asking anything in return.

MOLINA: I don't know about that . . .

VALENTIN: About what?

MOLINA: Don't get me wrong, but if I'm nice to you, well, it's because I want you to be my friend . . . and why not admit it? I want your affection. Just like I treat my mother well because she's a good person and I want her to love me. And you're a good person too, and unselfish because you're risking your life for an ideal . . . that I don't understand but, all the same, it's not just for yourself . . . Don't look away like that, are you embarrassed?

VALENTIN: A bit.

(*He looks* MOLINA *in the face.*)

MOLINA: And that's why I respect you and have warm feelings toward you . . . and why I want you to like me . . . because, you see, my mother's love is the only good thing I've felt in my life, because she likes me . . . just the way I am.

VALENTIN (*pointing to the loaf* MOLINA *put aside*): Can I cut the loaf for you?

MOLINA: Of course . . .

VALENTIN (*cutting the loaf*): And did you never have good friends that meant a lot to you?

MOLINA: My friends were all . . . screaming queens, like me, we never really count on each other because . . . how can I express it?—because we know we're so easily frightened off. We're always looking, you know, for friendship, or whatever, with somebody more serious, with a man, you see? And that just doesn't happen, right? Because what a man wants is a woman.

VALENTIN (*taking a slice of ham for* MOLINA's *sandwich*): And are all homosexuals like that?

MOLINA: Oh no, there are some who fall in love with each other. But me and my friends, we're women. One hundred percent. We don't go in for those little games. We're normal women; *we* only go to bed with men.

VALENTIN (*too absorbed to see the funny side of this*): Butter?

MOLINA: Yes, thanks. There's something I have to tell you.

VALENTIN: Of course, the movie . . .

MOLINA (*with cunning, but nervous all the same*): My lawyer said things were looking up.

VALENTIN: What a creep I am! I didn't ask you.

MOLINA: And when there's an appeal pending, the prisoner gets moved to another block in the prison. They'll probably shift me within a week or so.

VALENTIN (*upset by this but dissimulating*): That's terrific . . . You ought to be pleased.

MOLINA: I don't want to dwell on it too much, build my hopes . . . Have some coleslaw.

VALENTIN: Should I?

MOLINA: It's very good.

VALENTIN: Your news made me lose my appetite.

> (*He gets up.*)

MOLINA: Pretend I didn't say anything, nothing's settled yet.

VALENTIN: No, it all looks good for you, we should be happy.

MOLINA: Have some salad.

VALENTIN: I don't know what's wrong, but all of a sudden I don't feel too good.

MOLINA: Is your stomach hurting?

VALENTIN: No . . . it's my head. I'm all confused.

MOLINA: About what?

VALENTIN: Let me rest for a while.

> (VALENTIN *sits down again, resting his head in his palms. The light changes to indicate a shift to a different time—the two characters stay where they are: there is a special tension, a hypersensitivity in the air.*)

MOLINA: The guy is all muddled up, he doesn't know how to handle this freaky wife of his. She comes in, sees that he's dead serious and goes to the bathroom to put away her shoes, all dirty with mud. He says he went to the doctor's to look for her and found out that she didn't go anymore. Then she breaks into tears and tells him that she's just what she always feared, a madwoman with hallucinations or even worse, a panther-woman. Then he gives in and takes her in his arms, and you were right, she's really just a little girl for him, because when he sees her so defenseless and lost, he feels again he loves her with all his heart and tells her that everything will sort itself out . . .

> (MOLINA *sighs deeply.*) Ahhh . . . !

VALENTIN: What a sigh!

MOLINA: Life is so difficult . . .

VALENTIN: What's the matter?

MOLINA: I don't know, I'm afraid of building up my hopes of getting out of here . . . and that I'll get put in some other cell and spend my life there with God knows what sort of creep.

VALENTIN: Don't lose sight of this. Your mother's health is the most precious thing to you, right?

MOLINA: Yes . . .

VALENTIN: Think about her recovery. Period!

> (MOLINA *laughs involuntarily in his distress.*)

MOLINA: I don't want to think about it.

VALENTIN: What's wrong?

MOLINA: Nothing!

VALENTIN: Don't bury your head in the pillow . . . Are you hiding something from me?

MOLINA: It's . . .

VALENTIN: It's what . . . ? Look, when you get out of here, you're going to be a free man. You can join a political organization if you like.

MOLINA: You're crazy! They won't trust a fag.

VALENTIN: But I can tell you who to speak to . . .

MOLINA (*suddenly forceful, raising his head from the pillow*): Promise me on whatever you hold most dear, never, never, you understand, never tell me anything about your comrades.

VALENTIN: But who would ever think you're seeing them?

MOLINA: They could interrogate me, whatever, but if I know nothing, I say nothing.

VALENTIN: In any case, there are all kinds of groups, of political action; there are even some who just sit and talk. When you get out, things'll be different.

MOLINA: Things *won't* be different. That's the worst of it.

VALENTIN: How many times have I seen you cry? Come on, you annoy me with your snivelling.

MOLINA: It's just that I can't take any more . . . I've had nothing but bad luck . . . always.

(*The prison light goes out.*)

VALENTIN: Lights out already . . . ? In the first place, you must join a group, avoid being alone.

MOLINA: I don't understand any of that . . . (*suddenly grave*) . . . and I don't believe in it much either.

VALENTIN (*tough*): Then like it or lump it.

MOLINA (*still crying a little*): Let's . . . skip it.

VALENTIN (*conciliatory*): Come on, don't be like that . . .

(*He pats* MOLINA *on the back affectionately.*)

MOLINA: I'm asking you . . . please don't touch me.

VALENTIN: Can't a friend pat you on the back?

MOLINA: It makes it worse . . .

VALENTIN: Why . . . ? Tell me what's troubling you . . .

MOLINA (*with deep, deep feeling*): I'm so tired, Valentin . . . I'm tired of suffering. I hurt all over inside.

VALENTIN: Where does it hurt you?

MOLINA: Inside my chest and my throat . . . Why does sadness always get you there? It's choking me, like a knot . . .

VALENTIN: It's true, that's where people always feel it.

(MOLINA *is quiet.*)

Is it hurting you a lot, this knot?

MOLINA: Yes.

VALENTIN: Is it here?

MOLINA: Yes.

VALENTIN: Want me to stroke it . . . here?

MOLINA: Yes.

(*Short pause.*)

VALENTIN: This is relaxing . . .

MOLINA: Why relaxing, Valentin?

VALENTIN: Not to think about myself for a while. Thinking about you, that you need me, and I can be of some use to you.

MOLINA: You're always looking for explanations . . . You're crazy.

VALENTIN: I don't want events to get the better of me. I want to know why they happen.

MOLINA: Can I touch you?

VALENTIN: Yes . . .

MOLINA: I want to touch that mole—the little round one over your eye.
(MOLINA *touches the mole.*)
You're very kind.

VALENTIN: No, you're the one who's kind.

MOLINA: If you like, you can do what you want with me . . . because I want it too . . . If it won't disgust you . . .

VALENTIN: Don't say that—let's not say anything.
(VALENTIN *goes under* MOLINA's *top sheet.*)
Shift a bit closer to the wall . . . (*Pause.*) You can't see a thing, it's so dark.

MOLINA: Gently . . . (*Pause.*) No, it hurts too much like that. (*Pause.*) Slowly please . . . (*Pause.*) That's it . . . (*Pause.*) . . . thanks . . .

VALENTIN: Thank you, too. Are you feeling better?

MOLINA: Yes. And what about you, Valentin?

VALENTIN: Don't ask me . . . I don't know anything anymore . . .

MOLINA: Oh . . . it's beautiful . . .

VALENTIN: Don't say anything . . . not for now . . .

MOLINA: It's just that I feel . . . such strange things . . . Without thinking, I just lifted my hand to my eye, looking for that mole.

VALENTIN: What mole . . . ? I'm the one with the mole, not you.

MOLINA: I know, but I just lifted up my hand . . . to touch the mole . . . I don't have.

VALENTIN: Ssh, try and keep quiet for a while . . .

MOLINA: And do you know what else I felt, but only for a minute, no longer . . . ?

VALENTIN: Tell me, but keep still, like that . . .

MOLINA: For just a minute, it felt like I wasn't here . . . not in here, nor anywhere else . . . (*Pause.*) It felt like I wasn't here, there was just you . . . Or that I wasn't me any more. As if I was . . . you.

Scene Three

Day. MOLINA *and* VALENTIN *are in their beds.*

VALENTIN: Good morning.
(*He is reinvigorated, happy.* MOLINA *is also highly charged.*)

MOLINA: Good morning, Valentin.

VALENTIN: Did you sleep well?

MOLINA: Yes. (*calmly, not insisting*) Would you like tea or coffee?

VALENTIN: Coffee. To wake me up well—and study. Try to get back into the swing of things . . . What about you? Is the gloom over? Or not?

MOLINA: Yes it is, but I feel groggy. I can't think . . . my mind's blank.

VALENTIN: I don't want to think about anything either, so I'm going to read. That'll keep my mind off things.

MOLINA: Off what? Feeling guilty about what happened?

VALENTIN: I'm more and more convinced that sex is innocence itself.

MOLINA: Can I ask you a favor . . . ? Can we not analyze anything, just for today.

VALENTIN: Whatever you like.

MOLINA: I feel . . . fine and I don't want anything to rob me of that feeling. I haven't felt so good since I was a kid. Since my mother bought me some toy.

VALENTIN: Do you remember what toy you liked most?

MOLINA: A doll.

VALENTIN: Ay!

(*He starts to laugh.*)

MOLINA: What's funny about that?

VALENTIN: As a psychologist I would starve.

MOLINA: Why?

VALENTIN: Nothing . . . I was just wondering if there was any link between your favorite toy and . . . me.

MOLINA: (*playing along*) It was your own fault for asking.

VALENTIN: Are you sure it wasn't a boy doll?

MOLINA: Absolutely. She had blonde braids and a little Tyrolese folk dress. (*They laugh together, unselfconsciously.*)

VALENTIN: One question . . . Physically, you're as much a man as I am.

MOLINA: Ummm . . .

VALENTIN: Why then don't you behave like a man . . . ? I don't mean with women if you're not attracted to them, but with another man?

MOLINA: It's not me. I only enjoy myself like that.

VALENTIN: Well, if you like being a woman . . . you shouldn't feel diminished because of that.

(MOLINA *doesn't answer.*)

I mean you shouldn't feel you owe anyone, or feel obliged to them because that's what you happen to feel like . . . You shouldn't yield . . .

MOLINA: But if a man is . . . my husband, he has to be boss to feel good. That's only natural.

VALENTIN: No, the man and the woman should be equal partners inside the home. Otherwise, it's exploitation. Don't you see?

MOLINA: But there's no thrill like that.

VALENTIN: What?

MOLINA: Since you want to know about it . . . the thrill is that when a man embraces you, you're a little bit afraid.

VALENTIN: Who put that idea into your head? That's all crap.

MOLINA: But it's what I feel.

VALENTIN: No, it's not what you feel, it's what you've been taught to feel. Being a woman doesn't make you . . . how shall I say . . . ? A martyr. And if I didn't think it would hurt like hell, I'd ask you to do it to me, to show you that all this business about being macho doesn't give anyone rights over another person.

MOLINA (*now disturbed*): This is getting us nowhere.

VALENTIN: On the contrary, I want to talk about it.

MOLINA: Well, I don't, so that's it. I'm begging you, no more, please.

VALENTIN: As you like.

MOLINA: There is something I want to tell you, though . . . When you were here it was like I wasn't myself, it was such a relief. And then later, when you were back in your bed . . . I still wasn't me, it's so strange, I can't explain.

VALENTIN: Tell me . . . try . . .

MOLINA: Don't rush me, I have to concentrate . . . Yes . . . when I was alone in my bed, and I was no longer you, I still felt like I was somebody else, neither male nor female . . . what I felt was . . .

VALENTIN: . . . out of danger . . .

MOLINA: Yes! That's it, exactly. How did you know?

VALENTIN: Because it's just what I felt too.

MOLINA: Valentin, why should we feel like that?

VALENTIN: I don't know . . .

MOLINA: Valentin . . .

VALENTIN: Mmm . . .

MOLINA: I'm going to tell you something, but promise me you won't laugh.

VALENTIN: Tell me.

MOLINA: When you come to my bed, afterwards . . . I hope I'll never wake up anymore once I've fallen asleep. I'd be sorry for my mother, sure, because she'd be on her own . . . but if it was just me, then I wouldn't want to wake ever again. And this isn't just some half-baked notion that I've just dreamed up either, no, it's the honest truth . . .

VALENTIN: But first you have to finish the movie.

GUARD'S VOICE: Prisoner Luis Alberto Molina! To the visiting room!

WARDEN'S VOICE: Put me through to your boss, please . . . How's it going? Nothing this end. Yes, that's why I called. He's on his way here now . . . Yes, they need the information, I'm aware of that . . . and if Molina still hasn't found out anything, what should I do with him . . . ? Are you sure . . . ? Let him out . . . But why . . . ? Yes, of course, there's no time to lose. Quite, and if the other one gives him a message, Molina will lead us straight to the group . . . I've got it, yes, we'll give him just enough time

for the other to pass on the message . . . The tricky thing will be if Molina
catches on that he's under surveillance . . . It's hard to anticipate the reactions of someone like Molina: a pervert after all.

(*The cell door opens and* MOLINA *comes back in totally deflated.*)

MOLINA: Poor Valentin, you're looking at my hands.

VALENTIN: I didn't mean to.

MOLINA: Your eyes gave you away, poor love . . .

VALENTIN: Such language . . .

MOLINA: I didn't get a parcel. You'll have to forgive me . . . Ay! Valentin . . .

VALENTIN: What's wrong.

MOLINA: Ay, you can't imagine . . .

VALENTIN: What's up. Tell me.

MOLINA: I'm going.

VALENTIN: To another cell . . .

MOLINA: No, they're releasing me.

VALENTIN: No.

MOLINA: I'm out on parole.

VALENTIN (*exploding with unexpected happiness*): But that's incredible!

(MOLINA *is confused by the way* VALENTIN *is taking this.*)

MOLINA: You're very kind to be so pleased for me.

VALENTIN: I'm happy for you too, of course . . . but, it's terrific! And I guarantee there's not the slightest risk.

MOLINA: What are you saying?

VALENTIN: Listen . . . I had to get urgent information out to my people, and I
was dying with frustration because I couldn't do anything about it. I was
racking my brains trying to find a way . . . And you come and serve it to
me on a plate.

MOLINA (*as if he'd just had an electric shock*): I can't do that, you're out of your
head.

VALENTIN: You'll memorize it in a minute. That's how easy it is. All you have
to do is tell them that Number Three Command has been knocked out
and they have to go to Corrientes for new orders.

MOLINA: No, I'm on parole, they can lock me up again for anything.

VALENTIN: I give you my word there's no risk.

MOLINA: I'm pleading with you. I don't want to hear another word. Not who
they are or where they are. Nothing.

VALENTIN: Don't you want me to get out one day too?

MOLINA: Of here?

VALENTIN: Yes, to be free.

MOLINA: There's nothing I want more. But listen to me, I'm telling you this for
your own good . . . I'm not good at this sort of thing, if they catch me, I'll
spill everything.

VALENTIN: I'll answer for my comrades. You just have to wait a few days and
then call from a public telephone, and make an appointment with someone in some bogus place.

MOLINA: What do you mean "a bogus place"?

VALENTIN: You just give them a name in code, let's say the Ritz cinema, and that means a certain bench in a particular square.

MOLINA: I'm frightened.

VALENTIN: You won't be when I explain the procedure to you.

MOLINA: But if the phone's tapped, I'll get in trouble.

VALENTIN: Not from a public call-box and if you disguise your voice. It's the easiest thing in the world, I'll show you how to do it. There are millions of ways—a sweet in your mouth, or a toothpick under your tongue . . .

MOLINA: No.

VALENTIN: We'll discuss it later.

MOLINA: No!

VALENTIN: Whatever you say.

(MOLINA *flops on the bed, all done in, and buries his face in the pillow.*)

Look at me please.

MOLINA (*not looking at* VALENTIN): I made a promise, I don't know who to, maybe God, even though I don't much believe in that.

VALENTIN: Yes . . .

MOLINA: I swore that I'd sacrifice anything if I could only get out of here and look after my mother. And my wish has come true.

VALENTIN: It was very generous of you to put someone else first.

MOLINA: But where's the justice in it? I always get left with nothing . . .

VALENTIN: You have your mother and she needs you. You have to assume that responsibility.

MOLINA: Listen, my mother's already had her life, she's lived, been married, had a child . . . She's old now, and her life is almost finished . . .

VALENTIN: But she's still alive . . .

MOLINA: And so am I . . . But when is my life going to begin . . . ? When is it my turn for something good to happen? To have something for myself?

VALENTIN: You can start a new life outside . . .

MOLINA: All I want is to stay with you . . .

(VALENTIN *doesn't say anything.*)

Doesn't that embarrass you?

VALENTIN: No . . . er, well, yes . . .

MOLINA: Yes what?

VALENTIN: That . . . it makes me a little embarrassed . . . Molina, try to understand this. Everything in a man's life, which may be short or long, is only temporary. Nothing lasts forever.

MOLINA: Maybe . . . but why can't it last a little longer, just that at least . . . ? If I can relay the information, will you get out sooner?

VALENTIN: It's a way of helping the cause.

MOLINA: But you won't get out sooner. You just think it'll bring the revolution a bit closer.

VALENTIN: Yes, Molinita . . . Don't dwell on it, we'll discuss it later.

MOLINA: There's no time left to discuss.

VALENTIN: Besides, you have to finish the panther movie.

MOLINA: It's a sad ending.

VALENTIN: How?

MOLINA: She's a flawed woman ... (*with his usual irony*) All we flawed women come to a sad ending.

VALENTIN (*laughing*): And the psychoanalyst? Does he get her in the end?

MOLINA: She gets him! And good! No, it's not so terrible, she just tears him to pieces.

VALENTIN: Does she kill him?

MOLINA: In the movie, yes. In real life, no.

VALENTIN: Tell me.

MOLINA: Let's see. Irina goes from bad to worse, she's insanely jealous of the other girl and tries to kill her. But the other one's lucky like hell, and she gets away. Then one day the husband, who's at his wits' end now, arranges to meet the psychoanalyst at their house while she's out. But things get all muddled up, and when the psychoanalyst arrives, she's there on her own. He tries to take advantage of the situation and throws himself at her and kisses her. And right there she turns into a panther. By the time the husband gets home, the guy's bled to death. Meanwhile, Irina has made it to the zoo, and she sidles up to the panther's cage. She's all alone, in the night. That afternoon she got the key when the keeper left it in the lock. It's like Irina's in another world. The husband is on his way with the cops at top speed. Irina opens the panther's cage, and it pounces on her and mortally wounds her with the first blow. The animal is scared away by the police siren, it dashes out into the street, a car runs over it and kills it.

VALENTIN: I'm going to miss you, Molinita.

MOLINA: The movies, at least.

VALENTIN: At least.

MOLINA: I want to ask you for a going-away present. Something that we never did, although we got up to worse.

VALENTIN: What?

MOLINA: A kiss.

VALENTIN: It's true. We never did.

MOLINA: But right at the end, just as I'm leaving.

VALENTIN: Okay.

MOLINA: I'm curious ... Did the idea of kissing me disgust you?

VALENTIN: Ummm ... Maybe I was afraid you'd turn into a panther.

MOLINA: I'm not the panther-woman.

VALENTIN: I know.

MOLINA: It's not fun to be a panther-woman, no one can kiss you. Or anything else.

VALENTIN: You're the spider woman who traps men in her web.

MOLINA (*flattered*): How sweet! I like that!

VALENTIN: And now it's your turn to promise me something: that you'll make people respect you, that you won't let anybody take advantage of you . . . Promise me you won't let anybody degrade you.

GUARD'S VOICE: Prisoner Luis Alberto Molina, be ready with your belongings!

MOLINA: Valentin . . .

VALENTIN: What?

MOLINA: Nothing, it doesn't matter . . . (*Pause.*) Valentin . . .

VALENTIN: What is it?

MOLINA: Rubbish, skip it.

VALENTIN: Do you want . . . ?

MOLINA: What?

VALENTIN: The kiss.

MOLINA: No, it was something else.

VALENTIN: Don't you want your kiss now?

MOLINA: Yes, if it won't disgust you.

VALENTIN: Don't get me mad.

(*He walks over to* MOLINA *and timidly gives him a kiss on the mouth.*)

MOLINA: Thank you.

VALENTIN: Thank you.

(*Long pause.*)

MOLINA: And now give me the number of your comrades.

VALENTIN: If you want.

MOLINA: I'll get the message to them.

VALENTIN: Okay . . . Is that what you wanted to ask?

MOLINA: Yes.

(VALENTIN *kisses* MOLINA *one more time.*)

VALENTIN: You don't know how happy you've made me. It's 323–1025.

(*Bolero music starts playing; it chokes* VALENTIN's *voice as he gives his instructions.* MOLINA *and* VALENTIN *separate slowly.* MOLINA *puts all his belongings into a duffel bag. They are now openly broken-hearted:* MOLINA *can hardly keep his mind on what he's doing.* VALENTIN *looks at him in total helplessness. Their taped voices are heard as all this action takes place onstage.*)

MOLINA'S VOICE: What happened to me, Valentin, when I got out of here?

VALENTIN'S VOICE: The police kept you under constant surveillance, listened in on your phone, everything. The first call you got was from an uncle, your godfather; he told you not to dally with minors again. You told him what he deserved, that he should go to hell, because in jail you'd learned what dignity was. Your friends telephoned and you called each other Greta and Marlene and Marilyn, and the police thought maybe it was a secret code. You got a job as a window dresser, and then finally one day you called my comrades. You took your mother to the movies and bought her some fashion magazines. And one day you went to meet my friends, but the police were shadowing you and they arrested you. My friends opened fire and killed you from their getaway car as you'd asked them to if the police caught you. And that was all . . . And what about me, Molina, what happened to me?

MOLINA'S VOICE: They tortured you a lot . . . and then your wounds turned septic. A nurse took pity on you and secretly he gave you some morphine, and you had a dream.

VALENTIN'S VOICE: About what?

MOLINA'S VOICE: You dreamed that inside you, in your chest, you were carrying Marta and that you'd never ever be apart from one another. And she asked you if you regretted what happened to me, my death, which she said was your fault.

VALENTIN'S VOICE: And what did I answer her?

MOLINA'S VOICE: You replied that I had died for a noble and selfless ideal. And she said that wasn't true, she said that I had sacrificed myself just so I could die like the heroine in a movie. And you said that only I knew the answer. And you dreamed you were very hungry when you escaped from prison and that you ended up on a savage island, and in the middle of the jungle you met a spider woman who gave you food to eat. And she was so lonely there in the jungle, but you had to carry on with your struggle and go back to join your comrades, and your strength was restored by the food the spider woman gave you.

VALENTIN'S VOICE: And, at the end, did I get away from the police, or did they catch up with me?

MOLINA'S VOICE: No, at the end you left the island, you were glad to be reunited with your comrades in the struggle, because it was a short dream, but a pleasant one . . .

(*The door opens:* MOLINA *and* VALENTIN *embrace one another with infinite sadness.* MOLINA *exits. The door closes behind him.*)

CURTAIN

❋   **Discussion and Writing**

1. Examine the nature of the narrative of the panther woman; analyze the use of narration in furthering the action of the play.
2. Explore the development of the friendship between Molina and Valentin: do they change their beliefs; how do they influence each other?
3. Why does Valentin call Molina a spider woman and not a panther woman?
4. Analyze Puig's blending of the past, present, and future in this play. What is the significance of the last scene?

❋ Research and Comparison

This play is a dramatic adaptation of Puig's novel of the same name. Compare the novel, the film version, and the play.

Interdisciplinary Discussion Question: Survey the history of the treatment of homosexuality in literature from the earliest times in any culture. You may wish to also include the manifestation of this theme in different cultures in recent years.

Austin Clarke
(b. 1934)
Barbados

Austin Chesterfield Clarke was born in Barbados into a society that was rigidly structured according to fine distinctions of class. His father, a poet and painter, belonged to a lower status than did his mother; hence, they were forbidden to marry. Her family refused to allow her to see him, or to speak of him to his son. Raised by his mother and a stepfather, Clarke was sent to the best Barbadian schools, where all standards of excellence, culture, and intelligence were British, standards that his community held firmly. He taught in Barbados after graduating from Harrison College, then left to study economics at the University of Toronto. Although over the years he has served as the Barbadian cultural attaché to Washington as well as cultural officer in Barbados, and has taught at various universities in the United States, he has joined the expatriate West Indian communities living in a kind of exile in Canada. And his work reflects this sense of exile, both inside and outside Barbados: now satirizing Barbadian class consciousness, now examining a young man's search for his father, for his identity.

Leaving This Island Place

The faces at the grilled windows of the parish almshouse were looking out, on this hot Saturday afternoon, on a world of gray-flannel and cricket and cream shirts, a different world, as they had looked every afternoon from the long imprisonment of the wards. Something in those faces told me they were all going to die in the almshouse. Standing on the cricket field I searched for the face of my father. I knew he would never live to see the sun of day again.

It is not cricket, it is leaving the island that makes me think about my father. I am leaving the island. And as I walk across the green playing field and onto the driveway of the almshouse, its walkway speckled with spots of tar and white pebbles, and walk right up to the white spotless front of the building, I know it is too late now to think of saving him. It is too late to become involved with this dying man.

In the open veranda I can see the men, looking half-alive and half-dead, lying on the smudged canvas cots that were once white and cream as the cricketers' clothes, airing themselves. They have played, perhaps, in too many muddy tournaments, and are now soiled. But I am leaving. But I know before I leave there is some powerful tug which pulls me into this almshouse, grabbing me and almost swallowing me to make me enter these doors and slap me flat on the sore-back canvas cot beside a man in dying health. But I am leaving.

"You wasn't coming to visit this poor man, this poor father o' yourn?" It is Miss Brewster, the head nurse. She knew my father and she knew me. And she knew that I played cricket every Saturday on the field across the world from the almshouse. She is old and haggard. And she looks as if she has looked once too often on the face of death; and now she herself resembles a half-dead, dried-out flying fish, wrapped in the greaseproof paper of her nurse's uniform. "That man having fits and convulsions by the hour! Every day he asking for you. All the time, day in and day out. And you is such a poor-great, high-school educated bastard that you now acting *too proud* to come in here, because it is a almshouse and not a *private ward*, to see your own father! And you didn' even have the presence o' mind to bring along a orange, not even one, or a banana for that man, *your father!*"

She was now leading me through a long dark hallway, through rows of men on their sides, and some on their backs, lying like soldiers on a battle-field. They all looked at me as if I was dying. I tried to avoid their eyes, and I looked instead at their bones and the long fingernails and toenails, the thermometers of their long idle illness. The matted hair and the smell of men overdue for the bedpan: men too weary now to raise themselves to pass water even in a lonely gutter. They were dying slowly and surely, for the almshouse was crowded and it did not allow its patients to die too quickly. I passed them, miles out of my mind: the rotting clothes and sores, men of all colors, all ages, dressed like women in long blue sail-cloth-hard shirts that dropped right down to the scales on their toothpick legs. One face smiled at me, and I wondered whether the smile meant welcome.

"Wait here!" It was Miss Brewster again who had spoken. She opened the door of a room and pushed me inside as you would push a small boy into the headmaster's office for a caning; and straightaway the smell of stale urine and of sweat and feces whipped me in the face. When the door closed behind me I was alone with the dead, with the smells of the almshouse.

I am frightened. But I am leaving. I find myself think about the trimmed sandwiches and the whiskey-and-sodas waiting for me at the farewell party in honor of my leaving. Something inside me is saying I should pay some respect in my thoughts for this man, this dying man. I opened my eyes and thought of Cynthia. I thought of her beautiful face beside my father's face. And I tried to hold her face in the hands of my mind, and I squeezed it close to me and kept myself alive with the living outside world of cricket and cheers and "tea in the pavilion." There is death in this room and I am inside it. And Cynthia's voice is saying to me. Run run run! back through the smells, through the fallen lines of the men, through the front door and out into the green sunlight of the afternoon and the cricket and shouts; out into the applause.

"That's he laying-down there. Your father," the voice said. It was Miss Brewster. She too must have felt the power of death in the room, for she spoke in a whisper.

This is my father: more real than the occasional boundary hit by the cricket bat and the cheers that came with the boundary only. The two large eyeballs in the sunset of this room are my father.

"Boy?" It was the skeleton talking. I am leaving. He held out a hand to touch me. Dirt was under his fingernails like black moons. I saw the hand. A dead hand, a dirty hand, a hand of quarter-moons of dirt under the claws of its nails. ("You want to know something, son?" My godmother told me long ago. "I'll tell you something. That man that your mother tell you to call your father, he isn't your father, in truth. Your mother put the blame of your birth on him because once upon a time, long long ago in this island, that man was a man.")

I do not touch the hand. I am leaving this place.

And then the words, distant and meaningless from this departure of love because they came too late, began to turn the room on a side. Words and words and words. He must have talked this way each time he heard a door open or shut; or a footstep. ". . . is a good thing you going away, son, a good thing. I hear you going away, and that is a good thing . . . because I am going away . . . from this place. . . . Miss Brewster, she . . . but I am sorry . . . cannot go with you . . . " (Did my mother hate this man so much to drive him here? Did she drive him to such a stick of love that it broke his heart; and made him do foolish things with his young life on the village green of cricket near his house, that made him the playful enemy of Barrabas the policeman, whose delight, my godmother told me, was to drag my father the captain of the village team away drunk from victory and pleasure to throw him into the crowded jail to make him slip on the cold floor fast as a new cricket pitch with vomit . . . ("And it was then, my child, after all those times in the jail, that your father contract that sickness which nobody in this village don't call by name. It is so horrible a sickness.") . . . and I remember now that even before this time I was told by my mother that my father's name was not to be mentioned in her house which her husband made for me as my stepfather.

And she kept her word. For eighteen years. For eighteen years, his name was never mentioned; so he had died before this present visit. And there was not even a spasm of a reminiscence of his name. He was dead before this. But sometimes I would risk the lash of her hand and visit him, in his small shack on the fringe of Rudders Pasture where he lived out the riotous twenty-four years of middle life. ("Your mother never loved that bastard," my godmother said.) But I loved him, in a way. I loved him when he was rich enough to give me two shillings for a visit, for each visit. And although my mother had said he had come "from no family at-all, at-all," had had "no background," yet to me in those laughing days he held a family circle of compassion in his heart. I see him now, lying somewhere on a cot, and I know I am leaving this island.

In those days of cricket when I visited him, I visited him in his house: the pin-up girls of the screen, white and naked; and the photographs of black women he had taken with box camera (because "Your father is some kind o' genius, but in this island we call him a blasted madman, but he may be a real genius"), black women always dressed in their Sunday-best after church, dressed in too much clothes, and above them all, above all those pin-ups and photographs, the photographs of me, caught running in a record time, torn from the island's newspapers. And there was one of me he had framed, when I passed my examinations at Harrison College. And once, because in those days he was my best admirer, I gave him a silver cup which I had won for winning a race in a speed which no boy had done in twenty-five years, at the same school, in the history of the school. And all those, women on the walls, and some in real life, looking at me, and whispering under their breath so I might barely hear it, "That's his *son!*"; and some looking at me as if I had entered their bedroom of love at the wrong moment of hectic ecstasy, and he, like a child caught stealing, would hang his father's head in shame and apologize for them in a whisper, and would beg the women in a loud voice, "You don't see I am with *my son?* You can't behave yourself in his presence?" And once, standing in his house alone, when he went to buy a sugar cake for me, I was looking at the photograph of a naked woman on the wall and my eyes became full of mists and I saw coming out of the rainwater of vision my mother's face, and her neck and her shoulders and her breasts and her navel. And I shut my eyes tight, tight, tight, and ran into him returning with the sugar cake and ran screaming from his house. That was my last visit. This is my first visit after that. And I am leaving this island place.

After that last visit I gave myself headaches wondering if my mother had gone to his shack before she found herself big and heavy with the burden of me in her womb. ("Child, you have no idea what he do to that poor pretty girl, your mother, that she hates his guts even to this day!")

. . . and the days at Harrison College when the absence of his surname on my report card would remind me in the eyes of my classmates that I might be the best cricketer and the best runner, but that I was after all, among this cream of best blood and brains, only a bas——) ". . . this island is only a place, one place," his voice was saying. "The only saving thing is to escape." He was a pile of very old rags thrown around a stunted tree. Then he was talking again, in a new way. "Son, do not leave before you get somebody to say a prayer for me . . . somebody like Sister Christopher from the Nazarene Church . . . "

But Sister Christopher is dead. Dead and gone five years now. "When she was shouting at the Lord one night at a revival," my godmother said.

"She's dead."

"Dead?"

"Five years."

"But couldn' you still ask her to come, ask Miss Christo, Sister Christopher to come . . . "

There is no point listening to a dying man talk. I am going to leave. No point telling him that Sister Christopher is alive, because he is beyond that, beyond praying for, since he is going to die and he never was a Catholic. And I am going to leave. For I cannot forget the gray-flannel and the cream of the cricket field just because he is dying, and the sharp smell of the massage and the cheers of the men and women at the tape, which I have now made a part of my life. And the Saturday afternoon matinees with the wealthy middle-class girls from Queen's College, wealthy in looks and wealthy in books, with their boyfriends the growing-up leaders of the island. Forget all that? And forget the starched white shirt and the blue-and-gold Harrison College tie? Forget all this because a man is dying and because he tells you he is going to die?

Perhaps I should forget them. They form a part of the accident of my life, a life which—if there were any logic in life—ought to have been spent in the gutters round the Bath Corner, or in some foreign white woman's rose garden, or fielding tennis balls in the Garrison Savannah Tennis Club where those who played tennis could be bad tennis players but had to be white.

Let him die. I am leaving this island place. And let him die with his claim on my life. And let the claim be nailed in the coffin, which the poor authorities for the poor will authorize out of plain dealboard, without a minister or a prayer. And forget Sister Christopher who prefers to testify and shout on God; and call somebody else, perhaps, more in keeping with the gray-flannel and the cream of the cricket field and Saturday afternoon walks in the park and matinees at the Empire Theater. Call a canon. Call a canon to bury a pauper, call a canon to bury a pauper, ha-ha-haaaa! . . .

Throughout the laughter and the farewell speeches and the drinks that afternoon, all I did hear was the slamming of many heavy oak doors of the rectory when I went to ask the canon to bury the pauper. And I tried to prevent the slamming from telling me what it was telling me: that I was out of place here, that I belonged with the beginning in the almshouse. Each giggle, each toast, each rattle of drunken ice cubes in the whirling glass pointed a finger back to the almshouse. "Man, you not drinking?" a wealthy girl said. "Man, what's wrong with you, at all?" And someone else was saying, "Have any of you remember Freddie?" But Briggs said, "Remember that bitch? The fellar with the girl with the biggest bubbies in the whole Caribbean? And who uses to . . . man, Marcus! Marcus, I calling you! Godblummuh, Marcus, we come here to drink rum and you mean to tell me that you selling we *water,* instead o' rum?" And Joan Warton said, "But wait, look this lucky bastard though, saying he going up in Canada to university! Boy, you real lucky, in truth. I hear though that up there they possess some real inferior low-class rum that they does mix with water. Yak-yak-yak! From now on you'd be drinking Canadian rum-water, so stop playing the arse and drink this Bajan rum, man. We paying for this, yuh know!" I was leaving. I was thinking of tomorrow, and I was climbing the BOAC gang-plank on the plane bound for Canada, for hope, for school, for glory; and the sea and the distance had already eased the pain of conscience; and there was already much sea between me and the cause of conscience . . .

And when the party was over, Cynthia was with me on the sands of Gravesend Beach. And the beach was full of moonlight and love. There was laughter too; and the laughter of crabs scrambling among dead leaves and skeletons of other crabs caught unawares by someone running into the sea. And there was a tourist ship in the outer harbor. "Write! write, write, write, write me everyday of the week, every week of the year, and tell me what Canada is like, and think of me always, and don't forget to say nice things in your letters, and pray for me every night. And write poems, love poems like the ones you write in the college magazine; and when you write don't send the letters to the Rectory, because father would, well . . . send them to Auntie's address. You understand? You know how ministers and canons behave and think. I have to tell father, I have to tell him I love you, and that we are getting married when you graduate. And I shall tell him about us . . . when you leave tomorrow." Watching the sea and the moonlight on the sea; and watching to see if the sea was laughing; and the scarecrows of masts on the fishing boats now lifeless and boastless, taking a breather from the depths and the deaths of fishing; and the large incongruous luxury liner drunk-full of tourists. And all the time Cynthia chatting and chattering, ". . . but we should have got married, even secretly and eloped somewhere, even to Trinidad, or even to Tobago. Father won't've known, and won't've liked it, but we would've been married . . . Oh hell, man! This island stifles me, and I wish I was leaving with you. Sometimes I feel like a crab in a crab hole with a pile o' sand in front . . . "

"Remember how we used to build sandcastles on bank holidays?"

"And on Sundays, far far up the beach where nobody came . . ."

"Cynthia?"

"Darling?"

"My Old Man, my Old Man is dying right now . . . "

"You're too philosophical! Anyhow, where? Are you kidding? I didn' even know you had an Old Man." And she laughs.

"I was at the almshouse this afternoon, before the party."

"Is he really in the almshouse?"

"St. Michael's almshouse, near . . . "

"You must be joking. You *must* be joking!" She turned her back to me, and her face to the sea. "You aren't pulling my leg, eh?" she said. And before I could tell her more about my father, who he was, how kind a man he was, she was walking from me and we were in her father's Jaguar and speeding away from the beach.

And it is the next day, mid-morning, and I am sitting in the Seawell Airport terminal, waiting to be called to board the plane. I am leaving. My father, is he dead yet? A newspaper is lying on a bench without a man, or woman. Something advises me to look in the obituary column and see if . . . But my mother had said, as she packed my valises, making sure that the fried fish was in my briefcase which Cynthia had bought for me as a going-away present, my mother had said, "Look, boy, leave the dead to live with the blasted dead, do! Leave the dead in this damn islan' place!"

And I am thinking now of Cynthia who promised ("I promise, I promise, I promise. Man, you think I going let you leave this place, *leave Barbados?* and I not going be there at the airport?") to come to wave goodbye, to take a photograph waving goodbye from the terminal and the plane, to get her photograph taken for the social column waving goodbye at the airport, to kiss, to say goodbye and promise return in English, and say *"au revoir"* in French because she was the best student in French at Queen's College.

A man looks at the newspaper, and takes it up, and gives it to a man loaded-down as a new-traveller for a souvenir of the island. And the friend wraps two large bottles of Goddards Gold Braid rum in it, smuggling the rum and the newspaper out of the island, in memory of the island. And I know I will never find out how he died. Now there are only the fear and the tears and the handshakes of other people's saying goodbye and the weeping of departure. "Come back real soon again, man!" a fat, sweating man says. "And next time I going take you to some places that going make your head *curl!* Man, I intend to show you the whole islan', and give you some dolphin steaks that is more bigger than the ones we eat down in Nelson Street with the whores last night!" An old woman, who was crying, was saying goodbye to a younger woman who could have been her daughter, or her daughter-in-law, or her niece. "Don't take long to return back, child! Do not tarry too long. Come back again soon . . . and don't forget that you was borned right here, pon this rock, pon this island. This is a good decent island, so return back as soon as you get yuh learning, come back again soon, child . . ."

The plane is ready now. And Cynthia is not coming through the car park in her father's Jaguar. She has not come; she has not come as she promised. And I am leaving the island.

Below me on the ground are the ants of people, standing at an angle, near the terminal. And I can see the architect-models of houses and buildings, and the beautiful quiltwork patches of land under the plough . . . and then there is the sea, and the sea, and then the sea.

❈ Discussion and Writing

1. Describe the narrator's relationship with his father when the narrator was a child. Analyze the complex relationship between the father, the mother, and the son.
2. How does the almshouse relate to the cricket field? What is the significance of the description of the narrator's visit to the almshouse on the eve of his leaving the island?
3. Explain the function of such peripheral characters as Cynthia, the godmother, and the nurse.
4. Explore the narrator's disparate worlds. Examine his ambivalence toward each. What does his leaving the island symbolize?
5. Discuss the significance of such repeated motifs as death, decay, and distance. What does the image of the sea imply? What is the association of these motifs and images with the narrator's conscience?
6. Analyze Austin Clarke's treatment of time, place, and characters in structuring the narrative.

Earl Lovelace
(b. 1935)
Trinidad

Earl W. Lovelace, who was born in the village of Toco in Trinidad, was raised on the island of Tobago. He attended high school in Port-of-Spain in Trinidad, and then worked as a proofreader for the Trinidad Publishing Company. In the late 1960s he studied at Howard University for a year; and in the early 1970s he entered a writing program at Johns Hopkins University, only to find himself teaching the course when the professor left. Over the years, he has worked as a forest ranger and agricultural assistant in the Trinidad Department of Forestry, as a journalist, as a teacher, and most recently as writer in residence at the University of the West Indies. The island of Trinidad remains his home, nourishing his work. It is not only in the depiction of village characters and customs or in the use of language that this inspiration is obvious. Nor is the influence apparent only in Lovelace's concern regarding urban destructiveness and its impingement upon rural wholeness. His major theme—the search for one's self, for an integrity of one's own being, and the frequently poignant frustration of that search—derives from this same source.

The Fire Eater's Journey

One

That time in Cunaripo everybody was young, and life was sitting with the fellars on the railing at Cunaripo Junction on pay-day Friday and, amid the bedlam of blaring calypsos and cinema announcements and shopping bargains hailed over loudspeakers, and Indian songs blasted from roadside snackettes, watch the thick-fleshed district girls glide with slim briskness between the stalls of the bazaar which wayside vendors made of the stretch of pavement along the shopping area on Main Street, with cots stretched out and the sides of uncovered vans let down to display the clothing and the baskets and the pottery and the cheap wares which they travelled across the island to sell in rural towns on the day when workers got their pay. Life was football (soccer), and on a Sunday evening, trotting out with the fellars from underneath the shadow of a breadfruit tree down the hill from the half-built pavilion, into the sunlight of the recreation ground, in the blue jerseys of Penetrators Football Club, when the game was against Cross Winds of Mayaro or Ebonites from Biche, with the referee going to center the ball and the fellars stretching and prancing and leaping tall, and everybody ready, the ground full, and the girls clustered like bouquets of variegated croton between the clumps of vertivier grass sprouting from the terraced hillside, with the half-Chinese gambler who everybody called Japan, coming down the hill, one hand keeping up his trousers and the other uplifting a fistful of bills, shouting, "Who against Penetrators? Who against Penetrators?" And Big John and Sylvan, two huge Mayaro fishermen, barefooted and in short pants, standing up and bringing money from their pockets and calling, "Over here! Over here is Cross Winds!" And to hear the silence at a Cross Winds raid and to hear the girls' screams tingling the blood when Berris got the ball and Penetrators swept forward in an invasion, with Kelly and Kenny and Mervyn and Phonso and Blues, and everybody calling, everybody screaming, "Berris! Berris!" as Berris moved and darted and danced and spun, and Big John's huge hoarse voice thundered, "Oh Lord, Mayaro. Hold that man!"

Life was Bazaar Day, with the Roman Catholic school hung with palm leaves and old man's beard and frilly paper and balloons, and Joey Lewis band getting ready to play, the musicians picking up their instruments with a torturous slowness, and fellars, thirsty to dance, standing around in a deceptive nonchalance, not even looking at the girls who didn't get to go nowhere except to church and school except on this one day when the church who was organizing the Bazaar said it was okay, each man alert for the split-second bang of the piano to launch himself across the room to where the girls sit stewing in the perfumed heat of long-sleeved dresses and can-cans, each man's heart beating with the hope that he would get there on time to be the first to stretch out his hand to that girl that he dying whole day to dance with, and same time hoping that the tune would be a bolero or one of those calypsos with plenty of bounce in it, with space within the music to bring her in and sway with her and hold her gentle and let her go and spin her and make her smile and look up into his face so he could ask her name and tell her his and in that way lay claim to the next dance, and, if she was game, the next. And the next time she passed on Main Street, he would disentangle himself from the conversation on the railing and go to her and if it was all right, if she would smile, he would walk a little way with her, talking to her, the both of them bursting with fright and delight, the two of them too shy to look at the other's face, and in that kind of a magical way she would be his girl.

That was the life. The future? The future was a secret that none of the fellars talked about. When police constables were being recruited, those of them who met the height requirement would make the annual pilgrimage to the recruitment center to see if they would pass the physical and qualify to do the written test. In the evening, still wearing their best clothes, they would return to the railing and talk about the words they had misspelled and the meanings they had missed. I was their authority. Blues stood aside and listened. He wasn't in that because, for all his bulging chest and military bearing, even if he could have mastered the general knowledge and spelling, he was too short for the Police Force to accept him.

Like most of the fellars, Blues had not gone beyond primary school, had learned no trade; though, if you asked him what trade he knew, he would tell you he was a painter. A couple of years earlier, Oliver, a small contractor, had a job to paint some government buildings in the district, and, wanting to do it as cheaply as possible, had taken Blues on. It was his longest period of employment. He called himself a painter after that. And though there was little work in that area, it was a nice thing to say, it sort of located him. For employment, he would get a fortnight's work with the County Council on the road gang, around Christmas or just before Carnival, and once or twice I passed on my motorcycle and saw him waving a branch of green bush, directing traffic away from the area of road his gang was patching. In general, though, he picked up a few days with Berisford, mixing cement and sand to make a concrete foundation, or he would go and work for that scamp, Oliver, and have to run all over the place behind him to get the little money he was promised as pay, or he would go out with Poser, who doubled as a truck loader and cinema checker for the owners of Empress cinema, to give out handbills and stick up posters for the coming attractions.

But whatever the task, he would come back in time to play football or to sit with the fellars on the railing at the Junction with his bulging chest, square jaw and uncertain grin that gave to his rough sculptured face a look of undeserved wisdom.

Once, in a moment of idleness, he had followed Poser and slicked his hair, replacing the soft woolly fluff of it with a greasy messy mop that made him look a little like one of the Katzenjammer Kids, only black. He had used too much dye in the hair preparation and this had caused his hair to begin turning red. Later, with the same rashness, he had shaved off all his hair. He began to wear shirts with the sleeves torn off at the shoulders. With his bulging chest, he looked like a strong-man. It made us laugh. When his hair began to grow back, he started to groom it carefully, and now, he came among us there on the railing, with an almost comical neatness. His long-sleeved shirt was tucked into his trousers and his trousers were pulled up as far above his navel as the length of its crotch would allow, the waist coming to rest way up the rib-cage of his chest; and that chest, whose magnificence impressed even him, was thrown out as he swaggered with a splendid and grotesque elegance that made a boulevard of the ordinary Main Street of Cunaripo. His wasn't the strong tough walk of a desperado of the movies: not the toughness of a Bogart nor the brash brawling imperious ease of a John Wayne, but something more genteel, each step stiff, measured, strong, weighty as a weightlifter's but not as slow, purposeful yet unhurried, the way he would imagine it performed by someone more respectable.

Whenever someone gave him a cigarette, he smoked it with a studied, severe frown, holding it stiffly between index and middle fingers, placing it carefully between lips he had fixed to receive it, drawing in smoke in long, smooth pulls, blowing smoke out in great big puffs, shyly uplifting his eyelids that in inhaling he had closed down, as if he wanted to see who among us was attentive to his performance.

Fellars laughed at his antics; but I saw in them something more subversive.

"Give him a chance, Santo," Phonso said to me. "Don't condemn him just so. Listen to him. He have good ideas."

I couldn't believe that Phonso could be so taken in by Blues. I had listened hard to Blues. He spoke with a lot of superior smiling, in a self-important, put-on tone, his words barely intelligible, his talk weighed down with words he could not pronounce and phrases he did not understand. I could see that he was simply repeating what he had heard from sources he thought to be authoritative in order that the fellars would think him learned. The nonsense he was parroting wasn't even his own. His earlier performances had amused me; but he was over-doing it now. It vexed me that he should think it necessary to go through this kind of mimicry in order to impress fellars who would have accepted him anyway.

One night, I went to the Muslim school to see an acrobatic show put on by Boy Boy and Toy, two self-taught acrobats from Cunaripo. They had billed it as "The Greatest Show on Earth." They did some tumbles and flips, and the big event of the night was the high wire act in which Toy, balancing himself with a long pole, and with Boy shadowing him on the floor below to catch him if he should fall, walked across a length of wire stretched across the ceiling of the school. To give variety, they had three limbo dancers and a contortionist who hopped around on his hands, with his feet twined around his neck and shoulders. There was one other performer. He did two acts. His first was eating fire. He poured some gasoline into his mouth, put a lighted match to it and blew out a stream of flame. For his second act he came on stage wearing only bathing trunks and carrying a huge rice bag filled with broken bottles. The drums began to play as he emptied the contents of the bag onto the stage and smashed the bottle into smaller bits. The tempo of the drums quickened, and when the drumming reached a crescendo, he dashed himself onto the bed of broken bottle. As the drums continued their frenzied beat, he pranced and swam and rolled upon that bed of broken bottle. When the drums ceased, he stepped out without a scratch on his body. This last performer, the Fire Eater and Bottle Dancer, was, I could not believe it, Blues.

I was almost respectful when next I saw him, "Man, I didn't know you could do such things," I said. I was really stunned.

"You liked the show?" He was grinning from ear to ear, delighted that he had managed finally to impress me.

"Really, I didn't know that you were so . . . good."

He brushed aside my attempts at praise with an easy magnanimity, "Toy great, eh?" he said, glowing. "One of the best in the nation. And everything he learn, he learn right here. Right now we have to put on a little more polish, do a few more show, then we going on a tour. Toy working on it. Port-of-Spain first, then England."

"Great," I said. And, yes, the show was okay. It was all right. It was pretty good, especially for a remote town like Cunaripo. Port-of-Spain might find it interesting; but, England? I wasn't so sure about England. But now I understood Blues better. I felt relieved. I knew where he was coming from. And when he came on the railings with his antics now, I found myself smiling. We even became sorta friends.

Over the next two years, my last in Cunaripo, they held more shows and I went to all of them. They brought in a fellow who could husk a dry coconut with his teeth. They brought in Baboolal, the magician, who brought a lot of laughter, making people lay green eggs and pee coca-cola. They brought back the contortionist, Rubber Man. After each show, Blues would tell me confidentially, "We going on tour next month. Getting the contract fixed up. Port-of-Spain first, then England." I listened to him. What could I say?

One day he said to me, "Boy, these local people is hell. They want the show in England, but down here it have so much red tape tying up everything."

"Yeah," I said.

Not long after that, I left Cunaripo to go to work in Port-of-Spain. The red tape tying up Blues's tour had not been unravelled. I left Blues there.

Two

I am in Port-of-Spain now. I am going along Independence Square one day when there, coming toward me, through the crowd, not swept along by its bustle, but at his own independent gait, with the purposeful, self-admiring walk whose elegance had seemed so extravagant in Cunaripo, was Blues. His long sleeves were buttoned at the wrist. He held a folded newspaper in one hand and a cigarette stiffly between the fingers of the other. Our eyes met. Immediately my steps quickened. He too seemed to jump at sight of me; but only for a moment. As if he decided that to hurry would undermine the picture of sophistication he was projecting, he restrained himself and, taking a long pull on his cigarette, he strolled toward me.

I felt humbled, rebuked, elated. It all flashed home to me. Blues had not been trying to impress us at all. Blues had been practicing for this, preparing for the city. His grand gestures that had so chagrined me were not for Cunaripo; they were for Port-of-Spain.

He was standing before me now, with a restrained smile that gave an almost forgiving look to his face, holding himself as if on display, with the knowledge that he had turned the tables on me.

"Blues!" I stood paralyzed, in a kind of awe before him, and it was he who stretched out a hand for me to shake.

"So what you doing in the city, Santo?" he said, talking with that stilted affectation of superiority. "I hear you leave Forestry. You in journalism or something? Writing a lot of stories. I see your name in the papers. That's good. You was always a man with ambition. Always had brains. That's why I used to stick close to you. You was the only man in Cunaripo could understand what I say."

Even with his affectation, I had to admire Blues. I smiled, "Yes. I'm at *The Standard*. And you?"

"I'm down here with The Show, with Boy Boy and Toy." He was speaking a bit haltingly, the better to maintain control of the new rhythm of English he was attempting. "Playing at Paloma night club. They have us book down there. You don't see it in the papers? We have acrobats, calypsonians—Lord Christo, composer. Blakie does come in sometimes. Dancers: Madame Temptation, Rosetta Seduction. Strip tease, you know. It's a great show. The tour . . ." Almost as if he had read my mind, ". . . the tour frustrating everybody. The people in England want the show; but it have all this red tape to go through down here. Papers to fix, arrangements to make. Boy, when I tell you these local people slow." He had added an impressive raising of his eyebrows to his repertoire of gestures.

I didn't know how to begin to talk to him. I felt myself a traitor. I couldn't understand it. How could I not have seen that Blues had ambition beyond Cunaripo? It was hard to accept; but I had to accept it: I didn't know Blues at all. I had totally underestimated Blues.

He was still displaying himself. "Let's go and have a beer," he said. "Inn and Out," announcing the name of the place with a sense of familiarity that was supposed to impress me. "It's up Frederick Street."

Blues had been in Port-of-Spain a few months already; but, as we moved up the street, I could sense from him a genuine delight at being at last part of the people, part of the center of things, there among the shoppers and the newspaper hawkers and coconut vendors standing with feet apart like ancient charioteers hacking off the tops of green coconuts on coconut carts. With his chest thrust out, he strolled with an overpowering grandeur as if he were an honored guest at a festival with dancing, turning his head self-consciously now and again to see who was admiring him. Now and again he stopped to look in on a display window at the banlon jerseys and tweed jackets displayed on the torso of mannequins with pink faces and brown hair and his eyes would light up with delighted amazement as he saw reflected there the man in long sleeves with folded newspaper, carrying so effortlessly that magnificent chest. God, he was beautiful. God, he was strong. And he would turn with an exaggerated elegance and bow to the beautiful women that went by and turn with his still shining eyes to see if I had seen. A few of the women smiled. But it was sadder than it should have been to see the women he was saluting or that he had intended to charm hurry away with alarm, their eyes looking for a place to flee from a man they must have thought crazy. Even before we reached Inn and Out, I had the feeling that the city, after all, without a knowledge of Blues, might take his exuberance in the wrong spirit and might not be giving him the welcome his sincerity and delight merited. His glances at me asked for approval or comment. I didn't know how to tell him what I had seen.

"And how is Cunaripo?" I asked when we were seated.

"You should be telling me. Is nearly three months I down here. Time," he said, looking at his watch, a new acquisition. "Can't find the time to go up since I down here."

"They should be deep in the football season now," I said.

"The fellars going to miss you in the middle."

"They have Porrie," I said.

"Porrie?" He smiled disdainfully. "Dribble too much. No speed. Skylark too much. Speed and toughness, that is what you had. When a player see you coming, he know he had to play the ball or clear out the way. Cross Winds going to give us a good tussle this year."

"We still have Berris and Mervyn. Mosta the other fellars still there."

"Berris should be playing football down here in the city," he said. "I go to the Savannah and watch football there, I see fellars who they call stars playing there. Berris will run rings round them. Berris should be playing real football down here in the big league. But, you know," he said, almost sadly, "Berris will never leave Cunaripo. He stays up there. He feel the place so big.

And how he will leave? How the world will see him? You lucky, you have education. You travel." He grinned, "I watch you, you know. Yes. I watch you."

We sat in Inn and Out and talked about Berris and the fellars and football and Cunaripo and we drank beers and we talked about the Bazaar. Blues's gestures, his way of speaking, all had the quality of performance with which he had first greeted me. It amused me in the beginning. I took it to be a skill he was displaying, a sort of private demonstration of how accomplished he had become, how at ease he was in the new milieu of the city, and I had waited for him to revert to a more natural tone and manner with me. But, as we went on, it occurred to me that what he was revealing was the new persona which he had settled on for his stay in the city. I accepted his ambition. I accepted that he had a life that had to be acknowledged by me, by the whole world; but I believed that he needed to discard that grotesque performance and seek himself.

"You must come up and see the show," he said, when we were getting ready to leave. "Every night we on. Maybe you could even do a story on me. We have people marvelling at the club." With a smile, he added, "I doing a new number."

"Calypso?" I had my own smile.

Just before I left Cunaripo, Phonso had gotten the fellars together and organized a Calypso Tent in the community center on weekends. "Make the place bright for Carnival," Phonso had said, "Can't leave the place dead so." That was Phonso: always trying to get something organized, sports, dance, concert, play. He managed to talk a lot of the fellars into singing calypso. A couple of Sundays, he took the show to outlying districts. Starved for entertainment, the villagers lapped it up. They treated the fellars royally, like real stars. Blues was one of the hits of the show.

I saw him on the stage of the community center in Cunaripo one night in the role of calypsonian. He went on stage without a clear tune or thorough lyrics, just a theme, just a chorus: *Chong chiki chong chong.* It was a song about a Chinese man. How Blues did it, I don't know. He kept up with the musicians best way he could, or rather the musicians kept up with him, and he improvised every nonsense that came into his head, coming back to the chorus line: *Chong chiki chong chong kee chong.* He had everybody rolling.

"Not calypso. No," he said, chuckling, remembering too. "That is for Cunaripo. No. I breaking iron on my chest."

I looked at his chest bulging out strong, "Breaking iron on your chest?"

Seeing me so attentive, he smiled again, "The Iron Man, that is what they call me." In his eyes was a mischievous glee, "Santo, I not suppose to tell anybody, but I will tell you. What they do is heat the iron at a point, break it and rejoin it with solder." He made a circle with his fingers by way of demonstration. "When I go on stage and put the iron on my chest and start to strain and put force on it, it is pure acting. A child could break it." He grinned again. "The whole thing is one big act." To him it was a great joke.

"Look," he said, "Lemme show you something."

He took a wallet from his pocket and from it removed a photograph of himself in leopard skin tights, those with the one strap across the shoulder. His face in the picture was contorted and he was sweating and straining to break a bar of iron across his chest.

"That is me, the Iron Man. Heh heh heh! You can't see it in the photo, but, there," he pointed to a spot. "You see where the iron is breaking? No, you can't see the difference. Some color all over."

For a moment I was astonished that something like this could be happening. I was even more surprised that Blues should reveal this information to me. After all, it was secret. Why did he tell it to me?

Almost immediately, I realised that Blues was giving me another bit of information. It was this: that he had found Port-of-Spain out. The city was a lie, a sham, a con. It was appearance. It was in no way superior to him.

"You know what they want me to do?" He smiled as a man superior to everybody. He was taking another photograph from his wallet.

"Look at this one. This is Marcia. Dancer. Lovely woman, eh?"

Marcia was a shapely, big-boned creature with her long limbs growing immodestly out of the shiniest and flimsiest costume. She had big, big eyes of the most amazing softness.

"Yours?" I asked, when I could tug my eyes away from her figure.

"No no no!" he cried. But he was smiling with sufficient ambivalence to leave me in doubt. "No. She is the queen of the band."

"Which band?"

"That's what I'm telling you about. Paloma night club is bringing out a Carnival band. *The Rise of the Monguls.* They want me to play the king, Attila the Hun."

"The king? You?"

He was smiling. "All the girls from the club will be there. Dancers, tourists, everybody. Why don't you come and play with us? Everybody does have a real good time. Woman like peas."

"Play with you? These things cost money," I said. "Plenty money. I hope you know what you getting yourself in."

My voice must have been a little stern. I saw a shadow of hurt cross his sculptured face, and for a moment I could feel him struggling to compose himself.

"What happen, Santo? You think I can't handle myself in this town?" A note of reproach had leaked into his voice. "Anyhow, you always take me for a joker."

"Blues . . ." I began.

"Yes?" Now it was he who was stern. "Yes. You always take me for a joker."

"Is just . . . Is just that with me . . . With rent to pay and all my expenses, with my salary, I can't afford to play mas'."

"I have to play. They depending on me."

"But, can you afford it, Blues?"

"But that is the whole point, Santo. A man don't play a masquerade he can afford. Anyhow, they depending on me."

"Let me hear that again."

We were both smiling now.

"If I could afford a mas', then I don't have to play it. You don't see, Santo. I have to show them."

"Show who?"

"All those people in the club. They look up to me you know. I can't back out now."

"You right," I said, "you know the situation." I wasn't smiling now. "Anyhow, watch yourself. Don't make them stick you with the most expensive costume."

He patted me on the shoulder. In his eyes was a mischievous twinkle, "Santo, I know how to live. Don't frighten."

I wasn't convinced that Blues was in command of the situation. I had known many masquerade players who spent their life in debt. I had a feeling that he would find himself out of his depth in that band; but, I had already misjudged him. To lay too great a caution upon him now was to suggest that he didn't know what he was doing. I felt that I had said enough.

Against my protests that we at least split the bill, he paid it all, and we came out into the sunlight of Frederick Street.

"So where can I find you?" I asked. "What's your address?" For a moment he hesitated.

"Don't forget to come up to Paloma night club," he said. "Any night. Just ask at the door for me. And come alone," he added. "It have plenty nice woman up there. Heh heh heh."

We parted there in front of Inn and Out. As I watched him straighten himself and step off with his contrived gentility, I wished there was some more substantial way in which I could help. I hoped that he would be able to pay the price of the masquerade that he couldn't afford but was convinced that he had to play. I wanted to say something to him, but somehow I didn't feel I had the right. Maybe he really knew how to live.

❋ Discussion and Writing

1. What is the significance of the opening scene of life in Cunaripo? Comment on Santo's attitude to the life in the town.
2. Analyze Blues's character: what seems to motivate his behavior; in what different ways is Blues a fire eater?
3. Describe how Santo and Blues view each other. What is implied by Santo's changing reactions to Blues's demeanor?
4. What is the importance of the two secrets Blues shares with Santo?
5. What is the significance of the metaphor of the journey in the title? Explain the meaning of the last sentence.

Mario Vargas Llosa
(b. 1936)
Peru

Mario Vargas Llosa was born in Arequipa, Peru, but after his parents separated, he and his mother lived with his grandfather, a diplomat, in Cochabamba, Bolivia. When he was eight, they returned to Peru, to the northern desert city of Piura, for a year, and then with his parents' reconciliation, he moved to Lima. After attending a Catholic secondary school, he was sent to the government's Leoncio Prado military academy because his father was not happy about his literary inclinations. While still a student at the University of San Marcos in Lima, studying law and literature in opposition to his family's desire that he attend Catholic University, he married, and in order to earn money he took on many jobs, among them writing radio news broadcasts. He was also reading voraciously and writing short stories, one of which won him the prize of a two-week trip to Paris. This visit, his early marriage and radio work, his avid reading, the military school, his year in Piura (but not the happy first eight years with his grandfather), all became material for his fiction. Awarded a prize for his first novel, *The Time of the Hero* (1963), he also gained notoriety when a group of officers publicly burned it; the book attacked the military academy at which he had been a boarder.

Vargas Llosa's reputation grew when *The Green House* (1966) won the prestigious Romulo Gallegos Award. This novel plays with narrative technique even as it tells a straightforward tale, and it epitomizes his dominant subject: corruption and morality. In fact, the Green House is the name of the symbolic madhouse of Machado de Asis's famous novella "The Psychiatrist" (1881), an allusion that heightens the irony of the novel. "A Shadow of Gnats" is the self-contained first chapter of *The Green House.*

A Shadow of Gnats*

The Sergeant takes a look at Sister Patrocinio and the botfly is still there. The launch is pitching on the muddy waters, between two walls of trees that give off a burning, sticky mist. Huddled under the canopy, stripped to the waist, the soldiers are asleep, with the greenish, yellowish noonday sun above: Shorty's head is lying on Fats's stomach, Blondy is breathing in short bursts, Blacky has his mouth open and is grunting. A thin shadow of gnats is escorting the launch, and butterflies, wasps, horseflies take shape among the

---

*Translated by Gregory Rabassa

bodies. The motor is snoring evenly, it chokes, it snores, and Nieves the pilot is holding the rudder in his left hand as he uses his right to smoke with, and his face, deeply tanned, is unchanging under his straw hat. These savages weren't normal, why didn't they sweat like other people? Sitting stiffly in the stern, Sister Angelica has her eyes closed, there are at least a thousand wrinkles on her face, sometimes she sticks out the tip of her tongue, licks the sweat from her upper lip, and spits. Poor old woman, she wasn't up to these chores. The botfly moves its blue little wings, softly pushes off from Sister Patrocinio's flushed forehead, is lost as it circles off into the white light and the pilot goes to turn off the motor, they were getting there, Sergeant, Chicais was beyond that gorge. But he was telling the good Sergeant that there wouldn't be anybody there. The sound of the engine stops, the nuns and the soldiers open their eyes, raise their heads, look around. Standing up, Nieves the pilot moves the rudder pole from left to right, the launch silently approaches the shore, the soldiers get up, put on their shirts, their caps, fasten their leggings. The vegetable palisade on the right bank suddenly opens up beyond the bend in the river and there is a rise, a brief parenthesis of reddish earth that descends to a tiny inlet of mud, pebbles, reeds, and ferns. There is no canoe on the bank, no human figure on the top of the rise. The boat runs aground. Nieves and the soldiers jump out, slosh in the lead-colored mud. A cemetery, a person's feelings could always tell, the Mangaches, were right. The Sergeant leans over the prow, the pilot and the soldiers drag the launch up onto dry land. They should help the sisters, make a hand chair for them so they wouldn't get wet. Sister Angelica is very serious as she sits on the arms of Blacky and Fats, Sister Patrocinio hesitates as Shorty and Blondy put their hands together to receive her and, as she lets herself down, she turns red as a shrimp. The soldiers stagger across the shore and put the nuns down where the mud ends. The Sergeant jumps out, reaches the foot of the hill, and Sister Angelica is already climbing resolutely up the slope, followed by Sister Patrocinio, both are using their hands, they disappear among clouds of red dust. The soil on the hill is soft, it gives way with every step, the Sergeant and the soldiers go forward, sinking to their knees, hunched over, smothered in the dust, Fats is sneezing and spitting and holds his handkerchief over his mouth. At the top, they all brush off their uniforms and the Sergeant looks around: a circular clearing, a handful of huts with conical roofs, small plots of cassava and bananas, and thick under-growth all around. Among the huts, small trees with oval-shaped pockets hanging from the branches: paucar nests. He had told her, Sister Angelica, here was the proof, not a soul, now they could see for themselves. But Sister Angelica is walking around, she goes into a hut, comes out and sticks her head into the next one, shoos away the flies by clapping her hands, does not stop for a second, and in that way, seen from a distance, hazy in the dust, she is not an old woman but a walking habit, erect, an energetic shadow. Sister Patrocinio, on the other hand, does not move, her hands are hidden in her habit, and her eyes run back and forth over the empty village. A few branches shake and shrieks are heard, a squadron of green wings, black beaks, and blue breasts flies noisily over the deserted huts of Chicais, the soldiers and the nuns follow them with their eyes until the jungle swallows them up, the shrieking lasts for a moment. There were parrots around, good to know if they needed food. But they gave you diarrhea, Sister, I meant, they loosened up a person's stomach. A straw hat appears at the top of the hill, the tanned face of Nieves the pilot: that was why the Aguarunas were afraid, Sisters. They were so stubborn, you couldn't tell them not to pay any attention to him. Sister Angelica approaches, looks here and there with her little wrinkled eyes, and she shakes her gnarled, stiff hands with dark brown spots in the Sergeant's face: they were nearby, they hadn't taken away their things, they had to wait for them to come back. The soldiers look at each other, the Sergeant lights a cigarette, two paucars are coming and going through the air, their black and gold feathers giving off damp flashes. Birds too, there was everything in Chicais. Everything except Aguarunas and Fats laughs. Why wouldn't they attack unexpectedly? Sister Angelica is panting, maybe you didn't know them. Sister, the cluster of white hairs on her chin trembles slightly, they were afraid of people and they hid, they wouldn't think of coming back, while they were there they wouldn't even see their dust. Small, pudgy, Sister Patrocinio is there too, between Blondy and Blacky. But they hadn't hidden last year, they had come out to meet them and they had even given them a fresh gamitana,[1] didn't the Sergeant remember? But they hadn't known then, Sister Patrocinio, now they did. The soldiers and Nieves the pilot sit down on the ground, take off their shoes, Blacky opens his canteen, drinks and sighs. Sister Angelica raises her head: they should put up the tents. Sergeant, a withered face, he should have them put up the mosquito nettings, a liquid look, they would wait for them to come back, a cracked voice, and you shouldn't make that face, she had experience. The Sergeant throws away his cigarette, grinds it out, what difference did it make, you guys, you should move it. And just then there is a cackling and the bushes spit out a hen, Blondy and Shorty shout with glee, a black one, they chase it, with white spots, catch it, and Sister Angelica's eyes flash, bandits, what were they doing, she waves her fist in the air, did it belong to them?, they should let it go, and the Sergeant should tell them to let it go, but, Sisters, they were going to need food, they didn't feel like going hungry. Sister Angelica would not stand for any abuses, what kind of confidence would they have if we stole their animals? And Sister Patrocinio agrees, Sergeant, stealing it would be an offense against God, with her round and healthy face, didn't he know the commandments? The hen touches the ground, clucks, picks a flea from under her wing, waddles off, and the Sergeant shrugs his shoulders: why were they fooling themselves since they

---

[1] A kind of fish in the rivers of the jungle. [eds]

knew them as well or even better than he did. The soldiers go off toward the slope, the parrots and paucars are screeching in the trees again, there is a buzzing of insects, a light breeze shakes the yarina leaves that form the roofs of Chicais. The Sergeant loosens his leggings, mutters between his teeth, twists his mouth, and Nieves the pilot slaps him on the back, Sergeant: you shouldn't get upset, you should take things easy. And the Sergeant furtively points at the nuns, Don Adrian, little jobs like this were too much. Sister Angelica was very thirsty and probably a little feverish, her spirit was still eager, but her body was already getting weak. Sister Patrocinio and she did not, no, you shouldn't say that, Sister Angelica, as soon as the soldiers came back she would take a lemonade and she would feel better, you'd see. Were they whispering about him?, the Sergeant looks about with distant eyes, did they think he was a man or not?, he was fanning himself with his cap, that pair of buzzards!, and suddenly he turns toward Nieves the pilot; keeping secrets together was bad manners and anyone who saw them, Sergeant, the soldiers come back on the run. A canoe?, and Blacky yes, with Aguarunas?, and Blondy, yes Sergeant, and Shorty yes, and Fats and the nuns yes, yes, they come and ask questions and go off in all directions and the Sergeant has Blondy go back to the top of the hill and tell him if they are coming up, the others should hide and Nieves the pilot picks the leggings up off the ground and the rifles. The soldiers and the Sergeant go into a hut, the nuns are still in the open, Sisters, you should hide. Sister Patrocinio, quick, Sister Angelica. They look at each other, they whisper, they go into the hut opposite and, from the bushes where he is hiding, Blondy points at the river, they were getting out now, Sergeant, and he didn't know what he should do, you should come and hide, Blondy, you shouldn't fall asleep. Stretched out on their bellies, Fats and Shorty are spying out from behind the cross-hatching of the wall made out of tucuma strips; Blacky and Nieves are standing back in the hut and Blondy comes running, squats down beside the Sergeant. There they were, Sister Angelica, there they were now and Sister Angelica may have been old but she had good eyes, Sister Patrocinio, she could see them, there were six of them. The old woman, with long hair, is wearing a whitish loincloth and two tubes of soft dark flesh hang down to her waist. Behind her two men of indeterminate age, short, big-bellied, with skeletal legs, their sexes covered with pieces of ochre-colored cloth tied with thongs, their buttocks naked, their hair cut in bangs around their heads. They are carrying bunches of bananas. After them come two girls with straw head-bands, one has a ring in her nose, the other leather hoops on her ankles. They are naked, just as is the little boy who follows them, he looks younger and he is thinner. They look at the deserted clearing, the woman opens her mouth, the men shake their heads. Were they going to talk to them, Sister Angelica? and the Sergeant yes, there went the sisters, you should be on your toes, boys. The six heads turn at the same time, they remain fixed. The nuns advance toward the group with a steady pace, smiling, and, at the same time, almost imperceptibly, the Aguarunas draw together, soon form one earthen and compact group. The six pairs of eyes do not leave the two figures in dark folds that float toward them and if they resisted we would have to come out running, boys, no shooting, no scaring them. They were letting them approach, Sergeant, Blondy thought they would run away when they saw them. And the girls were nice and tender, young ones, right Sergeant?, there was no holding that Fats. The nuns stop and, at the same time, the girls draw back, they stretch out their hands, they clutch the legs of the old woman who begins to pat them on the shoulders, each pat makes her long breasts shake, makes them swing back and forth: might the Lord be with them. And Sister Angelica grunts, spits, pours out a flow of scratchy, rough, and sibilant sounds, interrupts herself to spit, and ostentatiously, martially, goes on grunting, her hands move about, they trace figures solemnly in the air before the motionless, pale, impassive Aguaruna faces. She was talking to them in pagan, boys, and the little old sister was spitting just like the redskins. They must have liked that, Sergeant, having a white woman talking their language, but not so much noise, boys, if they heard you they'd get scared. Sister Angelica's grunts reach the hut very clear, robust, out of tune, and now Blacky and the pilot too are spying on the clearing with their faces against the wall. She had them in her pocket, boys, the little old sister was smart, and the nuns and the two Aguarunas smile at each other, exchange bows. And she had a good education, did the Sergeant know that at the Mission they made them study all the time? They were most likely praying, Shorty, for the sins of the world. Sister Patrocinio smiles at the old woman, the woman turns her eyes away and is still serious, her hands on the girl's shoulders. I was wondering what they were saying, Sergeant, what they were talking about. Sister Angelica and the two men make faces, gesture, spit, interrupt each other and, suddenly, the three children leave the old woman, run about, laugh loudly. The kid was looking at them, boys, he wasn't taking his eyes off here. Look how skinny he was, did the Sergeant notice?, a great big round head and a skinny little body, he looked like a spider. From under his mat of hair, the boy's large eyes are staring at the hut. He is as dark as an ant, his legs are curved and sickly. He suddenly raises his hand, shouts, the little bastard, Sergeant and there is a violent agitation behind the wall, oaths, bumping into each other, and guttural shouts break out in the clearing as the soldiers invade it running and tripping. You should lower those rifles, you dunces, Sister Angelica shows the soldiers her angry hands, oh, the Lieutenant would hear about this. The two girls bury their heads on the old woman's chest, they flatten out her soft breasts, and the little boy is out of orbit, halfway between the soldiers and the nuns. One of the Aguarunas drops his bunch of bananas, the hen is cackling off somewhere. Nieves the pilot is standing in the doorway of the hut, his straw hat thrown back, a cigarette between his teeth. What did the Sergeant think he was doing, and Sister Angelica takes a little leap, why had you interfered if you hadn't been called? But if they lowered the rifles you wouldn't see them for their dust, Sister, she shows him her freckled fist and he, you should put down your Mausers, boys. Gently, she continues. Sister Angelica talks to the Aguarunas, her stiff hands sketch slow figures, persuasively, little by little the men lose their stiffness, now they answer with monosyllables and she, smiling, inexorable, keeps on grunting. The boy goes over to the soldiers, smells the rifles, touches them. Fats gives him a pat on the forehead, he crouches down and shrieks, he didn't trust him, the bastard, and the laugh shakes Fats's flabby waist, his jowls, his jawbones. Sister Patrocinio blushes, embarrassed, what was he saying, why was he disrespectful like that, the boor and Fats a thousand pardons, he shakes his confused ox head, it came out without his realizing it, Sister, he is tongue-tied. The girls and the little boy circulate among the soldiers, they examine them, touch them with their fingertips. Sister Angelica and the two men are grunting in a friendly way and the sun is still shining in the distance, but a cloak has come over the place, another forest of white and heady clouds is piling up over the forest: it was probably going to rain. Sister Angelica had insulted them before, Sister, and what had they said. Sister Patrocinio smiles, dunce wasn't an insult, just a kind of pointed hat just right for their heads and Sister Angelica turns toward the Sergeant: they were going to eat with them, they should bring up the gifts and the lemonade. He agrees, gives instructions to Shorty and Blondy, pointing at the hill, green bananas and raw fish, a banquet fit for a mother whore. The children sit in a circle around Fats, Blacky, and Nieves the pilot, and Sister Angelica, the men, and the old woman put banana leaves on the ground, go into the huts, bring out clay pots, cassavas, light a small fire, wrap catfish and bocachicas in leaves that they tie together with reeds and put them near the flames. Were they going to wait for the rest of them, Sergeant? It would never end and Nieves the pilot throws his cigarette away, the others weren't coming back, if they had gone away it meant that they didn't want any visitors and these here would leave too at the first chance they got. Yes, the Sergeant was aware, but it was no use fighting with the sisters. Shorty and Blondy come back with the bags and the thermos bottles. The nuns, the Aguarunas, and the soldiers are sitting in a circle facing the banana leaves and the old woman is shooing away the insects by clapping her hands. Sister Angelica distributes the gifts and the Aguarunas take them without showing any signs of enthusiasm, but then, when the nuns and the soldiers begin to eat small pieces of fish that they pick off with their fingers, the two men, without looking at each other, open the bags, fondle mirrors and necklaces, divide up the colored beads and greedy lights suddenly come on in the eyes of the old woman. The girls fight over a bottle, the little boy is chewing furiously, and the Sergeant was going to get sick to his stomach, god damn it, he was going to get diarrhea, he was going to swell up like a fat-bellied hualo, toad lumps would grow on his body, they would break and give off pus. He has the piece of fish next to his lips, his small eyes blink and Blacky, Shorty, and Blondy are screwing up their faces too, Sister Patrocinio closes her eyes, swallows, makes a face and only

Nieves the pilot and Sister Angelica keep reaching toward the banana leaves and with a kind of hasty delight break up the white meat, clean out the bones, put it in their mouths. All jungle people had a little redskin in them, even the nuns, the way they ate. The Sergeant belches, everybody looks at him and he coughs. The Aguarunas have put on the necklaces, they show them to each other. The glass beads are garnet-colored and contrast with the tattoo on the chest of the one who has six beaded bracelets on one arm, three on the other. What time were they going to leave, Sister Angelica? The soldiers watch the Sergeant, the Aguarunas stop chewing. The children stretch out their hands, they timidly touch the shiny necklaces, the bracelets. They had to wait for the rest of them. Sergeant. The Aguaruna with the tattoo grunts and Sister Angelica yes, Sergeant, did you see?, you should eat, they were offended with all the faces you were making. He was not hungry, but he wanted to say something, Sister, they couldn't stay in Chicais any longer. Sister Angelica's mouth is full, the Sergeant had come to help, her small and stony hand drains the lemonade from a thermos, not to give orders. Shorty had heard the Lieutenant, what had he said?, and he too that they should come back before a week was out, Sister. Five days had already gone by and how many would it take to get back, Don Adrian?, three days as long as it didn't rain, did you see?, they were orders, Sister, so she shouldn't be angry with him. Along with the sound of the conversation between the Sergeant and Sister Angelica there is another sound, a harsher one: the Aguarunas are conversing animatedly, they hit their arms and compare their bracelets. Sister Patrocinio swallows and opens her eyes, and if the others didn't come back?, and if they took a month in coming back? of course it was only an opinion, and she closes her eyes, maybe she was wrong, and swallows. Sister Angelica wrinkles her brow, new wrinkles appear on her face, her hand strokes the tuft of white hairs on her chin. The Sergeant takes a drink from his canteen: worse than a laxative, everything got hot in this region, it wasn't the kind of heat they had where he came from, the heat here rotted every-thing. Fats and Blondy are lying on their backs with their caps over their faces, and Shorty wanted to know if anyone was sure of that, Don Adrian, and Blacky really, Don Adrian should continue and tell some more. They were half fish and half women, they lived at the bottom of the lagoons wait-ing for people who had drowned and as soon as a canoe tipped over they would come and grab the people and take them down to their palaces. They would put them in hammocks that were not made out of jute but made out of snakes and they would have fun with them there and Sister Patrocinio were they talking about superstitions now?, and they, no, no, and did they call themselves Christians?, nothing like that, Sister, they were talking about whether it was going to rain. Sister Angelica leans toward the Aguarunas, grunting softly, smiling insistently, she has her hands clasped and the men, without moving from the spot, sit up little by little, stretch out their necks like cranes sunning themselves on a river bank when a steamboat comes along, and something frightens them, dilates their pupils, and one's chest puffs up, the tattoo grows clear, is erased, grows clear and they gradually approach Sister Angelica, very attent, serious, silent, and the long-haired old woman opens her arms and clasps the girls. The little boy is still eating, boys, the rough part was coming, you should stay awake. The pilot, Shorty, and Blacky are quiet. Blondy gets up with red eyes and shakes Fats, an Aguaruna looks at the Sergeant out of the corner of his eye, then at the sky, and now the old woman is hugging the girls, pressing them against her long and drooping breasts and the eyes of the little boy go back and forth between Sister Angelica and the men, from them to the old woman, from her to the soldiers and to Sister Angelica. The Aguaruna with the tattoo begins to speak, the other one follows him, the old woman, a storm of voices drowns out the voice of Sister Angelica who says no now with her head and with her hands and suddenly, without stopping their snorting and spitting, slowly, ceremoniously, the two men take off their necklaces, their bracelets, and there is a rain of glass beads on the banana leaves. The Aguarunas reach out toward the remains of the fish, across which a narrow river of brown ants is flowing. They were already getting a little wild, boys, but they were ready, Sergeant, whenever he gave the word. The Aguarunas clean off the remains of the blue and white flesh, catch the ants in their fingernails, squash them and very carefully wrap the food in the veiny leaves. Shorty and Blondy were to take care of the kids, the Sergeant orders and Fats the lucky guys. Sister Patrocinio is very pale, she moves her lips, her fingers close tightly over the black beads of her rosary and you should remember, Sergeant, they were little girls, he knew, he knew, and Fats and Blacky would keep the naked savages quiet and the Sister should not worry and Sister Patrocinio oh if they committed any brutalities and the pilot would take care of carrying the things, boys, no brutalities: Holy Mary, Mother of God. All of them look at the bloodless lips of Sister Patrocinio, and she Pray for us, is shedding the little black balls in her fingers and Sister Angelica, you should be calm, Sister, and the Sergeant now, now was the time. They get up slowly. Fats and Blacky dust off their pants, they squat down, pick-up their rifles, and now there is running, screams and at the hour, trampling, the little boy covers his face, of our death, and the two Aguarunas stay rigid amen, their teeth chatter and their eyes look perplexedly at the rifles that are pointed at them. But the old woman is on her feet struggling with Shorty and the girls are slippery as eels in Blondy's arms. Sister Angelica covers her mouth with a handkerchief, the dust cloud grows and thickens, Fats sneezes and the Sergeant ready, they should make it to the top of the hill, boys, Sister Angelica. And someone should help Blondy, Sergeant, couldn't you see that they were getting away from him? Shorty and the old woman are rolling around together on the ground, Blacky should go help him, the Sergeant would take his place, he'd keep his eyes on the naked savage. The nuns walk toward the hill holding each other's arm, Blondy drags along two intermingled and gesticulating figures and Blacky pulls the old woman furiously by the hair until she lets go of Shorty and he gets up. But the old woman jumps on them, catches them, scratches them and the Sergeant ready, Fats, they would slip away. Still keeping aim on the two men, they retreat, heel their way back and the Aguarunas get up at the same time and advance, as if attracted by the rifles. The old woman is dancing like a monkey, she falls and clutches two pairs of legs, Shorty and Blacky stumble, Mother of God, they fall down too and Sister Patrocinio should not shout like that. A sudden breeze comes up from the river, it scales the slope and brings up active, enveloping, orange-colored and thick grains of earth that fly like botflies. The two Aguarunas docilely face the rifles and the slope is very close. If they attacked him, would Fats shoot? and Sister Angelica stupid man, he was capable of killing them. Blondy takes one girl by the arm at the top of the hill, why didn't they go down. Sergeant?, he has the other one by the neck, they were getting away from him, they were getting away from him and they are not shouting but they are pulling and their heads, shoulders, feet, and legs struggle and kick and vibrate and Nieves the pilot goes by loaded down with thermos bottles: you should hurry up, Don Adrian, had you left anything behind? No, nothing, whenever the Sergeant wanted to. Shorty and Blacky are hold-ing the old woman by the shoulders and the hair and she sits down shriek-ing, sometimes she swats them weakly on the legs and blessed was the fruit. Mother, Mother, of her womb and they were getting away from Blondy, Jesus. The man with the tattoo looks at Fats's rifle, the old woman gives a hoot and cries, two wet threads open narrow channels on the crust of dust on her face and Fats should not act crazy. But if they attacked him, Sergeant, he would open up somebody's skull, only with his rifle butt, Sergeant, and the joke would be over. Sister Angelica takes the handkerchief away from her mouth: stupid, why were you saying such evil things?, why did the Sergeant allow it?, and Blondy, would he start going down?, those wild girls were skinning him alive. The girls' hands cannot reach Blondy's face, only his neck, already full of purple scratches, and they have torn his shirt and pulled off the buttons. Sometimes they seem to lose their spirit, their bodies go limp and they moan and they attack again, their naked feet kick at Blondy's leggings, he curses and shakes them, they follow along mutely and the Sister should go down, what was she waiting for, and Blondy too and Sister Angelica why was he holding them like that, they were only children, of her womb Jesus, Mother, Mother. If Shorty and Blacky let the old woman go, she would pounce on them, Sergeant, what were they going to do?, and Blondy she would grab them, you should see, Sister, couldn't she see how they were scratching him? The Sergeant shakes his rifle, the Aguarunas balk, take a step backward, and Shorty and Blacky let go of the old woman, they keep their hands ready to defend themselves, but she does not move, she only rubs her eyes and there is the little boy looking as if he were isolated by the whirlwinds: she squats down and buries her face between her flowing breasts. Shorty and Blacky are going downhill, a rose-colored wall of dust soon swallows them up and how in hell was Blondy going to carry them down all by himself, what was the matter with them, Sergeant, why were those guys leaving and Sister Angelica approaches him swinging her arms resolutely: she would help him. She stretches out her hands toward the girl on the slope but she does not touch her and she doubles over and the small fist hits out again and sinks into the habit and Sister Angelica gives a little cry and withdraws: what did he tell her, Blondy shakes the girl like a rag, Sister, wasn't she an animal? Pale and wrinkled, Sister Angelica tries again, she catches the arm with her two hands, Holy Mary, and now they howl, Mother of God, kick, Holy Mary, they scratch, they are all coughing, Mother of God and instead of so much praying they should have been going down, Sister Patrocinio, why in the world was she so frightened and how long, and how long, they should go down because the Sergeant was already getting hot, damn it. Sister Patrocinio spins, jumps down the slope, and disappears, Fats advances his rifle and the one with the tattoo draws back. The hate there was in his look, Sergeant, he looked angry, son of a whore, and proud: that was what the eyes of the chullachaqui devil must have been like, Sergeant. The heavy clouds that enveloped those descending are farther away, the old woman is crying, twisting around, and the two Aguarunas are watching the barrels, the butts, the round muzzles of the two rifles: Fats shouldn't get so excited. He wasn't getting excited, Sergeant, but what kind of a way was that to look at a person, damn it, what right did he have? Blondy, Sister Angelica, and the girls also disappear into the waves of dust and the old woman has crawled to the edge of the hill, she looks down toward the river, her nipples touch the ground and the little boy is making strange shouts, he howls like a mournful bird and Fats did not like to have them so close to the savages. Sergeant, how would they get down now that they were all alone. And then the motor on the launch snorts: the old woman grows silent and looks up, looks at the sky, the little boy follows her, the two Aguarunas do the same and the bastards were looking for a plane. Fats, they weren't watching, now was the time. They draw back their rifles and suddenly thrust them forward, the two men jump back and make signs and now the Sergeant and Fats go down backward, still aiming, sinking up to their knees and the sound of the hoarse motor is growing stronger and stronger, it pollutes the air with hiccups, gargling, vibrations, and shaking, and it is different on the slope from up on the clearing, there is no breeze, only a hot vapor and reddish and biting dust that makes one sneeze. Dimly, there on top of the hill, hairy heads are exploring the sky, they move softly back and forth, searching among the clouds, and the motor was going and the kids were crying, Fats, what about him?, Sergeant, he couldn't make it. They cross the mud on the run and when they reach the launch they are panting and their tongues are hanging out. It was time now, why had they taken so long? How did they think Fats was going to get on board, they had all got so comfortable, the devils, they should make room for him. But he had to lose some weight, they should just look at him, Fats was getting on board and the boat was sinking down and it was no time for jokes, they should get under way at once, Sergeant. They were leaving right away, Sister Angelica, Sister Angelica, of our death amen.

❋ Discussion and Writing

1. Note the naming of the various characters: What is the significance of the names; what is the impact of not having a name or having a vocation or traits as names?
2. Describe the setting, and examine the interaction of the characters against this background. What does Vargas Llosa accomplish by this interaction?
3. Comment on the description of the atmosphere. How is it related to the action?
4. Comment on the relationship between the Church, the state, and the Aguarunas depicted in this narrative.

❋ Research and Comparison

Examine the life and works of Mario Vargas Llosa and his involvement in his country's politics.

Interdisciplinary Discussion Question: Explore the history of the Church in Latin America and its influence on people's lives.

Maryse Conde
(b. 1937)
Guadeloupe

Maryse Boucolon Conde was born into the affluent Boucolon family in Guadeloupe. Although their first language was French rather than Creole, they took great pride in their African ancestry. Reading her way through her family's large library when she was a child, she determined to become an author who would reveal the painful aspects of life that people avoided examining, and she has held to that intention. She lived in West Africa for a good part of the 1960s—when she began publishing plays—and into the 1970s. During these years, she was actively engaged by the political and cultural questions of African heritage that were being widely discussed. However, the death of her sister's husband at the hands of Guinea's president, Sekou Toure, intensified her shift from an emphasis on racial identification to the problems of neocolonialism. In 1976, the year Conde received her Ph.D. in comparative literature from the Sorbonne, she published her first novel, *Heremakhonon*. She intended it to irritate, and it did, from her attacking ideas that had become cliche, such as *negritude* and Maoism, to her challenging Toure.

Insisting that the Caribbean experience, and thus its culture, is a unique entity, she returned to Guadeloupe. There she became active in the struggle for Guadeloupean independence, but also for the recognition of the cultural complexity and racial diversity of a Caribbean identity. In *Traversee de la mangrove* (Crossing the Mangrove, 1989), she turned to the Creole experience, as had Simone Schwarz-Bart, whom she admires; not only was Schwarz-Bart the first modern female Caribbean author, she was the first to transform the French in her writing to Creole. In similar fashion, just as a wake is one of the centers of Creole life, Conde placed a wake at the center of *Traversee de la mangrove*. In the novel, the separate episodes spin off from the wake, revealing each character.

*Mira**

One should go down to the Ravine at the close of the day, when the water is black, here tranquil, black upon the black of the void, there running, bouncing upon rocks that the eye does not perceive any more. As a child, I used to go down to the Ravine, each day, late in the afternoon, and stay there for hours. I had discovered how tasty the water feels at that time, when the blackness thickens little by little. I curled up under the leaves of the giant philodendron and I could hear their angry voices:

—Where could she be? We should keep her there!

—This child deserves a good beating. But her father does not let anyone lay a finger on her!

When the sound of voices became silent, I took off my dress and all my clothes. I slipped into the water which penetrated, scorching from the heat of the sun, to the depth of my body. I quivered under this brutal fondling. Then, I sat on the bank and dried myself in the wind.

One should go down into the Ravine at the close of the day, when the sky is round, hollow as a painted shell above our heads.

Sometimes, when I did not feel sleepy in the middle of the night, I tiptoed along the central corridor of the house. On the right, I could hear the snores of my father who was not yet remarried to Dinah, the woman from

---

Translated by Marie-Agnes Sourieau

Saint-Martin, and who had finished making love to Julia, our maid. On the left, a beam shone under the bedroom door of my brothers. One of them, Aristide, was undoubtedly reading some forbidden book. In the garden, the dogs came to me moaning and wagging their tails. They wanted to follow me. But I chased them away, because at night the Ravine belonged to me only. I hate the loud, purple sea which messes up the hair. I do not like much the rivers, their slow and cloudy waters. I only like the vivid, even violent ravines. I bathe in them. I sleep on their banks, populated with batrachians. I twist my ankles on their slippery rocks. It is my private domain, for myself alone. Ordinary people fear them, believing that they are haunted with spirits. Therefore you would never encounter anyone there. This is why, when I stumbled over his body, invisible in the darkness like a *cheval a diable*,[1] I believed that just like me, he had really come for me.

Solitude is my companion. It has cradled me and fed me. It has not left me until this very day. People talk, talk. They do not know what it is to come out burning from the already cold womb of your mother, to tell her farewell at the first moment of the world. My father wiped his red eyes. He had loved her, his Negress Rosalie, Rosalie Sorane, with her eggplant-like breast. The midwife kept telling him:

—Take heart, Monsieur Lameaulnes!

My father had no daughters. His first wife, Aurore Dugazon, who had since died from a fibroma, had given him only boys. Three boys, one after the other. Then, he took me in his arms and his warm tears ran down my face. But for me, since that time, I did not want his love. I did not want to give him mine. He was guilty.

Because, had he left her alone, Rosalie Sorane, had he let her sleep in the house of her mother who sat five times a week at the market on Hincelin street to resell tomatoes, okra and green beans, but who wanted her daughter to go studying in France and become a university graduate, she would not have died at age eighteen, emptied of all her young blood, lying with cold feet between two embroidered linen sheets.

My father swathed me in a blue cape because Rosalie Sorane had hoped for a boy and prepared all her layette of that color, and he laid me in the back of his huge American car. When we arrived at Riviere au Sel after a one-hour drive, it was in the evening. A cool wind slipped around the sides of the mountain, massive, outlined into a shadowgraph. Aurore Dugazon, pallid and sickly, was sitting on the porch. My father walked past her without a glance, as usual, and handed me over to Minerve, the maid, who had rushed out at the sound of the engine. He simply said to her:

—We shall christen her next Saturday.

The following Saturday, I was christened in the church of Petit Bourg: Almira (after my grandmother's name, my father's mother) Rosalie Sorane. Because, however on familiar terms my father may have been with all the

---

[1] Ordinary insect living in dark and humid places.

bank directors, the President of the Chamber of Commerce and the President of the Tourist Bureau, he could not transform an adulterine child into a legitimate one. In spite of that, I was never called differently than Mira Lameaulnes.

At five, I ran away for the first time. I could not understand that, for me, there was no mother anywhere in this world. I was convinced that she was hiding in the mountain, that she was protected by the giants of the dense forest, that she slept between the enormous toes of their roots. One day, looking for her since morning, I climbed up a track. I was too tired to put one foot in front of the other. Dead tired. Then I tripped on a rock and tumbled down to the bottom of a ravine, hidden under the mass of the plants. I never forgot this first encounter with the water, this flowing song, barely audible, and the smell of the decayed humus.

When they found me after a search of three days and three nights, my brother Aristide laughed at me:

—Your mother was a Negress who took men. How can you imagine that she is high up in the mountain? At this time, she must be under our feet, roasting in hell, her skin scorched like the rind of a pig.

Nevertheless, whatever he said, his nastiness did not affect me. I had found the maternal bed.

Since that day, each time that my heart is blood-soaked with the maliciousness of the people of Riviere au Sel who only know how to sharpen the knife of their slanderous gossip, I go down to the Ravine. I go down there every anniversary of the death of Rosalie Sorane which is also the anniversary of my birth and I try to imagine what life would be if she were here in the flesh to watch me grow, to welcome me on the porch when I return from school and to explain to me all the mysteries of the woman's body that I must discover by myself. Because if I had to rely on Dinah! One could think that it is through the workings of the Holy Spirit that she has had them, her three sons!

I liked Aurore Dugazon, Aristide's mother, so pallid, so pallid that we knew that she was condemned in this world. When she died, all the mirrors were covered with black and purple shawls so that she would not come to look at herself and mourn her lost youth. People said:

—Good God, she looks like a bride!

Aristide, as for him, had shut himself up in his room. It is my father who went to fetch him and threatened to beat him if he did not come to give her a last kiss before the cover of the coffin was nailed down.

I really believed that he was also going to die that day! It is because of all this that we were both prepared for Dinah, the second wife, she turned up one morning from Saint-Martin. Aristide had warned me;

—You are going to see how I am going to teach her her place!

But this has not been necessary. It is not us who trained her.

Ah, at the beginning, Dinah resembled a tuberose flower! In the morning, she used to sing in front of her window widely open to the freshness of the mountain. She had the entire house scrubbed with vetiver roots and greenery. The air was fragrant. In the evening, she told us stories.

Soon, alas, we watched her languishing, withering like the grass deprived of the morning dew. My father did not talk to her anymore. He walked past her without looking at her. At the table, he pushed away his plate after one bite. In the evening, he went out or he shut himself up in one of the garret bedrooms with some women picked up who knows where and we heard them laugh, laugh, behind the closed door. Because of this, when my gaze came to rest on him, he sniggered:

—You want to kill me, don't you?

It was true, hatred choked me, I was wondering what I could devise to hurt him. Aristide, this is why I have listened to him. Actually, I loved him only as a brother. But I believed that I could find happiness in embracing the evil, the forbidden.

Very soon, that was not enough for me anymore. Since I had been expelled from my fourth private school, I did not do anything and went to seed without joy. I had started to have a dream, always the same, night after night. I was shut up in a house with no door or window and I tried in vain to get out. Suddenly someone would knock at a wall which cracked, fell into pieces and I would find myself face to face with a stranger, sturdy like a *pie-bwa*[2] and who set me free.

I killed time during the days as well as I could. At one time Aristide had got it into his head to find work for me at the Nursery. I prepared sprays of flowers for the brides or wreaths for the dead. But when I was near them, men did nothing at all and they coveted me with their vicious eyes. So this could not last. Sometimes my father looked at me:

—I have to find you a husband! When I have time for you!

I did not even answer him.

Life started when I went down to the Ravine. An evening like the others, no more no less fireflies in the *serein*,[3] I took the familiar path I was about to come close to the water when I struck his invisible body under the philodendron leaves. He stood up and questioned:

—It's you? It's you?

With my flashlight, I outlined his face in the darkness. I recognized him immediately. Then I whispered:

—You were expecting me?

He stammered:

—Not so early!

I leaned over him:

—You think that it is too early? As for me, I have been waiting for you twenty-five years without seeing anything coming. I had lost hope.

He questioned:

---

[2]A tree.
[3]Evening.

—Twenty-five years? How come twenty-five years?

I put my hand on his shoulder. He was shaking all over and I questioned:

—What are you afraid of?

—But of you. How will you do?

I came close to him, very close and I pressed my mouth on his, dry lifeless and which did not answer me:

—Like this! . . .

After this kiss, he stared at me, his eyes filled with a mad terror which I did not understand.

—That's all?

I laughed:

—No! Let's go on if you want!

I unbuttoned his coarse fabric shirt, undid his tough leather belt. He did not breathe a word. He seemed like a child before an adult. We made love on the compost at the foot of the tree ferns. He let himself be led, not restive, but on the look-out for each of my movements, as if he believed that they were hiding lethal blows. Afterward, he remained a long time motionless, next to me, and then he said:

—My name is Francis Sancher.

I answered:

—That, I know, believe it or not.

He turned toward me:

—You are not the one I was expecting. Who are you?

I stood up and went down to the water which glittered black between the rocks, saying mockingly:

—You do not know who I am, how surprising! People of Riviere au Sel tell all kinds of stories about me.

—They avoid me like the plague. Nobody talks to me.

—Not even Maringoin?

—Maringoin?

I ran some water on my hair:

—Moise, if you prefer. It is how he is called, your friend the mailman! He has not told you about me?

He did not answer.

In the darkness, I could hear the heavy tread of the toads hunting for insects under the leaves. Suddenly, the wind fell down, chilled on my shoulders and I came out of the water to put on my clothes. He was still looking at me silently. As I walked away, he asked:

—Shall I see you again?

I retorted over my shoulder:

—You have got a liking for it, haven't you!

The people of Riviere au Sel do not like me. Women say their prayers to the Virgin Mary when they pass me. Men remember their nightly dreams when they have soaked their sheets and are ashamed. Then, they stare at me in defiance to hide their desires.

Why? No doubt I am too beautiful for their ugliness, too light for the blackness of their skins and hearts. My father, under his appearance, is afraid of me. He may pester his foremen and Haitian workers. He may rule his children of the second marriage with an iron hand, without talking about Dinah, lost ghost in front of him. He may fire the servants at the drop of a hat when he does not want them anymore or when they resist him. With me, it is a different matter. He knows that Rosalie Sorane's body is between us. Aristide is also afraid of me, to my fits of anger, of my bad "moons," as he puts it. When I arrived at Riviere au Sel, swathed in my blue cape, Aristide had just turned three. For me, he dropped his mother's hand. We have grown like two savages. We have no secrets from each other. Yet, I have never taken him to the Ravine. It belongs to me only. It is my realm, my refuge.

Aristide says that he could not live far from the mountain. Each morning, he sinks into its womb and comes back, his backpack full of yellow-footed thrushes, black woodpeckers, partridges and ringdoves that he smears with bird-lime in the ferns and encloses in bamboo cages at the far end of the Nursery. Along with the greenhouses of orchids, they are his realm, his very own. Those who say that his heart is made of stone do not know him. His heart is sensitive like a very small child's.

The day I met Francis Sancher in the Ravine, I found Aristide smoking on the porch. He grumbled:

—Where have you been hanging about this time?

I turned my back on him and headed for my room. He followed me and sat with all his weight on the rocking chair. I began to do my hair for the night. Then I questioned, being most careful of the tone of my voice, because I know his jealousy.

—What do people say about Francis Sancher?

He looked at me and his eyes burned me through:

—You are interested in him?

—Is not everybody here?

—People say that he is a Cuban. When Fidel opened the doors of the country, he left.

—Why did he come here where there is no work, nothing to do?

—This is the question!

There was a silence. Then he went on:

—Listen to me, I am going to tell you a story.

"One Sunday, at church, Ti-Mari saw a man that she did not know, all dressed in white, wearing a panama hat. Coming out of the church, she asked her godmother:

—Godmother, Godmother! You saw this handsome chap wearing a panama hat? Do you know his name?"

I shrugged my shoulders:

—Stop with your stories! You think I am a baby?

He got up and left without a word.

Night is not meant to sleep in a bed like a cart wheel sunk into the mud of a sugarcane field. It is meant to dream wide-awake. It is meant to bring back to life the poor joys of the days. I lived again the moments spent with Francis Sancher. Until now, I had never caressed but one familiar body, without mystery, as close to mine as the trunk of the gum tree is to the epiphyte philodendron. Now, I had to discover what this unknown form was hiding. As Ti-Mari, in love at first glance with her stranger wearing a panama hat, all dressed in white, I had to find out who he was.

At breakfast, my father stamped his feet like a vicious horse. He started with Joby, the oldest of the children of his second marriage, a pale boy and who is afraid of everything:

—Why do I spend my money to send you to school, eh? You are not worth more than the Haitian Negroes who cart along the manure in my Nursery.

For once, Dinah protested:

—Do not forget that he has had the *dengue*.[4] Until yesterday he was sick in bed!

He fumed at her:

—Shut up when I talk to my children!

Then he turned toward Aristide:

—What does that mean, goddammit? You are going to clear the savannah?

Aristide did not lose his cool and finished drinking his coffee quietly.

—I went to Martinique and visited the Balata garden. A guy has had the idea to grow all kinds of flowers and plants in the country estate of his grandmother. And the tourists come from all over and they pay for the visit. Why not us? We have land enough to spare and the right climate.

My father sniggered:

—Except that the tourists never come this way!

—They will come if there is something to see!

I knew that they were going to start twittering, tearing each other apart like two dogs, so I went out onto the porch. I prefer the morning. Leaves dance softly on the branches of trees just waking up under the sun. The air smells of water.

Curled up in the rocking chair where, from six o'clock in the evening, Dinah tames her loneliness, I saw Maringoin who handed the mail to Cornelia.

If somebody had followed me, spied on me with his crooked eyes, it is Maringoin. One day I was strolling on top of the Dillon plateau, because

---

[4]A type of malaria.

from there one can see the clouds running above the sea, I met him, wandering like a lost soul. He smiled at me:

—Good evening beauty! May I walk a bit of the way with you?

I did not even bother answering him. He swayed about for a while and then left sheepishly.

That morning, on the contrary, he appeared to me to be a gift of God and I ran to him:

—Take me to the shop, I am going to see if I find some stationery.

I did not know how to speak just like that about Francis Sancher when, in the basket where he put the mail in bundles tied up with rubber bands of different colors, I noticed a letter with an unusual name, coming from elsewhere, so different from those of the people of Riviere au Sel who are called Apollon, Saturne, Mercure, Boisfer, Boisgris, needless to say, the Masters must have had great fun naming them: "Francisco Alvarez Sanchez."

I understood immediately, but I feigned surprise:

—He is from Riviere au Sel, this one?

He shouted:

—Put down my letter! Don't you know that if you were in America, you would go to jail?

What does he know about America, this chap? Aristide went there once, to America. For an orchid exhibit in Monterey. He told me about the white birds and the trees that the great wind trimmed at its will.

I laid my hand on his knee, tough and sharp like a pebble in a river, he started shaking about to the point of inspiring my compassion for an ugly body which will never discover love.

—What do you know about him?

He tried to laugh, but his eyes shone like those of animals:

—What will you give me if I tell you what I know? A kiss?

I did not even answer. He stammered:

—His family comes from here and he is looking for his roots. They were *bekes*[5] who fled after the abolition.

—That's all?

I eyed him scornfully:

—Let me tell you. If you want your kiss, you'd do well to discover other things.

At that point, I got off his van slamming the door. Already, people were looking at us. But I waited one week, two weeks. Maringoin did not come to see me. Therefore, I went down every night to the Ravine. Francis Sancher did not come either.

Back home, I dismissed Aristide who did not understand anything and I drenched my pillow with salted water.

---

[5]Name of the first French white settlers in Martinique.

Love comes by surprise like death. It doesn't move forward beating the *gwo-ka*.[6] Its foot penetrates softly, softly in the loose soil of the hearts. All of a sudden, I lost my sleep, I lost all interest in eating or drinking. I could not think but of those moments spent at the Ravine which, apparently, I would not live again any more since he had forgotten me.

That Monday, it was a Monday I remember, because like each week, my father had gone to La Pointe and had had lunch at his cousin Edgar's, the cardiologist whom he cannot stand the sight of. Night had unbolted the door to the blowing wind. One should always mistrust the blowing wind, its insane voice which resounds and rebounds through the hills and savannahs, seeps into cracks, sows disorder even in the closed calabash of our heads. It is the wind which stuck that idea in my head. I was there, lying in bed, when it started to hang round me, to badger me:

—Come on! Come on! Go to him! Don't stay like this crying your eyes out!

I had just climbed back from the Ravine, deserted; its water had coiled up, like a shroud, around my scorned body. Why had he asked: "Shall I see you again?" if he did not know the meaning of those very words, if he did not know that it was a date that he was giving me?

All along the way, the oblong moon had walked ahead of me, mocking my sorrow:

—Mira, Mira Lameaulnes, what has become of you now? A rag doll who cries for a man.

Now that I know the rest of this story, my story, and that I ended up like Ti-Mari being consumed, I do not understand anymore why I had set all my hopes on that man whom I did not know from Adam. No doubt because he came from Elsewhere. From Elsewhere. On the other side of the water. He had not been born in our tittle-tattle island, abandoned to the cyclones and the devastations of the maliciousness of the Negroes' heart.

From Elsewhere.

Yes, it is the blowing window which stuck that idea in my head, under my mop of hair. Foolish idea, unreasonable idea since I was going to offer life and love to someone who was only expecting death.

Early morning, I jumbled up in a Caribbean basket all that I could find. And then, I went out. The blowing wind had dropped. The rain water streamed down, flattening the long grass to a bright green, freshly washed. Everything seemed to be waiting for the mood of the sun. For a while I was scared. I saw myself, crazy woman in a leafy-patterned dress, taking the road to disaster. I almost walked back. But I remembered the sad life that I was leaving behind my back and my desire to live, at last, in the sun, was stronger. I walked down the road.

---

[6]Tomtom.

❊ Discussion and Writing

1. What do the ravine and the sky symbolize? Analyze Mira's perception of them. What is implied by Mira's claim that the ravine belonged only to her?
2. Describe Mira's behavior toward her father, brother, the mailman, and Francis Sacher. What does each relationship reveal about her, her search, isolation, and sensitivity?
3. What is the role of women in this community? Explain Mira's understanding of them.
4. What is the political implication of the character of Monsieur Lameaulnes? Analyze the nature and the impact of colonization in the lives and minds of the people of Riviere au Sel.

❊ Research and Comparison

Interdisciplinary Discussion Question: Examine Conde's historical novels and the way she has restructured the cultural and political experiences of her African ancestors.

Nelida Pinon
(b. 1937)
Brazil

Nelida Pinon was born in Rio de Janeiro, Brazil; her father was Spanish and her mother Brazilian. While she worked briefly as a journalist and has taught occasional courses in universities, since 1955, she has concentrated on her writing. Her novels and stories are marked by a philosophical and religious undertone, by the search for identifying the condition of woman, and by a sense of solitude. Her work is also marked by a tightly enclosed, frequently elliptical, technique that often avoids transitions and more complexly developed descriptions of the state of mind of her characters.

Brief Flower*

Her inconsistency was racial. The sure orientation of her blood. Amidst a glass-like clarity, the softness of her steps as they passed through heaven and earth, such was her framework, her undirected drive. She had lost her direction among the admonitions of her friends, and she would laugh raucously

---

*Translated by Gregory Rabassa

at how funny stones were. She would even decipher them, unlocking secrets, for she had recently acquired the gift of words. She played at hiding, fascinating men, that would be her trick. They would always have to look for her, thinking that she was lost. The offense which they committed on her was funny, it made her vibrate and become aware of herself. In one way or another she would repair the shambles and put on a new dress, with the gamut of its material shining in the light of day.

On certain evenings, right there in front of the mirror, she would get rid of the discovery of her body. She would stare until she enjoyed it, the comfort and the feeling. She did not blush at the thought that she could be dazzled by that minute and exciting examination of her flesh. In that way an area that she had always imagined as dark and dirty was becoming clear and clean. As she mastered the miracle, she would run along the beach, the sand would come at her with the speed of the wind, a tickling that always irritates, even with innocence.

She sat down on a stone to think: now I can decipher any expectation there is. And she got a stomach-ache, just as when she had eaten too much chocolate, or when her body went through its modification, altering its flow of blood, the surprise of that initial abundance that upset her, the realization that she was becoming a woman. With that realization, she became shrewd and daring as she faced the exaggeration of the resources she had just received. She would guess at answers until she could learn and breathe.

Men would pass by thinking how nice a woman is when she is young like that, and I am destined to rule that thing that grows in her or in some other one, for I am meant to possess the one who is waiting for me to lead her into the green fields, and if it is not this girl, I will enjoy her in another one for just as long as I live.

She grew tired after eating some ice cream. Despite her courage to go on, for the sun was still shining. The company of small creatures, nervous things protected by a shell and who left a trail, a molecule betrayed by its own brilliance. So funny, and more than company, they offered her astonishment, at any moment she could discover an immediate world, one that had risen up and reached completion through its own precarious science, where guesses were all.

She picked up a periwinkle, with the urge to stick her tongue inside of it, into the restriction of that opening, to taste its savor and its grace. Suddenly taken by the torpor of the small thing and wanting to understand its trick, hiding there inside, so much the prisoner of itself that it became excited and lost, fleeing now into the way of its species and its mystery. And the girl, wanting to stick out her tongue, feared the encounter of her tongue with that soft thing to be undone, until she broke the secret, wresting away the fragility of the little creature, the intimate craving of one who opens her legs, without selection, engulfed in the vital flow of strange resources.

The girl was afraid that with the arrival of the time there would never be any impediments to procreation, better and more serious things, or lost things, which do not cede before the strength of grace and her whim, which is also perfection.

She threw the creature far away, its truth, after the necessary ripening of her inconsistent race. Later, other men, different from the first, tried more daring approaches, preparing for the advances that discipline races. As if they were going about tasks to dominate vague and circumspect women. Who let themselves be sheltered in spring by any domination whatsoever, after which they store up virtues in honey for sweet and strange palates.

My name is Pedro, one of them said to her, and he was boldly waiting for the falling of the fruits. Kicking at the ground, feigning embarrassment, distraction, he sat down beside her. The girl, changing stones, going from the highest one to the lowest, said nothing, Disdainful, the boy smoked a cigarette, and protected by the smoke, he shouted and yours, what's your name? Bewitchingly, she said: a girl is nameless. Like a serene horseman atop the restlessness of his mount, replete with code and shining sword, he answered her: from now on, even if you haven't got a name, you've got a master.

Afterwards she cleaned the house, took care of the wild plants, decorated the table in a dedication to life. Delicate with the cleaning of the objects. Until she was pregnant and pretty, the violence of growth. She had barely noticed it because she was simple, feeling its effects. Such was her modesty. Every day the boy would occupy the house, with a loss of ceremony and respect. He would scratch himself where the chair had abused him, after which he would drag her to bed. The girl, still fascinated, would let herself be led, somewhere between feeling irritated and exalted. As it became a habit, the man drained her of her will and urge. The orientations of her nature were scarcely defined.

And that was how they were becoming, until the child was born. Strong and daring like his father, continuously unfolding with no beauty in him now that would not later change. The boy decide to disappear, never to be seen again. That disturbed the girl profoundly. Even though she had experienced such violent flights, she would still look at the stars, the same intensity. She had a precarious intuition of the freedom of any worthiness that might comfort her, she would make use of the flour that ennobles man after it has received the delicate mixture of some ferment. She dedicated herself to the subtleties that memory suggests, until she attained the vulgarity of such rendering. Only then did she rest a little. To join a new companion in bed and at the table.

At first there was strangeness, the hesitations with a different body, the imposition of other habits. That yellow and dazzling laugh that would always dominate the man, even when they were making love, as if it too were part of the rite. Then his teeth began to fall out from being shown so much, and the girl found herself joined to an old man who, in addition to being ugly, was also imposing the sordidness of his now flabby flesh upon her. Even though it was difficult for her to show her disgust, the sight of those gums, she could barely hold her vomit back, the penury of intense cohabitation. She would run to the bathroom and give herself abundant relief there after the hope, after the abolition of so many things. Even so, the man's presence was strong, and in addition to her body, it filled the whole house, the lust for gold showing on his face. One day she took her son, quite large now, and left the house. Abandoning the city just as she had left shelters so often in the wake of new disturbances. For she had lost the essential notions of living together, and even in a search of kindness, she would release herself in a torment of really wanting to live.

When another man chose her, as one casually chooses something that he is prepared to discard at any moment, she accepted in confusion. She went off to raise chickens, healthy and early-rising, to take care of cows, stubbornly thrusting her hands into the full udders, until her life changed, just as the smell of her skin. Even in that way she was following the path of her star and its false brilliance, as if freedom could be experienced in that way, in its excess. Every morning she would massage the cows, after the man had massaged her body. She would delude herself by thinking that they would rest when they got old. But that was taking time and her son was growing in a rapid and exaggerated way, and the woman hesitated as she faced the innovation of that world that had detached itself from her womb, marginal and operative. The struggle seemed hard and wild.

One day, dragging her son along, she went to the city, where she had not been for a long time. They delicately watched the epic passing-by of men. And they had some ice cream, which she liked so much, giving in to that vital appreciation by closing their eyes and enjoying, the tongue as it slipped across, with no greater demands. As if she were teaching the boy procedures for the future when he would invade the realms of pleasure. And if the boy imitated his mother, it was because the intimacy of that face made him feel good, it had become a powerful presence, and by having to discover his own expression that acknowledged the pleasure he was to feel when, even carelessly, he would be unable to spare his body its necessary exhibitions. Later on there were other things, sordid and colorful, that touched bottom.

After that she could no longer tolerate at all either the man or the cows. It was a disquieting peace and she forgot the attributes of the earth. She admitted again her inborn inconsistency and she laughed in compensation as she met her ancestors. She woke up the boy cautiously, they put a few things into a suitcase and daringly slipped away. The man would never follow them or disturb the earth with his vain pursuit. They rested only when it grew light, and they continued on immediately after, oriented by a simple independence that lays out roads with the illusion of building new cities. Brief stops, the simple necessities of sleep and food. Mother and son were ruling the world with the insouciance of emperors, nothing disturbed them, neither fatigue nor the imperfection of exigent shapes.

At last they came to a house with high walls, surrounded by trees and a lawn. A nun dressed in black came out to greet them, her face protected by a veil. Inviting them to rest and have some hot soup. As one who dares to look so as to observe and appreciate, they entered. The boy looked at his mother as if in reprimand: really, was this what we had fled for? The mother closed her face and, illuminated, she had something that deformed her expression and her patience. In her whole life she had never recorded a deed that had been more heroic. After prayers they ate. Mother and son were still upset when they looked at each other, imprisoned in a modest cell, a common bed—this before they went to sleep. When bells pealed forth in place of the lowing of the cows, more than the sound, they could perceive the sadness of the prayers, and they arose as if wishing to flee, forgetting the caprice of miracles, changes that, even if they do not come about, dominate the world and make it marginal. But—the high wall and its locked gate—they waited, until the nun asked them: after all, you must be a religious woman, since you've always dreamed of stars. She could not resist the intensity of such wooing.

She went with the nun, her son following. She found herself to be an emotional pioneer, a torch-bearer, and her sudden adolescence was so color-ful with its fruits and shrouds. They shared everything, prayers and hates, women daring by the stimulus of prayer, confusing devotion and martyr-dom, for war had honest roots in the world, death and hunger were savage. The boy was dazzled by the freshness of the prayers and the women's work, as they scarcely allowed compliments, a distant trace of friendship, and if, perhaps, they thought of love, they reflected on it as a necessary privation.

The woman had learned to fulfill her human duty as her body inhabited others, and in this multiplicity, the combinations of revolving works, she accepted everything, because here, as before, she found herself convinced that she would rule the stars in their passage, in the briefness of their bril-liance. And as she ruled, she would dazzle herself with belief and faith, letting her son grow up among the women's austerity. Until when he was quite large and the mother superior warned her, you must leave, or you may stay and have your son discover the world. Sad and predestined, she looked at the son of her flesh, who was imposing successive sacrifices upon her, and in chapel or at the table, she would become upset. She asked her son: what do you think? He did not answer as he lit the candles in the chapel, one of his daily chores.

The mother saw pacification and love in that look, and she put the prob-lem aside. Later on, it rained so much one night that even though she could not bear it, she imagined him leaving, discovering the world and its deep rivers. She knocked at his door, careful not to startle him: even though he was grown now, she called to him in a whisper and told him: whenever you want, we will leave together, I will not be separated from you.

They took leave the next day, stifling a certain faith that can squelch necessary decisions, and even though they could see the beginning of a greater struggle. They walked on, the boy slowing down his pace now so that his mother would not sense her own weakness and become ashamed, and so that the age already showing on her face would not become the only point of interest for the two. Fear that the mother might take a look into some mirror after her dishonor in the life of a recluse. They would only stop when necessary, always talking and looking at the countryside. And they loved one another as never before, now that they were free from things and life had become more difficult. The son was always afraid that he might weep at any moment, and that too was the inconsistency of his race. He would look at his mother, he was learning.

The mother had kept her nun's habit and from time to time, children on the roads would run up and ask for her blessing, offering her bread and trinkets. They found a hut, ugly and in shambles. He took a job at the mill, amidst the thick, white flour. He would return to the house, grave and circumspect, while his mother took care of it, cooking and sweeping the floor. Even though the world around them had forced communication, wounded in their love and glory, they did not pay much attention. Until the woman's body began to pain, it was her spine which hurt. She could no longer walk, and this was followed by a violent trembling, and she was pitiful to see. Age had imposed itself. The boy carried her everywhere on his back, the way one takes a child, so that she could appreciate the changes in nature and would not forget that, in spite of her debilities, she was still alive.

The son liked to look at her white hair, for his eyes did nothing else, and then, of a different race, as they well knew, they found that other joys were strange. Until he became owner of the mill. But the mother could no longer stand the impatience of living in bed, coupled to her son's sight, and he was a compassionate and solitary person. Once she asked him for some gold coins, telling him, if you love me, throw them into the river for me, the time has come for you to begin to suffer and to free yourself. The son did as she asked. Sad, but not over losing the money. His arrogance was something else. He could recognize it in all that hesitation in the face of life of one who is soon to die. They hung in the water for a moment and the mother had given the first sign of her independence.

Later on they ate, and as they filled themselves, she could feel the restlessness of death. She found it strange to die before she had intensely assimilated her old age. Distracted still, she might have let a stranger into her bed and not be offended by any of the actions he might come to practice. Such a disposition seemed like youth to her. Her inconsistency was racial, and she understood, looking up, smiling at the ceiling, that she was approaching the strength of her star. Her son had also inherited from her the illness and gravity of life. They both knew from pungent and audacious attestations.

When her son buried her, he decorated her grave with the brevity of flowers.

❋ Discussion and Writing

1. What does Pinon imply in her description of the woman's body: what impact does the awareness of her body have on the woman; on the men?
2. Comment on the significance of the namelessness of the characters?
3. Analyze the woman's relationship with her mates and her son. What are the similarities and differences in her relationships with them?
4. What is the role of the nuns in the story?
5. Pinon refers to race in the first sentence and repeats the reference several times throughout the story. What is its implication?
6. Discuss the significance of the title.

❋ Research and Comparison

Compare and contrast the portrayal of feminist issues in this story with those portrayed in other selections in this anthology, preferably from different cultures. Examine their ideological variations as well as their distinctive styles.

Simone Schwarz-Bart
(b. 1938)
Guadeloupe

Simone Schwarz-Bart, whose mother was a school teacher, was born in Charente-Maritime in France and raised in Guadeloupe. During World War II, Vichy France occupied the French West Indies, resulting in the imposition of a blockade by the Allied forces. Since the blockade produced a scarcity of food, and since many of the men—her father included—left the islands to fight with the Free French forces, Schwarz-Bart grew up in a world of women who were determined to survive and who called on their traditional heritage to do so. After the war she studied in France, where she met and married the writer Andre Schwarz-Bart and established one of the noted literary marriages of the mid-twentieth century. They lived in Senegal and Switzerland for a time before returning to Goyave, the village of her childhood. *Pluie et vent sur Telumee miracle* (The Bridge of Beyond, 1972), which won the *Elle* literary prize, pays tribute to one of the resolute Goyave women. Through her, the novel commemorates the strong Guadeloupe women who survived slavery and, with the abolition of slavery in the French West Indian colonies in 1848, passed on a legacy of endurance and determination to their daughters. The inheritance is carried, in part, in the Creole sayings that inform the novel, underlining its vitality as well as its connection to a Caribbean aesthetic. "Toussine" is the first chapter of *The Bridge of Beyond*.

*Toussine**

A man's country may be cramped or vast according to the size of his heart. I've never found my country too small, though that isn't to say my heart is great. And if I could choose it's here in Guadeloupe that I'd be born again, suffer and die. Yet not long back my ancestors were slaves on this volcanic, hurricane-swept, mosquito-ridden, nasty-minded island. But I didn't come into the world to weigh the world's woe. I prefer to dream, on and on, standing in my garden, just like any other old woman of my age, till death comes and takes me as I dream, me and all my joy.

When I was a child my mother, Victory, often talked to me about my grandmother Toussine. She spoke of her with fervor and veneration: Toussine, she'd say, was a woman who helped you hold your head up, and people with this gift are rare. My mother's reverence for Toussine was such that I came to regard her as some mythical being not of this world, so that for me she was legendary even while still alive.

I got into the habit of calling her, as men called her, Queen Without a Name. But her maiden name had been Toussine Lougandor.

* * *

Her mother was Minerva, a fortunate woman freed by the abolition of slavery from a master notorious for cruelty and caprice. After the abolition Minerva wandered in search of a refuge far from the plantation and its vagaries, and she came to rest at L'Abandonnee. Some runaway slaves came there afterward, and a village grew up. The wanderers seeking refuge were countless, and many would not settle anywhere permanently for fear the old days might return. One Negro from Dominica vanished as soon as he learned he had sired a child, and those in L'Abandonnee whom Minerva had scorned now laughed at her swollen belly. But when dark-skinned Xango took on the shame of my great-grandmother Minerva, the laughter stopped dead, and those who had been amusing themselves at others' misfortunes choked on their own bile. Little Toussine came into the world, and Xango loved her as if she were his own. As the child grew, shooting up as gracefully as a sugarcane, she became the light of his eyes, the blood in his veins, the air in his lungs. Thus through the love and respect lavished on her by Xango, Minerva, now long dead, could walk without shame along the main street of the hamlet, head high, back arched, arms akimbo, and foul breath turned from her to blow over better pastures. And so life began for young Toussine, as delicately as dawn on a clear day.

They lived in a hamlet swept alternately by winds from the land and winds from the sea. A steep road ran along by cliffs and wastelands, leading,

---

**Translated by Barbara Bray*

it seemed, to nothing human. And that was why it was called the deserted village, L'Abandonnee. At certain times everyone there would be filled with dread, like travellers lost in a strange land. Still young and strong, always dressed in a worker's overall, Minerva had a glossy, light mahogany skin and black eyes brimming over with kindness. She had an unshakable faith in life. When things went wrong she would say that nothing, no one, would ever wear out the soul God had chosen out for her and put in her body. All the year round she fertilized vanilla, picked coffee, hoed the banana groves, and weeded the rows of sweet potatoes. And her daughter Toussine was no more given to dreaming than she. Almost as soon as she woke the child would make herself useful sweeping, gathering fruit, peeling vegetables. In the afternoon she would go to the forest to collect leaves for the rabbits, and sometimes the whim would take her to kneel in the shade of the mahoganies and look for the flat brightly coloured seeds that are made into necklaces. When she came back with a huge pile of greenstuff on her head, Xango delighted to see her with leaves hanging down over her face, and would fling both arms in the air and shout: "Hate me, so long as you love Toussine. Pinch me till you draw blood, but don't touch so much as the hem of her robe." And he would laugh and cry just to look at the radiant, frank-faced child whose features were said to be like those of the Negro from Dominica, whom he would have liked to meet once, just to see. But as yet she was not in full bloom. It was when she was fifteen that she stood out from all the other girls with the unexpected grace of a red canna growing on a mountain, so that the old folk said she in herself was the youth of L'Abandonnee.

There was also in L'Abandonnee at that time a young fisherman called Jeremiah who filled one's soul with the same radiance. But he paid no attention to girls, to whom his friends used to say, laughing, "When Jeremiah falls in love it will be with a mermaid." But this didn't make him any less handsome, and the girls' hearts shriveled up with vexation. He was nineteen and already the best fisherman in Caret cove. Where on earth did he get those hauls of vivaneaux, tazars, and blue balarous? Nowhere but from beneath his boat, the *Headwind,* in which he used to go off forever, from morn till night and night till morn; all he lived for was hearing the sound of the waves in his ears and feeling the tradewinds caressing his face. Such was Jeremiah when Toussine was for everyone a red canna growing on a high mountain.

On windless days when the sea was dead calm Jeremiah would go into the forest to cut the lianas he made into lobster pots. One afternoon when he left the beach for this purpose, Toussine appeared in his path, right in the middle of a wood. She was wearing one of her mother's old dresses that came down to her ankles, and with her heap of greenstuff coming down over her eyes and hiding her face, she looked as if she didn't know where she was going. The young man asked her, "Is this L'Abandonnee's latest fashion in donkeys?" She threw down her burden looked at him, and said in surprise, almost in tears: "A girl just goes to collect greenstuff from the forest, and here

I am, insulted." With that, she burst out laughing and scampered off into the shadow. It was then Jeremiah was caught in the finest lobster pot he ever saw. When he got back from his excursion his friends noticed he looked absentminded, but they did not ask any questions. Real fishermen, those who have taken the sea for their native country, often have that lost look. So his friends just thought dry land didn't agree with Jeremiah, and that his natural element was the water. But they sang a different tune in the days that followed, when they saw Jeremiah neglecting the *Headwind,* deserting her and leaving her high and dry on the beach. Consulting among themselves, they came to the conclusion he must be under the spell of the Guiablesse, the most wicked of spirits, the woman with the cloven hoof who feeds exclusively on your desire to live, and whose charms drive you sooner or later to suicide. They asked him if he hadn't met someone that ill-fated day when he went up into the forest. Eventually Jeremiah confessed: "The only Guiablesse I met that day," he said, "is called Toussine—Xango's Toussine." Then they said, chuckling, "Oh, so that's it! Now we see. But it's not such a problem as you might think; if you want our opinion there are no prince's daughters in L'Abandonnee that we know of. Fortunately we're only a pack of Negroes all in the same boat, without any fathers and mothers before God. Here everyone is everyone's else's equal, and none of our women can boast of having three eyes or two tourmalines sleeping in the hollow of her thighs. True, you'll say *she* isn't like all the others, the women you see everywhere, like lizards, protected by the very insipidity of their flesh. We answer: Jeremiah, you say well, as usual. For we too have eyes, and when Toussine brushes against our pupils our sight is refreshed. All these words to say just one thing, friend: Beautiful as she is, the girl is like you, and when you appear with her in the street you will be a good match for her. One more thing. When you go to tell her parents of your intentions, remember we don't have any cannibals here, and Xango and Minerva won't eat you."

Then they left Jeremiah to himself, so that he could make his decision like a man.

Thank God for my friends, thought Jeremiah the day he went to see Toussine's parents, dressed as usual and carrying a fine catch of pink crabs. As soon as they opened the door he told them he loved Toussine, and they asked him right in, without even consulting the young lady. Their behavior gave the impression they knew all about Jeremiah, what he did in life on land and sea, and that he was in a position to take a wife, have children, and bring up a family. It was the beginning of one of those warm Guadeloupe afternoons, lit up at the end by the arrival of Toussine with a tray spread with an embroidered cloth, with vermouth for the men and sapodilla syrup for the weaker sex. When Jeremiah left, Minerva told him the door of the cottage would be open to him day and night from now on, and he knew he could consider the vermouth and the invitation as marking definite victory: for in the case of such a choice morsel as Toussine it isn't usual for people to fall on someone's neck the first time of asking, as if they were trying to get rid of a beast that had something wrong with it. That evening, to celebrate this triumph, Jeremiah and his friends decided to go night fishing, and they brought back so much fish their expedition was long remembered in L'Abandonnee. But they had enjoyed catching those coulirous too much to sell them on the beach, so they gave them away, and that too remained everyone's memory. At noon that day the men, with glasses of rum in their hands, threw out their chests with satisfaction, tapped them three times, and exulted: "In spite of all, the race of men is not dead." The women shook their heads and whispered, "What one does a thousand undo." "But in the meanwhile," said one of them, as if reluctantly, "it does spread a little hope." And the sated tongues went full tilt, while inside Jeremiah's head the sound of the waves had started up again.

Jeremiah came every afternoon. He was treated not as a suitor but rather as if he were Toussine's brother, the son Minerva and Xango had never had. No acid had eaten into the young man's soul, and my poor great-grandmother couldn't take her eyes off him. Gay by temperament, she was doubly gay to see this scrap of her own country, the man sent by St. Anthony in person especially for her daughter. In the overflowing of her joy she would sometimes tease her. "I hope you're fond of fish, Miss Toussine. Come along, you lucky girl, and I'll teach you to make a court-bouillon that'll make Jeremiah lick the fingers of both hands, polite as he is."

Then she would hold out her wide yellow skirt and sing to her daughter:

I want a fisherman for a husband
To catch me fine sea bream

I don't know if you know
But I want a fisherman

O oar before, he pleases me
O oar behind, I die.

But Toussine scarcely listened. Since Jeremiah had taken to spending his afternoons with her his image danced continually in her mind's eye, and she spent the whole day admiring the one she loved, unsuspected, as she thought, by all the world. She looked at his figure and saw it was slim and supple. She looked at his fingers and saw they were nimble and slender, like coconut leaves in the wind. She gazed into his eyes, and her body was filled with a great peace. But what she liked best of all about the man St. Anthony had sent her was the satiny, iridescent skin like the juicy flesh of certain mauve coco plums, so delicious under one's teeth. Minerva with her song about the fisherman knew very well how her daughter passed her time, but she still sang and danced just for the pleasure of seeing Toussine go on dreaming.

Here, as everywhere else, reality was not made up entirely of laughing and singing, dancing and dreaming: for one ray of sun on one cottage there was a whole village still in the shade. All through the preparations for the wedding, L'Abandonnee remained full of the same surliness, the same typical human desire to bring the level of the world down a peg, the same heavy malice weighing down on the chambers of the heart. The breeze blowing over Minerva's cottage embittered the women, made them more unaccountable than ever, fierce, fanciful, always ready with some new shrewishness. "What I say is, Toussine's more for ornament than for use. Beauty's got no market value. The main thing is not getting married, but sticking together year in year out," said one. "They're laughing now, but after laughter come tears, and three months from now Minerva's happy band will find itself with six eyes to cry with," said another. The most savage of all were those living with a man on a temporary basis. They bejgrudged in advance the scrap of gold that was going to gleam on her finger, they wondered if she really possessed some unique and exceptional quality, some virtue or merit so great it elicited marriage. And to console themselves and soothe a deep-seated resentment, they would come right up to Minerva's cottage at dusk and mutter, with a kind of savage frenzy, incantations like:

Married today
Divorced tomorrow
But Mrs. just the same.

Minerva knew these women had nothing in their lives but a few planks balanced on four stones and a procession of men over their bellies. For these lost Negresses, marriage was the greatest and perhaps the only dignity. But when she couldn't stand hearing them any longer, Minerva would plant her hands on her hips and shout: "I'm not the only one with a daughter, my fine windbags, and I wish yours the same you wish my Toussine. For, under the sun, the saying has never gone unfulfilled. All they that take the sword shall perish with the sword." Then she would go inside and shut the doors and let the mad bitches yelp.

On the day of the wedding all the village paths were swept and decorated as for the local feast day. Xango and Minerva's cottage was surrounded by huts of woven coconut palm. The one reserved for the bridal couple was a great bouquet of hibiscus, mignonette, and orange blossom—the scent was intoxicating. Rows of tables stretched as far as the eye could see, and you were offered whatever drink you were thirsty for, whatever meat would tickle your palate. There was meat of pig, sheep, and cattle, and even poultry served in the liquor it was cooked in. Blood pudding rose up in shining coils; tiered cakes were weighed down with lacy frosting; every kind of water ice melted before your eyes—custard-apple, water-lemon, coconut. But for the Negroes of L'Abandonnee all this was nothing without some music, and when they saw the three bands, one for quadrilles and mazurkas, one for the fashionable beguine, and the traditional combination of drum, wind instruments, and horn, then they knew they'd really have something worth talking about at least once in their lives. And this assuaged the hearts swollen with jealousy. For three days everyone left behind hills and plateaus, troubles and indignities of every kind, to relax, dance, and salute the bridal couple, going to and fro before them in the flower-decked tent, congratulating Toussine on her luck and Jeremiah on his best of luck. It was impossible to count how many mouths uttered the word luck, for that was the theme they decided to adopt for telling their descendants, in later years, of the wedding of Toussine and Jermiah.

The years flowed over it all, and Toussine was still the same dragonfly with shimmering blue wings, Jeremiah still the same glossy-coated sea dog. He continued to go out alone, never bringing back an empty boat, however niggardly the sea. Scandalmongers said he used witchcraft and had a spirit go out fishing in his stead when no one else was about. But in fact his only secret was his enormous patience. When the fish would not bite at all, he dived for lambis. If there were no lambis, he put out long rods with hooks or live crabs to tempt the octopi. He knew the sea as the hunter knows the forest. When the wind had gone and the boat was hauled up on the shore, he would make for his little cottage, pour the money he'd earned into his wife's lap, and have a snack as he waited for the sun to abate. Then the two of them would go to tend their garden. While he dug, she would mark out the rows; while he burned weeds, she would sow. And the sudden dusk of the islands would come down over them, and Jeremiah would take advantage of the deepening dark to have a little hors d'oeuvre of his wife's body, there on the ground, murmuring all sorts of foolishness to her, as on the very first day. "I still don't know what it is I like best about you—one day it's your eyes, the next your woodland laugh, another your hair, and the day after the lightness of your step; another, the beauty spot on your temple, and then the day after that the grains of rice I glimpse when you smile at me." And to this air on the mandolin, Toussine, trembling with delight, would reply with a cool, rough little air on the flute: "My dear, anyone just seeing you in the street would give you the host without asking you to go to confession, but you're a dangerous man, and you'd have buried me long ago if people ever died of happiness." Then they would go indoors and Jeremiah would address the evening, casting a last look over the fields: "How can one help loving a garden?"

Their prosperity began with a grass path shaded by coconut palms and kept up as beautifully as if it led to a castle. In fact it led to a little wooden house with two rooms, a thatched roof, and a floor supported on four large cornerstones. There was a hut for cooking in, three blackened stones for a hearth, and a covered tank so that Toussine could do her washing without having to go and gossip with the neighbors by the river. As the women did their washing they would pick quarrels to give zest to the work, comparing their respective fates and filling their hearts with bitterness and rancor.

Meanwhile Toussine's linen would be boiling away in a pan in the back yard, and she took advantage of every minute to make her house more attractive. Right in front of the door she'd planted a huge bed of Indian poppies, which flowered all year round. To the right there was an orange tree with hummingbirds and to the left clumps of Congo cane from which she used to cut pieces to give to her daughters. Eloisine and Meranee, for their tea. She would go to and fro amid all this in a sort of permanent joy and richness, as if Indian poppies, Congo canes, hummingbirds, and orange trees were enough to fill a woman's heart with complete satisfaction. And because of the richness and joy she felt in return for so little, people envied and hated her. She could withdraw at will into the recesses of her own soul, but she was reserved, not disillusioned. And because she bloomed like that, in solitude, she was also accused of being an aristocrat stuck-up. Late every Sunday evening she would walk through the village on Jeremiah's arm to look at the place and the people and the animals just before they disappeared in the darkness. She was happy, herself part of all that spectacle, that close and familiar universe. She came to be the thorn in some people's flesh, the delight of others, and because she had a distant manner they thought she put on aristocratic airs.

After the grass path came a veranda, which surrounded the little house, giving constant cool and shade if you moved the bench according to the time of day. Then there were the two windows back and front, real windows with slatted shutters, so that you could close the door and shut yourself safely away from spirits and still breathe in the scents of evening. But the true sign of their prosperity was the bed they inherited from Minerva and Xango. It was a vast thing of locust wood with tall head posts and three mattresses, which took up the entire bedroom. Toussine used to put vetiver roots under the mattresses, and citronella leaves, so that whenever anyone lay down there were all sorts of delicious scents: the children said it was a magic bed. It was a great object of curiosity in that poor village, where everyone else still slept on old clothes laid down on the floor at night, carefully folded up in the morning, and spread in the sun to get rid of the fleas. People would come and weigh up the grass path, the real windows with slatted shutters, the bed with its oval-panelled headboard lording it beyond the open door, and the red-bordered counterpane, which seemed an additional insult. And some of the women would say with a touch of bitterness, "Who do they take themselves for, these wealthy Negroes? Toussine and Jeremiah, with their two-roomed house, their wooden veranda, their slatted shutters, and their bed with three mattresses and red borders—do they think all these things make them white?"

Later on Toussine also had a satin scarf, a broad necklace of gold and silver alloy, garnet earrings, and high-vamped slippers she wore twice a year, on Ash Wednesday and Christmas Day. And as the wave showed no sign of flagging, the time came when the other Negroes were no longer surprised, and talked about other things, other people, other pains and other wonders. They had got used to the prosperity as they had got used to their own poverty. The subject of Toussine and wealthy Negroes was a thing of the past; it had all become quite ordinary.

Woe to him who laughs once and gets into the habit, for the wickedness of life is limitless: if it gives you your heart's desire with one hand, it is only to trample on you with both feet and let loose on you that madwoman bad luck, who seizes and rends you and scatters your flesh to the crows.

Eloisine and Meranee, twins, were ten years old when luck forsook their mother Toussine. A school had just opened in the village, and a teacher came twice a week to teach the children their letters in exchange for a few penny-worth of foodstuff. One evening as they were learning their alphabet, Meranee said her sister had all the light and told her to move the lamp to the middle of the table. And so just one little word gave bad luck an opening. "Have it all, then!" said Eloisine, giving the light an angry shove. It was over in an instant: the china lamp was in pieces and the burning oil was spreading all over Meranee's legs and shoulders and hair. A living torch flew out into the darkness, and the evening breeze howled around it, fanning the flames. Toussine caught up a blanket and ran after the child, shouting to her to stand still, but she rushed madly hither and thither, leaving a luminous track behind her like a falling star. In the end she collapsed, and Toussine wrapped her in the blanket, picked her up, and went back toward the house, which was still burning. Jeremiah comforted Eloisine, and they all sat in the middle of their beautiful path, on the damp grass of evening, watching their sweat, their life, their joy, go up in flames. A big crowd had gathered: the Negroes stood there fascinated, dazzled by the magnitude of the disaster. They stared at the flames lighting up the sky, shifting from foot to foot, in two minds—they felt an impulse to pity, and yet saw the catastrophe as poetic justice. It made them forget their own fate and compare the cruelty of this misfortune with the ordinariness of their own. At any rate, it's one thing that won't happen to us, they said.

Meranee's suffering was terrible. Her body was one great wound attracting more and more flies as it decayed. Toussine, her eyes empty of all expression, fanned them away, put on soothing oil, and grew hoarse calling on death, which, being no doubt occupied elsewhere, refused to come. If anyone offered to replace Toussine at the bedside for a while, she would say, smiling gently: "Don't worry about me. However heavy a woman's breasts, her chest is always strong enough to carry them." She spent seventeen days and seventeen nights cajoling death, and then, ill luck having gone elsewhere, Meranee expired. Life went on as before, but without one vestige of heart left, like a flea feasting on your last drop of blood, delighting in leaving you senseless and sore, cursing heaven and earth and the womb that conceived you.

Against sorrow and the vanity of things, there is and will always be human fantasy. It was thanks to the fantasy of a white man that Toussine and Jeremiah found a roof. He was a Creole called Colbert Lanony, who in the old days just after the abolition of slavery had fallen in love with a strange and fascinating young Negress. Cast out by his own people, he had sought refuge in a desolate and inaccessible wasteland far from the eyes that looked askance at his love. Nothing remained of all that now but some fine blocks of stone moldering away in the wilderness, colonnades, worm-eaten ceilings, and tiles bearing witness still to the past and to an outlawed white man's fancy for a Negrees. To those who were surprised to find a house like that in such a place, the local people got into the habit of saying, "It's L'Abandonnee," and the name later came to be used for the hamlet itself. Only one room on the first floor was habitable, a sort of closet, where the window openings were covered with sheets of cardboard. When it rained the water trickled through a hole in the roof into a bucket, and at night the ground floor was the resort of toads, frogs, and bats. But none of this seemed to bother Toussine, who had gone to live there like a body without a soul, indifferent to such details. As was the custom, she was visited there the first nine evenings by all the people of the village, who came to pay their respects to the dead and to keep the living company. Toussine did not weep or complain, but sat upright on a bench in a corner as if every breath of air were poison. People did not want to desert a ship like Toussine, but the sight of her was so unbearable they cut the ceremony short, just coming in, greeting her, and leaving, full of pitying kindness, thinking she was lost forever.

The leaf that falls into the pond does not rot the same day, and Toussine's sorrow only grew worse with time, fulfilling all the gloomy predictions. At first Jeremiah still went to sea three times a week, but then only twice, then once, then not at all. The house looked as deserted as ever, as if there were no one living there. Toussine never left the room with the cardboard windows, and Jeremiah collected their food from the woods around—purslane, scurvy grass, pink makanga bananas. Before, the women going to market used to take a path that led by the ruined house; it was a shortcut to the main road and Basse-Terre, where they sold their wares. But now they were afraid, and they made a big detour through the forest rather than go near the pig-headed Toussine, who didn't speak, wouldn't even answer, but just sat staring into space, a bag of bones as good as dead. Every so often, when the conversation came around to her and Jeremiah and little Eloisine, a man would shin up a tree, peer toward the house, and report that it was still the same; nothing had changed, nothing had moved.

Three years went by before people began to talk about them again. As usual, a man climbed a tree and looked toward the ruins; but this time he didn't say anything, and showed no sign of coming down. When questioned he only signed for someone else to come up and look. It was the second man who announced that Toussine, the little stranded boat, the woman thought to be lost forever, had come out of her cardboard tower and was taking a little walk outside in the sun.

* * *

Glad as they were at this news, the Negroes still waited, hesitating to rejoice outright until the kid was safely caught and tethered and they were sure they hadn't sharpened their knives for nothing. And as they looked, this is what they saw: Toussine was cutting down the weeds around the ruined house. She shivered a moment, went in, then came out again almost at once and began to cut down brushwood and scrub with the furious energy of a woman with something urgent to do and not a minute to lose.

From that day on the place began to be a little less desolate and the market women went back to using the shortcut to Basse-Terre. Toussine had taken her family into prison with her, and now she brought them back to life again. First Eloisine was seen in the village again, as slight and brittle as a straw. Next poor Jeremiah came down to the beach, filled his eyes with the sea and stood staring, fascinated, then went back smiling up the hill as in the days when the song of the waves sounded in his head. It could be seen plainly written across his brow that he would go back to sea again. Toussine put curtains up at the windows, and planted Indian poppies around the ruin, Angola peas, root vegetables, and clumps of Congo cane for Eloisine. And then one day she planted the pip of a hummingbird orange. But the Negroes did not rejoice yet. They still watched and waited, from a distance. They thought of the old Toussine, in rags, and compared her with the Toussine of today—not a woman, for what is a woman? Nothing at all, they said, whereas Toussine was a bit of the world, a whole country, a plume of a Negress, the ship, sail, and wind, for she had not made a habit of sorrow. Then Toussine's belly swelled and burst and the child was called Victory. And then the Negroes did rejoice. On the day of the christening they came to Toussine and said:

"In the days of your silks and jewels we called you Queen Toussine. We were not far wrong, for you are truly a queen. But now, with your Victory, you may boast that you have put us in a quandary. We have tried and tried to think of a name for you, but in vain, for there isn't one that will do. And so from now on we shall call you 'Queen Without a Name!'"

And they ate, drank, and were merry, and from that day forth my grandmother was called the Queen Without a Name.

Queen Without a Name went on living in L'Abandonnee with her two daughters, Eloisine and my mother, Victory, until my grandfather died. Then, when her daughters came to have the wombs of women, she left them to steer the course of their lives under their own sail. She wanted to go away from the house where her fisher husband had loved and cherished her and kept her safe in her affliction, when her hair was unkempt and her dress in rags. She longed for solitude, so she had a little hut built in a place called Fond-Zombi, which was said to be very wild. An old childhood friend of hers, a famous witch called Ma Cia, lived nearby, and Toussine hoped she would put her in touch with Jeremiah. So Toussine lived in the woods, and came very seldom to L'Abandonee.

❈ Discussion and Writing

1. Describe the function of the prefatory paragraph.
2. Analyze the images used to portray Toussine and Jeremiah. How do these characters differ from the rest of the community?
3. Discuss the significance of the names, especially Xango and Minerva: what resonances do the names carry; what do the allusions suggest about the characters; how do the allusions affect the story?
4. Comment on the life people lead in L'Abandonnee: what is the source of their strength? Discuss the role of community in general; discuss the outlook of the people in L'Abandonnee.

❈ Research and Comparison

Interdisciplinary Discussion Question: Examine Schwarz-Bart's work and her treatment of women's issues in the context of the African Caribbean experience in particular and the African diaspora in general.

Olive Senior
(b. 1941)
Jamaica

Olive Senior was born and raised in the country, in the outlying limestone landscape of hilly western Jamaica. There she was shuttled back and forth among the parishes of Trelawny and Westmoreland, Hanover and St. James, journeys that epitomized the polarities of Jamaican society and its attitudes toward race and class. On the one hand, she spent part of her childhood in a poor family among ten children in a remote village in Trelawny, where customs brought from Africa prevailed. Here, by means of the oral tradition, she learned the pleasure in and power of language; she learned the delight and morality embodied in stories and their telling, as well as in preaching and testifying. On the other hand, she spent part of her childhood in the relatively affluent house in Westmoreland, where she was the only child and where the assimilation of European values was the established goal. During her high school days in Montego Bay, she began to write for *The Daily Gleaner,* Jamaica's major newspaper, and after graduation, she took a journalism degree at Carleton University in Ottawa, Canada. When she returned to Jamaica, she worked as a journalist and also in publishing, while writing poetry and short stories.

Olive Senior has been concerned about the difficulties Antillean writers face when trying to publish their work in the West Indies, and she has been disturbed by the splintering of the Caribbean community. Her dedication to Jamaica and to a concept of a Caribbean sensibility has informed her writing. In her focus on individual lives, she has affirmed the integrity of her Creole heritage. She has, moreover, attested to its inherent validity as an appropriate literary subject and to its right to be considered appropriate, despite centuries of entrenched colonial standards. In this way, she has confronted the legacy of colonialism.

Do Angels Wear Brassieres?

Beccka down on her knees ending her goodnight prayers and Cherry telling her softly, "And Ask God to bless Auntie Mary." Beccka vex that anybody could interrupt her private conversation with God so, say loud loud, "No. Not praying for nobody that tek weh mi best glassy eye marble."

"Beccka!" Cherry almost crying in shame, "Shhhhh! She wi hear you. Anyway she did tell you not to roll them on the floor when she have her headache."

"A hear her already"—this is the righteous voice of Auntie Mary in the next room—"But I am sure that God is not listening to the like of she. Blasphemous little wretch."

She add the last part under her breath and with much lifting of her eyes to heaven she turn back to her nightly reading of the Imitations of Christ.

"Oooh Beccka, Rebecca, see what yu do," Cherry whispering, crying in her voice.

Beccka just stick out her tongue at the world, wink at God who she know right now in the shape of a big fat anansi[1] in a corner of the roof, kiss her mother and get into bed.

As soon as her mother gone into Auntie Mary room to try make it up and the whole night come down with whispering, Beccka whip the flashlight from off the dressing table and settle down under the blanket to read. Beccka reading the Bible in secret from cover to cover not from any conviction the little wretch but because everybody round her always quoting that book and Beccka want to try and find flaw and question she can best them with.

Next morning Auntie Mary still vex. Auntie Mary out by the tank washing clothes and slapping them hard on the big rock. Fat sly-eye Katie from the next yard visiting and consoling her. Everybody visiting Auntie Mary these days and consoling her for the crosses she have to bear (that is Beccka they talking about). Fat Katie have a lot of time to walk bout consoling

---

[1] A spider; also, the trickster character in West African and Caribbean stories. [eds.)

because ever since hard time catch her son and him wife a town they come country to cotch[2] with Katie. And from the girl walk through the door so braps![3] Katie claim she too sickly to do any washing or housework. So while the daughter-in-law beating suds at her yard she over by Auntie Mary wash-pan say she keeping her company. Right now she consoling about Beccka who (as she telling Auntie Mary) every decent-living upright Christian soul who is everybody round here except that Dorcas Waite about whom one should not dirty one's mouth to talk yes every clean living person heart go out to Auntie Mary for with all due respect to a sweet mannersable child like Cherry her daughter is the devil own pickney.[4] Not that anybody saying a word about Cherry God know she have enough trouble on her head from she meet up that big hard back man though young little gal like that never shoulda have business with no married man. Katie take a breath long enough to ask question:

"But see here Miss Mary you no think Cherry buck up the devil own self when she carrying her? Plenty time that happen you know. Remember that woman over Allside that born the pickney with two head praise Jesus it did born dead. But see here you did know one day she was going down river to wash clothes and is the devil own self she meet. Yes'm. Standing right there in her way. She pop one big bawling before she faint weh and when everybody run come not a soul see him. Is gone he gone. But you no know where he did gone? No right inside that gal. Right inna her belly. And Miss Mary I telling you the living truth, just as the baby borning the midwife no see a shadow fly out of the mother and go right cross the room. She frighten so till she close her two eye tight and is so the devil escape."

"Well I dont know about that. Beccka certainly dont born with no two head or nothing wrong with her. Is just hard ears she hard ears."

"Den no so me saying?"

"The trouble is, Cherry is too soft to manage her. As you look hard at Cherry herself she start cry. She was never a strong child and she not a strong woman, her heart just too soft."

"All the same right is right and there is only one right way to bring up a child and that is by bus' ass pardon my french Miss Mary but hard things call for hard words. That child should be getting blows from the day she born. Then she wouldnt be so force-ripe[5] now. Who cant hear must feel for the rod and reproof bring wisdom but a child left to himself bringeth his mother to shame. Shame, Miss Mary."

"Is true. And you know I wouldnt mind if she did only get into mischief Miss Katie but what really hurt me is how the child know so much and show

---

[2]Support. [eds.]
[3]A sound suggesting suddenness or sudden cessation of motion. [eds.]
[4]Pickney or picknie: a child. [eds.]
[5]Prematurely ripened: used to castigate children who act above themselves. [eds.]

off. Little children have no right to have so many things in their brain. Guess what she ask me the other day nuh?—if me know how worms reproduce."

"Say what, maam?"

"As Jesus is me judge. Me big woman she come and ask that. Reproduce I say. Yes Auntie Mary she say as if I stupid. When the man worm and the lady worm come together and they have baby. You know how it happen?— Is so she ask me."

"What you saying maam? Jesus of Nazareth!"

"Yes, please. That is what the child ask me. Lightning come strike me dead if is lie I lie. In my own house. My own sister pickney. So help me I was so frighten that pickney could so impertinent that right away a headache strike me like autoclaps. But before I go lie down you see Miss Katie, I give her some licks so hot there she forget bout worm and reproduction."

"In Jesus name!"

"Yes. Is all those books her father pack her up with. Book is all him ever good for. Rather than buy food put in the pickney mouth or help Cherry find shelter his only contribution is book. Nuh his character stamp on her. No responsibility that man ever have. Look how him just take off for foreign without a word even to his lawful wife and children much less Cherry and hers. God knows where it going to end."

"Den Miss M. They really come to live with you for all time?"

"I dont know my dear. What are they to do? You know Cherry cant keep a job from one day to the next. From she was a little girl she so nervous she could never settle down long enough to anything. And you know since Papa and Mama pass away is me one she have to turn to. I tell you even if they eat me out of house and home and the child drive me to Bellevue I accept that this is the crosses that I put on this earth to bear ya Miss Katie."

"Amen. Anyway dont forget what I was saying to you about the devil. The child could have a devil inside her. No pickney suppose to come facety[6] and force-ripe so. You better ask the Archdeacon to check it out next time he come here."

"Well. All the same Miss Katie she not all bad you know. Sometime at night when she ready to sing and dance and make up play and perform for us we laugh so till! And those times when I watch her I say to myself, this is really a gifted child."

"Well my dear is your crosses. If is so you see it then is your sister child."

"Aie. I have one hope in God and that is the child take scholarship exam and God know she so bright she bound to pass. And you know what, Miss Katie, I put her name down for the three boarding school them that furthest from here. Make them teacher deal with her. That is what they get paid for."

Beccka hiding behind the tank listening to the conversation as usual. She think about stringing a wire across the track to trip fat Katie but she feeling

---

[6]Rude. [eds.]

too lazy today. Fat Katie will get her comeuppance on Judgment Day for she wont able to run quick enough to join the heavenly hosts. Beccka there thinking of fat Katie huffing and puffing arriving at the pasture just as the company of the faithful in their white robes are rising as one body on a shaft of light. She see Katie a-clutch at the hem of the gown of one of the faithful and miraculously, slowly, slowly, Katie start to rise. But her weight really too much and with a tearing sound that spoil the solemn moment the hem tear way from the garment and Katie fall back to earth with a big buff, shouting and wailing for them to wait on her. Beccka snickering so hard at the sight she have to scoot way quick before Auntie Mary and Katie hear her. They think the crashing about in the cocoa walk is mongoose.

Beccka in Auntie Mary room—which is forbidden—dress up in Auntie Mary bead, Auntie Mary high heel shoes, Auntie Mary shawl, and Auntie Mary big floppy hat which she only wear to wedding—all forbidden. Beccka mincing and prancing prancing and mincing in front of the three-way adjustable mirror in Auntie Mary vanity she brought all the way from Cuba with her hard-earned money. Beccka seeing herself as a beautiful lady on the arms of a handsome gentleman who look just like her father. They about to enter a nightclub neon sign flashing for Beccka know this is the second wickedest thing a woman can do. At a corner table lit by Chinese lantern soft music playing Beccka do the wickedest thing a woman can do— she take a drink. Not rum. One day Beccka went to wedding with Auntie Mary and sneak a drink of rum and stay sick for two days. Beccka thinking of all the bright-color drink she see advertise in the magazine Cherry get from a lady she use to work for in town a nice yellow drink in a tall frosted glass . . .

"Beccka, Rebecca O My god!" That is Cherry rushing into the room and wailing. "You know she wi mad like hell if she see you with her things you know you not to touch her things."

Cherry grab Auntie Mary things from off Beccka and fling them back into where she hope is the right place, adjust the mirror to what she hope is the right angle, and pray just pray that Auntie Mary won't find out that Beccka was messing with her things. Again. Though Auntie Mary so absolutely neat she always know if a pin out of place. "O God Beccka," Cherry moaning.

Beccka stripped of her fancy clothes dont pay no mind to her mother fluttering about her. She take the story in her head to the room next door though here the mirror much too high for Beccka to see the sweep of her gown as she does the third wickedest thing a woman can do which is dance all night.

Auntie Mary is a nervous wreck and Cherry weeping daily in excitement. The Archdeacon is coming. Auntie Mary so excited she cant sit cant stand cant do her embroidery cant eat she forgetting things the house going to the dog she dont even notice that Beccka been using her lipstick. Again. The Archdeacon coming Wednesday to the churches in the area and after-ward—as usual—Archdeacon sure to stop outside Auntie Mary gate even for one second—as usual—to get two dozen of Auntie Mary best roses and a bottle of pimento dram save from Christmas. And maybe just this one time Archdeacon will give in to Auntie Mary pleading and step inside her humble abode for tea. Just this one time.

Auntie Mary is due this honor at least once because she is head of Mothers Union and though a lot of them jealous and back-biting her because Archdeacon never stop outside their gate even once let them say anything to her face.

For Archdeacon's certain stop outside her gate Auntie Mary scrub the house from top to bottom put up back the freshly laundered Christmas Curtains and the lace tablecloth and the newly starch doilies and the anti-macassars clean all the windows in the house get the thick hibiscus hedge trim so you can skate across the top wash the dog whitewash every rock in the garden and the trunk of every tree paint the gate polish the silver and bring out the crystal cake-plate and glasses she bring from Cuba twenty-five years ago and is saving for her old age. Just in case Archdeacon can stop for tea Auntie Mary bake a fruitcake a upside-down cake a three-layer cake a chocolate cake for she dont know which he prefer also some coconut cookies for although the Archdeacon is an Englishman dont say he dont like his little Jamaican dainties. Everything will be pretty and nice for the Archdeacon just like the American lady she did work for in Cuba taught her to make them.

The only thing that now bothering Auntie Mary as she give a last look over her clean and well-ordered household is Beccka, dirty Beccka right now sitting on the kitchen steps licking out the mixing bowls. The thought of Beccka in the same house with Archdeacon bring on one of Auntie Mary headache. She think of asking Cherry to take Beccka somewhere else for the afternoon when Archdeacon coming but poor Cherry work so hard and is just excited about Archdeacon coming. Auntie Mary dont have the courage to send Beccka to stay with anyone for nobody know what that child is going to come out with next and a lot of people not so broadmind as Auntie Mary. She pray that Beccka will get sick enough to have to stay in bed she—O God forgive her but is for a worthy cause—she even consider drugging the child for the afternoon. But she don't have the heart. And anyway she dont know how. So Auntie Mary take two asprin and a small glass of tonic wine and pray hard that Beccka will vanish like magic on the afternoon that Archdeacon visit.

Now Archdeacon here and Beccka and everybody in their very best clothes. Beccka thank God also on her best behavior which can be very good so far in fact she really look like a little angel she so clean and behaving.

In fact Archdeacon is quite taken with Beccka and more and more please that this is the afternoon he decide to consent to come inside Auntie Mary parlor for one little cup of tea. Beccka behaving so well and talking so nice to the Archdeacon Auntie Mary feel her heart swell with pride and joy over everything. Beccka behaving so beautiful in fact that Auntie Mary and Cherry dont even think twice about leaving her to talk to Archdeacon in the parlor while they out in the kitchen preparing tea.

By now Beccka and the Archdeacon exchanging Bible knowledge. Beccka asking him question and he trying his best to answer but they never really tell him any of these things in theological college. First he go ask Beccka if she is a good little girl. Beccka say yes she read her Bible every day. Do you now say the Archdeacon, splendid. Beccka smile and look shy.

"Tell me my little girl, is there anything in the Bible you would like to ask me about?"

"Yes sir. Who in the Bible wrote big?"

"Who in the Bible wrote big. My dear child!"

This wasnt the kind of question Archdeacon expecting but him always telling himself how he have rapport with children so he decide to confess his ignorance.

"Tell me, who?"

"Paul!" Beccka shout.

"Paul?"

"Galations six eleven 'See with how large letters I write onto you with mine own hands.'"

"Ho Ho Ho Ho" Archdeacon laugh.—"Well done. Try me with another one."

Beccka decide to ease him up this time.

"What animal saw an angel?"

"What animal saw an angel? My word. What animal ... of course. Balaam's Ass."

"Yes you got it."

Beccka jumping up and down she so excited. She decide to ask the Archdeacon a trick question her father did teach her.

"What did Adam and Eve do when they were driven out of the garden?"

"Hm," the Archdeacon sputtered but could not think of a suitable answer.

"Raise Cain ha ha ha ha ha."

"They raised Cain Ho Ho Ho Ho Ho."

The Archdeacon promise himself to remember that one to tell the Deacon. All the same he not feeling strictly comfortable. It really don't seem dignified for an Archdeacon to be having this type of conversation with an eleven-year-old girl. But Beccka already in high gear with the next question and Archdeacon tense himself.

"Who is the shortest man in the Bible?"
Archdeacon groan.
"Peter. Because him sleep on his watch. Ha Ha Ha."
"Ho Ho Ho Ho Ho."
"What is the smallest insect in the Bible?"
"The widow's mite," Archdeacon shout.
"The wicked flee," Beccka cry.
"Ho Ho Ho Ho Ho Ho."

Archdeacon laughing so hard now he starting to cough. He cough and cough till the coughing bring him to his senses. He there looking down the passage where Auntie Mary gone and wish she would hurry come back. He sputter a few time into his handkerchief, wipe his eye, sit up straight and assume his most religious expression. Even Beccka impress.

"Now Rebecca. Hm. You are a very clever very entertaining little girl. Very. But what I had in mind were questions that are a bit more serious. Your aunt tells me you are being prepared for confirmation. Surely you must have some questions about doctrine hm, religion, that puzzle you. No serious questions?"

Beccka look at Archdeacon long and hard. "Yes," she say at long last in a small voice. Right away Archdeacon sit up straighter.

"What is it my little one?"

Beccka screwing up her face in concentration.

"Sir, what I want to know is this for I can't find it in the Bible. Please sir, do angels wear brassieres?"

Auntie Mary just that minute coming through the doorway with a full tea tray with Cherry carrying another big tray right behind her. Enough food and drink for ten Archdeacon. Auntie Mary stop braps in the doorway with fright when she hear Beccka question. She stop so sudden that Cherry bounce into her and spill and a whole pitcher of cold drink all down Auntie Mary back. As the coldness hit her Auntie Mary jump and half her tray throw way on the floor milk and sugar and sandwiches a rain down on Archdeacon. Archdeacon jump up with his handkerchief and start mop himself and Auntie Mary at the same time he trying to take the tray from her. Auntie Mary at the same time trying to mop up the Archdeacon with a napkin in her mortification not even noticing how Archdeacon relieve that so much confusion come at this time. Poor soft-hearted Cherry only see that her sister whole life ruin now she dont yet know the cause run and sit on the kitchen stool and throw kitchen cloth over her head and sit there bawling and bawling in sympathy.

Beccka win the scholarship to high school. She pass so high she getting to go to the school of Auntie Mary choice which is the one that is furthest away. Beccka vex because she dont want go no boarding school with no heap of girl. Beccka dont want to go to no school at all.

Everyone so please with Beccka. Auntie Mary even more please when she get letter from the headmistress setting out Rules and Regulation. She only sorry that the list not longer for she could think of many things she could add. She get another letter setting out uniform and right away Auntie Mary start sewing. Cherry take the bus to town one day with money coming from God know where for the poor child dont have no father to speak of and she buy shoes and socks and underwear and hair ribbon and towels and toothbrush and a suitcase for Beccka. Beccka normally please like puss with every new thing vain like peacock in ribbons and clothes. Now she hardly look at them. Beccka thinking. She dont want to go to no school. But how to get out of it. When Beccka think done she decide to run away and find her father who like a miracle have job now in a circus. And as Beccka find him so she get job in the circus as a tight-rope walker and in spangles and tights lipstick and powder (her own) Beccka perform every night before a cheering crowd in a blaze of light. Beccka and the circus go right round the world. Every now and then, dress up in furs and hats like Auntie Mary wedding hat Beccka come home to visit Cherry and Auntie Mary. She arrive in a chauffeur-driven limousine pile high with luggage. Beccka shower them with presents. The whole village. For fat Katie Beccka bring a years supply of diet pill and a exercise machine just like the one she see advertise in the magazine the lady did give to Cherry.

Now Beccka ready to run away. In the books, the picture always show children running away with their things tied in a bundle on a stick. The stick easy. Beccka take one of the walking stick that did belong to Auntie Mary's dear departed. Out of spite she take Auntie Mary silk scarf to wrap her things in for Auntie Mary is to blame for her going to school at all. She pack in the bundle Auntie Mary lipstick Auntie Mary face powder and a pair of Auntie Mary stockings for she need these for her first appearance as a tight rope walker. She take a slice of cake, her shiny eye marble and a yellow nicol which is her best taa in case she get a chance to play in the marble championship of the world. She also take the Bible. She want to find some real hard question for the Archdeacon next time he come to Auntie Mary house for tea.

When Auntie Mary and Cherry busy sewing her school clothes Beccka take off with her bundle and cut across the road into the field. Mr. O'Connor is her best friend and she know he won't mind if she walk across his pasture. Mr. O'Connor is her best friend because he is the only person Beccka can hold a real conversation with. Beccka start to walk toward the mountain that hazy in the distance. She plan to climb the mountain and when she is high enough she will look for a sign that will lead her to her father. Beccka walk and walk through the pasture divided by stone wall and wooden gates which she climb. Sometime a few trees tell her where a pond is. But it is very lonely. All Beccka see is john crow and cow and cattle egret blackbird and parrotlets that scream at her from the trees. But Beccka dont notice them. Her mind busy on how Auntie Mary and Cherry going to be sad now she gone and she composing letter she will write to tell them she safe and she forgive them everything. But the sun getting too high in the sky and Beccka thirsty. She eat the cake but she dont have water. Far in the distance she see a bamboo clump and hope is round a spring with water. But when she get to the bamboo all if offer is shade. In fact the dry bamboo leaves on the ground so soft and inviting that Beccka decide to sit and rest for a while. Is sleep Beccka sleep. When she wake she see a stand above her four horse leg and when she raise up and look, stirrups, boots, and sitting atop the horse her best friend, Mr. O'Connor.

"Well Beccka, taking a long walk?"

"Yes sir."

"Far from home eh?"

"Yes sir."

"Running away?"

"Yes sir."

"Hm. What are you taking with you?"

Beccka tell him what she have in the bundle. Mr. O'Connor shock.

"What, no money?"

"Oooh!"

Beccka shame like anything for she never remember anything about money.

"Well you need money for running away you know. How else you going to pay for trains and planes and taxis and buy ice cream and pindar cake?"

Beccka didnt think about any of these things before she run away. But now she see that is sense. Mr. O'Connor talking but she dont know what to do. So the two of them just stand up there for a while. They thinking hard.

"You know Beccka if I was you I wouldnt bother with the running away today. Maybe they dont find out you gone yet. So I would go back home and wait until I save enough money to finance my journey."

Beccka love how that sound. To finance my journey. She think about that a long time. Mr O'Connor say, "Tell you what. Why dont you let me give you a ride back and you can pretend this was just a practice and you can start saving your money to run away properly next time."

Beccka look at Mr. O'Connor. He looking off into the distance and she follow where he gazing and when she see the mountain she decide to leave it for another day. All the way back riding with Mr. O'Connor Beccka thinking and thinking and her smile getting bigger and bigger. Beccka cant wait to get home to dream up all the tricky question she could put to a whole school full of girl. Not to mention the teachers. Beccka laughing for half the way home. Suddenly she say—

"Mr. Connor, you know the Bible?"

"Well Beccka I read my Bible every day so I should think so."

"Promise you will answer a question."

"Promise."

"Mr. Connor, do angels wear brassieres?"
"Well Beccka, as far as I know only the lady angels need to."
Beccka laugh cant done. Wasnt that the answer she was waiting for?

❊ Discussion and Writing

1. What is implied by Auntie Mary's preparations for and fears about the English archdeacon's probable stop at her house?
2. Contrast Beccka's encounters with the archdeacon and Mr. O'Connor. What do these encounters reveal about Beccka?
3. What is the significance of her running away; of her fantasy about her father; of her search?
4. Analyze the use of language in the narration. Discuss the purpose and effect of using spoken language in literary writing.
5. What serious issues does the writer address in this humorous story? What is the significance of the question in the title?

❊ Research and Comparison

Interdisciplinary Discussion Question: Research the various patios and Creoles that are spoken throughout the Caribbean. Examine these languages in relation to the oral tradition, its vitality and role in the life of Caribbean communities.

Cesar Verduguez
(b. 1941)
Bolivia

Cesar Verduguez Gomez was born in La Paz, Bolivia. A painter and writer, he has worked as an art teacher at various schools in Cochabamba and at the Academy of Fine Arts. He has published studies about art as well as fiction. He received his most recent literary prize in 1992, when he was awarded first prize in the National Literature Competition of the City of Cochabamba for his subsequently published book of stories *Un Gato Encerrado en la Noche* (1993).

All his fiction is set within the context of the social problems of Bolivia and Latin America. Since his student days, he has personally identified with those who have endured injustice. He has said: "This world of those who suffer—the children, peasants, miners, those on the margins of small and large urban settlements—is the subject of my literary work." He is, thus, one of the outspoken critics of oppressive Latin American governments and dictatorships. Verduguez likens this repression—in which even the suggestion of opposition to governmental policy brought persecution—to the burning of people as witches during the Middle Ages. Confined for six months, although not affiliated with a political party, he has found himself among those who have been imprisoned or "disappeared." "The Scream in Your Silence" concerns *los desaparecidos* (the "disappeareds"), a nightmare known too well throughout Latin America and the Caribbean, especially during the decade of the 1970s when the term was coined.

*The Scream in Your Silence**

Any similarity to persons, institutions and events in real life is not coincidental but is a poor description of actual events beyond the imagination.

Zenon said, "I'm not surprised, this country is a bar of soap," Imelda remembered. He said it when we got the news. Who would have believed it possible. Nobody, but nobody could have imagined such a thing of Adalberto. A quiet boy, studious, nothing of a Don Juan, just one girlfriend, and he broke with her for I don't know what reason. Pamela says it was for another girl. I don't know, but nobody would have thought it of him. I can't believe it even now.

Everything was ready. Imelda couldn't say if it was the first, third, or fifth time. She went over her list, her traveling notes: the small suitcase, the toilet kit, the money and ticket, her pocketbook, the cake.

Zenon sat in silence. Imelda would have preferred him to talk, even if he made her head hurt with his strange remarks. His silence was more painful. "Febei" had a sad look, staring into the silence. Imelda was on the verge of tears, but she controlled herself. She could constrain herself in front of Zenon, her daughter, and anybody else, but not in front of her sister. I am the pillar of this house, the man, the woman, everything, she told herself. I have to do everything, I have to cook, I have to work, I have to look after family affairs, I have to go out and protest, because Zenon can't. If he weren't sick it would be different. Like it used to be. He has turned everything over to me. Before it would have been my place to cry, but not now. One must behave in keeping with one's place, and if I don't live up to my position, this house will go under. The brush, the wallet. Imelda had cried at Mildred's house. All right, she was told, you have to take this on alone, your husband is too sick

*Translated by Carolina Udovicki

to do anything. Anything, Imelda repeated with a sigh of infinite resignation. It's true, she went on after remembering that talk, and that's why the poor man must be suffering much more; he who always raised his voice against injustices and liked to protest and defend the people he saw victimized by the self-important, by some abuse. Getting old is killing, and even more so with his illness. And now he seems to be eating his own soul and innards with his silence. And there is nothing to be had from my Meritorious title, or from being retired, he had said, after almost a whole life of service to the state. Nothing, he repeated, with bitter conviction. It had been his idea to put the note in the dough before baking it. Imelda wasn't sure whether it was in the first, second, or fourth cake that she had baked. Everything happens for nothing, Zenon said. So much effort, so many years of sacrifice, for what? The state neither recognizes nor rewards service in the true measure of our dedication. It's always been like that. Always. So, why complain? And he sank back into silence. Tooth paste, soap, a towel, and clothes for Adalberto, a pair of pants, change of underwear, sweater. Mildred had said: you need all your strength now more than ever. Imelda had cried. When she was with Mildred, she cried like a baby. She cried anywhere, when there was no one to see her. But only Mildred had seen her tears.

"Febei" watched the door. I wonder if he's waiting for Adalberto to come in or for me to go out, thought Imelda. The animal, too, seemed to feel the heavy and gray atmosphere in the house. Pamela is the only one who has been able to adjust to Adalberto's absence, but she is still a child, Imelda said to herself. Here are the candies. Pamela had bought a bag of candy for Imelda to give to her brother in her name. You must go to the Undersecretary of the Ministry of Defense, Mildred told Imelda, and to Jorge Ramirez, too, he's a friend of mine, you tell him you're my sister, he's very nice and works in the Ministry of Defense, he can help you, go there, go here and there, to this and that place, to this one and that one, you have to say that you are the wife of a Meritorious, that your son was always first in his class in elementary and high school, that he won prizes and certificates of excellence. Take the certificates with you, just in case. And talk with Juan Balderrama also. He's our relative on our mother's side. His father was a cousin of our grandmother. In these cases you have to turn to everybody you can think of, and he holds a high position with lots of influence. Tell him this, and tell him that, as though I didn't know what I should say, Imelda thought. Or maybe in a situation like this you turn stupid without even realizing it. The truth is that since they gave me the news that day, I've been living in a daze. They told me and I felt I'd been hit in the chest. Imelda did her best to pull herself together and set herself to preparing the food, cooking coffee, readying a blanket, going out to buy cigarettes. She arrived at the offices of the Political Department. They did not let her see Adalberto, he was listed as being held in solitary confinement. Please, she asked, could you at least get these things to him? Yes, they answered, that we can do.

It's only food, coffee, and cigarettes, said Imelda. Just routine, senora, they answered, no notes, letters, newspapers or radios can be received.

Zenon, at home, hung between anger and sorrow. The same as always, the same as always. It's always been the same. It's not even a repetition. Mankind hasn't moved an inch, it's the same as it used to be despite all the scientific and technical advances, despite the increase in universities and schools, in men who are supposed to think. It remains stuck. Its habits, the way it operates and thinks, all the same as a thousand years ago: ambition, power, hate, love. Mankind is a point glued out there in space. It's not going anywhere. It's there and that's all.

Imelda, the next day, did the cooking early and went, together with Pamela, to the Political Department taking another dinner pail. Your son, senora, they told her, has been taken to the capital. Imelda asked the same question as the day before: Why? What were the reasons for his arrest, and now, for his transfer to the capital? We don't know anything, they answered. Orders from above. But, how is it possible? insisted Imelda. We have already told you, senora, we know nothing. Our job is to obey. The order came from the Ministry, that's where you have to inquire. Rocks covered their mouths. What could Adalberto have done? Imelda asked herself. I never noticed anything unusual in his university activities, nor heard a conversation either with even a hint about politics. Her thoughts went back to his childhood.

From his past she had a large album of photographs, dating back to his first month in the world. And for his future, she had opened a savings account to ensure his future, something to fall back on in his life ahead, as she put it to herself.

Zenon, on hearing of the new unfortunate turn, Adalberto's transfer, commented: We know nothing of the laws of government, they are laws which do not belong to the governed. We are not capacitated to know them. Pamela, as usual, hummed quietly. Imelda finished her preparations. Everything was ready: the clothes, the suitcase, the cake. From then on, Pamela would be the official cook in the house. She and Mildred were there to see off Imelda at the inter-city bus terminal. Imelda took a night bus.

After buying fruit and little meat pies, Imelda headed for the Ministry of the Interior. She was allowed entry on presentation of her ID card. Having explained why she was there, the ministry officials looked through some lists and told her: No, senora, we're holding nobody by that name. If he was brought from the interior, they might have taken him directly to the cells at the Political Department and they'd send his papers on to us later. Yes, yes, of course you can go.

At the Political Department, nobody could or would give her any information about Adalberto's whereabouts. We've never heard the name, and there is no university student here. From the interior? They must have gotten things mixed up or there's been a mistake, but he's not here. Or maybe they sent him to the City Jail. Have you inquired there? Sometimes for lack of room or for special reasons they send them there. She remembered Mildred: You're sure to have a lot of problems, run into a thousand difficulties. Your road won't be easy. Don't get discouraged. I know you have a strong character, but there are situations which break the spirit of even the strongest. Don't crack up. Remember you have a daughter and husband who depend on you.

She reached the City Jail with hope. But to her sorrow, he was not there either. No, senora, he's not here. Don't insist. We don't know. If he were here we'd have no reason for not letting you see him, but he isn't here. You have to ask at the Ministry. They don't know? That's not our fault. Imelda felt a terrible uneasiness. The flesh of her flesh could give her much more pain than any physical or spiritual suffering of her own. Where could Adalberto be? she asked herself. Somebody had to know, somebody had to have some knowledge of where he was, where he was being held. It just isn't possible, she said to herself, again in the street, her tears out of control, for a person to disappear just like that, in a civilized country, in the middle of the 20th century.

Zenon had said: If Adalberto got mixed up in some political movement, I don't know why he got involved. Why didn't he discuss these things with me? All political movements are a waste of time. What do they accomplish? Nothing. Before any one of them gets halfway down its road, it forgets what it's about, goes down another road, comes to a standstill, gets lost. And when you finally wake up, nothing has been done, you're right where you were at the start, you haven't moved an inch. The useless sacrifice of a few or of many thousand, to be forgotten in the end.

Once again at the Ministry, Imelda asked herself, which time is this? but could not answer her own question. How many times had she been up these stairs? ten, twenty, thirty? She had learned that in the basement under the stairs there were large cells, and she wondered if her son might not be just a few meters below her at that very moment, under heavy guard. She asked, yet again, to be received. She waited. How many hundreds of hours had she waited, seated on a wooden chair or in an armchair, to speak with the Undersecretary or Minister. Many people waited, struggling to have a few words with the Minister, and when it seemed her turn had come at last, office hours were over or some person of importance would go in without being announced, without having to wait, and stay forever. Other times, the Minister would leave, called by the President or on some other highly important, they claimed, business. Or he simply did not show up at all at his office, all day. And then there was that woman, the wife of an arrested factory worker, Imelda remembered, who advised her: Just in case, why don't you go to Viacha and Achocalla? They have political prisoners there, too. And they say they are held in a place called Chonchocoro which is somewhere in the middle of the Altiplano.

Of the package of fruit, meat pies, cake and bag of candy, only the last remained. I got on a bus for Viacha, a one hour ride. And it was the same: no Adalberto. I was told Chonchocoro was some seven to eight kilometers further on by foot. It was my bad luck that the bus passed only every other day and today was a day the bus didn't go by. I'd had no idea. So I went by foot, walking the whole way across the Altiplano. My tiredness would have disappeared if they'd told me Adalberto was there, but nothing. Heavy-hearted I had to walk back that whole distance. I got back to the city half-dead. The next day I went to Achocalla, two hours by bus, also in vain.

Imelda never did get to speak with the Minister, but she did see the Undersecretary. He told her coldly: There must be some mix up. Your son must still be in his hometown. As you yourself have established, senora, your son is not here. His name appears on none of our lists. Go back to your town, that's where he has to be.

On her return, her anxiety became the blood running through her veins, her pain became her flesh. Pamela wept, although later she was humming again. Mildred shed tears in silence. Zenon said: We live in circles. There is an intimate correspondence between events from a time in the past and those in the present, it's as though a point in history had come to an eternal standstill. That point is a sameness, and it exists, it is there, every time, yesterday, today and tomorrow. Which means that an event recurs in each turn of mankind's circular history, the same thing happens all over again.

The officials at the local Political Department told Imelda and Mildred: He's not in La Paz? How strange! But you can be sure he's not here. If you like we can let you see the cells. He isn't here. The same night of the day of his arrest, special agents sent by the Ministry took him away. They had top Government orders. They told us they were taking him to La Paz. But maybe they left him to be held for a while in Cochabamba or Oruro. So he must be in one of those places.

Tomorrow, I'll go to Cochabamba, Imelda told Zenon, and from there I'll go on to Oruro. And she went to bed in an effort to overcome the great fatigue weighing her down. That night, Imelda had a dream. She dreamt she was terribly hungry, that all her flesh was in pain from the torments she suffered at the break of each day, that there were many winters accumulated in her bones and that her cells were being penetrated by cement and steel. She felt icy rains soaking her naked body, and thunder and lightning explod-ing under her skin. Her nights were curdled by fear and horror, and she prayed the morning would come, but it never did. She felt with her hand in the dark for the dust she so often thought she had become. A river of firy winds and ice flowed over her and woke her up. She slept no more that night, telling herself over and over that the dream had been nothing more than the result of her feeling so discouraged and of her pessimistic imagina-tion. She tried to think of Adalberto as well, somewhere where he was being treated with the considerations due all human beings, with the respect required for a fellow man, that they were brothers even more because of the land, the country of their birth, brothers in the blood of their race, brothers in Adam and Eve, and, finally, brothers in the love of God. But the darkness of the room fed her doubts. She turned on the light on her night table.

Mildred told her: Make another cake to take to Adalberto. It's a way of preserving your self-confidence, optimism. And optimism is good for your spirits and for your whole being, and it also helps things turn out right.

Once again the hours of ceremony prior to traveling. The cake, the suitcase, the clothes. Zenon in his armchair, silent. Pamela checking the oven. "Febei" lying there, looking at that gray picture, that viscous silence expanding into every corner. Imelda, nervous, had a premonition of a scream, right there in the room, in the silence itself. It punctured her eardrums, that scream ... "Febei" moved his head without turning to look at the door. Zenon broke the oppressive silence and said: A revolution is like an arrow released into flight, shot into the air. Everybody thinks it will go somewhere, but no, wrong. It remains immobile. Because if we divide time and at each instant the arrow occupies a point in space, the point being occupied determines that the arrow, at that instant, is without movement.

Imelda traveled to Cochabamba, and from there to Oruro. In neither of the these cities was she given news of Adalberto. From Oruro she went on to La Paz. She looked up the people Mildred had recommended to ask for their help. It took her three days. They were not easy to find due to changes of address, unexpected trips, momentary absences. But finding them did no good. Those of us with government jobs are not permitted, are forbidden, to take up the defense of, to intercede for any political prisoner, one of them said. I'm sorry, I would like to help, but I have an important printing firm and it would compromise me to even visit your son, the other said. However, I will try to help in some other way. Do you, perhaps, need money?

Imelda decided to make the rounds again of the different facilities where prisoners were held. At the window of the Political Department, the officer asked, What's your son's name? Adalberto Vega. Let's see, let's see, yes, he's here, the officer said as he looked at some papers. The blood rushed to Imelda's head. A crushing joy invaded her like a torrent, overflowing through all the pores of her body. Ma-may I see him? Of course you can, only three minutes. Have you the required permit for a visit? Permit ... ? No, no, I don't. Where do I get it? At the Ministry. Imelda took a taxi. Hurry, hurry, please! The traffic jam, the snarl of vehicles made it almost impossible for the car to move. The driver blew his horn. It was 12 noon. When she got there, the offices were closed. On Monday, senora. Again she felt that terrible uneasiness. She took another taxi and went back to the building of the Political Department. Is there no other way I can get to see him? She saw other people entering with that permit to see their imprisoned relatives. Bring out Wilfredo Sanchez ... for his mother, an officer shouts. No, senora, there isn't. But, at least, will you give him these things I've brought for him. Yes of course. We'll hand them through. Imelda said, I'll be right back. And she hurried off to buy sardines, crackers, two cartons of cigarettes, fruit juices, canned milk, butter, cheese, bread, olives, cold cuts, jams, apples, bananas, oranges, roasted nuts, canned frankfurters. All of this, together with the candies from Pamela, the cake, by now quite stale, and Adalberto's clothes, she handed over to the officer at the visitor's window. Imelda drew a calmer breath. All she could do now was wait for the afternoon and tomorrow, Sunday, to pass.

For whom?, Imelda was asked when she arrived on Monday morning early at the Ministry to apply for a visitor's pass. For Adalberto Vega. Where is he being held? At the Political Department. Let's see, section "c," Vega, va, va, ve, there's no Vega here.

But that's not possible, Imelda exclaimed in alarm. She went to the highest police official, fourth or fifth in the Ministry hierarchy. I personally left food for my son on Saturday. Whom did you give it to, senora. To an officer. What was his name? I don't know his name, he was on duty at the window and he even received the clothes . . . His name, I asked? I don't know, I've already said. Find out and let us know, because your son's name is not listed. There is no entry, of arrest or release, with that name. You must have imagined it, the mind plays tricks, or maybe it was an error or mix-up of the Political Department.

Imelda rushed in despair to the Political Department. No, senora, there's no Adalberto Vega, university student. Where is the officer who attended me on Saturday? Which officer? He was dark, thin, between 30 and 35 years old. What was his name? I don't know, I don't know, but he told me my son was here and he accepted a bag of clothes and food for him. Senora, the three officers who were here on Saturday were drawn to do a turn in the interior. They'll be back in two weeks. You come back then, and have it out face-to-face with the officer you spoke to. But if he told me . . . No, senora, he is not here.

Zenon said: Everybody says the future will be beautiful, we will all live better in the future. Man will be another man, different, better, but nobody realizes that we never reach that future. As soon as we advance ten or one hundred years, the future also advances ten or a hundred years, and that is why we'll never catch up. The future will always be far away. In conclusion, man will always be the same.

Another trip. The baking of the cake was like a ritual of hope.

At the Ministry offices, Imelda watched, like in a theater, scenes of painful drama. Women who wept uncontrollably, pleading, some of then kneeling in front of a lame official. Get up, senora. Don't come crying here. Why didn't you keep a better check on your son; go make yourself another son. Your husband? You'd do better to find yourself a better one. Get up, senora, if you don't want us to lock you up, too. You are all also conspiring against the government, with your weeping you make the government look bad. Imelda held back her rage and swore she would never let them break her, bow so low as to let them mistreat her in this way. When her turn came at last to speak with the Undersecretary, he told her: The truth is, nothing is known about the university student Adalberto Vega Estrada. Since no document of his arrest or of his release is to be found in any of the files of the branches of this office, he obviously must have been released only a few hours after his arrest as soon as it was established that he had not participated in any act against the government. We truly believe your son must have run off with some girl and that they are now secretly living together. He'll show up. Don't worry so much, go get things ready, instead, for his return. Who knows, he may be needing a cradle. Maybe you're still young but you could be a grandmother. That's how young people are these day.

Imelda heard that Wilfredo Sanchez had been released, she remembered the name. He must have known Adalberto. Sanchez told her the following: Yes, senora, I met Adalberto Veguita, a nice boy, very nice. We were together for two weeks, maybe more. One night, at midnight, they came for him. I don't know where they took him. They're always transferring us from one place to another. I don't know where he might be now. The food? Not very good. No, he had no blanket nor a change of clothes. He arrived without anything. We had to loan him things. You sent him food and clothes? canned foods, cigarettes? No, senora, during the time I was with him he received nothing, absolutely nothing, Oh, yes, I remember now! He received a bag of candy.

The cake, the suitcase, Pamela humming a tune. Zenon said: History is all one, it never varies. Since the so-called dawn of civilization, there has always been the ambition for power, betrayal, crime. Cain and the blood of his brother live on forever. They have only changed clothes. A crime is committed and the people think it is something new, or a repetition of something, and they don't realize it is the same crime of a year ago, a decade ago, a century ago, an eon ago. They think it is a repetition, but the truth is it is the same crime as before. Why do they think there are amazing similarities? Because it's always the same event within the circular passage of time.

Imelda had dozed off on the night bus when she felt a spasmodic shudder, horribly intense and disagreeable. Wide awake, she thought the bus had run into a ditch or a hole in the road. She held back a scream. Looking out ahead she saw a truck illuminated in the headlights of her bus and had the sensation of a bitter taste, as though a mixture of acids and fermented juices were eating her stomach. Sleep, she thought, would restore her peace. But it was not easy. The bus jolted, the motor rumbled and images with no relation to anything, which made no sense, appeared before her eyes. A spider was spinning a thread of eggs of infinite length. A truck whose noise mixed with that in her ears, moved in a place of extreme darkness. The eggs burst, spattering excrement. The truck moved in reverse crushing chickens, ducks, dogs. From their midst a bird appeared and took flight, higher and higher. Suddenly, it was enveloped in a great radiance and fell. Its impact as it hit the ground sent a shudder through Imelda which seemed to give substance to an omen. Still she fought with all the strength of her mind against the message in the ominous meaning of an inexplicable anxiety, of a feeling that her flesh was coming apart slowly in pieces, that her days left to live were piling up in blood and being transformed into tiny beings rushing to devour her nerves. A kind of darkness turned to stone in her throat. Imelda continued trying to keep faith, with all her being, with her conviction that Adalberto was somewhere, a prisoner perhaps, in hiding, perhaps, after having escaped, but with his heart beating to the joy of his loved ones, to her joy, above all. I'd like Adalberto to be living in the dawn, and for him to appear someday with the sun. But, despite herself, she felt he was living now only in her thoughts.

She couldn't stand it any more and, in front of a Ministry official, she broke into tears: You too must have children, do it for them, tell me where my son is, please, I beg you.

Imelda made many trips, and it would have been hard on any budget. There is a last possibility, she thought, to pay. I have no more money but there is the money in Adalberto's savings account. As the mother of Adalberto, she was able to draw the funds after some minor red tape. Zenon had criticized her for her constant trips. It looks as though the boy is no more than an excuse for you to travel again, he said, the boy must be dead by now. No, no, no, he isn't, yelled Imelda, exasperated. And she could not stop herself. Of course, you with your rheumatoid arthritis are going around doing everything for my son's freedom so there's no need for me to travel. For you it's easier for him to be dead.

Well, dona[1] Imelda, as we agreed, here is what I have to tell you. I have investigated your son's case. There isn't much information or documentation. Many of the policemen of three years ago have been discharged or transferred to the interior. First of all, I want to show you the file I managed to sneak out; I have to return it to its place by early morning. See, somebody wrote in red, in big letters, ATTENTION. Here are some interesting scraps of papers. In this one, somebody denounces your son as an active member of the ELN,[2] an important person, it says, occupying a key position in the high command but operating under the cover of an ordinary student who never openly participates in public meetings or demonstrations. Imelda's eyes opened wide. Let me see. She studied the print of the typewriter used: small, italic, with large accents. And she noted the spacing errors between letters. It was the same print and typing as in a letter sent by Adalberto's ex-girl friend asking him to loan her certain books and calling him her beloved BIRD.

And here's this other note. Imelda recognized it. It was the one Zenon had slipped into the unbaked cake dough.

Adalberto, my son:

I don't know if (crossed out) you have really been involved in political activity. If the suspicions are false, have patience. Your mother has taken action to obtain your freedom and in a short time you will be, will be (repeated) with us again. Certain friends and my title of Meritorious will

---

[1] A title of respect used before a married or widowed woman's first name.
[2] *Ejercito de Liberation Nacional*, National Liberation Army.

help to have you free very soon. But should your involvement indeed be true, conduct yourself as the man we brought you up to be. I believe you embraced a (crossed out) just ideal and in that case I would prefer you to bite your tongue, until it is cut through, before you inform on your friends or comrades. I shall be, I am proud of you.

Ever affectionately
your father

From what I have been able to find out, your son was put on a plane and thrown—It is possible!—from the air into the middle of the jungle or of Lake Titicaca. I don't know who gave the order.

The man closes the door and locks it. Imelda sits down in a chair and opens her purse. She removes several bundles of bills of large denomination. At the bottom still, among her personal belongings, is the bank book of Adalberto's savings account.

"You are still young, dona Imelda. You must have had your son when you were 18."

"Isn't the money I'm going to give you enough? I can give you more."

"A deal is a deal. I've done my part".

From that moment, not one word is spoken by Imelda. The man waits for her to stop crying. She cries for a long time. She falls quiet. Quiet. The man approaches her. Imelda closes her eyes and fixes her mind on another moment, another place.

You hear the noise of doors opening. A slight tremor runs through you deep inside. It must be between three and five in the morning. The door to your cell opens and a voice orders: get ready, fast. In fact you are ready, you have no suitcase, no bundle, no blanket. You were sleeping without taking off your clothes, not even your shoes, curled up tight to fit into one half of the pallet, virtually coming apart in dirt and straw, and barely covering yourself with the other half. You get up and are ready. You remove a few straws from yourself. Out! the voice orders you. You run your fingers through your hair to straighten it and various things pass through your mind: you are being taken for a new round of questioning, with the usual punishment of every morning, or perhaps with something more painful to extract a confession. You are ready. What more can you tell them if you know nothing about the things they keep asking? You are sure there must be a misunderstanding, and yet they insist that you contradict yourself, or you don't want to tell them what you know so you talk about other things to throw them off. That is what they believe. And you don't know if you are crazy or if they are the crazy ones. Crazy. You go out into the street and they make you get into a van. So you know it's not the usual questioning but obviously a transfer.

"Would you like me to turn out the light? You don't want to talk?"

But a ride in a van at these hours can have other implications, like a solitary and far-off place where the law in cases of attempted escape can be applied. By the route the van is taking, you realize the airport is the most likely destination. And indeed, you arrive and are ordered into a plane. So it could be a detention camp or expulsion from the country. You are confused. The plane takes off. You don't know how long the flight has lasted but in the activity and words of the men guarding you there are enough clues to catch their real meaning and you grasp your hideous fate. At that moment, one of the men tells you: Take off your clothes. And I undress slowly, like an automaton. Then they say: Ready, this is the best place. And I don't know why but a terrible fear invades me and I tremble. I who always believed myself strong. They open the hatch and say: Jump! Jump you bastard! The wind howls, beating against the plane with all its force, it is deafening. I see darkness, in the distance the weak light of the breaking day. I fight in my desparation, grabbing at anything, and catch hold of a leg of one of the men. A cold sweat covers me. They hit at my arms until they succeed in making me let go . . . They are the stronger, they overcome me. I scream at the edge of insanity, they push me with all their might. They shove. The dawn is my tomb.

❀ Discussion and Writing

1. Discuss the role of Imelda and the impact of her tireless, innumerable trips to track down her son.
2. Explore the implications of Zenon's statements, including his letter to his son. What is his function in the narrative?
3. Reconstruct the story of Adalberto as it unfolds through Imelda's almost endless search.
4. What are the implications of the way the officers handle Imelda's search for her son? Comment on the depiction of bureaucracy and its relevance to the title of the story.

❀ Research and Comparison

Interdisciplinary Discussion Question: Research the political situation, governmental oppression, and bureaucracy in Latin America during the 1970s, examining the issue of the *desaparecidos*.

Isabel Allende
(b. 1942)
Chile

Isabel Allende was born in Peru, where her father, a diplomat, was posted, but she was raised in her grandparents' house in Santiago after her parents' divorce. The title she later gave to her first novel, the internationally acclaimed *The House of the Spirits* (1985), derives from her childhood. After her grandmother, an astrologer, died, her grandfather continued to summon and speak with her every day, and so the child felt she lived in a house of spirits. Isabel Allende was also close to her paternal uncle, Salvador Allende, the president of Chile, and like him, she supported democracy in Chile. His assassination caused her to flee the country.

*Our Secret**

She let herself be caressed, drops of sweat in the small of her back, her body exuding the scent of burnt sugar, silent, as if she divined that a single sound could nudge its way into memory and destroy everything, reducing to dust this instant in which he was a person like any other, a casual lover she had met that morning, another man without a past attracted to her wheat-colored hair, her freckled skin, the jangle of her gypsy bracelets, just a man who had spoken to her in the street and begun to walk with her aimlessly, commenting on the weather and the traffic, watching the crowd, with the slightly forced confidence of her countrymen in this foreign land, a man without sorrow or anger, without guilt, pure as ice, who merely wanted to spend the day with her, wandering through bookstores and parks, drinking coffee, celebrating the chance of having met, talking of old nostalgias, of how life had been when both were growing up in the same city, in the same barrio, when they were fourteen, you remember, winters of shoes soggy from frost, and paraffin stoves, summers of peach trees, there in the now forbidden country. Perhaps she was feeling a little lonely, or this seemed an opportunity to make love without complications, but, for whatever reason, at the end of the day, when they had run out of pretexts to walk any longer, she had taken his hand and led him to her house. She shared with other exiles a sordid apartment in a yellow building at the end of an alley filled with garbage cans. Her room was tiny: a mattress on the floor covered with a striped blanket, bookshelves improvised from boards stacked on two rows of bricks, books, posters, clothing on a chair, a suitcase in the corner. She had removed her clothes without preamble, with the attitude of a little girl eager to please. He tried to make love to her. He stroked her body patiently, slipping over her hills and valleys, discovering her secret routes, kneading her, soft clay upon the sheets, until she yielded, and opened to him. Then he retreated, mute, reserved. She gathered herself, and sought him, her head on his belly, her face hidden, as if constrained by modesty, as she fondled him, licked him, spurred him. He tried to lose himself; he closed his eyes and for a while let her do as she was doing, until he was defeated by sadness, or

---

*Translated Margaret Sayers Peden

shame, and pushed her away. They lighted another cigarette. There was no complicity now; the urgent anticipation that had united them during the day was lost, and all that was left were two vulnerable people lying on a mattress, without memory, floating in the terrible vacuum of unspoken words. When they had met that morning they had had no extraordinary expectations, they had had no particular plan, only companionship, and a little pleasure, that was all, but at the hour of their coming together they had been engulfed by melancholy. We're tired, she smiled, seeking excuses for the desolation that had settled over them. In a last attempt to buy time, he took her face in his hands and kissed her eyelids. They lay down side by side, holding hands, and talked about their lives in this country where they had met by chance, a green and generous land in which, nevertheless, they would forever be foreigners. He thought of putting on his clothes and saying goodbye, before the tarantula of his nightmares poisoned the air, but she looked so young and defenseless, and he wanted to be her friend. Her friend, he thought, not her lover; her friend, to share quiet moments, without demands or commitments; her friend, someone to be with, to help ward off fear. He did not leave, or let go her hand. A warm, tender feeling, an enormous compassion for himself and for her, made his eyes sting. The curtain puffed out like a sail, and she got up to close the window, thinking that darkness would help them recapture their desire to be together, to make love. But darkness was not good; he needed the rectangle of light from the street, because without it he felt trapped again in the abyss of the timeless ninety centimeters of his cell, fermenting in his own excrement, delirious. Leave the curtain open, I want to look at you, he lied, because he did not dare confide his night terrors to her, the wracking thirst, the bandage pressing upon his head like a crown of nails, the visions of caverns, the assault of so many ghosts. He could not talk to her about that, because one thing leads to another, and he would end up saying things that had never been spoken. She returned to the mattress, stroked him absently, ran her fingers over the small lines, exploring them. Don't worry, it's nothing contagious, they're just scars he laughed, almost with a sob. The girl perceived his anguish and stopped, the gesture suspended, alert. At that moment he should have told her that this was not the beginning of a new love, not even of a passing affair; it was merely an instant of truce, a brief moment of innocence, and soon, when she fell asleep, he would go; he should have told her that there was no future for them, no secret gestures, that they would not stroll hand in hand through the streets again, nor share lovers' games, but he could not speak, his voice was buried somewhere in his gut, like a claw. He knew he was sinking. He tried to cling to the reality that was slipping away from him, to anchor his mind on anything on the jumble of clothing on the chair, on the books piled on the floor, on the poster of Chile on the wall, or the coolness of this Caribbean night, on the distant street noises; he tried to concentrate on this body that had been offered him, think only of the girl's luxuriant hair, the caramel scent of her skin. He begged her voicelessly to help him save those seconds, while she observed him from the far edge of the bed, sitting cross-legged like a fakir, her pale breasts and the eye of her navel also observing him, registering his trembling, the chattering of his teeth, his moan. He thought he could hear the silence growing within him; he knew that he was coming apart, as he had so often before, and he gave up the struggle, releasing his last hold on the present, letting himself plunge down the endless precipice. He felt the crusted straps on his ankles and wrists, the brutal charge, the torn tendons, the insulting voices demanding names, the unforgettable screams of Ana, tortured beside him, and of the others, hanging by their arms in the courtyard.

What's the matter? For God's sake, what's wrong? Ana's voice was asking from far away. No, Ana was still bogged in the quicksands to the south. He thought he could make out a naked girl, shaking him and calling his name, but he could not get free of the shadows with their snaking whips and rippling flags. Hunched over, he tried to control the nausea. He began to weep for Ana and for all the others. What is it, what's the matter? Again the girl, calling him from somewhere. Nothing! Hold me! he begged, and she moved toward him timidly, and took him in her arms, lulled him like a baby, kissed his forehead, said, Go ahead, cry, cry all you want; she laid him flat on his back on the mattress and then, crucified, stretched out upon him.

For a thousand years they lay like that, together, until slowly the hallucinations faded and he returned to the room to find himself alive in spite of everything, breathing, pulsing, the girl's weight on his body, her head resting on his chest, her arms and legs atop his: two frightened orphans. And at that moment, as if she knew everything, she said to him, Fear is stronger than desire, than love or hatred or guilt or rage, stronger than loyalty. Fear is all-consuming . . . , and he felt her tears rolling down his neck. Everything stopped: she had touched his most deeply hidden wound. He had a presentiment that she was not just a girl willing to make love for the sake of pity but that she knew the thing that crouched beyond the silence, beyond absolute solitude, beyond the sealed box where he had hidden from the Colonel and his own treachery, beyond the memory of Ana Diaz and the other betrayed *companeros* being led in one by one with their eyes blindfolded. How could she know all that?

She sat up. As she groped for the switch, her slender arm was silhouetted against the pale haze of the window. She turned on the light and, one by one, removed her metal bracelets, dropping them noiselessly on the mattress. Her hair was half covering her face when she held out her hands to him. White scars circled her wrists, too. For a timeless instant he stared at them, unmoving, until he understood everything, love, and saw her strapped to the electric grid, and then they could embrace, and weep, hungry for pacts and confidences, for forbidden words, for promises of tomorrow, shared, finally, the most hidden secret.

✦ Discussion ansd Writing

1. What is implied by the namelessness of the two characters?
2. What interferes with the characters' love-making? When do they realize the secret they share? When does the reader realize it? Analyze the way Allende reveals the characters' discovery of each other.
3. What is the implication of her lying "crucified, stretched out upon him," and "(f)or a thousand years they lay like that"? Analyze the use of images and phrases in the narrative to further explore Allende's social and political stance.

✦ Research and Comparison

Compare and contrast this story to any other with a similar political background.

Interdisciplinary Discussion Question: Examine the political history of Chile, focusing on the twentieth century and particularly on the last half of the twentieth century.

Antonio Cisneros
(b. 1942)
Peru

Antonio Cisneros is among the group of young Peruvian poets who came to the forefront in the 1960s. Cisneros wrote *Comentarios Reales* (1964) when he was 22 and a student at the University of San Marcos, and its publication established his reputation in the circles of Latin American intellectuals and artists. Leaving behind the theories evolved by the older generations of Latin American writers, the younger poets took Cesar Vallejo's last works as their springboard. They explored the nature of Peru itself as a historical independent reality and themselves as Peruvian. In his examination of Peruvian history, Cisneros has looked at the accretions surrounding the actual events with an ironic eye that thrusts the events of the past into the present. The actual Battle of Ayacucho (1824) and the legend that accrued over time thus explode in the light of the mid-twentieth century.

After the Battle of Ayacucho: A Mother's Testimony*

Some soldiers who were drinking brandy
have told me that now this country
is ours.
They also said
I shouldn't wait for my sons.
So I must
exchange the wooden chairs
for a little oil & some bread.
The land is black as dead ants,
the soldiers said it was ours.
But when the rains begin
I'll have to sell
the shoes & ponchos
of my dead sons.

Some day I'll buy a longhaired mule
& go down to my fields
of black earth
to reap the fruit
of these broad dark lands.

❋ **Discussion and Writing**

1. Characterize the speaker in the poem. What are her concerns? Formulate a political statement that is conveyed in the poem through the speaker.
2. What does she see in the future? What are the implications?
3. How would a freedom fighter or a soldier react to the Battle of Ayacucho?

❋ **Research and Comparison**

Interdisciplinary Discussion Question: Examine the importance of the Battle of Ayacucho as it paved the way for eminent liberators in the fight for the independence of Spanish America.

---

*Translated by David Tipton

Rosario Ferre
(b. 1942)
Puerto Rico

Rosario Ferre was born and raised in the southern coastal city of Ponce, Puerto Rico, in the walled-in privacy of an affluent middle-class household. Her mother grew up in a country village; her father, an industrialist from Ponce, served as governor (1968–1972) and was a leader in the drive for statehood. As was fitting for young people of her social status, she did her undergraduate work in the United States. She also earned a master's degree at the University of Puerto Rico, and returned to the United States, where she received a doctorate at the University of Maryland. She wrote her thesis and dissertation on Latin American masters of the macabre and the fantastic, and her stories about her childhood reveal the same preoccupation with intense emotional states. She tells how her mother's brother died the year she was born; how her mother mourned his loss for ten years, taking her on weekly visits to place flowers in his crypt; how her mother competed with this brother's widow to see who brought the largest bouquet. She tells, too, how a lively 17-year-old nanny, who splashed bright lipstick across her mouth and sported brightly flowered dresses, helped dispel her mother's gloomy presence. This nanny arrived from the poor edge of town, near the sugar mill, when Ferre was seven, and the two girls devoured fairytales, for both were avid readers. These are among the contrasts and images that have fed her work.

Ferre began to write as a child in Puerto Rico, publishing articles while she was still in high school. In the early 1970s, she helped found and was editor of *Zona de carga y descarga,* a literary journal that published many of the young, subsequently important Puerto Rican writers. The journal published her work as well: her poems, stories, and essays, including an article protesting the exploitation of women both in the home and in the workplace. In her writing, she has attacked social and economic exploitation, the racism within the class structure, and the role of the United States in the economic and political life of Puerto Rico.

The Youngest Doll*

Early in the morning the maiden aunt had taken her rocking chair out onto the porch facing the canefields, as she always did whenever she woke up with the urge to make a doll. As a young woman, she had often bathed in the

---

Translated by Rosario Ferre and Diana Velez

river, but one day when the heavy rains had fed the dragontail current, she had a soft feeling of melting snow in the marrow of her bones. With her head nestled among the black rock's reverberations she could hear the slamming of salty foam on the beach mingled with the sound of the waves, and she suddenly thought that her hair had poured out to sea at last. At that very moment, she felt a sharp bite in her calf. Screaming, she was pulled out of the water, and, writhing in pain, was taken home in a stretcher.

The doctor who examined her assured her it was nothing, that she had probably been bitten by an angry river prawn. But the days passed and the scab would not heal. A month later, the doctor concluded that the prawn had worked its way into the soft flesh of her calf and had nestled there to grow. He prescribed a mustard plaster so that the heat would force it out. The aunt spent a whole week with her leg covered with mustard from thigh to ankle, but when the treatment was over, they found that the ulcer had grown even larger and that it was covered with a slimy, stonelike substance that couldn't be removed without endangering the whole leg. She then resigned herself to living with the prawn permanently curled up in her calf.

She had been very beautiful, but the prawn hidden under the long, gauzy folds of her skirt stripped her of all vanity. She locked herself up in her house, refusing to see any suitors. At first she devoted herself entirely to bringing up her sister's children, dragging her monstrous leg around the house quite nimbly. In those days, the family was nearly ruined; they lived surrounded by a past that was breaking up around them with the same impassive musicality with which the crystal chandelier crumbled on the frayed embroidered linen cloth of the dining-room table. Her nieces adored her. She would comb their hair, bathe and feed them, and when she read them stories, they would sit around her and furtively lift the starched ruffle of her skirt so as to sniff the aroma of ripe sweetsop that oozed from her leg when it was at rest.

As the girls grew up, the aunt devoted herself to making dolls for them to play with. At first they were just plain dolls, with cottony stuffing from the gourd tree in the garden and stray buttons sewn on for eyes. As time passed, though, she began to refine her craft more and more, thus earning the respect and admiration of the whole family. The birth of a new doll was always cause for a ritual celebration, which explains why it never occurred to the aunt to sell them for a profit, even when the girls had grown up and the family was beginning to fall into need. The aunt continued to increase the size of the dolls so that their height and other measurements conformed to those of each of the girls. There were nine of them, and the aunt would make one doll for each per year, so it became necessary to set aside a room for the dolls alone in the house. When the eldest girl turned eighteen, there were one hundred and twenty-six dolls of all ages in the room. Opening the door gave you the impression of entering a dovecote, or the ballroom in the czarina's palace, or a warehouse in which someone had spread out a row of tobacco leaves to dry. But the aunt didn't enter the room for any of these pleasures. Instead, she would unlatch the door and gently pick up each doll, murmuring a lullaby as she rocked it: "This is how you were when you were a year old, this is you at two, and like this at three," measuring out each year of their lives against the hollow they had left in her arms.

The day the eldest turned ten, the aunt sat down in her rocking chair facing the canefields and hardly ever got up again. She would rock away entire days on the porch, watching the patterns of rain shift like watercolor over the canefields, and coming out of her stupor only when the doctor would pay her a visit, or she awoke with the desire to make a doll. Then she would call out so that everyone in the house would come and help her. On that day, one could see the hired help making repeated trips to town like cheerful Inca messengers, bringing wax, porcelain clay, needles, spools of thread of every shade and color. While these preparations were taking place, the aunt would call the niece she had dreamt about the night before into her bedroom and take her measurements. Then she would make a wax mask of the child's face, covering it with plaster on both sides, like a living face sheathed in two dead ones. Then she would draw out an endless flaxen thread of melted wax through a pinpoint on her chin. The porcelain of the hands and face was always translucent; it had an ivory tint to it that formed a great contrast with the curdled whiteness of the bisque faces. For the body, the aunt would always send out to the garden for twenty glossy gourds. She would hold them in one hand and, with an expert twist of her knife, would slice them up and lean them against the railing of the balcony, so that the sun and wind would dry the cottony guano brains out. After a few days, she would scrape off the dried fluff with a teaspoon and, with infinite patience, feed it into the doll's mouth.

The only items the aunt would agree to use in the birth of a doll that were not made by her with whatever materials came to her from the land, were the glass eyeballs. They were mailed to her directly from Europe in all colors, but the aunt considered them useless until she had left them submerged at the bottom of the stream for a few days, so that they would learn to recognize the slightest stirring of the prawn's antennae. Only then would she carefully rinse them in ammonia water and place them, glossy as gems and nestled in a bed of cotton, at the bottom of one of her Dutch cookie tins. The dolls were always outfitted in the same way, even though the girls were growing up. She would dress the younger ones in Swiss embroidery and the older ones in silk guipure, and on each of their heads she would tie the same bow, wide and white and trembling like the breast of a dove.

The girls began to marry and leave home. On their wedding day, the aunt would give each of them their last doll, kissing them on the forehead and telling them with a smile, "Here is your Easter Sunday." She would reassure the grooms by explaining to them that the doll was merely a sentimental ornament, of the kind that people used to place on the lid of grand pianos in the old days. From the porch, the aunt would watch the girls walk down the fanlike staircase for the last time. They would carry a modest checkered cardboard suitcase in one hand, the other hand slipped around the waist of the exuberant doll made in their image and likeness, still wearing the same old-fashioned kid slippers and gloves, and with Valenciennes bloomers barely showing under their snowy, embroidered skirts. But the hands and faces of these new dolls looked less transparent than those of the old: they had the consistency of skim milk. This difference concealed a more subtle one: the wedding doll was never stuffed with cotton but was filled with honey.

All the girls had married, and only the youngest niece was left at home when the doctor paid his monthly visit to the aunt, bringing his son along this time, who had just returned from studying medicine up north. The young man lifted the starched ruffle of the aunt's skirt and looked intently at the huge ulcer which oozed a perfumed sperm from the tip of its greenish scales. He pulled out his stethoscope and listened to it carefully. The aunt thought he was listening for the prawn's breathing, to see if it was still alive, and so she fondly lifted his hand and placed it on the spot where he could feel the constant movement of the creature's antennae. The young man released the ruffle and looked fixedly at his father. "You could have cured this from the start," he told him. "That's true," his father answered, "but I just wanted you to come and see the prawn that has been paying for your education these twenty years."

From then on it was the young doctor who visited the old aunt every month. His interest in the youngest niece was evident from the start, so that the aunt was able to begin her last doll in plenty of time. He would always show up for the visit wearing a pair of brightly polished shoes, a starched collar, and an ostentatious tiepin of extravagant poor taste. After examining the aunt he would sit in the parlor, leaning his paper silhouette against the oval frame of the chair, and each time would hand the youngest an identical bouquet of purple forget-me-nots. She would offer him ginger cookies and would hold the bouquet with the tip of her fingers, as if she were holding a purple sea urchin turned inside out. She made up her mind to marry him because she was intrigued by his drowsy profile, and also because she was deathly curious to find out what dolphin flesh was like.

On her wedding day, as she was about to leave the house, the youngest was surprised to find that the doll the aunt had given her as a wedding present was warm. As she slipped her arm around her waist, she examined her attentively, but quickly forgot about it, so amazed was she at the excellence of the craft. The doll's face and hands were made of the most delicate Mikado porcelain, and in her half-open and slightly sad smile she recognized her full set of baby teeth. There was also another notable detail: the aunt had embedded her diamond eardrops in the doll's pupils.

The young doctor took off to live in town, in a square house that made one think of a cement block. Each day he made his wife sit out on the balcony, so that passersby would be sure to see that he had married into society. Motionless inside her cubicle of heat, the youngest began to suspect that it wasn't just her husband's silhouette that was made of paper, but his soul as well. Her suspicions were soon confirmed. One day he pried out the doll's eyes with the tip of his scalpel and pawned them for a fancy gold pocket watch with a long, embossed chain. From then on the doll remained seated as always on the lid of the grand piano, but with her gaze modestly lowered.

A few months later the doctor noticed the doll was missing from her usual place and asked the youngest what she'd done with it. A sisterhood of pious ladies had offered him a healthy sum for the porcelain hands and face, which they thought would be perfect for the image of the Veronica in the next Lenten procession. The youngest answered him that the ants had at last discovered the doll was filled with honey and, streaming over the piano, had devoured it in a single night. "Since the hands and face were made of Mikado porcelain and were as delicate as sugar," she said, "the ants have probably taken them to some underground burrow and at this very moment are probably wearing down their teeth, gnawing furiously at fingers and eyelids to no avail." That night the doctor dug up all the ground around the house, but could not find the doll.

As the years passed the doctor became a millionaire. He had slowly acquired the whole town as his clientele, people who didn't mind paying exorbitant fees in order to see a genuine member of the extinct sugarcane aristocracy up close. The youngest went on sitting in her chair out on the balcony, motionless in her muslin and lace, and always with lowered eyelids. Whenever her husband's patients, draped in necklaces and feathers and carrying elaborate handbags and canes, would sit beside her, perhaps coughing or sneezing, or shaking their doleful rolls of flesh with a jingling of coins, they would notice a strange scent that would involuntarily make them think of a slowly oozing sweetsop. They would then feel an uncontrollable urge to rub their hands together as if they were paws.

There was only one thing missing from the doctor's otherwise-perfect happiness. He noticed that, although he was aging naturally, the youngest still kept the same firm, porcelained skin she had had, when he had called on her at the big house on the plantation. One night he decided to go into her bedroom, to watch her as she slept. He noticed that her chest wasn't moving. He gently placed his stethoscope over her heart and heard a distant swish of water. Then the doll lifted up her eyelids, and out of the empty sockets of her eyes came the frenzied antennae of all those prawns.

❋ Discussion and Writing

1. Describe the incident pictured in the first paragraph. Examine the connections among the sea, the river, the prawn, and the aunt.
2. Analyze the symbolism involved in the doll-making, examine the components of the dolls themselves as well as the process and purpose of their creation.

3. What does doll-making indicate about the aunt's personality and her needs?
4. What is special about the youngest doll? Why did the aunt make this doll different from the others?
5. Discuss the roles of the two doctors; how and by whom are they challenged?
6. Analyze the transposition of the youngest doll and the niece. What is the significance of the final episode?

✹ Research and Comparison

Explore the use of the doll as a motif to represent women in any two literary traditions of different cultures.

Ana Lydia Vega
(b. 1946)
Puerto Rico

Ana Lydia Vega was born in Santurce, a district in San Juan, Puerto Rico and spent her childhood there in a much loved wooden house. During the 1940s, when many poor rural Puerto Ricans were migrating to the cities to find better-paying work, her father had come to the capital from the tiny mountain town of Coamo and her mother from the coastal town of Arroyo. He had never gone to school, while she had obtained her teaching diploma from the University of Puerto Rico, the first woman from Arroyo to do so. He studied the dictionary and built a large pool of words for use in the complicated poems he spun; she peppered her language with slang and built her conversation on proverbs. He saw to it that his daughters were formally educated, in part as a means of preventing dependency on a man. When the family moved to the urban environment of Rio Piedras, they sent Vega to a Catholic high school, where, under the guidance of an order of Irish-American nuns, she received the education her father respected and had missed. During the 1960s, she studied French literature at the University of Puerto Rico (where she has returned to teach French and Caribbean literature). This was the time of great political awakenings, and she became a *borinquena*—a proudly Puerto Rican woman activist— and a socialist. She then earned her master's degree and doctorate at the University of Provence, completing her dissertation on Francophone Caribbean literature in 1978, a study that spoke from and to her belief in a Caribbean consciousness.

Her writing, which had begun in high school with plays and mystery novels, took on new meaning in the political turmoil of the 1970s, when she composed several satiric narratives that centered on the experiences of contemporary women. She has continued to develop her satiric irreverence, now parodying conventional Western genres and narrative techniques, now protesting social and political conventions. The critics seem to have been waiting for just such a fresh voice and received her work with pleasure. She believes she has been fortunate, bearing out a prophecy disclosed at her birth: she was born with one tooth already present, and she tells the story that an old Arab woman warned, "either she'll die young or be lucky."

ADJ, Inc.*

Hate oppression; fear the oppressed.
V. S. Naipaul

I

On the second of December, 1990, Her Excellency the Magistrate blew a fuse. The rage she had been trying so hard to contain finally exploded. Pressing down hard on the intercom button, she had her secretary cancel all appointments and come in right away to take a letter. She then dictated the following urgent missive:

Honorable Supreme Benefactress:

Your letter of 27th November has more than chagrined us, it has unsettled us. But it gives me great pleasure to remind you that in seven years of uninterrupted operation under my leadership, the Agency has established an enviable record: 5,999 cases satisfactorily resolved. Our carefully monitored dossiers and the effusive letters of appreciation we receive almost daily from our clients attest to the fact that we aim to please and succeed admirably in doing so.

Statistics don't lie: 3,995 husbands rehabilitated and 1,994 corrected or neutralized. The Censor's Board was forced to recommend Final Solution in only ten cases, a tiny percentage considering the overwhelming success of our rehabilitation drive.

This brings me to the difficult subject of this letter, dear Benefactress, the purpose of which is to rid you of any doubts regarding the competence of either ADJ, Inc., or myself, its humble director. Case #6000 has monopolized our professional activity for the last four months. Due to its complexity and unique character, we are now undergoing a technical recycling of our operative personnel. In light of the surfacing of this case, which may well be the harbinger of a new social reality, we have considered setting up an Unresolved Questions Bureau to deal with this and similar cases.

Translated by Diana Velez

I trust this initiative will go some way toward restoring your confidence and that of the other members of the Social Benefactresses' Club so that we may once again enjoy a climate of mutual trust. This will allow your members to continue to provide us with generous and anonymous financial support as they have done in the past during our brief but efficient existence.

As per your request, we enclose photocopies of documents related to Case #6000. We sincerely appreciate the interest you have shown in the resolution of this most complex of cases, and we ask that you call on us for any additional information you might need in your deliberations.

Awaiting your wise decree, and on behalf of our entire team, I send you my best sisterly regards.

Cordially,
Barbara Z.
Magistrate
ADJ, Inc.

Appendix A: Case #6000
Client's Sworn Affidavit

I, Porcia M., duly sworn notary and complaint recorder of ADJ, Inc., hereinafter referred to as the Agency, declare that on September 15, 1990, there appeared before me a married woman, a housewife and resident of San Juan, Puerto Rico, whom, in the interest of privacy, we shall hereafter refer to as the Client. Client testified to us under oath that:

Whereas she has no cause for complaint regarding her husband, whose behavior to date has been exemplary; and

Whereas she thinks the vast majority of the nation's wives would envy her exceptional marital position since she is the unhappy owner of what she insists on calling the Ideal Husband; and

Whereas said Ideal Husband, hereafter referred to as the Accused, shares housework, is a good provider, is considerate, responsible, sweet, courteous, affectionate, serious, and faithful, as well as an efficient executor of all physical husbandly duties, lacking any defect other than his absolute perfection in every respect; and

Whereas the Accused's said perfection is an assault on the Client's self-image as it thereby calls attention implacably to her own imperfection; and

Whereas in the interest of her mental well-being the Client feels an urgent need to file for divorce; said Client, lacking even the faintest cause to justify such action, turns to the Agency in the hope that it will provide requisite pretext so that official rupture of the matrimonial bond may be initiated without further delay and with the celerity merited by the circumstances.

Sworn before me on this 15th day of September, year of our Lord, 1990.

Porcia M.
Principal Notary
Complaint Registry
ADJ, Inc.

Appendix B: Case #6000
Assessment and Training Division Report
Re: Operation Assault

A preliminary screening revealed that the Client had behaved in exemplary fashion during her ten years of marriage. Our conclusion was obvious: systematic subversion of this model behavior was necessary if the couple's stability was to be undermined.

Client therefore attended our Exasperation Techniques Workshops I and II. Our Division offers these workshops free of charge as a service to the community. Client passed with a grade of "A+" and subsequently launched into a four-week "Operation Assault" program custom-designed for her by our expert programmers.

There were four phases to the operation, each methodically designed to bring about a crisis in the domestic system. Outlined below are the Client's evaluative statements on each phase:

Domestic Sabotage

I took the opportunity afforded by my husband's business trip to cease and desist from all household cleaning. I let dirty dishes pile up in the sink. The bathtub had more than twelve rings in it. Bedsheets were rank with sweat and Vicks Vaporub. I piled dirty clothes everywhere. I disconnected the fridge, so that meat would thaw and the freezer would fill with maggots. I spread leftovers over the kitchen counters. The oven became a luxury condo for cruising roaches. . . .

Physiological Terrorism

Just as I expected, my husband returned and, before I could bat an eyelash, he had donned his plaid bermudas and pulled on a pair of rubber gloves. He put everything in order in a flash. But since forewarned is forearmed, I had already gotten into bed faking dizzy spells and other symptoms, complaining about phony aches and pains and refusing to see a doctor. The poor slob thought I was pregnant. The joy on his face was almost more than I could stomach. It gave me a special delight to show him my stained underwear the following week.

What followed constituted an enormous sacrifice on my part, meticulous as I am about personal hygiene. I stopped bathing, despite the unbearable September heat. I gave up brushing my teeth even after eating mangoes. I let my legs, thighs, and underarms grow Amazonic. I threw into the garbage all brushes and combs so as to not succumb to the temptation of taming the tangled and greasy mess I had for hair. Since my skin and scalp are naturally dry, it wasn't long before I was scaly as an iguana. I had never been so wonderfully frightful; it turned my own stomach; I don't know how he was able to put up with it.

Psychological Offensive

My husband's understanding and tenderness almost drove me insane during this phase. The phony tics which had been recommended came naturally. My eyes began to twitch, my nose jerked, and my mouth contracted into spasms. What's worse, for that long month of Operation Assault I couldn't even count on the Agency's moral support, as we had decided to cut off all communication to avoid any suspicion on his part.

By this time I found it relatively effortless to yell obscenities at him and subject him to all sorts of verbal abuse whenever he spoke a kind word to me. Whenever he tried to talk on any subject, I would yawn obviously and act annoyed. I would refuse to go out with him anywhere. And if he asked me why, I would let loose with all the verbal violence I could muster. Insults and curses were the order of the day. . . .

Sexual Strike

I've never much enjoyed the pleasures of the flesh, anyway. My main erogenous zone is definitely my brain. That's why the final phase was not as much of an effort as the others. I simply denied him any intimate contact, turning away from him as soon as my head hit the pillow. This strategy, which would have been misinterpreted and exploited by any other Puerto Rican husband, was actually my safest approach: his democratic principles kept him from taking rearguard action without my consent.

No king-sized bed had ever seemed so small to me before. In my overwrought state the sound of his regular breathing, his most discreet movement, his very heartbeat seemed like deafening drumming that wouldn't let me sleep a wink. After a month of this, he was looking younger and more handsome than ever. I, on the other hand, was on the verge of anorexia nervosa.

The Division's Recommendation

Urgent transfer of Case #6000 to Dirty Tricks Division.
    Medea H.
    Head Trainer II
    Assessment and Training Division

Appendix C. Case #6000
Dirty Tricks Division
Re: Operation No Holds Barred

Transcription of tape recorded by Olga the Vamp, *Agente PFrovocateur*

MAGISTRATE'S NOTE: The agency claims no solidarity *with*, and accepts no responsibility *for* the linguistic unruliness and the concomitant loose style that characterizes the jargon of the agents of this division.

I was having me a delicious and well-earned vacation in Boqueron after having had to screw about ten Accuseds in a row, each one a bigger mother than the one before him, when Dirty Tricks sent for me. Since I always put business before pleasure if I can't manage to combine the two, I gathered my duds and in a blink found myself getting a briefing from the girls in the Assessment and Training office. The Boss Lady gave me twenty-four hours to pull a workplan together. That didn't make me lose no sleep since I can check out any dude and tell you what makes him tick in two hours flat. After reading the statements and laying in some good brain time on it like I do, I checked out the photographs of the Accused in question. Especially the full-length shot. No two ways about it. No problem dealing with this one: nice graying sideburns and temples, cute face, firm body for someone his age. But definitely *not* my type.

My first thought was: "piece of cake." These tall, light-skinned types, kind of cute, you know, Clark Kent glasses, the whole bit—they're usually a cinch. Nine out of ten, it's a case of they've been stirring it up since they were fourteen and by the time they've been married a few years, they can't wait to let it all hang out. That's where I come in. The only thing that didn't fit in with this dude's image were the three large onyx rings on the three fingers of his right hand. I say three because the other two were missing. Vietnam vet, I figured. But since that detail wasn't in the records I'd been given, I filed it away for future reference.

One of the chicks in Corporal Sanctions followed him for me for a few days, so as to catch his moves, you know, so I wouldn't get screwed in the process. The guy was a case. He went from home to work, from work, home; no stops on the way. No bar, no pool hall, no health club, no liquor store, no chicks, no chums, no nothing. Straight. According to the file, he only traveled once a year and that was on bona fide business. Maybe he fooled around while he was in New York, but as far as the island goes, nothing. No two ways about it, if we were to catch him in the act it would have to be staged right here and that's that. I figured the best place for it was his office.

One of our informers who worked in the Office of Economic Development gave me the break I needed. As head of the unit, she figured out how to get me into his office by firing their receptionist and putting me in her place. I blew quite a wad on fine threads and makeup, and Assessment made me take a crash course in office protocol and a mini-finishing school-type program. But by November 1st there was yours truly at her post behind the reception desk with a low-cut skin-tight dress slit up almost to my belly button. Then I grabbed me one of those Bette Davis cigarette holders and was off and running. They don't call me Olga the Vamp for nothing.

About a week after I started, I swear on my mother each and every one of the dudes working there was after me to go out—even the janitor. But mostly they were after me to go *in*, you know. Everyone but the one I was after, the damned Accused. And it wasn't that he hadn't noticed me; it was impossible not to notice me. Besides, he had to go past my desk every morning after punching in. I would about split a lip smiling at him, batting my false lashes, and leaning forward so he could practically see my navel. Then I'd say "Good morning" to him in a voice that would make even a battalion of eunuchs get a hard-on. No dice. The only thing left for me to do was to hoist my ass on the desk to exhibit the rest of the merchandise made in Puerto Rico. Modesty aside, nature has been good to me, as those who know know. At work they all know there's nobody who can beat me at getting, processing, and dispensing with the male element. But the son of a bitch was something else. All I could get out of him were polite hellos and toothpaste commercial smiles.

Since I don't have a stupid bone in my body, I wouldn't miss a chance to sashay by his office, ass swinging and tits erect, during coffee breaks and on my way to the ladies' room. I tell you, I would swing that thing. None of the other guys could get any work done watching me take my swinging strolls. A broken pencil point, a few photocopies to be done, any little thing was an excuse to end up by his desk. Sometimes I'd wait as long as an hour just to ride down the crowded elevator with him, then I'd seize the time to establish some breast-to-back physical rapport. But none of it made a dent.

Then to top it all off, his secretary started giving me a hard time. She was one of those ambulatory antiques who'd noticed the moves I'd put on her boss and looked at me as if she had just bit into a sour mango every time she'd intercept my vibes. Every morning she would greet me with the scowl that launched a thousand shipwrecks, and one fine day she subjected me to an atomic barrage in the copying room: her boss was a decent family man and I'd better lay off, this, that and the other, including a few uncalled-for remarks about the morals of yours truly. I blew my stack and told her in no uncertain terms that what she really needed was a good macho to check her oil, and I knew just the guy who could do it for her. All hell broke loose. She turned purple, stammered, her jaw started quivering, and she threatened to slap me silly, to which I replied with "You and what fucking army?" which calmed her down some since she was a midget if I ever saw one. Good thing she didn't try anything because, though the Agency's policy is never to hit broads no matter how bitchy they get, that particular historical monument held all the numbers for the solid whack in the head I was raffling. . . .

They'd given me a deadline at the Agency and this mess with his secretary was slowing me down, so I had to take the bull by the horns and make my move. I went straight to the Accused and, in my huskiest voice, told him I needed to see him urgently when he was through with work. I licked my lips in slow motion so there would be no mistake about my meaning. He said, no problem, to wait for him at five, that he'd be there as soon as he finished "verifying some overdue accounts . . ."

I was still pacing around at quarter past six, waiting for that half-wit to finish putting x's and circles in his godforsaken columns. I was surprised at my own patience. But the best part was, the hag kept hanging around trying to see what I was up to in the interest of protecting her beloved boss's good name. Finally he says to her, "That's fine, Ms. Thelma, you can go home now. Good night," and she had no choice but to take off with steam blowing out her ears. I gave her my best smirk and a look that said, "Chalk one up for the Vamp."

To make a long story short, I exhausted all my tricks and hints, all my winks and leg crossings, and you know that when it comes to that, I'm the best there is. . . . Zilch. I probably could have taken a little longer with it, but when he asked me in that polite tone of his "what it was I wanted to ask him," I lost it. I pounced on him and started messing with his fly, panting into his ear, to see if at the moment of truth, he'd respond, if only to show he'd been put together right at the factory, shit. But before I could get more deeply into things he pushed me away, shifted into reverse, and took off carrying that silly attaché case of his, and with such a shit-eating grin on his face that I wanted to rip off his glasses, grind them into a fine dust with my heels, and paint his graying moustache red. And I would have done it, too, if it hadn't been that I was still figuring if I could get him to play ball.

Next day I was fired. That son of a bitch reported me to the personnel office for "sexual harassment." Never in all my years as *Agente Provocateur* Level III have I ever come across a specimen like this one. There's just no way to lay your hands on him!

As far as the Client is concerned, in my book she's either a moron or one of those types that gets off on being punished. Why don't they send this hot potato over to Corporal Sanctions? Let Chiqui the Fist handle him. She likes nothing better than to give a well-earned smack in the head to any jerk who deserves it.

Appendix D: Case #6000
Sexual Rehabilitation Division
Re: Operation Motel

At her age and considering the social costs involved in such an action, the idea of going to a motel with a strange man was not exactly to the Client's liking. But the impasse which had been reached, combined with her desperation, made her accept the plan. With the little that remained in the budget for this case we contracted the services of a well-known gigolo who was very popular in the resort areas. We hoped this would be the first and last time we would be forced to resort to the services of a member of the male gender in solving a case. We gave him money for clothes and rented him a car. We reserved a room in a motel on the Caguas Expressway, a motel famous as a place for illicit trysts. Assessment decided on a place called "Swing Butt Low," their reasoning being that the lower the class of the establishment chosen, the bigger the insult to marital honor.

On the 20th of November at three o'clock sharp, the contracted gigolo, one Sly Stick by name, drove up to the Client's house with the radio blaring.

He proceeded to honk boisterously and raised the volume of his radio as instructed, so the neighbors would have no choice but to peep through the blinds of their respective windows. The Client made Sly wait a few moments in order to create some suspense. When she finally came out she was wearing a skin-tight, most revealing crepe dress and mounted on stilt-like spike heels. She walked over to the door Sly was holding open and the two of them French-kissed for a full sixty seconds.

They then screeched out of the neighborhood and made their way to the aforementioned motel. While participating in joint action at the motel, they were guarded by Chiqui the Fist in case any violence ensued.

The Agency had sent several anonymous notes to the Accused before the date of the meeting. On the day itself, Chiqui the Fist made the necessary phone call from a pay phone. She disguised her voice with her chewing gum as she does on these occasions. She very politely asked to speak to the Accused. She covered herself by faking a heavy Cuban accent and using an alias. When he got on the line, she breathed hoarsely into the phone (verbatim quote): "Listen, jerk, your wife's getting it on with some pimp in Caguas. She's screaming so loud you can hear her three miles down the road."

Chiqui asserts that just when she was about to give him the name and address of the motel, she heard a sudden click. This report was subsequently confirmed. Not only didn't the expected action take place as a result of the call, but the Client reports that, upon her return home, looking as disheveled, disarrayed, and distraught as if she'd just spent the night performing sadomasochistic rituals with a band of banshees, she found the table set with their best silver candelabra and their finest china and stemware. He didn't even ask her where she'd been all afternoon as he was too busy with the supergourmet meal he was preparing for their tenth wedding anniversary.

We have been forced to come to the conclusion that results have been inversely proportional to the effort expended on this case by our division. The infallibility of our operations has been checkmated. I fear that Case #6000 has set an inauspicious precedent in the glorious history of ADJ, Inc.

Circe F.
Rehab Counselor IV
Sexual Rehab Division
ADJ, Inc.

II

The Honorable Supreme Benefactress shuffled through the documents one last time before putting them into a manila envelope marked in red with the number 6000. A thoughtful stroking of the salt-and-pepper mustache. A quick tap on the glasses to set them straight on the bridge of the nose. Plastic gloves slipped elegantly, expertly on the hands after depositing the three black rings on top of the desk.

The sheet of paper with its official letterhead carefully centered on the typewriter, he smiled with vague tenderness. Then his eight virtuoso fingers rested delicately on the keyboard to write, very carefully, on the very center of the sheet:

> **BURN FILE.**
> **SILENCE CLIENT.**
> **ASSIGN #6000 TO NEXT CASE.**

❀ Discussion and Writing

1. Describe the nature and function of ADJ, Inc. Discuss the significance of using a U.S. government agency as a model for ADJ, Inc.
2. Why is an ideal husband a threat, and to whom? What does he subvert? Discuss the presentation of the social norms; what is its effect?
3. What is implied by allusions to such characters as Porcia, Medea, Circe, and Clark Kent?
4. Comment on the functions of Olga the Vamp.
5. Why does Case #6000 remain unresolved? What are the implications of the Benefactress's final commands?
6. Analyze the varied levels of ironies and satire in this tale of gender roles. What is the relevance of the quotation from V. S. Naipaul?

❀ Research and Comparison

Interdisciplinary Discussion Questions: Research the political history of Puerto Rico since the Spanish-American War, when the island was ceded to the United States. Discuss the effect of this history on people's lives and the various political responses: statehood, independence, etc.

Rigoberta Menchu
(b. 1951)
Guatemala

Rigoberta Menchu was born in a small village in the mountains of the northwest province of El Quiche, Guatemala. Her parents were the leaders of the village; respected as the "parents" or "grandparents" of the community, they directed the customary practices. When her father could no longer tolerate the exploitation and humiliation inflicted by the landowners and their overseers on his people, he became one of the leaders in the fight for justice. The entire family joined the struggle. In *I, Rigoberta Menchu,* she tells the story of her childhood: the terrible poverty and the inability to escape the forced labor that was no different from slavery; the death of two brothers because of malnutrition and inadequate medical treatment; and her own experiences working on the *fincas* (the plantations) and as a maid. Her story reveals the change from cruel indifference, lies, injustice, and exploitation to unspeakable brutality as the people began to organize in their own defense. She describes how the village was forced to watch as over 20 people who had all been tortured—her younger, 16-year-old brother among them—were burned alive. She describes the separate deaths of her father and mother, equally merciless, and the legacy of the murders of her family and community: a deeper commitment to continue the battle. In 1992, Rigoberta Menchu won the Nobel Peace Prize for her efforts on behalf of the native peoples throughout Latin America who have suffered economic and social repression, deprivation, and discrimination.

The Death of Dona Petrona Chona*

Inhuman are their soldiers, cruel their fierce mastiffs.
CHILAM BALAM

There is something I didn't say before when I spoke about the landowners in my area—the Garcias and the Martinezes. I think I should say it now. I remember something I saw, now that I'm remembering things about other people's lives. In 1975, the Garcias had a market near where I lived and they tried to make all the Indians sell their maize and beans there so that they could buy it cheap, transport it to other places and sell it dear. They had a *finca*[1] where I used to work a lot when I was a child since it was near our house. I used to pick coffee. It was mostly coffee there. There were banana trees to shade the coffee but the landowner didn't let us pick the bananas because they were there for shade. The bananas rotted on their stalks while we were all hungry but couldn't pick them.

I had a friend called Petrona Chona. She had two children, the little boy would be about two and the little girl about three. She had a husband. Petrona was very young and so was her husband. They both worked in the Garcias' *finca.* Then one day the son of the landowner, his name was Carlos Garcia, began courting my friend. I hate him in the very depth of my being. He asked her if she'd be his mistress. She was an Indian. She said, "How can I, I'm a married woman." He said that he loved her, that he really loved her, that he adored her and all that. Then he started threatening her. The landowner's son came to the fields everyday, and as he didn't have anything else to do, he kept after her. One Friday she didn't go to work because her little boy was ill and she had to stay at home. They lived in the *finca.* They

*Translated by Ann Wright
[1]Plantation. [eds.]

paid rent and worked as *peones*[2] but they weren't paid. What they earned went for the rent of the land and the little house. She told me she was in despair because they had nothing to eat even though they worked all the time. One Friday she stayed at home and the landowner's son came to her house. He'd been to the fields and hadn't found her, so he went to the house, to her hut. And he began again asking her to be his mistress and to let him have his way with her. She was very worried about her little boy and kept saying no, and no. They argued for a long time but unfortunately we were all working a long way away. There were some *peones* near the house but they were working too. In the end she refused, and the landowner's son went away. But what that murderer Carlos Garcia did was to send his father's bodyguard to kill the woman in her house. But he told the bodyguard not to shoot her but to hack her to death with a machete. Naturally the bodyguard did as he was told and went to the woman's house and, catching her by surprise, hacked her up with his machete.

It was the first dead body I'd ever seen, and that's why I was saying that I'll have to talk about a lot more corpses, but this was the first one I'd ever touched. He hacked her to pieces and cut one of her baby's fingers off because she was carrying her on her back. The other child came running out of the house in fright. He took the baby off her back, put her on one side and hacked her into twenty-five pieces, if I'm not mistaken. She lay there in pieces. I won't forget it because my friend had talked to me earlier that morning and told me that they were leaving the *finca*. But they didn't have time. The woman had shouted, but none of the workers went near because they saw that first the landowner's son had been there and then the body-guard arrived. Which of them was going to interfere? He'd only be killed himself or dismissed from his job. So the woman was left in pieces. That same Friday afternoon, I went to see her body lying on the ground. The parts of her body were all there on one side. I couldn't believe it was Petrona lying there. There she stayed. No one could bear to lift her up. Not even our community. A lot of people came. But since many different people worked there, from many different areas, no one went near the young woman's body. Then my father came. He cried when he saw her. He said: "Petrona was such a good person." No one could believe it. We picked her little boy up and bandaged his finger so it wouldn't bleed so much. But we didn't know what to do. She stayed there all night. And all Saturday morning. Saturday night came and Sunday. No one would pick her up. Then my father said: "Well, it's up to us." She was already smelling very bad. The smell of her body carried a long way. My father said: "Yes, it's up to us to move her. We must do it." There is a law in Guatemala that you can't move a dead body until the authorities have been so we'd told the authorities immediately. They are in town and don't come until they have time, so they wouldn't get there until Monday. By Sunday the body was already covered with

---

[2]Laborers. [eds.]

flies and everything. It's a very hot place, so there was the smell and all that. My father said: "Well, it's up to us to move the body even if they think that we have committed the crime." We collected Dona Petrona up in baskets and her blood was congealed on the ground. Her hands, her head, every bit of her, all cut off. We picked her up in baskets, we put her in a box and buried her on Sunday. Many people came afterward, but a lot didn't come at all because it was a crime and nobody wanted to get involved in case the authorities accused them as well. We knew the landowners were capable of anything.

The mayor arrived on Monday. It was the first time that I felt, well, I don't know how to explain—like an invalid. I couldn't do anything. Just before the mayor arrived, the landowner talked to him and they were laughing. We didn't understand what they were saying. They didn't ask us to tell them what had happened, when it had happened, or at what time. Nothing. The mayor arrived as if it was nothing at all, and calmly went away again. They put the bodyguard into prison for fifteen days, just to smooth things over, so our people would say nothing. After fifteen days, he went back to work. Every time I remember it I get the same feeling. The first time I picked up a dead body. All in pieces. For about six years afterward perhaps, I dreamed about Dona Petrona. There wasn't a single night I didn't feel I'd dreamed about Dona Petrona. For a long time I couldn't go to sleep for thinking about her.

❀ Discussion and Writing

1. Comment on the Garcias' land-management and marketing strategies. What is the effect of this business policy on the lives of the indigenous people?
2. Examine the nature of Carlos Garcia's exploitation of Dona Petrona Chona, in terms of gender, race, and class.
3. Why do neighbors not get involved before Petrona is viciously murdered?
4. What are the problems in disposing of the dead body: why would people from different areas not touch the body; what is the legal restriction; why does the authorization get delayed?
5. What is the impact of witnessing Dona Petrona's body on young Rigoberta?
6. Discuss the nature of the inquiry into Dona Petrona's murder and the punishment.

❀ Research and Comparison

Interdisciplinary Discussion Question: Research Rigoberta Menchu's life and her work with her people. Examine her fight against discrimination and her contribution in alleviating the condition of her people.

Opal Palmer Adisa
(b. 1954)
Jamaica

Opal Palmer Adisa was born in Jamaica, a proud daughter of a proud, independent woman who rejected her husband because of his drinking instead of resigning herself to a life not of her choosing. The poet Louise Bennett—another courageous woman, whom Adisa claims as a spiritual mother and calls the Jamaican Queen Mother—dared to use the spoken language and rhythm of Jamaica in writing her poetry. Both women were censured for braving social mores; both have inspired Adisa's work. A politically committed woman, Opal Palmer Adisa has built her poetry and fiction on her respect for the vitality of the Creole heritage, its language and customs, and for the people's ability to endure. Consequently, she has taken issue with social conditions in Jamaica and the Caribbean. She has voiced concern that rural areas are still without running water; that care for poor women in public hospitals is inferior; that rape is increasing; that young men can find no employment. She has protested against neocolonialist expansion. Thus, when she spins old tales in the language of the countryside, she is paying a tribute, and she is insisting on her own and Caribbean independence.

Duppy Get Her

Duppy nuh wan yuh drop
* yuh picknie deh, guh home*
Duppy nuh wan yuh drop
* yuh picknie deh, guh home*
Duppy nuh wan yuh drop
* yuh picknie deh, guh home, gal*
tie yuh belly, gal, guh home.

Evening falls like dewdrops on oleander petals glistening under the sun. Oshun, goddess of love, is present, her orange-yellow skirt swaying coquettishly. Mosquitoes are like kiskode petals on skin, blown off by the lax odor whispering mischief in the air. Cane fields rustle in frolic; answered by the evening breeze, they dance the merenge, twirling to giddiness. What are the cane fields saying? What is uttered by the leaves? Listen! Listen—with wide eyes.

Suddenly the murmur of the cane fields—almost hypnotic—forces everyone to look in their direction. Swirling, they sing:

Steal away, steal away;
* duppy gwana get yuh, gal, steal away.*

Steal away, steal away;
   duppy a come get yuh, gal, steal away.

The labyrishers—gossipers—do not hear; they don't hear, save one—Lilly.

Lilly cleans house, cooks food, washes clothes, irons and does other domestic chores for her living. She has been since she was sixteen; she is eighteen, now, and with child due any day. She sits with Beatrice, her cousin, also a domestic; with Richard, her baby's father and a pot-boiler at the sugar estate; and with Basil and Errol, two other factory hands. They are gathered together, feeling content at being their own bosses for at least the next twelve hours.

The evening is rare in its simple grace. The sun, sinking beyond the cane fields, dominates the sky. All the land kneels in homage to this god of energy and sustainer of life—fully orange, gigantic and mystic, surrounded by black-purple haze. The clouds stand back, way off in respect. The sun, heedful of his power, gyrates and snarls. Lilly glances at him just as he flaps his ears, emitting fire from his nostrils; she checks her laughter. So awed is she by the sun's fire she scarcely breathes. After some moments, Lilly mumbles: "Lawd, de sun mitey tonite, sah. Look, im on im way home nuh." Suddenly, the turning of the child in her belly elicits a laugh that escapes deep from her womb.

Beatrice, seated by her, places her hand on Lilly's stomach, feeling the baby's position. "Dis a definite boy picknie yuh a guh ave. See how yuh belly pointed and de sonofabitch won gi yuh nuh peace."

"Im mus tek afta im fada."

Richard turns away in vexation; he chups,[1] kissing his teeth: "Is me yuh ave mout fah, nuh? Ooman neba satisfy. Wen dem nuh ave nutten else fi seh, dem chat stupidness." He moves to leave, but changes his mind; he chups again: "Nuh boda me backside dis evenin yah, gal, nuh boda me backside."

The breeze whistles by. The dogs cover their ears in embarrassment, while the frogs exchange glances which ask, "What's troubling him this nice evening, eh? What's troubling him?" A green lizard, in response, croaks; its bulging eyes are lit by the sun. There is silence amidst the gathering of two women and three men—maids, pot-boiler and factory-hands.

Silence dominates but the undercurrent there is anger mingled with amusement and foreboding. Again, the swishing of the cane fields seems to grab everyone's attention. Lilly is rocking. Suddenly noticing a flock of birds in the sky, she points like an excited child. Again, silence. The sun is almost gone. Lilly sees a star, and thinking it must be the very first one in the sky this evening, she quickly makes a wish, anxious for its fulfillment. She resumes her rocking, forgetting what it was she wished for. A rooster cackles

---

[1]The sound of sucking one's teeth. [eds.]

near the barbed wire fence separating them from the canal and the cane field beyond. Two dogs are stuck, one in the other.

Richard picks up a stone, throws it at them; he swears under his breath: "Damn dog—dem nuh ave nuh shame. Look how much bush bout de place, yet dem a fi come rite inna de open."

Beatrice snickers. Lilly retorts, "Nuh eberybode wait till nite fi cova dem act inna de darkness like yuh."

"Ooman, me nuh tell yuh nuh boda me soul-case. If yuh nuh ave nutten fi seh, shet yuh backside."

Beatrice comments, "Some people hot tonite, Lawd. Mus all dat boilin molasses. De sweetness keep de heat inna de body." Again silence. Beatrice fidgets in the chair, which is too small for her large behind. Suddenly, she starts singing, a mischievous smile on her face. Her voice is full and melodious, and her song is aimed at Richard, whom she always provokes to anger:

Gentle Jesas, meek an mile,
  look upon a trouble man.
Ease im soul an let im rest,
  for im is a soul distress.

Lilly bursts out in loud belly-laughter and Errol and Basil sputter. Richard's color is rising like the pink of a cat's tonque. Anger is clearly written on his face. A sudden wind blows dirt into Beatrice's eye, putting an end to her song.

Richard keenly observes the little gathering and feels excluded. He looks at the dark bodies, envying them. He is the "red nega" among them. All during his school days, the boys teased him, saying his mother had slept with a sailor. And even though he knew it wasn't true (although he was the fairest one in his family), he was still always hurt; he didn't care if his great-great-grandfather had married an Irish settler whom he resembled. He wanted to be purple-dark like the rest of them so his face wouldn't turn red like the color of sorrel fruit whenever he got angry. Staying out in the sun didn't help either; it only made his skin tomato. Lean and muscular, he stood out like a guinep[2] among star-apples.

Lately, however (that is, ever since meeting Lilly not yet twelve months ago), Richard has been relaxed. Lilly, lusted after by all the men, the gentlemen of the community included, chose him. Although every once in a while she teases him about his complexion and stings his hand to see her fingerprints revealed, he knows she cares for him.

Richard doesn't feel like being anyone's beating stick tonight, however. He looks from Lilly, sitting with a smile crowning her face, to Errol and Basil, with mischief twinkling in their eyes, to Beatrice, playing her usual pious role. Richard wants to remind Beatrice of the nightly utterances of her

---

[2]A tree. [eds.]

mattress and bedsprings, but he holds his tongue as he isn't sure whether it is Errol or Basil or both who pray to the Lord between her thighs at night. He chuckles, stomping the balls of his feet, and then chups, kissing his teeth, before turning to fidget with his bicycle. "One of des days oonuh gwane wan fi serious and kyan," he warns.

Richard catches a glimpse of the sun just before it disappears, and it whispers to him: "Steal away, steal away—duppy gwane box yuh, duppy nuh like yuh, steal away . . . " He looks over his shoulder to see if anyone else heard. No one did; the group is already onto something else.

The cane fields whimper, swishing to and fro. The evening is alive. All the creatures stop to say their piece. Sparkling fireflies called penewales dart in and out of the darkness; crickets are in argument. Even the water in the canal tastes the omen. It rumbles like a vexed child who is sent to sweep up the dirt and gather leaves; the task adds to the child's vexation when the twirling leaves blind his eyes while playing rounders with the breeze. So is the evening sweet yet wicked—as even the nicest woman can be.

The rustling of the cane fields is louder. Beatrice shivers. Blossoms from the ackee tree fall and the wind takes them, blowing them everywhere. Lilly tries to catch the blossoms, but the movement in her belly stops her. She relaxes and pats her stomach.

Beatrice feels her head growing big; it is a ton of bricks on her body. She rubs her arms, feeling the cold-bumps. Something is going to happen. She looks around at Richard, who is still angry, and Basil and Errol, who are sharing some private joke. Beatrice reaches over and rubs Lilly's belly, feeling the child inside kicking. She is certain it's a boy. Again, the murmur of the cane fields. Beatrice quickly blows into her cupped palms and throws the air over her left shoulder. It is her way of telling the duppies to step back. She cannot see the ghosts, but she senses their presence near. Again she cups her palms, blows, and throws her cupped hands over her right shoulder, cursing a bad-word with the motion before mumbling "De Lawd is me Shepherd, Ah fear nuh evil. . . ." Still she senses an outside force. Lilly is smiling to herself and rocking, one hand patting her stomach.

Beatrice's head swells; she feels it's much larger than her body, much larger than the veranda where they are sitting, much larger than the evening. She hugs her bosom and rocks, trying to put aside the fear that has crept upon her without invitation.

After her mother died when she was six and her father wandered to another town and another woman, Beatrice was taken in by Lilly's mother, who was her aunt. She was two years older than Lilly, so their lives followed similar paths until at fifteen Beatrice's was partially ruined by her Sunday school teacher. Fear made her keep her mouth shut; prayer made the child born dead. Soon thereafter she left, getting several jobs as domestic help before settling in this quiet community. Eight years ago, Beatrice and Lilly both attended their grandparents' funerals, three months apart. They were always close, so over the years, they kept in touch. When Lilly complained of being restless and wanting to leave the overprotective shield of her mother two years ago, Beatrice found her a job with her own employer, Mrs. Edwards. That was how they came to be together again.

Before Beatrice lost her child, she had promised the Lord that she would spread his name if he killed the life that was growing in her womb. When the child was born strangled, she kept her word, but it was already too late, because she had discovered the joy which lay buried between her legs. As she wasn't pretty, it was easy to have several men without ruining her reputation. No one wanted to boast of sleeping with the coarse, big busted, no ass, Jesus-crazy maid. This way she had it her way all the time, not really trusting any man in the first place.

Putting aside her reflections, Beatrice leans her head to hear what Basil is saying.

"Oonuh look like oonuh inna anoda world."

Richard is still fidgeting with his bicycle; Errol has gone to help him. Lilly, rocking on the seatless cane rocker, is hypnotized by the rustling cane field beyond. Beatrice and Basil notice her staring at what to them appears to be nothing. They feel her strangeness like silence between them. Pausing to take it in, they resume their conversation. An ackee blossom falls, disquieting Richard, and he curses: "See yah, Lawd, yuh nuh test me fait tuh dis yah nite."

A man and woman have crept out of the cane field. They stand right at the edge on the bank of the canal. To look at the woman is to see an older Lilly. The man is all gray. The woman wears a plaid dress gathered at the waist, and her feet are without shoes. Her husband wears rubber shoes and stained khaki pants turned up at the ankles. His faded shirt is partially unbuttoned, his arm is around his wife's waist. They exude a gentleness like the petals of roses. The woman uses her index finger to beckon to Lilly. Jumping as if pulled from her seat, Lilly bounds toward the man and woman by the cane field beyond the canal and beyond the barbed wire fence. She scrambles over Beatrice's feet.

Beatrice yells, "Lilly, Lilly, weh yuh a guh? Lilly! Is mad? Yuh mad? Min yuh fall down hurt yuhself. Lilly! Gal, weh yuh a guh?"

Richard runs after Lilly.

Beatrice repeats, "Lilly, gal, wha get inna yuh?"

Lilly: "Yuh rass-cloth, leabe me alone. Yuh nuh ear me granny a call me?" She points to what appears to be the canal.

They all stare, seeing no one, hearing nothing. Lilly is close to the fence, running, tearing off her clothes. Fearing that she is going to dive in, Richard reaches for her, but she clutches and attempts the barbed wire fence; Richard pulls at her. She boxes and derides him till he releases her. She tries scrambling through. Richard takes firm hold of her and pulls her safely from the fence. Beatrice is by their side; she helps with Lilly. Errol stands transfixed by the bicycle, while Basil cranes his neck from the veranda. Richard and Beatrice struggle with Lilly, pulling her away from the fence; they are breathless, but luckily, Lilly settles down for a moment.

The woman in the cane field beckons to Lilly, cajoling: "Lilly, me picknie, come kiss yuh granny and granpa; yuh nuh long fi see we?"

Lilly, strident, gesticulates wildly like a man cheated out of his paycheck. She calls, "Yes, Granny, me a come, me long fi see yuh."

Beatrice and Richard struggle with Lilly. Their fright and confusion are as loud as Lilly's screams. Richard tries to rough her up but she merely bucks him off. Beatrice's jaws work, sweat forms on her forehead, and her fleshy arms flail about, comical.

Again, she tries to reason with Lilly: "Lilly, gal, memba me and you did help dress Granny fah er funeral? Memba, memba, Lilly, how we did cry til we eye swell big? Granny dead. She nuh call yuh."

"Granny nuh dead; see, she stan deh wid granpa. Oonuh leh me guh." At this, Lilly spits at Beatrice and Richard and frees herself from their hold.

She rushes toward the cane field like a man afire in search of water. Richard seizes her, but she now has the strength of many persons; he hollers for Errol and Basil. Lilly rips off her blouse and brassiere, and her ample breasts flap about. Richard remembers the taste of her milk, only last night. More hands take hold of her; she bites, scratches and kicks. Miss Maud from next door, hearing the commotion, runs to her fence to learn all about it.

"Leh me guh, leh me guh! Yuh nuh see me granny a call me? Leh me guh."

Richard: "Lilly, shet yuh mout. Min Miss Edward ear yuh an yuh loose yuh wuk. Nuhbody nuh call yuh."

"Miss Edward bumbu-hole—Miss Edward rass-cloth. Oonuh leabe me alone mek me guh tuh me granny and granpa."

Beatrice scolds: "Lilly, gal, shet yuh mout. How yuh can speak suh bout Miss Edward? Gal, shet yuh mout for yuh loose yuh wuk."

"Oonuh rass-cloth, oonuh bumbu-hole, oonuh leabe me alone—mek me guh to me granny."

The four find it difficult to hold Lilly. She kicks, bucks and tears at her remaining clothes. The evening sings:

Steal away, steal away, duppy get yuh.
Steal away . . . duppy get yuh . . .

From across the fence, Miss Maud offers: "Lawd, God, duppy done mad me picknie, Lawd God. Jesas! Rub er up wid some frankincense and white rum; rub er up quick come." Before anyone can respond, she is climbing through the barbed wire fence which separates her yard from theirs, opening a bottle. In her haste, her dress catches on the fence, but she pulls it, ripping the hem. The pungent smell from the bottle vapors into the air.

Miss Maud rubs Lilly's hands, face and neck with the potion, then makes the sign of the cross in the air. Now she sprinkles some of the substance on the ground, muttering: "Steal away, duppy, steal away. De deed well done; steal away. . . ." She looks about her, pats her head and turns to Beatrice. "Fin piece a red rag, tie er head. Duppy fraid red, fraid red. Our Fada who in heaven, duppy fraid red. Dy kingdom come, tie er head. Dy will be done, tie er head. Ave mercy, Pupa Jesas."

Lilly breathes heavily; Richard, Errol and Basil hold her firmly.

Says Beatrice, "She kyan stay ere; dem nuh wan er stay ere."

Maud explains, "Dem jus wan er home. No arm will be done. Lawd ave mercy."

Richard stares at Lilly: "Who obeah me sweet Lilly? Who?"

Beatrice explodes: "Shet yuh mout, Richard, nuhbody nuh set nuh spell pan Lilly, nuhbody obeah er."

Steal away, chile, steal away.
Duppy nuh wan yuh ere, chile,
   duppy nuh wan yuh ere.
Dem nuh wan yuh ere.

It is generally agreed that Lilly must be returned to her place of birth—that for whatever reason, her dead grandparents don't want her where she is. Mrs. Edwards is consulted and a car is summoned. Kicking and frothing at the mouth, Lilly is forced into the back of the car, Richard to her right and Basil to her left. Beatrice sits up front with the driver armed with Miss Maud's flask of potion. The car pulls off, leaving a trail of dust.

Mrs. Edwards returns to her house; she fumbles inside her medicine cabinet and comes up with a brown vial, the contents of which she sprinkles at each doorway and window and in all four corners of every room. Then she goes back to her rocking chair, her hands folded in her lap, her eyes searching the gray sky.

Miss Maud, the community myalist—healer—returns to her backyard. Her lips are pouted and her eyes intent, as if seeking a shiny shilling in the road; she shakes her head from side to side.

Suddenly she is possessed; she twirls around her yard, her wide skirt billowing out, her hands lifted to the sky, her feet marching time to an invisible drum. Her voice, deep bass, echoes like a man's throughout the entire community:

Duppy nuh wan yuh drop
   yuh picknie deh, guh home
Duppy nuh wan yuh drop
   yuh picknie deh, guh home
Duppy nuh wan yuh drop
   yuh picknie deh, guh home, gal,

tie yuh belly, gal, guh home.
Yuh muma seh she neba raise
   nuh picknie fi guh lego
Yuh muma seh she neba raise
   nuh picknie fi guh lego
Yuh muma seh she neba raise
   nuh picknie fi guh lego
   tie yuh belly, guh home.
Duppy nuh wan yuh drop
   yuh picknie deh
   tie yuh belly, guh home.
Guh home.

Mrs. Edwards feels cold-bumps covering her arms as she watches Miss Maud twirling and singing in her yard. The swishing of the cane fields has stopped and suddenly, a sense of desolation—abandonment—takes over. The sky turns a deep mauve, a lone donkey somewhere in the distance brays, brays, brays and the night is on so fully all creep to the safety of their homes and pull the covers tightly over their heads. Only Mrs. Edwards sits for a long time on her veranda in the dark, rocking and rocking away the fear and doubt.

Upon returning from taking Lilly home, Beatrice reports that Lilly calmed gradually as she approached her place of birth. In fact, by the time she got home, she was reasonable enough to request from her mother a cup of water sweetened with condensed milk. After drinking the milk, Lilly hugged her mother and they both cried; no one had to restrain her thereafter. Nothing needed to be explained to Lilly's mother, who had been expecting them all day. It appeared she had had a dream from her dead mother the night before.

Prior to this incident, Lilly always claimed that she saw duppies in Mrs. Edwards's house and around the estate in general. Since no one else professed such powers, there was no way to verify her claim. Many came to her when they wanted to ask for protection from those in the other world. Often, when they were in Lilly's presence, they asserted that they felt their heads rise and swell to twice their size, but again, since this was only a feeling and nothing visible, nothing could be proven. There were others who wanted to be able to see duppies like Lilly and asked her how they could obtain such powers. Lilly's recommendations were the following: "Rub dog matta inna yuh eye or visit a graveyard wen de clock strike twelve midnite. Once dere, put yuh head between yuh legs, spit, then get up an walk, not lookin back. Afta dat, yuh will see duppy all de time."

It is not known if anyone ever followed Lilly's advice, although two women who went to see Lilly had taken to visiting the graveyard daily and were now in the habit of talking to themselves.

Lilly returns to Mrs. Edwards's employment exactly ten weeks after the incident, healthy and as sane as before, with her bubbling, carefree manner. She gave birth to a seven-and-a-half pound boy, the spitting image of Richard, the day after her departure. The child was left behind with her mother, who christened him Sam, after his deceased grandfather.

Now when Lilly looks into the cane field, nothing bursts forth and no dead are brought back to life, but every time people see her looking, they remember that evening and somehow, the cane field starts rustling and a voice much like Lilly's rings throughout the entire community, stopping people at their chores:

Leh me guh, leh me guh, oonuh rass-cloth!
Le me guh—me granny a call me, oonuh leh me guh.
Mrs. Edwards bumbu-hole; leh me guh.

No one referred to Mrs. Edwards, a highly respected member of her community, in such a manner before, and no one has after Lilly. Lilly, of course, apologized to Mrs. Edwards, who graciously forgave her as she was not in possession of herself at the time. And although Mrs. Edwards was committed to taking Lilly back in her employment after she gave birth, whenever Mrs. Edwards was around her, she was always full of trepidation.

Lilly goes off one other time since the cane field incident. Several years have passed; Lilly is getting married to Richard. This is the big day. She is dressed, waiting to be taken to the church. Her grandmother appears again, but this time alone. Lilly rips her bridal dress to shreds and runs naked to the river, cursing everyone she meets, while Richard waits by the altar. For nine days she has to be tied down with ropes. For nine days, the breeze sings:

Steal away, steal away.
Duppy seh nuh, duppy seh nuh.
Steal away . . .

Lilly's face is a dimpled cake pan. Her body is pleasing like a mango tree laden with fruits. She has eight children, now, six for her husband and two for Richard, the first two. Richard stole away after duppy boxed him the second time. The last that was heard of him, it was reported that he was seen walking and talking to himself, his hair matty and his skin black from dirt. Lilly now has a maid to help her with her many chores; her husband owns a fleet of trucks.

Beatrice has opened up a storefront church in another community far from where the main part of this story took place. Her congregation is said to be ninety-two percent sturdy black men. Basil is still working as a pot-boiler at the sugar factory. Errol went abroad to England, it could be Canada or

America as well, where he is said to have married an East Indian girl, so now he eats with his fingers.

After Lilly left Mrs. Edwards's employment, Mrs. Edwards swore confidentially to Mrs. Salmon, her best friend, that she would never again hire a maid from Agusta valley—that was the district from which Lilly came. Mrs. Edwards, of course, did not admit to a belief in local superstitions.

At least once a year, Miss Maud can still be heard singing at the top of her voice:

Duppy nuh wan yuh drop
  yuh picknie deh, guh home
Duppy nuh wan yuh drop
  yuh picknie deh, guh home
Duppy nuh wan yuh drop
  yuh picknie deh, guh home, gal,
  tie yuh belly, guh home

❋ Discussion and Writing

1. Analyze the images used in the description of the opening scene. What is accomplished by the repeated songs?
2. Comment on the function of the pervasive image of the cane field.
3. What is the role of the grandparents in the narrative?
4. Describe the cultural identity that emerges from the mixing of the indigenous and Christian traditions in the lives of the people.
5. Examine the impact of the use of spoken language in the narrative.

❋ Research and Comparison

Interdisciplinary Discussion Question: Research the issue of different Englishes in Anglophone countries where English is either the primary or the official language, or both, and where there has been a fusion of English with the local languages. Analyze how any one author from these countries experiments with these languages.

Appendix A

Alternate Table of Contents by Theme

The selections are listed alphabetically by author. While the readings can be cross-listed under several categories, here each is classified by a single over-arching theme. Many common themes such as time, love, war, and death are implicit in the classifications. Also, some themes overlap.

Sacrifice and Redemption

Asturias, Miguel Angel   Legend of "El Cadejo"   *Guatemala*   829

Borges, Jorge Luis   The Gospel According to Mark   *Argentina*   834

Easmon, R. Sarif   Bindeh's Gift   *Sierra Leone*   620

Enchi Fumiko   Boxcar of Chrysanthemums   *Japan*   77

Mahapatra, Jayanta   30 January 1982: A Story   *India*   320

Nyoongah, Mudrooroo (Colin Johnson)   Poem Two   *Australia*   379

Ogot, Grace   The Rain Came   *Kenya*   629

Rao, Raja   Companions   *India*   225

Rulfo, Juan   Tell them not to kill me   *Mexico*   950

Soyinka, Wole   The Strong Breed   *Nigeria*   700

Tagore, Rabindranath   Chandalika   *India*   208

Selfhood and Cultural Identity

Abe Kobo   The Red Cocoon   *Japan*   136

Achebe, Chinua   The Madman   *Nigeria*   613

Adnan, Etel   In the Heart of the Heart of Another Country   *Lebanon*   451

Allende, Isabel   Our Secret   *Chile*   1136

Ariyoshi Sawako   The Tomoshibi   *Japan*   157

Bitton, Erez   Something on Madness   *Israel*   507

Clarke, Austin   Leaving This Island Place   *Barbados*   1060

Damas, Leon   Poems   *French Guiana*   916
Das, Kamala   An Introduction   *India*   346
Hidayat, Sadiq   Seeking Absolution   *Iran*   426
Hirabayashi Taiko   A Man's Life   *Japan*   91
Idris, Yusuf   The Chair Carrier   *Egypt*   608
Joshi, Umashankar   The Universal Man   *India*   234
Kawabata Yasunari   The Silver Fifty-Sen Pieces   *Japan*   66
Lovelace, Earl   The Fire Eater's Journey   *Trinidad*   1068
McKay, Claude   Crazy Mary   *Jamaica*   820
Mungoshi, Charles   Shadows on the Wall   *Zimbabwe*   787
Puig, Manuel   Kiss of the Spider Woman   *Argentina*   1020
Queiroz, Rachel de   Tangerine Girl   *Brazil*   905
Walcott, Derek   I Once Gave My Daughters . . .   *Saint Lucia*
   1010
Yosano Akiko   Three modern *tanka*   *Japan*   16

Gender Roles and Power
Akutagawa Ryunosuke   In a Grove   *Japan*   36
Burgos, Julia de   To Julia de Burgos   *Puerto Rico*   932
Castellanos, Rosario   Daily Round of the Spinster   *Mexico*   993
Ch'i Chun   The Chignon   *Taiwan*   131
Deshpande, Shashi   My Beloved Charioteer   *India*   372
Devi, Mahasweta   Dhowli   *India*   291
Farrokhzad, Forugh   The Wind-Up Doll   *Iran*   477
Fonseca, Rubem   Night Drive   *Brazil*   968
Head, Bessie   The Collector of Treasures   *South Africa*   741
Khalid, Fawziyya Abu   A Pearl   *Saudi Arabia*   508
Mistral, Gabriela   Song   *Chile*   818
p'Bitek, Okot   Song of Lawino   *Uganda*   680
Pinon, Nelida   Brief Flower   *Brazil*   1097
Saadawi, Nawal El   She Has No Place in Paradise   *Egypt*   637
Santos, Bienvenido N.   Footnote to a Laundry List   *Philippines*
   236
Sutherland, Efua   New Life at Kyerefaso   *Ghana*   590
Tomioka Taeko   Just the Two of Us   *Japan*   174
Wicomb, Zoe   You Can't Get Lost in Cape Town   *South Africa*
   792
Yi Sang   Wings   *Korea*   105
Yosano Akiko   The Day When Mountains Move   *Japan*   16

Tradition and Modernity

Ahmad, Abd al-Hameed   Khlalah SEL   *United Arab Emirates*
511

Aidoo, Ama Ata   In the Cutting of a Drink   *Ghana*   777

Daguio, Amador   Wedding Dance   *Philippines*   245

Danishvar, Simin   The Half-Closed Eye   *Iran*   438

Desai, Anita   A Devoted Son   *India*   348

Djebar, Assia   There Is No Exile   *Algieria*   731

Ezekiel, Nissim   Night of the Scorpion   *India*   278

Kim Sowol   The Road   *Korea*   70

Laye, Camara   The Goldsmith   *Guinea*   585

Lu Xun   My Old Home   *China*   20

Mahfouz, Naguib   Half a Day   *Egypt*   536

Mao Dun   Spring Silkworms   *China*   46

Mapanje, Jack   On African Writing   *Malawi*   785

Nwapa, Flora   The Chief's Daughter   *Nigeria*   643

Ogundipe-Leslie, Molara   song at the african middle class
Nigeria   776

Pritam, Amrita   The Weed   *India*   258

Xiao Hong   The Crossroads   *China*   120

Nationalism and Colonialism

al-Maqalih, Abd al-Aziz   Sanaa Is Hungry   *Yemen*   490

al-Wali, Muhammad Abd   Abu Rubbiya   *Yemen*   492

Awoonor, Kofi   The Weaver Bird   *Ghana*   697

Brutus, Dennis   Nightsong: City   *South Africa*   583

Carter, Martin   Listening to the Land   *Guyana*   995

Diop, David   The Vultures   *Senegal*   606

Elkayam, Shelley   The Crusader Man   *Israel*   509

Faiz, Ahmed Faiz   Ghazal   *Pakistan*   231

Gilbert, Kevin (Wiradjuri)   Kiacatoo   *Australia*   343

Han Yongun   On Reading Tagore's "The Gardener"   *Korea*   18

Ho Chi Minh   Noon   *Vietnam*   219

Ho Chi Minh   Transferred to Nanning   *Vietnam*   219

Hussein, Abdullah   The Tale of the Old Fisherman   *Pakistan*
323

Hwang Sunwon   Cranes   *Korea*   125

Kenyatta, Jomo   The Gentlemen of the Jungle   *Kenya*   526

Kim Namjo   Having Come to the Mountain   *Korea*   156
Lara, Jesus   Incallajta Jarahui   *Bolivia*   827
Mao Zedong   Swimming   *China*   44
Morgan, Sally   Arthur Corunna's Story   *Australia*   401
Mphahlele, Es'kia   Interlude   *South Africa*   540
Neruda, Pablo   The Heights of Macchu Picchu, III   *Chile*   861
Neto, Augustinho   Kinaxixi   *Angola*   556
Sousa, Noemia de   If You Want to Know Me   *Mozambique*   604
Tagore, Rabindranath   Where the Mind Is Without Fear
  India   216
Thumboo, Edwin   Christmas Week, 1975
  Singapore/Malaysia   341
U Tam'si, Tchicaya   Brush-Fire   *Congo*   652
Vargas Llosa, Mario   A Shadow of Gnats   *Peru*   1077

Protest and Oppression
al-Baraduni, Abdallah   Answers to One Question
  Yemen   459
Andrade, Costa   Fourth Poem of a Canto of Accusation
  Angola   729
Aulaqi, Saeed   The Succession   *Yemen*   497
Bei Dao   Electric Shock   *China*   192
Bei Dao   Language   *China*   192
Bekederemo, J.P. Clarke   The Leader   *Nigeria*   698
Cardenal, Ernesto   The Filibusters   *Nicaragua*   991
Cesaire, Aime   To Africa   *Martinique*   925
Cisneros, Antonio   After the Battle of Ayacucho: A Mother's
  Testimony   *Peru*   1140
Coker, Syl Cheney   The Philosopher   *Sierra Leone*   784
Darwish, Mahmoud   Guests on the Sea   *Palestine*   504
Ding Ling   A Certain Night   *China*   72
Hikmet, Nazim   12 December 1945   *Turkey*   424
Kato Shuson   Three modern *haiku*   *Japan*   104
Kgositsile, Keorapetse   The Air I Hear   *South Africa*   757
Noonuccal, Oodgeroo (Kath Walker)   Municipal Gum
  Australia   264
Nuhman, M. A.   Murder   *Sri Lanka*   390
Okara, Gabriel   You Laughed and Laughed and Laughed
  Nigeria   554
Okigbo, Christopher   Come Thunder   *Nigeria*   568

Sembene Ousmane   The March of the Women   *Senegal*   570
Senghor, Leopold Sedar   Prayer to Masks   *Senegal*   534
Tuqan, Fadwa   Song of Becoming   *Palestine*   436
Verduguez, Cesar   The Scream in Your Silence   *Bolivia*   1125

Class-Caste-Race-Religion

Amado, Jorge   Of Dice and Unshakable Principles   *Brazil*   991
Ballas, Shimon   Imaginary Childhood   *Israel*   460
Conde, Maryse   Mira   *Guadeloupe*   1088
Donoso, Jose   Paseo   *Chile*   970
Fugard, Athol   The Island   *South Africa*   654
Gordimer, Nadine   Good Climate, Friendly Inhabitants   *South Africa*   557
Ihimaera, Witi   Yellow Brick Road   *New Zealand*   384
Kani, John   The Island   *South Africa*   654
Ko Un   Lee Chongnam   *Korea*   172
Lim, Catherine   Ah Bah's Money   *Singapore/Malaysia*   380
Manto, Saadat Hasan   The Dog of Titwal   *Pakistan*   253
Menchu, Rigoberta   The Death of Dona Petrona Chona   *Guatemala*   1156
Montenegro, Walter   The *Pepino*   *Bolivia*   918
Naipaul, V.S.   My Aunt Gold Teeth   *Trinidad*   1013
Neruda, Pablo   Chilean Forest   *Chile*   861
Ntshona, Winston   The Island   *South Africa*   654
Ocampo, Silvina   The Servant's Slaves   *Argentina*   843
Pai Hsien-yung   A Sea of Bloodred Azealeas   *Taiwan*   175
Peters, Lenrie   Isatou Died   *Gambia*   696
Rabearivelo, Jean-Joseph   Flute Players   *Madagascar*   530
Roumain, Jacques   Delira Delivrance   *Haiti*   871
Schwarz-Bart, Simone   Toussine   *Guadeloupe*   1104
Shamlu, Ahmad   The Gap   *Iran*   457
Thiong'o, Ngugi Wa   Wedding at the Cross   *Kenya*   758
Toer, Pramoedya   Inem   *Indonesia*   280
Yehoshua, Ya'akob   Childhood in Old Jerusalem   *Israel*   434
Zobel, Joseph   Mr. Medouze   *Martinique*   937

The Fantastic and the Factual

Adisa, Opal Palmer   Duppy Get Her   *Jamaica*   1159
Asghar, Khalida   The Wagon   *Pakistan*   361

Carpentier, Alejo Like the Night *Cuba* 850
Ferre, Rosario The Youngest Doll *Puerto Rico* 1141
Fuentes, Carlos Chac-Mool *Mexico* 996
Garcia Marquez, Gabriel The Handsomest Drowned Man in the World *Colombia* 1005
Golshiri, Hushang The Wolf *Iran* 484
Khudayyir, Mohammed Clocks Like Horses *Iraq* 466
Rubiao, Murilo Teleco, the Rabbit *Brazil* 943
Rushdie, Salman An Iff and a Butt *India* 392
So Chongju The Huge Wave *Korea* 130
Tanizaki Junichiro The Tattooer *Japan* 29
Telles, Lygia Fagundes The Ants *Brazil* 984
Walcott, Derek The Season of Phantasmal Peace *Saint Lucia* 1011

Mystical Quest

Bombal, Maria Luisa Sky, Sea and Earth *Chile* 902
Bravo, Antonio Gonzalez Kori Pilpintu *Bolivia* 816
Gibran, Kahlil On Children *Lebanon* 422
Guillen, Nicolas Arrival *Cuba* 841
Guimaraes Rosa, Joao The Third Bank of the River *Brazil* 879
Han Yongun Ferryboat and Traveler *Korea* 17
Haqqi, Yahya The Tavern Keeper *Egypt* 531
Harris, Wilson Yurokon *Guyana* 956
Kanafani, Ghassan The Slave Fort *Palestine* 479
Lubis, Mochtar Harimau! *Indonesia* 265
Maris, Hyllus Spiritual Song of the Aborigine *Australia* 322
Mishima Yukio The Damask Drum *Japan* 140
Obeyesekere, Ranjini Despair *Sri Lanka* 337
Onetti, Juan Carlos A Dream Come True *Uruguay* 891
Paz, Octavio Return *Mexico* 935
Peng, Tan Kong A Jungle Passage *Singapore/Malaysia* 331
Thich Nhat Hanh The Pine Gate *Vietnam* 312
Vallejo, Cesar The Eternal Dice *Peru* 826

Humor

Armah, Ayi Kwei Halfway to Nirvana *Ghana* 770
Bosch, Juan The Beautiful Soul of Don Damian *Dominican Republic* 884

Cortazar, Julio   Our Demeanor at Wakes   *Argentina*   928
Drummond de Andrade, Carlos   An Ox Looks at Man
 Brazil   839
Grace, Patricia   It Used to Be Green Once   *New Zealand*   357
Narayan, R. K.   Trail of the Green Blazer   *India*   220
Peng, Jialin   What's in a Name   *China*   186
Senior, Olive   Do Angels Wear Brassieres?   *Jamaica*   1115
Themba, Can   The Suit   *South Africa*   596
Tutuola, Amos   The Gentleman of Complete Parts   *Nigeria*   545
Vega, Ana Lydia   ADJ, Inc.   *Puerto Rico*   1147

Alternate Table of Contents by Country

The selections are arranged by region, then country, then chronologically according to the author's year of birth; this organization provides cultural and historical contexts for the readings.

East Asia

Japan

Yosano Akiko (1878–1942), Three modern *tanka;* The Day When Mountains Move   15

Tanizaki Junichiro (1886–1972), The Tattooer   28

Akutagawa Ryunosuke (1892–1927), In a Grove   35

Kawabata Yasunari (1899–1972), The Silver Fifty-Sen Pieces   65

Enchi Fumiko (1905–1986), Boxcar of Chrysanthemums   76

Hirabayashi Taiko (1905–1972), A Man's Life   90

Kato Shuson (b. 1905), Three modern *haiku*   103

Abe Kobo (1924–1993), The Red Cocoon   135

Mishima Yukio (1925–1970), The Damask Drum   139

Ariyoshi Sawako (1931–1984), The Tomoshibi   157

Tomioka Taeko (b. 1935), Just the Two of Us   173

Korea

Han Yongun (1879–1944), Ferryboat and Traveler; On Reading Tagore's "The Gardener"   17

Kim Sowol (1902–1934), The Road   70

Yi Sang (1910–1937), Wings   105

Hwang Sunwon (b. 1915), Cranes   124

So Chongju (b. 1915), The Huge Wave   129

Kim Namjo (b. 1927), Having Come to the Mountain   156

Ko Un (b. 1933), Lee Chongnam   171

China

Lu Xun (1881–1936), My Old Home   19
Mao Zedong (1893–1976), Swimming   43
Mao Dun (1896–1982), Spring Silkworms   45
Ding Ling (1904–1986), A Certain Night   71
Xiao Hong (1911–1942), The Crossroads   119
Jialin Peng (b. 1948), What's in a Name   185
Bei Dao (b. 1949), Electric Shock, Language   191

Taiwan

Ch'i Chun (b. 1918), The Chignon   130
Pai Hsien-Yung (b. 1948), A Sea of Bloodred Azaleas   175

Southeast Asia, Australia, and New Zealand

Vietnam

Ho Chi Minh (1890–1969), Noon; Transferred to Nanning   217
Thich Nhat Hanh (b. 1926), The Pine Gate   312

Philippines

Bienvenido N. Santos (b. 1911), Footnote to a Laundry List   235
Amador Daguio (1912–1966), Wedding Dance   245

Indonesia

Mochtar Lubis (b. 1922), Harimau!   264
Pramoedya Toer (b. 1925), Inem   279

Singapore/Malaysia

Tan Kong Peng (b. 1932), A Jungle Passage   331
Edwin Thumboo (b. 1933), Christmas Week, 1975   340
Catherine Lim (b. 1942), Ah Bah's Money   380

Australia

Oodgeroo Noonuccal (Kath Walker, 1920–1993), Municipal Gum
    263
Hyllus Maris (1930–1986), Spiritual Song of the Aborigine   322
Kevin Gilbert, Wiradjuri (b. 1933), Kiacatoo   343
Mudrooroo Nyoongah (Colin Johnson, b. 1938), Poem Two   378
Sally Morgan (b. 1951), Arthur Corunna's Story   400

New Zealand
Patricia Grace (b. 1937), It Used to Be Green Once   *356*
Witi Ihimaera (b. 1944), Yellow Brick Road   *384*

South Asia
India
Rabindranath Tagore (1861–1941), Chandalika; Where the Mind Is
  Without Fear   *207*
R. K. Narayan (b. 1906), Trail of the Green Blazer   *219*
Raja Rao (b. 1909), Companions   *224*
Umashankar Joshi (1911–1988), The Universal Man   *233*
Amrita Pritam (b. 1919), The Weed   *257*
Nissim Ezekiel (b. 1924), Night of the Scorpion   *277*
Mahasweta Devi (b. 1926), Dhowli   *290*
Jayanta Mahapatra (b. 1928), 30th January 1982: A Story   *320*
Kamala Das (b. 1934), An Introduction   *345*
Anita Desai (b. 1937), A Devoted Son   *348*
Shashi Deshpande (b. 1938), My Beloved Charioteer   *371*
Salman Rushdie (b. 1947), An Iff and a Butt   *391*

Pakistan
Faiz Ahmed Faiz (1911–1984), Ghazal   *231*
Saadat Hasan Manto (1912–1955), The Dog of Titwal   *252*
Abdullah Hussein (b. 1931), The Tale of the Old Fisherman   *323*
Khalida Ashgar (b. 1938), The Wagon   *361*

Sri Lanka
Ranjini Obeyesekere (b. 1933), Despair   *337*
M. A. Nuhman (b. 1944), Murder   *390*

Middle East
Iran
Sadiq Hidayat (1903–1951), Seeking Absolution   *425*
Simin Danishvar (b. 1921), The Half-Closed Eye   *437*
Ahmad Shamlu (b. 1925), The Gap   *457*
Forugh Farrokhzad (1935–1967), The Wind-Up Doll   *476*
Hushang Golshiri (b. 1937), The Wolf   *483*

Iraq
Mohammed Khudayyir (b. 1930?), Clocks Like Horses   *466*

Saudi Arabia
Fawziyya Abu Khalid (b. 1955), A Pearl   *508*

United Arab Emirates
Abd al-Hameed Ahmad (b. 1957), Khlalah SEL   *510*

Yemen
Abdallah al-Baraduni (b. 1929), Answers to One
  Question   *458*
Abd al-Aziz al-Maqalih (b. 1939), Sanaa Is Hungry   *490*
Muhammad Abd al-Wali (1940–1973), Abu Rubbiya   *491*
Saeed Aulaqi (b. 1940), The Succession   *496*

Israel
Ya'akob Yehoshua (b. 1905), Childhood in
  Old Jerusalem   *433*
Shimon Ballas (b. 1930), Imaginary Childhood   *459*
Erez Bitton (b. 1949), Something on Madness   *506*
Shelley Elkayam (b. 1956), The Crusader Man   *509*

Palestine
Fadwa Tuqan (b. 1917), Song of Becoming   *435*
Ghassan Kanafani (1936–1972), The Slave Fort   *479*
Mahmoud Darwish, (b. 1942) Guests on the Sea   *503*

Lebanon
Kahlil Gibran (1883–1931), On Children   *422*
Etel Adnan (b. 1925), In the Heart of the Heart of Another
  Country   *450*

Turkey
Nazim Hikmet (1902–1963), 12 December 1945   *423*

Africa
North and East Africa
Egypt
Yahya Haqqi (b. 1905), The Tavern Keeper   *531*
Naguib Mahfouz (b. 1911), Half a Day   *536*
Yusuf Idris (b. 1927), The Chair Carrier   *607*
Nawal el Saadawi (b. 1931), She Has No Place in Paradise   *637*

Algieria
Assia Djebar (b. 1936), There Is No Exile   *730*

Kenya
Jomo Kenyatta (1891–1978), The Gentlemen of the Jungle   *526*
Grace Ogot (b. 1930), The Rain Came   *628*
Ngugi Wa Thiong'o (b. 1938), Wedding at the Cross   *758*

Uganda
Okot p'Bitek (1931–1982), Song of Lawino   *679*

Southern Africa
Madagascar
Jean-Joseph Rabearivelo (1901–1937), Flute Players   *529*

Mozambique
Noemia de Sousa (b. 1927), If You Want to Know Me   *604*

Malawi
Jack Mapanje (b. 1945), On African Writing   *785*

South Africa
Es'kia Mphahlele (b. 1919), Interlude   *539*
Nadine Gordimer (b. 1923), Good Climate, Friendly Inhabitants
  557
Dennis Brutus (b. 1924), Nightsong: City   *582*
Can Themba (1924–1969), The Suit   *595*
Athol, Fugard (b. 1932), *John Kani (b. 1943)*, and
  Winston Ntshona (b. 1942), The Island   *653*
Bessie Head (1937–1986), The Collector of Treasures   *740*
Keorapetse Kgositsile (b. 1938), The Air I Hear   *757*
Zoe Wicomb (b. 1948), You Can't Get Lost in Cape Town   *791*

Zimbabwe
Charles Mungoshi (b. 1947), Shadows on the Wall   *786*

Central Africa
Angola
Augustinho Neto (1922–1979), Kinaxixi   *555*
Costa Andrade (b. 1936), Fourth Poem of a Canto of
  Accusation   *729*

Congo
Tchicoya U Tam'si (1931–1988), Brush-Fire   *651*

West Africa

Nigeria

Amos Tutuola (b. 1920), The Gentleman of Complete Parts   *545*
Gabriel Okara (b. 1921), You Laughed and Laughed and
   Laughed   *553*
Christopher Okigbo (1923–1967), Come Thunder   *568*
Chinua Achebe (b. 1930), The Madman   *612*
Flora Nwapa (1931–1993), The Chief's Daughter   *643*
J. P. Clarke Bekederemo (b. 1935), The Leader   *698*
Wole Soyinka (b. 1935), The Strong Breed   *699*
Molara Ogundipe-Leslie (b. 1940), song at the african middle class
   775

Ghana

Efua Sutherland (b. 1924), New Life at Kyerefaso   *589*
Kofi Awoonor (b. 1935), The Weaver Bird   *696*
Ayi Kwei Armah (b. 1939), Halfway to Nirvana   *770*
Ama Ata Aidoo (b. 1942), In the Cutting of a Drink   *777*

Sierra Leone

R. Sarif Easmon (b. 1930), Bindeh's Gift   *619*
Syl Cheney Coker (b. 1945), The Philosopher   *783*

Guinea

Camara Laye (1924–1980), The Goldsmith   *584*

Senegal

Leopold Sedar Senghor (b. 1906), Prayer to Masks   *534*
Sembeme Ousmane (b. 1923), March of the Women   *569*
David Diop (1927–1960), The Vultures   *606*

Gambia

Lenrie Peters (b. 1932), Isatou Died   *695*

Latin America

Argentina

Jorge Luis Borges (1899–1980), The Gospel According to Mark
   833
Silvina Ocampo (b. 1903), The Servant's Slaves   *842*

Julio Cortazar (1914–1984), Our Demeanor at Wakes   *927*
Manuel Puig (1932–1990), Kiss of the Spider Woman   *1020*

Uruguay
Juan Carlos Onetti (b. 1909), A Dream Come True   *890*

Chile
Gabriela Mistral (1889–1957), Song   *817*
Pablo Neruda (1904–1973), The Heights of Macchu Picchu, III; The
  Chilean Forest   *860*
Maria Luisa Bombal (1910–1980), Sky, Sea and Earth   *901*
Jose Donoso (b. 1924), Paseo   *969*
Isabel Allende (b. 1942), Our Secret   *1135*

Bolivia
Antonio Gonzalez Bravo (1885–1962), Kori Pilpintu   *816*
Jesus Lara (1898–1980), Incallajta Jarahui   *827*
Walter Montenegro (1912–1991), The *Pepino*   *917*
Cesar Verduguez (b. 1941), The Scream in Your Silence   *1124*

Brazil
Carlos Drummond de Andrade (1902–1987), An Ox Looks at
  Man   *839*
Joao Guimaraes Rosa (1908–1967), The Third Bank of the
  River   *878*
Rachel de Queiroz (b. 1910), The Tangerine Girl   *905*
Jorge Amado (b. 1912), Of Dice and Unshakable Principles   *910*
Murilo Rubiao (b. 1916), Teleco, the Rabbit   *942*
Rubem Fonseca (b. 1922), Night Drive   *967*
Lygia Fagundes Telles (b. 1924), The Ants   *983*
Nelida Pinon (b. 1937), Brief Flower   *1097*

Peru
Cesar Vallejo (1892–1938), The Eternal Dice   *825*
Mario Vargas Llosa (b. 1936), A Shadow of Gnats   *1077*
Antonio Cisneros (b. 1942), After the Battle of Ayacucho: A
  Mother's Testimony   *1139*

Colombia
Gabriel Garcia Marquez (b. 1928), The Handsomest Drowned Man
  in the World   *1004*

Nicaragua
Ernesto Cardenal (b. 1925), The Filibusters   990

Guatemala
Miguel Angel Asturias (1899–1974), The Legend of
  "El Cadejo"   828
Rigoberta Menchu (b. 1951), The Death of Dona Petrona
  Chona   1155

Mexico
Octavio Paz (b. 1914), Return   934
Juan Rulfo (1918–1986), Tell them not to kill me   950
Rosario Castellanos (1925–1978), Daily Round of the
  Spinster   992
Carlos Fuentes (b. 1928), Chac-Mool   995

The Caribbean
French Guiana
Leon Damas (1912–1978), Poems   915

Guyana
Wilson Harris (b. 1921), Yurokon   955
Martin Carter (b. 1927), Listening to the Land   994

Trinidad
V. S. Naipaul (b. 1932), My Aunt Gold Teeth   1012
Earl Lovelace (b. 1935), The Fire Eater's Journey   1067

Barbados
Austin Clarke (b. 1934), Leaving This Island Place   1060

Saint Lucia
Derek Walcott (b. 1930), I Once Gave My Daughters. . . ; The
  Season of Phantasmal Peace   1009

Martinique
Aime Cesaire (b. 1913), To Africa   924
Joseph Zobel (b. 1915), Mr. Medouze   937

Guadeloupe
Maryse Conde (b. 1937), Mira   *1087*
Simone Schwarz-Bart (b. 1938), Toussine   *1103*

Puerto Rico
Julia de Burgos (1914–1953), To Julia de Burgos   *931*
Rosario Ferre (b. 1942), The Youngest Doll   *1141*
Ana Lydia Vega (b. 1946), ADJ, Inc.   *1146*

Dominican Republic
Juan Bosch (b. 1909), The Beautiful Soul of Don Damian   *883*

Haiti
Jacques Roumain (1907–1944), Delira Delivrance   *870*

Cuba
Nicolas Guillen (b. 1902), Arrival   *840*
Alejo Carpentier (1904–1980), Like the Night   *849*

Jamaica
Claude McKay (1890–1948), Crazy Mary   *819*
Olive Senior (b. 1941), Do Angels Wear Brassieres?   *1114*
Opal Palmer Adisa (b. 1954), Duppy Get Her   *1159*

The selections are listed alphabetically by author.

Drama

Fugard, Athol, John Kani, & Winston Ntshona   The Island   *South Africa*   654

Mishima Yukio   The Damask Drum   *Japan*   140

Puig, Manuel   Kiss of the Spider Woman   *Argentina*   1020

Soyinka, Wole   The Strong Breed   *Nigeria*   700

Tagore, Rabindranath   Chandalika   *India*   208

Fiction

Abe Kobo   The Red Cocoon   *Japan*   136

Achebe, Chinua   The Madman   *Nigeria*   613

Adisa, Opal Palmer   Duppy Get Her   *Jamaica*   1159

Ahmad, Abd al-Hameed   Khlalah SEL   *United Arab Emirates*   511

Aidoo, Ama Ata   In the Cutting of a Drink   *Ghana*   777

Akutagawa Ryunosuke   In a Grove   *Japan*   36

al-Wali, Muhammad Abd   Abu Rubbiya   *Yemen*   492

Allende, Isabel   Our Secret   *Chile*   1136

Amado, Jorge   Of Dice and Unshakable Principles   *Brazil*   911

Ariyoshi Sawako   The Tomoshibi   *Japan*   157

Armah, Ayi Kwei   Halfway to Nirvana   *Ghana*   770

Asghar, Khalida   The Wagon   *Pakistan*   362

Asturias, Miguel Angel   Legend of "El Cadejo"   *Guatemala*   829

Aulaqi, Saeed   The Succession   *Yemen*   497

Ballas, Shimon Imaginary Childhood *Israel* 460
Bombal, Maria Luisa Sky, Sea and Earth *Chile* 902
Borges, Jorge Luis The Gospel According to Mark
  Argentina 834
Bosch, Juan The Beautiful Soul of Don Damian *Dominican*
  Republic 884
Carpentier, Alejo Like the Night *Cuba* 850
Ch'i Chun The Chignon *Taiwan* 131
Clarke, Austin Leaving This Island Place *Barbados* 1060
Conde, Maryse Mira *Guadeloupe* 1088
Cortazar, Julio Our Demeanor at Wakes *Argentina* 928
Daguio, Amador Wedding Dance *Philippines* 245
Danishvar, Simin The Half-Closed Eye *Iran* 438
Desai, Anita A Devoted Son *India* 348
Deshpande, Shashi My Beloved Charioteer *India* 372
Devi, Mahasweta Dhowli *India* 291
Ding Ling A Certain Night *China* 72
Djebar, Assia There Is No Exile *Algeria* 731
Donoso, Jose Paseo *Chile* 970
Easmon, R. Sarif Bindeh's Gift *Sierra Leone* 620
Enchi Fumiko Boxcar of Chrysanthemums *Japan* 77
Ferre, Rosario The Youngest Doll *Puerto Rico* 1141
Fonseca, Rubem Night Drive *Brazil* 968
Fuentes, Carlos Chac-Mool *Mexico* 996
Garcia Marquez, Gabriel The Handsomest Drowned Man in the
  World *Colombia* 1005
Golshiri, Hushang The Wolf *Iran* 484
Gordimer, Nadine Good Climate, Friendly Inhabitants *South*
  Africa 557
Grace, Patricia It Used to Be Green Once *New Zealand* 357
Guimaraes Rosa, Joao The Third Bank of the River *Brazil* 879
Haqqi, Yahya The Tavern Keeper *Egypt* 531
Harris, Wilson Yurokon *Guyana* 956
Head, Bessie The Collector of Treasures *South Africa* 741
Hidayat, Sadiq Seeking Absolution *Iran* 426
Hirabayashi Taiko A Man's Life *Japan* 91
Hussein, Abdullah The Tale of the Old Fisherman
  Pakistan 323
Hwang Sunwon Cranes *Korea* 125
Idris, Yusuf The Chair Carrier *Egypt* 608

Ihimaera, Witi   Yellow Brick Road   *New Zealand*   384
Kanafani, Ghassan   The Slave Fort   *Palestine*   479
Kawabata Yasunari   The Silver Fifty-Sen Pieces   *Japan*   66
Kenyatta, Jomo   The Gentlemen of the Jungle   *Kenya*   526
Khudayyir, Mohammed   Clocks Like Horses   *Iraq*   466
Lim, Catherine   Ah Bah's Money   *Singapore/Malaysia*   380
Lovelace, Earl   The Fire Eater's Journey   *Trinidad*   1068
Lu Xun (Lu Hsun)   My Old Home   *China*   20
Lubis, Mochtar   Harimau!   *Indonesia*   265
Mahfouz, Naguib   Half a Day   *Egypt*   536
Manto, Saadat Hasan   The Dog of Titwal   *Pakistan*   253
Mao Dun (Mao Tun)   Spring Silkworms   *China*   46
McKay, Claude   Crazy Mary   *Jamaica*   820
Montenegro, Walter   The *Pepino*   *Bolivia*   918
Mungoshi, Charles   Shadows on the Wall   *Zimbabwe*   787
Naipaul, V. S.   My Aunt Gold Teeth   *Trinidad*   1013
Narayan, R. K.   Trail of the Green Blazer   *India*   220
Nwapa, Flora   The Chief's Daughter   *Nigeria*   643
Obeyesekere, Ranjini   Despair   *Sri Lanka*   337
Ocampo, Silvina   The Servant's Slaves   *Argentina*   843
Ogot, Grace   The Rain Came   *Kenya*   629
Onetti, Juan Carlos   A Dream Come True   *Uruguay*   891
Pai Hsien-yung   A Sea of Bloodred Azealeas   *Taiwan*   175
Peng, Jialin   What's in a Name   *China*   186
Peng, Tan Kong   A Jungle Passage   *Singapore/Malaysia*   331
Pinon, Nelida   Brief Flower   *Brazil*   1097
Pritam, Amrita   The Weed   *India*   258
Queiroz, Rachel de   The Tangerine Girl   *Brazil*   905
Rao, Raja   Companions   *India*   225
Roumain, Jacques   Delira Delivrance   *Haiti*   871
Rubiao, Murilo   Teleco, the Rabbit   *Brazil*   943
Rulfo, Juan   Tell them not to kill me   *Mexico*   950
Rushdie, Salman   An Iff and a Butt   *India*   392
Saadawi, Nawal El   She Has No Place in Paradise   *Egypt*   637
Santos, Bienvenido N.   Footnote to a Laundry List   *Philippines* 236
Schwarz-Bart, Simone   Toussine   *Guadeloupe*   1104
Sembene Ousmane   March of the Women   *Senegal*   570
Senior, Olive   Do Angels Wear Brassieres?   *Jamaica*   1115
Sutherland, Efua   New Life at Kyerefaso   *Ghana*   590

Tanizaki Junichiro   The Tattooer   *Japan*   29
Telles, Lygia Fagundes   The Ants   *Brazil*   984
Themba, Can   The Suit   *South Africa*   596
Thich Nhat Hanh   The Pine Gate   *Vietnam*   312
Thiong'o, Ngugi Wa   Wedding at the Cross   *Kenya*   758
Toer, Pramoedya   Inem   *Indonesia*   280
Tutuola, Amos   The Gentleman of Complete Parts   *Nigeria*   545
Vargas Llosa, Mario   A Shadow of Gnats   *Peru*   1077
Vega, Ana Lydia   ADJ, Inc.   *Puerto Rico*   1147
Verduguez, Cesar   The Scream in Your Silence   *Bolivia*   1125
Wicomb, Zoe   You Can't Get Lost in Cape Town   *South Africa*
   792
Yi Sang   Wings   *Korea*   105
Zobel, Joseph   Mr. Medouze   *Martinique*   937

Memoir

Adnan, Etel   In the Heart of the Heart of Another Country
   Lebanon   451
Laye, Camara   The Goldsmith   *Guinea*   585
Menchu, Rigoberta   The Death of Dona Petrona Chona
   Guatemala   1156
Morgan, Sally   Arthur Corunna's Story   *Australia*   401
Mphahlele, Es'kia   Interlude   *South Africa*   540
Neruda, Pablo   The Chilean Forest   *Chile*   861
Xiao Hong   The Crossroads   *China*   120
Yehoshua, Ya'akob   Childhood in Old Jerusalem   *Israel*   434

Poetry

al-Baraduni, Abdallah   Answers to One Question   *Yemen*   459
al-Maqalih, Abd al-Aziz   Sanaa Is Hungry   *Yemen*   490
Andrade, Costa   Fourth Poem of a Canto of Accusation
   Angola   729
Awoonor, Kofi   The Weaver Bird   *Ghana*   697
Bei Dao   Electric Shock; Language   *China*   192
Bekederemo, Clarke J. P.   The Leader   *Nigeria*   698
Bitton, Erez   Something on Madness   *Israel*   507
Bravo, Antonio Gonzalez   Kori Pilpintu   *Bolivia*   816
Brutus, Dennis   Nightsong: City   *South Africa*   583
Burgos, Julia de   To Julia de Burgos   *Puerto Rico*   932

Cardenal, Ernesto   The Filibusters   *Nicaragua*   *991*
Carter, Martin   Listening to the Land   *Guyana*   *995*
Castellanos, Rosario   Daily Round of the Spinster   *Mexico*   *993*
Cesaire, Aime   To Africa   *Martinique*   *925*
Cisneros, Antonio   After the Battle of Ayacucho: a mother's testi-
mony   *Peru*   *1140*
Coker, Syl Cheney   The Philosopher   *Sierra Leone*   *784*
Damas, Leon   Poems   *French Guiana*   *916*
Darwish, Mahmoud   Guests on the Sea   *Palestine*   *504*
Das, Kamala   An Introduction   *India*   *346*
Diop, David   The Vultures   *Senegal*   *606*
Drummond de Andrade, Carlos   An Ox Looks at Man
Brazil   *839*
Elkayam, Shelley   The Crusader Man   *Israel*   *509*
Ezekiel, Nissim   Night of the Scorpion   *India*   *278*
Faiz, Ahmed Faiz   Ghazal   *Pakistan*   *231*
Farrokhzad, Forugh   The Wind-Up Doll   *Iran*   *477*
Gilbert, Kevin (Wiradjuri)   Kiacatoo   *Australia*   *343*
Gibran, Kahlil   On Children   *Lebanon*   *422*
Guillen, Nicolas   Arrival   *Cuba*   *841*
Han Yongun   Ferryboat and Traveler   *Korea*   *17*
Han Yongun   On Reading Tagore's "The Gardener"   *Korea*   *18*
Hikmet, Nazim   12 December 1945   *Turkey*   *424*
Ho Chi Minh   Noon; Transferred to Nanning   *Vietnam*   *219*
Joshi, Umashankar   The Universal Man   *India*   *234*
Kato Shuson   Three modern *haiku*   *Japan*   *104*
Kgositsile, Keorapetse   The Air I Hear   *South Africa*   *757*
Khalid, Fawziyya Abu   A Pearl   *Saudi Arabia*   *508*
Kim Namjo   Having Come to the Mountain   *Korea*   *156*
Kim Sowol   The Road   *Korea*   *70*
Ko Un   Lee Chongnam   *Korea*   *172*
Lara, Jesus   Incallajta Jarahui   *Bolivia*   *827*
Mahapatra, Jayanta   30 January 1982: A Story   *India*   *320*
Mao Zedong (Mao Tse Tung)   Swimming   *China*   *44*
Mapanje, Jack   On African Writing   *Malawi*   *785*
Maris, Hyllus   Spirtual Song of the Aborigine   *Australia*   *322*
Mistral, Gabriela   Song   *Chile*   *818*
Neruda, Pablo   The Heights of Macchu Picchu, III   *Chile*   *861*
Neto, Augustinho   Kinaxixi   *Angola*   *556*
Noonuccal, Oodgeroo (Kath Walker)   Municipal Gum
Australia   *264*

Nuhman, M. A. Murder *Sri Lanka* 390
Nyoongah, Mudrooroo (Colin Johnson) Poem Two
Australia 379
Ogundipe-Leslie, Molara song at the african middle class
Nigeria 776
Okara, Gabriel You Laughed and Laughed and Laughed
Nigeria 554
Okigbo, Christopher Come Thunder *Nigeria* 568
p'Bitek, Okot Song of Lawino *Uganda* 680
Paz, Octavio Return *Mexico* 935
Peters, Lenrie Isatou Died *Gambia* 696
Rabearivelo, Jean-Joseph Flute Players *Madagascar* 529
Senghor, Leopold Sedar Prayer to Masks *Senegal* 534
Shamlu, Ahmad The Gap *Iran* 457
So Chongju The Huge Wave *Korea* 130
Sousa, Noemia de If You Want to Know Me *Mozambique* 604
Tagore, Rabindranath Where the Mind Is Without Fear
India 216
Thumboo, Edwin Christmas Week, 1975
Singapore/Malaysia 341
Tomioka Taeko Just the Two of Us *Japan* 174
Tuqan, Fadwa Song of Becoming *Palestine* 436
U Tam'si, Tchicaya Brush-Fire *Congo* 652
Vallejo, Cesar The Eternal Dice *Peru* 826
Walcott, Derek I Once Gave My Daughters . . .
Saint Lucia 1010
Walcott, Derek The Season of Phantasmal Peace
Saint Lucia 1011
Yosano Akiko Three modern *tanka* *Japan* 16
Yosano Akiko The Day When Mountains Move *Japan* 16

Appendix D

Selected Further Readings

General Bio-Bibliographical References

The following texts indicate primary and secondary sources for many of the authors included in this anthology:

Berrian, Brenda F. *Bibliography of African Women Writers and Journalists.* Washington, D.C.: Three Continents Press, 1985.

Dance, Daryl Cumber. *Fifty Caribbean Writers: A Bio-Bibliographical Critical Sourcebook.* Westport, Conn.: Greenwood Press, 1986.

Foster, David William. *Handbook of Latin American Literature.* 2nd ed. New York: Garland, 1992.

Foster, David William, and Virginia Ramos Foster, eds. *Modern Latin American Literature.* Vols. 1 and 2. New York: Frederick Ungar, 1975.

Green, John. *Iranian Short Story Authors: A Bio-Bibliographic Survey.* Costa Mesa, Calif.: Mazda, 1989.

Herdeck, Donald E. *African Authors.* Washington, D.C.: Black Orpheus Press, 1974–.

———. *Caribbean Authors.* Washington, D.C.: Three Continents Press, 1979.

Klein, Leonard S., ed. *Encyclopedia of World Literature in the 20th Century.* Rev. ed. New York: Ungar, 1984.

Marting, Diane E., ed. *Spanish American Women Writers: A Bio-bibliographical Source Book.* New York: Greenwood Press, 1990.

Page, James A. *Selected Black American, African, and Caribbean Authors.* Littleton, Colo.: Libraries Unlimited, 1985.

Rimer, Thomas J. *A Reader's Guide to Japanese Literature.* Tokyo: Kodansha International, 1988.

General References

Ashcroft, Bill, Gareth Griffiths, and Helen Tiffin. *The Empire Writes Back: Theory and Practice in Post-Colonial Literatures.* London and New York: Routledge, 1989.

Calvino, Italo. *The Uses of Literature.* New York: Norton, 1979.

Clifford, James, and George E. Marcus, eds. *Writing Culture: The Poetics and Politics of Ethnography.* Berkeley: University of California Press, 1986.

Eagleton, Terry. *Literary Theory: An Introduction.* Minneapolis: University of Minnesota Press, 1983.

El Saadawi, Nawal. *The Hidden Face of Eve: Women in the Arab World.* Boston: Beacon, 1981.

Fanon, Frantz. *Black Skin, White Masks.* New York: Grove, 1968.

————. *The Wretched of the Earth.* New York: Grove, 1968.

Hall, Stuart, et al., eds., *Culture, Media, Language.* London: Hutchinson, 1984.

Harlow, Barbara. *Resistance Literature.* New York: Methuen, 1987.

Hopfe, Lewis M. *Religions of the World.* 7th ed. New York: Macmillan, 1993.

Mohanty, Chandra Talpade, Ann Russo, and Lourdes Torres, eds., *Third World Women and the Politics of Feminism.* Bloomington: Indiana University Press, 1991.

Nandy, Ashis. *The Intimate Enemy: Loss and Recovery of Self Under Colonialism.* New York: Oxford University Press, 1989.

Nasta, Susheila, ed. *Motherlands: Black Women's Writing from Africa, the Caribbean, and South Asia.* New Brunswick, N.J.: Rutgers University Press, 1992.

Ngugi Wa Thiong'o. *Moving the Center.* Portsmouth, N.H.: Heinemann, 1993.

Rosaldo, Michelle Zimbalist, and Louise Lamphere, eds. *Woman, Culture, and Society.* Stanford: Stanford University Press, 1974.

Said, Edward. *Culture and Imperialism.* London: Chatto and Windus; New York: Knopf, 1993.

————. *Orientalism.* New York: Vintage-Random, 1979.

Soyinka, Wole. *Art, Dialogue and Outrage: Essays on Literature and Culture.* Ibadan: New Horn Press, 1988.

Spivak, Gayatri Chakravorty. *In Other Worlds: Essays in Cultural Politics.* New York: Methuen, 1987.

Asia

Japan

Historical, Cultural, and Literary Resources

Blyth, R. H. *History of Haiku*. Vol. 2. Tokyo: Hoku Seido Press, 1964.

Duus, Peter, ed. *The Cambridge History of Japan*. Vol. 6: The Twentieth Century. New York: Cambridge University Press, 1988.

Keene, Donald. *The Pleasures of Japanese Literature*. New York: Columbia University Press, 1993.

Minear, Richard H., ed. and trans. *Hiroshima: Three Witnesses*. Princeton: Princeton University Press, 1990.

Miner, Earl. *Comparative Poetics: An Intercultural Essay on Theories of Literature*. Princeton: Princeton University Press, 1990.

Rimer, Thomas J. *Modern Japanese Fiction and Its Tradition*. Princeton: Princeton University Press, 1976.

———. *Pilgrimages: Aspects of Japanese Literature and Culture*. Honolulu: University of Hawaii Press, 1988.

Tiedemann, Arthur E., ed., *An Introduction to Japanese Civilization*. New York: Columbia University Press, 1974.

Ueda, Makota. *Modern Japanese Writers and the Nature of Literature*. Stanford: Stanford University Press, 1976.

Anthologies

Dunlop, Lane, ed. and trans. *A Late Chrysanthemum: Twenty-one Stories from the Japanese*. Tokyo: Tuttle, 1988.

Hibbett, Howard, ed. *Contemporary Japanese Literature: An Anthology of Fiction, Film, and Other Writing Since 1945*. New York: Knopf, 1977.

Keene, Donald, ed. and trans. *Anthology of Japanese Literature*. New York: Grove, 1955.

Lippit, Norkio Mizuta, and Kyoko Iriye Selden, eds. and trans. *Japanese Women Writers: Twentieth Century Short Fiction*. Armonk, N.Y.: M. E. Sharpe, 1991.

Morris, Ivan, ed. *Modern Japanese Stories: An Anthology*. Rutland, VT.: Tuttle, 1989.

Rexroth, Kenneth, and Ikuko Atsumi, eds. and trans. *Women Poets of Japan*. New York: New Directions, 1977.

Sato, Hiroaki, and Burton Watson, eds. and trans. *From the Country of Eight Islands: An Anthology of Japanese Poetry*. New York: Columbia University Press, 1986.

Shimer, Dorothy Blair, ed. *Rice Bowl Women: Writings by and about the Women of China and Japan.* New York: NAL, 1982.

Takaya, Ted T., ed. and trans. *Modern Japanese Drama: An Anthology.* New York: Columbia University Press, 1979.

Tanaka, Yukiko, and Elizabeth Hanson, eds. *This Kind of Woman: Ten Stories by Japanese Women Writers, 1960–1976.* New York: Wideview/Perigee, 1984.

Ueda, Makota, ed. *The Mother of Dreams and Other Short Stories: Portrayals of Women in Modern Japanese Fiction.* Tokyo: Kodansha, 1989.

China

Historical, Cultural, and Literary Resources

Anderson, Marston. *The Limits of Realism: Chinese Fiction in the Revolutionary Period.* Berkeley: University of California Press, 1990.

Gentzler, J. Mason. *A Syllabus of Chinese Civilization.* 2nd ed. New York: Columbia University Press, 1972.

Goldman, Merle, ed. *Modern Chinese Literature in the May Fourth Era.* Cambridge: Harvard University Press, 1982.

Hinton, William. *Fanshen: A Documentary of Revolution in a Chinese Village.* New York: Vintage, 1966.

Hsia, C. T. *A History of Modern Chinese Fiction.* 2nd ed. New Haven: Yale University Press, 1971.

Kinkley, Jeffrey C., ed. *After Mao: Chinese Literature and Society: 1978–1981.* Cambridge: Harvard University Press, 1985.

Kristeva, Julia. *About Chinese Women.* New York: Urizen Books, 1977.

Lee, Yee. *The New Realism: Writings from China After the Cultural Revolution.* New York: Hippocrene, 1985.

Spence, Jonathan D. *The Gate of Heavenly Peace: The Chinese and Their Revolution, 1895–1980.* New York: Viking, 1981.

———. *The Search for Modern China.* New York: Norton, 1990.

Yeh, Michelle. *Modern Chinese Poetry.* New Haven: Yale University Press, 1991.

Wolf, Margery, and Roxane Witke, eds. *Women in Chinese Society.* Stanford: Stanford University Press, 1975.

Anthologies

Carver, Ann, and Sung-Sheng Yvonne Chang, eds. *Bamboo Shoots after the Rain: Contemporary Stories by Women Writers of Taiwan.* New York: Feminist Press, 1990.

Cheung, Dominic, ed. and trans. *The Isle Full of Noises: Modern Chinese Poetry from Taiwan.* New York: Columbia University Press, 1987.

Duke, Michael, ed. *Worlds of Modern Chinese Fiction: Short Stories and Novellas from the People's Republic, Taiwan, and Hong Kong.* Armonk, N.Y.: M. E. Sharpe, 1991.

Hsia, C. T., and Joseph S. M. Lau, eds. *Twentieth-Century Chinese Stories.* New York: Columbia University Press, 1971.

Link, Perry, ed. *Roses and Thorns: The Second Blooming of the Hundred Flowers in Chinese Fiction: 1979–1980.* Berkeley: University of California Press, 1984.

Rexroth, Kenneth, and Liung Chung, eds. *The Orchid Boat: Women Poets of China.* New York: McGraw-Hill, 1972.

Tai, Jeanne, ed. and trans. *Spring Bamboo: A Collection of Contemporary Chinese Short Stories.* New York: Random House, 1989.

Yang, Gladys, ed. *Seven Contemporary Chinese Women Writers.* Beijing: Panda, 1985.

Korea

Historical, Cultural, and Literary Resources

Kim, Yong-jik, and Sung Chan-kyung, eds. *Making of Korean Literature.* Seoul: Korean Culture and Arts Foundation, 1986.

Sym, Myung-ho. *The Making of Modern Korean Poetry: Foreign Influence and Native Creativity.* Seoul: Seoul National University Press, 1982.

Lee, Peter H. *Songs of Flying Dragons: A Critical Reading.* Cambridge: Harvard University Press, 1975.

Anthologies

Hollman, Martin, ed. *Shadows of a Sound.* San Francisco: Mercury House, 1990.

Lee, Peter H., ed. *Flowers of Fire: Twentieth-Century Korean Stories.* Honolulu: University of Hawaii Press, 1986.

———. *Modern Korean Literature: An Anthology.* Honolulu: University of Hawaii Press, 1990.

———. *The Silence of Love: Twentieth-Century Korean Poetry.* Honolulu: University of Hawaii Press, 1980.

McCann, David R., ed. *Black Crane: An Anthology of Korean Literature.* Ithaca: China-Japan Program, Cornell University, 1980.

Southeast Asia, Australia, and New Zealand

Historical, Cultural, and Literary Resources

Becker, A. L., ed. *Writing on the Tongue.* Ann Arbor: University of Michigan, 1989.

Davis, Jack, and Bob Hodge, eds. *Aboriginal Writing Today.* Canberra: Australian Institute of Aboriginal Studies, 1985.

Durand, Maurice M. *An Introduction to Vietnamese Literature.* New York: Columbia University Press, 1985.

Herbert, Patricia, and Anthony Milner, eds. *South-East Asia: Languages and Literatures: A Select Guide.* Honolulu: University of Hawaii Press, 1989.

McGregor, Graham, and Mark Williams, eds. *Dirty Silence: Aspects of Language and Literature in New Zealand.* Aukland: Oxford University Press, 1991.

Montague, Ashley. *Coming into Being among the Australian Aborigines.* London: Routledge and Keegan Paul, 1974.

Muecke, Stephen. *Textual Spaces: Aboriginality and Cultural Studies.* Kensington, NSW: New South Wales University Press, 1992.

Narogin, Mudrooroo. *Writing from the Fringe: A study of Modern Aboriginal Literature.* South Yarra, Melbourne: Hyland House, 1990.

Pearson, Bill. *Fretful Sleepers and Other Essays.* London: Heinemann, 1974.

Rutherford, Anna, ed. *Aboriginal Culture Today.* Sydney, Australia: Dangaroo Press, 1988.

San Juan, E. *Toward a People's Literature.* Honolulu: University of Hawaii Press, 1985.

Shoemaker, Adam. *Black Words, White Page: Aboriginal Literature 1929–1988.* St. Lucia, Qld.: University of Queensland Press, 1989.

Simms, Norman. *Silence and Invisibility: A Study of the Literatures of the Pacific, Australia, and New Zealand.* Washington, D.C.: Three Continents Press, 1986.

Singh, Kirpal, ed. *The Writer's Sense of the Past: Essays on Southeast Asia and Australasian Literature.* Singapore: Singapore University Press, 1987.

Tarling, Nicholas, ed. *The Cambridge History of Southeast Asia.* Vol. 2. Cambridge: Cambridge University Press, 1992.

Thornton, Agathe. *Maori Oral Literature.* Dunedin, N.Z.: University of Otago Press, 1987.

Thumboo, Edwin, ed. *Literature and Liberation.* Manila, Philippines: Solidaridad Publishing House, 1988.

———. *Perceiving Other Worlds.* Singapore: Times Academic Press, 1991.

Weedon, Chris. *Culture, Race, and Identity: Australian Aboriginal Writing.* London: University of London, 1990.

Wicks, Peter. *Literary Perspectives on Southeast Asia.* Toowoomba, Qld.: USQ Press, 1991.

Anthologies

Cong-Huy en-Ton-Nu, Nha-Trang. *Favourite Stories from Vietnam.* Hong Kong: Heinemann Asia, 1979.

Davis, Jack, et al., eds. *A Collection of Black Australian Writings.* St. Lucia, Qld.: University of Queensland Press, 1990.

Gilbert, Kevin, ed. *Inside Black Australia: An Anthology of Aboriginal Poetry.* Victoria, Australia: Penguin Books, 1988.

Glass, Colleen, and Archie Weller, eds. *Us Fellas: An Anthology of Aboriginal Writing.* Perth, W. A.: Artlook Books, 1987.

Orbell, Margaret Rose, ed. *Contemporary Maori Writing.* Wellington: Reed, 1970.

Thompson, Liz, ed. *Aboriginal Voices: Contemporary Aboriginal Artists, Writers, and Performers.* Brookvale, NSW: Simon & Schuster Australia, 1990.

War and Exile: A Vietnamese Anthology. Vietnamese PEN abroad, USA 1989.

Yabes, Leopoldo Y., ed., *Philippine Short Stories, 1941–1955.* Honolulu: University of Hawaii Press, 1981.

South Asia

Historical, Cultural, and Literary Resources

De Souza, Alfred. *Women in Contemporary India and South Asia.* 2nd ed. Columbia, Mo.: South Asia Books, 1981.

Dhawan, R. K., and P. V. Dhamija, and A. K. Srivastava, *Recent Commonwealth Literature.* Vols. I and II. New Delhi: Prestige Books, 1989.

Iyengar, K. R. Srinivas, ed. *Indian Literature since Independence: A Symposium.* New Delhi: Sahitya Akademi, 1973.

Johnson, Gordon, gen. ed. *The Cambridge History of India.* Vols. 3–4. Cambridge: Cambridge University Press, 1989–.

Jussawalla, Feroza, and Reed Way Dasenbrock, eds. *Interviews with Writers of the Post-Colonial World.* Miss.: University Press of Mississippi, 1992.

Kachru, Braj B. *The Indianization of English: The English Language in India.* Delhi: Oxford University Press, 1981.

Liddle, Joanna, and Rama Joshi, eds., *Daughters of Independence: Gender, Caste and Class in India*. New Brunswick, N.J.: Rutgers University Press, 1986.

Mohan, Chandra. ed., *Aspects of Comparative Literature: Current Approaches*. New Delhi: India Publishers and Distributors, 1989.

Mukherjee, Meenakshi. *The Twice-Born Fiction*. London: Heinemann, 1971.

―――. *Realism and Reality: The Novel and Society in India*. New York: Oxford University Press, 1985.

Narasimhan, C. D., ed. *Indian Literature of the Past Fifty Years*. Mysore, India: University of Mysore, 1970.

Naik, M. K. *A History of Indian Writing in English*. Delhi: Sahitya Akademi, 1981.

Rao, A. Ramakrishna, ed. *Comparative Perspectives on Indian Literature*. New Delhi: Prestige, 1992.

Singh, Sushila, ed. *Feminism and Recent Fiction in English*. New Delhi: Prestige, 1991.

Spear, Percival. *A History of India*. Vol. 2. London: Penguin, 1990.

Thapar, Romila. *A History of India*. Vol. 1. London: Penguin, 1990.

Walsh, William. *Indian Literature in English*. London: Longman, 1990.

Anthologies

Alter, Stephen, and Wimal Dissanayake, eds. *The Penguin Book of Modern Indian Short Stories*. Delhi: Penguin Books, India, 1990.

Bardhan, Kalpana, ed. and trans. *Of Women, Outcastes, Peasants, and Rebels: A Selection of Bengali Short Stories*. Berkeley: University of California Press, 1990.

Ezekiel, Nissim, and Meenakshi Mukherjee, eds. *Another India: An Anthology of Contemporary Indian Fiction and Poetry*. Delhi: Penguin Books, India, 1990.

Goonetilleke, D. C. R. A., ed. *The Penguin New Writing in Sri Lanka*. New Delhi: Penguin Books, India, 1992.

Holmstrom, Lakshmi, ed. *The Inner Courtyard: Stories by Indian Women*. London: Virago, 1991.

Kali for Women, ed. *Truth Tales: Contemporary Writing by Indian Women*. New York: Feminist Press, 1990.

Khwaja, Waqas Ahmad, ed. *Pakistani Short Stories*. New Delhi: UBS Publisher, 1992.

Mehrotra, Arvind Krishna, ed. *The Oxford India Anthology of Twelve Modern Indian Poets*. Delhi: Oxford University Press, 1992.

Memon, Muhammad Umar, ed. and trans. *The Colour of Nothingness: Modern Urdu Short Stories*. Delhi: Penguin Books, India, 1991.

———. *The Tale of the Old Fisherman: Contemporary Urdu Short Stories*. Washington, D.C.: Three Continents Press, 1991.

Ray, David, and Amritjit Singh, eds. *India: An Anthology of Contemporary Writing*. Athens: Ohio University Press, 1983.

Tharu, Susie, and K. Lalita, eds. *Women Writers of India: 600 B.C. to the Present*. Vol. II. New York: Feminist Press, 1993.

Middle East

Historical, Cultural, and Literary Resources

Adonis. *An Introduction to Arab Poetics*. Austin: University of Texas Press, 1990.

Alcalay, Ammiel. *After Jews and Arabs: Remaking Levantine Culture*. Minneapolis: University of Minnesota Press, 1993.

Badawi, M. M. *A Critical Introduction to Modern Arabic Poetry*. Cambridge: Cambridge University Press, 1975.

———, ed. *Modern Arabic Literature*. Cambridge: Cambridge University Press, 1992.

Boullata, Issa J., ed. *Critical Perspectives on Modern Arabic Literature*. Washington, D.C.: Three Continents Press, 1980.

Fernea, Elizabeth, ed. *Women and Family in the Middle East: New Voices of Change*. Austin: University of Texas Press, 1985.

Hourani, Albert. *A History of the Arab People*. Cambridge: Harvard University Press, 1991.

Malti-Douglas, Fedwa. *Woman's Body, Woman's Word: Gender and Discourse in Arabo-Islamic Writing*. Princeton: Princeton University Press, 1991.

Milani, Farzaneh. *Veils and Words: The Emerging Voices of Iranian Women Writers*. Syracuse: Syracuse University Press, 1992.

Moosa, Matti. *The Origins of Modern Arabic Fiction*. Washington, D.C.: Three Continents Press, 1983.

Segev, Tom. *1949: The First Israelis*. New York: Free Press, 1986.

Sulaiman, Khalid A. *Palestine and Modern Arab Poetry*. London: Zed Books, 1984.

Anthologies

Anderson, Elliott, ed. *Contemporary Israeli Literature: An Anthology*. Philadelphia: Jewish Publication Society of America, 1977.

Boullata, Kamal, ed. and trans. *Women of the Fertile Crescent: Modern Poetry by Arab Women.* Washington, D.C.: Three Continents Press, 1978.

Carmi, T., ed. *Penguin Book of Hebrew Verse.* New York: Penguin, 1981.

Davies, Denys Johnson, ed. and trans. *Arabic Short Stories.* New York: Quartet Books, 1983.

———. *Egyptian Short Stories.* London: Heinemann, 1978.

Ghanoonparvar, M. R., and John Green, eds. *Iranian Drama: An Anthology.* Costa Mesa, Calif.: Mazda, 1989.

Halman, Talat Sait, ed. *Contemporary Turkish Literature.* Rutherford, N.J.: Fairleigh Dickinson University Press, 1982.

Hamalian, Leo, and John D. Yohannan, eds. *New Writing from the Middle East.* New York: Ungar, 1978.

Jayyusi, Salma Khadra, ed. *The Literature of Modern Arabia: An Anthology.* Austin: University of Texas Press, 1990.

———. *Modern Arabic Poetry: An Anthology.* New York: Columbia University Press, 1987.

———. *Modern Palestinian Literature: An Anthology.* New York: Columbia University Press, 1992.

Karimi-Hakkak, Ahmad, ed. and trans. *An Anthology of Modern Persian Poetry.* Boulder, Colo.: Westview Press, 1978.

Kassem, Ceza, and Malak Haashem, eds. *Flights and Fantasy: Arabic Short Stories.* Cairo: Elias Modern Publishing House, 1985.

Moayyad, Heshmat, ed. *Stories from Iran: A Chicago Anthology 1921–1991.* Washington, D.C.: Mage Publishers, 1991.

Africa
Historical, Cultural, and Literary Resources

Achebe, Chinua. *Hopes and Impediments: Selected Essays.* New York: Anchor, 1989.

Amuta, Chidi. *The Theory of African Literature.* London: Zed Books, 1989.

Berrian, Brenda, ed. *Critical Perspectives on Women Writers from Africa.* Washington, D.C.: Three Continents Press, 1992.

Cartey, Wilfred. *Whispers from a Continent: The Literature of Contemporary Black Africa.* New York: Vintage, 1969.

Chinweizu, Onwuchekwa Jamie, and Ihechukwu Madubuike, eds. *Toward the Decolonization of African Literature.* Washington, D.C.: Howard University Press, 1983.

Davidson, Basil. *Let Freedom Come: Africa in Modern History.* Boston: Little, Brown, 1978.

Davies, Carole Boyce, and Anne Adams Graves, eds. *Ngambika: Studies of Women in African Literature.* Trenton, N.J.: Africa World Press, 1986.

Gikandi, Simon. *Reading the African Novel.* London: James Currey, 1987.

Irele, Abiola. *The African Experience in Literature and Ideology.* Bloomington: Indiana University Press, 1990.

Jahn, Janheinz. *Muntu.* 14th ed. New York: Grove, 1979.

James, Adeola, ed. *In Their Own Voices: African Women Writers Talk.* London: James Currey, 1990.

Jones, Eldred Durosimi, ed. *Oral and Written Poetry in African Literature Today: A Review.* London: Currey; Trenton, N.J.: Africa World Press, 1988.

———. *Women in African Literature Today: A Review.* London: Currey; Trenton, N.J.: Africa World Press, 1987.

July, R. *An African Voice: The Role of the Humanities in African Independence.* Prospect Heights, Ill.: Waveland Press, 1992.

Mazrui, Ali M. *The African Condition.* London: Heinemann, 1980.

Mbiti, John S. *African Religions and Philosophy.* New York: Anchor, 1970.

Moore, Gerald. *Twelve African Writers.* Bloomington: Indiana University Press, 1980.

Mphahlele, Ezekiel. *The African Image.* London: Faber, 1974.

Ngugi Wa Thiong'o. *Decolonising the Mind: The Politics of Language in African Literature.* London: Heinemann, 1986.

Nichols, Lee. *Conversations With African Writers.* Washington, D.C.: Voice of America, 1981.

Okpaku, Joseph Ohiomogben, Alfred Esimatemi Opubor, and Benjamin Olatunji Oloruntimehin, gen. eds. *The Arts and Civilization of Black and African Peoples.* Vol. 3. Lagos: Third Press International, 1986.

Okpewho, Isidore. *African Oral Literature: Backgrounds, Characters, and Continuity.* Bloomington: Indiana University Press, 1992.

Soyinka, Wole. *Myth, Literature and the African World.* Cambridge: Cambridge University Press, 1976.

Wilkinson, Jane, ed. *Talking with African Writers: Interviews with African Poets, Playwrights, and Novelists.* London: James Currey; Portsmouth, N.H.: Heinemann, 1992.

Ziegler, Wedad Zenie, ed. *In Search of Shadows: Conversations with Egyptian Women.* London: Zed Books, 1988.

Anthologies

Achebe, Chinua, and C. L. Innes, eds. *African Short Stories.* London: Heinemann, 1985.

Anyidoho, Kofi, Peter Porter, and Musaemura Zimunya, eds. *The Fate of Vultures: New Poetry of Africa.* Oxford: Heinemann International, 1989.

Bruner, Charlotte H., ed. *Unwinding Threads: Writing by Women in Africa.* London: Heinemann, 1983.

———. *Heinemann Book of African Women's Writing.* London: Heinemann, 1993.

Busby, Margaret, ed. *Daughters of Africa.* New York: Pantheon, 1992.

Chinweizu, ed. *Voices from Twentieth-Century Africa: Griots and Towncriers.* London: Faber, 1988.

Maja-Pearce, Adewale, ed. *The Heinemann Book of African Poetry in English.* Oxford: Heinemann International, 1990.

Moore, Gerald, and Ulli Beier, eds. *The Penguin Book of Modern African Poetry.* 3rd ed. London: Penguin, 1984.

Okpewho, Isidore, ed. *The Heritage of African Poetry: An Anthology of Oral and Written Poetry.* London: Longman, 1985.

Obradovic, Nadezda, ed. *Looking for a Rain God: An Anthology of Contemporary African Short Stories.* New York: Simon and Schuster/Fireside, 1990.

Latin America and the Caribbean

Historical, Cultural, and Literary Resources

Abrahams, Roger D. *The Man-of-Words in the West Indies: Performance and the Emergence of Creole Culture.* Baltimore: Johns Hopkins University Press, 1983.

Bethell, Leslie, ed. *The Cambridge History of Latin America.* 9 vols. Cambridge: Cambridge University Press, 1984–.

Brathwaite, Edward Kamau. *English in the Caribbean* [microform] Notes on Nation, Language and Poetry. Jamaica: Savacou Publication, 1982.

Burnett, Paula. Introduction to *Penguin Book of Caribbean Verse.* Middlesex, England: Penguin, 1986.

Cartey, Wilfred. *Whispers from the Caribbean: I Going Away, I Going Home.* Los Angeles: Center for Afro-American Studies, University of California, 1991.

Cudjoe, Selwyn, ed. *Caribbean Women Writers: Essays from the First International Conference.* Wellesley, Mass.: Calaloux, 1990.

Dash, Michael J. Introduction to *Masters of the Dew* by Jacques Roumain. London: Heinemann, 1986.

———. *Literature and Ideology in Haiti: 1915–1961.* London: Macmillan, 1981.

Davies, Carole Boyce, and Elaine Savory Fido, eds. *Out of the Kumbla: Caribbean Women and Literature.* Trenton, N.J.: Africa World Press, 1990.

Donoso, José. *The Boom in Spanish American Literature.* New York: Columbia University Press, 1977.

González Echevarria, Roberto, and Enrique Pupo-Walker, eds. *The Cambridge History of Latin American Literature.* Cambridge: Cambridge University Press, 1995.

Mintz, Sidney, and Sally Price, eds. *Caribbean Contours.* Baltimore: Johns Hopkins University Press, 1985.

Ormerod, Beverly. *An Introduction to the French Caribbean Novel.* London: Heinemann, 1985.

Pinto, Magdalena Garcia. *Women Writers of Latin America: Intimate Histories.* Austin: University of Texas Press, 1991.

Ramchand, Kenneth. *The West Indian Novel and Its Background.* 2nd ed. London: Heinemann, 1983.

Saakana, Amon Saba. *The Colonial Legacy in Caribbean Literature.* Vol. 1. Trenton, N.J.: Africa World Press, 1987.

Sunshine, Catherine. *The Caribbean: Survival, Struggle and Sovereignty.* 2nd ed. Washington, D.C.: Epica, 1988.

Taylor, Patrick. *The Narrative of Liberation: Perspectives on Afro-Caribbean Literature, Popular Culture and Politics.* Ithaca: Cornell University Press, 1989.

Anthologies

Agosin, Marjorie, ed. *Landscapes of a New Land: Short Fiction by Latin American Women.* Buffalo: White Pine Press, 1989.

———. *Secret Weavers: Stories of the Fantastic by Women of Argentina and Chile.* Fredonia, N.Y.: White Pine Press, 1992.

Burnett, Paula, ed. *Penguin Book of Caribbean Verse.* Middlesex, England: Penguin, 1986.

Colchie, Thomas, ed. *A Hammock Beneath the Mangoes: Stories from Latin America.* New York: Penguin, 1991.

Crow, Mary, ed. *Woman Who Has Sprouted Wings: Poems by Contemporary Latin American Women Poets.* Pittsburgh: Latin American Literary Review Press, 1988.

Donoso, Jose, and William A. Henken, eds. *The Tri-Quarterly Anthology of Contemporary Latin American Literature.* New York: Dutton, 1969.

Esteves, Carmen C., and Lisa Paravisini-Gebert, eds. *Green Cane and Juicy Flotsam: Short Stories by Caribbean Women.* New Brunswick, N.J.: Rutgers University Press, 1991.

Flores, Angel, and Kate Flores, eds. *The Defiant Muse: Hispanic Feminist Poems from the Middle Ages to the Present*. New York: Feminist Press, 1986.

Grossman, William L., ed. and trans. *Modern Brazilian Short Stories*. Berkeley: University of California Press, 1967.

Howe, Barbara, ed. *The Eye of the Heart: Short Stories from Latin America*. New York: Avon, 1983.

Mordecai, Pamela, and Betty Wilson, eds. *Her True-True Name: An Anthology of Women's Writing from the Caribbean*. Oxford: Heinemann International, 1990.

Morris, Mervyn. ed. *The Faber Book of Contemporary Caribbean Short Stories*. London: Faber, 1990.

Rodriguez Monegal, Emir, ed. with the assistance of Thomas Colchie. *The Borzoi Anthology of Latin American Literature*. Vol. 2. New York: Knopf, 1977.

Credits

University Press. Copyright © 1953 by the Board of Trustees of the Leland Stanford Junior University.

Saadat Hasan Manto, "The Dog of Titwal," from *Kingdom's End*. Reprinted by permission of Verso Books.

Amrita Pritam, "The Weed," translated by Raj Gill, from *Aerial and other Stories*. Copyright © 1978 by United Writers. Reprinted by permission of the Author.

Oodgeroo Noonuccal, "Municipal Gum," from *My People*, by Oodjeroo of the tribe Noonuccal, Custodian of the land Minjerribah. Published by Jacaranda Wiley Ltd. Reprinted by permission of Jacaranda Wiley Ltd.

Mochtar Lubis, "Harimau!", as it appeared in *Tiger!*, translated by Florence Lamoreux, Singapore: Select Books, 1991.

Nissim Ezekial, "Night of the Scorpion" (pp.130-131), from *Collected Poems*. Reprinted by permission of Oxford University Press.

Pramoedya Anana Toer, "Inem," from *From Surabaya to Armageddon*, edited and translated by Harry Aveling. Reprinted by permission of Heinemann Asia/Reed International (Singapore) Pte Ltd.

Mahasweta Devi, "Dhowli," from *Of Women, Outcastes, Peasants, and Rebels: A Selection of Bengali Short Stories*, edited by Kalpana Bardhan. Copyright © 1990 The Regents of the University of California. Reprinted by permission of the University of California Press.

Thich Nhat Hanh, "The Pine Gate," from *The Pine Gate*, translated by Vo-Dinh Mai and Mobi Ho. Copyright © 1988 by Thich Nhat Hanh and White Pine Press. Reprinted by permission of White Pine Press.

Jayanta Mahapatra, "30th January, 1982: A Story" from *Indian Literature Journal*. Copyright © 1985 by National Academy of Letters. Reprinted by permission of National Academy of Letters.

Hyllus Maris, "Spiritual Song of the Aborigine," from *Inside Black Australia*, edited by Kevin Gilbert. Reprinted by permission of Penguin Books Australia Ltd.

Abdullah Hussain, "The Tale of the Old Fisherman," from *Journal of South Asian Literature*. Copyright © 1965. Reprinted by permission of *Journal of South Asian Literature*.

Tan Kong Peng, "A Jungle Passage," from *Malagan Chinese Stories*, edited by R. Sinko. Reprinted by permission of Heinemann Asia/Reed International (Singapore) Pte Ltd.

Ranjini Obeyesekere, "Despair," from *The Penguin New Writing in Sri Lanka*, edited by D. C. R. A. Goonetilleke. Copyright © 1991, 1992 by Penguin Books India (P) Ltd. Reprinted by permission of D. C. R. A. Goonetilleke.

Edwin Thumboo, "Christmas Week 1975," from *Gods Can Die*. Reprinted by permission of the author.

Kevin Gilbert, "Kiacatoo," from *Inside Black Australia*. Reprinted by permission of Penguin Books Australia Ltd.

Kamala Das, "An Introduction," from *Summer in Calcutta*, published in 1965. Reprinted by permission of the author.

Anita Desai. "A Devoted Son," from *Games at Twilight and Other Stories*. Copyright © 1978 by Anita Desai. Reprinted by permission of HarperCollins Publishers, Inc. and Rogers, Coleridge & White Ltd.

Patricia Grace, "It Used to Be Green Once," from *The Dream Sleepers and Other Stories*. Reprinted by permission by Longman Paul Limited.

Khalida Asghar, "The Wagon," from *Indian Literature Journal*. Copyright © 1976 by National Academy of Letters. Reprinted by permission of National Academy of Letters.

Shashi Deshpande, "My Beloved Charioteer," as it appeared in *The Inner Courtyard: Stories by Indian Women*, ed. Lakshmi Holstrom, Calcutta: Rupa & Co., 1991.

Mudrooroo Nyoongah, "Poem Two," from *The Garden of Gethsemane*. Copyright © 1991 by Hyland House Publishing Pty Ltd. Reprinted by permission of Hyland House Publishing Pty Ltd.

Catherine Lim, "Ah Bah's Money," from *Or Else, The Lightning God & Other Stories*. Reprinted by permission of Heinemann Asia/Reed International (Singapore) Pte Ltd.

Index

Abe Kobo, 135–139
  The Red Cocoon, 136–139
Abu Rubbiya, 492–496
Achebe, Chinua, 612–619
  The Madman, 613–619
Adisa, Opal Palmer, 1159–1168
  Duppy Get Her, 1159–1168
ADJ, Inc., 1147–1155
Adnan, Etel, 450–457
  *In the Heart of the Heart of Another
  Country*, 451–457
*After the Battle of Ayacucho: A mother's
  testimony*, 1140
Ah Bah's Money, 380–383
Ahmad, Abd al-Hameed, 510–518
  Khlalah SEL, 511–518
Aidoo, Ama Ata, 777–783
  In the Cutting of a Drink, 777–783
Air I Hear, The, 757
Akutagawa Ryunosuke, 35–43
  In a Grove, 36–43
al-Baraduni, Abdallah, 458–459
  Answers to One Question, 459
al-Wali, Muhammad Abd, 491–496
  Abu Rubbiya, 492–496
Allende, Isabel, 1135–1139
  Our Secret, 1136–1139
al-Maqalih, Abd al-Aziz, 490–491
  Sanaa Is Hungry, 490–491
Amado, Jorge, 910–915
  Of Dice and Unshakable Principles,
  911–915
Andrade, Carlos Drummond De,
  839–840
  Ox Looks at Man, An, 839–840
Andrade, Costa, 729–730
  Fourth Poem of a Canto of Accusation,
  729–730

Answers to One Question, 459
Ants, The, 984–989
Ariyoshi Sawako, 157–171
  The Tomoshibi, 157–171
Armah, Ayi Kwei, 770–775
  Halfway to Nirvana, 770–775
Arrival, 841–842
Arthur Corunna's Story, 401–414
Asghar, Khalida, 361–371
  The Wagon, 362–371
Asturias, Miguel Angel, 828–833
  Legend of "El Cadejo," 829–833
Aulaqi, Saeed, 496–503
  The Succession, 497–503
Awoonor, Kofi, 696–698
  The Weaver Bird, 697–698

Ballas, Shimon, 459–466
  Imaginary Childhood, 460–466
Beautiful Soul of Don Damian, The,
  884–890
Bei Dao, 191–193
  Electric Shock, 192–193
  Language, 192–193
Bindeh's Gift, 620–628
Bitton, Erez, 506–508
  Something on Madness, 507–508
Bombal Maria Luisa, 901–904
  Sky, Sea and Earth, 902–904
Borges, Jorge Luis, 833–838
  The Gospel According to Mark,
  834–838
Bosch, Juan, 883–890
  The Beautiful Soul of Don Damian,
  884–890
Boxcar of Chrysanthemums, 77–90
Bravo, Antonio Gonzalez, 816–817
  Kori Pilpintu, 816–817

Brief Flower, 1097–1103
Brush-Fire, 652–653
Brutus, Dennis, 582–584
  Nightsong: City, 583–584
Burgos, Julia de, 931–934
    To Julia de Burgos, 932–934

Cardenal, Ernesto, 990–992
  The Filibusters, 991–992
Carpentier, Alejo, 849–859
  Like the Night, 850–859
Carter, Martin, 994–995
  Listening to the Land, 995
Castellanos, Rosario, 992–994
  Daily Round of the Spinster, 993–994
Certain Night, A, 72–76
Cesaire, Aime, 924–927
  To Africa, 925–927
Ch'i Chun, 130–135
  The Chignon, 131–135
Chac-Mool, 996–1003
Chair Carrier, The, 608–612
Chandalika, 208–216
Chief's Daughter, The, 643–651
Chignon, The, 131–135
Childhood in Old Jerusalem, 434–435
Chilean Forest, The, 861–869
Christmas Week 1975, 341–343
Cisneros, Antonio, 1139–1140
    After the Battle of Ayacucho: A mother's testimony, 1140
Clarke Bekederemo, J.P., 698–699
  The Leader, 698–699
Clarke, Austin, 1060–1067
  Leaving This Island Place, 1060–1067
Clocks Like Horses, 466–476
Coker, Syl Cheney, 783–784
  The Philosopher, 784
Collector of Treasures, The, 741–756
Come Thunder, 568–569
Companions, 225–230
Conde, Maryse, 1087–1097
  Mira, 1088–1097
Cortazar, Julio, 927–931
  Our Demeanor at Wakes, 928–931
Cranes, 125–129
Crazy Mary, 820–825
Crossroads, The, 120–124
Crusader Man, The, 509–510

Daguio, Amador, 245–252
  Wedding Dance, 245–252
Daily Round of the Spinster, 993–994
Damas, Leon, 915–917
  Poems, 916–917
Damask Drum, The, 140–155
Danishvar, Simin, 437–450
  The Half-Closed Eye, 438–450
Darwish, Mahmoud, 503–506
  Guests on the Sea, 504–506
Das, Kamala, 345–348
  An Introduction, 346–348
Day When Mountains Move, The, 16
Death of Dona Petrona Chona, The, 1156–1158
Delira Delivrance, 871–878
Desai, Anita, 348–356
  A Devoted Son, 348–356
Deshpande, Shashi, 371–378
  My Beloved Charioteer, 372–378
Despair, 337–340
Devi, Mahasweta, 290–312
  Dhowli, 291–312
Devoted Son, A, 348–356
Dhowli, 291–312
Ding Ling, 71–76
  A Certain Night, 72–76
Diop, David, 606–607
  The Vultures, 606–607
Djebar, Assia, 730–740
  There Is No Exile, 731–740
Do Angels Wear Brassieres?, 1115–1124
Dog of Titwal, The, 253–257
Donoso, Jose, 969–983
  Paseo, 970–983
Dream Come True, A, 891–901
Duppy Get Her, 1159–1168

Easmon, R. Sarif, 619–628
  Bindeh's, Gift, 620–628
Electric Shock, 192–193
Elkayam, Shelley, 509–510
  The Crusader Man, 509–510
Enchi Fumiko, 76–90
  Boxcar of Chrysanthemums, 77–90
Eternal Dice, The, 826–827
Ezekiel, Nissim, 277–279
  Night of the Scorpion, 278–279

Faiz, Faiz Ahmed, 231–233
  Ghazal, 231–233
Farrokhzad, Forugh, 476–478
  The Wind-Up Doll, 477–478
Ferre, Rosario, 1141–1146
  The Youngest Doll, 1141–1146
Ferryboat and Traveler, 17–18
Filibusters, The, 991–992
Fire Eater's Journey, The, 1068–1076
Flute Players, 529–530
Fonseca, Rubem, 967–969
  Night Drive, 968–969
Footnote to a Laundry List, 236–244
Fourth Poem of a Canto of Accusation,
  729–730
Fuentes, Carlos, 995–1003
  Chac-Mool, 996–1003
Fugard, Athol, 653–679
  The Island, 654–679

Gap, The, 457–458
Gentleman of Complete Parts, The,
  545–553
Gentlemen of the Jungle, The, 526–529
Ghazal, 231–233
Gibran, Kahlil Gibran, 422–423
  On Children, 422–423
Gilbert, Kevin—Wiradjuri, 343–345
  Kiacatoo, 343–345
Goldsmith, The, 585–589
Golshiri, Hushang, 483–490
  The Wolf, 484–490
Good Climate, Friendly Inhabitants,
  557–568
Gordimer, Nadine, 557–568
  Good Climate, Friendly Inhabitants,
  557–568
Gospel According to Mark, The, 834–838
Grace, Patricia, 356–361
  It Used to Be Green Once, 357–361
Guests on the Sea, 504–506
Guillen, Nicolas, 840–842
  Arrival, 841–842

Half a Day, 536–539
Half-Closed Eye, The, 438–450
Halfway to Nirvana, 770–775

Han Yongun, 16–18
  Ferryboat and Traveler, 17
  On Reading Tagore's "The Gardener,"
  18
*Handsomest Drowned Man in the World,
  The*, 1005–1009
Haqqi, Yahya, 531–533
  The Tavern Keeper, 531–533
Harimau!, 265–277
Harris, Wilson, 955–967
  Yorokon, 956–967
Having Come to the Mountain, 156–157
Head, Bessie, 740–756
  The Collector of Treasures, 741–756
Heights of Macchu Picchu, III, The, 861
Hidayat, Sadiq, 425–433
  Seeking Absolution, 426–433
Hikmet, Nazim, 423–425
  12 December 1945, 424–425
Hirabayashi Taiko, 90–103
  A Man's Life, 91–103
Ho Chi Minh, 217–219
  Noon, 219
  Transferred to Nanning, 219
Huge Wave, The, 130
Hussein, Abdullah, 323–331
  The Tale of the Old Fisherman, 323–331
Hwang SunWon, 124–129
  Cranes, 125–129

I once gave my daughters . . ., 1010–1011
Idris, Yusuf, 607–612
  The Chair Carrier, 608–612
If You Want to Know Me, 604–605
Ihimaera, Witi, 384–390
  Yellow Brick Road, 384–390
Imaginary Childhood, 460–466
In a Grove, 36–43
In the Cutting of a Drink, 777–783
*In the Heart of the Heart of Another
  Country*, 451–457
Incallajta Jarahui, 827–828
Inem, 280–290
Interlude, 540–544
Introduction, An, 346–348
Isatou Died, 696
Island, The, 654–679
It Used to Be Green Once, 357–361

Jialin Peng, 185–191
 What's in a Name, 186–191
Joshi, Umashankar, 233–235
 The Universal Man, 234–235
Jungle Passage, A, 331–336
Just the Two of Us, 174–175

Kanafani, Ghassan, 479–483
 The Slave Fort, 479–483
Kato Shuson, 103–104
 Three Modern Haiku, 104
Kawabata Yasunari, 65–69
 The Silver Fifty-Sen Pieces, 66–69
Kenyatta, Jomo, 526–529
 The Gentlemen of the Jungle, 526–529
Kgositsile, Keorapetse, 757
 The Air I Hear, 757
Khalid, Fawziyya Abu, 508–509
 A Pearl, 508–509
Khlalah SEL, 511–518,
Khudayyir, Mohammed, 466–476
 Clocks Like Horses, 466–476
Kiacatoo, 343–345
Kim Namjo, 156–157
 Having Come to the Mountain,
  156–157
Kim Sowol, 70–71
 The Road, 70–71
Kinaxixi, 556
Kiss of the Spider Woman, 1020–1059
Ko Un, 171–173
 Lee Chongnam, 172–173
Kori Pilpintu, 816–817

Language, 192–193
Lara, Jesus, 827–828
 Incallajta Jarahui, 827–828
Laye, Camara, 584–589
 The Goldsmith, 585–589
Leader, The, 698–699
Leaving This Island Place, 1060–1067
Lee Chongnam, 172–173
Legend of "El Cadejo," 829–833
Like the Night, 850–859
Lim, Catherine, 380–383
 Ah Bah's Money, 380–383
Listening to the Land, 995

Llosa, Mario Vargas, 1077–1087
 A Shadow of Gnats, 1077–1087
Lovelace, Earl, 1067–1076
 The Fire Eater's Journey, 1068–1076
Lu Xun (Lu Hsun), 19–28
 My Old Home, 20–28
Lubis, Mochtar, 264–277
 Harimau!, 265–277

McKay, Claude, 819–825
 Crazy Mary, 820–825
Madman, The, 613–619
Mahapatra, Jayanta, 320–321
 30 January 1982: A Story, 320–321
Mahfouz, Naguib, 536–539
 Half a Day, 536–539
Man's Life, A, 91–103
Manto, Saadat Hasan, 252–257
 The Dog of Titwal, 253–257
Mao Dun (Mao Tun), 45–65
 Spring Silkworms, 46–65
Mao Zedong (Mao Tse Tung), 43–45
 Swimming, 44–45
Mapanje, Jack, 785–786
 On African Writing, 785–786
March of the Women, The, 570–582
Maris, Hyllus, 322
 Spiritual Song of the Aborigine, 322
Marquez, Gabriel Garcia, 1004–1009
 *The Handsomest Drowned Man in the
  World*, 1005–1009
Menchu, Rigoberta, 1155–1158
 The Death of Dona Petrona Chona,
  1156–1158
Mira, 1088–1097
Mishima Yukio, 139–155
 The Damask Drum, 140–155
Mistral, Gabriela, 817–819
 Song, 818–819
Montenegro, Walter, 917–924
 The Pepino, 918–924
Morgan, Sally, 400–414
 Arthur Corunna's Story, 401–414
Mphahlele, Es'kia, 539–544
 Interlude, 540–544
Mr. Medouze, 937–942
Mungoshi, Charles, 786–791
 Shadows on the Wall, 787–791

Municipal Gum, 264
Murder, 390–391
My Aunt Gold Teeth, 1013–1020
My Beloved Charioteer, 372–378
My Old Home, 20–28

Naipaul, V.S., 1012–1020
  My Aunt Gold Teeth, 1013–1020
Narayan, R. K., 219–224
  Trail of the Green Blazer, 220–224
Neruda, Pablo, 860–869
  The Heights of Macchu Picchu III, 861
  The Chilean Forest, 861–869
Neto, Augustinoh, 555–556
  Kinaxixi, 556
New Life at Kyerefaso, 590–595
Night Drive, 968–969
Night of the Scorpion, 278–279
Nightsong: City, 583–584
Noon, 219
Noonuccal, Oodjeroo (Kath Walker),
    263–264
  Municipal Gum, 264
Nuhman, M. A., 390–391
  Murder, 390–391
Nwapa, Flora, 643–651
  The Chief's Daughter, 643–651
Nyoongah, Mudrooroo (Colin
    Johnson), 378–379
  Poem Two, 379

Obeyesekere, Ranjini, 337–340
  Despair, 337–340
Ocampo, Silvina, 842–849
  The Servant's Slaves, 843–849
Of Dice and Unshakable Principles,
    911–915
Ogot, Grace, 628–637
  The Rain Came, 629–637
Ogundipe-Leslie, Molara, 775–776
  song at the african middle class, 776
Okara, Gabriel, 553–555
  You Laughed and Laughed and Laughed,
    554–555
Okigbo, Christopher, 568–569
  Come Thunder, 568–569
On African Writing, 785–786

On Children, 422–423
On Reading Tagore's "The Gardener," 18
Onetti, Juan Carlos, 890–901
  A Dream Come True, 891–901
Our Demeanor at Wakes, 928–931
Our Secret, 1136–1139
Ox Looks at Man, An, 839–840

p'Bitek, Okot, 679–695
  Song of Lawino, 680–695
Pai Hsien–yung, 175–185
  A Sea of Bloodred Azeleas, 175–185
Paseo, 970–983
Paz, Octavio, 934–937
  Return, 935–937
Pearl, A, 508–509
Peng, Tan Kong, 331–336
  A Jungle Passage, 331–336
Pepino,The, 918–924
Peters, Lenrie, 695–696
  Isatou Died, 696
Philosopher, The, 784
Pine Gate, The, 312–319
Pinon, Nelida, 1097–1103
  Brief Flower, 1097–1103
Poem Two, 379
Poems, 916–917
Prayer to Masks, 534–536
Pritam, Amrita, 257–263
  The Weed, 258–263
Puig, Manuel, 1020–1060
  Kiss of the Spider Woman, 1020–1060

Queiroz, Rachel de, 905–910
  Tangerine Girl, 905–910

Rabearivelo, Jean-Joseph, 529–530
  Flute Players, 529–530
Rain Came, The, 629–637
Rao, Raja, 224–230
  Companions, 225–230
Red Cocoon, The, 136–139
Return, 935–937
Road, The, 70–71
Rosa, Joao Guimaraes, 878–883
  The Third Bank of the River, 879–883
Roumain, Jacques, 870–878
  Delira Delivrance, 871–878

Rubiao, Murilo, 942–949
   Teleco, the Rabbit, 943–949
Rulfo, Juan, 949–955
   Tell them not to kill me, 950–955
Rushdie, Salman, 391–400
   An Iff and a Butt, 392–400

Saadawi, Nawal El, 637–642
   She Has No Place in Paradise, 637–642
Sanaa Is Hungry, 490–491
Santos, Bienvenido N., 235–244
   Footnote to a Laundry List, 236–244
Schwarz–Bart, Simone, 1103–1114
   Toussine, 1104–1114
Scream in Your Silence, The, 1125–1135
Sea of Bloodred Azealeas, A, 175–185
Season of Phantasmal Peace, The,
   1011–1012
Seeking Absolution, 426–433
Sembene Ousmene, 569–582
   The March of the Women, 570–582
Senghor, Leopold Sedar, 534–536
   Prayer to Masks, 534–536
Senior, Olive, 1114–1124
   Do Angels Wear Brassieres?, 1115–1124
Servant's Slaves, The, 843–849
Shadow of Gnats, A, 1077–1087
Shadows on the Wall, 787–791
Shamlu, Ahmad, 457–458
   The Gap, 457–458
She Has No Place in Paradise, 637–642
Silver Fifty-Sen Pieces, The, 66–69
Sky, Sea and Earth, 902–904
Slave Fort, The, 479–483
So Chong–Ju, 129–130
   The Huge Wave, 130
Something on Madness, 507–508
Song, 818–819
song at the african middle class, 776
Song of Becoming, 436–437
Song of Lawino, 680–695
Sousa, Noemia, de, 604–606
   If You Want to Know Me, 604–605
Soyinka, Wole, 699–729
   The Strong Breed, 700–729
Spirtual Song of the Aborigine, 322
Spring Silkworms, 46–65
Strong Breed, The, 700–729
Succession, The, 497–503

Suit, The, 596–604
Sutherland, Efua, 589–595
   New Life at Kyerefaso, 590–595
Swimming, 44–45

Tagore, Rabindranath, 207–217
   Chandalika, 208–216
   Where the Mind Is Without Fear,
   216–217
Tale of the Old Fisherman, The,
   323–331
Taleco, the Rabbit, 943–949
Tangerine Girl, 905–910
Tanizaki Junichiro, 28–34
   The Tattooer, 29–34
Tattooer, The, 29–34
Tavern Keeper, The, 531–533
Telles, Lygia Fagundes, 983–989
   The Ants, 984–989
Tell them not to kill me, 950–955
Themba, Can, 595–604
   The Suit, 596–604
There Is No Exile, 731–740
Thich Nhat Hanh, 312–319
   The Pine Gate, 312–319
Thiong'o, Ngugi Wa, 758–769
   Wedding at the Cross, 758–769
Third Bank of the River, The, 879–883
30 January 1982: A Story, 320–321
Three modern haiku, 104
Three modern tanka, 15
Thumboo, Edwin, 341–343
   Christams Week 1975, 341–343
To Africa, 925–927
To Julia de Burgos, 932–934
Toer, Pramoedya, 279–290
   Inem, 280–290
Tomioka Taeko, 173–175
   Just the Two of Us, 174–175
Tomoshibi, The, 157–171
Toussine, 1104–1114
Trail of the Green Blazer, 220–224
Transferred to Nanning, 219
Tuqan, Fadwa, 435–437
   Song of Becoming, 436–437
Tutuola, Amos, 545–553
   The Gentleman of Complete Parts,
   545–553
12 December 1945, 424–425

U Tam'si, Tchicaya, 651–653
   Brush-Fire, 652–653
Universal Man, The, 234–235

Vallejo, Cesar, 825–827
   The Eternal Dice, 826–827
Vega, Ana Lydia, 1146–1155
   ADJ, Inc, 1147–1155
Verduguez, Cesar, 1124–1135
   The Scream in Your Silence, 1125–1135
Vultures, The, 606–607

Wagon, The, 362–371
Walcott, Derek, 1009–1012
   I once gave my daughters . . ., 1010–1012
   The Season of Phantasmal Peace,
      1011–1012
Weaver Bird, The, 697–698
Wedding at the Cross, 758–769
Wedding Dance, 245–252
Weed, The, 258–263
What's in a Name, 186–191
Where the Mind Is Without Fear, 216–217
Wicomb, Zoe, 791–804
   You Can't Get Lost in Cape Town,
      792–804

Wind-Up Doll, The, 477–478
Wings, 105–119
Wolf, The, 484–490

Xiao Hong, 119–124
   The Crossroads, 120–124

Yehoshua, Ya'akob, 433–435
   Childhood in Old Jerusalem, 434–435
Yellow Brick Road, 384–390
Yi Sang, 105–119
      Wings, 105–119
Yosano Akiko, 15–16
   Three modern tanka, 15
   The Day When Mountains Move, 16
You Can't Get Lost in Cape Town,
      792–804
You Laughed and Laughed and Laughed,
      554–555
Youngest Doll, The, 1141–1146
Yurokon, 956–967

Zobel, Joseph, 937–942
   Mr. Medouze, 937–942